S0-BIP-253

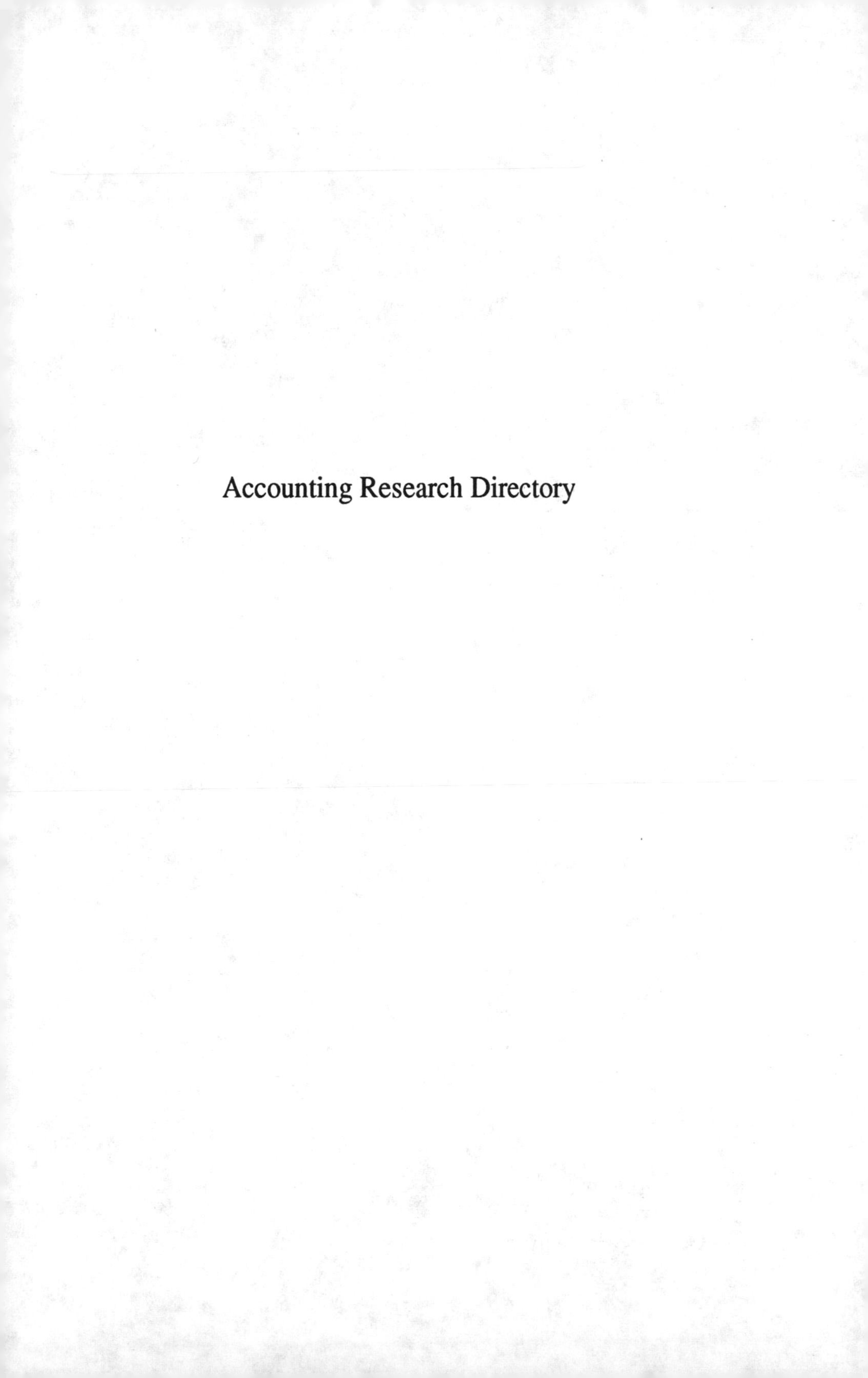

Accounting Research Directory

ACCOUNTING RESEARCH DIRECTORY

The Database of Accounting Literature

THIRD EDITION

LAWRENCE D. BROWN
State University of New York at Buffalo

JOHN C. GARDNER
State University of New York at Binghamton

MIKLOS A. VASARHELYI
Rutgers University

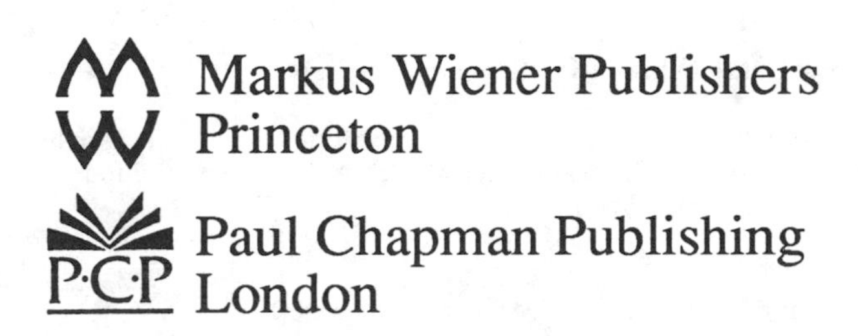

For information write to:
Markus Wiener Publishers
114 Jefferson Road, Princeton, NJ 08540

Distributed exclusively in the United Kingdom and Continental Europe by:
Paul Chapman Publishing, Ltd.
144 Liverpool Road, London N1 1LA
Tel: 071-609-5315 Fax: 071-700-1057

Library of Congress Cataloging-in-Publication Data

Brown, Lawrence D. (Lawrence David), 1946-
Accounting research directory: database of accounting literature/
Lawrence D. Brown, John C. Gardner, Miklos A. Vasarhelyi—3rd ed.
Includes index.
ISBN 1-55876-068-7
1. Accounting—Bibliography. I. Gardner, John Consul.
II. Vasarhelyi, Miklos A. III. Title.
Z7164.C81B884
[HF5635]
016.657—dc20 93-21572
CIP

British Library Cataloguing-in-Publication Data

Accounting Research Directory: Database of Accounting Literature. –3Rev.ed
I. Brown, Lawrence D. II. Vasarhelyi, Miklos A. III. Gardner, John
016.657 ISBN 1-85396-248-1

Printed in the United States of America on acid-free paper.

CONTENTS

INTRODUCTION viii

PART I: LISTING OF ALL ARTICLES 1

PART II: ARTICLES CLASSIFIED FOUR WAYS 421

I. MODE OF REASONING (METHOD)

1.1 MODE OF REASONING(METHOD)=QUANTITATIVE: DESCRIPTIVE STATS 422
1.2 MODE OF REASONING(METHOD)=QUANTITATIVE: REGRESSION 434
1.3 MODE OF REASONING(METHOD)=QUANTITATIVE: ANOVA 456
1.4 MODE OF REASONING(METHOD)=QUANTITATIVE: FACT.ANAL,MDA,LOGIT,PROBIT,DIS.....................................460
1.5 MODE OF REASONING(METHOD)=QUANTITATIVE: MARKOV 461
1.6 MODE OF REASONING(METHOD)=QUANTITATIVE: NON-PARAMETRIC 461
1.7 MODE OF REASONING(METHOD)=QUANTITATIVE: CORRELATION................463
1.8 MODE OF REASONING(METHOD)=QUANTITATIVE: ANALYTICAL 465
1.9 MODE OF REASONING(METHOD)=MIXED 473
1.10 MODE OF REASONING(METHOD)=QUALITATIVE......................................475

2. RESEARCH METHOD

2.1 RESEARCH METHOD=ANALYTICAL – INTERNAL LOGIC 489
2.2 RESEARCH METHOD=ANALYTICAL – SIMULATION....................................516
2.3 RESEARCH METHOD=ARCHIVAL – PRIMARY 518
2.4 RESEARCH METHOD=ARCHIVAL – SECONDARY 537
2.5 RESEARCH METHOD=EMPIRICAL – CASE 541
2.6 RESEARCH METHOD=EMPIRICAL – FIELD 542
2.7 RESEARCH METHOD=EMPIRICAL – LAB..544
2.8 RESEARCH METHOD=OPINION – SURVEY...552
2.9 RESEARCH METHOD=OPINION – MIXED..556

3. SCHOOL OF THOUGHT

3.1 SCHOOL OF THOUGHT=BEHAVIORAL – HIPS 557
3.2 SCHOOL OF THOUGHT=BEHAVIORAL – OTHER 562
3.3 SCHOOL OF THOUGHT=STAT.MODEL – EMH...569
3.4 SCHOOL OF THOUGHT=STAT.MODEL – TIME SERIES 578
3.5 SCHOOL OF THOUGHT=STAT.MODEL – INFO ECON./AGENCY....................580
3.6 SCHOOL OF THOUGHT=STAT.MODEL – MATH. PROGRAMMING 585
3.7 SCHOOL OF THOUGHT=STAT.MODEL – OTHER 587
3.8 SCHOOL OF THOUGHT=ACCOUNTING THEORY 597
3.9 SCHOOL OF THOUGHT=ACCOUNTING HISTORY 611
3.10 SCHOOL OF THOUGHT=INSTITUTIONAL 613
3.11 SCHOOL OF THOUGHT=OTHER 617
3.12 SCHOOL OF THOUGHT=EXPERT SYSTEMS...621

4. TREATMENTS

4.1 TREATMENTS=FINANCIAL ACCOUNTING METHODS 621
4.2 TREATMENTS=CASH 627
4.3 TREATMENTS=INVENTORY 627
4.4 TREATMENTS=OTHER CURRENT ASSETS 629
4.5 TREATMENTS=PROP,PLANT & EQUIP / DEPR 629
4.6 TREATMENTS=OTHER NON-CURRENT ASSETS 630
4.7 TREATMENTS=LEASES 631
4.8 TREATMENTS=LONG TERM DEBT 631
4.9 TREATMENTS=TAXES 632
4.10 TREATMENTS=OTHER LIABILITIES 634
4.11 TREATMENTS=VALUATION (INFLATION) 634
4.12 TREATMENTS=SPECIAL ITEMS 638
4.13 TREATMENTS=REVENUE RECOGNITION 638
4.14 TREATMENTS=ACCTG CHANGES 639
4.15 TREATMENTS=BUSINESS COMBINATIONS 640
4.16 TREATMENTS=INTERIM REPORTING 641
4.17 TREATMENTS=AMORTIZATION/DEPLETION 641
4.18 TREATMENTS=SEGMENT REPORTS 642
4.19 TREATMENTS=FOREIGN CURRENCY 642
4.20 TREATMENTS=DIVIDENDS – CASH 642
4.21 TREATMENTS=DIVIDENDS – STOCK 642
4.22 TREATMENTS=PENSION (FUNDS) 643
4.23 TREATMENTS=OTHER -FIN.ACCGT 643
4.24 TREATMENTS=FIN. STATEMENT TIMING 644
4.25 TREATMENTS=R&D 645
4.26 TREATMENTS=OIL & GAS 645
4.27 TREATMENTS=AUDITING 646
4.28 TREATMENTS=OPINION 647
4.29 TREATMENTS=SAMPLING 648
4.30 TREATMENTS=LIABILITY 650
4.31 TREATMENTS=RISK 650
4.32 TREATMENTS=INDEPENDENCE 651
4.33 TREATMENTS=ANALYTICAL REVIEW 651
4.34 TREATMENTS=INTERNAL CONTROL 652
4.35 TREATMENTS=TIMING 653
4.36 TREATMENTS=MATERIALITY 653
4.37 TREATMENTS=EDP AUDIT 654
4.38 TREATMENTS=ORGANIZATION 654
4.39 TREATMENTS=INTERNAL AUDIT 655
4.40 TREATMENTS=ERRORS 656
4.41 TREATMENTS=TRAIL 656
4.42 TREATMENTS=JUDGMENT 656
4.43 TREATMENTS=PLANNING 657
4.44 TREATMENTS=EFFICIENCY – OPERATIONAL 658
4.45 TREATMENTS=AUDIT THEORY 658

4.46 TREATMENTS=CONFIRMATIONS 658
4.47 TREATMENTS=MANAGERIAL 659
4.48 TREATMENTS=TRANSFER PRICING 661
4.49 TREATMENTS=BREAKEVEN, CVPA 661
4.50 TREATMENTS=BUDGETING & PLANNING 662
4.51 TREATMENTS=RELEVANT COSTS 664
4.52 TREATMENTS=RESPONSIBILITY ACCTG 665
4.53 TREATMENTS=COST ALLOCS 665
4.54 TREATMENTS=CAPITAL BUDGETING 666
4.55 TREATMENTS=TAX (TAX PLANNING) 666
4.56 TREATMENTS=OVERHEAD ALLOCS 666
4.57 TREATMENTS=HRA-SOCIAL ACCTG 667
4.58 TREATMENTS=VARIANCES 668
4.59 TREATMENTS=EXEC.COMPENSATION 669
4.60 TREATMENTS=OTHER 670
4.61 TREATMENTS=SUBMISSN TO THE FASB ETC 673
4.62 TREATMENTS=MANAGER DECISION CHARS 674
4.63 TREATMENTS=INFO STRCTRS (DISCL) 674
4.64 TREATMENTS=AUDITOR TRAINING 677
4.65 TREATMENTS=INSIDER TRADING RULES 677
4.66 TREATMENTS=PROBABILITY ELICITATION 677
4.67 TREATMENTS=INTL DIFFERENCES 678
4.68 TREATMENTS=FORM OF ORG. (PARTNER.) 678
4.69 TREATMENTS=AUDITOR BEHAVIOR 678
4.70 TREATMENTS=METHODOLOGY 680
4.71 TREATMENTS=BUSINESS FAILURE 683
4.72 TREATMENTS=EDUCATION 684
4.73 TREATMENTS=PROF.RESPONSIBILITIES 684
4.74 TREATMENTS=FORECASTS 685
4.75 TREATMENTS=DECISION AIDS 687
4.76 TREATMENTS=ORGANIZATION ~ ENVIRONMENT 687
4.77 TREATMENTS=LITIGATION 689

5.1 ABBREVIATIONS **689**

5.2 GLOSSARY **693**

INTRODUCTION

The purpose of the Accounting Research Directory [ARD] is to help facilitate the research efforts of accounting academics and practitioners by listing, evaluating, and categorizing the major articles published between 1963 and 1992 in seven leading accounting journals. The third edition of the ARD includes four more years (1989-92) and one more journal (Contemporary Accounting Research) than the second edition. Some applications of the ARD include:

1. aiding professors in selecting pertinent articles to assign to students;
2. helping accounting practitioners identify relevant articles when preparing responses to FASB Discussion Memoranda; and
3. facilitating the selection of papers in a particular subject area, mode of reasoning, research method, or school of thought.

Part I of the ARD is a complete listing of all major articles published during the thirty-year period, 1963-1992, in seven accounting journals:

- The Accounting Review (TAR)
- Accounting, Organizations and Society (AOS)
- Auditing: A Journal of Theory and Practice (AUD)
- Contemporary Accounting Research (CAR)
- Journal of Accounting and Economics (JAE)
- Journal of Accounting Research (JAR)
- Journal of Accounting, Auditing & Finance (JAA).

It is organized alphabetically by author; each article is listed as many times as there are coauthors. Thus, an article by R. Ball and P. Brown will appear twice in the first part of the ARD.

Each entry in Part I consists of three (or four, if more than three authors) lines:

1. Author's surname and initials; other coauthors' surnames and initials; and the order in which the other coauthors' names appear in the article. Citation index (discussed below).
2. Complete title of the paper, abbreviated only when necessitated by space constraints.

3. Journal, issue, year, volume, pages. Part II cross-reference (discussed below).

For example, the Autumn (AU) 1968 JAR paper, by R. Ball and P. Brown, is listed in Part I under P. Brown as:

BROWN, P ; FIRS: BALL, R CIT: 8.35
AN EMPIRICAL EVALUATION OF ACCOUNTING INCOME NUMBERS
JAR AU 68 VOL: 6 PG: 159-178; NON-PAR.: PRIM.: EMH :FIN.METH.

Part II of the ARD organizes all articles contained in Part I according to four taxonomies:

1. Mode of Reasoning (key method of analysis)
2. Research Method
3. School of Thought
4. Treatment (subject area).

The Table of Contents lists the groupings within the taxonomies, along with their abbreviations, and the Glossary defines the terms.

The Autumn 1968 JAR article by Ball and Brown appears in Part II four times, corresponding to its grouping within each of the above four taxonomies:

1. Mode of Reasoning: NON-PAR.
2. Research Method: PRIM.
3. School of Thought: EMH
4. Treatment: FIN.METH.

Note that the terms, NON-PAR., PRIM., EMH and FIN.METH., for the four taxonomies, are the same as those listed on the third line of the bibliographic reference in Part I. Each listing in Part II contains a citation index, which indicates the number of times per year that the paper has been cited since its year of publication (or 1976, whichever is later) by "contemporary accounting research," where the latter is defined as all major articles published in five accounting journals during the seventeen year period, 1976 though 1992: TAR, AOS, CAR, JAE, and JAR. As two examples of how the citation index is determined, the Autumn 1968 JAR article by Ball and Brown has been cited 142 times, giving it a citation index of 142/(1993-1976), or 8.35; the Spring 1985 JAR article by R. Atiase has been cited 39 times, giving it a citation index of 39/(1993-1985), or 4.86. Within each taxonomy grouping, all articles are listed in decreasing order of citation index.

Each listing in Part II has nine columns:

- CITE INDEX (citation index)
- FIRST AUTHOR (surname, initials of first author)
- ISSUE (e.g., month of publication)
- YEAR (year of publication)
- JOURNAL (TAR, AOS, AUD, CAR, JAE, JAR, or JAA)
- SECOND AUTHOR (surname, initials of second author)
- THIRD AUTHOR (surname, initials of third author)
- PAGE BEG (beginning page number).
- PAGE END (ending page number)

For example, the AU 1968 JAR paper by R. Ball and P. Brown appears in Part II of the ARD in Sections PRIM., NON-PAR., EMH, AND FIN.METH. as:

8.35	BALL, R	AU	1968	JAR	BROWN, P		159	178

The citation index is also included in the first line of each article in Part I, abbreviated as CIT. This directory has been helping researchers to locate articles in specific areas quickly and efficiently, and to move ahead with their research. The authors expect that the use of this guide will result in further publications, which will be listed in future editions of this book.

ACKNOWLEDGEMENT: We greatly appreciate the assistance provided by Rimona Palas, Keith Donnelly, and Ranjan Banerji.

Lawrence D. Brown, *SUNY-Buffalo*
John C. Gardner, *Binghamton University*
Miklos A. Vasarhelyi, *Rutgers University*

August 1993

PART I

Complete Listing of All Major Articles Published in Six Accounting Journals

ABARBANELL,JS CIT: 0
DO ANALYSTS' EARNINGS FORECASTS INCORPORATE INFORMATION IN PRIOR STOCK PRICE CHANGES?
JAE JN 91 VOL: 14 PG:147 - 165 :: REGRESS. :PRIM. :OTH.STAT. :FOREC.

ABDEL-KHALIK,AR CIT: 0.33
SPECIFICATION PROBLEMS WITH INFORMATION CONTENT OF EARNINGS: REVISIONS AND RATIONALITY OF EXPECTATIONS AND SELF-SELECTION BIAS
CAR AU 90 VOL: 7 PG:142 - 172 :: DES.STAT. :PRIM. :TIME SER. :METHOD.

ABDEL-KHALIK,AR CIT: 0.67
THE JOINTNESS OF AUDIT FEES AND DEMAND FOR MAS: A SELF-SELECTION ANALYSIS
CAR SP 90 VOL: 6 PG:295 - 322 :: REGRESS. :PRIM. :OTH.STAT. :ORG.

ABDEL-KHALIK,AR CIT: 0.6
INCENTIVES FOR ACCRUING COSTS AND EFFICIENCY IN REGULATED MONOPOLIES SUBJECT TO ROE CONSTRAINT
JAR ST 88 VOL: 26 PG:144 - 181 :: REGRESS. :PRIM. :INF.ECO./AG. :EXEC.COMP.

ABDEL-KHALIK,AR ; SEC: CHI ,C ; THIR: GHICAS,D CIT: 0.33
REATIONALITY OF EXECUTIVE COMPENSATION SCHEMES AND REAL ACCOUNTING CHANGES
CAR AU 87 VOL: 4 PG:32 - 60 :: REGRESS. :PRIM. :INF.ECO./AG. :ACC.CHNG.

ABDEL-KHALIK,AR CIT: 0
A CRITIQUE OF "MARKET REACTIONS TO MANDATED INTEREST CAPITALIZATION"
CAR SP 86 VOL: 2 PG:242 - 251 :: REGRESS. :SEC. :EMH :FIN.METH.

ABDEL-KHALIK,AR ; SEC: GRAUL ,PR ; THIR: NEWTON,JD CIT: 0
REPORTING UNCERTAINTY AND ASSESSMENT OF RISK: REPLICATION AND EXTENSION IN A CANADIAN SETTING
JAR AU 86 VOL: 24 PG:372 - 382 :: REGRESS. :LAB. :HIPS :OPIN.

ABDEL-KHALIK,AR CIT: 1.75
THE EFFECT OF LIFO-SWITCHING AND FIRM OWNERSHIP ON EXECUTIVES' PAY
JAR AU 85 VOL: 23 PG:427 - 447 :: REGRESS. :PRIM. :OTH.STAT. :INV.

ABDEL-KHALIK,AR CIT: 0.1
OVERFITTING BIAS IN THE MODELS ASSESSING THE PREDICTIVE POWER OF QUARTERLY REPORTS
JAR SP 83 VOL: 21 PG:293 - 296 :: MIXED :PRIM. :TIME SER. :METHOD.

ABDEL-KHALIK,AR ; SEC: SNOWBALL,D ; THIR: WRAGGE,JH CIT: 0.4
THE EFFECTS OF CERTAIN INTERNAL AUDIT VARIABLES ON THE PLANNING OF EXTERNAL AUDIT PROGRAMS
TAR AP 83 VOL: 58 PG:215 - 227 :: ANOVA :LAB. :OTH.BEH. :INT.AUD.

ABDEL-KHALIK,AR ; SEC: AJINKYA,BB CIT: 0.45
RETURNS TO INFORMATIONAL ADVANTAGES: THE CASE OF ANALYSTS' FORECAST REVISIONS
TAR OC 82 VOL: 57 PG:661 - 680 :: REGRESS. :PRIM. :EMH :FOREC.

ABDEL-KHALIK,AR ; SEC: EL-SHESHAI,KM CIT: 0.92
INFORMATION CHOICE AND UTILIZATION IN AN EXPERIMENT ON DEFAULT PREDICTION
JAR AU 80 VOL: 18 PG:325 - 342 :: DES.STAT. :LAB. :HIPS :BUS.FAIL.

ABDEL-KHALIK,AR ; SEC: ESPEJO,J CIT: 0.6
EXPECTATIONS DATA AND THE PREDICTIVE VALUE OF INTERIM REPORTING

JAR SP 78 VOL: 16 PG:1 - 13 :: REGRESS. :LAB. :TIME SER. :FOREC.

ABDEL-KHALIK,AR ; SEC: MCKEOWN,JC CIT: 0.27
DISCLOSURE OF ESTIMATES OF HOLDING GAINS AND THE ASSESSMENT OF SYSTEMATIC RISK
JAR ST 78 VOL: 16 PG:46 - 77 :: ANOVA :PRIM. :EMH :VALUAT.(INFL.)

ABDEL-KHALIK,AR ; SEC: MCKEOWN,JC CIT: 1.27
UNDERSTANDING ACCOUNTING CHANGES IN AN EFFICIENT MARKET: EVIDENCE OF DIFFERENTIAL REACTION
TAR OC 78 VOL: 53 PG:851 - 868 :: ANOVA :PRIM. :EMH :INV.

ABDEL-KHALIK,AR CIT: 0.12
ADVERTISING EFFECTIVENESS AND ACCOUNTING POLICY
TAR OC 75 VOL: 50 PG:657 - 670 :: REGRESS. :PRIM. :TIME SER. :OTH. NON-C/A

ABDEL-KHALIK,AR ; SEC: LUSK ,EJ CIT: 0.76
TRANSFER PRICING - A SYNTHESIS
TAR JA 74 VOL: 49 PG:8 - 23 :: QUAL. :SEC. :N/A :TRANS.PRIC.

ABDEL-KHALIK,AR CIT: 0.24
THE ENTROPY LAW, ACCOUNTING DATA, AND RELEVANCE TO DECISION-MAKING
TAR AP 74 VOL: 49 PG:271 - 283 :: CORR. :FIELD :INF.ECO./AG. :FIN.ST.TIM.

ABDEL-KHALIK,AR CIT: 1
ON THE EFFICIENCY OF SUBJECT SURROGATION IN ACCOUNTING RESEARCH
TAR OC 74 VOL: 49 PG:743 - 750 :: NON-PAR. :LAB. :N/A :METHOD.

ABDEL-KHALIK,AR CIT: 0.71
THE EFFECT OF AGGREGATING ACCOUNTING REPORTS ON THE QUALITY OF THE LENDING DECISION: AN EMPIRICAL INVESTIGATION
JAR ST 73 VOL: 11 PG:104 - 138 :: ANOVA :LAB. :OTH. :PROF.RESP.

ABDEL-KHALIK,AR CIT: 0.24
USER PREFERENCE ORDERING VALUE
TAR JL 71 VOL: 46 PG:457 - 471 :: ANAL. :INT. LOG. :N/A :FIN.METH.

ABDEL-KHALIK,AR CIT: 0
CONTROLLERSHIP IN EGYPT
JAR SP 66 VOL: 4 PG:37 - 46 :: QUAL. :INT. LOG. :INSTIT. :PROF.RESP.

ABDEL-MAGID,MF CIT: 0
TOWARD A BETTER UNDERSTANDING OF THE ROLE OF MEASUREMENT IN ACCOUNTING
TAR AP 79 VOL: 54 PG:346 - 357 :: QUAL. :INT. LOG. :OTH.STAT. :FIN.METH.

ABDOLMOHAMMADI,MJ CIT: 0
FACTORS AFFECTING AUDITORS' PERCEPTIONS OF APPLICABLE DECISION AIDS FOR VARIOUS AUDIT TASKS
CAR SP 91 VOL: 7 PG:535 - 548 :: REGRESS. :LAB. :HIPS :DEC.AIDS

ABDOLMOHAMMADI,MJ ; SEC: WRIGHT,A CIT: 3
AN EXAMINATION OF THE EFFECTS OF EXPERIENCE AND TASK COMPLEXITY ON AUDIT JUDGMENTS
TAR JA 87 VOL: 62 PG:1 - 13 :: REGRESS. :LAB. :OTH.BEH. :JUDG.

ABDOLMOHAMMADI,MJ CIT: 0.29
EFFICIENCY OF THE BAYESIAN APPROACH IN COMPLIANCE TESTING: SOME EMPIRICAL EVIDENCE

AUD SP 86 VOL: 5 PG:1 - 16 :: REGRESS. :LAB. :OTH.BEH. :SAMP.

ABDOLMOHAMMADI,MJ ; SEC: BERGER,PD CIT: 0
A TEST OF THE ACCURACY OF PROBABILITY ASSESSMENT TECHNIQUES IN AUDITING
CAR AU 86 VOL: 3 PG:149 - 165 :: REGRESS. :LAB. :HIPS :PROB.ELIC.

ABDOLMOHAMMADI,MJ CIT: 0.38
BAYESIAN INFERENCE RESEARCH IN AUDITING: SOME METHODOLOGICAL SUGGESTIONS
CAR AU 85 VOL: 2 PG:76 - 94 :: DES.STAT. :INT. LOG. :MATH.PROG. :JUDG.

ABDULKADER,AA ; FIRS: LOREK ,KS ; SEC: ICERMAN,JD CIT: 0
FURTHER DESCRIPTIVE AND PREDICTIVE EVIDENCE ON ALTERNATIVE TIME-SERIES MODELS FOR QUARTERLY EARNINGS
JAR SP 83 VOL: 21 PG:317 - 328 :: REGRESS. :PRIM. :TIME SER. :FOREC.

ABEL ,R CIT: 0.06
A COMPARATIVE SIMULATION OF GERMAN AND U.S. ACCOUNTING PRINCIPLES
JAR SP 69 VOL: 7 PG:1 - 11 :: QUAL. :SIM. :OTH. :INT.DIFF.

ABERNETHY,MA ; SEC: STOELWINDER,JU CIT: 0
BUDGET USE, TASK UNCERTAINTY, SYSTEM GOAL ORIENTATION AND SUBUNIT PERFORMANCE: A TEST OF THE 'FIT' HYPOTHESIS IN NOT-FOR-PROFIT
AOS 02 91 VOL: 16 PG:105 - 120 :: REGRESS. :SURV. :OTH.BEH. :BUDG.& PLAN.

ABRANOVIC,WA CIT: 0
PROBABILITY PLOTTING FOR ESTIMATING TIME-TO-PAYMENT CHARACTERISTICS FOR COLLECTIONS ON ACCOUNTS RECEIVABLE
TAR OC 76 VOL: 51 PG:863 - 874 :: ANAL. :INT. LOG. :OTH.STAT. :OTH.C/A

ACLAND,D CIT: 0.12
THE EFFECTS OF BEHAVIORAL INDICATORS ON INVESTOR DECISIONS: AN EXPLORATORY STUDY
AOS 23 76 VOL: 1 PG:133 - 142 :: NON-PAR. :LAB. :OTH.BEH. :HRA

ADAMS ,KD CIT: 0
HEDGE ACCOUNTING FOR ANTICIPATORY HEDGES OF SHORT-TERM LIABILITIES
JAA WI 84 VOL: 7 PG:151 - 163 :: QUAL. :INT. LOG. :THEORY :FIN.METH.

ADAMS ,SJ ; FIRS: LIGHTNER,SM ; THIR: LIGHTNER,KM CIT: 0.36
THE INFLUENCE OF SITUATIONAL, ETHICAL, AND EXPECTANCY THEORY VARIABLES ON ACCOUNTANTS' UNDERREPORTING BEHAVIOR
AUD AU 82 VOL: 2 PG:1 - 12 :: DES.STAT. :SURV. :OTH.STAT. :ORG.

ADAMS ,SJ ; FIRS: WHITTINGTON,OR CIT: 0
TEMPORARY BREAKDOWNS OF INTERNAL CONTROL: IMPLICATIONS FOR EXTERNAL AND INTERNAL AUDITORS
JAA SU 82 VOL: 5 PG:310 - 319 :: QUAL. :INT. LOG. :OTH. :N/A

ADAR ,Z ; SEC: BARNEA,A ; THIR: LEV ,B CIT: 0.19
A COMPREHENSIVE COST-VOLUME-PROFIT ANALYSIS UNDER UNCERTAINTY
TAR JA 77 VOL: 52 PG:137 - 149 :: QUAL. :INT. LOG. :THEORY :TAXES

ADDY JR,ND ; FIRS: MAYPER,AG CIT: 0
THE RELIABILITY OF THE DISCLOSURE OF AUDITOR CHANGES BY THE PUBLIC ACCOUNTING REPORT
AUD SP 91 VOL: 10 PG:136 - 144 :: REGRESS. :PRIM. :INSTIT. :ORG.

ADELBERG,AH CIT: 0.21
A METHODOLOGY FOR MEASURING THE UNDERSTANDABILITY OF FINANCIAL REPORT MESSAGES

JAR AU 79 VOL: 17 PG:565 - 592 :: ANOVA :PRIM. :OTH.BEH. :FIN.METH.

ADESI ,GB ; SEC: TALWAR,PP CIT: 0
STATIONARITY TESTS OF THE MARKET MODEL FOR SECURITY RETURNS
JAA SU 92 VOL: 7 PG:369 - 378 :: DES.STAT. :SIM. :OTH.STAT. :METHOD.

AFFLECK-GRAVES,J ; SEC: DAVIS ,LR ; THIR: MENDENHALL,RR CIT: 0
FORECASTS OF EARNINGS PER SHARE: POSSIBLE SOURCES OF ANALYST SUPERIORITY AND BIAS
CAR SP 90 VOL: 6 PG:501 - 517 :: REGRESS. :LAB. :TIME SER. :FOREC.

AGGARWAL,R CIT: 0.07
FASB NO.8 AND REPORTED RESULTS OF MULTINATIONAL OPERATIONS: HAZARD FOR MANAGERS AND INVESTORS
JAA SP 78 VOL: 1 PG:197 - 216 :: MIXED :INT. LOG. :THEORY :FOR.CUR.

AGRAWAL,SP ; SEC: HALLBAUER,RC ; THIR: PERRITT,GW CIT: 0
MEASUREMENT OF THE CURRENT COST OF EQUIVALENT PRODUCTIVE CAPACITY
JAA WI 80 VOL: 3 PG:163 - 173 :: ANAL. :INT. LOG. :OTH.STAT. :VALUAT.(INFL.)

AGRAWAL,SP CIT: 0
ACCOUNTING FOR THE IMPACT OF INFLATION ON A BUSINESS ENTERPRISE
TAR OC 77 VOL: 52 PG:789 - 809 :: ANAL. :INT. LOG. :THEORY :VALUAT.(INFL.)

AHARONI,A ; FIRS: RONEN ,J CIT: 0.25
THE CHOICE AMONG ACCOUNTING ALTERNATIVES AND MANAGEMENT COMPENSATION: EFFECTS OF CORPORATE TAX
TAR JA 89 VOL: 64 PG:69 - 86 :: REGRESS. :SURV. :OTH.BEH. :TAX PLNG.

AHARONI,Y ; FIRS: BEJA ,A CIT: 0
SOME ASPECTS OF CONVENTIONAL ACCOUNTING PROFITS IN AN INFLATIONARY ENVIRONMENT
JAR AU 77 VOL: 15 PG:169 - 178 :: ANAL. :INT. LOG. :THEORY :VALUAT.(INFL.)

AHARONI,Y ; SEC: OPHIR ,T CIT: 0
ACCOUNTING FOR LINKED LOANS
JAR SP 67 VOL: 5 PG:1 - 26 :: QUAL. :INT. LOG. :THEORY :FIN.METH.

AHARONY,J ; SEC: BAR-YOSEF,S CIT: 0.33
TESTS OF THE IMPACT OF LIFO ADOPTION ON STOCKHOLDERS: A STOCHASTIC DOMINANCE APPROACH
CAR SP 87 VOL: 3 PG:430 - 444 :: REGRESS. :PRIM. :EMH :INV.

AHITUV,N ; SEC: HALPERN,J ; THIR: WILL ,H CIT: 0.13
AUDIT PLANNING: AN ALGORITHMIC APPROACH
CAR AU 85 VOL: 2 PG:95 - 110 :: DES.STAT. :INT. LOG. :MATH.PROG. :PLAN.

AIKEN ,ME ; FIRS: COVALESKI,M CIT: 0.29
ACCOUNTING AND THEORIES OF ORGANIZATIONS: SOME PRELIMINARY CONSIDERATIONS
AOS 45 86 VOL: 11 PG:297 - 320 :: ANOVA :INT. LOG. :THEORY :ORG.& ENVIR.

AIKEN ,ME ; SEC: BLACKETT,LA ; THIR: ISAACS,G CIT: 0.06
MODELING BEHAVIOURAL INTERDEPENDENCIES FOR STEWARDSHIP REPORTING
TAR JL 75 VOL: 50 PG:544 - 562 :: ANAL. :INT. LOG. :THEORY :OTH.MANAG.

AJINKYA,BB ; SEC: ATIASE,RK ; THIR: GIFT ,MJ CIT: 0
VOLUME OF TRADING AND THE DISPERSION OF FINANCIAL ANALYSTS' EARNINGS FORECASTS
TAR AP 91 VOL: 66 PG:389 - 401 :: REGRESS. :PRIM. :EMH :AUD.BEH.

AJINKYA,BB ; SEC: JAIN ,PC CIT: 0.5
THE BEHAVIOR OF DAILY STOCK MARKET TRADING VOLUME
JAE NV 89 VOL: 11 PG:331 - 359 :: REGRESS. :PRIM. :EMH :METHOD.

AJINKYA,BB ; SEC: GIFT ,MJ CIT: 1.56
CORPORATE MANAGERS' EARNINGS FORECASTS AND SYMMETRICAL ADJUSTMENTS OF MARKET EXPECTATIONS
JAR AU 84 VOL: 22 PG:425 - 444 :: ANOVA :PRIM. :EMH :FOREC.

AJINKYA,BB ; FIRS: ABDEL-KHALIK,AR CIT: 0.45
RETURNS TO INFORMATIONAL ADVANTAGES: THE CASE OF ANALYSTS' FORECAST REVISIONS
TAR OC 82 VOL: 57 PG:661 - 680 :: REGRESS. :PRIM. :EMH :FOREC.

AJINKYA,BB CIT: 0.23
AN EMPIRICAL EVALUATION OF LINE-OF-BUSINESS REPORTING
JAR AU 80 VOL: 18 PG:343 - 361 :: ANOVA :PRIM. :EMH :SEG.REP.

ALBRECHT,WS ; SEC: LOOKABILL,LL ; THIR: MCKEOWN,JC CIT: 2.25
THE TIME-SERIES PROPERTIES OF ANNUAL EARNINGS
JAR AU 77 VOL: 15 PG:226 - 244 :: MIXED :PRIM. :TIME SER. :FOREC.

ALBRECHT,WS CIT: 0.06
ESTIMATION ERROR IN INCOME DETERMINATION
TAR OC 76 VOL: 51 PG:824 - 837 :: MIXED :CASE :OTH.STAT. :PROB.ELIC.

ALDERMAN,CW ; SEC: DEITRICK,JW CIT: 0.36
AUDITORS' PERCEPTIONS OF TIME BUDGET PRESSURES AND PREMATURE SIGN-OFFS: A REPLICATION AND EXTENSION
AUD WI 82 VOL: 1 PG:54 - 68 :: DES.STAT. :SURV. :OTH.BEH. :ERRORS

ALDERMAN,CW ; FIRS: ROBERTSON,JC CIT: 0
COMPARATIVE AUDITING STANDARDS
JAA WI 81 VOL: 4 PG:144 - 161 :: QUAL. :INT. LOG. :THEORY :ORG.

ALDERMAN,CW ; FIRS: DEITRICK,JW CIT: 0
INTERIM REPORTING DEVELOPMENTS: A STEP TOWARD THE AUDITOR-OF-RECORD CONCEPT
JAA SU 79 VOL: 2 PG:316 - 328 :: QUAL. :INT. LOG. :INSTIT. :AUD.

ALFORD,AW CIT: 0
THE EFFECT OF THE SET OF COMPARABLE FIRMS ON THE ACCURACY OF THE PRICE-EARNINGS VALUATION METHOD
JAR SP 92 VOL: 30 PG:94 - 108 :: REGRESS. :PRIM. :OTH.STAT. :VALUAT.(INFL.)

ALFORD,MR ; SEC: EDMONDS,TP CIT: 0.08
A REPLICATION: DOES AUDIT INVOLVEMENT AFFECT THE QUALITY OF INTERIM REPORT NUMBERS?
JAA SP 81 VOL: 4 PG:255 - 264 :: DES.STAT. :SEC. :THEORY :INT.REP.

ALFRED,AM CIT: 0.06
INVESTMENT IN THE DEVELOPMENT DISTRICTS OF THE UNITED KINGDOM: TAX AND DISCOUNTED CASH FLOW
JAR AU 64 VOL: 2 PG:172 - 182 :: QUAL. :INT. LOG. :THEORY :TAXES

ALI ,A ; SEC: ZAROWIN,P CIT: 2
PERMANENT VERSUS TRANSITORY COMPONENTS OF ANNUAL EARNINGS AND ESTIMATION ERROR IN EARNINGS RESPONSE COEFFICIENTS

JAE JN 92 VOL: 15 PG:249 - 264 :: REGRESS. :PRIM. :EMH :FIN.METH.

ALI ,A ; SEC: KLEIN ,A ; THIR: ROSENFELD,J CIT: 0
ANALYSTS' USE OF INFORMATION ABOUT PERMANENT AND TRANSITORY EARNINGS COMPONENTS IN FORECASTING ANNUAL EPS
TAR JA 92 VOL: 67 PG:183 - 198 :: REGRESS. :PRIM. :TIME SER. :FOREC.

ALIBER,RZ ; SEC: STICKNEY,CP CIT: 0.12
ACCOUNTING MEASURES OF FOREIGN EXCHANGE EXPOSURE: THE LONG AND SHORT OF IT
TAR JA 75 VOL: 50 PG:44 - 57 :: QUAL. :INT. LOG. :INSTIT. :FOR.CUR.

ALLEN ,G ; FIRS: GARSOMBKE,HP CIT: 0
DID SFAS NO.19 LEAD TO OIL AND GAS COMPANY MERGERS?
JAA SU 83 VOL: 6 PG:285 - 298 :: NON-PAR. :PRIM. :THEORY :OIL & GAS

ALLEN ,S ; SEC: RAMANAN,R CIT: 0
EARNINGS SURPRISES AND PRIOR INSIDER TRADING: TESTS OF JOINT INFORMATIVENESS
CAR SP 90 VOL: 6 PG:518 - 543 :: REGRESS. :PRIM. :EMH :INS.TRAD.

ALLYN ,RG CIT: 0
ACCREDITATION OF ACCOUNTING CURRICULUMS
TAR AP 66 VOL: 41 PG:303 - 311 :: QUAL. :INT. LOG. :INSTIT. :OTH.MANAG.

ALLYN ,RG CIT: 0
PLANNING FOR THE CPA EXAMINATION IN THE UNITED STATES
TAR JA 64 VOL: 39 PG:121 - 127 :: QUAL. :INT. LOG. :INSTIT. :OTH.MANAG.

ALM ,J CIT: 0.5
A PERSPECTIVE ON THE EXPERIMENTAL ANALYSIS OF TAXPAYER REPORTING
TAR JL 91 VOL: 66 PG:577 - 594 :: DES.STAT. :SURV. :OTH.BEH. :TAX PLNG.

ALTMAN,EI CIT: 0.36
ACCOUNTING IMPLICATIONS OF FAILURE PREDICTION MODELS
JAA AU 82 VOL: 6 PG:4 - 19 :: OTH.QUANT. :PRIM. :OTH.STAT. :FIN.METH.

ALVEY ,KL CIT: 0
ALTERNATIVE DERIVATION OF FORMULAS FOR THE INCOME TAX PROBLEM
TAR JA 63 VOL: 38 PG:124 - 125 :: ANAL. :INT. LOG. :THEORY :TAXES

ALY ,HF ; SEC: DUBOFF,JI CIT: 0.06
STATISTICAL VS. JUDGMENT SAMPLING: AN EMPIRICAL STUDY OF AUDITING THE ACCOUNTS RECEIVABLE OF A SMALL RETAIL STORE
TAR JA 71 VOL: 46 PG:119 - 128 :: ANOVA :CASE :OTH.STAT. :SAMP.

ALY ,IM ; SEC: BARLOW,HA ; THIR: JONES ,RW CIT: 0
THE USEFULNESS OF SFAS NO. 82 INFORMATION IN DISCRIMINATING BUSINESS FAILURE: AN EMPIRICAL STUDY
JAA SP 92 VOL: 7 PG:217 - 230 :: REGRESS. :PRIM. :OTH.STAT. :BUS.FAIL.

AMATO ,HN ; SEC: ANDERSON,EE ; THIR: HARVEY,DW CIT: 0.06
A GENERAL MODEL OF FUTURE PERIOD WARRANTY COSTS
TAR OC 76 VOL: 51 PG:854 - 862 :: ANAL. :INT. LOG. :OTH. :SPEC.ITEMS

AMERNIC,J ; FIRS: ARANYA,N ; SEC: LACHMAN,R CIT: 0.27
ACCOUNTANTS' JOB SATISFACTION: A PATH ANALYSIS
AOS 03 82 VOL: 7 PG:201 - 216 :: CORR. :SURV. :OTH.BEH. :N/A

AMERNIC,J ; FIRS: ARANYA,N ; SEC: POLLOCK,J CIT: 0.25
AN EXAMINATION OF PROFESSIONAL COMMITMENT IN PUBLIC ACCOUNTING

AOS 04 81 VOL: 6 PG:271 - 280 :: MIXED :LAB. :OTH.BEH. :PROF.RESP.

AMERSHI,AH ; SEC: CHENG ,P CIT: 0.67
INTRAFIRM RESOURCE ALLOCATION: THE ECONOMICS OF TRANSFER PRICING AND COST ALLOCATIONS IN ACCOUNTING
CAR AU 90 VOL: 7 PG:61 - 99 :: DES.STAT. :INT. LOG. :INF.ECO./AG. :TRANS.PRIC.

AMERSHI,AH ; SEC: BANKER,RD ; THIR: DATAR ,SM CIT: 0
ECONOMIC SUFFICIENCY AND STATISTICAL SUFFICIENCY IN THE AGGREGATION OF ACCOUNTING SIGNALS
TAR JA 90 VOL: 65 PG:113 - 130 :: DES.STAT. :INT. LOG. :INF.ECO./AG. :MANAG.

AMERSHI,AH ; SEC: CHENG ,P CIT: 0.25
ON THE DEMAND FOR HISTORICAL EVENTS RECORDING AND MAINTENANCE OF AUDIT TRAILS
CAR AU 89 VOL: 6 PG:72 - 90 :: DES.STAT. :INT. LOG. :INF.ECO./AG. :AUD.TRAIL

AMERSHI,AH ; SEC: CHENG ,P CIT: 0.6
IMPLEMENTABLE EQUILIBRIA IN ACCOUNTING CONTEXTS: AN EXPLORATORY STUDY
CAR SP 88 VOL: 4 PG:515 - 563 :: DES.STAT. :INT. LOG. :INF.ECO./AG. :EXEC.COMP.

AMERSHI,AH ; SEC: SUNDER,S CIT: 0.5
FAILURE OF STOCK PRICES TO DISCIPLINE MANAGERS IN A RATIONAL EXPECTATIONS ECONOMY
JAR AU 87 VOL: 25 PG:177 - 195 :: DES.STAT. :INT. LOG. :INF.ECO./AG. :INV.

AMERSHI,AH ; SEC: DEMSKI,JS ; THIR: FELLINGHAM,J CIT: 0.38
SEQUENTIAL BAYESIAN ANALYSIS IN ACCOUNTING
CAR SP 85 VOL: 1 PG:176 - 192 :: DES.STAT. :INT. LOG. :INF.ECO./AG. :DEC.AIDS

AMEY ,LR ; SEC: GOFFIN,JL CIT: 0
JOINT PRODUCT DECISIONS: THE VARIABLE PROPORTIONS CASE
CAR AU 88 VOL: 5 PG:174 - 198 :: DES.STAT. :INT. LOG. :INF.ECO./AG. :REL.COSTS

AMEY ,LR CIT: 0
TERBORGH'S ASSET REPLACEMENT FORMULA RECONSIDERED
CAR AU 84 VOL: 1 PG:64 - 76 :: ANOVA :INT. LOG. :MATH.PROG. :DEC.AIDS

AMEY ,LR CIT: 0.07
TOWARDS A NEW PERSPECTIVE ON ACCOUNTING CONTROL
AOS 04 79 VOL: 4 PG:247 - 258 :: QUAL. :INT. LOG. :OTH. :MANAG.

AMIHUD,Y ; SEC: MENDELSON,H CIT: 0
INDEX AND INDEX-FUTURES RETURNS
JAA AU 89 VOL: 4 PG:415 - 431 :: REGRESS. :PRIM. :EMH :OTH.FIN.ACC.

AMIHUD,Y ; SEC: MENDELSON,H CIT: 0
LIQUIDITY, VOLATILITY, AND EXCHANGE AUTOMATION
JAA AU 88 VOL: 3 PG:369 - 395 :: DES.STAT. :INT. LOG. :EMH :ORG.& ENVIR.

AMIT ,R ; SEC: LIVNAT,J ; THIR: ZAROWIN,P CIT: 0
A CLASSIFICATION OF MERGERS AND ACQUISITIONS BY MOTIVES: ANALYSIS OF MARKET RESPONSES
CAR AU 89 VOL: 6 PG:143 - 158 :: REGRESS. :PRIM. :EMH :BUS.COMB.

AMIT ,R ; SEC: LIVNAT,J CIT: 0
DIVERSIFICATION, CAPITAL STRUCTURE, AND SYSTEMATIC RISK: AN EMPIRICAL INVESTIGATION
JAA WI 88 VOL: 03 PG:19 - 43 :: REGRESS. :PRIM. :EMH :OTH.FIN.ACC.

ANDERSON JR,KE CIT: 0
A HORIZONTAL EQUITY ANALYSIS OF THE MINIMUM TAX PROVISIONS: AN EMPIRICAL STUDY
TAR JL 85 VOL: 60 PG:357 - 371 :: REGRESS. :PRIM. :THEORY :TAXES

ANDERSON JR,TN ; SEC: KIDA ,TE CIT: 0
THE CROSS-LAGGED RESEARCH APPROACH: DESCRIPTION AND ILLUSTRATION
JAR AU 82 VOL: 20 PG:403 - 414 :: CORR. :LAB. :OTH.BEH. :MAN.DEC.CHAR.

ANDERSON,EE ; FIRS: AMATO ,HN ; THIR: HARVEY,DW CIT: 0.06
A GENERAL MODEL OF FUTURE PERIOD WARRANTY COSTS
TAR OC 76 VOL: 51 PG:854 - 862 :: ANAL. :INT. LOG. :OTH. :SPEC.ITEMS

ANDERSON,HM ; SEC: GIESE ,J ; THIR: BOOKER,J CIT: 0.12
SOME PROPOSITIONS ABOUT AUDITING
TAR JL 70 VOL: 45 PG:524 - 531 :: QUAL. :INT. LOG. :INSTIT. :AUD.

ANDERSON,HM ; SEC: GRIFFIN,FB CIT: 0
THE ACCOUNTING CURRICULUM AND POSTGRADUATE ACHIEVEMENT
TAR OC 63 VOL: 38 PG:813 - 818 :: QUAL. :INT. LOG. :THEORY :EDUC.

ANDERSON,JA ; FIRS: ST.PIERRE,K CIT: 1.33
AN ANALYSIS OF THE FACTORS ASSOCIATED WITH LAWSUITS AGAINST PUBLIC ACCOUNTANTS
TAR AP 84 VOL: 59 PG:242 - 263 :: DES.STAT. :PRIM. :INSTIT. :LIAB.

ANDERSON,JA ; FIRS: ST.PIERRE,K CIT: 0
AN ANALYSIS OF AUDIT FAILURES BASED ON DOCUMENTED LEGAL CASES
JAA SP 82 VOL: 5 PG:229 - 247 :: DES.STAT. :PRIM. :OTH. :ERRORS

ANDERSON,JA CIT: 0.13
THE POTENTIAL IMPACT OF KNOWLEDGE OF MARKET EFFICIENCY ON THE LEGAL LIABILITY OF AUDITORS
TAR AP 77 VOL: 52 PG:417 - 426 :: QUAL. :INT. LOG. :EMH :LIAB.

ANDERSON,JA CIT: 0
INFORMATION INTERACTIONS AND ACCOUNTING INFORMATION USER REACTIONS
TAR JL 75 VOL: 50 PG:509 - 511 :: ANAL. :INT. LOG. :N/A :FIN.METH.

ANDERSON,JC ; SEC: KAPLAN,SE ; THIR: RECKERS,PMJ CIT: 0
THE EFFECTS OF OUTPUT INTERFERENCE ON ANALYTICAL PROCEDURES JUDGMENTS
AUD AU 92 VOL: 11 PG:1 - 13 :: REGRESS. :LAB. :HIPS :ANAL.REV.

ANDERSON,JC ; SEC: KRAUSHAAR,JM CIT: 0.14
MEASUREMENT ERROR AND STATISTICAL SAMPLING IN AUDITING: THE POTENTIAL EFFECTS
TAR JL 86 VOL: 61 PG:379 - 399 :: DES.STAT. :SIM. :OTH.STAT. :SAMP.

ANDERSON,JC ; SEC: FRANKLE,AW CIT: 0.31
VOLUNTARY SOCIAL REPORTING: AN ISO-BETA PORTFOLIO ANALYSIS
TAR JL 80 VOL: 55 PG:467 - 479 :: REGRESS. :PRIM. :EMH :HRA

ANDERSON,JJ CIT: 0
INTEGRATED INSTRUCTION IN COMPUTERS AND ACCOUNTING
TAR JL 67 VOL: 42 PG:583 - 588 :: QUAL. :INT. LOG. :N/A :OTH.MANAG.

ANDERSON,JM CIT: 0
DILEMMAS IN MODERN ACCOUNTING RESEARCH

JAR AU 64 VOL: 2 PG:236 - 238 :: QUAL. :INT. LOG. :THEORY :N/A

ANDERSON,MJ ; SEC: ANDERSON,U ; THIR: HELLELOID,R ; FOUR: JOYCE ,E ; FIFT: SCHADEWALD,M CIT: 0
INTERNAL REVENUE SERVICE ACCESS TO TAX ACCRUAL WORKPAPERS: A LABORATORY INVESTIGATION
TAR OC 90 VOL: 65 PG:857 - 874 :: REGRESS. :LAB. :MATH.PROG. :AUD.

ANDERSON,MJ CIT: 0.2
A COMPARATIVE ANALYSIS OF INFORMATION SEARCH AND EVALUATION BEHAVIOR OF PROFESSIONAL AND NON-PROFESSIONAL FINANCIAL ANALYSTS
AOS 05 88 VOL: 13 PG:431 - 446 :: REGRESS. :LAB. :HIPS :MAN.DEC.CHAR.

ANDERSON,MJ CIT: 0.38
SOME EVIDENCE ON THE EFFECT OF VERBALIZATION ON PROCESS: A METHODOLOGICAL NOTE
JAR AU 85 VOL: 23 PG:843 - 852 :: REGRESS. :LAB. :HIPS :METHOD.

ANDERSON,PF ; FIRS: MARTIN,JD ; THIR: KEOWN ,AJ CIT: 0
LEASE CAPITALIZATION AND STOCK PRICE STABILITY: IMPLICATIONS FOR ACCOUNTING
JAA WI 79 VOL: 2 PG:151 - 164 :: REGRESS. :PRIM. :EMH :LEASES

ANDERSON,U ; FIRS: ANDERSON,MJ ; THIR: HELLELOID,R ; FOUR: JOYCE ,E ; FIFT: SCHADEWALD,M CIT: 0
INTERNAL REVENUE SERVICE ACCESS TO TAX ACCRUAL WORKPAPERS: A LABORATORY INVESTIGATION
TAR OC 90 VOL: 65 PG:857 - 874 :: REGRESS. :LAB. :MATH.PROG. :AUD.

ANDERSON,U ; SEC: MARCHANT,G CIT: 0
THE AUDITOR'S ASSESSMENT OF COMPETENCE AND INTEGRITY OF AUDITEE PERSONNEL
AUD 89 VOL: 8 PG:101 - 115 :: REGRESS. :LAB. :HIPS :JUDG.

ANDERSON,U ; SEC: YOUNG ,RA CIT: 0
INTERNAL AUDIT PLANNING IN AN INTERACTIVE ENVIRONMENT
AUD AU 88 VOL: 08 PG:23 - 42 :: DES.STAT. :INT. LOG. :OTH.BEH. :TIM.

ANDREWS JR,WT ; FIRS: FRANCIS,JR ; THIR: SIMON ,DT CIT: 0
VOLUNTARY PEER REVIEWS, AUDIT QUALITY, AND PROPOSALS FOR MANDATORY PEER REVIEWS
JAA SU 90 VOL: 5 PG:369 - 378 :: REGRESS. :MIXED :OTH.STAT. :OPER.AUD.

ANDREWS,RW ; FIRS: GODFREY,JT CIT: 0.36
A FINITE POPULATION BAYESIAN MODEL FOR COMPLIANCE TESTING
JAR AU 82 VOL: 20 PG:304 - 315 :: ANAL. :INT. LOG. :OTH.STAT. :SAMP.

ANDREWS,VL ; FIRS: MEHTA ,DR CIT: 0
A NOTE ON INSTALLMENT REPORTING OF INCOME, PROFITABILITY, AND FUND FLOWS
JAR SP 68 VOL: 6 PG:50 - 57 :: DES.STAT. :SIM. :OTH.STAT. :TAXES

ANDREWS,WT ; FIRS: ROSE ,PS ; THIR: GIROUX,GA CIT: 0
PREDICTING BUSINESS FAILURE: A MACROECONOMIC PERSPECTIVE
JAA AU 82 VOL: 6 PG:20 - 31 :: REGRESS. :PRIM. :TIME SER. :BUS.FAIL.

ANELL ,B CIT: 0.13
EXERCISES IN ARBITRARINESS AND AMBIGUITY - A STUDY OF TWELVE COST BENEFIT ANALYSES OF INDUSTRIAL DISINVESTMENT DECISIONS
AOS 04 85 VOL: 10 PG:479 - 492 :: REGRESS. :PRIM. :THEORY :BUS.FAIL.

ANSARI,SL ; SEC: EUSKE ,KJ CIT: 1.17
RATIONAL, RATIONALIZING, AND REIFYING USES OF ACCOUNTING DATA IN ORGANIZATIONS

AOS 06 87 VOL: 12 PG:549 - 570 :: REGRESS. :SURV. :OTH.BEH. :COST.ALLOC.

ANSARI,SL ; SEC: MCDONOUGH,JJ CIT: 0.15
INTERSUBJECTIVITY - THE CHALLENGE AND OPPORTUNITY FOR ACCOUNTING
AOS 01 80 VOL: 5 PG:129 - 142 :: QUAL. :INT. LOG. :THEORY :N/A

ANSARI,SL CIT: 0.57
TOWARDS AN OPEN SYSTEMS APPROACH TO BUDGETING
AOS 03 79 VOL: 4 PG:149 - 162 :: QUAL. :INT. LOG. :OTH.BEH. :BUDG.& PLAN.

ANSARI,SL CIT: 0.88
AN INTEGRATED APPROACH TO CONTROL SYSTEM DESIGN
AOS 02 77 VOL: 2 PG:101 - 112 :: QUAL. :INT. LOG. :OTH. :N/A

ANSARI,SL CIT: 0.41
BEHAVIOURAL FACTORS IN VARIANCE CONTROL: REPORT ON A LABORATORY EXPERIMENT
JAR AU 76 VOL: 14 PG:189 - 211 :: ANOVA :LAB. :OTH.BEH. :VAR.

ANTAL ,AB ; FIRS: DIERKES,M CIT: 0.13
THE USEFULNESS AND USE OF SOCIAL REPORTING INFORMATION
AOS 01 85 VOL: 10 PG:29 - 34 :: DES.STAT. :INT. LOG. :OTH.BEH. :HRA

ANTHONY,JH ; SEC: RAMESH,K CIT: 1
ASSOCIATION BETWEEN ACCOUNTING PERFORMANCE MEASURES AND STOCK PRICES: A TEST OF THE LIFE CYCLE HYPOTHESIS
JAE JN 92 VOL: 15 PG:203 - 227 :: REGRESS. :PRIM. :EMH :FIN.METH.

ANTHONY,JH CIT: 0
THE EFFECT OF INFORMATION ANNOUNCEMENTS ON BID/ASK SPREADS IN THE CALL OPTIONS MARKET
CAR SP 87 VOL: 3 PG:460 - 475 :: REGRESS. :PRIM. :INF.ECO./AG. :FIN.METH.

ANTLE ,R ; SEC: DEMSKI,JS CIT: 0.5
CONTRACTING FRICTIONS, REGULATION, AND THE STRUCTURE OF CPA FIRMS
JAR ST 91 VOL: 29 PG:1 - 30 :: DES.STAT. :INT. LOG. :INF.ECO./AG. :ORG.

ANTLE ,R ; SEC: NALEBUFF,B CIT: 0.5
CONSERVATISM AND AUDITOR-CLIENT NEGOTIATIONS
JAR ST 91 VOL: 29 PG:31 - 59 :: DES.STAT. :INT. LOG. :INF.ECO./AG. :FIN.METH.

ANTLE ,R ; SEC: FELLINGHAM,J CIT: 0
RESOURCE RATIONING AND ORGANIZATIONAL SLACK IN A TWO-PERIOD MODEL
JAR SP 90 VOL: 28 PG:1 - 24 :: DES.STAT. :INT. LOG. :INF.ECO./AG. :EXEC.COMP.

ANTLE ,R ; SEC: DEMSKI,JS CIT: 0.75
REVENUE RECOGNITION
CAR SP 89 VOL: 5 PG:423 - 451 :: DES.STAT. :INT. LOG. :INF.ECO./AG. :REV.REC.

ANTLE ,R ; SEC: SMITH ,A CIT: 2.43
AN EMPIRICAL INVESTIGATION OF THE RELATIVE PERFORMANCE EVALUATION OF CORPORATE EXECUTIVES
JAR SP 86 VOL: 24 PG:1 - 39 :: REGRESS. :PRIM. :OTH.STAT. :EXEC.COMP.

ANTLE ,R ; SEC: SMITH ,A CIT: 1
MEASURING EXECUTIVE COMPENSATION: METHODS AND AN APPLICATION
JAR SP 85 VOL: 23 PG:296 - 325 :: REGRESS. :PRIM. :OTH.STAT. :EXEC.COMP.

ANTLE ,R CIT: 1
AUDITOR INDEPENDENCE
JAR SP 84 VOL: 22 PG:1 - 20 :: ANAL. :INT. LOG. :INF.ECO./AG. :INDEP.

ANTLE ,R CIT: 0.73
THE AUDITOR AS AN ECONOMIC AGENT
JAR AU 82 VOL: 20 PG:504 - 527 :: ANAL. :INT. LOG. :INF.ECO./AG. :AUD.BEH.

ANTON ,HR ; FIRS: BRIEF ,RP CIT: 0
AN INDEX OF GROWTH DUE TO DEPRECIATION
CAR SP 87 VOL: 3 PG:394 - 407 :: DES.STAT. :INT. LOG. :OTH.STAT. :PP&E / DEPR

ANTON ,HR CIT: 0.18
SOME ASPECTS OF MEASUREMENT AND ACCOUNTING
JAR SP 64 VOL: 2 PG:1 - 9 :: QUAL. :INT. LOG. :THEORY :N/A

APOSTOLOU,NG ; FIRS: ROBBINS,WA ; THIR: STRAWSER,RH CIT: 0
MUNICIPAL ANNUAL REPORTS AND THE INFORMATION NEEDS OF INVESTORS
JAA SU 85 VOL: 8 PG:279 - 292 :: REGRESS. :PRIM. :THEORY :FIN.METH.

APOSTOLOU,NG ; SEC: GIROUX,GA ; THIR: WELKER,RB CIT: 0
THE INFORMATION CONTENT OF MUNICIPAL SPENDING RATE DATA
JAR AU 85 VOL: 23 PG:853 - 858 :: REGRESS. :PRIM. :INSTIT. :LTD

ARANYA,N ; SEC: WHEELER,JT CIT: 0.14
ACCOUNTANTS' PERSONALITY TYPES AND THEIR COMMITMENT TO ORGANIZATION AND PROFESSION
CAR AU 86 VOL: 3 PG:184 - 199 :: REGRESS. :LAB. :OTH.BEH. :AUD.BEH.

ARANYA,N ; SEC: FERRIS,KR CIT: 0.78
A REEXAMINATION OF ACCOUNTANTS' ORGANIZATIONAL-PROFESSIONAL CONFLICT
TAR JA 84 VOL: 59 PG:1 - 15 :: ANOVA :SURV. :OTH.BEH. :PROF.RESP.

ARANYA,N ; SEC: LACHMAN,R ; THIR: AMERNIC,J CIT: 0.27
ACCOUNTANTS' JOB SATISFACTION: A PATH ANALYSIS
AOS 03 82 VOL: 7 PG:201 - 216 :: CORR. :SURV. :OTH.BEH. :N/A

ARANYA,N ; SEC: POLLOCK,J ; THIR: AMERNIC,J CIT: 0.25
AN EXAMINATION OF PROFESSIONAL COMMITMENT IN PUBLIC ACCOUNTING
AOS 04 81 VOL: 6 PG:271 - 280 :: MIXED :LAB. :OTH.BEH. :PROF.RESP.

ARCHIBALD,TR CIT: 0.88
STOCK MARKET REACTION TO THE DEPRECIATION SWITCH-BACK
TAR JA 72 VOL: 47 PG:22 - 30 :: REGRESS. :PRIM. :EMH :PP&E / DEPR

ARCHIBALD,TR CIT: 0.53
THE RETURN TO STRAIGHT-LINE DEPRECIATION: AN ANALYSIS OF A CHANGE IN ACCOUNTING METHOD
JAR ST 67 VOL: 5 PG:164 - 186 :: DES.STAT. :PRIM. :THEORY :PP&E / DEPR

ARCHIBALD,TR ; FIRS: SORTER,GH ; SEC: BECKER,S ; FOUR: BEAVER,WH CIT: 0.35
CORPORATE PERSONALITY AS REFLECTED IN ACCOUNTING DECISIONS: SOME PRELIMINARY FINDINGS
JAR AU 64 VOL: 2 PG:183 - 196 :: ANOVA :SURV. :THEORY :ORG.FORM

ARGYRIS,C CIT: 0
THE DILEMMA OF IMPLEMENTING CONTROLS: THE CASE OF MANAGERIAL ACCOUNTING
AOS 06 90 VOL: 15 PG:503 - 511 :: DES.STAT. :INT. LOG. :THEORY :MANAG.

ARGYRIS,C CIT: 1.06
ORGANIZATIONAL LEARNING AND MANAGEMENT INFORMATION SYSTEMS
AOS 02 77 VOL: 2 PG:113 - 124 :: QUAL. :INT. LOG. :OTH.BEH. :N/A

ARMSTRONG,P CIT: 0.5
CONTRADICTION AND SOCIAL DYNAMICS IN THE CAPITALIST AGENCY RELATIONSHIP
AOS 01 91 VOL: 16 PG:1 - 25 :: ANOVA :SEC. :INF.ECO./AG. :HRA

ARMSTRONG,P ; FIRS: HOPPER,T CIT: 0
COST ACCOUNTING, CONTROLLING LABOUR AND THE RISE OF CONGLOMERATES
AOS 05 91 VOL: 16 PG:405 - 438 :: ANOVA :SEC. :HIST. :MANAG.

ARMSTRONG,P CIT: 3.33
THE RISE OF ACCOUNTING CONTROLS IN BRITISH CAPITALIST ENTERPRISES
AOS 05 87 VOL: 12 PG:415 - 436 :: REGRESS. :INT. LOG. :HIST. :FIN.METH.

ARMSTRONG,P CIT: 1.5
CHANGING MANAGEMENT CONTROL STRATEGIES: THE ROLE OF COMPETITION BETWEEN ACCOUNTANCY AND OTHER ORGANIZATIONAL PROFESSIONS
AOS 02 85 VOL: 10 PG:129 - 148 :: REGRESS. :INT. LOG. :INSTIT. :ORG.& ENVIR.

ARNETT,HE CIT: 0
TAXABLE INCOME VS. FINANCIAL INCOME: HOW MUCH UNIFORMITY CAN WE STAND?
TAR JL 69 VOL: 44 PG:482 - 494 :: QUAL. :INT. LOG. :INSTIT. :FIN.METH.

ARNETT,HE CIT: 0.06
THE CONCEPT OF FAIRNESS
TAR AP 67 VOL: 42 PG:291 - 297 :: QUAL. :INT. LOG. :THEORY :OTH.FIN.ACC.

ARNETT,HE CIT: 0
APPLICATION OF THE CAPITAL GAINS AND LOSSES CONCEPT IN PRACTICE
TAR JA 65 VOL: 40 PG:54 - 64 :: DES.STAT. :PRIM. :THEORY :INFO.STRUC.

ARNETT,HE CIT: 0
RECOGNITION AS A FUNCTION OF MEASUREMENT IN THE REALIZATION CONCEPT
TAR OC 63 VOL: 38 PG:733 - 741 :: QUAL. :INT. LOG. :THEORY :VALUAT.(INFL.)

ARNOLD,DF ; SEC: PONEMON,LA CIT: 0
INTERNAL AUDITORS' PERCEPTIONS OF WHISTLE-BLOWING AND THE INFLUENCE OF MORAL REASONING: AN EXPERIMENT
AUD AU 91 VOL: 10 PG:1 - 15 :: REGRESS. :LAB. :HIPS :PROF.RESP.

ARNOLD,DF ; SEC: HUEFNER,RJ CIT: 0.06
MEASURING AND EVALUATING REPLACEMENT COSTS: AN APPLICATION
JAR AU 77 VOL: 15 PG:245 - 252 :: QUAL. :FIELD :THEORY :VALUAT.(INFL.)

ARNOLD,DF ; SEC: HUMANN,TE CIT: 0.06
EARNINGS PER SHARE: AN EMPIRICAL TEST OF THE MARKET PARITY AND THE INVESTMENT VALUE METHODS
TAR JA 73 VOL: 48 PG:23 - 33 :: NON-PAR. :PRIM. :OTH.STAT. :LTD

ARNOLD,PJ CIT: 0
ACCOUNTING AND THE STATE: CONSEQUENCES OF MERGER AND ACQUISITION ACCOUNTING IN THE U.S. HOSPITAL INDUSTRY
AOS 02 91 VOL: 16 PG:121 - 140 :: REGRESS. :PRIM. :OTH. :ORG.& ENVIR.

ARRINGTON,CE ; SEC: SCHWEIKER,W CIT: 0
THE RHETORIC AND RATIONALITY OF ACCOUNTING RESEARCH
AOS 06 92 VOL: 17 PG:511 - 533 :: REGRESS. :SEC. :OTH. :METHOD.

ARRINGTON,CE ; SEC: FRANCIS,JR CIT: 2.75
LETTING THE CHAT OUT OF THE BAG: DECONSTRUCTION, PRIVILEGE AND ACCOUNTING RESEARCH
AOS 02 89 VOL: 14 PG:1 - 28 :: DES.STAT. :SEC. :THEORY :METHOD.

ARRINGTON,CE ; FIRS: HASSELL,JM CIT: 0
A COMPARATIVE ANALYSIS OF THE CONSTRUCT VALIDITY OF COEFFICIENTS IN PARAMORPHIC MODELS OF ACCOUNTING JUDGMENTS: A REPLICATION AND EXTENSION
AOS 06 89 VOL: 14 PG:527 - 537 :: REGRESS. :LAB. :HIPS :JUDG.

ARRINGTON,CE ; SEC: BAILEY,CD ; THIR: HOPWOOD,WS CIT: 0.25
AN ATTRIBUTION ANALYSIS OF RESPONSIBILITY ASSESSMENT FOR AUDIT PERFORMANCE
JAR SP 85 VOL: 23 PG:1 - 20 :: REGRESS. :LAB. :OTH.BEH. :AUD.

ARRINGTON,CE ; SEC: HILLISON,WA ; THIR: JENSEN,RE CIT: 0.44
AN APPLICATION OF ANALYTICAL HIERARCHY PROCESS TO MODEL EXPERT JUDGMENTS ON ANALYTICAL REVIEW PROCEDURES
JAR SP 84 VOL: 22 PG:298 - 312 :: OTH.QUANT. :LAB. :HIPS :ANAL.REV.

ARTMAN,JT ; FIRS: LIBBY ,R ; THIR: WILLINGHAM,JJ CIT: 0.75
PROCESS SUSCEPTIBILITY, CONTROL RISK, AND AUDIT PLANNING
TAR AP 85 VOL: 60 PG:212 - 230 :: REGRESS. :LAB. :HIPS :INT.CONT.

ASARE ,SK CIT: 0
THE AUDITOR'S GOING-CONCERN DECISION: INTERACTION OF TASK VARIABLES AND THE SEQUENTIAL PROCESSING OF EVIDENCE
TAR AP 92 VOL: 67 PG:379 - 393 :: REGRESS. :FIELD :HIPS :AUD.BEH.

ASHMORE,M ; FIRS: PINCH ,T ; SEC: MULKAY,M CIT: 1
CLINICAL BUDGETING: EXPERIMENTATION IN THE SOCIAL SCIENCES: A DRAMA IN FIVE ACTS
AOS 03 89 VOL: 14 PG:271 - 301 :: REGRESS. :SURV. :OTH.BEH. :BUDG.& PLAN.

ASHTON,AH CIT: 1
EXPERIENCE AND ERROR FREQUENCY KNOWLEDGE AS POTENTIAL DETERMINANTS OF AUDIT EXPERTISE
TAR AP 91 VOL: 66 PG:218 - 239 :: ANOVA :LAB. :HIPS :AUD.BEH.

ASHTON,AH ; SEC: ASHTON,RH CIT: 2.4
SEQUENTIAL BELIEF REVISION IN AUDITING
TAR OC 88 VOL: 63 PG:623 - 641 :: REGRESS. :LAB. :HIPS :JUDG.

ASHTON,AH CIT: 1.25
DOES CONSENSUS IMPLY ACCURACY IN ACCOUNTING DECISION MAKING?
TAR AP 85 VOL: 60 PG:173 - 185 :: REGRESS. :LAB. :HIPS :FOREC.

ASHTON,AH CIT: 0.11
A FIELD TEST OF IMPLICATIONS OF LABORATORY STUDIES OF DECISION MAKING
TAR JL 84 VOL: 59 PG:361 - 375 :: REGRESS. :FIELD :HIPS :BUDG.& PLAN.

ASHTON,AH CIT: 0.27
THE DESCRIPTIVE VALIDITY OF NORMATIVE DECISION THEORY IN AUDITING CONTEXTS
JAR AU 82 VOL: 20 PG:415 - 428 :: ANOVA :LAB. :OTH.BEH. :METHOD.

ASHTON,RH CIT: 0.67
PRESSURE AND PERFORMANCE IN ACCOUNTING DECISION SETTINGS: PARADOXICAL EFFECTS OF INCENTIVES, FEEDBACK, AND JUSTIFICATION
JAR ST 90 VOL: 28 PG:148 - 186 :: REGRESS. :LAB. :HIPS :AUD.BEH.

ASHTON,RH ; SEC: GRAUL ,PR ; THIR: NEWTON,JD CIT: 0
AUDIT DELAY AND THE TIMELINESS OF CORPORATE REPORTING
CAR SP 89 VOL: 5 PG:657 - 673 :: REGRESS. :PRIM. :OTH.STAT. :TIM.

ASHTON,RH ; FIRS: WRIGHT,A CIT: 1
IDENTIFYING AUDIT ADJUSTMENTS WITH ATTENTION-DIRECTING PROCEDURES
TAR OC 89 VOL: 64 PG:710 - 728 :: DES.STAT. :SURV. :OTH.BEH. :ANAL.REV.

ASHTON,RH ; FIRS: ASHTON,AH CIT: 2.4
SEQUENTIAL BELIEF REVISION IN AUDITING
TAR OC 88 VOL: 63 PG:623 - 641 :: REGRESS. :LAB. :HIPS :JUDG.

ASHTON,RH ; SEC: WILLINGHAM,JJ ; THIR: ELLIOTT,RK CIT: 0.33
AN EMPIRICAL ANALYSIS OF AUDIT DELAY
JAR AU 87 VOL: 25 PG:275 - 292 :: REGRESS. :SURV. :INSTIT. :TIM.

ASHTON,RH ; FIRS: HYLAS ,RE CIT: 1.45
AUDIT DETECTION OF FINANCIAL STATEMENT ERRORS
TAR OC 82 VOL: 57 PG:751 - 765 :: DES.STAT. :FIELD :N/A :ERRORS

ASHTON,RH ; SEC: HYLAS ,RE CIT: 0
INCREASING CONFIRMATION RESPONSE RATES
AUD SU 81 VOL: 1 PG:12 - 22 :: ANOVA :FIELD :OTH. :CONF.

ASHTON,RH ; SEC: HYLAS ,RE CIT: 0
A STUDY OF THE RESPONSE TO BALANCE AND INVOICE CONFIRMATION REQUESTS
JAA SU 81 VOL: 4 PG:325 - 332 :: DES.STAT. :FIELD :OTH. :OPER.AUD.

ASHTON,RH CIT: 0.5
A DESCRIPTIVE STUDY OF INFORMATION EVALUATION
JAR SP 81 VOL: 19 PG:42 - 61 :: REGRESS. :LAB. :HIPS :MANAG.

ASHTON,RH ; FIRS: KESSLER,L CIT: 0.42
FEEDBACK AND PREDICTION ACHIEVEMENT IN FINANCIAL ANALYSIS
JAR SP 81 VOL: 19 PG:146 - 162 :: ANOVA :LAB. :HIPS :BUDG.& PLAN.

ASHTON,RH ; SEC: KRAMER,SS CIT: 1.85
STUDENTS AS SURROGATES IN BEHAVIOURAL ACCOUNTING RESEARCH: SOME EVIDENCE
JAR SP 80 VOL: 18 PG:1 - 15 :: NON-PAR. :LAB. :HIPS :METHOD.

ASHTON,RH ; SEC: BROWN ,PR CIT: 0.69
DESCRIPTIVE MODELING OF AUDITORS' INTERNAL CONTROL JUDGMENTS: REPLICATION AND EXTENSION
JAR SP 80 VOL: 18 PG:269 - 277 :: NON-PAR. :LAB. :HIPS :INT.CONT.

ASHTON,RH CIT: 0.25
OBJECTIVITY OF ACCOUNTING MEASURES: A MULTIRULE-MULTIMEASURER APPROACH
TAR JL 77 VOL: 52 PG:567 - 575 :: QUAL. :INT. LOG. :HIPS :OTH.FIN.ACC.

ASHTON,RH CIT: 0.29
DEVIATION-AMPLIFYING FEEDBACK AND UNINTENDED CONSEQUENCES OF MANAGEMENT ACCOUNTING SYSTEMS
AOS 04 76 VOL: 1 PG:289 - 300 :: QUAL. :INT. LOG. :OTH.BEH. :N/A

ASHTON,RH CIT: 1
COGNITIVE CHANGES INDUCED BY ACCOUNTING CHANGES: EXPERIMENTAL EVIDENCE ON THE FUNCTIONAL FIXATION HYPOTHESIS
JAR ST 76 VOL: 14 PG:1 - 17 :: NON-PAR. :LAB. :HIPS :MANAG.

ASHTON,RH CIT: 0.53
USER PREDICTION MODELS IN ACCOUNTING: AN ALTERNATIVE USE
TAR OC 75 VOL: 50 PG:710 - 722 :: QUAL. :SEC. :HIPS :BUDG.& PLAN.

ASHTON,RH CIT: 2.71
AN EXPERIMENTAL STUDY OF INTERNAL CONTROL JUDGMENTS
JAR SP 74 VOL: 12 PG:143 - 157 :: MIXED :LAB. :HIPS :INT.CONT.

ASHTON,RH CIT: 0.88
THE PREDICTIVE-ABILITY CRITERION AND USER PREDICTION MODELS
TAR OC 74 VOL: 49 PG:719 - 732 :: QUAL. :INT. LOG. :HIPS :FIN.METH.

ASKARI,H ; SEC: CAIN ,P ; THIR: SHAW ,R CIT: 0
A GOVERNMENT TAX SUBSIDY
TAR AP 76 VOL: 51 PG:331 - 334 :: DES.STAT. :PRIM. :N/A :TAX PLNG.

ASQUITH,P ; SEC: HEALY ,P ; THIR: PALEPU,K CIT: 0
EARNINGS AND STOCK SPLITS
TAR JL 89 VOL: 64 PG:387 - 403 :: REGRESS. :PRIM. :EMH :STK.DIV.

ATIASE,RK ; FIRS: AJINKYA,BB ; THIR: GIFT ,MJ CIT: 0
VOLUME OF TRADING AND THE DISPERSION OF FINANCIAL ANALYSTS' EARNINGS FORECASTS
TAR AP 91 VOL: 66 PG:389 - 401 :: REGRESS. :PRIM. :EMH :AUD.BEH.

ATIASE,RK ; SEC: BAMBER,LS ; THIR: TSE ,S CIT: 0.5
TIMELINESS OF FINANCIAL REPORTING, THE FIRM SIZE EFFECT, AND STOCK PRICE REACTIONS TO ANNUAL EARNINGS ANNOUNCEMENTS
CAR SP 89 VOL: 5 PG:526 - 552 :: REGRESS. :PRIM. :EMH :FIN.ST.TIM.

ATIASE,RK CIT: 0.83
MARKET IMPLICATIONS OF PREDISCLOSURE INFORMATION: SIZE AND EXCHANGE EFFECTS
JAR SP 87 VOL: 25 PG:168 - 176 :: REGRESS. :PRIM. :EMH :INFO.STRUC.

ATIASE,RK CIT: 4.88
PREDISCLOSURE INFORMATION, FIRM CAPITALIZATION, AND SECURITY PRICE BEHAVIOR AROUND EARNINGS ANNOUNCEMENTS
JAR SP 85 VOL: 23 PG:21 - 36 :: REGRESS. :PRIM. :EMH :FIN.METH.

ATKINSON,AA CIT: 0.43
INFORMATION INCENTIVES IN A STANDARD-SETTING MODEL OF CONTROL
JAR SP 79 VOL: 17 PG:1 - 22 :: ANAL. :INT. LOG. :INF.ECO./AG. :MANAG.

AUSTIN,KR ; FIRS: ROBBINS,WA CIT: 0.14
DISCLOSURE QUALITY IN GOVERNMENT FINANCIAL REPORTS: AN ASSESSMENT OF THE APPROPRIATENESS OF A COMPOUND MEASURE
JAR AU 86 VOL: 24 PG:412 - 421 :: REGRESS. :SURV. :THEORY :METHOD.

AWASTHI,V ; SEC: PRATT ,J CIT: 0.67
THE EFFECTS OF MONETARY INCENTIVES ON EFFORT AND DECISION PERFORMANCE: THE ROLE OF COGNITIVE CHARACTERISTICS
TAR OC 90 VOL: 65 PG:797 - 811 :: REGRESS. :LAB. :HIPS :DEC.AIDS

AYRES ,FL ; SEC: JACKSON,BR ; THIR: HITE ,PS CIT: 0.25
THE ECONOMIC BENEFITS OF REGULATION: EVIDENCE FROM PROFESSIONAL TAX PREPARERS
TAR AP 89 VOL: 64 PG:300 - 312 :: REGRESS. :FIELD :HIPS :TAXES

AYRES ,FL CIT: 1.43
CHARACTERISTICS OF FIRMS ELECTING EARLY ADOPTION OF SFAS 52
JAE JN 86 VOL: 8 PG:143 - 158 :: REGRESS. :PRIM. :OTH.STAT. :FOR.CUR.

AYRES ,FL CIT: 0
A COMMENT ON CORPORATE PREFERENCES FOR FOREIGN CURRENCY ACCOUNTING STANDARDS
JAR SP 86 VOL: 24 PG:166 - 169 :: REGRESS. :PRIM. :THEORY :FOR.CUR.

BABAD ,YM ; SEC: BALACHANDRAN,BV CIT: 0
OPERATIONAL MATRIX ACCOUNTING
CAR SP 89 VOL: 5 PG:775 - 792 :: DES.STAT. :INT. LOG. :MATH.PROG. :FIN.METH.

BABER ,WR ; SEC: FAIRFIELD,PM ; THIR: HAGGARD,JA CIT: 0
THE EFFECT OF CONCERN ABOUT REPORTED INCOME DISCRETIONARY SPENDING DECISIONS: THE CASE OF RESEARCH AND DEVELOPMENT
TAR OC 91 VOL: 66 PG:818 - 829 :: REGRESS. :PRIM. :INF.ECO./AG. :R & D

BABER ,WR ; SEC: BROOKS,EH ; THIR: RICKS ,WE CIT: 0.67
AN EMPIRICAL INVESTIGATION OF THE MARKET FOR AUDIT SERVICES IN THE PUBLIC SECTOR
JAR AU 87 VOL: 25 PG:293 - 305 :: REGRESS. :PRIM. :OTH.STAT. :ORG.

BABER ,WR CIT: 0
A FRAMEWORK FOR MAKING A CLASS OF INTERNAL ACCOUNTING CONTROL DECISIONS
JAR SP 85 VOL: 23 PG:360 - 369 :: REGRESS. :INT. LOG. :OTH.STAT. :INT.CONT.

BABER ,WR CIT: 0
BUDGET-BASED COMPENSATION AND DISCRETIONARY SPENDING
TAR JA 85 VOL: 60 PG:1 - 9 :: DES.STAT. :INT. LOG. :INF.ECO./AG. :BUDG.& PLAN.

BABER ,WR CIT: 0.5
TOWARD UNDERSTANDING THE ROLE OF AUDITING IN THE PUBLIC SECTOR
JAE DE 83 VOL: 5 PG:213 - 227 :: REGRESS. :INT. LOG. :OTH.STAT. :AUD.

BACHAR,J CIT: 0.25
AUDITING QUALITY, SIGNALING, AND UNDERWRITING CONTRACTS
CAR AU 89 VOL: 6 PG:216 - 241 :: DES.STAT. :INT. LOG. :INF.ECO./AG. :OPER.AUD.

BACHAR,J CIT: 0
OPTIMAL UNDERWRITING CONTRACTS AND UNDERPRICING OF NEW ISSUES
JAA AU 89 VOL: 4 PG:432 - 459 :: DES.STAT. :INT. LOG. :INF.ECO./AG. :VALUAT.(INFL.)

BACKER,M CIT: 0
COMMENTS ON THE VALUE OF THE SEC'S ACCOUNTING DISCLOSURE REQUIREMENTS
TAR JL 69 VOL: 44 PG:533 - 538 :: QUAL. :INT. LOG. :INSTIT. :INFO.STRUC.

BAGGETT,WD CIT: 0
INTERNAL CONTROL: INSIGHT FROM A GENERAL SYSTEMS THEORY PERSPECTIVE
JAA SP 83 VOL: 6 PG:227 - 233 :: QUAL. :INT. LOG. :OTH. :N/A

BAGINSKI,SP ; SEC: HASSELL,JM CIT: 0
THE MARKET INTERPRETATION OF MANAGEMENT EARNINGS FORECASTS AS A PREDICTOR OF SUBSEQUENT FINANCIAL ANALYST FORECAST REVISION
TAR JA 90 VOL: 65 PG:175 - 190 :: REGRESS. :PRIM. :EMH :FOREC.

BAGINSKI,SP CIT: 0.83
INTRAINDUSTRY INFORMATION TRANSFERS ASSOCIATED WITH MANAGEMENT FORECASTS OF EARNINGS
JAR AU 87 VOL: 25 PG:196 - 216 :: REGRESS. :PRIM. :OTH.STAT. :INV.

BAGLIONI,AJ ; FIRS: HASKINS,ME ; THIR: COOPER,CL CIT: 0.67
AN INVESTIGATION OF THE SOURCES, MODERATORS, AND PSYCHOLOGICAL SYMPTOMS OF STRESS AMONG AUDIT SENIORS
CAR SP 90 VOL: 6 PG:361 - 385 :: REGRESS. :LAB. :HIPS :AUD.BEH.

BAILEY JR,AD ; FIRS: KO ,CE ; SEC: NACHTSHEIM,CJ ; THIR: DUKE ,GL CIT: 0
ON THE ROBUSTNESS OF MODEL-BASED SAMPLING IN AUDITING
AUD SP 88 VOL: 07 PG:119 - 136 :: DES.STAT. :SIM. :OTH.STAT. :SAMP.

BAILEY JR,AD ; FIRS: DANOS ,P ; SEC: HOLT ,DL CIT: 0
THE INTERACTION OF SCIENCE AND ATTESTATION STANDARD FORMATION
AUD SP 87 VOL: 6 PG:134 - 149 :: DES.STAT. :INT. LOG. :THEORY :OPIN.

BAILEY JR,AD ; FIRS: MESERVY,RD ; THIR: JOHNSON,PE CIT: 0.57
INTERNAL CONTROL EVALUATION: A COMPUTATIONAL MODEL OF THE REVIEW PROCESS
AUD AU 86 VOL: 6 PG:44 - 74 :: DES.STAT. :LAB. :EXP.SYST. :INT.CONT.

BAILEY JR,AD ; SEC: DUKE ,GL ; THIR: GERLACH,JH ; FOUR: KO ,CE ; FIFT: MESERVY,RD ; SIX: WHINSTON,AB CIT: 0.38
TICOM AND THE ANALYSIS OF INTERNAL CONTROLS
TAR AP 85 VOL: 60 PG:186 - 201 :: CORR. :INT. LOG. :OTH. :INT.CONT.

BAILEY JR,AD ; FIRS: VASARHELYI,MA ; THIR: CAMARDESSE JR,JE ; FOUR: GROOMER,SM ; FIFT: LAMPE ,JC CIT: 0
THE USAGE OF COMPUTERS IN AUDITING TEACHING AND RESEARCH
AUD SP 84 VOL: 3 PG:98 - 103 :: QUAL. :SIM. :OTH. :EDP AUD.

BAILEY JR,AD ; FIRS: CASH JR,JI ; THIR: WHINSTON,AB CIT: 0.13
A SURVEY OF TECHNIQUES FOR AUDITING EDP-BASED ACCOUNTING INFORMATION SYSTEMS
TAR OC 77 VOL: 52 PG:813 - 832 :: QUAL. :SEC. :N/A :ANAL.REV.

BAILEY JR,AD ; SEC: BOE ,WJ CIT: 0.12
GOAL AND RESOURCE TRANSFERS IN THE MULTIGOAL ORGANIZATION
TAR JL 76 VOL: 51 PG:559 - 573 :: QUAL. :INT. LOG. :MATH.PROG. :TRANS.PRIC.

BAILEY JR,AD CIT: 0.06
A DYNAMIC PROGRAMMING APPROACH TO THE ANALYSIS OF DIFFERENT COSTING METHODS IN ACCOUNTING FOR INVENTORIES
TAR JL 73 VOL: 48 PG:560 - 574 :: ANAL. :INT. LOG. :MATH.PROG. :INV.

BAILEY JR,AD ; SEC: GRAY ,J CIT: 0
A STUDY OF THE IMPORTANCE OF THE PLANNING HORIZON ON REPORTS UTILIZING DISCOUNTED FUTURE CASH FLOWS
JAR SP 68 VOL: 6 PG:98 - 105 :: DES.STAT. :SIM. :N/A :CAP.BUDG.

BAILEY,AP ; SEC: MCAFEE,RP ; THIR: WHINSTON,AB CIT: 0.17
AN APPLICATION OF COMPLEXITY THEORY TO THE ANALYSIS OF INTERNAL CONTROL SYSTEMS
AUD SU 81 VOL: 1 PG:38 - 52 :: ANAL. :INT. LOG. :OTH.STAT. :INT.CONT.

BAILEY,CD ; SEC: MCINTYRE,EV CIT: 0
SOME EVIDENCE ON THE NATURE OF RELEARNING CURVES
TAR AP 92 VOL: 67 PG:368 - 378 :: REGRESS. :LAB. :HIPS :EDUC.

BAILEY,CD ; SEC: BALLARD,G CIT: 0
IMPROVING RESPONSE RATES TO ACCOUNTS RECEIVABLE CONFIRMATIONS: AN EXPERIMENT USING FOUR TECHNIQUES
AUD SP 86 VOL: 5 PG:77 - 85 :: REGRESS. :LAB. :OTH.BEH. :CONF.

BAILEY,CD ; FIRS: ARRINGTON,CE ; THIR: HOPWOOD,WS CIT: 0.25
AN ATTRIBUTION ANALYSIS OF RESPONSIBILITY ASSESSMENT FOR AUDIT PERFORMANCE
JAR SP 85 VOL: 23 PG:1 - 20 :: REGRESS. :LAB. :OTH.BEH. :AUD.

BAILEY,D CIT: 0
ACCOUNTING IN THE SHADOW OF STALINISM
AOS 06 90 VOL: 15 PG:513 - 525 :: REGRESS. :SEC. :HIST. :ORG.& ENVIR.

BAILEY,KE ; SEC: BYLINSKI,JH ; THIR: SHIELDS,MD CIT: 0
EFFECTS OF AUDIT REPORT WORDING CHANGES ON THE PERCEIVED MESSAGE
JAR AU 83 VOL: 21 PG:355 - 370 :: OTH.QUANT. :LAB. :OTH.BEH. :OPIN.

BAILEY,WT CIT: 0
THE EFFECTS OF AUDIT REPORTS ON CHARTERED FINANCIAL ANALYSTS' PERCEPTIONS OF THE SOURCES OF FINANCIAL STATEMENT AND AUDIT-REPORT
TAR OC 81 VOL: 56 PG:882 - 896 :: MIXED :LAB. :OTH.BEH. :OPIN.

BAIMAN,S ; SEC: EVANS III,JH ; THIR: NAGARAJAN,NJ CIT: 0.5
COLLUSION IN AUDITING
JAR SP 91 VOL: 29 PG:1 - 18 :: DES.STAT. :INT. LOG. :INF.ECO./AG. :AUD.BEH.

BAIMAN,S ; SEC: SIVARAMAKRISHNAN,K CIT: 0
THE VALUE OF PRIVATE PRE-DECISION INFORMATION IN A PRINCIPLE-AGENT CONTEXT
TAR OC 91 VOL: 66 PG:747 - 767 :: DES.STAT. :INT. LOG. :INF.ECO./AG. :MANAG.

BAIMAN,S CIT: 0.33
AGENCY RESEARCH IN MANAGERIAL ACCOUNTING: A SECOND LOOK
AOS 04 90 VOL: 15 PG:341 - 371 :: DES.STAT. :SEC. :INF.ECO./AG. :EXEC.COMP.

BAIMAN,S ; SEC: MAY ,JH ; THIR: MUKHERJI,A CIT: 0.33
OPTIMAL EMPLOYMENT CONTRACTS AND THE RETURNS TO MONITORING IN A PRINCIPAL-AGENT CONTEXT
CAR SP 90 VOL: 6 PG:761 - 799 :: DES.STAT. :INT. LOG. :INF.ECO./AG. :EXEC.COMP.

BAIMAN,S ; SEC: LEWIS ,BL CIT: 1.25
AN EXPERIMENT TESTING THE BEHAVIORAL EQUIVALENCE OF STRATEGICALLY EQUIVALENT CONTRACTS
JAR SP 89 VOL: 27 PG:1 - 20 :: REGRESS. :LAB. :HIPS :EXEC.COMP.

BAIMAN,S ; SEC: EVANS III,JH ; THIR: NOEL ,J CIT: 1.67
OPTIMAL CONTRACTS WITH A UTILITY-MAXIMIZING AUDITOR
JAR AU 87 VOL: 25 PG:217 - 244 :: ANAL. :INT. LOG. :INF.ECO./AG. :AUD.BEH.

BAIMAN,S ; SEC: NOEL ,J CIT: 0.75
NONCONTROLLABLE COSTS AND RESPONSIBILITY ACCOUNTING
JAR AU 85 VOL: 23 PG:486 - 501 :: ANAL. :INT. LOG. :INF.ECO./AG. :RESP.ACC.

BAIMAN,S ; SEC: EVANS III,JH CIT: 2.5
PRE-DECISION INFORMATION AND PARTICIPATIVE MANAGEMENT CONTROL SYSTEMS
JAR AU 83 VOL: 21 PG:371 - 395 :: ANAL. :INT. LOG. :INF.ECO./AG. :MANAG.

BAIMAN,S ; SEC: DEMSKI,JS CIT: 1.92
ECONOMICALLY OPTIMAL PERFORMANCE EVALUATION AND CONTROL SYSTEMS
JAR ST 80 VOL: 18 PG:184 - 220 :: ANAL. :INT. LOG. :OTH. :MANAG.

BAIMAN,S CIT: 0.53
THE EVALUATION AND CHOICE OF INTERNAL INFORMATION SYSTEMS WITHIN A MULTIPERSON WORLD
JAR SP 75 VOL: 13 PG:1 - 15 :: ANAL. :INT. LOG. :INF.ECO./AG. :INFO.STRUC.

BAINBRIDGE,DR CIT: 0
IS DOLLAR-VALUE LIFO CONSISTENT WITH AUTHORITATIVE GAAP?
JAA SU 84 VOL: 7 PG:334 - 346 :: ANAL. :INT. LOG. :THEORY :INV.

BAKER ,CR CIT: 0.08
LEASING AND THE SETTING OF ACCOUNTING STANDARDS: MAPPING THE LABYRINTH
JAA SP 80 VOL: 3 PG:197 - 206 :: QUAL. :INT. LOG. :INSTIT. :LEASES

BAKER ,CR CIT: 0.38
MANAGEMENT STRATEGY IN A LARGE ACCOUNTING FIRM
TAR JL 77 VOL: 52 PG:576 - 586 :: QUAL. :CASE :OTH.BEH. :AUD.BEH.

BAKER ,RE CIT: 0
INCOME OF LIFE INSURANCE COMPANIES
TAR JA 66 VOL: 41 PG:98 - 105 :: QUAL. :INT. LOG. :N/A :REV.REC.

BAKER ,RE CIT: 0
THE PENSION COST PROBLEM
TAR JA 64 VOL: 39 PG:52 - 61 :: QUAL. :INT. LOG. :THEORY :PENS.

BALACHANDRAN,BV ; SEC: PADMARAJ,RA CIT: 0
A GENERALIZED TRANSSHIPMENT MODEL FOR CASH MANAGEMENT
JAA WI 91 VOL: 6 PG:1 - 28 :: DES.STAT. :INT. LOG. :MATH.PROG. :COST.ALLOC.

BALACHANDRAN,BV ; FIRS: CHANDRA,R CIT: 1
A SYNTHESIS OF ALTERNATIVE TESTING PROCEDURES FOR EVENT STUDIES
CAR SP 90 VOL: 6 PG:611 - 640 :: DES.STAT. :SEC. :TIME SER. :METHOD.

BALACHANDRAN,BV ; FIRS: DYE ,RA ; THIR: MAGEE ,RP CIT: 1
CONTINGENT FEES FOR AUDIT FIRMS
JAR AU 90 VOL: 28 PG:239 - 266 :: DES.STAT. :INT. LOG. :INF.ECO./AG. :AUD.BEH.

BALACHANDRAN,BV ; FIRS: BABAD ,YM CIT: 0
OPERATIONAL MATRIX ACCOUNTING
CAR SP 89 VOL: 5 PG:775 - 792 :: DES.STAT. :INT. LOG. :MATH.PROG. :FIN.METH.

BALACHANDRAN,BV ; SEC: RAMANAN,R CIT: 0
OPTIMAL INTERNAL CONTROL STRATEGY UNDER DYNAMIC CONDITIONS
JAA WI 88 VOL: 03 PG:1 - 13 :: DES.STAT. :INT. LOG. :INF.ECO./AG. :INT.CONT.

BALACHANDRAN,BV ; SEC: LI ,L ; THIR: MAGEE ,RP CIT: 0.33
ON THE ALLOCATION OF FIXED AND VARIABLE COSTS FROM SERVICE DEPARTMENTS
CAR AU 87 VOL: 4 PG:164 - 185 :: DES.STAT. :INT. LOG. :INF.ECO./AG. :COST.ALLOC.

BALACHANDRAN,BV ; SEC: NAGARAJAN,NJ CIT: 0.5
IMPERFECT INFORMATION, INSURANCE, AND AUDITORS' LEGAL LIABILITY
CAR SP 87 VOL: 3 PG:281 - 301 :: DES.STAT. :INT. LOG. :INF.ECO./AG. :LIAB.

BALACHANDRAN,BV ; SEC: RAMAKRISHNAN,RT CIT: 0.33
A THEORY OF AUDIT PARTNERSHIPS: AUDIT FIRM SIZE AND FEES
JAR SP 87 VOL: 25 PG:111 - 126 :: DES.STAT. :INT. LOG. :INF.ECO./AG. :ORG.

BALACHANDRAN,BV CIT: 0
DISCUSSION OF: "AN ANALYSIS OF THE AUDITOR'S UNCERTAINTY ABOUT PROBABILITIES"
CAR SP 86 VOL: 2 PG:282 - 287 :: DES.STAT. :SEC. :HIPS :JUDG.

BALACHANDRAN,BV ; SEC: RAMAKRISHNAN,RT CIT: 0.08
JOINT COST ALLOCATION: A UNIFIED APPROACH
TAR JA 81 VOL: 56 PG:85 - 96 :: ANAL. :INT. LOG. :MATH.PROG. :COST.ALLOC.

BALACHANDRAN,BV ; SEC: ZOLTNERS,AA CIT: 0
AN INTERACTIVE AUDIT-STAFF SCHEDULING DECISION SUPPORT SYSTEM
TAR OC 81 VOL: 56 PG:801 - 812 :: ANAL. :INT. LOG. :OTH.STAT. :AUD.BEH.

BALACHANDRAN,BV ; SEC: RAMAKRISHNAN,RT CIT: 0.23
INTERNAL CONTROL AND EXTERNAL AUDITING FOR INCENTIVE COMPENSATION SCHEDULES
JAR ST 80 VOL: 18 PG:140 - 171 :: ANAL. :INT. LOG. :INF.ECO./AG. :AUD.

BALACHANDRAN,KR ; SEC: MACHMEYER,RA CIT: 0
ACCOUNTING FOR PRODUCT WEAR OUT COST
JAA WI 92 VOL: 7 PG:49 - 64 :: DES.STAT. :INT. LOG. :OTH.STAT. :REL.COSTS

BALACHANDRAN,KR ; FIRS: RONEN ,J CIT: 0.4
AN APPROACH TO TRANSFER PRICING UNDER UNCERTAINTY
JAR AU 88 VOL: 26 PG:300 - 314 :: ANAL. :INT. LOG. :INF.ECO./AG. :TRANS.PRIC.

BALACHANDRAN,KR ; SEC: SRINIDHI,BN CIT: 0
A RATIONALE FOR FIXED CHARGE APPLICATION
JAA SP 87 VOL: 2 PG:151 - 169 :: DES.STAT. :INT. LOG. :MATH.PROG. :COST.ALLOC.

BALACHANDRAN,KR ; SEC: STEUER,RE CIT: 0.09
AN INTERACTIVE MODEL FOR THE CPA FIRM AUDIT STAFF PLANNING PROBLEM WITH MULTIPLE OBJECTIVES
TAR JA 82 VOL: 57 PG:125 - 140 :: ANAL. :INT. LOG. :N/A :AUD.

BALACHANDRAN,KR ; SEC: MASCHMEYER,R ; THIR: LIVINGSTONE,JL CIT: 0.08
PRODUCT WARRANTY PERIOD: A MARKOVIAN APPROACH TO ESTIMATION AND ANALYSIS OF REPAIR AND REPLACEMENT COSTS
TAR JA 81 VOL: 56 PG:115 - 124 :: MARKOV :INT. LOG. :OTH.STAT. :SPEC.ITEMS

BALACHANDRAN,KR ; SEC: LIVINGSTONE,JL CIT: 0
COST AND EFFECTIVENESS OF PHYSICIAN PEER REVIEW IN REDUCING MEDICARE OVERUTILIZATION
AOS 02 77 VOL: 2 PG:153 - 164 :: DES.STAT. :PRIM. :OTH.STAT. :MANAG.

BALADOUNI,V CIT: 0.06
THE ACCOUNTING PERSPECTIVE RE-EXAMINED
TAR AP 66 VOL: 41 PG:215 - 225 :: QUAL. :INT. LOG. :INSTIT. :OTH.MANAG.

BALAKRISHNAN,R CIT: 0
THE VALUE OF COMMUNICATION IN RESOURCE ALLOCATION DECISIONS
CAR SP 92 VOL: 8 PG:353 - 373 :: DES.STAT. :INT. LOG. :INF.ECO./AG. :COST.ALLOC.

BALAKRISHNAN,R CIT: 0.5
INFORMATION ACQUISITION AND RESOURCE ALLOCATION DECISIONS
TAR JA 91 VOL: 66 PG:120 - 140 :: REGRESS. :INT. LOG. :INF.ECO./AG. :MAN.DEC.CHAR.

BALAKRISHNAN,R CIT: 0
THE ROLE OF BUDGETS AND VARIANCES IN REPEATED INVESTMENT DECISIONS
CAR AU 90 VOL: 7 PG:105 - 122 :: DES.STAT. :INT. LOG. :INF.ECO./AG. :VAR.

BALAKRISHNAN,R ; SEC: HARRIS,TS ; THIR: SEN ,PK CIT: 0
THE PREDICTIVE ABILITY OF GEOGRAPHIC SEGMENT DISCLOSURES
JAR AU 90 VOL: 28 PG:305 - 325 :: REGRESS. :PRIM. :TIME SER. :SEG.REP.

BALDWIN,BA CIT: 0.56
SEGMENT EARNINGS DISCLOSURE AND THE ABILITY OF SECURITY ANALYSTS TO FORECAST EARNINGS PER SHARE
TAR JL 84 VOL: 59 PG:376 - 389 :: OTH.QUANT. :PRIM. :OTH.STAT. :SEG.REP.

BALDWIN,J ; SEC: GLEZEN,GW CIT: 0
BANKRUPTCY PREDICTION USING QUARTERLY FINANCIAL STATEMENT DATA
JAA SU 92 VOL: 7 PG:269 - 285 :: REGRESS. :PRIM. :TIME SER. :BUS.FAIL.

BALL ,R CIT: 0
THE EARNINGS-PRICE ANOMALY
JAE JN 92 VOL: 15 PG:309 - 345 :: DES.STAT. :SEC. :EMH :FIN.METH.

BALL ,R ; SEC: KOTHARI,SP CIT: 1
SECURITY RETURNS AROUND EARNINGS ANNOUNCEMENTS
TAR OC 91 VOL: 66 PG:718 - 738 :: REGRESS. :PRIM. :EMH :FIN.ST.TIM.

BALL ,R ; SEC: FOSTER,G CIT: 2.82
CORPORATE FINANCIAL REPORTING: A METHODOLOGICAL REVIEW OF EMPIRICAL RESEARCH
JAR ST 82 VOL: 20 PG:161 - 234 :: MIXED :SEC. :OTH. :FIN.METH.

BALL ,R ; SEC: LEV ,B ; THIR: WATTS ,RL CIT: 0.24
INCOME VARIATION AND BALANCE SHEET COMPOSITIONS
JAR SP 76 VOL: 14 PG:1 - 9 :: REGRESS. :PRIM. :OTH.STAT. :REV.REC.

BALL ,R CIT: 2.29
CHANGES IN ACCOUNTING TECHNIQUES AND STOCK PRICES
JAR ST 72 VOL: 10 PG:1 - 38 :: REGRESS. :PRIM. :EMH :ACC.CHNG.

BALL ,R CIT: 0.12
INDEX OF EMPIRICAL RESEARCH IN ACCOUNTING
JAR SP 71 VOL: 9 PG:1 - 31 :: QUAL. :SEC. :OTH. :METHOD.

BALL ,R ; SEC: BROWN ,P CIT: 8.35
AN EMPIRICAL EVALUATION OF ACCOUNTING INCOME NUMBERS
JAR AU 68 VOL: 6 PG:159 - 178 :: NON-PAR. :PRIM. :EMH :FIN.METH.

BALL ,R ; FIRS: BROWN ,P CIT: 0.94
SOME PRELIMINARY FINDINGS ON THE ASSOCIATION BETWEEN THE EARNINGS OF A FIRM, ITS INDUSTRY, AND THE ECONOMY
JAR ST 67 VOL: 5 PG:55 - 77 :: CORR. :PRIM. :EMH :REV.REC.

BALLARD,G ; FIRS: BAILEY,CD CIT: 0
IMPROVING RESPONSE RATES TO ACCOUNTS RECEIVABLE CONFIRMATIONS: AN EXPERIMENT USING FOUR TECHNIQUES
AUD SP 86 VOL: 5 PG:77 - 85 :: REGRESS. :LAB. :OTH.BEH. :CONF.

BALLEW,V ; FIRS: SPICER,BH CIT: 0.9
MANAGEMENT ACCOUNTING SYSTEMS AND THE ECONOMICS OF INTERNAL ORGANIZATION
AOS 01 83 VOL: 8 PG:73 - 98 :: QUAL. :INT. LOG. :THEORY :MANAG.

BALLEW,V CIT: 0.27
TECHNOLOGICAL ROUTINENESS AND INTRA-UNIT STRUCTURE IN CPA FIRMS
TAR JA 82 VOL: 57 PG:88 - 104 :: REGRESS. :LAB. :OTH.STAT. :ORG.

BALOFF,N ; SEC: KENNELLY,JW CIT: 0.18
ACCOUNTING IMPLICATIONS OF PRODUCT AND PROCESS START-UPS
JAR AU 67 VOL: 5 PG:131 - 143 :: REGRESS. :CASE :TIME SER. :COST.ALLOC.

BALVERS,RJ ; SEC: MCDONALD,B ; THIR: MILLER,RE CIT: 0.8
UNDERPRICING OF NEW ISSUES AND THE CHOICE OF AUDITOR AS A SIGNAL OF INVESTMENT BANKER REPUTATION
TAR OC 88 VOL: 63 PG:605 - 622 :: REGRESS. :PRIM. :MATH.PROG. :AUD.THEOR.

BAMBER,EM ; SEC: SNOWBALL,D ; THIR: TUBBS ,RM CIT: 0.5
AUDIT STRUCTURE AND ITS RELATION TO ROLE CONFLICT AND ROLE AMBIGUITY: AN EMPIRICAL INVESTIGATION
TAR AP 89 VOL: 64 PG:285 - 299 :: REGRESS. :FIELD :HIPS :AUD.

BAMBER,EM ; SEC: BAMBER,LS ; THIR: BYLINSKI,JH CIT: 0
A DESCRIPTIVE STUDY OF AUDIT MANAGERS' WORKING PAPER REVIEW
AUD SP 88 VOL: 07 PG:137 - 149 :: REGRESS. :LAB. :HIPS :AUD.BEH.

BAMBER,EM ; SEC: SNOWBALL,D CIT: 0
AN EXPERIMENTAL STUDY OF THE EFFECTS OF AUDIT STRUCTURE IN UNCERTAIN TASK ENVIRONMENTS
AUD JL 88 VOL: 63 PG:490 - 504 :: REGRESS. :LAB. :OTH.BEH. :JUDG.

BAMBER,EM ; SEC: BYLINSKI,JH CIT: 0
THE EFFECTS OF THE PLANNING MEMORANDUM, TIME PRESSURE AND INDIVIDUAL AUDITOR CHARACTERISTICS ON AUDIT MANAGERS' REVIEW TIME JUDGMENTS
CAR AU 87 VOL: 4 PG:127 - 143 :: REGRESS. :LAB. :HIPS :JUDG.

BAMBER,EM CIT: 0.2
EXPERT JUDGMENT IN THE AUDIT TEAM: A SOURCE RELIABILITY APPROACH
JAR AU 83 VOL: 21 PG:396 - 412 :: ANOVA :LAB. :HIPS :JUDG.

BAMBER,LS ; FIRS: ATIASE,RK ; THIR: TSE ,S CIT: 0.5
TIMELINESS OF FINANCIAL REPORTING, THE FIRM SIZE EFFECT, AND STOCK PRICE REACTIONS TO ANNUAL EARNINGS ANNOUNCEMENTS
CAR SP 89 VOL: 5 PG:526 - 552 :: REGRESS. :PRIM. :EMH :FIN.ST.TIM.

BAMBER,LS ; FIRS: BAMBER,EM ; THIR: BYLINSKI,JH CIT: 0
A DESCRIPTIVE STUDY OF AUDIT MANAGERS' WORKING PAPER REVIEW
AUD SP 88 VOL: 07 PG:137 - 149 :: REGRESS. :LAB. :HIPS :AUD.BEH.

BAMBER,LS CIT: 1.5
UNEXPECTED EARNINGS, FIRM SIZE, AND TRADING VOLUME AROUND QUARTERLY EARNINGS ANNOUNCEMENTS
TAR JL 87 VOL: 62 PG:510 - 532 :: REGRESS. :PRIM. :EMH :FIN.METH.

BAMBER,LS CIT: 1.71
THE INFORMATION CONTENT OF ANNUAL EARNINGS RELEASES: A TRADING VOLUME APPROACH
JAR SP 86 VOL: 24 PG:40 - 56 :: REGRESS. :PRIM. :EMH :FIN.METH.

BANBURY,J ; SEC: NAHAPIET,JE CIT: 0.86
TOWARDS A FRAMEWORK FOR THE STUDY OF THE ANTECEDENTS AND CONSEQUENCES OF INFORMATION SYSTEMS IN ORGANIZATIONS
AOS 03 79 VOL: 4 PG:163 - 178 :: QUAL. :INT. LOG. :OTH. :N/A

BANKER,RD ; SEC: DATAR ,SM CIT: 1
OPTIMAL TRANSFER PRICING UNDER POSTCONTRACT INFORMATION
CAR SP 92 VOL: 8 PG:329 - 352 :: DES.STAT. :INT. LOG. :INF.ECO./AG. :TRANS.PRIC.

BANKER,RD CIT: 1
SELECTION OF EFFICIENCY EVALUATION MODELS
CAR AU 92 VOL: 9 PG:343 - 354 :: DES.STAT. :INT. LOG. :MATH.PROG. :MANAG.

BANKER,RD ; SEC: COOPER,WW ; THIR: POTTER,G CIT: 0
A PERSPECTIVE ON RESEARCH IN GOVERNMENTAL ACCOUNTING
TAR JL 92 VOL: 67 PG:496 - 510 :: REGRESS. :SEC. :THEORY :N/A

BANKER,RD ; SEC: DATAR ,SM ; THIR: MAZUR ,MJ CIT: 0
TESTING THE OPTIMALITY OF A PERCENTAGE EVALUATION MEASURE FOR A GAIN SHARING CONTRACT
CAR SP 90 VOL: 6 PG:809 - 824 :: DES.STAT. :INT. LOG. :INF.ECO./AG. :EXEC.COMP.

BANKER,RD ; FIRS: AMERSHI,AH ; THIR: DATAR ,SM CIT: 0
ECONOMIC SUFFICIENCY AND STATISTICAL SUFFICIENCY IN THE AGGREGATION OF ACCOUNTING SIGNALS
TAR JA 90 VOL: 65 PG:113 - 130 :: DES.STAT. :INT. LOG. :INF.ECO./AG. :MANAG.

BANKER,RD ; SEC: DATAR ,SM ; THIR: KAPLAN,RS CIT: 0
PRODUCTIVITY MEASUREMENT AND MANAGEMENT ACCOUNTING
JAA AU 89 VOL: 4 PG:528 - 554 :: DES.STAT. :CASE :OTH.STAT. :REL.COSTS

BANKER,RD ; SEC: DATAR ,SM CIT: 1
SENSITIVITY, PRECISION, AND LINEAR AGGREGATION OF SIGNALS FOR PERFORMANCE EVALUATION
JAR SP 89 VOL: 27 PG:21 - 39 :: DES.STAT. :INT. LOG. :INF.ECO./AG. :EXEC.COMP.

BANKER,RD ; SEC: DATAR ,SM ; THIR: MAINDIRATTA,A CIT: 0.4
UNOBSERVABLE OUTCOMES AND MULTIATTRIBUTE PREFERENCES IN THE EVALUATION OF MANAGERIAL PERFORMANCE
CAR AU 88 VOL: 5 PG:96 - 124 :: DES.STAT. :INT. LOG. :INF.ECO./AG. :EXEC.COMP.

BANKER,RD ; SEC: DATAR ,SM ; THIR: KEKRE ,S CIT: 0
RELEVANT COSTS, CONGESTION AND STOCHASTICITY IN PRODUCTION ENVIRONMENTS
JAE JL 88 VOL: 10 PG:171 - 197 :: DES.STAT. :INT. LOG. :OTH.STAT. :REL.COSTS

BANKER,RD ; SEC: DATAR ,SM ; THIR: RAJAN ,MV CIT: 0.33
MEASUREMENT OF PRODUCTIVITY IMPROVEMENTS: AN EMPIRICAL ANALYSIS
JAA AU 87 VOL: 2 PG:319 - 347 :: DES.STAT. :FIELD :OTH.STAT. :MANAG.

BANKS ,DW ; SEC: KINNEY JR,WR CIT: 0.55
LOSS CONTINGENCY REPORTS AND STOCK PRICES: AN EMPIRICAL STUDY
JAR SP 82 VOL: 20 PG:240 - 254 :: REGRESS. :PRIM. :EMH :SPEC.ITEMS

BAO ,BE ; SEC: BAO ,DA CIT: 0
LIFO ADOPTION: A TECHNOLOGY DIFFUSION ANALYSIS
AOS 04 89 VOL: 14 PG:303 - 319 :: REGRESS. :PRIM. :OTH.STAT. :INV.

BAO ,BE ; SEC: BAO ,DA ; THIR: VASARHELYI,MA CIT: 0
A STOCHASTIC MODEL OF PROFESSIONAL ACCOUNTANT TURNOVER
AOS 03 86 VOL: 11 PG:289 - 296 :: DES.STAT. :PRIM. :OTH.BEH. :ORG.

BAO ,DA ; FIRS: BAO ,BE CIT: 0
LIFO ADOPTION: A TECHNOLOGY DIFFUSION ANALYSIS
AOS 04 89 VOL: 14 PG:303 - 319 :: REGRESS. :PRIM. :OTH.STAT. :INV.

BAO ,DA ; FIRS: BAO ,BE ; THIR: VASARHELYI,MA CIT: 0
A STOCHASTIC MODEL OF PROFESSIONAL ACCOUNTANT TURNOVER
AOS 03 86 VOL: 11 PG:289 - 296 :: DES.STAT. :PRIM. :OTH.BEH. :ORG.

BAR-YOSEF,S ; SEC: SEN ,PK CIT: 0
ON OPTIMAL CHOICE OF INVENTORY ACCOUNTING METHOD
TAR AP 92 VOL: 67 PG:320 - 336 :: DES.STAT. :INT. LOG. :INF.ECO./AG. :INV.

BAR-YOSEF,S ; FIRS: AHARONY,J CIT: 0.33
TESTS OF THE IMPACT OF LIFO ADOPTION ON STOCKHOLDERS: A STOCHASTIC DOMINANCE APPROACH
CAR SP 87 VOL: 3 PG:430 - 444 :: REGRESS. :PRIM. :EMH :INV.

BARAN ,A ; SEC: LAKONISHOK,J ; THIR: OFER ,AR CIT: 0.15
THE INFORMATION CONTENT OF GENERAL PRICE LEVEL ADJUSTED EARNINGS: SOME EMPIRICAL EVIDENCE
TAR JA 80 VOL: 55 PG:22 - 35 :: REGRESS. :PRIM. :HIPS :VALUAT.(INFL.)

BAREFIELD,RM CIT: 0.88
THE EFFECT OF AGGREGATION ON DECISION MAKING SUCCESS: A LABORATORY STUDY
JAR AU 72 VOL: 10 PG:229 - 242 :: ANOVA :LAB. :HIPS :INFO.STRUC.

BAREFIELD,RM ; SEC: COMISKEY,EE CIT: 0.24
THE SMOOTHING HYPOTHESIS: AN ALTERNATIVE TEST
TAR AP 72 VOL: 47 PG:291 - 298 :: NON-PAR. :PRIM. :TIME SER. :FIN.METH.

BAREFIELD,RM ; SEC: COMISKEY,EE CIT: 0.18
DEPRECIATION POLICY AND THE BEHAVIOR OF CORPORATE PROFITS
JAR AU 71 VOL: 9 PG:351 - 358 :: NON-PAR. :PRIM. :TIME SER. :PP&E / DEPR

BAREFIELD,RM CIT: 0.12
A MODEL OF FORECAST BIASING BEHAVIOR
TAR JL 70 VOL: 45 PG:490 - 501 :: ANAL. :INT. LOG. :MATH.PROG. :FOREC.

BARENBAUM,L ; FIRS: MONAHAN,TF CIT: 0
THE USE OF CONSTANT DOLLAR INFORMATION TO PREDICT BOND RATING CHANGES
JAA SU 83 VOL: 6 PG:325 - 340 :: OTH.QUANT. :PRIM. :OTH.STAT. :VALUAT.(INFL.)

BARIFF,ML ; SEC: GALBRAITH,JR CIT: 0.67
INTRAORGANIZATIONAL POWER CONSIDERATIONS FOR DESIGNING INFORMATION SYSTEMS
AOS 01 78 VOL: 3 PG:15 - 28 :: QUAL. :INT. LOG. :OTH.BEH. :ORG.FORM

BARKMAN,A CIT: 0
WITHIN-ITEM VARIATION: A STOCHASTIC APPROACH TO AUDIT UNCERTAINTY
TAR JA 77 VOL: 52 PG:450 - 464 :: DES.STAT. :SIM. :OTH.STAT. :RISK

BARLEV,B ; SEC: FRIED ,D ; THIR: LIVNAT,J CIT: 0
ECONOMIC AND FINANCIAL REPORTING EFFECTS OF INVENTORY TAX ALLOWANCES
CAR SP 86 VOL: 2 PG:288 - 310 :: REGRESS. :INT. LOG. :MATH.PROG. :INV.

BARLEV,B CIT: 0
CONTINGENT EQUITY AND THE DILUTIVE EFFECT ON EPS
TAR AP 83 VOL: 58 PG:385 - 393 :: ANAL. :INT. LOG. :OTH. :FIN.METH.

BARLEV,B ; SEC: LEVY ,H CIT: 0.07
ON THE VARIABILITY OF ACCOUNTING INCOME NUMBERS
JAR AU 79 VOL: 17 PG:305 - 315 :: DES.STAT. :PRIM. :TIME SER. :FIN.METH.

BARLEV,B ; FIRS: GOLDMAN,A CIT: 0.35
THE AUDITOR-FIRM CONFLICT OF INTERESTS: ITS IMPLICATIONS FOR INDEPENDENCE
TAR OC 74 VOL: 49 PG:707 - 718 :: QUAL. :INT. LOG. :INSTIT. :INDEP.

BARLEV,B ; SEC: LIVNAT,J CIT: 0
THE INFORMATION CONTENT OF FUNDS STATEMENT RATIOS
JAA SU 90 VOL: 5 PG:411 - 433 :: REGRESS. :PRIM. :TIME SER. :OTH.FIN.ACC.

BARLOW,HA ; FIRS: ALY ,IM ; THIR: JONES ,RW CIT: 0
THE USEFULNESS OF SFAS NO. 82 INFORMATION IN DISCRIMINATING BUSINESS FAILURE: AN EMPIRICAL STUDY
JAA SP 92 VOL: 7 PG:217 - 230 :: REGRESS. :PRIM. :OTH.STAT. :BUS.FAIL.

BARNEA,A ; FIRS: ADAR ,Z ; THIR: LEV ,B CIT: 0.19
A COMPREHENSIVE COST-VOLUME-PROFIT ANALYSIS UNDER UNCERTAINTY
TAR JA 77 VOL: 52 PG:137 - 149 :: QUAL. :INT. LOG. :THEORY :TAXES

BARNEA,A ; SEC: RONEN ,J ; THIR: SADAN ,S CIT: 0.29
CLASSIFICATORY SMOOTHING OF INCOME WITH EXTRAORDINARY ITEMS
TAR JA 76 VOL: 51 PG:110 - 122 :: REGRESS. :PRIM. :TIME SER. :INFO.STRUC.

BARNEA,A ; SEC: RONEN ,J ; THIR: SADAN ,S CIT: 0.24
THE IMPLEMENTATION OF ACCOUNTING OBJECTIVES: AN APPLICATION TO EXTRAORDINARY ITEMS
TAR JA 75 VOL: 50 PG:58 - 68 :: ANAL. :INT. LOG. :THEORY :SPEC.ITEMS

BARNES,P ; SEC: WEBB ,J CIT: 0.43
MANAGEMENT INFORMATION CHANGES AND FUNCTIONAL FIXATION: SOME EXPERIMENTAL EVIDENCE FROM THE PUBLIC SECTOR
AOS 01 86 VOL: 11 PG:1 - 18 :: REGRESS. :LAB. :HIPS :COST.ALLOC.

BARNISEL,TS ; FIRS: SPENCER,CH CIT: 0
A DECADE OF PRICE-LEVEL CHANGES - THE EFFECT ON THE FINANCIAL STATEMENTS OF CUMMINS ENGINE COMPANY
TAR JA 65 VOL: 40 PG:144 - 153 :: DES.STAT. :CASE :THEORY :VALUAT.(INFL.)

BARNIV,R CIT: 0
ACCOUNTING PROCEDURES, MARKET DATA, CASH-FLOW FIGURES, AND INSOLVENCY CLASSIFICATION: THE CASE OF THE INSURANCE INDUSTRY
TAR JL 90 VOL: 65 PG:578 - 605 :: DES.STAT. :FIELD :MATH.PROG. :BUS.FAIL.

BARON ,CD ; FIRS: KING ,RR CIT: 0.06
AN INTEGRATED ACCOUNT STRUCTURE FOR GOVERNMENTAL ACCOUNTING AND FINANCIAL REPORTING
TAR JA 74 VOL: 49 PG:76 - 87 :: QUAL. :INT. LOG. :THEORY :FIN.METH.

BARRETT,ME CIT: 0.24
FINANCIAL REPORTING PRACTICES: DISCLOSURE AND COMPREHENSIVENESS IN AN INTERNATIONAL SETTING
JAR SP 76 VOL: 14 PG:10 - 26 :: DES.STAT. :PRIM. :THEORY :INT.DIFF.

BARRETT,ME CIT: 0.29
ACCOUNTING FOR INTERCORPORATE INVESTMENTS: A BEHAVIOR FIELD STUDY
JAR ST 71 VOL: 9 PG:50 - 65 :: NON-PAR. :LAB. :OTH.BEH. :N/A

BARRETT,WB CIT: 0
A FUNCTIONAL APPROACH TO ACCOUNTING
TAR JA 68 VOL: 43 PG:105 - 112 :: QUAL. :INT. LOG. :THEORY :FIN.METH.

BARRON,FH ; FIRS: EMERY ,DR ; THIR: MESSIER JR,WF CIT: 0.09
CONJOINT MEASUREMENT AND THE ANALYSIS OF NOISY DATA: A COMMENT
JAR AU 82 VOL: 20 PG:450 - 458 :: NON-PAR. :SIM. :HIPS :METHOD.

BARRON,FH ; FIRS: MORIARITY,S CIT: 0.57
A JUDGMENT-BASED DEFINITION OF MATERIALITY
JAR ST 79 VOL: 17 PG:114 - 135 :: OTH.QUANT. :LAB. :OTH.STAT. :MAT.

BARRON,FH ; FIRS: MORIARITY,S CIT: 0.88
MODELING THE MATERIALITY JUDGMENTS OF AUDIT PARTNERS
JAR AU 76 VOL: 14 PG:320 - 341 :: MIXED :LAB. :OTH.BEH. :MAT.

BARTCZAK,N ; FIRS: CASEY JR,CJ CIT: 0.13
USING OPERATING CASH FLOW DATA TO PREDICT FINANCIAL DISTRESS: SOME EXTENSIONS
JAR SP 85 VOL: 23 PG:384 - 401 :: REGRESS. :PRIM. :MATH.PROG. :BUS.FAIL.

BARTH ,ME ; SEC: BEAVER,WH ; THIR: LANDSMAN,WR CIT: 0
THE MARKET VALUATION IMPLICATIONS OF NET PERIODIC PENSION COST COMPONENTS
JAE MR 92 VOL: 15 PG:27 - 61 :: REGRESS. :PRIM. :EMH :PENS.

BARTH ,ME ; SEC: BEAVER,WH ; THIR: STINSON,CH CIT: 1
SUPPLEMENTAL DATA AND THE STRUCTURE OF THRIFT SHARE PRICES
TAR JA 91 VOL: 66 PG:56 - 66 :: REGRESS. :PRIM. :TIME SER. :FIN.METH.

BARTH ,ME CIT: 0
RELATIVE MEASUREMENT ERRORS AMONG ALTERNATIVE PENSION ASSET AND LIABILITY MEASURES
TAR JL 91 VOL: 66 PG:516 - 534 :: REGRESS. :PRIM. :THEORY :PENS.

BARTLETT,RW ; FIRS: SEILER,RE CIT: 0.18
PERSONALITY VARIABLES AS PREDICTORS OF BUDGET SYSTEM CHARACTERISTICS
AOS 04 82 VOL: 7 PG:381 - 404 :: OTH.QUANT. :SURV. :OTH.BEH. :BUDG.& PLAN.

BARTON,AD CIT: 0.24
EXPECTATIONS AND ACHIEVEMENTS IN INCOME THEORY
TAR OC 74 VOL: 49 PG:664 - 681 :: QUAL. :INT. LOG. :THEORY :VALUAT.(INFL.)

BARTON,RF CIT: 0
AN EXPERIMENTAL STUDY ON THE IMPACT OF COMPETITIVE PRESSURES ON OVERHEAD ALLOCATION BIDS
JAR SP 69 VOL: 7 PG:116 - 122 :: DES.STAT. :LAB. :OTH.BEH. :OVER.ALLOC.

BARTOV,E CIT: 0
PATTERNS IN UNEXPECTED EARNINGS AS AN EXPLANATION FOR POST-ANNOUNCEMENT DRIFT
TAR JL 92 VOL: 67 PG:610 - 622 :: REGRESS. :PRIM. :EMH :TIM.

BARTOV,E CIT: 1.5
OPEN-MARKET STOCK REPURCHASES AS SIGNALS FOR EARNINGS AND RISK CHANGES
JAE SE 91 VOL: 14 PG:275 - 293 :: REGRESS. :PRIM. :EMH :BUS.COMB.

BASI ,BA ; SEC: CAREY ,KJ ; THIR: TWARK ,RD CIT: 0.82
A COMPARISON OF THE ACCURACY OF CORPORATE AND SECURITY ANALYSTS' FORECASTS
TAR AP 76 VOL: 51 PG:244 - 254 :: ANOVA :PRIM. :TIME SER. :FOREC.

BASKIN,EF ; FIRS: BOATSMAN,JR CIT: 0.17
ASSET VALUATION WITH INCOMPLETE MARKETS
TAR JA 81 VOL: 56 PG:38 - 53 :: ANAL. :INT. LOG. :EMH :FIN.METH.

BASKIN,EF ; FIRS: DAVIS ,DW ; SEC: BOATSMAN,JR CIT: 0.07
ON GENERALIZING STOCK MARKET RESEARCH TO A BROADER CLASS OF MARKETS
TAR JA 78 VOL: 53 PG:1 - 10 :: MIXED :PRIM. :EMH :FIN.METH.

BASKIN,EF CIT: 0.41
THE COMMUNICATIVE EFFECTIVENESS OF CONSISTENCY EXCEPTIONS
TAR JA 72 VOL: 47 PG:38 - 51 :: MIXED :PRIM. :EMH :ACC.CHNG.

BASTABLE,CW ; SEC: BEAMS ,FA CIT: 0
CASH FLOWS AND CASH COWS
JAA SP 81 VOL: 4 PG:248 - 254 :: ANAL. :INT. LOG. :OTH. :DEC.AIDS

BASU ,S CIT: 0.2
THE EFFECT OF EARNINGS YIELD ON ASSESSMENTS OF THE ASSOCIATION BETWEEN ANNUAL ACCOUNTING INCOME NUMBERS AND SECURITY PRICES
TAR JL 78 VOL: 53 PG:599 - 625 :: ANOVA :PRIM. :EMH :FIN.METH.

BATHKE,AW ; SEC: LOREK ,KS ; THIR: WILLINGER,GL CIT: 0
FIRM-SIZE AND THE PREDICTIVE ABILITY OF QUARTERLY EARNINGS DATA
TAR JA 89 VOL: 64 PG:49 - 68 :: REGRESS. :PRIM. :TIME SER. :INT.REP.

BATHKE,AW ; FIRS: LOREK ,KS CIT: 0.11
A TIME-SERIES ANALYSIS OF NONSEASONAL QUARTERLY EARNINGS DATA
JAR SP 84 VOL: 22 PG:369 - 379 :: CORR. :PRIM. :TIME SER. :FOREC.

BATHKE,AW ; SEC: LOREK ,KS CIT: 0.56
THE RELATIONSHIP BETWEEN TIME-SERIES MODELS AND THE SECURITY MARKET'S EXPECTATION OF QUARTERLY EARNINGS
TAR AP 84 VOL: 59 PG:163 - 176 :: REGRESS. :PRIM. :TIME SER. :FOREC.

BATTISTEL,GP ; FIRS: GAVER ,JJ ; SEC: GAVER ,KM CIT: 0
THE STOCK MARKET REACTION TO PERFORMANCE PLAN ADOPTIONS
TAR JA 92 VOL: 67 PG:172 - 182 :: REGRESS. :PRIM. :EMH :EXEC.COMP.

BAUMLER,JV ; FIRS: JIAMBALVO,J ; SEC: WATSON,DJ CIT: 0.6
AN EXAMINATION OF PERFORMANCE EVALUATION DECISIONS IN CPA FIRM SUBUNITS
AOS 01 83 VOL: 8 PG:13 - 30 :: REGRESS. :LAB. :OTH.BEH. :ORG.

BAUMLER,JV ; FIRS: WATSON,DJ CIT: 0.65
TRANSFER PRICING: A BEHAVIOURAL CONTEXT
TAR JL 75 VOL: 50 PG:466 - 474 :: QUAL. :INT. LOG. :OTH.BEH. :TRANS.PRIC.

BAUMOL,WJ CIT: 0
QUALITY CHANGES AND PRODUCTIVITY MEASUREMENT: HEDONICS AND AN ALTERNATIVE
JAA WI 90 VOL: 5 PG:105 - 117 :: DES.STAT. :INT. LOG. :OTH. :OTH.MANAG.

BAVISHI,VB ; FIRS: HUSSEIN,ME ; THIR: GANGOLLY,JS CIT: 0
INTERNATIONAL SIMILARITIES AND DIFFERENCES IN THE AUDITOR'S REPORT
AUD AU 86 VOL: 6 PG:124 - 133 :: DES.STAT. :PRIM. :INSTIT. :INT.DIFF.

BAXTER,WT ; SEC: CARRIER,NH CIT: 0.06
DEPRECIATION, REPLACEMENT PRICE, AND COST OF CAPITAL
JAR AU 71 VOL: 9 PG:189 - 214 :: ANAL. :INT. LOG. :THEORY :VALUAT.(INFL.)

BAZERMAN,MH ; FIRS: MURNIGHAN,JK CIT: 0
A PERSPECTIVE ON NEGOTIATION RESEARCH IN ACCOUNTING AND AUDITING
TAR JL 90 VOL: 65 PG:642 - 657 :: DES.STAT. :SEC. :OTH.BEH. :MANAG.

BEACH ,LR ; SEC: FREDERICKSON,JR CIT: 0
IMAGE THEORY: AN ALTERNATIVE DESCRIPTION OF AUDIT DECISIONS
AOS 02 89 VOL: 14 PG:101 - 112 :: DES.STAT. :SEC. :HIPS :METHOD.

BEAMS ,FA ; FIRS: BASTABLE,CW CIT: 0
CASH FLOWS AND CASH COWS
JAA SP 81 VOL: 4 PG:248 - 254 :: ANAL. :INT. LOG. :OTH. :DEC.AIDS

BEAMS ,FA CIT: 0
INDICATIONS OF PRAGMATISM AND EMPIRICISM IN ACCOUNTING THOUGHT
TAR AP 69 VOL: 44 PG:382 - 388 :: QUAL. :INT. LOG. :THEORY :FIN.METH.

BEATTY,RP ; SEC: HAND ,JRM CIT: 0
THE CAUSES AND EFFECTS OF MANDATED ACCOUNTING STANDARDS: SFAS NO. 94 AS A TEST OF THE LEVEL PLAYING FIELD THEORY
JAA AU 92 VOL: 7 PG:509 - 530 :: REGRESS. :PRIM. :EMH :FASB SUBM.

BEATTY,RP ; SEC: VERRECCHIA,RE CIT: 0
THE EFFECT OF A MANDATED ACCOUNTING CHANGE ON THE CAPITALIZATION PROCESS
CAR SP 89 VOL: 5 PG:472 - 493 :: REGRESS. :PRIM. :TIME SER. :R & D

BEATTY,RP CIT: 0.5
AUDITOR REPUTATION AND THE PRICING OF INITIAL PUBLIC OFFERINGS
TAR OC 89 VOL: 64 PG:693 - 709 :: REGRESS. :PRIM. :INSTIT. :AUD.BEH.

BEATTY,RP ; SEC: JOHNSON,SB CIT: 0
A MARKET-BASED METHOD OF CLASSIFYING CONVERTIBLE SECURITIES
JAA WI 85 VOL: 8 PG:112 - 124 :: REGRESS. :PRIM. :EMH :LTD

BEAULIEU,P ; FIRS: PRATT ,J CIT: 0
ORGANIZATIONAL CULTURE IN PUBLIC ACCOUNTING: SIZE, TECHNOLOGY, RANK, AND FUNCTIONAL AREA
AOS 92 VOL: 17 PG:667 - 684 :: REGRESS. :SURV. :OTH.BEH. :ORG.

BEAVER,WH ; FIRS: BARTH ,ME ; THIR: LANDSMAN,WR CIT: 0
THE MARKET VALUATION IMPLICATIONS OF NET PERIODIC PENSION COST COMPONENTS
JAE MR 92 VOL: 15 PG:27 - 61 :: REGRESS. :PRIM. :EMH :PENS.

BEAVER,WH ; FIRS: BARTH ,ME ; THIR: STINSON,CH CIT: 1
SUPPLEMENTAL DATA AND THE STRUCTURE OF THRIFT SHARE PRICES
TAR JA 91 VOL: 66 PG:56 - 66 :: REGRESS. :PRIM. :TIME SER. :FIN.METH.

BEAVER,WH ; SEC: EGER ,C ; THIR: RYAN ,S ; FOUR: WOLFSON,M CIT: 1
FINANCIAL REPORTING, SUPPLEMENTAL DISCLOSURES, AND BANK SHARE PRICES
JAR AU 89 VOL: 27 PG:157 - 178 :: REGRESS. :PRIM. :OTH.STAT. :INFO.STRUC.

BEAVER,WH ; SEC: LAMBERT,RA ; THIR: RYAN ,SG CIT: 3.33
THE INFORMATION CONTENT OF SECURITY PRICES: A SECOND LOOK
JAE JL 87 VOL: 9 PG:139 - 157 :: REGRESS. :PRIM. :EMH :FOREC.

BEAVER,WH CIT: 0.67
THE PROPERTIES OF SEQUENTIAL REGRESSIONS WITH MULTIPLE EXPLANATORY VARIABLES
TAR JA 87 VOL: 62 PG:137 - 144 :: DES.STAT. :INT. LOG. :EMH :METHOD.

BEAVER,WH ; SEC: GRIFFIN,PA ; THIR: LANDSMAN,WR CIT: 0
TESTING FOR INCREMENTAL INFORMATION CONTENT IN THE PRESENCE OF COLLINEARITY :A COMMENT
JAE DE 84 VOL: 6 PG:219 - 223 :: QUAL. :INT. LOG. :OTH.STAT. :METHOD.

BEAVER,WH ; SEC: GRIFFIN,PA ; THIR: LANDSMAN,WR CIT: 2.55
THE INCREMENTAL INFORMATION CONTENT OF REPLACEMENT COST EARNINGS
JAE JL 82 VOL: 4 PG:15 - 39 :: MIXED :PRIM. :EMH :VALUAT.(INFL.)

BEAVER,WH ; SEC: WOLFSON,MA CIT: 0.09
FOREIGN CURRENCY TRANSLATION AND CHANGING PRICES IN PERFECT AND COMPLETE MARKETS
JAR AU 82 VOL: 20 PG:528 - 550 :: ANAL. :INT. LOG. :OTH.STAT. :VALUAT.(INFL.)

BEAVER,WH ; SEC: LANDSMAN,WR CIT: 0
NOTE ON THE BEHAVIOR OF RESIDUAL SECURITY RETURNS FOR WINNER AND LOSER PORTFOLIOS
JAE DE 81 VOL: 3 PG:233 - 241 :: DES.STAT. :PRIM. :EMH :N/A

BEAVER,WH CIT: 1.08
ECONOMETRIC PROPERTIES OF ALTERNATIVE SECURITY RETURN METHODS
JAR SP 81 VOL: 19 PG:163 - 184 :: ANAL. :INT. LOG. :EMH :METHOD.

BEAVER,WH CIT: 0.33
MARKET EFFICIENCY
TAR JA 81 VOL: 56 PG:23 - 37 :: ANAL. :INT. LOG. :EMH :FIN.METH.

BEAVER,WH ; SEC: LAMBERT,RA ; THIR: MORSE ,D CIT: 4.31
THE INFORMATION CONTENT OF SECURITY PRICES
JAE MR 80 VOL: 2 PG:3 - 28 :: REGRESS. :PRIM. :EMH :FOREC.

BEAVER,WH ; SEC: CHRISTIE,AA ; THIR: GRIFFIN,PA CIT: 1.62
THE INFORMATION CONTENT OF SEC ACCOUNTING SERIES RELEASE NO.190
JAE AG 80 VOL: 2 PG:127 - 157 :: REGRESS. :PRIM. :EMH :VALUAT.(INFL.)

BEAVER,WH ; SEC: CLARKE,R ; THIR: WRIGHT,WF CIT: 4.93
THE ASSOCIATION BETWEEN UNSYSTEMATIC SECURITY RETURNS AND THE MAGNITUDE OF EARNINGS FORECAST ERRORS
JAR AU 79 VOL: 17 PG:316 - 340 :: NON-PAR. :PRIM. :EMH :FIN.METH.

BEAVER,WH ; SEC: DEMSKI,JS CIT: 1.5
THE NATURE OF INCOME MEASUREMENT
TAR JA 79 VOL: 54 PG:38 - 46 :: QUAL. :INT. LOG. :INF.ECO./AG. :OTH.FIN.ACC.

BEAVER,WH ; SEC: DUKES ,RE CIT: 0.12
DELTA-DEPRECIATION METHODS: SOME ANALYTICAL RESULTS
JAR AU 74 VOL: 12 PG:205 - 215 :: ANAL. :INT. LOG. :OTH.STAT. :PP&E / DEPR

BEAVER,WH ; SEC: DEMSKI,JS CIT: 0.71
THE NATURE OF FINANCIAL ACCOUNTING OBJECTIVES: A SUMMARY AND SYNTHESIS
JAR ST 74 VOL: 12 PG:170 - 187 :: ANAL. :SEC. :THEORY :FIN.METH.

BEAVER,WH ; SEC: DUKES ,RE CIT: 0.71
INTERPERIOD TAX ALLOCATION AND DELTA-DEPRECIATION METHODS: SOME EMPIRICAL RESULTS
TAR JL 73 VOL: 48 PG:549 - 559 :: REGRESS. :PRIM. :EMH :PP&E / DEPR

BEAVER,WH ; SEC: DUKES ,RE CIT: 1.59
INTERPERIOD TAX ALLOCATION, EARNINGS EXPECTATIONS, AND THE BEHAVIOR OF SECURITY PRICES
TAR AP 72 VOL: 47 PG:320 - 332 :: REGRESS. :PRIM. :EMH :PP&E / DEPR

BEAVER,WH CIT: 1.35
THE TIME SERIES BEHAVIOR OF EARNINGS
JAR ST 70 VOL: 8 PG:62 - 99 :: MIXED :PRIM. :TIME SER. :FIN.METH.

BEAVER,WH ; FIRS: ROSE ,R ; THIR: BECKER,S ; FOUR: SORTER,GH CIT: 0.65
TOWARD AN EMPIRICAL MEASURE OF MATERIALITY
JAR ST 70 VOL: 8 PG:138 - 148 :: DES.STAT. :LAB. :OTH.BEH. :MAT.

BEAVER,WH ; SEC: KETTLER,P ; THIR: SCHOLES,M CIT: 1.82
THE ASSOCIATION BETWEEN MARKET DETERMINED AND ACCOUNTING DETERMINED RISK MEA
TAR OC 70 VOL: 45 PG:654 - 682 :: REGRESS. :PRIM. :TIME SER. :FIN.METH.

BEAVER,WH CIT: 0.41
MARKET PRICES, FINANCIAL RATIOS, AND THE PREDICTION OF FAILURE
JAR AU 68 VOL: 6 PG:179 - 192 :: DES.STAT. :PRIM. :TIME SER. :BUS.FAIL.

BEAVER,WH CIT: 5.35
THE INFORMATION CONTENT OF ANNUAL EARNINGS ANNOUNCEMENTS
JAR ST 68 VOL: 6 PG:67 - 92 :: REGRESS. :PRIM. :EMH :FIN.METH.

BEAVER,WH CIT: 0.53
ALTERNATIVE ACCOUNTING MEASURES AS PREDICTORS OF FAILURE
TAR JA 68 VOL: 43 PG:113 - 122 :: DES.STAT. :PRIM. :N/A :BUS.FAIL.

BEAVER,WH ; SEC: KENNELLY,JW ; THIR: VOSS ,WM CIT: 0.94
PREDICTIVE ABILITY AS A CRITERION FOR THE EVALUATION OF ACCOUNTING DATA
TAR OC 68 VOL: 43 PG:675 - 683 :: QUAL. :INT. LOG. :THEORY :FIN.METH.

BEAVER,WH CIT: 1.24
FINANCIAL RATIOS AS PREDICTORS OF FAILURE
JAR ST 66 VOL: 4 PG:71 - 111 :: DES.STAT. :PRIM. :OTH.STAT. :BUS.FAIL.

BEAVER,WH ; FIRS: SORTER,GH ; SEC: BECKER,S ; THIR: ARCHIBALD,TR CIT: 0.35
CORPORATE PERSONALITY AS REFLECTED IN ACCOUNTING DECISIONS: SOME PRELIMINARY FINDINGS
JAR AU 64 VOL: 2 PG:183 - 196 :: ANOVA :SURV. :THEORY :ORG.FORM

BECK ,PJ ; SEC: DAVIS ,JS ; THIR: JUNG ,W-O CIT: 0
EXPERIMENTAL EVIDENCE ON AN ECONOMIC MODEL OF TAXPAYER AGGRESSION UNDER STRATEGIC AND NON-STRATEGIC AUDITS
CAR AU 92 VOL: 9 PG:86 - 112 :: REGRESS. :LAB. :OTH.BEH. :TAXES

BECK ,PJ ; SEC: DAVIS ,JS ; THIR: JUNG ,W CIT: 0.5
EXPERIMENTAL EVIDENCE ON TAXPAYER REPORTING UNDER UNCERTAINTY
TAR JL 91 VOL: 66 PG:535 - 558 :: REGRESS. :LAB. :INF.ECO./AG. :TAX PLNG.

BECK ,PJ ; SEC: JUNG ,W CIT: 0.5
TAXPAYERS' REPORTING DECISIONS AND AUDITING UNDER INFORMATION ASYMMETRY
TAR JL 89 VOL: 64 PG:468 - 487 :: REGRESS. :INT. LOG. :INF.ECO./AG. :TAXES

BECK ,PJ ; SEC: SOLOMON,I CIT: 0.38
EX POST SAMPLING RISKS AND DECISION RULE CHOICE IN SUBSTANTIVE TESTING
AUD SP 85 VOL: 4 PG:1 - 10 :: DES.STAT. :INT. LOG. :OTH.STAT. :SAMP.

BECK ,PJ ; SEC: SOLOMON,I ; THIR: TOMASSINI,LA CIT: 0.38
SUBJECTIVE PRIOR PROBABILITY DISTRIBUTIONS AND AUDIT RISK
JAR SP 85 VOL: 23 PG:37 - 56 :: REGRESS. :INT. LOG. :OTH.BEH. :RISK

BECK ,PJ CIT: 0.15
A CRITICAL ANALYSIS OF THE REGRESSION ESTIMATOR IN AUDIT SAMPLING
JAR SP 80 VOL: 18 PG:16 - 37 :: MIXED :SIM. :OTH.STAT. :METHOD.

BECKER,S ; SEC: RONEN ,J ; THIR: SORTER,GH CIT: 0.35
OPPORTUNITY COSTS - AN EXPERIMENTAL APPROACH
JAR AU 74 VOL: 12 PG:317 - 329 :: ANOVA :LAB. :OTH.BEH. :REL.COSTS

BECKER,S ; FIRS: ROSE ,R ; SEC: BEAVER,WH ; FOUR: SORTER,GH CIT: 0.65
TOWARD AN EMPIRICAL MEASURE OF MATERIALITY
JAR ST 70 VOL: 8 PG:138 - 148 :: DES.STAT. :LAB. :OTH.BEH. :MAT.

BECKER,S ; FIRS: SORTER,GH ; THIR: ARCHIBALD,TR ; FOUR: BEAVER,WH CIT: 0.35
CORPORATE PERSONALITY AS REFLECTED IN ACCOUNTING DECISIONS: SOME PRELIMINARY FINDINGS
JAR AU 64 VOL: 2 PG:183 - 196 :: ANOVA :SURV. :THEORY :ORG.FORM

BEDARD,JC ; SEC: BIGGS ,SF CIT: 0
THE EFFECT OF DOMAIN-SPECIFIC EXPERIENCE ON EVALUATION OF MANAGEMENT REPRESENTATIONS IN ANALYTICAL PROCEDURES
AUD 91 VOL: 10 PG:77 - 90 :: REGRESS. :LAB. :HIPS :ANAL.REV.

BEDARD,JC ; SEC: BIGGS ,SF CIT: 0.5
PATTERN RECOGNITION, HYPOTHESES GENERATION, AND AUDITOR PERFORMANCE IN AN ANALYTICAL TASK
TAR JL 91 VOL: 66 PG:622 - 642 :: REGRESS. :LAB. :HIPS :ERRORS

BEDARD,JC CIT: 1.25
EXPERTISE IN AUDITING: MYTH OR REALITY?
AOS 02 89 VOL: 14 PG:113 - 131 :: REGRESS. :SEC. :HIPS :AUD.BEH.

BEDARD,JC CIT: 0
AN ARCHIVAL INVESTIGATION OF AUDIT PROGRAM PLANNING
AUD AU 89 VOL: 9 PG:57 - 71 :: REGRESS. :SURV. :THEORY :PLAN.

BEDFORD,NM ; SEC: ZIEGLER,RE CIT: 0.06
THE CONTRIBUTIONS OF A.C. LITTLETON TO ACCOUNTING THOUGHT AND PRACTICE
TAR JL 75 VOL: 50 PG:435 - 443 :: QUAL. :SEC. :THEORY :FIN.METH.

BEDFORD,NM ; SEC: MCKEOWN,JC CIT: 0
COMPARATIVE ANALYSIS OF NET REALIZABLE VALUE AND REPLACEMENT COSTING
TAR AP 72 VOL: 47 PG:333 - 338 :: QUAL. :INT. LOG. :THEORY :VALUAT.(INFL.)

BEDFORD,NM ; FIRS: LEE ,LC CIT: 0
AN INFORMATION THEORY ANALYSIS OF THE ACCOUNTING PROCESS
TAR AP 69 VOL: 44 PG:256 - 275 :: ANAL. :INT. LOG. :INF.ECO./AG. :OTH.MANAG.

BEDFORD,NM ; SEC: IINO ,T CIT: 0.06
CONSISTENCY REEXAMINED
TAR JL 68 VOL: 43 PG:453 - 458 :: QUAL. :INT. LOG. :THEORY :OTH.FIN.ACC.

BEDFORD,NM CIT: 0
THE NATURE OF FUTURE ACCOUNTING THEORY
TAR JA 67 VOL: 42 PG:82 - 85 :: QUAL. :INT. LOG. :THEORY :FIN.METH.

BEECHY,TH CIT: 0
QUASI-DEBT ANALYSIS OF FINANCIAL LEASES
TAR AP 69 VOL: 44 PG:375 - 381 :: QUAL. :INT. LOG. :N/A :LEASES

BEEDLES,W ; FIRS: SMITH ,DB ; SEC: STETTLER,HF CIT: 0.22
AN INVESTIGATION OF THE INFORMATION CONTENT OF FOREIGN SENSITIVE PAYMENT DISCLOSURES
JAE AG 84 VOL: 6 PG:153 - 162 :: REGRESS. :PRIM. :EMH :N/A

BEGLEY,J CIT: 0.67
DEBT COVENANTS AND ACCOUNTING CHOICE
JAE JA 90 VOL: 12 PG:125 - 139 :: DES.STAT. :SEC. :THEORY :FIN.METH.

BEIDLEMAN,CR CIT: 0.53
INCOME SMOOTHING: THE ROLE OF MANAGEMENT
TAR OC 73 VOL: 48 PG:653 - 667 :: REGRESS. :PRIM. :TIME SER. :FIN.METH.

BEJA ,A ; SEC: AHARONI,Y CIT: 0
SOME ASPECTS OF CONVENTIONAL ACCOUNTING PROFITS IN AN INFLATIONARY ENVIRONMENT
JAR AU 77 VOL: 15 PG:169 - 178 :: ANAL. :INT. LOG. :THEORY :VALUAT.(INFL.)

BELKAOUI,A CIT: 0
SLACK BUDGETING, INFORMATION DISTORTION AND SELF-ESTEEM
CAR AU 85 VOL: 2 PG:111 - 123 :: REGRESS. :LAB. :HIPS :BUDG.& PLAN.

BELKAOUI,A CIT: 0.08
THE RELATIONSHIP BETWEEN SELF-DISCLOSURE STYLE AND ATTITUDES TO RESPONSIBILITY ACCOUNTING
AOS 04 81 VOL: 6 PG:281 - 290 :: OTH.QUANT. :SURV. :OTH.BEH. :RESP.ACC.

BELKAOUI,A CIT: 0.31
THE IMPACT OF SOCIO-ECONOMIC ACCOUNTING STATEMENTS ON THE INVESTMENT DECISION: AN EMPIRICAL STUDY
AOS 03 80 VOL: 5 PG:263 - 284 :: ANOVA :LAB. :OTH.BEH. :HRA

BELKAOUI,A CIT: 0.31
THE INTERPROFESSIONAL LINGUISTIC COMMUNICATION OF ACCOUNTING CONCEPTS: AN EXPERIMENT IN SOCIO LINGUISTICS
JAR AU 80 VOL: 18 PG:362 - 374 :: REGRESS. :SURV. :OTH.BEH. :FIN.METH.

BELKAOUI,A CIT: 0.47
LINGUISTIC RELATIVITY IN ACCOUNTING
AOS 02 78 VOL: 3 PG:97 - 104 :: QUAL. :INT. LOG. :OTH. :N/A

BELL ,J ; FIRS: LEWIS ,BL CIT: 0
DECISIONS INVOLVING SEQUENTIAL EVENTS: REPLICATIONS AND EXTENSIONS
JAR SP 85 VOL: 23 PG:228 - 239 :: REGRESS. :LAB. :HIPS :INFO.STRUC.

BELL ,PW CIT: 0
ACCOUNTING AS A DISCIPLINE FOR STUDY AND PRACTICE: 1986
CAR SP 87 VOL: 3 PG:338 - 367 :: DES.STAT. :INT. LOG. :THEORY :METHOD.

BELL ,TB ; SEC: TABOR ,RH CIT: 0
EMPIRICAL ANALYSIS OF AUDIT UNCERTAINTY QUALIFICATIONS
JAR AU 91 VOL: 29 PG:350 - 370 :: REGRESS. :PRIM. :OTH.STAT. :OPIN.

BELL ,TB ; FIRS: MCKEE ,AJ ; THIR: BOATSMAN,JR CIT: 0.56
MANAGEMENT PREFERENCES OVER ACCOUNTING STANDARDS: A REPLICATION AND ADDITIONAL TESTS
TAR OC 84 VOL: 59 PG:647 - 659 :: OTH.QUANT. :PRIM. :INSTIT. :FASB SUBM.

BELL ,TB CIT: 0.6
MARKET REACTION TO RESERVE RECOGNITION ACCOUNTING
JAR SP 83 VOL: 21 PG:1 - 17 :: REGRESS. :PRIM. :EMH :OIL & GAS

BENBASAT,I ; SEC: DEXTER,AS CIT: 0.18
INDIVIDUAL DIFFERENCES IN THE USE OF DECISION SUPPORT AIDS
JAR SP 82 VOL: 20 PG:1 - 11 :: ANOVA :LAB. :HIPS :DEC.AIDS

BENBASAT,I ; SEC: DEXTER,AS CIT: 0.93
VALUE AND EVENTS APPROACHES TO ACCOUNTING: AN EXPERIMENTAL EVALUATION
TAR OC 79 VOL: 54 PG:735 - 749 :: ANOVA :LAB. :HIPS :INFO.STRUC.

BENISHAY,H CIT: 0
THE PRATT-ARROW REQUIREMENT IN A FOURTH DEGREE POLYNOMIAL UTILITY FUNCTION
JAA WI 92 VOL: 7 PG:97 - 112 :: DES.STAT. :INT. LOG. :INF.ECO./AG. :METHOD.

BENISHAY,H CIT: 0
A FORTH-DEGREE POLYNOMIAL UTILITY FUNCTION AND ITS IMPLICATIONS FOR INVESTORS' RESPONSES TOWARD FOUR MOMENTS OF THE WEALTH DISTRIBUTION
JAA SU 87 VOL: 2 PG:203 - 238 :: DES.STAT. :INT. LOG. :INF.ECO./AG. :METHOD.

BENISHAY,H CIT: 0.12
MANAGERIAL CONTROLS OF ACCOUNTS RECEIVABLE: A DETERMINISTIC APPROACH
JAR SP 65 VOL: 3 PG:114 - 132 :: ANAL. :INT. LOG. :THEORY :OTH.C/A

BENJAMIN,JJ ; SEC: GROSSMAN,SD ; THIR: WIGGIN,CE CIT: 0
THE IMPACT OF FOREIGN CURRENCY TRANSLATION ON REPORTING DURING THE PHASE-IN OF SFAS NO.52
JAA SU 86 VOL: 1 PG:177 - 184 :: REGRESS. :PRIM. :THEORY :FOR.CUR.

BENKE ,RL ; SEC: RHODE ,JG CIT: 0.31
THE JOB SATISFACTION OF HIGHER LEVEL EMPLOYEES IN LARGE CERTIFIED PUBLIC ACCOUNTING FIRMS
AOS 02 80 VOL: 5 PG:187 - 202 :: OTH.QUANT. :SURV. :OTH.BEH. :ORG.

BENNINGER,LJ CIT: 0
ACCOUNTING THEORY AND COST ACCOUNTING
TAR JL 65 VOL: 40 PG:547 - 557 :: QUAL. :INT. LOG. :THEORY :MANAG.

BENSON,ED ; SEC: MARKS ,BR ; THIR: RAMAN ,KK CIT: 0
THE EFFECT OF VOLUNTARY GAAP COMPLIANCE AND FINANCIAL DISCLOSURE ON GOVERNMENTAL BORROWING COSTS
JAA SU 91 VOL: 6 PG:303 - 319 :: REGRESS. :PRIM. :INSTIT. :FIN.METH.

BENSTON,GJ CIT: 0.5
THE SELF-SERVING MANAGEMENT HYPOTHESIS: SOME EVIDENCE
JAE AP 85 VOL: 7 PG:67 - 84 :: DES.STAT. :PRIM. :THEORY :EXEC.COMP.

BENSTON,GJ CIT: 0.44
ON THE VALUE AND LIMITATIONS OF FINANCIAL ACCOUNTING
CAR AU 84 VOL: 1 PG:47 - 57 :: ANOVA :SEC. :THEORY :ACC.CHNG.

BENSTON,GJ CIT: 0.09
ACCOUNTING AND CORPORATE ACCOUNTABILITY
AOS 02 82 VOL: 7 PG:87 - 106 :: QUAL. :SURV. :THEORY :HRA

BENSTON,GJ ; SEC: KRASNEY,MA CIT: 0.33
DAAM: THE DEMAND FOR ALTERNATIVE ACCOUNTING MEASUREMENTS
JAR ST 78 VOL: 16 PG:1 - 30 :: REGRESS. :SURV. :OTH.STAT. :VALUAT.(INFL.)

BENSTON,GJ CIT: 0
PUBLIC (U.S.) COMPARED TO PRIVATE (U.K.) REGULATION OF CORPORATE FINANCIAL DISCLOSURE
TAR JL 76 VOL: 51 PG:483 - 498 :: QUAL. :INT. LOG. :INSTIT. :DEC.AIDS

BENSTON,GJ CIT: 0.65
THE VALUE OF THE SEC'S ACCOUNTING DISCLOSURE REQUIREMENTS
TAR JL 69 VOL: 44 PG:515 - 532 :: ANAL. :PRIM. :INSTIT. :INFO.STRUC.

BENSTON,GJ CIT: 0.35
PUBLISHED CORPORATE ACCOUNTING DATA AND STOCK PRICES
JAR ST 67 VOL: 5 PG:1 - 54 :: REGRESS. :PRIM. :EMH :FIN.METH.

BENSTON,GJ CIT: 0.18
MULTIPLE REGRESSION ANALYSIS OF COST BEHAVIOR
TAR OC 66 VOL: 41 PG:657 - 672 :: REGRESS. :INT. LOG. :TIME SER. :BUDG.& PLAN.

BENSTON,GJ CIT: 0.41
THE ROLE OF THE FIRM'S ACCOUNTING SYSTEM FOR MOTIVATION
TAR AP 63 VOL: 38 PG:347 - 354 :: QUAL. :INT. LOG. :OTH.BEH. :BUDG.& PLAN.

BERANEK,W CIT: 0
A NOTE ON THE EQUIVALENCE OF CERTAIN CAPITAL BUDGETING CRITERIA
TAR OC 64 VOL: 39 PG:914 - 916 :: ANAL. :INT. LOG. :N/A :CAP.BUDG.

BERG ,KB ; SEC: COURSEY,D ; THIR: DICKHAUT,J CIT: 1.33
EXPERIMENTAL METHODS IN ACCOUNTING: A DISCUSSION OF RECURRING ISSUES
CAR SP 90 VOL: 6 PG:825 - 849 :: DES.STAT. :SEC. :INF.ECO./AG. :METHOD.

BERG ,KB ; SEC: MUELLER,FJ CIT: 0
ACCOUNTING FOR INVESTMENT CREDITS
TAR JL 63 VOL: 38 PG:554 - 561 :: QUAL. :INT. LOG. :THEORY :TAXES

BERGER,PD ; FIRS: ABDOLMOHAMMADI,MJ CIT: 0
A TEST OF THE ACCURACY OF PROBABILITY ASSESSMENT TECHNIQUES IN AUDITING
CAR AU 86 VOL: 3 PG:149 - 165 :: REGRESS. :LAB. :HIPS :PROB.ELIC.

BERKOW,WF CIT: 0
NEED FOR ENGINEERING INFLUENCE UPON ACCOUNTING PROCEDURE
TAR AP 64 VOL: 39 PG:377 - 386 :: QUAL. :INT. LOG. :N/A :REL.COSTS

BERKOWITCH,E ; SEC: VENEZIA,I CIT: 0
TERM VS. WHOLE LIFE INSURANCE
JAA SP 92 VOL: 7 PG:241 - 250 :: DES.STAT. :INT. LOG. :INF.ECO./AG. :N/A

BERKOWITZ,B ; FIRS: BRANCH,B CIT: 0
THE PREDICTIVE ACCURACY OF THE BUSINESS WEEK EARNINGS FORECASTS
JAA SP 81 VOL: 4 PG:215 - 219 :: REGRESS. :SEC. :OTH.STAT. :FOREC.

BERNARD,VL ; SEC: NOEL ,J CIT: 0
DO INVENTORY DISCLOSURES PREDICT SALES AND EARNINGS?
JAA SP 91 VOL: 6 PG:145 - 181 :: REGRESS. :PRIM. :OTH.STAT. :INV.

BERNARD,VL ; SEC: THOMAS,JK CIT: 2.67
EVIDENCE THAT STOCK PRICES DO NOT FULLY REFLECT THE IMPLICATIONS OF CURRENT EARNINGS FOR FUTURE EARNINGS
JAE DE 90 VOL: 13 PG:305 - 340 :: REGRESS. :PRIM. :EMH :FIN.METH.

BERNARD,VL ; SEC: THOMAS,JK CIT: 3.5
POST-EARNINGS-ANNOUNCEMENT DRIFT: DELAYED PRICE RESPONSE OR RISK PREMIUM?
JAR ST 89 VOL: 27 PG:1 - 36 :: REGRESS. :PRIM. :EMH :FIN.METH.

BERNARD,VL ; SEC: STOBER,TL CIT: 1.25
THE NATURE AND AMOUNT OF INFORMATION IN CASH FLOWS AND ACCRUALS
TAR OC 89 VOL: 64 PG:624 - 652 :: REGRESS. :PRIM. :EMH :OTH.FIN.ACC.

BERNARD,VL CIT: 4.5
CROSS-SECTIONAL DEPENDENCE AND PROBLEMS IN INFERENCE IN MARKET-BASED ACCOUNTING RESEARCH
JAR SP 87 VOL: 25 PG:1 - 48 :: REGRESS. :PRIM. :EMH :METHOD.

BERNARD,VL ; SEC: RULAND,RG CIT: 0.17
THE INCREMENTAL INFORMATION CONTENT OF HISTORICAL COST OME NUMBERS: TIME-SERIES ANALYSES FOR 1962-1980
TAR OC 87 VOL: 62 PG:707 - 722 :: REGRESS. :PRIM. :EMH :VALUAT.(INFL.)

BERNARD,VL CIT: 0.11
THE USE OF MARKET DATA AND ACCOUNTING DATA IN HEDGING AGAINST CONSUMER PRICE INFLATION
JAR AU 84 VOL: 22 PG:445 - 466 :: REGRESS. :PRIM. :HIPS :VALUAT.(INFL.)

BERNHARDT,I ; SEC: COPELAND,RM CIT: 0.12
SOME PROBLEMS IN APPLYING AN INFORMATION THEORY APPROACH TO ACCOUNTING AGGREGATION
JAR SP 70 VOL: 8 PG:95 - 98 :: QUAL. :INT. LOG. :INF.ECO./AG. :INFO.STRUC.

BERNSTEIN,LA CIT: 0.29
THE CONCEPT OF MATERIALITY
TAR JA 67 VOL: 42 PG:86 - 95 :: DES.STAT. :INT. LOG. :THEORY :MAT.

BERRY ,AJ ; SEC: CAPPS ,T ; THIR: COOPER,D ; FOUR: FERGUSON,P ; FIFT: HOPPER,T ; SIX: LOWE ,EA CIT: 3
MANAGEMENT CONTROL IN AN AREA OF THE NCB: RATIONALES OF ACCOUNTING PRACTICES IN A PUBLIC ENTERPRISE
AOS 01 85 VOL: 10 PG:3 - 28 :: REGRESS. :FIELD :OTH.BEH. :MANAG.

BERRY ,AJ ; FIRS: OTLEY ,DT CIT: 1.08
CONTROL, ORGANIZATION AND ACCOUNTING
AOS 02 80 VOL: 5 PG:231 - 246 :: QUAL. :INT. LOG. :OTH.BEH. :N/A

BERRY ,LE ; SEC: HARWOOD,GB ; THIR: KATZ ,JL CIT: 0.17
PERFORMANCE OF AUDITING PROCEDURES BY GOVERNMENTAL AUDITORS: SOME PRELIMINARY EVIDENCE
TAR JA 87 VOL: 62 PG:14 - 28 :: DES.STAT. :SURV. :OTH.STAT. :AUD.

BERRYMAN,RG ; FIRS: JOHNSON,PE ; SEC: JAMAL ,K CIT: 0.5
AUDIT JUDGMENT RESEARCH
AOS 02 89 VOL: 14 PG:83 - 99 :: REGRESS. :SEC. :HIPS :JUDG.

BERRYMAN,RG ; FIRS: COGLITORE,F CIT: 0
ANALYTICAL PROCEDURES: A DEFENSIVE NECESSITY
AUD SP 88 VOL: 07 PG:150 - 163 :: REGRESS. :SIM. :THEORY :ANAL.REV.

BERTIN,WJ ; FIRS: TORABZADEH,KM CIT: 0
ABNORMAL RETURNS TO STOCKHOLDERS OF FIRMS ACQUIRED IN BUSINESS COMBINATIONS AND LEVERAGED BUYOUTS
JAA SP 92 VOL: 7 PG:231 - 240 :: REGRESS. :PRIM. :EMH :BUS.COMB.

BHAGAT,S ; FIRS: BRICKLEY,JA ; THIR: LEASE ,RC CIT: 0.63
THE IMPACT OF LONG-RANGE MANAGERIAL COMPENSATION PLANS ON SHAREHOLDER WEALTH
JAE AP 85 VOL: 7 PG:115 - 130 :: REGRESS. :PRIM. :EMH :EXEC.COMP.

BHUSHAN,R ; FIRS: O'BRIEN,PC CIT: 0.67
ANALYST FOLLOWING AND INSTITUTIONAL OWNERSHIP
JAR ST 90 VOL: 28 PG:055 - 82 :: REGRESS. :PRIM. :INSTIT. :ORG.& ENVIR.

BHUSHAN,R CIT: 1
COLLECTION OF INFORMATION ABOUT PUBLICLY TRADED FIRMS: THEORY AND EVIDENCE
JAE JL 89 VOL: 11 PG:183 - 206 :: REGRESS. :PRIM. :EMH :FIN.METH.

BHUSHAN,R CIT: 0.5
FIRM CHARACTERISTICS AND ANALYST FOLLOWING
JAE JL 89 VOL: 11 PG:255 - 274 :: REGRESS. :PRIM. :OTH.STAT. :FOREC.

BIDDLE,GC ; SEC: SEOW ,GS CIT: 1
THE ESTIMATION AND DETERMINANTS OF ASSOCIATIONS BETWEEN RETURNS AND EARNINGS: EVIDENCE FROM CROSS-INDUSTRY COMPARISONS
JAA SP 91 VOL: 6 PG:183 - 232 :: REGRESS. :PRIM. :EMH :FIN.METH.

BIDDLE,GC ; SEC: BRUTON,CM ; THIR: SIEGEL,AF CIT: 0
COMPUTER-INTENSIVE METHODS IN AUDITING: BOOTSTRAP DIFFERENCE AND RATIO ESTIMATION
AUD AU 90 VOL: 9 PG:92 - 114 :: DES.STAT. :SIM. :OTH.STAT. :SAMP.

BIDDLE,GC ; SEC: RICKS ,WE CIT: 0.2
ANALYST FORECAST ERRORS AND STOCK PRICE BEHAVIOR NEAR THE EARNINGS ANNOUNCEMENT DATES OF LIFO ADOPTERS
JAR AU 88 VOL: 26 PG:169 - 194 :: REGRESS. :PRIM. :EMH :INV.

BIDDLE,GC ; SEC: MARTIN,RK CIT: 0.25
INFLATION, TAXES, AND OPTIMAL INVENTORY POLICIES
JAR SP 85 VOL: 23 PG:57 - 83 :: REGRESS. :SIM. :OTH.STAT. :INV.

BIDDLE,GC ; SEC: LINDAHL,FW CIT: 2.36
STOCK PRICE REACTIONS TO LIFO ADOPTIONS: THE ASSOCIATION BETWEEN EXCESS RETURNS AND LIFO TAX SAVINGS
JAR AU 82 VOL: 20 PG:551 - 588 :: MIXED :PRIM. :EMH :INV.

BIDDLE,GC ; FIRS: JOYCE ,EJ CIT: 1.58
ANCHORING AND ADJUSTMENT IN PROBABILISTIC INFERENCE IN AUDITING
JAR SP 81 VOL: 19 PG:120 - 145 :: ANOVA :LAB. :OTH.BEH. :DEC.AIDS

BIDDLE,GC ; FIRS: JOYCE ,EJ CIT: 1.42
ARE AUDITORS' JUDGMENTS SUFFICIENTLY REGRESSIVE?
JAR AU 81 VOL: 19 PG:323 - 349 :: ANOVA :LAB. :HIPS :PLAN.

BIDDLE,GC CIT: 1.85
ACCOUNTING METHODS AND MANAGEMENT DECISIONS: THE CASE OF INVENTORY COSTING AND INVENTORY POLICY
JAR ST 80 VOL: 18 PG:235 - 280 :: NON-PAR. :PRIM. :OTH. :INV.

BIDWELL III,CM ; SEC: RIDDLE JR,JR CIT: 0
MARKET INEFFICIENCIES - OPPORTUNITIES FOR PROFITS
JAA SP 81 VOL: 4 PG:198 - 214 :: REGRESS. :PRIM. :EMH :INFO.STRUC.

BIERMAN JR,H CIT: 0
COMMON STOCK EQUIVALENTS, EARNINGS PER SHARE AND STOCK VALUATION
JAA WI 86 VOL: 1 PG:62 - 70 :: DES.STAT. :INT. LOG. :THEORY :LTD

BIERMAN JR,H CIT: 0
DEPRECIATION AND INCOME TAX ALLOCATION
JAA SP 85 VOL: 8 PG:184 - 194 :: DES.STAT. :INT. LOG. :THEORY :TAXES

BIERMAN JR,H CIT: 0.06
REGULATION, IMPLIED REVENUE REQUIREMENTS, AND METHOD DEPRECIATION
TAR JL 74 VOL: 49 PG:448 - 454 :: ANAL. :INT. LOG. :N/A :PP&E / DEPR

BIERMAN JR,H CIT: 0
DISCOUNTED CASH FLOWS, PRICE LEVEL ADJUSTMENTS AND EXPECTATIONS
TAR OC 71 VOL: 46 PG:693 - 700 :: ANAL. :INT. LOG. :THEORY :VALUAT.(INFL.)

BIERMAN JR,H CIT: 0
INVESTMENT DECISIONS AND TAXES
TAR OC 70 VOL: 45 PG:690 - 697 :: ANAL. :INT. LOG. :N/A :TAX PLNG.

BIERMAN JR,H CIT: 0
ACCELERATED DEPRECIATION AND RATE REGULATION
TAR JA 69 VOL: 44 PG:65 - 78 :: QUAL. :INT. LOG. :N/A :PP&E / DEPR

BIERMAN JR,H ; SEC: DAVIDSON,S CIT: 0
THE INCOME CONCEPT-VALUE-INCREMENT OR EARNINGS PREDICTOR
TAR AP 69 VOL: 44 PG:239 - 246 :: QUAL. :INT. LOG. :THEORY :FIN.METH.

BIERMAN JR,H ; SEC: LIU ,E CIT: 0
THE COMPUTATION OF EARNINGS PER SHARE
TAR JA 68 VOL: 43 PG:62 - 67 :: QUAL. :INT. LOG. :THEORY :PENS.

BIERMAN JR,H CIT: 0
THE TERM STRUCTURE OF INTEREST RATES AND ACCOUNTING FOR DEBT
TAR OC 68 VOL: 43 PG:657 - 661 :: ANAL. :INT. LOG. :THEORY :LTD

BIERMAN JR,H ; SEC: SMIDT ,S CIT: 0
ACCOUNTING FOR DEBT AND COSTS OF LIQUIDITY UNDER CONDITIONS OF UNCERTAINTY
JAR AU 67 VOL: 5 PG:144 - 153 :: ANAL. :INT. LOG. :THEORY :LTD

BIERMAN JR,H CIT: 0
INVENTORY VALUATION: THE USE OF MARKET PRICES
TAR OC 67 VOL: 42 PG:731 - 737 :: ANAL. :INT. LOG. :THEORY :INV.

BIERMAN JR,H CIT: 0.06
A FURTHER STUDY OF DEPRECIATION
TAR AP 66 VOL: 41 PG:271 - 274 :: ANAL. :INT. LOG. :THEORY :PP&E / DEPR

BIERMAN JR,H CIT: 0
MYTHS AND ACCOUNTANTS
TAR JL 65 VOL: 40 PG:541 - 546 :: QUAL. :INT. LOG. :THEORY :FIN.METH.

BIERMAN JR,H CIT: 0
RECORDING OBSOLESCENCE
JAR AU 64 VOL: 2 PG:229 - 235 :: MIXED :INT. LOG. :THEORY :AMOR./DEPL.

BIERMAN JR,H CIT: 0
A PROBLEM IN EXPENSE RECOGNITION
TAR JA 63 VOL: 38 PG:61 - 63 :: QUAL. :INT. LOG. :THEORY :N/A

BIERMAN JR,H CIT: 0.12
MEASUREMENT AND ACCOUNTING
TAR JL 63 VOL: 38 PG:501 - 507 :: QUAL. :INT. LOG. :THEORY :FIN.METH.

BIGGS ,SF ; FIRS: BEDARD,JC CIT: 0
THE EFFECT OF DOMAIN-SPECIFIC EXPERIENCE ON EVALUATION OF MANAGEMENT REPRESENTATIONS IN ANALYTICAL PROCEDURES
AUD 91 VOL: 10 PG:77 - 90 :: REGRESS. :LAB. :HIPS :ANAL.REV.

BIGGS ,SF ; FIRS: BEDARD,JC CIT: 0.5
PATTERN RECOGNITION, HYPOTHESES GENERATION, AND AUDITOR PERFORMANCE IN AN ANALYTICAL TASK
TAR JL 91 VOL: 66 PG:622 - 642 :: REGRESS. :LAB. :HIPS :ERRORS

BIGGS ,SF ; FIRS: WILD ,JJ CIT: 0
STRATEGIC CONSIDERATIONS FOR UNAUDITED ACCOUNT VALUES IN ANALYTICAL REVIEW
TAR JA 90 VOL: 65 PG:227 241 :: DES.STAT. :INT. LOG. :OTH. :ANAL.REV.

BIGGS ,SF ; SEC: MOCK ,TJ ; THIR: WATKINS,PR CIT: 1.4
AUDITOR'S USE OF ANALYTICAL REVIEW IN AUDIT PROGRAM DESIGN
TAR JA 88 VOL: 63 PG:148 - 162 :: REGRESS. :LAB. :OTH.BEH. :ANAL.REV.

BIGGS ,SF ; SEC: MESSIER JR,WF ; THIR: HANSEN,JV CIT: 0.5
A DESCRIPTIVE ANALYSIS OF COMPUTER AUDIT SPECIALISTS' DECISION MAKING
AUD SP 87 VOL: 6 PG:1 - 21 :: REGRESS. :LAB. :HIPS :EDP AUD.

BIGGS ,SF ; SEC: WILD ,JJ CIT: 0.5
AN INVESTIGATION OF AUDITOR JUDGMENT IN ANALYTICAL REVIEW
TAR OC 85 VOL: 60 PG:607 - 633 :: REGRESS. :LAB. :HIPS :ANAL.REV.

BIGGS ,SF CIT: 0.22
FINANCIAL ANALYSTS' INFORMATION SEARCH IN THE ASSESSMENT OF CORPORATE EARNING POWER
AOS 34 84 VOL: 9 PG:313 - 323 :: DES.STAT. :LAB. :HIPS :N/A

BIGGS ,SF ; SEC: WILD ,JJ CIT: 0.22
A NOTE ON THE PRACTICE OF ANALYTICAL REVIEW
AUD SP 84 VOL: 3 PG:68 - 79 :: CORR. :SURV. :OTH.STAT. :ANAL.REV.

BIGGS ,SF ; SEC: MOCK ,TJ CIT: 1.1
AN INVESTIGATION OF AUDITOR DECISION PROCESSES IN THE EVALUATION OF INTERNAL CONTROLS AND AUDIT SCOPE DECISIONS
JAR SP 83 VOL: 21 PG:234 - 255 :: DES.STAT. :LAB. :HIPS :INT.CONT.

BILDERSEE,JS ; SEC: RONEN ,J CIT: 0.17
STOCK RETURNS AND REAL ACTIVITY IN AN INFLATIONARY ENVIRONMENT: THE INFORMATIONAL IMPACT OF FAS NO. 33
CAR AU 87 VOL: 4 PG:89 - 110 :: REGRESS. :PRIM. :EMH :VALUAT.(INFL.)

BILDERSEE,JS ; SEC: KAHN ,N CIT: 0
A PRELIMINARY TEST OF THE PRESENCE OF WINDOW DRESSING: EVIDENCE FROM
JAA SU 87 VOL: 2 PG:239 - 256 :: REGRESS. :PRIM. :OTH.STAT. :INFO.STRUC.

BILDERSEE,JS CIT: 0.29
THE ASSOCIATION BETWEEN A MARKET-DETERMINED MEASURE OF RISK AND ALTERNATIVE MEASURES OF RISK
TAR JA 75 VOL: 50 PG:81 - 98 :: REGRESS. :PRIM. :EMH :FIN.METH.

BILLERA,LJ ; SEC: HEATH ,DC ; THIR: VERRECCHIA,RE CIT: 0.25
A UNIQUE PROCEDURE FOR ALLOCATING COMMON COSTS FROM A PRODUCTION PROCESS
JAR SP 81 VOL: 19 PG:185 - 196 :: ANAL. :INT. LOG. :INF.ECO./AG. :N/A

BINDER,JJ CIT: 0
ON THE USE OF THE MULTIVARIATE REGRESSION MODEL IN EVENT STUDIES
JAR SP 85 VOL: 23 PG:370 - 383 :: REGRESS. :PRIM. :EMH :METHOD.

BIRD ,FA ; SEC: DAVIDSON,LF ; THIR: SMITH ,CH CIT: 0.12
PERCEPTIONS OF EXTERNAL ACCOUNTING TRANSFERS UNDER ENTITY AND PROPRIETARY THEORY
TAR AP 74 VOL: 49 PG:233 - 244 :: QUAL. :INT. LOG. :THEORY :FIN.METH.

BIRD ,PA CIT: 0.06
TAX INCENTIVES TO CAPITAL INVESTMENT
JAR SP 65 VOL: 3 PG:1 - 11 :: QUAL. :INT. LOG. :THEORY :INT.DIFF.

BIRNBERG,JG ; SEC: SNODGRASS,C CIT: 0.6
CULTURE AND CONTROL: A FIELD STUDY
AOS 05 88 VOL: 13 PG:447 - 464 :: REGRESS. :SURV. :OTH.BEH. :INT.DIFF.

BIRNBERG,JG ; FIRS: WILNER,N CIT: 0.43
METHODOLOGICAL PROBLEMS IN FUNCTIONAL FIXATION RESEARCH: CRITICISM AND SUGGESTIONS
AOS 01 86 VOL: 11 PG:71 - 82 :: REGRESS. :INT. LOG. :HIPS :METHOD.

BIRNBERG,JG ; SEC: SHIELDS,MD CIT: 0.44
THE ROLE OF ATTENTION AND MEMORY IN ACCOUNTING DECISIONS
AOS 34 84 VOL: 9 PG:365 - 382 :: QUAL. :INT. LOG. :HIPS :N/A

BIRNBERG,JG ; SEC: TUROPOLEC,L ; THIR: YOUNG ,SM CIT: 1.7
THE ORGANIZATIONAL CONTEXT OF ACCOUNTING
AOS 23 83 VOL: 8 PG:111 - 130 :: QUAL. :SEC. :OTH.BEH. :REL.COSTS

BIRNBERG,JG ; FIRS: SHIELDS,MD ; THIR: FRIEZE,IH CIT: 0.42
ATTRIBUTIONS, COGNITIVE PROCESSES AND CONTROL SYSTEMS
AOS 01 81 VOL: 6 PG:69 - 96 :: ANOVA :LAB. :OTH.BEH. :BUDG.& PLAN.

BIRNBERG,JG CIT: 0
THE ROLE OF ACCOUNTING IN FINANCIAL DISCLOSURE
AOS 01 80 VOL: 5 PG:71 - 80 :: QUAL. :INT. LOG. :HIPS :N/A

BIRNBERG,JG ; FIRS: MCGHEE,W ; SEC: SHIELDS,MD CIT: 1
THE EFFECTS OF PERSONALITY ON A SUBJECT'S INFORMATION PROCESSING
TAR JL 78 VOL: 53 PG:681 - 697 :: ANOVA :LAB. :HIPS :OTH.MANAG.

BIRNBERG,JG ; SEC: FRIEZE,IH ; THIR: SHIELDS,MD CIT: 0.38
THE ROLE OF ATTRIBUTION THEORY IN CONTROL SYSTEMS
AOS 03 77 VOL: 2 PG:189 - 200 :: QUAL. :INT. LOG. :OTH.BEH. :MANAG.

BIRNBERG,JG ; SEC: GANDHI,NM CIT: 0.06
TOWARD DEFINING THE ACCOUNTANT'S ROLE IN THE EVALUATION OF SOCIAL PROGRAMS
AOS 01 76 VOL: 1 PG:5 - 10 :: QUAL. :INT. LOG. :THEORY :HRA

BIRNBERG,JG ; SEC: NATH ,R CIT: 0.47
LABORATORY EXPERIMENTATION IN ACCOUNTING RESEARCH
TAR JA 68 VOL: 43 PG:38 - 45 :: QUAL. :INT. LOG. :N/A :METHOD.

BIRNBERG,JG ; SEC: NATH ,R CIT: 0.18
IMPLICATIONS OF BEHAVIOURAL SCIENCE FOR MANAGERIAL ACCOUNTING
TAR JL 67 VOL: 42 PG:468 - 479 :: QUAL. :SEC. :OTH.BEH. :MANAG.

BIRNBERG,JG ; FIRS: DOPUCH,N ; THIR: DEMSKI,JS CIT: 0.12
AN EXTENSION OF STANDARD COST VARIANCE ANALYSIS
TAR JL 67 VOL: 42 PG:526 - 536 :: ANAL. :INT. LOG. :OTH.STAT. :VAR.

BIRNBERG,JG CIT: 0.06
THE REPORTING OF EXECUTORY CONTRACTS
TAR OC 65 VOL: 40 PG:814 - 820 :: QUAL. :INT. LOG. :THEORY :INFO.STRUC.

BIRNBERG,JG CIT: 0
AN INFORMATION ORIENTED APPROACH TO THE PRESENTATION OF COMMON SHAREHOLDERS' EQUITY
TAR OC 64 VOL: 39 PG:963 - 971 :: QUAL. :INT. LOG. :N/A :OTH.FIN.ACC.

BISHOP,RA ; FIRS: WALLER,WS CIT: 0.33
AN EXPERIMENTAL STUDY OF INCENTIVE PAY SCHEMES, COMMUNICATION, AND INTRAFIRM RESOURCE ALLOCATION
TAR OC 90 VOL: 65 PG:812 - 836 :: REGRESS. :FIELD :INF.ECO./AG. :COST.ALLOC.

BJORN-ANDERSEN,N ; SEC: PEDERSEN,PH CIT: 0
COMPUTER FACILITATED CHANGES IN THE MANAGEMENT POWER STRUCTURE
AOS 02 80 VOL: 5 PG:203 - 216 :: QUAL. :CASE :OTH.BEH. :N/A

BLACCONIERE,WG CIT: 0
MARKET REACTIONS TO ACCOUNTING REGULATIONS IN THE SAVINGS AND LOAN INDUSTRY
JAE MR 91 VOL: 14 PG:91 - 113 :: REGRESS. :PRIM. :EMH :ACC.CHNG.

BLACCONIERE,WG ; SEC: BOWEN ,RM ; THIR: SEFCIK,SE ; FOUR: STINSON,CH CIT: 0
DETERMINANTS OF THE USE OF REGULATORY ACCOUNTING PRINCIPLES BY SAVINGS AND LOANS
JAE JN 91 VOL: 14 PG:167 - 201 :: REGRESS. :PRIM. :OTH.STAT. :ACC.CHNG.

BLACKBURN,JO ; FIRS: DICKENS,RL CIT: 0.06
HOLDING GAINS ON FIXED ASSETS: AN ELEMENT OF BUSINESS INCOME?
TAR AP 64 VOL: 39 PG:312 - 329 :: ANAL. :INT. LOG. :THEORY :VALUAT.(INFL.)

BLACKETT,LA ; FIRS: AIKEN ,ME ; THIR: ISAACS,G CIT: 0.06
MODELING BEHAVIOURAL INTERDEPENDENCIES FOR STEWARDSHIP REPORTING
TAR JL 75 VOL: 50 PG:544 - 562 :: ANAL. :INT. LOG. :THEORY :OTH.MANAG.

BLAKELY,EJ ; SEC: KNUTSON,PH CIT: 0
LIFO OR LOFI - WHICH?
TAR JA 63 VOL: 38 PG:75 - 86 :: QUAL. :INT. LOG. :THEORY :N/A

BLANCHARD,GA ; SEC: CHOW ,CW ; THIR: NOREEN,EW CIT: 0
INFORMATION ASYMMETRY, INCENTIVE SCHEMES, AND INFORMATION BIASING: THE CASE OF HOSPITAL BUDGETING UNDER RATE REGULATION
TAR JA 86 VOL: 61 PG:1 - 15 :: REGRESS. :PRIM. :N/A :BUDG.& PLAN.

BLAZENKO,GW ; SEC: SCOTT ,WR CIT: 0.29
A MODEL OF STANDARD SETTING IN AUDITING
CAR AU 86 VOL: 3 PG:68 - 92 :: DES.STAT. :INT. LOG. :INF.ECO./AG. :AUD.

BLOCHER,E ; SEC: COOPER,JC CIT: 0
A STUDY OF AUDITORS' ANALYTICAL REVIEW PERFORMANCE
AUD SP 88 VOL: 07 PG:1 - 28 :: REGRESS. :LAB. :OTH.BEH. :ANAL.REV.

BLOCHER,E ; SEC: MOFFIE,RP ; THIR: ZMUD ,RW CIT: 0.14
REPORT FORMAT AND TASK COMPLEXITY: INTERACTION IN RISK JUDGMENTS
AOS 06 86 VOL: 11 PG:457 - 470 :: REGRESS. :LAB. :HIPS :INFO.STRUC.

BLOCHER,E ; SEC: BYLINSKI,JH CIT: 0
THE INFLUENCE OF SAMPLE CHARACTERISTICS IN SAMPLE EVALUATION
AUD AU 85 VOL: 5 PG:79 - 90 :: REGRESS. :LAB. :OTH.BEH. :SAMP.

BLOCHER,E ; SEC: ESPOSITO,RS ; THIR: WILLINGHAM,JJ CIT: 0.1
AUDITOR'S ANALYTICAL REVIEW JUDGMENTS FOR PAYROLL EXPENSE
AUD AU 83 VOL: 3 PG:75 - 91 :: DES.STAT. :LAB. :OTH.BEH. :ANAL.REV.

BLOCHER,E CIT: 0.21
PERFORMANCE EFFECTS OF DIFFERENT AUDIT STAFF ASSIGNMENT STRATEGIES
TAR JL 79 VOL: 54 PG:563 - 573 :: DES.STAT. :CASE :OTH.BEH. :ORG.

BLOOM ,R ; SEC: ELGERS,PT ; THIR: MURRAY,D CIT: 0.11
FUNCTIONAL FIXATION IN PRODUCT PRICING: A COMPARISON OF INDIVIDUALS AND GROUPS
AOS 01 84 VOL: 9 PG:1 - 11 :: MIXED :LAB. :HIPS :PP&E / DEPR

BLUM ,M CIT: 0.29
FAILING COMPANY DISCRIMINANT ANALYSIS
JAR SP 74 VOL: 12 PG:1 - 25 :: OTH.QUANT. :PRIM. :OTH.STAT. :BUS.COMB.

BOARD ,JLG ; SEC: WALKER,M CIT: 0
INTERTEMPORAL AND CROSS-SECTIONAL VARIATION IN THE ASSOCIATION BETWEEN UNEXPECTED ACCOUNTING RATES OF RETURN AND ABNORMAL RETURNS
JAR SP 90 VOL: 28 PG:182 - 192 :: REGRESS. :PRIM. :EMH :METHOD.

BOATSMAN,JR ; SEC: GRASSO,LP ; THIR: ORMISTON,MB ; FOUR: RENEAU,JH CIT: 0
A PERSPECTIVE ON THE USE OF LABORATORY MARKET EXPERIMENTATION IN AUDITING RESEARCH
TAR JA 92 VOL: 67 PG:148 - 156 :: ANOVA :SEC. :INF.ECO./AG. :METHOD.

BOATSMAN,JR ; SEC: DOWELL,CD ; THIR: KIMBRELL,JI CIT: 0
VALUING STOCK USED FOR A BUSINESS COMBINATION
JAA AU 84 VOL: 8 PG:35 - 43 :: ANAL. :INT. LOG. :OTH.STAT. :BUS.COMB.

BOATSMAN,JR ; FIRS: MCKEE ,AJ ; SEC: BELL ,TB CIT: 0.56
MANAGEMENT PREFERENCES OVER ACCOUNTING STANDARDS: A REPLICATION AND ADDITIONAL TESTS
TAR OC 84 VOL: 59 PG:647 - 659 :: OTH.QUANT. :PRIM. :INSTIT. :FASB SUBM.

BOATSMAN,JR ; SEC: BASKIN,EF CIT: 0.17
ASSET VALUATION WITH INCOMPLETE MARKETS
TAR JA 81 VOL: 56 PG:38 - 53 :: ANAL. :INT. LOG. :EMH :FIN.METH.

BOATSMAN,JR ; FIRS: GHEYARA,K CIT: 1.31
MARKET REACTION TO THE 1976 REPLACEMENT COST DISCLOSURES
JAE AG 80 VOL: 2 PG:107 - 125 :: MIXED :PRIM. :EMH :VALUAT.(INFL.)

BOATSMAN,JR ; FIRS: DAVIS ,DW ; THIR: BASKIN,EF CIT: 0.07
ON GENERALIZING STOCK MARKET RESEARCH TO A BROADER CLASS OF MARKETS
TAR JA 78 VOL: 53 PG:1 - 10 :: MIXED :PRIM. :EMH :FIN.METH.

BOATSMAN,JR ; SEC: ROBERTSON,JC CIT: 1
POLICY-CAPTURING ON SELECTED MATERIALITY JUDGMENTS
TAR AP 74 VOL: 49 PG:342 - 352 :: OTH.QUANT. :LAB. :OTH.STAT. :OTH.FIN.ACC.

BOATSMAN,JR ; FIRS: PATZ ,DH CIT: 0.18
ACCOUNTING PRINCIPLE FORMULATION IN AN EFFICIENT MARKETS ENVIRONMENT
JAR AU 72 VOL: 10 PG:392 - 403 :: ANOVA :PRIM. :EMH :OIL & GAS

BODNAR,G ; SEC: LUSK ,EJ CIT: 0.06
MOTIVATIONAL CONSIDERATIONS IN COST ALLOCATION SYSTEMS: A CONDITIONING THEORY APPROACH
TAR OC 77 VOL: 52 PG:857 - 868 :: ANAL. :INT. LOG. :OTH.BEH. :OVER.ALLOC.

BODNAR,G CIT: 0.47
RELIABILITY MODELING OF INTERNAL CONTROL SYSTEMS
TAR OC 75 VOL: 50 PG:747 - 757 :: ANAL. :INT. LOG. :OTH.STAT. :INT.CONT.

BOE ,WJ ; FIRS: BAILEY JR,AD CIT: 0.12
GOAL AND RESOURCE TRANSFERS IN THE MULTIGOAL ORGANIZATION
TAR JL 76 VOL: 51 PG:559 - 573 :: QUAL. :INT. LOG. :MATH.PROG. :TRANS.PRIC.

BOER ,G CIT: 0
REPLACEMENT COST: A HISTORICAL LOOK
TAR JA 66 VOL: 41 PG:92 - 97 :: QUAL. :INT. LOG. :HIST. :VALUAT.(INFL.)

BOGART,FO CIT: 0
TAX CONSIDERATIONS IN PARTNERSHIP AGREEMENTS
TAR OC 65 VOL: 40 PG:834 - 838 :: QUAL. :INT. LOG. :N/A :TAXES

BOLAND,LA ; SEC: GORDON,IM CIT: 0
CRITICIZING POSITIVE ACCOUNTING THEORY
CAR AU 92 VOL: 9 PG:142 - 170 :: DES.STAT. :SEC. :THEORY :FIN.METH.

BOLAND,RJ ; SEC: PONDY ,LR CIT: 0.57
THE MICRO DYNAMICS OF A BUDGET-CUTTING PROCESS: MODES, MODELS AND STRUCTURE
AOS 45 86 VOL: 11 PG:403 - 422 :: REGRESS. :FIELD :HIPS :BUDG.& PLAN.

BOLAND,RJ ; SEC: PONDY ,LR CIT: 2.1
ACCOUNTING IN ORGANIZATIONS: A UNION OF NATURAL AND RATIONAL PERSPECTIVES
AOS 23 83 VOL: 8 PG:223 - 234 :: QUAL. :CASE :OTH. :OTH.MANAG.

BOLAND,RJ CIT: 0.17
A STUDY IN SYSTEM DESIGN: C. WEST CHURCHMAN AND CHRIS ARGYRIS
AOS 02 81 VOL: 6 PG:109 - 118 :: QUAL. :INT. LOG. :OTH. :N/A

BOLAND,RJ CIT: 1
CONTROL, CAUSALITY AND INFORMATION SYSTEM REQUIREMENTS
AOS 04 79 VOL: 4 PG:259 - 272 :: QUAL. :INT. LOG. :OTH. :MANAG.

BOLCE ,WJ ; FIRS: HEARD ,JE CIT: 0
THE POLITICAL SIGNIFICANCE OF CORPORATE SOCIAL REPORTING IN THE U.S.A.
AOS 03 81 VOL: 6 PG:247 - 254 :: QUAL. :INT. LOG. :OTH. :HRA

BOLLOM,WJ CIT: 0.06
TOWARDS A THEORY OF INTERIM REPORTING FOR A SEASONAL BUSINESS: A BEHAVIOURAL APPROACH
TAR JA 73 VOL: 48 PG:12 - 22 :: ANOVA :LAB. :THEORY :INT.REP.

BOLLOM,WJ ; SEC: WEYGANDT,JJ CIT: 0.06
AN EXAMINATION OF SOME INTERIM REPORTING THEORIES FOR A SEASONAL BUSINESS
TAR JA 72 VOL: 47 PG:75 - 84 :: QUAL. :SEC. :THEORY :INT.REP.

BONETT,DG ; SEC: CLUTE ,RD CIT: 0
AUDIT SAMPLING WITH NONSAMPLING ERRORS OF THE FIRST TYPE
CAR SP 90 VOL: 6 PG:432 - 445 :: DES.STAT. :SIM. :OTH.STAT. :SAMP.

BONNER,SE ; SEC: LEWIS ,BL CIT: 0.67
DETERMINANTS OF AUDITOR EXPERTISE
JAR ST 90 VOL: 28 PG:001 - 28 :: REGRESS. :LAB. :HIPS :AUD.BEH.

BONNER,SE CIT: 1.67
EXPERIENCE EFFECTS IN AUDITING: THE ROLE OF TASK-SPECIFIC KNOWLEDGE
TAR JA 90 VOL: 65 PG:72 - 92 :: REGRESS. :LAB. :HIPS :AUD.BEH.

BONNIER,KA ; SEC: BRUNER,RF CIT: 0
AN ANALYSIS OF STOCK PRICE REACTION TO MANAGEMENT CHANGE IN DISTRESSED FIRMS
JAE FB 89 VOL: 11 PG:95 - 106 :: REGRESS. :PRIM. :EMH :N/A

BOOCKHOLDT,JL ; FIRS: FINLEY,DR CIT: 0
A CONTINUOUS CONSTRAINED OPTIMIZATION MODEL FOR AUDIT SAMPLING
AUD SP 87 VOL: 6 PG:22 - 39 :: DES.STAT. :SIM. :OTH.STAT. :SAMP.

BOOKER,J ; FIRS: ANDERSON,HM ; SEC: GIESE ,J CIT: 0.12
SOME PROPOSITIONS ABOUT AUDITING
TAR JL 70 VOL: 45 PG:524 - 531 :: QUAL. :INT. LOG. :INSTIT. :AUD.

BORITZ,JE ; SEC: WENSLEY,AKP CIT: 0
EVALUATING EXPERT SYSTEMS WITH COMPLEX OUTPUTS: THE CASE OF AUDIT PLANNING
AUD AU 92 VOL: 11 PG:14 - 29 :: REGRESS. :LAB. :EXP.SYST. :PLAN.

BORITZ,JE ; SEC: CIT: 0
STRUCTURING THE ASSESSMENT OF AUDIT EVIDENCE-AN EXPERT SYSTEMS APPROACH
AUD 90 VOL: 9 PG:49 - 87 :: DES.STAT. :MIXED :EXP.SYST. :JUDG.

BORITZ,JE ; SEC: GABER ,BG ; THIR: LEMON ,WM CIT: 0
AN EXPERIMENTAL STUDY OF THE EFFECTS OF ELICITATION METHODS ON REVIEW OF PRELIMINARY AUDIT STRATEGY BY EXTERNAL AUDITORS
CAR SP 88 VOL: 4 PG:392 - 411 :: REGRESS. :LAB. :HIPS :METHOD.

BORITZ,JE ; SEC: BROCA ,DS CIT: 0.29
SCHEDULING INTERNAL AUDIT ACTIVITIES
AUD AU 86 VOL: 6 PG:1 - 19 :: DES.STAT. :SIM. :OTH.STAT. :INT.AUD.

BORITZ,JE CIT: 0.29
THE EFFECT OF RESEARCH METHOD ON AUDIT PLANNING AND REVIEW JUDGMENTS
JAR AU 86 VOL: 24 PG:335 - 348 :: REGRESS. :LAB. :HIPS :PLAN.

BORITZ,JE CIT: 0.13
THE EFFECT OF INFORMATION PRESENTATION STRUCTURES ON AUDIT PLANNING AND REVIEW JUDGMENTS
CAR SP 85 VOL: 1 PG:193 - 218 :: DES.STAT. :LAB. :HIPS :JUDG.

BOTTS ,RR CIT: 0
INTEREST AND THE TRUTH-IN-LENDING BILL
TAR OC 63 VOL: 38 PG:789 - 795 :: QUAL. :INT. LOG. :THEORY :N/A

BOUGEN,P ; FIRS: OGDEN ,S CIT: 0.63
A RADICAL PERSPECTIVE ON THE DISCLOSURE OF ACCOUNTING INFORMATION TO TRADE UNIONS
AOS 02 85 VOL: 10 PG:211 - 226 :: DES.STAT. :INT. LOG. :INSTIT. :METHOD.

BOUGEN,PD ; SEC: OGDEN ,SG ; THIR: OUTRAM,Q CIT: 0
THE APPEARANCE AND DISAPPEARANCE OF ACCOUNTING: WAGE DETERMINATION IN THE U.K. COAL INDUSTRY
AOS 03 90 VOL: 15 PG:149 - 170 :: REGRESS. :SEC. :HIST. :ORG.& ENVIR.

BOUGEN,PD CIT: 0.5
THE EMERGENCE, ROLES AND CONSEQUENCES OF AN ACCOUNTING-INDUSTRIAL RELATIONS INTERACTION
AOS 03 89 VOL: 14 PG:203 - 234 :: REGRESS. :CASE :THEORY :MANAG.

BOURN ,AM CIT: 0
TRAINING FOR THE ACCOUNTANCY PROFESSION IN ENGLAND AND WALES
JAR AU 66 VOL: 4 PG:213 - 223 :: QUAL. :INT. LOG. :OTH. :EDUC.

BOURN ,M ; FIRS: EZZAMEL,M CIT: 0
THE ROLES OF ACCOUNTING INFORMATION SYSTEMS IN AN ORGANIZATION EXPERIENCING FINANCIAL CRISIS
AOS 05 90 VOL: 15 PG:399 - 424 :: REGRESS. :CASE :EXP.SYST. :MAN.DEC.CHAR.

BOUTELL,WS CIT: 0
BUSINESS-ORIENTED COMPUTERS: A FRAME OF REFERENCE
TAR AP 64 VOL: 39 PG:305 - 311 :: QUAL. :INT. LOG. :N/A :OTH.MANAG.

BOUWMAN,MJ ; SEC: FRISHKOFF,PA ; THIR: FRISHKOFF,P CIT: 1
HOW DO FINANCIAL ANALYSTS MAKE DECISIONS? A PROCESS MODEL OF THE INVESTMENT SCREENING DECISION
AOS 01 87 VOL: 12 PG:1 - 30 :: REGRESS. :LAB. :HIPS :OTH.FIN.ACC.

BOUWMAN,MJ CIT: 0.56
EXPERT VS. NOVICE DECISION MAKING IN ACCOUNTING: A SUMMARY
AOS 34 84 VOL: 9 PG:325 - 327 :: MIXED :LAB. :HIPS :N/A

BOUWMAN,MJ ; FIRS: FRISHKOFF,P ; SEC: FRISHKOFF,PA CIT: 0
USE OF ACCOUNTING DATA IN SCREENING BY FINANCIAL ANALYSTS
JAA AU 84 VOL: 8 PG:44 - 53 :: DES.STAT. :LAB. :HIPS :INFO.STRUC.

BOWEN ,EK CIT: 0
MATHEMATICS IN THE UNDERGRADUATE BUSINESS CURRICULUM
TAR OC 67 VOL: 42 PG:782 - 787 :: QUAL. :INT. LOG. :N/A :OTH.MANAG.

BOWEN ,RM ; SEC: JOHNSON,MF ; THIR: SHEVLIN,T ; FOUR: SHORES,D CIT: 0
DETERMINANTS OF THE TIMING OF QUARTERLY EARNINGS ANNOUNCEMENTS
JAA AU 92 VOL: 7 PG:395 - 422 :: REGRESS. :PRIM. :TIME SER. :FIN.ST.TIM.

BOWEN ,RM ; FIRS: BLACCONIERE,WG ; THIR: SEFCIK,SE ; FOUR: STINSON,CH CIT: 0
DETERMINANTS OF THE USE OF REGULATORY ACCOUNTING PRINCIPLES BY SAVINGS AND LOANS
JAE JN 91 VOL: 14 PG:167 - 201 :: REGRESS. :PRIM. :OTH.STAT. :ACC.CHNG.

BOWEN ,RM ; SEC: JOHNSON,MF ; THIR: SHEVLIN,T CIT: 0.25
INFORMATIONAL EFFICIENCY AND THE INFORMATION CONTENT OF EARNINGS DURING THE MARKET CRASH OF OCTOBER 1987
JAE JL 89 VOL: 11 PG:225 - 254 :: REGRESS. :PRIM. :EMH :FIN.METH.

BOWEN ,RM ; SEC: PFEIFFER,GM CIT: 0
THE YEAR-END LIFO PURCHASE DECISION: THE CASE OF FARMER BROTHERS COMPANY
TAR JA 89 VOL: 64 PG:152 - 171 :: REGRESS. :CASE :HIST. :INV.

BOWEN ,RM ; SEC: BURGSTAHLER,D ; THIR: DALEY ,LA CIT: 1.67
THE INCREMENTAL INFORMATION CONTENT OF ACCRUAL VERSUS CASH FLOWS
TAR OC 87 VOL: 62 PG:723 - 747 :: REGRESS. :PRIM. :EMH :FIN.METH.

BOWEN ,RM ; SEC: BURGSTAHLER,D ; THIR: DALEY ,LA CIT: 0.71
EVIDENCE ON THE RELATIONSHIPS BETWEEN VARIOUS EARNINGS MEASURES OF CASH FLOW
TAR OC 86 VOL: 61 PG:713 - 725 :: REGRESS. :PRIM. :OTH.STAT. :REV.REC.

BOWEN ,RM ; SEC: SUNDEM,GL CIT: 0
EDITORIAL AND PUBLICATION LAGS IN THE ACCOUNTING AND FINANCE LITERATURE
TAR OC 82 VOL: 57 PG:778 - 784 :: DES.STAT. :PRIM. :OTH. :N/A

BOWEN ,RM ; SEC: NOREEN,EW ; THIR: LACEY ,JM CIT: 4
DETERMINANTS OF THE CORPORATE DECISION TO CAPITALIZE INTEREST
JAE AG 81 VOL: 3 PG:151 - 179 :: DES.STAT. :INT. LOG. :INF.ECO./AG. :SPEC.ITEMS

BOWEN ,RM CIT: 0.67
VALUATION OF EARNINGS COMPONENTS IN THE ELECTRIC UTILITY INDUSTRY
TAR JA 81 VOL: 56 PG:1 - 22 :: REGRESS. :PRIM. :EMH :FIN.METH.

BOWER ,JB ; SEC: SCHLOSSER,RE CIT: 0
INTERNAL CONTROL - ITS TRUE NATURE
TAR AP 65 VOL: 40 PG:338 - 344 :: QUAL. :INT. LOG. :INSTIT. :INT.CONT.

BOWER ,RS ; SEC: HERRINGER,F ; THIR: WILLIAMSON,JP CIT: 0
LEASE EVALUATION
TAR AP 66 VOL: 41 PG:257 - 265 :: ANAL. :INT. LOG. :OTH.STAT. :LEASES

BOWMAN,EH ; SEC: HAIRE ,M CIT: 0.18
SOCIAL IMPACT DISCLOSURE AND CORPORATE ANNUAL REPORTS
AOS 01 76 VOL: 1 PG:11 - 22 :: DES.STAT. :PRIM. :THEORY :HRA

BOWMAN,RG CIT: 0.38
THE IMPORTANCE OF A MARKET-VALUE MEASUREMENT OF DEBT IN ASSESSING LEVERAGE
JAR SP 80 VOL: 18 PG:242 - 254 :: ANOVA :PRIM. :EMH :LTD

BOWMAN,RG CIT: 0.15
THE DEBT EQUIVALENCE OF LEASES: AN EMPIRICAL INVESTIGATION
TAR AP 80 VOL: 55 PG:237 - 253 :: REGRESS. :PRIM. :EMH :LEASES

BOWSHER,CA CIT: 0
REDUCING THE FEDERAL DEFICIT: A CRITICAL CHALLENGE
JAA WI 86 VOL: 1 PG:7 - 16 :: DES.STAT. :INT. LOG. :OTH. :ORG.& ENVIR.

BOYLE ,PP CIT: 0
ACCOUNTING FOR EQUITY INVESTMENTS OF LIFE INSURANCE COMPANIES
CAR SP 85 VOL: 1 PG:116 - 144 :: DES.STAT. :INT. LOG. :MATH.PROG. :FIN.METH.

BOZE ,KM CIT: 0
ACCOUNTING FOR OPTIONS, FORWARDS AND FUTURES CONTRACTS
JAA AU 90 VOL: 5 PG:627 - 638 :: DES.STAT. :MIXED :THEORY :FIN.METH.

BRADBURY,ME ; SEC: CALDERWOOD,SC CIT: 0
EQUITY ACCOUNTING FOR RECIPROCAL STOCKHOLDINGS
TAR AP 88 VOL: 63 PG:330 - 347 :: DES.STAT. :INT. LOG. :THEORY :BUS.COMB.

BRADFORD,WD CIT: 0.06
PRICE-LEVEL RESTATED ACCOUNTING AND THE MEASUREMENT OF INFLATION GAINS AND LOSSES
TAR AP 74 VOL: 49 PG:296 - 305 :: ANAL. :INT. LOG. :THEORY :VALUAT.(INFL.)

BRADISH,RD CIT: 0.06
CORPORATE REPORTING AND THE FINANCIAL ANALYST
TAR OC 65 VOL: 40 PG:757 - 766 :: QUAL. :SURV. :INSTIT. :FIN.METH.

BRADLEY,G ; FIRS: TROTMAN,KT CIT: 0.5
ASSOCIATIONS BETWEEN SOCIAL RESPONSIBILITY DISCLOSURE AND CHARACTERISTICS OF COMPANIES
AOS 04 81 VOL: 6 PG:355 - 362 :: NON-PAR. :PRIM. :OTH. :HRA

BRANCH,B ; SEC: BERKOWITZ,B CIT: 0
THE PREDICTIVE ACCURACY OF THE BUSINESS WEEK EARNINGS FORECASTS
JAA SP 81 VOL: 4 PG:215 - 219 :: REGRESS. :SEC. :OTH.STAT. :FOREC.

BRANDI,JT ; FIRS: BROWN ,BC CIT: 0
SECURITY PRICE REACTIONS TO CHANGES IN FOREIGN CURRENCY TRANSLATION
JAA SU 86 VOL: 1 PG:185 - 205 :: REGRESS. :PRIM. :EMH :FOR.CUR.

BRANSON,BC ; FIRS: LOREK ,KS ; THIR: ICERMAN,RC CIT: 0
ON THE USE OF TIME-SERIES MODELS AS ANALYTICAL PROCEDURES
AUD AU 92 VOL: 11 PG:66 - 88 :: DES.STAT. :PRIM. :TIME SER. :ANAL.REV.

BRAVENEC,LL ; SEC: EPSTEIN,MJ ; THIR: CRUMBLEY,DL CIT: 0
TAX IMPACT IN CORPORATE SOCIAL RESPONSIBILITY DECISIONS AND REPORTING
AOS 02 77 VOL: 2 PG:131 - 140 :: QUAL. :INT. LOG. :THEORY :HRA

BREMSER,WG ; FIRS: HECK ,JL CIT: 0
SIX DECADES OF THE ACCOUNTING REVIEW: A SUMMARY OF AUTHOR AND INSTITUTIONAL CONTRIBUTORS
TAR OC 86 VOL: 61 PG:735 - 744 :: REGRESS. :SEC. :HIST. :METHOD.

BREMSER,WG CIT: 0.24
THE EARNINGS CHARACTERISTICS OF FIRMS REPORTING DISCRETIONARY ACCOUNTING CHANGES
TAR JL 75 VOL: 50 PG:563 - 573 :: ANOVA :PRIM. :N/A :ACC.CHNG.

BRENNAN,MJ CIT: 0
A PERSPECTIVE ON ACCOUNTING AND STOCK PRICES
TAR JA 91 VOL: 66 PG:67 - 79 :: ANOVA :SEC. :EMH :INT.REP.

BRENNER,VC ; SEC: CARMACK,CW ; THIR: WEINSTEIN,MG CIT: 0
AN EMPIRICAL TEST OF THE MOTIVATION-HYGIENE THEORY
JAR AU 71 VOL: 9 PG:359 - 366 :: CORR. :SURV. :OTH.BEH. :AUD.BEH.

BRENNER,VC CIT: 0.24
FINANCIAL STATEMENT USERS' VIEWS OF THE DESIRABILITY OF REPORTING CURRENT COST INFORMATION
JAR AU 70 VOL: 8 PG:159 - 166 :: NON-PAR. :SURV. :OTH. :VALUAT.(INFL.)

BRICKER,R CIT: 0
AN EMPIRICAL INVESTIGATION OF THE STRUCTURE OF ACCOUNTING RESEARCH
JAR AU 89 VOL: 27 PG:246 - 262 :: REGRESS. :SEC. :THEORY :METHOD.

BRICKLEY,JA ; SEC: VAN DRUNEN,LD CIT: 0.33
INTERNAL CORPORATE RESTRUCTURING: AN EMPIRICAL ANALYSIS
JAE JA 90 VOL: 12 PG:251 - 280 :: REGRESS. :PRIM. :OTH.STAT. :ORG.& ENVIR.

BRICKLEY,JA ; SEC: BHAGAT,S ; THIR: LEASE ,RC CIT: 0.63
THE IMPACT OF LONG-RANGE MANAGERIAL COMPENSATION PLANS ON SHAREHOLDER WEALTH
JAE AP 85 VOL: 7 PG:115 - 130 :: REGRESS. :PRIM. :EMH :EXEC.COMP.

BRIDEN,GE ; FIRS: REBELE,JE ; SEC: HEINTZ,JA CIT: 0
INDEPENDENT AUDITOR SENSITIVITY TO EVIDENCE RELIABILITY
AUD AU 88 VOL: 08 PG:43 - 52 :: REGRESS. :LAB. :OTH.BEH. :JUDG.

BRIEF ,AP ; FIRS: UECKER,WC ; THIR: KINNEY JR,WR CIT: 0.33
PERCEPTION OF THE INTERNAL AND EXTERNAL AUDITOR AS A DETERRENT TO CORPORATE IRREGULARITIES
TAR JL 81 VOL: 56 PG:465 - 478 :: ANOVA :LAB. :OTH.BEH. :AUD.BEH.

BRIEF ,RP ; SEC: LAWSON,RA CIT: 0
THE ROLE OF THE ACCOUNTING RATE OF RETURN IN FINANCIAL STATEMENT ANALYSIS
TAR AP 92 VOL: 67 PG:411 - 426 :: DES.STAT. :INT. LOG. :OTH.STAT. :CAP.BUDG.

BRIEF ,RP ; SEC: ANTON ,HR CIT: 0
AN INDEX OF GROWTH DUE TO DEPRECIATION
CAR SP 87 VOL: 3 PG:394 - 407 :: DES.STAT. :INT. LOG. :OTH.STAT. :PP&E / DEPR

BRIEF ,RP CIT: 0
A NOTE ON REDISCOVERY AND THE RULE OF 69
TAR OC 77 VOL: 52 PG:810 - 812 :: QUAL. :SEC. :HIST. :PP&E / DEPR

BRIEF ,RP CIT: 0.12
THE ACCOUNTANT'S RESPONSIBILITY IN HISTORICAL PERSPECTIVE
TAR AP 75 VOL: 50 PG:285 - 297 :: QUAL. :INT. LOG. :THEORY :N/A

BRIEF ,RP ; SEC: OWEN ,J CIT: 0.12
A REFORMULATION OF THE ESTIMATION PROBLEM
JAR SP 73 VOL: 11 PG:1 - 15 :: ANAL. :INT. LOG. :OTH.STAT. :PP&E / DEPR

BRIEF ,RP ; SEC: OWEN ,J CIT: 0.06
PRESENT VALUE MODELS AND THE MULTI-ASSET PROBLEM
TAR OC 73 VOL: 48 PG:690 - 695 :: QUAL. :INT. LOG. :THEORY :PP&E / DEPR

BRIEF ,RP ; SEC: OWEN ,J CIT: 0.18
THE ESTIMATION PROBLEM IN FINANCIAL ACCOUNTING
JAR AU 70 VOL: 8 PG:167 - 177 :: ANAL. :INT. LOG. :OTH.STAT. :PP&E / DEPR

BRIEF ,RP ; SEC: OWEN ,J CIT: 0
ON THE BIAS IN ACCOUNTING ALLOCATIONS UNDER UNCERTAINTY
JAR SP 69 VOL: 7 PG:12 - 16 :: ANAL. :INT. LOG. :OTH.STAT. :COST.ALLOC.

BRIEF ,RP CIT: 0
AN ECONOMETRIC ANALYSIS OF GOODWILL: SOME FINDINGS IN A SEARCH FOR VALUATION RULES
TAR JA 69 VOL: 44 PG:20 - 26 :: REGRESS. :PRIM. :TIME SER. :OTH. NON-C/A

BRIEF ,RP ; SEC: OWEN ,J CIT: 0
A LEAST SQUARES ALLOCATION MODEL
JAR AU 68 VOL: 6 PG:193 - 199 :: ANAL. :INT. LOG. :MATH.PROG. :COST.ALLOC.

BRIEF ,RP ; SEC: OWEN ,J CIT: 0
DEPRECIATION AND CAPITAL GAINS: A NEW APPROACH
TAR AP 68 VOL: 43 PG:367 - 372 :: ANAL. :INT. LOG. :THEORY :PP&E / DEPR

BRIEF ,RP CIT: 0.06
A LATE NINETEENTH CENTURY CONTRIBUTION TO THE THEORY OF DEPRECIATION
JAR SP 67 VOL: 5 PG:27 - 38 :: QUAL. :SEC. :HIST. :PP&E / DEPR

BRIEF ,RP CIT: 0.12
NINETEENTH CENTURY ACCOUNTING ERROR
JAR SP 65 VOL: 3 PG:12 - 31 :: QUAL. :INT. LOG. :HIST. :N/A

BRIERS,M ; SEC: HIRST ,M CIT: 0.33
THE ROLE OF BUDGETARY INFORMATION IN PERFORMANCE EVALUATION
AOS 04 90 VOL: 15 PG:373 - 398 :: REGRESS. :SEC. :OTH.BEH. :BUDG.& PLAN.

BRIGHAM,EF ; SEC: NANTELL,TJ CIT: 0
NORMALIZATION VERSUS FLOW THROUGH FOR UTILITY COMPANIES USING LIBERALIZED TAX DEPRECIATION
TAR JL 74 VOL: 49 PG:436 - 447 :: ANAL. :SIM. :OTH.STAT. :TAXES

BRIGHAM,EF CIT: 0
THE EFFECTS OF ALTERNATIVE DEPRECIATION POLICIES ON REPORTED PROFITS
TAR JA 68 VOL: 43 PG:46 - 61 :: ANAL. :SIM. :OTH.STAT. :PP&E / DEPR

BRIGHTON,GD CIT: 0
ACCRUED EXPENSE TAX REFORM - NOT READY IN 1954 - READY IN 1969?
TAR JA 69 VOL: 44 PG:137 - 144 :: QUAL. :SEC. :HIST. :SPEC.ITEMS

BRIGHTON,GD ; FIRS: BRUGEMAN,DC CIT: 0
INSTITUTIONAL ACCOUNTING - HOW IT DIFFERS FROM COMMERCIAL ACCOUNTING
TAR OC 63 VOL: 38 PG:764 - 770 :: QUAL. :INT. LOG. :THEORY :N/A

BRILOFF,AJ CIT: 0
DIRTY POOLING
TAR JL 67 VOL: 42 PG:489 - 496 :: QUAL. :INT. LOG. :THEORY :BUS.COMB.

BRILOFF,AJ CIT: 0.12
OLD MYTHS AND NEW REALITIES IN ACCOUNTANCY
TAR JL 66 VOL: 41 PG:484 - 495 :: DES.STAT. :SURV. :INSTIT. :AUD.

BRILOFF,AJ CIT: 0.06
NEEDED: A REVOLUTION IN THE DETERMINATION AND APPLICATION OF ACCOUNTING PRINCIPLES
TAR JA 64 VOL: 39 PG:12 - 15 :: QUAL. :INT. LOG. :THEORY :FIN.METH.

BROCA ,DS ; FIRS: BORITZ,JE CIT: 0.29
SCHEDULING INTERNAL AUDIT ACTIVITIES
AUD AU 86 VOL: 6 PG:1 - 19 :: DES.STAT. :SIM. :OTH.STAT. :INT.AUD.

BROCKETT,P ; SEC: CHARNES,A ; THIR: COOPER,WW ; FOUR: SHIN ,HC CIT: 0
A CHANCE-CONSTRAINED PROGRAMMING APPROACH TO COST-VOLUME-PROFIT ANALYSIS
TAR JL 84 VOL: 59 PG:474 - 487 :: ANAL. :INT. LOG. :MATH.PROG. :C-V-P-A

BROCKHOFF,K CIT: 0.14
A NOTE ON EXTERNAL SOCIAL REPORTING BY GERMAN COMPANIES: A SURVEY OF 1973 COMPANY REPORTS
AOS 12 79 VOL: 4 PG:77 - 86 :: DES.STAT. :PRIM. :THEORY :HRA

BROMAN,AJ ; FIRS: MAHER ,MW ; SEC: TIESSEN,P ; THIR: COLSON,R CIT: 0
COMPETITION AND AUDIT FEES
TAR JA 92 VOL: 67 PG:199 - 211 :: REGRESS. :PRIM. :OTH. :ORG.

BROMWICH,M CIT: 0
THE CASE FOR STRATEGIC MANAGEMENT ACCOUNTING: THE ROLE OF ACCOUNTING INFORMATION FOR STRATEGY IN COMPETITIVE MARKETS
AOS 02 90 VOL: 15 PG:27 - 46 :: DES.STAT. :SEC. :OTH. :MANAG.

BROMWICH,M CIT: 0.15
THE POSSIBILITY OF PARTIAL ACCOUNTING STANDARDS
TAR AP 80 VOL: 55 PG:288 - 300 :: ANAL. :INT. LOG. :INSTIT. :FASB SUBM.

BROMWICH,M CIT: 0.13
THE USE OF PRESENT VALUE VALUATION MODELS IN PUBLISHED ACCOUNTING REPORTS
TAR JL 77 VOL: 52 PG:587 - 596 :: QUAL. :INT. LOG. :THEORY :VALUAT.(INFL.)

BROOKS,EH ; FIRS: BABER ,WR ; THIR: RICKS ,WE CIT: 0.67
AN EMPIRICAL INVESTIGATION OF THE MARKET FOR AUDIT SERVICES IN THE PUBLIC SECTOR
JAR AU 87 VOL: 25 PG:293 - 305 :: REGRESS. :PRIM. :OTH.STAT. :ORG.

BROWN ,BC ; SEC: BRANDI,JT CIT: 0
SECURITY PRICE REACTIONS TO CHANGES IN FOREIGN CURRENCY TRANSLATION
JAA SU 86 VOL: 1 PG:185 - 205 :: REGRESS. :PRIM. :EMH :FOR.CUR.

BROWN ,C CIT: 0
DIAGNOSTIC INFERENCE IN PERFORMANCE EVALUATION: EFFECTS OF CAUSE AND EVENT COVARIATION AND SIMILARITY
CAR AU 87 VOL: 4 PG:111 - 126 :: REGRESS. :LAB. :OTH.BEH. :VAR.

BROWN ,C ; SEC: SOLOMON,I CIT: 0.5
EFFECTS OF OUTCOME INFORMATION ON EVALUATIONS OF MANAGERIAL DECISIONS
TAR JL 87 VOL: 62 PG:564 - 577 :: REGRESS. :LAB. :OTH.BEH. :BUDG.& PLAN.

BROWN ,C CIT: 0.25
CASUAL REASONING IN PERFORMANCE ASSESSMENT: EFFECTS OF CAUSE AND EFFECT TEMPORAL ORDER AND COVARIATION
AOS 03 85 VOL: 10 PG:255 - 266 :: REGRESS. :LAB. :OTH.BEH. :VAR.

BROWN ,C CIT: 0.1
EFFECTS OF DYNAMIC TASK ENVIRONMENT ON THE LEARNING OF STANDARD COST VARIANCE SIGNIFICANCE
JAR AU 83 VOL: 21 PG:413 - 431 :: ANOVA :LAB. :HIPS :ORG.& ENVIR.

BROWN ,C CIT: 0.33
HUMAN INFORMATION PROCESSING FOR DECISIONS TO INVESTIGATE COST VARIANCES
JAR SP 81 VOL: 19 PG:62 - 85 :: ANOVA :LAB. :HIPS :VAR.

BROWN ,CE ; SEC: SOLOMON,I CIT: 0.5
CONFIGURAL INFORMATION PROCESSING IN AUDITING: THE ROLE OF DOMAIN-SPECIFIC KNOWLEDGE
TAR JA 91 VOL: 66 PG:100 - 119 :: REGRESS. :LAB. :HIPS :AUD.

BROWN ,CE ; SEC: SOLOMON,I CIT: 0.33
AUDITOR CONFIGURAL INFORMATION PROCESSING IN CONTROL RISK ASSESSMENT
AUD AU 90 VOL: 9 PG:17 - 38 :: REGRESS. :LAB. :HIPS :RISK

BROWN ,JR ; FIRS: MEHREZ,A ; THIR: KHOUJA,M CIT: 1
AGGREGATE EFFICIENCY MEASURES AND SIMPSON'S PARADOX
CAR AU 92 VOL: 9 PG:329 - 342 :: DES.STAT. :INT. LOG. :MATH.PROG. :MANAG.

BROWN ,LD ; SEC: HAN ,JCY CIT: 0
THE IMPACT OF ANNUAL EARNINGS ANNOUNCEMENTS ON CONVERGENCE OF BELIEFS
TAR OC 92 VOL: 67 PG:862 - 875 :: REGRESS. :PRIM. :EMH :AUD.BEH.

BROWN ,LD ; SEC: RICHARDSON,GD ; THIR: TRZCINKA,CA CIT: 0.5
STRONG-FORM EFFICIENCY ON THE TORONTO STOCK EXCHANGE: AN EXAMINATION OF ANALYST PRICE FORECASTS
CAR SP 91 VOL: 7 PG:323 - 346 :: REGRESS. :PRIM. :EMH :FOREC.

BROWN ,LD ; SEC: KIM ,SK CIT: 0
TIMELY AGGREGATE ANALYST FORECASTS AS BETTER PROXIES FOR MARKET EARNINGS EXPECTATIONS
JAR AU 91 VOL: 29 PG:382 - 385 :: DES.STAT. :PRIM. :EMH :METHOD.

BROWN ,LD ; SEC: GARDNER,JC ; THIR: VASARHELYI,MA CIT: 0
ATTRIBUTES OF ARTICLES IMPACTING CONTEMPORARY ACCOUNTING LITERATURE
CAR SP 89 VOL: 5 PG:793 - 815 :: REGRESS. :SEC. :THEORY :METHOD.

BROWN ,LD ; SEC: GARDNER,JC ; THIR: VASARHELYI,MA CIT: 0.5
AN ANALYSIS OF THE RESEARCH CONTRIBUTIONS OF ACCOUNTING, ORGANIZATIONS AND SOCIETY, 1976-1984
AOS 02 87 VOL: 12 PG:193 - 204 :: REGRESS. :SEC. :HIST. :METHOD.

BROWN ,LD ; SEC: ZMIJEWSKI,MA CIT: 0.17
THE EFFECT OF LABOR STRIKES ON SECURITY ANALYSTS' FORECAST SUPERIORITY AND ON THE ASSOCIATION BETWEEN RISK-ADJUSTED STOCK RETURN
CAR AU 87 VOL: 4 PG:61 - 75 :: REGRESS. :PRIM. :TIME SER. :FOREC.

BROWN ,LD ; SEC: GRIFFIN,PA ; THIR: HAGERMAN,RL ; FOUR: ZMIJEWSKI,ME CIT: 4.5
SECURITY ANALYST SUPERIORITY RELATIVE TO UNIVARIATE TIME-SERIES MODELS IN FORECASTING QUARTERLY EARNINGS
JAE AP 87 VOL: 9 PG:61 - 87 :: REGRESS. :PRIM. :TIME SER. :FOREC.

BROWN ,LD ; SEC: GRIFFIN,PA ; THIR: HAGERMAN,RL ; FOUR: ZMIJEWSKI,ME CIT: 5.17
AN EVALUATION OF ALTERNATIVE PROXIES FOR THE MARKET'S ASSESSMENT OF UNEXPECTED EARNINGS
JAE JL 87 VOL: 9 PG:159 - 193 :: REGRESS. :PRIM. :TIME SER. :METHOD.

BROWN ,LD ; SEC: RICHARDSON,GD ; THIR: SCHWAGER,SJ CIT: 1.5
AN INFORMATION INTERPRETATION OF FINANCIAL ANALYST SUPERIORITY IN FORECASTING EARNINGS
JAR SP 87 VOL: 25 PG:49 - 67 :: REGRESS. :PRIM. :TIME SER. :FOREC.

BROWN ,LD CIT: 0
DISCUSSION OF: "MARKET REACTIONS TO MANDATED INTEREST CAPITALIZATION"
CAR SP 86 VOL: 2 PG:252 - 258 :: DES.STAT. :SEC. :EMH :FIN.METH.

BROWN ,LD ; SEC: GARDNER,JC CIT: 0.75
USING CITATION ANALYSIS TO ASSESS THE IMPACT OF JOURNALS AND ARTICLES ON CONTEMPORARY ACCOUNTING RESEARCH (CAR)
JAR SP 85 VOL: 23 PG:84 - 109 :: REGRESS. :SEC. :HIST. :METHOD.

BROWN ,LD ; SEC: GARDNER,JC CIT: 0.88
APPLYING CITATION ANALYSIS TO EVALUATE THE RESEARCH CONTRIBUTIONS OF ACCOUNTING FACULTY AND DOCTORAL PROGRAMS
TAR AP 85 VOL: 60 PG:262 - 277 :: REGRESS. :SEC. :OTH.STAT. :METHOD.

BROWN ,LD CIT: 0.1
ACCOUNTING CHANGES AND THE ACCURACY OF ANALYSTS' EARNINGS FORECASTS
JAR AU 83 VOL: 21 PG:432 - 443 :: NON-PAR. :PRIM. :OTH.STAT. :ACC.CHNG.

BROWN ,LD ; SEC: HUGHES,JS ; THIR: ROZEFF,MS ; FOUR: VANDERWEIDE,JH CIT: 0.08
EXPECTATIONS DATA AND THE PREDICTIVE VALUE OF INTERIM REPORTING: A COMMENT
JAR SP 80 VOL: 18 PG:278 - 288 :: REGRESS. :PRIM. :TIME SER. :FOREC.

BROWN ,LD ; SEC: ROZEFF,MS CIT: 2.07
UNIVARIATE TIME-SERIES MODELS OF QUARTERLY ACCOUNTING EARNINGS PER SHARE: A PROPOSED MODEL
JAR SP 79 VOL: 17 PG:179 - 189 :: MIXED :PRIM. :TIME SER. :FOREC.

BROWN ,LD ; SEC: ROZEFF,MS CIT: 0.86
ADAPTIVE EXPECTATIONS, TIME-SERIES MODELS, AND ANALYST FORECAST REVISION
JAR AU 79 VOL: 17 PG:341 - 351 :: REGRESS. :PRIM. :TIME SER. :FOREC.

BROWN ,LD ; SEC: ROZEFF,MS CIT: 0.21
THE PREDICTIVE VALUE OF INTERIM REPORTS FOR IMPROVING FORECASTS OF FUTURE QUARTERLY EARNINGS
TAR JL 79 VOL: 54 PG:585 - 591 :: NON-PAR. :INT. LOG. :TIME SER. :FOREC.

BROWN ,P ; FIRS: BALL ,R CIT: 8.35
AN EMPIRICAL EVALUATION OF ACCOUNTING INCOME NUMBERS
JAR AU 68 VOL: 6 PG:159 - 178 :: NON-PAR. :PRIM. :EMH :FIN.METH.

BROWN ,P ; SEC: BALL ,R CIT: 0.94
SOME PRELIMINARY FINDINGS ON THE ASSOCIATION BETWEEN THE EARNINGS OF A FIRM, ITS INDUSTRY, AND THE ECONOMY
JAR ST 67 VOL: 5 PG:55 - 77 :: CORR. :PRIM. :EMH :REV.REC.

BROWN ,PR ; SEC: KARAN ,V CIT: 0.43
ONE APPROACH FOR ASSESSING THE OPERATIONAL NATURE OF AUDITING STANDARDS: AN ANALYSIS OF SAS NO. 9
AUD AU 86 VOL: 6 PG:134 - 147 :: ANOVA :LAB. :INSTIT. :INT.AUD.

BROWN ,PR CIT: 0.3
INDEPENDENT AUDITOR JUDGMENT IN THE EVALUATION OF INTERNAL AUDIT FUNCTIONS
JAR AU 83 VOL: 21 PG:444 - 455 :: NON-PAR. :LAB. :HIPS :INT.AUD.

BROWN ,PR CIT: 0
FASB RESPONSIVENESS TO CORPORATE INPUT
JAA SU 82 VOL: 5 PG:282 - 290 :: DES.STAT. :PRIM. :INSTIT. :FASB SUBM.

BROWN ,PR CIT: 0.58
A DESCRIPTIVE ANALYSIS OF SELECT INPUT BASES OF THE FINANCIAL ACCOUNTING STANDARDS BOARD
JAR SP 81 VOL: 19 PG:232 - 246 :: OTH.QUANT. :PRIM. :INSTIT. :FASB SUBM.

BROWN ,PR ; FIRS: ASHTON,RH CIT: 0.69
DESCRIPTIVE MODELING OF AUDITORS' INTERNAL CONTROL JUDGMENTS: REPLICATION AND EXTENSION
JAR SP 80 VOL: 18 PG:269 - 277 :: NON-PAR. :LAB. :HIPS :INT.CONT.

BROWN ,RM CIT: 1.31
SHORT-RANGE MARKET REACTION TO CHANGES TO LIFO ACCOUNTING USING PRELIMINARY EARNINGS ANNOUNCEMENT DATES
JAR SP 80 VOL: 18 PG:38 - 63 :: REGRESS. :PRIM. :EMH :INV.

BROWN ,SH ; FIRS: COPELAND,RM ; SEC: TAYLOR,RL CIT: 0.08
OBSERVATION ERROR AND BIAS IN ACCOUNTING RESEARCH
JAR SP 81 VOL: 19 PG:197 - 207 :: ANOVA :LAB. :OTH.BEH. :METHOD.

BROWNELL,P ; SEC: DUNK ,AS CIT: 0
TASK UNCERTAINTY AND ITS INTERACTION WITH BUDGETARY PARTICIPATION AND BUDGET EMPHASIS: SOME METHODOLOGICAL ISSUES AND EMPIRICAL INVESTIGATION
AOS 91 VOL: 16 PG:693 - 703 :: REGRESS. :SURV. :OTH.BEH. :BUDG.& PLAN.

BROWNELL,P ; FIRS: CHENHALL,RH CIT: 0.6
THE EFFECT OF PARTICIPATIVE BUDGETING ON JOB SATISFACTION AND PERFORMANCE: ROLE AMBIGUITY AS AN INTERVENING VARIABLE
AOS 03 88 VOL: 13 PG:225 - 233 :: ANOVA :SURV. :EMH :BUDG.& PLAN.

BROWNELL,P ; SEC: HIRST ,MK CIT: 1.14
RELIANCE ON ACCT. INFO., BUDGETARY PARTICIPATION, AND TASK UNCERTAINTY: TESTS OF A THREE-WAY INTERACTION
JAR AU 86 VOL: 24 PG:241 - 249 :: REGRESS. :SURV. :OTH.BEH. :BUDG.& PLAN.

BROWNELL,P ; SEC: MCINNES,M CIT: 1.57
BUDGETARY PARTICIPATION, MOTIVATION, AND MANAGERIAL PERFORMANCE
TAR OC 86 VOL: 61 PG:587 - 600 :: REGRESS. :SURV. :OTH.BEH. :BUDG.& PLAN.

BROWNELL,P CIT: 0.88
BUDGETARY SYSTEMS AND THE CONTROL OF FUNCTIONALLY DIFFERENTIATED ORGANIZATIONAL ACTIVITIES
JAR AU 85 VOL: 23 PG:502 - 512 :: REGRESS. :SURV. :OTH.BEH. :BUDG.& PLAN.

BROWNELL,P CIT: 0.3
LEADERSHIP STYLE, BUDGETARY PARTICIPATION AND MANAGERIAL BEHAVIOR
AOS 04 83 VOL: 8 PG:307 - 322 :: ANOVA :SURV. :OTH.BEH. :BUDG.& PLAN.

BROWNELL,P CIT: 0.5
THE MOTIVATIONAL IMPACT OF MANAGEMENT-BY-EXCEPTION IN A BUDGETARY CONTEXT
JAR AU 83 VOL: 21 PG:456 - 472 :: REGRESS. :SURV. :OTH.BEH. :BUDG.& PLAN.

BROWNELL,P CIT: 2.18
THE ROLE OF ACCOUNTING DATA IN PERFORMANCE EVALUATION, BUDGETARY PARTICIPATION, AND ORGANIZATIONAL EFFECTIVENESS
JAR SP 82 VOL: 20 PG:12 - 27 :: REGRESS. :LAB. :OTH.BEH. :BUDG.& PLAN.

BROWNELL,P CIT: 0.18
A FIELD STUDY EXAMINATION OF BUDGETARY PARTICIPATION AND LOCUS OF CONTROL
TAR OC 82 VOL: 57 PG:766 - 777 :: MIXED :FIELD :OTH.BEH. :BUDG.& PLAN.

BROWNELL,P CIT: 1.5
PARTICIPATION IN BUDGETING, LOCUS OF CONTROL AND ORGANIZATIONAL EFFECTIVENESS
TAR OC 81 VOL: 56 PG:844 - 860 :: REGRESS. :LAB. :OTH.BEH. :BUDG.& PLAN.

BRUGEMAN,DC ; SEC: BRIGHTON,GD CIT: 0
INSTITUTIONAL ACCOUNTING - HOW IT DIFFERS FROM COMMERCIAL ACCOUNTING
TAR OC 63 VOL: 38 PG:764 - 770 :: QUAL. :INT. LOG. :THEORY :N/A

BRUGGE,WG CIT: 0
THE ACCOUNTANCY PROFESSION IN GREECE
TAR JL 63 VOL: 38 PG:596 - 600 :: QUAL. :INT. LOG. :THEORY :FIN.METH.

BRUMMET,RL ; SEC: FLAMHOLTZ,EG ; THIR: PYLE ,WC CIT: 0.41
HUMAN RESOURCE MEASUREMENT - A CHALLENGE FOR ACCOUNTANTS
TAR AP 68 VOL: 43 PG:217 - 224 :: QUAL. :INT. LOG. :OTH.BEH. :HRA

BRUNDAGE,MV ; SEC: LIVINGSTONE,JL CIT: 0
SIMULATION ON A TIME-SHARING COMPUTER UTILITY SYSTEM
TAR JL 69 VOL: 44 PG:539 - 545 :: ANAL. :SIM. :N/A :OTH.MANAG.

BRUNER,RF ; FIRS: BONNIER,KA CIT: 0
AN ANALYSIS OF STOCK PRICE REACTION TO MANAGEMENT CHANGE IN DISTRESSED FIRMS
JAE FB 89 VOL: 11 PG:95 - 106 :: REGRESS. :PRIM. :EMH :N/A

BRUNS JR,WJ ; SEC: WATERHOUSE,JH CIT: 3.18
BUDGETARY CONTROL AND ORGANIZATION STRUCTURE
JAR AU 75 VOL: 13 PG:177 - 203 :: OTH.QUANT. :FIELD :OTH.BEH. :ORG.FORM

BRUNS JR,WJ CIT: 0.29
ACCOUNTING INFORMATION AND DECISION-MAKING: SOME BEHAVIOURAL HYPOTHESES
TAR JL 68 VOL: 43 PG:469 - 480 :: QUAL. :INT. LOG. :OTH.BEH. :MANAG.

BRUNS JR,WJ CIT: 0.06
THE ACCOUNTING PERIOD CONCEPT AND ITS EFFECT ON MANAGEMENT DECISIONS
JAR ST 66 VOL: 4 PG:1 - 14 :: DES.STAT. :LAB. :OTH.BEH. :INT.REP.

BRUNS JR,WJ CIT: 0.24
INVENTORY VALUATION AND MANAGEMENT DECISIONS
TAR AP 65 VOL: 40 PG:345 - 357 :: NON-PAR. :LAB. :N/A :INV.

BRUNSSON,N CIT: 0
DECIDING FOR RESPONSIBILITY AND LEGITIMATION: ALTERNATIVE INTERPRETATIONS OF ORGANIZATIONAL DECISION-MAKING
AOS 02 90 VOL: 15 PG:47 - 59 :: DES.STAT. :INT. LOG. :HIPS :ORG.& ENVIR.

BRUTON,CM ; FIRS: BIDDLE,GC ; THIR: SIEGEL,AF CIT: 0
COMPUTER-INTENSIVE METHODS IN AUDITING: BOOTSTRAP DIFFERENCE AND RATIO ESTIMATION
AUD AU 90 VOL: 9 PG:92 - 114 :: DES.STAT. :SIM. :OTH.STAT. :SAMP.

BRYER ,RA CIT: 0.5
ACCOUNTING FOR THE "RAILWAY MANIA" OF 1845 - A GREAT RAILWAY SWINDLE?
AOS 05 91 VOL: 16 PG:439 - 486 :: REGRESS. :SEC. :HIST. :ORG.& ENVIR.

BUBLITZ,B ; FIRS: JONES ,CP CIT: 0
MARKET REACTIONS TO THE INFORMATION CONTENT OF EARNINGS OVER ALTERNATIVE QUARTERS
JAA AU 90 VOL: 5 PG:549 - 566 :: REGRESS. :PRIM. :TIME SER. :INT.REP.

BUBLITZ,B ; SEC: ETTREDGE,M CIT: 0.5
THE INFORMATION IN DISCRETIONARY OUTLAYS: ADVERTISING, RESEARCH, AND DEVELOPMENT
TAR JA 89 VOL: 64 PG:108 - 124 :: REGRESS. :PRIM. :HIPS :R & D

BUBLITZ,B ; SEC: FRECKA,TJ ; THIR: MCKEOWN,JC CIT: 1.38
MARKET ASSOCIATION TESTS AND FASB STATEMENT NO. 33 DISCLOSURES: A REEXAMINATION
JAR ST 85 VOL: 23 PG:1 - 23 :: REGRESS. :PRIM. :EMH :VALUAT.(INFL.)

BUBLITZ,B ; SEC: KEE ,R CIT: 0
DO WE NEED SUNSET REQUIREMENTS FOR FASB PRONOUNCEMENTS?
JAA WI 84 VOL: 7 PG:123 - 137 :: QUAL. :INT. LOG. :INSTIT. :FASB SUBM.

BUBLITZ,B ; FIRS: STONE ,M CIT: 0.11
AN ANALYSIS OF THE RELIABILITY OF THE FASB DATA BANK OF CHANGING PRICE AND PENSION INFORMATION
TAR JL 84 VOL: 59 PG:469 - 473 :: DES.STAT. :PRIM. :OTH. :METHOD.

BUCHMAN,TA CIT: 0.25
AN EFFECT OF HINDSIGHT ON PREDICTING BANKRUPTCY WITH ACCOUNTING INFORMATION
AOS 03 85 VOL: 10 PG:267 - 286 :: REGRESS. :LAB. :OTH.BEH. :BUS.FAIL.

BUCHMAN,TA CIT: 0
THE RELIABILITY OF INTERNAL AUDITORS' WORKING PAPERS
AUD AU 83 VOL: 3 PG:92 - 103 :: NON-PAR. :SURV. :OTH.BEH. :INT.AUD.

BUCKLESS,FA ; SEC: RAVENSCROFT,SP CIT: 0
CONTRAST CODING: A REFINEMENT OF ANOVA IN BEHAVIORAL ANALYSIS
TAR OC 90 VOL: 65 PG:933 - 945 :: REGRESS. :SEC. :HIPS :METHOD.

BUCKLEY,JW CIT: 0
POLICY MODELS IN ACCOUNTING: A CRITICAL COMMENTARY
AOS 01 80 VOL: 5 PG:49 - 64 :: QUAL. :SEC. :THEORY :N/A

BUCKLEY,JW ; SEC: KIRCHER,P ; THIR: MATHEWS,RL CIT: 0.06
METHODOLOGY IN ACCOUNTING THEORY
TAR AP 68 VOL: 43 PG:274 - 283 :: QUAL. :INT. LOG. :THEORY :FIN.METH.

BUCKLEY,JW CIT: 0
PROGRAMMED INSTRUCTION: WITH EMPHASIS ON ACCOUNTING
TAR JL 67 VOL: 42 PG:572 - 582 :: QUAL. :INT. LOG. :N/A :OTH.MANAG.

BUCKLEY,JW CIT: 0
MEDICARE AND ACCOUNTING
TAR JA 66 VOL: 41 PG:75 - 82 :: QUAL. :SEC. :N/A :FIN.METH.

BUCKMAN,AG ; SEC: MILLER,BL CIT: 0
OPTIMAL INVESTIGATION OF A MULTIPLE COST PROCESSES SYSTEM
JAR SP 82 VOL: 20 PG:28 - 41 :: ANAL. :INT. LOG. :OTH.STAT. :N/A

BUCKMAN,AG ; FIRS: OHLSON,JA CIT: 0.42
TOWARD A THEORY OF FINANCIAL ACCOUNTING: WELFARE AND PUBLIC INFORMATION
JAR AU 81 VOL: 19 PG:399 - 433 :: ANAL. :INT. LOG. :THEORY :N/A

BULLEN,ML ; SEC: FLAMHOLTZ,EG CIT: 0.13
A THEORETICAL AND EMPIRICAL INVESTIGATION OF JOB SATISFACTION AND INTENDED TURNOVER IN THE LARGE CPA FIRM
AOS 03 85 VOL: 10 PG:287 - 302 :: REGRESS. :SURV. :OTH.BEH. :ORG.

BULLOCH,J ; FIRS: DUVALL,RM CIT: 0
ADJUSTING RATE OF RETURN AND PRESENT VALUE FOR PRICE-LEVEL CHANGES
TAR JL 65 VOL: 40 PG:569 - 573 :: ANAL. :INT. LOG. :OTH.STAT. :OTH.MANAG.

BULLOCK,CL CIT: 0.06
RECONCILING ECONOMIC DEPRECIATION WITH TAX ALLOCATION
TAR JA 74 VOL: 49 PG:98 - 103 :: ANAL. :INT. LOG. :THEORY :PP&E / DEPR

BURCHELL,S ; SEC: CLUBB ,C ; THIR: HOPWOOD,AG CIT: 3.75
ACCOUNTING IN ITS SOCIAL CONTEXT: TOWARDS A HISTORY OF VALUE ADDED IN THE UNITED KINGDOM
AOS 04 85 VOL: 10 PG:381 - 414 :: DES.STAT. :INT. LOG. :THEORY :HRA

BURCHELL,S ; SEC: CLUBB ,C ; THIR: HOPWOOD,AG ; FOUR: HUGHES,JS ; FIFT: NAHAPIET,JE CIT: 4.92
THE ROLES OF ACCOUNTING IN ORGANIZATIONS AND SOCIETY
AOS 01 80 VOL: 5 PG:5 - 27 :: QUAL. :INT. LOG. :THEORY :N/A

BURGHER,PH CIT: 0
PERT AND THE AUDITOR
TAR JA 64 VOL: 39 PG:103 - 120 :: ANAL. :INT. LOG. :OTH.STAT. :INT.AUD.

BURGSTAHLER,D ; SEC: JIAMBALVO,J ; THIR: NOREEN,E CIT: 0.25
CHANGES IN THE PROBABILITY OF BANKRUPTCY AND EQUITY VALUE
JAE JL 89 VOL: 11 PG:207 - 224 :: REGRESS. :PRIM. :OTH.STAT. :BUS.FAIL.

BURGSTAHLER,D ; FIRS: BOWEN ,RM ; THIR: DALEY ,LA CIT: 1.67
THE INCREMENTAL INFORMATION CONTENT OF ACCRUAL VERSUS CASH FLOWS
TAR OC 87 VOL: 62 PG:723 - 747 :: REGRESS. :PRIM. :EMH :FIN.METH.

BURGSTAHLER,D ; SEC: NOREEN,EW CIT: 0
DETECTING CONTEMPORANEOUS SECURITY MARKET REACTIONS TO A SEQUENCE OF RELATED EVENTS
JAR SP 86 VOL: 24 PG:170 - 186 :: REGRESS. :PRIM. :EMH :METHOD.

BURGSTAHLER,D ; SEC: JIAMBALVO,J CIT: 0.43
SAMPLE ERROR CHARACTERISTICS AND PROJECTION OF ERROR TO AUDIT POPULATIONS
TAR AP 86 VOL: 61 PG:233 - 248 :: REGRESS. :LAB. :HIPS :ERRORS

BURGSTAHLER,D ; FIRS: BOWEN ,RM ; THIR: DALEY ,LA CIT: 0.71
EVIDENCE ON THE RELATIONSHIPS BETWEEN VARIOUS EARNINGS MEASURES OF CASH FLOW
TAR OC 86 VOL: 61 PG:713 - 725 :: REGRESS. :PRIM. :OTH.STAT. :REV.REC.

BURKE ,EJ CIT: 0.06
OBJECTIVITY AND ACCOUNTING
TAR OC 64 VOL: 39 PG:837 - 849 :: QUAL. :INT. LOG. :THEORY :OTH.FIN.ACC.

BURKE ,WL CIT: 0
COST ALLOCATION AND DISTRIBUTION - MERCHANDISE ACCOUNTING
TAR OC 63 VOL: 38 PG:802 - 812 :: QUAL. :INT. LOG. :THEORY :N/A

BURNS ,JS ; SEC: JAEDICKE,RK ; THIR: SANGSTER,JM CIT: 0
FINANCIAL REPORTING OF PURCHASE CONTRACTS USED TO GUARANTEE LARGE INVESTMENTS
TAR JA 63 VOL: 38 PG:1 - 13 :: QUAL. :INT. LOG. :THEORY :SPEC.ITEMS

BURRELL,G CIT: 0.83
NO ACCOUNTING FOR SEXUALITY
AOS 01 87 VOL: 12 PG:89 - 102 :: DES.STAT. :INT. LOG. :INSTIT. :ORG.& ENVIR.

BURT ,OR CIT: 0
A UNIFIED THEORY OF DEPRECIATION
JAR SP 72 VOL: 10 PG:28 - 57 :: ANAL. :INT. LOG. :THEORY :PP&E / DEPR

BURTON,JC ; SEC: FAIRFIELD,P CIT: 0.36
AUDITING EVOLUTION IN A CHANGING ENVIRONMENT
AUD WI 82 VOL: 1 PG:1 - 22 :: DES.STAT. :INT. LOG. :INSTIT. :ORG.

BUSHMAN,R ; FIRS: KANODIA,C ; THIR: DICKHAUT,J CIT: 1
ESCALATION ERRORS AND THE SUNK COST EFFECT: AN EXPLANATION BASED ON REPUTATION AN INFORMATION ASYMMETRIES
JAR SP 89 VOL: 27 PG:59 - 77 :: DES.STAT. :INT. LOG. :INF.ECO./AG. :EXEC.COMP.

BUSHMAN,RM CIT: 0.5
PUBLIC DISCLOSURE AND THE STRUCTURE OF PRIVATE INFORMATION MARKETS
JAR AU 91 VOL: 29 PG:261 - 276 :: DES.STAT. :INT. LOG. :INF.ECO./AG. :INFO.STRUC.

BUTLER,SA ; FIRS: REIMERS,JL CIT: 0
THE EFFECT OF OUTCOME KNOWLEDGE ON AUDITORS' JUDGMENTAL EVALUATIONS
AOS 02 92 VOL: 17 PG:185 - 194 :: REGRESS. :LAB. :HIPS :JUDG.

BUTLER,SA CIT: 0.14
ANCHORING IN THE JUDGMENTAL EVALUATION OF AUDIT SAMPLES
TAR JA 86 VOL: 61 PG:101 - 111 :: REGRESS. :LAB. :HIPS :RISK

BUTLER,SA CIT: 0.25
APPLICATION OF A DECISION AID IN THE JUDGMENTAL EVALUATION OF SUBSTANTIVE TEST OF DETAILS SAMPLES
JAR AU 85 VOL: 23 PG:513 - 526 :: REGRESS. :LAB. :HIPS :DEC.AIDS

BUTT ,JL ; SEC: CAMPBELL,TL CIT: 0.75
THE EFFECTS OF INFORMATION ORDER AND HYPOTHESIS-TESTING STRATEGIES ON AUDITORS' JUDGMENTS
AOS 06 89 VOL: 14 PG:471 - 479 :: REGRESS. :LAB. :HIPS :JUDG.

BUTT ,JL CIT: 1.2
FREQUENCY JUDGMENTS IN AN AUDITING-RELATED TASK
JAR AU 88 VOL: 26 PG:315 - 330 :: REGRESS. :LAB. :OTH.BEH. :JUDG.

BUTTERWORTH,JE CIT: 0.53
THE ACCOUNTING SYSTEM AS AN INFORMATION FUNCTION
JAR SP 72 VOL: 10 PG:1 - 27 :: ANAL. :INT. LOG. :INF.ECO./AG. :INFO.STRUC.

BUTTERWORTH,JE ; SEC: SIGLOCH,BA CIT: 0.06
A GENERALIZED MULTI-STAGE INPUT-OUTPUT MODEL AND SOME DERIVED EQUIVALENT SYSTEMS
TAR OC 71 VOL: 46 PG:701 - 716 :: ANAL. :INT. LOG. :MATH.PROG. :MANAG.

BUZBY ,SL ; SEC: FALK ,H CIT: 0.29
DEMAND FOR SOCIAL RESPONSIBILITY INFORMATION BY UNIVERSITY INVESTORS
TAR JA 79 VOL: 54 PG:23 - 37 :: DES.STAT. :SURV. :INSTIT. :HRA

BUZBY ,SL ; SEC: FALK ,H CIT: 0.2
A SURVEY OF THE INTEREST IN SOCIAL RESPONSIBILITY INFORMATION BY MUTUAL FUNDS
AOS 34 78 VOL: 3 PG:191 - 202 :: DES.STAT. :SURV. :OTH.BEH. :METHOD.

BUZBY ,SL CIT: 0.06
COMPANY SIZE, LISTED VERSUS UNLISTED STOCKS, AND THE EXTENT OF FINANCIAL DISCLOSURE
JAR SP 75 VOL: 13 PG:16 - 37 :: NON-PAR. :SURV. :THEORY :N/A

BUZBY ,SL CIT: 0.35
EXTENDING THE APPLICABILITY OF PROBABILISTIC MANAGEMENT PLANNING AND CONTROL MODELS
TAR JA 74 VOL: 49 PG:42 - 49 :: ANAL. :INT. LOG. :OTH.STAT. :C-V-P-A

BUZBY ,SL CIT: 0.59
SELECTED ITEMS OF INFORMATION AND THEIR DISCLOSURE IN ANNUAL REPORTS
TAR JL 74 VOL: 49 PG:423 - 435 :: DES.STAT. :SURV. :N/A :INFO.STRUC.

BUZBY ,SL ; FIRS: MORRISON,TA CIT: 0
EFFECT OF THE INVESTMENT TAX CREDIT ON THE CAPITALIZE-EXPENSE DECISION
TAR JL 68 VOL: 43 PG:517 - 521 :: ANAL. :INT. LOG. :N/A :TAX PLNG.

BYLINSKI,JH ; FIRS: BAMBER,EM ; SEC: BAMBER,LS CIT: 0
A DESCRIPTIVE STUDY OF AUDIT MANAGERS' WORKING PAPER REVIEW
AUD SP 88 VOL: 07 PG:137 - 149 :: REGRESS. :LAB. :HIPS :AUD.BEH.

BYLINSKI,JH ; FIRS: BAMBER,EM CIT: 0
THE EFFECTS OF THE PLANNING MEMORANDUM, TIME PRESSURE AND INDIVIDUAL AUDITOR CHARACTERISTICS ON AUDIT MANAGERS' REVIEW TIME JUDG
CAR AU 87 VOL: 4 PG:127 - 143 :: REGRESS. :LAB. :HIPS :JUDG.

BYLINSKI,JH ; FIRS: BLOCHER,E CIT: 0
THE INFLUENCE OF SAMPLE CHARACTERISTICS IN SAMPLE EVALUATION
AUD AU 85 VOL: 5 PG:79 - 90 :: REGRESS. :LAB. :OTH.BEH. :SAMP.

BYLINSKI,JH ; FIRS: BAILEY,KE ; THIR: SHIELDS,MD CIT: 0
EFFECTS OF AUDIT REPORT WORDING CHANGES ON THE PERCEIVED MESSAGE
JAR AU 83 VOL: 21 PG:355 - 370 :: OTH.QUANT. :LAB. :OTH.BEH. :OPIN.

BYRNE ,R ; SEC: CHARNES,A ; THIR: COOPER,WW ; FOUR: KORTANEK,KO CIT: 0
SOME NEW APPROACHES TO RISK
TAR JA 68 VOL: 43 PG:18 - 37 :: ANAL. :INT. LOG. :MATH.PROG. :BUDG.& PLAN.

BYUN ,YH ; FIRS: LEVY ,H CIT: 0
AN EMPIRICAL TEST OF THE BLACK-SCHOLES OPTION PRICING MODEL AND THE IMPLIED VARIANCE: A CONFIDENCE INTERVAL APPROACH
JAA AU 87 VOL: 2 PG:355 - 369 :: DES.STAT. :PRIM. :OTH. :OTH.MANAG.

CAHAN ,SF CIT: 0
THE EFFECT OF ANTITRUST INVESTIGATIONS ON DISCRETIONARY ACCRUALS: A REFINED TEST OF THE POLITICAL-COST HYPOTHESIS
TAR JA 92 VOL: 67 PG:77 - 96 :: REGRESS. :PRIM. :OTH. :FIN.METH.

CAIN ,P ; FIRS: ASKARI,H ; THIR: SHAW ,R CIT: 0
A GOVERNMENT TAX SUBSIDY
TAR AP 76 VOL: 51 PG:331 - 334 :: DES.STAT. :PRIM. :N/A :TAX PLNG.

CALDERON,TG ; FIRS: LAMBERT,JC ; SEC: LAMBERT III,SJ CIT: 0
COMMUNICATION BETWEEN SUCCESSOR AND PREDECESSOR AUDITORS
AUD SP 91 VOL: 10 PG:97 - 109 :: REGRESS. :SURV. :OTH.STAT. :ORG.

CALDERWOOD,SC ; FIRS: BRADBURY,ME CIT: 0
EQUITY ACCOUNTING FOR RECIPROCAL STOCKHOLDINGS
TAR AP 88 VOL: 63 PG:330 - 347 :: DES.STAT. :INT. LOG. :THEORY :BUS.COMB.

CALL ,DV CIT: 0
SOME SALIENT FACTORS OFTEN OVERLOOKED IN STOCK OPTIONS
TAR OC 69 VOL: 44 PG:711 - 719 :: ANAL. :INT. LOG. :N/A :OTH.MANAG.

CALLAHAN,C ; FIRS: ELGERS,P ; THIR: STROCK,E CIT: 0.17
THE EFFECT OF EARNINGS YIELDS UPON THE ASSOCIATION BETWEEN UNEXPECTED
EARNINGS AND SECURITY RETURNS; A RE-EXAMINATION
TAR OC 87 VOL: 62 PG:763 - 773 :: REGRESS. :PRIM. :EMH :FIN.METH.

CALLEN,JL CIT: 0
AN INDEX NUMBER THEORY OF ACCOUNTING COST VARIANCES
JAA SP 88 VOL: 03 PG:87 - 108 :: DES.STAT. :INT. LOG. :OTH.STAT. :VAR.

CALLEN,JL CIT: 0.2
FINANCIAL COST ALLOCATIONS: A GAME THEORETIC APPROACH
TAR AP 78 VOL: 53 PG:303 - 308 :: ANAL. :INT. LOG. :OTH.STAT. :COST.ALLOC.

CALOMME,GJ ; FIRS: MILTZ ,D ; THIR: WILLIKENS,M CIT: 0
A RISK-BASED ALLOCATION OF INTERNAL AUDIT TIME: A CASE STUDY
AUD AU 91 VOL: 10 PG:49 - 61 :: REGRESS. :CASE :OTH.STAT. :RISK

CAMARDESSE JR,JE ; FIRS: VASARHELYI,MA ; SEC: BAILEY JR,AD ; FOUR: GROOMER,SM ; FIFT: LAMPE ,JC CIT: 0
THE USAGE OF COMPUTERS IN AUDITING TEACHING AND RESEARCH
AUD SP 84 VOL: 3 PG:98 - 103 :: QUAL. :SIM. :OTH. :EDP AUD.

CAMMANN,C CIT: 0.35
EFFECTS OF THE USE OF CONTROL SYSTEMS
AOS 04 76 VOL: 1 PG:301 - 314 :: REGRESS. :CASE :OTH.BEH. :BUDG.& PLAN.

CAMPBELL,DR CIT: 0
AN ANALYSIS OF THE GROWTH IN PUBLIC ACCOUNTING: IMPLICATIONS FOR FUTURE
PLANNING STRATEGIES
JAA SP 83 VOL: 6 PG:196 - 211 :: DES.STAT. :PRIM. :OTH. :PROF.RESP.

CAMPBELL,JE CIT: 0.22
AN APPLICATION OF PROTOCOL ANALYSIS TO THE LITTLE GAAP CONTROVERSY
AOS 34 84 VOL: 9 PG:329 - 342 :: DES.STAT. :LAB. :HIPS :MAN.DEC.CHAR.

CAMPBELL,TL ; FIRS: BUTT ,JL CIT: 0.75
THE EFFECTS OF INFORMATION ORDER AND HYPOTHESIS-TESTING STRATEGIES ON
AUDITORS' JUDGMENTS
AOS 06 89 VOL: 14 PG:471 - 479 :: REGRESS. :LAB. :HIPS :JUDG.

CAMPFIELD,WL CIT: 0
TOWARD MAKING ACCOUNTING EDUCATION ADAPTIVE AND NORMATIVE
TAR OC 70 VOL: 45 PG:683 - 689 :: QUAL. :INT. LOG. :N/A :OTH.MANAG.

CAMPFIELD,WL CIT: 0
PROFESSIONAL STATUS FOR INTERNAL AUDITORS
TAR JL 65 VOL: 40 PG:594 - 598 :: QUAL. :INT. LOG. :INSTIT. :OTH.MANAG.

CAMPFIELD,WL CIT: 0
CRITICAL PATHS FOR PROFESSIONAL ACCOUNTANTS DURING THE NEW MANAGEMENT REVOLUTION
TAR JL 63 VOL: 38 PG:521 - 527 :: QUAL. :INT. LOG. :INSTIT. :PROF.RESP.

CAPLAN,EM CIT: 0.18
BEHAVIOURAL ASSUMPTIONS OF MANAGEMENT ACCOUNTING - REPORT OF A FIELD STUDY
TAR AP 68 VOL: 43 PG:342 - 362 :: DES.STAT. :SURV. :OTH.BEH. :MANAG.

CAPLAN,EM CIT: 0.65
BEHAVIOURAL ASSUMPTIONS OF MANAGEMENT ACCOUNTING
TAR JL 66 VOL: 41 PG:496 - 509 :: QUAL. :INT. LOG. :OTH.BEH. :MANAG.

CAPPS ,T ; FIRS: BERRY ,AJ ; THIR: COOPER,D ; FOUR: FERGUSON,P ; FIFT: HOPPER,T ; SIX: LOWE ,EA CIT: 3
MANAGEMENT CONTROL IN AN AREA OF THE NCB: RATIONALES OF ACCOUNTING PRACTICES IN A PUBLIC ENTERPRISE
AOS 01 85 VOL: 10 PG:3 - 28 :: REGRESS. :FIELD :OTH.BEH. :MANAG.

CARCELLO,JV ; SEC: HERMANSON,RH ; THIR: MCGRATH,NT CIT: 0
AUDIT QUALITY ATTRIBUTES: THE PERCEPTIONS OF AUDIT PARTNERS, PREPARERS, AND FINANCIAL STATEMENT USERS
AUD SP 92 VOL: 11 PG:1 - 15 :: REGRESS. :SURV. :OTH.BEH. :OPER.AUD.

CAREY ,JL CIT: 0
TEACHERS AND PRACTITIONERS
TAR JA 69 VOL: 44 PG:79 - 85 :: QUAL. :INT. LOG. :INSTIT. :OTH.MANAG.

CAREY ,JL CIT: 0
WHAT IS THE PROFESSIONAL PRACTICE OF ACCOUNTING?
TAR JA 68 VOL: 43 PG:1 - 9 :: QUAL. :INT. LOG. :INSTIT. :AUD.

CAREY ,KJ ; FIRS: BASI ,BA ; THIR: TWARK ,RD CIT: 0.82
A COMPARISON OF THE ACCURACY OF CORPORATE AND SECURITY ANALYSTS' FORECASTS
TAR AP 76 VOL: 51 PG:244 - 254 :: ANOVA :PRIM. :TIME SER. :FOREC.

CARLISLE,HM CIT: 0
COST ACCOUNTING FOR ADVANCED TECHNOLOGY PROGRAMS
TAR JA 66 VOL: 41 PG:115 - 120 :: QUAL. :INT. LOG. :N/A :MANAG.

CARLSON,ML ; SEC: LAMB ,JW CIT: 0
CONSTRUCTING A THEORY OF ACCOUNTING - AN AXIOMATIC APPROACH
TAR JL 81 VOL: 56 PG:554 - 573 :: ANAL. :INT. LOG. :THEORY :N/A

CARLSSON,J ; SEC: EHN ,P ; THIR: ERLANDER,B ; FOUR: PERBY ,M ; FIFT: SANDBERG,A CIT: 0.07
PLANNING AND CONTROL FROM THE PERSPECTIVE OF LABOR: A SHORT REPRESENTATION OF THE DEMOS PROJECT
AOS 34 78 VOL: 3 PG:249 - 260 :: QUAL. :FIELD :OTH. :BUDG.& PLAN.

CARMACK,CW ; FIRS: BRENNER,VC ; THIR: WEINSTEIN,MG CIT: 0
AN EMPIRICAL TEST OF THE MOTIVATION-HYGIENE THEORY
JAR AU 71 VOL: 9 PG:359 - 366 :: CORR. :SURV. :OTH.BEH. :AUD.BEH.

CARMICHAEL,DR ; SEC: WHITTINGTON,OR CIT: 0
THE AUDITOR'S CHANGING ROLE IN FINANCIAL REPORTING
JAA SU 84 VOL: 7 PG:347 - 361 :: QUAL. :INT. LOG. :OTH. :PROF.RESP.

CARMICHAEL,DR CIT: 0
THE COHEN COMMISSION IN PERSPECTIVE: ACTIONS AND REACTIONS
JAA SU 79 VOL: 2 PG:294 - 306 :: QUAL. :INT. LOG. :INSTIT. :AUD.

CARMICHAEL,DR CIT: 0.35
BEHAVIOURAL HYPOTHESES OF INTERNAL CONTROL
TAR AP 70 VOL: 45 PG:235 - 245 :: QUAL. :INT. LOG. :OTH.BEH. :INT.CONT.

CARMICHAEL,DR ; SEC: SWIERINGA,RJ CIT: 0.06
THE COMPATIBILITY OF AUDITING INDEPENDENCE AND MANAGEMENT SERVICES: AN IDENTIFICATION OF ISSUES
TAR OC 68 VOL: 43 PG:697 - 705 :: QUAL. :INT. LOG. :INSTIT. :INDEP.

CARPENTER,BW ; SEC: DIRSMITH,MW CIT: 0
EARLY DEBT EXTINGUISHMENT TRANSACTIONS AND AUDITOR MATERIALITY JUDGMENTS: A BOUNDED RATIONALITY PERSPECTIVE
AOS 92 VOL: 17 PG:709 - 739 :: REGRESS. :LAB. :HIPS :MAT.

CARPENTER,CG ; SEC: STRAWSER,RH CIT: 0
A STUDY OF THE JOB SATISFACTION OF ACADEMIC ACCOUNTANTS
TAR JL 71 VOL: 46 PG:509 - 518 :: NON-PAR. :SURV. :INSTIT. :OTH.MANAG.

CARPENTER,VL ; SEC: FEROZ ,EH CIT: 0
GAAP AS A SYMBOL OF LEGITIMACY: NEW YORK STATE'S DECISION TO ADOPT GENERALLY ACCEPTED ACCOUNTING PRINCIPLES
AOS 92 VOL: 17 PG:613 - 643 :: REGRESS. :MIXED :HIST. :ORG.& ENVIR.

CARPER,WB ; SEC: POSEY ,JM CIT: 0.06
THE VALIDITY OF SELECTED SURROGATE MEASURES OF HUMAN RESOURCE VALUE: A FIELD STUDY
AOS 23 76 VOL: 1 PG:143 - 152 :: NON-PAR. :SURV. :OTH.BEH. :HRA

CARRIER,NH ; FIRS: BAXTER,WT CIT: 0.06
DEPRECIATION, REPLACEMENT PRICE, AND COST OF CAPITAL
JAR AU 71 VOL: 9 PG:189 - 214 :: ANAL. :INT. LOG. :THEORY :VALUAT.(INFL.)

CARROLL,R ; FIRS: HOLT ,RN CIT: 0.31
CLASSIFICATION OF COMMERCIAL BANK LOANS THROUGH POLICY CAPTURING
AOS 03 80 VOL: 5 PG:285 - 296 :: OTH.QUANT. :LAB. :HIPS :BUS.FAIL.

CARSBERG,BV CIT: 0
ON THE LINEAR PROGRAMMING APPROACH TO ASSET VALUATION
JAR AU 69 VOL: 7 PG:165 - 182 :: ANAL. :INT. LOG. :MATH.PROG. :PP&E / DEPR

CARSBERG,BV CIT: 0.06
THE CONTRIBUTION OF P.D. LEAKE TO THE THEORY OF GOODWILL VALUATION
JAR SP 66 VOL: 4 PG:1 - 15 :: QUAL. :INT. LOG. :HIST. :OTH. NON-C/A

CARSLAW,C CIT: 0.2
ANOMALIES IN INCOME NUMBERS: EVIDENCE OF GOAL ORIENTED BEHAVIOR
TAR AP 88 VOL: 63 PG:321 - 327 :: REGRESS. :PRIM. :OTH. :METHOD.

CARSON,AB CIT: 0
CASH MOVEMENT: THE HEART OF INCOME MEASUREMENT
TAR AP 65 VOL: 40 PG:334 - 337 :: QUAL. :INT. LOG. :THEORY :FIN.METH.

CARTER,WK CIT: 0
A BENEFITS APPROACH TO CERTAIN ACCOUNTING POLICY CHOICES
TAR JA 81 VOL: 56 PG:108 - 114 :: QUAL. :INT. LOG. :THEORY :FIN.METH.

CASEY JR,CJ ; SEC: MCGEE ,VE ; THIR: STICKNEY,CP CIT: 0.43
DISCRIMINATING BETWEEN REORGANIZED AND LIQUIDATED FIRMS IN BANKRUPTCY
TAR AP 86 VOL: 61 PG:249 - 262 :: REGRESS. :PRIM. :OTH.STAT. :BUS.FAIL.

CASEY JR,CJ ; SEC: SELLING,T CIT: 0.14
THE EFFECT OF TASK PREDICTABILITY AND PRIOR PROBABILITY DISCLOSURE ON JUDGMENT QUALITY AND CONFIDENCE
TAR AP 86 VOL: 61 PG:302 - 317 :: REGRESS. :LAB. :HIPS :BUS.FAIL.

CASEY JR,CJ ; SEC: BARTCZAK,N CIT: 0.13
USING OPERATING CASH FLOW DATA TO PREDICT FINANCIAL DISTRESS: SOME EXTENSIONS
JAR SP 85 VOL: 23 PG:384 - 401 :: REGRESS. :PRIM. :MATH.PROG. :BUS.FAIL.

CASEY JR,CJ CIT: 0.1
PRIOR PROBABILITY DISCLOSURE AND LOAN OFFICERS' JUDGMENTS: SOME EVIDENCE OF THE IMPACT
JAR SP 83 VOL: 21 PG:300 - 307 :: OTH.QUANT. :PRIM. :OTH.BEH. :N/A

CASEY JR,CJ CIT: 0.85
VARIATION IN ACCOUNTING INFORMATION LOAD: THE EFFECT ON LOAN OFFICERS' PREDICTIONS OF BANKRUPTCY
TAR JA 80 VOL: 55 PG:36 - 49 :: ANOVA :LAB. :HIPS :BUS.FAIL.

CASH JR,JI ; SEC: BAILEY JR,AD ; THIR: WHINSTON,AB CIT: 0.13
A SURVEY OF TECHNIQUES FOR AUDITING EDP-BASED ACCOUNTING INFORMATION SYSTEMS
TAR OC 77 VOL: 52 PG:813 - 832 :: QUAL. :SEC. :N/A :ANAL.REV.

CASLER,DJ ; FIRS: HALL ,TW CIT: 0
USING INDEXING TO ESTIMATE CURRENT COSTS - COMPOSITE OR MULTIPLE INDEXES?
JAA SP 85 VOL: 8 PG:210 - 224 :: REGRESS. :PRIM. :THEORY :VALUAT.(INFL.)

CASLER,DJ ; SEC: HALL ,TW CIT: 0.38
FIRM-SPECIFIC ASSET VALUATION ACCURACY USING A COMPOSITE PRICE INDEX
JAR SP 85 VOL: 23 PG:110 - 122 :: REGRESS. :SIM. :OTH.STAT. :VALUAT.(INFL.)

CASPARI,JA CIT: 0
WHEREFORE ACCOUNTING DATA-EXPLANATION, PREDICTION AND DECISIONS
TAR OC 76 VOL: 51 PG:739 - 746 :: ANAL. :INT. LOG. :THEORY :OTH.MANAG.

CASSIDY,DB CIT: 0
INVESTOR EVALUATION OF ACCOUNTING INFORMATION: SOME ADDITIONAL EMPIRICAL EVIDENCE
JAR AU 76 VOL: 14 PG:212 - 229 :: REGRESS. :PRIM. :EMH :N/A

CASTER,P CIT: 0
AN EMPIRICAL STUDY OF ACCOUNTS RECEIVABLE CONFIRMATIONS AS AUDIT EVIDENCE
AUD AU 90 VOL: 9 PG:75 - 91 :: REGRESS. :LAB. :HIPS :CONF.

CAUSEY JR,DY CIT: 0.12
NEWLY EMERGING STANDARDS OF AUDITOR RESPONSIBILITY
TAR JA 76 VOL: 51 PG:19 - 30 :: QUAL. :SEC. :INSTIT. :LIAB.

CAUSEY JR,DY CIT: 0
FORESEEABILITY AS A DETERMINANT OF AUDIT RESPONSIBILITY
TAR AP 73 VOL: 48 PG:258 - 267 :: QUAL. :INT. LOG. :OTH. :N/A

CERF ,AR CIT: 0
ACCOUNTING FOR RETAIL LAND SALES
TAR JL 75 VOL: 50 PG:451 - 465 :: ANAL. :INT. LOG. :THEORY :REV.REC.

CHALOS,P ; SEC: CHERIAN,J ; THIR: HARRIS,D CIT: 0
FINANCIAL DISCLOSURE EFFECTS ON LABOR CONTRACTS: A NASH ANALYSIS
CAR SP 91 VOL: 7 PG:431 - 448 :: REGRESS. :PRIM. :OTH.BEH. :INFO.STRUC.

CHALOS,P ; SEC: HAKA ,S CIT: 0.33
TRANSFER PRICING UNDER BILATERAL BARGAINING
TAR JL 90 VOL: 65 PG:624 - 641 :: REGRESS. :LAB. :OTH.BEH. :TRANS.PRIC.

CHALOS,P CIT: 0
FINANCIAL DISTRESS: A COMPARATIVE STUDY OF INDIVIDUAL, MODEL, AND COMMITTEE ASSESSMENTS
JAR AU 85 VOL: 23 PG:527 - 543 :: REGRESS. :LAB. :OTH.BEH. :BUS.FAIL.

CHAMBERS,AE ; SEC: PENMAN,SH CIT: 3.33
TIMELINESS OF REPORTING AND THE STOCK PRICE REACTION TO EARNINGS ANNOUNCEMENTS
JAR SP 84 VOL: 22 PG:21 - 47 :: REGRESS. :PRIM. :EMH :FIN.ST.TIM.

CHAMBERS,RJ CIT: 0.33
ACCOUNTING "ONE OF THE FINEST INVENTIONS OF THE HUMAN SPIRIT"
CAR AU 84 VOL: 1 PG:1 - 22 :: ANOVA :SEC. :THEORY :ACC.CHNG.

CHAMBERS,RJ CIT: 0.11
PURSUIT OF AN IDEAL
CAR AU 84 VOL: 1 PG:58 - 63 :: ANOVA :SEC. :THEORY :ACC.CHNG.

CHAMBERS,RJ CIT: 0.08
THE MYTHS AND SCIENCE OF ACCOUNTING
AOS 01 80 VOL: 5 PG:167 - 180 :: QUAL. :INT. LOG. :THEORY :N/A

CHAMBERS,RJ CIT: 0
CANNING'S THE ECONOMICS OF ACCOUNTANCY - AFTER 50 YEARS
TAR OC 79 VOL: 54 PG:764 - 775 :: QUAL. :INT. LOG. :HIST. :N/A

CHAMBERS,RJ CIT: 0
MEASUREMENT IN CURRENT ACCOUNTING PRACTICES: A CRITIQUE
TAR JL 72 VOL: 47 PG:488 - 509 :: ANAL. :INT. LOG. :THEORY :OTH.FIN.ACC.

CHAMBERS,RJ CIT: 0
MEASURES AND VALUES
TAR AP 68 VOL: 43 PG:239 - 247 :: QUAL. :INT. LOG. :THEORY :VALUAT.(INFL.)

CHAMBERS,RJ CIT: 0
PROSPECTIVE ADVENTURES IN ACCOUNTING IDEAS
TAR AP 67 VOL: 42 PG:241 - 253 :: QUAL. :INT. LOG. :THEORY :FIN.METH.

CHAMBERS,RJ CIT: 0.12
CONTINUOUSLY CONTEMPORARY ACCOUNTING - ADDITIVITY AND ACTION
TAR OC 67 VOL: 42 PG:751 - 757 :: QUAL. :INT. LOG. :THEORY :VALUAT.(INFL.)

CHAMBERS,RJ CIT: 0.12
A MATTER OF PRINCIPLE
TAR JL 66 VOL: 41 PG:443 - 457 :: QUAL. :INT. LOG. :THEORY :FIN.METH.

CHAMBERS,RJ CIT: 0.12
MEASUREMENT IN ACCOUNTING
JAR SP 65 VOL: 3 PG:32 - 62 :: QUAL. :INT. LOG. :THEORY :VALUAT.(INFL.)

CHAMBERS,RJ CIT: 0.12
THE PRICE LEVEL PROBLEM AND SOME INTELLECTUAL GROOVES
JAR AU 65 VOL: 3 PG:242 - 252 :: ANAL. :INT. LOG. :THEORY :VALUAT.(INFL.)

CHAMBERS,RJ CIT: 0.18
EDWARDS AND BELL ON BUSINESS INCOME
TAR OC 65 VOL: 40 PG:731 - 741 :: QUAL. :INT. LOG. :THEORY :VALUAT.(INFL.)

CHAMBERS,RJ CIT: 0.18
MEASUREMENT AND OBJECTIVITY IN ACCOUNTING
TAR AP 64 VOL: 39 PG:264 - 274 :: QUAL. :INT. LOG. :THEORY :OTH.FIN.ACC.

CHAMBERS,RJ CIT: 0.12
WHY BOTHER WITH POSTULATES?
JAR SP 63 VOL: 1 PG:3 - 15 :: QUAL. :INT. LOG. :THEORY :N/A

CHAN ,H ; SEC: SMIELIAUSKAS,W CIT: 0
FURTHER TESTS OF THE MODIFIED MOMENT BOUND IN AUDIT SAMPLING OF ACCOUNTING POPULATIONS
AUD AU 90 VOL: 9 PG:167 - 182 :: REGRESS. :SIM. :OTH.STAT. :SAMP.

CHAN ,JL CIT: 0.07
CORPORATE DISCLOSURE IN OCCUPATIONAL SAFETY AND HEALTH: SOME EMPIRICAL EVIDENCE
AOS 04 79 VOL: 4 PG:273 - 282 :: DES.STAT. :PRIM. :THEORY :HRA

CHAN ,JL CIT: 0
ORGANIZATIONAL CONSENSUS REGARDING THE RELATIVE IMPORTANCE OF RESEARCH OUTPUT INDICATORS
TAR AP 78 VOL: 53 PG:309 - 323 :: NON-PAR. :CASE :HIPS :MANAG.

CHAN ,KH ; SEC: DODIN ,B CIT: 0
A DECISION SUPPORT SYSTEM FOR AUDIT-STAFF SCHEDULING WITH PRECEDENCE CONSTRAINTS
TAR OC 86 VOL: 61 PG:726 - 734 :: DES.STAT. :INT. LOG. :MATH.PROG. :ORG.

CHAN ,KH ; SEC: CHENG ,TT CIT: 0
THE RECOVERY OF NUCLEAR POWER PLANT DECOMMISSIONING COSTS
JAA WI 84 VOL: 7 PG:164 - 177 :: QUAL. :INT. LOG. :THEORY :COST.ALLOC.

CHAN ,YK ; FIRS: CHOW ,CW ; SEC: SHIELDS,MD CIT: 0
THE EFFECTS OF MANAGEMENT CONTROLS AND NATIONAL CULTURE ON MANUFACTURING PERFORMANCE: AN EXPERIMENTAL INVESTIGATION
AOS 03 91 VOL: 16 PG:209 - 226 :: REGRESS. :LAB. :OTH.STAT. :ORG.& ENVIR.

CHANDLER,AD ; SEC: DAEMS ,H CIT: 0.71
ADMINISTRATIVE COORDINATION, ALLOCATION AND MONITORING: A COMPARATIVE ANALYSIS OF EMERGENCE OF ACCOUNTING AND ORGANIZATIONS IN THE USA AND EUROPE
AOS 12 79 VOL: 4 PG:3 - 20 :: QUAL. :INT. LOG. :HIST. :N/A

CHANDLER,JS ; FIRS: LIANG ,T-P ; THIR: HAN ,I ; FOUR: ROAN ,J CIT: 0
AN EMPIRICAL INVESTIGATION OF SOME DATA EFFECTS ON THE CLASSIFICATION ACCURACY OF PROBIT, ID3 AND NEURAL NETWORKS
CAR AU 92 VOL: 9 PG:306 - 328 :: DES.STAT. :PRIM. :OTH.STAT. :METHOD.

CHANDRA,G CIT: 0.24
A STUDY OF THE CONSENSUS ON DISCLOSURE AMONG PUBLIC ACCOUNTANTS AND SECURITY ANALYSTS
TAR OC 74 VOL: 49 PG:733 - 742 :: DES.STAT. :LAB. :N/A :INFO.STRUC.

CHANDRA,R ; SEC: ROHRBACH,KJ ; THIR: WILLINGER,GL CIT: 0
LONGITUDINAL RANK TESTS FOR DETECTING LOCATION SHIFT IN THE DISTRIBUTION OF ABNORMAL RETURNS: AN EXTENSION
CAR AU 92 VOL: 9 PG:296 - 305 :: DES.STAT. :SIM. :TIME SER. :METHOD.

CHANDRA,R ; SEC: ROHRBACH,K CIT: 0.33
A METHODOLOGICAL NOTE ON DETECTING A LOCATION SHIFT IN THE DISTRIBUTION OF ABNORMAL RETURNS: A NONPARAMETRIC APPROACH
CAR AU 90 VOL: 7 PG:123 - 141 :: DES.STAT. :SIM. :EMH :METHOD.

CHANDRA,R ; SEC: BALACHANDRAN,BV CIT: 1
A SYNTHESIS OF ALTERNATIVE TESTING PROCEDURES FOR EVENT STUDIES
CAR SP 90 VOL: 6 PG:611 - 640 :: DES.STAT. :SEC. :TIME SER. :METHOD.

CHANEY,PK ; SEC: JETER ,DC CIT: 0
THE EFFECT OF SIZE ON THE MAGNITUDE OF LONG-WINDOW EARNINGS RESPONSE COEFFICIENTS
CAR SP 92 VOL: 8 PG:540 - 560 :: REGRESS. :PRIM. :EMH :FIN.METH.

CHANG ,OH ; SEC: NICHOLS,DR CIT: 0
TAX INCENTIVES AND CAPITAL STRUCTURES: THE CASE OF THE DIVIDEND REINVESTMENT PLAN
JAR SP 92 VOL: 30 PG:109 - 125 :: REGRESS. :PRIM. :OTH.STAT. :TAXES

CHAPMAN,G ; FIRS: KROSS ,W ; THIR: STRAND,KH CIT: 0
FULLY DILUTED EARNINGS PER SHARE AND SECURITY RETURNS: SOME ADDITIONAL EVIDENCE
JAA AU 80 VOL: 4 PG:36 - 46 :: CORR. :SEC. :EMH :CASH DIV.

CHARITOU,A ; SEC: KETZ ,JE CIT: 0
VALUATION OF EARNINGS, CASH FLOWS, AND THEIR COMPONENTS: AN EMPIRICAL INVESTIGATION
JAA AU 90 VOL: 5 PG:475 - 497 :: REGRESS. :PRIM. :EMH :VALUAT.(INFL.)

CHARNES,A ; FIRS: BROCKETT,P ; THIR: COOPER,WW ; FOUR: SHIN ,HC CIT: 0
A CHANCE-CONSTRAINED PROGRAMMING APPROACH TO COST-VOLUME-PROFIT ANALYSIS
TAR JL 84 VOL: 59 PG:474 - 487 :: ANAL. :INT. LOG. :MATH.PROG. :C-V-P-A

CHARNES,A ; SEC: COOPER,WW CIT: 0.08
AUDITING AND ACCOUNTING FOR PROBLEM EFFICIENCY AND MANAGEMENT EFFICIENCY IN NOT-FOR PROFIT ENTITIES
AOS 01 80 VOL: 5 PG:87 - 107 :: MIXED :PRIM. :OTH.STAT. :AUD.

CHARNES,A ; SEC: COLANTONI,CS ; THIR: COOPER,WW CIT: 0
A FUTUROLOGICAL JUSTIFICATION FOR HISTORICAL COST AND MULTI-DIMENSIONAL ACCOUNTING
AOS 04 76 VOL: 1 PG:315 - 338 :: ANAL. :INT. LOG. :MATH.PROG. :HRA

CHARNES,A ; SEC: COLANTONI,CS ; THIR: COOPER,WW ; FOUR: KORTANEK,KO CIT: 0.06
ECONOMIC SOCIAL AND ENTERPRISE ACCOUNTING AND MATHEMATICAL MODELS
TAR JA 72 VOL: 47 PG:85 - 108 :: ANAL. :INT. LOG. :MATH.PROG. :FIN.METH.

CHARNES,A ; FIRS: BYRNE ,R ; THIR: COOPER,WW ; FOUR: KORTANEK,KO CIT: 0
SOME NEW APPROACHES TO RISK
TAR JA 68 VOL: 43 PG:18 - 37 :: ANAL. :INT. LOG. :MATH.PROG. :BUDG.& PLAN.

CHARNES,A ; SEC: COOPER,WW CIT: 0.06
SOME NETWORK CHARACTERIZATIONS FOR MATHEMATICAL PROGRAMMING AND ACCOUNTING APPROACHES TO PLANNING AND CONTROL
TAR JA 67 VOL: 42 PG:24 - 52 :: ANAL. :INT. LOG. :MATH.PROG. :MANAG.

CHARNES,A ; SEC: DAVIDSON,HJ ; THIR: KORTANEK,KO CIT: 0
ON A MIXED-SEQUENTIAL ESTIMATING PROCEDURE WITH APPLICATION TO AUDIT TESTS IN ACCOUNTING
TAR AP 64 VOL: 39 PG:241 - 250 :: ANAL. :INT. LOG. :OTH.STAT. :SAMP.

CHARNES,A ; SEC: COOPER,WW ; THIR: IJIRI ,Y CIT: 0.06
BREAKEVEN BUDGETING AND PROGRAMMING TO GOALS
JAR SP 63 VOL: 1 PG:16 - 43 :: ANAL. :INT. LOG. :MATH.PROG. :C-V-P-A

CHASTEEN,LG CIT: 0
IMPLICIT FACTORS IN THE EVALUATION OF LEASE VS. BUY ALTERNATIVES
TAR OC 73 VOL: 48 PG:764 - 767 :: ANAL. :INT. LOG. :N/A :LEASES

CHASTEEN,LG CIT: 0.18
AN EMPIRICAL STUDY OF DIFFERENCES IN ECONOMIC CIRCUMSTANCES AS A JUSTIFICATION FOR ALTERNATIVE INVENTORY PRICING METHODS
TAR JL 71 VOL: 46 PG:504 - 508 :: ANOVA :PRIM. :N/A :INV.

CHATFIELD,M CIT: 0
THE ACCOUNTING REVIEW'S FIRST FIFTY YEARS
TAR JA 75 VOL: 50 PG:1 - 6 :: QUAL. :SEC. :HIST. :N/A

CHEN ,AH ; FIRS: HSIEH ,S-J ; SEC: FERRIS,KR CIT: 0.33
SECURITIES MARKET RESPONSE TO PENSION FUND TERMINATION
CAR SP 90 VOL: 6 PG:550 - 572 :: REGRESS. :PRIM. :EMH :PENS.

CHEN ,JT ; SEC: MANES ,RP CIT: 0
DISTINGUISHING THE TWO FORMS OF THE CONSTANT PERCENTAGE LEARNING CURVE MODEL
CAR SP 85 VOL: 1 PG:242 - 252 :: REGRESS. :SEC. :MATH.PROG. :MANAG.

CHEN ,JT CIT: 0.2
COST ALLOCATION AND EXTERNAL ACQUISITION OF SERVICES WHEN SELF-SERVICES EXIST
TAR JL 83 VOL: 58 PG:600 - 605 :: ANAL. :INT. LOG. :OTH.STAT. :COST.ALLOC.

CHEN ,K ; SEC: SUMMERS,EL CIT: 0.17
A STUDY OF REPORTING PROBABILISTIC ACCOUNTING FIGURES
AOS 01 81 VOL: 6 PG:1 - 16 :: ANOVA :LAB. :HIPS :MANAG.

CHEN ,KCW ; SEC: CHURCH,BK CIT: 0
DEFAULT ON DEBT OBLIGATIONS AND THE ISSUANCE OF GOING-CONCERN OPINIONS
AUD AU 92 VOL: 11 PG:30 - 49 :: REGRESS. :PRIM. :OTH.STAT. :OPIN.

CHEN ,RS CIT: 0.29
SOCIAL AND FINANCIAL STEWARDSHIP
TAR JL 75 VOL: 50 PG:533 - 543 :: QUAL. :INT. LOG. :THEORY :OTH.MANAG.

CHENG ,CSA ; SEC: HOPWOOD,WS ; THIR: MCKEOWN,JC CIT: 1
NON-LINEARITY AND SPECIFICATION PROBLEMS IN UNEXPECTED EARNINGS RESPONSE REGRESSION MODEL
TAR JL 92 VOL: 67 PG:579 - 598 :: REGRESS. :PRIM. :EMH :METHOD.

CHENG ,P ; FIRS: AMERSHI,AH CIT: 0.67
INTRAFIRM RESOURCE ALLOCATION: THE ECONOMICS OF TRANSFER PRICING AND COST ALLOCATIONS IN ACCOUNTING
CAR AU 90 VOL: 7 PG:61 - 99 :: DES.STAT. :INT. LOG. :INF.ECO./AG. :TRANS.PRIC.

CHENG ,P ; FIRS: AMERSHI,AH CIT: 0.25
ON THE DEMAND FOR HISTORICAL EVENTS RECORDING AND MAINTENANCE OF AUDIT TRAILS
CAR AU 89 VOL: 6 PG:72 - 90 :: DES.STAT. :INT. LOG. :INF.ECO./AG. :AUD.TRAIL

CHENG ,P ; FIRS: AMERSHI,AH CIT: 0.6
IMPLEMENTABLE EQUILIBRIA IN ACCOUNTING CONTEXTS: AN EXPLORATORY STUDY
CAR SP 88 VOL: 4 PG:515 - 563 :: DES.STAT. :INT. LOG. :INF.ECO./AG. :EXEC.COMP.

CHENG ,TT CIT: 0
STANDARD SETTING AND SECURITY RETURNS: A TIME SERIES ANALYSIS OF FAS NO. 8 EVENTS
CAR AU 86 VOL: 3 PG:226 - 241 :: REGRESS. :PRIM. :TIME SER. :FOR.CUR.

CHENG ,TT ; FIRS: CHAN ,KH CIT: 0
THE RECOVERY OF NUCLEAR POWER PLANT DECOMMISSIONING COSTS
JAA WI 84 VOL: 7 PG:164 - 177 :: QUAL. :INT. LOG. :THEORY :COST.ALLOC.

CHENHALL,R ; SEC: MORRIS,D CIT: 0
THE EFFECT OF COGNITIVE STYLE AND SPONSORSHIP BIAS ON THE TREATMENT OF OPPORTUNITY COSTS IN RESOURCE ALLOCATION DECISIONS
AOS 01 91 VOL: 16 PG:27 - 46 :: REGRESS. :LAB. :HIPS :COST.ALLOC.

CHENHALL,RH ; SEC: BROWNELL,P CIT: 0.6
THE EFFECT OF PARTICIPATIVE BUDGETING ON JOB SATISFACTION AND PERFORMANCE:
AOS 03 88 VOL: 13 PG:225 - 233 :: ANOVA :SURV. :EMH :BUDG.& PLAN.

CHENHALL,RH ; SEC: MORRIS,D CIT: 0.86
THE IMPACT OF STRUCTURE, ENVIRONMENT, AND INTERDEPENDENCE ON THE PERCEIVED USEFULNESS OF MANAGEMENT ACCOUNTING SYSTEMS
TAR JA 86 VOL: 61 PG:16 - 35 :: REGRESS. :SURV. :OTH.STAT. :ORG.& ENVIR.

CHENHALL,RH CIT: 0
AUTHORITARIANISM AND PARTICIPATIVE BUDGETING - A DYADIC ANALYSIS
TAR AP 86 VOL: 61 PG:263 - 272 :: REGRESS. :SURV. :OTH.BEH. :BUDG.& PLAN.

CHERIAN,J ; FIRS: CHALOS,P ; THIR: HARRIS,D CIT: 0
FINANCIAL DISCLOSURE EFFECTS ON LABOR CONTRACTS: A NASH ANALYSIS
CAR SP 91 VOL: 7 PG:431 - 448 :: REGRESS. :PRIM. :OTH.BEH. :INFO.STRUC.

CHERNS,AB CIT: 0.27
ALIENATION AND ACCOUNTANCY
AOS 02 78 VOL: 3 PG:105 - 114 :: QUAL. :INT. LOG. :OTH. :N/A

CHERRINGTON,DJ ; SEC: CHERRINGTON,JO CIT: 0.82
APPROPRIATE REINFORCEMENT CONTINGENCIES IN THE BUDGETING PROCESS
JAR ST 73 VOL: 11 PG:225 - 253 :: ANOVA :LAB. :OTH.BEH. :BUDG.& PLAN.

CHERRINGTON,JO ; FIRS: CHERRINGTON,DJ CIT: 0.82
APPROPRIATE REINFORCEMENT CONTINGENCIES IN THE BUDGETING PROCESS
JAR ST 73 VOL: 11 PG:225 - 253 :: ANOVA :LAB. :OTH.BEH. :BUDG.& PLAN.

CHESLEY,GR CIT: 0.14
INTERPRETATION OF UNCERTAINTY EXPRESSIONS
CAR SP 86 VOL: 2 PG:179 - 199 :: REGRESS. :LAB. :HIPS :JUDG.

CHESLEY,GR ; FIRS: LARSSON,S CIT: 0.14
AN ANALYSIS OF THE AUDITOR'S UNCERTAINTY ABOUT PROBABILITIES
CAR SP 86 VOL: 2 PG:259 - 282 :: REGRESS. :SURV. :HIPS :JUDG.

CHESLEY,GR CIT: 0.4
SUBJECTIVE PROBABILITY ELICITATION TECHNIQUES: A PERFORMANCE COMPARISON
JAR AU 78 VOL: 16 PG:225 - 241 :: ANOVA :LAB. :HIPS :PROB.ELIC.

CHESLEY,GR CIT: 0.56
SUBJECTIVE PROBABILITY ELICITATION: THE EFFECT OF CONGRUITY OF DATUM AND RESPONSE MODE ON PERFORMANCE
JAR SP 77 VOL: 15 PG:1 - 11 :: NON-PAR. :LAB. :HIPS :PROB.ELIC.

CHESLEY,GR ; FIRS: HEIMANN,SR CIT: 0.25
AUDIT SAMPLE SIZES FOR AGGREGATED STATEMENT ACCOUNTS
JAR AU 77 VOL: 15 PG:193 - 206 :: ANAL. :INT. LOG. :MATH.PROG. :SAMP.

CHESLEY,GR CIT: 0.59
THE ELICITATION OF SUBJECTIVE PROBABILITIES: A LABORATORY STUDY IN AN ACCOUNTING CONTEXT
JAR SP 76 VOL: 14 PG:27 - 48 :: ANOVA :LAB. :HIPS :PROB.ELIC.

CHESLEY,GR CIT: 1
ELICITATION OF SUBJECTIVE PROBABILITIES: A REVIEW
TAR AP 75 VOL: 50 PG:325 - 337 :: QUAL. :SEC. :OTH.BEH. :PROB.ELIC.

CHEUNG,JK CIT: 0
THE VALUATION SIGNIFICANCE OF EXIT VALUES: A CONTINGENT-CLAIM ANALYSIS
CAR SP 90 VOL: 6 PG:724 - 737 :: DES.STAT. :INT. LOG. :MATH.PROG. :VALUAT.(INFL.)

CHEUNG,JK ; SEC: HEANEY,J CIT: 0
A CONTINGENT-CLAIM INTEGRATION OF COST-VOLUME-PROFIT ANALYSIS
CAR SP 90 VOL: 6 PG:738 - 760 :: DES.STAT. :INT. LOG. :THEORY :C-V-P-A

CHEUNG,JK CIT: 0.25
ON THE NATURE OF DEFERRED INCOME TAXES
CAR SP 89 VOL: 5 PG:625 - 641 :: DES.STAT. :INT. LOG. :MATH.PROG. :TAXES

CHEUNG,JK ; FIRS: WHALEY,RE CIT: 0.09
ANTICIPATION OF QUARTERLY EARNINGS ANNOUNCEMENTS: A TEST OF OPTION MARKET EFFICIENCY
JAE OC 82 VOL: 4 PG:57 - 83 :: REGRESS. :SEC. :EMH :INT.REP.

CHEWNING,E ; FIRS: HARRELL,A ; SEC: TAYLOR,M CIT: 0.5
AN EXAMINATION OF MANAGEMENT'S ABILITY TO BIAS THE PROFESSIONAL OBJECTIVITY OF INTERNAL AUDITORS
AOS 03 89 VOL: 14 PG:259 - 269 :: REGRESS. :LAB. :HIPS :INT.AUD.

CHEWNING,EG ; FIRS: MITTELSTAEDT,HF ; SEC: REGIER,PR ; FOUR: PANY ,K CIT: 0
DO CONSISTENCY MODIFICATIONS PROVIDE INFORMATION TO EQUITY MARKETS?
AUD SP 92 VOL: 11 PG:83 - 98 :: REGRESS. :PRIM. :OTH.STAT. :OPIN.

CHEWNING,EG ; SEC: HARRELL,AM CIT: 0
THE EFFECT OF INFORMATION LOAD ON DECISION MAKERS' CUE UTILIZATION LEVELS AND DECISION QUALITY IN A FINANCIAL DISTRESS DECISION
AOS 06 90 VOL: 15 PG:527 - 542 :: REGRESS. :LAB. :HIPS :AUD.BEH.

CHEWNING,EG ; FIRS: HARRELL,AM ; THIR: TAYLOR,M CIT: 0
ORGANIZATIONAL-PROFESSIONAL CONFLICT AND THE JOB SATISFACTION AND TURNOVER INTENTIONS OF INTERNAL AUDITORS
AUD SP 86 VOL: 5 PG:111 - 121 :: REGRESS. :SURV. :OTH.BEH. :AUD.TRAIL

CHEWNING,EG ; FIRS: INGRAM,RW CIT: 0.1
THE EFFECT OF FINANCIAL DISCLOSURE REGULATION ON SECURITY MARKET BEHAVIOR
TAR JL 83 VOL: 58 PG:562 - 580 :: REGRESS. :PRIM. :EMH :FIN.METH.

CHEWNING,G ; SEC: PANY ,K ; THIR: WHEELER,S CIT: 0.5
AUDITOR REPORTING DECISIONS INVOLVING ACCOUNTING PRINCIPLE CHANGES: SOME EVIDENCE ON MATERIALITY THRESHOLDS
JAR SP 89 VOL: 27 PG:78 - 96 :: REGRESS. :PRIM. :OTH.STAT. :MAT.

CHI ,C ; FIRS: ABDEL-KHALIK,AR ; THIR: GHICAS,D CIT: 0.33
REATIONALITY OF EXECUTIVE COMPENSATION SCHEMES AND REAL ACCOUNTING CHANGES
CAR AU 87 VOL: 4 PG:32 - 60 :: REGRESS. :PRIM. :INF.ECO./AG. :ACC.CHNG.

CHIU ,JS ; SEC: DECOSTER,DT CIT: 0
MULTIPLE PRODUCT COSTING BY MULTIPLE CORRELATION ANALYSIS
TAR OC 66 VOL: 41 PG:673 - 680 :: REGRESS. :INT. LOG. :TIME SER. :COST.ALLOC.

CHOI ,FD CIT: 0.18
FINANCIAL DISCLOSURE AND ENTRY TO THE EUROPEAN CAPITAL MARKET
JAR AU 73 VOL: 11 PG:159 - 175 :: NON-PAR. :PRIM. :INSTIT. :INFO.STRUC.

CHOI ,SK ; SEC: JETER ,DC CIT: 0
THE EFFECTS OF QUALIFIED AUDIT OPINIONS ON EARNINGS RESPONSE COEFFICIENTS
JAE JN 92 VOL: 15 PG:229 - 247 :: REGRESS. :PRIM. :EMH :OPIN.

CHOO ,F ; SEC: TROTMAN,KT CIT: 0.5
THE RELATIONSHIP BETWEEN KNOWLEDGE STRUCTURE AND JUDGMENTS FOR EXPERIENCED AND INEXPERIENCED AUDITORS
TAR JL 91 VOL: 66 PG:464 - 485 :: REGRESS. :LAB. :HIPS :JUDG.

CHOO ,F CIT: 0
COGNITIVE SCRIPTS IN AUDITING AND ACCOUNTING BEHAVIOR
AOS 06 89 VOL: 14 PG:481 - 493 :: DES.STAT. :SEC. :HIPS :METHOD.

CHOO ,F CIT: 0.57
JOB STRESS, JOB PERFORMANCE, AND AUDITOR PERSONALITY CHARACTERISTICS
AUD SP 86 VOL: 5 PG:17 - 34 :: REGRESS. :SURV. :HIPS :AUD.BEH.

CHOTTINER,S ; SEC: YOUNG ,AE CIT: 0.06
A TEST OF THE AICPA DIFFERENTIATION BETWEEN STOCK DIVIDENDS AND STOCK SPLITS
JAR AU 71 VOL: 9 PG:367 - 374 :: DES.STAT. :PRIM. :OTH. :STK.DIV.

CHOUDHURY,N CIT: 1
THE SEEKING OF ACCOUNTING WHERE IT IS NOT: TOWARDS A THEORY OF NON-ACCOUNTING IN ORGANIZATIONAL SETTINGS
AOS 06 88 VOL: 13 PG:549 - 557 :: DES.STAT. :INT. LOG. :THEORY :ORG.& ENVIR.

CHOW ,CW ; SEC: SHIELDS,MD ; THIR: CHAN ,YK CIT: 0
THE EFFECTS OF MANAGEMENT CONTROLS AND NATIONAL CULTURE ON MANUFACTURING PERFORMANCE: AN EXPERIMENTAL INVESTIGATION
AOS 03 91 VOL: 16 PG:209 - 226 :: REGRESS. :LAB. :OTH.STAT. :ORG.& ENVIR.

CHOW ,CW ; SEC: COOPER,JC ; THIR: WALLER,WS CIT: 0.8
PARTICIPATIVE BUDGETING: EFFECTS OF A TRUTH-INDUCING PAY SCHEME AND INFORMATION ASYMMETRY ON SLACK AND PERFORMANCE
TAR JA 88 VOL: 63 PG:111 - 122 :: REGRESS. :LAB. :OTH.BEH. :BUDG.& PLAN.

CHOW ,CW ; SEC: MCNAMEE,AH ; THIR: PLUMLEE,RD CIT: 0.5
PRACTITIONERS' PERCEPTIONS OF AUDIT STEP DIFFICULTY AND CRITICALNESS: IMPLICATIONS FOR AUDIT RESEARCH
AUD SP 87 VOL: 6 PG:123 - 133 :: REGRESS. :SURV. :OTH.STAT. :AUD.THEOR.

CHOW ,CW ; SEC: WONG-BOREN,A CIT: 0.17
VOLUNTARY FINANCIAL DISCLOSURE BY MEXICAN CORPORATIONS
TAR JL 87 VOL: 62 PG:533 - 541 :: REGRESS. :PRIM. :OTH.STAT. :FIN.METH.

CHOW ,CW ; FIRS: BLANCHARD,GA ; THIR: NOREEN,EW CIT: 0
INFORMATION ASYMMETRY, INCENTIVE SCHEMES, AND INFORMATION BIASING: THE CASE OF HOSPITAL BUDGETING UNDER RATE REGULATION
TAR JA 86 VOL: 61 PG:1 - 15 :: REGRESS. :PRIM. :N/A :BUDG.& PLAN.

CHOW ,CW ; FIRS: WALLER,WS CIT: 0.75
THE SELF-SELECTION AND EFFORT EFFECTS OF STANDARD-BASED EMPLOYEE CONTRACTS: A FRAMEWORK AND SOME EMPIRICAL EVIDENCE
TAR JL 85 VOL: 60 PG:458 - 476 :: REGRESS. :LAB. :OTH.BEH. :EXEC.COMP.

CHOW ,CW CIT: 0.3
THE IMPACTS OF ACCOUNTING REGULATION ON BONDHOLDER AND SHAREHOLDER WEALTH: THE CASE OF THE SECURITIES ACTS
TAR JL 83 VOL: 58 PG:485 - 520 :: REGRESS. :PRIM. :EMH :FIN.METH.

CHOW ,CW CIT: 1
THE EFFECTS OF JOB STANDARD TIGHTNESS AND COMPENSATION SCHEME ON PERFORMANCE: AN EXPLORATION OF LINKAGES
TAR OC 83 VOL: 58 PG:667 - 685 :: ANOVA :LAB. :OTH.STAT. :BUDG.& PLAN.

CHOW ,CW ; SEC: RICE ,SJ CIT: 0.36
QUALIFIED AUDIT OPINIONS AND SHARE PRICES - AN INVESTIGATION
AUD WI 82 VOL: 1 PG:35 - 53 :: MIXED :PRIM. :EMH :OPIN.

CHOW ,CW CIT: 0.91
THE DEMAND FOR EXTERNAL AUDITING: SIZE, DEBT AND OWNERSHIP INFLUENCES
TAR AP 82 VOL: 57 PG:272 - 291 :: DES.STAT. :PRIM. :INF.ECO./AG. :AUD.

CHOW ,CW ; SEC: RICE ,SJ CIT: 1
QUALIFIED AUDIT OPINIONS AND AUDITOR SWITCHING
TAR AP 82 VOL: 57 PG:326 - 335 :: DES.STAT. :PRIM. :OTH. :OPIN.

CHOW,CW ; SEC: COOPER,JC ; THIR: HADDAD,K CIT: 0
THE EFFECTS OF PAY SCHEMES AND RATCHETS ON BUDGETARY SLACK AND PERFORMANCE: A MULTIPERIOD EXPERIMENT
AOS 01 91 VOL: 16 PG:47 - 60 :: REGRESS. :LAB. :OTH.BEH. :BUDG.& PLAN.

CHRISTENSEN,J CIT: 1.18
THE DETERMINATION OF PERFORMANCE STANDARDS AND PARTICIPATION
JAR AU 82 VOL: 20 PG:589 - 603 :: ANAL. :INT. LOG. :INF.ECO./AG. :BUDG.& PLAN.

CHRISTENSEN,PO ; FIRS: FELTHAM,GA CIT: 0.2
FIRM-SPECIFIC INFORMATION AND EFFICIENT RESOURCE ALLOCATION
CAR AU 88 VOL: 5 PG:133 - 169 :: DES.STAT. :INT. LOG. :INF.ECO./AG. :EXEC.COMP.

CHRISTENSON,C CIT: 2
THE METHODOLOGY OF POSITIVE ACCOUNTING
TAR JA 83 VOL: 58 PG:1 - 22 :: QUAL. :SEC. :OTH. :METHOD.

CHRISTIE,AA CIT: 2.33
AGGREGATION OF TEST STATISTICS: AN EVALUATION OF THE EVIDENCE ON CONTRACTING AND SIZE HYPOTHESES
JAE JA 90 VOL: 12 PG:15 - 36 :: REGRESS. :SEC. :EMH :FIN.METH.

CHRISTIE,AA CIT: 4.17
ON CROSS-SECTIONAL ANALYSIS IN ACCOUNTING RESEARCH
JAE DE 87 VOL: 9 PG:231 - 258 :: DES.STAT. :INT. LOG. :EMH :METHOD.

CHRISTIE,AA ; SEC: KENNELLEY,MD ; THIR: KING ,JW ; FOUR: SCHAEFER,TF CIT: 1
TESTING FOR INCREMENTAL INFORMATION CONTENT IN THE PRESENCE OF COLLINEARITY
JAE DE 84 VOL: 6 PG:205 - 217 :: ANAL. :INT. LOG. :OTH.STAT. :METHOD.

CHRISTIE,AA ; FIRS: BEAVER,WH ; THIR: GRIFFIN,PA CIT: 1.62
THE INFORMATION CONTENT OF SEC ACCOUNTING SERIES RELEASE NO.190
JAE AG 80 VOL: 2 PG:127 - 157 :: REGRESS. :PRIM. :EMH :VALUAT.(INFL.)

CHUA ,WF CIT: 0.71
THEORETICAL CONSTRUCTIONS OF AND BY THE REAL
AOS 06 86 VOL: 11 PG:583 - 598 :: DES.STAT. :INT. LOG. :THEORY :FASB SUBM.

CHUA ,WF CIT: 2.14
RADICAL DEVELOPMENTS IN ACCOUNTING THOUGHT
TAR OC 86 VOL: 61 PG:601 - 632 :: DES.STAT. :INT. LOG. :THEORY :METHOD.

CHUMACHENKO,NG CIT: 0
ONCE AGAIN: THE VOLUME-MIX-PRICE/COST BUDGET VARIANCE ANALYSIS
TAR OC 68 VOL: 43 PG:753 - 762 :: ANAL. :INT. LOG. :N/A :VAR.

CHUNG ,DY ; SEC: LINDSAY,WD CIT: 0
THE PRICING OF AUDIT SERVICES: THE CANADIAN PERSPECTIVE
CAR AU 88 VOL: 5 PG:19 - 46 :: REGRESS. :PRIM. :OTH.STAT. :ORG.

CHURCH,BK ; FIRS: CHEN ,KCW CIT: 0
DEFAULT ON DEBT OBLIGATIONS AND THE ISSUANCE OF GOING-CONCERN OPINIONS
AUD AU 92 VOL: 11 PG:30 - 49 :: REGRESS. :PRIM. :OTH.STAT. :OPIN.

CHURCH,BK CIT: 0.5
AN EXAMINATION OF THE EFFECT THAT COMMITMENT TO A HYPOTHESIS HAS ON AUDITORS' EVALUATIONS OF CONFIRMING AND DISCONFIRMING EVIDENCE
CAR SP 91 VOL: 7 PG:513 - 534 :: REGRESS. :LAB. :HIPS :AUD.BEH.

CHURCHILL,NC ; SEC: COOPER,WW ; THIR: GOVINDARAJAN,V CIT: 0
EFFECTS OF AUDITS ON THE BEHAVIOR OF MEDICAL PROFESSIONALS UNDER THE BENNETT AMENDMENT
AUD WI 82 VOL: 1 PG:69 - 91 :: ANOVA :PRIM. :OTH.STAT. :OPER.AUD.

CHURCHILL,NC ; SEC: SHANK ,JK CIT: 0.12
ACCOUNTING FOR AFFIRMATIVE ACTION PROGRAMS: A STOCHASTIC FLOW APPROACH
TAR OC 75 VOL: 50 PG:643 - 656 :: ANOVA :FIELD :OTH.STAT. :HRA

CHURCHILL,NC CIT: 0.06
AUDIT RECOMMENDATIONS AND MANAGEMENT AUDITING: A CASE STUDY AND SOME REMARKS
JAR ST 66 VOL: 4 PG:128 - 156 :: QUAL. :CASE :THEORY :AUD.

CHURCHILL,NC ; SEC: COOPER,WW CIT: 0.12
A FIELD STUDY OF INTERNAL AUDITING
TAR OC 65 VOL: 40 PG:767 - 781 :: DES.STAT. :FIELD :OTH.BEH. :AUD.

CHURCHILL,NC CIT: 0.12
LINEAR ALGEBRA AND COST ALLOCATIONS: SOME EXAMPLES
TAR OC 64 VOL: 39 PG:894 - 904 :: ANAL. :INT. LOG. :MATH.PROG. :COST.ALLOC.

CHURCHMAN,CW CIT: 0
ON THE FACILITY, FELICITY, AND MORALITY OF MEASURING SOCIAL CHANGE
TAR JA 71 VOL: 46 PG:30 - 35 :: QUAL. :INT. LOG. :INSTIT. :HRA

CIANCIOLO,ST ; FIRS: NURNBERG,H CIT: 0
THE MEASUREMENT VALUATION ALLOWANCE: HELP FOR DEFERRED TAXES
JAA AU 85 VOL: 9 PG:50 - 59 :: DES.STAT. :INT. LOG. :THEORY :TAXES

CLANCY,DK ; SEC: COLLINS,F CIT: 0.29
INFORMAL ACCOUNTING INFORMATION SYSTEMS: SOME TENTATIVE FINDINGS
AOS 12 79 VOL: 4 PG:21 - 30 :: OTH.QUANT. :SURV. :THEORY :N/A

CLARK ,JJ ; SEC: ELGERS,PT CIT: 0
FORECASTED INCOME STATEMENTS: AN INVESTOR PERSPECTIVE
TAR OC 73 VOL: 48 PG:668 - 678 :: CORR. :CASE :OTH.STAT. :BUDG.& PLAN.

CLARK ,TN CIT: 0
FISCAL MANAGEMENT OF AMERICAN CITIES: FUNDS FLOW INDICATORS
JAR ST 77 VOL: 15 PG:54 - 94 :: REGRESS. :PRIM. :OTH.STAT. :OTH.MANAG.

CLARKE,CK ; FIRS: PESANDO,JE CIT: 0
ECONOMIC MODELS OF THE LABOR MARKET AND PENSION ACCOUNTING: AN EXPLORATORY ANALYSIS
TAR OC 83 VOL: 58 PG:733 - 748 :: ANAL. :INT. LOG. :OTH.STAT. :PENS.

CLARKE,R ; FIRS: BEAVER,WH ; THIR: WRIGHT,WF CIT: 4.93
THE ASSOCIATION BETWEEN UNSYSTEMATIC SECURITY RETURNS AND THE MAGNITUDE OF EARNINGS FORECAST ERRORS
JAR AU 79 VOL: 17 PG:316 - 340 :: NON-PAR. :PRIM. :EMH :FIN.METH.

CLARKE,RW ; FIRS: ROBERTSON,JC CIT: 0.12
VERIFICATION OF MANAGEMENT REPRESENTATIONS: A FIRST STEP TOWARD INDEPENDENT AUDITS OF MANAGEMENT
TAR JL 71 VOL: 46 PG:562 - 571 :: DES.STAT. :PRIM. :N/A :AUD.

CLARKE,RW CIT: 0.06
EXTENSION OF THE CPA'S ATTEST FUNCTION IN CORPORATE ANNUAL REPORTS
TAR OC 68 VOL: 43 PG:769 - 776 :: QUAL. :INT. LOG. :INSTIT. :OPIN.

CLARKSON,PM ; SEC: DONTOH,A ; THIR: RICHARDSON,G ; FOUR: SEFCIK,SE CIT: 0
THE VOLUNTARY INCLUSION OF EARNINGS FORECASTS IN IPO PROSPECTUSES
CAR SP 92 VOL: 8 PG:601 - 625 :: REGRESS. :PRIM. :TIME SER. :VALUAT.(INFL.)

CLAY JR,RJ ; FIRS: SUMNERS,GE ; SEC: WHITE ,RA CIT: 0
THE USE OF ENGAGEMENT LETTERS IN AUDIT, REVIEW, AND COMPILATION ENGAGEMENTS: AN EMPIRICAL STUDY
AUD SP 87 VOL: 6 PG:116 - 122 :: REGRESS. :SURV. :OTH.BEH. :ORG.

CLINCH,G ; SEC: MAGLIOLO,J CIT: 0
MARKET PERCEPTIONS OF RESERVE DISCLOSURES UNDER SFAS NO. 69
TAR OC 92 VOL: 67 PG:843 - 861 :: REGRESS. :PRIM. :MATH.PROG. :OIL & GAS

CLINCH,G CIT: 0
EMPLOYEE COMPENSATION AND FIRMS' RESEARCH AND DEVELOPMENT ACTIVITY
JAR SP 91 VOL: 29 PG:59 - 78 :: REGRESS. :PRIM. :OTH.STAT. :R & D

CLINCH,GJ ; SEC: SINCLAIR,NA CIT: 0.67
INTRA-INDUSTRY INFORMATION RELEASES: A RECURSIVE SYSTEMS APPROACH
JAE AP 87 VOL: 9 PG:89 - 106 :: REGRESS. :PRIM. :EMH :FIN.METH.

CLOUSE,ML ; FIRS: SELTO ,FH CIT: 0.25
AN INVESTIGATION OF MANAGERS' ADAPTATIONS TO SFAS NO. 2: ACCOUNTING FOR RESEARCH AND DEVELOPMENT COSTS
JAR AU 85 VOL: 23 PG:700 - 717 :: REGRESS. :PRIM. :EMH :R & D

CLUBB ,C ; FIRS: BURCHELL,S ; THIR: HOPWOOD,AG CIT: 3.75
ACCOUNTING IN ITS SOCIAL CONTEXT: TOWARDS A HISTORY OF VALUE ADDED IN THE UNITED KINGDOM
AOS 04 85 VOL: 10 PG:381 - 414 :: DES.STAT. :INT. LOG. :THEORY :HRA

CLUBB ,C ; FIRS: BURCHELL,S ; THIR: HOPWOOD,AG ; FOUR: HUGHES,JS ; FIFT: NAHAPIET,JE CIT: 4.92
THE ROLES OF ACCOUNTING IN ORGANIZATIONS AND SOCIETY
AOS 01 80 VOL: 5 PG:5 - 27 :: QUAL. :INT. LOG. :THEORY :N/A

CLUTE ,RD ; FIRS: BONETT,DG CIT: 0
AUDIT SAMPLING WITH NONSAMPLING ERRORS OF THE FIRST TYPE
CAR SP 90 VOL: 6 PG:432 - 445 :: DES.STAT. :SIM. :OTH.STAT. :SAMP.

COASE ,RH CIT: 0
ACCOUNTING AND THE THEORY OF THE FIRM
JAE JA 90 VOL: 12 PG:3 - 13 :: DES.STAT. :SEC. :HIST. :ORG.& ENVIR.

COATES,R CIT: 0.35
THE PREDICTIVE CONTENT OF INTERIM REPORTS - A TIME SERIES ANALYSIS
JAR ST 72 VOL: 10 PG:132 - 144 :: MIXED :PRIM. :TIME SER. :INT.REP.

COE ,TL CIT: 0
AN ANALYSIS OF THE SEC MONITORING OF PROSPECT USES
JAA SP 79 VOL: 2 PG:244 - 253 :: DES.STAT. :PRIM. :INSTIT. :OTH.MANAG.

COGGER,KO ; FIRS: EMERY ,GW CIT: 0.09
THE MEASUREMENT OF LIQUIDITY
JAR AU 82 VOL: 20 PG:290 - 303 :: ANAL. :PRIM. :OTH.STAT. :BUS.FAIL.

COGGER,KO ; SEC: RULAND,W CIT: 0.09
A NOTE ON ALTERNATIVE TESTS FOR INDEPENDENCE OF FINANCIAL TIME SERIES
JAR AU 82 VOL: 20 PG:733 - 737 :: CORR. :PRIM. :TIME SER. :METHOD.

COGGER,KO CIT: 0.17
A TIME-SERIES ANALYTIC APPROACH TO AGGREGATION ISSUES IN ACCOUNTING DATA
JAR AU 81 VOL: 19 PG:285 - 298 :: ANAL. :INT. LOG. :TIME SER. :INFO.STRUC.

COGLITORE,F ; SEC: BERRYMAN,RG CIT: 0
ANALYTICAL PROCEDURES: A DEFENSIVE NECESSITY
AUD SP 88 VOL: 07 PG:150 - 163 :: REGRESS. :SIM. :THEORY :ANAL.REV.

COHEN ,J ; SEC: KIDA ,T CIT: 0.5
THE IMPACT OF ANALYTICAL REVIEW RESULTS, INTERNAL CONTROL RELIABILITY, AND EXPERIENCE ON AUDITORS' USE OF ANALYTICAL REVIEW
JAR AU 89 VOL: 27 PG:263 - 276 :: REGRESS. :LAB. :HIPS :ANAL.REV.

COHEN ,MA ; SEC: HALPERIN,R CIT: 0.23
OPTIMAL INVENTORY ORDER POLICY FOR A FIRM USING THE LIFO INVENTORY COSTING METHOD
JAR AU 80 VOL: 18 PG:375 - 389 :: ANAL. :SIM. :MATH.PROG. :INV.

COHEN ,MF CIT: 0
CURRENT DEVELOPMENTS AT THE SEC
TAR JA 65 VOL: 40 PG:1 - 8 :: QUAL. :SEC. :INSTIT. :AUD.

COHEN ,SI ; SEC: LOEB ,M CIT: 0.2
IMPROVING PERFORMANCE THROUGH COST ALLOCATION
CAR AU 88 VOL: 5 PG:70 - 95 :: DES.STAT. :INT. LOG. :INF.ECO./AG. :COST.ALLOC.

COHEN ,SI ; SEC: LOEB ,M CIT: 0.09
PUBLIC GOODS, COMMON INPUTS, AND THE EFFICIENCY OF FULL COST ALLOCATIONS
TAR AP 82 VOL: 57 PG:336 - 347 :: ANAL. :INT. LOG. :OTH.STAT. :COST.ALLOC.

COLANTONI,CS ; FIRS: CHARNES,A ; THIR: COOPER,WW CIT: 0
A FUTUROLOGICAL JUSTIFICATION FOR HISTORICAL COST AND MULTI-DIMENSIONAL ACCOUNTING
AOS 04 76 VOL: 1 PG:315 - 338 :: ANAL. :INT. LOG. :MATH.PROG. :HRA

COLANTONI,CS ; FIRS: CHARNES,A ; THIR: COOPER,WW ; FOUR: KORTANEK,KO CIT: 0.06
ECONOMIC SOCIAL AND ENTERPRISE ACCOUNTING AND MATHEMATICAL MODES
TAR JA 72 VOL: 47 PG:85 - 108 :: ANAL. :INT. LOG. :MATH.PROG. :FIN.METH.

COLANTONI,CS ; SEC: MANES ,RP ; THIR: WHINSTON,AB CIT: 0.41
A UNIFIED APPROACH TO THE THEORY OF ACCOUNTING AND INFORMATION SYSTEMS
TAR JA 71 VOL: 46 PG:90 - 102 :: QUAL. :INT. LOG. :N/A :MANAG.

COLANTONI,CS ; SEC: MANES ,RP ; THIR: WHINSTON,AB CIT: 0.06
PROGRAMMING, PROFIT RATES AND PRICING DECISIONS
TAR JL 69 VOL: 44 PG:467 - 481 :: ANAL. :INT. LOG. :MATH.PROG. :REL.COSTS

COLBERT,JL CIT: 0
INHERENT RISK: AN INVESTIGATION OF AUDITORS' JUDGMENTS
AOS 02 88 VOL: 13 PG:111 - 121 :: REGRESS. :LAB. :HIPS :JUDG.

COLDWELL,S ; FIRS: HORVITZ,JS CIT: 0
ANALYSIS OF THE ARTHUR YOUNG DECISION AND ITS POTENTIAL IMPACT ON PUBLIC ACCOUNTING
JAA WI 85 VOL: 8 PG:86 - 99 :: REGRESS. :CASE :THEORY :LITIG.

COLIGNON,R ; SEC: COVALESKI,M CIT: 0.5
A WEBERIAN FRAMEWORK IN THE STUDY OF ACCOUNTING
AOS 02 91 VOL: 16 PG:141 - 157 :: DES.STAT. :SEC. :THEORY :ORG.& ENVIR.

COLIGNON,R ; SEC: COVALESKI,M CIT: 0.2
AN EXAMINATION OF MANAGERIAL ACCOUNTING PRACTICES AS A PROCESS OF MUTUAL ADJUSTMENT
AOS 06 88 VOL: 13 PG:559 - 579 :: REGRESS. :CASE :THEORY :BUDG.& PLAN.

COLLINS,DW ; SEC: DeANGELO,L CIT: 1.67
ACCOUNTING INFORMATION AND CORPORATE GOVERNANCE: MARKET AND ANALYST REACTIONS TO EARNINGS OF FIRMS ENGAGED IN PROXY CONTESTS
JAE OC 90 VOL: 13 PG:213 - 247 :: REGRESS. :PRIM. :TIME SER. :BUS.COMB.

COLLINS,DW ; SEC: KOTHARI,SP CIT: 5.5
AN ANALYSIS OF INTERTEMPORAL AND CROSS-SECTIONAL DETERMINANTS OF EARNINGS RESPONSE COEFFICIENTS
JAE JL 89 VOL: 11 PG:143 - 181 :: REGRESS. :PRIM. :EMH :FIN.METH.

COLLINS,DW ; FIRS: DORAN ,BM ; THIR: DHALIWAL,DS CIT: 1
THE INFORMATION OF HISTORICAL COST EARNINGS RELATIVE TO SUPPLEMENTAL RESERVE-BASED ACCOUNTING DATA IN THE EXTRACTIVE PETROLEUM INDUSTRY
TAR JL 88 VOL: 63 PG:389 - 413 :: REGRESS. :PRIM. :EMH :OIL & GAS

COLLINS,DW ; SEC: KOTHARI,SP ; THIR: RAYBURN,JD CIT: 4.33
FIRM SIZE AND THE INFORMATION CONTENT OF PRICES WITH RESPECT TO EARNINGS
JAE JL 87 VOL: 9 PG:111 - 138 :: REGRESS. :PRIM. :EMH :ORG.& ENVIR.

COLLINS,DW ; SEC: DENT ,WT CIT: 1.44
A COMPARISON OF ALTERNATIVE TESTING METHODOLOGIES USED IN CAPITAL MARKET RESEARCH
JAR SP 84 VOL: 22 PG:48 - 84 :: MIXED :SIM. :EMH :METHOD.

COLLINS,DW ; SEC: ROZEFF,MS ; THIR: SALATKA,WK CIT: 0.73
THE SEC'S REJECTION OF SFAS NO.19: TESTS OF MARKET PRICE REVERSAL
TAR JA 82 VOL: 57 PG:1 - 17 :: CORR. :PRIM. :EMH :OIL & GAS

COLLINS,DW ; SEC: ROZEFF,MS ; THIR: DHALIWAL,DS CIT: 3.33
THE ECONOMIC DETERMINANTS OF THE MARKET REACTION TO PROPOSED MANDATORY ACCOUNTING CHANGES IN THE OIL AND GAS INDUSTRY: A CROSS-SECTIONAL ANALYSIS
JAE MR 81 VOL: 3 PG:37 - 71 :: REGRESS. :PRIM. :EMH :OIL & GAS

COLLINS,DW ; SEC: DENT ,WT CIT: 2.64
THE PROPOSED ELIMINATION OF FULL COST ACCOUNTING IN THE EXTRACTIVE PETROLEUM INDUSTRY: AN EMPIRICAL ASSESSMENT OF MARKET CONSEQUENCES
JAE MR 79 VOL: 1 PG:3 - 44 :: NON-PAR. :PRIM. :EMH :OIL & GAS

COLLINS,DW ; SEC: SIMONDS,RR CIT: 0.36
SEC LINE-OF-BUSINESS DISCLOSURE AND MARKET RISK ADJUSTMENTS
JAR AU 79 VOL: 17 PG:352 - 383 :: MIXED :PRIM. :EMH :SEG.REP.

COLLINS,F ; SEC: MUNTER,P ; THIR: FINN ,DW CIT: 0.5
THE BUDGETING GAMES PEOPLE PLAY
TAR JA 87 VOL: 62 PG:29 - 49 :: REGRESS. :SURV. :OTH.BEH. :BUDG.& PLAN.

COLLINS,F CIT: 0.45
MANAGERIAL ACCOUNTING SYSTEMS AND ORGANIZATIONAL CONTROL: A ROLE PERSPECTIVE
AOS 02 82 VOL: 7 PG:107 - 122 :: QUAL. :SURV. :OTH.BEH. :N/A

COLLINS,F ; FIRS: CLANCY,DK CIT: 0.29
INFORMAL ACCOUNTING INFORMATION SYSTEMS: SOME TENTATIVE FINDINGS
AOS 12 79 VOL: 4 PG:21 - 30 :: OTH.QUANT. :SURV. :THEORY :N/A

COLLINS,F CIT: 1.07
THE INTERACTION OF BUDGET CHARACTERISTICS AND PERSONALITY VARIABLES WITH BUDGETARY RESPONSE ATTITUDES
TAR AP 78 VOL: 53 PG:324 - 335 :: REGRESS. :FIELD :OTH.BEH. :BUDG.& PLAN.

COLLINS,JH ; SEC: PLUMLEE,RD CIT: 0.5
THE TAXPAYER'S LABOR AND REPORTING DECISION: THE EFFECT OF AUDIT SCHEMES
TAR JL 91 VOL: 66 PG:559 - 576 :: REGRESS. :SEC. :INF.ECO./AG. :TAX PLNG.

COLLINS,KM ; SEC: KILLOUGH,LN CIT: 0
AN EMPIRICAL EXAMINATION OF STRESS IN PUBLIC ACCOUNTING
AOS 06 92 VOL: 17 PG:535 - 547 :: REGRESS. :LAB. :OTH.BEH. :ORG.

COLLINS,WA ; SEC: HOPWOOD,WS ; THIR: MCKEOWN,JC CIT: 0.44
THE PREDICTABILITY OF INTERIM EARNINGS OVER ALTERNATIVE QUARTERS
JAR AU 84 VOL: 22 PG:467 - 479 :: NON-PAR. :PRIM. :TIME SER. :INT.REP.

COLLINS,WA ; SEC: HOPWOOD,WS CIT: 1.31
A MULTIVARIATE ANALYSIS OF ANNUAL EARNINGS FORECASTS GENERATED FROM QUARTERLY FORECASTS OF FINANCIAL ANALYSTS AND UNIVARIATE TIME-SERIES MODELS
JAR AU 80 VOL: 18 PG:390 - 406 :: ANOVA :PRIM. :TIME SER. :FOREC.

COLLINSON,D ; FIRS: KNIGHTS,D CIT: 1.17
DISCIPLINING THE SHOPFLOOR: A COMPARISON OF THE DISCIPLINARY EFFECTS
AOS 05 87 VOL: 12 PG:457 - 477 :: DES.STAT. :INT. LOG. :THEORY :HRA

COLSON,R ; FIRS: MAHER ,MW ; SEC: TIESSEN,P ; FOUR: BROMAN,AJ CIT: 0
COMPETITION AND AUDIT FEES
TAR JA 92 VOL: 67 PG:199 - 211 :: REGRESS. :PRIM. :OTH. :ORG.

COLVILLE,I CIT: 1.25
RECONSTRUCTING BEHAVIOURAL ACCOUNTING
AOS 02 81 VOL: 6 PG:119 - 132 :: QUAL. :INT. LOG. :OTH.BEH. :N/A

COMISKEY,EE ; FIRS: MULFORD,CW CIT: 0
INVESTMENT DECISIONS AND THE EQUITY ACCOUNTING STANDARD
TAR JL 86 VOL: 61 PG:519 - 525 :: REGRESS. :PRIM. :OTH.STAT. :BUS.COMB.

COMISKEY,EE ; FIRS: BAREFIELD,RM CIT: 0.24
THE SMOOTHING HYPOTHESIS: AN ALTERNATIVE TEST
TAR AP 72 VOL: 47 PG:291 - 298 :: NON-PAR. :PRIM. :TIME SER. :FIN.METH.

COMISKEY,EE ; FIRS: BAREFIELD,RM CIT: 0.18
DEPRECIATION POLICY AND THE BEHAVIOR OF CORPORATE PROFITS
JAR AU 71 VOL: 9 PG:351 - 358 :: NON-PAR. :PRIM. :TIME SER. :PP&E / DEPR

COMISKEY,EE CIT: 0.29
MARKET RESPONSE TO CHANGES IN DEPRECIATION ACCOUNTING
TAR AP 71 VOL: 46 PG:279 - 285 :: ANOVA :PRIM. :N/A :PP&E / DEPR

COMISKEY,EE ; SEC: MLYNARCZYK,FA CIT: 0
RECOGNITION OF INCOME BY FINANCE COMPANIES
TAR AP 68 VOL: 43 PG:248 - 256 :: ANAL. :SIM. :THEORY :REV.REC.

COMISKEY,EE CIT: 0.06
COST CONTROL BY REGRESSION ANALYSIS
TAR AP 66 VOL: 41 PG:235 - 238 :: REGRESS. :INT. LOG. :OTH.STAT. :VAR.

CONROY,R ; SEC: HUGHES,JS CIT: 0
ON THE OBSERVABILITY OF OWNERSHIP RETENTION BY ENTREPRENEURS WITH PRIVATE INFORMATION IN THE MARKET FOR NEW ISSUES
CAR AU 89 VOL: 6 PG:159 - 176 :: DES.STAT. :INT. LOG. :INF.ECO./AG. :BUS.COMB.

CONROY,RM ; SEC: HUGHES,JS CIT: 0.33
DELEGATING INFORMATION GATHERING DECISIONS
TAR JA 87 VOL: 62 PG:50 - 66 :: DES.STAT. :INT. LOG. :INF.ECO./AG. :MANAG.

COOK ,DM CIT: 0.47
THE EFFECT OF FREQUENCY OF FEEDBACK ON ATTITUDES AND PERFORMANCE
JAR ST 67 VOL: 5 PG:213 - 224 :: ANOVA :LAB. :OTH.BEH. :BUDG.& PLAN.

COOK ,E ; FIRS: FLAMHOLTZ,EG CIT: 0.4
CONNOTATIVE MEANING AND ITS ROLE IN ACCOUNTING CHANGE: A FIELD STUDY
AOS 02 78 VOL: 3 PG:115 - 140 :: OTH.QUANT. :FIELD :OTH.BEH. :METHOD.

COOK ,FX ; FIRS: MAXIM ,LD ; SEC: CULLEN,PE CIT: 0
OPTIMAL ACCEPTANCE SAMPLING PLANS FOR AUDITING BATCHED STOP AND GO VS. CONVENTIONAL SINGLE-STAGE ATTRIBUTES
TAR JA 76 VOL: 51 PG:97 - 109 :: ANAL. :INT. LOG. :OTH.STAT. :SAMP.

COOK ,JS ; SEC: HOLZMANN,OJ CIT: 0.06
CURRENT COST AND PRESENT VALUE IN INCOME THEORY
TAR OC 76 VOL: 51 PG:778 - 787 :: ANAL. :INT. LOG. :THEORY :VALUAT.(INFL.)

COOMBS,RW ; FIRS: PRESTON,AM ; SEC: COOPER,DJ CIT: 1
FABRICATING BUDGETS: A STUDY OF PRODUCTION OF MANAGEMENT BUDGETING IN THE NATIONAL HEALTH SERVICE
AOS 06 92 VOL: 17 PG:561 - 593 :: REGRESS. :CASE :OTH.BEH. :BUDG.& PLAN.

COOPER,CL ; FIRS: HASKINS,ME ; SEC: BAGLIONI,AJ CIT: 0.67
AN INVESTIGATION OF THE SOURCES, MODERATORS, AND PSYCHOLOGICAL SYMPTOMS OF STRESS AMONG AUDIT SENIORS
CAR SP 90 VOL: 6 PG:361 - 385 :: REGRESS. :LAB. :HIPS :AUD.BEH.

COOPER,D ; FIRS: BERRY ,AJ ; SEC: CAPPS ,T ; FOUR: FERGUSON,P ; FIFT: HOPPER,T ; SIX: LOWE ,EA CIT: 3
MANAGEMENT CONTROL IN AN AREA OF THE NCB: RATIONALES OF ACCOUNTING PRACTICES IN A PUBLIC ENTERPRISE
AOS 01 85 VOL: 10 PG:3 - 28 :: REGRESS. :FIELD :OTH.BEH. :MANAG.

COOPER,DJ ; FIRS: PRESTON,AM ; THIR: COOMBS,RW CIT: 1
FABRICATING BUDGETS: A STUDY OF PRODUCTION OF MANAGEMENT BUDGETING IN THE NATIONAL HEALTH SERVICE
AOS 06 92 VOL: 17 PG:561 - 593 :: REGRESS. :CASE :OTH.BEH. :BUDG.& PLAN.

COOPER,DJ ; FIRS: PUXTY ,AG ; SEC: WILLMOTT,HC ; FOUR: LOWE ,T CIT: 1.33
MODES OF REGULATION IN ADVANCED CAPITALISM: LOCATING ACCOUNTANCY IN FOUR COUNTRIES
AOS 03 87 VOL: 12 PG:273 - 291 :: DES.STAT. :INT. LOG. :THEORY :ORG.& ENVIR.

COOPER,DJ ; SEC: HOPPER,TM CIT: 0.17
CRITICAL STUDIES IN ACCOUNTING
AOS 05 87 VOL: 12 PG:407 - 414 :: DES.STAT. :INT. LOG. :THEORY :FIN.METH.

COOPER,DJ ; SEC: SHERER,MJ CIT: 2.78
THE VALUE OF CORPORATE ACCOUNTING REPORTS: ARGUMENTS FOR A POLITICAL ECONOMY OF ACCOUNTING
AOS 34 84 VOL: 9 PG:207 - 232 :: QUAL. :SURV. :THEORY :N/A

COOPER,DJ CIT: 1.8
TIDINESS, MUDDLE AND THINGS: COMMONALITIES AND DIVERGENCIES IN TWO APPROACHES TO MANAGEMENT ACCOUNTING RESEARCH
AOS 23 83 VOL: 8 PG:269 - 286 :: QUAL. :SEC. :OTH. :MANAG.

COOPER,DJ ; SEC: HAYES ,DC ; THIR: WOLF ,FM CIT: 1.08
ACCOUNTING IN ORGANIZED ANARCHIES: UNDERSTANDING AND DESIGNING ACCOUNTING SYSTEMS IN AMBIGUOUS SITUATIONS
AOS 03 81 VOL: 6 PG:175 - 192 :: QUAL. :INT. LOG. :THEORY :N/A

COOPER,DJ ; SEC: ESSEX ,S CIT: 0.31
ACCOUNTING INFORMATION AND EMPLOYEE DECISION MAKING
AOS 03 77 VOL: 2 PG:201 - 218 :: DES.STAT. :SURV. :OTH.BEH. :HRA

COOPER,JC ; FIRS: CHOW,CW ; THIR: HADDAD,K CIT: 0
THE EFFECTS OF PAY SCHEMES AND RATCHETS ON BUDGETARY SLACK AND PERFORMANCE: A MULTIPERIOD EXPERIMENT
AOS 01 91 VOL: 16 PG:47 - 60 :: REGRESS. :LAB. :OTH.BEH. :BUDG.& PLAN.

COOPER,JC ; SEC: SELTO ,FH CIT: 0
AN EXPERIMENTAL EXAMINATION OF THE EFFECTS OF SFAS NO. 2 ON R&D INVESTMENT DECISIONS
AOS 03 91 VOL: 16 PG:227 - 242 :: REGRESS. :LAB. :THEORY :R & D

COOPER,JC ; FIRS: BLOCHER,E CIT: 0
A STUDY OF AUDITORS' ANALYTICAL REVIEW PERFORMANCE
AUD SP 88 VOL: 07 PG:1 - 28 :: REGRESS. :LAB. :OTH.BEH. :ANAL.REV.

COOPER,JC ; FIRS: CHOW ,CW ; THIR: WALLER,WS CIT: 0.8
PARTICIPATIVE BUDGETING: EFFECTS OF A TRUTH-INDUCING PAY SCHEME AND INFORMATION ASYMMETRY ON SLACK AND PERFORMANCE
TAR JA 88 VOL: 63 PG:111 - 122 :: REGRESS. :LAB. :OTH.BEH. :BUDG.& PLAN.

COOPER,T CIT: 0
REPLACEMENT COST AND BETA: A FINANCIAL MODEL
JAA WI 80 VOL: 3 PG:138 - 146 :: MIXED :SEC. :EMH :VALUAT.(INFL.)

COOPER,WW ; FIRS: BANKER,RD ; THIR: POTTER,G CIT: 0
A PERSPECTIVE ON RESEARCH IN GOVERNMENTAL ACCOUNTING
TAR JL 92 VOL: 67 PG:496 - 510 :: REGRESS. :SEC. :THEORY :N/A

COOPER,WW ; SEC: HO ,JL ; THIR: HUNTER,JE ; FOUR: RODGERS,RC CIT: 0
THE IMPACT OF THE FOREIGN CORRUPT PRACTICES ACT ON INTERNAL CONTROL PRACTICES
JAA AU 85 VOL: 9 PG:22 - 39 :: REGRESS. :SEC. :THEORY :INT.CONT.

COOPER,WW ; FIRS: BROCKETT,P ; SEC: CHARNES,A ; FOUR: SHIN ,HC CIT: 0
A CHANCE-CONSTRAINED PROGRAMMING APPROACH TO COST-VOLUME-PROFIT ANALYSIS
TAR JL 84 VOL: 59 PG:474 - 487 :: ANAL. :INT. LOG. :MATH.PROG. :C-V-P-A

COOPER,WW ; FIRS: CHURCHILL,NC ; THIR: GOVINDARAJAN,V CIT: 0
EFFECTS OF AUDITS ON THE BEHAVIOR OF MEDICAL PROFESSIONALS UNDER THE BENNETT AMENDMENT
AUD WI 82 VOL: 1 PG:69 - 91 :: ANOVA :PRIM. :OTH.STAT. :OPER.AUD.

COOPER,WW ; FIRS: CHARNES,A CIT: 0.08
AUDITING AND ACCOUNTING FOR PROBLEM EFFICIENCY AND MANAGEMENT EFFICIENCY IN NOT-FOR PROFIT ENTITIES
AOS 01 80 VOL: 5 PG:87 - 107 :: MIXED :PRIM. :OTH.STAT. :AUD.

COOPER,WW ; FIRS: CHARNES,A ; SEC: COLANTONI,CS CIT: 0
A FUTUROLOGICAL JUSTIFICATION FOR HISTORICAL COST AND MULTI-DIMENSIONAL ACCOUNTING
AOS 04 76 VOL: 1 PG:315 - 338 :: ANAL. :INT. LOG. :MATH.PROG. :HRA

COOPER,WW ; FIRS: CHARNES,A ; SEC: COLANTONI,CS ; FOUR: KORTANEK,KO CIT: 0.06
ECONOMIC SOCIAL AND ENTERPRISE ACCOUNTING AND MATHEMATICAL MODES
TAR JA 72 VOL: 47 PG:85 - 108 :: ANAL. :INT. LOG. :MATH.PROG. :FIN.METH.

COOPER,WW ; FIRS: BYRNE ,R ; SEC: CHARNES,A ; FOUR: KORTANEK,KO CIT: 0
SOME NEW APPROACHES TO RISK
TAR JA 68 VOL: 43 PG:18 - 37 :: ANAL. :INT. LOG. :MATH.PROG. :BUDG.& PLAN.

COOPER,WW ; SEC: DOPUCH,N ; THIR: KELLER,TF CIT: 0.06
BUDGETARY DISCLOSURE AND OTHER SUGGESTIONS FOR IMPROVING ACCOUNTING REPORTS
TAR OC 68 VOL: 43 PG:640 - 648 :: QUAL. :INT. LOG. :THEORY :FIN.METH.

COOPER,WW ; FIRS: CHARNES,A CIT: 0.06
SOME NETWORK CHARACTERIZATIONS FOR MATHEMATICAL PROGRAMMING AND ACCOUNTING APPROACHES TO PLANNING AND CONTROL
TAR JA 67 VOL: 42 PG:24 - 52 :: ANAL. :INT. LOG. :MATH.PROG. :MANAG.

COOPER,WW ; FIRS: CHURCHILL,NC CIT: 0.12
A FIELD STUDY OF INTERNAL AUDITING
TAR OC 65 VOL: 40 PG:767 - 781 :: DES.STAT. :FIELD :OTH.BEH. :AUD.

COOPER,WW ; FIRS: CHARNES,A ; THIR: IJIRI ,Y CIT: 0.06
BREAKEVEN BUDGETING AND PROGRAMMING TO GOALS
JAR SP 63 VOL: 1 PG:16 - 43 :: ANAL. :INT. LOG. :MATH.PROG. :C-V-P-A

COPELAND,RM ; SEC: INGRAM,RW CIT: 0.36
THE ASSOCIATION BETWEEN MUNICIPAL ACCOUNTING INFORMATION AND BOND RATING CHANGES
JAR AU 82 VOL: 20 PG:275 - 289 :: OTH.QUANT. :PRIM. :OTH.STAT. :FIN.METH.

COPELAND,RM ; FIRS: INGRAM,RW CIT: 0.27
MUNICIPAL MARKET MEASURES AND REPORTING PRACTICES: AN EXTENSION
JAR AU 82 VOL: 20 PG:766 - 772 :: REGRESS. :PRIM. :OTH.STAT. :FIN.METH.

COPELAND,RM ; SEC: TAYLOR,RL ; THIR: BROWN ,SH CIT: 0.08
OBSERVATION ERROR AND BIAS IN ACCOUNTING RESEARCH
JAR SP 81 VOL: 19 PG:197 - 207 :: ANOVA :LAB. :OTH.BEH. :METHOD.

COPELAND,RM ; FIRS: INGRAM,RW CIT: 0.25
MUNICIPAL ACCOUNTING INFORMATION AND VOTING BEHAVIOR
TAR OC 81 VOL: 56 PG:830 - 843 :: OTH.QUANT. :PRIM. :INSTIT. :N/A

COPELAND,RM ; SEC: FRANCIA,AJ ; THIR: STRAWSER,RH CIT: 0.53
STUDENTS AS SUBJECTS IN BEHAVIOURAL BUSINESS RESEARCH
TAR AP 73 VOL: 48 PG:365 - 374 :: QUAL. :SURV. :OTH.BEH. :METHOD.

COPELAND,RM ; FIRS: SHANK ,JK CIT: 0.29
CORPORATE PERSONALITY THEORY AND CHANGES IN ACCOUNTING METHODS: AN EMPIRICAL TEST
TAR JL 73 VOL: 48 PG:494 - 501 :: NON-PAR. :PRIM. :OTH.STAT. :ORG.FORM

COPELAND,RM ; FIRS: DASCHER,PE CIT: 0.18
SOME FURTHER EVIDENCE ON CRITERIA FOR JUDGING DISCLOSURE IMPROVEMENT
JAR SP 71 VOL: 9 PG:32 - 39 :: ANOVA :LAB. :OTH.BEH. :SEG.REP.

COPELAND,RM ; SEC: SHANK ,JK CIT: 0.35
LIFO AND THE DIFFUSION OF INNOVATION
JAR ST 71 VOL: 9 PG:196 - 224 :: DES.STAT. :PRIM. :THEORY :INV.

COPELAND,RM ; FIRS: BERNHARDT,I CIT: 0.12
SOME PROBLEMS IN APPLYING AN INFORMATION THEORY APPROACH TO ACCOUNTING AGGREGATION
JAR SP 70 VOL: 8 PG:95 - 98 :: QUAL. :INT. LOG. :INF.ECO./AG. :INFO.STRUC.

COPELAND,RM ; SEC: WOJDAK,JF CIT: 0.12
INCOME MANIPULATION AND THE PURCHASE-POOLING CHOICE
JAR AU 69 VOL: 7 PG:188 - 195 :: DES.STAT. :PRIM. :OTH. :BUS.COMB.

COPELAND,RM ; SEC: FREDERICKS,W CIT: 0.12
EXTENT OF DISCLOSURE
JAR SP 68 VOL: 6 PG:106 - 113 :: NON-PAR. :PRIM. :THEORY :INFO.STRUC.

COPELAND,RM CIT: 0.59
INCOME SMOOTHING
JAR ST 68 VOL: 6 PG:101 - 116 :: NON-PAR. :PRIM. :N/A :REV.REC.

COPELAND,RM ; SEC: LICASTRO,RD CIT: 0.18
A NOTE ON INCOME SMOOTHING
TAR JL 68 VOL: 43 PG:540 - 545 :: ANOVA :PRIM. :TIME SER. :CASH DIV.

COPELAND,TE CIT: 0
EFFICIENT CAPITAL MARKETS: EVIDENCE AND IMPLICATIONS FOR FINANCIAL REPORTING
JAA AU 78 VOL: 2 PG:33 - 48 :: QUAL. :SEC. :EMH :FIN.METH.

COPPOCK,R CIT: 0.19
LIFE AMONG THE ENVIRONMENTALISTS: AN ELABORATION ON WILDAVSKY'S ECONOMICS AND ENVIRONMENT/RATIONALITY AND RITUAL
AOS 02 77 VOL: 2 PG:125 - 130 :: QUAL. :INT. LOG. :OTH. :N/A

CORBIN,DA CIT: 0
ON THE FEASIBILITY OF DEVELOPING CURRENT COST INFORMATION
TAR OC 67 VOL: 42 PG:635 - 641 :: QUAL. :INT. LOG. :THEORY :VALUAT.(INFL.)

CORBIN,DA CIT: 0
COMMENTS ON THE ACCRETION CONCEPT OF INCOME
TAR OC 63 VOL: 38 PG:742 - 744 :: QUAL. :INT. LOG. :THEORY :VALUAT.(INFL.)

CORCORAN,AW ; SEC: LEININGER,WE CIT: 0.06
STOCHASTIC PROCESS COSTING MODELS
TAR JA 73 VOL: 48 PG:105 - 114 :: ANAL. :INT. LOG. :MATH.PROG. :COST.ALLOC.

CORCORAN,AW CIT: 0
COMPUTERS VERSUS MATHEMATICS
TAR AP 69 VOL: 44 PG:359 - 374 :: ANAL. :INT. LOG. :N/A :OTH.MANAG.

CORCORAN,AW ; SEC: KWANG ,CW CIT: 0
A SET THEORY APPROACH TO FUNDS-FLOW ANALYSIS
JAR AU 65 VOL: 3 PG:206 - 217 :: ANAL. :INT. LOG. :THEORY :PP&E / DEPR

CORDERY,C ; FIRS: LOUDDER,ML ; SEC: KHURANA,IK ; THIR: SAWYERS,RB ; FIFT: JOHNSON,C ; SIX: LOWE ,J CIT: 0
THE INFORMATION CONTENT OF AUDIT QUALIFICATIONS
AUD SP 92 VOL: 11 PG:69 - 82 :: REGRESS. :PRIM. :OTH.STAT. :OPIN.

CORLESS,JC CIT: 1.18
ASSESSING PRIOR DISTRIBUTIONS FOR APPLYING BAYESIAN STATISTICS IN AUDITING
TAR JL 72 VOL: 47 PG:556 - 566 :: DES.STAT. :LAB. :OTH.STAT. :SAMP.

CORNELL,B ; SEC: LANDSMAN,W ; THIR: SHAPIRO,AC CIT: 0
CROSS-SECTIONAL REGULARITIES IN THE RESPONSE OF STOCK PRICES TO BOND RATING CHANGES
JAA AU 89 VOL: 4 PG:460 - 479 :: REGRESS. :PRIM. :EMH :OTH.C/A

CORNELL,B ; SEC: LANDSMAN,WR CIT: 1.25
SECURITY PRICE RESPONSE TO QUARTERLY EARNINGS ANNOUNCEMENTS AND ANALYSTS' FORECAST REVISIONS
TAR OC 89 VOL: 64 PG:680 - 692 :: REGRESS. :PRIM. :EMH :AUD.BEH.

COTTELL JR,PG CIT: 0
LIFO LAYER LIQUIDATIONS: SOME EMPIRICAL EVIDENCE
JAA WI 86 VOL: 1 PG:30 - 45 :: REGRESS. :SURV. :THEORY :INV.

COTTON,W ; FIRS: WELLS ,MC CIT: 0
HOLDING GAINS ON FIXED ASSETS
TAR OC 65 VOL: 40 PG:829 - 833 :: QUAL. :INT. LOG. :THEORY :VALUAT.(INFL.)

COUGHLAN,AT ; SEC: SCHMIDT,RM CIT: 1.25
EXECUTIVE COMPENSATION, MANAGEMENT TURNOVER, AND FIRM PERFORMANCE: AN EMPIRICAL INVESTIGATION
JAE AP 85 VOL: 7 PG:43 - 66 :: REGRESS. :PRIM. :OTH.STAT. :EXEC.COMP.

COURSEY,D ; FIRS: BERG ,KB ; THIR: DICKHAUT,J CIT: 1.33
EXPERIMENTAL METHODS IN ACCOUNTING: A DISCUSSION OF RECURRING ISSUES
CAR SP 90 VOL: 6 PG:825 - 849 :: DES.STAT. :SEC. :INF.ECO./AG. :METHOD.

COUTTS,JA ; FIRS: ROBERTS,J CIT: 0
FEMINIZATION AND PROFESSIONALIZATION: A REVIEW OF AN EMERGING LITERATURE ON THE DEVELOPMENT OF ACCOUNTING IN THE UNITED KINGDOM
AOS 04 92 VOL: 17 PG:379 - 395 :: REGRESS. :SEC. :HIST. :ORG.& ENVIR.

COVALESKI,M ; FIRS: COLIGNON,R CIT: 0.5
A WEBERIAN FRAMEWORK IN THE STUDY OF ACCOUNTING
AOS 02 91 VOL: 16 PG:141 - 157 :: DES.STAT. :SEC. :THEORY :ORG.& ENVIR.

COVALESKI,M ; FIRS: COLIGNON,R CIT: 0.2
AN EXAMINATION OF MANAGERIAL ACCOUNTING PRACTICES AS A PROCESS OF MUTUAL ADJUSTMENT
AOS 06 88 VOL: 13 PG:559 - 579 :: REGRESS. :CASE :THEORY :BUDG.& PLAN.

COVALESKI,M ; SEC: AIKEN ,ME CIT: 0.29
ACCOUNTING AND THEORIES OF ORGANIZATIONS: SOME PRELIMINARY CONSIDERATIONS
AOS 45 86 VOL: 11 PG:297 - 320 :: ANOVA :INT. LOG. :THEORY :ORG.& ENVIR.

COVALESKI,MA ; SEC: DIRSMITH,MW CIT: 1
DIALECTIC TENSION, DOUBLE REFLEXIVITY AND THE EVERDAY ACCOUNTING RESEARCHER: ON USING QUALITATIVE METHODS
AOS 06 90 VOL: 15 PG:543 - 573 :: DES.STAT. :INT. LOG. :THEORY :METHOD.

COVALESKI,MA ; SEC: DIRSMITH,MW CIT: 1.8
THE USE OF BUDGETARY SYMBOLS IN THE POLITICAL ARENA: AN HISTORICALLY INFORMED FIELD STUDY
AOS 01 88 VOL: 13 PG:1 - 24 :: REGRESS. :CASE :THEORY :BUDG.& PLAN.

COVALESKI,MA ; SEC: DIRSMITH,MW ; THIR: WHITE ,CE CIT: 0.17
ECONOMIC CONSEQUENCES: THE RELATIONSHIP BETWEEN FINANCIAL REPORTING AND STRATEGIC PLANNING, MANAGEMENT AND OPERATING CONTROL DECISIONS
CAR SP 87 VOL: 3 PG:408 - 429 :: REGRESS. :LAB. :HIPS :FIN.METH.

COVALESKI,MA ; SEC: DIRSMITH,MW CIT: 1.14
THE BUDGETARY PROCESS OF POWER AND POLITICS
AOS 03 86 VOL: 11 PG:193 - 214 :: REGRESS. :SURV. :OTH.BEH. :BUDG.& PLAN.

COVALESKI,MA ; FIRS: DIRSMITH,MW CIT: 0.63
INFORMAL COMMUNICATIONS, NONFORMAL COMMUNICATIONS AND MENTORING IN PUBLIC ACCOUNTING FIRMS
AOS 02 85 VOL: 10 PG:149 - 170 :: REGRESS. :INT. LOG. :INSTIT. :ORG.

COVALESKI,MA ; FIRS: DIRSMITH,MW ; THIR: MCALLISTER,JP CIT: 0.5
OF PARADIGMS AND METAPHORS IN AUDITING THOUGHT
CAR AU 85 VOL: 2 PG:46 - 68 :: REGRESS. :SURV. :THEORY :AUD.TRAIN.

COVALESKI,MA ; FIRS: DIRSMITH,MW CIT: 0.38
PRACTICE MANAGEMENT ISSUES IN PUBLIC ACCOUNTING FIRMS
JAA AU 85 VOL: 9 PG:5 - 21 :: REGRESS. :SURV. :OTH. :ORG.

COVALESKI,MA ; SEC: DIRSMITH,MW CIT: 0.5
BUDGETING AS A MEANS FOR CONTROL AND LOOSE COUPLING
AOS 04 83 VOL: 8 PG:323 - 340 :: CORR. :SURV. :OTH.BEH. :BUDG.& PLAN.

COWAN ,TK CIT: 0
A PRAGMATIC APPROACH TO ACCOUNTING THEORY
TAR JA 68 VOL: 43 PG:94 - 100 :: QUAL. :INT. LOG. :THEORY :FIN.METH.

COWAN ,TK CIT: 0
A RESOURCES THEORY OF ACCOUNTING
TAR JA 65 VOL: 40 PG:9 - 20 :: QUAL. :INT. LOG. :THEORY :FIN.METH.

COWAN ,TK CIT: 0.06
ARE TRUTH AND FAIRNESS GENERALLY ACCEPTABLE?
TAR OC 65 VOL: 40 PG:788 - 794 :: QUAL. :INT. LOG. :INSTIT. :FIN.METH.

COWEN ,SS ; SEC: FERRERI,LB ; THIR: PARKER,LD CIT: 0.33
THE IMPACT OF CORPORATE CHARACTERISTICS ON SOCIAL RESPONSIBILITY DISCLOSURE: A TYPOLOGY AND FREQUENCY-BASED ANALYSIS
AOS 02 87 VOL: 12 PG:111 - 122 :: REGRESS. :PRIM. :THEORY :HRA

COWIE ,JB ; SEC: FREMGEN,JM CIT: 0
COMPUTERS VERSUS MATHEMATICS: ROUND 2
TAR JA 70 VOL: 45 PG:27 - 37 :: QUAL. :INT. LOG. :N/A :OTH.MANAG.

COX ,CT CIT: 0.13
FURTHER EVIDENCE ON THE REPRESENTATIVENESS OF MANAGEMENT EARNINGS FORECASTS
TAR OC 85 VOL: 60 PG:692 - 701 :: REGRESS. :PRIM. :EMH :FOREC.

CRAIG ,PW ; FIRS: GROBSTEIN,M CIT: 0.78
A RISK ANALYSIS APPROACH TO AUDITING
AUD SP 84 VOL: 3 PG:1 - 16 :: QUAL. :INT. LOG. :OTH. :RISK

CRAMER JR,JJ ; SEC: NEYHART,CA CIT: 0
A COMPREHENSIVE ACCOUNTING FRAMEWORK FOR EVALUATING EXECUTORY CONTRACTS
JAA WI 79 VOL: 2 PG:135 - 150 :: QUAL. :INT. LOG. :THEORY :N/A

CRAMER JR,JJ ; SEC: SCHRADER,WJ CIT: 0
DEPRECIATION ACCOUNTING AND THE ANOMALOUS SELF-INSURANCE COST
TAR OC 70 VOL: 45 PG:698 - 703 :: QUAL. :INT. LOG. :THEORY :PP&E / DEPR

CRAMER JR,JJ CIT: 0
LEGAL INFLUENCES ON PENSION TRUST ACCOUNTING
TAR JL 65 VOL: 40 PG:606 - 616 :: QUAL. :INT. LOG. :INSTIT. :FIN.METH.

CRAMER JR,JJ CIT: 0
A NOTE ON PENSION TRUST ACCOUNTINGS
TAR OC 64 VOL: 39 PG:869 - 875 :: QUAL. :INT. LOG. :N/A :FIN.METH.

CRANDALL,RH CIT: 0
INFORMATION ECONOMICS AND ITS IMPLICATIONS FOR THE FURTHER DEVELOPMENT OF ACCOUNTING THEORY
TAR JL 69 VOL: 44 PG:457 - 466 :: QUAL. :INT. LOG. :INF.ECO./AG. :OTH.MANAG.

CREADY,WM ; SEC: RAMANAN,R CIT: 0
THE POWER OF TESTS EMPLOYING LOG-TRANSFORMED VOLUME IN DETECTING ABNORMAL TRADING
JAE JN 91 VOL: 14 PG:203 - 214 :: DES.STAT. :SIM. :OTH.STAT. :METHOD.

CREADY,WM ; SEC: MYNATT,PG CIT: 0.5
THE INFORMATION CONTENT OF ANNUAL REPORTS: A PRICE AND TRADING RESPONSE ANALYSIS
TAR AP 91 VOL: 66 PG:291 - 312 :: REGRESS. :PRIM. :EMH :N/A

CREADY,WM CIT: 0.4
INFORMATION VALUE AND INVESTOR WEALTH: THE CASE OF EARNINGS ANNOUNCEMENTS
JAR SP 88 VOL: 26 PG:1 - 27 :: REGRESS. :PRIM. :EMH :FIN.METH.

CREADY,WM ; SEC: SHANK ,JK CIT: 0
UNDERSTANDING ACCOUNTING CHANGES IN AN EFFICIENT MARKET: A COMMENT REGULATION, AND RE-INTERPRETATION
TAR JL 87 VOL: 62 PG:589 - 596 :: REGRESS. :PRIM. :EMH :ACC.CHNG.

CRICHFIELD,T ; SEC: DYCKMAN,TR ; THIR: LAKONISHOK,J CIT: 0.93
AN EVALUATION OF SECURITY ANALYSTS' FORECASTS
TAR JL 78 VOL: 53 PG:651 - 668 :: ANOVA :PRIM. :TIME SER. :FOREC.

CROSBY,MA CIT: 0.13
THE DEVELOPMENT OF BAYESIAN DECISION THEORETIC CONCEPTS IN ATTRIBUTE SAMPLING
AUD SP 85 VOL: 4 PG:118 - 132 :: REGRESS. :SEC. :OTH.STAT. :SAMP.

CROSBY,MA CIT: 0.75
BAYESIAN STATISTICS IN AUDITING: A COMPARISON OF PROBABILITY ELICITATION TECHNIQUES
TAR AP 81 VOL: 56 PG:355 - 365 :: DES.STAT. :LAB. :OTH.BEH. :PROB.ELIC.

CROSBY,MA CIT: 0.46
IMPLICATIONS OF PRIOR PROBABILITY ELICITATION ON AUDITOR SAMPLE SIZE DECISIONS
JAR AU 80 VOL: 18 PG:585 - 593 :: ANAL. :INT. LOG. :OTH.BEH. :PROB.ELIC.

CRUMBLEY,DL ; FIRS: BRAVENEC,LL ; SEC: EPSTEIN,MJ CIT: 0
TAX IMPACT IN CORPORATE SOCIAL RESPONSIBILITY DECISIONS AND REPORTING
AOS 02 77 VOL: 2 PG:131 - 140 :: QUAL. :INT. LOG. :THEORY :HRA

CRUMBLEY,DL ; SEC: SAVICH,RS CIT: 0
USE OF HUMAN RESOURCE ACCOUNTING IN TAXATION
TAR JA 75 VOL: 50 PG:112 - 117 :: QUAL. :INT. LOG. :THEORY :HRA

CRUMBLEY,DL CIT: 0.24
BEHAVIOURAL IMPLICATIONS OF TAXATION
TAR OC 73 VOL: 48 PG:759 - 763 :: QUAL. :INT. LOG. :INSTIT. :TAXES

CRUMBLEY,DL CIT: 0
NARROWING THE TAXABLE AND ACCOUNTING INCOME GAP FOR CONSOLIDATIONS
TAR JL 68 VOL: 43 PG:554 - 564 :: QUAL. :INT. LOG. :N/A :BUS.COMB.

CRUSE ,RB ; SEC: SUMMERS,EL CIT: 0
ECONOMICS, ACCOUNTING PRACTICE AND ACCOUNTING RESEARCH STUDY NO.3
TAR JA 65 VOL: 40 PG:82 - 88 :: QUAL. :INT. LOG. :THEORY :FIN.METH.

CULLEN,PE ; FIRS: MAXIM ,LD ; THIR: COOK ,FX CIT: 0
OPTIMAL ACCEPTANCE SAMPLING PLANS FOR AUDITING BATCHED STOP AND GO VS. CONVENTIONAL SINGLE-STAGE ATTRIBUTES
TAR JA 76 VOL: 51 PG:97 - 109 :: ANAL. :INT. LOG. :OTH.STAT. :SAMP.

CULPEPPER,RC CIT: 0.06
A STUDY OF SOME RELATIONSHIPS BETWEEN ACCOUNTING AND DECISION-MAKING PROCESSES
TAR AP 70 VOL: 45 PG:322 - 332 :: ANOVA :PRIM. :INSTIT. :FIN.METH.

CUMMING,J CIT: 0.06
AN EMPIRICAL EVALUATION OF POSSIBLE EXPLANATIONS FOR THE DIFFERING TREATMENT OF APPARENTLY SIMILAR UNUSUAL EVENTS
JAR ST 73 VOL: 11 PG:60 - 95 :: NON-PAR. :SURV. :OTH.BEH. :SPEC.ITEMS

CURATOLA,AP ; FIRS: SAMI ,H ; THIR: TRAPNELL,JE CIT: 0
EVIDENCE ON THE PREDICTIVE ABILITY OF INFLATION-ADJUSTED EARNINGS MEASURES
CAR SP 89 VOL: 5 PG:556 - 574 :: REGRESS. :PRIM. :EMH :VALUAT.(INFL.)

CURLEY,AJ CIT: 0
CONGLOMERATE EARNINGS PER SHARE: REAL AND TRANSITORY GROWTH
TAR JL 71 VOL: 46 PG:519 - 528 :: ANAL. :INT. LOG. :N/A :BUS.COMB.

CURRY ,DW CIT: 0.06
OPINION 15 VS. A COMPREHENSIVE FINANCIAL REPORTING METHOD FOR CONVERTIBLE DEBT
TAR JL 71 VOL: 46 PG:490 - 503 :: QUAL. :INT. LOG. :THEORY :LTD

CUSHING,BE ; SEC: LECLERE,MJ CIT: 1
EVIDENCE ON THE DETERMINANTS OF INVENTORY ACCOUNTING POLICY CHOICE
TAR AP 92 VOL: 67 PG:355 - 367 :: REGRESS. :MIXED :OTH.STAT. :INV.

CUSHING,BE ; SEC: LOEBBECKE,JK CIT: 1.3
ANALYTICAL APPROACHES TO AUDIT RISK: A SURVEY AND ANALYSIS
AUD AU 83 VOL: 3 PG:23 - 41 :: ANAL. :SEC. :OTH.STAT. :RISK

CUSHING,BE ; SEC: SEARFOSS,DG ; THIR: RANDALL,RH CIT: 0.36
MATERIALITY ALLOCATION IN AUDIT PLANNING: A FEASIBILITY STUDY
JAR ST 79 VOL: 17 PG:172 - 216 :: DES.STAT. :FIELD :OTH.STAT. :PLAN.

CUSHING,BE CIT: 0.38
ON THE POSSIBILITY OF OPTIMAL ACCOUNTING PRINCIPLES
TAR AP 77 VOL: 52 PG:308 - 321 :: ANAL. :INT. LOG. :INSTIT. :FIN.METH.

CUSHING,BE CIT: 0.65
A MATHEMATICAL APPROACH TO THE ANALYSIS AND DESIGN OF INTERNAL CONTROL SYSTEMS
TAR JA 74 VOL: 49 PG:24 - 41 :: ANAL. :INT. LOG. :OTH.STAT. :INT.CONT.

CUSHING,BE CIT: 0.76
AN EMPIRICAL STUDY OF CHANGES IN ACCOUNTING POLICY
JAR AU 69 VOL: 7 PG:196 - 203 :: DES.STAT. :PRIM. :OTH. :ACC.CHNG.

CUSHING,BE CIT: 0
SOME OBSERVATIONS ON DEMSKI'S EX POST ACCOUNTING SYSTEM
TAR OC 68 VOL: 43 PG:668 - 671 :: QUAL. :INT. LOG. :INF.ECO./AG. :VAR.

CYERT ,RM ; SEC: IJIRI ,Y CIT: 0.18
PROBLEMS OF IMPLEMENTING THE TRUEBLOOD OBJECTIVES REPORT
JAR ST 74 VOL: 12 PG:29 - 42 :: QUAL. :INT. LOG. :THEORY :FIN.METH.

CZARNIAWSKA-,B CIT: 0
DYNAMICS OF ORGANIZATIONAL CONTROL: THE CASE OF BEROL KEMI AB
AOS 04 88 VOL: 13 PG:415 - 430 :: REGRESS. :CASE :HIST. :MANAG.

CZARNIAWSKA-JOERGES ; SEC: JACOBSSON,B CIT: 0
BUDGET IN A COLD CLIMATE
AOS 02 89 VOL: 14 PG:29 - 39 :: REGRESS. :SEC. :HIST. :ORG.& ENVIR.

DAEMS ,H ; FIRS: CHANDLER,AD CIT: 0.71
ADMINISTRATIVE COORDINATION, ALLOCATION AND MONITORING: A COMPARATIVE ANALYSIS OF EMERGENCE OF ACCOUNTING AND ORGANIZATIONS IN U
AOS 12 79 VOL: 4 PG:3 - 20 :: QUAL. :INT. LOG. :HIST. :N/A

DAFT ,RL ; FIRS: MACINTOSH,NB CIT: 0.67
MANAGEMENT CONTROL SYSTEMS AND DEPARTMENTAL INTERDEPENDENCIES: AN EMPIRICAL STUDY
AOS 01 87 VOL: 12 PG:49 - 61 :: REGRESS. :SURV. :OTH.BEH. :ORG.& ENVIR.

DAFT ,RL ; FIRS: GIROUX,GA ; SEC: MAYPER,AG CIT: 0
ORGANIZATION SIZE, BUDGET CYCLE, AND BUDGET RELATED INFLUENCE IN CITY GOVERNMENTS: AN EMPIRICAL STUDY
AOS 06 86 VOL: 11 PG:499 - 520 :: REGRESS. :SURV. :OTH.STAT. :BUDG.& PLAN.

DAILY ,RA CIT: 0.47
THE FEASIBILITY OF REPORTING FORECASTED INFORMATION
TAR OC 71 VOL: 46 PG:686 - 692 :: CORR. :PRIM. :N/A :FOREC.

DALEY ,LA ; SEC: SENKOW,DW ; THIR: VIGELAND,RL CIT: 0.4
ANALYSTS' FORECASTS, EARNINGS VARIABILITY, AND OPTION PRICING: EMPIRICAL EVIDENCE
TAR OC 88 VOL: 63 PG:563 - 585 :: REGRESS. :PRIM. :TIME SER. :FOREC.

DALEY ,LA ; FIRS: BOWEN ,RM ; SEC: BURGSTAHLER,D CIT: 1.67
THE INCREMENTAL INFORMATION CONTENT OF ACCRUAL VERSUS CASH FLOWS
TAR OC 87 VOL: 62 PG:723 - 747 :: REGRESS. :PRIM. :EMH :FIN.METH.

DALEY ,LA ; FIRS: BOWEN ,RM ; SEC: BURGSTAHLER,D CIT: 0.71
EVIDENCE ON THE RELATIONSHIPS BETWEEN VARIOUS EARNINGS MEASURES OF CASH FLOW
TAR OC 86 VOL: 61 PG:713 - 725 :: REGRESS. :PRIM. :OTH.STAT. :REV.REC.

DALEY ,LA CIT: 0.89
THE VALUATION OF REPORTED PENSION MEASURES FOR FIRMS SPONSORING DEFINED BENEFIT PLANS
TAR AP 84 VOL: 59 PG:177 - 198 :: REGRESS. :PRIM. :OTH.STAT. :PENS.

DALEY ,LA ; SEC: VIGELAND,RL CIT: 2
THE EFFECTS OF DEBT COVENANTS AND POLITICAL COSTS ON THE CHOICE OF ACCOUNTING METHODS: THE CASE OF ACCOUNTING FOR R & D COSTS
JAE DE 83 VOL: 5 PG:195 - 211 :: OTH.QUANT. :PRIM. :OTH.STAT. :R & D

DALTON,FE ; SEC: MINER ,JB CIT: 0.06
THE ROLE OF ACCOUNTING TRAINING IN TOP MANAGEMENT DECISION MAKING
TAR JA 70 VOL: 45 PG:134 - 139 :: ANOVA :LAB. :N/A :AUD.TRAIN.

DALY ,BA ; SEC: OMER ,T CIT: 0
A COMMENT ON "A BEHAVIORAL STUDY OF THE MEANING AND INFLUENCE OF TAX COMPLEXITY"
JAR SP 90 VOL: 28 PG:193 - 197 :: REGRESS. :LAB. :OTH.BEH. :TAXES

DAMENS,J ; FIRS: GRAHAM,LE ; THIR: VAN NESS,G CIT: 0
DEVELOPING RISK ADVISOR: AN EXPERT SYSTEM FOR RISK IDENTIFICATION
AUD SP 91 VOL: 10 PG:69 - 96 :: REGRESS. :LAB. :EXP.SYST. :RISK

DAMODARAN,A ; FIRS: LANDSMAN,WR CIT: 0.25
USING SHRINKAGE ESTIMATORS TO IMPROVE UPON TIME-SERIES MODEL PROXIES FOR THE SECURITY MARKET'S EXPECTATION OF EARNINGS
JAR SP 89 VOL: 27 PG:97 - 115 :: DES.STAT. :PRIM. :TIME SER. :METHOD.

DANIEL,SJ ; SEC: REITSPERGER,WD CIT: 0
LINKING QUALITY STRATEGY WITH MANAGEMENT CONTROL SYSTEMS: EMPIRICAL EVIDENCE FROM JAPANESE INDUSTRY
AOS 91 VOL: 16 PG:601 - 618 :: REGRESS. :FIELD :OTH.STAT. :MANAG.

DANIEL,SJ CIT: 0
SOME EMPIRICAL EVIDENCE ABOUT THE ASSESSMENT OF AUDIT RISK IN PRACTICE
AUD SP 88 VOL: 07 PG:174 - 181 :: REGRESS. :LAB. :OTH. :RISK

DANN ,LY ; SEC: MASULIS,RW ; THIR: MAYERS,D CIT: 1
REPURCHASE TENDER OFFERS AND EARNINGS INFORMATION
JAE SE 91 VOL: 14 PG:217 - 251 :: REGRESS. :PRIM. :TIME SER. :BUS.COMB.

DANOS ,P ; SEC: HOLT ,DL ; THIR: IMHOFF JR,EA CIT: 0.25
THE USE OF ACCOUNTING INFORMATION IN BANK LENDING DECISIONS
AOS 03 89 VOL: 14 PG:235 - 246 :: REGRESS. :LAB. :HIPS :OTH.FIN.ACC.

DANOS ,P ; SEC: EICHENSEHER,JW ; THIR: HOLT ,DL CIT: 0
SPECIALIZED KNOWLEDGE AND ITS COMMUNICATION IN AUDITING
CAR AU 89 VOL: 6 PG:91 - 109 :: REGRESS. :SURV. :OTH.BEH. :OPER.AUD.

DANOS ,P ; SEC: HOLT ,DL ; THIR: BAILEY JR,AD CIT: 0
THE INTERACTION OF SCIENCE AND ATTESTATION STANDARD FORMATION
AUD SP 87 VOL: 6 PG:134 - 149 :: DES.STAT. :INT. LOG. :THEORY :OPIN.

DANOS ,P ; SEC: EICHENSEHER,JW CIT: 0.57
LONG-TERM TRENDS TOWARD SELLER CONCENTRATION IN THE US AUDIT MARKET
TAR OC 86 VOL: 61 PG:633 - 650 :: REGRESS. :PRIM. :OTH.STAT. :ORG.& ENVIR.

DANOS ,P ; SEC: HOLT ,DL ; THIR: IMHOFF JR,EA CIT: 0.33
BOND RATERS' USE OF MANAGEMENT FINANCIAL FORECASTS: EXPERIMENT IN EXPERT JUDGMENT
TAR OC 84 VOL: 59 PG:547 - 573 :: ANOVA :LAB. :OTH.BEH. :FOREC.

DANOS ,P ; SEC: IMHOFF JR,EA CIT: 0.1
FACTORS AFFECTING AUDITORS' EVALUATIONS OF FORECASTS
JAR AU 83 VOL: 21 PG:473 - 494 :: ANOVA :LAB. :OTH.BEH. :JUDG.

DANOS ,P ; SEC: IMHOFF JR,EA CIT: 0.27
FORECAST SYSTEMS, CONSTRUCTION AND ATTESTATION
AUD WI 82 VOL: 1 PG:23 - 34 :: DES.STAT. :LAB. :OTH.BEH. :FOREC.

DANOS ,P ; SEC: EICHENSEHER,JW CIT: 0.73
AUDIT INDUSTRY DYNAMICS: FACTORS AFFECTING CHANGES IN CLIENT-INDUSTRY MARKETSHARES
JAR AU 82 VOL: 20 PG:604 - 616 :: ANOVA :PRIM. :OTH.STAT. :ORG.

DANOS ,P ; SEC: IMHOFF JR,EA CIT: 0.45
AUDITOR REVIEW OF FINANCIAL FORECASTS: AN ANALYSIS OF FACTORS AFFECTING REASONABLENESS JUDGMENTS
TAR JA 82 VOL: 57 PG:39 - 54 :: ANOVA :LAB. :OTH.BEH. :AUD.

DANOS ,P ; FIRS: EICHENSEHER,JW CIT: 1
THE ANALYSIS OF INDUSTRY-SPECIFIC AUDITOR CONCENTRATION: TOWARDS AN EXPLANATORY MODEL
TAR JL 81 VOL: 56 PG:479 - 492 :: MIXED :PRIM. :OTH.STAT. :ORG.

DAROCA,FP ; SEC: HOLDER,WW CIT: 0.25
THE USE OF ANALYTICAL PROCEDURES IN REVIEW AND AUDIT ENGAGEMENTS
AUD SP 85 VOL: 4 PG:80 - 92 :: REGRESS. :SURV. :INSTIT. :ANAL.REV.

DAROCA,FP CIT: 0.11
INFORMATIONAL INFLUENCES ON GROUP DECISION MAKING IN A PARTICIPATIVE BUDGETING CONTEXT
AOS 01 84 VOL: 9 PG:13 - 32 :: ANOVA :LAB. :OTH.BEH. :BUDG.& PLAN.

DARROUGH,MN ; SEC: STOUGHTON,NM CIT: 1.33
FINANCIAL DISCLOSURE POLICY IN AN ENTRY GAME
JAE JA 90 VOL: 12 PG:219 - 243 :: DES.STAT. :INT. LOG. :INF.ECO./AG. :INFO.STRUC.

DARROUGH,MN CIT: 0
VARIANCE ANALYSIS: A UNIFYING COST FUNCTION APPROACH
CAR AU 88 VOL: 5 PG:199 - 221 :: DES.STAT. :INT. LOG. :INF.ECO./AG. :VAR.

DAS ,H CIT: 0
ORGANIZATIONAL AND DECISION CHARACTERISTICS AND PERSONALITY AS DETERMINANTS OF CONTROL ACTIONS: A LABORATORY EXPERIMENT
AOS 03 86 VOL: 11 PG:215 - 232 :: REGRESS. :LAB. :OTH.BEH. :INT.CONT.

DAS ,TK ; FIRS: FLAMHOLTZ,EG ; THIR: TSUI ,AS CIT: 0.13
TOWARD AN INTEGRATIVE FRAMEWORK OF ORGANIZATIONAL CONTROL
AOS 01 85 VOL: 10 PG:35 - 50 :: DES.STAT. :INT. LOG. :OTH.BEH. :HRA

DASCHER,PE ; SEC: COPELAND,RM CIT: 0.18
SOME FURTHER EVIDENCE ON CRITERIA FOR JUDGING DISCLOSURE IMPROVEMENT
JAR SP 71 VOL: 9 PG:32 - 39 :: ANOVA :LAB. :OTH.BEH. :SEG.REP.

DASCHER,PE ; SEC: MALCOM,RE CIT: 0.24
A NOTE ON INCOME SMOOTHING IN THE CHEMICAL INDUSTRY
JAR AU 70 VOL: 8 PG:253 - 259 :: DES.STAT. :PRIM. :TIME SER. :FIN.METH.

DATAR ,SM ; FIRS: BANKER,RD CIT: 1
OPTIMAL TRANSFER PRICING UNDER POSTCONTRACT INFORMATION
CAR SP 92 VOL: 8 PG:329 - 352 :: DES.STAT. :INT. LOG. :INF.ECO./AG. :TRANS.PRIC.

DATAR ,SM ; SEC: FELTHAM,GA ; THIR: HUGHES,JS CIT: 1.5
THE ROLE OF AUDITS AND AUDIT QUALITY IN VALUING NEW ISSUES
JAE MR 91 VOL: 14 PG:3 - 49 :: DES.STAT. :INT. LOG. :INF.ECO./AG. :VALUAT.(INFL.)

DATAR ,SM ; FIRS: BANKER,RD ; THIR: MAZUR ,MJ CIT: 0
TESTING THE OPTIMALITY OF A PERCENTAGE EVALUATION MEASURE FOR A GAIN SHARING CONTRACT
CAR SP 90 VOL: 6 PG:809 - 824 :: DES.STAT. :INT. LOG. :INF.ECO./AG. :EXEC.COMP.

DATAR ,SM ; FIRS: AMERSHI,AH ; SEC: BANKER,RD CIT: 0
ECONOMIC SUFFICIENCY AND STATISTICAL SUFFICIENCY IN THE AGGREGATION OF ACCOUNTING SIGNALS
TAR JA 90 VOL: 65 PG:113 - 130 :: DES.STAT. :INT. LOG. :INF.ECO./AG. :MANAG.

DATAR ,SM ; FIRS: BANKER,RD ; THIR: KAPLAN,RS CIT: 0
PRODUCTIVITY MEASUREMENT AND MANAGEMENT ACCOUNTING
JAA AU 89 VOL: 4 PG:528 - 554 :: DES.STAT. :CASE :OTH.STAT. :REL.COSTS

DATAR ,SM ; FIRS: BANKER,RD CIT: 1
SENSITIVITY, PRECISION, AND LINEAR AGGREGATION OF SIGNALS FOR PERFORMANCE EVALUATION
JAR SP 89 VOL: 27 PG:21 - 39 :: DES.STAT. :INT. LOG. :INF.ECO./AG. :EXEC.COMP.

DATAR ,SM ; FIRS: BANKER,RD ; THIR: MAINDIRATTA,A CIT: 0.4
UNOBSERVABLE OUTCOMES AND MULTIATTRIBUTE PREFERENCES IN THE EVALUATION OF MANAGERIAL PERFORMANCE
CAR AU 88 VOL: 5 PG:96 - 124 :: DES.STAT. :INT. LOG. :INF.ECO./AG. :EXEC.COMP.

DATAR ,SM ; FIRS: BANKER,RD ; THIR: KEKRE ,S CIT: 0
RELEVANT COSTS, CONGESTION AND STOCHASTICITY IN PRODUCTION ENVIRONMENTS
JAE JL 88 VOL: 10 PG:171 - 197 :: DES.STAT. :INT. LOG. :OTH.STAT. :REL.COSTS

DATAR ,SM ; FIRS: BANKER,RD ; THIR: RAJAN ,MV CIT: 0.33
MEASUREMENT OF PRODUCTIVITY IMPROVEMENTS: AN EMPIRICAL ANALYSIS
JAA AU 87 VOL: 2 PG:319 - 347 :: DES.STAT. :FIELD :OTH.STAT. :MANAG.

DAVIDSON,HJ ; SEC: NETER ,J ; THIR: PETRAN,AS CIT: 0.12
ESTIMATING THE LIABILITY FOR UNREDEEMED STAMPS
JAR AU 67 VOL: 5 PG:186 - 207 :: ANAL. :INT. LOG. :OTH.STAT. :SPEC.ITEMS

DAVIDSON,HJ ; FIRS: CHARNES,A ; THIR: KORTANEK,KO CIT: 0
ON A MIXED-SEQUENTIAL ESTIMATING PROCEDURE WITH APPLICATION TO AUDIT TESTS IN ACCOUNTING
TAR AP 64 VOL: 39 PG:241 - 250 :: ANAL. :INT. LOG. :OTH.STAT. :SAMP.

DAVIDSON,LF ; FIRS: KELLER,SB CIT: 1.1
AN ASSESSMENT OF INDIVIDUAL INVESTOR REACTION TO CERTAIN QUALIFIED AUDIT OPINIONS
AUD AU 83 VOL: 3 PG:1 22 :: ANOVA :PRIM. :EMH :OPIN.

DAVIDSON,LF ; FIRS: BIRD ,FA ; THIR: SMITH ,CH CIT: 0.12
PERCEPTIONS OF EXTERNAL ACCOUNTING TRANSFERS UNDER ENTITY AND PROPRIETARY THEORY
TAR AP 74 VOL: 49 PG:233 - 244 :: QUAL. :INT. LOG. :THEORY :FIN.METH.

DAVIDSON,S ; SEC: WEIL ,RL CIT: 0.07
INCOME TAX IMPLICATIONS OF VARIOUS METHODS OF ACCOUNTING FOR CHANGING PRICE
JAR ST 78 VOL: 16 PG:154 - 233 :: DES.STAT. :PRIM. :OTH.STAT. :VALUAT.(INFL.)

DAVIDSON,S ; FIRS: BIERMAN JR,H CIT: 0
THE INCOME CONCEPT-VALUE-INCREMENT OR EARNINGS PREDICTOR
TAR AP 69 VOL: 44 PG:239 - 246 :: QUAL. :INT. LOG. :THEORY :FIN.METH.

DAVIDSON,S ; SEC: KOHLMEIER,JM CIT: 0.06
A MEASURE OF THE IMPACT OF SOME FOREIGN ACCOUNTING PRINCIPLES
JAR AU 66 VOL: 4 PG:183 - 212 :: DES.STAT. :SIM. :OTH.STAT. :INT.DIFF.

DAVIDSON,S CIT: 0.06
THE DAY OF RECKONING: ACCOUNTING THEORY AND MANAGEMENT ANALYSIS
JAR AU 63 VOL: 1 PG:117 - 126 :: QUAL. :INT. LOG. :THEORY :N/A

DAVIDSON,S CIT: 0
OLD WINE INTO NEW BOTTLES
TAR AP 63 VOL: 38 PG:278 - 284 :: QUAL. :SEC. :HIST. :OVER.ALLOC.

DAVIS ,DW ; SEC: BOATSMAN,JR ; THIR: BASKIN,EF CIT: 0.07
ON GENERALIZING STOCK MARKET RESEARCH TO A BROADER CLASS OF MARKETS
TAR JA 78 VOL: 53 PG:1 - 10 :: MIXED :PRIM. :EMH :FIN.METH.

DAVIS ,FG ; FIRS: PEI ,BKW CIT: 0
THE IMPACT OF ORGANIZATIONAL STRUCTURE ON INTERNAL AUDITOR ORGANIZATIONAL-PROFESSIONAL CONFLICT AND STRESS: AN EXPLORATION OF LINKAGES
AUD SP 89 VOL: 8 PG:101 - 112 :: REGRESS. :LAB. :HIPS :ORG.& ENVIR.

DAVIS ,GB ; SEC: WEBER ,R CIT: 0.14
THE IMPACT OF ADVANCED COMPUTER SYSTEMS ON CONTROLS AND AUDIT PROCEDURES: A THEORY AND AN EMPIRICAL TEST
AUD SP 86 VOL: 5 PG:35 - 49 :: REGRESS. :LAB. :OTH.STAT. :EDP AUD.

DAVIS ,GB CIT: 0
THE APPLICATION OF NETWORK TECHNIQUES (PERT/CPM) TO THE PLANNING AND CONTROL OF AN AUDIT
JAR SP 63 VOL: 1 PG:96 - 101 :: ANAL. :INT. LOG. :MATH.PROG. :AUD.

DAVIS ,HZ ; SEC: KAHN ,N ; THIR: ROZEN ,E CIT: 0
LIFO INVENTORY LIQUIDATIONS: AN EMPIRICAL STUDY
JAR AU 84 VOL: 22 PG:480 - 490 :: NON-PAR. :PRIM. :OTH.STAT. :INV.

DAVIS ,HZ ; SEC: KAHN ,N CIT: 0
SOME ADDITIONAL EVIDENCE ON THE LIFO-FIFO CHOICE USING REPLACEMENT COST DATA
JAR AU 82 VOL: 20 PG:738 - 744 :: NON-PAR. :PRIM. :OTH.STAT. :INV.

DAVIS ,JS ; FIRS: BECK ,PJ ; THIR: JUNG ,W-O CIT: 0
EXPERIMENTAL EVIDENCE ON AN ECONOMIC MODEL OF TAXPAYER AGGRESSION UNDER STRATEGIC AND NON-STRATEGIC AUDITS
CAR AU 92 VOL: 9 PG:86 - 112 :: REGRESS. :LAB. :OTH.BEH. :TAXES

DAVIS ,JS ; FIRS: BECK ,PJ ; THIR: JUNG ,W CIT: 0.5
EXPERIMENTAL EVIDENCE ON TAXPAYER REPORTING UNDER UNCERTAINTY
TAR JL 91 VOL: 66 PG:535 - 558 :: REGRESS. :LAB. :INF.ECO./AG. :TAX PLNG.

DAVIS ,LR ; SEC: SIMON ,DT CIT: 0
THE IMPACT OF SEC DISCIPLINARY ACTIONS ON AUDIT FEES
AUD SP 92 VOL: 11 PG:58 - 68 :: REGRESS. :PRIM. :INSTIT. :ORG.

DAVIS ,LR ; FIRS: AFFLECK-GRAVES,J ; THIR: MENDENHALL,RR CIT: 0
FORECASTS OF EARNINGS PER SHARE: POSSIBLE SOURCES OF ANALYST SUPERIORITY AND BIAS
CAR SP 90 VOL: 6 PG:501 - 517 :: REGRESS. :LAB. :TIME SER. :FOREC.

DAVIS ,LR CIT: 0
REPORT FORMAT AND THE DECISION MAKER'S TASK: AN EXPERIMENTAL INVESTIGATION
AOS 06 89 VOL: 14 PG:495 - 508 :: REGRESS. :LAB. :HIPS :AUD.BEH.

DAVIS ,ML CIT: 0
DIFFERENTIAL MARKET REACTION TO POOLING AND PURCHASE METHODS
TAR JL 90 VOL: 65 PG:696 - 709 :: REGRESS. :PRIM. :THEORY :BUS.COMB.

DAVIS ,ML ; SEC: LARGAY III,JA CIT: 0
REPORTING CONSOLIDATED GAINS AND LOSSES ON SUBSIDIARY STOCK ISSUANCES
TAR AP 88 VOL: 63 PG:348 - 363 :: REGRESS. :PRIM. :THEORY :BUS.COMB.

DAVIS ,PM CIT: 0
MARGINAL ANALYSIS OF CREDIT SALES
TAR JA 66 VOL: 41 PG:121 - 126 :: ANAL. :INT. LOG. :N/A :MANAG.

DAVIS ,RR CIT: 0.18
AN EMPIRICAL EVALUATION OF AUDITORS' 'SUBJECT-TO' OPINIONS
AUD AU 82 VOL: 2 PG:13 - 32 :: REGRESS. :PRIM. :EMH :OPIN.

DAVIS ,SW ; SEC: MENON ,K ; THIR: MORGAN,G CIT: 0.55
THE IMAGES THAT HAVE SHAPED ACCOUNTING THEORY
AOS 04 82 VOL: 7 PG:307 - 318 :: QUAL. :INT. LOG. :THEORY :N/A

DAVISON,AG ; SEC: STENING,BW ; THIR: WAI ,WT CIT: 0
AUDITOR CONCENTRATION AND THE IMPACT OF INTERLOCKING DIRECTORATES
JAR SP 84 VOL: 22 PG:313 - 317 :: CORR. :PRIM. :OTH. :ORG.& ENVIR.

DAY ,P ; FIRS: ROSENBERG,D ; SEC: TOMKINS,L CIT: 0.18
A WORK ROLE PERSPECTIVE OF ACCOUNTANTS IN LOCAL GOVERNMENT SERVICE DEPARTMENTS
AOS 02 82 VOL: 7 PG:123 - 138 :: QUAL. :SURV. :OTH.BEH. :N/A

DEAKIN,EB CIT: 0.25
RATIONAL ECONOMIC BEHAVIOR AND LOBBYING ON ACCOUNTING ISSUES: EVIDENCE FROM THE OIL AND GAS INDUSTRY
TAR JA 89 VOL: 64 PG:137 - 151 :: REGRESS. :PRIM. :INSTIT. :FIN.METH.

DEAKIN,EB CIT: 1
AN ANALYSIS OF DIFFERENCES BETWEEN NON-MAJOR OIL FIRMS USING SUCCESSFUL EFFORTS AND FULL COST METHODS
TAR OC 79 VOL: 54 PG:722 - 734 :: OTH.QUANT. :PRIM. :OTH.STAT. :OIL & GAS

DEAKIN,EB CIT: 0.29
DISTRIBUTIONS OF FINANCIAL ACCOUNTING RATIOS: SOME EMPIRICAL EVIDENCE
TAR JA 76 VOL: 51 PG:90 - 96 :: ANOVA :PRIM. :OTH.STAT. :FIN.METH.

DEAKIN,EB CIT: 0.18
ACCOUNTING REPORTS, POLICY INTERVENTIONS AND THE BEHAVIOR OF SECURITIES RETURNS
TAR JL 76 VOL: 51 PG:590 - 603 :: REGRESS. :PRIM. :EMH :FIN.METH.

DEAKIN,EB ; SEC: GRANOF,MH CIT: 0.35
REGRESSION ANALYSIS AS A MEANS OF DETERMINING AUDIT SAMPLE SIZE
TAR OC 74 VOL: 49 PG:764 - 771 :: REGRESS. :INT. LOG. :OTH.STAT. :SAMP.

DEAKIN,EB CIT: 1.24
A DISCRIMINANT ANALYSIS OF PREDICTORS OF BUSINESS FAILURE
JAR SP 72 VOL: 10 PG:167 - 179 :: OTH.QUANT. :PRIM. :EMH :BUS.FAIL.

DEAN ,J ; SEC: HARRISS,CL CIT: 0
RAILROAD ACCOUNTING UNDER THE NEW DEPRECIATION GUIDELINES AND INVESTMENT TAX CREDIT
TAR AP 63 VOL: 38 PG:229 - 242 :: QUAL. :INT. LOG. :THEORY :TAXES

DEAN ,RA ; SEC: FERRIS,KR ; THIR: KONSTANS,C CIT: 0.4
OCCUPATIONAL REALITY SHOCK AND ORGANIZATIONAL COMMITMENT: EVIDENCE FROM THE ACCOUNTING PROFESSION
AOS 03 88 VOL: 13 PG:235 - 250 :: REGRESS. :SURV. :OTH.BEH. :AUD.BEH.

DEANGELO,LE CIT: 0.67
EQUITY VALUATION AND CORPORATE CONTROL
TAR JA 90 VOL: 65 PG:93 - 112 :: REGRESS. :MIXED :EMH :VALUAT.(INFL.)

DEANGELO,LE CIT: 1.6
MANAGERIAL COMPETITION, INFORMATION COSTS, AND CORPORATE GOVERNANCE: THE USE OF ACCOUNTING PERFORMANCE MEASURES IN PROXY CONTESTS
JAE JA 88 VOL: 10 PG:3 - 36 :: REGRESS. :PRIM. :EMH :BUS.COMB.

DEANGELO,LE CIT: 1.43
ACCOUNTING NUMBERS AS MARKET VALUATION SUBSTITUTES: A STUDY OF MANAGEMENT BUYOUT OF PUBLIC STOCKHOLDERS
TAR JL 86 VOL: 61 PG:400 - 420 :: REGRESS. :PRIM. :THEORY :INFO.STRUC.

DEANGELO,LE CIT: 0.45
MANDATED SUCCESSFUL EFFORTS AND AUDITOR CHOICE
JAE DE 82 VOL: 4 PG:171 - 203 :: DES.STAT. :SEC. :THEORY :OIL & GAS

DEANGELO,LE CIT: 2.25
AUDITOR INDEPENDENCE, 'LOW BALLING', AND DISCLOSURE REGULATION
JAE AG 81 VOL: 3 PG:113 - 127 :: ANAL. :INT. LOG. :TIME SER. :INDEP.

DEANGELO,LE CIT: 2.08
AUDITOR SIZE AND AUDIT QUALITY
JAE DE 81 VOL: 3 PG:183 - 199 :: QUAL. :INT. LOG. :THEORY :JUDG.

DECHOW,PM ; SEC: SLOAN ,RG CIT: 0
EXECUTIVE INCENTIVES AND THE HORIZON PROBLEM: AN EMPIRICAL INVESTIGATION
JAE MR 91 VOL: 14 PG:1 - 89 :: REGRESS. :PRIM. :INF.ECO./AG. :R & D

DECOSTER,DT ; FIRS: FORAN ,MF CIT: 0.71
AN EXPER. STUDY OF THE EFFECTS OF PARTICIP., AUTHORITARIANISM, AND FEEDBACK ON COGNITIVE DISSONANCE IN A STANDARD SETTING SITUATION
TAR OC 74 VOL: 49 PG:751 - 763 :: ANOVA :LAB. :OTH.BEH. :BUDG.& PLAN.

DECOSTER,DT ; SEC: RHODE ,JG CIT: 0.12
THE ACCOUNTANT'S STEREOTYPE: REAL OR IMAGINED, DESERVED OR UNWARRANTED
TAR OC 71 VOL: 46 PG:651 - 664 :: ANOVA :SURV. :OTH.BEH. :AUD.

DECOSTER,DT ; FIRS: ROSEN ,LS CIT: 0
FUNDS STATEMENTS: A HISTORICAL PERSPECTIVE
TAR JA 69 VOL: 44 PG:124 - 136 :: QUAL. :SEC. :HIST. :FIN.METH.

DECOSTER,DT ; SEC: FERTAKIS,JP CIT: 1.35
BUDGET-INDUCED PRESSURE AND ITS RELATIONSHIP TO SUPERVISORY BEHAVIOR
JAR AU 68 VOL: 6 PG:237 - 246 :: DES.STAT. :SURV. :OTH.BEH. :BUDG.& PLAN.

DECOSTER,DT CIT: 0
MEASUREMENT OF THE IDLE-CAPACITY VARIANCE
TAR AP 66 VOL: 41 PG:297 - 302 :: QUAL. :INT. LOG. :N/A :VAR.

DECOSTER,DT ; FIRS: CHIU ,JS CIT: 0
MULTIPLE PRODUCT COSTING BY MULTIPLE CORRELATION ANALYSIS
TAR OC 66 VOL: 41 PG:673 - 680 :: REGRESS. :INT. LOG. :TIME SER. :COST.ALLOC.

DEFEO ,VJ ; SEC: LAMBER,RA ; THIR: LARCKER,DF CIT: 0.75
EXECUTIVE COMPENSATION EFFECTS OF EQUITY-FOR-DEBT SWAPS
TAR AP 89 VOL: 64 PG:201 - 227 :: REGRESS. :PRIM. :INF.ECO./AG. :LTD

DEFEO ,VJ CIT: 0.14
AN EMPIRICAL INVESTIGATION OF THE SPEED OF THE MARKET REACTION TO EARNINGS ANNOUNCEMENTS
JAR AU 86 VOL: 24 PG:349 - 363 :: ANOVA :PRIM. :EMH :FIN.METH.

DEFLIESE,PL CIT: 0
A PRACTITIONER'S VIEW OF THE REALIZATION CONCEPT
TAR JL 65 VOL: 40 PG:517 - 521 :: QUAL. :INT. LOG. :THEORY :VALUAT.(INFL.)

DEFOND,ML CIT: 0
THE ASSOCIATION BETWEEN CHANGES IN CLIENT FIRM AGENCY COSTS AND AUDITOR SWITCHING
AUD SP 92 VOL: 11 PG:16 - 31 :: REGRESS. :PRIM. :INF.ECO./AG. :OPER.AUD.

DEFOND,ML ; SEC: JIAMBALVO,J CIT: 0
INCIDENCE AND CIRCUMSTANCES OF ACCOUNTING ERRORS
TAR JL 91 VOL: 66 PG:643 - 655 :: REGRESS. :FIELD :INF.ECO./AG. :ERRORS

DEINZER,HT CIT: 0
EXPLANATION STRAINS IN FINANCIAL ACCOUNTING
TAR JA 66 VOL: 41 PG:21 - 31 :: QUAL. :INT. LOG. :THEORY :OTH.MANAG.

DEIS JR,DR ; SEC: GIROUX,GA CIT: 0
DETERMINANTS OF AUDIT QUALITY IN THE PUBLIC SECTOR
TAR JL 92 VOL: 67 PG:462 - 479 :: REGRESS. :MIXED :INSTIT. :INDEP.

DEITRICK,JW ; FIRS: ALDERMAN,CW CIT: 0.36
AUDITORS' PERCEPTIONS OF TIME BUDGET PRESSURES AND PREMATURE SIGN-OFFS: A REPLICATION AND EXTENSION
AUD WI 82 VOL: 1 PG:54 - 68 :: DES.STAT. :SURV. :OTH.BEH. :ERRORS

DEITRICK,JW ; SEC: ALDERMAN,CW CIT: 0
INTERIM REPORTING DEVELOPMENTS: A STEP TOWARD THE AUDITOR-OF-RECORD CONCEPT
JAA SU 79 VOL: 2 PG:316 - 328 :: QUAL. :INT. LOG. :INSTIT. :AUD.

DEJONG,DV ; SEC: FORSYTHE,R CIT: 0
A PERSPECTIVE ON THE USE OF LABORATORY MARKET EXPERIMENTATION IN AUDITING RESEARCH
TAR JA 92 VOL: 67 PG:157 - 171 :: ANOVA :SEC. :INF.ECO./AG. :METHOD.

DEJONG,DV ; SEC: FORSYTHE,R ; THIR: KIM ,JA ; FOUR: UECKER,WC CIT: 0.25
A LABORATORY INVESTIGATION OF ALTERNATIVE TRANSFER PRICING MECHANISMS
AOS 02 89 VOL: 14 PG:41 - 64 :: REGRESS. :LAB. :OTH.BEH. :TRANS.PRIC.

DEJONG,DV ; SEC: FORSYTHE,R ; THIR: UECKER,WC CIT: 1.25
THE METHODOLOGY OF LABORATORY MARKETS AND ITS IMPLICATIONS FOR AGENCY RESEARCH IN ACCOUNTING AND AUDITING
JAR AU 85 VOL: 23 PG:753 - 793 :: REGRESS. :LAB. :INF.ECO./AG. :METHOD.

DEJONG,DV ; SEC: FORSYTHE,R ; THIR: LUNDHOLM,RJ ; FOUR: UECKER,WC CIT: 0.88
A LABORATORY INVESTIGATION OF THE MORAL HAZARD PROBLEM IN AN AGENCY RELATIONSHIP
JAR ST 85 VOL: 23 PG:81 - 120 :: REGRESS. :LAB. :INF.ECO./AG. :MAN.DEC.CHAR.

DEJONG,DV ; SEC: SMITH ,JH CIT: 0.11
THE DETERMINATION OF AUDIT RESPONSIBILITIES: AN APPLICATION OF AGENCY THEORY
AUD AU 84 VOL: 4 PG:20 - 34 :: QUAL. :INT. LOG. :INF.ECO./AG. :LIAB.

DEKKER,HC ; FIRS: HUIZING,A CIT: 1
THE ENVIRONMENTAL ISSUE ON THE DUTCH POLITICAL MARKET
AOS 05 92 VOL: 17 PG:427 - 448 :: REGRESS. :CASE :HIST. :ORG.& ENVIR.

DEKKER,HC ; FIRS: HUIZING,A CIT: 0
HELPING TO PULL OUR PLANET OUT OF THE RED: AN ENVIRONMENTAL REPORT OF BSO/ORIGIN
AOS 05 92 VOL: 17 PG:449 - 458 :: REGRESS. :CASE :OTH. :ORG.& ENVIR.

DEMARIS,EJ CIT: 0
SUCCESS INDICATOR FUNCTION OF INCOME CONCEPT ARGUES ITS FURTHER DEVELOPMENT
TAR JA 63 VOL: 38 PG:37 - 45 :: QUAL. :INT. LOG. :THEORY :REV.REC.

DEMING,WE CIT: 0
ON A PROBLEM IN STANDARDS OF AUDITING FROM THE VIEWPOINT OF STATISTICAL PRACTICE
JAA SP 79 VOL: 2 PG:197 - 208 :: ANAL. :INT. LOG. :OTH.STAT. :SAMP.

DEMPSEY,SJ CIT: 0
PREDISCLOSURE INFORMATION SEARCH INCENTIVES, ANALYST FOLLOWING, AND EARNINGS ANNOUNCEMENT PRICE RESPONSE
TAR OC 89 VOL: 64 PG:748 - 757 :: REGRESS. :PRIM. :TIME SER. :FOREC.

DEMSKI,JS ; SEC: SAPPINGTON,DEM CIT: 0
FURTHER THOUGHTS ON FULLY REVEALING INCOME MEASUREMENT
TAR JL 92 VOL: 67 PG:628 - 630 :: DES.STAT. :INT. LOG. :THEORY :INFO.STRUC.

DEMSKI,JS ; SEC: MAGEE ,RP CIT: 0
A PERSPECTIVE ON ACCOUNTING FOR DEFENSE CONTRACTS
TAR OC 92 VOL: 67 PG:732 - 740 :: DES.STAT. :SEC. :INF.ECO./AG. :MANAG.

DEMSKI,JS ; FIRS: ANTLE ,R CIT: 0.5
CONTRACTING FRICTIONS, REGULATION, AND THE STRUCTURE OF CPA FIRMS
JAR ST 91 VOL: 29 PG:1 - 30 :: DES.STAT. :INT. LOG. :INF.ECO./AG. :ORG.

DEMSKI,JS ; SEC: SAPPINGTON,DEM CIT: 0
FULLY REVEALING INCOME MEASUREMENT
TAR AP 90 VOL: 65 PG:363 - 383 :: DES.STAT. :INT. LOG. :THEORY :VALUAT.(INFL.)

DEMSKI,JS ; FIRS: ANTLE ,R CIT: 0.75
REVENUE RECOGNITION
CAR SP 89 VOL: 5 PG:423 - 451 :: DES.STAT. :INT. LOG. :INF.ECO./AG. :REV.REC.

DEMSKI,JS ; SEC: SAPPINGTON,DEM CIT: 0.75
HIERARCHICAL STRUCTURE AND RESPONSIBILITY ACCOUNTING
JAR SP 89 VOL: 27 PG:40 - 58 :: DES.STAT. :INT. LOG. :INF.ECO./AG. :EXEC.COMP.

DEMSKI,JS ; SEC: SAPPINGTON,DEM CIT: 1.33
DELEGATED EXPERTISE
JAR SP 87 VOL: 25 PG:68 - 89 :: DES.STAT. :INT. LOG. :INF.ECO./AG. :MANAG.

DEMSKI,JS ; SEC: SAPPINGTON,DEM CIT: 0.71
LINE-ITEM REPORTING, FACTOR ACQUISITION, AND SUBCONTRACTING
JAR AU 86 VOL: 24 PG:250 - 269 :: ANAL. :INT. LOG. :INF.ECO./AG. :INFO.STRUC.

DEMSKI,JS CIT: 0
ACCOUNTING RESEARCH: 1985
CAR AU 85 VOL: 2 PG:69 - 75 :: ANOVA :SEC. :THEORY :FIN.METH.

DEMSKI,JS ; FIRS: AMERSHI,AH ; THIR: FELLINGHAM,J CIT: 0.38
SEQUENTIAL BAYESIAN ANALYSIS IN ACCOUNTING
CAR SP 85 VOL: 1 PG:176 - 192 :: DES.STAT. :INT. LOG. :INF.ECO./AG. :DEC.AIDS

DEMSKI,JS ; SEC: PATELL,JM ; THIR: WOLFSON,MA CIT: 1.56
DECENTRALIZED CHOICE OF MONITORING SYSTEMS
TAR JA 84 VOL: 59 PG:16 - 34 :: ANAL. :INT. LOG. :INF.ECO./AG. :MANAG.

DEMSKI,JS ; SEC: KREPS ,DM CIT: 1
MODELS IN MANAGERIAL ACCOUNTING
JAR ST 82 VOL: 20 PG:117 - 148 :: QUAL. :SEC. :OTH.STAT. :METHOD.

DEMSKI,JS ; FIRS: BAIMAN,S CIT: 1.92
ECONOMICALLY OPTIMAL PERFORMANCE EVALUATION AND CONTROL SYSTEMS
JAR ST 80 VOL: 18 PG:184 - 220 :: ANAL. :INT. LOG. :OTH. :MANAG.

DEMSKI,JS ; FIRS: BEAVER,WH CIT: 1.5
THE NATURE OF INCOME MEASUREMENT
TAR JA 79 VOL: 54 PG:38 - 46 :: QUAL. :INT. LOG. :INF.ECO./AG. :OTH.FIN.ACC.

DEMSKI,JS ; SEC: FELTHAM,GA CIT: 2.8
ECONOMIC INCENTIVES IN BUDGETARY CONTROL SYSTEMS
TAR AP 78 VOL: 53 PG:336 - 359 :: ANAL. :INT. LOG. :INF.ECO./AG. :BUDG.& PLAN.

DEMSKI,JS CIT: 0.59
UNCERTAINTY AND EVALUATION BASED ON CONTROLLABLE PERFORMANCE
JAR AU 76 VOL: 14 PG:230 - 245 :: ANAL. :INT. LOG. :INF.ECO./AG. :MANAG.

DEMSKI,JS ; FIRS: BEAVER,WH CIT: 0.71
THE NATURE OF FINANCIAL ACCOUNTING OBJECTIVES: A SUMMARY AND SYNTHESIS
JAR ST 74 VOL: 12 PG:170 - 187 :: ANAL. :SEC. :THEORY :FIN.METH.

DEMSKI,JS CIT: 0.76
CHOICE AMONG FINANCIAL REPORTING ALTERNATIVES
TAR AP 74 VOL: 49 PG:221 - 232 :: ANAL. :INT. LOG. :INF.ECO./AG. :FIN.METH.

DEMSKI,JS ; SEC: SWIERINGA,RJ CIT: 0.47
A COOPERATIVE FORMULATION OF THE AUDIT CHOICE PROBLEM
TAR JL 74 VOL: 49 PG:506 - 513 :: ANAL. :INT. LOG. :OTH.STAT. :AUD.

DEMSKI,JS CIT: 0.12
RATIONAL CHOICE OF ACCOUNTING METHOD FOR A CLASS OF PARTNERSHIPS
JAR AU 73 VOL: 11 PG:176 - 190 :: ANAL. :INT. LOG. :OTH.STAT. :FIN.METH.

DEMSKI,JS CIT: 1.06
THE GENERAL IMPOSSIBILITY OF NORMATIVE ACCOUNTING STANDARDS
TAR OC 73 VOL: 48 PG:718 - 723 :: QUAL. :INT. LOG. :THEORY :FIN.METH.

DEMSKI,JS CIT: 0.35
INFORMATION IMPROVEMENT BOUNDS
JAR SP 72 VOL: 10 PG:58 - 76 :: ANAL. :INT. LOG. :INF.ECO./AG. :INFO.STRUC.

DEMSKI,JS CIT: 0.53
OPTIMAL PERFORMANCE MEASUREMENT
JAR AU 72 VOL: 10 PG:243 - 258 :: ANAL. :INT. LOG. :INF.ECO./AG. :MANAG.

DEMSKI,JS ; SEC: FELTHAM,GA CIT: 0.47
FORECAST EVALUATION
TAR JL 72 VOL: 47 PG:533 - 548 :: MIXED :SIM. :INF.ECO./AG. :BUDG.& PLAN.

DEMSKI,JS CIT: 0.12
IMPLEMENTATION EFFECTS OF ALTERNATIVE PERFORMANCE MEASUREMENT MODELS IN A MULTIVARIABLE CONTEXT
TAR AP 71 VOL: 46 PG:268 - 278 :: ANAL. :SIM. :INF.ECO./AG. :BUDG.& PLAN.

DEMSKI,JS CIT: 0.18
SOME DECOMPOSITION RESULTS FOR INFORMATION EVALUATION
JAR AU 70 VOL: 8 PG:178 - 198 :: ANAL. :INT. LOG. :INF.ECO./AG. :MANAG.

DEMSKI,JS CIT: 0.18
THE DECISION IMPLEMENTATION INTERFACE: EFFECTS OF ALTERNATIVE PERFORMANCE MEASUREMENT MODELS
TAR JA 70 VOL: 45 PG:76 - 87 :: ANAL. :SIM. :OTH.STAT. :VAR.

DEMSKI,JS ; FIRS: FELTHAM,GA CIT: 0.76
THE USE OF MODELS IN INFORMATION EVALUATION
TAR OC 70 VOL: 45 PG:623 - 640 :: ANAL. :INT. LOG. :INF.ECO./AG. :MANAG.

DEMSKI,JS CIT: 0
PREDICTIVE ABILITY OF ALTERNATIVE PERFORMANCE MEASUREMENT MODELS
JAR SP 69 VOL: 7 PG:96 - 115 :: REGRESS. :SIM. :OTH.STAT. :VAR.

DEMSKI,JS CIT: 0.12
DECISION-PERFORMANCE CONTROL
TAR OC 69 VOL: 44 PG:669 - 679 :: ANAL. :INT. LOG. :INF.ECO./AG. :MANAG.

DEMSKI,JS ; FIRS: DOPUCH,N ; SEC: BIRNBERG,JG CIT: 0.12
AN EXTENSION OF STANDARD COST VARIANCE ANALYSIS
TAR JL 67 VOL: 42 PG:526 - 536 :: ANAL. :INT. LOG. :OTH.STAT. :VAR.

DEMSKI,JS CIT: 0.35
AN ACCOUNTING SYSTEM STRUCTURED ON A LINEAR PROGRAMMING MODEL
TAR OC 67 VOL: 42 PG:701 - 712 :: ANAL. :INT. LOG. :INF.ECO./AG. :MANAG.

DENT ,AS CIT: 0
ACCOUNTING AND ORGANIZATIONAL CULTURES: A FIELD STUDY OF THE EMERGENCE OF NEW ORGANIZATIONAL REALITY
AOS 91 VOL: 16 PG:705 - 732 :: REGRESS. :CASE :OTH.BEH. :ORG.

DENT ,JF CIT: 0.33
STATEGY, ORGANIZATION AND CONTROL: SOME POSSIBILITIES FOR ACCOUNTING RESEARCH
AOS 02 90 VOL: 15 PG:3 - 25 :: REGRESS. :SEC. :OTH. :METHOD.

DENT ,WT ; FIRS: COLLINS,DW CIT: 1.44
A COMPARISON OF ALTERNATIVE TESTING METHODOLOGIES USED IN CAPITAL MARKET RESEARCH
JAR SP 84 VOL: 22 PG:48 - 84 :: MIXED :SIM. :EMH :METHOD.

DENT ,WT ; FIRS: COLLINS,DW CIT: 2.64
THE PROPOSED ELIMINATION OF FULL COST ACCOUNTING IN THE EXTRACTIVE PETROLEUM INDUSTRY: AN EMPIRICAL ASSESSMENT OF MARKET CONSEQU
JAE MR 79 VOL: 1 PG:3 - 44 :: NON-PAR. :PRIM. :EMH :OIL & GAS

DERMER,J CIT: 0
THE STRATEGIC AGENDA: ACCOUNTING FOR ISSUES AND SUPPORT
AOS 02 90 VOL: 15 PG:67 - 76 :: DES.STAT. :SEC. :OTH. :ORG.& ENVIR.

DERMER,JD CIT: 0.2
CONTROL AND ORGANIZATIONAL ORDER
AOS 01 88 VOL: 13 PG:25 - 36 :: DES.STAT. :INT. LOG. :INSTIT. :ORG.FORM

DERMER,JD ; SEC: LUCAS ,RG CIT: 0.14
THE ILLUSION OF MANAGERIAL CONTROL
AOS 06 86 VOL: 11 PG:471 - 482 :: DES.STAT. :INT. LOG. :THEORY :INT.CONT.

DERMER,JD ; SEC: SIEGEL,JP CIT: 0.12
THE ROLE OF BEHAVIOURAL MEASURES IN ACCOUNTING FOR HUMAN RESOURCES
TAR JA 74 VOL: 49 PG:88 - 97 :: CORR. :LAB. :OTH.BEH. :HRA

DERMER,JD CIT: 1.24
COGNITIVE CHARACTERISTICS AND THE PERCEIVED IMPORTANCE OF INFORMATION
TAR JL 73 VOL: 48 PG:511 - 519 :: CORR. :LAB. :OTH.BEH. :MAN.DEC.CHAR.

DERSTINE,RP ; SEC: HUEFNER,RJ CIT: 0.41
LIFO-FIFO, ACCOUNTING RATIOS AND MARKET RISK
JAR AU 74 VOL: 12 PG:216 - 234 :: NON-PAR. :PRIM. :OTH. :INV.

DERY ,D CIT: 0
ERRING AND LEARNING: AN ORGANIZATIONAL ANALYSIS
AOS 03 82 VOL: 7 PG:217 - 224 :: QUAL. :INT. LOG. :OTH. :N/A

DESAI ,HB ; FIRS: SINGHVI,SS CIT: 0.35
AN EMPIRICAL ANALYSIS OF THE QUALITY OF CORPORATE FINANCIAL DISCLOSURE
TAR JA 71 VOL: 46 PG:129 - 138 :: DES.STAT. :PRIM. :N/A :INFO.STRUC.

DESANCTIS,G ; SEC: JARVENPAA,SL CIT: 0
GRAPHICAL PRESENTATION OF ACCOUNTING DATA FOR FINANCIAL FORECASTING: AN EXPERIMENTAL INVESTIGATION
AOS 06 89 VOL: 14 PG:509 - 525 :: REGRESS. :LAB. :HIPS :FOREC.

DESKINS,JW ; FIRS: SUMMERS,EL CIT: 0
A CLASSIFICATION SCHEMA OF METHODS FOR REPORTING EFFECTS OF RESOURCE PRICE CHANGES
JAR SP 70 VOL: 8 PG:113 - 117 :: QUAL. :INT. LOG. :THEORY :VALUAT.(INFL.)

DESKINS,JW CIT: 0
ON THE NATURE OF THE PUBLIC INTEREST
TAR JA 65 VOL: 40 PG:76 - 81 :: ANAL. :INT. LOG. :INSTIT. :N/A

DEVINE,CT CIT: 0
PROFESSIONAL RESPONSIBILITIES - AN EMPIRICAL SUGGESTION
JAR ST 66 VOL: 4 PG:160 - 176 :: DES.STAT. :SURV. :OTH. :PROF.RESP.

DEVINE,CT CIT: 0.12
THE RULE OF CONSERVATISM REEXAMINED
JAR AU 63 VOL: 1 PG:127 - 138 :: QUAL. :INT. LOG. :THEORY :N/A

DEWHIRST,JF CIT: 0
A CONCEPTUAL APPROACH TO PENSION ACCOUNTING
TAR AP 71 VOL: 46 PG:365 - 373 :: QUAL. :INT. LOG. :THEORY :PENS.

DEXTER,AS ; FIRS: BENBASAT,I CIT: 0.18
INDIVIDUAL DIFFERENCES IN THE USE OF DECISION SUPPORT AIDS
JAR SP 82 VOL: 20 PG:1 - 11 :: ANOVA :LAB. :HIPS :DEC.AIDS

DEXTER,AS ; FIRS: BENBASAT,I CIT: 0.93
VALUE AND EVENTS APPROACHES TO ACCOUNTING: AN EXPERIMENTAL EVALUATION
TAR OC 79 VOL: 54 PG:735 - 749 :: ANOVA :LAB. :HIPS :INFO.STRUC.

DHALIWAL,D ; SEC: WANG ,S CIT: 0
THE EFFECT OF BOOK INCOME ADJUSTMENT IN THE 1986 ALTERNATIVE MINIMUM TAX ON CORPORATE FINANCIAL REPORTING
JAE MR 92 VOL: 15 PG:7 - 25 :: REGRESS. :PRIM. :OTH.STAT. :TAXES

DHALIWAL,DS ; FIRS: JOHNSON,WB CIT: 0.6
LIFO ABANDONMENT
JAR AU 88 VOL: 26 PG:236 - 272 :: REGRESS. :PRIM. :EMH :INV.

DHALIWAL,DS ; FIRS: DORAN ,BM ; SEC: COLLINS,DW CIT: 1
THE INFORMATION OF HISTORICAL COST EARNINGS RELATIVE TO SUPPLEMENTAL RESERVE-BASED ACCOUNTING DATA IN THE EXTRACTIVE PETROLEUM I
TAR JL 88 VOL: 63 PG:389 - 413 :: REGRESS. :PRIM. :EMH :OIL & GAS

DHALIWAL,DS CIT: 0.43
MEASUREMENT OF FIN. LEVERAGE IN THE PRESENCE OF UNFUNDED PENSION OBLIGATIONS
TAR OC 86 VOL: 61 PG:651 - 661 :: REGRESS. :PRIM. :EMH :PENS.

DHALIWAL,DS ; SEC: SALAMON,GL ; THIR: SMITH ,ED CIT: 2.18
THE EFFECT OF OWNER VERSUS MANAGEMENT CONTROL ON THE CHOICE OF ACCOUNTING METHODS
JAE JL 82 VOL: 4 PG:41 - 53 :: NON-PAR. :SEC. :TIME SER. :AMOR./DEPL.

DHALIWAL,DS ; FIRS: COLLINS,DW ; SEC: ROZEFF,MS CIT: 3.33
THE ECONOMIC DETERMINANTS OF THE MARKET REACTION TO PROPOSED MANDATORY ACCOUNTING CHANGES IN THE OIL AND GAS INDUSTRY: A CROSS-S
JAE MR 81 VOL: 3 PG:37 - 71 :: REGRESS. :PRIM. :EMH :OIL & GAS

DHAR ,V ; FIRS: PETERS,JM ; SEC: LEWIS ,BL CIT: 0
ASSESSING INHERENT RISK DURING AUDIT PLANNING: THE DEVELOPMENT OF A KNOWLEDGE BASED MODEL
AOS 04 89 VOL: 14 PG:359 - 378 :: ANOVA :SURV. :EXP.SYST. :PLAN.

DHARAN,BG ; SEC: MASCARENHAS,B CIT: 0
DETERMINANTS OF ACCOUNTING CHANGE: AN INDUSTRY ANALYSIS OF DEPRECIATION CHANGE
JAA WI 92 VOL: 7 PG:1 - 21 :: REGRESS. :PRIM. :OTH.STAT. :OIL & GAS

DHARAN,BG CIT: 0
THE EFFECT OF SALES AND COLLECTION DISCLOSURES ON CASH FLOW FORECASTING AND INCOME SMOOTHING
CAR SP 87 VOL: 3 PG:445 - 459 :: DES.STAT. :SIM. :OTH.STAT. :REV.REC.

DHARAN,BG CIT: 0.33
EXPECTATION MODELS AND POTENTIAL INFORMATION CONTENT OF OIL AND GAS RESERVE VALUE DISCLOSURES
TAR AP 84 VOL: 59 PG:199 - 217 :: NON-PAR. :PRIM. :OTH.STAT. :OIL & GAS

DHARAN,BG CIT: 0.2
IDENTIFICATION AND ESTIMATION ISSUES FOR A CAUSAL EARNINGS MODEL
JAR SP 83 VOL: 21 PG:18 - 41 :: ANAL. :SIM. :TIME SER. :FOREC.

DHARAN,BG CIT: 0
EMPIRICAL IDENTIFICATION PROCEDURES FOR EARNINGS MODELS
JAR SP 83 VOL: 21 PG:256 - 270 :: NON-PAR. :PRIM. :TIME SER. :METHOD.

DHAVALE,DG CIT: 0
A NOTE ON A VARIABLE ERROR RATE MODEL IN COMPLIANCE TESTING
AUD SP 91 VOL: 10 PG:159 - 166 :: DES.STAT. :INT. LOG. :OTH.STAT. :SAMP.

DIAS ,FJB ; FIRS: OTLEY ,DT CIT: 0.18
ACCOUNTING AGGREGATION AND DECISION-MAKING PERFORMANCE: AN EXPERIMENTAL INVESTIGATION
JAR SP 82 VOL: 20 PG:171 - 188 :: ANOVA :LAB. :HIPS :INFO.STRUC.

DICKENS,RL ; SEC: BLACKBURN,JO CIT: 0.06
HOLDING GAINS ON FIXED ASSETS: AN ELEMENT OF BUSINESS INCOME?
TAR AP 64 VOL: 39 PG:312 - 329 :: ANAL. :INT. LOG. :THEORY :VALUAT.(INFL.)

DICKHAUT,J ; FIRS: BERG ,KB ; SEC: COURSEY,D CIT: 1.33
EXPERIMENTAL METHODS IN ACCOUNTING: A DISCUSSION OF RECURRING ISSUES
CAR SP 90 VOL: 6 PG:825 - 849 :: DES.STAT. :SEC. :INF.ECO./AG. :METHOD.

DICKHAUT,J ; FIRS: KANODIA,C ; SEC: BUSHMAN,R CIT: 1
ESCALATION ERRORS AND THE SUNK COST EFFECT: AN EXPLANATION BASED ON REPUTATION AN INFORMATION ASYMMETRIES
JAR SP 89 VOL: 27 PG:59 - 77 :: DES.STAT. :INT. LOG. :INF.ECO./AG. :EXEC.COMP.

DICKHAUT,JW ; SEC: LERE ,JC CIT: 0.2
COMPARISON OF ACCOUNTING SYSTEMS AND HEURISTICS IN SELECTING ECONOMIC OPTIMA
JAR AU 83 VOL: 21 PG:495 - 513 :: ANAL. :INT. LOG. :INF.ECO./AG. :INFO.STRUC.

DICKHAUT,JW ; FIRS: EGER ,C CIT: 0.45
AN EXAMINATION OF THE CONSERVATIVE INFORMATION PROCESSING BIAS IN AN ACCOUNTING FRAMEWORK
JAR AU 82 VOL: 20 PG:711 - 723 :: REGRESS. :LAB. :HIPS :MAN.DEC.CHAR.

DICKHAUT,JW ; FIRS: MAGEE ,RP CIT: 0.47
EFFECTS OF COMPENSATION PLANS ON HEURISTICS IN COST VARIANCE INVESTIGATIONS
JAR AU 78 VOL: 16 PG:294 - 314 :: ANOVA :LAB. :HIPS :VAR.

DICKHAUT,JW ; SEC: EGGLETON,IRC CIT: 0.41
AN EXAMINATION OF THE PROCESSES UNDERLYING COMPARATIVE JUDGMENTS OF NUMERICAL STIMULI
JAR SP 75 VOL: 13 PG:38 - 72 :: DES.STAT. :LAB. :HIPS :N/A

DICKHAUT,JW CIT: 0.71
ALTERNATIVE INFORMATION STRUCTURES AND PROBABILITY REVISIONS
TAR JA 73 VOL: 48 PG:61 - 79 :: ANOVA :LAB. :HIPS :INFO.STRUC.

DIERKES,M ; SEC: ANTAL ,AB CIT: 0.13
THE USEFULNESS AND USE OF SOCIAL REPORTING INFORMATION
AOS 01 85 VOL: 10 PG:29 - 34 :: DES.STAT. :INT. LOG. :OTH.BEH. :HRA

DIERKES,M CIT: 0.14
CORPORATE SOCIAL REPORTING IN GERMANY: CONCEPTUAL DEVELOPMENTS AND PRACTICAL EXPERIENCE
AOS 12 79 VOL: 4 PG:87 - 108 :: DES.STAT. :PRIM. :THEORY :HRA

DIERKES,M ; SEC: PRESTON,LE CIT: 0.38
CORPORATE SOCIAL ACCOUNTING REPORTING FOR THE PHYSICAL ENVIRONMENT: A CRITICAL REVIEW AND IMPLEMENTATION PROPOSAL
AOS 01 77 VOL: 2 PG:3 - 22 :: QUAL. :INT. LOG. :THEORY :HRA

DIETRICH,JR ; FIRS: THOMPSON,RB ; SEC: OLSEN ,C CIT: 0.4
THE INFLUENCE OF ESTIMATION PERIOD NEWS EVENTS ON STANDARDIZED MARKET MODEL PREDICTION ERRORS
TAR JL 88 VOL: 63 PG:448 - 471 :: REGRESS. :PRIM. :EMH :METHOD.

DIETRICH,JR ; FIRS: THOMPSON II,RB ; SEC: OLSEN ,C CIT: 1.17
ATTRIBUTES OF NEWS ABOUT FIRMS: AN ANALYSIS OF FIRM-SPECIFIC NEWS REPORTED IN THE WALL STREET JOURNAL INDEX
JAR AU 87 VOL: 25 PG:245 - 274 :: REGRESS. :PRIM. :INSTIT. :INFO.STRUC.

DIETRICH,JR ; FIRS: OLSEN ,C CIT: 0.75
VERTICAL INFORMATION TRANSFERS: THE ASSOCIATION BETWEEN RETAILERS' SALES ANNOUNCEMENTS AND SUPPLIERS' SECURITY RETURNS
JAR ST 85 VOL: 23 PG:144 - 166 :: REGRESS. :PRIM. :EMH :FIN.METH.

DIETRICH,JR CIT: 0.11
EFFECTS OF EARLY BOND REFUNDINGS: AN EMPIRICAL INVESTIGATION OF SECURITY RETURNS
JAE AP 84 VOL: 6 PG:67 - 96 :: REGRESS. :PRIM. :EMH :LTD

DIETRICH,JR ; FIRS: HARRISON JR,WT ; SEC: TOMASSINI,LA CIT: 0.2
THE USE OF CONTROL GROUPS IN CAPITAL MARKET RESEARCH
JAR SP 83 VOL: 21 PG:65 - 77 :: NON-PAR. :PRIM. :EMH :METHOD.

DIETRICH,JR ; SEC: KAPLAN,RS CIT: 0.55
EMPIRICAL ANALYSIS OF THE COMMERCIAL LOAN CLASSIFICATION DECISION
TAR JA 82 VOL: 57 PG:18 - 38 :: REGRESS. :PRIM. :OTH.STAT. :BUS.FAIL.

DILLA ,WN CIT: 0
INFORMATION EVALUATION IN A COMPETITIVE ENVIRONMENT: CONTEXT AND TASK EFFECTS
TAR JL 89 VOL: 64 PG:404 - 432 :: REGRESS. :LAB. :INF.ECO./AG. :MAN.DEC.CHAR.

DILLARD,JF ; SEC: KAUFFMAN,NL ; THIR: SPIRES,EE CIT: 0
EVIDENCE ORDER AND BELIEF REVISION IN MANAGEMENT ACCOUNTING DECISIONS
AOS 91 VOL: 16 PG:619 - 633 :: REGRESS. :LAB. :HIPS :AUD.BEH.

DILLARD,JF CIT: 0
COGNITIVE SCIENCE AND DECISION MAKING RESEARCH IN ACCOUNTING
AOS 34 84 VOL: 9 PG:343 - 354 :: QUAL. :INT. LOG. :HIPS :N/A

DILLARD,JF CIT: 0.25
A LONGITUDINAL EVALUATION OF AN OCCUPATIONAL GOAL-EXPECTANCY MODEL IN PROFESSIONAL ACCOUNTING ORGANIZATIONS
AOS 01 81 VOL: 6 PG:17 - 26 :: MIXED :SURV. :OTH.BEH. :ORG.

DILLARD,JF ; FIRS: FERRIS,KR ; THIR: NETHERCOTT,L CIT: 0.08
A COMPARISON OF V-I-E MODEL PREDICTIONS: A CROSS-NATIONAL STUDY IN PROFESSIONAL ACCOUNTING FIRMS
AOS 04 80 VOL: 5 PG:361 - 368 :: DES.STAT. :LAB. :OTH.BEH. :INT.DIFF.

DILLARD,JF CIT: 0.21
VALENCE-INSTRUMENTALITY-EXPECTANCY MODEL VALIDATION USING SELECTED ACCOUNTING GROUPS
AOS 12 79 VOL: 4 PG:31 - 38 :: OTH.QUANT. :SURV. :OTH.BEH. :AUD.BEH.

DILLARD,JF ; SEC: FERRIS,KR CIT: 0.57
SOURCES OF PROFESSIONAL STAFF TURNOVER IN PUBLIC ACCOUNTING FIRMS: SOME FURTHER EVIDENCE
AOS 03 79 VOL: 4 PG:179 - 186 :: OTH.QUANT. :SURV. :OTH.BEH. :AUD.BEH.

DILLON,RD ; SEC: NASH ,JF CIT: 0.2
THE TRUE RELEVANCE OF RELEVANT COSTS
TAR JA 78 VOL: 53 PG:11 - 17 :: QUAL. :INT. LOG. :THEORY :REL.COSTS

DIRSMITH,MW ; FIRS: CARPENTER,BW CIT: 0
EARLY DEBT EXTINGUISHMENT TRANSACTIONS AND AUDITOR MATERIALITY JUDGMENTS: A BOUNDED RATIONALITY PERSPECTIVE
AOS 92 VOL: 17 PG:709 - 739 :: REGRESS. :LAB. :HIPS :MAT.

DIRSMITH,MW ; SEC: HASKINS,ME CIT: 0
INHERENT RISK ASSESSMENT AND AUDIT FIRM TECHNOLOGY: A CONTRAST IN WORLD THEORIES
AOS 01 91 VOL: 16 PG:61 - 90 :: REGRESS. :FIELD :HIPS :DEC.AIDS

DIRSMITH,MW ; FIRS: COVALESKI,MA CIT: 1
DIALECTIC TENSION, DOUBLE REFLEXIVITY AND THE EVERDAY ACCOUNTING RESEARCHER: USING QUALITATIVE METHODS
AOS 06 90 VOL: 15 PG:543 - 573 :: DES.STAT. :INT. LOG. :THEORY :METHOD.

DIRSMITH,MW ; FIRS: COVALESKI,MA CIT: 1.8
THE USE OF BUDGETARY SYMBOLS IN THE POLITICAL ARENA: AN HISTORICALLY INFORMED FIELD STUDY
AOS 01 88 VOL: 13 PG:1 - 24 :: REGRESS. :CASE :THEORY :BUDG.& PLAN.

DIRSMITH,MW ; FIRS: WILLIAMS,DD CIT: 0.2
THE EFFECTS OF AUDIT TECHNOLOGY ON AUDITOR EFFICIENCY: AUDITING AND THE TIMELINESS OF CLIENT EARNINGS ANNOUNCEMENTS
AOS 05 88 VOL: 13 PG:487 - 508 :: REGRESS. :PRIM. :INSTIT. :OPER.AUD.

DIRSMITH,MW ; FIRS: COVALESKI,MA ; THIR: WHITE ,CE CIT: 0.17
ECONOMIC CONSEQUENCES: THE RELATIONSHIP BETWEEN FINANCIAL REPORTING AND STRATEGIC PLANNING, MANAGEMENT AND OPERATING CONTROL DEC
CAR SP 87 VOL: 3 PG:408 - 429 :: REGRESS. :LAB. :HIPS :FIN.METH.

DIRSMITH,MW ; FIRS: COVALESKI,MA CIT: 1.14
THE BUDGETARY PROCESS OF POWER AND POLITICS
AOS 03 86 VOL: 11 PG:193 - 214 :: REGRESS. :SURV. :OTH.BEH. :BUDG.& PLAN.

DIRSMITH,MW ; SEC: COVALESKI,MA CIT: 0.63
INFORMAL COMMUNICATIONS, NONFORMAL COMMUNICATIONS AND MENTORING IN PUBLIC ACCOUNTING FIRMS
AOS 02 85 VOL: 10 PG:149 - 170 :: REGRESS. :INT. LOG. :INSTIT. :ORG.

DIRSMITH,MW ; SEC: COVALESKI,MA ; THIR: MCALLISTER,JP CIT: 0.5
OF PARADIGMS AND METAPHORS IN AUDITING THOUGHT
CAR AU 85 VOL: 2 PG:46 - 68 :: REGRESS. :SURV. :THEORY :AUD.TRAIN.

DIRSMITH,MW ; SEC: COVALESKI,MA CIT: 0.38
PRACTICE MANAGEMENT ISSUES IN PUBLIC ACCOUNTING FIRMS
JAA AU 85 VOL: 9 PG:5 - 21 :: REGRESS. :SURV. :OTH. :ORG.

DIRSMITH,MW ; FIRS: COVALESKI,MA CIT: 0.5
BUDGETING AS A MEANS FOR CONTROL AND LOOSE COUPLING
AOS 04 83 VOL: 8 PG:323 - 340 :: CORR. :SURV. :OTH.BEH. :BUDG.& PLAN.

DIRSMITH,MW ; SEC: LEWIS ,BL CIT: 0.09
THE EFFECT OF EXTERNAL REPORTING ON MANAGERIAL DECISION-MAKING: SOME ANTECEDENT CONDITIONS
AOS 04 82 VOL: 7 PG:319 - 336 :: NON-PAR. :SURV. :HIPS :FIN.METH.

DIRSMITH,MW ; SEC: MCALLISTER,JP CIT: 0.45
THE ORGANIC VS. THE MECHANISTIC AUDIT: PROBLEMS AND PITFALLS (PART II)
JAA AU 82 VOL: 6 PG:60 - 74 :: QUAL. :INT. LOG. :OTH. :AUD.

DIRSMITH,MW ; SEC: MCALLISTER,JP CIT: 0.45
THE ORGANIC VS. THE MECHANISTIC AUDIT
JAA SP 82 VOL: 5 PG:214 - 228 :: QUAL. :INT. LOG. :OTH. :AUD.

DIRSMITH,MW ; SEC: JABLONSKY,SF CIT: 0.36
MBO, POLITICAL RATIONALITY AND INFORMATION INDUCTANCE
AOS 12 79 VOL: 4 PG:39 - 52 :: QUAL. :INT. LOG. :OTH. :N/A

DIRSMITH,MW ; SEC: JABLONSKY,SF CIT: 0.27
THE PATTERN OF PPB REJECTION: SOMETHING ABOUT ORGANIZATIONS, SOMETHING ABOUT PPB
AOS 34 78 VOL: 3 PG:215 - 226 :: QUAL. :INT. LOG. :THEORY :BUDG.& PLAN.

DITTMAN,DA ; SEC: PRAKASH,P CIT: 0.29
COST VARIANCE INVESTIGATION: MARKOVIAN CONTROL VERSUS OPTIMAL CONTROL
TAR AP 79 VOL: 54 PG:358 - 373 :: DES.STAT. :SIM. :OTH.STAT. :VAR.

DITTMAN,DA ; SEC: PRAKASH,P CIT: 0.33
COST VARIANCE INVESTIGATION: MARKOVIAN CONTROL OF MARKOV PROCESSES
JAR SP 78 VOL: 16 PG:14 - 25 :: ANAL. :INT. LOG. :OTH.STAT. :VAR.

DITTMAN,DA ; SEC: JURIS ,HA ; THIR: REVSINE,L CIT: 0.29
ON THE EXISTENCE OF UNRECORDED HUMAN ASSETS: AN ECONOMIC PERSPECTIVE
JAR SP 76 VOL: 14 PG:49 - 65 :: ANAL. :INT. LOG. :OTH.BEH. :HRA

DOCKWEILER,RC CIT: 0.12
THE PRACTICABILITY OF DEVELOPING MULTIPLE FINANCIAL STATEMENTS: A CASE STUDY
TAR OC 69 VOL: 44 PG:729 - 742 :: QUAL. :CASE :THEORY :VALUAT.(INFL.)

DODD ,P ; SEC: DOPUCH,N ; THIR: HOLTHAUSEN,RW ; FOUR: LEFTWICH,R CIT: 1.56
QUALIFIED AUDIT OPINIONS AND STOCK PRICES: INFORMATION CONTENT, ANNOUNCEMENT DATES, AND CONCURRENT DISCLOSURES
JAE AP 84 VOL: 6 PG:3 - 38 :: REGRESS. :PRIM. :EMH :OPIN.

DODIN ,B ; FIRS: CHAN ,KH CIT: 0
A DECISION SUPPORT SYSTEM FOR AUDIT-STAFF SCHEDULING WITH PRECEDENCE CONSTRAINTS
TAR OC 86 VOL: 61 PG:726 - 734 :: DES.STAT. :INT. LOG. :MATH.PROG. :ORG.

DOLPHIN,R ; FIRS: SOPER ,FJ CIT: 0.06
READABILITY AND CORPORATE ANNUAL REPORTS
TAR AP 64 VOL: 39 PG:358 - 362 :: DES.STAT. :PRIM. :N/A :OTH.MANAG.

DONEGAN,J ; SEC: SUNDER,S CIT: 0
CONTRACT THEORETIC ANALYSIS OF OFF-BALANCE SHEET FINANCING
JAA SP 89 VOL: 4 PG:203 - 216 :: REGRESS. :SEC. :INSTIT. :OTH.C/A

DONEY ,LD ; FIRS: WILKINSON,JR CIT: 0.06
EXTENDING AUDIT AND REPORTING BOUNDARIES
TAR OC 65 VOL: 40 PG:753 - 756 :: QUAL. :INT. LOG. :INSTIT. :AUD.

DONTOH,A ; FIRS: CLARKSON,PM ; THIR: RICHARDSON,G ; FOUR: SEFCIK,SE CIT: 0
THE VOLUNTARY INCLUSION OF EARNINGS FORECASTS IN IPO PROSPECTUSES
CAR SP 92 VOL: 8 PG:601 - 625 :: REGRESS. :PRIM. :TIME SER. :VALUAT.(INFL.)

DONTOH,A CIT: 0.5
VOLUNTARY DISCLOSURE
JAA AU 89 VOL: 4 PG:480 - 511 :: DES.STAT. :INT. LOG. :INF.ECO./AG. :INFO.STRUC.

DONTOH,A ; SEC: RICHARDSON,G CIT: 0
ON INTERIM INFORMATION AND THE INFORMATION CONTENT OF FIRM EARNINGS: A STATE VARIABLE APPROACH
CAR SP 88 VOL: 4 PG:450 - 469 :: ANOVA :PRIM. :EMH :INT.REP.

DOPUCH,N CIT: 0
ANOTHER PERSPECTIVE ON THE USE OF DECEPTION IN AUDITING EXPERIMENTS
AUD AU 92 VOL: 11 PG:109 - 112 :: DES.STAT. :INT. LOG. :HIPS :METHOD.

DOPUCH,N ; SEC: KING ,RR CIT: 1
NEGLIGENCE VERSUS STRICT LIABILITY REGIMES IN AUDITING: AN EXPERIMENTAL INVESTIGATION
TAR JA 92 VOL: 67 PG:97 - 120 :: REGRESS. :LAB. :OTH.BEH. :LIAB.

DOPUCH,N ; SEC: KING ,RR CIT: 0
THE IMPACT OF MAS ON AUDITORS' INDEPENDENCE: AN EXPERIMENTAL MARKETS STUDY
JAR ST 91 VOL: 29 PG:60 - 106 :: REGRESS. :LAB. :OTH.STAT. :INDEP.

DOPUCH,N ; SEC: KING ,RR ; THIR: WALLIN,DE CIT: 0.25
THE USE OF EXPERIMENTAL MARKETS IN AUDITING RESEARCH: SOME INITIAL FINDINGS
AUD 89 VOL: 8 PG:98 - 127 :: REGRESS. :LAB. :INF.ECO./AG. :MAN.DEC.CHAR.

DOPUCH,N CIT: 0.5
THE IMPACT OF REGULATIONS ON FINANCIAL ACCOUNTING RESEARCH
CAR SP 89 VOL: 5 PG:494 - 500 :: REGRESS. :INT. LOG. :HIST. :METHOD.

DOPUCH,N CIT: 0
IMPLICATIONS OF TORTS RULES OF THE ACCOUNTANT'S LIABILITY FOR THE ACCOUNTING MODEL
JAA SU 88 VOL: 03 PG:245 - 250 :: DES.STAT. :INT. LOG. :INSTIT. :LIAB.

DOPUCH,N ; SEC: PINCUS,M CIT: 1.2
EVIDENCE ON THE CHOICE OF INVENTORY ACCOUNTING METHODS: LIFO VERSUS FIFO
JAR SP 88 VOL: 26 PG:28 - 59 :: REGRESS. :PRIM. :OTH.STAT. :INV.

DOPUCH,N ; SEC: HOLTHAUSEN,RW ; THIR: LEFTWICH,RW CIT: 1
PREDICTING AUDIT QUALIFICATIONS WITH FINANCIAL AND MARKET VARIABLES
TAR JL 87 VOL: 62 PG:431 - 454 :: REGRESS. :PRIM. :EMH :OPIN.

DOPUCH,N ; SEC: HOLTHAUSEN,RW ; THIR: LEFTWICH,RW CIT: 0.57
ABNORMAL STOCK RETURNS ASSOCIATED WITH MEDIA DISCLOSURES OF 'SUBJECT TO' QUALIFIED AUDIT OPINIONS
JAE JN 86 VOL: 8 PG:93 - 118 :: REGRESS. :PRIM. :EMH :OPIN.

DOPUCH,N ; FIRS: DODD ,P ; THIR: HOLTHAUSEN,RW ; FOUR: LEFTWICH,R CIT: 1.56
QUALIFIED AUDIT OPINIONS AND STOCK PRICES: INFORMATION CONTENT, ANNOUNCEMENT DATES, AND CONCURRENT DISCLOSURES
JAE AP 84 VOL: 6 PG:3 - 38 :: REGRESS. :PRIM. :EMH :OPIN.

DOPUCH,N ; SEC: SUNDER,S CIT: 0.46
FASB'S STATEMENTS ON OBJECTIVES AND ELEMENTS OF FINANCIAL ACCOUNTING: A REVIEW
TAR JA 80 VOL: 55 PG:1 - 21 :: QUAL. :INT. LOG. :INSTIT. :FASB SUBM.

DOPUCH,N ; FIRS: GONEDES,NJ CIT: 0.5
ECONOMIC ANALYSES AND ACCOUNTING TECHNIQUES: PERSPECTIVES AND PROPOSALS
JAR AU 79 VOL: 17 PG:384 - 410 :: QUAL. :INT. LOG. :THEORY :METHOD.

DOPUCH,N ; FIRS: GONEDES,NJ ; THIR: PENMAN,SH CIT: 2.41
DISCLOSURE RULES, INFORMATION-PRODUCTION, AND CAPITAL MARKET EQUILIBRIUM: THE CASE OF FORECAST DISCLOSURE RULES
JAR SP 76 VOL: 14 PG:89 - 137 :: NON-PAR. :PRIM. :EMH :FOREC.

DOPUCH,N ; FIRS: GONEDES,NJ CIT: 4.12
CAPITAL MARKET EQUILIBRIUM, INFORMATION PRODUCTION, AND SELECTING ACCOUNTING TECHNIQUES: THEORETICAL FRAMEWORK AND REVIEW OF EMPIRICAL WORK
JAR ST 74 VOL: 12 PG:48 - 129 :: ANAL. :SEC. :EMH :FIN.METH.

DOPUCH,N ; SEC: RONEN ,J CIT: 0.47
THE EFFECTS OF ALTERNATIVE INVENTORY VALUATION METHODS - AN EXPERIMENTAL STUDY
JAR AU 73 VOL: 11 PG:191 - 211 :: DES.STAT. :LAB. :THEORY :INV.

DOPUCH,N ; SEC: WATTS ,RL CIT: 0.94
USING TIME-SERIES MODELS TO ASSESS THE SIGNIFICANCE OF ACCOUNTING CHANGES
JAR SP 72 VOL: 10 PG:180 - 194 :: MIXED :PRIM. :TIME SER. :ACC.CHNG.

DOPUCH,N ; FIRS: COOPER,WW ; THIR: KELLER,TF CIT: 0.06
BUDGETARY DISCLOSURE AND OTHER SUGGESTIONS FOR IMPROVING ACCOUNTING REPORTS
TAR OC 68 VOL: 43 PG:640 - 648 :: QUAL. :INT. LOG. :THEORY :FIN.METH.

DOPUCH,N ; SEC: BIRNBERG,JG ; THIR: DEMSKI,JS CIT: 0.12
AN EXTENSION OF STANDARD COST VARIANCE ANALYSIS
TAR JL 67 VOL: 42 PG:526 - 536 :: ANAL. :INT. LOG. :OTH.STAT. :VAR.

DOPUCH,N ; SEC: DRAKE ,DF CIT: 0.12
THE EFFECT OF ALTERNATIVE ACCOUNTING RULES FOR NONSUBSIDIARY INVESTMENTS
JAR ST 66 VOL: 4 PG:192 - 219 :: DES.STAT. :PRIM. :THEORY :FIN.METH.

DOPUCH,N ; FIRS: DRAKE ,DF CIT: 0.47
ON THE CASE FOR DICHOTOMIZING INCOME
JAR AU 65 VOL: 3 PG:192 - 205 :: QUAL. :INT. LOG. :THEORY :REV.REC.

DOPUCH,N ; SEC: DRAKE ,DF CIT: 0.18
ACCOUNTING IMPLICATIONS OF A MATHEMATICAL PROGRAMMING APPROACH TO THE TRANSFER PRICE PROBLEM
JAR SP 64 VOL: 2 PG:10 - 24 :: ANAL. :INT. LOG. :MATH.PROG. :TRANS.PRIC.

DOPUCH,N CIT: 0
MATHEMATICAL PROGRAMMING AND ACCOUNTING APPROACHES TO INCREMENTAL COST ANALYSIS
TAR OC 63 VOL: 38 PG:745 - 753 :: ANAL. :INT. LOG. :MATH.PROG. :N/A

DORAN ,BM ; SEC: COLLINS,DW ; THIR: DHALIWAL,DS CIT: 1
THE INFORMATION OF HISTORICAL COST EARNINGS RELATIVE TO SUPPLEMENTAL RESERVE-BASED ACCOUNTING DATA IN THE EXTRACTIVE PETROLEUM I
TAR JL 88 VOL: 63 PG:389 - 413 :: REGRESS. :PRIM. :EMH :OIL & GAS

DORAN ,DT ; SEC: NACHTMANN,R CIT: 0
THE ASSOCIATION OF STOCK DISTRIBUTION ANNOUNCEMENTS AND EARNINGS PERFORMANCE
JAA SP 88 VOL: 03 PG:113 - 132 :: REGRESS. :PRIM. :EMH :STK.DIV.

DOUCET,MS ; FIRS: MAYPER,AG ; THIR: WARREN,CS CIT: 0.25
AUDITORS' MATERIALITY JUDGMENTS OF INTERNAL ACCOUNTING CONTROL WEAKNESSES
AUD AU 89 VOL: 9 PG:72 - 86 :: REGRESS. :LAB. :HIPS :MAT.

DOWELL,CD ; FIRS: BOATSMAN,JR ; THIR: KIMBRELL,JI CIT: 0
VALUING STOCK USED FOR A BUSINESS COMBINATION
JAA AU 84 VOL: 8 PG:35 - 43 :: ANAL. :INT. LOG. :OTH.STAT. :BUS.COMB.

DOWELL,CD ; SEC: HALL ,JA CIT: 0
EDP CONTROLS WITH AUDIT COST IMPLICATIONS
JAA AU 81 VOL: 5 PG:30 - 40 :: QUAL. :SURV. :THEORY :EDP AUD.

DOWNES,D ; SEC: DYCKMAN,TR CIT: 0.29
A CRITICAL LOOK AT THE EFFICIENT MARKET EMPIRICAL RESEARCH LITERATURE AS IT RELATES TO ACCOUNTING INFORMATION
TAR AP 73 VOL: 48 PG:300 - 317 :: MIXED :SEC. :EMH :FIN.METH.

DRAKE ,DF ; FIRS: DOPUCH,N CIT: 0.12
THE EFFECT OF ALTERNATIVE ACCOUNTING RULES FOR NONSUBSIDIARY INVESTMENTS
JAR ST 66 VOL: 4 PG:192 - 219 :: DES.STAT. :PRIM. :THEORY :FIN.METH.

DRAKE ,DF ; SEC: DOPUCH,N CIT: 0.47
ON THE CASE FOR DICHOTOMIZING INCOME
JAR AU 65 VOL: 3 PG:192 - 205 :: QUAL. :INT. LOG. :THEORY :REV.REC.

DRAKE ,DF ; FIRS: DOPUCH,N CIT: 0.18
ACCOUNTING IMPLICATIONS OF A MATHEMATICAL PROGRAMMING APPROACH TO THE TRANSFER PRICE PROBLEM
JAR SP 64 VOL: 2 PG:10 - 24 :: ANAL. :INT. LOG. :MATH.PROG. :TRANS.PRIC.

DREBIN,AR CIT: 0
A FALLACY OF DEPRECIATION TRANSLATION
JAR AU 69 VOL: 7 PG:204 - 214 :: ANAL. :INT. LOG. :OTH. :VALUAT.(INFL.)

DREBIN,AR CIT: 0
THE INVENTORY CALCULUS
JAR SP 66 VOL: 4 PG:68 - 86 :: ANAL. :INT. LOG. :OTH.STAT. :INV.

DREBIN,AR CIT: 0
ACCOUNTING FOR PROPRIETARY RESEARCH
TAR JL 66 VOL: 41 PG:413 - 425 :: ANAL. :INT. LOG. :THEORY :OTH. NON-C/A

DREBIN,AR CIT: 0.06
PRICE LEVEL ADJUSTMENTS AND INVENTORY FLOW ASSUMPTIONS
TAR JA 65 VOL: 40 PG:154 - 162 :: ANAL. :INT. LOG. :THEORY :INV.

DREBIN,AR CIT: 0
CASH-FLOWITIS: MALADY OR SYNDROME?
JAR SP 64 VOL: 2 PG:25 - 34 :: QUAL. :INT. LOG. :THEORY :N/A

DREBIN,AR CIT: 0
RECOGNIZING IMPLICIT INTEREST IN NON-FUNDED PENSION PLANS
TAR JL 63 VOL: 38 PG:579 - 583 :: QUAL. :INT. LOG. :THEORY :SPEC.ITEMS

DRINKWATER,D ; SEC: EDWARDS,JD CIT: 0
THE NATURE OF TAXES AND THE MATCHING PRINCIPLE
TAR JL 65 VOL: 40 PG:579 - 582 :: QUAL. :INT. LOG. :THEORY :TAXES

DRIVER,MJ ; SEC: MOCK ,TJ CIT: 1.65
HUMAN INFORMATION PROCESSING, DECISION STYLE THEORY, AND ACCOUNTING INFORMATION SYSTEMS
TAR JL 75 VOL: 50 PG:490 - 508 :: MIXED :LAB. :HIPS :INFO.STRUC.

DRTINA,RE ; FIRS: THODE ,SF ; THIR: LARGAY III,JA CIT: 0
OPERATING CASH FLOWS: A GROWING NEED FOR SEPARATE REPORTING
JAA WI 86 VOL: 1 PG:46 - 61 :: REGRESS. :PRIM. :EMH :OTH.FIN.ACC.

DUBOFF,JI ; FIRS: ALY ,HF CIT: 0.06
STATISTICAL VS. JUDGMENT SAMPLING: AN EMPIRICAL STUDY OF AUDITING THE ACCOUNTS RECEIVABLE OF A SMALL RETAIL STORE
TAR JA 71 VOL: 46 PG:119 - 128 :: ANOVA :CASE :OTH.STAT. :SAMP.

DUGAN ,MT ; SEC: GENTRY,JA ; THIR: SHRIVER,KA CIT: 0
THE X-11 MODEL: A NEW ANALYTICAL REVIEW TECHNIQUE FOR THE AUDITOR
AUD SP 85 VOL: 4 PG:11 - 22 :: DES.STAT. :INT. LOG. :TIME SER. :ANAL.REV.

DUKE ,D CIT: 0
THIRD WORLD LOANS BY U.S. MONEY CENTER BANKS
JAA WI 91 VOL: 6 PG:135 - 142 :: DES.STAT. :PRIM. :OTH. :FIN.METH.

DUKE ,GL ; FIRS: KO ,CE ; SEC: NACHTSHEIM,CJ ; FOUR: BAILEY JR,AD CIT: 0
ON THE ROBUSTNESS OF MODEL-BASED SAMPLING IN AUDITING
AUD SP 88 VOL: 07 PG:119 - 136 :: DES.STAT. :SIM. :OTH.STAT. :SAMP.

DUKE ,GL ; FIRS: BAILEY JR,AD ; THIR: GERLACH,JH ; FOUR: KO ,CE ; FIFT: MESERVY,RD ; SIX: WHINSTON,AB CIT: 0.38
TICOM AND THE ANALYSIS OF INTERNAL CONTROLS
TAR AP 85 VOL: 60 PG:186 - 201 :: CORR. :INT. LOG. :OTH. :INT.CONT.

DUKE ,GL ; SEC: NETER ,J ; THIR: LEITCH,RA CIT: 1.09
POWER CHARACTERISTICS OF TEST STATISTICS IN THE AUDITING ENVIRONMENT: AN EMPIRICAL STUDY
JAR SP 82 VOL: 20 PG:42 - 67 :: MIXED :PRIM. :OTH.STAT. :ERRORS

DUKE ,JC ; SEC: HUNT III,HG CIT: 3
AN EMPIRICAL EXAMINATION OF DEBT COVENANT RESTRICTIONS AND ACCOUNTING-RELATED DEBT PROXIES
JAE JA 90 VOL: 12 PG:45 - 63 :: REGRESS. :PRIM. :OTH.STAT. :LTD

DUKES ,RE ; FIRS: ELLIOTT,JA ; SEC: RICHARDSON,G ; THIR: DYCKMAN,TR CIT: 1
THE IMPACT OF SFAS NO.2 ON FIRM EXPENDITURES ON RESEARCH AND DEVELOPMENT: REPLICATIONS AND EXTENSIONS
JAR SP 84 VOL: 22 PG:85 - 102 :: NON-PAR. :PRIM. :EMH :R & D

DUKES ,RE ; SEC: DYCKMAN,TR ; THIR: ELLIOTT,JA CIT: 1.38
ACCOUNTING FOR RESEARCH AND DEVELOPMENT COSTS: THE IMPACT ON RESEARCH AND DEVELOPMENT EXPENDITURES
JAR ST 80 VOL: 18 PG:1 - 26 :: NON-PAR. :PRIM. :THEORY :R & D

DUKES ,RE ; FIRS: BEAVER,WH CIT: 0.12
DELTA-DEPRECIATION METHODS: SOME ANALYTICAL RESULTS
JAR AU 74 VOL: 12 PG:205 - 215 :: ANAL. :INT. LOG. :OTH.STAT. :PP&E / DEPR

DUKES ,RE ; FIRS: BEAVER,WH CIT: 0.71
INTERPERIOD TAX ALLOCATION AND DELTA-DEPRECIATION METHODS: SOME EMPIRICAL RESULTS
TAR JL 73 VOL: 48 PG:549 - 559 :: REGRESS. :PRIM. :EMH :PP&E / DEPR

DUKES ,RE ; FIRS: BEAVER,WH CIT: 1.59
INTERPERIOD TAX ALLOCATION, EARNINGS EXPECTATIONS, AND THE BEHAVIOR OF SECURITY PRICES
TAR AP 72 VOL: 47 PG:320 - 332 :: REGRESS. :PRIM. :EMH :PP&E / DEPR

DUNK ,AS CIT: 0
RELIANCE ON BUDGETARY CONTROL, MANUFACTURING PROCESS AUTOMATION AND PRODUCTION SUBUNIT PERFORMANCE: A RESEARCH NOTE
AOS 04 92 VOL: 17 PG:195 - 203 :: REGRESS. :SURV. :OTH.BEH. :BUDG.& PLAN.

DUNK ,AS ; FIRS: BROWNELL,P CIT: 0
TASK UNCERTAINTY AND ITS INTERACTION WITH BUDGETARY PARTICIPATION AND BUDGET EMPHASIS: SOME METHODOLOGICAL ISSUES AND EMPIRICAL
AOS 91 VOL: 16 PG:693 - 703 :: REGRESS. :SURV. :OTH.BEH. :BUDG.& PLAN.

DUNK ,AS CIT: 0
BUDGETARY PARTICIPATION, AGREEMENT ON EVALUATION CRITERIA AND MANAGERIAL PERFORMANCE: A RESEARCH NOTE
AOS 03 90 VOL: 15 PG:171 - 178 :: REGRESS. :SURV. :OTH.BEH. :BUDG.& PLAN.

DUNK ,AS CIT: 0.5
BUDGET EMPHASIS, BUDGETARY PARTICIPATION AND MANAGERIAL PERFORMANCE: A NOTE
AOS 04 89 VOL: 14 PG:321 - 324 :: REGRESS. :SURV. :OTH.BEH. :BUDG.& PLAN.

DUNMORE,PV CIT: 0.14
ON THE COMPARISON OF DOLLAR-UNIT AND STRATIFIED MEAN-PER-UNIT ESTIMATORS
CAR AU 86 VOL: 3 PG:125 - 148 :: DES.STAT. :INT. LOG. :OTH.STAT. :SAMP.

DUVALL,RM ; SEC: BULLOCH,J CIT: 0
ADJUSTING RATE OF RETURN AND PRESENT VALUE FOR PRICE-LEVEL CHANGES
TAR JL 65 VOL: 40 PG:569 - 573 :: ANAL. :INT. LOG. :OTH.STAT. :OTH.MANAG.

DWORIN,L ; SEC: GRIMLUND,RA CIT: 0
A COMPREHENSIVE HYPOTHESIS TESTING APPROACH TO DOLLAR UNIT SAMPLING
CAR SP 89 VOL: 5 PG:674 - 691 :: DES.STAT. :SIM. :OTH.STAT. :SAMP.

DWORIN,L ; SEC: GRIMLUND,RA CIT: 0.71
DOLLAR-UNIT SAMPLING: A COMPARISON OF THE QUASI-BAYESIAN AND MOMENT BOUNDS
TAR JA 86 VOL: 61 PG:36 - 57 :: DES.STAT. :SIM. :OTH.STAT. :SAMP.

DWORIN,L ; SEC: GRIMLUND,RA CIT: 0.89
DOLLAR UNIT SAMPLING FOR ACCOUNTS RECEIVABLE AND INVENTORY
TAR AP 84 VOL: 59 PG:218 - 241 :: MIXED :SIM. :OTH.STAT. :SAMP.

DYCKMAN,TR ; FIRS: ELLIOTT,JA ; SEC: RICHARDSON,G ; FOUR: DUKES ,RE CIT: 1
THE IMPACT OF SFAS NO.2 ON FIRM EXPENDITURES ON RESEARCH AND DEVELOPMENT: REPLICATIONS AND EXTENSIONS
JAR SP 84 VOL: 22 PG:85 - 102 :: NON-PAR. :PRIM. :EMH :R & D

DYCKMAN,TR ; SEC: ZEFF ,SA CIT: 1
TWO DECADES OF THE JOURNAL OF ACCOUNTING RESEARCH
JAR SP 84 VOL: 22 PG:225 - 297 :: DES.STAT. :SEC. :INSTIT. :METHOD.

DYCKMAN,TR ; SEC: PHILBRICK,D ; THIR: STEPHAN,J CIT: 0.89
A COMPARISON OF EVENT STUDY METHODOLOGIES USING DAILY STOCK RETURNS: A SIMULATION APPROACH
JAR ST 84 VOL: 22 PG:1 - 30 :: REGRESS. :SIM. :OTH.BEH. :METHOD.

DYCKMAN,TR ; SEC: HOSKIN,RE ; THIR: SWIERINGA,RJ CIT: 0.36
AN ACCOUNTING CHANGE AND INFORMATION PROCESSING CHANGES
AOS 01 82 VOL: 7 PG:1 - 12 :: REGRESS. :LAB. :HIPS :ACC.CHNG.

DYCKMAN,TR CIT: 0.17
THE INTELLIGENCE OF AMBIGUITY
AOS 04 81 VOL: 6 PG:291 - 300 :: QUAL. :INT. LOG. :THEORY :N/A

DYCKMAN,TR ; FIRS: DUKES ,RE ; THIR: ELLIOTT,JA CIT: 1.38
ACCOUNTING FOR RESEARCH AND DEVELOPMENT COSTS: THE IMPACT ON RESEARCH AND DEVELOPMENT EXPENDITURES
JAR ST 80 VOL: 18 PG:1 - 26 :: NON-PAR. :PRIM. :THEORY :R & D

DYCKMAN,TR ; SEC: SMITH ,AJ CIT: 2.21
FINANCIAL ACCOUNTING AND REPORTING BY OIL AND GAS PRODUCING COMPANIES: A STUDY OF INFORMATION EFFECTS
JAE MR 79 VOL: 1 PG:45 - 75 :: NON-PAR. :PRIM. :EMH :OIL & GAS

DYCKMAN,TR ; FIRS: CRICHFIELD,T ; THIR: LAKONISHOK,J CIT: 0.93
AN EVALUATION OF SECURITY ANALYSTS' FORECASTS
TAR JL 78 VOL: 53 PG:651 - 668 :: ANOVA :PRIM. :TIME SER. :FOREC.

DYCKMAN,TR ; FIRS: DOWNES,D CIT: 0.29
A CRITICAL LOOK AT THE EFFICIENT MARKET EMPIRICAL RESEARCH LITERATURE AS IT RELATES TO ACCOUNTING INFORMATION
TAR AP 73 VOL: 48 PG:300 - 317 :: MIXED :SEC. :EMH :FIN.METH.

DYCKMAN,TR ; FIRS: OZAN ,T CIT: 0.24
A NORMATIVE MODEL FOR INVESTIGATION DECISIONS INVOLVING MULTI-ORIGIN COST VARIANCES
JAR SP 71 VOL: 9 PG:88 - 115 :: ANAL. :INT. LOG. :MATH.PROG. :VAR.

DYCKMAN,TR CIT: 0.53
THE INVESTIGATION OF COST VARIANCES
JAR AU 69 VOL: 7 PG:215 - 244 :: ANAL. :INT. LOG. :MATH.PROG. :VAR.

DYCKMAN,TR CIT: 0.41
THE EFFECTS OF ALTERNATIVE ACCOUNTING TECHNIQUES ON CERTAIN MANAGEMENT DECISIONS
JAR SP 64 VOL: 2 PG:91 - 107 :: NON-PAR. :LAB. :OTH.BEH. :INV.

DYCKMAN,TR CIT: 0.24
ON THE INVESTMENT DECISION
TAR AP 64 VOL: 39 PG:285 - 295 :: NON-PAR. :LAB. :N/A :INV.

DYE ,RA CIT: 2
RELATIVE PERFORMANCE EVALUATION AND PROJECT SELECTION
JAR SP 92 VOL: 30 PG:27 - 52 :: DES.STAT. :INT. LOG. :INF.ECO./AG. :EXEC.COMP.

DYE ,RA CIT: 0
INFORMALLY MOTIVATED AUDITOR REPLACEMENT
JAE DE 91 VOL: 14 PG:347 - 373 :: DES.STAT. :INT. LOG. :INF.ECO./AG. :ORG.

DYE ,RA ; SEC: BALACHANDRAN,BV ; THIR: MAGEE ,RP CIT: 1
CONTINGENT FEES FOR AUDIT FIRMS
JAR AU 90 VOL: 28 PG:239 - 266 :: DES.STAT. :INT. LOG. :INF.ECO./AG. :AUD.BEH.

DYE ,RA CIT: 1
MANDATORY VERSUS VOLUNTARY DISCLOSURES: THE CASES OF FINANCIAL AND REAL EXTERNALITIES
TAR JA 90 VOL: 65 PG:1 - 24 :: DES.STAT. :INT. LOG. :INF.ECO./AG. :INFO.STRUC.

DYE ,RA CIT: 0.8
EARNINGS MANAGEMENT IN AN OVERLAPPING GENERATIONS MODEL
JAR AU 88 VOL: 26 PG:195 - 235 :: DES.STAT. :INT. LOG. :INF.ECO./AG. :REV.REC.

DYE ,RA CIT: 2.38
DISCLOSURE OF NONPROPRIETARY INFORMATION
JAR SP 85 VOL: 23 PG:123 - 145 :: REGRESS. :INT. LOG. :INF.ECO./AG. :FIN.METH.

DYE ,RA CIT: 0.5
STRATEGIC ACCOUNTING CHOICE AND THE EFFECTS OF ALTERNATIVE FINANCIAL REPORTING REQUIREMENTS
JAR AU 85 VOL: 23 PG:544 - 574 :: REGRESS. :INT. LOG. :THEORY :INFO.STRUC.

DYE ,RA CIT: 1.5
COMMUNICATION AND POST-DECISION INFORMATION
JAR AU 83 VOL: 21 PG:514 - 533 :: ANAL. :INT. LOG. :INF.ECO./AG. :MAN.DEC.CHAR.

DYER ,JC ; SEC: MCHUGH,AJ CIT: 0.47
THE TIMELINESS OF THE AUSTRALIAN ANNUAL REPORT
JAR AU 75 VOL: 13 PG:204 - 219 :: NON-PAR. :PRIM. :OTH.STAT. :TIM.

DYKXHOORN,HJ ; SEC: SINNING,KE CIT: 0
PERCEPTIONS OF AUDITOR INDEPENDENCE: ITS PERCEIVED EFFECT ON THE LOAN AND INVESTMENT DECISIONS OF GERMAN FINANCIAL STATEMENT USE
AOS 04 82 VOL: 7 PG:337 - 348 :: ANOVA :LAB. :HIPS :INDEP.

DYKXHOORN,HJ ; SEC: SINNING,KE CIT: 0
WIRTSCHAFTSPRUFER PERCEPTION OF AUDITOR INDEPENDENCE
TAR JA 81 VOL: 56 PG:97 - 107 :: NON-PAR. :SURV. :OTH.BEH. :INDEP.

DYL ,EA ; SEC: LILLY ,MS CIT: 0.13
A NOTE ON INSTITUTIONAL CONTRIBUTIONS TO THE ACCOUNTING LITERATURE
AOS 02 85 VOL: 10 PG:171 - 176 :: REGRESS. :SEC. :INSTIT. :METHOD.

DEANGELO,L ; FIRS: COLLINS,DW CIT: 1.67
ACCOUNTING INFORMATION AND CORPORATE GOVERNANCE: MARKET AND ANALYST REACTIONS TO EARNINGS OF FIRMS ENGAGED IN PROXY CONTESTS
JAE OC 90 VOL: 13 PG:213 - 247 :: REGRESS. :PRIM. :TIME SER. :BUS.COMB.

EASTON,PD ; SEC: HARRIS,TS ; THIR: OHLSON,JA CIT: 2
AGGREGATE ACCOUNTING EARNINGS CAN EXPLAIN MOST OF SECURITY RETURNS: THE CASE OF LONG RETURN INTERVALS
JAE JN 92 VOL: 15 PG:119 - 142 :: REGRESS. :PRIM. :EMH :FIN.METH.

EASTON,PD ; SEC: HARRIS,TS CIT: 3.5
EARNINGS AS AN EXPLANATORY VARIABLE FOR RETURNS
JAR SP 91 VOL: 29 PG:19 - 36 :: REGRESS. :PRIM. :EMH :FIN.METH.

EASTON,PD ; SEC: ZMIJEWSKI,ME CIT: 5.5
CROSS-SECTIONAL VARIATION IN THE STOCK MARKET RESPONSE TO ACCOUNTING EARNINGS ANNOUNCEMENTS
JAE JL 89 VOL: 11 PG:117 - 141 :: REGRESS. :PRIM. :EMH :FIN.METH.

EASTON,PD CIT: 0.63
ACCOUNTING EARNINGS AND SECURITY VALUATION: EMPIRICAL EVIDENCE OF THE FUNDAMENTAL LINKS
JAR ST 85 VOL: 23 PG:54 - 77 :: REGRESS. :PRIM. :EMH :CASH DIV.

EAVES ,BC CIT: 0.18
OPERATIONAL AXIOMATIC ACCOUNTING MECHANICS
TAR JL 66 VOL: 41 PG:426 - 442 :: ANAL. :INT. LOG. :THEORY :FIN.METH.

ECKEL ,LG CIT: 0.06
ARBITRARY AND INCORRIGIBLE ALLOCATIONS
TAR OC 76 VOL: 51 PG:764 - 777 :: QUAL. :INT. LOG. :THEORY :COST.ALLOC.

EDEY ,HC CIT: 0
COMPANY ACCOUNTS IN BRITAIN: THE JENKINS REPORT
TAR AP 63 VOL: 38 PG:262 - 265 :: QUAL. :INT. LOG. :INSTIT. :FIN.METH.

EDGAR ,SM ; FIRS: PEAVY ,JW CIT: 0
RATING ELECTRIC UTILITY COMMERCIAL PAPER
JAA WI 85 VOL: 8 PG:125 - 135 :: REGRESS. :PRIM. :OTH.STAT. :LTD

EDMONDS,TP ; FIRS: ALFORD,MR CIT: 0.08
A REPLICATION: DOES AUDIT INVOLVEMENT AFFECT THE QUALITY OF INTERIM REPORT NUMBERS?
JAA SP 81 VOL: 4 PG:255 - 264 :: DES.STAT. :SEC. :THEORY :INT.REP.

EDWARDS,EO CIT: 0.12
THE STATE OF CURRENT VALUE ACCOUNTING
TAR AP 75 VOL: 50 PG:235 - 245 :: QUAL. :INT. LOG. :THEORY :VALUAT.(INFL.)

EDWARDS,JD ; FIRS: DRINKWATER,D CIT: 0
THE NATURE OF TAXES AND THE MATCHING PRINCIPLE
TAR JL 65 VOL: 40 PG:579 - 582 :: QUAL. :INT. LOG. :THEORY :TAXES

EGER ,C ; FIRS: BEAVER,WH ; THIR: RYAN ,S ; FOUR: WOLFSON,M CIT: 1
FINANCIAL REPORTING, SUPPLEMENTAL DISCLOSURES, AND BANK SHARE PRICES
JAR AU 89 VOL: 27 PG:157 - 178 :: REGRESS. :PRIM. :OTH.STAT. :INFO.STRUC.

EGER ,C ; SEC: DICKHAUT,JW CIT: 0.45
AN EXAMINATION OF THE CONSERVATIVE INFORMATION PROCESSING BIAS IN AN ACCOUNTING FRAMEWORK
JAR AU 82 VOL: 20 PG:711 - 723 :: REGRESS. :LAB. :HIPS :MAN.DEC.CHAR.

EGGLETON,IRC ; FIRS: LUCKETT,PF CIT: 0
FEEDBACK AND MANAGEMENT ACCOUNTING: A REVIEW OF RESEARCH INTO BEHAVIOURAL CONSEQUENCES
AOS 04 91 VOL: 16 PG:371 - 394 :: REGRESS. :SEC. :HIPS :AUD.BEH.

EGGLETON,IRC CIT: 0.18
INTUITIVE TIME-SERIES EXTRAPOLATION
JAR SP 82 VOL: 20 PG:68 - 102 :: DES.STAT. :LAB. :HIPS :BUDG.& PLAN.

EGGLETON,IRC ; SEC: PENMAN,SH ; THIR: TWOMBLY,JR CIT: 0.82
ACCOUNTING CHANGES AND STOCK PRICES: AN EXAMINATION OF SELECTED UNCONTROLLED VARIABLES
JAR SP 76 VOL: 14 PG:66 - 88 :: NON-PAR. :PRIM. :EMH :ACC.CHNG.

EGGLETON,IRC CIT: 0.35
PATTERNS, PROTOTYPES, AND PREDICTIONS: AN EXPLORATORY STUDY
JAR ST 76 VOL: 14 PG:68 - 131 :: ANOVA :LAB. :HIPS :N/A

EGGLETON,IRC ; FIRS: DICKHAUT,JW CIT: 0.41
AN EXAMINATION OF THE PROCESSES UNDERLYING COMPARATIVE JUDGMENTS OF NUMERICAL STIMULI
JAR SP 75 VOL: 13 PG:38 - 72 :: DES.STAT. :LAB. :HIPS :N/A

EHN ,P ; FIRS: CARLSSON,J ; THIR: ERLANDER,B ; FOUR: PERBY ,M ; FIFT: SANDBERG,A CIT: 0.07
PLANNING AND CONTROL FROM THE PERSPECTIVE OF LABOR: A SHORT REPRESENTATION OF THE DEMOS PROJECT
AOS 34 78 VOL: 3 PG:249 - 260 :: QUAL. :FIELD :OTH. :BUDG.& PLAN.

EHRENREICH,K ; FIRS: GROVE ,HD ; SEC: MOCK ,TJ CIT: 0.06
A REVIEW OF HUMAN RESOURCE ACCOUNTING MEASUREMENT SYSTEMS FROM A MEASUREMENT THEORY PERSPECTIVE
AOS 03 77 VOL: 2 PG:219 - 236 :: QUAL. :SEC. :OTH.BEH. :HRA

EICHENSEHER,JW ; SEC: HAGIGI,M ; THIR: SHIELDS,D CIT: 0.25
MARKET REACTION TO AUDITOR CHANGES BY OTC COMPANIES
AUD AU 89 VOL: 9 PG:29 - 40 :: REGRESS. :PRIM. :EMH :OTH.MANAG.

EICHENSEHER,JW ; FIRS: DAMOS ,P ; THIR: HOLT ,DL CIT: 0
SPECIALIZED KNOWLEDGE AND ITS COMMUNICATION IN AUDITING
CAR AU 89 VOL: 6 PG:91 - 109 :: REGRESS. :SURV. :OTH.BEH. :OPER.AUD.

EICHENSEHER,JW ; FIRS: DANOS ,P CIT: 0.57
LONG-TERM TRENDS TOWARD SELLER CONCENTRATION IN THE US AUDIT MARKET
TAR OC 86 VOL: 61 PG:633 - 650 :: REGRESS. :PRIM. :OTH.STAT. :ORG.& ENVIR.

EICHENSEHER,JW CIT: 0.13
THE EFFECTS OF FOREIGN OPERATIONS ON DOMESTIC AUDITOR SELECTION
JAA SP 85 VOL: 8 PG:195 - 209 :: REGRESS. :PRIM. :OTH. :SEG.REP.

EICHENSEHER,JW ; SEC: SHIELDS,D CIT: 1.3
THE CORRELATES OF CPA-FIRM CHANGE FOR PUBLICLY-HELD CORPORATIONS
AUD SP 83 VOL: 2 PG:23 - 37 :: NON-PAR. :SURV. :OTH.BEH. :ORG.

EICHENSEHER,JW ; FIRS: DANOS ,P CIT: 0.73
AUDIT INDUSTRY DYNAMICS: FACTORS AFFECTING CHANGES IN CLIENT-INDUSTRY MARKETSHARES
JAR AU 82 VOL: 20 PG:604 - 616 :: ANOVA :PRIM. :OTH.STAT. :ORG.

EICHENSEHER,JW ; SEC: DANOS ,P CIT: 1
THE ANALYSIS OF INDUSTRY-SPECIFIC AUDITOR CONCENTRATION: TOWARDS AN EXPLANATORY MODEL
TAR JL 81 VOL: 56 PG:479 - 492 :: MIXED :PRIM. :OTH.STAT. :ORG.

EICKHOFF,R ; FIRS: HARRELL,AM CIT: 0
AUDITORS' INFLUENCE ORIENTATION AND THEIR AFFECTIVE RESPONSES TO THE BIG EIGHT WORK ENVIRONMENT
AUD SP 88 VOL: 07 PG:105 - 118 :: REGRESS. :SURV. :OTH.BEH. :AUD.BEH.

EIGEN ,MM CIT: 0
IS POOLING REALLY NECESSARY?
TAR JL 65 VOL: 40 PG:536 - 540 :: QUAL. :INT. LOG. :THEORY :BUS.COMB.

EINHORN,HJ ; SEC: HOGARTH,RM CIT: 1.17
BEHAVIOURAL DECISION THEORY: PROCESSES OF JUDGMENT AND CHOICE
JAR SP 81 VOL: 19 PG:1 - 31 :: QUAL. :SEC. :HIPS :N/A

EINHORN,HJ CIT: 0.94
A SYNTHESIS: ACCOUNTING AND BEHAVIOURAL SCIENCE
JAR ST 76 VOL: 14 PG:196 - 206 :: QUAL. :INT. LOG. :HIPS :METHOD.

EINING,MM ; FIRS: LOEBBECKE,JK ; THIR: WILLINGHAM,JJ CIT: 0.5
AUDITORS' EXPERIENCE WITH MATERIAL IRREGULARITIES: FREQUENCY, NATURE, AND DETECTABILITY
AUD AU 89 VOL: 9 PG:1 - 28 :: REGRESS. :SURV. :OTH.STAT. :PLAN.

EL-GAZZAR,S ; SEC: LILIEN,S ; THIR: PASTENA,V CIT: 0.25
THE USE OF OFF-BALANCE SHEET FINANCING TO CIRCUMVENT FINANCIAL COVENANT RESTRICTIONS
JAA SP 89 VOL: 4 PG:217 - 231 :: REGRESS. :PRIM. :OTH.STAT. :SPEC.ITEMS

EL-GAZZAR,S ; SEC: LILIEN,S ; THIR: PASTENA,V CIT: 0.86
ACCOUNTING FOR LEASES BY LESSEES
JAE OC 86 VOL: 8 PG:217 - 238 :: REGRESS. :PRIM. :OTH.STAT. :LEASES

EL-SHESHAI,KM ; FIRS: ABDEL-KHALIK,AR CIT: 0.92
INFORMATION CHOICE AND UTILIZATION IN AN EXPERIMENT ON DEFAULT PREDICTION
JAR AU 80 VOL: 18 PG:325 - 342 :: DES.STAT. :LAB. :HIPS :BUS.FAIL.

ELAM ,R ; FIRS: NIKOLAI,LA CIT: 0
THE POLLUTION CONTROL TAX INCENTIVE: A NON-INCENTIVE
TAR JA 79 VOL: 54 PG:119 - 131 :: ANAL. :SIM. :OTH.STAT. :TAXES

ELAM ,R CIT: 0.41
THE EFFECT OF LEASE DATA ON THE PREDICTIVE ABILITY OF FINANCIAL RATIOS
TAR JA 75 VOL: 50 PG:25 - 43 :: NON-PAR. :PRIM. :OTH. :BUS.FAIL.

ELGERS,PT ; SEC: MURRAY,D CIT: 0
THE RELATIVE AND COMPLEMENTARY PERFORMANCE OF ANALYST AND SECURITY-PRICE-BASED MEASURES OF EXPECTED EARNINGS
JAE JN 92 VOL: 15 PG:303 - 316 :: REGRESS. :PRIM. :OTH.STAT. :FOREC.

ELGERS,P ; SEC: CALLAHAN,C ; THIR: STROCK,E CIT: 0.17
THE EFFECT OF EARNINGS YIELDS UPON THE ASSOCIATION BETWEEN UNEXPECTED EARNINGS AND SECURITY RETURNS; A RE-EXAMINATION
TAR OC 87 VOL: 62 PG:763 - 773 :: REGRESS. :PRIM. :EMH :FIN.METH.

ELGERS,PT ; FIRS: BLOOM ,R ; THIR: MURRAY,D CIT: 0.11
FUNCTIONAL FIXATION IN PRODUCT PRICING: A COMPARISON OF INDIVIDUALS AND GROUPS
AOS 01 84 VOL: 9 PG:1 - 11 :: MIXED :LAB. :HIPS :PP&E / DEPR

ELGERS,PT ; SEC: MURRAY,D CIT: 0
THE IMPACT OF THE CHOICE OF MARKET INDEX ON THE EMPIRICAL EVALUATION OF ACCOUNTING DETERMINED RISK MEASURES
TAR AP 82 VOL: 57 PG:358 - 375 :: REGRESS. :PRIM. :EMH :N/A

ELGERS,PT CIT: 0
ACCOUNTING-BASED RISK PREDICTIONS: A RE-EXAMINATION
TAR JL 80 VOL: 55 PG:389 - 408 :: REGRESS. :PRIM. :EMH :FOREC.

ELGERS,PT ; FIRS: CLARK ,JJ CIT: 0
FORECASTED INCOME STATEMENTS: AN INVESTOR PERSPECTIVE
TAR OC 73 VOL: 48 PG:668 - 678 :: CORR. :CASE :OTH.STAT. :BUDG.& PLAN.

ELIAS ,N CIT: 0.67
THE EFFECTS OF FINANCIAL INFORMATION SYMMETRY ON CONFLICT RESOLUTION: AN EXPERIMENT IN THE CONTEXT OF LABOR NEGOTIATIONS
TAR JL 90 VOL: 65 PG:606 - 623 :: REGRESS. :LAB. :OTH.BEH. :ORG.& ENVIR.

ELIAS ,N CIT: 0.82
THE EFFECTS OF HUMAN ASSET STATEMENTS ON THE INVESTMENT DECISION: AN EXPERIMENT
JAR ST 72 VOL: 10 PG:215 - 233 :: ANOVA :LAB. :OTH.BEH. :HRA

ELITZUR,RR CIT: 0
A MODEL OF TRANSLATION OF FOREIGN FINANCIAL STATEMENTS UNDER INFLATION IN THE U.S. AND CANADA
CAR SP 91 VOL: 7 PG:466 - 484 :: DES.STAT. :INT. LOG. :THEORY :FOR.CUR.

ELLIOTT,EL ; SEC: LARREA,J ; THIR: RIVERA,JM CIT: 0
ACCOUNTING AID TO DEVELOPING COUNTRIES: SOME ADDITIONAL CONSIDERATIONS
TAR OC 68 VOL: 43 PG:763 - 768 :: QUAL. :INT. LOG. :INSTIT. :OTH.MANAG.

ELLIOTT,JA ; SEC: HANNA ,JD ; THIR: SHAW ,WH CIT: 0
TE EVALUATION BY THE FINANCIAL MARKETS OF CHANGES IN BANK LOAN LOSS RESERVE LEVELS
TAR OC 91 VOL: 66 PG:847 - 861 :: REGRESS. :PRIM. :EMH :OTH. NON-C/A

ELLIOTT,JA ; SEC: PHILBRICK,DR CIT: 0
ACCOUNTING CHANGES AND EARNINGS PREDICTABILITY
TAR JA 90 VOL: 65 PG:157 - 174 :: REGRESS. :PRIM. :OTH. :ACC.CHNG.

ELLIOTT,JA ; SEC: SHAW,WH CIT: 0.2
WRITE-OFFS AS ACCOUNTING PROCEDURES TO MANAGE PERCEPTIONS
JAR ST 88 VOL: 26 PG:91 - 126 :: REGRESS. :PRIM. :EMH :REV.REC.

ELLIOTT,JA ; SEC: RICHARDSON,G ; THIR: DYCKMAN,TR ; FOUR: DUKES ,RE CIT: 1
THE IMPACT OF SFAS NO.2 ON FIRM EXPENDITURES ON RESEARCH AND DEVELOPMENT: REPLICATIONS AND EXTENSIONS
JAR SP 84 VOL: 22 PG:85 - 102 :: NON-PAR. :PRIM. :EMH :R & D

ELLIOTT,JA CIT: 1
SUBJECT TO AUDIT OPINIONS AND ABNORMAL SECURITY RETURNS: OUTCOMES AND AMBIGUITIES
JAR AU 82 VOL: 20 PG:617 - 638 :: REGRESS. :PRIM. :EMH :OPIN.

ELLIOTT,JA ; FIRS: DUKES ,RE ; SEC: DYCKMAN,TR CIT: 1.38
ACCOUNTING FOR RESEARCH AND DEVELOPMENT COSTS: THE IMPACT ON RESEARCH AND DEVELOPMENT EXPENDITURES
JAR ST 80 VOL: 18 PG:1 - 26 :: NON-PAR. :PRIM. :THEORY :R & D

ELLIOTT,JW ; SEC: UPHOFF,HL CIT: 0.12
PREDICTING THE NEAR TERM PROFIT AND LOSS STATEMENT WITH AN ECONOMETRIC MODEL: A FEASIBILITY STUDY
JAR AU 72 VOL: 10 PG:259 - 274 :: MIXED :PRIM. :TIME SER. :BUDG.& PLAN.

ELLIOTT,RK ; FIRS: ASHTON,RH ; SEC: WILLINGHAM,JJ CIT: 0.33
AN EMPIRICAL ANALYSIS OF AUDIT DELAY
JAR AU 87 VOL: 25 PG:275 - 292 :: REGRESS. :SURV. :INSTIT. :TIM.

ELLIOTT,RK CIT: 1.1
UNIQUE AUDIT METHODS: PEAT MARWICK INTERNATIONAL
AUD SP 83 VOL: 2 PG:1 - 12 :: QUAL. :INT. LOG. :OTH. :AUD.THEOR.

ELNICKI,RA CIT: 0
HOSPITAL WORKING CAPITAL: AN EMPIRICAL STUDY
JAR ST 77 VOL: 15 PG:209 - 218 :: REGRESS. :PRIM. :TIME SER. :OTH.MANAG.

ELY ,KM CIT: 0.5
INTERINDUSTRY DIFFERENCES IN THE RELATION BETWEEN COMPENSATION AND FIRM PERFORMANCE VARIABLES
JAR SP 91 VOL: 29 PG:37 - 58 :: REGRESS. :PRIM. :TIME SER. :ORG.& ENVIR.

EMBY ,C ; SEC: GIBBINS,M CIT: 0
GOOD JUDGMENT IN PUBLIC ACCOUNTING: QUALITY AND JUSTIFICATION
CAR SP 88 VOL: 4 PG:287 - 313 :: REGRESS. :SURV. :HIPS :JUDG.

EMERY ,DR ; SEC: BARRON,FH ; THIR: MESSIER JR,WF CIT: 0.09
CONJOINT MEASUREMENT AND THE ANALYSIS OF NOISY DATA: A COMMENT
JAR AU 82 VOL: 20 PG:450 - 458 :: NON-PAR. :SIM. :HIPS :METHOD.

EMERY ,GW ; SEC: COGGER,KO CIT: 0.09
THE MEASUREMENT OF LIQUIDITY
JAR AU 82 VOL: 20 PG:290 - 303 :: ANAL. :PRIM. :OTH.STAT. :BUS.FAIL.

ENG ,R ; FIRS: WIESEN,JL CIT: 0
CORPORATE PERKS: DISCLOSURE AND TAX CONSIDERATIONS
JAA WI 79 VOL: 2 PG:101 - 121 :: QUAL. :INT. LOG. :THEORY :TAXES

ENGLE ,TJ CIT: 0
INCREASING CONFIRMATION RESPONSE RATES: PRENOTIFICATIONS, MONETARY INCENTIVES AND ADDRESSEE DIFFERENCES
JAA WI 91 VOL: 6 PG:109 - 121 :: REGRESS. :FIELD :OTH. :SPEC.ITEMS

ENGLEBRECHT,TD ; SEC: JAMISON,RW CIT: 0.07
AN EMPIRICAL INQUIRY INTO THE ROLE OF THE TAX COURT IN THE VALUATION OF PROPERTY FOR CHARITABLE CONTRIBUTION PURPOSES
TAR JL 79 VOL: 54 PG:554 - 562 :: REGRESS. :PRIM. :OTH.STAT. :TAXES

ENGSTROM,JH CIT: 0
THE GOVERNMENTAL REPORTING ENTITY
JAA SU 85 VOL: 8 PG:305 - 318 :: REGRESS. :SURV. :THEORY :FIN.METH.

ENGSTROM,JH CIT: 0
PENSION REPORTING BY MUNICIPALITIES
JAA SP 84 VOL: 7 PG:197 - 211 :: DES.STAT. :INT. LOG. :THEORY :PENS.

ENIS ,CR CIT: 0.2
THE IMPACT OF CURRENT-VALUED DATA ON THE PREDICTIVE JUDGMENTS OF INVESTORS
AOS 02 88 VOL: 13 PG:123 - 145 :: REGRESS. :LAB. :HIPS :VALUAT.(INFL.)

EPSTEIN,MJ ; FIRS: BRAVENEC,LL ; THIR: CRUMBLEY,DL CIT: 0
TAX IMPACT IN CORPORATE SOCIAL RESPONSIBILITY DECISIONS AND REPORTING
AOS 02 77 VOL: 2 PG:131 - 140 :: QUAL. :INT. LOG. :THEORY :HRA

EPSTEIN,MJ ; SEC: FLAMHOLTZ,EG ; THIR: MCDONOUGH,JJ CIT: 0.41
CORPORATE SOCIAL ACCOUNTING IN THE U.S.A.: STATE OF THE ART AND FUTURE PROSPECTS
AOS 01 76 VOL: 1 PG:23 - 42 :: QUAL. :SEC. :THEORY :HRA

ERLANDER,B ; FIRS: CARLSSON,J ; SEC: EHN ,P ; FOUR: PERBY ,M ; FIFT: SANDBERG,A CIT: 0.07
PLANNING AND CONTROL FROM THE PERSPECTIVE OF LABOR: A SHORT REPRESENTATION OF THE DEMOS PROJECT
AOS 34 78 VOL: 3 PG:249 - 260 :: QUAL. :FIELD :OTH. :BUDG.& PLAN.

ESKEW ,RK CIT: 0.14
THE FORECASTING ABILITY OF ACCOUNTING RISK MEASURES: SOME ADDITIONAL EVIDENCE
TAR JA 79 VOL: 54 PG:107 - 118 :: ANOVA :PRIM. :OTH.STAT. :FIN.METH.

ESKEW ,RK CIT: 0.18
AN EXAMINATION OF THE ASSOCIATION BETWEEN ACCOUNTING AND SHARE PRICE DATA IN THE EXTRACTIVE PETROLEUM INDUSTRY
TAR AP 75 VOL: 50 PG:316 - 324 :: REGRESS. :PRIM. :EMH :FIN.METH.

ESPAHBODI,H ; SEC: STROCK,E ; THIR: TEHRANIAN,H CIT: 0
IMPACT ON EQUITY PRICES OF PRONOUNCEMENTS RELATED TO NONPENSION POST RETIREMENT BENEFITS
JAE DE 91 VOL: 14 PG:323 - 345 :: REGRESS. :PRIM. :EMH :PENS.

ESPAHBODI,R ; SEC: TEHRANIAN,H CIT: 0.25
STOCK MARKET REACTIONS TO THE ISSUANCE OF FAS 33 AND ITS PRECEDING EXPOSURE DRAFTS
CAR SP 89 VOL: 5 PG:575 - 591 :: REGRESS. :PRIM. :EMH :VALUAT.(INFL.)

ESPEJO,J ; FIRS: ABDEL-KHALIK,AR CIT: 0.6
EXPECTATIONS DATA AND THE PREDICTIVE VALUE OF INTERIM REPORTING
JAR SP 78 VOL: 16 PG:1 - 13 :: REGRESS. :LAB. :TIME SER. :FOREC.

ESPELAND,WN ; SEC: HIRSCH,PM CIT: 0.33
OWNERSHIP CHANGES, ACCOUNTING PRACTICE AND THE REDEFINITION OF THE CORPORATION
AOS 02 90 VOL: 15 PG:77 - 96 :: REGRESS. :SEC. :HIST. :ORG.& ENVIR.

ESPOSITO,RS ; FIRS: BLOCHER,E ; THIR: WILLINGHAM,JJ CIT: 0.1
AUDITOR'S ANALYTICAL REVIEW JUDGMENTS FOR PAYROLL EXPENSE
AUD AU 83 VOL: 3 PG:75 - 91 :: DES.STAT. :LAB. :OTH.BEH. :ANAL.REV.

ESQUIBEL,AK ; FIRS: LANZILLOTTI,RF CIT: 0
MEASURING DAMAGES IN COMMERCIAL LITIGATION: PRESENT VALUE OF LOST OPPORTUNITIES
JAA WI 90 VOL: 5 PG:125 - 142 :: DES.STAT. :INT. LOG. :OTH. :LITIG.

ESSEX ,S ; FIRS: COOPER,DJ CIT: 0.31
ACCOUNTING INFORMATION AND EMPLOYEE DECISION MAKING
AOS 03 77 VOL: 2 PG:201 - 218 :: DES.STAT. :SURV. :OTH.BEH. :HRA

ESTES ,RW CIT: 0.41
SOCIO-ECONOMIC ACCOUNTING AND EXTERNAL DISECONOMIES
TAR AP 72 VOL: 47 PG:284 - 290 :: QUAL. :INT. LOG. :INSTIT. :HRA

ESTES ,RW CIT: 0.06
AN ASSESSMENT OF THE USEFULNESS OF CURRENT COST AND PRICE-LEVEL INFORMATION BY FINANCIAL STATEMENT USERS
JAR AU 68 VOL: 6 PG:200 - 207 :: NON-PAR. :SURV. :N/A :VALUAT.(INFL.)

ESTRIN,TL ; FIRS: MOCK ,TJ ; THIR: VASARHELYI,MA CIT: 0.71
LEARNING PATTERNS, DECISION APPROACH, AND VALUE OF INFORMATION
JAR SP 72 VOL: 10 PG:129 - 153 :: ANOVA :LAB. :HIPS :INFO.STRUC.

ETTENSON,RT ; FIRS: KROGSTAD,JL ; THIR: SHANTEAU,J CIT: 0.67
CONTEXT AND EXPERIENCE IN AUDITORS' MATERIALITY JUDGMENTS
AUD AU 84 VOL: 4 PG:54 - 74 :: ANOVA :LAB. :OTH.BEH. :MAT.

ETTREDGE,M ; SEC: GREENBERG,R CIT: 0.67
DETERMINANTS OF FEE CUTTING ON INITIAL AUDIT ENGAGEMENTS
JAR SP 90 VOL: 28 PG:198 - 210 :: REGRESS. :PRIM. :OTH.STAT. :ORG.

ETTREDGE,M ; FIRS: BUBLITZ,B CIT: 0.5
THE INFORMATION IN DISCRETIONARY OUTLAYS: ADVERTISING, RESEARCH, AND DEVELOPMENT
TAR JA 89 VOL: 64 PG:108 - 124 :: REGRESS. :PRIM. :HIPS :R & D

ETTREDGE,M ; SEC: SHANE ,PB ; THIR: SMITH ,D CIT: 0
AUDIT FIRM SIZE AND THE ASSOCIATION BETWEEN REPORTED EARNINGS AND SECURITY RETURNS
AUD SP 88 VOL: 07 PG:29 - 42 :: REGRESS. :PRIM. :EMH :AUD.THEOR.

ETZIONI,A CIT: 0.25
A MATTER OF GOALS: HIGH GROWTH-OR DEFICIT REDUCTION?
JAA AU 89 VOL: 4 PG:555 - 570 :: DES.STAT. :INT. LOG. :OTH. :ORG.& ENVIR.

EUDY ,KH ; FIRS: HOLDER,WW CIT: 0
A FRAMEWORK FOR BUILDING AN ACCOUNTING CONSTITUTION
JAA WI 82 VOL: 5 PG:110 - 125 :: QUAL. :INT. LOG. :THEORY :FASB SUBM.

EUSKE ,KJ ; FIRS: ANSARI,SL CIT: 1.17
RATIONAL, RATIONALIZING, AND REIFYING USES OF ACCOUNTING DATA IN ORGANIZATIONS
AOS 06 87 VOL: 12 PG:549 - 570 :: REGRESS. :SURV. :OTH.BEH. :COST.ALLOC.

EVANS III,JH ; FIRS: BAIMAN,S ; THIR: NAGARAJAN,NJ CIT: 0.5
COLLUSION IN AUDITING
JAR SP 91 VOL: 29 PG:1 - 18 :: DES.STAT. :INT. LOG. :INF.ECO./AG. :AUD.BEH.

EVANS III,JH ; FIRS: BAIMAN,S ; THIR: NOEL ,J CIT: 1.67
OPTIMAL CONTRACTS WITH A UTILITY-MAXIMIZING AUDITOR
JAR AU 87 VOL: 25 PG:217 - 244 :: ANAL. :INT. LOG. :INF.ECO./AG. :AUD.BEH.

EVANS III,JH ; SEC: PATTON,JM CIT: 0.83
SIGNALING AND MONITORING IN PUBLIC-SECTOR ACCOUNTING
JAR ST 87 VOL: 25 PG:130 - 164 :: MIXED :SURV. :INF.ECO./AG. :FIN.METH.

EVANS III,JH ; SEC: LEWIS ,BL ; THIR: PATTON,JM CIT: 0.14
AN ECONOMIC MODELING APPROACH TO CONTINGENCY THEORY AND MANAGEMENT CONTROL
AOS 06 86 VOL: 11 PG:483 - 498 :: DES.STAT. :INT. LOG. :INF.ECO./AG. :INT.CONT.

EVANS III,JH ; SEC: PATTON,JM CIT: 1.1
AN ECONOMIC ANALYSIS OF PARTICIPATION IN THE MUNICIPAL FINANCE OFFICERS ASSOCIATION CERTIFICATE OF CONFORMANCE PROGRAM
JAE AG 83 VOL: 5 PG:151 - 175 :: OTH.QUANT. :PRIM. :INSTIT. :FIN.METH.

EVANS III,JH ; FIRS: BAIMAN,S CIT: 2.5
PRE-DECISION INFORMATION AND PARTICIPATIVE MANAGEMENT CONTROL SYSTEMS
JAR AU 83 VOL: 21 PG:371 - 395 :: ANAL. :INT. LOG. :INF.ECO./AG. :MANAG.

EVANS III,JH CIT: 0.54
OPTIMAL CONTRACTS WITH COSTLY CONDITIONAL AUDITING
JAR ST 80 VOL: 18 PG:108 - 128 :: ANAL. :INT. LOG. :INF.ECO./AG. :AUD.

EVEREST,GL ; SEC: WEBER ,R CIT: 0.25
A RELATIONAL APPROACH TO ACCOUNTING MODELS
TAR AP 77 VOL: 52 PG:340 - 359 :: ANAL. :INT. LOG. :OTH.STAT. :N/A

EVERETT,JO ; SEC: PORTER,GA CIT: 0
SAFE-HARBOR LEASING - UNRAVELING THE TAX IMPLICATIONS
JAA SP 84 VOL: 7 PG:241 - 256 :: MIXED :INT. LOG. :THEORY :LEASES

EWUSI-MENSAH,K CIT: 0.42
THE EXTERNAL ORGANIZATIONAL ENVIRONMENT AND ITS IMPACT ON MANAGEMENT INFORMATION SYSTEMS
AOS 04 81 VOL: 6 PG:301 - 316 :: QUAL. :INT. LOG. :OTH. :N/A

EZZAMEL,M ; SEC: BOURN ,M CIT: 0
THE ROLES OF ACCOUNTING INFORMATION SYSTEMS IN AN ORGANIZATION EXPERIENCING FINANCIAL CRISIS
AOS 05 90 VOL: 15 PG:399 - 424 :: REGRESS. :CASE :EXP.SYST. :MAN.DEC.CHAR.

FAGERBERG,P CIT: 0
CONCERNING THREE MISCHIEVOUS ACCOUNTS
TAR JL 72 VOL: 47 PG:454 - 457 :: QUAL. :INT. LOG. :N/A :FIN.METH.

FAIRCLOTH,AW ; SEC: RICCHIUTE,DN CIT: 0
AMBIGUITY INTOLERANCE AND FINANCIAL REPORTING ALTERNATIVES
AOS 01 81 VOL: 6 PG:53 - 68 :: DES.STAT. :SURV. :HIPS :FIN.METH.

FAIRFIELD,P ; FIRS: BURTON,JC CIT: 0.36
AUDITING EVOLUTION IN A CHANGING ENVIRONMENT
AUD WI 82 VOL: 1 PG:1 - 22 :: DES.STAT. :INT. LOG. :INSTIT. :ORG.

FAIRFIELD,PM ; FIRS: BABER ,WR ; THIR: HAGGARD,JA CIT: 0
THE EFFECT OF CONCERN ABOUT REPORTED INCOME DISCRETIONARY SPENDING DECISIONS: THE CASE OF RESEARCH AND DEVELOPMENT
TAR OC 91 VOL: 66 PG:818 - 829 :: REGRESS. :PRIM. :INF.ECO./AG. :R & D

FALK ,G ; FIRS: RONEN ,J CIT: 0.12
ACCOUNTING AGGREGATION AND THE ENTROPY MEASURE: AN EXPERIMENTAL APPROACH
TAR OC 73 VOL: 48 PG:696 - 717 :: NON-PAR. :LAB. :INF.ECO./AG. :INFO.STRUC.

FALK ,H CIT: 0
TOWARDS A FRAMEWORK FOR NOT-FOR-PROFIT ACCOUNTING
CAR SP 92 VOL: 8 PG:468 - 499 :: DES.STAT. :INT. LOG. :THEORY :FIN.METH.

FALK ,H CIT: 0.25
CONTEMPORARY ACCOUNTING RESEARCH: THE FIRST FIVE YEARS
CAR SP 89 VOL: 5 PG:816 - 825 :: REGRESS. :SEC. :THEORY :METHOD.

FALK ,H ; FIRS: BUZBY ,SL CIT: 0.29
DEMAND FOR SOCIAL RESPONSIBILITY INFORMATION BY UNIVERSITY INVESTORS
TAR JA 79 VOL: 54 PG:23 - 37 :: DES.STAT. :SURV. :INSTIT. :HRA

FALK ,H ; FIRS: BUZBY ,SL CIT: 0.2
A SURVEY OF THE INTEREST IN SOCIAL RESPONSIBILITY INFORMATION BY MUTUAL FUNDS
AOS 34 78 VOL: 3 PG:191 - 202 :: DES.STAT. :SURV. :OTH.BEH. :METHOD.

FALK ,H ; SEC: MILLER,JC CIT: 0.06
AMORTIZATION OF ADVERTISING EXPENDITURES
JAR SP 77 VOL: 15 PG:12 - 22 :: REGRESS. :PRIM. :OTH.STAT. :AMOR./DEPL.

FALK ,H ; SEC: HEINTZ,JA CIT: 0
ASSESSING INDUSTRY RISK BY RATIO ANALYSIS
TAR OC 75 VOL: 50 PG:758 - 779 :: NON-PAR. :PRIM. :N/A :FIN.METH.

FALK ,H ; SEC: OPHIR ,T CIT: 0.18
THE INFLUENCE OF DIFFERENCES IN ACCOUNTING POLICIES ON INVESTMENT DECISIONS
JAR SP 73 VOL: 11 PG:108 - 116 :: DES.STAT. :LAB. :OTH.BEH. :FIN.METH.

FALK ,H ; SEC: OPHIR ,T CIT: 0.12
THE EFFECT OF RISK ON USE OF FINANCIAL STATEMENTS BY INVESTMENT DECISION-MAKERS: A CASE STUDY
TAR AP 73 VOL: 48 PG:323 - 338 :: NON-PAR. :CASE :THEORY :N/A

FALK ,H CIT: 0
ASSESSING THE EFFECTIVENESS OF ACCOUNTING COURSES THROUGH FACET ANALYSIS
JAR AU 72 VOL: 10 PG:359 - 375 :: MIXED :FIELD :OTH.STAT. :EDUC.

FARAG ,SM CIT: 0
A PLANNING MODEL FOR THE DIVISIONALIZED ENTERPRISE
TAR AP 68 VOL: 43 PG:312 - 320 :: ANAL. :INT. LOG. :MATH.PROG. :BUDG.& PLAN.

FARBER,A ; FIRS: GOMBERG,M CIT: 0
THE BALANCE SHEET OF THE FUTURE
TAR JL 64 VOL: 39 PG:615 - 617 :: QUAL. :INT. LOG. :THEORY :FIN.METH.

FARMAN,WL CIT: 0
NATIONAL FLOW-OF-FUNDS: AN ACCOUNTING ANALYSIS
TAR AP 64 VOL: 39 PG:392 - 404 :: QUAL. :INT. LOG. :INSTIT. :HRA

FARMAN,WL ; SEC: HOU ,C CIT: 0
THE BALANCE OF PAYMENTS: AN ACCOUNTING ANALYSIS
TAR JA 63 VOL: 38 PG:133 - 141 :: QUAL. :INT. LOG. :THEORY :INT.DIFF.

FARMER,TA ; SEC: RITTENBERG,LE ; THIR: TROMPETER,GM CIT: 0.5
AN INVESTIGATION OF THE IMPACT OF ECONOMIC AND ORGANIZATIONAL FACTORS
AUD AU 87 VOL: 7 PG:1 - 14 :: REGRESS. :LAB. :OTH.BEH. :INDEP.

FARRELY,GE ; SEC: FERRIS,KR ; THIR: REICHENSTEIN,WR CIT: 0
PERCEIVED RISK, MARKET RISK, AND ACCOUNTING-DETERMINED RISK MEASURES
TAR AP 85 VOL: 60 PG:278 - 288 :: REGRESS. :SURV. :OTH.STAT. :FOREC.

FEINSCHREIBER,R CIT: 0
ACCELERATED DEPRECIATION: A PROPOSED NEW METHOD
JAR SP 69 VOL: 7 PG:17 - 21 :: DES.STAT. :SIM. :INSTIT. :PP&E / DEPR

FEKRAT,MA CIT: 0.06
THE CONCEPTUAL FOUNDATIONS OF ABSORPTION COSTING
TAR AP 72 VOL: 47 PG:351 - 355 :: QUAL. :INT. LOG. :THEORY :OVER.ALLOC.

FELIX JR,WL ; SEC: GRIMLUND,RA ; THIR: KOSTER,FJ ; FOUR: ROUSSEY,RS CIT: 0
ARTHUR ANDERSEN'S NEW MONETARY UNIT SAMPLING APPROACH
AUD AU 90 VOL: 9 PG:1 - 16 :: DES.STAT. :SIM. :EXP.SYST. :SAMP.

FELIX JR,WL ; FIRS: WALLER,WS CIT: 0
AUDITORS' CAUSAL JUDGMENTS: EFFECTS OF FORWARD VS BACKWARD INFERENCE ON INFORMATION PROCESSING
AOS 02 89 VOL: 14 PG:179 - 200 :: REGRESS. :LAB. :HIPS :JUDG.

FELIX JR,WL ; SEC: NILES ,MS CIT: 0
RESEARCH IN INTERNAL CONTROL EVALUATION
AUD SP 88 VOL: 07 PG:43 - 60 :: DES.STAT. :SEC. :THEORY :INT.CONT.

FELIX JR,WL ; FIRS: WALLER,WS CIT: 0.5
AUDITORS' COVARIATION JUDGMENTS
TAR AP 87 VOL: 62 PG:275 - 292 :: REGRESS. :LAB. :HIPS :JUDG.

FELIX JR,WL ; FIRS: GRIMLUND,RA CIT: 0.5
SIMULATION EVIDENCE AND ANALYSIS OF ALTERNATIVE METHODS OF EVALUATING DOLLAR-UNIT SAMPLES
TAR JL 87 VOL: 62 PG:455 - 479 :: DES.STAT. :SIM. :OTH.STAT. :SAMP.

FELIX JR,WL ; FIRS: WALLER,WS CIT: 2.22
THE AUDITOR AND LEARNING FROM EXPERIENCE: SOME CONJECTURES
AOS 34 84 VOL: 9 PG:383 - 406 :: QUAL. :INT. LOG. :HIPS :N/A

FELIX JR,WL ; FIRS: WALLER,WS CIT: 0.22
THE EFFECTS OF INCOMPLETE OUTCOME FEEDBACK ON AUDITORS' SELF-PERCEPTIONS OF JUDGMENT ABILITY
TAR OC 84 VOL: 59 PG:637 - 646 :: ANOVA :LAB. :HIPS :JUDG.

FELIX JR,WL ; SEC: KINNEY JR,WR CIT: 1.91
RESEARCH IN THE AUDITOR'S OPINION FORMULATION PROCESS: STATE OF THE ART
TAR AP 82 VOL: 57 PG:245 - 271 :: QUAL. :SEC. :OTH. :N/A

FELIX JR,WL ; SEC: GRIMLUND,RA CIT: 1.19
A SAMPLING MODEL FOR AUDIT TESTS OF COMPOSITE ACCOUNTS
JAR SP 77 VOL: 15 PG:23 - 41 :: ANAL. :INT. LOG. :OTH.STAT. :SAMP.

FELIX JR,WL CIT: 1.06
EVIDENCE ON ALTERNATIVE MEANS OF ASSESSING PRIOR PROBABILITY DISTRIBUTIONS FOR AUDIT DECISION MAKING
TAR OC 76 VOL: 51 PG:800 - 807 :: DES.STAT. :LAB. :OTH.STAT. :PROB.ELIC.

FELIX JR,WL CIT: 0
ESTIMATING THE RELATIONSHIP BETWEEN TECHNICAL CHANGE AND REPORTED PERFORMANCE
TAR JA 72 VOL: 47 PG:52 - 63 :: REGRESS. :PRIM. :TIME SER. :AUD.BEH.

FELLINGHAM,J ; FIRS: ANTLE ,R CIT: 0
RESOURCE RATIONING AND ORGANIZATIONAL SLACK IN A TWO-PERIOD MODEL
JAR SP 90 VOL: 28 PG:1 - 24 :: DES.STAT. :INT. LOG. :INF.ECO./AG. :EXEC.COMP.

FELLINGHAM,J ; FIRS: AMERSHI,AH ; SEC: DEMSKI,JS CIT: 0.38
SEQUENTIAL BAYESIAN ANALYSIS IN ACCOUNTING
CAR SP 85 VOL: 1 PG:176 - 192 :: DES.STAT. :INT. LOG. :INF.ECO./AG. :DEC.AIDS

FELLINGHAM,JC ; SEC: YOUNG ,RA CIT: 0
THE VALUE OF SELF-REPORTED COSTS IN REPEATED INVESTMENT DECISIONS
TAR OC 90 VOL: 65 PG:837 - 856 :: DES.STAT. :INT. LOG. :INF.ECO./AG. :DEC.AIDS

FELLINGHAM,JC ; SEC: NEWMAN,DP ; THIR: PATTERSON,ER CIT: 0.5
SAMPLING INFORMATION IN STRATEGIC AUDIT SETTINGS
AUD SP 89 VOL: 8 PG:1 - 21 :: DES.STAT. :INT. LOG. :INF.ECO./AG. :SAMP.

FELLINGHAM,JC ; SEC: YOUNG ,RA CIT: 0
SPECIAL ALLOCATIONS, INVESTMENT DECISIONS, AND TRANSACTIONS COSTS IN PARTNERSHIPS
JAR AU 89 VOL: 27 PG:179 - 200 :: DES.STAT. :INT. LOG. :INF.ECO./AG. :ORG.FORM

FELLINGHAM,JC ; SEC: WOLFSON,MA CIT: 0.5
TAXES AND RISK SHARING
TAR JA 85 VOL: 60 PG:10 - 17 :: DES.STAT. :INT. LOG. :INF.ECO./AG. :TAXES

FELLINGHAM,JC ; SEC: NEWMAN,DP CIT: 1
STRATEGIC CONSIDERATIONS IN AUDITING
TAR OC 85 VOL: 60 PG:634 - 650 :: REGRESS. :INT. LOG. :OTH.STAT. :PLAN.

FELTHAM,GA ; SEC: GIGLER,FB ; THIR: HUGHES,JS CIT: 0
THE EFFECTS OF LINE-OF-BUSINESS REPORTING ON COMPETITION IN OLIGOPOLY SETTINGS
CAR AU 92 VOL: 9 PG:1 - 23 :: DES.STAT. :INT. LOG. :INF.ECO./AG. :SEG.REP.

FELTHAM,GA ; SEC: XIE ,JZ CIT: 1
VOLUNTARY FINANCIAL DISCLOSURE IN AN ENTRY GAME WITH CONTINUA OF TYPES
CAR AU 92 VOL: 9 PG:46 - 80 :: DES.STAT. :INT. LOG. :INF.ECO./AG. :INFO.STRUC.

FELTHAM,GA ; FIRS: DATAR ,SM ; THIR: HUGHES,JS CIT: 1.5
THE ROLE OF AUDITS AND AUDIT QUALITY IN VALUING NEW ISSUES
JAE MR 91 VOL: 14 PG:3 - 49 :: DES.STAT. :INT. LOG. :INF.ECO./AG. :VALUAT.(INFL.)

FELTHAM,GA ; SEC: HUGHES,JS ; THIR: SIMUNIC,DA CIT: 0.5
EMPIRICAL ASSESSMENT OF THE IMPACT OF AUDITOR QUALITY ON THE VALUATION OF NEW ISSUES
JAE DE 91 VOL: 14 PG:375 - 399 :: REGRESS. :PRIM. :EMH :OPER.AUD.

FELTHAM,GA ; SEC: CHRISTENSEN,PO CIT: 0.2
FIRM-SPECIFIC INFORMATION AND EFFICIENT RESOURCE ALLOCATION
CAR AU 88 VOL: 5 PG:133 - 169 :: DES.STAT. :INT. LOG. :INF.ECO./AG. :EXEC.COMP.

FELTHAM,GA CIT: 0
JOHN BUTTERWORTH'S PIONEERING CONTRIBUTIONS TO THE ACCOUNTING AND INFORMATION ECONOMICS LITERATURE
CAR AU 84 VOL: 1 PG:87 - 98 :: REGRESS. :SEC. :THEORY :OTH.MANAG.

FELTHAM,GA ; FIRS: DEMSKI,JS CIT: 2.8
ECONOMIC INCENTIVES IN BUDGETARY CONTROL SYSTEMS
TAR AP 78 VOL: 53 PG:336 - 359 :: ANAL. :INT. LOG. :INF.ECO./AG. :BUDG.& PLAN.

FELTHAM,GA CIT: 0.38
COST AGGREGATION: AN INFORMATION ECONOMIC ANALYSIS
JAR SP 77 VOL: 15 PG:42 - 70 :: MIXED :SIM. :INF.ECO./AG. :INFO.STRUC.

FELTHAM,GA ; FIRS: DEMSKI,JS CIT: 0.47
FORECAST EVALUATION
TAR JL 72 VOL: 47 PG:533 - 548 :: MIXED :SIM. :INF.ECO./AG. :BUDG.& PLAN.

FELTHAM,GA CIT: 0.06
SOME QUANTITATIVE APPROACHES TO PLANNING FOR MULTIPRODUCT PRODUCTION SYSTEMS
TAR JA 70 VOL: 45 PG:11 - 26 :: ANAL. :INT. LOG. :MATH.PROG. :BUDG.& PLAN.

FELTHAM,GA ; SEC: DEMSKI,JS CIT: 0.76
THE USE OF MODELS IN INFORMATION EVALUATION
TAR OC 70 VOL: 45 PG:623 - 640 :: ANAL. :INT. LOG. :INF.ECO./AG. :MANAG.

FELTHAM,GA CIT: 0.47
THE VALUE OF INFORMATION
TAR OC 68 VOL: 43 PG:684 - 696 :: ANAL. :INT. LOG. :THEORY :INFO.STRUC.

FELTON,S ; SEC: MANN ,H CIT: 0
ACCOUNTING FOR A BREWERY OF LOUISBOURG
CAR AU 90 VOL: 7 PG:261 - 277 :: REGRESS. :CASE :HIST. :FIN.METH.

FERGUSON,P ; FIRS: BERRY ,AJ ; SEC: CAPPS ,T ; THIR: COOPER,D ; FIFT: HOPPER,T ; SIX: LOWE ,EA CIT: 3
MANAGEMENT CONTROL IN AN AREA OF THE NCB: RATIONALES OF ACCOUNTING PRACTICES IN A PUBLIC ENTERPRISE
AOS 01 85 VOL: 10 PG:3 - 28 :: REGRESS. :FIELD :OTH.BEH. :MANAG.

FEROZ ,EH ; FIRS: CARPENTER,VL CIT: 0
GAAP AS A SYMBOL OF LEGITIMACY: NEW YORK STATE'S DECISION TO ADOPT GENERALLY ACCEPTED ACCOUNTING PRINCIPLES
AOS 92 VOL: 17 PG:613 - 643 :: REGRESS. :MIXED :HIST. :ORG.& ENVIR.

FEROZ ,EH ; SEC: WILSON,ER CIT: 0
MARKET SEGMENTATION AND THE ASSOCIATION BETWEEN MUNICIPAL FINANCIAL DISCLOSURE AND NET INTEREST COSTS
TAR JL 92 VOL: 67 PG:480 495 :: REGRESS. :PRIM. :INSTIT. :LTD

FEROZ ,EH ; SEC: PARK ,K ; THIR: PASTENA,VS CIT: 0.5
THE FINANCIAL AND MARKET EFFECTS OF THE SEC'S ACCOUNTING AND AUDITING ENFORCEMENT RELEASES
JAR ST 91 VOL: 29 PG:107 - 148 :: REGRESS. :PRIM. :EMH :ORG.& ENVIR.

FERRARA,WL CIT: 0
PROBABILISTIC APPROACHES TO RETURN ON INVESTMENT AND RESIDUAL INCOME
TAR JL 77 VOL: 52 PG:597 - 604 :: ANAL. :SIM. :OTH.STAT. :RESP.ACC.

FERRARA,WL ; SEC: HAYYA ,JC ; THIR: NACHMAN,DA CIT: 0.24
NORMALCY OF PROFIT IN THE JAEDICKE-ROBICHEK MODEL
TAR AP 72 VOL: 47 PG:299 - 307 :: ANAL. :SIM. :OTH.STAT. :C-V-P-A

FERRARA,WL CIT: 0
SHOULD INVESTMENT AND FINANCING DECISIONS BE SEPARATED?
TAR JA 66 VOL: 41 PG:106 - 114 :: ANAL. :INT. LOG. :N/A :BUDG.& PLAN.

FERRARA,WL CIT: 0
RELEVANT COSTING - TWO POINTS OF VIEW
TAR OC 63 VOL: 38 PG:719 - 722 :: QUAL. :INT. LOG. :THEORY :REL.COSTS

FERRERI,LB ; FIRS: COWEN ,SS ; THIR: PARKER,LD CIT: 0.33
THE IMPACT OF CORPORATE CHARACTERISTICS ON SOCIAL RESPONSIBILITY DISCLOSURE: A TYPOLOGY AND FREQUENCY-BASED ANALYSIS
AOS 02 87 VOL: 12 PG:111 - 122 :: REGRESS. :PRIM. :THEORY :HRA

FERRIS,KR ; FIRS: HSIEH ,S-J ; THIR: CHEN ,AH CIT: 0.33
SECURITIES MARKET RESPONSE TO PENSION FUND TERMINATION
CAR SP 90 VOL: 6 PG:550 - 572 :: REGRESS. :PRIM. :EMH :PENS.

FERRIS,KR ; FIRS: DEAN ,RA ; THIR: KONSTANS,C CIT: 0.4
OCCUPATIONAL REALITY SHOCK AND ORGANIZATIONAL COMMITMENT: EVIDENCE FROM THE ACCOUNTING PROFESSION
AOS 03 88 VOL: 13 PG:235 - 250 :: REGRESS. :SURV. :OTH.BEH. :AUD.BEH.

FERRIS,KR ; FIRS: FARRELY,GE ; THIR: REICHENSTEIN,WR CIT: 0
PERCEIVED RISK, MARKET RISK, AND ACCOUNTING-DETERMINED RISK MEASURES
TAR AP 85 VOL: 60 PG:278 - 288 :: REGRESS. :SURV. :OTH.STAT. :FOREC.

FERRIS,KR ; SEC: TENNANT,KL CIT: 0.33
AN INVESTIGATION OF THE IMPACT OF THE QUALITATIVE NATURE OF COMPLIANCE ERRORS ON INTERNAL CONTROL ASSESSMENTS
AUD SP 84 VOL: 3 PG:31 - 43 :: NON-PAR. :LAB. :OTH.STAT. :INT.CONT.

FERRIS,KR ; FIRS: ARANYA,N CIT: 0.78
A REEXAMINATION OF ACCOUNTANTS' ORGANIZATIONAL-PROFESSIONAL CONFLICT
TAR JA 84 VOL: 59 PG:1 - 15 :: ANOVA :SURV. :OTH.BEH. :PROF.RESP.

FERRIS,KR ; SEC: LARCKER,DF CIT: 0.3
EXPLANATORY VARIABLES OF AUDITOR PERFORMANCE IN A LARGE PUBLIC ACCOUNTING FIRM
AOS 01 83 VOL: 8 PG:1 - 12 :: CORR. :SURV. :OTH.BEH. :ORG.

FERRIS,KR CIT: 0
PERCEIVED ENVIRONMENTAL UNCERTAINTY, ORGANIZATIONAL ADAPTATION AND EMPLOYEE PERFORMANCE: A LONGITUDINAL STUDY IN PROFESSIONAL AC
AOS 01 82 VOL: 7 PG:13 - 26 :: ANOVA :SURV. :OTH.BEH. :ORG.

FERRIS,KR CIT: 0
EDUCATIONAL PREDICTORS OF PROFESSIONAL PAY AND PERFORMANCE
AOS 03 82 VOL: 7 PG:225 - 230 :: REGRESS. :SURV. :OTH.BEH. :EDUC.

FERRIS,KR CIT: 0.17
ORGANIZATIONAL COMMITMENT AND PERFORMANCE IN A PROFESSIONAL ACCOUNTING FIRM
AOS 04 81 VOL: 6 PG:317 - 326 :: CORR. :SURV. :OTH.BEH. :AUD.BEH.

FERRIS,KR ; SEC: DILLARD,JF ; THIR: NETHERCOTT,L CIT: 0.08
A COMPARISON OF V-I-E MODEL PREDICTIONS: A CROSS-NATIONAL STUDY IN PROFESSIONAL ACCOUNTING FIRMS
AOS 04 80 VOL: 5 PG:361 - 368 :: DES.STAT. :LAB. :OTH.BEH. :INT.DIFF.

FERRIS,KR ; FIRS: DILLARD,JF CIT: 0.57
SOURCES OF PROFESSIONAL STAFF TURNOVER IN PUBLIC ACCOUNTING FIRMS: SOME FURTHER EVIDENCE
AOS 03 79 VOL: 4 PG:179 - 186 :: OTH.QUANT. :SURV. :OTH.BEH. :AUD.BEH.

FERRIS,KR CIT: 0.13
PERCEIVED UNCERTAINTY AND JOB SATISFACTION IN THE ACCOUNTING ENVIRONMENT
AOS 01 77 VOL: 2 PG:23 - 28 :: CORR. :SURV. :OTH.BEH. :OTH.MANAG.

FERRIS,KR CIT: 1.13
A TEST OF THE EXPECTANCY THEORY OF MOTIVATION IN AN ACCOUNTING ENVIRONMENT
TAR JL 77 VOL: 52 PG:605 - 615 :: REGRESS. :FIELD :OTH.BEH. :AUD.BEH.

FERTAKIS,JP CIT: 0
EMPIRICAL EVIDENCE - A REPLY
TAR JL 70 VOL: 45 PG:509 - 512 :: QUAL. :INT. LOG. :OTH.BEH. :INFO.STRUC.

FERTAKIS,JP CIT: 0.29
ON COMMUNICATION, UNDERSTANDING, AND RELEVANCE IN ACCOUNTING REPORTING
TAR OC 69 VOL: 44 PG:680 - 691 :: QUAL. :INT. LOG. :OTH.BEH. :INFO.STRUC.

FERTAKIS,JP ; FIRS: DECOSTER,DT CIT: 1.35
BUDGET-INDUCED PRESSURE AND ITS RELATIONSHIP TO SUPERVISORY BEHAVIOR
JAR AU 68 VOL: 6 PG:237 - 246 :: DES.STAT. :SURV. :OTH.BEH. :BUDG.& PLAN.

FESS ,PE CIT: 0
THE WORKING CAPITAL CONCEPT
TAR AP 66 VOL: 41 PG:266 - 270 :: QUAL. :INT. LOG. :THEORY :INFO.STRUC.

FESS ,PE CIT: 0
THE RELEVANT COSTING CONCEPT FOR INCOME MEASUREMENT - CAN IT BE DEFENDED?
TAR OC 63 VOL: 38 PG:723 - 732 :: QUAL. :INT. LOG. :THEORY :REL.COSTS

FIELD ,JE CIT: 0.06
TOWARD A MULTI-LEVEL, MULTI-GOAL INFORMATION SYSTEM
TAR JL 69 VOL: 44 PG:593 - 599 :: QUAL. :INT. LOG. :OTH.BEH. :MANAG.

FIELDS,LP ; SEC: WILKINS,MS CIT: 0
THE INFORMATION CONTENT OF WITHDRAWN AUDIT QUALIFICATIONS: NEW EVIDENCE ON THE VALUE OF "SUBJECT-TO" OPINIONS
AUD AU 91 VOL: 10 PG:62 - 69 :: REGRESS. :PRIM. :EMH :OPIN.

FIENBERG,SE ; FIRS: NETER ,J ; SEC: LEITCH,RA CIT: 0.73
DOLLAR UNIT SAMPLING: MULTINOMIAL BOUNDS FOR TOTAL OVERSTATEMENT AND UNDERSTATEMENT ERRORS
TAR JA 78 VOL: 53 PG:77 - 93 :: NON-PAR. :SIM. :MATH.PROG. :SAMP.

FINLEY,DR CIT: 0
DECISION THEORY ANALYSIS OF AUDIT DISCOVERY SAMPLING
CAR SP 89 VOL: 5 PG:692 - 719 :: DES.STAT. :SIM. :OTH.STAT. :SAMP.

FINLEY,DR ; SEC: BOOCKHOLDT,JL CIT: 0
A CONTINUOUS CONSTRAINED OPTIMIZATION MODEL FOR AUDIT SAMPLING
AUD SP 87 VOL: 6 PG:22 - 39 :: DES.STAT. :SIM. :OTH.STAT. :SAMP.

FINLEY,DR ; FIRS: THAKKAR,RB ; THIR: LIAO ,WM CIT: 0.11
A STOCHASTIC DEMAND CVP MODEL WITH RETURN ON INVESTMENT CRITERION
CAR AU 84 VOL: 1 PG:77 - 86 :: DES.STAT. :INT. LOG. :MATH.PROG. :C-V-P-A

FINLEY,DR CIT: 0.2
NORMAL FORM DECISION THEORY DEVELOPMENT OF THE AUDIT SAMPLING MODEL
AUD AU 83 VOL: 3 PG:104 - 116 :: MIXED :INT. LOG. :OTH.STAT. :SAMP.

FINN ,DW ; FIRS: COLLINS,F ; SEC: MUNTER,P CIT: 0.5
THE BUDGETING GAMES PEOPLE PLAY
TAR JA 87 VOL: 62 PG:29 - 49 :: REGRESS. :SURV. :OTH.BEH. :BUDG.& PLAN.

FIRMIN,PA ; SEC: GOODMAN,SS ; THIR: HENDRICKS,TE ; FOUR: LINN ,JJ CIT: 0
UNIVERSITY COST STRUCTURE AND BEHAVIOR: AN EMPIRICAL STUDY
JAR ST 68 VOL: 6 PG:122 - 155 :: DES.STAT. :SIM. :OTH.STAT. :MANAG.

FIRMIN,PA ; SEC: LINN ,JJ CIT: 0.06
INFORMATION SYSTEMS AND MANAGERIAL ACCOUNTING
TAR JA 68 VOL: 43 PG:75 - 82 :: QUAL. :INT. LOG. :N/A :OTH.MANAG.

FIRMIN,PA CIT: 0
DOLLAR-VALUE LIFO: LEGITIMATE OR NOT?
TAR AP 63 VOL: 38 PG:270 - 277 :: QUAL. :INT. LOG. :THEORY :INV.

FIRTH ,MA ; FIRS: MEAR ,RWT CIT: 0
A PARSIMONIOUS DESCRIPTION OF INDIVIDUAL DIFFERENCES IN FINANCIAL ANALYST JUDGMENT
JAA AU 90 VOL: 5 PG:501 - 520 :: REGRESS. :LAB. :HIPS :JUDG.

FIRTH ,MA ; FIRS: MEAR ,R CIT: 0
ASSESSING THE ACCURACY OF FINANCIAL ANALYST SECURITY RETURN PREDICTIONS
AOS 04 87 VOL: 12 PG:331 - 340 :: REGRESS. :PRIM. :HIPS :FOREC.

FIRTH ,MA ; FIRS: MEAR ,R CIT: 0
CUE USAGE AND SELF-INSIGHT OF FINANCIAL ANALYSTS
TAR JA 87 VOL: 62 PG:176 - 182 :: REGRESS. :LAB. :HIPS :MAN.DEC.CHAR.

FIRTH ,MA CIT: 0.25
AN ANALYSIS OF AUDIT FEES AND THEIR DETERMINATION IN NEW ZEALAND
AUD SP 85 VOL: 4 PG:23 - 37 :: REGRESS. :PRIM. :OTH.STAT. :ORG.

FIRTH ,MA CIT: 0
THE RELATIVE INFORMATION CONTENT OF THE RELEASE OF FINANCIAL RESULTS DATA
JAR AU 81 VOL: 19 PG:521 - 529 :: REGRESS. :PRIM. :EMH :N/A

FIRTH ,MA CIT: 0.08
PERCEPTIONS OF AUDITOR INDEPENDENCE AND OFFICIAL ETHICAL GUIDELINES
TAR JL 80 VOL: 55 PG:451 - 466 :: ANOVA :SURV. :OTH. :INDEP.

FIRTH ,MA CIT: 0.29
CONSENSUS VIEWS AND JUDGMENT MODELS IN MATERIALITY DECISIONS
AOS 04 79 VOL: 4 PG:283 - 296 :: ANOVA :LAB. :HIPS :MAT.

FIRTH ,MA CIT: 0.53
QUALIFIED AUDIT REPORTS: THEIR IMPACT ON INVESTMENT DECISIONS
TAR JL 78 VOL: 53 PG:642 - 650 :: ANOVA :PRIM. :EMH :OPIN.

FIRTH ,MA CIT: 0
AN EMPIRICAL EXAMINATION OF THE APPLICABILITY OF ADOPTING THE AICPA AND NYSE REGULATIONS ON FREE SHARE DISTRIBUTIONS IN THE U.K.
JAR SP 73 VOL: 11 PG:16 - 24 :: OTH.QUANT. :PRIM. :OTH. :STK.DIV.

FISHBURN,PC ; FIRS: LIBBY ,R CIT: 0.75
BEHAVIOURAL MODELS OF RISK TAKING IN BUSINESS DECISIONS: A SURVEY AND EVALUATION
JAR AU 77 VOL: 15 PG:272 - 292 :: QUAL. :SEC. :OTH.BEH. :OTH.MANAG.

FISHER,M CIT: 0
INTERNAL CONTROLS: GUIDELINES FOR MANAGEMENT ACTION
JAA SU 78 VOL: 1 PG:349 - 360 :: QUAL. :INT. LOG. :INSTIT. :INT.CONT.

FISHER,MH CIT: 0
THE EFFECTS OF REPORTING AUDITOR MATERIALITY LEVELS PUBLICLY, PRIVATELY, OR NOT AT ALL IN AN EXPERIMENTAL MARKETS SETTING
AUD 90 VOL: 9 PG:184 - 223 :: REGRESS. :LAB. :OTH.BEH. :MAT.

FITZGERALD,RD ; SEC: KELLEY,EM CIT: 0
INTERNATIONAL DISCLOSURE STANDARDS - THE UNITED NATIONS POSITION
JAA AU 79 VOL: 3 PG:5 - 20 :: QUAL. :INT. LOG. :INSTIT. :INT.DIFF.

FLAHERTY,RE ; SEC: SCHWARTZ,BN CIT: 0.08
EARNINGS PER SHARE: COMPLIANCE AND UNDERSTANDABILITY
JAA AU 80 VOL: 4 PG:47 - 56 :: DES.STAT. :SEC. :THEORY :INFO.STRUC.

FLAHERTY,RE ; FIRS: STERLING,RR ; SEC: TOLLEFSON,SO CIT: 0
EXCHANGE VALUATION: AN EMPIRICAL TEST
TAR OC 72 VOL: 47 PG:709 - 721 :: DES.STAT. :LAB. :THEORY :VALUAT.(INFL.)

FLAHERTY,RE ; FIRS: STERLING,RR CIT: 0
THE ROLE OF LIQUIDITY IN EXCHANGE VALUATION
TAR JL 71 VOL: 46 PG:441 - 456 :: ANAL. :INT. LOG. :THEORY :VALUAT.(INFL.)

FLAMHOLTZ,EG CIT: 0
VALUATION OF HUMAN ASSETS IN A SECURITIES BROKERAGE FIRM: AN EMPIRICAL STUDY
AOS 04 87 VOL: 12 PG:309 - 318 :: DES.STAT. :FIELD :OTH.BEH. :HRA

FLAMHOLTZ,EG ; SEC: DAS ,TK ; THIR: TSUI ,AS CIT: 0.13
TOWARD AN INTEGRATIVE FRAMEWORK OF ORGANIZATIONAL CONTROL
AOS 01 85 VOL: 10 PG:35 - 50 :: DES.STAT. :INT. LOG. :OTH.BEH. :HRA

FLAMHOLTZ,EG ; FIRS: BULLEN,ML CIT: 0.13
A THEORETICAL AND EMPIRICAL INVESTIGATION OF JOB SATISFACTION AND INTENDED TURNOVER IN THE LARGE CPA FIRM
AOS 03 85 VOL: 10 PG:287 - 302 :: REGRESS. :SURV. :OTH.BEH. :ORG.

FLAMHOLTZ,EG CIT: 0.7
ACCOUNTING, BUDGETING AND CONTROL SYSTEMS IN THEIR ORGANIZATIONAL CONTEXT: THEORETICAL AND EMPIRICAL PERSPECTIVES
AOS 23 83 VOL: 8 PG:153 - 170 :: QUAL. :FIELD :OTH.BEH. :BUDG.& PLAN.

FLAMHOLTZ,EG CIT: 0.08
THE PROCESS OF MEASUREMENT IN MANAGERIAL ACCOUNTING: A PSYCHO-TECHNICAL SYSTEMS PERSPECTIVE
AOS 01 80 VOL: 5 PG:31 - 42 :: QUAL. :INT. LOG. :THEORY :MANAG.

FLAMHOLTZ,EG ; SEC: COOK ,E CIT: 0.4
CONNOTATIVE MEANING AND ITS ROLE IN ACCOUNTING CHANGE: A FIELD STUDY
AOS 02 78 VOL: 3 PG:115 - 140 :: OTH.QUANT. :FIELD :OTH.BEH. :METHOD.

FLAMHOLTZ,EG ; FIRS: EPSTEIN,MJ ; THIR: MCDONOUGH,JJ CIT: 0.41
CORPORATE SOCIAL ACCOUNTING IN THE U.S.A.: STATE OF THE ART AND FUTURE PROSPECTS
AOS 01 76 VOL: 1 PG:23 - 42 :: QUAL. :SEC. :THEORY :HRA

FLAMHOLTZ,EG CIT: 0.41
THE IMPACT OF HUMAN RESOURCE VALUATION ON MANAGEMENT DECISIONS: A LABORATORY EXPERIMENT
AOS 23 76 VOL: 1 PG:153 - 166 :: NON-PAR. :LAB. :OTH.BEH. :HRA

FLAMHOLTZ,EG CIT: 0.24
ASSESSING THE VALIDITY OF A THEORY OF HUMAN RESOURCE VALUE: A FIELD STUDY
JAR ST 72 VOL: 10 PG:241 - 266 :: NON-PAR. :FIELD :OTH.BEH. :HRA

FLAMHOLTZ,EG CIT: 0.35
TOWARD A THEORY OF HUMAN RESOURCE VALUE IN FORMAL ORGANIZATIONS
TAR OC 72 VOL: 47 PG:666 - 678 :: QUAL. :INT. LOG. :OTH.BEH. :HRA

FLAMHOLTZ,EG CIT: 0.59
A MODEL FOR HUMAN RESOURCE VALUATION: A STOCHASTIC PROCESS WITH SERVICE REWARDS
TAR AP 71 VOL: 46 PG:253 - 267 :: QUAL. :INT. LOG. :OTH.BEH. :HRA

FLAMHOLTZ,EG ; FIRS: BRUMMET,RL ; THIR: PYLE ,WC CIT: 0.41
HUMAN RESOURCE MEASUREMENT - A CHALLENGE FOR ACCOUNTANTS
TAR AP 68 VOL: 43 PG:217 - 224 :: QUAL. :INT. LOG. :OTH.BEH. :HRA

FLEISCHMAN,RK ; SEC: PARKER,LD CIT: 0
BRITISH ENTREPRENEURS AND PRE-INDUSTRIAL REVOLUTION EVIDENCE OF COST MANAGEMENT
TAR AP 91 VOL: 66 PG:361 - 375 :: REGRESS. :PRIM. :HIST. :MANAG.

FLESHER,DL ; FIRS: MOODY ,SM CIT: 0
ANALYSIS OF FASB VOTING PATTERNS: STATEMENT NOS. 1-86
JAA AU 86 VOL: 1 PG:319 - 330 :: REGRESS. :PRIM. :INSTIT. :FASB SUBM.

FLESHER,DL ; SEC: FLESHER,TK CIT: 0.14
IVER KREUGER'S CONTRIBUTION TO U.S. FINANCIAL REPORTING
TAR JL 86 VOL: 61 PG:421 - 434 :: REGRESS. :SEC. :HIST. :BUS.FAIL.

FLESHER,DL ; SEC: FLESHER,TK CIT: 0
MANAGERIAL ACCOUNTING IN AN EARLY 19TH CENTURY GERMAN-AMERICAN RELIGIOUS COMMUNE
AOS 04 79 VOL: 4 PG:297 - 304 :: QUAL. :INT. LOG. :HIST. :N/A

FLESHER,TK ; FIRS: FLESHER,DL CIT: 0.14
IVER KREUGER'S CONTRIBUTION TO U.S. FINANCIAL REPORTING
TAR JL 86 VOL: 61 PG:421 - 434 :: REGRESS. :SEC. :HIST. :BUS.FAIL.

FLESHER,TK ; FIRS: FLESHER,DL CIT: 0
MANAGERIAL ACCOUNTING IN AN EARLY 19TH CENTURY GERMAN-AMERICAN RELIGIOUS COMMUNE
AOS 04 79 VOL: 4 PG:297 - 304 :: QUAL. :INT. LOG. :HIST. :N/A

FLORY ,SM ; SEC: PHILLIPS JR,TJ ; THIR: REIDENBACH,RE ; FOUR: ROBIN ,DP CIT: 0
A MULTIDIMENSIONAL ANALYSIS OF SELECTED ETHICAL ISSUES IN ACCOUNTING
TAR AP 92 VOL: 67 PG:284 - 302 :: REGRESS. :SURV. :HIPS :JUDG.

FLOWER,JF CIT: 0.06
THE CASE OF THE PROFITABLE BLOODHOUND
JAR SP 66 VOL: 4 PG:16 - 36 :: QUAL. :CASE :INSTIT. :MANAG.

FOGARTY,JA ; FIRS: HOUGHTON,CW CIT: 0
INHERENT RISK
AUD SP 91 VOL: 10 PG:1 - 21 :: REGRESS. :PRIM. :THEORY :ERRORS

FOGARTY,TJ CIT: 0
ORGANIZATIONAL SOCIALIZATION IN ACCOUNTING FIRMS: A THEORETICAL FRAMEWORK AND AGENDA FOR FUTURE RESEARCH
AOS 02 92 VOL: 17 PG:129 - 149 :: DES.STAT. :SEC. :OTH.BEH. :ORG.

FOGELBERG,G CIT: 0.06
INTERIM INCOME DETERMINATION: AN EXAMINATION OF THE EFFECTS OF ALTERNATIVE MEASUREMENT TECHNIQUES
JAR AU 71 VOL: 9 PG:215 - 235 :: DES.STAT. :CASE :THEORY :INT.REP.

FOGLER,HR CIT: 0
RANKING TECHNIQUES AND CAPITAL BUDGETING
TAR JA 72 VOL: 47 PG:134 - 143 :: ANAL. :INT. LOG. :MATH.PROG. :CAP.BUDG.

FORAN ,MF ; SEC: DECOSTER,DT CIT: 0.71
AN EXPER. STUDY OF THE EFFECTS OF PARTICIP., AUTHORITARIANISM, AND FEEDBACK ON COGNITIVE DISSONANCE IN A STANDARD SETTING SITUAT
TAR OC 74 VOL: 49 PG:751 - 763 :: ANOVA :LAB. :OTH.BEH. :BUDG.& PLAN.

FORD ,A CIT: 0
TRAVEL EXPENSES FOR A VISITING PROFESSOR
TAR AP 75 VOL: 50 PG:338 - 344 :: QUAL. :INT. LOG. :OTH. :N/A

FORD ,A CIT: 0
SHOULD COST BE ASSIGNED TO CONVERSION VALUE?
TAR OC 69 VOL: 44 PG:818 - 822 :: QUAL. :INT. LOG. :THEORY :LTD

FORSYTHE,R ; FIRS: DEJONG,DV CIT: 0
A PERSPECTIVE ON THE USE OF LABORATORY MARKET EXPERIMENTATION IN AUDITING RESEARCH
TAR JA 92 VOL: 67 PG:157 - 171 :: ANOVA :SEC. :INF.ECO./AG. :METHOD.

FORSYTHE,R ; FIRS: DEJONG,DV CIT: 0
A PERSPECTIVE ON THE USE OF LABORATORY MARKET EXPERIMENTATION IN AUDITING RESEARCH
TAR JA 92 VOL: 67 PG:157 - 171 :: ANOVA :SEC. :INF.ECO./AG. :METHOD.

FORSYTHE,R ; FIRS: DEJONG,DV ; THIR: KIM ,JA ; FOUR: UECKER,WC CIT: 0.25
A LABORATORY INVESTIGATION OF ALTERNATIVE TRANSFER PRICING MECHANISMS
AOS 02 89 VOL: 14 PG:41 - 64 :: REGRESS. :LAB. :OTH.BEH. :TRANS.PRIC.

FORSYTHE,R ; FIRS: DEJONG,DV ; THIR: UECKER,WC CIT: 1.25
THE METHODOLOGY OF LABORATORY MARKETS AND ITS IMPLICATIONS FOR AGENCY RESEARCH IN ACCOUNTING AND AUDITING
JAR AU 85 VOL: 23 PG:753 - 793 :: REGRESS. :LAB. :INF.ECO./AG. :METHOD.

FORSYTHE,R ; FIRS: DEJONG,DV ; THIR: LUNDHOLM,RJ ; FOUR: UECKER,WC CIT: 0.88
A LABORATORY INVESTIGATION OF THE MORAL HAZARD PROBLEM IN AN AGENCY RELATIONSHIP
JAR ST 85 VOL: 23 PG:81 - 120 :: REGRESS. :LAB. :INF.ECO./AG. :MAN.DEC.CHAR.

FOSSUM,RL ; FIRS: ZEFF ,SA CIT: 0.29
AN ANALYSIS OF LARGE AUDIT CLIENTS
TAR AP 67 VOL: 42 PG:298 - 320 :: DES.STAT. :PRIM. :INSTIT. :AUD.

FOSTER III,TW ; SEC: KOOGLER,PR ; THIR: VICKREY,D CIT: 0
VALUATION OF EXECUTIVE STOCK OPTIONS AND THE FASB PROPOSAL
TAR JL 91 VOL: 66 PG:595 - 610 :: DES.STAT. :INT. LOG. :INF.ECO./AG. :EXEC.COMP.

FOSTER III,TW ; SEC: VICKREY,DW CIT: 0.07
THE INFORMATION CONTENT OF STOCK DIVIDEND ANNOUNCEMENTS
TAR AP 78 VOL: 53 PG:360 - 370 :: REGRESS. :PRIM. :EMH :STK.DIV.

FOSTER III,TW ; SEC: VICKREY,DW CIT: 0.6
THE INCREMENTAL INFORMATION CONTENT OF THE 10-K
TAR OC 78 VOL: 53 PG:921 - 934 :: ANOVA :PRIM. :EMH :FIN.METH.

FOSTER,G ; SEC: GUPTA ,M CIT: 0
MANUFACTURING OVERHEAD COST DRIVER ANALYSIS
JAE JA 90 VOL: 12 PG:309 - 337 :: REGRESS. :FIELD :OTH.STAT. :OVER.ALLOC.

FOSTER,G ; SEC: OLSEN ,C ; THIR: SHEVLIN,T CIT: 2.89
EARNINGS RELEASES, ANOMALIES, AND THE BEHAVIOR OF SECURITY RETURNS
TAR OC 84 VOL: 59 PG:574 - 603 :: REGRESS. :PRIM. :EMH :FIN.METH.

FOSTER,G ; FIRS: BALL ,R CIT: 2.82
CORPORATE FINANCIAL REPORTING: A METHODOLOGICAL REVIEW OF EMPIRICAL RESEARCH
JAR ST 82 VOL: 20 PG:161 - 234 :: MIXED :SEC. :OTH. :FIN.METH.

FOSTER,G CIT: 2.17
INTRA-INDUSTRY INFORMATION TRANSFERS ASSOCIATED WITH EARNINGS RELEASES
JAE DE 81 VOL: 3 PG:201 - 232 :: CORR. :PRIM. :EMH :FIN.METH.

FOSTER,G CIT: 3.15
ACCOUNTING POLICY DECISIONS AND CAPITAL MARKET RESEARCH
JAE MR 80 VOL: 2 PG:29 - 62 :: ANAL. :SEC. :EMH :OIL & GAS

FOSTER,G CIT: 4.31
QUARTERLY ACCOUNTING DATA: TIME-SERIES PROPERTIES AND PREDICTIVE-ABILITY RESULTS
TAR JA 77 VOL: 52 PG:1 - 21 :: MIXED :PRIM. :TIME SER. :FOREC.

FOSTER,G CIT: 0.29
SECURITY PRICE REVALUATION IMPLICATIONS OF SUB-EARNINGS DISCLOSURE
JAR AU 75 VOL: 13 PG:283 - 292 :: REGRESS. :PRIM. :EMH :FIN.METH.

FOSTER,G CIT: 0.47
ACCOUNTING EARNINGS AND STOCK PRICES OF INSURANCE COMPANIES
TAR OC 75 VOL: 50 PG:686 - 698 :: MIXED :PRIM. :EMH :FIN.METH.

FOSTER,G CIT: 1.12
STOCK MARKET REACTION TO ESTIMATES OF EARNINGS PER SHARE BY COMPANY OFFICIALS
JAR SP 73 VOL: 11 PG:25 - 37 :: REGRESS. :PRIM. :EMH :FOREC.

FRANCIA,AJ ; FIRS: COPELAND,RM ; THIR: STRAWSER,RH CIT: 0.53
STUDENTS AS SUBJECTS IN BEHAVIOURAL BUSINESS RESEARCH
TAR AP 73 VOL: 48 PG:365 - 374 :: QUAL. :SURV. :OTH.BEH. :METHOD.

FRANCIS,J ; SEC: PAGACH,D ; THIR: STEPHAN,J CIT: 0
THE STOCK MARKET RESPONSE TO EARNINGS ANNOUNCEMENTS RELEASED DURING TRADING VERSUS NONTRADING PERIODS
JAR AU 92 VOL: 30 PG:165 - 184 :: REGRESS. :PRIM. :EMH :FIN.ST.TIM.

FRANCIS,J CIT: 0
CORPORATE COMPLIANCE WITH DEBT COVENANTS
JAR AU 90 VOL: 28 PG:326 - 347 :: REGRESS. :PRIM. :OTH.STAT. :SPEC.ITEMS

FRANCIS,J CIT: 0
ACCOUNTING FOR FUTURES CONTRACTS AND THE EFFECT ON EARNINGS VARIABILITY
TAR OC 90 VOL: 65 PG:891 - 911 :: REGRESS. :SIM. :MATH.PROG. :N/A

FRANCIS,JR ; SEC: ANDREWS JR,WT ; THIR: SIMON ,DT CIT: 0
VOLUNTARY PEER REVIEWS, AUDIT QUALITY, AND PROPOSALS FOR MANDATORY PEER REVIEWS
JAA SU 90 VOL: 5 PG:369 - 378 :: REGRESS. :MIXED :OTH.STAT. :OPER.AUD.

FRANCIS,JR ; FIRS: ARRINGTON,CE CIT: 2.75
LETTING THE CHAT OUT OF THE BAG: DECONSTRUCTION, PRIVILEGE AND ACCOUNTING RESEARCH
AOS 02 89 VOL: 14 PG:1 - 28 :: DES.STAT. :SEC. :THEORY :METHOD.

FRANCIS,JR ; FIRS: SIMON ,DT CIT: 1.4
THE EFFECTS OF AUDITOR CHANGE ON AUDIT FEES: TESTS OF PRICE CUTTING AND PRICE RECOVERY
TAR AP 88 VOL: 63 PG:255 - 269 :: REGRESS. :PRIM. :OTH.STAT. :ORG.

FRANCIS,JR ; SEC: WILSON,ER CIT: 0.6
AUDITOR CHANGES: A JOINT TEST OF THEORIES RELATING TO AGENCY COSTS AND AUDITOR DIFFERENTIATION
TAR OC 88 VOL: 63 PG:663 - 682 :: REGRESS. :PRIM. :OTH.STAT. :ORG.

FRANCIS,JR ; SEC: REITER,SA CIT: 1.33
DETERMINANTS OF CORPORATE PENSION FUNDING STRATEGY
JAE AP 87 VOL: 9 PG:35 - 59 :: REGRESS. :PRIM. :OTH.STAT. :PENS.

FRANCIS,JR ; SEC: SIMON ,DT CIT: 1.5
A TEST OF AUDIT PRICING IN THE SMALL-CLIENT SEGMENT OF THE U.S. AUDIT MARKET
TAR JA 87 VOL: 62 PG:145 - 157 :: REGRESS. :SURV. :OTH.STAT. :ORG.

FRANCIS,JR ; SEC: STOKES,DJ CIT: 0.43
AUDIT PRICES, PRODUCT DIFFERENTIATION, AND SCALE ECONOMIES: FURTHER EVIDENCE FROM THE AUSTRALIAN MARKET
JAR AU 86 VOL: 24 PG:383 - 393 :: REGRESS. :PRIM. :OTH.STAT. :OPER.AUD.

FRANCIS,JR CIT: 1
THE EFFECT OF AUDIT FIRM SIZE ON AUDIT PRICES: A STUDY OF THE AUSTRALIAN MARKET
JAE AG 84 VOL: 6 PG:133 - 151 :: REGRESS. :PRIM. :OTH.STAT. :ORG.

FRANCIS,ME CIT: 0.06
ACCOUNTING AND THE EVALUATION OF SOCIAL PROGRAMS: A CRITICAL COMMENT
TAR AP 73 VOL: 48 PG:245 - 257 :: QUAL. :INT. LOG. :THEORY :HRA

FRANK ,WG ; FIRS: NAIR ,RD CIT: 0.23
THE IMPACT OF DISCLOSURE AND MEASUREMENT PRACTICES ON INTERNATIONAL ACCOUNTING CLASSIFICATIONS
TAR JL 80 VOL: 55 PG:426 - 450 :: OTH.QUANT. :PRIM. :OTH.STAT. :INT.DIFF.

FRANK ,WG CIT: 0.14
AN EMPIRICAL ANALYSIS OF INTERNATIONAL ACCOUNTING PRINCIPLES
JAR AU 79 VOL: 17 PG:593 - 605 :: OTH.QUANT. :PRIM. :INSTIT. :FIN.METH.

FRANK ,WG ; SEC: WEYGANDT,JJ CIT: 0.06
A PREDICTION MODEL FOR CONVERTIBLE DEBENTURES
JAR SP 71 VOL: 9 PG:116 - 126 :: OTH.QUANT. :PRIM. :OTH. :LTD

FRANK ,WG ; SEC: WEYGANDT,JJ CIT: 0.12
CONVERTIBLE DEBT AND EARNINGS PER SHARE: PRAGMATISM VS. GOOD THEORY
TAR AP 70 VOL: 45 PG:280 - 289 :: DES.STAT. :PRIM. :N/A :PENS.

FRANK ,WG CIT: 0.18
A STUDY OF THE PREDICTIVE SIGNIFICANCE OF TWO INCOME MEASURES
JAR SP 69 VOL: 7 PG:123 - 136 :: NON-PAR. :PRIM. :OTH. :VALUAT.(INFL.)

FRANK ,WG ; SEC: MANES ,RP CIT: 0.06
A STANDARD COST APPLICATION OF MATRIX ALGEBRA
TAR JL 67 VOL: 42 PG:516 - 525 :: ANAL. :INT. LOG. :MATH.PROG. :VAR.

FRANK ,WG CIT: 0
A COMPUTER APPLICATION IN PROCESS COST ACCOUNTING

TAR OC 65 VOL: 40 PG:854 - 862 :: QUAL. :INT. LOG. :N/A :OTH.MANAG.
FRANKFURTER,GM ; SEC: YOUNG ,AE CIT: 0
FINANCIAL THEORY: ITS MESSAGE TO THE ACCOUNTANT
JAA SU 83 VOL: 6 PG:314 - 324 :: QUAL. :INT. LOG. :OTH. :N/A

FRANKFURTER,GM ; SEC: HORWITZ,BN CIT: 0.06
THE EFFECTS OF ACCOUNTING PRINCIPLES BOARD OPINION NO.15 ON EARNINGS PER SHARE: A SIMULATION STUDY
TAR AP 72 VOL: 47 PG:245 - 259 :: DES.STAT. :SIM. :THEORY :FIN.METH.

FRANKLE,AW ; FIRS: ANDERSON,JC CIT: 0.31
VOLUNTARY SOCIAL REPORTING: AN ISO-BETA PORTFOLIO ANALYSIS
TAR JL 80 VOL: 55 PG:467 - 479 :: REGRESS. :PRIM. :EMH :HRA

FRANKS,DD ; FIRS: SORENSEN,JE CIT: 0.18
THE RELATIVE CONTRIBUTION OF ABILITY, SELF-ESTEEM AND EVALUATIVE FEEDBACK TO PERFORMANCE: IMPLICATIONS FOR ACCOUNTING SYSTEMS
TAR OC 72 VOL: 47 PG:735 - 746 :: ANOVA :FIELD :OTH.BEH. :OTH.MANAG.

FRAZIER,KB ; FIRS: MURRAY,D CIT: 0.43
A WITHIN-SUBJECTS TEST OF EXPECTANCY THEORY IN A PUBLIC ACCOUNTING ENVIRONMENT
JAR AU 86 VOL: 24 PG:400 - 404 :: REGRESS. :LAB. :OTH.BEH. :INFO.STRUC.

FRAZIER,KB ; SEC: INGRAM,RW ; THIR: TENNYSON,BM CIT: 0.22
A METHODOLOGY FOR THE ANALYSIS OF NARRATIVE ACCOUNTING DISCLOSURES
JAR SP 84 VOL: 22 PG:318 - 331 :: OTH.QUANT. :PRIM. :OTH.STAT. :FOREC.

FRECKA,TJ ; FIRS: BUBLITZ,B ; THIR: MCKEOWN,JC CIT: 1.38
MARKET ASSOCIATION TESTS AND FASB STATEMENT NO. 33 DISCLOSURES: A REEXAMINATION
JAR ST 85 VOL: 23 PG:1 - 23 :: REGRESS. :PRIM. :EMH :VALUAT.(INFL.)

FRECKA,TJ ; SEC: LEE ,CF CIT: 0
GENERALIZED FINANCIAL RATIO ADJUSTMENT PROCESSES AND THEIR IMPLICATIONS
JAR SP 83 VOL: 21 PG:308 - 316 :: REGRESS. :PRIM. :EMH :N/A

FRECKA,TJ ; SEC: HOPWOOD,WS CIT: 0.6
THE EFFECTS OF OUTLIERS ON THE CROSS-SECTIONAL DISTRIBUTIONAL PROPERTIES OF FINANCIAL RATIOS
TAR JA 83 VOL: 58 PG:115 - 128 :: DES.STAT. :LAB. :OTH.STAT. :METHOD.

FREDERICK,DM CIT: 2
AUDITORS' REPRESENTATION AND RETRIEVAL OF INTERNAL CONTROL KNOWLEDGE
TAR AP 91 VOL: 66 PG:240 - 258 :: REGRESS. :FIELD :HIPS :AUD.BEH.

FREDERICK,DM ; FIRS: LIBBY ,R CIT: 2.33
EXPERIENCE AND THE ABILITY TO EXPLAIN AUDIT FINDINGS
JAR AU 90 VOL: 28 PG:348 - 367 :: REGRESS. :LAB. :HIPS :AUD.BEH.

FREDERICK,DM ; SEC: LIBBY ,R CIT: 2
EXPERTISE AND AUDITORS' JUDGMENTS OF CONJUNCTIVE EVENTS
JAR AU 86 VOL: 24 PG:270 - 290 :: REGRESS. :LAB. :HIPS :JUDG.

FREDERICKS,W ; FIRS: COPELAND,RM CIT: 0.12
EXTENT OF DISCLOSURE
JAR SP 68 VOL: 6 PG:106 - 113 :: NON-PAR. :PRIM. :THEORY :INFO.STRUC.

FREDERICKSON,JR CIT: 0
RELATIVE PERFORMANCE INFORMATION: THE EFFECTS OF COMMON UNCERTAINTY AND CONTRACT TYPE OF AGENT EFFORT
TAR OC 92 VOL: 67 PG:647 - 670 :: REGRESS. :LAB. :INF.ECO./AG. :MANAG.

FREDERICKSON,JR ; FIRS: BEACH ,LR CIT: 0
IMAGE THEORY: AN ALTERNATIVE DESCRIPTION OF AUDIT DECISIONS
AOS 02 89 VOL: 14 PG:101 - 112 :: DES.STAT. :SEC. :HIPS :METHOD.

FREDRIKSON,EB CIT: 0
ON THE MEASUREMENT OF FOREIGN INCOME
JAR AU 68 VOL: 6 PG:208 - 221 :: DES.STAT. :SIM. :THEORY :CASH

FREEMAN,R ; SEC: TSE ,S CIT: 0
AN EARNINGS PREDICTION APPROACH TO EXAMINING INTERCOMPANY INFORMATION TRANSFERS
JAE DE 92 VOL: 15 PG:509 - 523 :: REGRESS. :PRIM. :EMH :FIN.ST.TIM.

FREEMAN,RN ; SEC: TSE ,SY CIT: 1
A NONLINEAR MODEL OF SECURITY PRICE RESPONSES TO UNEXPECTED EARNINGS
JAR AU 92 VOL: 30 PG:185 - 209 :: REGRESS. :PRIM. :EMH :REV.REC.

FREEMAN,RN ; SEC: TSE ,S CIT: 1.75
THE MULTIPERIOD INFORMATION CONTENT OF ACCOUNTING EARNINGS: CONFIRMATIONS AND CONTRADICTIONS OF PREVIOUS EARNINGS REPORTS
JAR ST 89 VOL: 27 PG:49 - 79 :: REGRESS. :PRIM. :EMH :REV.REC.

FREEMAN,RN CIT: 4.5
THE ASSOCIATION BETWEEN ACCOUNTING EARNINGS AND SECURITY RETURNS FOR LARGE AND SMALL FIRMS
JAE JL 87 VOL: 9 PG:195 - 228 :: REGRESS. :PRIM. :EMH :FIN.METH.

FREEMAN,RN CIT: 0.5
ALTERNATIVE MEASURES OF PROFIT MARGIN: AN EMPIRICAL STUDY OF THE POTENTIAL INFORMATION CONTENT OF CURRENT COST ACCOUNTING
JAR SP 83 VOL: 21 PG:42 - 64 :: REGRESS. :PRIM. :EMH :VALUAT.(INFL.)

FREEMAN,RN ; SEC: OHLSON,JA ; THIR: PENMAN,SH CIT: 1.27
BOOK RATE-OF-RETURN AND PREDICTION OF EARNINGS CHANGES: AN EMPIRICAL INVESTIGATION
JAR AU 82 VOL: 20 PG:639 - 653 :: REGRESS. :PRIM. :EMH :FOREC.

FREEMAN,RN CIT: 0
ON THE ASSOCIATION BETWEEN NET MONETARY POSITION AND EQUITY SECURITY PRICES
JAR ST 78 VOL: 16 PG:111 - 145 :: REGRESS. :PRIM. :EMH :CASH

FREMGEN,JM ; FIRS: COWIE ,JB CIT: 0
COMPUTERS VERSUS MATHEMATICS: ROUND 2
TAR JA 70 VOL: 45 PG:27 - 37 :: QUAL. :INT. LOG. :N/A :OTH.MANAG.

FREMGEN,JM CIT: 0.06
THE GOING CONCERN ASSUMPTION: A CRITICAL APPRAISAL
TAR OC 68 VOL: 43 PG:649 - 656 :: QUAL. :INT. LOG. :THEORY :OTH.FIN.ACC.

FREMGEN,JM CIT: 0
UTILITY AND ACCOUNTING PRINCIPLES
TAR JL 67 VOL: 42 PG:457 - 467 :: QUAL. :INT. LOG. :THEORY :FIN.METH.

FREMGEN,JM CIT: 0
THE DIRECT COSTING CONTROVERSY - AN IDENTIFICATION OF ISSUES
TAR JA 64 VOL: 39 PG:43 - 51 :: QUAL. :INT. LOG. :THEORY :COST.ALLOC.

FRIBERG,RA CIT: 0.18
PROBABILISTIC DEPRECIATION WITH A VARYING SALVAGE VALUE
TAR JA 73 VOL: 48 PG:50 - 60 :: ANAL. :INT. LOG. :OTH.STAT. :PP&E / DEPR

FRIED ,D ; SEC: HOSLER,C CIT: 0
S&LS, REPORTING CHANGES AND THE IMPACT ON THE GNMA MARKET
JAA WI 87 VOL: 2 PG:5 - 23 :: REGRESS. :PRIM. :THEORY :LTD

FRIED ,D ; FIRS: BARLEV,B ; THIR: LIVNAT,J CIT: 0
ECONOMIC AND FINANCIAL REPORTING EFFECTS OF INVENTORY TAX ALLOWANCES
CAR SP 86 VOL: 2 PG:288 - 310 :: REGRESS. :INT. LOG. :MATH.PROG. :INV.

FRIED ,D ; SEC: GIVOLY,D CIT: 2.73
FINANCIAL ANALYSTS' FORECASTS OF EARNINGS: A BETTER SURROGATE FOR MARKET EXPECTATIONS
JAE OC 82 VOL: 4 PG:85 - 107 :: OTH.QUANT. :SEC. :TIME SER. :FOREC.

FRIED ,D CIT: 0.08
COMPENSATING FOR INFLATION: SHORTER LIFE VS. ACCELERATED DEPRECIATION METHODS
JAA SU 81 VOL: 4 PG:295 - 308 :: ANAL. :INT. LOG. :OTH.STAT. :PP&E / DEPR

FRIED ,D ; SEC: SCHIFF,A CIT: 0.42
CPA SWITCHES AND ASSOCIATED MARKET REACTIONS
TAR AP 81 VOL: 56 PG:326 - 341 :: NON-PAR. :PRIM. :EMH :OTH.MANAG.

FRIED ,D ; SEC: LIVNAT,J CIT: 0.08
INTERIM STATEMENTS: AN ANALYTICAL EXAMINATION OF ALTERNATIVE ACCOUNTING TECHNIQUES
TAR JL 81 VOL: 56 PG:493 - 509 :: ANAL. :INT. LOG. :TIME SER. :N/A

FRIEDLOB,GT CIT: 0
HOW ECONOMIC STATISTICIANS VIEW ACCOUNTING PROFITS
JAA WI 83 VOL: 6 PG:100 - 107 :: DES.STAT. :PRIM. :THEORY :REV.REC.

FRIEDMAN,A ; SEC: LEV ,B CIT: 0.24
A SURROGATE MEASURE FOR THE FIRM'S INVESTMENT IN HUMAN RESOURCES
JAR AU 74 VOL: 12 PG:235 - 250 :: ANAL. :INT. LOG. :OTH.BEH. :HRA

FRIEDMAN,L ; FIRS: HAKA ,S ; THIR: JONES ,V CIT: 0.29
FUNCTIONAL FIXATION AND INTERFERENCE THEORY: A THEORETICAL AND EMPIRICAL INVESTIGATION
TAR JL 86 VOL: 61 PG:455 - 474 :: REGRESS. :LAB. :HIPS :REL.COSTS

FRIEDMAN,LA ; SEC: NEUMANN,BR CIT: 0.23
EFFECTS OF OPPORTUNITY COSTS ON PROJECT INVESTMENT DECISIONS: A REPLICATION AND EXTENSION
JAR AU 80 VOL: 18 PG:407 - 419 :: ANOVA :LAB. :OTH.BEH. :MANAG.

FRIEDMAN,LA ; FIRS: NEUMANN,BR CIT: 0.4
OPPORTUNITY COSTS: FURTHER EVIDENCE THROUGH AN EXPERIMENTAL REPLICATION
JAR AU 78 VOL: 16 PG:400 - 410 :: ANOVA :LAB. :OTH.BEH. :REL.COSTS

FRIEDMAN,LA CIT: 0
AN EXIT-PRICE INCOME STATEMENT
TAR JA 78 VOL: 53 PG:18 - 30 :: QUAL. :INT. LOG. :THEORY :VALUAT.(INFL.)

FRIEDMAN,LA CIT: 0
EXIT-PRICE LIABILITIES: AN ANALYSIS OF THE ALTERNATIVES
TAR OC 78 VOL: 53 PG:895 - 909 :: QUAL. :INT. LOG. :THEORY :VALUAT.(INFL.)

FRIEZE,IH ; FIRS: SHIELDS,MD ; SEC: BIRNBERG,JG CIT: 0.42
ATTRIBUTIONS, COGNITIVE PROCESSES AND CONTROL SYSTEMS
AOS 01 81 VOL: 6 PG:69 - 96 :: ANOVA :LAB. :OTH.BEH. :BUDG.& PLAN.

FRIEZE,IH ; FIRS: BIRNBERG,JG ; THIR: SHIELDS,MD CIT: 0.38
THE ROLE OF ATTRIBUTION THEORY IN CONTROL SYSTEMS
AOS 03 77 VOL: 2 PG:189 - 200 :: QUAL. :INT. LOG. :OTH.BEH. :MANAG.

FRISHKOFF,P ; FIRS: BOUWMAN,MJ ; SEC: FRISHKOFF,PA CIT: 1
HOW DO THE FIN. ANALYSTS MAKE DECISIONS? A PROCESS MODEL OF THE INVESTMENT SCREENING DECISION
AOS 01 87 VOL: 12 PG:1 - 30 :: REGRESS. :LAB. :HIPS :OTH.FIN.ACC.

FRISHKOFF,P ; SEC: FRISHKOFF,PA ; THIR: BOUWMAN,MJ CIT: 0
USE OF ACCOUNTING DATA IN SCREENING BY FINANCIAL ANALYSTS
JAA AU 84 VOL: 8 PG:44 - 53 :: DES.STAT. :LAB. :HIPS :INFO.STRUC.

FRISHKOFF,P CIT: 0.53
AN EMPIRICAL INVESTIGATION OF THE CONCEPT OF MATERIALITY IN ACCOUNTING
JAR ST 70 VOL: 8 PG:116 - 129 :: OTH.QUANT. :PRIM. :THEORY :MAT.

FRISHKOFF,PA ; FIRS: BOUWMAN,MJ ; THIR: FRISHKOFF,P CIT: 1
HOW DO THE FIN. ANALYSTS MAKE DECISIONS? A PROCESS MODEL OF THE INVESTMENT SCREENING DECISION
AOS 01 87 VOL: 12 PG:1 - 30 :: REGRESS. :LAB. :HIPS :OTH.FIN.ACC.

FRISHKOFF,PA ; FIRS: FRISHKOFF,P ; THIR: BOUWMAN,MJ CIT: 0
USE OF ACCOUNTING DATA IN SCREENING BY FINANCIAL ANALYSTS
JAA AU 84 VOL: 8 PG:44 - 53 :: DES.STAT. :LAB. :HIPS :INFO.STRUC.

FROST ,CA CIT: 0.75
THE ROLE OF DEBT COVENANTS IN ASSESSING THE ECONOMIC CONSEQUENCES OF LIMITING CAPITALIZATION OF EXPLORATION COSTS
TAR OC 89 VOL: 64 PG:788 - 808 :: REGRESS. :PRIM. :EMH :OIL & GAS

FROST ,PA ; SEC: TAMURA,H CIT: 0
ACCURACY OF AUXILIARY INFORMATION INTERVAL ESTIMATION IN STATISTICAL AUDITING
JAR SP 86 VOL: 24 PG:57 - 75 :: DES.STAT. :SIM. :OTH.STAT. :SAMP.

FROST ,PA ; FIRS: TAMURA,H CIT: 0.14
TIGHTENING CAV (DUS) BOUNDS BY USING A PARAMETRIC MODEL
JAR AU 86 VOL: 24 PG:364 - 371 :: DES.STAT. :SIM. :OTH.STAT. :SAMP.

FROST ,PA ; SEC: TAMURA,H CIT: 0.55
JACKKNIFED RATIO ESTIMATION IN STATISTICAL AUDITING
JAR SP 82 VOL: 20 PG:103 - 120 :: DES.STAT. :SIM. :OTH.STAT. :SAMP.

FRUGOT,V ; SEC: SHEARON,WT CIT: 0
BUDGETARY PARTICIPATION, LOCUS OF CONTROL, AND MEXICAN MANAGERIAL PERFORMANCE AND JOB SATISFACTION
TAR JA 91 VOL: 66 PG:80 - 99 :: REGRESS. :FIELD :OTH.BEH. :BUDG.& PLAN.

FU ,P CIT: 0
GOVERNMENTAL ACCOUNTING IN CHINA DURING THE CHOU DYNASTY (1122 B.C.-256 B.C.)
JAR SP 71 VOL: 9 PG:40 - 51 :: QUAL. :PRIM. :HIST. :OTH.MANAG.

FULMER,JG ; SEC: MOON ,JE CIT: 0
TESTS FOR COMMON STOCK EQUIVALENCY
JAA AU 84 VOL: 8 PG:5 - 14 :: NON-PAR. :PRIM. :OTH.STAT. :FIN.METH.

FURLONG,WL CIT: 0
MINIMIZING FOREIGN EXCHANGE LOSSES
TAR AP 66 VOL: 41 PG:244 - 252 :: QUAL. :INT. LOG. :N/A :SPEC.ITEMS

GAA ,JC CIT: 0.29
USER PRIMACY IN FINANCIAL REPORTING: A SOCIAL CONTRACT APPROACH
TAR JL 86 VOL: 61 PG:435 - 454 :: DES.STAT. :INT. LOG. :THEORY :ORG.& ENVIR.

GAA ,JC ; SEC: SMITH ,CH CIT: 0
AUDITORS AND DECEPTIVE FINANCIAL STATEMENTS: ASSIGNING RESPONSIBILITY AND BLAME
CAR SP 85 VOL: 1 PG:219 - 241 :: ANOVA :SURV. :INSTIT. :ERRORS

GABER ,BG ; FIRS: BORITZ,JE ; THIR: LEMON ,WM CIT: 0
AN EXPERIMENTAL STUDY OF THE EFFECTS OF ELICITATION METHODS ON REVIEW OF PRELIMINARY AUDIT STRATEGY BY EXTERNAL AUDITORS
CAR SP 88 VOL: 4 PG:392 - 411 :: REGRESS. :LAB. :HIPS :METHOD.

GABHART,DRL ; FIRS: PONEMON,LA CIT: 0.67
AUDITOR INDEPENDENCE JUDGMENTS: A COGNITIVE-DEVELOPMENTAL MODEL AND EXPERIMENTAL EVIDENCE
CAR AU 90 VOL: 7 PG:227 - 251 :: REGRESS. :LAB. :HIPS :INDEP.

GAGNON,JM CIT: 0.18
THE PURCHASE-POOLING CHOICE: SOME EMPIRICAL EVIDENCE
JAR SP 71 VOL: 9 PG:52 - 72 :: NON-PAR. :PRIM. :OTH. :BUS.COMB.

GAGNON,JM CIT: 0.65
PURCHASE VERSUS POOLING OF INTERESTS: THE SEARCH FOR A PREDICTOR
JAR ST 67 VOL: 5 PG:187 - 204 :: DES.STAT. :PRIM. :THEORY :BUS.COMB.

GALBRAITH,JR ; FIRS: BARIFF,ML CIT: 0.67
INTRAORGANIZATIONAL POWER CONSIDERATIONS FOR DESIGNING INFORMATION SYSTEMS
AOS 01 78 VOL: 3 PG:15 - 28 :: QUAL. :INT. LOG. :OTH.BEH. :ORG.FORM

GALLHOFER,S ; SEC: HASLAM,J CIT: 0
THE AURA OF ACCOUNTING IN THE CONTEXT OF A CRISIS: GERMANY AND THE FIRST WORLD WAR
AOS 05 91 VOL: 16 PG:487 - 520 :: REGRESS. :SEC. :HIST. :ORG.& ENVIR.

GAMBLE,GO CIT: 0
PROPERTY RIGHTS THEORY AND THE FORMULATION OF FINANCIAL STATEMENTS
JAA SP 86 VOL: 1 PG:102 - 117 :: DES.STAT. :INT. LOG. :INSTIT. :FASB SUBM.

GAMBLE,GO CIT: 0
AN APPLICATION OF CURRENT VALUE THEORY TO ACCOUNTING FOR INVESTMENTS IN BONDS
JAA SU 82 VOL: 5 PG:320 - 326 :: QUAL. :INT. LOG. :THEORY :VALUAT.(INFL.)

GAMBLE,GO CIT: 0
CONCEPTS OF CAPITAL MAINTENANCE
JAA SP 81 VOL: 4 PG:220 - 237 :: QUAL. :INT. LOG. :THEORY :METHOD.

GAMBLING,T CIT: 0.17
ACCOUNTING FOR RITUALS
AOS 04 87 VOL: 12 PG:319 - 329 :: DES.STAT. :INT. LOG. :THEORY :ORG.& ENVIR.

GAMBLING,T CIT: 0.13
THE ACCOUNTANT'S GUIDE TO THE GALAXY, INCLUDING THE PROFESSION AT THE END OF THE UNIVERSE
AOS 04 85 VOL: 10 PG:415 - 426 :: DES.STAT. :INT. LOG. :THEORY :HRA

GAMBLING,TE CIT: 1.06
MAGIC, ACCOUNTING AND MORALE
AOS 02 77 VOL: 2 PG:141 - 152 :: QUAL. :INT. LOG. :THEORY :N/A

GAMBLING,TE CIT: 0.06
SYSTEMS DYNAMICS AND HUMAN RESOURCE ACCOUNTING
AOS 23 76 VOL: 1 PG:167 - 174 :: QUAL. :INT. LOG. :OTH.BEH. :HRA

GAMBLING,TE ; SEC: NOUR ,A CIT: 0
A NOTE ON INPUT-OUTPUT ANALYSIS: ITS USES IN MACRO-ECONOMICS AND MICRO-ECONOMICS
TAR JA 70 VOL: 45 PG:98 - 102 :: ANAL. :INT. LOG. :OTH.STAT. :BUDG.& PLAN.

GANDHI,NM ; FIRS: BIRNBERG,JG CIT: 0.06
TOWARD DEFINING THE ACCOUNTANT'S ROLE IN THE EVALUATION OF SOCIAL PROGRAMS
AOS 01 76 VOL: 1 PG:5 - 10 :: QUAL. :INT. LOG. :THEORY :HRA

GANGOLLY,JS ; FIRS: HUSSEIN,ME ; SEC: BAVISHI,VB CIT: 0
INTERNATIONAL SIMILARITIES AND DIFFERENCES IN THE AUDITOR'S REPORT
AUD AU 86 VOL: 6 PG:124 - 133 :: DES.STAT. :PRIM. :INSTIT. :INT.DIFF.

GANGOLLY,JS CIT: 0.08
ON JOINT COST ALLOCATION: INDEPENDENT COST PROPORTIONAL SCHEME (ICPS) AND ITS PROPERTIES
JAR AU 81 VOL: 19 PG:299 - 312 :: ANAL. :INT. LOG. :OTH.STAT. :COST.ALLOC.

GANS ,MS ; FIRS: SORTER,GH CIT: 0
OPPORTUNITIES AND IMPLICATIONS OF THE REPORT ON OBJECTIVES OF FINANCIAL STATEMENTS
JAR ST 74 VOL: 12 PG:1 - 12 :: QUAL. :INT. LOG. :THEORY :FIN.METH.

GARDNER,JC ; FIRS: BROWN ,LD ; THIR: VASARHELYI,MA CIT: 0
ATTRIBUTES OF ARTICLES IMPACTING CONTEMPORARY ACCOUNTING LITERATURE
CAR SP 89 VOL: 5 PG:793 - 815 :: REGRESS. :SEC. :THEORY :METHOD.

GARDNER,JC ; FIRS: SWANSON,GA CIT: 0
NOT-FOR-PROFIT ACCOUNTING AND AUDITING IN THE EARLY EIGHTEENTH CENTURY: SOME ARCHIVAL EVIDENCE
TAR JL 88 VOL: 63 PG:436 - 447 :: REGRESS. :INT. LOG. :HIST. :AUD.

GARDNER,JC ; FIRS: BROWN ,LD ; THIR: VASARHELYI,MA CIT: 0.5
AN ANALYSIS OF THE RESEARCH CONTRIBUTIONS OF ACCOUNTING, ORGANIZATIONS AND SOCIETY, 1976-1984
AOS 02 87 VOL: 12 PG:193 - 204 :: REGRESS. :SEC. :HIST. :METHOD.

GARDNER,JC ; FIRS: BROWN ,LD CIT: 0.75
USING CITATION ANALYSIS TO ASSESS THE IMPACT OF JOURNALS AND ARTICLES ON CONTEMPORARY ACCOUNTING RESEARCH (CAR)
JAR SP 85 VOL: 23 PG:84 - 109 :: REGRESS. :SEC. :HIST. :METHOD.

GARDNER,JC ; FIRS: BROWN ,LD CIT: 0.88
APPLYING CITATION ANALYSIS TO EVALUATE THE RESEARCH CONTRIBUTIONS OF ACCOUNTING FACULTY AND DOCTORAL PROGRAMS
TAR AP 85 VOL: 60 PG:262 - 277 :: REGRESS. :SEC. :OTH.STAT. :METHOD.

GARMAN,MB ; SEC: OHLSON,JA CIT: 1.15
INFORMATION AND THE SEQUENTIAL VALUATION OF ASSETS IN ARBITRAGE-FREE ECONOMIES
JAR AU 80 VOL: 18 PG:420 - 440 :: ANAL. :INT. LOG. :OTH. :OTH.MANAG.

GARSOMBKE,HP ; SEC: ALLEN ,G CIT: 0
DID SFAS NO.19 LEAD TO OIL AND GAS COMPANY MERGERS?
JAA SU 83 VOL: 6 PG:285 - 298 :: NON-PAR. :PRIM. :THEORY :OIL & GAS

GARSTKA,SJ ; SEC: OHLSON,PA CIT: 0.57
RATIO ESTIMATION IN ACCOUNTING POPULATIONS WITH PROBABILITIES OF SAMPLE SELECTION PROPORTIONAL TO SIZE OF BOOK VALUES
JAR SP 79 VOL: 17 PG:23 - 59 :: DES.STAT. :SIM. :OTH.STAT. :SAMP.

GARSTKA,SJ CIT: 0.19
MODELS FOR COMPUTING UPPER ERROR LIMITS IN DOLLAR-UNIT SAMPLING
JAR AU 77 VOL: 15 PG:179 - 192 :: DES.STAT. :SIM. :OTH.STAT. :SAMP.

GAUMNITZ,BR ; SEC: NUNAMAKER,TR ; THIR: SURDICK,JJ ; FOUR: THOMAS,MF CIT: 0.64
AUDITOR CONSENSUS IN INTERNAL CONTROL EVALUATION AND AUDIT PROGRAM PLANNING
JAR AU 82 VOL: 20 PG:745 - 755 :: CORR. :LAB. :HIPS :INT.CONT.

GAVER ,JJ CIT: 0
INCENTIVE EFFECTS AND MANAGERIAL COMPENSATION CONTRACTS: A STUDY OF PERFORMANCE PLAN ADOPTIONS
JAA SP 92 VOL: 7 PG:137 - 156 :: REGRESS. :PRIM. :OTH.STAT. :EXEC.COMP.

GAVER ,JJ ; SEC: GAVER ,KM ; THIR: BATTISTEL,GP CIT: 0
THE STOCK MARKET REACTION TO PERFORMANCE PLAN ADOPTIONS
TAR JA 92 VOL: 67 PG:172 - 182 :: REGRESS. :PRIM. :EMH :EXEC.COMP.

GAVER ,KM ; FIRS: GAVER ,JJ ; THIR: BATTISTEL,GP CIT: 0
THE STOCK MARKET REACTION TO PERFORMANCE PLAN ADOPTIONS
TAR JA 92 VOL: 67 PG:172 - 182 :: REGRESS. :PRIM. :EMH :EXEC.COMP.

GEIGER,MA CIT: 0
THE NEW AUDIT REPORT: AN ANALYSIS OF EXPOSURE DRAFT COMMENTS
AUD SP 89 VOL: 8 PG:40 - 63 :: REGRESS. :SURV. :INSTIT. :FASB SUBM.

GELFAND,J ; FIRS: PETRI ,E CIT: 0
THE PRODUCTION FUNCTION: A NEW PERSPECTIVE IN CAPITAL MAINTENANCE
TAR AP 79 VOL: 54 PG:330 - 345 :: ANAL. :INT. LOG. :OTH. :OTH.MANAG.

GENTRY,JA ; FIRS: DUGAN ,MT ; THIR: SHRIVER,KA CIT: 0
THE X-11 MODEL: A NEW ANALYTICAL REVIEW TECHNIQUE FOR THE AUDITOR
AUD SP 85 VOL: 4 PG:11 - 22 :: DES.STAT. :INT. LOG. :TIME SER. :ANAL.REV.

GENTRY,JA ; SEC: NEWBOLD,P ; THIR: WHITFORD,DT CIT: 0.38
CLASSIFYING BANKRUPT FIRMS WITH FUNDS FLOW COMPONENTS
JAR SP 85 VOL: 23 PG:146 - 160 :: REGRESS. :PRIM. :OTH.STAT. :BUS.FAIL.

GEORGE,NE ; FIRS: RULAND,W ; SEC: TUNG ,S CIT: 0
FACTORS ASSOCIATED WITH THE DISCLOSURE OF MANAGERS' FORECASTS
TAR JL 90 VOL: 65 PG:710 - 721 :: REGRESS. :PRIM. :HIPS :FOREC.

GERBOTH,DL CIT: 0.18
RESEARCH, INTUITION, AND POLITICS IN ACCOUNTING INQUIRY
TAR JL 73 VOL: 48 PG:475 - 482 :: QUAL. :INT. LOG. :INSTIT. :METHOD.

GERLACH,JH CIT: 0
A MODEL FOR TESTING THE RELIABILITY OF COMPUTER PROGRAMS AND EDP MANAGEMENT :INTERNAL CONTROL IMPLICATIONS
AUD SP 88 VOL: 07 PG:61 - 76 :: DES.STAT. :SIM. :OTH.STAT. :INT.CONT.

GERLACH,JH ; FIRS: BAILEY JR,AD ; SEC: DUKE ,GL ; FOUR: KO ,CE ; FIFT: MESERVY,RD ; SIX: WHINSTON,AB CIT: 0.38
TICOM AND THE ANALYSIS OF INTERNAL CONTROLS
TAR AP 85 VOL: 60 PG:186 - 201 :: CORR. :INT. LOG. :OTH. :INT.CONT.

GHEYARA,K ; SEC: BOATSMAN,JR CIT: 1.31
MARKET REACTION TO THE 1976 REPLACEMENT COST DISCLOSURES
JAE AG 80 VOL: 2 PG:107 - 125 :: MIXED :PRIM. :EMH :VALUAT.(INFL.)

GHICAS,D ; SEC: PASTENA,V CIT: 0.5
THE ACQUISITION VALUE OF OIL AND GAS FIRMS: THE ROLE OF HISTORICAL COSTS, RESERVE RECOGNITION ACCOUNTING, AND ANALYSTS' APPRAISALS
CAR AU 89 VOL: 6 PG:125 - 142 :: REGRESS. :PRIM. :EMH :OIL & GAS

GHICAS,D ; FIRS: ABDEL-KHALIK,AR ; SEC: CHI ,C CIT: 0.33
RATIONALITY OF EXECUTIVE COMPENSATION SCHEMES AND REAL ACCOUNTING CHANGES
CAR AU 87 VOL: 4 PG:32 - 60 :: REGRESS. :PRIM. :INF.ECO./AG. :ACC.CHNG.

GHICAS,DC CIT: 0
DETERMINANTS OF ACTUARIAL COST METHOD CHANGES FOR PENSION ACCOUNTING AND FUNDING
TAR AP 90 VOL: 65 PG:384 - 405 :: REGRESS. :PRIM. :OTH.STAT. :PENS.

GIACCOTTO,C CIT: 0
ACCOUNTS RECEIVABLE POLICY UNDER STOCHASTIC INFLATION
JAA SU 92 VOL: 7 PG:291 - 310 :: DES.STAT. :PRIM. :TIME SER. :OTH.C/A

GIBBINS,M ; SEC: RICHARDSON,A ; THIR: WATERHOUSE,J CIT: 0.33
THE MANAGEMENT OF CORPORATE FINANCIAL DISCLOSURES: OPPORTUNISM, RITUALISM, POLICIES, AND PROCESSES
JAR SP 90 VOL: 28 PG:121 - 143 :: REGRESS. :SURV. :OTH.BEH. :INFO.STRUC.

GIBBINS,M ; FIRS: EMBY ,C CIT: 0
GOOD JUDGMENT IN PUBLIC ACCOUNTING: QUALITY AND JUSTIFICATION
CAR SP 88 VOL: 4 PG:287 - 313 :: REGRESS. :SURV. :HIPS :JUDG.

GIBBINS,M CIT: 3.11
PROPOSITIONS ABOUT THE PSYCHOLOGY OF PROFESSIONAL JUDGMENT IN PUBLIC ACCOUNTING
JAR SP 84 VOL: 22 PG:103 - 125 :: QUAL. :INT. LOG. :HIPS :JUDG.

GIBBINS,M CIT: 0.18
REGRESSION AND OTHER STATISTICAL IMPLICATIONS FOR RESEARCH ON JUDGMENT USING INTERCORRELATED DATA SOURCES
JAR SP 82 VOL: 20 PG:121 - 138 :: ANAL. :INT. LOG. :HIPS :METHOD.

GIBBINS,M ; SEC: WOLF ,FM CIT: 0.73
AUDITORS' SUBJECTIVE DECISION ENVIRONMENT - THE CASE OF A NORMAL EXTERNAL AUDIT
TAR JA 82 VOL: 57 PG:105 - 124 :: DES.STAT. :SURV. :OTH.BEH. :AUD.

GIBBINS,M ; FIRS: SWIERINGA,RJ ; THIR: LARSSON,L ; FOUR: SWEENEY,JL CIT: 1.41
EXPERIMENTS IN THE HEURISTICS OF HUMAN INFORMATION PROCESSING
JAR ST 76 VOL: 14 PG:159 - 187 :: MIXED :LAB. :HIPS :MANAG.

GIBBONS,M CIT: 0
DECEPTION: A TRICKY ISSUE FOR BEHAVIORAL RESEARCH IN ACCOUNTING AND AUDITING
AUD AU 92 VOL: 11 PG:113 - 126 :: DES.STAT. :INT. LOG. :HIPS :METHOD.

GIBBS ,G CIT: 0
PROFESSORS' TAXABLE INCOME AND DEDUCTIONS
TAR OC 64 VOL: 39 PG:004 - 007 :: QUAL. :SEC. :N/A :OTH.MANAG.

GIBSON,JL CIT: 0
ACCOUNTING IN THE DECISION-MAKING PROCESS: SOME EMPIRICAL EVIDENCE
TAR JL 63 VOL: 38 PG:492 - 500 :: QUAL. :CASE :THEORY :MANAG.

GIBSON,RW CIT: 0
COMPARATIVE PROFESSIONAL ACCOUNTANCY - AUSTRALIA
TAR JA 65 VOL: 40 PG:196 - 203 :: QUAL. :INT. LOG. :INSTIT. :AUD.

GIESE ,J ; FIRS: ANDERSON,HM ; THIR: BOOKER,J CIT: 0.12
SOME PROPOSITIONS ABOUT AUDITING
TAR JL 70 VOL: 45 PG:524 - 531 :: QUAL. :INT. LOG. :INSTIT. :AUD.

GIFT ,MJ ; FIRS: AJINKYA,BB ; SEC: ATIASE,RK CIT: 0
VOLUME OF TRADING AND THE DISPERSION OF FINANCIAL ANALYSTS' EARNINGS FORECASTS
TAR AP 91 VOL: 66 PG:389 - 401 :: REGRESS. :PRIM. :EMH :AUD.BEH.

GIFT ,MJ ; FIRS: AJINKYA,BB CIT: 1.56
CORPORATE MANAGERS' EARNINGS FORECASTS AND SYMMETRICAL ADJUSTMENTS OF MARKET EXPECTATIONS
JAR AU 84 VOL: 22 PG:425 - 444 :: ANOVA :PRIM. :EMH :FOREC.

GIGLER,FB ; FIRS: FELTHAM,GA ; THIR: HUGHES,JS CIT: 0
THE EFFECTS OF LINE-OF-BUSINESS REPORTING ON COMPETITION IN OLIGOPOLY SETTINGS
CAR AU 92 VOL: 9 PG:1 - 23 :: DES.STAT. :INT. LOG. :INF.ECO./AG. :SEG.REP.

GILLES JR,LH CIT: 0
STATUTORY DEPLETION - SUBSIDY IN DISGUISE?
TAR OC 63 VOL: 38 PG:776 - 784 :: QUAL. :INT. LOG. :THEORY :AMOR./DEPL.

GINZBERG,MJ CIT: 0.62
AN ORGANIZATIONAL CONTINGENCIES VIEW OF ACCOUNTING AND INFORMATION SYSTEMS IMPLEMENTATION
AOS 04 80 VOL: 5 PG:369 - 382 :: QUAL. :INT. LOG. :OTH. :AUD.BEH.

GIRARD,D ; FIRS: HAWKINS,CA CIT: 0
REPLACEMENT DECISIONS UNDER THE ACCELERATED COST RECOVERY SYSTEM
JAA SP 84 VOL: 7 PG:225 - 240 :: MIXED :INT. LOG. :THEORY :PP&E / DEPR

GIROUX,GA ; FIRS: DEIS JR,DR CIT: 0
DETERMINANTS OF AUDIT QUALITY IN THE PUBLIC SECTOR
TAR JL 92 VOL: 67 PG:462 - 479 :: REGRESS. :MIXED :INSTIT. :INDEP.

GIROUX,GA ; SEC: MAYPER,AG ; THIR: DAFT ,RL CIT: 0
ORGANIZATION SIZE, BUDGET CYCLE, AND BUDGET RELATED INFLUENCE IN CITY GOVERNMENTS: AN EMPIRICAL STUDY
AOS 06 86 VOL: 11 PG:499 - 520 :: REGRESS. :SURV. :OTH.STAT. :BUDG.& PLAN.

GIROUX,GA ; FIRS: APOSTOLOU,NG ; THIR: WELKER,RB CIT: 0
THE INFORMATION CONTENT OF MUNICIPAL SPENDING RATE DATA
JAR AU 85 VOL: 23 PG:853 - 858 :: REGRESS. :PRIM. :INSTIT. :LTD

GIROUX,GA ; FIRS: ROSE ,PS ; SEC: ANDREWS,WT CIT: 0
PREDICTING BUSINESS FAILURE: A MACROECONOMIC PERSPECTIVE
JAA AU 82 VOL: 6 PG:20 - 31 :: REGRESS. :PRIM. :TIME SER. :BUS.FAIL.

GIVENS,HR CIT: 0
BASIC ACCOUNTING POSTULATES
TAR JL 66 VOL: 41 PG:458 - 463 :: QUAL. :INT. LOG. :THEORY :FIN.METH.

GIVOLY,D ; SEC: HAYN ,C CIT: 0
THE VALUATION OF THE DEFERRED TAX LIABILITY: EVIDENCE FROM THE STOCK MARKET
TAR AP 92 VOL: 67 PG:394 - 410 :: REGRESS. :PRIM. :EMH :SPEC.ITEMS

GIVOLY,D ; SEC: LAKONISHOK,J CIT: 0
AGGREGATE EARNINGS EXPECTATIONS AND STOCK MARKET BEHAVIOR
JAA SP 87 VOL: 2 PG:117 - 137 :: REGRESS. :PRIM. :EMH :FOREC.

GIVOLY,D CIT: 0.63
THE FORMATION OF EARNINGS EXPECTATIONS
TAR JL 85 VOL: 60 PG:372 - 386 :: REGRESS. :PRIM. :N/A :FOREC.

GIVOLY,D ; FIRS: FRIED ,D CIT: 2.73
FINANCIAL ANALYSTS' FORECASTS OF EARNINGS: A BETTER SURROGATE FOR MARKET EXPECTATIONS
JAE OC 82 VOL: 4 PG:85 - 107 :: OTH.QUANT. :SEC. :TIME SER. :FOREC.

GIVOLY,D ; SEC: PALMON,D CIT: 1.64
TIMELINESS OF ANNUAL EARNINGS ANNOUNCEMENTS: SOME EMPIRICAL EVIDENCE
TAR JL 82 VOL: 57 PG:486 - 508 :: REGRESS. :PRIM. :EMH :FIN.ST.TIM.

GIVOLY,D ; SEC: PALMON,D CIT: 0
CLASSIFICATION OF CONVERTIBLE DEBT AS COMMON STOCK EQUIVALENTS: SOME EMPIRICAL EVIDENCE ON THE EFFECTS OF APB OPINION 15
JAR AU 81 VOL: 19 PG:530 - 543 :: CORR. :PRIM. :EMH :LTD

GIVOLY,D ; SEC: LAKONISHOK,J CIT: 1.14
THE INFORMATION CONTENT OF FINANCIAL ANALYSTS' FORECASTS OF EARNINGS: SOME EVIDENCE ON SEMI-STRONG INEFFICIENCY
JAE DE 79 VOL: 1 PG:165 - 185 :: DES.STAT. :PRIM. :EMH :FOREC.

GIVOLY,D ; SEC: RONEN ,J ; THIR: SCHIFF,A CIT: 0.07
DOES AUDIT INVOLVEMENT AFFECT THE QUALITY OF INTERIM REPORT NUMBERS?
JAA SU 78 VOL: 1 PG:361 - 372 :: ANOVA :PRIM. :INSTIT. :AUD.

GJESDAL,F CIT: 1.5
ACCOUNTING FOR STEWARDSHIP
JAR SP 81 VOL: 19 PG:208 - 231 :: ANAL. :INT. LOG. :INF.ECO./AG. :INFO.STRUC.

GLATZER,W CIT: 0
AN OVERVIEW OF THE INTERNATIONAL DEVELOPMENT IN MACRO SOCIAL INDICATORS
AOS 03 81 VOL: 6 PG:219 - 234 :: QUAL. :INT. LOG. :OTH. :HRA

GLEZEN,GW ; FIRS: BALDWIN,J CIT: 0
BANKRUPTCY PREDICTION USING QUARTERLY FINANCIAL STATEMENT DATA
JAA SU 92 VOL: 7 PG:269 - 285 :: REGRESS. :PRIM. :TIME SER. :BUS.FAIL.

GLEZEN,GW ; FIRS: ROBERTS,RW ; THIR: JONES ,TW CIT: 0.67
DETERMINANTS OF AUDIT CHANGE IN THE PUBLIC SECTOR
JAR SP 90 VOL: 28 PG:220 - 228 :: REGRESS. :PRIM. :OTH.STAT. :ORG.

GLEZEN,GW ; FIRS: WILSON,AC CIT: 0
REGRESSION ANALYSIS IN AUDITING: A COMPARISON OF ALTERNATIVE INVESTIGATION RULES-SOME FURTHER EVIDENCE
AUD SP 89 VOL: 8 PG:90 - 100 :: DES.STAT. :PRIM. :OTH.STAT. :ANAL.REV.

GLEZEN,GW ; SEC: MILLAR,JA CIT: 0
AN EMPIRICAL INVESTIGATION OF STOCKHOLDER REACTION TO DISCLOSURES REQUIREDBY ASR NO. 150
JAR AU 85 VOL: 23 PG:859 - 870 :: REGRESS. :PRIM. :INSTIT. :ORG.

GLICK ,R ; SEC: PLAUT ,SE CIT: 0
MONEY DEMAND AND OFF-BALANCE SHEET LIQUIDITY: EMPIRICAL ANALYSIS AND IMPLICATIONS FOR MONETARY POLICY
JAA SP 89 VOL: 4 PG:147 - 159 :: REGRESS. :PRIM. :OTH.STAT. :SPEC.ITEMS

GLOVER,F CIT: 0
MANAGEMENT DECISION AND INTEGER PROGRAMMING
TAR AP 69 VOL: 44 PG:300 - 303 :: ANAL. :INT. LOG. :MATH.PROG. :LTD

GODFREY,J ; FIRS: WURST ,J ; SEC: NETER ,J CIT: 0
EFFECTIVENESS OF RECTIFICATION IN AUDIT SAMPLING
TAR AP 91 VOL: 66 PG:333 - 347 :: DES.STAT. :SIM. :OTH.STAT. :ERRORS

GODFREY,JT ; FIRS: KIM ,HS ; SEC: NETER ,J CIT: 0.17
BEHAVIOR OF STATISTICAL ESTIMATORS IN MULTILOCATION AUDIT SAMPLING
AUD SP 87 VOL: 6 PG:40 - 58 :: DES.STAT. :SIM. :OTH.STAT. :SAMP.

GODFREY,JT ; FIRS: ROSHWALB,A ; SEC: WRIGHT,RL CIT: 0
A NEW APPROACH FOR STRATIFIED SAMPLING IN INVENTORY COST ESTIMATION
AUD AU 87 VOL: 7 PG:54 - 70 :: DES.STAT. :SIM. :OTH.STAT. :SAMP.

GODFREY,JT ; SEC: NETER ,J CIT: 0.78
BAYESIAN BOUNDS FOR MONETARY UNIT SAMPLING IN ACCOUNTING AND AUDITING
JAR AU 84 VOL: 22 PG:497 - 525 :: ANAL. :SIM. :OTH.STAT. :SAMP.

GODFREY,JT ; SEC: ANDREWS,RW CIT: 0.36
A FINITE POPULATION BAYESIAN MODEL FOR COMPLIANCE TESTING
JAR AU 82 VOL: 20 PG:304 - 315 :: ANAL. :INT. LOG. :OTH.STAT. :SAMP.

GODFREY,JT ; SEC: PRINCE,TR CIT: 0.12
THE ACCOUNTING MODEL FROM AN INFORMATION SYSTEMS PERSPECTIVE
TAR JA 71 VOL: 46 PG:75 - 89 :: QUAL. :INT. LOG. :INF.ECO./AG. :MANAG.

GODFREY,JT CIT: 0
SHORT-RUN PLANNING IN A DECENTRALIZED FIRM
TAR AP 71 VOL: 46 PG:286 - 297 :: ANAL. :INT. LOG. :MATH.PROG. :BUDG.& PLAN.

GOETZ ,BE CIT: 0.12
PROFESSORIAL OBSOLESCENCE
TAR JA 67 VOL: 42 PG:53 - 61 :: QUAL. :INT. LOG. :INSTIT. :OTH.MANAG.

GOETZ ,BE CIT: 0
TRANSFER PRICES: AN EXERCISE IN RELEVANCY AND GOAL CONGRUENCE
TAR JL 67 VOL: 42 PG:435 - 440 :: QUAL. :INT. LOG. :N/A :TRANS.PRIC.

GOETZ-JR,JF ; SEC: MORROW,PC ; THIR: MCELROY,JC CIT: 0
THE EFFECT OF ACCOUNTING FIRM SIZE AND MEMBER RANK ON PROFESSIONALISM
AOS 02 91 VOL: 16 PG:159 - 165 :: REGRESS. :SURV. :OTH.BEH. :ORG.

GOFFIN,JL ; FIRS: AMEY ,LR CIT: 0
JOINT PRODUCT DECISIONS: THE VARIABLE PROPORTIONS CASE
CAR AU 88 VOL: 5 PG:174 - 198 :: DES.STAT. :INT. LOG. :INF.ECO./AG. :REL.COSTS

GOGGANS,TP CIT: 0
THE ACCOUNTANT'S ROLE IN WAGE NEGOTIATIONS
TAR JL 64 VOL: 39 PG:627 - 630 :: QUAL. :INT. LOG. :INSTIT. :OTH.MANAG.

GOLDBERG,L CIT: 0
THE PRESENT STATE OF ACCOUNTING THEORY
TAR JL 63 VOL: 38 PG:457 - 469 :: QUAL. :INT. LOG. :THEORY :OTH.MANAG.

GOLDIN,HJ CIT: 0.25
CHANGES IN MUNICIPAL ACCOUNTING: THE NEW YORK CITY COMPTROLLER'S OVERVIEW
JAA SU 85 VOL: 8 PG:269 - 278 :: DES.STAT. :INT. LOG. :THEORY :FIN.METH.

GOLDMAN,A ; SEC: BARLEV,B CIT: 0.35
THE AUDITOR-FIRM CONFLICT OF INTERESTS: ITS IMPLICATIONS FOR INDEPENDENCE
TAR OC 74 VOL: 49 PG:707 - 718 :: QUAL. :INT. LOG. :INSTIT. :INDEP.

GOLDSCHMIDT,Y ; SEC: SHASHUA,L CIT: 0
DISTORTION OF INCOME BY SFAS NO.33
JAA AU 84 VOL: 8 PG:54 - 67 :: QUAL. :INT. LOG. :THEORY :VALUAT.(INFL.)

GOLDSCHMIDT,Y ; SEC: SMIDT ,S CIT: 0
VALUING THE FIRM'S DURABLE ASSETS FOR MANAGERIAL INFORMATION
TAR AP 69 VOL: 44 PG:317 - 329 :: QUAL. :INT. LOG. :THEORY :VALUAT.(INFL.)

GOLDWASSER,DL CIT: 0
POLICY CONSIDERATIONS IN ACCOUNTANTS' LIABILITY TO THIRD PARTIES FOR NEGLIGENCE
JAA SU 88 VOL: 03 PG:217 - 232 :: DES.STAT. :INT. LOG. :INSTIT. :LIAB.

GOLEMBIEWSKI,RT CIT: 0.29
ACCOUNTANCY AS A FUNCTION OF ORGANIZATION THEORY
TAR AP 64 VOL: 39 PG:333 - 341 :: QUAL. :INT. LOG. :OTH.BEH. :OTH.MANAG.

GOMBERG,M ; SEC: FARBER,A CIT: 0
THE BALANCE SHEET OF THE FUTURE
TAR JL 64 VOL: 39 PG:615 - 617 :: QUAL. :INT. LOG. :THEORY :FIN.METH.

GOMBOLA,MJ ; SEC: KETZ ,JE CIT: 0.1
A NOTE ON CASH FLOW AND CLASSIFICATION PATTERNS OF FINANCIAL RATIOS
TAR JA 83 VOL: 58 PG:105 - 114 :: OTH.QUANT. :LAB. :OTH.STAT. :SPEC.ITEMS

GONEDES,NJ CIT: 0.38
PUBLIC DISCLOSURE RULES, PRIVATE INFORMATION-PRODUCTION DECISIONS AND CAPITAL MARKET EQUILIBRIUM
JAR AU 80 VOL: 18 PG:441 - 476 :: ANAL. :INT. LOG. :INF.ECO./AG. :INFO.STRUC.

GONEDES,NJ ; SEC: DOPUCH,N CIT: 0.5
ECONOMIC ANALYSES AND ACCOUNTING TECHNIQUES: PERSPECTIVES AND PROPOSALS
JAR AU 79 VOL: 17 PG:384 - 410 :: QUAL. :INT. LOG. :THEORY :METHOD.

GONEDES,NJ CIT: 1.53
CORPORATE SIGNALING, EXTERNAL ACCOUNTING, AND CAPITAL MARKET EQUILIBRIUM: EVIDENCE ON DIVIDENDS, INCOME, AND EXTRAORDINARY ITEMS
JAR SP 78 VOL: 16 PG:26 - 79 :: MIXED :PRIM. :EMH :CASH DIV.

GONEDES,NJ ; SEC: DOPUCH,N ; THIR: PENMAN,SH CIT: 2.41
DISCLOSURE RULES, INFORMATION-PRODUCTION, AND CAPITAL MARKET EQUILIBRIUM: THE CASE OF FORECAST DISCLOSURE RULES
JAR SP 76 VOL: 14 PG:89 - 137 :: NON-PAR. :PRIM. :EMH :FOREC.

GONEDES,NJ CIT: 1.88
RISK, INFORMATION, AND THE EFFECTS OF SPECIAL ACCOUNTING ITEMS ON CAPITAL MARKET EQUILIBRIUM
JAR AU 75 VOL: 13 PG:220 - 256 :: REGRESS. :PRIM. :EMH :SPEC.ITEMS

GONEDES,NJ CIT: 0.94
CAPITAL MARKET EQUILIBRIUM AND ANNUAL ACCOUNTING NUMBERS: EMPIRICAL EVIDENCE
JAR SP 74 VOL: 12 PG:26 - 62 :: REGRESS. :PRIM. :EMH :FIN.METH.

GONEDES,NJ ; SEC: IJIRI ,Y CIT: 0.35
IMPROVING SUBJECTIVE PROBABILITY ASSESSMENT FOR PLANNING AND CONTROL IN TEAM-LIKE ORGANIZATIONS
JAR AU 74 VOL: 12 PG:251 - 269 :: ANAL. :INT. LOG. :INF.ECO./AG. :PROB.ELIC.

GONEDES,NJ ; SEC: DOPUCH,N CIT: 4.12
CAPITAL MARKET EQUILIBRIUM, INFORMATION PRODUCTION, AND SELECTING ACCOUNTING TECHNIQUES: THEORETICAL FRAMEWORK AND REVIEW OF EMP
JAR ST 74 VOL: 12 PG:48 - 129 :: ANAL. :SEC. :EMH :FIN.METH.

GONEDES,NJ CIT: 0.94
PROPERTIES OF ACCOUNTING NUMBERS: MODELS AND TESTS
JAR AU 73 VOL: 11 PG:212 - 237 :: REGRESS. :PRIM. :TIME SER. :FIN.METH.

GONEDES,NJ CIT: 0.41
EFFICIENT CAPITAL MARKETS AND EXTERNAL ACCOUNTING
TAR JA 72 VOL: 47 PG:11 - 21 :: QUAL. :INT. LOG. :EMH :FIN.METH.

GONEDES,NJ CIT: 0.12
OPTIMAL TIMING OF CONTROL MESSAGES FOR A TWO-STATE MARKOV PROCESS
JAR AU 71 VOL: 9 PG:236 - 252 :: MARKOV :INT. LOG. :OTH.STAT. :MANAG.

GONEDES,NJ CIT: 0
SOME EVIDENCE ON INVESTOR ACTIONS AND ACCOUNTING MESSAGES - PART I
TAR AP 71 VOL: 46 PG:320 - 328 :: ANAL. :INT. LOG. :TIME SER. :FIN.METH.

GONEDES,NJ CIT: 0
SOME EVIDENCE ON INVESTOR ACTIONS AND ACCOUNTING MESSAGES - PART II
TAR JL 71 VOL: 46 PG:535 - 551 :: REGRESS. :PRIM. :EMH :FIN.METH.

GONEDES,NJ CIT: 0.06
ACCOUNTING FOR MANAGERIAL CONTROL: AN APPLICATION OF CHANCE-CONSTRAINED PROGRAMMING
JAR SP 70 VOL: 8 PG:1 - 20 :: ANAL. :INT. LOG. :MATH.PROG. :MANAG.

GONEDES,NJ CIT: 0
THE SIGNIFICANCE OF SELECTED ACCOUNTING PROCEDURES: A STATISTICAL TEST
JAR ST 69 VOL: 7 PG:90 - 113 :: REGRESS. :PRIM. :EMH :FIN.METH.

GONEDES,NJ ; FIRS: LARSON,KD CIT: 0.06
BUSINESS COMBINATIONS: AN EXCHANGE RATIO DETERMINATION MODEL
TAR OC 69 VOL: 44 PG:720 - 728 :: ANAL. :INT. LOG. :N/A :BUS.COMB.

GOODMAN,SS ; FIRS: FIRMIN,PA ; THIR: HENDRICKS,TE ; FOUR: LINN ,JJ CIT: 0
UNIVERSITY COST STRUCTURE AND BEHAVIOR: AN EMPIRICAL STUDY
JAR ST 68 VOL: 6 PG:122 - 155 :: DES.STAT. :SIM. :OTH.STAT. :MANAG.

GORDON,DA ; SEC: GORDON,MJ CIT: 0
THE INTEREST RATE COMPONENT OF SYSTEMATIC RISK
JAA AU 90 VOL: 5 PG:573 - 588 :: REGRESS. :PRIM. :EMH :LTD

GORDON,FE ; SEC: RHODE ,JG ; THIR: MERCHANT,KA CIT: 0.19
THE EFFECTS OF SALARY AND HUMAN RESOURCE ACCOUNTING DISCLOSURES ON SMALL GROUP RELATIONS AND PERFORMANCE
AOS 04 77 VOL: 2 PG:295 - 306 :: ANOVA :LAB. :OTH.BEH. :HRA

GORDON,IM ; FIRS: BOLAND,LA CIT: 0
CRITICIZING POSITIVE ACCOUNTING THEORY
CAR AU 92 VOL: 9 PG:142 - 170 :: DES.STAT. :SEC. :THEORY :FIN.METH.

GORDON,LA ; SEC: SMITH ,KJ CIT: 0
POSTAUDITING CAPITAL EXPENDITURES AND FIRM PERFORMANCE: THE ROLE OF ASYMMETRIC INFORMATION
AOS 92 VOL: 17 PG:741 - 757 :: REGRESS. :PRIM. :OTH.BEH. :CAP.BUDG.

GORDON,LA ; FIRS: SCHICK,AG ; THIR: HAKA ,S CIT: 0
INFORMATION OVERLOAD: A TEMPORAL APPROACH
AOS 03 90 VOL: 15 PG:199 - 220 :: REGRESS. :SEC. :HIPS :DEC.AIDS

GORDON,LA CIT: 0.25
BENEFIT-COST ANALYSIS AND RESOURCE ALLOCATION DECISIONS
AOS 03 89 VOL: 14 PG:247 - 258 :: REGRESS. :PRIM. :OTH.BEH. :COST.ALLOC.

GORDON,LA ; SEC: HAMER ,MH CIT: 0
RATES OF RETURN AND CASH FLOW PROFILES: AN EXTENSION
AUD JL 88 VOL: 63 PG:514 - 521 :: DES.STAT. :INT. LOG. :THEORY :FIN.METH.

GORDON,LA ; FIRS: HAKA ,SF ; THIR: PINCHES,GE CIT: 0.63
SOPHISTICATED CAPITAL BUDGETING SELECTION TECHNIQUES AND FIRM PERFORMANCE
TAR OC 85 VOL: 60 PG:651 - 669 :: REGRESS. :PRIM. :EMH :CAP.BUDG.

GORDON,LA ; SEC: NARAYANAN,VK CIT: 0.89
MANAGEMENT ACCOUNTING SYSTEMS, PERCEIVED ENVIRONMENTAL UNCERTAINTY AND ORGANIZATION STRUCTURE: AN EMPIRICAL INVESTIGATION
AOS 01 84 VOL: 9 PG:33 - 47 :: CORR. :SURV. :OTH. :ORG.FORM

GORDON,LA ; SEC: HAKA ,S ; THIR: SCHICK,AG CIT: 0.11
STRATEGIES FOR INFORMATION SYSTEMS IMPLEMENTATION: THE CASE OF ZERO BASE BUDGETING
AOS 02 84 VOL: 9 PG:111 - 123 :: NON-PAR. :PRIM. :OTH. :BUDG.& PLAN.

GORDON,LA ; SEC: LARCKER,DF ; THIR: TUGGLE,FD CIT: 0.67
STRATEGIC DECISION PROCESSES AND THE DESIGN OF ACCOUNTING INFORMATION SYSTEMS: CONCEPTUAL LINKAGES
AOS 34 78 VOL: 3 PG:203 - 214 :: QUAL. :INT. LOG. :OTH. :INFO.STRUC.

GORDON,LA ; SEC: MILLER,D CIT: 1.53
A CONTINGENCY FRAMEWORK FOR THE DESIGN OF ACCOUNTING INFORMATION SYSTEMS
AOS 01 76 VOL: 1 PG:59 - 70 :: QUAL. :INT. LOG. :OTH.BEH. :INFO.STRUC.

GORDON,MJ ; FIRS: GORDON,DA CIT: 0
THE INTEREST RATE COMPONENT OF SYSTEMATIC RISK
JAA AU 90 VOL: 5 PG:573 - 588 :: REGRESS. :PRIM. :EMH :LTD

GORDON,MJ CIT: 0.12
A METHOD OF PRICING FOR A SOCIALIST ECONOMY
TAR JL 70 VOL: 45 PG:427 - 443 :: ANAL. :INT. LOG. :N/A :TRANS.PRIC.

GORDON,MJ CIT: 0.88
POSTULATES, PRINCIPLES AND RESEARCH IN ACCOUNTING
TAR AP 64 VOL: 39 PG:251 - 263 :: QUAL. :INT. LOG. :THEORY :OTH.FIN.ACC.

GORMLEY,RJ CIT: 0.2
DEVELOPMENTS IN ACCOUNTANTS' LIABILITY TO NONCLIENTS FOR NEGLIGENCE
JAA SU 88 VOL: 03 PG:185 - 212 :: REGRESS. :PRIM. :INSTIT. :LIAB.

GORMLEY,RJ CIT: 0
RICO AND THE PROFESSIONAL ACCOUNTANT
JAA AU 82 VOL: 6 PG:51 - 59 :: QUAL. :INT. LOG. :OTH. :PROF.RESP.

GORMLEY,RJ CIT: 0
PROFESSIONAL RISKS IN PURCHASE AUDITS AND REVIEWS
JAA SU 80 VOL: 3 PG:293 - 312 :: QUAL. :INT. LOG. :THEORY :RISK

GORTON,G ; SEC: PENNACCHI,G CIT: 0
ARE LOAN SALES REALLY OFF-BALANCE SHEET?
JAA SP 89 VOL: 4 PG:125 - 145 :: REGRESS. :PRIM. :TIME SER. :SPEC.ITEMS

GOSMAN,ML CIT: 0.71
CHARACTERISTICS OF FIRMS MAKING ACCOUNTING CHANGES
TAR JA 73 VOL: 48 PG:1 - 11 :: DES.STAT. :PRIM. :OTH.BEH. :AUD.BEH.

GOVINDARAJ,S CIT: 0
LINEAR VALUATION MODELS IN CONTINUOUS TIME WITH ACCOUNTING INFORMATION
JAA AU 92 VOL: 7 PG:485 - 508 :: DES.STAT. :INT. LOG. :EMH :METHOD.

GOVINDARAJAN,V ; FIRS: STEPHENS,RG CIT: 0
ON ASSESSING A FIRM'S CASH GENERATING ABILITY
TAR JA 90 VOL: 65 PG:242 - 257 :: REGRESS. :CASE :HIPS :FIN.METH.

GOVINDARAJAN,V ; SEC: GUPTA ,AK CIT: 1.38
LINKING CONTROL SYSTEMS TO BUSINESS UNIT STRATEGY: IMPACT ON PERFORMANCE
AOS 01 85 VOL: 10 PG:51 - 66 :: REGRESS. :SURV. :OTH.BEH. :MANAG.

GOVINDARAJAN,V CIT: 1.67
APPROPRIATENESS OF ACCOUNTING DATA IN PERFORMANCE EVALUATION: AN EMPIRICAL EXAMINATION OF ENVIRONMENTAL UNCERTAINTY AS AN INTERVENING VARIABLE
AOS 02 84 VOL: 9 PG:125 - 135 :: DES.STAT. :SURV. :OTH.BEH. :ORG.& ENVIR.

GOVINDARAJAN,V ; FIRS: SAN MIGUEL,JG CIT: 0
THE CONTINGENT RELATIONSHIP BETWEEN THE CONTROLLER AND INTERNAL AUDIT FUNCTIONS IN LARGE ORGANIZATIONS
AOS 02 84 VOL: 9 PG:179 - 188 :: NON-PAR. :SURV. :OTH.BEH. :INT.AUD.

GOVINDARAJAN,V ; FIRS: CHURCHILL,NC ; SEC: COOPER,WW CIT: 0
EFFECTS OF AUDITS ON THE BEHAVIOR OF MEDICAL PROFESSIONALS UNDER THE BENNETT AMENDMENT
AUD WI 82 VOL: 1 PG:69 - 91 :: ANOVA :PRIM. :OTH.STAT. :OPER.AUD.

GOVINDARAJAN,V CIT: 0
THE OBJECTIVES OF FINANCIAL STATEMENTS: AN EMPIRICAL STUDY OF THE USE OF CASH FLOW AND EARNINGS BY SECURITY ANALYSTS
AOS 04 80 VOL: 5 PG:383 - 392 :: DES.STAT. :PRIM. :THEORY :CASH

GOVINDARAJAN,V CIT: 0
OBJECTIVES OF FINANCIAL REPORTING BY BUSINESS ENTERPRISES: SOME EVIDENCE OF USER PREFERENCE
JAA SU 79 VOL: 2 PG:339 - 343 :: DES.STAT. :PRIM. :THEORY :FIN.METH.

GOVINDARAJAN,V ; FIRS: SAN MIGUEL,JG ; SEC: SHANK ,JK CIT: 0.06
EXTENDING CORPORATE ACCOUNTABILITY: A SURVEY AND FRAMEWORK FOR ANALYSIS
AOS 04 77 VOL: 2 PG:333 - 348 :: DES.STAT. :PRIM. :OTH. :AUD.

GRADY ,P CIT: 0
INVENTORY OF GENERALLY ACCEPTED ACCOUNTING PRINCIPLES IN THE U.S.A.
TAR JA 65 VOL: 40 PG:21 - 30 :: QUAL. :SEC. :THEORY :FIN.METH.

GRAESE,CE CIT: 0
RESPONSIBILITY REPORTING TO MANAGEMENT
TAR AP 64 VOL: 39 PG:387 - 391 :: QUAL. :INT. LOG. :N/A :RESP.ACC.

GRAHAM,LE ; SEC: DAMENS,J ; THIR: VAN NESS,G CIT: 0
DEVELOPING RISK ADVISOR: AN EXPERT SYSTEM FOR RISK IDENTIFICATION
AUD SP 91 VOL: 10 PG:69 - 96 :: REGRESS. :LAB. :EXP.SYST. :RISK

GRAHAM,LE ; FIRS: SHPILBERG,D CIT: 0.57
DEVELOPING EXPERTAX: AN EXPERT SYSTEM FOR CORPORATE TAX ACCRUAL
AUD AU 86 VOL: 6 PG:75 - 94 :: QUAL. :LAB. :EXP.SYST. :TAXES

GRAHAM,LE ; FIRS: NETER ,J ; SEC: KIM ,HS CIT: 0.11
ON COMBINING STRINGER BOUNDS FOR INDEPENDENT MONETARY UNIT SAMPLES FROM SEVERAL POPULATIONS
AUD AU 84 VOL: 4 PG:75 - 88 :: ANAL. :INT. LOG. :OTH.STAT. :SAMP.

GRANOF,MH ; SEC: SHORT ,DG CIT: 0.22
WHY DO COMPANIES REJECT LIFO?
JAA SU 84 VOL: 7 PG:323 - 333 :: DES.STAT. :SURV. :THEORY :INV.

GRANOF,MH ; FIRS: DEAKIN,EB CIT: 0.35
REGRESSION ANALYSIS AS A MEANS OF DETERMINING AUDIT SAMPLE SIZE
TAR OC 74 VOL: 49 PG:764 - 771 :: REGRESS. :INT. LOG. :OTH.STAT. :SAMP.

GRANT ,EB CIT: 2
MARKET IMPLICATIONS OF DIFFERENTIAL AMOUNTS OF INTERIM INFORMATION
JAR SP 80 VOL: 18 PG:255 - 268 :: REGRESS. :PRIM. :EMH :INT.REP.

GRASSO,LP ; FIRS: BOATSMAN,JR ; THIR: ORMISTON,MB ; FOUR: RENEAU,JH CIT: 0
A PERSPECTIVE ON THE USE OF LABORATORY MARKET EXPERIMENTATION IN AUDITING RESEARCH
TAR JA 92 VOL: 67 PG:148 - 156 :: ANOVA :SEC. :INF.ECO./AG. :METHOD.

GRAUL ,PR ; FIRS: ASHTON,RH ; THIR: NEWTON,JD CIT: 0
AUDIT DELAY AND THE TIMELINESS OF CORPORATE REPORTING
CAR SP 89 VOL: 5 PG:657 - 673 :: REGRESS. :PRIM. :OTH.STAT. :TIM.

GRAUL ,PR ; FIRS: ABDEL-KHALIK,AR ; THIR: NEWTON,JD CIT: 0
REPORTING UNCERTAINTY AND ASSESSMENT OF RISK: REPLICATION AND EXTENSION IN
JAR AU 86 VOL: 24 PG:372 - 382 :: REGRESS. :LAB. :HIPS :OPIN.

GRAWOIG,DE ; FIRS: NICHOLS,AC CIT: 0
ACCOUNTING REPORTS WITH TIME AS A VARIABLE
TAR OC 68 VOL: 43 PG:631 - 639 :: QUAL. :INT. LOG. :THEORY :OTH.MANAG.

GRAY ,D CIT: 0
CORPORATE PREFERENCES FOR FOREIGN CURRENCY ACCOUNTING STANDARDS
JAR AU 84 VOL: 22 PG:760 - 764 :: DES.STAT. :PRIM. :THEORY :FOR.CUR.

GRAY ,J ; FIRS: PURDY ,CR ; SEC: SMITH JR,JM CIT: 0
THE VISIBILITY OF THE AUDITOR'S DISCLOSURE OF DEVIANCE FROM APB OPINION: AN EMPIRICAL TEST
JAR ST 69 VOL: 7 PG:1 - 18 :: ANOVA :LAB. :OTH.BEH. :INFO.STRUC.

GRAY ,J ; FIRS: SIMMONS,JK CIT: 0.35
AN INVESTIGATION OF THE EFFECT OF DIFFERING ACCOUNTING FRAMEWORKS ON THE PREDICTION OF NET INCOME
TAR OC 69 VOL: 44 PG:757 - 776 :: ANAL. :SIM. :THEORY :VALUAT.(INFL.)

GRAY ,J ; FIRS: BAILEY JR,AD CIT: 0
A STUDY OF THE IMPORTANCE OF THE PLANNING HORIZON ON REPORTS UTILIZING DISCOUNTED FUTURE CASH FLOWS
JAR SP 68 VOL: 6 PG:98 - 105 :: DES.STAT. :SIM. :N/A :CAP.BUDG.

GRAY ,J ; SEC: WILLINGHAM,JJ ; THIR: JOHNSTON,K CIT: 0
A BUSINESS GAME FOR THE INTRODUCTORY COURSE IN ACCOUNTING
TAR AP 63 VOL: 38 PG:336 - 346 :: QUAL. :INT. LOG. :OTH. :EDUC.

GRAY ,R CIT: 1
ACCOUNTING AND ENVIRONMENTALISM: AN EXPLORATION OF THE CHALLENGE OF GENTLY ACCOUNTING FOR ACCOUNTABILITY, TRANSPARENCY AND SUSTAINABILITY
AOS 05 92 VOL: 17 PG:399 - 425 :: DES.STAT. :INT. LOG. :THEORY :ORG.& ENVIR.

GRAY ,SJ ; SEC: RADEBAUGH,LH CIT: 0
INTERNATIONAL SEGMENT DISCLOSURES BY U.S. AND U.K. MULTINATIONAL ENTERPRISES: A DESCRIPTIVE STUDY
JAR SP 84 VOL: 22 PG:351 - 360 :: DES.STAT. :PRIM. :THEORY :INT.DIFF.

GRAY ,SJ CIT: 0.15
THE IMPACT OF INTERNATIONAL ACCOUNTING DIFFERENCES FROM A SECURITY-ANALYSIS PERSPECTIVE: SOME EUROPEAN EVIDENCE
JAR SP 80 VOL: 18 PG:64 - 76 :: ANOVA :PRIM. :OTH. :INT.DIFF.

GRAY ,SJ CIT: 0.07
SEGMENT REPORTING AND THE EEC MULTINATIONALS
JAR AU 78 VOL: 16 PG:242 - 253 :: DES.STAT. :PRIM. :THEORY :INT.DIFF.

GREEN ,D ; SEC: SEGALL,J CIT: 0.47
THE PREDICTIVE POWER OF FIRST-QUARTER EARNINGS REPORTS: A REPLICATION
JAR ST 66 VOL: 4 PG:21 - 36 :: DES.STAT. :PRIM. :OTH.STAT. :INT.REP.

GREEN ,D CIT: 0.12
EVALUATING THE ACCOUNTING LITERATURE
TAR JA 66 VOL: 41 PG:52 - 64 :: QUAL. :INT. LOG. :N/A :OTH.MANAG.

GREEN ,D CIT: 0.06
TOWARDS A THEORY OF INTERIM REPORTS
JAR SP 64 VOL: 2 PG:35 - 49 :: QUAL. :INT. LOG. :THEORY :INT.REP.

GREEN ,SL ; FIRS: LEWIS ,BL ; SEC: PATTON,JM CIT: 0.2
THE EFFECTS OF INFORMATION CHOICE AND INFORMATION USE ON ANALYSTS' PREDICTIONS OF MUNICIPAL BOND RATING CHANGES
TAR AP 88 VOL: 63 PG:270 282 :: REGRESS. :LAB. :OTH.STAT. :FOREC.

GREENBALL,MN CIT: 0.12
A STATISTICAL MODEL OF EARNINGS ESTIMATION
JAR ST 71 VOL: 9 PG:172 - 190 :: MIXED :PRIM. :TIME SER. :N/A

GREENBALL,MN CIT: 0.06
APPRAISING ALTERNATIVE METHODS OF ACCOUNTING FOR ACCELERATED TAX DEPRECIATION: A RELATIVE-ACCURACY APPROACH
JAR AU 69 VOL: 7 PG:262 - 289 :: ANAL. :INT. LOG. :OTH.STAT. :TAXES

GREENBALL,MN CIT: 0.12
THE ACCURACY OF DIFFERENT METHODS OF ACCOUNTING FOR EARNINGS - A SIMULATION APPROACH
JAR SP 68 VOL: 6 PG:114 - 129 :: DES.STAT. :SIM. :OTH.STAT. :VALUAT.(INFL.)

GREENBALL,MN CIT: 0
EVALUATION OF THE USEFULNESS TO INVESTORS OF DIFFERENT ACCOUNTING ESTIMATORS OF EARNINGS: A SIMULATION APPROACH
JAR ST 68 VOL: 6 PG:27 - 49 :: DES.STAT. :SIM. :THEORY :FIN.METH.

GREENBERG,R ; FIRS: ETTREDGE,M CIT: 0.67
DETERMINANTS OF FEE CUTTING ON INITIAL AUDIT ENGAGEMENTS
JAR SP 90 VOL: 28 PG:198 - 210 :: REGRESS. :PRIM. :OTH.STAT. :ORG.

GREENBERG,R CIT: 0
ADAPTIVE ESTIMATION: AN ALTERNATIVE TO THE TRADITIONAL STATIONARITY ASSUMPTION
JAR AU 84 VOL: 22 PG:719 - 730 :: NON-PAR. :PRIM. :TIME SER. :FOREC.

GREENBERG,RR ; SEC: JOHNSON,GL ; THIR: RAMESH,K CIT: 0
EARNINGS VERSUS CASH FLOW AS A PREDICTOR OF FUTURE CASH FLOW MEASURES
JAA AU 86 VOL: 1 PG:266 - 277 :: REGRESS. :PRIM. :THEORY :SPEC.ITEMS

GREENE,ED CIT: 0.06
CHANGING FROM DECLINING BALANCE TO STRAIGHT-LINE DEPRECIATION
TAR AP 63 VOL: 38 PG:355 - 362 :: QUAL. :INT. LOG. :INSTIT. :PP&E / DEPR

GREENWALD,B ; SEC: STIGLITZ,JE CIT: 0
IMPACT OF THE CHANGING TAX ENVIRONMENT ON INVESTMENTS AND PRODUCTIVITY: FINANCIAL STRUCTURE AND THE CORPORATION INCOME TAX
JAA SU 89 VOL: 4 PG:281 - 297 :: DES.STAT. :INT. LOG. :INF.ECO./AG. :TAXES

GREER ,HC CIT: 0
THE CORPORATION STOCKHOLDER - ACCOUNTING'S FORGOTTEN MAN
TAR JA 64 VOL: 39 PG:22 - 31 :: QUAL. :INT. LOG. :THEORY :FIN.METH.

GREER JR,WR ; SEC: MORRISSEY,LE CIT: 0
ACCOUNTING RULE-MAKING IN A WORLD OF EFFICIENT MARKETS
JAA AU 78 VOL: 2 PG:49 - 57 :: QUAL. :INT. LOG. :INSTIT. :FIN.METH.

GREER JR,WR CIT: 0.06
THEORY VERSUS PRACTICE IN RISK ANALYSIS: AN EMPIRICAL STUDY
TAR JL 74 VOL: 49 PG:496 - 505 :: NON-PAR. :LAB. :N/A :CAP.BUDG.

GREER JR,WR CIT: 0.12
CAPITAL BUDGETING ANALYSIS WITH THE TIMING OF EVENTS UNCERTAIN
TAR JA 70 VOL: 45 PG:103 - 114 :: ANAL. :INT. LOG. :OTH.STAT. :CAP.BUDG.

GREIG ,AC CIT: 3
FUNDAMENTAL ANALYSIS AND SUBSEQUENT STOCK RETURNS
JAE JN 92 VOL: 15 PG:413 - 442 :: REGRESS. :PRIM. :EMH :FIN.METH.

GRIFFIN,CH ; FIRS: WILLIAMS,TH CIT: 0
INCOME DEFINITION AND MEASUREMENT: A STRUCTURAL APPROACH
TAR OC 67 VOL: 42 PG:642 - 649 :: QUAL. :INT. LOG. :THEORY :OTH.MANAG.

GRIFFIN,CH ; FIRS: WILLIAMS,TH CIT: 0.12
MATRIX THEORY AND COST ALLOCATION
TAR JL 64 VOL: 39 PG:671 - 678 :: ANAL. :INT. LOG. :MATH.PROG. :COST.ALLOC.

GRIFFIN,FB ; FIRS: ANDERSON,HM CIT: 0
THE ACCOUNTING CURRICULUM AND POSTGRADUATE ACHIEVEMENT
TAR OC 63 VOL: 38 PG:813 - 818 :: QUAL. :INT. LOG. :THEORY :EDUC.

GRIFFIN,PA ; SEC: WALLACH,SJR CIT: 0
LATIN AMERICAN LENDING BY MAJOR U.S. BANKS: THE EFFECTS OF DISCLOSURES ABOUT NONACCRUAL LOANS AND LOAN LOSS PROVISIONS
TAR OC 91 VOL: 66 PG:830 - 846 :: REGRESS. :PRIM. :EMH :OTH. NON-C/A

GRIFFIN,PA ; FIRS: BROWN ,LD ; THIR: HAGERMAN,RL ; FOUR: ZMIJEWSKI,ME CIT: 4.5
SECURITY ANALYST SUPERIORITY RELATIVE TO UNIVARIATE TIME-SERIES MODELS IN FORECASTING QUARTERLY EARNINGS
JAE AP 87 VOL: 9 PG:61 - 87 :: REGRESS. :PRIM. :TIME SER. :FOREC.

GRIFFIN,PA ; FIRS: BROWN ,LD ; THIR: HAGERMAN,RL ; FOUR: ZMIJEWSKI,ME CIT: 5.17
AN EVALUATION OF ALTERNATIVE PROXIES FOR THE MARKET'S ASSESSMENT OF UNEXPECTED EARNINGS
JAE JL 87 VOL: 9 PG:159 - 193 :: REGRESS. :PRIM. :TIME SER. :METHOD.

GRIFFIN,PA ; FIRS: BEAVER,WH ; THIR: LANDSMAN,WR CIT: 0
TESTING FOR INCREMENTAL INFORMATION CONTENT IN THE PRESENCE OF COLLINEARITY :A COMMENT
JAE DE 84 VOL: 6 PG:219 - 223 :: QUAL. :INT. LOG. :OTH.STAT. :METHOD.

GRIFFIN,PA ; FIRS: BEAVER,WH ; THIR: LANDSMAN,WR CIT: 2.55
THE INCREMENTAL INFORMATION CONTENT OF REPLACEMENT COST EARNINGS
JAE JL 82 VOL: 4 PG:15 - 39 :: MIXED :PRIM. :EMH :VALUAT.(INFL.)

GRIFFIN,PA ; FIRS: BEAVER,WH ; SEC: CHRISTIE,AA CIT: 1.62
THE INFORMATION CONTENT OF SEC ACCOUNTING SERIES RELEASE NO.190
JAE AG 80 VOL: 2 PG:127 - 157 :: REGRESS. :PRIM. :EMH :VALUAT.(INFL.)

GRIFFIN,PA CIT: 2.19
THE TIME-SERIES BEHAVIOR OF QUARTERLY EARNINGS: PRELIMINARY EVIDENCE
JAR SP 77 VOL: 15 PG:71 - 83 :: MIXED :PRIM. :TIME SER. :FOREC.

GRIFFIN,PA CIT: 0.12
THE ASSOCIATION BETWEEN RELATIVE RISK AND RISK ESTIMATES DERIVED FROM QUARTERLY EARNINGS AND DIVIDENDS
TAR JL 76 VOL: 51 PG:499 - 515 :: REGRESS. :PRIM. :EMH :TAXES

GRIMLUND,RA ; FIRS: RAGHUNANDAN,K ; THIR: SCHEPANSKI,A CIT: 0
AUDITOR EVALUATION OF LOSS CONTINGENCIES
CAR SP 91 VOL: 7 PG:549 - 568 :: REGRESS. :LAB. :HIPS :VALUAT.(INFL.)

GRIMLUND,RA ; FIRS: FELIX JR,WL ; THIR: KOSTER,FJ ; FOUR: ROUSSEY,RS CIT: 0
ARTHUR ANDERSEN'S NEW MONETARY UNIT SAMPLING APPROACH
AUD AU 90 VOL: 9 PG:1 - 16 :: DES.STAT. :SIM. :EXP.SYST. :SAMP.

GRIMLUND,RA ; FIRS: WILSON JR,TE CIT: 0.67
AN EXAMINATION OF THE IMPORTANCE OF AN AUDITOR'S REPUTATION
AUD SP 90 VOL: 9 PG:43 - 59 :: REGRESS. :PRIM. :THEORY :AUD.

GRIMLUND,RA CIT: 0
COMBINED MONETARY UNIT SAMPLING FROM SEVERAL INDEPENDENT POPULATIONS: SAMPLE SIZE PLANNING AND SAMPLE EVALUATION WITH THE MOMENT
CAR SP 90 VOL: 6 PG:446 - 484 :: DES.STAT. :SIM. :OTH.STAT. :SAMP.

GRIMLUND,RA ; FIRS: DWORIN,L CIT: 0
A COMPREHENSIVE HYPOTHESIS TESTING APPROACH TO DOLLAR UNIT SAMPLING
CAR SP 89 VOL: 5 PG:674 - 691 :: DES.STAT. :SIM. :OTH.STAT. :SAMP.

GRIMLUND,RA ; SEC: SCHROEDER,MS CIT: 0.6
ON THE CURRENT USE OF THE STRINGER METHOD OF MUS: SOME NEW DIRECTIONS
AUD AU 88 VOL: 08 PG:53 - 62 :: REGRESS. :SIM. :OTH.STAT. :SAMP.

GRIMLUND,RA CIT: 0.2
SAMPLE SIZE PLANNING FOR THE MOMENT METHOD OF MUS: INCORPORATING AUDIT JUDGMENTS
AUD SP 88 VOL: 07 PG:77 - 104 :: DES.STAT. :SIM. :OTH.STAT. :SAMP.

GRIMLUND,RA ; SEC: FELIX JR,WL CIT: 0.5
SIMULATION EVIDENCE AND ANALYSIS OF ALTERNATIVE METHODS OF EVALUATING
TAR JL 87 VOL: 62 PG:455 - 479 :: DES.STAT. :SIM. :OTH.STAT. :SAMP.

GRIMLUND,RA ; FIRS: DWORIN,L CIT: 0.71
DOLLAR-UNIT SAMPLING: A COMPARISON OF THE QUASI-BAYESIAN AND MOMENT BOUNDS
TAR JA 86 VOL: 61 PG:36 - 57 :: DES.STAT. :SIM. :OTH.STAT. :SAMP.

GRIMLUND,RA CIT: 0
A PROPOSAL FOR IMPLEMENTING THE FASB'S REASONABLY POSSIBLE DISCLOSURE PROVISION FOR PRODUCT WARRANTY LIABILITIES
JAR AU 85 VOL: 23 PG:575 - 594 :: DES.STAT. :SIM. :OTH.STAT. :SPEC.ITEMS

GRIMLUND,RA ; FIRS: DWORIN,L CIT: 0.89
DOLLAR UNIT SAMPLING FOR ACCOUNTS RECEIVABLE AND INVENTORY
TAR AP 84 VOL: 59 PG:218 - 241 :: MIXED :SIM. :OTH.STAT. :SAMP.

GRIMLUND,RA CIT: 0.64
AN INTEGRATION OF INTERNAL CONTROL SYSTEM AND ACCOUNT BALANCE EVIDENCE
JAR AU 82 VOL: 20 PG:316 - 342 :: ANAL. :INT. LOG. :OTH.STAT. :SAMP.

GRIMLUND,RA ; FIRS: FELIX JR,WL CIT: 1.19
A SAMPLING MODEL FOR AUDIT TESTS OF COMPOSITE ACCOUNTS
JAR SP 77 VOL: 15 PG:23 - 41 :: ANAL. :INT. LOG. :OTH.STAT. :SAMP.

GROBSTEIN,M ; SEC: CRAIG ,PW CIT: 0.78
A RISK ANALYSIS APPROACH TO AUDITING
AUD SP 84 VOL: 3 PG:1 - 16 :: QUAL. :INT. LOG. :OTH. :RISK

GROFF ,JE ; FIRS: WRIGHT,CJ CIT: 0.29
USES OF INDEXES AND DATA BASES FOR INFORMATION RELEASE ANALYSIS
TAR JA 86 VOL: 61 PG:91 - 100 :: REGRESS. :PRIM. :EMH :METHOD.

GROJER,JE ; SEC: STARK ,A CIT: 0.25
SOCIAL ACCOUNTING: A SWEDISH ATTEMPT
AOS 04 77 VOL: 2 PG:349 - 385 :: QUAL. :CASE :THEORY :HRA

GRONLUND,A ; FIRS: JONSSON,S CIT: 0
LIFE WITH A SUB-CONTRACTOR: NEW TECHNOLOGY AND MANAGEMENT ACCOUNTING
AOS 05 88 VOL: 13 PG:513 - 532 :: DES.STAT. :CASE :THEORY :MANAG.

GROOMER,SM ; FIRS: VASARHELYI,MA ; SEC: BAILEY JR,AD ; THIR: CAMARDESSE JR,JE ; FIFT: LAMPE ,JC CIT: 0
THE USAGE OF COMPUTERS IN AUDITING TEACHING AND RESEARCH
AUD SP 84 VOL: 3 PG:98 - 103 :: QUAL. :SIM. :OTH. :EDP AUD.

GROSS ,H CIT: 0
MAKE OR BUY DECISIONS IN GROWING FIRMS
TAR OC 66 VOL: 41 PG:745 - 753 :: QUAL. :INT. LOG. :N/A :REL.COSTS

GROSSMAN,SD ; FIRS: BENJAMIN,JJ ; THIR: WIGGIN,CE CIT: 0
THE IMPACT OF FOREIGN CURRENCY TRANSLATION ON REPORTING DURING THE PHASE-IN OF SFAS NO.52
JAA SU 86 VOL: 1 PG:177 - 184 :: REGRESS. :PRIM. :THEORY :FOR.CUR.

GROSSMAN,SD ; SEC: KRATCHMAN,SH ; THIR: WELKER,RB CIT: 0
COMMENT: THE EFFECT OF REPLACEMENT COST DISCLOSURES ON SECURITY PRICES
JAA WI 81 VOL: 4 PG:136 - 143 :: DES.STAT. :PRIM. :EMH :VALUAT.(INFL.)

GROVE ,HD ; FIRS: SELTO ,FH CIT: 0
THE PREDICTIVE POWER OF VOTING POWER INDICES: FASB VOTING ON STATEMENTS OF FINANCIAL ACCOUNTING STANDARDS NOS. 45-69
JAR AU 83 VOL: 21 PG:619 - 622 :: NON-PAR. :PRIM. :INSTIT. :FASB SUBM.

GROVE ,HD ; FIRS: SELTO ,FH CIT: 0.09
VOTING POWER INDICES AND THE SETTING OF FINANCIAL ACCOUNTING STANDARDS: EXTENSIONS
JAR AU 82 VOL: 20 PG:676 - 688 :: DES.STAT. :PRIM. :INSTIT. :FASB SUBM.

GROVE ,HD ; SEC: SAVICH,RS CIT: 0.21
ATTITUDE RESEARCH IN ACCOUNTING: A MODEL FOR RELIABILITY AND VALIDITY CONSIDERATIONS
TAR JL 79 VOL: 54 PG:522 - 537 :: QUAL. :SEC. :OTH.BEH. :METHOD.

GROVE ,HD ; SEC: MOCK ,TJ ; THIR: EHRENREICH,K CIT: 0.06
A REVIEW OF HUMAN RESOURCE ACCOUNTING MEASUREMENT SYSTEMS FROM A MEASUREMENT THEORY PERSPECTIVE
AOS 03 77 VOL: 2 PG:219 - 236 :: QUAL. :SEC. :OTH.BEH. :HRA

GROVE ,HD ; FIRS: SORENSEN,JE CIT: 0.06
COST-OUTCOME AND COST-EFFECTIVENESS ANALYSIS: EMERGING NONPROFIT PERFORMANCE EVALUATION TECHNIQUES
TAR JL 77 VOL: 52 PG:658 - 675 :: ANAL. :SEC. :OTH.STAT. :REL.COSTS

GROVES,R ; FIRS: TOMKINS,C CIT: 2.4
THE EVERYDAY ACCOUNTANT AND RESEARCHING HIS REALITY
AOS 04 83 VOL: 8 PG:361 - 374 :: QUAL. :INT. LOG. :THEORY :METHOD.

GROVES,R ; SEC: MANES ,RP ; THIR: SORENSEN,R CIT: 0.06
THE APPLICATION OF THE HIRSCH-DANTZIG FIXED CHARGE ALGORITHM TO PROFIT PLANNING: A FORMAL STATEMENT OF PRODUCT PROFITABILITY ANALYSIS
TAR JL 70 VOL: 45 PG:481 - 489 :: ANAL. :INT. LOG. :MATH.PROG. :BUDG.& PLAN.

GRUNDFEST,JA ; SEC: SHOVEN,JB CIT: 0
ADVERSE IMPLICATIONS OF A SECURITIES TRANSACTIONS EXCISE TAX
JAA AU 91 VOL: 6 PG:409 - 442 :: DES.STAT. :INT. LOG. :OTH. :ORG.& ENVIR.

GUENTHER,DA CIT: 0
TAXES AND ORGANIZATIONAL FORM: A COMPARISON OF CORPORATIONS AND MASTER LIMITED PARTNERSHIPS
TAR JA 92 VOL: 67 PG:17 - 45 :: REGRESS. :PRIM. :OTH. :ORG.FORM

GUL ,FA CIT: 0
AN EMPIRICAL STUDY OF THE USEFULNESS OF HUMAN RESOURCES TURNOVER COSTS IN AUSTRALIAN ACCOUNTING FIRMS
AOS 34 84 VOL: 9 PG:233 - 239 :: NON-PAR. :LAB. :OTH.BEH. :HRA

GUL ,FA CIT: 0.33
THE JOINT AND MODERATING ROLE OF PERSONALITY AND COGNITIVE STYLE ON DECISION MAKING
TAR AP 84 VOL: 59 PG:264 - 277 :: ANOVA :LAB. :HIPS :N/A

GUNN ,S ; FIRS: JOHNSON,O CIT: 0
CONFLICT RESOLUTION: THE MARKET AND/OR ACCOUNTING?
TAR OC 74 VOL: 49 PG:649 - 663 :: QUAL. :INT. LOG. :INSTIT. :FIN.METH.

GUPTA ,AK ; FIRS: GOVINDARAJAN,V CIT: 1.38
LINKING CONTROL SYSTEMS TO BUSINESS UNIT STRATEGY: IMPACT ON PERFORMANCE
AOS 01 85 VOL: 10 PG:51 - 66 :: REGRESS. :SURV. :OTH.BEH. :MANAG.

GUPTA ,M ; FIRS: FOSTER,G CIT: 0
MANUFACTURING OVERHEAD COST DRIVER ANALYSIS
JAE JA 90 VOL: 12 PG:309 - 337 :: REGRESS. :FIELD :OTH.STAT. :OVER.ALLOC.

GUPTA ,MC ; SEC: HUEFNER,RJ CIT: 0.18
A CLUSTER ANALYSIS STUDY OF FINANCIAL RATIOS AND INDUSTRY CHARACTERISTICS
JAR SP 72 VOL: 10 PG:77 - 95 :: OTH.QUANT. :PRIM. :OTH.STAT. :N/A

GUSTAVSON,SG ; FIRS: SCHULTZ JR,JJ CIT: 0.53
ACTUARIES' PERCEPTIONS OF VARIABLES AFFECTING THE INDEPENDENT AUDITOR'S LEGAL LIABILITY
TAR JL 78 VOL: 53 PG:626 - 641 :: ANOVA :LAB. :HIPS :LIAB.

GUTBERLET,LG CIT: 0
AN OPPORTUNITY-DIFFERENTIAL STANDARDS
JAA AU 83 VOL: 7 PG:16 - 28 :: QUAL. :INT. LOG. :THEORY :FASB SUBM.

GUTBERLET,LG CIT: 0
COMPILATION AND REVIEW OF FINANCIAL STATEMENTS BY AN ACCOUNTANT
JAA SU 80 VOL: 3 PG:313 - 338 :: QUAL. :INT. LOG. :THEORY :PROF.RESP.

GYNTHER,MM CIT: 0.06
FUTURE GROWTH ASPECTS OF THE CASH FLOW COMPUTATION
TAR OC 68 VOL: 43 PG:706 - 718 :: ANAL. :SIM. :OTH.STAT. :PP&E / DEPR

GYNTHER,RS CIT: 0.12
CAPITAL MAINTENANCE, PRICE CHANGES, AND PROFIT DETERMINATION
TAR OC 70 VOL: 45 PG:712 - 730 :: QUAL. :INT. LOG. :THEORY :VALUAT.(INFL.)

GYNTHER,RS CIT: 0
SOME CONCEPTUALIZING ON GOODWILL
TAR AP 69 VOL: 44 PG:247 - 255 :: QUAL. :INT. LOG. :THEORY :OTH. NON-C/A

GYNTHER,RS CIT: 0.24
ACCOUNTING CONCEPTS AND BEHAVIOURAL HYPOTHESES
TAR AP 67 VOL: 42 PG:274 - 290 :: QUAL. :INT. LOG. :OTH.BEH. :FIN.METH.

HACKENBRACK,K CIT: 0
IMPLICATIONS OF SEEMINGLY IRRELEVANT EVIDENCE IN AUDIT JUDGMENT
JAR SP 92 VOL: 30 PG:126 - 136 :: REGRESS. :LAB. :HIPS :JUDG.

HADDAD,K ; FIRS: CHOW,CW ; SEC: COOPER,JC CIT: 0
THE EFFECTS OF PAY SCHEMES AND RATCHETS ON BUDGETARY SLACK AND PERFORMANCE: A MULTIPERIOD EXPERIMENT
AOS 01 91 VOL: 16 PG:47 - 60 :: REGRESS. :LAB. :OTH.BEH. :BUDG.& PLAN.

HAFNER,GF CIT: 0
AUDITING EDP
TAR OC 64 VOL: 39 PG:979 - 982 :: QUAL. :INT. LOG. :N/A :AUD.

HAGERMAN,RL ; FIRS: BROWN ,LD ; SEC: GRIFFIN,PA ; FOUR: ZMIJEWSKI,ME CIT: 4.5
SECURITY ANALYST SUPERIORITY RELATIVE TO UNIVARIATE TIME-SERIES MODELS IN FORECASTING QUARTERLY EARNINGS
JAE AP 87 VOL: 9 PG:61 - 87 :: REGRESS. :PRIM. :TIME SER. :FOREC.

HAGERMAN,RL ; FIRS: BROWN ,LD ; SEC: GRIFFIN,PA ; FOUR: ZMIJEWSKI,ME CIT: 5.17
AN EVALUATION OF ALTERNATIVE PROXIES FOR THE MARKET'S ASSESSMENT OF UNEXPECTED EARNINGS
JAE JL 87 VOL: 9 PG:159 - 193 :: REGRESS. :PRIM. :TIME SER. :METHOD.

HAGERMAN,RL ; SEC: ZMIJEWSKI,ME ; THIR: SHAH ,P CIT: 1.11
THE ASSOCIATION BETWEEN THE MAGNITUDE OF QUARTERLY EARNINGS FORECAST ERRORS AND RISK-ADJUSTED STOCK RETURNS
JAR AU 84 VOL: 22 PG:526 - 540 :: REGRESS. :PRIM. :EMH :FOREC.

HAGERMAN,RL ; FIRS: ZMIJEWSKI,ME CIT: 3.33
AN INCOME STRATEGY APPROACH TO THE POSITIVE THEORY OF ACCOUNTING STANDARD SETTING/CHOICE
JAE AG 81 VOL: 3 PG:129 - 149 :: OTH.QUANT. :SEC. :OTH.STAT. :METHOD.

HAGERMAN,RL ; SEC: ZMIJEWSKI,ME CIT: 3.79
SOME ECONOMIC DETERMINANTS OF ACCOUNTING POLICY CHOICE
JAE AG 79 VOL: 1 PG:141 - 161 :: OTH.QUANT. :PRIM. :OTH.STAT. :ACC.CHNG.

HAGERMAN,RL CIT: 0.24
A TEST OF GOVERNMENT REGULATION OF ACCOUNTING PRINCIPLES
TAR OC 75 VOL: 50 PG:699 - 709 :: MIXED :PRIM. :EMH :FIN.METH.

HAGG ,J ; SEC: HEDLUND,G CIT: 0.36
CASE STUDIES IN ACCOUNTING RESEARCH
AOS 12 79 VOL: 4 PG:135 - 143 :: QUAL. :INT. LOG. :OTH. :METHOD.

HAGGARD,JA ; FIRS: BABER ,WR ; SEC: FAIRFIELD,PM CIT: 0
THE EFFECT OF CONCERN ABOUT REPORTED INCOME DISCRETIONARY SPENDING DECISIONS: THE CASE OF RESEARCH AND DEVELOPMENT
TAR OC 91 VOL: 66 PG:818 - 829 :: REGRESS. :PRIM. :INF.ECO./AG. :R & D

HAGIGI,M ; FIRS: EICHENSEHER,JW ; THIR: SHIELDS,D CIT: 0.25
MARKET REACTION TO AUDITOR CHANGES BY OTC COMPANIES
AUD AU 89 VOL: 9 PG:29 - 40 :: REGRESS. :PRIM. :EMH :OTH.MANAG.

HAIN ,HP CIT: 0
CASTING THE ACCOUNT
JAR AU 67 VOL: 5 PG:154 - 163 :: QUAL. :SEC. :HIST. :MAN.DEC.CHAR.

HAIN ,HP CIT: 0
ACCOUNTING CONTROL IN THE ZENON PAPYRI
TAR OC 66 VOL: 41 PG:699 - 703 :: QUAL. :PRIM. :HIST. :FIN.METH.

HAINKEL,M ; FIRS: HORVITZ,JS CIT: 0
THE IRS SUMMONS POWER AND ITS EFFECT ON THE INDEPENDENT AUDITOR
JAA WI 81 VOL: 4 PG:114 - 127 :: QUAL. :CASE :INSTIT. :PROF.RESP.

HAIRE ,M ; FIRS: BOWMAN,EH CIT: 0.18
SOCIAL IMPACT DISCLOSURE AND CORPORATE ANNUAL REPORTS
AOS 01 76 VOL: 1 PG:11 - 22 :: DES.STAT. :PRIM. :THEORY :HRA

HAKA ,S ; FIRS: SCHICK,AG ; SEC: GORDON,LA CIT: 0
INFORMATION OVERLOAD: A TEMPORAL APPROACH
AOS 03 90 VOL: 15 PG:199 - 220 :: REGRESS. :SEC. :HIPS :DEC.AIDS

HAKA ,S ; FIRS: CHALOS,P CIT: 0.33
TRANSFER PRICING UNDER BILATERAL BARGAINING
TAR JL 90 VOL: 65 PG:624 - 641 :: REGRESS. :LAB. :OTH.BEH. :TRANS.PRIC.

HAKA ,S ; SEC: FRIEDMAN,L ; THIR: JONES ,V CIT: 0.29
FUNCTIONAL FIXATION AND INTERFERENCE THEORY: A THEORETICAL AND EMPIRICAL INVESTIGATION
TAR JL 86 VOL: 61 PG:455 - 474 :: REGRESS. :LAB. :HIPS :REL.COSTS

HAKA ,S ; FIRS: GORDON,LA ; THIR: SCHICK,AG CIT: 0.11
STRATEGIES FOR INFORMATION SYSTEMS IMPLEMENTATION: THE CASE OF ZERO BASE BUDGETING
AOS 02 84 VOL: 9 PG:111 - 123 :: NON-PAR. :PRIM. :OTH. :BUDG.& PLAN.

HAKA ,SF CIT: 0.33
CAPITAL BUDGETING TECHNIQUES AND FIRM SPECIFIC CONTINGENCIES: A CORRELATIONAL ANALYSIS
AOS 01 87 VOL: 12 PG:31 - 48 :: REGRESS. :SURV. :OTH.BEH. :BUDG.& PLAN.

HAKA ,SF ; SEC: GORDON,LA ; THIR: PINCHES,GE CIT: 0.63
SOPHISTICATED CAPITAL BUDGETING SELECTION TECHNIQUES AND FIRM PERFORMANCE
TAR OC 85 VOL: 60 PG:651 - 669 :: REGRESS. :PRIM. :EMH :CAP.BUDG.

HAKANSSON,NH CIT: 0
WHY IS FINANCIAL REPORTING SO INEFFICIENT?
JAA WI 90 VOL: 5 PG:33 - 53 :: DES.STAT. :INT. LOG. :INF.ECO./AG. :INFO.STRUC.

HAKANSSON,NH CIT: 0.42
ON THE POLICIES OF ACCOUNTING DISCLOSURE AND MEASUREMENT: AN ANALYSIS OF ECONOMIC INCENTIVES
JAR ST 81 VOL: 19 PG:1 - 35 :: ANAL. :INT. LOG. :INSTIT. :INFO.STRUC.

HAKANSSON,NH CIT: 0.07
WHERE WE ARE IN ACCOUNTING: A REVIEW OF STATEMENT ON ACCOUNTING THEORY AND THEORY ACCEPTANCE
TAR JL 78 VOL: 53 PG:717 - 725 :: QUAL. :INT. LOG. :THEORY :FIN.METH.

HAKANSSON,NH CIT: 0.81
INTERIM DISCLOSURE AND PUBLIC FORECASTS: AN ECONOMIC ANALYSIS AND A FRAMEWORK FOR CHOICE
TAR AP 77 VOL: 52 PG:396 - 416 :: ANAL. :INT. LOG. :THEORY :INT.REP.

HAKANSSON,NH CIT: 0
ON THE RELEVANCE OF PRICE-LEVEL ACCOUNTING
JAR SP 69 VOL: 7 PG:11 - 31 :: ANAL. :INT. LOG. :OTH.STAT. :VALUAT.(INFL.)

HAKANSSON,NH CIT: 0
AN INDUCED THEORY OF ACCOUNTING UNDER RISK
TAR JL 69 VOL: 44 PG:495 - 514 :: ANAL. :INT. LOG. :INF.ECO./AG. :INFO.STRUC.

HALL ,JA ; FIRS: DOWELL,CD CIT: 0
EDP CONTROLS WITH AUDIT COST IMPLICATIONS
JAA AU 81 VOL: 5 PG:30 - 40 :: QUAL. :SURV. :THEORY :EDP AUD.

HALL ,TP ; FIRS: ROBINSON,LA CIT: 0
SYSTEMS EDUCATION AND THE ACCOUNTING CURRICULUM
TAR JA 64 VOL: 39 PG:62 - 69 :: QUAL. :INT. LOG. :N/A :OTH.MANAG.

HALL ,TW ; SEC: SHRIVER,KA CIT: 0.33
ECONOMETRIC PROPERTIES OF ASSET VALUATION RULES UNDER PRICE MOVEMENT AND MEASUREMENT ERRORS: AN EMPIRICAL TEST
TAR JL 90 VOL: 65 PG:537 - 556 :: DES.STAT. :LAB. :INF.ECO./AG. :VALUAT.(INFL.)

HALL ,TW ; SEC: PIERCE,BJ ; THIR: ROSS ,WR CIT: 0
PLANNING SAMPLE SIZES FOR STRINGER-METHOD MONETARY UNIT AND SINGLE-STAGE ATTRIBUTE SAMPLING PLANS
AUD SP 89 VOL: 8 PG:64 - 89 :: DES.STAT. :SIM. :OTH.STAT. :SAMP.

HALL ,TW ; SEC: CASLER,DJ CIT: 0
USING INDEXING TO ESTIMATE CURRENT COSTS - COMPOSITE OR MULTIPLE INDEXES?
JAA SP 85 VOL: 8 PG:210 - 224 :: REGRESS. :PRIM. :THEORY :VALUAT.(INFL.)

HALL ,TW ; FIRS: CASLER,DJ CIT: 0.38
FIRM-SPECIFIC ASSET VALUATION ACCURACY USING A COMPOSITE PRICE INDEX
JAR SP 85 VOL: 23 PG:110 - 122 :: REGRESS. :SIM. :OTH.STAT. :VALUAT.(INFL.)

HALL ,TW CIT: 0.1
INFLATION AND RATES OF EXCHANGE: SUPPORT FOR SFAS NO.52
JAA SU 83 VOL: 6 PG:299 - 313 :: REGRESS. :PRIM. :THEORY :FOR.CUR.

HALL ,TW CIT: 0.55
AN EMPIRICAL TEST OF THE EFFECT OF ASSET AGGREGATION ON VALUATION ACCURACY
JAR SP 82 VOL: 20 PG:139 - 151 :: ANOVA :PRIM. :OTH.STAT. :PP&E / DEPR

HALLBAUER,RC ; FIRS: AGRAWAL,SP ; THIR: PERRITT,GW CIT: 0
MEASUREMENT OF THE CURRENT COST OF EQUIVALENT PRODUCTIVE CAPACITY
JAA WI 80 VOL: 3 PG:163 - 173 :: ANAL. :INT. LOG. :OTH.STAT. :VALUAT.(INFL.)

HALPER,FB ; FIRS: VASARHELYI,MA CIT: 0
THE CONTINUOUS AUDIT OF ONLINE SYSTEMS
AUD SP 91 VOL: 10 PG:110 - 125 :: REGRESS. :LAB. :EXP.SYST. :INT.AUD.

HALPERIN,R ; SEC: MAINDIRATTA,A CIT: 0
ON THE LINK BETWEEN TAXES AND INCENTIVES IN THE CHOICE OF BUSINESS FORM
JAA SU 89 VOL: 4 PG:345 - 366 :: DES.STAT. :INT. LOG. :INF.ECO./AG. :ORG.FORM

HALPERIN,R ; SEC: LANEN ,WN CIT: 0
THE EFFECTS OF THE THOR POWER TOOL DECISION ON THE LIFO/FIFO CHOICE
TAR AP 87 VOL: 62 PG:378 - 384 :: REGRESS. :PRIM. :EMH :INV.

HALPERIN,R ; SEC: SRINIDHI,BN CIT: 0
THE EFFECTS OF THE U.S. INCOME TAX REGULATIONS' TRANSFER PRICING RULE
TAR OC 87 VOL: 62 PG:686 - 706 :: REGRESS. :INT. LOG. :THEORY :TRANS.PRIC.

HALPERIN,R ; SEC: TZUR ,J CIT: 0.13
MONETARY COMPENSATION AND NONTAXABLE EMPLOYEE BENEFITS: AN ANALYTICAL PERSPECTIVE
TAR OC 85 VOL: 60 PG:670 - 680 :: REGRESS. :INT. LOG. :THEORY :EXEC.COMP.

HALPERIN,R ; FIRS: COHEN ,MA CIT: 0.23
OPTIMAL INVENTORY ORDER POLICY FOR A FIRM USING THE LIFO INVENTORY COSTING METHOD
JAR AU 80 VOL: 18 PG:375 - 389 :: ANAL. :SIM. :MATH.PROG. :INV.

HALPERIN,R CIT: 0.29
THE EFFECTS OF LIFO INVENTORY COSTING ON RESOURCE ALLOCATION: A PUBLIC POLICY PERSPECTIVE
TAR JA 79 VOL: 54 PG:58 - 71 :: ANAL. :INT. LOG. :N/A :INV.

HALPERIN,RM ; SEC: SRINIDHI,B CIT: 0
U.S. INCOME TAX TRANSFER-PRICING RULES AND RESOURCE ALLOCATION: THE CASE OF DECENTRALIZED MULTINATIONAL FIRMS
TAR JA 91 VOL: 66 PG:141 - 157 :: REGRESS. :INT. LOG. :INF.ECO./AG. :TRANS.PRIC.

HALPERN,J ; FIRS: AHITUV,N ; THIR: WILL ,H CIT: 0.13
AUDIT PLANNING: AN ALGORITHMIC APPROACH
CAR AU 85 VOL: 2 PG:95 - 110 :: DES.STAT. :INT. LOG. :MATH.PROG. :PLAN.

HAM ,J ; SEC: LOSELL,D ; THIR: SMIELIAUSKAS,W CIT: 0.33
SOME EMPIRICAL EVIDENCE ON THE STABILITY OF ACCOUNTING ERROR CHARACTERISTICS OVER TIME
CAR AU 87 VOL: 4 PG:210 - 226 :: REGRESS. :PRIM. :TIME SER. :ERRORS

HAM ,J ; SEC: LOSELL,D ; THIR: SMIELIAUSKAS,W CIT: 0
A NOTE ON THE NEUTRALITY OF INTERNAL CONTROL SYSTEMS IN AUDIT PRACTICE
CAR SP 86 VOL: 2 PG:311 - 317 :: DES.STAT. :FIELD :HIST. :AUD.

HAM ,J ; SEC: LOSELL,D ; THIR: SMIELIAUSKAS,W CIT: 0.88
AN EMPIRICAL STUDY OF ERROR CHARACTERISTICS IN ACCOUNTING POPULATIONS
TAR JL 85 VOL: 60 PG:387 - 406 :: REGRESS. :PRIM. :OTH.STAT. :ERRORS

HAMER ,MH ; FIRS: GORDON,LA CIT: 0
RATES OF RETURN AND CASH FLOW PROFILES: AN EXTENSION
AUD JL 88 VOL: 63 PG:514 - 521 :: DES.STAT. :INT. LOG. :THEORY :FIN.METH.

HAMILTON,RE ; SEC: WRIGHT,WF CIT: 1.36
INTERNAL CONTROL JUDGMENTS AND EFFECTS OF EXPERIENCE: REPLICATIONS AND EXTENSIONS
JAR AU 82 VOL: 20 PG:756 - 765 :: MIXED :LAB. :HIPS :INT.CONT.

HAMLEN,SS ; SEC: HAMLEN,WA ; THIR: TSCHIRHART,JT CIT: 0.08
THE USE OF THE GENERALIZED SHAPLEY ALLOCATION IN JOINT COST ALLOCATION
TAR AP 80 VOL: 55 PG:269 - 287 :: ANAL. :INT. LOG. :OTH.STAT. :INT.CONT.

HAMLEN,SS CIT: 0.31
A CHANCE-CONSTRAINED MIXED INTEGER PROGRAMMING MODEL FOR INTERNAL CONTROL DESIGN
TAR OC 80 VOL: 55 PG:578 - 593 :: ANAL. :INT. LOG. :MATH.PROG. :MANAG.

HAMLEN,SS ; SEC: HAMLEN,WA ; THIR: TSCHIRHART,JT CIT: 0.63
THE USE OF CORE THEORY IN EVALUATING JOINT COST ALLOCATION SCHEMES
TAR JL 77 VOL: 52 PG:616 - 627 :: ANAL. :INT. LOG. :MATH.PROG. :COST.ALLOC.

HAMLEN,WA ; FIRS: HAMLEN,SS ; THIR: TSCHIRHART,JT CIT: 0.08
THE USE OF THE GENERALIZED SHAPLEY ALLOCATION IN JOINT COST ALLOCATION
TAR AP 80 VOL: 55 PG:269 - 287 :: ANAL. :INT. LOG. :OTH.STAT. :INT.CONT.

HAMLEN,WA ; FIRS: HAMLEN,SS ; THIR: TSCHIRHART,JT CIT: 0.63
THE USE OF CORE THEORY IN EVALUATING JOINT COST ALLOCATION SCHEMES
TAR JL 77 VOL: 52 PG:616 - 627 :: ANAL. :INT. LOG. :MATH.PROG. :COST.ALLOC.

HAMRE ,JC ; FIRS: O'CONNOR,MC CIT: 0
ALTERNATIVE METHODS OF ACCOUNTING FOR LONG-TERM NONSUBSIDIARY INTERCORPORATE INVESTMENTS IN COMMON STOCK
TAR AP 72 VOL: 47 PG:308 - 319 :: QUAL. :INT. LOG. :THEORY :BUS.COMB.

HAN ,BH ; SEC: JENNINGS,R ; THIR: NOEL ,J CIT: 0
COMMUNICATION OF NONEARNINGS INFORMATION AT THE FINANCIAL STATEMENTS RELEASE DATE
JAE MR 92 VOL: 15 PG:63 - 85 :: REGRESS. :PRIM. :EMH :BUS.FAIL.

HAN ,I ; FIRS: LIANG ,T-P ; SEC: CHANDLER,JS ; FOUR: ROAN ,J CIT: 0
AN EMPIRICAL INVESTIGATION OF SOME DATA EFFECTS ON THE CLASSIFICATION ACCURACY OF PROBIT, ID3 AND NEURAL NETWORKS
CAR AU 92 VOL: 9 PG:306 - 328 :: DES.STAT. :PRIM. :OTH.STAT. :METHOD.

HAN ,JCY ; FIRS: BROWN ,LD CIT: 0
THE IMPACT OF ANNUAL EARNINGS ANNOUNCEMENTS ON CONVERGENCE OF BELIEFS
TAR OC 92 VOL: 67 PG:862 - 875 :: REGRESS. :PRIM. :EMH :AUD.BEH.

HAN ,JCY ; SEC: WILD ,JJ CIT: 0
STOCK PRICE BEHAVIOR ASSOCIATED WITH MANAGERS' EARNINGS AND REVENUE FORECASTS
JAR SP 91 VOL: 29 PG:79 - 95 :: REGRESS. :PRIM. :EMH :FOREC.

HAN ,JCY ; SEC: WILD ,JJ CIT: 0.33
UNEXPECTED EARNINGS AND INTRAINDUSTRY INFORMATION TRANSFERS: FURTHER EVIDENCE
JAR SP 90 VOL: 28 PG:211 - 219 :: REGRESS. :PRIM. :EMH :METHOD.

HAN ,JCY ; SEC: WILD ,JJ ; THIR: RAMESH,K CIT: 1.25
MANAGERS' EARNINGS FORECASTS AND INTRA-INDUSTRY INFORMATION TRANSFERS
JAE FB 89 VOL: 11 PG:3 - 33 :: REGRESS. :PRIM. :EMH :FOREC.

HAND ,JRM ; FIRS: BEATTY,RP CIT: 0
THE CAUSES AND EFFECTS OF MANDATED ACCOUNTING STANDARDS: SFAS NO. 94 AS A TEST OF THE LEVEL PLAYING FIELD THEORY
JAA AU 92 VOL: 7 PG:509 - 530 :: REGRESS. :PRIM. :EMH :FASB SUBM.

HAND ,JRM CIT: 0
EXTENDED FUNCTIONAL FIXATION AND SECURITY RETURNS AROUND EARNINGS ANNOUNCEMENTS: A REPLY TO BALL AND KOTHARI
TAR OC 91 VOL: 66 PG:739 - 746 :: REGRESS. :PRIM. :EMH :FIN.METH.

HAND ,JRM CIT: 0
A TEST OF THE EXTENDED FUNCTIONAL FIXATION HYPOTHESIS
TAR OC 90 VOL: 65 PG:739 - 763 :: REGRESS. :PRIM. :EMH :LTD

HAND ,JRM CIT: 1.5
DID FIRMS UNDERTAKE DEBT-EQUITY SWAPS FOR AN ACCOUNTING PAPER PROFIT OR TRUE FINANCIAL GAIN?
TAR OC 89 VOL: 64 PG:587 - 623 :: REGRESS. :PRIM. :TIME SER. :LTD

HANNA ,JD ; FIRS: ELLIOTT,JA ; THIR: SHAW ,WH CIT: 0
THE EVALUATION BY THE FINANCIAL MARKETS OF CHANGES IN BANK LOAN LOSS RESERVE LEVELS
TAR OC 91 VOL: 66 PG:847 - 861 :: REGRESS. :PRIM. :EMH :OTH. NON-C/A

HANNUM,WH ; SEC: WASSERMAN,W CIT: 0
GENERAL ADJUSTMENTS AND PRICE LEVEL MEASUREMENT
TAR AP 68 VOL: 43 PG:295 - 302 :: QUAL. :INT. LOG. :THEORY :VALUAT.(INFL.)

HANSEN,DR ; SEC: SHAFTEL,TL CIT: 0
SAMPLING FOR INTEGRATED AUDITING OBJECTIVES
TAR JA 77 VOL: 52 PG:109 - 123 :: ANAL. :INT. LOG. :MATH.PROG. :SAMP.

HANSEN,ES CIT: 0
MUNICIPAL FINANCES IN PERSPECTIVE: A LOOK AT INTER JURISDICTIONAL SPENDING AND REVENUE PATTERNS
JAR ST 77 VOL: 15 PG:156 - 201 :: QUAL. :PRIM. :INSTIT. :OTH.MANAG.

HANSEN,JV ; FIRS: BIGGS ,SF ; SEC: MESSIER JR,WF CIT: 0.5
A DESCRIPTIVE ANALYSIS OF COMPUTER AUDIT SPECIALISTS' DECISION MAKING
AUD SP 87 VOL: 6 PG:1 - 21 :: REGRESS. :LAB. :HIPS :EDP AUD.

HANSEN,JV ; FIRS: MESSIER JR,WF CIT: 0.33
EXPERT SYSTEMS IN AUDITING: THE STATE OF THE ART
AUD AU 87 VOL: 7 PG:94 - 105 :: REGRESS. :SURV. :EXP.SYST. :JUDG.

HANSEN,JV ; SEC: MESSIER JR,WF CIT: 0.57
A PRELIMINARY INVESTIGATION OF EDP-XPERT
AUD AU 86 VOL: 6 PG:109 - 123 :: ANAL. :LAB. :EXP.SYST. :EDP AUD.

HANSON,EI CIT: 0.12
THE BUDGETARY CONTROL FUNCTION
TAR AP 66 VOL: 41 PG:239 - 243 :: QUAL. :INT. LOG. :HIPS :BUDG.& PLAN.

HARIED,AA CIT: 0.65
MEASUREMENT OF MEANING IN FINANCIAL REPORTS
JAR SP 73 VOL: 11 PG:117 - 145 :: DES.STAT. :SURV. :OTH.BEH. :FIN.METH.

HARIED,AA CIT: 0.65
THE SEMANTIC DIMENSIONS OF FINANCIAL STATEMENTS
JAR AU 72 VOL: 10 PG:376 - 391 :: CORR. :LAB. :OTH.STAT. :METHOD.

HARMELINK,PJ CIT: 0.12
AN EMPIRICAL EXAMINATION OF THE PREDICTIVE ABILITY OF ALTERNATE SETS OF INSURANCE COMPANY ACCOUNTING DATA
JAR SP 73 VOL: 11 PG:146 - 158 :: OTH.QUANT. :PRIM. :OTH. :OTH.C/A

HARMON,WK CIT: 0
EARNINGS VS. FUNDS FLOWS: AN EMPIRICAL INVESTIGATION OF MARKET REACTION
JAA AU 84 VOL: 8 PG:24 - 34 :: REGRESS. :PRIM. :EMH :FIN.METH.

HARPER JR,RM ; SEC: STRAWSER,JR ; THIR: TANG ,K CIT: 0
ESTABLISHING INVESTIGATION THRESHOLDS FOR PRELIMINARY ANALYTICAL PROCEDURES
AUD AU 90 VOL: 9 PG:115 - 133 :: DES.STAT. :PRIM. :OTH.STAT. :ANAL.REV.

HARPER JR,RM ; SEC: MISTER,WG ; THIR: STRAWSER,JR CIT: 0
THE IMPACT OF NEW PENSION DISCLOSURE RULES ON PERCEPTIONS OF DEBT
JAR AU 87 VOL: 25 PG:327 - 330 :: REGRESS. :LAB. :OTH.STAT. :PENS.

HARRELL,A ; FIRS: RASCH ,RH CIT: 0
THE IMPACT OF PERSONAL CHARACTERISTICS ON THE TURNOVER BEHAVIOR OF ACCOUNTING PROFESSIONALS
AUD SP 90 VOL: 9 PG:90 - 102 :: REGRESS. :SURV. :OTH.BEH. :ORG.

HARRELL,A ; SEC: WRIGHT,A CIT: 0
EMPIRICAL EVIDENCE ON THE VALIDITY AND RELIABILITY OF BEHAVIORALLY ANCHORED RATING SCALES FOR AUDITORS
AUD AU 90 VOL: 9 PG:134 - 149 :: REGRESS. :FIELD :OTH.BEH. :AUD.BEH.

HARRELL,A ; SEC: TAYLOR,M ; THIR: CHEWNING,E CIT: 0.5
AN EXAMINATION OF MANAGEMENT'S ABILITY TO BIAS THE PROFESSIONAL OBJECTIVITY OF INTERNAL AUDITORS
AOS 03 89 VOL: 14 PG:259 - 269 :: REGRESS. :LAB. :HIPS :INT.AUD.

HARRELL,AM ; FIRS: CHEWNING,EG CIT: 0
THE EFFECT OF INFORMATION LOAD ON DECISION MAKERS' CUE UTILIZATION LEVELS AND DECISION QUALITY IN A FINANCIAL DISTRESS DECISION
AOS 06 90 VOL: 15 PG:527 - 542 :: REGRESS. :LAB. :HIPS :AUD.BEH.

HARRELL,AM ; SEC: EICKHOFF,R CIT: 0
AUDITORS' INFLUENCE ORIENTATION AND THEIR AFFECTIVE RESPONSES TO THE BIG EIGHT WORK ENVIRONMENT
AUD SP 88 VOL: 07 PG:105 - 118 :: REGRESS. :SURV. :OTH.BEH. :AUD.BEH.

HARRELL,AM ; SEC: CHEWNING,EG ; THIR: TAYLOR,M CIT: 0
ORGANIZATIONAL-PROFESSIONAL CONFLICT AND THE JOB SATISFACTION AND TURNOVER INTENTIONS OF INTERNAL AUDITORS
AUD SP 86 VOL: 5 PG:111 - 121 :: REGRESS. :SURV. :OTH.BEH. :AUD.TRAIL

HARRELL,AM ; SEC: STAHL ,MJ CIT: 0
MCCLELLAND'S TRICHOTOMY OF NEEDS THEORY AND THE JOB SATISFACTION AND WORK PERFORMANCE OF CPA FIRM PROFESSIONALS
AOS 34 84 VOL: 9 PG:241 - 252 :: CORR. :LAB. :OTH.BEH. :AUD.BEH.

HARRELL,AM ; SEC: KLICK ,HD CIT: 0.15
COMPARING THE IMPACT OF MONETARY AND NONMONETARY HUMAN ASSET MEASURES ON EXECUTIVE DECISION MAKING
AOS 04 80 VOL: 5 PG:393 - 400 :: REGRESS. :LAB. :OTH.BEH. :HRA

HARRELL,AM CIT: 0.63
THE DECISION-MAKING BEHAVIOR OF AIR FORCE OFFICERS AND THE MANAGEMENT CONTROL PROCESS
TAR OC 77 VOL: 52 PG:833 - 841 :: ANOVA :LAB. :HIPS :RESP.ACC.

HARRIS,D ; FIRS: CHALOS,P ; SEC: CHERIAN,J CIT: 0
FINANCIAL DISCLOSURE EFFECTS ON LABOR CONTRACTS: A NASH ANALYSIS
CAR SP 91 VOL: 7 PG:431 - 448 :: REGRESS. :PRIM. :OTH.BEH. :INFO.STRUC.

HARRIS,RS ; FIRS: MARSTON,F CIT: 0
SUITABILITY OF LEASES AND DEBT IN CORPORATE CAPITAL STRUCTURES
JAA SP 88 VOL: 03 PG:147 - 164 :: REGRESS. :PRIM. :EMH :LEASES

HARRIS,TS ; FIRS: EASTON,PD ; THIR: OHLSON,JA CIT: 2
AGGREGATE ACCOUNTING EARNINGS CAN EXPLAIN MOST OF SECURITY RETURNS: TH CASE OF LONG RETURN INTERVALS
JAE JN 92 VOL: 15 PG:119 - 142 :: REGRESS. :PRIM. :EMH :FIN.METH.

HARRIS,TS ; FIRS: EASTON,PD CIT: 3.5
EARNINGS AS AN EXPLANATORY VARIABLE FOR RETURNS
JAR SP 91 VOL: 29 PG:19 - 36 :: REGRESS. :PRIM. :EMH :FIN.METH.

HARRIS,TS ; FIRS: BALAKRISHNAN,R ; THIR: SEN ,PK CIT: 0
THE PREDICTIVE ABILITY OF GEOGRAPHIC SEGMENT DISCLOSURES
JAR AU 90 VOL: 28 PG:305 - 325 :: REGRESS. :PRIM. :TIME SER. :SEG.REP.

HARRIS,TS ; SEC: OHLSON,JA CIT: 0.67
ACCOUNTING DISCLOSURES AND THE MARKET'S VALUATION OF OIL AND GAS PROPERTIES: EVALUATION OF MARKET EFFICIENCY AND FUNCTIONAL FIXATION
TAR OC 90 VOL: 65 PG:764 - 780 :: REGRESS. :PRIM. :HIPS :OIL & GAS

HARRIS,TS ; SEC: OHLSON,JA CIT: 1.5
ACCOUNTING DISCLOSURES AND THE MARKET'S VALUATION OF OIL AND GAS PROPERTIES
TAR OC 87 VOL: 62 PG:651 - 670 :: REGRESS. :PRIM. :EMH :OIL & GAS

HARRISON JR,WT ; SEC: TOMASSINI,LA ; THIR: DIETRICH,JR CIT: 0.2
THE USE OF CONTROL GROUPS IN CAPITAL MARKET RESEARCH
JAR SP 83 VOL: 21 PG:65 - 77 :: NON-PAR. :PRIM. :EMH :METHOD.

HARRISON,GL CIT: 0
THE CROSS-CULTURAL GENERALIZABILITY OF THE RELATION BETWEEN PARTICIPATION, PARTICIPATION, BUDGET EMPHASIS AND JOB RELATED ATTITUDES
AOS 01 92 VOL: 17 PG:1 - 15 :: REGRESS. :SURV. :OTH.BEH. :BUDG.& PLAN.

HARRISON,GL ; SEC: MCKINNON,JL CIT: 0.14
CULTURE AND ACCOUNTING CHANGE: A NEW PROSPECTIVE ON CORPORATE REPORTING REGULATION AND ACCOUNTING POLICY FORMULATION
AOS 03 86 VOL: 11 PG:233 - 252 :: DES.STAT. :INT. LOG. :INSTIT. :FASB SUBM.

HARRISON,KE ; SEC: TOMASSINI,LA CIT: 0.25
JUDGING THE PROBABILITY OF A CONTINGENT LOSS: AN EMPIRICAL STUDY
CAR SP 89 VOL: 5 PG:642 - 648 :: REGRESS. :LAB. :HIPS :PROB.ELIC.

HARRISON,PD ; SEC: WEST ,SG ; THIR: RENEAU,JH CIT: 0.2
INITIAL ATTRIBUTIONS AND INFORMATION-SEEKING BY SUPERIORS AND SUBORDINATES IN PRODUCTION VARIANCE INVESTIGATIONS
TAR AP 88 VOL: 63 PG:307 - 320 :: REGRESS. :LAB. :OTH.BEH. :VAR.

HARRISON,T CIT: 1.06
DIFFERENT MARKET REACTIONS TO DISCRETIONARY AND NONDISCRETIONARY ACCOUNTING CHANGES
JAR SP 77 VOL: 15 PG:84 - 107 :: REGRESS. :PRIM. :EMH :ACC.CHNG.

HARRISS,CL ; FIRS: DEAN ,J CIT: 0
RAILROAD ACCOUNTING UNDER THE NEW DEPRECIATION GUIDELINES AND INVESTMENT TAX CREDIT
TAR AP 63 VOL: 38 PG:229 - 242 :: QUAL. :INT. LOG. :THEORY :TAXES

HARTE ,GF ; SEC: OWEN ,DL CIT: 0.5
FIGHTING DE-INDUSTRIALIZATION: THE ROLE OF LOCAL GOVERNMENT SOCIAL AUDITS
AOS 02 87 VOL: 12 PG:123 - 142 :: REGRESS. :INT. LOG. :THEORY :ORG.& ENVIR.

HARTLEY,RV CIT: 0.18
DECISION MAKING WHEN JOINT PRODUCTS ARE INVOLVED
TAR OC 71 VOL: 46 PG:746 - 755 :: ANAL. :INT. LOG. :MATH.PROG. :BUDG.& PLAN.

HARTLEY,RV CIT: 0.06
SOME EXTENSIONS OF SENSITIVITY ANALYSIS
TAR AP 70 VOL: 45 PG:223 - 234 :: ANAL. :INT. LOG. :MATH.PROG. :BUDG.& PLAN.

HARTLEY,RV CIT: 0
OPERATIONS RESEARCH AND ITS IMPLICATIONS FOR THE ACCOUNTING PROFESSION
TAR AP 68 VOL: 43 PG:321 - 332 :: QUAL. :INT. LOG. :MATH.PROG. :MANAG.

HARVEY,DW ; SEC: RHODE ,JG ; THIR: MERCHANT,KA CIT: 0.14
ACCOUNTING AGGREGATION: USER PREFERENCES AND DECISION MAKING
AOS 03 79 VOL: 4 PG:187 - 210 :: ANOVA :LAB. :OTH.BEH. :N/A

HARVEY,DW CIT: 0.06
FINANCIAL PLANNING INFORMATION FOR PRODUCTION START-UPS
TAR OC 76 VOL: 51 PG:838 - 845 :: ANAL. :INT. LOG. :OTH.STAT. :MANAG.

HARVEY,DW ; FIRS: AMATO ,HN ; SEC: ANDERSON,EE CIT: 0.06
A GENERAL MODEL OF FUTURE PERIOD WARRANTY COSTS
TAR OC 76 VOL: 51 PG:854 - 862 :: ANAL. :INT. LOG. :OTH. :SPEC.ITEMS

HARWOOD,GB ; FIRS: BERRY ,LE ; THIR: KATZ ,JL CIT: 0.17
PERFORMANCE OF AUDITING PROCEDURES BY GOVERNMENTAL AUDITORS: SOME PRELIMINARY EVIDENCE
TAR JA 87 VOL: 62 PG:14 - 28 :: DES.STAT. :SURV. :OTH.STAT. :AUD.

HASEMAN,WC CIT: 0
AN INTERPRETIVE FRAMEWORK FOR COST
TAR OC 68 VOL: 43 PG:738 - 752 :: QUAL. :INT. LOG. :THEORY :MANAG.

HASEMAN,WD ; SEC: WHINSTON,AB CIT: 0.41
DESIGN OF A MULTIDIMENSIONAL ACCOUNTING SYSTEM
TAR JA 76 VOL: 51 PG:65 - 79 :: ANAL. :INT. LOG. :N/A :MANAG.

HASKINS,M CIT: 0.67
CLIENT CONTROL ENVIRONMENTS: AN EXAMINATION OF AUDITORS' PERCEPTIONS
TAR JL 87 VOL: 62 PG:542 - 563 :: REGRESS. :SURV. :OTH.BEH. :INT.CONT.

HASKINS,ME ; FIRS: DIRSMITH,MW CIT: 0
INHERENT RISK ASSESSMENT AND AUDIT FIRM TECHNOLOGY: A CONTRAST IN WORLD THEORIES
AOS 01 91 VOL: 16 PG:61 - 90 :: REGRESS. :FIELD :HIPS :DEC.AIDS

HASKINS,ME ; SEC: WILLIAMS,DD CIT: 0
A CONTINGENT MODEL OF INTRA-BIG EIGHT AUDITOR CHANGES
AUD AU 90 VOL: 9 PG:55 - 74 :: REGRESS. :PRIM. :INSTIT. :ORG.

HASKINS,ME ; SEC: BAGLIONI,AJ ; THIR: COOPER,CL CIT: 0.67
AN INVESTIGATION OF THE SOURCES, MODERATORS, AND PSYCHOLOGICAL SYMPTOMS OF STRESS AMONG AUDIT SENIORS
CAR SP 90 VOL: 6 PG:361 - 385 :: REGRESS. :LAB. :HIPS :AUD.BEH.

HASLAM,J ; FIRS: GALLHOFER,S CIT: 0
THE AURA OF ACCOUNTING IN THE CONTEXT OF A CRISIS: GERMANY AND THE FIRST WORLD WAR
AOS 05 91 VOL: 16 PG:487 - 520 :: REGRESS. :SEC. :HIST. :ORG.& ENVIR.

HASSELBACK,JR CIT: 0
AN EMPIRICAL EXAMINATION OF ANNUAL REPORT PRESENTATION OF THE CORPORATE INCOME TAX EXPENSE
TAR AP 76 VOL: 51 PG:269 - 276 :: ANOVA :INT. LOG. :INSTIT. :TAXES

HASSELDINE,CR CIT: 0.18
MIX AND YIELD VARIANCES
TAR JL 67 VOL: 42 PG:497 - 515 :: ANAL. :INT. LOG. :OTH.STAT. :VAR.

HASSELL,JM ; FIRS: BAGINSKI,SP CIT: 0
THE MARKET INTERPRETATION OF MANAGEMENT EARNINGS FORECASTS AS A PREDICTOR OF SUBSEQUENT FINANCIAL ANALYST FORECAST REVISION
TAR JA 90 VOL: 65 PG:175 - 190 :: REGRESS. :PRIM. :EMH :FOREC.

HASSELL,JM ; SEC: ARRINGTON,CE CIT: 0
A COMPARATIVE ANALYSIS OF THE CONSTRUCT VALIDITY OF COEFFICIENTS IN PARAMORPHIC MODELS OF ACCOUNTING JUDGMENTS: A REPLICATION AN
AOS 06 89 VOL: 14 PG:527 - 537 :: REGRESS. :LAB. :HIPS :JUDG.

HASSELL,JM ; SEC: JENNINGS,RH CIT: 0.57
RELATIVE FORECAST ACCURACY AND THE TIMING OF EARNINGS FORECAST ANNOUNCEMENTS
TAR JA 86 VOL: 61 PG:58 - 75 :: REGRESS. :PRIM. :TIME SER. :FOREC.

HATFIELD,HR CIT: 0
SOME VARIATIONS IN ACCOUNTING PRACTICE IN ENGLAND, FRANCE, GERMANY AND THE UNITED STATES
JAR AU 66 VOL: 4 PG:169 - 182 :: QUAL. :INT. LOG. :THEORY :INT.DIFF.

HAW ,I ; SEC: KIM ,W CIT: 0
FIRM SIZE AND DIVIDEND ANNOUNCEMENT EFFECT
JAA SU 91 VOL: 6 PG:325 - 344 :: REGRESS. :PRIM. :EMH :CASH DIV.

HAW ,I ; SEC: JUNG ,K ; THIR: LILIEN,SB CIT: 0
OVERFUNDED DEFINED BENEFIT PENSION PLAN SETTLEMENTS WITHOUT ASSET REVERSIONS
JAE SE 91 VOL: 14 PG:295 - 320 :: REGRESS. :PRIM. :TIME SER. :PENS.

HAW ,I ; SEC: PASTENA,VS ; THIR: LILIEN,SB CIT: 0.33
MARKET MANIFESTATION OF NONPUBLIC INFORMATION PRIOR TO MERGERS: THE EFFECT OF OWNERSHIP STRUCTURE
TAR AP 90 VOL: 65 PG:432 - 451 :: REGRESS. :PRIM. :EMH :BUS.COMB.

HAW ,IM ; SEC: LUSTGARTEN,S CIT: 0.4
EVIDENCE ON INCOME MEASUREMENT PROPERTIES OF ASR NO. 190 AND SFAS NO. 33 DATA
JAR AU 88 VOL: 26 PG:331 - 352 :: REGRESS. :PRIM. :EMH :VALUAT.(INFL.)

HAW ,IM ; SEC: PASTENA,V ; THIR: LILIEN,S CIT: 0
THE ASSOCIATION BETWEEN MARKET-BASED MERGER PREMIUMS AND FIRMS' FINANCIAL POSITION PRIOR TO MERGER
JAA WI 87 VOL: 2 PG:24 - 42 :: REGRESS. :PRIM. :EMH :BUS.COMB.

HAWKINS,CA ; SEC: GIRARD,D CIT: 0
REPLACEMENT DECISIONS UNDER THE ACCELERATED COST RECOVERY SYSTEM
JAA SP 84 VOL: 7 PG:225 - 240 :: MIXED :INT. LOG. :THEORY :PP&E / DEPR

HAYES ,DC CIT: 1.5
ACCOUNTING FOR ACCOUNTING: A STORY ABOUT MANAGERIAL ACCOUNTING
AOS 23 83 VOL: 8 PG:241 - 250 :: QUAL. :INT. LOG. :INF.ECO./AG. :MANAG.

HAYES ,DC ; FIRS: COOPER,DJ ; THIR: WOLF ,FM CIT: 1.08
ACCOUNTING IN ORGANIZED ANARCHIES: UNDERSTANDING AND DESIGNING ACCOUNTING SYSTEMS IN AMBIGUOUS SITUATIONS
AOS 03 81 VOL: 6 PG:175 - 192 :: QUAL. :INT. LOG. :THEORY :N/A

HAYES ,DC CIT: 2.56
THE CONTINGENCY THEORY OF MANAGERIAL ACCOUNTING
TAR JA 77 VOL: 52 PG:22 - 39 :: OTH.QUANT. :FIELD :OTH.STAT. :RESP.ACC.

HAYES ,RD ; SEC: MILLAR,JA CIT: 0
MEASURING PRODUCTION EFFICIENCY IN A NOT-FOR-PROFIT SETTING
TAR JL 90 VOL: 65 PG:505 - 519 :: ANOVA :LAB. :INF.ECO./AG. :OPER.AUD.

HAYES ,SC ; FIRS: TAUSSIG,RA CIT: 0
CASH TAKE-OVERS AND ACCOUNTING VALUATIONS
TAR JA 68 VOL: 43 PG:68 - 74 :: ANOVA :PRIM. :N/A :INV.

HAYN ,C ; FIRS: GIVOLY,D CIT: 0
THE VALUATION OF THE DEFERRED TAX LIABILITY: EVIDENCE FROM THE STOCK MARKET
TAR AP 92 VOL: 67 PG:394 - 410 :: REGRESS. :PRIM. :EMH :SPEC.ITEMS

HAYYA ,JC ; FIRS: FERRARA,WL ; THIR: NACHMAN,DA CIT: 0.24
NORMALCY OF PROFIT IN THE JAEDICKE-ROBICHEK MODEL
TAR AP 72 VOL: 47 PG:299 - 307 :: ANAL. :SIM. :OTH.STAT. :C-V-P-A

HEALY ,P ; FIRS: ASQUITH,P ; THIR: PALEPU,K CIT: 0
EARNINGS AND STOCK SPLITS
TAR JL 89 VOL: 64 PG:387 - 403 :: REGRESS. :PRIM. :EMH :STK.DIV.

HEALY ,PM ; SEC: MODIGLIANI,F CIT: 0
DIVIDEND DECISIONS AND EARNINGS
JAA WI 90 VOL: 5 PG:3 - 25 :: REGRESS. :PRIM. :OTH.STAT. :CASH DIV.

HEALY ,PM ; SEC: PALEPU,KG CIT: 1.33
EFFECTIVENESS OF ACCOUNTING-BASED DIVIDEND COVENANTS
JAE JA 90 VOL: 12 PG:97 - 123 :: REGRESS. :PRIM. :OTH.STAT. :CASH DIV.

HEALY ,PM ; SEC: PALEPU,KG CIT: 0.67
EARNINGS AND RISK CHANGES SURROUNDING PRIMARY STOCK OFFERS
JAR SP 90 VOL: 28 PG:25 - 48 :: REGRESS. :PRIM. :EMH :INFO.STRUC.

HEALY ,PM ; SEC: KANG ,SH ; THIR: PALEPU,KG CIT: 1.5
THE EFFECT OF ACCOUNTING PROCEDURE CHANGES ON CEOS' CASH SALARY AND BONUS COMPENSATION
JAE AP 87 VOL: 9 PG:7 - 34 :: REGRESS. :PRIM. :OTH.STAT. :INV.

HEALY ,PM CIT: 6
THE EFFECT OF BONUS SCHEMES ON ACCOUNTING DECISIONS
JAE AP 85 VOL: 7 PG:85 - 108 :: REGRESS. :PRIM. :OTH.STAT. :EXEC.COMP.

HEANEY,J ; FIRS: CHEUNG,JK CIT: 0
A CONTINGENT-CLAIM INTEGRATION OF COST-VOLUME-PROFIT ANALYSIS
CAR SP 90 VOL: 6 PG:738 - 760 :: DES.STAT. :INT. LOG. :THEORY :C-V-P-A

HEARD ,JE ; SEC: BOLCE ,WJ CIT: 0
THE POLITICAL SIGNIFICANCE OF CORPORATE SOCIAL REPORTING IN THE U.S.A.
AOS 03 81 VOL: 6 PG:247 - 254 :: QUAL. :INT. LOG. :OTH. :HRA

HEATH ,DC ; FIRS: BILLERA,LJ ; THIR: VERRECCHIA,RE CIT: 0.25
A UNIQUE PROCEDURE FOR ALLOCATING COMMON COSTS FROM A PRODUCTION PROCESS
JAR SP 81 VOL: 19 PG:185 - 196 :: ANAL. :INT. LOG. :INF.ECO./AG. :N/A

HEATH ,LC CIT: 0.06
DISTINGUISHING BETWEEN MONETARY AND NONMONETARY ASSETS AND LIABILITIES IN GENERAL PRICE-LEVEL ACCOUNTING
TAR JL 72 VOL: 47 PG:458 - 468 :: QUAL. :INT. LOG. :THEORY :VALUAT.(INFL.)

HECK ,JL ; SEC: BREMSER,WG CIT: 0
SIX DECADES OF THE ACCOUNTING REVIEW: A SUMMARY OF AUTHOR AND INSTITUTIONAL CONTRIBUTORS
TAR OC 86 VOL: 61 PG:735 - 744 :: REGRESS. :SEC. :HIST. :METHOD.

HECK ,WR CIT: 0.06
ACCOUNTING FOR WARRANTY COSTS
TAR JL 63 VOL: 38 PG:577 - 578 :: QUAL. :INT. LOG. :THEORY :SPEC.ITEMS

HEDBERG,B ; SEC: JONSSON,S CIT: 1.93
DESIGNING SEMI-CONFUSING INFORMATION SYSTEMS FOR ORGANIZATIONS IN CHANGING ENVIRONMENTS
AOS 01 78 VOL: 3 PG:47 - 64 :: QUAL. :INT. LOG. :OTH. :N/A

HEDLUND,G ; FIRS: HAGG ,J CIT: 0.36
CASE STUDIES IN ACCOUNTING RESEARCH
AOS 12 79 VOL: 4 PG:135 - 143 :: QUAL. :INT. LOG. :OTH. :METHOD.

HEEBINK,DV CIT: 0
THE OPTIMUM CAPITAL BUDGET
TAR JA 64 VOL: 39 PG:90 - 93 :: ANAL. :INT. LOG. :N/A :CAP.BUDG.

HEIMAN,VB CIT: 0.67
AUDITORS' ASSESSMENTS OF THE LIKELIHOOD OF ERROR EXPLANATIONS IN ANALYTICAL REVIEW
TAR OC 90 VOL: 65 PG:875 - 890 :: REGRESS. :FIELD :HIPS :ANAL.REV.

HEIMANN,SR ; SEC: CHESLEY,GR CIT: 0.25
AUDIT SAMPLE SIZES FOR AGGREGATED STATEMENT ACCOUNTS
JAR AU 77 VOL: 15 PG:193 - 206 :: ANAL. :INT. LOG. :MATH.PROG. :SAMP.

HEIMANN,SR ; SEC: LUSK ,EJ CIT: 0.06
DECISION FLEXIBILITY: AN ALTERNATIVE EVALUATION CRITERION
TAR JA 76 VOL: 51 PG:51 - 64 :: ANAL. :INT. LOG. :OTH.STAT. :MANAG.

HEIN ,LW CIT: 0
NEW BRITISH ACCOUNTING RECOMMENDATIONS
TAR AP 63 VOL: 38 PG:252 - 261 :: QUAL. :INT. LOG. :INSTIT. :FIN.METH.

HEIN ,LW CIT: 0
THE AUDITOR AND THE BRITISH COMPANIES ACTS
TAR JL 63 VOL: 38 PG:508 - 520 :: QUAL. :INT. LOG. :HIST. :OTH.MANAG.

HEINS ,EB CIT: 0
A SURVEY OF ACCOUNTING IN JUNIOR COLLEGES
TAR AP 66 VOL: 41 PG:323 - 326 :: QUAL. :SURV. :N/A :OTH.MANAG.

HEINTZ,JA ; SEC: WHITE ,GB CIT: 0
AUDITOR JUDGMENT IN ANALYTICAL REVIEW-SOME FURTHER EVIDENCE
AUD SP 89 VOL: 8 PG:22 - 39 :: REGRESS. :LAB. :HIPS :ANAL.REV.

HEINTZ,JA ; FIRS: REBELE,JE ; THIR: BRIDEN,GE CIT: 0
INDEPENDENT AUDITOR SENSITIVITY TO EVIDENCE RELIABILITY
AUD AU 88 VOL: 08 PG:43 - 52 :: REGRESS. :LAB. :OTH.BEH. :JUDG.

HEINTZ,JA ; FIRS: FALK ,H CIT: 0
ASSESSING INDUSTRY RISK BY RATIO ANALYSIS
TAR OC 75 VOL: 50 PG:758 - 779 :: NON-PAR. :PRIM. :N/A :FIN.METH.

HEINTZ,JA CIT: 0.24
PRICE-LEVEL RESTATED FINANCIAL STATEMENTS AND INVESTMENT DECISION MAKING
TAR OC 73 VOL: 48 PG:679 - 689 :: DES.STAT. :LAB. :THEORY :VALUAT.(INFL.)

HELLELOID,R ; FIRS: ANDERSON,MJ ; SEC: ANDERSON,U ; FOUR: JOYCE ,E ; FIFT: SCHADEWALD,M CIT: 0
INTERNAL REVENUE SERVICE ACCESS TO TAX ACCRUAL WORKPAPERS: A LABORATORY INVESTIGATION
TAR OC 90 VOL: 65 PG:857 - 874 :: REGRESS. :LAB. :MATH.PROG. :AUD.

HELMKAMP,JG CIT: 0
TECHNICAL INFORMATION CENTER MANAGEMENT: AN ACCOUNTING DEFICIENCY
TAR JL 69 VOL: 44 PG:605 - 610 :: QUAL. :INT. LOG. :N/A :MANAG.

HENDRICKS,JA CIT: 0.41
THE IMPACT OF HUMAN RESOURCE ACCOUNTING INFORMATION AND STOCK INVESTMENT DECISIONS: AN EMPIRICAL STUDY
TAR AP 76 VOL: 51 PG:292 - 305 :: CORR. :LAB. :THEORY :HRA

HENDRICKS,TE ; FIRS: FIRMIN,PA ; SEC: GOODMAN,SS ; FOUR: LINN ,JJ CIT: 0
UNIVERSITY COST STRUCTURE AND BEHAVIOR: AN EMPIRICAL STUDY
JAR ST 68 VOL: 6 PG:122 - 155 :: DES.STAT. :SIM. :OTH.STAT. :MANAG.

HENDRIKSEN,ES CIT: 0
PURCHASING POWER AND REPLACEMENT COST CONCEPTS - ARE THEY RELATED?
TAR JL 63 VOL: 38 PG:483 - 491 :: QUAL. :INT. LOG. :THEORY :VALUAT.(INFL.)

HENDRICKSON,HS CIT: 0
SOME COMMENTS ON DIRTY POOLING
TAR AP 68 VOL: 43 PG:363 - 366 :: QUAL. :INT. LOG. :THEORY :REV.REC.

HENNESSY,VC CIT: 0
ACCOUNTING FOR PENSION LIABILITIES CREATED BY ERISA
JAA SU 78 VOL: 1 PG:317 - 330 :: QUAL. :INT. LOG. :THEORY :SPEC.ITEMS

HERBERT,L CIT: 0
A PERSPECTIVE OF ACCOUNTING
TAR JL 71 VOL: 46 PG:433 - 440 :: QUAL. :INT. LOG. :HIST. :OTH.MANAG.

HERMANSON,RH ; FIRS: CARCELLO,JV ; THIR: MCGRATH,NT CIT: 0
AUDIT QUALITY ATTRIBUTES: THE PERCEPTIONS OF AUDIT PARTNERS, PREPARERS, AND FINANCIAL STATEMENT USERS
AUD SP 92 VOL: 11 PG:1 - 15 :: REGRESS. :SURV. :OTH.BEH. :OPER.AUD.

HERRINGER,F ; FIRS: BOWER ,RS ; THIR: WILLIAMSON,JP CIT: 0
LEASE EVALUATION
TAR AP 66 VOL: 41 PG:257 - 265 :: ANAL. :INT. LOG. :OTH.STAT. :LEASES

HERTOG,FD ; SEC: WIELINGA,C CIT: 0
CONTROL SYSTEMS IN DISSONANCE: THE COMPUTER AS AN INK BLOT
AOS 02 92 VOL: 17 PG:103 - 128 :: REGRESS. :CASE :OTH.BEH. :ORG.& ENVIR.

HERTOG,JF CIT: 0.47
THE ROLE OF INFORMATION AND CONTROL SYSTEMS IN THE PROCESS OF ORGANIZATIONAL RENEWAL: ROADBLOCK OR ROAD BRIDGE?
AOS 01 78 VOL: 3 PG:29 - 46 :: QUAL. :INT. LOG. :OTH.BEH. :ORG.FORM

HERTZER,M ; SEC: JAIN ,PC CIT: 1
EARNINGS AND RISK CHANGES AROUND STOCK REPURCHASE TENDER OFFERS
JAE SE 91 VOL: 14 PG:253 - 273 :: REGRESS. :PRIM. :EMH :BUS.COMB.

HESSEL,CA ; SEC: NORMAN,M CIT: 0
FINANCIAL CHARACTERISTICS OF NEGLECTED AND INSTITUTIONALLY HELD STOCKS
JAA SU 92 VOL: 7 PG:313 - 330 :: REGRESS. :PRIM. :OTH.STAT. :ORG.& ENVIR.

HICKS ,EL CIT: 0.06
MATERIALITY
JAR AU 64 VOL: 2 PG:158 - 171 :: QUAL. :INT. LOG. :THEORY :MAT.

HICKS JR,JO CIT: 0.27
AN EXAMINATION OF ACCOUNTING INTEREST GROUPS' DIFFERENTIAL PERCEPTIONS OF INNOVATIONS
TAR AP 78 VOL: 53 PG:371 - 388 :: ANOVA :SURV. :INSTIT. :N/A

HICKS ,SA CIT: 0
CHOOSING THE FORM FOR BUSINESS TAX INCENTIVES
TAR JL 78 VOL: 53 PG:708 - 716 :: QUAL. :INT. LOG. :N/A :TAXES

HILKE ,JC CIT: 0.14
REGULATORY COMPLIANCE COSTS AND LIFO: NO WONDER SMALL COMPANIES HAVEN'T SWITCHED
JAA WI 86 VOL: 1 PG:17 - 29 :: REGRESS. :SURV. :THEORY :INV.

HILL ,HP CIT: 0
RATIONAL EXPECTATIONS AND ACCOUNTING PRINCIPLES
JAA WI 82 VOL: 5 PG:99 - 109 :: QUAL. :INT. LOG. :THEORY :FASB SUBM.

HILL ,JW ; SEC: INGRAM,RW CIT: 1
SELECTION OF GAAP OR RAP IN THE SAVINGS AND LOAN INDUSTRY
TAR OC 89 VOL: 64 PG:667 - 679 :: REGRESS. :PRIM. :HIST. :FIN.METH.

HILLIARD,JE ; SEC: LEITCH,RA CIT: 0.41
COST-VOLUME-PROFIT ANALYSIS UNDER UNCERTAINTY: A LOG NORMAL APPROACH
TAR JA 75 VOL: 50 PG:69 - 80 :: ANAL. :INT. LOG. :OTH.STAT. :C-V-P-A

HILLISON,WA ; FIRS: ICERMAN,RC CIT: 0
DISPOSITION OF AUDIT-DETECTED ERRORS: SOME EVIDENCE ON EVALUATIVE MATERIALITY
AUD SP 91 VOL: 10 PG:22 - 34 :: REGRESS. :PRIM. :HIPS :MAT.

HILLISON,WA ; FIRS: ICERMAN,RC CIT: 0
DISTRIBUTION OF AUDIT-DETECTED ERRORS PARTITIONED BY INTERNAL CONTROL
JAA AU 90 VOL: 5 PG:527 - 543 :: REGRESS. :FIELD :OTH.STAT. :ERRORS

HILLISON,WA ; FIRS: ARRINGTON,CE ; THIR: JENSEN,RE CIT: 0.44
AN APPLICATION OF ANALYTICAL HIERARCHY PROCESS TO MODEL EXPERT JUDGMENTS ON ANALYTICAL REVIEW PROCEDURES
JAR SP 84 VOL: 22 PG:298 - 312 :: OTH.QUANT. :LAB. :HIPS :ANAL.REV.

HILLISON,WA CIT: 0.07
EMPIRICAL INVESTIGATION OF GENERAL PURCHASING POWER ADJUSTMENTS ON EARNINGS PER SHARE AND THE MOVEMENT OF SECURITY PRICES
JAR SP 79 VOL: 17 PG:60 - 73 :: REGRESS. :PRIM. :EMH :VALUAT.(INFL.)

HILLMAN,AP ; FIRS: WOLK ,HI CIT: 0.12
MATERIALS MIX AND YIELD VARIANCES: A SUGGESTED IMPROVEMENT
TAR JL 72 VOL: 47 PG:549 - 555 :: ANAL. :INT. LOG. :MATH.PROG. :VAR.

HILTON,RW ; FIRS: TURNER,MJ CIT: 0.25
USE OF ACCOUNTING PRODUCT-COSTING SYSTEMS IN MAKING PRODUCTION DECISIONS
JAR AU 89 VOL: 27 PG:297 - 312 :: REGRESS. :LAB. :OTH.BEH. :REL.COSTS

HILTON,RW ; SEC: SWIERINGA,RJ ; THIR: TURNER,MJ CIT: 0.2
PRODUCT PRICING, ACCOUNTING COSTS AND USE OF PRODUCT-COSTING SYSTEMS
TAR AP 88 VOL: 63 PG:195 - 218 :: REGRESS. :LAB. :OTH.BEH. :REL.COSTS

HILTON,RW CIT: 0
INTERDEPENDENCE BETWEEN THE INFORMATION EVALUATOR AND THE DECISION MAKER
CAR AU 86 VOL: 3 PG:50 - 67 :: DES.STAT. :INT. LOG. :INF.ECO./AG. :INFO.STRUC.

HILTON,RW ; SEC: SWIERINGA,RJ ; THIR: HOSKIN,RE CIT: 0.58
PERCEPTION OF ACCURACY AS A DETERMINANT OF INFORMATION VALUE
JAR SP 81 VOL: 19 PG:86 - 108 :: ANOVA :LAB. :OTH.BEH. :MANAG.

HILTON,RW ; SEC: SWIERINGA,RJ CIT: 0.42
PERCEPTION OF INITIAL UNCERTAINTY AS A DETERMINANT OF INFORMATION VALUE
JAR SP 81 VOL: 19 PG:109 - 119 :: ANOVA :LAB. :HIPS :OTH.MANAG.

HILTON,RW CIT: 0.77
INTEGRATING NORMATIVE AND DESCRIPTIVE THEORIES OF INFORMATION PROCESSING
JAR AU 80 VOL: 18 PG:477 - 505 :: ANAL. :INT. LOG. :HIPS :OTH.MANAG.

HILTON,RW CIT: 0.29
THE DETERMINANTS OF COST INFORMATION VALUE: AN ILLUSTRATIVE ANALYSIS
JAR AU 79 VOL: 17 PG:411 - 435 :: ANAL. :INT. LOG. :INF.ECO./AG. :C-V-P-A

HINES ,RD CIT: 0
ACCOUNTING: FILLING THE NEGATIVE SPACE
AOS 04 92 VOL: 17 PG:313 - 341 :: DES.STAT. :SEC. :THEORY :ORG.& ENVIR.

HINES ,RD CIT: 1
THE FASB'S CONCEPTUAL FRAMEWORK, FINANCIAL ACCOUNTING AND THE MAINTENANCE OF THE SOCIAL WORLD
AOS 04 91 VOL: 16 PG:313 - 331 :: REGRESS. :SEC. :INSTIT. :FIN.METH.

HINES ,RD CIT: 1.8
FINANCIAL ACCOUNTING: IN COMMUNICATING REALITY, WE CONSTRUCT REALITY
AOS 03 88 VOL: 13 PG:251 - 261 :: ANOVA :INT. LOG. :THEORY :FIN.METH.

HINES ,RD CIT: 0.6
POPPER'S METHODOLOGY OF FALSIFICATIONISM AND ACCOUNTING RESEARCH
TAR OC 88 VOL: 63 PG:642 - 656 :: DES.STAT. :INT. LOG. :THEORY :METHOD.

HINES JR,JR CIT: 0
THE FLIGHT PATHS OF MIGRATORY CORPORATIONS
JAA AU 91 VOL: 6 PG:447 - 479 :: REGRESS. :CASE :OTH.STAT. :TAXES

HININGS,CR ; FIRS: WILLIAMS,JJ CIT: 0
A NOTE ON MATCHING CONTROL SYSTEM IMPLICATIONS WITH ORGANIZATIONAL CHARACTERISTICS: ZBB AND MBO REVISITED
AOS 02 88 VOL: 13 PG:191 - 198 :: REGRESS. :SURV. :OTH.BEH. :BUDG.& PLAN.

HINOMOTO,H CIT: 0.12
OPTIMUM STRATEGIES FOR MANAGEMENT INFORMATION PROCESSING AND CONTROL
JAR AU 71 VOL: 9 PG:253 - 267 :: ANAL. :INT. LOG. :MATH.PROG. :MANAG.

HIRSCH JR,ML CIT: 0.2
DISAGGREGATED PROBABILISTIC ACCOUNTING INFORMATION: THE EFFECT OF SEQUENTIAL EVENTS ON EXPECTED VALUE MAXIMIZATION DECISIONS
JAR AU 78 VOL: 16 PG:254 - 269 :: ANOVA :LAB. :OTH.STAT. :INFO.STRUC.

HIRSCH,AJ CIT: 0
ACCOUNTING FOR FIXED ASSETS: A NEW PERSPECTIVE
TAR OC 64 VOL: 39 PG:972 - 978 :: QUAL. :INT. LOG. :THEORY :PP&E / DEPR

HIRSCH,PM ; FIRS: ESPELAND,WN CIT: 0.33
OWNERSHIP CHANGES, ACCOUNTING PRACTICE AND THE REDEFINITION OF THE CORPORATION
AOS 02 90 VOL: 15 PG:77 - 96 :: REGRESS. :SEC. :HIST. :ORG.& ENVIR.

HIRSCHEY,M ; SEC: WEYGANDT,JJ CIT: 0.5
AMORTIZATION POLICY FOR ADVERTISING AND RESEARCH AND DEVELOPMENT EXPENDITURES
JAR SP 85 VOL: 23 PG:326 - 335 :: REGRESS. :PRIM. :TIME SER. :R & D

HIRSCHMAN,RW CIT: 0
DIRECT COSTING AND THE LAW
TAR JA 65 VOL: 40 PG:176 - 183 :: QUAL. :INT. LOG. :THEORY :INV.

HIRST ,M ; FIRS: BRIERS,M CIT: 0.33
THE ROLE OF BUDGETARY INFORMATION IN PERFORMANCE EVALUATION
AOS 04 90 VOL: 15 PG:373 - 398 :: REGRESS. :SEC. :OTH.BEH. :BUDG.& PLAN.

HIRST ,MK ; SEC: LOWY ,SM CIT: 0
THE LINEAR ADDITIVE AND INTERACTIVE EFFECTS OF BUDGETARY GOAL DIFFICULTY AND FEEDBACK ON PERFORMANCE
AOS 05 90 VOL: 15 PG:425 - 436 :: REGRESS. :SURV. :OTH.BEH. :BUDG.& PLAN.

HIRST ,MK ; FIRS: LUCKETT,PF CIT: 0.25
THE IMPACT OF FEEDBACK ON INTER-RATER AGREEMENT AND SELF INSIGHT IN PERFORMANCE EVALUATION DECISIONS
AOS 06 89 VOL: 14 PG:379 - 387 :: REGRESS. :LAB. :HIPS :AUD.BEH.

HIRST ,MK CIT: 0.33
THE EFFECT OF SETTING BUDGET GOALS AND TASK UNCERTAINTY ON PERFORMANCE: A THEORETICAL ANALYSIS
TAR OC 87 VOL: 62 PG:774 - 784 :: DES.STAT. :INT. LOG. :OTH.BEH. :BUDG.& PLAN.

HIRST ,MK ; FIRS: BROWNELL,P CIT: 1.14
RELIANCE ON ACCT. INFO., BUDGETARY PARTICIPATION, AND TASK UNCERTAINTY: TESTS OF A THREE-WAY INTERACTION
JAR AU 86 VOL: 24 PG:241 - 249 :: REGRESS. :SURV. :OTH.BEH. :BUDG.& PLAN.

HIRST ,MK CIT: 0.6
RELIANCE ON ACCOUNTING PERFORMANCE MEASURES, TASK UNCERTAINTY, AND DISFUNCTIONAL BEHAVIOR: SOME EXTENSIONS
JAR AU 83 VOL: 21 PG:596 - 605 :: REGRESS. :SURV. :OTH.BEH. :ORG.& ENVIR.

HIRST ,MK CIT: 0.92
ACCOUNTING INFORMATION AND THE EVALUATION OF SUBORDINATE PERFORMANCE: A SITUATIONAL APPROACH
TAR OC 81 VOL: 56 PG:771 - 784 :: QUAL. :INT. LOG. :OTH.BEH. :N/A

HITE ,GL ; SEC: LONG ,MS CIT: 0.45
TAXES AND EXECUTIVE STOCK OPTIONS
JAE JL 82 VOL: 4 PG:3 - 14 :: QUAL. :INT. LOG. :THEORY :TAXES

HITE ,PS ; FIRS: AYRES ,FL ; SEC: JACKSON,BR CIT: 0.25
THE ECONOMIC BENEFITS OF REGULATION: EVIDENCE FROM PROFESSIONAL TAX PREPARERS
TAR AP 89 VOL: 64 PG:300 - 312 :: REGRESS. :FIELD :HIPS :TAXES

HO ,JL ; FIRS: COOPER,WW ; THIR: HUNTER,JE ; FOUR: RODGERS,RC CIT: 0
THE IMPACT OF THE FOREIGN CORRUPT PRACTICES ACT ON INTERNAL CONTROL PRACTICES
JAA AU 85 VOL: 9 PG:22 - 39 :: REGRESS. :SEC. :THEORY :INT.CONT.

HOBBS ,JB CIT: 0
VOLUME-MIX-PRICE/COST BUDGET VARIANCE ANALYSIS: A PROPER APPROACH
TAR OC 64 VOL: 39 PG:905 - 913 :: ANAL. :INT. LOG. :OTH.STAT. :VAR.

HOFSTEDE,G CIT: 0.42
MANAGEMENT CONTROL OF PUBLIC AND NOT-FOR-PROFIT ACTIVITIES
AOS 03 81 VOL: 6 PG:193 - 216 :: QUAL. :INT. LOG. :OTH. :BUDG.& PLAN.

HOFSTEDT,TR ; SEC: HUGHES,GD CIT: 0.81
AN EXPERIMENTAL STUDY OF THE JUDGMENT ELEMENT IN DISCLOSURE DECISIONS
TAR AP 77 VOL: 52 PG:379 - 395 :: MIXED :LAB. :HIPS :INFO.STRUC.

HOFSTEDT,TR CIT: 0.29
BEHAVIOURAL ACCOUNTING RESEARCH: PATHOLOGIES, PARADIGMS AND PRESCRIPTIONS
AOS 01 76 VOL: 1 PG:43 - 58 :: DES.STAT. :SEC. :OTH.BEH. :MANAG.

HOFSTEDT,TR CIT: 0.65
SOME BEHAVIOURAL PARAMETERS OF FINANCIAL ANALYSIS
TAR OC 72 VOL: 47 PG:679 - 692 :: ANOVA :LAB. :OTH.BEH. :INFO.STRUC.

HOFSTEDT,TR ; SEC: WEST ,RR CIT: 0.06
THE APB, YIELD INDICES, AND PREDICTIVE ABILITY
TAR AP 71 VOL: 46 PG:329 - 337 :: DES.STAT. :PRIM. :OTH.STAT. :PENS.

HOFSTEDT,TR ; SEC: KINARD,JC CIT: 0.35
A STRATEGY FOR BEHAVIOURAL ACCOUNTING RESEARCH
TAR JA 70 VOL: 45 PG:38 - 54 :: QUAL. :INT. LOG. :OTH.BEH. :OTH.MANAG.

HOGARTH,RM CIT: 0.5
A PERSPECTIVE ON COGNITIVE RESEARCH IN AUDITING
TAR AP 91 VOL: 66 PG:277 - 290 :: DES.STAT. :SEC. :HIPS :JUDG.

HOGARTH,RM ; FIRS: EINHORN,HJ CIT: 1.17
BEHAVIOURAL DECISION THEORY: PROCESSES OF JUDGMENT AND CHOICE
JAR SP 81 VOL: 19 PG:1 - 31 :: QUAL. :SEC. :HIPS :N/A

HOGLER,RL ; FIRS: HUNT-III,HG CIT: 0
AGENCY THEORY AS IDEOLOGY: A COMPARATIVE ANALYSIS BASED ON CRITICAL LEGAL THEORY AND RADICAL ACCOUNTING
AOS 05 90 VOL: 15 PG:437 - 454 :: DES.STAT. :SEC. :INF.ECO./AG. :ORG.& ENVIR.

HOLDER,WW ; FIRS: DAROCA,FP CIT: 0.25
THE USE OF ANALYTICAL PROCEDURES IN REVIEW AND AUDIT ENGAGEMENTS
AUD SP 85 VOL: 4 PG:80 - 92 :: REGRESS. :SURV. :INSTIT. :ANAL.REV.

HOLDER,WW CIT: 0.2
ANALYTICAL REVIEW PROCEDURES IN PLANNING THE AUDIT: AN APPLICATION STUDY
AUD SP 83 VOL: 2 PG:100 - 108 :: DES.STAT. :LAB. :OTH. :ANAL.REV.

HOLDER,WW ; SEC: EUDY ,KH CIT: 0
A FRAMEWORK FOR BUILDING AN ACCOUNTING CONSTITUTION
JAA WI 82 VOL: 5 PG:110 - 125 :: QUAL. :INT. LOG. :THEORY :FASB SUBM.

HOLDREN,GC CIT: 0
LIFO AND RATIO ANALYSIS
TAR JA 64 VOL: 39 PG:70 - 85 :: DES.STAT. :PRIM. :N/A :INV.

HOLMES,W CIT: 0
GOVERNMENT ACCOUNTING IN COLONIAL MASSACHUSETTS
TAR JA 79 VOL: 54 PG:47 - 57 :: QUAL. :SEC. :HIST. :FIN.METH.

HOLSTRUM,GL ; SEC: MESSIER JR,WF CIT: 0.73
A REVIEW AND INTEGRATION OF EMPIRICAL RESEARCH ON MATERIALITY
AUD AU 82 VOL: 2 PG:45 - 63 :: QUAL. :SEC. :OTH. :MAT.

HOLSTRUM,GL CIT: 0.24
THE EFFECT OF BUDGET ADAPTIVENESS AND TIGHTNESS ON MANAGERIAL DECISION BEHAVIOR
JAR AU 71 VOL: 9 PG:268 - 277 :: ANOVA :LAB. :OTH.BEH. :BUDG.& PLAN.

HOLT ,DL ; SEC: MORROW,PC CIT: 0
RISK ASSESSMENT JUDGMENTS OF AUDITORS AND BANK LENDERS: A COMPARATIVE ANALYSIS OF CONFORMANCE TO BAYES' THEOREM
AOS 06 92 VOL: 17 PG:549 - 559 :: REGRESS. :LAB. :HIPS :RISK

HOLT ,DL ; FIRS: DAMOS ,P ; THIR: IMHOFF JR,EA CIT: 0.25
THE USE OF ACCOUNTING INFORMATION IN BANK LENDING DECISIONS
AOS 03 89 VOL: 14 PG:235 - 246 :: REGRESS. :LAB. :HIPS :OTH.FIN.ACC.

HOLT ,DL ; FIRS: DAMOS ,P ; SEC: EICHENSEHER,JW CIT: 0
SPECIALIZED KNOWLEDGE AND ITS COMMUNICATION IN AUDITING
CAR AU 89 VOL: 6 PG:91 - 109 :: REGRESS. :SURV. :OTH.BEH. :OPER.AUD.

HOLT ,DL CIT: 0.17
AUDITORS AND BASE RATES REVISITED
AOS 06 87 VOL: 12 PG:571 - 578 :: REGRESS. :LAB. :HIPS :JUDG.

HOLT ,DL ; FIRS: DANOS ,P ; THIR: BAILEY JR,AD CIT: 0
THE INTERACTION OF SCIENCE AND ATTESTATION STANDARD FORMATION
AUD SP 87 VOL: 6 PG:134 - 149 :: DES.STAT. :INT. LOG. :THEORY :OPIN.

HOLT ,DL ; FIRS: DANOS ,P ; THIR: IMHOFF JR,EA CIT: 0.33
BOND RATERS' USE OF MANAGEMENT FINANCIAL FORECASTS: EXPERIMENT IN EXPERT JUDGMENT
TAR OC 84 VOL: 59 PG:547 - 573 :: ANOVA :LAB. :OTH.BEH. :FOREC.

HOLT ,RN ; FIRS: SHOCKLEY,RA CIT: 0.4
A BEHAVIOURAL INVESTIGATION OF SUPPLIER DIFFERENTIATION IN THE MARKET FOR AUDIT SERVICES
JAR AU 83 VOL: 21 PG:545 - 564 :: OTH.QUANT. :LAB. :INSTIT. :ORG.

HOLT ,RN ; SEC: CARROLL,R CIT: 0.31
CLASSIFICATION OF COMMERCIAL BANK LOANS THROUGH POLICY CAPTURING
AOS 03 80 VOL: 5 PG:285 - 296 :: OTH.QUANT. :LAB. :HIPS :BUS.FAIL.

HOLTHAUSEN,RW ; SEC: LARCKER,DF CIT: 2
THE PREDICTION OF STOCK RETURNS USING FINANCIAL STATEMENT INFORMATION
JAE JN 92 VOL: 15 PG:373 - 411 :: REGRESS. :PRIM. :EMH :FIN.METH.

HOLTHAUSEN,RW CIT: 0.33
ACCOUNTING METHOD CHOICE: OPPORTUNISTIC BEHAVIOR, EFFICIENT CONTRACTING, AND INFORMATION PERSPECTIVES
JAE JA 90 VOL: 12 PG:207 - 218 :: DES.STAT. :SEC. :THEORY :FIN.METH.

HOLTHAUSEN,RW ; SEC: VERRECCHIA,RE CIT: 1.33
THE EFFECT OF INFORMEDNESS AND CONSENSUS ON PRICE AND VOLUME BEHAVIOR
TAR JA 90 VOL: 65 PG:191 - 208 :: DES.STAT. :INT. LOG. :INF.ECO./AG. :INFO.STRUC.

HOLTHAUSEN,RW ; SEC: VERRECCHIA,RE CIT: 2.2
THE EFFECT OF SEQUENTIAL INFORMATION RELEASES ON THE VARIANCE OF PRICE CHANGES IN AN INTERTEMPORAL MULTI-ASSET MARKET
JAR SP 88 VOL: 26 PG:82 - 106 :: ANAL. :INT. LOG. :INF.ECO./AG. :INFO.STRUC.

HOLTHAUSEN,RW ; FIRS: DOPUCH,N ; THIR: LEFTWICH,RW CIT: 1
PREDICTING AUDIT QUALIFICATIONS WITH FINANCIAL AND MARKET VARIABLES
TAR JL 87 VOL: 62 PG:431 - 454 :: REGRESS. :PRIM. :EMH :OPIN.

HOLTHAUSEN,RW ; FIRS: DOPUCH,N ; THIR: LEFTWICH,RW CIT: 0.57
ABNORMAL STOCK RETURNS ASSOCIATED WITH MEDIA DISCLOSURES OF 'SUBJECT TO' QUALIFIED AUDIT OPINIONS
JAE JN 86 VOL: 8 PG:93 - 118 :: REGRESS. :PRIM. :EMH :OPIN.

HOLTHAUSEN,RW ; FIRS: DODD ,P ; SEC: DOPUCH,N ; FOUR: LEFTWICH,R CIT: 1.56
QUALIFIED AUDIT OPINIONS AND STOCK PRICES: INFORMATION CONTENT, ANNOUNCEMENT DATES, AND CONCURRENT DISCLOSURES
JAE AP 84 VOL: 6 PG:3 - 38 :: REGRESS. :PRIM. :EMH :OPIN.

HOLTHAUSEN,RW ; SEC: LEFTWICH,RW CIT: 5.2
THE ECONOMIC CONSEQUENCES OF ACCOUNTING CHOICES: IMPLICATIONS OF COSTLY CONTRACTING AND MONITORING
JAE AG 83 VOL: 5 PG:77 - 117 :: QUAL. :SEC. :EMH :METHOD.

HOLTHAUSEN,RW CIT: 3.33
EVIDENCE ON THE EFFECT OF BOND COVENANTS AND MANAGEMENT COMPENSATION CONTRACTS ON THE CHOICE OF ACCOUNTING TECHNIQUES: CASE OF DEPRECIATION SWITCHBACK
JAE MR 81 VOL: 3 PG:73 - 109 :: REGRESS. :PRIM. :EMH :AMOR./DEPL.

HOLZER,HP ; SEC: SCHONFELD,HM CIT: 0
THE FUNKTIONALE KONTORECHNUNG OF WALTER THOMS
TAR AP 64 VOL: 39 PG:405 - 413 :: QUAL. :INT. LOG. :THEORY :FIN.METH.

HOLZER,HP ; SEC: SCHONFELD,HM CIT: 0
THE GERMAN SOLUTION OF THE POST-WAR PRICE LEVEL PROBLEM
TAR AP 63 VOL: 38 PG:377 - 381 :: QUAL. :INT. LOG. :HIST. :FIN.METH.

HOLZER,HP ; SEC: SCHONFELD,HM CIT: 0
THE FRENCH APPROACH TO THE POST-WAR PRICE LEVEL PROBLEM
TAR AP 63 VOL: 38 PG:382 - 388 :: QUAL. :INT. LOG. :HIST. :FIN.METH.

HOLZMANN,OJ ; SEC: MEANS ,KM CIT: 0
ACCOUNTING FOR SAVINGS AND LOAN MERGERS: CONFLICT AND ACCOUNTING ERROR
JAA WI 84 VOL: 7 PG:138 - 150 :: QUAL. :INT. LOG. :THEORY :BUS.COMB.

HOLZMANN,OJ ; FIRS: COOK ,JS CIT: 0.06
CURRENT COST AND PRESENT VALUE IN INCOME THEORY
TAR OC 76 VOL: 51 PG:778 - 787 :: ANAL. :INT. LOG. :THEORY :VALUAT.(INFL.)

HONG ,BG ; FIRS: STEIN ,JL CIT: 0
PRICE VOLATILITY AND SPECULATION
JAA SP 90 VOL: 5 PG:277 - 300 :: DES.STAT. :INT. LOG. :INF.ECO./AG. :OTH.MANAG.

HONG ,H ; SEC: KAPLAN,RS ; THIR: MANDELKER,G CIT: 0.93
POOLING VS. PURCHASE: THE EFFECTS OF ACCOUNTING FOR MERGERS ON STOCK PRICES
TAR JA 78 VOL: 53 PG:31 - 47 :: MIXED :PRIM. :EMH :BUS.COMB.

HONIG ,LE CIT: 0
THEORY VS. PRACTICE: PARSIMONY AS REFEREE
JAA SP 78 VOL: 1 PG:231 - 236 :: DES.STAT. :SURV. :OTH. :METHOD.

HOOKS ,KL CIT: 0
GENDER EFFECTS AND LABOR SUPPLY IN PUBLIC ACCOUNTING: AN AGENDA OF RESEARCH ISSUES
AOS 04 92 VOL: 17 PG:343 - 366 :: DES.STAT. :SEC. :HIST. :METHOD.

HOPPER,T ; FIRS: MILLER,P ; THIR: LAUGHLIN,R CIT: 0
THE NEW ACCOUNTING HISTORY: AN INTRODUCTION
AOS 05 91 VOL: 16 PG:395 - 403 :: REGRESS. :SEC. :HIST. :METHOD.

HOPPER,T ; SEC: ARMSTRONG,P CIT: 0
COST ACCOUNTING, CONTROLLING LABOUR AND THE RISE OF CONGLOMERATES
AOS 05 91 VOL: 16 PG:405 - 438 :: ANOVA :SEC. :HIST. :MANAG.

HOPPER,T ; SEC: STOREY,J ; THIR: WILLMOTT,H CIT: 1.17
ACCOUNTING FOR ACCOUNTING: TOWARDS THE DEVELOPMENT OF A DIALECTICAL VIEW
AOS 05 87 VOL: 12 PG:437 - 456 :: DES.STAT. :INT. LOG. :THEORY :MANAG.

HOPPER,T ; FIRS: BERRY ,AJ ; SEC: CAPPS ,T ; THIR: COOPER,D ; FOUR: FERGUSON,P ; SIX: LOWE ,EA CIT: 3
MANAGEMENT CONTROL IN AN AREA OF THE NCB: RATIONALES OF ACCOUNTING PRACTICES IN A PUBLIC ENTERPRISE
AOS 01 85 VOL: 10 PG:3 - 28 :: REGRESS. :FIELD :OTH.BEH. :MANAG.

HOPPER,TM ; FIRS: COOPER,DJ CIT: 0.17
CRITICAL STUDIES IN ACCOUNTING
AOS 05 87 VOL: 12 PG:407 - 414 :: DES.STAT. :INT. LOG. :THEORY :FIN.METH.

HOPPER,TM CIT: 0.08
ROLE CONFLICTS OF MANAGEMENT ACCOUNTANTS AND THEIR POSITION WITHIN ORGANIZATION STRUCTURES
AOS 04 80 VOL: 5 PG:401 - 412 :: NON-PAR. :FIELD :OTH.BEH. :BUDG.& PLAN.

HOPWOOD,AG CIT: 0.83
ACCOUNTING AND GENDER: AN INTRODUCTION
AOS 01 87 VOL: 12 PG:65 - 70 :: DES.STAT. :INT. LOG. :INSTIT. :ORG.& ENVIR.

HOPWOOD,AG CIT: 6
THE ARCHEOLOGY OF ACCOUNTING SYSTEMS
AOS 03 87 VOL: 12 PG:207 - 234 :: DES.STAT. :INT. LOG. :HIST. :ORG.& ENVIR.

HOPWOOD,AG CIT: 1.13
THE TALE OF A COMMITTEE THAT NEVER REPORTED: DISAGREEMENTS ON INTERTWINING ACCOUNTING WITH THE SOCIAL
AOS 03 85 VOL: 10 PG:361 - 376 :: REGRESS. :INT. LOG. :INSTIT. :FASB SUBM.

HOPWOOD,AG ; FIRS: BURCHELL,S ; SEC: CLUBB ,C CIT: 3.75
ACCOUNTING IN ITS SOCIAL CONTEXT: TOWARDS A HISTORY OF VALUE ADDED IN THE UNITED KINGDOM
AOS 04 85 VOL: 10 PG:381 - 414 :: DES.STAT. :INT. LOG. :THEORY :HRA

HOPWOOD,AG CIT: 3.1
ON TRYING TO STUDY ACCOUNTING IN THE CONTEXTS IN WHICH IT OPERATES
AOS 23 83 VOL: 8 PG:287 - 305 :: QUAL. :INT. LOG. :THEORY :ORG.& ENVIR.

HOPWOOD,AG ; FIRS: BURCHELL,S ; SEC: CLUBB ,C ; FOUR: HUGHES,JS ; FIFT: NAHAPIET,JE CIT: 4.92
THE ROLES OF ACCOUNTING IN ORGANIZATIONS AND SOCIETY
AOS 01 80 VOL: 5 PG:5 - 27 :: QUAL. :INT. LOG. :THEORY :N/A

HOPWOOD,AG CIT: 2.2
TOWARDS AN ORGANIZATIONAL PERSPECTIVE FOR THE STUDY OF ACCOUNTING AND INFORMATION SYSTEMS
AOS 01 78 VOL: 3 PG:3 - 14 :: QUAL. :SEC. :OTH. :AUD.BEH.

HOPWOOD,AG CIT: 1.06
LEADERSHIP CLIMATE AND THE USE OF ACCOUNTING DATA IN PERFORMANCE EVALUATION
TAR JL 74 VOL: 49 PG:485 - 495 :: NON-PAR. :FIELD :OTH.BEH. :BUDG.& PLAN.

HOPWOOD,AG CIT: 2.18
AN EMPIRICAL STUDY OF THE ROLE OF ACCOUNTING DATA IN PERFORMANCE EVALUATION
JAR ST 72 VOL: 10 PG:156 - 182 :: MIXED :FIELD :OTH.BEH. :MAN.DEC.CHAR.

HOPWOOD,W ; FIRS: MCKEOWN,JC ; SEC: MUTCHLER,JF CIT: 0
TOWARDS AN EXPLANATION OF AUDITOR FAILURE TO MODIFY THE AUDIT OPINIONS OF BANKRUPT COMPANIES
AUD 91 VOL: 10 PG:1 - 13 :: REGRESS. :PRIM. :OTH.STAT. :BUS.FAIL.

HOPWOOD,W ; SEC: MCKEOWN,J ; THIR: MUTCHLER,J CIT: 0.25
A TEST OF THE INCREMENTAL EXPLANATORY POWER OF OPINIONS QUALIFIED FOR CONSISTENCY AND UNCERTAINTY
TAR JA 89 VOL: 64 PG:28 - 48 :: REGRESS. :PRIM. :THEORY :BUS.FAIL.

HOPWOOD,W ; SEC: SCHAEFER,T CIT: 0
FIRM-SPECIFIC RESPONSIVENESS TO INPUT PRICE CHANGES AND THE INCREMENTAL INFORMATION IN CURRENT COST INCOME
TAR AP 89 VOL: 64 PG:313 - 328 :: REGRESS. :PRIM. :EMH :FIN.METH.

HOPWOOD,W ; SEC: MCKEOWN,J ; THIR: MUTCHLER,J CIT: 0
THE SENSITIVITY OF FINANCIAL DISTRESS PREDICTION MODELS TO DEPARTURES FROM NORMALITY
CAR AU 88 VOL: 5 PG:284 - 298 :: REGRESS. :PRIM. :OTH.STAT. :METHOD.

HOPWOOD,WS ; FIRS: CHENG ,CSA ; THIR: MCKEOWN,JC CIT: 1
NON-LINEARITY AND SPECIFICATION PROBLEMS IN UNEXPECTED EARNINGS RESPONSE REGRESSION MODEL
TAR JL 92 VOL: 67 PG:579 - 598 :: REGRESS. :PRIM. :EMH :METHOD.

HOPWOOD,WS ; SEC: MCKEOWN,JC CIT: 0
EVIDENCE ON SURROGATES FOR EARNINGS EXPECTATIONS WITHIN A CAPITAL MARKET CONTEXT
JAA SU 90 VOL: 5 PG:339 - 363 :: REGRESS. :PRIM. :TIME SER. :FOREC.

HOPWOOD,WS ; SEC: SCHAEFER,TF CIT: 0
INCREMENTAL INFORMATION CONTENT OF EARNINGS AND NONEARNINGS BASED FINANCIAL RATIOS
CAR AU 88 VOL: 5 PG:318 - 342 :: REGRESS. :PRIM. :EMH :FIN.METH.

HOPWOOD,WS ; FIRS: ARRINGTON,CE ; SEC: BAILEY,CD CIT: 0.25
AN ATTRIBUTION ANALYSIS OF RESPONSIBILITY ASSESSMENT FOR AUDIT PERFORMANCE
JAR SP 85 VOL: 23 PG:1 - 20 :: REGRESS. :LAB. :OTH.BEH. :AUD.

HOPWOOD,WS ; SEC: MCKEOWN,JC CIT: 0.25
THE INCREMENTAL INFORMATIONAL CONTENT OF INTERIM EXPENSES OVER INTERIM SALES
JAR SP 85 VOL: 23 PG:161 - 174 :: REGRESS. :PRIM. :EMH :TAXES

HOPWOOD,WS ; FIRS: COLLINS,WA ; THIR: MCKEOWN,JC CIT: 0.44
THE PREDICTABILITY OF INTERIM EARNINGS OVER ALTERNATIVE QUARTERS
JAR AU 84 VOL: 22 PG:467 - 479 :: NON-PAR. :PRIM. :TIME SER. :INT.REP.

HOPWOOD,WS ; FIRS: FRECKA,TJ CIT: 0.6
THE EFFECTS OF OUTLIERS ON THE CROSS-SECTIONAL DISTRIBUTIONAL PROPERTIES OF FINANCIAL RATIOS
TAR JA 83 VOL: 58 PG:115 - 128 :: DES.STAT. :LAB. :OTH.STAT. :METHOD.

HOPWOOD,WS ; SEC: MCKEOWN,JC ; THIR: NEWBOLD,P CIT: 0.55
THE ADDITIONAL INFORMATION CONTENT OF QUARTERLY EARNINGS REPORTS: INTERTEMPORAL DISAGGREGATION
JAR AU 82 VOL: 20 PG:343 - 349 :: REGRESS. :PRIM. :TIME SER. :FOREC.

HOPWOOD,WS ; SEC: NEWBOLD,P ; THIR: SILHAN,PA CIT: 0.36
THE POTENTIAL FOR GAINS IN PREDICTIVE ABILITY THROUGH DISAGGREGATION: SEGMENTED ANNUAL EARNINGS
JAR AU 82 VOL: 20 PG:724 - 732 :: DES.STAT. :PRIM. :TIME SER. :SEG.REP.

HOPWOOD,WS ; SEC: MCKEOWN,JC CIT: 0.42
AN EVALUATION OF UNIVARIATE TIME-SERIES EARNINGS MODELS AND THEIR GENERALIZATION TO A SINGLE INPUT TRANSFER FUNCTION
JAR AU 81 VOL: 19 PG:313 - 322 :: CORR. :PRIM. :TIME SER. :FOREC.

HOPWOOD,WS CIT: 0.23
THE TRANSFER FUNCTION RELATIONSHIP BETWEEN EARNINGS AND MARKET-INDUSTRY INDICES: AN EMPIRICAL STUDY
JAR SP 80 VOL: 18 PG:77 - 90 :: MIXED :PRIM. :TIME SER. :METHOD.

HOPWOOD,WS CIT: 0.08
ON THE AUTOMATION OF THE BOX-JENKINS MODELING PROCEDURES: AN ALGORITHM WITH AN EMPIRICAL TEST
JAR SP 80 VOL: 18 PG:289 - 296 :: MIXED :PRIM. :TIME SER. :FOREC.

HOPWOOD,WS ; FIRS: COLLINS,WA CIT: 1.31
A MULTIVARIATE ANALYSIS OF ANNUAL EARNINGS FORECASTS GENERATED FROM QUARTERLY FORECASTS OF FINANCIAL ANALYSTS AND UNIVARIATE TIM
JAR AU 80 VOL: 18 PG:390 - 406 :: ANOVA :PRIM. :TIME SER. :FOREC.

HORNE ,JC CIT: 0
A LOOK AT THE LOSS CARRY-FORWARD
TAR JA 63 VOL: 38 PG:56 - 60 :: QUAL. :INT. LOG. :THEORY :TAXES

HORNGREN,CT CIT: 0.06
THE ACCOUNTING DISCIPLINE IN 1999
TAR JA 71 VOL: 46 PG:1 - 11 :: QUAL. :INT. LOG. :INSTIT. :OTH.MANAG.

HORNGREN,CT CIT: 0
CAPACITY UTILIZATION AND THE EFFICIENCY VARIANCE
TAR JA 69 VOL: 44 PG:86 - 89 :: QUAL. :INT. LOG. :N/A :VAR.

HORNGREN,CT CIT: 0
A CONTRIBUTION MARGIN APPROACH TO THE ANALYSIS OF CAPACITY UTILIZATION
TAR AP 67 VOL: 42 PG:254 - 264 :: QUAL. :INT. LOG. :N/A :VAR.

HORNGREN,CT CIT: 0.12
HOW SHOULD WE INTERPRET THE REALIZATION CONCEPT?
TAR AP 65 VOL: 40 PG:323 - 333 :: QUAL. :INT. LOG. :THEORY :VALUAT.(INFL.)

HORNGREN,CT ; SEC: SORTER,GH CIT: 0
AN EVALUATION OF SOME CRITICISMS OF RELEVANT COSTING
TAR AP 64 VOL: 39 PG:417 - 420 :: QUAL. :INT. LOG. :N/A :COST.ALLOC.

HORRIGAN,JO CIT: 0.06
A SHORT HISTORY OF FINANCIAL RATIO ANALYSIS
TAR AP 68 VOL: 43 PG:284 - 294 :: QUAL. :SEC. :HIST. :FIN.METH.

HORRIGAN,JO CIT: 0.53
THE DETERMINATION OF LONG-TERM CREDIT STANDING WITH FINANCIAL RATIOS
JAR ST 66 VOL: 4 PG:44 - 62 :: CORR. :PRIM. :OTH.STAT. :LTD

HORRIGAN,JO CIT: 0
SOME EMPIRICAL BASES OF FINANCIAL RATIO ANALYSIS
TAR JL 65 VOL: 40 PG:558 - 568 :: DES.STAT. :PRIM. :N/A :OTH.MANAG.

HORVITZ,JS ; SEC: COLDWELL,S CIT: 0
ANALYSIS OF THE ARTHUR YOUNG DECISION AND ITS POTENTIAL IMPACT ON PUBLIC ACCOUNTING
JAA WI 85 VOL: 8 PG:86 - 99 :: REGRESS. :CASE :THEORY :LITIG.

HORVITZ,JS ; SEC: HAINKEL,M CIT: 0
THE IRS SUMMONS POWER AND ITS EFFECT ON THE INDEPENDENT AUDITOR
JAA WI 81 VOL: 4 PG:114 - 127 :: QUAL. :CASE :INSTIT. :PROF.RESP.

HORWITZ,B ; SEC: NORMOLLE,D CIT: 0
FEDERAL AGENCY R&D CONTRACT AWARDS AND THE FASB RULE FOR PRIVATELY-FUNDED R&D
TAR JL 88 VOL: 63 PG:414 - 435 :: REGRESS. :PRIM. :OTH.STAT. :R & D

HORWITZ,BN ; SEC: KOLODNY,R CIT: 0.08
THE IMPACT OF RULE MAKING ON R & D INVESTMENTS OF SMALL HIGH-TECHNOLOGY FIRMS
JAA WI 81 VOL: 4 PG:102 - 113 :: NON-PAR. :SURV. :THEORY :ACC.CHNG.

HORWITZ,BN ; SEC: KOLODNY,R CIT: 0
SEGMENT REPORTING: HINDSIGHT AFTER TEN YEARS
JAA AU 80 VOL: 4 PG:20 - 35 :: QUAL. :INT. LOG. :THEORY :SEG.REP.

HORWITZ,BN ; SEC: KOLODNY,R CIT: 0.77
THE ECONOMIC EFFECTS OF INVOLUNTARY UNIFORMITY IN THE FINANCIAL REPORTING OF R & D EXPENDITURES
JAR ST 80 VOL: 18 PG:38 - 74 :: NON-PAR. :PRIM. :OTH. :R & D

HORWITZ,BN ; SEC: YOUNG ,AE CIT: 0
AN EMPIRICAL STUDY OF ACCOUNTING POLICY AND TENDER OFFERS
JAR SP 72 VOL: 10 PG:96 - 107 :: DES.STAT. :PRIM. :OTH.STAT. :BUS.COMB.

HORWITZ,BN ; FIRS: FRANKFURTER,GM CIT: 0.06
THE EFFECTS OF ACCOUNTING PRINCIPLES BOARD OPINION NO.15 ON EARNINGS PER SHARE: A SIMULATION STUDY
TAR AP 72 VOL: 47 PG:245 - 259 :: DES.STAT. :SIM. :THEORY :FIN.METH.

HORWITZ,BN ; SEC: SHABAHANG,R CIT: 0.29
PUBLISHED CORPORATE ACCOUNTING DATA AND GENERAL WAGE INCREASES OF THE FIRM
TAR AP 71 VOL: 46 PG:243 - 252 :: CORR. :PRIM. :N/A :FIN.METH.

HORWITZ,BN CIT: 0
DEPRECIATION AND COST STABILITY IN SOVIET ACCOUNTING
TAR OC 63 VOL: 38 PG:819 - 826 :: QUAL. :INT. LOG. :THEORY :PP&E / DEPR

HORWITZ,RM CIT: 0
THE INVESTMENT CREDIT, DEFERRED INCOME TAXES AND ACCOUNTING MEASUREMENT
TAR JL 64 VOL: 39 PG:618 - 621 :: QUAL. :INT. LOG. :THEORY :TAXES

HOSKIN,KW ; SEC: MACVE ,RH CIT: 1.8
THE GENESIS OF ACCOUNTABILITY: THE WEST POINT CONNECTIONS
AOS 01 88 VOL: 13 PG:37 - 73 :: DES.STAT. :INT. LOG. :THEORY :OTH.MANAG.

HOSKIN,KW ; SEC: MACVE ,RH CIT: 3
ACCOUNTING AND THE EXAMINATION: A GENEALOGY OF DISCIPLINARY POWER
AOS 02 86 VOL: 11 PG:105 - 136 :: DES.STAT. :INT. LOG. :HIST. :FASB SUBM.

HOSKIN,RE ; SEC: HUGHES,JS ; THIR: RICKS ,WE CIT: 1.43
EVIDENCE ON THE INCREMENTAL INFORMATION CONTENT OF ADDITIONAL FIRM DISCLOSURES MADE CONCURRENTLY WITH EARNINGS
JAR ST 86 VOL: 24 PG:1 - 36 :: REGRESS. :PRIM. :EMH :SPEC.ITEMS

HOSKIN,RE CIT: 0.4
OPPORTUNITY COST AND BEHAVIOR
JAR SP 83 VOL: 21 PG:78 - 95 :: ANOVA :LAB. :OTH.BEH. :REL.COSTS

HOSKIN,RE ; FIRS: DYCKMAN,TR ; THIR: SWIERINGA,RJ CIT: 0.36
AN ACCOUNTING CHANGE AND INFORMATION PROCESSING CHANGES
AOS 01 82 VOL: 7 PG:1 - 12 :: REGRESS. :LAB. :HIPS :ACC.CHNG.

HOSKIN,RE ; FIRS: HILTON,RW ; SEC: SWIERINGA,RJ CIT: 0.58
PERCEPTION OF ACCURACY AS A DETERMINANT OF INFORMATION VALUE
JAR SP 81 VOL: 19 PG:86 - 108 :: ANOVA :LAB. :OTH.BEH. :MANAG.

HOSLER,C ; FIRS: FRIED ,D CIT: 0
S&LS, REPORTING CHANGES AND THE IMPACT ON THE GNMA MARKET
JAA WI 87 VOL: 2 PG:5 - 23 :: REGRESS. :PRIM. :THEORY :LTD

HOU ,C ; FIRS: FARMAN,WL CIT: 0
THE BALANCE OF PAYMENTS: AN ACCOUNTING ANALYSIS
TAR JA 63 VOL: 38 PG:133 - 141 :: QUAL. :INT. LOG. :THEORY :INT.DIFF.

HOUGHTON,CW ; SEC: FOGARTY,JA CIT: 0
INHERENT RISK
AUD SP 91 VOL: 10 PG:1 - 21 :: REGRESS. :PRIM. :THEORY :ERRORS

HOUGHTON,KA CIT: 0
THE MEASUREMENT OF MEANING IN ACCOUNTING: A CRITICAL ANALYSIS OF THE PRINCIPAL EVIDENCE
AOS 03 88 VOL: 13 PG:263 - 280 :: REGRESS. :LAB. :OTH.BEH. :METHOD.

HOUGHTON,KA CIT: 0.17
TRUE AND FAIR VIEW: AN EMPIRICAL STUDY OF CONNOTATIVE MEANING
AOS 02 87 VOL: 12 PG:143 - 152 :: REGRESS. :LAB. :OTH.BEH. :MAN.DEC.CHAR.

HOUGHTON,KA CIT: 0
ACCOUNTING DATA AND THE PREDICTION OF BUSINESS FAILURE: THE SETTING OF PRIORS AND THE AGE OF DATA
JAR SP 84 VOL: 22 PG:361 - 368 :: DES.STAT. :PRIM. :OTH.BEH. :BUS.FAIL.

HOUGHTON,KA ; SEC: SENGUPTA,R CIT: 0
THE EFFECT OF PRIOR PROBABILITY DISCLOSURE AND INFORMATION SET CONSTRUCTION ON BANKERS' ABILITY TO PREDICT FAILURE
JAR AU 84 VOL: 22 PG:768 - 775 :: DES.STAT. :LAB. :HIPS :BUS.FAIL.

HOWARD,TP ; FIRS: WILSON,ER CIT: 0.56
THE ASSOCIATION BETWEEN MUNICIPAL MARKET MEASURES AND SELECTED FINANCIAL REPORTING PRACTICES: ADDITIONAL EVIDENCE
JAR SP 84 VOL: 22 PG:207 - 224 :: REGRESS. :PRIM. :OTH.STAT. :N/A

HOWARD,TP ; SEC: NIKOLAI,LA CIT: 0.5
ATTITUDE MEASUREMENT AND PERCEPTIONS OF ACCOUNTING FACULTY PUBLICATION OUTLETS
TAR OC 83 VOL: 58 PG:765 - 776 :: DES.STAT. :SURV. :OTH. :METHOD.

HSIEH ,DA ; FIRS: LEE ,CJ CIT: 1.38
CHOICE OF INVENTORY ACCOUNTING METHODS: COMPARATIVE ANALYSES OF ALTERNATIVE HYPOTHESES
JAR AU 85 VOL: 23 PG:468 - 485 :: REGRESS. :PRIM. :OTH.STAT. :INV.

HSIEH ,S-J ; SEC: FERRIS,KR ; THIR: CHEN ,AH CIT: 0.33
SECURITIES MARKET RESPONSE TO PENSION FUND TERMINATION
CAR SP 90 VOL: 6 PG:550 - 572 :: REGRESS. :PRIM. :EMH :PENS.

HUDSON,D ; FIRS: WILSON,AC CIT: 0
AN EMPIRICAL STUDY OF REGRESSION ANALYSIS AS AN ANALYTICAL PROCEDURE
CAR AU 89 VOL: 6 PG:196 - 215 :: REGRESS. :PRIM. :THEORY :ANAL.REV.

HUDSON,J ; FIRS: MCROBERTS,HA CIT: 0
AUDITING PROGRAM EVALUATIONS: THE CANADIAN CASE
AOS 04 85 VOL: 10 PG:493 - 502 :: REGRESS. :FIELD :INSTIT. :OPER.AUD.

HUDSON,RR CIT: 0
ACCOUNTING FOR UNEARNED DISCOUNT OF FINANCE COMPANIES
TAR OC 63 VOL: 38 PG:796 - 801 :: QUAL. :INT. LOG. :THEORY :REV.REC.

HUEFNER,RJ ; FIRS: ARNOLD,DF CIT: 0.06
MEASURING AND EVALUATING REPLACEMENT COSTS: AN APPLICATION
JAR AU 77 VOL: 15 PG:245 - 252 :: QUAL. :FIELD :THEORY :VALUAT.(INFL.)

HUEFNER,RJ ; FIRS: DERSTINE,RP CIT: 0.41
LIFO-FIFO, ACCOUNTING RATIOS AND MARKET RISK
JAR AU 74 VOL: 12 PG:216 - 234 :: NON-PAR. :PRIM. :OTH. :INV.

HUEFNER,RJ ; FIRS: GUPTA ,MC CIT: 0.18
A CLUSTER ANALYSIS STUDY OF FINANCIAL RATIOS AND INDUSTRY CHARACTERISTICS
JAR SP 72 VOL: 10 PG:77 - 95 :: OTH.QUANT. :PRIM. :OTH.STAT. :N/A

HUEFNER,RJ CIT: 0.06
ANALYZING AND REPORTING SENSITIVITY DATA
TAR OC 71 VOL: 46 PG:717 - 732 :: ANAL. :INT. LOG. :OTH.STAT. :OTH.MANAG.

HUEFNER,RJ ; FIRS: JEN ,FC CIT: 0.12
DEPRECIATION BY PROBABILITY-LIFE
TAR AP 70 VOL: 45 PG:290 - 298 :: ANAL. :INT. LOG. :OTH.STAT. :PP&E / DEPR

HUGHES,GD ; FIRS: HOFSTEDT,TR CIT: 0.81
AN EXPERIMENTAL STUDY OF THE JUDGMENT ELEMENT IN DISCLOSURE DECISIONS
TAR AP 77 VOL: 52 PG:379 - 395 :: MIXED :LAB. :HIPS :INFO.STRUC.

HUGHES,JS ; FIRS: FELTHAM,GA ; SEC: GIGLER,FB CIT: 0
THE EFFECTS OF LINE-OF-BUSINESS REPORTING ON COMPETITION IN OLIGOPOLY SETTINGS
CAR AU 92 VOL: 9 PG:1 - 23 :: DES.STAT. :INT. LOG. :INF.ECO./AG. :SEG.REP.

HUGHES,JS ; FIRS: DATAR ,SM ; SEC: FELTHAM,GA CIT: 1.5
THE ROLE OF AUDITS AND AUDIT QUALITY IN VALUING NEW ISSUES
JAE MR 91 VOL: 14 PG:3 - 49 :: DES.STAT. :INT. LOG. :INF.ECO./AG. :VALUAT.(INFL.)

HUGHES,JS ; FIRS: FELTHAM,GA ; THIR: SIMUNIC,DA CIT: 0.5
EMPIRICAL ASSESSMENT OF THE IMPACT OF AUDITOR QUALITY ON THE VALUATION OF NEW ISSUES
JAE DE 91 VOL: 14 PG:375 - 399 :: REGRESS. :PRIM. :EMH :OPER.AUD.

HUGHES,JS ; FIRS: CONROY,R CIT: 0
ON THE OBSERVABILITY OF OWNERSHIP RETENTION BY ENTREPRENEURS WITH PRIVATE INFORMATION IN THE MARKET FOR NEW ISSUES
CAR AU 89 VOL: 6 PG:159 - 176 :: DES.STAT. :INT. LOG. :INF.ECO./AG. :BUS.COMB.

HUGHES,JS ; FIRS: CONROY,RM CIT: 0.33
DELEGATING INFORMATION GATHERING DECISIONS
TAR JA 87 VOL: 62 PG:50 - 66 :: DES.STAT. :INT. LOG. :INF.ECO./AG. :MANAG.

HUGHES,JS ; SEC: RICKS ,WE CIT: 1
ASSOCIATIONS BETWEEN FORECAST ERRORS AND EXCESS RETURNS NEAR TO EARNINGS ANNOUNCEMENTS
TAR JA 87 VOL: 62 PG:158 - 175 :: REGRESS. :PRIM. :EMH :FOREC.

HUGHES,JS ; SEC: RICKS ,WE CIT: 0
MARKET REACTIONS TO MANDATED INTEREST CAPITALIZATION
CAR SP 86 VOL: 2 PG:222 - 241 :: REGRESS. :PRIM. :EMH :FIN.METH.

HUGHES,JS ; FIRS: HOSKIN,RE ; THIR: RICKS ,WE CIT: 1.43
EVIDENCE ON THE INCREMENTAL INFORMATION CONTENT OF ADDITIONAL FIRM DISCLOSURES MADE CONCURRENTLY WITH EARNINGS
JAR ST 86 VOL: 24 PG:1 - 36 :: REGRESS. :PRIM. :EMH :SPEC.ITEMS

HUGHES,JS ; FIRS: RICKS ,WE CIT: 0.25
MARKET REACTIONS TO A NON-DISCRETIONARY ACCOUNTING CHANGE: THE CASE OF LONG-TERM INVESTMENTS
TAR JA 85 VOL: 60 PG:33 - 52 :: ANOVA :PRIM. :EMH :ACC.CHNG.

HUGHES,JS ; SEC: RICKS ,WE CIT: 0.89
ACCOUNTING FOR RETAIL LAND SALES: ANALYSIS OF A MANDATED CHANGE
JAE AG 84 VOL: 6 PG:101 - 132 :: REGRESS. :PRIM. :EMH :ACC.CHNG.

HUGHES,JS ; FIRS: BURCHELL,S ; SEC: CLUBB ,C ; THIR: HOPWOOD,AG ; FIFT: NAHAPIET,JE CIT: 4.92
THE ROLES OF ACCOUNTING IN ORGANIZATIONS AND SOCIETY
AOS 01 80 VOL: 5 PG:5 - 27 :: QUAL. :INT. LOG. :THEORY :N/A

HUGHES,JS ; FIRS: BROWN ,LD ; THIR: ROZEFF,MS ; FOUR: VANDERWEIDE,JH CIT: 0.08
EXPECTATIONS DATA AND THE PREDICTIVE VALUE OF INTERIM REPORTING: A COMMENT
JAR SP 80 VOL: 18 PG:278 - 288 :: REGRESS. :PRIM. :TIME SER. :FOREC.

HUGHES,JS CIT: 0.13
TOWARD A CONTRACT BASIS OF VALUATION IN ACCOUNTING
TAR OC 78 VOL: 53 PG:882 - 894 :: ANAL. :INT. LOG. :THEORY :SPEC.ITEMS

HUGHES,JS CIT: 0.25
OPTIMAL INTERNAL AUDIT TIMING
TAR JA 77 VOL: 52 PG:56 - 68 :: ANAL. :INT. LOG. :OTH.STAT. :TIM.

HUGHES,MA ; SEC: KWON ,SO CIT: 0.33
AN INTEGRATIVE FRAMEWORK FOR THEORY CONSTRUCTION AND TESTING
AOS 03 90 VOL: 15 PG:179 - 191 :: DES.STAT. :SEC. :OTH.BEH. :METHOD.

HUGHES,PJ ; SEC: SCHWARTZ,ES CIT: 0.4
THE LIFO/FIFO CHOICE: AN ASYMMETRIC INFORMATION APPROACH
JAR ST 88 VOL: 26 PG:41 - 62 :: ANOVA :INT. LOG. :INF.ECO./AG. :INV.

HUGHES,PJ CIT: 2.14
SIGNALLING BY DIRECT DISCLOSURE UNDER ASYMMETRIC INFORMATION
JAE JN 86 VOL: 8 PG:119 - 142 :: DES.STAT. :INT. LOG. :INF.ECO./AG. :INFO.STRUC.

HUIZING,A ; SEC: DEKKER,HC CIT: 1
THE ENVIRONMENTAL ISSUE ON THE DUTCH POLITICAL MARKET
AOS 05 92 VOL: 17 PG:427 - 448 :: REGRESS. :CASE :HIST. :ORG.& ENVIR.

HUIZING,A ; SEC: DEKKER,HC CIT: 0
HELPING TO PULL OUR PLANET OUT OF THE RED: AN ENVIRONMENTAL REPORT OF BSO/ORIGIN
AOS 05 92 VOL: 17 PG:449 - 458 :: REGRESS. :CASE :OTH. :ORG.& ENVIR.

HUMANN,TE ; FIRS: ARNOLD,DF CIT: 0.06
EARNINGS PER SHARE: AN EMPIRICAL TEST OF THE MARKET PARITY AND THE INVESTMENT VALUE METHODS
TAR JA 73 VOL: 48 PG:23 - 33 :: NON-PAR. :PRIM. :OTH.STAT. :LTD

HUME ,LJ CIT: 0.06
THE DEVELOPMENT OF INDUSTRIAL ACCOUNTING: THE BENTHAMS' CONTRIBUTION
JAR SP 70 VOL: 8 PG:21 - 33 :: QUAL. :PRIM. :HIST. :OTH.MANAG.

HUNT III,HG ; FIRS: DUKE ,JC CIT: 3
AN EMPIRICAL EXAMINATION OF DEBT COVENANT RESTRICTIONS AND ACCOUNTING-RELATED DEBT PROXIES
JAE JA 90 VOL: 12 PG:45 - 63 :: REGRESS. :PRIM. :OTH.STAT. :LTD

HUNT III,HG CIT: 1.5
POTENTIAL DETERMINANTS OF CORPORATE INVENTORY ACCOUNTING DECISIONS
JAR AU 85 VOL: 23 PG:448 - 467 :: REGRESS. :PRIM. :EMH :INV.

HUNT-III,HG ; SEC: HOGLER,RL CIT: 0
AGENCY THEORY AS IDEOLOGY: A COMPARATIVE ANALYSIS BASED ON CRITICAL LEGAL THEORY AND RADICAL ACCOUNTING
AOS 05 90 VOL: 15 PG:437 - 454 :: DES.STAT. :SEC. :INF.ECO./AG. :ORG.& ENVIR.

HUNTER,JE ; FIRS: COOPER,WW ; SEC: HO ,JL ; FOUR: RODGERS,RC CIT: 0
THE IMPACT OF THE FOREIGN CORRUPT PRACTICES ACT ON INTERNAL CONTROL PRACTICES
JAA AU 85 VOL: 9 PG:22 - 39 :: REGRESS. :SEC. :THEORY :INT.CONT.

HUSS ,HF ; SEC: JACOBS,FA CIT: 0
RISK CONTAINMENT: EXPLORING AUDITOR DECISIONS IN THE ENGAGEMENT PROCESS
AUD AU 91 VOL: 10 PG:16 - 32 :: REGRESS. :FIELD :HIPS :RISK

HUSS ,HF ; SEC: ZHAO ,J CIT: 0
AN INVESTIGATION OF ALTERNATIVE TREATMENTS OF DEFERRED TAXES IN BOND RATERS' JUDGMENTS
JAA WI 91 VOL: 6 PG:53 - 66 :: REGRESS. :PRIM. :OTH.BEH. :TAXES

HUSS ,HF ; FIRS: TRADER,RL CIT: 0
AN INVESTIGATION OF THE POSSIBLE EFFECTS OF NONSAMPLING ERROR ON INFERENCE IN AUDITING: A BAYESIAN ANALYSIS
CAR AU 87 VOL: 4 PG:227 - 239 :: DES.STAT. :SIM. :OTH.STAT. :ERRORS

HUSS ,HF ; SEC: TRADER,RL CIT: 0.14
A NOTE ON OPT. SAM. SIZE IN COMPLIANCE TESTS USING A FORMAL BAYESIAN DECISION THEORETIC APPROACH FOR FINITE AND INFINITE POPULATIONS
JAR AU 86 VOL: 24 PG:394 - 399 :: DES.STAT. :SIM. :OTH.STAT. :SAMP.

HUSS ,HF CIT: 0
A CONTINGENCY APPROACH TO ACCOUNTING FOR INCOME TAXES
JAA AU 85 VOL: 9 PG:60 - 66 :: DES.STAT. :INT. LOG. :THEORY :TAXES

HUSSEIN,ME ; SEC: BAVISHI,VB ; THIR: GANGOLLY,JS CIT: 0
INTERNATIONAL SIMILARITIES AND DIFFERENCES IN THE AUDITOR'S REPORT
AUD AU 86 VOL: 6 PG:124 - 133 :: DES.STAT. :PRIM. :INSTIT. :INT.DIFF.

HUSSEIN,ME CIT: 0.25
THE INNOVATIVE PROCESS IN FINANCIAL ACCOUNTING STANDARDS SETTING
AOS 01 81 VOL: 6 PG:27 - 38 :: MIXED :SURV. :INSTIT. :FASB SUBM.

HUSSEIN,ME ; SEC: KETZ ,JE CIT: 0.23
RULING ELITES OF THE FASB: A STUDY OF THE BIG EIGHT
JAA SU 80 VOL: 3 PG:354 - 367 :: DES.STAT. :SEC. :OTH.STAT. :FASB SUBM.

HUTH ,WL ; SEC: MARIS ,BA CIT: 0
LARGE AND SMALL FIRM STOCK PRICE RESPONSE TO "HEARD ON THE STREET" RECOMMENDATIONS
JAA WI 92 VOL: 7 PG:27 - 44 :: REGRESS. :PRIM. :TIME SER. :OTH.MANAG.

HYLAS ,RE ; SEC: ASHTON,RH CIT: 1.45
AUDIT DETECTION OF FINANCIAL STATEMENT ERRORS
TAR OC 82 VOL: 57 PG:751 - 765 :: DES.STAT. :FIELD :N/A :ERRORS

HYLAS ,RE ; FIRS: ASHTON,RH CIT: 0
INCREASING CONFIRMATION RESPONSE RATES
AUD SU 81 VOL: 1 PG:12 - 22 :: ANOVA :FIELD :OTH. :CONF.

HYLAS ,RE ; FIRS: ASHTON,RH CIT: 0
A STUDY OF THE RESPONSE TO BALANCE AND INVOICE CONFIRMATION REQUESTS
JAA SU 81 VOL: 4 PG:325 - 332 :: DES.STAT. :FIELD :OTH. :OPER.AUD.

HYLTON,DP CIT: 0
ON MATCHING REVENUE WITH EXPENSE
TAR OC 65 VOL: 40 PG:824 - 828 :: QUAL. :INT. LOG. :THEORY :REV.REC.

HYLTON,DP CIT: 0
ARE CONSULTING AND AUDITING COMPATIBLE? - A CONTRARY VIEW
TAR JL 64 VOL: 39 PG:667 - 670 :: QUAL. :INT. LOG. :N/A :OTH.MANAG.

HYON ,YH ; FIRS: KENNEDY,DT CIT: 0
DO RRA EARNINGS IMPROVE THE USEFULNESS OF REPORTED EARNINGS IN REFLECTING THE PERFORMANCE OF OIL AND GAS PRODUCING FIRMS?
JAA SU 92 VOL: 7 PG:335 - 356 :: REGRESS. :PRIM. :OTH.STAT. :OIL & GAS

ICERMAN,JD ; FIRS: LOREK ,KS ; THIR: ABDULKADER,AA CIT: 0
FURTHER DESCRIPTIVE AND PREDICTIVE EVIDENCE ON ALTERNATIVE TIME-SERIES MODELS FOR QUARTERLY EARNINGS
JAR SP 83 VOL: 21 PG:317 - 328 :: REGRESS. :PRIM. :TIME SER. :FOREC.

ICERMAN,RC ; FIRS: LOREK ,KS ; SEC: BRANSON,BC CIT: 0
ON THE USE OF TIME-SERIES MODELS AS ANALYTICAL PROCEDURES
AUD AU 92 VOL: 11 PG:66 - 88 :: DES.STAT. :PRIM. :TIME SER. :ANAL.REV.

ICERMAN,RC ; SEC: HILLISON,WA CIT: 0
DISPOSITION OF AUDIT-DETECTED ERRORS: SOME EVIDENCE ON EVALUATIVE MATERIALITY
AUD SP 91 VOL: 10 PG:22 - 34 :: REGRESS. :PRIM. :HIPS :MAT.

ICERMAN,RC ; SEC: HILLISON,WA CIT: 0
DISTRIBUTION OF AUDIT-DETECTED ERRORS PARTITIONED BY INTERNAL CONTROL
JAA AU 90 VOL: 5 PG:527 - 543 :: REGRESS. :FIELD :OTH.STAT. :ERRORS

IINO ,T ; FIRS: BEDFORD,NM CIT: 0.06
CONSISTENCY REEXAMINED
TAR JL 68 VOL: 43 PG:453 - 458 :: QUAL. :INT. LOG. :THEORY :OTH.FIN.ACC.

IJIRI ,Y CIT: 0
A FRAMEWORK FOR TRIPLE-ENTRY BOOKKEEPING
TAR OC 86 VOL: 61 PG:745 - 760 :: DES.STAT. :INT. LOG. :THEORY :INFO.STRUC.

IJIRI ,Y ; SEC: NOEL ,J CIT: 0.33
A RELIABILITY COMPARISON OF THE MEASUREMENT OF WEALTH, INCOME AND FORCE
TAR JA 84 VOL: 59 PG:52 - 63 :: ANAL. :INT. LOG. :THEORY :REV.REC.

IJIRI ,Y ; SEC: KELLY ,EC CIT: 0
MULTIDIMENSIONAL ACCOUNTING AND DISTRIBUTED DATABASES: THEIR IMPLICATIONS FOR ORGANIZATIONS AND SOCIETY
AOS 01 80 VOL: 5 PG:115 - 123 :: QUAL. :INT. LOG. :THEORY :INFO.STRUC.

IJIRI ,Y ; SEC: LEITCH,RA CIT: 0.23
STEIN'S PARADOX AND AUDIT SAMPLING
JAR SP 80 VOL: 18 PG:91 - 108 :: MIXED :INT. LOG. :OTH.STAT. :N/A

IJIRI ,Y CIT: 0.2
CASH-FLOW ACCOUNTING AND ITS STRUCTURE
JAA SU 78 VOL: 1 PG:331 - 348 :: QUAL. :INT. LOG. :THEORY :FIN.METH.

IJIRI ,Y CIT: 0.12
THE PRICE-LEVEL RESTATEMENT AND ITS DUAL INTERPRETATION
TAR AP 76 VOL: 51 PG:227 - 243 :: ANAL. :INT. LOG. :THEORY :VALUAT.(INFL.)

IJIRI ,Y ; FIRS: GONEDES,NJ CIT: 0.35
IMPROVING SUBJECTIVE PROBABILITY ASSESSMENT FOR PLANNING AND CONTROL IN TEAM-LIKE ORGANIZATIONS
JAR AU 74 VOL: 12 PG:251 - 269 :: ANAL. :INT. LOG. :INF.ECO./AG. :PROB.ELIC.

IJIRI ,Y ; FIRS: CYERT ,RM CIT: 0.18
PROBLEMS OF IMPLEMENTING THE TRUEBLOOD OBJECTIVES REPORT
JAR ST 74 VOL: 12 PG:29 - 42 :: QUAL. :INT. LOG. :THEORY :FIN.METH.

IJIRI ,Y ; SEC: ITAMI ,H CIT: 0.24
QUADRATIC COST-VOLUME RELATIONSHIP AND TIMING OF DEMAND INFORMATION
TAR OC 73 VOL: 48 PG:724 - 737 :: ANAL. :INT. LOG. :OTH.STAT. :C-V-P-A

IJIRI ,Y CIT: 0
MEASUREMENT IN CURRENT ACCOUNTING PRACTICES: A REPLY
TAR JL 72 VOL: 47 PG:510 - 526 :: QUAL. :INT. LOG. :THEORY :OTH.FIN.ACC.

IJIRI ,Y ; SEC: KAPLAN,RS CIT: 0.29
A MODEL FOR INTEGRATING SAMPLING OBJECTIVES IN AUDITING
JAR SP 71 VOL: 9 PG:73 - 87 :: CORR. :INT. LOG. :OTH. :SAMP.

IJIRI ,Y ; SEC: KAPLAN,RS CIT: 0.06
SEQUENTIAL MODELS IN PROBABILISTIC DEPRECIATION
JAR SP 70 VOL: 8 PG:34 - 46 :: ANAL. :INT. LOG. :OTH.STAT. :PP&E / DEPR

IJIRI ,Y ; SEC: THOMPSON,GL CIT: 0
APPLICATIONS OF MATHEMATICAL CONTROL THEORY TO ACCOUNTING AND BUDGETING (THE CONTINUOUS WHEAT TRADING MODEL)
TAR AP 70 VOL: 45 PG:246 - 258 :: ANAL. :INT. LOG. :OTH.STAT. :BUDG.& PLAN.

IJIRI ,Y ; SEC: KAPLAN,RS CIT: 0.24
PROBABILISTIC DEPRECIATION AND ITS IMPLICATIONS FOR GROUP DEPRECIATION
TAR OC 69 VOL: 44 PG:743 - 756 :: ANAL. :INT. LOG. :OTH.STAT. :PP&E / DEPR

IJIRI ,Y ; SEC: KINARD,JC ; THIR: PUTNEY,FB CIT: 0.47
AN INTEGRATED EVALUATION SYSTEM FOR BUDGET FORECASTING AND OPERATING PERFORMANCE WITH A CLASSIFIED BUDGETING BIBLIOGRAPHY
JAR SP 68 VOL: 6 PG:1 - 28 :: QUAL. :SEC. :OTH.BEH. :BUDG.& PLAN.

IJIRI ,Y CIT: 0
ON BUDGETING PRINCIPLES AND BUDGET-AUDITING STANDARDS
TAR OC 68 VOL: 43 PG:662 - 667 :: QUAL. :INT. LOG. :THEORY :AUD.

IJIRI ,Y ; SEC: JAEDICKE,RK CIT: 0.65
RELIABILITY AND OBJECTIVITY OF ACCOUNTING MEASUREMENTS
TAR JL 66 VOL: 41 PG:474 - 483 :: ANAL. :INT. LOG. :OTH.STAT. :OTH.FIN.ACC.

IJIRI ,Y ; SEC: JAEDICKE,RK ; THIR: LIVINGSTONE,JL CIT: 0.12
THE EFFECT OF INVENTORY COSTING METHODS ON FULL AND DIRECT COSTING
JAR SP 65 VOL: 3 PG:63 - 74 :: ANAL. :INT. LOG. :THEORY :MANAG.

IJIRI ,Y CIT: 0
AXIOMS AND STRUCTURES OF CONVENTIONAL ACCOUNTING MEASUREMENT
TAR JA 65 VOL: 40 PG:36 - 53 :: ANAL. :INT. LOG. :THEORY :FIN.METH.

IJIRI ,Y ; FIRS: CHARNES,A ; SEC: COOPER,WW CIT: 0.06
BREAKEVEN BUDGETING AND PROGRAMMING TO GOALS
JAR SP 63 VOL: 1 PG:16 - 43 :: ANAL. :INT. LOG. :MATH.PROG. :C-V-P-A

IJIRI ,Y ; SEC: LEVY ,FK ; THIR: LYON ,RC CIT: 0.12
A LINEAR PROGRAMMING MODEL FOR BUDGETING AND FINANCIAL PLANNING
JAR AU 63 VOL: 1 PG:198 - 212 :: ANAL. :INT. LOG. :MATH.PROG. :BUDG.& PLAN.

IMDIEKE,LF ; FIRS: SCHROEDER,RG CIT: 0.19
LOCAL-COSMOPOLITAN AND BUREAUCRATIC PERCEPTIONS IN PUBLIC ACCOUNTING FIRMS
AOS 01 77 VOL: 2 PG:39 - 46 :: DES.STAT. :INT. LOG. :OTH.STAT. :ORG.

IMDIEKE,LF ; SEC: WEYGANDT,JJ CIT: 0
CLASSIFICATION OF CONVERTIBLE DEBT
TAR OC 69 VOL: 44 PG:798 - 805 :: QUAL. :INT. LOG. :THEORY :LTD

IMHOFF JR,EA ; SEC: LOBO ,GJ CIT: 1
THE EFFECT OF EX ANTE EARNINGS UNCERTAINTY ON EARNINGS RESPONSE COEFFICIENTS
TAR AP 92 VOL: 67 PG:427 - 439 :: REGRESS. :PRIM. :EMH :N/A

IMHOFF JR,EA ; FIRS: DAMOS ,P ; SEC: HOLT ,DL CIT: 0.25
THE USE OF ACCOUNTING INFORMATION IN BANK LENDING DECISIONS
AOS 03 89 VOL: 14 PG:235 - 246 :: REGRESS. :LAB. :HIPS :OTH.FIN.ACC.

IMHOFF JR,EA CIT: 0
A COMPARISON OF ANALYSTS' ACCOUNTING QUALITY JUDGMENTS AMONG CPA FIRMS' CLIENTS
AUD SP 88 VOL: 07 PG:182 - 191 :: REGRESS. :SURV. :INSTIT. :ORG.

IMHOFF JR,EA ; SEC: LOBO ,GJ CIT: 0.56
INFORMATION CONTENT OF ANALYSTS' COMPOSITE FORECAST REVISIONS
JAR AU 84 VOL: 22 PG:541 - 554 :: REGRESS. :PRIM. :EMH :FOREC.

IMHOFF JR,EA ; FIRS: DANOS ,P ; SEC: HOLT ,DL CIT: 0.33
BOND RATERS' USE OF MANAGEMENT FINANCIAL FORECASTS: EXPERIMENT IN EXPERT JUDGMENT
TAR OC 84 VOL: 59 PG:547 - 573 :: ANOVA :LAB. :OTH.BEH. :FOREC.

IMHOFF JR,EA ; FIRS: DANOS ,P CIT: 0.1
FACTORS AFFECTING AUDITORS' EVALUATIONS OF FORECASTS
JAR AU 83 VOL: 21 PG:473 - 494 :: ANOVA :LAB. :OTH.BEH. :JUDG.

IMHOFF JR,EA ; FIRS: DANOS ,P CIT: 0.27
FORECAST SYSTEMS, CONSTRUCTION AND ATTESTATION
AUD WI 82 VOL: 1 PG:23 - 34 :: DES.STAT. :LAB. :OTH.BEH. :FOREC.

IMHOFF JR,EA ; SEC: PARE ,PV CIT: 0.82
ANALYSIS AND COMPARISON OF EARNINGS FORECAST AGENTS
JAR AU 82 VOL: 20 PG:429 - 439 :: DES.STAT. :PRIM. :TIME SER. :METHOD.

IMHOFF JR,EA ; FIRS: DANOS ,P CIT: 0.45
AUDITOR REVIEW OF FINANCIAL FORECASTS: AN ANALYSIS OF FACTORS AFFECTING REASONABLENESS JUDGMENTS
TAR JA 82 VOL: 57 PG:39 - 54 :: ANOVA :LAB. :OTH.BEH. :AUD.

IMHOFF JR,EA CIT: 0
ANALYTICAL REVIEW OF INCOME ELEMENTS
JAA SU 81 VOL: 4 PG:333 - 351 :: REGRESS. :PRIM. :OTH.STAT. :ANAL.REV.

IMHOFF JR,EA CIT: 0.53
THE REPRESENTATIVENESS OF MANAGEMENT EARNINGS FORECASTS
TAR OC 78 VOL: 53 PG:836 - 850 :: NON-PAR. :PRIM. :OTH. :FOREC.

IMHOFF JR,EA CIT: 0
EMPLOYMENT EFFECTS ON AUDITOR INDEPENDENCE
TAR OC 78 VOL: 53 PG:869 - 881 :: NON-PAR. :SURV. :INSTIT. :INDEP.

IMHOFFJR,EA ; SEC: THOMAS,JK CIT: 0
ECONOMIC CONSEQUENCES OF ACCOUNTING STANDARDS: THE LEASE DISCLOSURE RULE CHANGE
JAE DE 88 VOL: 10 PG:277 - 310 :: REGRESS. :PRIM. :INSTIT. :LEASES

IMKE ,FJ CIT: 0
RELATIONSHIPS IN ACCOUNTING THEORY
TAR AP 66 VOL: 41 PG:318 - 322 :: QUAL. :INT. LOG. :THEORY :OTH.MANAG.

IMOISILI,OA CIT: 0
THE ROLE OF BUDGET DATA IN THE EVALUATION OF MANAGERIAL PERFORMANCE
AOS 04 89 VOL: 14 PG:325 - 335 :: REGRESS. :SURV. :OTH.BEH. :BUDG.& PLAN.

INDJEJIKIAN,RJ CIT: 0.5
THE IMPACT OF COSTLY INFORMATION INTERPRETATION ON FIRM DISCLOSURE DECISIONS
JAR AU 91 VOL: 29 PG:277 - 301 :: DES.STAT. :INT. LOG. :INF.ECO./AG. :INFO.STRUC.

INGBERMAN,M ; FIRS: SORTER,GH CIT: 0
THE IMPLICIT CRITERIA FOR THE RECOGNITION, QUANTIFICATION , AND REPORTING O F ACCOUNTING EVENTS
JAA SP 87 VOL: 2 PG:99 - 116 :: DES.STAT. :INT. LOG. :THEORY :REV.REC.

INGBERMAN,M CIT: 0
THE EVOLUTION OF REPLACEMENT COST ACCOUNTING
JAA WI 80 VOL: 3 PG:101 - 112 :: QUAL. :INT. LOG. :HIST. :VALUAT.(INFL.)

INGBERMAN,M ; SEC: SORTER,GH CIT: 0
THE ROLE OF FINANCIAL STATEMENTS IN AN EFFICIENT MARKET
JAA AU 78 VOL: 2 PG:58 - 62 :: QUAL. :INT. LOG. :INSTIT. :FIN.METH.

INGRAM,RW ; SEC: RAMAN ,KK ; THIR: WILSON,ER CIT: 0
THE INFORMATION IN GOVERNMENTAL ANNUAL REPORTS: A CONTEMPORANEOUS PRICE REACTION APPROACH
TAR AP 89 VOL: 64 PG:250 - 268 :: REGRESS. :INT. LOG. :EMH :LTD

INGRAM,RW ; FIRS: HILL ,JW CIT: 1
SELECTION OF GAAP OR RAP IN THE SAVINGS AND LOAN INDUSTRY
TAR OC 89 VOL: 64 PG:667 - 679 :: REGRESS. :PRIM. :HIST. :FIN.METH.

INGRAM,RW CIT: 0
TESTS OF THE FUND ACCOUNTING MODEL FOR LOCAL GOVERNMENTS
CAR AU 86 VOL: 3 PG:200 - 221 :: REGRESS. :PRIM. :INSTIT. :FIN.METH.

INGRAM,RW CIT: 0.25
A DESCRIPTIVE ANALYSIS OF MUNICIPAL BOND PRICE DATA FOR USE IN ACCOUNTING RESEARCH
JAR AU 85 VOL: 23 PG:595 - 618 :: REGRESS. :PRIM. :EMH :LTD

INGRAM,RW CIT: 0.56
ECONOMIC INCENTIVES AND THE CHOICE OF STATE GOVERNMENT ACCOUNTING PRACTICES
JAR SP 84 VOL: 22 PG:126 - 144 :: MIXED :PRIM. :INSTIT. :ORG.& ENVIR.

INGRAM,RW ; FIRS: FRAZIER,KB ; THIR: TENNYSON,BM CIT: 0.22
A METHODOLOGY FOR THE ANALYSIS OF NARRATIVE ACCOUNTING DISCLOSURES
JAR SP 84 VOL: 22 PG:318 - 331 :: OTH.QUANT. :PRIM. :OTH.STAT. :FOREC.

INGRAM,RW ; SEC: CHEWNING,EG CIT: 0.1
THE EFFECT OF FINANCIAL DISCLOSURE REGULATION ON SECURITY MARKET BEHAVIOR
TAR JL 83 VOL: 58 PG:562 - 580 :: REGRESS. :PRIM. :EMH :FIN.METH.

INGRAM,RW ; FIRS: COPELAND,RM CIT: 0.36
THE ASSOCIATION BETWEEN MUNICIPAL ACCOUNTING INFORMATION AND BOND RATING CHANGES
JAR AU 82 VOL: 20 PG:275 - 289 :: OTH.QUANT. :PRIM. :OTH.STAT. :FIN.METH.

INGRAM,RW ; SEC: COPELAND,RM CIT: 0.27
MUNICIPAL MARKET MEASURES AND REPORTING PRACTICES: AN EXTENSION
JAR AU 82 VOL: 20 PG:766 - 772 :: REGRESS. :PRIM. :OTH.STAT. :FIN.METH.

INGRAM,RW ; SEC: COPELAND,RM CIT: 0.25
MUNICIPAL ACCOUNTING INFORMATION AND VOTING BEHAVIOR
TAR OC 81 VOL: 56 PG:830 - 843 :: OTH.QUANT. :PRIM. :INSTIT. :N/A

INGRAM,RW CIT: 0.4
AN INVESTIGATION OF THE INFORMATION CONTENT OF (CERTAIN) SOCIAL RESPONSIBILITY DISCLOSURES
JAR AU 78 VOL: 16 PG:270 - 285 :: ANOVA :PRIM. :OTH.STAT. :HRA

ISAACS,G ; FIRS: AIKEN ,ME ; SEC: BLACKETT,LA CIT: 0.06
MODELING BEHAVIOURAL INTERDEPENDENCIES FOR STEWARDSHIP REPORTING
TAR JL 75 VOL: 50 PG:544 - 562 :: ANAL. :INT. LOG. :THEORY :OTH.MANAG.

ISELIN,ER CIT: 0.4
THE EFFECTS OF INFORMATION LOAD AND INFORMATION DIVERSITY ON DECISION QUALITY IN A STRUCTURED DECISION TASK
AOS 02 88 VOL: 13 PG:147 - 164 :: REGRESS. :LAB. :HIPS :INFO.STRUC.

ISELIN,ER CIT: 0.06
CHAMBERS ON ACCOUNTING THEORY
TAR AP 68 VOL: 43 PG:231 - 238 :: QUAL. :INT. LOG. :THEORY :VALUAT.(INFL.)

ISMAIL,BE ; SEC: KIM ,MK CIT: 0
ON THE ASSOCIATION OF CASH FLOW VARIABLES WITH MARKET RISK: FURTHER EVIDENCE
TAR JA 89 VOL: 64 PG:125 - 136 :: REGRESS. :PRIM. :TIME SER. :OTH.FIN.ACC.

ISMAIL,BE CIT: 0
SOME TIME SERIES PROPERTIES OF CORPORATE CASH RECOVERY RATES
CAR AU 87 VOL: 4 PG:76 - 88 :: REGRESS. :PRIM. :TIME SER. :CASH

ITAMI ,H CIT: 0.59
EVALUATION MEASURES AND GOAL CONGRUENCE UNDER UNCERTAINTY
JAR SP 75 VOL: 13 PG:73 - 96 :: ANAL. :INT. LOG. :INF.ECO./AG. :MANAG.

ITAMI ,H ; FIRS: IJIRI ,Y CIT: 0.24
QUADRATIC COST-VOLUME RELATIONSHIP AND TIMING OF DEMAND INFORMATION
TAR OC 73 VOL: 48 PG:724 - 737 :: ANAL. :INT. LOG. :OTH.STAT. :C-V-P-A

IVES ,M CIT: 0
THE GASB: A FRESH LOOK AT GOVERNMENTAL ACCOUNTING AND FINANCIAL REPORTING
JAA SU 85 VOL: 8 PG:253 - 268 :: DES.STAT. :INT. LOG. :THEORY :FIN.METH.

JABLONSKY,SF ; FIRS: DIRSMITH,MW CIT: 0.36
MBO, POLITICAL RATIONALITY AND INFORMATION INDUCTANCE
AOS 12 79 VOL: 4 PG:39 - 52 :: QUAL. :INT. LOG. :OTH. :N/A

JABLONSKY,SF ; FIRS: DIRSMITH,MW CIT: 0.27
THE PATTERN OF PPB REJECTION: SOMETHING ABOUT ORGANIZATIONS, SOMETHING ABOUT PPB
AOS 34 78 VOL: 3 PG:215 - 226 :: QUAL. :INT. LOG. :THEORY :BUDG.& PLAN.

JACKSON,BR ; FIRS: AYRES ,FL ; THIR: HITE ,PS CIT: 0.25
THE ECONOMIC BENEFITS OF REGULATION: EVIDENCE FROM PROFESSIONAL TAX PREPARERS
TAR AP 89 VOL: 64 PG:300 - 312 :: REGRESS. :FIELD :HIPS :TAXES

JACKSON,MW CIT: 0
GOETHE'S ECONOMY OF NATURE AND THE NATURE OF HIS ECONOMY
AOS 05 92 VOL: 17 PG:459 - 469 :: REGRESS. :SEC. :HIST. :ORG.& ENVIR.

JACKSON-COX,J ; SEC: THIRKELL,JE ; THIR: MCQUEENEY,J CIT: 0.33
THE DISCLOSURE OF COMPANY INFORMATION TO TRADE UNIONS: THE RELEVANCE OF THE ACAS CODE OF PRACTICE ON DISCLOSURE
AOS 34 84 VOL: 9 PG:253 - 273 :: QUAL. :SURV. :INSTIT. :N/A

JACOBS,FA ; FIRS: HUSS ,HF CIT: 0
RISK CONTAINMENT: EXPLORING AUDITOR DECISIONS IN THE ENGAGEMENT PROCESS
AUD AU 91 VOL: 10 PG:16 - 32 :: REGRESS. :FIELD :HIPS :RISK

JACOBS,FH ; SEC: MARSHALL,RM CIT: 0.17
A RECIPROCAL SERVICE COST APPROXIMATION
TAR JA 87 VOL: 62 PG:67 - 78 :: DES.STAT. :INT. LOG. :THEORY :COST.ALLOC.

JACOBS,FH CIT: 0.07
AN EVALUATION OF THE EFFECTIVENESS OF SOME COST VARIANCE INVESTIGATION MODELS
JAR SP 78 VOL: 16 PG:190 - 203 :: DES.STAT. :FIELD :OTH.STAT. :VAR.

JACOBSEN,LE CIT: 0
THE ANCIENT INCA EMPIRE OF PERU AND THE DOUBLE ENTRY ACCOUNTING CONCEPT
JAR AU 64 VOL: 2 PG:221 - 228 :: QUAL. :INT. LOG. :HIST. :N/A

JACOBSEN,LE CIT: 0
THE RISE OF THE PROFIT DEFERRAL NOTION - THE CONCEPT AND PRACTICE OF OPTIMEASUREMENT
TAR AP 63 VOL: 38 PG:285 - 292 :: QUAL. :INT. LOG. :THEORY :REV.REC.

JACOBSSON,B ; FIRS: CZARNIAWSKA-JOERGES CIT: 0
BUDGET IN A COLD CLIMATE
AOS 02 89 VOL: 14 PG:29 - 39 :: REGRESS. :SEC. :HIST. :ORG.& ENVIR.

JAEDICKE,RK ; FIRS: IJIRI ,Y CIT: 0.65
RELIABILITY AND OBJECTIVITY OF ACCOUNTING MEASUREMENTS
TAR JL 66 VOL: 41 PG:474 - 483 :: ANAL. :INT. LOG. :OTH.STAT. :OTH.FIN.ACC.

JAEDICKE,RK ; FIRS: IJIRI ,Y ; THIR: LIVINGSTONE,JL CIT: 0.12
THE EFFECT OF INVENTORY COSTING METHODS ON FULL AND DIRECT COSTING
JAR SP 65 VOL: 3 PG:63 - 74 :: ANAL. :INT. LOG. :THEORY :MANAG.

JAEDICKE,RK ; SEC: ROBICHEK,AA CIT: 0.47
COST-VOLUME-PROFIT ANALYSIS UNDER CONDITIONS OF UNCERTAINTY
TAR OC 64 VOL: 39 PG:917 - 926 :: ANAL. :INT. LOG. :OTH.STAT. :C-V-P-A

JAEDICKE,RK ; FIRS: BURNS ,JS ; THIR: SANGSTER,JM CIT: 0
FINANCIAL REPORTING OF PURCHASE CONTRACTS USED TO GUARANTEE LARGE INVESTMENTS
TAR JA 63 VOL: 38 PG:1 - 13 :: QUAL. :INT. LOG. :THEORY :SPEC.ITEMS

JAENICKE,HR CIT: 0.06
ACCOUNTING FOR RESTRICTED STOCK PLANS AND DEFERRED STOCK PLANS
TAR JA 70 VOL: 45 PG:115 - 128 :: QUAL. :INT. LOG. :N/A :STK.DIV.

JAGGI ,B CIT: 0.27
A NOTE ON THE INFORMATION CONTENT OF CORPORATE ANNUAL EARNINGS FORECASTS
TAR OC 78 VOL: 53 PG:961 - 967 :: REGRESS. :PRIM. :EMH :FOREC.

JAGGI ,B ; SEC: LAU ,HS CIT: 0.29
TOWARD A MODEL FOR HUMAN RESOURCE VALUATION
TAR AP 74 VOL: 49 PG:321 - 329 :: MARKOV :INT. LOG. :OTH.STAT. :HRA

JAIN ,PC ; FIRS: HERTZER,M CIT: 1
EARNINGS AND RISK CHANGES AROUND STOCK REPURCHASE TENDER OFFERS
JAE SE 91 VOL: 14 PG:253 - 273 :: REGRESS. :PRIM. :EMH :BUS.COMB.

JAIN ,PC ; FIRS: AJINKYA,BB CIT: 0.5
THE BEHAVIOR OF DAILY STOCK MARKET TRADING VOLUME
JAE NV 89 VOL: 11 PG:331 - 359 :: REGRESS. :PRIM. :EMH :METHOD.

JAIN ,PC CIT: 0.43
ANALYSES OF THE DISTRIBUTION OF SECURITY MARKET MODEL PREDICTION ERRORS FOR DAILY RETURNS DATA
JAR SP 86 VOL: 24 PG:76 - 96 :: REGRESS. :PRIM. :EMH :METHOD.

JAIN ,PC CIT: 0.14
RELATION BETWEEN MARKET MODEL PREDICTION ERRORS AND OMITTED VARIABLES
JAR SP 86 VOL: 24 PG:187 - 193 :: REGRESS. :INT. LOG. :EMH :METHOD.

JAIN ,PC CIT: 0
THE IMPACT OF ACCOUNTING REGULATION ON THE STOCK MARKET: THE CASE OF OIL AND GAS COMPANIES - SOME ADDITIONAL RESULTS
TAR JL 83 VOL: 58 PG:633 - 638 :: REGRESS. :PRIM. :EMH :OIL & GAS

JAIN ,PC CIT: 0.82
CROSS-SECTIONAL ASSOCIATION BETWEEN ABNORMAL RETURNS AND FIRM SPECIFIC VARIABLES
JAE DE 82 VOL: 4 PG:205 - 228 :: REGRESS. :PRIM. :EMH :SPEC.ITEMS

JAIN ,TN CIT: 0.29
ALTERNATIVE METHODS OF ACCOUNTING AND DECISION MAKING: A PSYCHO-LINGUISTICAL ANALYSIS
TAR JA 73 VOL: 48 PG:95 - 104 :: QUAL. :INT. LOG. :HIPS :FIN.METH.

JAMAL ,K ; FIRS: JOHNSON,PE ; THIR: BERRYMAN,RG CIT: 0.5
AUDIT JUDGMENT RESEARCH
AOS 02 89 VOL: 14 PG:83 - 99 :: REGRESS. :SEC. :HIPS :JUDG.

JAMES ,C CIT: 0
OFF-BALANCE SHEET ACTIVITIES AND THE UNDERINVESTMENT PROBLEM IN BANKING
JAA SP 89 VOL: 4 PG:111 - 124 :: DES.STAT. :INT. LOG. :OTH.STAT. :SPEC.ITEMS

JAMISON,RW ; FIRS: ENGLEBRECHT,TD CIT: 0.07
AN EMPIRICAL INQUIRY INTO THE ROLE OF THE TAX COURT IN THE VALUATION OF PROPERTY FOR CHARITABLE CONTRIBUTION PURPOSES
TAR JL 79 VOL: 54 PG:554 - 562 :: REGRESS. :PRIM. :OTH.STAT. :TAXES

JANAKIRAMAN,SN ; SEC: LAMBERT,RA ; THIR: LARCKER,DF CIT: 1
AN EMPIRICAL INVESTIGATION OF THE RELATIVE PERFORMANCE EVALUATION HYPOTHESIS
JAR SP 92 VOL: 30 PG:53 - 69 :: REGRESS. :PRIM. :INF.ECO./AG. :EXEC.COMP.

JANG ,HJ ; SEC: RO ,BT CIT: 0.25
TRADING VOLUME THEORIES AND THEIR IMPLICATIONS FOR EMPIRICAL INFORMATION CONTENT STUDIES
CAR AU 89 VOL: 6 PG:242 - 262 :: DES.STAT. :INT. LOG. :MATH.PROG. :METHOD.

JANSON,EC ; FIRS: WYER ,JC ; SEC: WHITE ,GT CIT: 0.2
AUDITS OF PUBLIC COMPANIES BY SMALLER CPA FIRMS: CLIENTS, REPORTS, AND QUALITY
AUD SP 88 VOL: 07 PG:164 - 173 :: REGRESS. :PRIM. :INSTIT. :ORG.

JARRELL,GA CIT: 0.57
PRO-PRODUCER REGULATION AND ACCOUNTING FOR ASSETS: THE CASE OF ELECTRIC UTILITIES
JAE AG 79 VOL: 1 PG:93 - 116 :: REGRESS. :SEC. :INF.ECO./AG. :PP&E / DEPR

JARRETT,JE CIT: 0
BIAS IN ADJUSTING ASSET VALUES FOR CHANGES IN THE PRICE LEVEL: AN APPLICATION OF ESTIMATION THEORY
JAR SP 74 VOL: 12 PG:63 - 66 :: ANAL. :INT. LOG. :THEORY :VALUAT.(INFL.)

JARRETT,JE CIT: 0
NOTES ON THE ESTIMATION PROBLEM IN FINANCIAL ACCOUNTING
JAR SP 72 VOL: 10 PG:108 - 112 :: ANAL. :INT. LOG. :OTH.STAT. :N/A

JARVENPAA,SL ; FIRS: DESANCTIS,G CIT: 0
GRAPHICAL PRESENTATION OF ACCOUNTING DATA FOR FINANCIAL FORECASTING: AN EXPERIMENTAL INVESTIGATION
AOS 06 89 VOL: 14 PG:509 - 525 :: REGRESS. :LAB. :HIPS :FOREC.

JAWORKSI,BJ ; SEC: YOUNG ,SM CIT: 0
DYSFUNCTIONAL BEHAVIOR AND MANAGEMENT CONTROL: AN EMPIRICAL STUDY OF MARKETING MANAGERS
AOS 01 92 VOL: 17 PG:17 - 35 :: REGRESS. :SURV. :OTH.BEH. :INT.CONT.

JEFFREY,C CIT: 0
THE RELATION OF JUDGMENT, PERSONAL INVOLVEMENT, AND EXPERIENCE IN THE AUDIT OF BANK LOANS
TAR OC 92 VOL: 67 PG:802 - 820 :: REGRESS. :LAB. :HIPS :JUDG.

JEN ,FC ; SEC: HUEFNER,RJ CIT: 0.12
DEPRECIATION BY PROBABILITY-LIFE
TAR AP 70 VOL: 45 PG:290 - 298 :: ANAL. :INT. LOG. :OTH.STAT. :PP&E / DEPR

JENKINS,DO CIT: 0
ACCOUNTING FOR FUNDED INDUSTRIAL PENSION PLANS
TAR JL 64 VOL: 39 PG:648 - 653 :: QUAL. :INT. LOG. :THEORY :PENS.

JENNINGS,M ; SEC: KNEER ,DC ; THIR: RECKERS,PMJ CIT: 0.33
A REEXAMINATION OF THE CONCEPT OF MATERIALITY: VIEWS OF AUDITORS, USERS AND OFFICERS OF THE COURT
AUD SP 87 VOL: 6 PG:104 - 115 :: REGRESS. :LAB. :OTH.BEH. :MAT.

JENNINGS,MM ; SEC: KNEER ,DC ; THIR: RECKERS,PMJ CIT: 0
SELECTED AUDITOR COMMUNICATIONS AND PERCEPTIONS OF LEGAL LIABILITY
CAR SP 91 VOL: 7 PG:449 - 465 :: REGRESS. :LAB. :HIPS :LIAB.

JENNINGS,R ; FIRS: HAN ,BH ; THIR: NOEL ,J CIT: 0
COMMUNICATION OF NONEARNINGS INFORMATION AT THE FINANCIAL STATEMENTS RELEASE DATE
JAE MR 92 VOL: 15 PG:63 - 85 :: REGRESS. :PRIM. :EMH :BUS.FAIL.

JENNINGS,R ; SEC: MEST ,DP ; THIR: THOMPSON II,RB CIT: 0
INVESTOR REACTION TO DISCLOSURES OF 1974-75 LIFO ADOPTION DECISIONS
TAR AP 92 VOL: 67 PG:337 - 354 :: REGRESS. :PRIM. :INF.ECO./AG. :ACC.CHNG.

JENNINGS,R CIT: 0
A NOTE ON INTERPRETING "INCREMENTAL INFORMATION CONTENT"
TAR OC 90 VOL: 65 PG:925 - 932 :: REGRESS. :SEC. :EMH :METHOD.

JENNINGS,R CIT: 0.83
UNSYSTEMATIC SECURITY PRICE MOVEMENTS, MANAGEMENT EARNINGS FORECASTS, AND REVISIONS IN CONSENSUS ANALYST EARNINGS FORECASTS
JAR SP 87 VOL: 25 PG:90 - 110 :: REGRESS. :PRIM. :EMH :FOREC.

JENNINGS,R ; SEC: STARKS,L CIT: 0.38
INFORMATION CONTENT AND THE SPEED OF STOCK PRICE ADJUSTMENT
JAR SP 85 VOL: 23 PG:336 - 350 :: REGRESS. :PRIM. :EMH :N/A

JENNINGS,RH ; FIRS: HASSELL,JM CIT: 0.57
RELATIVE FORECAST ACCURACY AND THE TIMING OF EARNINGS FORECAST ANNOUNCEMENTS
TAR JA 86 VOL: 61 PG:58 - 75 :: REGRESS. :PRIM. :TIME SER. :FOREC.

JENSEN,DL CIT: 0.5
A CLASS OF MUTUALLY SATISFACTORY ALLOCATIONS
TAR OC 77 VOL: 52 PG:842 - 856 :: ANAL. :INT. LOG. :MATH.PROG. :OVER.ALLOC.

JENSEN,DL CIT: 0.06
THE ROLE OF COST IN PRICING JOINT PRODUCTS: A CASE OF PRODUCTION IN FIXED PROPORTIONS
TAR JL 74 VOL: 49 PG:465 - 476 :: ANAL. :INT. LOG. :N/A :REL.COSTS

JENSEN,HL ; SEC: WYNDELTS,RW CIT: 0
THROUGH THE LOOKING GLASS: AN EMPIRICAL LOOK AT DISCRIMINATION IN THE FEDERAL INCOME TAX RATE STRUCTURE
TAR OC 76 VOL: 51 PG:846 - 853 :: ANAL. :SIM. :INSTIT. :OTH.MANAG.

JENSEN,MC ; SEC: ZIMMERMAN,JL CIT: 0
MANAGEMENT COMPENSATION AND THE MANAGERIAL LABOR MARKET
JAE AP 85 VOL: 7 PG:3 - 10 :: REGRESS. :INT. LOG. :THEORY :EXEC.COMP.

JENSEN,RE ; FIRS: ARRINGTON,CE ; SEC: HILLISON,WA CIT: 0.44
AN APPLICATION OF ANALYTICAL HIERARCHY PROCESS TO MODEL EXPERT JUDGMENTS ON ANALYTICAL REVIEW PROCEDURES
JAR SP 84 VOL: 22 PG:298 - 312 :: OTH.QUANT. :LAB. :HIPS :ANAL.REV.

JENSEN,RE ; FIRS: MANES ,RP ; SEC: PARK ,SH CIT: 0.09
RELEVANT COSTS OF INTERMEDIATE GOODS AND SERVICES
TAR JL 82 VOL: 57 PG:594 - 606 :: ANAL. :INT. LOG. :MATH.PROG. :N/A

JENSEN,RE CIT: 0.06
A CLUSTER ANALYSIS STUDY OF FINANCIAL PERFORMANCE OF SELECTED BUSINESS FIRMS
TAR JA 71 VOL: 46 PG:36 - 56 :: OTH.QUANT. :PRIM. :OTH.STAT. :AUD.BEH.

JENSEN,RE CIT: 0
EMPIRICAL EVIDENCE FROM THE BEHAVIOURAL SCIENCES: FISH OUT OF WATER
TAR JL 70 VOL: 45 PG:502 - 508 :: QUAL. :INT. LOG. :OTH.BEH. :INFO.STRUC.

JENSEN,RE ; SEC: THOMSEN,CT CIT: 0
STATISTICAL ANALYSIS IN COST MEASUREMENT AND CONTROL
TAR JA 68 VOL: 43 PG:83 - 93 :: ANAL. :INT. LOG. :OTH.STAT. :VAR.

JENSEN,RE CIT: 0
SENSITIVITY ANALYSIS AND INTEGER LINEAR PROGRAMMING
TAR JL 68 VOL: 43 PG:425 - 446 :: ANAL. :INT. LOG. :MATH.PROG. :BUDG.& PLAN.

JENSEN,RE CIT: 0.06
A MULTIPLE REGRESSION MODEL FOR COST CONTROL - ASSUMPTIONS AND LIMITATIONS
TAR AP 67 VOL: 42 PG:265 - 273 :: REGRESS. :INT. LOG. :TIME SER. :BUDG.& PLAN.

JENSEN,RE CIT: 0.41
AN EXPERIMENTAL DESIGN FOR STUDY OF EFFECTS OF ACCOUNTING VARIATIONS IN DECISION MAKING
JAR AU 66 VOL: 4 PG:224 - 238 :: ANOVA :LAB. :HIPS :INFO.STRUC.

JENTZ ,GA CIT: 0
TEN-YEAR REVIEW OF THE CPA LAW EXAMINATION
TAR AP 67 VOL: 42 PG:362 - 365 :: QUAL. :SEC. :N/A :OTH.MANAG.

JENTZ ,GA CIT: 0
THE CASE AGAINST THE PRESENT CPA COMMERCIAL LAW EXAMINATION
TAR JL 66 VOL: 41 PG:535 - 541 :: QUAL. :INT. LOG. :INSTIT. :OTH.MANAG.

JERSTON,JE CIT: 0
ANALYST'S VIEW OF DEFERRED INCOME TAXES
TAR OC 65 VOL: 40 PG:812 - 813 :: QUAL. :INT. LOG. :THEORY :TAXES

JETER ,DC ; FIRS: CHANEY,PK CIT: 0
THE EFFECT OF SIZE ON THE MAGNITUDE OF LONG-WINDOW EARNINGS RESPONSE COEFFICIENTS
CAR SP 92 VOL: 8 PG:540 - 560 :: REGRESS. :PRIM. :EMH :FIN.METH.

JETER ,DC ; FIRS: CHOI ,SK CIT: 0
THE EFFECTS OF QUALIFIED AUDIT OPINIONS ON EARNINGS RESPONSE COEFFICIENTS
JAE JN 92 VOL: 15 PG:229 - 247 :: REGRESS. :PRIM. :EMH :OPIN.

JEYNES,PH CIT: 0
A DISCIPLINE FOR INVESTMENT DECISIONS
TAR JA 65 VOL: 40 PG:105 - 118 :: QUAL. :INT. LOG. :N/A :CAP.BUDG.

JIAMBALVO,J ; FIRS: DEFOND,ML CIT: 0
INCIDENCE AND CIRCUMSTANCES OF ACCOUNTING ERRORS
TAR JL 91 VOL: 66 PG:643 - 655 :: REGRESS. :FIELD :INF.ECO./AG. :ERRORS

JIAMBALVO,J ; FIRS: BURGSTAHLER,D ; THIR: NOREEN,E CIT: 0.25
CHANGES IN THE PROBABILITY OF BANKRUPTCY AND EQUITY VALUE
JAE JL 89 VOL: 11 PG:207 - 224 :: REGRESS. :PRIM. :OTH.STAT. :BUS.FAIL.

JIAMBALVO,J ; FIRS: BURGSTAHLER,D CIT: 0.43
SAMPLE ERROR CHARACTERISTICS AND PROJECTION OF ERROR TO AUDIT POPULATIONS
TAR AP 86 VOL: 61 PG:233 - 248 :: REGRESS. :LAB. :HIPS :ERRORS

JIAMBALVO,J ; SEC: WILNER,N CIT: 0.38
AUDITOR EVALUATION OF CONTINGENT CLAIMS
AUD AU 85 VOL: 5 PG:1 - 11 :: REGRESS. :SURV. :OTH.STAT. :AUD.

JIAMBALVO,J ; SEC: WALLER,WS CIT: 0.11
DECOMPOSITION AND ASSESSMENTS OF AUDIT RISK
AUD SP 84 VOL: 3 PG:80 - 88 :: NON-PAR. :LAB. :OTH.STAT. :RISK

JIAMBALVO,J ; SEC: WATSON,DJ ; THIR: BAUMLER,JV CIT: 0.6
AN EXAMINATION OF PERFORMANCE EVALUATION DECISIONS IN CPA FIRM SUBUNITS
AOS 01 83 VOL: 8 PG:13 - 30 :: REGRESS. :LAB. :OTH.BEH. :ORG.

JIAMBALVO,J ; FIRS: PRATT ,J CIT: 0
DETERMINANTS OF LEADER BEHAVIOR IN AN AUDIT ENVIRONMENT
AOS 04 82 VOL: 7 PG:369 - 380 :: NON-PAR. :SURV. :HIPS :AUD.BEH.

JIAMBALVO,J CIT: 0.27
MEASURES OF ACCURACY AND CONGRUENCE IN THE PERFORMANCE EVALUATION OF CPA PERSONNEL: REPLICATION AND EXTENSIONS
JAR SP 82 VOL: 20 PG:152 - 161 :: DES.STAT. :LAB. :OTH.BEH. :ERRORS

JIAMBALVO,J ; SEC: PRATT ,J CIT: 0.09
TASK COMPLEXITY AND LEADERSHIP EFFECTIVENESS IN CPA FIRMS
TAR OC 82 VOL: 57 PG:734 - 750 :: ANOVA :LAB. :OTH.BEH. :ORG.

JIAMBALVO,J ; FIRS: PRATT ,J CIT: 0.33
RELATIONSHIPS BETWEEN LEADER BEHAVIORS AND AUDIT TEAM PERFORMANCE
AOS 02 81 VOL: 6 PG:133 - 142 :: CORR. :FIELD :OTH.BEH. :AUD.BEH.

JIAMBALVO,J CIT: 1.43
PERFORMANCE EVALUATION AND DIRECTED JOB EFFORT: MODEL DEVELOPMENT AND ANALYSIS IN A CPA FIRM SETTING
JAR AU 79 VOL: 17 PG:436 - 455 :: REGRESS. :LAB. :OTH.BEH. :AUD.BEH.

JOHN ,K ; SEC: RONEN ,J CIT: 0
EVOLUTION OF INFORMATION STRUCTURES, OPTIMAL CONTRACTS AND THE THEORY OF THE FIRM
JAA WI 90 VOL: 5 PG:61 - 95 :: DES.STAT. :INT. LOG. :INF.ECO./AG. :INFO.STRUC.

JOHNSON,C ; FIRS: LOUDDER,ML ; SEC: KHURANA,IK ; THIR: SAWYERS,RB ; FOUR: CORDERY,C ; SIX: LOWE ,J CIT: 0
THE INFORMATION CONTENT OF AUDIT QUALIFICATIONS
AUD SP 92 VOL: 11 PG:69 - 82 :: REGRESS. :PRIM. :OTH.STAT. :OPIN.

JOHNSON,DA ; SEC: PANY ,K CIT: 0
FORECASTS, AUDITOR REVIEW, AND BANK LOAN DECISIONS
JAR AU 84 VOL: 22 PG:731 - 743 :: ANOVA :LAB. :OTH.BEH. :FOREC.

JOHNSON,DA ; SEC: PANY ,K ; THIR: WHITE ,RA CIT: 0
AUDIT REPORTS AND THE LOAN DECISION: ACTIONS AND PERCEPTIONS
AUD SP 83 VOL: 2 PG:38 - 51 :: ANOVA :LAB. :OTH.BEH. :OPIN.

JOHNSON,GL ; FIRS: GREENBERG,RR ; THIR: RAMESH,K CIT: 0
EARNINGS VERSUS CASH FLOW AS A PREDICTOR OF FUTURE CASH FLOW MEASURES
JAA AU 86 VOL: 1 PG:266 - 277 :: REGRESS. :PRIM. :THEORY :SPEC.ITEMS

JOHNSON,GL ; SEC: SIMIK ,SS CIT: 0.12
THE USE OF PROBABILITY INEQUALITIES IN MULTIPRODUCT C-V-P ANALYSIS UNDER UNCERTAINTY
JAR SP 74 VOL: 12 PG:67 - 79 :: ANAL. :INT. LOG. :OTH.STAT. :C-V-P-A

JOHNSON,GL ; SEC: SIMIK ,SS CIT: 0.12
MULTIPRODUCT C-V-P ANALYSIS UNDER UNCERTAINTY
JAR AU 71 VOL: 9 PG:278 - 286 :: ANAL. :INT. LOG. :OTH.STAT. :C-V-P-A

JOHNSON,GL ; SEC: NEWTON,SW CIT: 0
TAX CONSIDERATIONS IN EQUIPMENT REPLACEMENT DECISIONS
TAR OC 67 VOL: 42 PG:738 - 746 :: ANAL. :INT. LOG. :N/A :CAP.BUDG.

JOHNSON,GL CIT: 0
FUNDS-FLOW EQUATIONS
TAR JL 66 VOL: 41 PG:510 - 517 :: ANAL. :INT. LOG. :OTH.STAT. :FIN.METH.

JOHNSON,GL CIT: 0
THE MONETARY AND NONMONETARY DISTINCTION
TAR OC 65 VOL: 40 PG:821 - 823 :: QUAL. :INT. LOG. :THEORY :FIN.METH.

JOHNSON,HT CIT: 0.9
THE SEARCH FOR GAIN IN MARKETS AND FIRMS: A REVIEW OF THE HISTORICAL EMERGENCE OF MANAGEMENT ACCOUNTING SYSTEMS
AOS 23 83 VOL: 8 PG:139 - 146 :: QUAL. :INT. LOG. :HIST. :MANAG.

JOHNSON,HT CIT: 0.5
TOWARD A NEW UNDERSTANDING OF NINETEENTH-CENTURY COST ACCOUNTING
TAR JL 81 VOL: 56 PG:510 - 518 :: QUAL. :INT. LOG. :HIST. :N/A

JOHNSON,HT CIT: 0.24
THE ROLE OF ACCOUNTING HISTORY IN THE STUDY OF MODERN BUSINESS ENTERPRISE
TAR JL 75 VOL: 50 PG:444 - 450 :: QUAL. :INT. LOG. :HIST. :OTH.MANAG.

JOHNSON,JR ; SEC: LEITCH,RA ; THIR: NETER ,J CIT: 1.83
CHARACTERISTICS OF ERRORS IN ACCOUNTS RECEIVABLE AND INVENTORY AUDITS
TAR AP 81 VOL: 56 PG:270 - 293 :: DES.STAT. :PRIM. :OTH. :ERRORS

JOHNSON,MF ; FIRS: BOWEN ,RM ; THIR: SHEVLIN,T ; FOUR: SHORES,D CIT: 0
DETERMINANTS OF THE TRADING OF QUARTERLY EARNINGS ANNOUNCEMENTS
JAA AU 92 VOL: 7 PG:395 - 422 :: REGRESS. :PRIM. :TIME SER. :FIN.ST.TIM.

JOHNSON,MF ; FIRS: BOWEN ,RM ; THIR: SHEVLIN,T CIT: 0.25
INFORMATIONAL EFFICIENCY AND THE INFORMATION CONTENT OF EARNINGS DURING THE MARKET CRASH OF OCTOBER 1987
JAE JL 89 VOL: 11 PG:225 - 254 :: REGRESS. :PRIM. :EMH :FIN.METH.

JOHNSON,O CIT: 0
BUSINESS JUDGMENT V. AUDIT JUDGMENT: WHY THE LEGAL DISTINCTION?
AOS 04 92 VOL: 17 PG:205 - 222 :: REGRESS. :SEC. :INSTIT. :LITIG.

JOHNSON,O CIT: 0
SOME IMPLICATIONS OF THE UNITED STATES CONSTITUTION FOR ACCOUNTING INSTITUTION ALTERNATIVES
JAR ST 81 VOL: 19 PG:89 - 119 :: QUAL. :INT. LOG. :INSTIT. :N/A

JOHNSON,O CIT: 0
CONTRA-EQUITY ACCOUNTING FOR R&D
TAR OC 76 VOL: 51 PG:808 - 823 :: DES.STAT. :PRIM. :THEORY :OTH. NON-C/A

JOHNSON,O ; SEC: GUNN ,S CIT: 0
CONFLICT RESOLUTION: THE MARKET AND/OR ACCOUNTING?
TAR OC 74 VOL: 49 PG:649 - 663 :: QUAL. :INT. LOG. :INSTIT. :FIN.METH.

JOHNSON,O CIT: 0.06
ON TAXONOMY AND ACCOUNTING RESEARCH
TAR JA 72 VOL: 47 PG:64 - 74 :: QUAL. :INT. LOG. :N/A :METHOD.

JOHNSON,O CIT: 0.12
TOWARD AN EVENTS THEORY OF ACCOUNTING
TAR OC 70 VOL: 45 PG:641 - 653 :: ANAL. :INT. LOG. :THEORY :FIN.METH.

JOHNSON,O CIT: 0.06
TWO GENERAL CONCEPTS OF DEPRECIATION
JAR SP 68 VOL: 6 PG:29 - 37 :: ANAL. :INT. LOG. :THEORY :PP&E / DEPR

JOHNSON,O CIT: 0
SOME RESERVATIONS ON THE SIGNIFICANCE OF PROSPECTIVE INCOME DATA
TAR JL 68 VOL: 43 PG:546 - 548 :: QUAL. :INT. LOG. :THEORY :PP&E / DEPR

JOHNSON,O CIT: 0.12
A CONSEQUENTIAL APPROACH TO ACCOUNTING FOR R&D
JAR AU 67 VOL: 5 PG:164 - 172 :: CORR. :PRIM. :TIME SER. :R & D

JOHNSON,O CIT: 0
CORPORATE GIVING: A NOTE ON PROFIT MAXIMIZATION AND ACCOUNTING DISCLOSURE
JAR SP 65 VOL: 3 PG:75 - 85 :: QUAL. :INT. LOG. :THEORY :N/A

JOHNSON,PE ; SEC: JAMAL ,K ; THIR: BERRYMAN,RG CIT: 0.5
AUDIT JUDGMENT RESEARCH
AOS 02 89 VOL: 14 PG:83 - 99 :: REGRESS. :SEC. :HIPS :JUDG.

JOHNSON,PE ; FIRS: MESERVY,RD ; SEC: BAILEY JR,AD CIT: 0.57
INTERNAL CONTROL EVALUATION: A COMPUTATIONAL MODEL OF THE REVIEW PROCESS
AUD AU 86 VOL: 6 PG:44 - 74 :: DES.STAT. :LAB. :EXP.SYST. :INT.CONT.

JOHNSON,R ; FIRS: MURRAY,D CIT: 0
DIFFERENTIAL GAAP AND THE FASB'S CONCEPTUAL FRAMEWORK
JAA AU 83 VOL: 7 PG:4 - 15 :: QUAL. :INT. LOG. :THEORY :FASB SUBM.

JOHNSON,SB ; FIRS: BEATTY,RP CIT: 0
A MARKET-BASED METHOD OF CLASSIFYING CONVERTIBLE SECURITIES
JAA WI 85 VOL: 8 PG:112 - 124 :: REGRESS. :PRIM. :EMH :LTD

JOHNSON,SB ; SEC: MESSIER JR,WF CIT: 0
THE NATURE OF ACCOUNTING STANDARDS SETTING: AN ALTERNATIVE EXPLANATION
JAA SP 82 VOL: 5 PG:195 - 213 :: QUAL. :INT. LOG. :INSTIT. :FASB SUBM.

JOHNSON,VE ; SEC: KAPLAN,SE CIT: 0
EXPERIMENTAL EVIDENCE ON THE EFFECTS OF ACCOUNTABILITY ON AUDITOR JUDGMENTS
AUD 91 VOL: 10 PG:96 - 107 :: REGRESS. :LAB. :HIPS :JUDG.

JOHNSON,WB ; SEC: LYS ,T CIT: 1
THE MARKET FOR AUDIT SERVICES: EVIDENCE FROM VOLUNTARY AUDITOR CHANGES
JAE JA 90 VOL: 12 PG:281 - 308 :: REGRESS. :PRIM. :INF.ECO./AG. :ORG.

JOHNSON,WB ; SEC: DHALIWAL,DS CIT: 0.6
LIFO ABANDONMENT
JAR AU 88 VOL: 26 PG:236 - 272 :: REGRESS. :PRIM. :EMH :INV.

JOHNSON,WB ; SEC: RAMANAN,R CIT: 0.4
DISCRETIONARY ACCOUNTING CHANGES FROM SUCCESSFUL EFFORTS TO FULL COST METHODS
TAR JA 88 VOL: 63 PG:96 - 110 :: REGRESS. :PRIM. :OTH.STAT. :OIL & GAS

JOHNSON,WB ; SEC: MAGEE ,RP ; THIR: NAGARAJAN,NJ ; FOUR: NEWMAN,HA CIT: 0.13
AN ANALYSIS OF THE STOCK PRICE REACTION TO SUDDEN EXECUTIVE DEATHS: IMPLICATIONS FOR THE MANAGEMENT LABOR MARKET
JAE AP 85 VOL: 7 PG:151 - 174 :: REGRESS. :PRIM. :EMH :OTH.MANAG.

JOHNSON,WB CIT: 0.2
REPRESENTATIVENESS IN JUDGMENTAL PREDICTIONS OF CORPORATE BANKRUPTCY
TAR JA 83 VOL: 58 PG:78 - 97 :: ANOVA :LAB. :HIPS :BUS.FAIL.

JOHNSON,WB CIT: 0
THE IMPACT OF CONFIDENCE INTERVAL INFORMATION ON PROBABILITY JUDGMENTS
AOS 04 82 VOL: 7 PG:349 - 368 :: ANOVA :LAB. :OTH.BEH. :PROB.ELIC.

JOHNSTON,DJ ; SEC: LEMON ,WM ; THIR: NEUMANN,FL CIT: 0
THE CANADIAN STUDY OF THE ROLE OF THE AUDITOR
JAA SP 80 VOL: 3 PG:251 - 263 :: QUAL. :INT. LOG. :THEORY :PROF.RESP.

JOHNSTON,K ; FIRS: GRAY ,J ; SEC: WILLINGHAM,JJ CIT: 0
A BUSINESS GAME FOR THE INTRODUCTORY COURSE IN ACCOUNTING
TAR AP 63 VOL: 38 PG:336 - 346 :: QUAL. :INT. LOG. :OTH. :EDUC.

JOLIVET,V CIT: 0
THE CURRENT FRENCH APPROACH TO INVENTORY PRICE LEVEL PROBLEMS
TAR JL 64 VOL: 39 PG:689 - 692 :: QUAL. :INT. LOG. :THEORY :VALUAT.(INFL.)

JONES ,CP ; SEC: BUBLITZ,B CIT: 0
MARKET REACTIONS TO THE INFORMATION CONTENT OF EARNINGS OVER ALTERNATIVE QUARTERS
JAA AU 90 VOL: 5 PG:549 - 566 :: REGRESS. :PRIM. :TIME SER. :INT.REP.

JONES ,CS CIT: 0
THE ATTITUDES OF OWNER-MANAGERS TOWARDS ACCOUNTING CONTROL SYSTEMS FOLLOWING MANAGEMENT BUYOUT
AOS 02 92 VOL: 17 PG:151 - 168 :: REGRESS. :SURV. :HIPS :INT.CONT.

JONES ,CS CIT: 0.13
AN EMPIRICAL STUDY OF THE ROLE OF MANAGEMENT ACCOUNTING SYSTEMS FOLLOWING TAKEOVER OR MERGER
AOS 02 85 VOL: 10 PG:177 - 200 :: REGRESS. :SURV. :THEORY :BUS.COMB.

JONES ,CS CIT: 0.13
AN EMPIRICAL STUDY OF THE EVIDENCE FOR CONTINGENCY THEORIES OF MANAGEMENT ACCOUNTING SYSTEMS IN CONDITIONS OF RAPID CHANGE
AOS 03 85 VOL: 10 PG:303 - 328 :: REGRESS. :SURV. :THEORY :BUS.COMB.

JONES ,JJ CIT: 0.5
EARNINGS MANAGEMENT DURING IMPORT RELIEF INVESTIGATIONS
JAR AU 91 VOL: 29 PG:193 - 228 :: REGRESS. :PRIM. :OTH.STAT. :FIN.METH.

JONES ,RW ; FIRS: ALY ,IM ; SEC: BARLOW,HA CIT: 0
THE USEFULNESS OF SFAS NO. 82 INFORMATION IN DISCRIMINATING BUSINESS FAILURE: AN EMPIRICAL STUDY
JAA SP 92 VOL: 7 PG:217 - 230 :: REGRESS. :PRIM. :OTH.STAT. :BUS.FAIL.

JONES ,TW ; FIRS: ROBERTS,RW ; SEC: GLEZEN,GW CIT: 0.67
DETERMINANTS OF AUDIT CHANGE IN THE PUBLIC SECTOR
JAR SP 90 VOL: 28 PG:220 - 228 :: REGRESS. :PRIM. :OTH.STAT. :ORG.

JONES ,V ; FIRS: HAKA ,S ; SEC: FRIEDMAN,L CIT: 0.29
FUNCTIONAL FIXATION AND INTERFERENCE THEORY: A THEORETICAL AND EMPIRICAL INVESTIGATION
TAR JL 86 VOL: 61 PG:455 - 474 :: REGRESS. :LAB. :HIPS :REL.COSTS

JONSON,LC ; SEC: JONSSON,B ; THIR: SVENSSON,G CIT: 0
THE APPLICATION OF SOCIAL ACCOUNTING TO ABSENTEEISM AND PERSONNEL TURNOVER
AOS 34 78 VOL: 3 PG:261 - 268 :: DES.STAT. :CASE :OTH.BEH. :METHOD.

JONSSON,B ; FIRS: JONSON,LC ; THIR: SVENSSON,G CIT: 0
THE APPLICATION OF SOCIAL ACCOUNTING TO ABSENTEEISM AND PERSONNEL TURNOVER
AOS 34 78 VOL: 3 PG:261 - 268 :: DES.STAT. :CASE :OTH.BEH. :METHOD.

JONSSON,S CIT: 0
ROLE MAKING FOR ACCOUNTING WHILE THE STATE IS WATCHING
AOS 05 91 VOL: 16 PG:521 - 546 :: REGRESS. :SEC. :HIST. :ORG.& ENVIR.

JONSSON,S ; SEC: GRONLUND,A CIT: 0
LIFE WITH A SUB-CONTRACTOR: NEW TECHNOLOGY AND MANAGEMENT ACCOUNTING
AOS 05 88 VOL: 13 PG:513 - 532 :: DES.STAT. :CASE :THEORY :MANAG.

JONSSON,S CIT: 0.45
BUDGETARY BEHAVIOR
AOS 03 82 VOL: 7 PG:287 - 304 :: QUAL. :CASE :OTH. :BUDG.& PLAN.

JONSSON,S ; FIRS: HEDBERG,B CIT: 1.93
DESIGNING SEMI-CONFUSING INFORMATION SYSTEMS FOR ORGANIZATIONS IN CHANGING ENVIRONMENTS
AOS 01 78 VOL: 3 PG:47 - 64 :: QUAL. :INT. LOG. :OTH. :N/A

JORDAN,JS CIT: 0.67
ACCOUNTING-BASED DIVISIONAL PERFORMANCE MEASUREMENT: INCENTIVES FOR PROFIT MAXIMIZATION
CAR SP 90 VOL: 6 PG:903 - 921 :: DES.STAT. :INT. LOG. :MATH.PROG. :COST.ALLOC.

JORGENSON,DW ; SEC: YUN ,K CIT: 0
THE EXCESS BURDEN OF TAXATION IN THE UNITED STATES
JAA AU 91 VOL: 6 PG:487 - 508 :: DES.STAT. :SIM. :TIME SER. :TAXES

JOSE ,ML ; FIRS: STEVENS,JL CIT: 0
THE EFFECTS OF DIVIDEND PAYOUT, STABILITY, AND SMOOTHING ON FIRM VALUE
JAA SP 92 VOL: 7 PG:195 - 212 :: REGRESS. :PRIM. :EMH :CASH DIV.

JOY ,OM ; SEC: LITZENBERGER,RH ; THIR: MCENALLY,RW CIT: 0.81
THE ADJUSTMENT OF STOCK PRICES TO ANNOUNCEMENTS OF UNANTICIPATED CHANGES IN QUARTERLY EARNINGS
JAR AU 77 VOL: 15 PG:207 - 225 :: REGRESS. :PRIM. :EMH :FIN.METH.

JOYCE ,E ; FIRS: ANDERSON,MJ ; SEC: ANDERSON,U ; THIR: HELLELOID,R ; FIFT: SCHADEWALD,M CIT: 0
INTERNAL REVENUE SERVICE ACCESS TO TAX ACCRUAL WORKPAPERS: A LABORATORY INVESTIGATION
TAR OC 90 VOL: 65 PG:857 - 874 :: REGRESS. :LAB. :MATH.PROG. :AUD.

JOYCE ,EJ ; SEC: LIBBY ,R ; THIR: SUNDER,S CIT: 0.09
USING THE FASB'S QUALITATIVE CHARACTERISTICS IN ACCOUNTING POLICY CHOICES
JAR AU 82 VOL: 20 PG:654 - 675 :: DES.STAT. :SURV. :INSTIT. :FASB SUBM.

JOYCE ,EJ ; SEC: BIDDLE,GC CIT: 1.58
ANCHORING AND ADJUSTMENT IN PROBABILISTIC INFERENCE IN AUDITING
JAR SP 81 VOL: 19 PG:120 - 145 :: ANOVA :LAB. :OTH.BEH. :DEC.AIDS

JOYCE ,EJ ; SEC: BIDDLE,GC CIT: 1.42
ARE AUDITORS' JUDGMENTS SUFFICIENTLY REGRESSIVE?
JAR AU 81 VOL: 19 PG:323 - 349 :: ANOVA :LAB. :HIPS :PLAN.

JOYCE ,EJ ; SEC: LIBBY ,R CIT: 0.33
SOME ACCOUNTING IMPLICATIONS OF BEHAVIOURAL DECISION THEORY: PROCESSES OF JUDGMENT AND CHOICE
JAR AU 81 VOL: 19 PG:544 - 550 :: QUAL. :INT. LOG. :HIPS :MANAG.

JOYCE ,EJ CIT: 2.35
EXPERT JUDGMENT IN AUDIT PROGRAM PLANNING
JAR ST 76 VOL: 14 PG:29 - 60 :: ANOVA :LAB. :HIPS :PLAN.

JUNG ,K ; FIRS: HAW ,I ; THIR: LILIEN,SB CIT: 0
OVERFUNDED DEFINED BENEFIT PENSION PLAN SETTLEMENTS WITHOUT ASSET REVERSIONS
JAE SE 91 VOL: 14 PG:295 - 320 :: REGRESS. :PRIM. :TIME SER. :PENS.

JUNG ,W ; FIRS: BECK ,PJ ; SEC: DAVIS ,JS CIT: 0.5
EXPERIMENTAL EVIDENCE ON TAXPAYER REPORTING UNDER UNCERTAINTY
TAR JL 91 VOL: 66 PG:535 - 558 :: REGRESS. :LAB. :INF.ECO./AG. :TAX PLNG.

JUNG ,W ; FIRS: BECK ,PJ CIT: 0.5
TAXPAYERS' REPORTING DECISIONS AND AUDITING UNDER INFORMATION ASYMMETRY
TAR JL 89 VOL: 64 PG:468 - 487 :: REGRESS. :INT. LOG. :INF.ECO./AG. :TAXES

JUNG ,WO ; FIRS: BECK ,PJ ; SEC: DAVIS ,JS CIT: 0
EXPERIMENTAL EVIDENCE ON AN ECONOMIC MODEL OF TAXPAYER AGGRESSION UNDER STRATEGIC AND NON-STRATEGIC AUDITS
CAR AU 92 VOL: 9 PG:86 - 112 :: REGRESS. :LAB. :OTH.BEH. :TAXES

JUNG ,WO CIT: 0
STRATEGIC CHOICE OF INVENTORY ACCOUNTING MODELS
CAR AU 89 VOL: 6 PG:1 - 25 :: DES.STAT. :INT. LOG. :MATH.PROG. :INV.

JUNG ,WO ; SEC: KWON ,YK CIT: 0.6
DISCLOSURE WHEN THE MARKET IS UNSURE OF INFORMATION ENDOWMENT OF MANAGERS
JAR SP 88 VOL: 26 PG:146 - 153 :: DES.STAT. :INT. LOG. :INF.ECO./AG. :INFO.STRUC.

JURIS ,HA ; FIRS: DITTMAN,DA ; THIR: REVSINE,L CIT: 0.29
ON THE EXISTENCE OF UNRECORDED HUMAN ASSETS: AN ECONOMIC PERSPECTIVE
JAR SP 76 VOL: 14 PG:49 - 65 :: ANAL. :INT. LOG. :OTH.BEH. :HRA

KABBES,SM CIT: 0
IS ACCOUNTING MEETING THE CHALLENGE IN EUROPE?
TAR AP 65 VOL: 40 PG:395 - 400 :: QUAL. :INT. LOG. :INSTIT. :FIN.METH.

KACHELMEIER,SJ CIT: 0
A LABORATORY MARKET INVESTIGATION OF THE DEMAND FOR STRATEGIC AUDITING
AUD 91 VOL: 10 PG:25 - 48 :: REGRESS. :LAB. :INF.ECO./AG. :AUD.BEH.

KACHELMEIER,SJ ; SEC: LIMBERG,ST ; THIR: SCHADEWALD,MS CIT: 0
A LABORATORY MARKET EXAMINATION OF THE CONSUMER PRICE RESPONSE TO INFORMATION ABOUT PRODUCERS' COSTS AND PROFITS
TAR OC 91 VOL: 66 PG:694 - 717 :: REGRESS. :LAB. :HIPS :N/A

KACHELMEIER,SJ ; SEC: MESSIER JR,WF CIT: 0.67
AN INVESTIGATION OF THE INFLUENCE OF A NONSTATISTICAL DECISION AID ON AUDITOR SAMPLE SIZE DECISIONS
TAR JA 90 VOL: 65 PG:209 - 226 :: REGRESS. :LAB. :HIPS :DEC.AIDS

KACZKA,E ; FIRS: MORRISON,TA CIT: 0.06
A NEW APPLICATION OF CALCULUS AND RISK ANALYSIS TO COST-VOLUME-PROFIT CHANGES
TAR AP 69 VOL: 44 PG:330 - 343 :: ANAL. :INT. LOG. :OTH.STAT. :C-V-P-A

KAHN ,N ; FIRS: BILDERSEE,JS CIT: 0
A PRELIMINARY TEST OF THE PRESENCE OF WINDOW DRESSING: EVIDENCE FROMINSTITUTIONAL STOCK TRADING
JAA SU 87 VOL: 2 PG:239 - 256 :: REGRESS. :PRIM. :OTH.STAT. :INFO.STRUC.

KAHN ,N ; SEC: SCHIFF,A CIT: 0
TANGIBLE EQUITY CHANGE AND THE EVOLUTION OF THE FASB'S DEFINITION OF INCOME
JAA AU 85 VOL: 9 PG:40 - 49 :: REGRESS. :INT. LOG. :THEORY :REV.REC.

KAHN ,N ; FIRS: DAVIS ,HZ ; THIR: ROZEN ,E CIT: 0
LIFO INVENTORY LIQUIDATIONS: AN EMPIRICAL STUDY
JAR AU 84 VOL: 22 PG:480 - 490 :: NON-PAR. :PRIM. :OTH.STAT. :INV.

KAHN ,N CIT: 0
CORPORATE MOTIVATION FOR CONVERTIBLE BOND DEBT EXCHANGES
JAA SU 82 VOL: 5 PG:327 - 337 :: DES.STAT. :PRIM. :OTH.STAT. :LTD

KAHN ,N ; FIRS: DAVIS ,HZ CIT: 0
SOME ADDITIONAL EVIDENCE ON THE LIFO-FIFO CHOICE USING REPLACEMENT COST DATA
JAR AU 82 VOL: 20 PG:738 - 744 :: NON-PAR. :PRIM. :OTH.STAT. :INV.

KALINSKI,BD CIT: 0
A CASE OF OVER-ACCOUNTING
TAR JL 63 VOL: 38 PG:591 - 595 :: QUAL. :INT. LOG. :INSTIT. :OTH.MANAG.

KAMIN ,JY ; SEC: RONEN ,J CIT: 0.2
THE SMOOTHING OF INCOME NUMBERS: SOME EMPIRICAL EVIDENCE OF SYSTEMATIC DIFFERENCES AMONG MANAGEMENT AND OWNER-CONTROLLED FIRMS
AOS 02 78 VOL: 3 PG:141 - 160 :: ANOVA :PRIM. :OTH.STAT. :N/A

KANG ,SH ; FIRS: HEALY ,PM ; THIR: PALEPU,KG CIT: 1.5
THE EFFECT OF ACCOUNTING PROCEDURE CHANGES ON CEOS' CASH SALARY AND BONUS COMPENSATION
JAE AP 87 VOL: 9 PG:7 - 34 :: REGRESS. :PRIM. :OTH.STAT. :INV.

KANODIA,C ; SEC: BUSHMAN,R ; THIR: DICKHAUT,J CIT: 1
ESCALATION ERRORS AND THE SUNK COST EFFECT: AN EXPLANATION BASED ON REPUTATION AND INFORMATION ASYMMETRIES
JAR SP 89 VOL: 27 PG:59 - 77 :: DES.STAT. :INT. LOG. :INF.ECO./AG. :EXEC.COMP.

KANODIA,CS CIT: 0.25
STOCHASTIC MONITORING AND MORAL HAZARD
JAR SP 85 VOL: 23 PG:175 - 193 :: ANAL. :INT. LOG. :INF.ECO./AG. :MANAG.

KANODIA,CS CIT: 0.29
RISK SHARING AND TRANSFER PRICE SYSTEMS UNDER UNCERTAINTY
JAR SP 79 VOL: 17 PG:74 - 98 :: ANAL. :INT. LOG. :MATH.PROG. :BUDG.& PLAN.

KAPLAN,HG ; SEC: SOLOMON,KI CIT: 0
REGULATION OF THE ACCOUNTING PROFESSION IN ISRAEL
TAR JA 64 VOL: 39 PG:145 - 149 :: QUAL. :INT. LOG. :INSTIT. :OTH.MANAG.

KAPLAN,RS ; FIRS: BANKER,RD ; SEC: DATAR ,SM CIT: 0
PRODUCTIVITY MEASUREMENT AND MANAGEMENT ACCOUNTING
JAA AU 89 VOL: 4 PG:528 - 554 :: DES.STAT. :CASE :OTH.STAT. :REL.COSTS

KAPLAN,RS CIT: 0.86
THE ROLE FOR EMPIRICAL RESEARCH IN MANAGEMENT ACCOUNTING
AOS 45 86 VOL: 11 PG:429 - 452 :: REGRESS. :INT. LOG. :THEORY :METHOD.

KAPLAN,RS CIT: 3
THE EVOLUTION OF MANAGEMENT ACCOUNTING
TAR JL 84 VOL: 59 PG:390 - 418 :: QUAL. :INT. LOG. :THEORY :MANAG.

KAPLAN,RS CIT: 0
A FINANCIAL PLANNING MODEL FOR AN ANALYTIC REVIEW: THE CASE OF A SAVINGS AND LOAN ASSOCIATION
AUD SP 83 VOL: 2 PG:52 - 65 :: REGRESS. :CASE :OTH.STAT. :ANAL.REV.

KAPLAN,RS CIT: 2.3
MEASURING MANUFACTURING PERFORMANCE: A NEW CHALLENGE FOR MANAGERIAL ACCOUNTING RESEARCH
TAR OC 83 VOL: 58 PG:686 - 705 :: QUAL. :INT. LOG. :THEORY :METHOD.

KAPLAN,RS ; FIRS: DIETRICH,JR CIT: 0.55
EMPIRICAL ANALYSIS OF THE COMMERCIAL LOAN CLASSIFICATION DECISION
TAR JA 82 VOL: 57 PG:18 - 38 :: REGRESS. :PRIM. :OTH.STAT. :BUS.FAIL.

KAPLAN,RS ; FIRS: HONG ,H ; THIR: MANDELKER,G CIT: 0.93
POOLING VS. PURCHASE: THE EFFECTS OF ACCOUNTING FOR MERGERS ON STOCK PRICES
TAR JA 78 VOL: 53 PG:31 - 47 :: MIXED :PRIM. :EMH :BUS.COMB.

KAPLAN,RS CIT: 0.25
PURCHASING POWER GAINS ON DEBT: THE EFFECT OF EXPECTED AND UNEXPECTED INFLATION
TAR AP 77 VOL: 52 PG:369 - 378 :: ANAL. :INT. LOG. :THEORY :VALUAT.(INFL.)

KAPLAN,RS CIT: 0.53
SAMPLE SIZE COMPUTATIONS FOR DOLLAR-UNIT SAMPLING
JAR ST 75 VOL: 13 PG:126 - 133 :: ANAL. :INT. LOG. :OTH.STAT. :SAMP.

KAPLAN,RS ; SEC: WELAM ,VP CIT: 0.47
OVERHEAD ALLOCATION WITH IMPERFECT MARKETS AND NONLINEAR TECHNOLOGY
TAR JL 74 VOL: 49 PG:477 - 484 :: ANAL. :INT. LOG. :MATH.PROG. :OVER.ALLOC.

KAPLAN,RS CIT: 0.65
A STOCHASTIC MODEL FOR AUDITING
JAR SP 73 VOL: 11 PG:38 - 46 :: ANAL. :INT. LOG. :OTH.STAT. :SAMP.

KAPLAN,RS CIT: 1.29
STATISTICAL SAMPLING IN AUDITING WITH AUXILIARY INFORMATION ESTIMATORS
JAR AU 73 VOL: 11 PG:238 - 258 :: NON-PAR. :SIM. :OTH.STAT. :SAMP.

KAPLAN,RS CIT: 0.29
VARIABLE AND SELF-SERVICE COSTS IN RECIPROCAL ALLOCATION MODELS
TAR OC 73 VOL: 48 PG:738 - 748 :: ANAL. :INT. LOG. :MATH.PROG. :COST.ALLOC.

KAPLAN,RS ; FIRS: IJIRI ,Y CIT: 0.29
A MODEL FOR INTEGRATING SAMPLING OBJECTIVES IN AUDITING
JAR SP 71 VOL: 9 PG:73 - 87 :: CORR. :INT. LOG. :OTH. :SAMP.

KAPLAN,RS ; SEC: THOMPSON,GL CIT: 0.47
OVERHEAD ALLOCATION VIA MATHEMATICAL PROGRAMMING MODELS
TAR AP 71 VOL: 46 PG:352 - 364 :: ANAL. :INT. LOG. :MATH.PROG. :OVER.ALLOC.

KAPLAN,RS ; FIRS: IJIRI ,Y CIT: 0.06
SEQUENTIAL MODELS IN PROBABILISTIC DEPRECIATION
JAR SP 70 VOL: 8 PG:34 - 46 :: ANAL. :INT. LOG. :OTH.STAT. :PP&E / DEPR

KAPLAN,RS CIT: 0.59
OPTIMAL INVESTIGATION STRATEGIES WITH IMPERFECT INFORMATION
JAR SP 69 VOL: 7 PG:32 - 43 :: ANAL. :INT. LOG. :MATH.PROG. :VAR.

KAPLAN,RS ; FIRS: IJIRI ,Y CIT: 0.24
PROBABILISTIC DEPRECIATION AND ITS IMPLICATIONS FOR GROUP DEPRECIATION
TAR OC 69 VOL: 44 PG:743 - 756 :: ANAL. :INT. LOG. :OTH.STAT. :PP&E / DEPR

KAPLAN,SE ; FIRS: ANDERSON,JC ; THIR: RECKERS,PMJ CIT: 0
THE EFFECTS OF OUTPUT INTERFERENCE ON ANALYTICAL PROCEDURES JUDGMENTS
AUD AU 92 VOL: 11 PG:1 - 13 :: REGRESS. :LAB. :HIPS :ANAL.REV.

KAPLAN,SE ; SEC: MOECKEL,C ; THIR: WILLIAMS,JD CIT: 0
AUDITORS' HYPOTHESIS PLAUSIBILITY ASSESSMENTS IN AN ANALYTICAL REVIEW SETTING
AUD AU 92 VOL: 11 PG:50 - 65 :: REGRESS. :LAB. :HIPS :ANAL.REV.

KAPLAN,SE ; FIRS: JOHNSON,VE CIT: 0
EXPERIMENTAL EVIDENCE ON THE EFFECTS OF ACCOUNTABILITY ON AUDITOR JUDGMENTS
AUD 91 VOL: 10 PG:96 - 107 :: REGRESS. :LAB. :HIPS :JUDG.

KAPLAN,SE ; SEC: RECKERS,PMJ CIT: 0
AN EXAMINATION OF INFORMATION SEARCH DURING INITIAL AUDIT PLANNING
AOS 06 89 VOL: 14 PG:539 - 550 :: REGRESS. :LAB. :HIPS :PLAN.

KAPLAN,SE ; SEC: RECKERS,PMJ ; THIR: ROARK ,SJ CIT: 0
AN ATTRIBUTION THEORY ANALYSIS OF TAX EVASION RELATED JUDGMENTS
AOS 04 88 VOL: 13 PG:371 - 379 :: REGRESS. :LAB. :OTH.BEH. :TAXES

KAPLAN,SE CIT: 0.13
AN EXAMINATION OF THE EFFECTS OF ENVIRONMENT AND EXPLICIT INTERNAL CONTROL EVALUATION ON PLANNED AUDIT HOURS
AUD AU 85 VOL: 5 PG:12 - 25 :: REGRESS. :LAB. :OTH.STAT. :PLAN.

KAPLAN,SE CIT: 0.13
THE EFFECT OF COMBINING COMPLIANCE AND SUBSTANTIVE TASKS ON AUDITOR CONSENSUS
JAR AU 85 VOL: 23 PG:871 - 877 :: REGRESS. :LAB. :HIPS :INT.CONT.

KAPLAN,SE ; SEC: RECKERS,PMJ CIT: 0.78
AN EMPIRICAL EXAMINATION OF AUDITORS' INITIAL PLANNING PROCESSES
AUD AU 84 VOL: 4 PG:1 - 19 :: ANOVA :LAB. :OTH.BEH. :PLAN.

KARAN ,V ; FIRS: BROWN ,PR CIT: 0.43
ONE APPROACH FOR ASSESSING THE OPERATIONAL NATURE OF AUDITING STANDARDS: AN ANALYSIS OF SAS NO. 9
AUD AU 86 VOL: 6 PG:134 - 147 :: ANOVA :LAB. :INSTIT. :INT.AUD.

KARLINSKY,SS CIT: 0
NEW TAX LAWS IMPACT ON CORPORATE FINANCIAL REPORTING
JAA AU 83 VOL: 7 PG:65 - 76 :: QUAL. :INT. LOG. :THEORY :TAXES

KARLINSKY,SS CIT: 0
CAPITAL GAINS PROVISIONS: CHANGED BY THE TAX ACT OF 1981, BUT NO LESS COMPLEX
JAA WI 83 VOL: 6 PG:157 - 167 :: QUAL. :INT. LOG. :THEORY :TAXES

KATZ ,BG ; SEC: OWEN ,J CIT: 0
INITIAL PUBLIC OFFERINGS: AN EQUILIBRIUM MODEL OF PRICE DETERMINATION
JAA SU 87 VOL: 2 PG:266 - 298 :: DES.STAT. :INT. LOG. :THEORY :SPEC.ITEMS

KATZ ,JL ; FIRS: BERRY ,LE ; SEC: HARWOOD,GB CIT: 0.17
PERFORMANCE OF AUDITING PROCEDURES BY GOVERNMENTAL AUDITORS: SOME PRELIMINARY EVIDENCE
TAR JA 87 VOL: 62 PG:14 - 28 :: DES.STAT. :SURV. :OTH.STAT. :AUD.

KAUFMAN,F CIT: 0
PROFESSIONAL CONSULTING BY CPA'S
TAR OC 67 VOL: 42 PG:713 - 720 :: QUAL. :INT. LOG. :INSTIT. :OTH.MANAG.

KAY ,RS CIT: 0
THE COHEN COMMISSION REPORT: SOME COMPLIMENTS, SOME CRITICISMS
JAA SU 79 VOL: 2 PG:307 - 315 :: QUAL. :INT. LOG. :INSTIT. :AUD.

KEASEY,K ; SEC: WATSON,R CIT: 0.25
CONSENSUS AND ACCURACY IN ACCOUNTING STUDIES OF DECISION-MAKING: A NOTE ON A NEW MEASURE OF CONSENSUS
AOS 04 89 VOL: 14 PG:337 - 345 :: REGRESS. :LAB. :HIPS :AUD.BEH.

KEE ,R ; FIRS: BUBLITZ,B CIT: 0
DO WE NEED SUNSET REQUIREMENTS FOR FASB PRONOUNCEMENTS?
JAA WI 84 VOL: 7 PG:123 - 137 :: QUAL. :INT. LOG. :INSTIT. :FASB SUBM.

KEISTER JR,OR CIT: 0
THE INCAN QUIPU
TAR AP 64 VOL: 39 PG:414 - 416 :: QUAL. :INT. LOG. :HIST. :FIN.METH.

KEISTER JR,OR CIT: 0.06
COMMERCIAL RECORD-KEEPING IN ANCIENT MESOPOTAMIA
TAR AP 63 VOL: 38 PG:371 - 376 :: QUAL. :INT. LOG. :HIST. :OTH.MANAG.

KEKRE ,S ; FIRS: BANKER,RD ; SEC: DATAR ,SM CIT: 0
RELEVANT COSTS, CONGESTION AND STOCHASTICITY IN PRODUCTION ENVIRONMENTS
JAE JL 88 VOL: 10 PG:171 - 197 :: DES.STAT. :INT. LOG. :OTH.STAT. :REL.COSTS

KELL ,WG CIT: 0
PUBLIC ACCOUNTING'S IRRESISTIBLE FORCE AND IMMOVABLE OBJECT
TAR AP 68 VOL: 43 PG:266 - 273 :: QUAL. :INT. LOG. :INSTIT. :INDEP.

KELLER,SB ; SEC: DAVIDSON,LF CIT: 1.1
AN ASSESSMENT OF INDIVIDUAL INVESTOR REACTION TO CERTAIN QUALIFIED AUDIT OPINIONS
AUD AU 83 VOL: 3 PG:1 - 22 :: ANOVA :PRIM. :EMH :OPIN.

KELLER,TF ; FIRS: COOPER,WW ; SEC: DOPUCH,N CIT: 0.06
BUDGETARY DISCLOSURE AND OTHER SUGGESTIONS FOR IMPROVING ACCOUNTING REPORTS
TAR OC 68 VOL: 43 PG:640 - 648 :: QUAL. :INT. LOG. :THEORY :FIN.METH.

KELLER,TF CIT: 0
THE INVESTMENT TAX CREDIT AND THE ANNUAL TAX CHARGE
TAR JA 65 VOL: 40 PG:184 - 189 :: QUAL. :INT. LOG. :THEORY :TAXES

KELLEY,EM ; FIRS: FITZGERALD,RD CIT: 0
INTERNATIONAL DISCLOSURE STANDARDS - THE UNITED NATIONS POSITION
JAA AU 79 VOL: 3 PG:5 - 20 :: QUAL. :INT. LOG. :INSTIT. :INT.DIFF.

KELLOGG,RL CIT: 0.89
ACCOUNTING ACTIVITIES, SECURITY PRICES, AND CLASS ACTION LAWSUITS
JAE DE 84 VOL: 6 PG:185 - 204 :: REGRESS. :PRIM. :EMH :LITIG.

KELLY ,AS ; SEC: MOHRWEIS,CS CIT: 0
BANKERS' AND INVESTORS' PERCEPTIONS OF THE AUDITOR'S ROLE IN FINANCIAL STATEMENT REPORTING: THE IMPACT OF SAS NO. 58
AUD AU 89 VOL: 9 PG:87 - 97 :: REGRESS. :LAB. :HIPS :FASB SUBM.

KELLY ,EC ; FIRS: IJIRI ,Y CIT: 0
MULTIDIMENSIONAL ACCOUNTING AND DISTRIBUTED DATABASES: THEIR IMPLICATIONS FOR ORGANIZATIONS AND SOCIETY
AOS 01 80 VOL: 5 PG:115 - 123 :: QUAL. :INT. LOG. :THEORY :INFO.STRUC.

KELLY ,LK CIT: 0.08
A SOCIOLOGICAL INVESTIGATION OF THE U.S.A. MANDATE FOR REPLACEMENT COST DISCLOSURES
AOS 03 80 VOL: 5 PG:311 - 322 :: OTH.QUANT. :PRIM. :OTH.STAT. :VALUAT.(INFL.)

KELLY ,LK CIT: 0.13
THE RISK FACTOR IN MATERIALITY DECISIONS
TAR JA 77 VOL: 52 PG:97 - 108 :: DES.STAT. :LAB. :THEORY :MAT.

KELLY ,R CIT: 0.38
CORPORATE MANAGEMENT LOBBYING ON FAS NO. 8: SOME FURTHER EVIDENCE
JAR AU 85 VOL: 23 PG:619 - 632 :: REGRESS. :PRIM. :THEORY :FASB SUBM.

KELLY ,T ; SEC: MARGHEIM,L CIT: 0.67
THE IMPACT OF TIME BUDGET PRESSURE, PERSONALITY, AND LEADERSHIP VARIABLES ON DYSFUNCTIONAL AUDIT BEHAVIOR
AUD SP 90 VOL: 9 PG:21 - 42 :: REGRESS. :SURV. :HIPS :AUD.BEH.

KELSEY,RL ; FIRS: RHODE ,JG ; SEC: WHITSELL,GM CIT: 0.29
AN ANALYSIS OF CLIENT-INDUSTRY CONCENTRATIONS FOR LARGE PUBLIC ACCOUNTING FIRMS
TAR OC 74 VOL: 49 PG:772 - 787 :: DES.STAT. :PRIM. :INSTIT. :AUD.

KEMP ,PS CIT: 0.06
THE AUTHORITY OF THE ACCOUNTING PRINCIPLES BOARD
TAR OC 65 VOL: 40 PG:782 - 787 :: QUAL. :INT. LOG. :INSTIT. :FIN.METH.

KEMP ,PS CIT: 0
CONTROVERSIES ON THE CONSTRUCTION OF FINANCIAL STATEMENTS
TAR JA 63 VOL: 38 PG:126 - 132 :: QUAL. :INT. LOG. :THEORY :N/A

KEMPER,EL ; FIRS: THOMPSON,WW CIT: 0
PROBABILITY MEASURES FOR ESTIMATED DATA
TAR JL 65 VOL: 40 PG:574 - 578 :: ANAL. :INT. LOG. :N/A :PROB.ELIC.

KENIS ,I CIT: 1.93
EFFECTS OF BUDGETARY GOAL CHARACTERISTICS ON MANAGERIAL ATTITUDES AND PERFORMANCE
TAR OC 79 VOL: 54 PG:707 - 721 :: CORR. :SURV. :OTH.BEH. :BUDG.& PLAN.

KENNEDY,D ; SEC: LAKONISHOK,J ; THIR: SHAW ,WH CIT: 0
ACCOMODATING OUTLIERS AND NONLINEARITY IN DECISION MODELS
JAA SP 92 VOL: 7 PG:161 - 190 :: REGRESS. :PRIM. :OTH.STAT. :METHOD.

KENNEDY,DB CIT: 0
CLASSIFICATION TECHNIQUES IN ACCOUNTING RESEARCH: EMPIRICAL EVIDENCE OF COMPARATIVE PERFORMANCE
CAR SP 92 VOL: 8 PG:419 - 442 :: DES.STAT. :SIM. :OTH.STAT. :METHOD.

KENNEDY,DT ; SEC: HYON ,YH CIT: 0
DO RRA EARNINGS IMPROVE THE USEFULNESS OF REPORTED EARNINGS IN REFLECTING THE PERFORMANCE OF OIL AND GAS PRODUCING FIRMS?
JAA SU 92 VOL: 7 PG:335 - 356 :: REGRESS. :PRIM. :OTH.STAT. :OIL & GAS

KENNEDY,HA CIT: 0.59
A BEHAVIOURAL STUDY OF THE USEFULNESS OF FOUR FINANCIAL RATIOS
JAR SP 75 VOL: 13 PG:97 - 116 :: DES.STAT. :LAB. :HIPS :BUS.FAIL.

KENNELLEY,M ; FIRS: SCHAEFER,T CIT: 0
ALTERNATIVE CASH FLOW MEASURES AND RISK-ADJUSTED RETURNS
JAA AU 86 VOL: 1 PG:278 - 287 :: REGRESS. :PRIM. :EMH :SPEC.ITEMS

KENNELLEY,MD ; FIRS: CHRISTIE,AA ; THIR: KING ,JW ; FOUR: SCHAEFER,TF CIT: 1
TESTING FOR INCREMENTAL INFORMATION CONTENT IN THE PRESENCE OF COLLINEARITY
JAE DE 84 VOL: 6 PG:205 - 217 :: ANAL. :INT. LOG. :OTH.STAT. :METHOD.

KENNELLY,JW ; FIRS: BEAVER,WH ; THIR: VOSS ,WM CIT: 0.94
PREDICTIVE ABILITY AS A CRITERION FOR THE EVALUATION OF ACCOUNTING DATA
TAR OC 68 VOL: 43 PG:675 - 683 :: QUAL. :INT. LOG. :THEORY :FIN.METH.

KENNELLY,JW ; FIRS: BALOFF,N CIT: 0.18
ACCOUNTING IMPLICATIONS OF PRODUCT AND PROCESS START-UPS
JAR AU 67 VOL: 5 PG:131 - 143 :: REGRESS. :CASE :TIME SER. :COST.ALLOC.

KEOWN ,AJ ; FIRS: MARTIN,JD ; SEC: ANDERSON,PF CIT: 0
LEASE CAPITALIZATION AND STOCK PRICE STABILITY: IMPLICATIONS FOR ACCOUNTING
JAA WI 79 VOL: 2 PG:151 - 164 :: REGRESS. :PRIM. :EMH :LEASES

KESSLER,L ; SEC: ASHTON,RH CIT: 0.42
FEEDBACK AND PREDICTION ACHIEVEMENT IN FINANCIAL ANALYSIS
JAR SP 81 VOL: 19 PG:146 - 162 :: ANOVA :LAB. :HIPS :BUDG.& PLAN.

KETTLER,P ; FIRS: BEAVER,WH ; THIR: SCHOLES,M CIT: 1.82
THE ASSOCIATION BETWEEN MARKET DETERMINED AND ACCOUNTING DETERMINED RISK MEASURES
TAR OC 70 VOL: 45 PG:654 - 682 :: REGRESS. :PRIM. :TIME SER. :FIN.METH.

KETZ ,JE ; FIRS: CHARITOU,A CIT: 0
VALUATION OF EARNINGS, CASH FLOWS, AND THEIR COMPONENTS: AN EMPIRICAL INVESTIGATION
JAA AU 90 VOL: 5 PG:475 - 497 :: REGRESS. :PRIM. :EMH :VALUAT.(INFL.)

KETZ ,JE ; SEC: WYATT ,AR CIT: 0
THE FASB IN A WORLD WITH PARTIALLY EFFICIENT MARKETS
JAA AU 83 VOL: 7 PG:29 - 43 :: QUAL. :INT. LOG. :EMH :OTH.MANAG.

KETZ ,JE ; FIRS: GOMBOLA,MJ CIT: 0.1
A NOTE ON CASH FLOW AND CLASSIFICATION PATTERNS OF FINANCIAL RATIOS
TAR JA 83 VOL: 58 PG:105 - 114 :: OTH.QUANT. :LAB. :OTH.STAT. :SPEC.ITEMS

KETZ ,JE ; FIRS: HUSSEIN,ME CIT: 0.23
RULING ELITES OF THE FASB: A STUDY OF THE BIG EIGHT
JAA SU 80 VOL: 3 PG:354 - 367 :: DES.STAT. :SEC. :OTH.STAT. :FASB SUBM.

KETZ ,JE CIT: 0.2
THE EFFECT OF GENERAL PRICE-LEVEL ADJUSTMENTS ON THE PREDICTIVE ABILITY OF FINANCIAL RATIOS
JAR ST 78 VOL: 16 PG:273 - 284 :: OTH.QUANT. :PRIM. :EMH :VALUAT.(INFL.)

KETZ ,JE CIT: 0.4
THE VALIDATION OF SOME GENERAL PRICE LEVEL ESTIMATING MODELS
TAR OC 78 VOL: 53 PG:952 - 960 :: ANAL. :SEC. :OTH.STAT. :VALUAT.(INFL.)

KEYS ,DE CIT: 0.27
CONFIDENCE INTERVAL FINANCIAL STATEMENTS: AN EMPIRICAL INVESTIGATION
JAR AU 78 VOL: 16 PG:389 - 399 :: ANOVA :LAB. :OTH.STAT. :PROB.ELIC.

KHANDWALLA,PN CIT: 1.12
THE EFFECT OF DIFFERENT TYPES OF COMPETITION ON THE USE OF MANAGEMENT CONTROLS
JAR AU 72 VOL: 10 PG:275 - 285 :: CORR. :SURV. :OTH. :MANAG.

KHEMAKHEM,A CIT: 0
A SIMULATION OF MANAGEMENT-DECISION BEHAVIOR: FUNDS AND INCOME
TAR JL 68 VOL: 43 PG:522 - 534 :: ANOVA :LAB. :N/A :FIN.METH.

KHOUJA,M ; FIRS: MEHREZ,A ; SEC: BROWN ,JR CIT: 1
AGGREGATE EFFICIENCY MEASURES AND SIMPSON'S PARADOX
CAR AU 92 VOL: 9 PG:329 - 342 :: DES.STAT. :INT. LOG. :MATH.PROG. :MANAG.

KHOURY,SJ CIT: 0
THE NATURE OF INTEREST SWAPS AND THE PRICING OF THEIR RISKS
JAA SU 90 VOL: 5 PG:459 - 473 :: DES.STAT. :INT. LOG. :OTH.STAT. :MANAG.

KHURANA,I CIT: 0
SECURITY MARKET EFFECTS ASSOCIATED WITH SFAS NO. 94 CONCERNING CONSOLIDATION POLICY
TAR JL 91 VOL: 66 PG:611 - 621 :: REGRESS. :INT. LOG. :TIME SER. :BUS.COMB.

KHURANA,IK ; FIRS: LOUDDER,ML ; THIR: SAWYERS,RB ; FOUR: CORDERY,C ; FIFT: JOHNSON,C ; SIX: LOWE ,J CIT: 0
THE INFORMATION CONTENT OF AUDIT QUALIFICATIONS
AUD SP 92 VOL: 11 PG:69 - 82 :: REGRESS. :PRIM. :OTH.STAT. :OPIN.

KIDA ,T ; FIRS: COHEN ,J CIT: 0.5
THE IMPACT OF ANALYTICAL REVIEW RESULTS, INTERNAL CONTROL RELIABILITY, AND EXPERIENCE ON AUDITORS' USE OF ANALYTICAL REVIEW
JAR AU 89 VOL: 27 PG:263 - 276 :: REGRESS. :LAB. :HIPS :ANAL.REV.

KIDA ,TE CIT: 0.22
PERFORMANCE EVALUATION AND REVIEW MEETING CHARACTERISTICS IN PUBLIC ACCOUNTING FIRMS
AOS 02 84 VOL: 9 PG:137 - 147 :: NON-PAR. :SURV. :HIPS :AUD.BEH.

KIDA ,TE CIT: 0.22
THE EFFECT OF CAUSALITY AND SPECIFICITY ON DATA USE
JAR SP 84 VOL: 22 PG:145 - 152 :: ANOVA :LAB. :HIPS :BUS.FAIL.

KIDA ,TE CIT: 0.78
THE IMPACT OF HYPOTHESIS-TESTING STRATEGIES ON AUDITORS' USE OF JUDGMENT DATA
JAR SP 84 VOL: 22 PG:332 - 340 :: ANOVA :LAB. :HIPS :JUDG.

KIDA ,TE ; FIRS: ANDERSON JR,TN CIT: 0
THE CROSS-LAGGED RESEARCH APPROACH: DESCRIPTION AND ILLUSTRATION
JAR AU 82 VOL: 20 PG:403 - 414 :: CORR. :LAB. :OTH.BEH. :MAN.DEC.CHAR.

KIDA ,TE CIT: 0.69
AN INVESTIGATION INTO AUDITORS' CONTINUITY AND RELATED QUALIFICATION JUDGMENTS
JAR AU 80 VOL: 18 PG:506 - 523 :: NON-PAR. :LAB. :OTH.BEH. :OPIN.

KIGER ,JE ; FIRS: SCHEINER,JH CIT: 0.09
AN EMPIRICAL INVESTIGATION OF AUDITOR INVOLVEMENT IN NON-AUDIT SERVICES
JAR AU 82 VOL: 20 PG:482 - 496 :: DES.STAT. :PRIM. :HIPS :PROF.RESP.

KIGER ,JE CIT: 0.12
VOLATILITY IN QUARTERLY ACCOUNTING DATA
TAR JA 74 VOL: 49 PG:1 - 7 :: DES.STAT. :PRIM. :TIME SER. :INT.REP.

KIGER ,JE CIT: 0.41
AN EMPIRICAL INVESTIGATION OF NYSE VOLUME AND PRICE REACTIONS TO THE ANNOUNCEMENT OF QUARTERLY EARNINGS
JAR SP 72 VOL: 10 PG:113 - 128 :: NON-PAR. :PRIM. :EMH :INT.REP.

KILLOUGH,LN ; FIRS: COLLINS,KM CIT: 0
AN EMPIRICAL EXAMINATION OF STRESS IN PUBLIC ACCOUNTING
AOS 06 92 VOL: 17 PG:535 - 547 :: REGRESS. :LAB. :OTH.BEH. :ORG.

KILLOUGH,LN ; SEC: SOUDERS,TL CIT: 0.24
A GOAL PROGRAMMING MODEL FOR PUBLIC ACCOUNTING FIRMS
TAR AP 73 VOL: 48 PG:268 - 279 :: ANAL. :INT. LOG. :MATH.PROG. :ORG.

KILMANN,RH CIT: 0.2
THE COSTS OF ORGANIZATION STRUCTURE: DISPELLING THE MYTHS OF INDEPENDENT DIVISIONS AND ORGANIZATION-WIDE DECISION MAKING
AOS 04 83 VOL: 8 PG:341 - 360 :: QUAL. :INT. LOG. :THEORY :ORG.FORM

KIM ,DC CIT: 0
RISK PREFERENCES IN PATICIPATIVE BUDGETING
TAR AP 92 VOL: 67 PG:303 - 319 :: REGRESS. :LAB. :HIPS :BUDG.& PLAN.

KIM ,DH ; SEC: ZIEBART,DA CIT: 0
AN INVESTIGATION OF THE PRICE AND TRADING REACTIONS TO THE ISSUANCE OF SFAS NO. 52
JAA WI 91 VOL: 6 PG:35 - 47 :: REGRESS. :PRIM. :EMH :FOR.CUR.

KIM ,DH ; FIRS: ZIEBART,DA CIT: 0.17
AN EXAMINATION OF THE MARKET REACTIONS ASSOCIATED WITH SFAS NO. 8 AND SFAS NO. 52
TAR AP 87 VOL: 62 PG:343 - 357 :: REGRESS. :PRIM. :EMH :FOR.CUR.

KIM ,HS ; SEC: NETER ,J ; THIR: GODFREY,JT CIT: 0.17
BEHAVIOR OF STATISTICAL ESTIMATORS IN MULTILOCATION AUDIT SAMPLING
AUD SP 87 VOL: 6 PG:40 - 58 :: DES.STAT. :SIM. :OTH.STAT. :SAMP.

KIM ,HS ; FIRS: NETER ,J ; THIR: GRAHAM,LE CIT: 0.11
ON COMBINING STRINGER BOUNDS FOR INDEPENDENT MONETARY UNIT SAMPLES FROM SEVERAL POPULATIONS
AUD AU 84 VOL: 4 PG:75 - 88 :: ANAL. :INT. LOG. :OTH.STAT. :SAMP.

KIM ,JA ; FIRS: DEJONG,DV ; SEC: FORSYTHE,R ; FOUR: UECKER,WC CIT: 0.25
A LABORATORY INVESTIGATION OF ALTERNATIVE TRANSFER PRICING MECHANISMS
AOS 02 89 VOL: 14 PG:41 - 64 :: REGRESS. :LAB. :OTH.BEH. :TRANS.PRIC.

KIM ,KK CIT: 0.4
ORGANIZATIONAL COORDINATION AND PERFORMANCE IN HOSPITAL ACCOUNTING INFORMATION SYSTEMS: AN EMPIRICAL INVESTIGATION
TAR JL 88 VOL: 63 PG:472 - 489 :: REGRESS. :SURV. :OTH.BEH. :INFO.STRUC.

KIM ,M ; SEC: MOORE ,G CIT: 0.4
ECONOMIC VS. ACCOUNTING DEPRECIATION
JAE AP 88 VOL: 10 PG:111 - 125 :: REGRESS. :PRIM. :THEORY :PP&E / DEPR

KIM ,MK ; FIRS: ISMAIL,BE CIT: 0
ON THE ASSOCIATION OF CASH FLOW VARIABLES WITH MARKET RISK: FURTHER EVIDENCE
TAR JA 89 VOL: 64 PG:125 - 136 :: REGRESS. :PRIM. :TIME SER. :OTH.FIN.ACC.

KIM ,O ; SEC: VERRECCHIA,RE CIT: 1
TRADING VOLUME AND PRICE REACTIONS TO PUBLIC ANNOUNCEMENTS
JAR AU 91 VOL: 29 PG:302 - 321 :: DES.STAT. :INT. LOG. :INF.ECO./AG. :INFO.STRUC.

KIM ,SK ; FIRS: BROWN ,LD CIT: 0
TIMELY AGGREGATE ANALYST FORECASTS AS BETTER PROXIES FOR MARKET EARNINGS EXPECTATIONS
JAR AU 91 VOL: 29 PG:382 - 385 :: DES.STAT. :PRIM. :EMH :METHOD.

KIM ,W ; FIRS: HAW ,I CIT: 0
FIRM SIZE AND DIVIDEND ANNOUNCEMENT EFFECT
JAA SU 91 VOL: 6 PG:325 - 344 :: REGRESS. :PRIM. :EMH :CASH DIV.

KIMBRELL,JI ; FIRS: BOATSMAN,JR ; SEC: DOWELL,CD CIT: 0
VALUING STOCK USED FOR A BUSINESS COMBINATION
JAA AU 84 VOL: 8 PG:35 - 43 :: ANAL. :INT. LOG. :OTH.STAT. :BUS.COMB.

KINARD,JC ; FIRS: HOFSTEDT,TR CIT: 0.35
A STRATEGY FOR BEHAVIOURAL ACCOUNTING RESEARCH
TAR JA 70 VOL: 45 PG:38 - 54 :: QUAL. :INT. LOG. :OTH.BEH. :OTH.MANAG.

KINARD,JC ; FIRS: IJIRI ,Y ; THIR: PUTNEY,FB CIT: 0.47
AN INTEGRATED EVALUATION SYSTEM FOR BUDGET FORECASTING AND OPERATING PERFORMANCE WITH A CLASSIFIED BUDGETING BIBLIOGRAPHY
JAR SP 68 VOL: 6 PG:1 - 28 :: QUAL. :SEC. :OTH.BEH. :BUDG.& PLAN.

KING ,JW ; FIRS: CHRISTIE,AA ; SEC: KENNELLEY,MD ; FOUR: SCHAEFER,TF CIT: 1
TESTING FOR INCREMENTAL INFORMATION CONTENT IN THE PRESENCE OF COLLINEARITY
JAE DE 84 VOL: 6 PG:205 - 217 :: ANAL. :INT. LOG. :OTH.STAT. :METHOD.

KING ,R ; SEC: POWNALL,G ; THIR: WAYMIRE,G CIT: 0
CORPORATE DISCLOSURE AND PRICE DISCOVERY ASSOCIATED WITH NYSE TEMPORARY TRADING HALTS
CAR SP 92 VOL: 8 PG:509 - 531 :: REGRESS. :PRIM. :EMH :INFO.STRUC.

KING ,RD ; SEC: O'KEEFE,TB CIT: 0
LOBBYING ACTIVITIES AND INSIDER TRADING
TAR JA 86 VOL: 61 PG:76 - 90 :: REGRESS. :PRIM. :OTH.STAT. :OIL & GAS

KING ,RD CIT: 0
THE EFFECT OF CONVERTIBLE BOND EQUITY VALUES ON DILUTION AND LEVERAGE
TAR JL 84 VOL: 59 PG:419 - 431 :: DES.STAT. :PRIM. :OTH.STAT. :LTD

KING ,RR ; FIRS: DOPUCH,N CIT: 1
NEGLIGENCE VERSUS STRICT LIABILITY REGIMES IN AUDITING: AN EXPERIMENTAL INVESTIGATION
TAR JA 92 VOL: 67 PG:97 - 120 :: REGRESS. :LAB. :OTH.BEH. :LIAB.

KING ,RR ; SEC: WALLIN,DE CIT: 1
VOLUNTARY DISCLOSURES WHEN SELLER'S LEVEL OF INFORMATION IS UNKNOWN
JAR SP 91 VOL: 29 PG:96 - 108 :: REGRESS. :LAB. :OTH.BEH. :INFO.STRUC.

KING ,RR ; FIRS: DOPUCH,N CIT: 0
THE IMPACT OF MAS ON AUDITORS' INDEPENDENCE: AN EXPERIMENTAL MARKETS STUDY
JAR ST 91 VOL: 29 PG:60 - 106 :: REGRESS. :LAB. :OTH.STAT. :INDEP.

KING ,RR ; SEC: WALLIN,DE CIT: 1
THE EFFECTS OF ANTIFRAUD RULES AND EX POST VERIFIABILITY ON MANAGERIAL DISCLOSURES
CAR SP 90 VOL: 6 PG:859 - 892 :: REGRESS. :LAB. :OTH.BEH. :RESP.ACC.

KING ,RR ; FIRS: DOPUCH,N ; THIR: WALLIN,DE CIT: 0.25
THE USE OF EXPERIMENTAL MARKETS IN AUDITING RESEARCH: SOME INITIAL FINDINGS
AUD 89 VOL: 8 PG:98 - 127 :: REGRESS. :LAB. :INF.ECO./AG. :MAN.DEC.CHAR.

KING ,RR ; SEC: BARON ,CD CIT: 0.06
AN INTEGRATED ACCOUNT STRUCTURE FOR GOVERNMENTAL ACCOUNTING AND FINANCIAL REPORTING
TAR JA 74 VOL: 49 PG:76 - 87 :: QUAL. :INT. LOG. :THEORY :FIN.METH.

KING ,TE ; SEC: ORTEGREN,AK CIT: 0
ACCOUNTING FOR HYBRID SECURITIES: THE CASE OF ADJUSTABLE RATE CONVERTIBLE NOTES
AUD JL 88 VOL: 63 PG:522 - 535 :: DES.STAT. :INT. LOG. :THEORY :SPEC.ITEMS

KING ,TE CIT: 0
ACCOUNTING STANDARDS FOR REPORTING UNINCORPORATED PARTNERSHIPS IN CORPORATE FINANCIAL STATEMENTS
JAA SP 79 VOL: 2 PG:209 - 223 :: QUAL. :INT. LOG. :THEORY :BUS.COMB.

KINNEY JR,WR CIT: 0
ACHIEVED AUDIT RISK AND THE AUDIT OUTCOME SPACE
AUD 89 VOL: 8 PG:67 - 84 :: N/A :SIM. :MATH.PROG. :RISK

KINNEY JR,WR CIT: 0.8
ATTESTATION RESEARCH OPPORTUNITIES: 1987
CAR SP 88 VOL: 4 PG:416 - 425 :: DES.STAT. :INT. LOG. :THEORY :METHOD.

KINNEY JR,WR CIT: 0.5
ATTENTION-DIRECTING ANALYTICAL REVIEW USING ACCOUNTING RATIOS: A CASE STUDY
AUD SP 87 VOL: 6 PG:59 - 73 :: DES.STAT. :CASE :OTH.STAT. :ANAL.REV.

KINNEY JR,WR CIT: 2.14
AUDIT TECHNOLOGY AND PREFERENCES FOR AUDITING STANDARDS
JAE MR 86 VOL: 8 PG:73 - 89 :: REGRESS. :PRIM. :INSTIT. :FASB SUBM.

KINNEY JR,WR CIT: 0.5
A NOTE ON COMPOUNDING PROBABILITIES IN AUDITING
AUD SP 83 VOL: 2 PG:13 - 22 :: ANAL. :INT. LOG. :OTH.STAT. :RISK

KINNEY JR,WR ; FIRS: BANKS ,DW CIT: 0.55
LOSS CONTINGENCY REPORTS AND STOCK PRICES: AN EMPIRICAL STUDY
JAR SP 82 VOL: 20 PG:240 - 254 :: REGRESS. :PRIM. :EMH :SPEC.ITEMS

KINNEY JR,WR ; SEC: SALAMON,GL CIT: 0.18
REGRESSION ANALYSIS IN AUDITING: A COMPARISON OF ALTERNATIVE INVESTIGATION RULES
JAR AU 82 VOL: 20 PG:350 - 366 :: REGRESS. :SIM. :OTH.STAT. :ANAL.REV.

KINNEY JR,WR ; SEC: UECKER,WC CIT: 1
MITIGATING THE CONSEQUENCES OF ANCHORING IN AUDITOR JUDGMENTS
TAR JA 82 VOL: 57 PG:55 - 69 :: DES.STAT. :LAB. :HIPS :ANAL.REV.

KINNEY JR,WR ; FIRS: FELIX JR,WL CIT: 1.91
RESEARCH IN THE AUDITOR'S OPINION FORMULATION PROCESS: STATE OF THE ART
TAR AP 82 VOL: 57 PG:245 - 271 :: QUAL. :SEC. :OTH. :N/A

KINNEY JR,WR CIT: 0
PREDICTING AUDITOR-INITIATED ADJUSTMENTS USING PAIRED BALANCE METHODS
JAA AU 81 VOL: 5 PG:5 - 17 :: MIXED :SEC. :OTH.STAT. :ANAL.REV.

KINNEY JR,WR ; FIRS: UECKER,WC ; SEC: BRIEF ,AP CIT: 0.33
PERCEPTION OF THE INTERNAL AND EXTERNAL AUDITOR AS A DETERRENT TO CORPORATE IRREGULARITIES
TAR JL 81 VOL: 56 PG:465 - 478 :: ANOVA :LAB. :OTH.BEH. :AUD.BEH.

KINNEY JR,WR CIT: 0.36
INTEGRATING AUDIT TESTS: REGRESSION ANALYSIS AND PARTITIONED DOLLAR-UNIT SAMPLING
JAR AU 79 VOL: 17 PG:456 - 475 :: REGRESS. :SIM. :OTH.STAT. :SAMP.

KINNEY JR,WR CIT: 1.14
THE PREDICTIVE POWER OF LIMITED INFORMATION IN PRELIMINARY ANALYTICAL REVIEW: AN EMPIRICAL STUDY
JAR ST 79 VOL: 17 PG:148 - 165 :: DES.STAT. :PRIM. :OTH.STAT. :ANAL.REV.

KINNEY JR,WR CIT: 0.87
ARIMA AND REGRESSION IN ANALYTICAL REVIEW: AN EMPIRICAL TEST
TAR JA 78 VOL: 53 PG:48 - 60 :: REGRESS. :PRIM. :TIME SER. :ANAL.REV.

KINNEY JR,WR ; FIRS: UECKER,WC CIT: 0.69
JUDGMENTAL EVALUATION OF SAMPLE RESULTS: A STUDY OF THE TYPE AND SEVERITY OF ERRORS MADE BY PRACTICING CPAS
AOS 03 77 VOL: 2 PG:269 - 275 :: DES.STAT. :LAB. :OTH.STAT. :SAMP.

KINNEY JR,WR CIT: 1.29
A DECISION THEORY APPROACH TO THE SAMPLING PROBLEM IN AUDITING
JAR SP 75 VOL: 13 PG:117 - 132 :: ANAL. :INT. LOG. :INF.ECO./AG. :SAMP.

KINNEY JR,WR CIT: 0.94
DECISION THEORY ASPECTS OF INTERNAL CONTROL SYSTEM DESIGN/COMPLIANCE AND SUBSTANTIVE TESTS
JAR ST 75 VOL: 13 PG:14 - 29 :: ANAL. :INT. LOG. :OTH.STAT. :SAMP.

KINNEY JR,WR CIT: 0.12
COVARIABILITY OF SEGMENT EARNINGS AND MULTISEGMENT COMPANY RETURNS
TAR AP 72 VOL: 47 PG:339 - 345 :: CORR. :PRIM. :EMH :SEG.REP.

KINNEY JR,WR CIT: 0.82
PREDICTING EARNINGS: ENTITY VERSUS SUBENTITY DATA
JAR SP 71 VOL: 9 PG:127 - 136 :: ANOVA :PRIM. :TIME SER. :SEG.REP.

KINNEY JR,WR CIT: 0.06
AN ENVIRONMENTAL MODEL FOR PERFORMANCE MEASUREMENT IN MULTI-OUTLET BUSINESSES
JAR SP 69 VOL: 7 PG:44 - 52 :: ANAL. :INT. LOG. :TIME SER. :OPIN.

KINNEYJR,WR ; SEC: MCDANIEL,LS CIT: 1
CHARACTERISTICS OF FIRMS CORRECTING PREVIOUSLY REPORTED QUARTERLY EARNINGS
JAE FB 89 VOL: 11 PG:71 - 93 :: REGRESS. :PRIM. :OTH.STAT. :AUD.

KIRBY ,AJ CIT: 0
INCENTIVE COMPENSATION SCHEMES: EXPERIMENTAL CALIBRATION OF THE RATIONALITY HYPOTHESIS
CAR SP 92 VOL: 8 PG:374 - 408 :: REGRESS. :LAB. :INF.ECO./AG. :EXEC.COMP.

KIRBY ,AJ ; SEC: REICHELSTEIN,S ; THIR: SEN ,PK ; FOUR: PAIK ,TY CIT: 1.5
PARTICIPATION, SLACK, AND BUDGET-BASED PERFORMANCE EVALUATION
JAR SP 91 VOL: 29 PG:109 - 128 :: DES.STAT. :INT. LOG. :OTH.BEH. :BUDG.& PLAN.

KIRCHER,P ; FIRS: BUCKLEY,JW ; THIR: MATHEWS,RL CIT: 0.06
METHODOLOGY IN ACCOUNTING THEORY
TAR AP 68 VOL: 43 PG:274 - 283 :: QUAL. :INT. LOG. :THEORY :FIN.METH.

KIRCHER,P CIT: 0
CLASSIFICATION AND CODING OF ACCOUNTING INFORMATION
TAR JL 67 VOL: 42 PG:537 - 543 :: QUAL. :INT. LOG. :THEORY :OTH.MANAG.

KIRCHER,P CIT: 0
CODING ACCOUNTING PRINCIPLES
TAR OC 65 VOL: 40 PG:742 - 752 :: QUAL. :INT. LOG. :THEORY :OTH.MANAG.

KIRKHAM,LM CIT: 1
INTEGRATING HERSTORY AND HISTORY IN ACCOUNTING
AOS 04 92 VOL: 17 PG:287 - 297 :: REGRESS. :SEC. :HIST. :ORG.& ENVIR.

KISSINGER,JN CIT: 0
IN DEFENSE OF INTERPERIOD INCOME TAX ALLOCATION
JAA SP 86 VOL: 1 PG:90 - 101 :: REGRESS. :INT. LOG. :THEORY :TAX PLNG.

KISSINGER,JN CIT: 0
AUDIT TIMING DECISIONS: A NORMATIVE MODEL, A PRACTICAL HEURISTIC, AND SOME EMPIRICAL EVIDENCE
AUD AU 83 VOL: 3 PG:42 - 54 :: MIXED :PRIM. :OTH. :TIM.

KISSINGER,JN CIT: 0.25
A GENERAL THEORY OF EVIDENCE AS THE CONCEPTUAL FOUNDATION IN AUDITING THEORY: SOME COMMENTS AND EXTENSIONS
TAR AP 77 VOL: 52 PG:322 - 339 :: ANAL. :INT. LOG. :THEORY :OPIN.

KISTLER,LH CIT: 0
STOCK OPTION DISCLOSURES ARE INADEQUATE
TAR OC 67 VOL: 42 PG:758 - 766 :: QUAL. :CASE :N/A :STK.DIV.

KISTNER,KP ; SEC: SALMI ,T CIT: 0
GENERAL PRICE LEVEL ACCOUNTING AND INVENTORY VALUATION: A COMMENT
JAR SP 80 VOL: 18 PG:297 - 311 :: ANAL. :INT. LOG. :THEORY :VALUAT.(INFL.)

KLAASSEN,J ; FIRS: SCHREUDER,H CIT: 0.11
CONFIDENTIAL REVENUE AND PROFIT FORECASTS BY MANAGEMENT AND FINANCIAL ANALYSTS: EVIDENCE FROM THE NETHERLANDS
TAR JA 84 VOL: 59 PG:64 - 77 :: NON-PAR. :PRIM. :OTH.STAT. :FOREC.

KLAMMER,T CIT: 0.41
THE ASSOCIATION OF CAPITAL BUDGETING TECHNIQUES WITH FIRM PERFORMANCE
TAR AP 73 VOL: 48 PG:353 - 364 :: REGRESS. :SURV. :EMH :CAP.BUDG.

KLEESPIE,DC ; FIRS: WINBORNE,MG CIT: 0
TAX ALLOCATION IN PERSPECTIVE
TAR OC 66 VOL: 41 PG:737 - 744 :: QUAL. :INT. LOG. :N/A :TAXES

KLEIN ,A ; FIRS: ALI ,A ; THIR: ROSENFELD,J CIT: 0
ANALYSTS' USE OF INFORMATION ABOUT PERMANENT AND TRANSITORY EARNINGS COMPONENTS IN FORECASTING ANNUAL EPS
TAR JA 92 VOL: 67 PG:183 - 198 :: REGRESS. :PRIM. :TIME SER. :FOREC.

KLERSEY,GF ; SEC: MOCK ,TJ CIT: 0.25
VERBAL PROTOCOL RESEARCH IN AUDITING
AOS 02 89 VOL: 14 PG:133 - 151 :: REGRESS. :SEC. :HIPS :METHOD.

KLICK ,HD ; FIRS: HARRELL,AM CIT: 0.15
COMPARING THE IMPACT OF MONETARY AND NONMONETARY HUMAN ASSET MEASURES ON EXECUTIVE DECISION MAKING
AOS 04 80 VOL: 5 PG:393 - 400 :: REGRESS. :LAB. :OTH.BEH. :HRA

KNAPP ,MC CIT: 0
FACTORS THAT AUDIT COMMITTEE MEMBERS USE AS SURROGATES FOR AUDIT QUALITY
AUD SP 91 VOL: 10 PG:35 - 52 :: REGRESS. :LAB. :OTH.BEH. :OPER.AUD.

KNAPP ,MC CIT: 0
AN EMPIRICAL STUDY OF AUDIT COMMITTEE SUPPORT FOR AUDITORS INVOLVED IN TECHNICAL DISPUTES WITH CLIENT MANAGEMENT
TAR JL 87 VOL: 62 PG:578 - 588 :: REGRESS. :LAB. :OTH.BEH. :AUD.

KNAPP ,MC CIT: 0.38
AUDIT CONFLICT: AN EMPIRICAL STUDY OF THE PERCEIVED ABILITY OF AUDITORS TO RESIST MANAGEMENT PRESSURE
TAR AP 85 VOL: 60 PG:202 - 211 :: REGRESS. :LAB. :OTH.BEH. :OPIN.

KNAUF ,JB ; SEC: VASARHELYI,MA CIT: 0
EMPIRICAL CHARACTERISTICS OF DEBENTURE CONVERSIONS: THE ISSUE OF EQUIVALENCY
JAA WI 87 VOL: 2 PG:43 - 64 :: REGRESS. :PRIM. :THEORY :LTD

KNECHEL,WR ; SEC: MESSIER JR,WF CIT: 0.33
SEQUENTIAL AUDITOR DECISION MAKING: INFORMATION SEARCH AND EVIDENCE EVALUATION
CAR SP 90 VOL: 6 PG:386 - 406 :: REGRESS. :LAB. :HIPS :AUD.BEH.

KNECHEL,WR ; FIRS: TUBBS ,RM ; SEC: MESSIER JR,WF CIT: 1.67
RECENCY EFFECTS IN THE AUDITOR'S BELIEF-REVISION PROCESS
TAR AP 90 VOL: 65 PG:452 - 460 :: REGRESS. :LAB. :HIPS :AUD.BEH.

KNECHEL,WR CIT: 0.2
THE EFFECTIVENESS OF NONSTATISTICAL ANALYTICAL REVIEW PROCEDURES USED AS SUBSTANTIVE AUDIT TESTS
AUD AU 88 VOL: 08 PG:87 - 107 :: DES.STAT. :SIM. :OTH.STAT. :ANAL.REV.

KNECHEL,WR CIT: 0.4
THE EFFECTIVENESS OF STATISTICAL ANALYTICAL REVIEW AS A SUBSTANTIVE AUDITING PROCEDURE: A SIMULATION ANALYSIS
TAR JA 88 VOL: 63 PG:74 - 95 :: DES.STAT. :SIM. :OTH.STAT. :ANAL.REV.

KNECHEL,WR CIT: 0.25
A SIMULATION MODEL FOR EVALUATING ACCOUNTING SYSTEM RELIABILITY
AUD SP 85 VOL: 4 PG:38 - 62 :: REGRESS. :SIM. :OTH.STAT. :INT.CONT.

KNECHEL,WR CIT: 0.13
AN ANALYSIS OF ALTERNATIVE ERROR ASSUMPTIONS IN MODELING THE RELIABILITY OF ACCOUNTING SYSTEMS
JAR SP 85 VOL: 23 PG:194 - 212 :: REGRESS. :SIM. :OTH.STAT. :ERRORS

KNEER ,DC ; FIRS: JENNINGS,MM ; THIR: RECKERS,PMJ CIT: 0
SELECTED AUDITOR COMMUNICATIONS AND PERCEPTIONS OF LEGAL LIABILITY
CAR SP 91 VOL: 7 PG:449 - 465 :: REGRESS. :LAB. :HIPS :LIAB.

KNEER ,DC ; FIRS: JENNINGS,M ; THIR: RECKERS,PMJ CIT: 0.33
A REEXAMINATION OF THE CONCEPT OF MATERIALITY: VIEWS OF AUDITORS, USERS AND OFFICERS OF THE COURT
AUD SP 87 VOL: 6 PG:104 - 115 :: REGRESS. :LAB. :OTH.BEH. :MAT.

KNIGHTS,D ; SEC: COLLINSON,D CIT: 1.17
DISCIPLINING THE SHOPFLOOR: A COMPARISON OF THE DISCIPLINARY EFFECTS
AOS 05 87 VOL: 12 PG:457 - 477 :: DES.STAT. :INT. LOG. :THEORY :HRA

KNOBLETT,JA ; FIRS: LEVITAN,AS CIT: 0.25
INDICATORS OF EXCEPTIONS TO THE GOING CONCERN ASSUMPTION
AUD AU 85 VOL: 5 PG:26 - 39 :: REGRESS. :PRIM. :OTH.STAT. :OPIN.

KNUTSON,PH CIT: 0
AN EMPIRICAL STUDY OF THE COSTS OF CONVERTIBLE SECURITIES
JAR ST 71 VOL: 9 PG:99 - 112 :: DES.STAT. :PRIM. :THEORY :LTD

KNUTSON,PH CIT: 0.12
INCOME DISTRIBUTION: THE KEY TO EARNINGS PER SHARE
TAR JA 70 VOL: 45 PG:55 - 68 :: QUAL. :INT. LOG. :THEORY :INFO.STRUC.

KNUTSON,PH ; FIRS: BLAKELY,EJ CIT: 0
LIFO OR LOFI - WHICH?
TAR JA 63 VOL: 38 PG:75 - 86 :: QUAL. :INT. LOG. :THEORY :N/A

KO ,CE ; SEC: NACHTSHEIM,CJ ; THIR: DUKE ,GL ; FOUR: BAILEY JR,AD CIT: 0
ON THE ROBUSTNESS OF MODEL-BASED SAMPLING IN AUDITING
AUD SP 88 VOL: 07 PG:119 - 136 :: DES.STAT. :SIM. :OTH.STAT. :SAMP.

KO ,CE ; FIRS: BAILEY JR,AD ; SEC: DUKE ,GL ; THIR: GERLACH,JH ; FIFT: MESERVY,RD ; SIX: WHINSTON,AB CIT: 0.38
TICOM AND THE ANALYSIS OF INTERNAL CONTROLS
TAR AP 85 VOL: 60 PG:186 - 201 :: CORR. :INT. LOG. :OTH. :INT.CONT.

KOCH ,BS ; FIRS: PEI ,BKW ; SEC: REED ,SA CIT: 0
AUDITOR BELIEF REVISIONS IN A PERFORMANCE AUDITING SETTING: AN APPLICATION OF THE BELIEF-ADJUSTMENT MODEL
AOS 02 92 VOL: 17 PG:169 - 183 :: REGRESS. :LAB. :HIPS :AUD.BEH.

KOCH ,BS ; FIRS: MERINO,BD ; THIR: MACRITCHIE,KL CIT: 0
HISTORICAL ANALYSIS- A DIAGNOSTIC TOOL FOR EVENTS STUDIES: THE IMPACT OF T
TAR OC 87 VOL: 62 PG:748 - 762 :: REGRESS. :INT. LOG. :HIST. :FIN.METH.

KOCH ,BS CIT: 0.08
INCOME SMOOTHING: AN EXPERIMENT
TAR JL 81 VOL: 56 PG:574 - 586 :: ANOVA :LAB. :THEORY :REV.REC.

KOCHANEK,RF CIT: 0.24
SEGMENTAL FINANCIAL DISCLOSURE BY DIVERSIFIED FIRMS AND SECURITY PRICES
TAR AP 74 VOL: 49 PG:245 - 258 :: MIXED :PRIM. :OTH.STAT. :SEG.REP.

KOHLER,EL CIT: 0
THE JENKINS REPORT
TAR AP 63 VOL: 38 PG:266 - 269 :: QUAL. :INT. LOG. :INSTIT. :FIN.METH.

KOHLMEIER,JM ; FIRS: DAVIDSON,S CIT: 0.06
A MEASURE OF THE IMPACT OF SOME FOREIGN ACCOUNTING PRINCIPLES
JAR AU 66 VOL: 4 PG:183 - 212 :: DES.STAT. :SIM. :OTH.STAT. :INT.DIFF.

KOLLARITSCH,FP CIT: 0
INTERNATIONAL ACCOUNTING PRACTICES
TAR AP 65 VOL: 40 PG:382 - 385 :: QUAL. :INT. LOG. :INSTIT. :FIN.METH.

KOLODNY,R ; FIRS: HORWITZ,BN CIT: 0.08
THE IMPACT OF RULE MAKING ON R & D INVESTMENTS OF SMALL HIGH-TECHNOLOGY FIRMS
JAA WI 81 VOL: 4 PG:102 - 113 :: NON-PAR. :SURV. :THEORY :ACC.CHNG.

KOLODNY,R ; FIRS: HORWITZ,BN CIT: 0
SEGMENT REPORTING: HINDSIGHT AFTER TEN YEARS
JAA AU 80 VOL: 4 PG:20 - 35 :: QUAL. :INT. LOG. :THEORY :SEG.REP.

KOLODNY,R ; FIRS: HORWITZ,BN CIT: 0.77
THE ECONOMIC EFFECTS OF INVOLUNTARY UNIFORMITY IN THE FINANCIAL REPORTING OFR & D EXPENDITURES
JAR ST 80 VOL: 18 PG:38 - 74 :: NON-PAR. :PRIM. :OTH. :R & D

KONSTANS,C ; FIRS: DEAN ,RA ; SEC: FERRIS,KR CIT: 0.4
OCCUPATIONAL REALITY SHOCK AND ORGANIZATIONAL COMMITMENT: EVIDENCE FROM THE ACCOUNTING PROFESSION
AOS 03 88 VOL: 13 PG:235 - 250 :: REGRESS. :SURV. :OTH.BEH. :AUD.BEH.

KOOGLER,PR ; FIRS: FOSTER III,TW ; THIR: VICKREY,D CIT: 0
VALUATION OF EXECUTIVE STOCK OPTIONS AND THE FASB PROPOSAL
TAR JL 91 VOL: 66 PG:595 - 610 :: DES.STAT. :INT. LOG. :INF.ECO./AG. :EXEC.COMP.

KOONCE,L CIT: 0
EXPLANATION AND COUNTER EXPLANATION DURING AUDIT ANALYTICAL REVIEW
TAR JA 92 VOL: 67 PG:59 - 76 :: REGRESS. :LAB. :HIPS :ANAL.REV.

KORKIE,B ; SEC: LAISS ,B CIT: 0
OPTIMAL PORTFOLIO RULES AND MAXIMUM GAINS FROM ECONOMIC EVENTS
JAA AU 90 VOL: 5 PG:593 - 617 :: DES.STAT. :INT. LOG. :EMH :FIN.METH.

KORNBLUTH,JS CIT: 0.12
ACCOUNTING IN MULTIPLE OBJECTIVE LINEAR PROGRAMMING
TAR AP 74 VOL: 49 PG:284 - 295 :: ANAL. :INT. LOG. :MATH.PROG. :MANAG.

KORTANEK,KO ; FIRS: CHARNES,A ; SEC: COLANTONI,CS ; THIR: COOPER,WW CIT: 0.06
ECONOMIC SOCIAL AND ENTERPRISE ACCOUNTING AND MATHEMATICAL MODES
TAR JA 72 VOL: 47 PG:85 - 108 :: ANAL. :INT. LOG. :MATH.PROG. :FIN.METH.

KORTANEK,KO ; FIRS: BYRNE ,R ; SEC: CHARNES,A ; THIR: COOPER,WW CIT: 0
SOME NEW APPROACHES TO RISK
TAR JA 68 VOL: 43 PG:18 - 37 :: ANAL. :INT. LOG. :MATH.PROG. :BUDG.& PLAN.

KORTANEK,KO ; FIRS: CHARNES,A ; SEC: DAVIDSON,HJ CIT: 0
ON A MIXED-SEQUENTIAL ESTIMATING PROCEDURE WITH APPLICATION TO AUDIT TESTS IN ACCOUNTING
TAR AP 64 VOL: 39 PG:241 - 250 :: ANAL. :INT. LOG. :OTH.STAT. :SAMP.

KOSTER,FJ ; FIRS: FELIX JR,WL ; SEC: GRIMLUND,RA ; FOUR: ROUSSEY,RS CIT: 0
ARTHUR ANDERSEN'S NEW MONETARY UNIT SAMPLING APPROACH
AUD AU 90 VOL: 9 PG:1 - 16 :: DES.STAT. :SIM. :EXP.SYST. :SAMP.

KOSTOLANSKY,JW ; FIRS: WERNER,CA CIT: 0
ACCOUNTING LIABILITIES UNDER THE MULTIEMPLOYER PENSION PLAN AMENDMENTS ACT
JAA SP 84 VOL: 7 PG:212 - 224 :: QUAL. :INT. LOG. :THEORY :PENS.

KOSTOLANSKY,JW ; FIRS: WERNER,CA CIT: 0
ACCOUNTING LIABILITIES UNDER ERISA
JAA AU 83 VOL: 7 PG:54 - 64 :: QUAL. :INT. LOG. :THEORY :PENS.

KOTHARI,SP ; SEC: SLAON ,RG CIT: 2
INFORMATION IN PRICES ABOUT FUTURE EARNINGS: IMPLICATIONS FOR EARNINGS RESPONSE COEFFICIENTS
JAE JN 92 VOL: 15 PG:143 - 171 :: REGRESS. :PRIM. :EMH :FIN.METH.

KOTHARI,SP CIT: 0
PRICE-EARNINGS REGRESSIONS IN THE PRESENCE OF PRICES LEADING EARNINGS: EARNINGS LEVEL VERSUS CHANGE SPECIFICATIONS AND ALTERNATIVE DEFLATORS
JAE JN 92 VOL: 15 PG:173 - 202 :: REGRESS. :PRIM. :EMH :FIN.METH.

KOTHARI,SP ; FIRS: BALL ,R CIT: 1
SECURITY RETURNS AROUND EARNINGS ANNOUNCEMENTS
TAR OC 91 VOL: 66 PG:718 - 738 :: REGRESS. :PRIM. :EMH :FIN.ST.TIM.

KOTHARI,SP ; FIRS: COLLINS,DW CIT: 5.5
AN ANALYSIS OF INTERTEMPORAL AND CROSS-SECTIONAL DETERMINANTS OF EARNINGS RESPONSE COEFFICIENTS
JAE JL 89 VOL: 11 PG:143 - 181 :: REGRESS. :PRIM. :EMH :FIN.METH.

KOTHARI,SP ; SEC: WASLEY,CE CIT: 0.5
MEASURING SECURITY PRICE PERFORMANCE IN SIZE-CLUSTERED SAMPLES
TAR AP 89 VOL: 64 PG:228 - 249 :: REGRESS. :SIM. :TIME SER. :OTH.FIN.ACC.

KOTHARI,SP ; SEC: LYS ,T ; THIR: SMITH ,CW ; FOUR: WATTS ,RL CIT: 0.6
AUDITOR LIABILITY AND INFORMATION DISCLOSURE
JAA AU 88 VOL: 3 PG:307 - 340 :: DES.STAT. :INT. LOG. :OTH. :LIAB.

KOTHARI,SP ; FIRS: COLLINS,DW ; THIR: RAYBURN,JD CIT: 4.33
FIRM SIZE AND THE INFORMATION CONTENT OF PRICES WITH RESPECT TO EARNINGS
JAE JL 87 VOL: 9 PG:111 - 138 :: REGRESS. :PRIM. :EMH :ORG.& ENVIR.

KOTTAS,JF ; SEC: LAU ,AH ; THIR: LAU ,HS CIT: 0.27
A GENERAL APPROACH TO STOCHASTIC MANAGEMENT PLANNING MODELS: AN OVERVIEW
TAR AP 78 VOL: 53 PG:389 - 401 :: ANAL. :INT. LOG. :MATH.PROG. :C-V-P-A

KOTTAS,JF ; SEC: LAU ,HS CIT: 0.07
DIRECT SIMULATION IN STOCHASTIC CVP ANALYSIS
TAR JL 78 VOL: 53 PG:698 - 707 :: QUAL. :INT. LOG. :OTH.STAT. :C-V-P-A

KRAMER,JL ; FIRS: NORDHAUSER,SL CIT: 0
REPEAL OF THE DEFERRAL PRIVILEGE FOR EARNINGS FROM DIRECT FOREIGN INVESTMENTS: AN ANALYSIS
TAR JA 81 VOL: 56 PG:54 - 69 :: ANAL. :INT. LOG. :OTH.STAT. :BUS.COMB.

KRAMER,SS CIT: 0
BLOCKAGE: VALUATION OF LARGE BLOCKS OF PUBLICLY TRADED STOCKS FOR TAX PURPOSES
TAR JA 82 VOL: 57 PG:70 - 87 :: REGRESS. :PRIM. :EMH :TAXES

KRAMER,SS ; FIRS: ASHTON,RH CIT: 1.85
STUDENTS AS SURROGATES IN BEHAVIOURAL ACCOUNTING RESEARCH: SOME EVIDENCE
JAR SP 80 VOL: 18 PG:1 - 15 :: NON-PAR. :LAB. :HIPS :METHOD.

KRASNEY,MA ; FIRS: BENSTON,GJ CIT: 0.33
DAAM: THE DEMAND FOR ALTERNATIVE ACCOUNTING MEASUREMENTS
JAR ST 78 VOL: 16 PG:1 - 30 :: REGRESS. :SURV. :OTH.STAT. :VALUAT.(INFL.)

KRATCHMAN,SH ; FIRS: GROSSMAN,SD ; THIR: WELKER,RB CIT: 0
COMMENT: THE EFFECT OF REPLACEMENT COST DISCLOSURES ON SECURITY PRICES
JAA WI 81 VOL: 4 PG:136 - 143 :: DES.STAT. :PRIM. :EMH :VALUAT.(INFL.)

KRATCHMAN,SH ; SEC: MALCOM,RE ; THIR: TWARK ,RD CIT: 0.06
AN INTRA-INDUSTRY COMPARISON OF ALTERNATIVE INCOME CONCEPTS AND RELATIVE PERFORMANCE EVALUATIONS
TAR OC 74 VOL: 49 PG:682 - 689 :: NON-PAR. :PRIM. :N/A :VALUAT.(INFL.)

KRAUSHAAR,JM ; FIRS: ANDERSON,JC CIT: 0.14
MEASUREMENT ERROR AND STATISTICAL SAMPLING IN AUDITING: THE POTENTIAL
TAR JL 86 VOL: 61 PG:379 - 399 :: DES.STAT. :SIM. :OTH.STAT. :SAMP.

KREISER,L CIT: 0
MAINTAINING AND IMPROVING THE AUDIT COMPETENCE OF CPAS: CPA AND SELECTED USER REACTION
TAR AP 77 VOL: 52 PG:427 - 437 :: DES.STAT. :SURV. :N/A :AUD.TRAIN.

KREN ,L CIT: 0
BUDGETARY PARTICIPATION AND MANAGERIAL PERFORMANCE: THE IMPACT OF INFORMATION AND ENVIRONMENTAL VOLATILITY
TAR JL 92 VOL: 67 PG:511 - 526 :: REGRESS. :SURV. :OTH.BEH. :BUDG.& PLAN.

KREPS ,DM ; FIRS: DEMSKI,JS CIT: 1
MODELS IN MANAGERIAL ACCOUNTING
JAR ST 82 VOL: 20 PG:117 - 148 :: QUAL. :SEC. :OTH.STAT. :METHOD.

KREUTZFELDT,RW ; FIRS: WALLACE,WA CIT: 0
DISTINCTIVE CHARACTERISTICS OF ENTITIES WITH AN INTERNAL AUDIT DEPARTMENT AND THE ASSOCIATION OF THE QUALITY OF SUCH DEPARTMENTS WITH ERRORS
CAR SP 91 VOL: 7 PG:485 - 512 :: REGRESS. :PRIM. :OTH.STAT. :INT.AUD.

KREUTZFELDT,RW ; SEC: WALLACE,WA CIT: 0
CONTROL RISK ASSESSMENTS: DO THEY RELATE TO ERRORS?
AUD 90 VOL: 9 PG:1 - 26 :: REGRESS. :PRIM. :OTH.STAT. :ERRORS

KREUTZFELDT,RW ; SEC: WALLACE,WA CIT: 1.14
ERROR CHARACTERISTICS IN AUDIT POPULATIONS: THEIR PROFILE AND RELATIONSHIP TO ENVIRONMENTAL FACTORS
AUD AU 86 VOL: 6 PG:20 - 43 :: DES.STAT. :SURV. :OTH.STAT. :ERRORS

KRIEGER,AM ; FIRS: RAMAGE,JG ; THIR: SPERO ,LL CIT: 0.79
AN EMPIRICAL STUDY OF ERROR CHARACTERISTICS IN AUDIT POPULATIONS
JAR ST 79 VOL: 17 PG:72 - 102 :: DES.STAT. :PRIM. :OTH.STAT. :ERRORS

KRINSKY,I ; SEC: ROTENBERG,W CIT: 0
THE VALUATION OF INITIAL PUBLIC OFFERINGS
CAR SP 89 VOL: 5 PG:501 - 515 :: REGRESS. :PRIM. :EMH :VALUAT.(INFL.)

KRIPKE,H CIT: 0
REFLECTIONS ON THE FASB'S CONCEPTUAL FRAMEWORK FOR ACCOUNTING AND ON AUDITING
JAA WI 89 VOL: 4 PG:3 - 65 :: REGRESS. :SEC. :INSTIT. :FASB SUBM.

KRIPKE,H CIT: 0
WHERE ARE WE ON SECURITIES DISCLOSURE AFTER THE ADVISORY COMMITTEE REPORT?
JAA AU 78 VOL: 2 PG:4 - 32 :: QUAL. :INT. LOG. :INSTIT. :OTH.MANAG.

KROGSTAD,JL ; FIRS: SMITH ,G CIT: 0
SOURCES AND USES OF AUDITING: A JOURNAL OF PRACTICE & THEORY'S LITERATURE: THE FIRST DECADE
AUD AU 91 VOL: 10 PG:84 - 97 :: REGRESS. :SEC. :HIST. :AUD.

KROGSTAD,JL ; SEC: ETTENSON,RT ; THIR: SHANTEAU,J CIT: 0.67
CONTEXT AND EXPERIENCE IN AUDITORS' MATERIALITY JUDGMENTS
AUD AU 84 VOL: 4 PG:54 - 74 :: ANOVA :LAB. :OTH.BEH. :MAT.

KROGSTAD,JL ; FIRS: SMITH ,G CIT: 0.11
IMPACT OF SOURCES AND AUTHORS ON AUDITING: A JOURNAL OF PRACTICE & THEORY - A CITATION ANALYSIS
AUD AU 84 VOL: 4 PG:107 - 117 :: DES.STAT. :SEC. :OTH.STAT. :METHOD.

KROGSTAD,JL ; FIRS: SOLOMON,I ; THIR: ROMNEY,MB ; FOUR: TOMASSINI,LA CIT: 0.64
AUDITORS' PRIOR PROBABILITY DISTRIBUTIONS FOR ACCOUNT BALANCES
AOS 01 82 VOL: 7 PG:27 - 42 :: DES.STAT. :LAB. :HIPS :PROB.ELIC.

KROSS ,W ; SEC: RO ,B ; THIR: SCHROEDER,D CIT: 0.67
EARNINGS EXPECTATIONS: THE ANALYSTS' INFORMATION ADVANTAGE
TAR AP 90 VOL: 65 PG:461 - 476 :: REGRESS. :PRIM. :TIME SER. :FOREC.

KROSS ,W ; SEC: SCHROEDER,DA CIT: 1.56
AN EMPIRICAL INVESTIGATION OF THE EFFECT OF QUARTERLY EARNINGS ANNOUNCEMENT TIMING ON STOCK RETURNS
JAR SP 84 VOL: 22 PG:153 - 176 :: REGRESS. :PRIM. :EMH :FIN.ST.TIM.

KROSS ,W CIT: 0
STOCK RETURNS AND OIL AND GAS PRONOUNCEMENTS: REPLICATION AND EXTENSION
JAR AU 82 VOL: 20 PG:459 - 471 :: NON-PAR. :PRIM. :EMH :FIN.METH.

KROSS ,W ; SEC: CHAPMAN,G ; THIR: STRAND,KH CIT: 0
FULLY DILUTED EARNINGS PER SHARE AND SECURITY RETURNS: SOME ADDITIONAL EVIDENCE
JAA AU 80 VOL: 4 PG:36 - 46 :: CORR. :SEC. :EMH :CASH DIV.

KUBLIN,M CIT: 0
ACCEPTABILITY OF A PROFESSIONAL SCHOOL OF ACCOUNTANCY
TAR JL 65 VOL: 40 PG:626 - 635 :: DES.STAT. :SURV. :INSTIT. :OTH.MANAG.

KUNITAKE,WK ; SEC: WHITE JR,CE CIT: 0
ETHICS FOR INDEPENDENT AUDITORS
JAA SU 86 VOL: 1 PG:222 - 231 :: DES.STAT. :INT. LOG. :INSTIT. :PROF.RESP.

KUNITZKY,S ; FIRS: LEV ,B CIT: 0.35
ON THE ASSOCIATION BETWEEN SMOOTHING MEASURES AND THE RISK OF COMMON STOCKS
TAR AP 74 VOL: 49 PG:259 - 270 :: CORR. :PRIM. :TIME SER. :FIN.METH.

KWANG ,CW ; FIRS: CORCORAN,AW CIT: 0
A SET THEORY APPROACH TO FUNDS-FLOW ANALYSIS
JAR AU 65 VOL: 3 PG:206 - 217 :: ANAL. :INT. LOG. :THEORY :PP&E / DEPR

KWATINETZ,M ; FIRS: PALMON,D CIT: 0.08
THE SIGNIFICANT ROLE INTERPRETATION PLAYS IN THE IMPLEMENTATION OF SFAS NO.13
JAA SP 80 VOL: 3 PG:207 - 226 :: QUAL. :INT. LOG. :THEORY :LEASES

KWON ,SO ; FIRS: HUGHES,MA CIT: 0.33
AN INTEGRATIVE FRAMEWORK FOR THEORY CONSTRUCTION AND TESTING
AOS 03 90 VOL: 15 PG:179 - 191 :: DES.STAT. :SEC. :OTH.BEH. :METHOD.

KWON ,YK ; FIRS: JUNG ,WO CIT: 0.6
DISCLOSURE WHEN THE MARKET IS UNSURE OF INFORMATION ENDOWMENT OF MANAGERS
JAR SP 88 VOL: 26 PG:146 - 153 :: DES.STAT. :INT. LOG. :INF.ECO./AG. :INFO.STRUC.

L'HER ,JF ; SEC: SURET ,J-M CIT: 0.5
THE REACTION OF CANADIAN SECURITIES TO REVISIONS OF EARNINGS FORECASTS
CAR SP 91 VOL: 7 PG:378 - 406 :: REGRESS. :PRIM. :EMH :FOREC.

LABELLE,R CIT: 0
BOND COVENANTS AND CHANGES IN ACCOUNTING POLICY: CANADIAN EVIDENCE
CAR SP 90 VOL: 6 PG:677 - 698 :: REGRESS. :PRIM. :OTH.STAT. :ACC.CHNG.

LACEY ,JM ; FIRS: BOWEN ,RM ; SEC: NOREEN,EW CIT: 4
DETERMINANTS OF THE CORPORATE DECISION TO CAPITALIZE INTEREST
JAE AG 81 VOL: 3 PG:151 - 179 :: DES.STAT. :INT. LOG. :INF.ECO./AG. :SPEC.ITEMS

LACHMAN,R ; FIRS: ARANYA,N ; THIR: AMERNIC,J CIT: 0.27
ACCOUNTANTS' JOB SATISFACTION: A PATH ANALYSIS
AOS 03 82 VOL: 7 PG:201 - 216 :: CORR. :SURV. :OTH.BEH. :N/A

LAIBSTAIN,S CIT: 0
A NEW LOOK AT ACCOUNTING FOR OPERATING LOSS CARRYFORWARDS
TAR AP 71 VOL: 46 PG:342 - 351 :: QUAL. :INT. LOG. :THEORY :TAXES

LAISS ,B ; FIRS: KORKIE,B CIT: 0
OPTIMAL PORTFOLIO RULES AND MAXIMUM GAINS FROM ECONOMIC EVENTS
JAA AU 90 VOL: 5 PG:593 - 617 :: DES.STAT. :INT. LOG. :EMH :FIN.METH.

LAKONISHOK,J ; FIRS: KENNEDY,D ; THIR: SHAW ,WH CIT: 0
ACCOMODATING OUTLIERS AND NONLINEARITY IN DECISION MODELS
JAA SP 92 VOL: 7 PG:161 - 190 :: REGRESS. :PRIM. :OTH.STAT. :METHOD.

LAKONISHOK,J ; FIRS: GIVOLY,D CIT: 0
AGGREGATE EARNINGS EXPECTATIONS AND STOCK MARKET BEHAVIOR
JAA SP 87 VOL: 2 PG:117 - 137 :: REGRESS. :PRIM. :EMH :FOREC.

LAKONISHOK,J ; FIRS: BARAN ,A ; THIR: OFER ,AR CIT: 0.15
THE INFORMATION CONTENT OF GENERAL PRICE LEVEL ADJUSTED EARNINGS: SOME EMPIRICAL EVIDENCE
TAR JA 80 VOL: 55 PG:22 - 35 :: REGRESS. :PRIM. :HIPS :VALUAT.(INFL.)

LAKONISHOK,J ; FIRS: GIVOLY,D CIT: 1.14
THE INFORMATION CONTENT OF FINANCIAL ANALYSTS' FORECASTS OF EARNINGS: SOME EVIDENCE ON SEMI-STRONG INEFFICIENCY
JAE DE 79 VOL: 1 PG:165 - 185 :: DES.STAT. :PRIM. :EMH :FOREC.

LAKONISHOK,J ; FIRS: CRICHFIELD,T ; SEC: DYCKMAN,TR CIT: 0.93
AN EVALUATION OF SECURITY ANALYSTS' FORECASTS
TAR JL 78 VOL: 53 PG:651 - 668 :: ANOVA :PRIM. :TIME SER. :FOREC.

LAMB ,JW ; FIRS: CARLSON,ML CIT: 0
CONSTRUCTING A THEORY OF ACCOUNTING - AN AXIOMATIC APPROACH
TAR JL 81 VOL: 56 PG:554 - 573 :: ANAL. :INT. LOG. :THEORY :N/A

LAMBERT,RA ; FIRS: DEFEO ,VJ ; THIR: LARCKER,DF CIT: 0.75
EXECUTIVE COMPENSATION EFFECTS OF EQUITY-FOR-DEBT SWAPS
TAR AP 89 VOL: 64 PG:201 - 227 :: REGRESS. :PRIM. :INF.ECO./AG. :LTD

LAMBERT III,SJ ; FIRS: LAMBERT,JC ; THIR: CALDERON,TG CIT: 0
COMMUNICATION BETWEEN SUCCESSOR AND PREDECESSOR AUDITORS
AUD SP 91 VOL: 10 PG:97 - 109 :: REGRESS. :SURV. :OTH.STAT. :ORG.

LAMBERT,JC ; SEC: LAMBERT III,SJ ; THIR: CALDERON,TG CIT: 0
COMMUNICATION BETWEEN SUCCESSOR AND PREDECESSOR AUDITORS
AUD SP 91 VOL: 10 PG:97 - 109 :: REGRESS. :SURV. :OTH.STAT. :ORG.

LAMBERT,RA ; FIRS: JANAKIRAMAN,SN ; THIR: LARCKER,DF CIT: 1
AN EMPIRICAL INVESTIGATION OF THE RELATIVE PERFORMANCE EVALUATION HYPOTHESIS
JAR SP 92 VOL: 30 PG:53 - 69 :: REGRESS. :PRIM. :INF.ECO./AG. :EXEC.COMP.

LAMBERT,RA ; SEC: LARCKER,DF ; THIR: VERRECCHIA,RE CIT: 0.5
PORTFOLIO CONSIDERATIONS IN VALUING EXECUTIVE COMPENSATION
JAR SP 91 VOL: 29 PG:129 - 149 :: DES.STAT. :SIM. :INF.ECO./AG. :EXEC.COMP.

LAMBERT,RA ; SEC: LARCKER,DF CIT: 0
ESTIMATING THE MARGINAL COSTS OF OPERATING A SERVICE DEPARTMENT WHEN RECIPROCAL SERVICES EXIST
TAR JL 89 VOL: 64 PG:449 - 467 :: DES.STAT. :INT. LOG. :MATH.PROG. :COST.ALLOC.

LAMBERT,RA ; FIRS: BEAVER,WH ; THIR: RYAN ,SG CIT: 3.33
THE INFORMATION CONTENT OF SECURITY PRICES: A SECOND LOOK
JAE JL 87 VOL: 9 PG:139 - 157 :: REGRESS. :PRIM. :EMH :FOREC.

LAMBERT,RA ; SEC: LARCKER,DF CIT: 1.67
AN ANALYSIS OF THE USE OF ACCOUNTING AND MARKET MEASURES OF PERFORMANCE IN EXECUTIVE COMPENSATION CONTRACTS
JAR ST 87 VOL: 25 PG:85 - 125 :: REGRESS. :PRIM. :EMH :EXEC.COMP.

LAMBERT,RA ; SEC: LARCKER,DF CIT: 0.25
GOLDEN PARACHUTES, EXECUTIVE DECISION-MAKING, AND SHAREHOLDER WEALTH
JAE AP 85 VOL: 7 PG:179 - 204 :: REGRESS. :PRIM. :EMH :EXEC.COMP.

LAMBERT,RA CIT: 0.38
VARIANCE INVESTIGATION IN AGENCY SETTINGS
JAR AU 85 VOL: 23 PG:633 - 647 :: REGRESS. :INT. LOG. :INF.ECO./AG. :VAR.

LAMBERT,RA CIT: 0.89
INCOME SMOOTHING AS RATIONAL EQUILIBRIUM BEHAVIOR
TAR OC 84 VOL: 59 PG:604 - 618 :: ANAL. :INT. LOG. :EMH :REV.REC.

LAMBERT,RA ; FIRS: BEAVER,WH ; THIR: MORSE ,D CIT: 4.31
THE INFORMATION CONTENT OF SECURITY PRICES
JAE MR 80 VOL: 2 PG:3 - 28 :: REGRESS. :PRIM. :EMH :FOREC.

LAMDEN,CW CIT: 0
THE FUNCTION OF THE STATE BOARD OF ACCOUNTANCY IN IMPROVING REPORTING STANDARDS IN CALIFORNIA
TAR JA 64 VOL: 39 PG:128 - 132 :: QUAL. :INT. LOG. :INSTIT. :OTH.MANAG.

LAMPE ,JC ; FIRS: VASARHELYI,MA ; SEC: BAILEY JR,AD ; THIR: CAMARDESSE JR,JE ; FOUR: GROOMER,SM CIT: 0
THE USAGE OF COMPUTERS IN AUDITING TEACHING AND RESEARCH
AUD SP 84 VOL: 3 PG:98 - 103 :: QUAL. :SIM. :OTH. :EDP AUD.

LANDSITTEL,DL ; SEC: SERLIN,JE CIT: 0.09
EVALUATING THE MATERIALITY OF ERRORS IN FINANCIAL STATEMENTS
JAA SU 82 VOL: 5 PG:291 - 300 :: QUAL. :INT. LOG. :OTH. :MAT.

LANDSMAN,W ; FIRS: CORNELL,B ; THIR: SHAPIRO,AC CIT: 0
CROSS-SECTIONAL REGULARITIES IN THE RESPONSE OF STOCK PRICES TO BOND RATING CHANGES
JAA AU 89 VOL: 4 PG:460 - 479 :: REGRESS. :PRIM. :EMH :OTH.C/A

LANDSMAN,WR ; FIRS: BARTH ,ME ; SEC: BEAVER,WH CIT: 0
THE MARKET VALUATION IMPLICATIONS OF NET PERIODIC PENSION COST COMPONENTS
JAE MR 92 VOL: 15 PG:27 - 61 :: REGRESS. :PRIM. :EMH :PENS.

LANDSMAN,WR ; SEC: OHLSON,JA CIT: 0.33
EVALUATION OF MARKET EFFICIENCY FOR SUPPLEMENTARY ACCOUNTING DISCLOSURES: THE CASE OF PENSION ASSETS AND LIABILITIES
CAR AU 90 VOL: 7 PG:185 - 198 :: REGRESS. :PRIM. :EMH :PENS.

LANDSMAN,WR ; SEC: DAMODARAN,A CIT: 0.25
USING SHRINKAGE ESTIMATORS TO IMPROVE UPON TIME-SERIES MODEL PROXIES FOR THE SECURITY MARKET'S EXPECTATION OF EARNINGS
JAR SP 89 VOL: 27 PG:97 - 115 :: DES.STAT. :PRIM. :TIME SER. :METHOD.

LANDSMAN,WR ; FIRS: CORNELL,B CIT: 1.25
SECURITY PRICE RESPONSE TO QUARTERLY EARNINGS ANNOUNCEMENTS AND ANALYSTS' FORECAST REVISIONS
TAR OC 89 VOL: 64 PG:680 - 692 :: REGRESS. :PRIM. :EMH :AUD.BEH.

LANDSMAN,WR ; SEC: MAGLIOLO,J CIT: 0.8
CROSS-SECTIONAL CAPITAL MARKET RESEARCH AND MODEL SPECIFICATION
TAR OC 88 VOL: 63 PG:586 - 604 :: DES.STAT. :INT. LOG. :EMH :METHOD.

LANDSMAN,WR CIT: 1.14
AN EMPIRICAL INVESTIGATION OF PENSION AND PROPERTY RIGHTS
TAR OC 86 VOL: 61 PG:662 - 691 :: REGRESS. :PRIM. :EMH :PENS.

LANDSMAN,WR ; FIRS: BEAVER,WH ; SEC: GRIFFIN,PA CIT: 0
TESTING FOR INCREMENTAL INFORMATION CONTENT IN THE PRESENCE OF COLLINEARITY: A COMMENT
JAE DE 84 VOL: 6 PG:219 - 223 :: QUAL. :INT. LOG. :OTH.STAT. :METHOD.

LANDSMAN,WR ; FIRS: BEAVER,WH ; SEC: GRIFFIN,PA CIT: 2.55
THE INCREMENTAL INFORMATION CONTENT OF REPLACEMENT COST EARNINGS
JAE JL 82 VOL: 4 PG:15 - 39 :: MIXED :PRIM. :EMH :VALUAT.(INFL.)

LANDSMAN,WR ; FIRS: BEAVER,WH CIT: 0
NOTE ON THE BEHAVIOR OF RESIDUAL SECURITY RETURNS FOR WINNER AND LOSER PORTFOLIOS
JAE DE 81 VOL: 3 PG:233 - 241 :: DES.STAT. :PRIM. :EMH :N/A

LANEN ,WN ; SEC: LARCKER,DF CIT: 0
EXECUTIVE COMPENSATION CONTRACT ADOPTION IN THE ELECTRIC UTILITY INDUSTRY
JAR SP 92 VOL: 30 PG:70 - 93 :: REGRESS. :PRIM. :INF.ECO./AG. :EXEC.COMP.

LANEN ,WN ; SEC: THOMPSON,R CIT: 0.4
STOCK PRICE REACTIONS AS SURROGATES FOR THE NET CASH FLOW EFFECTS OF CORPORATE POLICY DECISIONS
JAE DE 88 VOL: 10 PG:311 - 334 :: REGRESS. :PRIM. :EMH :MAN.DEC.CHAR.

LANEN ,WN ; FIRS: VERRECCHIA,RE CIT: 0.17
OPERATING DECISIONS AND THE DISCLOSURE OF MANAGEMENT ACCOUNTING INFORMATION
JAR ST 87 VOL: 25 PG:165 - 189 :: ANAL. :INT. LOG. :THEORY :MANAG.

LANEN ,WN ; FIRS: HALPERIN,R CIT: 0
THE EFFECTS OF THE THOR POWER TOOL DECISION ON THE LIFO/FIFO CHOICE
TAR AP 87 VOL: 62 PG:378 - 384 :: REGRESS. :PRIM. :EMH :INV.

LANG ,M CIT: 0
TIME-VARYING STOCK PRICE RESPONSE TO EARNINGS INDUCED BY UNCERTAINTY ABOUT THE TIME-SERIES PROCESS OF EARNINGS
JAR AU 91 VOL: 29 PG:229 - 257 :: REGRESS. :PRIM. :TIME SER. :FIN.ST.TIM.

LANGENDERFER,HQ ; SEC: ROBERTSON,JC CIT: 0.06
A THEORETICAL STRUCTURE FOR INDEPENDENT AUDITS OF MANAGEMENT
TAR OC 69 VOL: 44 PG:777 - 787 :: QUAL. :INT. LOG. :INSTIT. :OTH.MANAG.

LANGHOLM,O CIT: 0
COST STRUCTURE AND COSTING METHOD: AN EMPIRICAL STUDY
JAR AU 65 VOL: 3 PG:218 - 227 :: ANAL. :INT. LOG. :THEORY :N/A

LANIER,RA ; FIRS: SMITH ,CH ; THIR: TAYLOR,ME CIT: 0.12
THE NEED FOR AND SCOPE OF THE AUDIT OF MANAGEMENT: A SURVEY OF ATTITUDES
TAR AP 72 VOL: 47 PG:270 - 283 :: DES.STAT. :SURV. :INSTIT. :AUD.

LANZILLOTTI,RF ; SEC: ESQUIBEL,AK CIT: 0
MEASURING DAMAGES IN COMMERCIAL LITIGATION: PRESENT VALUE OF LOST OPPORTUNITIES
JAA WI 90 VOL: 5 PG:125 - 142 :: DES.STAT. :INT. LOG. :OTH. :LITIG.

LARCHER,DF ; FIRS: LAMBERT,RA CIT: 0
ESTIMATING THE MARGINAL COSTS OF OPERATING A SERVICE DEPARTMENT WHEN RECIPROCAL SERVICES EXIST
TAR JL 89 VOL: 64 PG:449 - 467 :: DES.STAT. :INT. LOG. :MATH.PROG. :COST.ALLOC.

LARCKER,DF ; FIRS: HOLTHAUSEN,RW CIT: 2
THE PREDICTION OF STOCK RETURNS USING FINANCIAL STATEMENT INFORMATION
JAE JN 92 VOL: 15 PG:373 - 411 :: REGRESS. :PRIM. :EMH :FIN.METH.

LARCKER,DF ; FIRS: JANAKIRAMAN,SN ; SEC: LAMBERT,RA CIT: 1
AN EMPIRICAL INVESTIGATION OF THE RELATIVE PERFORMANCE EVALUATION HYPOTHESIS
JAR SP 92 VOL: 30 PG:53 - 69 :: REGRESS. :PRIM. :INF.ECO./AG. :EXEC.COMP.

LARCKER,DF ; FIRS: LANEN ,WN CIT: 0
EXECUTIVE COMPENSATION CONTRACT ADOPTION IN THE ELECTRIC UTILITY INDUSTRY
JAR SP 92 VOL: 30 PG:70 - 93 :: REGRESS. :PRIM. :INF.ECO./AG. :EXEC.COMP.

LARCKER,DF ; FIRS: LAMBERT,RA ; THIR: VERRECCHIA,RE CIT: 0.5
PORTFOLIO CONSIDERATIONS IN VALUING EXECUTIVE COMPENSATION
JAR SP 91 VOL: 29 PG:129 - 149 :: DES.STAT. :SIM. :INF.ECO./AG. :EXEC.COMP.

LARCKER,DF ; FIRS: DEFEO ,VJ ; SEC: LAMBER,RA CIT: 0.75
EXECUTIVE COMPENSATION EFFECTS OF EQUITY-FOR-DEBT SWAPS
TAR AP 89 VOL: 64 PG:201 - 227 :: REGRESS. :PRIM. :INF.ECO./AG. :LTD

LARCKER,DF ; FIRS: LAMBERT,RA CIT: 1.67
AN ANALYSIS OF THE USE OF ACCOUNTING AND MARKET MEASURES OF PERFORMANCE IN EXECUTIVE COMPENSATION CONTRACTS
JAR ST 87 VOL: 25 PG:85 - 125 :: REGRESS. :PRIM. :EMH :EXEC.COMP.

LARCKER,DF ; FIRS: LAMBERT,RA CIT: 0.25
GOLDEN PARACHUTES, EXECUTIVE DECISION-MAKING, AND SHAREHOLDER WEALTH
JAE AP 85 VOL: 7 PG:179 - 204 :: REGRESS. :PRIM. :EMH :EXEC.COMP.

LARCKER,DF ; FIRS: FERRIS,KR CIT: 0.3
EXPLANATORY VARIABLES OF AUDITOR PERFORMANCE IN A LARGE PUBLIC ACCOUNTING FIRM
AOS 01 83 VOL: 8 PG:1 - 12 :: CORR. :SURV. :OTH.BEH. :ORG.

LARCKER,DF CIT: 2.4
THE ASSOCIATION BETWEEN PERFORMANCE PLAN ADOPTION AND CORPORATE CAPITAL INVESTMENT
JAE AP 83 VOL: 5 PG:3 - 30 :: REGRESS. :PRIM. :EMH :EXEC.COMP.

LARCKER,DF ; SEC: LESSIG,VP CIT: 0.4
AN EXAMINATION OF THE LINEAR AND RETROSPECTIVE PROCESS TRACING APPROACHES TO JUDGMENT MODELING
TAR JA 83 VOL: 58 PG:58 - 77 :: OTH.QUANT. :LAB. :HIPS :METHOD.

LARCKER,DF ; SEC: REDER ,RE ; THIR: SIMON ,DT CIT: 0.3
TRADES BY INSIDERS AND MANDATED ACCOUNTING STANDARDS
TAR JL 83 VOL: 58 PG:606 - 620 :: NON-PAR. :INT. LOG. :EMH :OIL & GAS

LARCKER,DF ; SEC: REVSINE,L CIT: 0.5
THE OIL AND GAS ACCOUNTING CONTROVERSY: AN ANALYSIS OF ECONOMIC CONSEQUENCES
TAR OC 83 VOL: 58 PG:706 - 732 :: REGRESS. :PRIM. :EMH :OIL & GAS

LARCKER,DF CIT: 0.58
THE PERCEIVED IMPORTANCE OF SELECTED INFORMATION CHARACTERISTICS FOR STRATEGIC CAPITAL BUDGETING DECISIONS
TAR JL 81 VOL: 56 PG:519 - 538 :: ANOVA :LAB. :OTH.BEH. :CAP.BUDG.

LARCKER,DF ; FIRS: GORDON,LA ; THIR: TUGGLE,FD CIT: 0.67
STRATEGIC DECISION PROCESSES AND THE DESIGN OF ACCOUNTING INFORMATION SYSTEMS: CONCEPTUAL LINKAGES
AOS 34 78 VOL: 3 PG:203 - 214 :: QUAL. :INT. LOG. :OTH. :INFO.STRUC.

LARGAY III,JA ; FIRS: DAVIS ,ML CIT: 0
REPORTING CONSOLIDATED GAINS AND LOSSES ON SUBSIDIARY STOCK ISSUANCES
TAR AP 88 VOL: 63 PG:348 - 363 :: REGRESS. :PRIM. :THEORY :BUS.COMB.

LARGAY III,JA ; FIRS: THODE ,SF ; SEC: DRTINA,RE CIT: 0
OPERATING CASH FLOWS: A GROWING NEED FOR SEPARATE REPORTING
JAA WI 86 VOL: 1 PG:46 - 61 :: REGRESS. :PRIM. :EMH :OTH.FIN.ACC.

LARGAY III,JA CIT: 0
SFAS NO.52: EXPEDIENCY OR PRINCIPLE?
JAA AU 83 VOL: 7 PG:44 - 53 :: QUAL. :INT. LOG. :THEORY :FOR.CUR.

LARGAY III,JA CIT: 0
MICROECONOMIC FOUNDATIONS OF VARIABLE COSTING
TAR JA 73 VOL: 48 PG:115 - 119 :: QUAL. :INT. LOG. :N/A :INV.

LARKIN,PD ; FIRS: NICHOLS,DR ; SEC: TSAY ,JJ CIT: 0
INVESTOR TRADING RESPONSES TO DIFFERING CHARACTERISTICS OF VOLUNTARILY DISCLOSED EARNINGS FORECASTS
TAR AP 79 VOL: 54 PG:376 - 382 :: NON-PAR. :PRIM. :EMH :FOREC.

LARREA,J ; FIRS: ELLIOTT,EL ; THIR: RIVERA,JM CIT: 0
ACCOUNTING AID TO DEVELOPING COUNTRIES: SOME ADDITIONAL CONSIDERATIONS
TAR OC 68 VOL: 43 PG:763 - 768 :: QUAL. :INT. LOG. :INSTIT. :OTH.MANAG.

LARSON,KD CIT: 0.12
IMPLICATIONS OF MEASUREMENT THEORY ON ACCOUNTING CONCEPT FORMULATION
TAR JA 69 VOL: 44 PG:38 - 47 :: QUAL. :INT. LOG. :THEORY :OTH.FIN.ACC.

LARSON,KD ; SEC: GONEDES,NJ CIT: 0.06
BUSINESS COMBINATIONS: AN EXCHANGE RATIO DETERMINATION MODEL
TAR OC 69 VOL: 44 PG:720 - 728 :: ANAL. :INT. LOG. :N/A :BUS.COMB.

LARSON,KD CIT: 0.06
DESCRIPTIVE VALIDITY OF ACCOUNTING CALCULATIONS
TAR JL 67 VOL: 42 PG:480 - 488 :: QUAL. :INT. LOG. :THEORY :OTH.FIN.ACC.

LARSON,KD ; SEC: SCHATTKE,RW CIT: 0
CURRENT CASH EQUIVALENT, ADDITIVITY, AND FINANCIAL ACTION
TAR OC 66 VOL: 41 PG:634 - 641 :: QUAL. :INT. LOG. :THEORY :VALUAT.(INFL.)

LARSSON,L ; FIRS: SWIERINGA,RJ ; SEC: GIBBINS,M ; FOUR: SWEENEY,JL CIT: 1.41
EXPERIMENTS IN THE HEURISTICS OF HUMAN INFORMATION PROCESSING
JAR ST 76 VOL: 14 PG:159 - 187 :: MIXED :LAB. :HIPS :MANAG.

LARSSON,S ; SEC: CHESLEY,GR CIT: 0.14
AN ANALYSIS OF THE AUDITOR'S UNCERTAINTY ABOUT PROBABILITIES
CAR SP 86 VOL: 2 PG:259 - 282 :: REGRESS. :SURV. :HIPS :JUDG.

LAU ,AH CIT: 0
A FIVE-STATE FINANCIAL DISTRESS PREDICTION MODEL
JAR SP 87 VOL: 25 PG:127 - 138 :: REGRESS. :PRIM. :OTH.STAT. :BUS.FAIL.

LAU ,AH ; SEC: LAU ,HS CIT: 0
SOME PROPOSED APPROACHES FOR WRITING OFF CAPITALIZED HUMAN RESOURCE ASSETS
JAR SP 78 VOL: 16 PG:80 - 102 :: ANAL. :INT. LOG. :OTH.BEH. :HRA

LAU ,AH ; FIRS: KOTTAS,JF ; THIR: LAU ,HS CIT: 0.27
A GENERAL APPROACH TO STOCHASTIC MANAGEMENT PLANNING MODELS: AN OVERVIEW
TAR AP 78 VOL: 53 PG:389 - 401 :: ANAL. :INT. LOG. :MATH.PROG. :C-V-P-A

LAU ,AHL ; SEC: LAU ,HS CIT: 0
CVP ANALYSIS WITH STOCHASTIC PRICE-DEMAND FUNCTIONS AND SHORTAGE-SURPLUS COSTS
CAR AU 87 VOL: 4 PG:194 - 209 :: DES.STAT. :INT. LOG. :OTH.STAT. :C-V-P-A

LAU ,HS ; FIRS: LAU ,AHL CIT: 0
CVP ANALYSIS WITH STOCHASTIC PRICE-DEMAND FUNCTIONS AND SHORTAGE-SURPLUS COSTS
CAR AU 87 VOL: 4 PG:194 - 209 :: DES.STAT. :INT. LOG. :OTH.STAT. :C-V-P-A

LAU ,HS ; FIRS: LAU ,AH CIT: 0
SOME PROPOSED APPROACHES FOR WRITING OFF CAPITALIZED HUMAN RESOURCE ASSETS
JAR SP 78 VOL: 16 PG:80 - 102 :: ANAL. :INT. LOG. :OTH.BEH. :HRA

LAU ,HS ; FIRS: KOTTAS,JF ; SEC: LAU ,AH CIT: 0.27
A GENERAL APPROACH TO STOCHASTIC MANAGEMENT PLANNING MODELS: AN OVERVIEW
TAR AP 78 VOL: 53 PG:389 - 401 :: ANAL. :INT. LOG. :MATH.PROG. :C-V-P-A

LAU ,HS ; FIRS: KOTTAS,JF CIT: 0.07
DIRECT SIMULATION IN STOCHASTIC CVP ANALYSIS
TAR JL 78 VOL: 53 PG:698 - 707 :: QUAL. :INT. LOG. :OTH.STAT. :C-V-P-A

LAU ,HS ; FIRS: JAGGI ,B CIT: 0.29
TOWARD A MODEL FOR HUMAN RESOURCE VALUATION
TAR AP 74 VOL: 49 PG:321 - 329 :: MARKOV :INT. LOG. :OTH.STAT. :HRA

LAUGHLIN,R ; FIRS: MILLER,P ; SEC: HOPPER,T CIT: 0
THE NEW ACCOUNTING HISTORY: AN INTRODUCTION
AOS 05 91 VOL: 16 PG:395 - 403 :: REGRESS. :SEC. :HIST. :METHOD.

LAUGHLIN,RC CIT: 0.33
ACCOUNTING SYSTEMS IN ORGANIZATIONAL CONTEXTS: A CASE FOR CRITICAL THEORY
AOS 05 87 VOL: 12 PG:479 - 502 :: DES.STAT. :INT. LOG. :THEORY :OTH.MANAG.

LAUVER,RC CIT: 0
THE CASE FOR POOLINGS
TAR JA 66 VOL: 41 PG:65 - 74 :: QUAL. :INT. LOG. :THEORY :BUS.COMB.

LAVALLE,IH ; SEC: RAPPAPORT,A CIT: 0
ON THE ECONOMICS OF ACQUIRING INFORMATION OF IMPERFECT RELIABILITY
TAR AP 68 VOL: 43 PG:225 - 230 :: ANAL. :INT. LOG. :INF.ECO./AG. :REL.COSTS

LAVIN ,D CIT: 0.19
SOME EFFECTS OF THE PERCEIVED INDEPENDENCE OF THE AUDITOR
AOS 03 77 VOL: 2 PG:237 - 244 :: QUAL. :SEC. :OTH.BEH. :INDEP.

LAVIN ,D CIT: 0.35
PERCEPTIONS OF THE INDEPENDENCE OF THE AUDITOR
TAR JA 76 VOL: 51 PG:41 - 50 :: ANOVA :SURV. :INSTIT. :INDEP.

LAVOIE,D CIT: 1
THE ACCOUNTING OF INTERPRETATIONS AND THE INTERPRETATION OF ACCOUNTS: THE COMMUNICATIVE FUNCTION OF THE LANGUAGE OF BUSINESS
AOS 06 87 VOL: 12 PG:579 - 604 :: DES.STAT. :INT. LOG. :THEORY :FIN.METH.

LAWLER III,EE ; FIRS: MIRVIS,PH CIT: 0.2
SYSTEMS ARE NOT SOLUTIONS: ISSUES IN CREATING INFORMATION SYSTEMS THAT ACCOUNT FOR THE HUMAN ORGANIZATION
AOS 23 83 VOL: 8 PG:175 - 190 :: QUAL. :FIELD :OTH.BEH. :ORG.& ENVIR.

LAWLER III,EE ; FIRS: RHODE ,JG ; SEC: SORENSEN,JE CIT: 0.69
SOURCES OF PROFESSIONAL STAFF TURNOVER IN PUBLIC ACCOUNTING FIRMS REVEALED BY THE EXIT INTERVIEW
AOS 02 77 VOL: 2 PG:165 - 176 :: NON-PAR. :SURV. :OTH. :ORG.

LAWLER,J CIT: 0
THE QUEST FOR ACCOUNTING PHILOSOPHERS
JAR ST 67 VOL: 5 PG:86 - 92 :: QUAL. :SURV. :THEORY :N/A

LAWRENCE,EC CIT: 0.1
REPORTING DELAYS FOR FAILED FIRMS
JAR AU 83 VOL: 21 PG:606 - 610 :: DES.STAT. :PRIM. :EMH :FIN.ST.TIM.

LAWSON,RA ; FIRS: BRIEF ,RP CIT: 0
THE ROLE OF THE ACCOUNTING RATE OF RETURN IN FINANCIAL STATEMENT ANALYSIS
TAR AP 92 VOL: 67 PG:411 - 426 :: DES.STAT. :INT. LOG. :OTH.STAT. :CAP.BUDG.

LEA ,RB CIT: 0
RECOMMENDATIONS OF THE COMMISSION ON AUDITOR'S RESPONSIBILITIES - AN ANALYSIS OF THE PROFESSION'S RESPONSES
AUD SU 81 VOL: 1 PG:53 - 94 :: QUAL. :INT. LOG. :INSTIT. :ORG.

LEA ,RB CIT: 0
A NOTE ON THE DEFINITION OF COST COEFFICIENTS IN A LINEAR PROGRAMMING MODEL
TAR AP 72 VOL: 47 PG:346 - 350 :: ANAL. :INT. LOG. :MATH.PROG. :MANAG.

LEASE ,RC ; FIRS: BRICKLEY,JA ; SEC: BHAGAT,S CIT: 0.63
THE IMPACT OF LONG-RANGE MANAGERIAL COMPENSATION PLANS ON SHAREHOLDER WEALTH
JAE AP 85 VOL: 7 PG:115 - 130 :: REGRESS. :PRIM. :EMH :EXEC.COMP.

LECLERE,MJ ; FIRS: CUSHING,BE CIT: 1
EVIDENCE ON THE DETERMINANTS OF INVENTORY ACCOUNTING POLICY CHOICE
TAR AP 92 VOL: 67 PG:355 - 367 :: REGRESS. :MIXED :OTH.STAT. :INV.

LEE ,CF ; SEC: WU ,C CIT: 0
EXPECTATION FORMATION AND FINANCIAL RATIO ADJUSTMENT PROCESSES
TAR AP 88 VOL: 63 PG:292 - 306 :: DES.STAT. :PRIM. :OTH.STAT. :METHOD.

LEE ,CF ; FIRS: FRECKA,TJ CIT: 0
GENERALIZED FINANCIAL RATIO ADJUSTMENT PROCESSES AND THEIR IMPLICATIONS
JAR SP 83 VOL: 21 PG:308 - 316 :: REGRESS. :PRIM. :EMH :N/A

LEE ,CJ CIT: 0.2
INVENTORY ACCOUNTING AND EARNINGS/PRICE RATIOS: A PUZZLE
CAR AU 88 VOL: 5 PG:371 - 388 :: REGRESS. :PRIM. :EMH :INV.

LEE ,CJ CIT: 0.25
STOCHASTIC PROPERTIES OF CROSS-SECTIONAL FINANCIAL DATA
JAR SP 85 VOL: 23 PG:213 - 227 :: REGRESS. :PRIM. :EMH :METHOD.

LEE ,CJ ; SEC: HSIEH ,DA CIT: 1.38
CHOICE OF INVENTORY ACCOUNTING METHODS: COMPARATIVE ANALYSES OF ALTERNATIVE HYPOTHESES
JAR AU 85 VOL: 23 PG:468 - 485 :: REGRESS. :PRIM. :OTH.STAT. :INV.

LEE ,CJ CIT: 0.11
THE SPEED OF ADJUSTMENT OF FINANCIAL RATIOS: AN ERROR-IN-VARIABLE PROBLEM
JAR AU 84 VOL: 22 PG:776 - 781 :: ANAL. :INT. LOG. :OTH. :METHOD.

LEE ,CMC CIT: 1
EARNINGS NEWS AND SMALL TRADERS: AN INTRADAY ANALYSIS
JAE JN 92 VOL: 15 PG:265 - 302 :: REGRESS. :PRIM. :EMH :FIN.METH.

LEE ,CWJ ; SEC: PETRUZZI,CR CIT: 0.5
INVENTORY ACCOUNTING SWITCH AND UNCERTAINTY
JAR AU 89 VOL: 27 PG:277 - 296 :: REGRESS. :PRIM. :OTH.STAT. :INV.

LEE ,GA CIT: 0
THE FRANCIS WILLUGHBY EXECUTORSHIP ACCOUNTS, 1672-1682: AN EARLY DOUBLE-ENTRY SYSTEM IN ENGLAND
TAR JL 81 VOL: 56 PG:539 - 553 :: QUAL. :INT. LOG. :HIST. :N/A

LEE ,GA CIT: 0
THE FLORENTINE BANK LEDGER FRAGMENTS OF 1211: SOME NEW INSIGHTS
JAR SP 73 VOL: 11 PG:47 - 61 :: QUAL. :INT. LOG. :HIST. :OTH.MANAG.

LEE ,LC ; SEC: BEDFORD,NM CIT: 0
AN INFORMATION THEORY ANALYSIS OF THE ACCOUNTING PROCESS
TAR AP 69 VOL: 44 PG:256 - 275 :: ANAL. :INT. LOG. :INF.ECO./AG. :OTH.MANAG.

LEE ,SS CIT: 0
KOREAN ACCOUNTING REVALUATION LAWS
TAR JL 65 VOL: 40 PG:622 - 625 :: QUAL. :INT. LOG. :THEORY :VALUAT.(INFL.)

LEFTWICH,R CIT: 0.33
AGGREGATION OF TEST STATISTICS: STATISTICS VS. ECONOMICS
JAE JA 90 VOL: 12 PG:37 - 44 :: REGRESS. :SEC. :EMH :FIN.METH.

LEFTWICH,R ; FIRS: DODD ,P ; SEC: DOPUCH,N ; THIR: HOLTHAUSEN,RW CIT: 1.56
QUALIFIED AUDIT OPINIONS AND STOCK PRICES: INFORMATION CONTENT, ANNOUNCEMENT DATES, AND CONCURRENT DISCLOSURES
JAE AP 84 VOL: 6 PG:3 - 38 :: REGRESS. :PRIM. :EMH :OPIN.

LEFTWICH,RW ; FIRS: DOPUCH,N ; SEC: HOLTHAUSEN,RW CIT: 1
PREDICTING AUDIT QUALIFICATIONS WITH FINANCIAL AND MARKET VARIABLES
TAR JL 87 VOL: 62 PG:431 - 454 :: REGRESS. :PRIM. :EMH :OPIN.

LEFTWICH,RW ; FIRS: DOPUCH,N ; SEC: HOLTHAUSEN,RW CIT: 0.57
ABNORMAL STOCK RETURNS ASSOCIATED WITH MEDIA DISCLOSURES OF 'SUBJECT TO' QUALIFIED AUDIT OPINIONS
JAE JN 86 VOL: 8 PG:93 - 118 :: REGRESS. :PRIM. :EMH :OPIN.

LEFTWICH,RW ; FIRS: HOLTHAUSEN,RW CIT: 5.2
THE ECONOMIC CONSEQUENCES OF ACCOUNTING CHOICES: IMPLICATIONS OF COSTLY CONTRACTING AND MONITORING
JAE AG 83 VOL: 5 PG:77 - 117 :: QUAL. :SEC. :EMH :METHOD.

LEFTWICH,RW CIT: 2.2
ACCOUNTING INFORMATION IN PRIVATE MARKETS: EVIDENCE FROM PRIVATE LENDING AGREEMENTS
TAR JA 83 VOL: 58 PG:23 - 42 :: DES.STAT. :PRIM. :THEORY :FASB SUBM.

LEFTWICH,RW CIT: 3.58
EVIDENCE OF THE IMPACT OF MANDATORY CHANGES IN ACCOUNTING PRINCIPLES ON CORPORATE LOAN AGREEMENTS
JAE MR 81 VOL: 3 PG:3 - 36 :: MIXED :PRIM. :EMH :ACC.CHNG.

LEFTWICH,RW ; SEC: WATTS ,RL ; THIR: ZIMMERMAN,JL CIT: 0.58
VOLUNTARY CORPORATE DISCLOSURE: THE CASE OF INTERIM REPORTING
JAR ST 81 VOL: 19 PG:50 - 77 :: ANAL. :PRIM. :OTH.STAT. :INT.REP.

LEFTWICH,RW CIT: 0.62
MARKET FAILURE FALLACIES AND ACCOUNTING INFORMATION
JAE DE 80 VOL: 2 PG:193 - 211 :: QUAL. :INT. LOG. :INF.ECO./AG. :METHOD.

LEFTWICH,RW ; FIRS: WATTS ,RL CIT: 2.63
THE TIME SERIES OF ANNUAL ACCOUNTING EARNINGS
JAR AU 77 VOL: 15 PG:253 - 271 :: MIXED :PRIM. :TIME SER. :FOREC.

LEHMAN,C ; SEC: TINKER,T CIT: 2.5
THE REAL CULTURAL SIGNIFICANCE OF ACCOUNTS
AOS 05 87 VOL: 12 PG:503 - 522 :: DES.STAT. :SEC. :HIST. :OTH.MANAG.

LEHMAN,CR CIT: 1
"HERSTORY" IN ACCOUNTING: THE FIRST EIGHTY YEARS
AOS 04 92 VOL: 17 PG:261 - 285 :: REGRESS. :SEC. :HIST. :ORG.& ENVIR.

LEININGER,WE ; FIRS: CORCORAN,AW CIT: 0.06
STOCHASTIC PROCESS COSTING MODELS
TAR JA 73 VOL: 48 PG:105 - 114 :: ANAL. :INT. LOG. :MATH.PROG. :COST.ALLOC.

LEITCH,RA ; FIRS: PLANTE,R ; SEC: NETER ,J CIT: 0.25
COMPARATIVE PERFORMANCE OF MULTINOMIAL, CELL, AND STRINGER BOUNDS
AUD AU 85 VOL: 5 PG:40 - 56 :: DES.STAT. :SIM. :OTH.STAT. :SAMP.

LEITCH,RA ; FIRS: DUKE ,GL ; SEC: NETER ,J CIT: 1.09
POWER CHARACTERISTICS OF TEST STATISTICS IN THE AUDITING ENVIRONMENT: AN EMPIRICAL STUDY
JAR SP 82 VOL: 20 PG:42 - 67 :: MIXED :PRIM. :OTH.STAT. :ERRORS

LEITCH,RA ; SEC: NETER ,J ; THIR: PLANTE,R ; FOUR: SINHA ,P CIT: 0.91
MODIFIED MULTINOMIAL BOUNDS FOR LARGER NUMBERS OF ERRORS IN AUDITS
TAR AP 82 VOL: 57 PG:384 - 400 :: DES.STAT. :SIM. :OTH.STAT. :SAMP.

LEITCH,RA ; FIRS: JOHNSON,JR ; THIR: NETER ,J CIT: 1.83
CHARACTERISTICS OF ERRORS IN ACCOUNTS RECEIVABLE AND INVENTORY AUDITS
TAR AP 81 VOL: 56 PG:270 - 293 :: DES.STAT. :PRIM. :OTH. :ERRORS

LEITCH,RA ; FIRS: IJIRI ,Y CIT: 0.23
STEIN'S PARADOX AND AUDIT SAMPLING
JAR SP 80 VOL: 18 PG:91 - 108 :: MIXED :INT. LOG. :OTH.STAT. :N/A

LEITCH,RA ; FIRS: NETER ,J ; THIR: FIENBERG,SE CIT: 0.73
DOLLAR UNIT SAMPLING: MULTINOMIAL BOUNDS FOR TOTAL OVERSTATEMENT AND UNDERSTATEMENT ERRORS
TAR JA 78 VOL: 53 PG:77 - 93 :: NON-PAR. :SIM. :MATH.PROG. :SAMP.

LEITCH,RA ; FIRS: HILLIARD,JE CIT: 0.41
COST-VOLUME-PROFIT ANALYSIS UNDER UNCERTAINTY: A LOG NORMAL APPROACH
TAR JA 75 VOL: 50 PG:69 - 80 :: ANAL. :INT. LOG. :OTH.STAT. :C-V-P-A

LEMBKE,VC ; SEC: TOOLE ,HR CIT: 0
DIFFERENCES IN DEPRECIATION METHODS AND THE ANALYSIS OF SUPPLEMENTAL CURRENT-COST AND REPLACEMENT COST DATA
JAA WI 81 VOL: 4 PG:128 - 135 :: ANAL. :INT. LOG. :THEORY :VALUAT.(INFL.)

LEMBKE,VC ; SEC: SMITH ,JH CIT: 0
REPLACEMENT COSTS: AN ANALYSIS OF FINANCIAL STATEMENT AND TAX POLICY EFFECTS
JAA WI 80 VOL: 3 PG:147 - 162 :: DES.STAT. :PRIM. :THEORY :VALUAT.(INFL.)

LEMBKE,VC CIT: 0
SOME CONSIDERATIONS IN ACCOUNTING FOR DIVISIVE REORGANIZATIONS
TAR JL 70 VOL: 45 PG:458 - 464 :: QUAL. :INT. LOG. :THEORY :FIN.METH.

LEMKE ,KW ; SEC: PAGE ,MJ CIT: 0
ECONOMIC DETERMINANTS OF ACCOUNTING POLICY CHOICE: THE CASE OF CURRENT COST ACCOUNTING IN THE U.K.
JAE MR 92 VOL: 15 PG:87 - 114 :: REGRESS. :PRIM. :OTH.STAT. :ACC.CHNG.

LEMKE ,KW CIT: 0.06
THE EVALUATION OF LIQUIDITY: AN ANALYTICAL STUDY
JAR SP 70 VOL: 8 PG:47 - 77 :: ANAL. :INT. LOG. :OTH.STAT. :FIN.METH.

LEMKE ,KW CIT: 0.12
ASSET VALUATION AND INCOME THEORY
TAR JA 66 VOL: 41 PG:32 - 41 :: QUAL. :INT. LOG. :THEORY :VALUAT.(INFL.)

LEMON ,WM ; FIRS: BORITZ,JE ; SEC: GABER ,BG CIT: 0
AN EXPERIMENTAL STUDY OF THE EFFECTS OF ELICITATION METHODS ON REVIEW OF PRELIMINARY AUDIT STRATEGY BY EXTERNAL AUDITORS
CAR SP 88 VOL: 4 PG:392 - 411 :: REGRESS. :LAB. :HIPS :METHOD.

LEMON ,WM ; FIRS: JOHNSTON,DJ ; THIR: NEUMANN,FL CIT: 0
THE CANADIAN STUDY OF THE ROLE OF THE AUDITOR
JAA SP 80 VOL: 3 PG:251 - 263 :: QUAL. :INT. LOG. :THEORY :PROF.RESP.

LENGERMANN,JJ CIT: 0.18
SUPPOSED AND ACTUAL DIFFERENCES IN PROFESSIONAL AUTONOMY AMONG CPAS AS RELATED TO TYPE OF WORK ORGANIZATION AND SIZE OF FIRM
TAR OC 71 VOL: 46 PG:665 - 675 :: ANOVA :SURV. :OTH.BEH. :AUD.

LENTILHON,RW CIT: 0
DIRECT COSTING - EITHER ... OR?
TAR OC 64 VOL: 39 PG:880 - 883 :: QUAL. :INT. LOG. :THEORY :OVER.ALLOC.

LENWAY,S ; FIRS: RAYBURN,J CIT: 0
AN INVESTIGATION OF THE BEHAVIOR OF ACCRUALS IN THE SEMICONDUCTOR INDUSTRY: 1985
CAR AU 92 VOL: 9 PG:237 - 251 :: REGRESS. :PRIM. :OTH. :REV.REC.

LERE ,JC CIT: 0
PRODUCT PRICING BASED ON ACCOUNTING COSTS
TAR AP 86 VOL: 61 PG:318 - 324 :: DES.STAT. :INT. LOG. :THEORY :COST.ALLOC.

LERE ,JC ; FIRS: DICKHAUT,JW CIT: 0.2
COMPARISON OF ACCOUNTING SYSTEMS AND HEURISTICS IN SELECTING ECONOMIC OPTIMA
JAR AU 83 VOL: 21 PG:495 - 513 :: ANAL. :INT. LOG. :INF.ECO./AG. :INFO.STRUC.

LESSARD,DR ; SEC: LORANGE,P CIT: 0
CURRENCY CHANGES AND MANAGEMENT CONTROL: RESOLVING THE CENTRALIZATION/DECENTRALIZATION DILEMMA
TAR JL 77 VOL: 52 PG:628 - 637 :: QUAL. :INT. LOG. :THEORY :TRANS.PRIC.

LESSEM,R CIT: 0.13
CORPORATE SOCIAL REPORTING IN ACTION: AN EVALUATION OF BRITISH, EUROPEAN AND AMERICAN PRACTICE
AOS 04 77 VOL: 2 PG:279 - 294 :: QUAL. :PRIM. :THEORY :HRA

LESSIG,VP ; FIRS: LARCKER,DF CIT: 0.4
AN EXAMINATION OF THE LINEAR AND RETROSPECTIVE PROCESS TRACING APPROACHES TO JUDGMENT MODELING
TAR JA 83 VOL: 58 PG:58 - 77 :: OTH.QUANT. :LAB. :HIPS :METHOD.

LEV ,B ; SEC: PENMAN,SH CIT: 1.33
VOLUNTARY FORECAST DISCLOSURE, NONDISCLOSURE, AND STOCK PRICES
JAR SP 90 VOL: 28 PG:49 - 76 :: REGRESS. :PRIM. :EMH :FOREC.

LEV ,B CIT: 2
ON THE USEFULNESS OF EARNINGS AND EARNINGS RESEARCH: LESSONS AND DIRECTIONS FROM TWO DECADES OF EMPIRICAL RESEARCH
JAR ST 89 VOL: 27 PG:153 - 192 :: REGRESS. :SEC. :EMH :FIN.METH.

LEV ,B CIT: 2
TOWARD A THEORY OF EQUITABLE AND EFFICIENT ACCOUNTING POLICY
TAR JA 88 VOL: 63 PG:1 - 22 :: ANAL. :INT. LOG. :THEORY :FIN.METH.

LEV ,B CIT: 0.4
SOME ECONOMIC DETERMINANTS OF TIME-SERIES PROPERTIES OF EARNINGS
JAE AP 83 VOL: 5 PG:31 - 48 :: CORR. :PRIM. :EMH :METHOD.

LEV ,B ; SEC: OHLSON,JA CIT: 3.27
MARKET-BASED EMPIRICAL RESEARCH IN ACCOUNTING: A REVIEW, INTERPRETATION, AND EXTENSION
JAR ST 82 VOL: 20 PG:249 - 322 :: QUAL. :SEC. :EMH :METHOD.

LEV ,B CIT: 0.31
ON THE USE OF INDEX MODELS IN ANALYTICAL REVIEWS BY AUDITORS
JAR AU 80 VOL: 18 PG:524 - 550 :: REGRESS. :PRIM. :TIME SER. :ANAL.REV.

LEV ,B ; SEC: TAYLOR,KW CIT: 0
ACCOUNTING RECOGNITION OF IMPUTED INTEREST ON EQUITY: AN EMPIRICAL INVESTIGATION
JAA SP 79 VOL: 2 PG:232 - 243 :: REGRESS. :PRIM. :EMH :FIN.METH.

LEV ,B ; SEC: SUNDER,S CIT: 0.79
METHODOLOGICAL ISSUES IN THE USE OF FINANCIAL RATIOS
JAE DE 79 VOL: 1 PG:187 - 210 :: QUAL. :INT. LOG. :OTH.STAT. :METHOD.

LEV ,B CIT: 1.93
THE IMPACT OF ACCOUNTING REGULATION ON THE STOCK MARKET: THE CASE OF OIL AND GAS COMPANIES
TAR JL 79 VOL: 54 PG:485 - 503 :: REGRESS. :PRIM. :EMH :OIL & GAS

LEV ,B ; SEC: THEIL ,H CIT: 0
A MAXIMUM ENTROPY APPROACH TO THE CHOICE OF ASSET DEPRECIATION
JAR AU 78 VOL: 16 PG:286 - 293 :: ANAL. :INT. LOG. :THEORY :PP&E / DEPR

LEV ,B ; FIRS: ADAR ,Z ; SEC: BARNEA,A CIT: 0.19
A COMPREHENSIVE COST-VOLUME-PROFIT ANALYSIS UNDER UNCERTAINTY
TAR JA 77 VOL: 52 PG:137 - 149 :: QUAL. :INT. LOG. :THEORY :TAXES

LEV ,B ; FIRS: BALL ,R ; THIR: WATTS ,RL CIT: 0.24
INCOME VARIATION AND BALANCE SHEET COMPOSITIONS
JAR SP 76 VOL: 14 PG:1 - 9 :: REGRESS. :PRIM. :OTH.STAT. :REV.REC.

LEV ,B ; FIRS: FRIEDMAN,A CIT: 0.24
A SURROGATE MEASURE FOR THE FIRM'S INVESTMENT IN HUMAN RESOURCES
JAR AU 74 VOL: 12 PG:235 - 250 :: ANAL. :INT. LOG. :OTH.BEH. :HRA

LEV ,B ; SEC: KUNITZKY,S CIT: 0.35
ON THE ASSOCIATION BETWEEN SMOOTHING MEASURES AND THE RISK OF COMMON STOCKS
TAR AP 74 VOL: 49 PG:259 - 270 :: CORR. :PRIM. :TIME SER. :FIN.METH.

LEV ,B ; SEC: SCHWARTZ,A CIT: 0.65
ON THE USE OF THE ECONOMIC CONCEPT OF HUMAN CAPITAL IN FINANCIAL STATEMENTS
TAR JA 71 VOL: 46 PG:103 - 112 :: ANAL. :INT. LOG. :THEORY :HRA

LEV ,B CIT: 0.12
THE INFORMATIONAL APPROACH TO AGGREGATION IN FINANCIAL STATEMENTS: EXTENSIONS
JAR SP 70 VOL: 8 PG:78 - 94 :: ANAL. :INT. LOG. :INF.ECO./AG. :INFO.STRUC.

LEV ,B CIT: 0
A COMMENT ON BUSINESS COMBINATIONS: AN EXCHANGE RATIO DETERMINATION MODEL
TAR JL 70 VOL: 45 PG:532 - 534 :: ANAL. :INT. LOG. :N/A :BUS.COMB.

LEV ,B CIT: 0.24
INDUSTRY AVERAGES AS TARGETS FOR FINANCIAL RATIOS
JAR AU 69 VOL: 7 PG:290 - 299 :: REGRESS. :PRIM. :TIME SER. :LEASES

LEV ,B CIT: 0
TESTING A PREDICTION METHOD FOR MULTIVARIATE BUDGETS
JAR ST 69 VOL: 7 PG:182 - 197 :: DES.STAT. :PRIM. :OTH.STAT. :BUDG.& PLAN.

LEV ,B CIT: 0
AN INFORMATION THEORY ANALYSIS OF BUDGET VARIANCES
TAR OC 69 VOL: 44 PG:704 - 710 :: ANAL. :INT. LOG. :INF.ECO./AG. :VAR.

LEV ,B CIT: 0.29
THE AGGREGATION PROBLEM IN FINANCIAL STATEMENTS: AN INFORMATIONAL APPROACH
JAR AU 68 VOL: 6 PG:247 - 261 :: ANAL. :INT. LOG. :INF.ECO./AG. :INFO.STRUC.

LEVITAN,AS ; SEC: KNOBLETT,JA CIT: 0.25
INDICATORS OF EXCEPTIONS TO THE GOING CONCERN ASSUMPTION
AUD AU 85 VOL: 5 PG:26 - 39 :: REGRESS. :PRIM. :OTH.STAT. :OPIN.

LEVY ,FK ; FIRS: IJIRI ,Y ; THIR: LYON ,RC CIT: 0.12
A LINEAR PROGRAMMING MODEL FOR BUDGETING AND FINANCIAL PLANNING
JAR AU 63 VOL: 1 PG:198 - 212 :: ANAL. :INT. LOG. :MATH.PROG. :BUDG.& PLAN.

LEVY ,H CIT: 0
SMALL FIRM EFFECT: ARE THERE ABNORMAL RETURNS IN THE MARKET
JAA SP 90 VOL: 5 PG:235 - 270 :: REGRESS. :PRIM. :EMH :ORG.& ENVIR.

LEVY ,H ; SEC: BYUN ,YH CIT: 0
AN EMPIRICAL TEST OF THE BLACK-SCHOLES OPTION PRICING MODEL AND THE IMPLIED VARIANCE: A CONFIDENCE INTERVAL APPROACH
JAA AU 87 VOL: 2 PG:355 - 369 :: DES.STAT. :PRIM. :OTH. :OTH.MANAG.

LEVY ,H ; FIRS: BARLEV,B CIT: 0.07
ON THE VARIABILITY OF ACCOUNTING INCOME NUMBERS
JAR AU 79 VOL: 17 PG:305 - 315 :: DES.STAT. :PRIM. :TIME SER. :FIN.METH.

LEWELLEN,W ; SEC: LODERER,C ; THIR: MARTIN,K CIT: 0.5
EXECUTIVE COMPENSATION AND EXECUTIVE INCENTIVE PROBLEMS: AN EMPIRICAL ANALYSIS
JAE DE 87 VOL: 9 PG:287 - 310 :: REGRESS. :PRIM. :OTH.STAT. :EXEC.COMP.

LEWELLEN,W ; SEC: LODERER,C ; THIR: ROSENFELD,A CIT: 0.5
MERGER DECISIONS AND EXECUTIVE STOCK OWNERSHIP IN ACQUIRING FIRMS
JAE AP 85 VOL: 7 PG:209 - 232 :: REGRESS. :PRIM. :OTH.STAT. :BUS.COMB.

LEWIN ,AY ; FIRS: SCHIFF,M CIT: 1.29
THE IMPACT OF PEOPLE ON BUDGETS
TAR AP 70 VOL: 45 PG:259 - 268 :: QUAL. :INT. LOG. :OTH.BEH. :BUDG.& PLAN.

LEWIS ,BL ; FIRS: BONNER,SE CIT: 0.67
DETERMINANTS OF AUDITOR EXPERTISE
JAR ST 90 VOL: 28 PG:001 - 28 :: REGRESS. :LAB. :HIPS :AUD.BEH.

LEWIS ,BL ; FIRS: PETERS,JM ; THIR: DHAR ,V CIT: 0
ASSESSING INHERENT RISK DURING AUDIT PLANNING: THE DEVELOPMENT OF A KNOWLEDGE BASED MODEL
AOS 04 89 VOL: 14 PG:359 - 378 :: ANOVA :SURV. :EXP.SYST. :PLAN.

LEWIS ,BL ; FIRS: BAIMAN,S CIT: 1.25
AN EXPERIMENT TESTING THE BEHAVIORAL EQUIVALENCE OF STRATEGICALLY EQUIVALENT CONTRACTS
JAR SP 89 VOL: 27 PG:1 - 20 :: REGRESS. :LAB. :HIPS :EXEC.COMP.

LEWIS ,BL ; SEC: PATTON,JM ; THIR: GREEN ,SL CIT: 0.2
THE EFFECTS OF INFORMATION CHOICE AND INFORMATION USE ON ANALYSTS' PREDICTIONS OF MUNICIPAL BOND RATING CHANGES
TAR AP 88 VOL: 63 PG:270 - 282 :: REGRESS. :LAB. :OTH.STAT. :FOREC.

LEWIS ,BL ; FIRS: EVANS III,JH ; THIR: PATTON,JM CIT: 0.14
AN ECONOMIC MODELING APPROACH TO CONTINGENCY THEORY AND MANAGEMENT CONTROL
AOS 06 86 VOL: 11 PG:483 - 498 :: DES.STAT. :INT. LOG. :INF.ECO./AG. :INT.CONT.

LEWIS ,BL ; SEC: BELL ,J CIT: 0
DECISIONS INVOLVING SEQUENTIAL EVENTS: REPLICATIONS AND EXTENSIONS
JAR SP 85 VOL: 23 PG:228 - 239 :: REGRESS. :LAB. :HIPS :INFO.STRUC.

LEWIS ,BL ; SEC: SHIELDS,MD ; THIR: YOUNG ,SM CIT: 0.9
EVALUATING HUMAN JUDGMENTS AND DECISION AIDS
JAR SP 83 VOL: 21 PG:271 - 285 :: DES.STAT. :LAB. :HIPS :ORG.& ENVIR.

LEWIS ,BL ; FIRS: LIBBY ,R CIT: 2.55
HUMAN INFORMATION PROCESSING RESEARCH IN ACCOUNTING: THE STATE OF THE ART IN 1982
AOS 03 82 VOL: 7 PG:231 - 286 :: QUAL. :SEC. :HIPS :MANAG.

LEWIS ,BL ; FIRS: DIRSMITH,MW CIT: 0.09
THE EFFECT OF EXTERNAL REPORTING ON MANAGERIAL DECISION-MAKING: SOME ANTECEDENT CONDITIONS
AOS 04 82 VOL: 7 PG:319 - 336 :: NON-PAR. :SURV. :HIPS :FIN.METH.

LEWIS ,BL CIT: 0.85
EXPERT JUDGMENT IN AUDITING: AN EXPECTED UTILITY APPROACH
JAR AU 80 VOL: 18 PG:594 - 602 :: ANOVA :LAB. :HIPS :JUDG.

LEWIS ,BL ; FIRS: LIBBY ,R CIT: 2.5
HUMAN INFORMATION PROCESSING RESEARCH IN ACCOUNTING: THE STATE OF THE ART
AOS 03 77 VOL: 2 PG:245 - 268 :: QUAL. :SEC. :HIPS :MANAG.

LEWIS ,CD CIT: 0
TAX DEDUCTIBILITY OF EDUCATORS' TRAVEL EXPENSES
TAR JA 67 VOL: 42 PG:96 - 105 :: QUAL. :SEC. :N/A :TAXES

LEWIS ,NR ; SEC: PARKER,LD ; THIR: SUTCLIFFE,P CIT: 0
FINANCIAL REPORTING TO EMPLOYEES: THE PATTERN OF DEVELOPMENT 1919 TO 1979
AOS 34 84 VOL: 9 PG:275 - 289 :: DES.STAT. :SEC. :HIST. :HRA

LI ,DH CIT: 0
THE OBJECTIVES OF THE CORPORATION UNDER THE ENTITY CONCEPT
TAR OC 64 VOL: 39 PG:946 - 950 :: QUAL. :INT. LOG. :THEORY :OTH.MANAG.

LI ,DH CIT: 0
THE SEMANTIC ASPECT OF COMMUNICATION THEORY AND ACCOUNTANCY
JAR SP 63 VOL: 1 PG:102 - 107 :: QUAL. :INT. LOG. :THEORY :N/A

LI ,DH CIT: 0
ALTERNATIVE ACCOUNTING PROCEDURES AND THE ENTITY CONCEPT
TAR JA 63 VOL: 38 PG:52 - 55 :: QUAL. :INT. LOG. :THEORY :N/A

LI ,DH CIT: 0
THE FUNDS STATEMENT UNDER THE ENTITY CONCEPT
TAR OC 63 VOL: 38 PG:771 - 775 :: QUAL. :INT. LOG. :THEORY :N/A

LI ,L ; FIRS: BALACHANDRAN,BV ; THIR: MAGEE ,RP CIT: 0.33
ON THE ALLOCATION OF FIXED AND VARIABLE COSTS FROM SERVICE DEPARTMENTS
CAR AU 87 VOL: 4 PG:164 - 185 :: DES.STAT. :INT. LOG. :INF.ECO./AG. :COST.ALLOC.

LIANG ,T-P ; SEC: CHANDLER,JS ; THIR: HAN ,I ; FOUR: ROAN ,J CIT: 0
AN EMPIRICAL INVESTIGATION OF SOME DATA EFFECTS ON THE CLASSIFICATION
ACCURACY OF PROBIT, ID3 AND NEURAL NETWORKS
CAR AU 92 VOL: 9 PG:306 - 328 :: DES.STAT. :PRIM. :OTH.STAT. :METHOD.

LIAO ,M CIT: 0.35
MODEL SAMPLING: A STOCHASTIC COST-VOLUME-PROFIT ANALYSIS
TAR OC 75 VOL: 50 PG:780 - 790 :: ANAL. :INT. LOG. :OTH.STAT. :C-V-P-A

LIAO ,WM ; FIRS: THAKKAR,RB ; SEC: FINLEY,DR CIT: 0.11
A STOCHASTIC DEMAND CVP MODEL WITH RETURN ON INVESTMENT CRITERION
CAR AU 84 VOL: 1 PG:77 - 86 :: DES.STAT. :INT. LOG. :MATH.PROG. :C-V-P-A

LIBBY ,PA ; FIRS: LIBBY ,R CIT: 0.75
EXPERT MEASUREMENT AND MECHANICAL COMBINATION IN CONTROL RELIANCE DECISIONS
TAR OC 89 VOL: 64 PG:729 - 747 :: DES.STAT. :FIELD :HIPS :JUDG.

LIBBY ,R ; SEC: LIPE ,MG CIT: 0
INCENTIVES, EFFORT, AND THE COGNITIVE PROCESSES INVOLVED IN
ACCOUNTING-RELATED JUDGMENTS
JAR AU 92 VOL: 30 PG:249 - 273 :: REGRESS. :LAB. :HIPS :JUDG.

LIBBY ,R ; SEC: FREDERICK,DM CIT: 2.33
EXPERIENCE AND THE ABILITY TO EXPLAIN AUDIT FINDINGS
JAR AU 90 VOL: 28 PG:348 - 367 :: REGRESS. :LAB. :HIPS :AUD.BEH.

LIBBY ,R ; SEC: LIBBY ,PA CIT: 0.75
EXPERT MEASUREMENT AND MECHANICAL COMBINATION IN CONTROL RELIANCE DECISIONS
TAR OC 89 VOL: 64 PG:729 - 747 :: DES.STAT. :FIELD :HIPS :JUDG.

LIBBY ,R ; FIRS: FREDERICK,DM CIT: 2
EXPERTISE AND AUDITORS' JUDGMENTS OF CONJUNCTIVE EVENTS
JAR AU 86 VOL: 24 PG:270 - 290 :: REGRESS. :LAB. :HIPS :JUDG.

LIBBY ,R CIT: 3
AVAILABILITY AND THE GENERATION OF HYPOTHESES IN ANALYTICAL REVIEW
JAR AU 85 VOL: 23 PG:648 - 667 :: REGRESS. :LAB. :HIPS :ANAL.REV.

LIBBY ,R ; SEC: ARTMAN,JT ; THIR: WILLINGHAM,JJ CIT: 0.75
PROCESS SUSCEPTIBILITY, CONTROL RISK, AND AUDIT PLANNING
TAR AP 85 VOL: 60 PG:212 - 230 :: REGRESS. :LAB. :HIPS :INT.CONT.

LIBBY ,R ; SEC: LEWIS ,BL CIT: 2.55
HUMAN INFORMATION PROCESSING RESEARCH IN ACCOUNTING: THE STATE OF THE ART IN1982
AOS 03 82 VOL: 7 PG:231 - 286 :: QUAL. :SEC. :HIPS :MANAG.

LIBBY ,R ; FIRS: JOYCE ,EJ ; THIR: SUNDER,S CIT: 0.09
USING THE FASB'S QUALITATIVE CHARACTERISTICS IN ACCOUNTING POLICY CHOICES
JAR AU 82 VOL: 20 PG:654 - 675 :: DES.STAT. :SURV. :INSTIT. :FASB SUBM.

LIBBY ,R ; FIRS: JOYCE ,EJ CIT: 0.33
SOME ACCOUNTING IMPLICATIONS OF BEHAVIOURAL DECISION THEORY: PROCESSES OF JUDGMENT AND CHOICE
JAR AU 81 VOL: 19 PG:544 - 550 :: QUAL. :INT. LOG. :HIPS :MANAG.

LIBBY ,R CIT: 0.64
BANKERS' AND AUDITORS' PERCEPTIONS OF THE MESSAGE COMMUNICATED BY THE AUDIT REPORT
JAR SP 79 VOL: 17 PG:99 - 122 :: OTH.QUANT. :LAB. :HIPS :OPIN.

LIBBY ,R CIT: 0.57
THE IMPACT OF UNCERTAINTY REPORTING ON THE LOAN DECISION
JAR ST 79 VOL: 17 PG:35 - 57 :: ANOVA :LAB. :HIPS :OPIN.

LIBBY ,R ; SEC: LEWIS ,BL CIT: 2.5
HUMAN INFORMATION PROCESSING RESEARCH IN ACCOUNTING: THE STATE OF THE ART
AOS 03 77 VOL: 2 PG:245 - 268 :: QUAL. :SEC. :HIPS :MANAG.

LIBBY ,R ; SEC: FISHBURN,PC CIT: 0.75
BEHAVIOURAL MODELS OF RISK TAKING IN BUSINESS DECISIONS: A SURVEY AND EVALUATION
JAR AU 77 VOL: 15 PG:272 - 292 :: QUAL. :SEC. :OTH.BEH. :OTH.MANAG.

LIBBY ,R CIT: 1.06
ACCOUNTING RATIOS AND THE PREDICTION OF FAILURE: SOME BEHAVIOURAL EVIDENCE
JAR SP 75 VOL: 13 PG:150 - 161 :: MIXED :LAB. :HIPS :BUS.FAIL.

LIBBY ,R CIT: 1.41
THE USE OF SIMULATED DECISION MAKERS IN INFORMATION EVALUATION
TAR JL 75 VOL: 50 PG:475 - 489 :: ANOVA :LAB. :HIPS :OTH.MANAG.

LIBERTY,SE ; SEC: ZIMMERMAN,JL CIT: 1.71
LABOR UNION CONTRACT NEGOTIATIONS AND ACCOUNTING CHOICES
TAR OC 86 VOL: 61 PG:692 - 712 :: REGRESS. :PRIM. :OTH.STAT. :INFO.STRUC.

LICASTRO,RD ; FIRS: COPELAND,RM CIT: 0.18
A NOTE ON INCOME SMOOTHING
TAR JL 68 VOL: 43 PG:540 - 545 :: ANOVA :PRIM. :TIME SER. :CASH DIV.

LICATA,MP ; SEC: STRAWSER,RH ; THIR: WELKER,RB CIT: 0.14
A NOTE ON PARTICIPATION IN BUDGETING AND LOCUS OF CONTROL
TAR JA 86 VOL: 61 PG:112 - 117 :: REGRESS. :LAB. :OTH.BEH. :BUDG.& PLAN.

LICHTENBERG,FR CIT: 0
A PERSPECTIVE ON ACCOUNTING FOR DEFENSE CONTRACTS
TAR OC 92 VOL: 67 PG:741 - 752 :: REGRESS. :PRIM. :INF.ECO./AG. :COST.ALLOC.

LIEBERMAN,AZ ; SEC: WHINSTON,AB CIT: 0.41
A STRUCTURING OF AN EVENTS-ACCOUNTING INFORMATION SYSTEM
TAR AP 75 VOL: 50 PG:246 - 258 :: QUAL. :INT. LOG. :OTH.STAT. :N/A

LIGHTNER,KM ; FIRS: LIGHTNER,SM ; SEC: ADAMS ,SJ CIT: 0.36
THE INFLUENCE OF SITUATIONAL, ETHICAL, AND EXPECTANCY THEORY VARIABLES ON ACCOUNTANTS' UNDERREPORTING BEHAVIOR
AUD AU 82 VOL: 2 PG:1 - 12 :: DES.STAT. :SURV. :OTH.STAT. :ORG.

LIGHTNER,SM ; SEC: ADAMS ,SJ ; THIR: LIGHTNER,KM CIT: 0.36
THE INFLUENCE OF SITUATIONAL, ETHICAL, AND EXPECTANCY THEORY VARIABLES ON ACCOUNTANTS' UNDERREPORTING BEHAVIOR
AUD AU 82 VOL: 2 PG:1 - 12 :: DES.STAT. :SURV. :OTH.STAT. :ORG.

LILIEN,S ; FIRS: EL-GAZZAR,S ; THIR: PASTENA,V CIT: 0.25
THE USE OF OFF-BALANCE SHEET FINANCING TO CIRCUMVENT FINANCIAL COVENANT RESTRICTIONS
JAA SP 89 VOL: 4 PG:217 - 231 :: REGRESS. :PRIM. :OTH.STAT. :SPEC.ITEMS

LILIEN,S ; SEC: MELLMAN,M ; THIR: PASTENA,V CIT: 0.6
ACCOUNTING CHANGES: SUCCESSFUL VERSUS UNSUCCESSFUL FIRMS
TAR OC 88 VOL: 63 PG:642 - 656 :: REGRESS. :PRIM. :THEORY :ACC.CHNG.

LILIEN,S ; FIRS: HAW ,IM ; SEC: PASTENA,V CIT: 0
THE ASSOCIATION BETWEEN MARKET-BASED MERGER PREMIUMS AND FIRMS' FINANCIAL POSITION PRIOR TO MERGER
JAA WI 87 VOL: 2 PG:24 - 42 :: REGRESS. :PRIM. :EMH :BUS.COMB.

LILIEN,S ; FIRS: EL-GAZZAR,S ; THIR: PASTENA,V CIT: 0.86
ACCOUNTING FOR LEASES BY LESSEES
JAE OC 86 VOL: 8 PG:217 - 238 :: REGRESS. :PRIM. :OTH.STAT. :LEASES

LILIEN,S ; SEC: PASTENA,V CIT: 1.82
DETERMINANTS OF INTRAMETHOD CHOICE IN THE OIL AND GAS INDUSTRY
JAE DE 82 VOL: 4 PG:145 - 170 :: REGRESS. :PRIM. :OTH.STAT. :OIL & GAS

LILIEN,SB ; FIRS: HAW ,I ; SEC: JUNG ,K CIT: 0
OVERFUNDED DEFINED BENEFIT PENSION PLAN SETTLEMENTS WITHOUT ASSET REVERSIONS
JAE SE 91 VOL: 14 PG:295 - 320 :: REGRESS. :PRIM. :TIME SER. :PENS.

LILIEN,SB ; FIRS: HAW ,I ; SEC: PASTENA,VS CIT: 0.33
MARKET MANIFESTATION OF NONPUBLIC INFORMATION PRIOR TO MERGERS: THE EFFECT PF OWNERSHIP STRUCTURE
TAR AP 90 VOL: 65 PG:432 - 451 :: REGRESS. :PRIM. :EMH :BUS.COMB.

LILLESTOL,J CIT: 0
A NOTE ON COMPUTING UPPER ERROR LIMITS IN DOLLAR-UNIT SAMPLING
JAR SP 81 VOL: 19 PG:263 - 267 :: ANAL. :SIM. :OTH.STAT. :LIAB.

LILLIS,A ; FIRS: WILLIAMS,DJ CIT: 0
EDP AUDITS OF OPERATING SYSTEMS - AN EXPLORATORY STUDY OF THE DETERMINANTS OF THE PRIOR PROBABILITY RISK
AUD SP 85 VOL: 4 PG:110 - 117 :: REGRESS. :SURV. :OTH.STAT. :EDP AUD.

LILLY ,MS ; FIRS: DYL ,EA CIT: 0.13
A NOTE ON INSTITUTIONAL CONTRIBUTIONS TO THE ACCOUNTING LITERATURE
AOS 02 85 VOL: 10 PG:171 - 176 :: REGRESS. :SEC. :INSTIT. :METHOD.

LIM ,R CIT: 0.12
THE MATHEMATICAL PROPRIETY OF ACCOUNTING MEASUREMENTS AND CALCULATIONS
TAR OC 66 VOL: 41 PG:642 - 651 :: ANAL. :INT. LOG. :OTH.STAT. :OTH.FIN.ACC.

LIM ,SS ; SEC: SUNDER,S CIT: 0
EFFICIENCY OF ASSET VALUATION RULES UNDER PRICE MOVEMENT AND MEASUREMENT ERRORS
TAR OC 91 VOL: 66 PG:669 - 693 :: DES.STAT. :INT. LOG. :MATH.PROG. :VALUAT.(INFL.)

LIMBERG,ST ; FIRS: KACHELMEIER,SJ ; THIR: SCHADEWALD,MS CIT: 0
A LABORATORY MARKET EXAMINATION OF THE CONSUMER PRICE RESPONSE TO INFORMATION ABOUT PRODUCERS' COSTS AND PROFITS
TAR OC 91 VOL: 66 PG:694 - 717 :: REGRESS. :LAB. :HIPS :N/A

LIN ,WT ; SEC: MOCK ,TJ ; THIR: WRIGHT,A CIT: 0.33
THE USE OF ANALYTIC HIERARCHY PROCESS AS AN AID IN PLANNING THE NATURE AND EXTENT OF AUDIT PROCEDURES
AUD AU 84 VOL: 4 PG:89 - 99 :: ANAL. :INT. LOG. :OTH.STAT. :PLAN.

LIN ,WT CIT: 0.13
MULTIPLE OBJECTIVE BUDGETING MODELS: A SIMULATION
TAR JA 78 VOL: 53 PG:61 - 76 :: ANOVA :SIM. :MATH.PROG. :BUDG.& PLAN.

LINDAHL,FW CIT: 0.75
DYNAMIC ANALYSIS OF INVENTORY ACCOUNTING CHOICE
JAR AU 89 VOL: 27 PG:201 - 226 :: REGRESS. :PRIM. :OTH.STAT. :INV.

LINDAHL,FW ; FIRS: BIDDLE,GC CIT: 2.36
STOCK PRICE REACTIONS TO LIFO ADOPTIONS: THE ASSOCIATION BETWEEN EXCESS RETURNS AND LIFO TAX SAVINGS
JAR AU 82 VOL: 20 PG:551 - 588 :: MIXED :PRIM. :EMH :INV.

LINDGREN,JH ; FIRS: PEARSON,MA ; THIR: MYERS ,BL CIT: 0.07
A PRELIMINARY ANALYSIS OF AUDSEC VOTING PATTERNS
JAA WI 79 VOL: 2 PG:122 - 134 :: OTH.QUANT. :PRIM. :INSTIT. :FASB SUBM.

LINDHE,R CIT: 0.12
ACCELERATED DEPRECIATION FOR INCOME TAX PURPOSES - A STUDY OF THE DECISION AND SOME FIRMS WHO MADE IT
JAR AU 63 VOL: 1 PG:139 - 148 :: DES.STAT. :PRIM. :THEORY :PP&E / DEPR

LINDSAY,WD ; FIRS: CHUNG ,DY CIT: 0
THE PRICING OF AUDIT SERVICES: THE CANADIAN PERSPECTIVE
CAR AU 88 VOL: 5 PG:19 - 46 :: REGRESS. :PRIM. :OTH.STAT. :ORG.

LINN ,JJ ; FIRS: FIRMIN,PA ; SEC: GOODMAN,SS ; THIR: HENDRICKS,TE CIT: 0
UNIVERSITY COST STRUCTURE AND BEHAVIOR: AN EMPIRICAL STUDY
JAR ST 68 VOL: 6 PG:122 - 155 :: DES.STAT. :SIM. :OTH.STAT. :MANAG.

LINN ,JJ ; FIRS: FIRMIN,PA CIT: 0.06
INFORMATION SYSTEMS AND MANAGERIAL ACCOUNTING
TAR JA 68 VOL: 43 PG:75 - 82 :: QUAL. :INT. LOG. :N/A :OTH.MANAG.

LINOWES,DF CIT: 0
FUTURE OF THE ACCOUNTING PROFESSION
TAR JA 65 VOL: 40 PG:97 - 104 :: QUAL. :INT. LOG. :INSTIT. :OTH.MANAG.

LINSMEIER,TJ ; FIRS: WARFIELD,TD CIT: 0
TAX PLANNING, EARNINGS MANAGEMENT, AND THE DIFFERENTIAL INFORMATION CONTENT OF BANK EARNINGS COMPONENTS
TAR JL 92 VOL: 67 PG:546 - 562 :: REGRESS. :PRIM. :EMH :FIN.METH.

LIPE ,MG ; FIRS: LIBBY ,R CIT: 0
INCENTIVES, EFFORT, AND THE COGNITIVE PROCESSES INVOLVED IN ACCOUNTING-RELATED JUDGMENTS
JAR AU 92 VOL: 30 PG:249 - 273 :: REGRESS. :LAB. :HIPS :JUDG.

LIPE ,R CIT: 3.67
THE RELATION BETWEEN STOCK RETURNS AND ACCOUNTING EARNINGS GIVEN ALTERNATIVE INFORMATION
TAR JA 90 VOL: 65 PG:49 - 71 :: REGRESS. :PRIM. :EMH :FIN.METH.

LIPE ,RC CIT: 2.86
THE INFORMATION CONTAINED IN THE COMPONENTS OF EARNINGS
JAR ST 86 VOL: 24 PG:37 - 68 :: REGRESS. :PRIM. :EMH :FIN.METH.

LITTLETON,AC CIT: 0
FACTORS LIMITING ACCOUNTING
TAR JL 70 VOL: 45 PG:476 - 480 :: QUAL. :INT. LOG. :THEORY :REV.REC.

LITZENBERGER,RH ; SEC: TALMOR,E CIT: 0
THE IRRELEVANCY OF CORPORATE TAXES FOR CAPITAL STRUCTURE AND INVESTMENT DECISIONS
JAA SU 89 VOL: 4 PG:305 - 316 :: DES.STAT. :INT. LOG. :INF.ECO./AG. :TAXES

LITZENBERGER,RH ; FIRS: JOY ,OM ; THIR: MCENALLY,RW CIT: 0.81
THE ADJUSTMENT OF STOCK PRICES TO ANNOUNCEMENTS OF UNANTICIPATED CHANGES IN QUARTERLY EARNINGS
JAR AU 77 VOL: 15 PG:207 - 225 :: REGRESS. :PRIM. :EMH :FIN.METH.

LIU ,E ; FIRS: BIERMAN JR,H CIT: 0
THE COMPUTATION OF EARNINGS PER SHARE
TAR JA 68 VOL: 43 PG:62 - 67 :: QUAL. :INT. LOG. :THEORY :PENS.

LIVINGSTONE,JL ; FIRS: BALACHANDRAN,KR ; SEC: MASCHMEYER,R CIT: 0.08
PRODUCT WARRANTY PERIOD: A MARKOVIAN APPROACH TO ESTIMATION AND ANALYSIS OF REPAIR AND REPLACEMENT COSTS
TAR JA 81 VOL: 56 PG:115 - 124 :: MARKOV :INT. LOG. :OTH.STAT. :SPEC.ITEMS

LIVINGSTONE,JL ; FIRS: BALACHANDRAN,KR CIT: 0
COST AND EFFECTIVENESS OF PHYSICIAN PEER REVIEW IN REDUCING MEDICARE OVERUTILIZATION
AOS 02 77 VOL: 2 PG:153 - 164 :: DES.STAT. :PRIM. :OTH.STAT. :MANAG.

LIVINGSTONE,JL ; FIRS: RONEN ,J CIT: 1.65
AN EXPECTANCY THEORY APPROACH TO THE MOTIVATIONAL IMPACTS OF BUDGETS
TAR OC 75 VOL: 50 PG:671 - 685 :: QUAL. :INT. LOG. :OTH.BEH. :BUDG.& PLAN.

LIVINGSTONE,JL ; SEC: SALAMON,GL CIT: 0.12
RELATIONSHIP BETWEEN THE ACCOUNTING AND THE INTERNAL RATE OF RETURN MEASURES: A SYNTHESIS AND AN ANALYSIS
JAR AU 70 VOL: 8 PG:199 - 216 :: DES.STAT. :SIM. :OTH.STAT. :FIN.METH.

LIVINGSTONE,JL CIT: 0.06
ACCELERATED DEPRECIATION, TAX ALLOCATION, AND CYCLICAL ASSET EXPENDITURES OF LARGE MANUFACTURING COMPANIES
JAR AU 69 VOL: 7 PG:245 - 256 :: REGRESS. :SIM. :OTH.STAT. :TAXES

LIVINGSTONE,JL CIT: 0.06
INPUT-OUTPUT ANALYSIS FOR COST ACCOUNTING, PLANNING AND CONTROL
TAR JA 69 VOL: 44 PG:48 - 64 :: ANAL. :INT. LOG. :MATH.PROG. :COST.ALLOC.

LIVINGSTONE,JL ; FIRS: BRUNDAGE,MV CIT: 0
SIMULATION ON A TIME-SHARING COMPUTER UTILITY SYSTEM
TAR JL 69 VOL: 44 PG:539 - 545 :: ANAL. :SIM. :N/A :OTH.MANAG.

LIVINGSTONE,JL CIT: 0.12
MATRIX ALGEBRA AND COST ALLOCATION
TAR JL 68 VOL: 43 PG:503 - 508 :: ANAL. :INT. LOG. :MATH.PROG. :COST.ALLOC.

LIVINGSTONE,JL CIT: 0
ACCELERATED DEPRECIATION, CYCLICAL ASSET EXPENDITURES AND DEFERRED TAXES
JAR SP 67 VOL: 5 PG:77 - 94 :: DES.STAT. :PRIM. :TIME SER. :PP&E / DEPR

LIVINGSTONE,JL CIT: 0
ACCELERATED DEPRECIATION AND DEFERRED TAXES: AN EMPIRICAL STUDY OF FLUCTUATING ASSET EXPENDITURES
JAR ST 67 VOL: 5 PG:93 - 123 :: REGRESS. :PRIM. :OTH.STAT. :PP&E / DEPR

LIVINGSTONE,JL CIT: 0.24
ELECTRIC UTILITY PLANT REPLACEMENT COSTS
TAR AP 67 VOL: 42 PG:233 - 240 :: DES.STAT. :PRIM. :THEORY :VALUAT.(INFL.)

LIVINGSTONE,JL CIT: 0
A BEHAVIOURAL STUDY OF TAX ALLOCATION IN ELECTRIC UTILITY REGULATION
TAR JL 67 VOL: 42 PG:544 - 552 :: ANOVA :PRIM. :N/A :TAXES

LIVINGSTONE,JL ; FIRS: IJIRI ,Y ; SEC: JAEDICKE,RK CIT: 0.12
THE EFFECT OF INVENTORY COSTING METHODS ON FULL AND DIRECT COSTING
JAR SP 65 VOL: 3 PG:63 - 74 :: ANAL. :INT. LOG. :THEORY :MANAG.

LIVNAT,J ; FIRS: BARLEY,B CIT: 0
THE INFORMATION CONTENT OF FUNDS STATEMENT RATIOS
JAA SU 90 VOL: 5 PG:411 - 433 :: REGRESS. :PRIM. :TIME SER. :OTH.FIN.ACC.

LIVNAT,J ; FIRS: AMIT ,R ; THIR: ZAROWIN,P CIT: 0
A CLASSIFICATION OF MERGERS AND ACQUISITIONS BY MOTIVES: ANALYSIS OF MARKET RESPONSES
CAR AU 89 VOL: 6 PG:143 - 158 :: REGRESS. :PRIM. :EMH :BUS.COMB.

LIVNAT,J ; FIRS: AMIT ,R CIT: 0
DIVERSIFICATION, CAPITAL STRUCTURE, AND SYSTEMATIC RISK: AN EMPIRICAL INVESTIGATION
JAA WI 88 VOL: 03 PG:19 - 43 :: REGRESS. :PRIM. :EMH :OTH.FIN.ACC.

LIVNAT,J ; FIRS: BARLEV,B ; SEC: FRIED ,D CIT: 0
ECONOMIC AND FINANCIAL REPORTING EFFECTS OF INVENTORY TAX ALLOWANCES
CAR SP 86 VOL: 2 PG:288 - 310 :: REGRESS. :INT. LOG. :MATH.PROG. :INV.

LIVNAT,J CIT: 0
A GENERALIZATION OF THE API METHODOLOGY AS A WAY OF MEASURING THE ASSOCIATION BETWEEN INCOME AND STOCK PRICES
JAR AU 81 VOL: 19 PG:350 - 359 :: REGRESS. :PRIM. :EMH :METHOD.

LIVNAT,J ; FIRS: RONEN ,J CIT: 0.17
INCENTIVES FOR SEGMENT REPORTING
JAR AU 81 VOL: 19 PG:459 - 481 :: ANAL. :INT. LOG. :EMH :SEG.REP.

LIVNAT,J ; FIRS: FRIED ,D CIT: 0.08
INTERIM STATEMENTS: AN ANALYTICAL EXAMINATION OF ALTERNATIVE ACCOUNTING TECHNIQUES
TAR JL 81 VOL: 56 PG:493 - 509 :: ANAL. :INT. LOG. :TIME SER. :N/A

LIVOCK,DM CIT: 0
THE ACCOUNTS OF THE CORPORATION OF BRISTOL: 1532 TO 1835
JAR SP 65 VOL: 3 PG:86 - 102 :: QUAL. :INT. LOG. :HIST. :N/A

LLOYD ,AJ ; FIRS: OWEN ,DL CIT: 0.38
THE USE OF FINANCIAL INFORMATION BY TRADE UNION NEGOTIATORS IN PLANT LEVEL COLLECTIVE BARGAINING
AOS 03 85 VOL: 10 PG:329 - 352 :: DES.STAT. :INT. LOG. :THEORY :ORG.& ENVIR.

LLOYD ,BM ; SEC: WEYGANDT,JJ CIT: 0
MARKET VALUE INFORMATION FOR NON SUBSIDIARY INVESTMENTS
TAR OC 71 VOL: 46 PG:756 - 764 :: DES.STAT. :PRIM. :N/A :BUS.COMB.

LOBO ,GJ ; FIRS: IMHOFF JR,EA CIT: 1
THE EFFECT OF EX ANTE EARNINGS UNCERTAINTY ON EARNINGS RESPONSE COEFFICIENTS
TAR AP 92 VOL: 67 PG:427 - 439 :: REGRESS. :PRIM. :EMH :N/A

LOBO ,GJ ; SEC: SONG ,I CIT: 0.5
THE INCREMENTAL INFORMATION IN SFAS NO. 33 INCOME DISCLOSURES OVER HISTORICAL COST INCOME AND ITS CASH AND ACCRUAL COMPONENTS
TAR AP 89 VOL: 64 PG:329 - 343 :: REGRESS. :PRIM. :EMH :FIN.METH.

LOBO ,GJ ; FIRS: IMHOFF JR,EA CIT: 0.56
INFORMATION CONTENT OF ANALYSTS' COMPOSITE FORECAST REVISIONS
JAR AU 84 VOL: 22 PG:541 - 554 :: REGRESS. :PRIM. :EMH :FOREC.

LOBO ,GL ; SEC: MAHMOUD,AAW CIT: 0.5
RELATIONSHIP BETWEEN DIFFERENTIAL AMOUNTS OF PRIOR INFORMATION AND SECURITY RETURN VARIABILITY
JAR SP 89 VOL: 27 PG:116 - 134 :: REGRESS. :PRIM. :EMH :INFO.STRUC.

LODERER,C ; FIRS: LEWELLEN,W ; THIR: MARTIN,K CIT: 0.5
EXECUTIVE COMPENSATION AND EXECUTIVE INCENTIVE PROBLEMS: AN EMPIRICAL ANALYSIS
JAE DE 87 VOL: 9 PG:287 - 310 :: REGRESS. :PRIM. :OTH.STAT. :EXEC.COMP.

LODERER,C ; FIRS: LEWELLEN,W ; THIR: ROSENFELD,A CIT: 0.5
MERGER DECISIONS AND EXECUTIVE STOCK OWNERSHIP IN ACQUIRING FIRMS
JAE AP 85 VOL: 7 PG:209 - 232 :: REGRESS. :PRIM. :OTH.STAT. :BUS.COMB.

LOEB ,M ; FIRS: COHEN ,SI CIT: 0.2
IMPROVING PERFORMANCE THROUGH COST ALLOCATION
CAR AU 88 VOL: 5 PG:70 - 95 :: DES.STAT. :INT. LOG. :INF.ECO./AG. :COST.ALLOC.

LOEB ,M ; FIRS: COHEN ,SI CIT: 0.09
PUBLIC GOODS, COMMON INPUTS, AND THE EFFICIENCY OF FULL COST ALLOCATIONS
TAR AP 82 VOL: 57 PG:336 - 347 :: ANAL. :INT. LOG. :OTH.STAT. :COST.ALLOC.

LOEB ,M ; SEC: MAGAT ,WA CIT: 0.4
SOVIET SUCCESS INDICATORS AND THE EVALUATION OF DIVISIONAL MANAGEMENT
JAR SP 78 VOL: 16 PG:103 - 121 :: ANAL. :INT. LOG. :INF.ECO./AG. :INT.DIFF.

LOEB ,SE CIT: 0.12
ENFORCEMENT OF THE CODE OF ETHICS: A SURVEY
TAR JA 72 VOL: 47 PG:1 - 10 :: DES.STAT. :PRIM. :INSTIT. :OTH.MANAG.

LOEB ,SE CIT: 0.24
A SURVEY OF ETHICAL BEHAVIOR IN THE ACCOUNTING PROFESSION
JAR AU 71 VOL: 9 PG:287 - 306 :: MIXED :SURV. :OTH.BEH. :AUD.BEH.

LOEBBECKE,JK ; SEC: EINING,MM ; THIR: WILLINGHAM,JJ CIT: 0.5
AUDITORS' EXPERIENCE WITH MATERIAL IRREGULARITIES: FREQUENCY, NATURE, AND DETECTABILITY
AUD AU 89 VOL: 9 PG:1 - 28 :: REGRESS. :SURV. :OTH.STAT. :PLAN.

LOEBBECKE,JK ; SEC: STEINBART,PJ CIT: 0.33
AN INVESTIGATION OF THE USE OF PRELIMINARY ANALYTICAL REVIEW TO PROVIDE SUBSTANTIVE AUDIT EVIDENCE
AUD SP 87 VOL: 6 PG:74 - 89 :: REGRESS. :SIM. :OTH.STAT. :ANAL.REV.

LOEBBECKE,JK ; FIRS: CUSHING,BE CIT: 1.3
ANALYTICAL APPROACHES TO AUDIT RISK: A SURVEY AND ANALYSIS
AUD AU 83 VOL: 3 PG:23 - 41 :: ANAL. :SEC. :OTH.STAT. :RISK

LOEBBECKE,JK ; SEC: NETER ,J CIT: 0.18
CONSIDERATIONS IN CHOOSING STATISTICAL SAMPLING PROCEDURES IN AUDITING
JAR ST 75 VOL: 13 PG:38 - 52 :: QUAL. :INT. LOG. :OTH.STAT. :SAMP.

LOFT ,A CIT: 0
ACCOUNTANCY AND THE GENDERED DIVISION OF LABOUR: A REVIEW ESSAY
AOS 04 92 VOL: 17 PG:367 - 378 :: REGRESS. :SEC. :HIST. :ORG.& ENVIR.

LOFT ,A CIT: 4.14
TOWARDS A CRITICAL UNDERSTANDING OF ACCOUNTING: THE CASE OF COST ACCOUNTING IN THE U.K., 1914-1925
AOS 02 86 VOL: 11 PG:137 - 170 :: DES.STAT. :INT. LOG. :HIST. :COST.ALLOC.

LONG ,MS ; FIRS: HITE ,GL CIT: 0.45
TAXES AND EXECUTIVE STOCK OPTIONS
JAE JL 82 VOL: 4 PG:3 - 14 :: QUAL. :INT. LOG. :THEORY :TAXES

LONGSTRETH,B CIT: 0
THE SEC'S ROLE IN FINANCIAL DISCLOSURE
JAA WI 84 VOL: 7 PG:110 - 122 :: QUAL. :INT. LOG. :INSTIT. :FIN.METH.

LOOKABILL,LL ; FIRS: ALBRECHT,WS ; THIR: MCKEOWN,JC CIT: 2.25
THE TIME-SERIES PROPERTIES OF ANNUAL EARNINGS
JAR AU 77 VOL: 15 PG:226 - 244 :: MIXED :PRIM. :TIME SER. :FOREC.

LOOKABILL,LL CIT: 0.47
SOME ADDITIONAL EVIDENCE ON THE TIME SERIES PROPERTIES OF ACCOUNTING EARNINGS
TAR OC 76 VOL: 51 PG:724 - 738 :: REGRESS. :PRIM. :TIME SER. :FOREC.

LORANGE,P ; FIRS: LESSARD,DR CIT: 0
CURRENCY CHANGES AND MANAGEMENT CONTROL: RESOLVING THE CENTRALIZATION/DECENTRALIZATION DILEMMA
TAR JL 77 VOL: 52 PG:628 - 637 :: QUAL. :INT. LOG. :THEORY :TRANS.PRIC.

LORD ,AT CIT: 0
PRESSURE: A METHODOLOGICAL CONSIDERATION FOR BEHAVIORAL RESEARCH IN AUDITING
AUD AU 92 VOL: 11 PG:89 - 108 :: REGRESS. :LAB. :HIPS :AUD.BEH.

LOREK ,KS ; SEC: BRANSON,BC ; THIR: ICERMAN,RC CIT: 0
ON THE USE OF TIME-SERIES MODELS AS ANALYTICAL PROCEDURES
AUD AU 92 VOL: 11 PG:66 - 88 :: DES.STAT. :PRIM. :TIME SER. :ANAL.REV.

LOREK ,KS ; FIRS: BATHKE,AW ; THIR: WILLINGER,GL CIT: 0
FIRM-SIZE AND THE PREDICTIVE ABILITY OF QUARTERLY EARNINGS DATA
TAR JA 89 VOL: 64 PG:49 - 68 :: REGRESS. :PRIM. :TIME SER. :INT.REP.

LOREK ,KS ; SEC: BATHKE,AW CIT: 0.11
A TIME-SERIES ANALYSIS OF NONSEASONAL QUARTERLY EARNINGS DATA
JAR SP 84 VOL: 22 PG:369 - 379 :: CORR. :PRIM. :TIME SER. :FOREC.

LOREK ,KS ; FIRS: BATHKE,AW CIT: 0.56
THE RELATIONSHIP BETWEEN TIME-SERIES MODELS AND THE SECURITY MARKET'S EXPECTATION OF QUARTERLY EARNINGS
TAR AP 84 VOL: 59 PG:163 - 176 :: REGRESS. :PRIM. :TIME SER. :FOREC.

LOREK ,KS ; SEC: ICERMAN,JD ; THIR: ABDULKADER,AA CIT: 0
FURTHER DESCRIPTIVE AND PREDICTIVE EVIDENCE ON ALTERNATIVE TIME-SERIES MODELS FOR QUARTERLY EARNINGS
JAR SP 83 VOL: 21 PG:317 - 328 :: REGRESS. :PRIM. :TIME SER. :FOREC.

LOREK ,KS CIT: 0.71
PREDICTING ANNUAL NET EARNINGS WITH QUARTERLY EARNINGS TIME SERIES MODELS
JAR SP 79 VOL: 17 PG:190 - 204 :: REGRESS. :PRIM. :TIME SER. :FOREC.

LOREK ,KS ; SEC: MCDONALD,CL ; THIR: PATZ ,DH CIT: 0.65
A COMPARATIVE EXAMINATION OF MANAGEMENT FORECASTS AND BOX-JENKINS FORECASTS OF EARNINGS
TAR AP 76 VOL: 51 PG:321 - 330 :: REGRESS. :PRIM. :TIME SER. :METHOD.

LORIG ,AN CIT: 0.12
SOME BASIC CONCEPTS OF ACCOUNTING AND THEIR IMPLICATIONS
TAR JL 64 VOL: 39 PG:563 - 573 :: QUAL. :INT. LOG. :THEORY :FIN.METH.

LORIG ,AN CIT: 0
SUGGESTED IMPROVEMENTS IN GOVERNMENTAL ACCOUNTING
TAR OC 63 VOL: 38 PG:759 - 763 :: QUAL. :INT. LOG. :THEORY :N/A

LOSELL,D ; FIRS: HAM ,J ; THIR: SMIELIAUSKAS,W CIT: 0.33
SOME EMPIRICAL EVIDENCE ON THE STABILITY OF ACCOUNTING ERROR CHARACTERISTICS OVER TIME
CAR AU 87 VOL: 4 PG:210 - 226 :: REGRESS. :PRIM. :TIME SER. :ERRORS

LOSELL,D ; FIRS: HAM ,J ; THIR: SMIELIAUSKAS,W CIT: 0
A NOTE ON THE NEUTRALITY OF INTERNAL CONTROL SYSTEMS IN AUDIT PRACTICE
CAR SP 86 VOL: 2 PG:311 - 317 :: DES.STAT. :FIELD :HIST. :AUD.

LOSELL,D ; FIRS: HAM ,J ; THIR: SMIELIAUSKAS,W CIT: 0.88
AN EMPIRICAL STUDY OF ERROR CHARACTERISTICS IN ACCOUNTING POPULATIONS
TAR JL 85 VOL: 60 PG:387 - 406 :: REGRESS. :PRIM. :OTH.STAT. :ERRORS

LOUDDER,ML ; SEC: KHURANA,IK ; THIR: SAWYERS,RB ; FOUR: CORDERY,C ; FIFT: JOHNSON,C ; SIX: LOWE ,J CIT: 0
THE INFORMATION CONTENT OF AUDIT QUALIFICATIONS
AUD SP 92 VOL: 11 PG:69 - 82 :: REGRESS. :PRIM. :OTH.STAT. :OPIN.

LOUDERBACK,JG CIT: 0
PROJECTABILITY AS A CRITERION FOR INCOME DETERMINATION METHODS
TAR AP 71 VOL: 46 PG:298 - 305 :: QUAL. :INT. LOG. :THEORY :FIN.METH.

LOVATA,LM CIT: 0
THE UTILIZATION OF GENERALIZED AUDIT SOFTWARE
AUD AU 88 VOL: 08 PG:72 - 86 :: REGRESS. :SURV. :OTH. :EDP AUD.

LOWE ,EA ; FIRS: BERRY ,AJ ; SEC: CAPPS ,T ; THIR: COOPER,D ; FOUR: FERGUSON,P FIFT: HOPPER,T CIT: 3
MANAGEMENT CONTROL IN AN AREA OF THE NCB: RATIONALES OF ACCOUNTING PRACTICES IN A PUBLIC ENTERPRISE
AOS 01 85 VOL: 10 PG:3 - 28 :: REGRESS. :FIELD :OTH.BEH. :MANAG.

LOWE ,HD CIT: 0
ACCOUNTING AID FOR DEVELOPING COUNTRIES
TAR AP 67 VOL: 42 PG:356 - 360 :: QUAL. :INT. LOG. :INSTIT. :OTH.MANAG.

LOWE ,HD CIT: 0
THE ESSENTIALS OF A GENERAL THEORY OF DEPRECIATION
TAR AP 63 VOL: 38 PG:293 - 301 :: ANAL. :INT. LOG. :THEORY :PP&E / DEPR

LOWE ,J ; FIRS: LOUDDER,ML ; SEC: KHURANA,IK ; THIR: SAWYERS,RB ; FOUR: CORDERY,C FIFT: JOHNSON,C CIT: 0
THE INFORMATION CONTENT OF AUDIT QUALIFICATIONS
AUD SP 92 VOL: 11 PG:69 - 82 :: REGRESS. :PRIM. :OTH.STAT. :OPIN.

LOWE ,RE CIT: 0
PUBLIC ACCOUNTING INTERNSHIPS
TAR OC 65 VOL: 40 PG:839 - 846 :: DES.STAT. :SURV. :INSTIT. :OTH.MANAG.

LOWE ,T ; FIRS: PUXTY ,AG ; SEC: WILLMOTT,HC ; THIR: COOPER,DJ CIT: 1.33
MODES OF REGULATION IN ADVANCED CAPITALISM: LOCATING ACCOUNTANCY IN
AOS 03 87 VOL: 12 PG:273 - 291 :: DES.STAT. :INT. LOG. :THEORY :ORG.& ENVIR.

LOWY ,SM ; FIRS: HIRST ,MK CIT: 0
THE LINEAR ADDITIVE AND INTERACTIVE EFFECTS OF BUDGETARY GOAL DIFFICULTY AND FEEDBACK ON PERFORMANCE
AOS 05 90 VOL: 15 PG:425 - 436 :: REGRESS. :SURV. :OTH.BEH. :BUDG.& PLAN.

LOY ,LD ; SEC: TOOLE ,HR CIT: 0.08
ACCOUNTING FOR DISCOUNTED CONVERTIBLE BOND EXCHANGES: A SURVEY OF RESULTS
JAA SP 80 VOL: 3 PG:227 - 243 :: DES.STAT. :PRIM. :OTH. :METHOD.

LUCAS ,HC CIT: 0
THE USE OF AN ACCOUNTING INFORMATION SYSTEM, ACTION AND ORGANIZATIONAL PERFORMANCE
TAR OC 75 VOL: 50 PG:735 - 746 :: REGRESS. :FIELD :OTH.BEH. :OTH.MANAG.

LUCAS ,RG ; FIRS: DERMER,JD CIT: 0.14
THE ILLUSION OF MANAGERIAL CONTROL
AOS 06 86 VOL: 11 PG:471 - 482 :: DES.STAT. :INT. LOG. :THEORY :INT.CONT.

LUCKETT,PF ; SEC: EGGLETON,IRC CIT: 0
FEEDBACK AND MANAGEMENT ACCOUNTING: A REVIEW OF RESEARCH INTO BEHAVIOURAL CONSEQUENCES
AOS 04 91 VOL: 16 PG:371 - 394 :: REGRESS. :SEC. :HIPS :AUD.BEH.

LUCKETT,PF ; SEC: HIRST ,MK CIT: 0.25
THE IMPACT OF FEEDBACK ON INTER-RATER AGREEMENT AND SELF INSIGHT IN PERFORMANCE EVALUATION DECISIONS
AOS 06 89 VOL: 14 PG:379 - 387 :: REGRESS. :LAB. :HIPS :AUD.BEH.

LUDMAN,EA CIT: 0
INSIDER TRADING: THE CASE FOR REGULATION
JAA SP 86 VOL: 1 PG:118 - 124 :: DES.STAT. :INT. LOG. :THEORY :LITIG.

LUH ,FS CIT: 0.12
CONTROLLED COST: AN OPERATIONAL CONCEPT AND STATISTICAL APPROACH TO STANDARD COSTING
TAR JA 68 VOL: 43 PG:123 - 132 :: ANAL. :INT. LOG. :OTH.STAT. :VAR.

LUKKA ,K CIT: 0.6
BUDGETARY BIASING IN ORGANIZATIONS: THEORETICAL FRAMEWORK AND EMPIRICAL EVIDENCE
AOS 03 88 VOL: 13 PG:281 - 301 :: REGRESS. :CASE :OTH.BEH. :BUDG.& PLAN.

LUNDHOLM,RJ CIT: 0
PUBLIC SIGNALS AND THE EQUILIBRIUM ALLOCATION OF PRIVATE INFORMATION
JAR AU 91 VOL: 29 PG:322 - 349 :: DES.STAT. :INT. LOG. :INF.ECO./AG. :INFO.STRUC.

LUNDHOLM,RJ CIT: 0
WHAT AFFECTS THE EFFICIENCY OF MARKET?
TAR JL 91 VOL: 66 PG:486 - 515 :: REGRESS. :LAB. :EMH :INFO.STRUC.

LUNDHOLM,RJ CIT: 0.4
PRICE-SIGNAL RELATIONS IN THE PRESENCE OF CORRELATED PUBLIC AND PRIVATE INFORMATION
JAR SP 88 VOL: 26 PG:107 - 118 :: ANAL. :INT. LOG. :INF.ECO./AG. :INFO.STRUC.

LUNDHOLM,RJ ; FIRS: DEJONG,DV ; SEC: FORSYTHE,R ; FOUR: UECKER,WC CIT: 0.88
A LABORATORY INVESTIGATION OF THE MORAL HAZARD PROBLEM IN AN AGENCY RELATIONSHIP
JAR ST 85 VOL: 23 PG:81 - 120 :: REGRESS. :LAB. :INF.ECO./AG. :MAN.DEC.CHAR.

LUNESKI,C CIT: 0
CONTINUOUS VERSUS DISCRETE COMPOUNDING FOR CAPITAL BUDGETING DECISIONS
TAR OC 67 VOL: 42 PG:767 - 771 :: ANAL. :INT. LOG. :N/A :OTH.MANAG.

LUNESKI,C CIT: 0
SOME ASPECTS OF THE MEANING OF CONTROL
TAR JL 64 VOL: 39 PG:591 - 597 :: QUAL. :INT. LOG. :N/A :MANAG.

LUSK ,EJ ; FIRS: BODNAR,G CIT: 0.06
MOTIVATIONAL CONSIDERATIONS IN COST ALLOCATION SYSTEMS: A CONDITIONING THEORY APPROACH
TAR OC 77 VOL: 52 PG:857 - 868 :: ANAL. :INT. LOG. :OTH.BEH. :OVER.ALLOC.

LUSK ,EJ ; FIRS: HEIMANN,SR CIT: 0.06
DECISION FLEXIBILITY: AN ALTERNATIVE EVALUATION CRITERION
TAR JA 76 VOL: 51 PG:51 - 64 :: ANAL. :INT. LOG. :OTH.STAT. :MANAG.

LUSK ,EJ ; FIRS: ABDEL-KHALIK,AR CIT: 0.76
TRANSFER PRICING - A SYNTHESIS
TAR JA 74 VOL: 49 PG:8 - 23 :: QUAL. :SEC. :N/A :TRANS.PRIC.

LUSK ,EJ CIT: 0.47
COGNITIVE ASPECTS OF ANNUAL REPORTS: FIELD INDEPENDENCE/DEPENDENCE
JAR ST 73 VOL: 11 PG:191 - 202 :: NON-PAR. :LAB. :HIPS :INFO.STRUC.

LUSK ,EJ CIT: 0.06
DISCRIMINANT ANALYSIS AS APPLIED TO THE RESOURCE ALLOCATION DECISION
TAR JL 72 VOL: 47 PG:567 - 575 :: OTH.QUANT. :INT. LOG. :OTH.STAT. :CAP.BUDG.

LUSTGARTEN,S ; FIRS: PYO ,Y CIT: 0
DIFFERENTIAL INTRA-INDUSTRY INFORMATION TRANSFER ASSOCIATED WITH MANAGEMENT EARNINGS FORECASTS
JAE DE 90 VOL: 13 PG:365 - 379 :: REGRESS. :PRIM. :EMH :FIN.METH.

LUSTGARTEN,S ; FIRS: HAW ,IM CIT: 0.4
EVIDENCE ON INCOME MEASUREMENT PROPERTIES OF ASR NO. 190 AND SFAS NO. 33 DATA
JAR AU 88 VOL: 26 PG:331 - 352 :: REGRESS. :PRIM. :EMH :VALUAT.(INFL.)

LUSTGARTEN,S CIT: 1
THE IMPACT OF REPLACEMENT COST DISCLOSURE ON SECURITY PRICES: NEW EVIDENCE
JAE OC 82 VOL: 4 PG:121 - 141 :: REGRESS. :PRIM. :EMH :VALUAT.(INFL.)

LYNN ,ES CIT: 0
EDUCATION FOR THE PROFESSION
TAR AP 64 VOL: 39 PG:371 - 376 :: QUAL. :INT. LOG. :INSTIT. :OTH.MANAG.

LYON ,JD ; SEC: SCHROEDER,DA CIT: 0
FIRM GROWTH AND THE VALUATION RELEVANCE OF EARNINGS LEVELS, EARNINGS INNOVATIONS, AND DIVIDENDS
JAA AU 92 VOL: 7 PG:531 - 552 :: REGRESS. :PRIM. :OTH.STAT. :VALUAT.(INFL.)

LYON ,RC ; FIRS: IJIRI ,Y ; SEC: LEVY ,FK CIT: 0.12
A LINEAR PROGRAMMING MODEL FOR BUDGETING AND FINANCIAL PLANNING
JAR AU 63 VOL: 1 PG:198 - 212 :: ANAL. :INT. LOG. :MATH.PROG. :BUDG.& PLAN.

LYS ,T ; FIRS: JOHNSON,WB CIT: 1
THE MARKET FOR AUDIT SERVICES: EVIDENCE FROM VOLUNTARY AUDITOR CHANGES
JAE JA 90 VOL: 12 PG:281 - 308 :: REGRESS. :PRIM. :INF.ECO./AG. :ORG.

LYS ,T ; SEC: SOHN ,S CIT: 1
THE ASSOCIATION BETWEEN REVISIONS OF FINANCIAL ANALYSTS' EARNINGS FORECASTS AND SECURITY-PRICE CHANGES
JAE DE 90 VOL: 13 PG:341 - 363 :: REGRESS. :PRIM. :OTH.STAT. :FOREC.

LYS ,T ; FIRS: KOTHARI,SP ; THIR: SMITH ,CW ; FOUR: WATTS ,RL CIT: 0.6
AUDITOR LIABILITY AND INFORMATION DISCLOSURE
JAA AU 88 VOL: 3 PG:307 - 340 :: DES.STAT. :INT. LOG. :OTH. :LIAB.

LYS ,T ; SEC: SIVARAMAKRISHNAN,K CIT: 0.4
EARNINGS EXPECTATIONS AND CAPITAL RESTRUCTURING: THE CASE OF EQUITY-FOR-DEBT SWAPS
JAR AU 88 VOL: 26 PG:273 - 299 :: REGRESS. :PRIM. :EMH :LTD

LYS ,T CIT: 1.89
MANDATED ACCOUNTING CHANGES AND DEBT COVENANTS: THE CASE OF OIL AND GAS ACCOUNTING
JAE AP 84 VOL: 6 PG:39 - 65 :: REGRESS. :PRIM. :EMH :OIL & GAS

MABERT,VA ; SEC: RADCLIFFE,RC CIT: 0.06
A FORECASTING METHODOLOGY AS APPLIED TO FINANCIAL TIME SERIES
TAR JA 74 VOL: 49 PG:61 - 75 :: REGRESS. :INT. LOG. :TIME SER. :BUDG.& PLAN.

MACHMEYER,RA ; FIRS: BALACHANDRAN,KR CIT: 0
ACCOUNTING FOR PRODUCT WEAR OUT COST
JAA WI 92 VOL: 7 PG:49 - 64 :: DES.STAT. :INT. LOG. :OTH.STAT. :REL.COSTS

MACINTOSH,NB ; FIRS: WILLIAMS,JJ ; THIR: MOORE ,JC CIT: 0.33
BUDGET-RELATED BEHAVIOR IN PUBLIC SECTOR ORGANIZATIONS: SOME EMPIRICAL EVIDENCE
AOS 03 90 VOL: 15 PG:221 - 246 :: REGRESS. :SURV. :OTH.BEH. :BUDG.& PLAN.

MACINTOSH,NB ; SEC: SCAPENS,RW CIT: 0.33
STRUCTURATION THEORY IN MANAGEMENT ACCOUNTING
AOS 05 90 VOL: 15 PG:455 - 477 :: REGRESS. :CASE :OTH.BEH. :HRA

MACINTOSH,NB ; SEC: DAFT ,RL CIT: 0.67
MANAGEMENT CONTROL SYSTEMS AND DEPARTMENTAL INTERDEPENDENCIES: AN EMPIRICAL STUDY
AOS 01 87 VOL: 12 PG:49 - 61 :: REGRESS. :SURV. :OTH.BEH. :ORG.& ENVIR.

MACINTOSH,NB CIT: 0.83
A CONTEXTUAL MODEL OF INFORMATION SYSTEMS
AOS 01 81 VOL: 6 PG:39 - 52 :: QUAL. :INT. LOG. :OTH. :N/A

MACKENZIE,O CIT: 0
ACCREDITATION OF ACCOUNTING CURRICULA
TAR AP 64 VOL: 39 PG:363 - 370 :: QUAL. :INT. LOG. :INSTIT. :OTH.MANAG.

MACNAUGHTON,A CIT: 0
FRINGE BENEFITS AND EMPLOYEE EXPENSES: TAX PLANNING AND NEUTRAL TAX POLICY
CAR AU 92 VOL: 9 PG:113 - 137 :: DES.STAT. :INT. LOG. :INF.ECO./AG. :TAXES

MACRITCHIE,KL ; FIRS: MERINO,BD ; SEC: KOCH ,BS CIT: 0
HISTORICAL ANALYSIS- A DIAGNOSTIC TOOL FOR EVENTS STUDIES: THE IMPACT OF THE SECURITIES ACT OF 1933
TAR OC 87 VOL: 62 PG:748 - 762 :: REGRESS. :INT. LOG. :HIST. :FIN.METH.

MACVE ,RH ; FIRS: HOSKIN,KW CIT: 1.8
THE GENESIS OF ACCOUNTABILITY: THE WEST POINT CONNECTIONS
AOS 01 88 VOL: 13 PG:37 - 73 :: DES.STAT. :INT. LOG. :THEORY :OTH.MANAG.

MACVE ,RH ; FIRS: HOSKIN,KW CIT: 3
ACCOUNTING AND THE EXAMINATION: A GENEALOGY OF DISCIPLINARY POWER
AOS 02 86 VOL: 11 PG:105 - 136 :: DES.STAT. :INT. LOG. :HIST. :FASB SUBM.

MACY ,BA ; SEC: MIRVIS,PH CIT: 0.18
ACCOUNTING FOR THE COSTS AND BENEFITS OF HUMAN RESOURCE DEVELOPMENT PROGRAMS: AN INTERDISCIPLINARY APPROACH
AOS 23 76 VOL: 1 PG:179 - 194 :: QUAL. :CASE :OTH.BEH. :HRA

MADDALA,GS CIT: 0
A PERSPECTIVE ON THE USE OF LIMITED-DEPENDENT AND QUALITATIVE VARIABLES MODELS IN ACCOUNTING RESEARCH
TAR OC 91 VOL: 66 PG:788 - 808 :: DES.STAT. :SEC. :THEORY :METHOD.

MADEO ,SA ; SEC: SCHEPANSKI,A ; THIR: UECKER,WC CIT: 0
MODELING JUDGMENTS OF TAXPAYER COMPLIANCE
TAR AP 87 VOL: 62 PG:323 - 342 :: REGRESS. :LAB. :OTH.STAT. :TAXES

MADEO ,SA ; SEC: PINCUS,M CIT: 0.25
STOCK MARKET BEHAVIOR AND TAX RULE CHANGES: THE CASE OF THE DISALLOWANCE OF CERTAIN INTEREST DEDUCTIONS CLAIMED BY BANKS
TAR JL 85 VOL: 60 PG:407 - 429 :: REGRESS. :LAB. :EMH :TAXES

MADEO ,SA CIT: 0.07
AN EMPIRICAL ANALYSIS OF TAX COURT DECISIONS IN ACCUMULATED EARNINGS CASES
TAR JL 79 VOL: 54 PG:538 - 553 :: OTH.QUANT. :PRIM. :OTH.STAT. :TAXES

MAGAT ,WA ; FIRS: LOEB ,M CIT: 0.4
SOVIET SUCCESS INDICATORS AND THE EVALUATION OF DIVISIONAL MANAGEMENT
JAR SP 78 VOL: 16 PG:103 - 121 :: ANAL. :INT. LOG. :INF.ECO./AG. :INT.DIFF.

MAGEE ,RP ; FIRS: DEMSKI,JS CIT: 0
A PERSPECTIVE ON ACCOUNTING FOR DEFENSE CONTRACTS
TAR OC 92 VOL: 67 PG:732 - 740 :: DES.STAT. :SEC. :INF.ECO./AG. :MANAG.

MAGEE ,RP ; FIRS: DYE ,RA ; SEC: BALACHANDRAN,BV CIT: 1
CONTINGENT FEES FOR AUDIT FIRMS
JAR AU 90 VOL: 28 PG:239 - 266 :: DES.STAT. :INT. LOG. :INF.ECO./AG. :AUD.BEH.

MAGEE ,RP ; SEC: TSENG ,M CIT: 1.33
AUDIT PRICING AND INDEPENDENCE
TAR AP 90 VOL: 65 PG:315 - 336 :: DES.STAT. :INT. LOG. :INF.ECO./AG. :INDEP.

MAGEE ,RP CIT: 0.2
VARIABLE COST ALLOCATION IN A PRINCIPAL/AGENT SETTING
TAR JA 88 VOL: 63 PG:42 - 54 :: DES.STAT. :INT. LOG. :INF.ECO./AG. :COST.ALLOC.

MAGEE ,RP ; FIRS: BALACHANDRAN,BV ; SEC: LI ,L CIT: 0.33
ON THE ALLOCATION OF FIXED AND VARIABLE COSTS FROM SERVICE DEPARTMENTS
CAR AU 87 VOL: 4 PG:164 - 185 :: DES.STAT. :INT. LOG. :INF.ECO./AG. :COST.ALLOC.

MAGEE ,RP ; FIRS: JOHNSON,WB ; THIR: NAGARAJAN,NJ ; FOUR: NEWMAN,HA CIT: 0.13
AN ANALYSIS OF THE STOCK PRICE REACTION TO SUDDEN EXECUTIVE DEATHS: IMPLICATIONS FOR THE MANAGEMENT LABOR MARKET
JAE AP 85 VOL: 7 PG:151 - 174 :: REGRESS. :PRIM. :EMH :OTH.MANAG.

MAGEE ,RP CIT: 0.62
EQUILIBRIA IN BUDGET PARTICIPATION
JAR AU 80 VOL: 18 PG:551 - 573 :: ANAL. :INT. LOG. :INF.ECO./AG. :BUDG.& PLAN.

MAGEE ,RP ; SEC: DICKHAUT,JW CIT: 0.47
EFFECTS OF COMPENSATION PLANS ON HEURISTICS IN COST VARIANCE INVESTIGATIONS
JAR AU 78 VOL: 16 PG:294 - 314 :: ANOVA :LAB. :HIPS :VAR.

MAGEE ,RP CIT: 0.06
COST CONTROL WITH IMPERFECT PARAMETER KNOWLEDGE
TAR JA 77 VOL: 52 PG:190 - 199 :: DES.STAT. :SIM. :MATH.PROG. :COST.ALLOC.

MAGEE ,RP CIT: 0.13
THE USEFULNESS OF COMMONALITY INFORMATION IN COST CONTROL DECISIONS
TAR OC 77 VOL: 52 PG:869 - 880 :: ANAL. :SIM. :INF.ECO./AG. :COST.ALLOC.

MAGEE ,RP CIT: 0.65
A SIMULATION ANALYSIS OF ALTERNATIVE COST VARIANCE INVESTIGATION MODELS
TAR JL 76 VOL: 51 PG:529 - 544 :: ANAL. :SIM. :INF.ECO./AG. :VAR.

MAGEE ,RP CIT: 0.18
COST-VOLUME-PROFIT ANALYSIS, UNCERTAINTY AND CAPITAL MARKET EQUILIBRIUM
JAR AU 75 VOL: 13 PG:257 - 266 :: ANAL. :INT. LOG. :EMH :C-V-P-A

MAGEE ,RP CIT: 0.47
INDUSTRY-WIDE COMMONALITIES IN EARNINGS
JAR AU 74 VOL: 12 PG:270 - 287 :: ANOVA :PRIM. :EMH :FIN.METH.

MAGLIOLO,J ; FIRS: CLINCH,G CIT: 0
MARKET PERCEPTIONS OF RESERVE DISCLOSURES UNDER SFAS NO. 69
TAR OC 92 VOL: 67 PG:843 - 861 :: REGRESS. :PRIM. :MATH.PROG. :OIL & GAS

MAGLIOLO,J ; FIRS: LANDSMAN,WR CIT: 0.8
CROSS-SECTIONAL CAPITAL MARKET RESEARCH AND MODEL SPECIFICATION
TAR OC 88 VOL: 63 PG:586 - 604 :: DES.STAT. :INT. LOG. :EMH :METHOD.

MAGLIOLO,J CIT: 0.71
CAPITAL MARKET ANALYSIS OF RESERVE RECOGNITION ACCOUNTING
JAR ST 86 VOL: 24 PG:69 - 111 :: REGRESS. :PRIM. :EMH :OIL & GAS

MAHER ,JJ CIT: 0
PENSION OBLIGATIONS AND THE BOND CREDIT MARKET: AN EMPIRICAL ANALYSIS OF ACCOUNTING NUMBERS
TAR OC 87 VOL: 62 PG:785 - 798 :: REGRESS. :PRIM. :OTH.STAT. :PENS.

MAHER ,MW ; SEC: TIESSEN,P ; THIR: COLSON,R ; FOUR: BROMAN,AJ CIT: 0
COMPETITION AND AUDIT FEES
TAR JA 92 VOL: 67 PG:199 - 211 :: REGRESS. :PRIM. :OTH. :ORG.

MAHER ,MW ; SEC: NANTELL,TJ CIT: 0
THE TAX EFFECTS OF INFLATION: DEPRECIATION, DEBT, AND MILLER'S EQUILIBRIUM TAX RATES
JAR SP 83 VOL: 21 PG:329 - 340 :: ANAL. :INT. LOG. :THEORY :VALUAT.(INFL.)

MAHER ,MW CIT: 0.17
THE IMPACT OF REGULATION ON CONTROLS: FIRMS' RESPONSE TO THE FOREIGN CORRUPT PRACTICES ACT
TAR OC 81 VOL: 56 PG:751 - 770 :: DES.STAT. :PRIM. :INSTIT. :N/A

MAHER ,MW ; SEC: RAMANATHAN,KV ; THIR: PETERSON,RB CIT: 0.29
PREFERENCE CONGRUENCE, INFORMATION ACCURACY, AND EMPLOYEE PERFORMANCE: A FIELD STUDY
JAR AU 79 VOL: 17 PG:476 - 503 :: ANOVA :FIELD :OTH.BEH. :AUD.BEH.

MAHMOUD,AAW ; FIRS: LOBO ,GL CIT: 0.5
RELATIONSHIP BETWEEN DIFFERENTIAL AMOUNTS OF PRIOR INFORMATION AND SECURITY RETURN VARIABILITY
JAR SP 89 VOL: 27 PG:116 - 134 :: REGRESS. :PRIM. :EMH :INFO.STRUC.

MAINDIRATTA,A ; FIRS: HALPERIN,R CIT: 0
ON THE LINK BETWEEN TAXES AND INCENTIVES IN THE CHOICE OF BUSINESS FORM
JAA SU 89 VOL: 4 PG:345 - 366 :: DES.STAT. :INT. LOG. :INF.ECO./AG. :ORG.FORM

MAINDIRATTA,A ; FIRS: BANKER,RD ; SEC: DATAR ,SM CIT: 0.4
UNOBSERVABLE OUTCOMES AND MULTIATTRIBUTE PREFERENCES IN THE EVALUATION OF MANAGERIAL PERFORMANCE
CAR AU 88 VOL: 5 PG:96 - 124 :: DES.STAT. :INT. LOG. :INF.ECO./AG. :EXEC.COMP.

MAINES,LA CIT: 0
THE EFFECT OF FORECAST REDUNDANCY ON JUDGMENTS OF A CONSENSUS FORECAST'S EXPECTED ACCURACY
JAR ST 90 VOL: 28 PG:029 - 54 :: REGRESS. :LAB. :HIPS :FOREC.

MAITRE,P CIT: 0
THE MEASUREMENT OF THE CREATION AND DISTRIBUTION OF WEALTH IN A FIRM BY THE METHOD OF SURPLUS ACCOUNTS
AOS 34 78 VOL: 3 PG:227 - 236 :: ANAL. :INT. LOG. :THEORY :FIN.METH.

MAKSY ,MM CIT: 0
ARTICULATION PROBLEMS BETWEEN THE BALANCE SHEET AND THE FUNDS STATEMENT
TAR OC 88 VOL: 63 PG:683 - 699 :: REGRESS. :INT. LOG. :THEORY :FIN.METH.

MALCOM,RE ; FIRS: KRATCHMAN,SH ; THIR: TWARK ,RD CIT: 0.06
AN INTRA-INDUSTRY COMPARISON OF ALTERNATIVE INCOME CONCEPTS AND RELATIVE PERFORMANCE EVALUATIONS
TAR OC 74 VOL: 49 PG:682 - 689 :: NON-PAR. :PRIM. :N/A :VALUAT.(INFL.)

MALCOM,RE ; FIRS: DASCHER,PE CIT: 0.24
A NOTE ON INCOME SMOOTHING IN THE CHEMICAL INDUSTRY
JAR AU 70 VOL: 8 PG:253 - 259 :: DES.STAT. :PRIM. :TIME SER. :FIN.METH.

MALMQUIST,DH CIT: 0.67
EFFICIENT CONTRACTING AND THE CHOICE OF ACCOUNTING METHOD IN THE OIL AND GAS INDUSTRY
JAE JA 90 VOL: 12 PG:173 - 205 :: REGRESS. :PRIM. :OTH.STAT. :OIL & GAS

MANDELKER,G ; FIRS: HONG ,H ; SEC: KAPLAN,RS CIT: 0.93
POOLING VS. PURCHASE: THE EFFECTS OF ACCOUNTING FOR MERGERS ON STOCK PRICES
TAR JA 78 VOL: 53 PG:31 - 47 :: MIXED :PRIM. :EMH :BUS.COMB.

MANEGOLD,JG CIT: 0
SMALL-COMPANY INITIAL PUBLIC OFFERINGS: THE IMPACT OF SEC REGISTRATION FORM S-18
JAA SU 86 VOL: 1 PG:206 - 221 :: REGRESS. :PRIM. :THEORY :SPEC.ITEMS

MANEGOLD,JG ; FIRS: MCNICHOLS,M CIT: 1
THE EFFECT OF THE INFORMATION ENVIRONMENT ON THE RELATIONSHIP BETWEEN FINANCIAL DISCLOSURE AND SECURITY PRICE VARIABILITY
JAE AP 83 VOL: 5 PG:49 - 74 :: MIXED :PRIM. :EMH :INT.REP.

MANEGOLD,JG CIT: 0.08
TIME-SERIES PROPERTIES OF EARNINGS: A COMPARISON OF EXTRAPOLATIVE AND COMPONENT MODELS
JAR AU 81 VOL: 19 PG:360 - 373 :: REGRESS. :PRIM. :TIME SER. :FOREC.

MANES ,RP ; FIRS: CHEN ,JT CIT: 0
DISTINGUISHING THE TWO FORMS OF THE CONSTANT PERCENTAGE LEARNING CURVE MODEL
CAR SP 85 VOL: 1 PG:242 - 252 :: REGRESS. :SEC. :MATH.PROG. :MANAG.

MANES ,RP ; SEC: PARK ,SH ; THIR: JENSEN,RE CIT: 0.09
RELEVANT COSTS OF INTERMEDIATE GOODS AND SERVICES
TAR JL 82 VOL: 57 PG:594 - 606 :: ANAL. :INT. LOG. :MATH.PROG. :N/A

MANES ,RP ; FIRS: COLANTONI,CS ; THIR: WHINSTON,AB CIT: 0.41
A UNIFIED APPROACH TO THE THEORY OF ACCOUNTING AND INFORMATION SYSTEMS
TAR JA 71 VOL: 46 PG:90 - 102 :: QUAL. :INT. LOG. :N/A :MANAG.

MANES ,RP ; FIRS: GROVES,R ; THIR: SORENSEN,R CIT: 0.06
THE APPLICATION OF THE HIRSCH-DANTZIG FIXED CHARGE ALGORITHM TO PROFIT PLANNING: A FORMAL STATEMENT OF PRODUCT PROFITABILITY A
TAR JL 70 VOL: 45 PG:481 - 489 :: ANAL. :INT. LOG. :MATH.PROG. :BUDG.& PLAN.

MANES ,RP ; FIRS: COLANTONI,CS ; THIR: WHINSTON,AB CIT: 0.06
PROGRAMMING, PROFIT RATES AND PRICING DECISIONS
TAR JL 69 VOL: 44 PG:467 - 481 :: ANAL. :INT. LOG. :MATH.PROG. :REL.COSTS

MANES ,RP ; SEC: SAMUELS,JM ; THIR: SMYTH ,DJ CIT: 0
INVENTORIES AND SALES: A CROSS SECTION STUDY
JAR ST 67 VOL: 5 PG:139 - 156 :: REGRESS. :PRIM. :THEORY :INV.

MANES ,RP ; FIRS: FRANK ,WG CIT: 0.06
A STANDARD COST APPLICATION OF MATRIX ALGEBRA
TAR JL 67 VOL: 42 PG:516 - 525 :: ANAL. :INT. LOG. :MATH.PROG. :VAR.

MANES ,RP CIT: 0.06
A NEW DIMENSION TO BREAKEVEN ANALYSIS
JAR SP 66 VOL: 4 PG:87 - 100 :: ANAL. :INT. LOG. :OTH.STAT. :C-V-P-A

MANES ,RP ; SEC: SMITH ,VL CIT: 0
ECONOMIC JOINT COST THEORY AND ACCOUNTING PRACTICE
TAR JA 65 VOL: 40 PG:31 - 35 :: ANAL. :INT. LOG. :N/A :COST.ALLOC.

MANES ,RP CIT: 0
THE GRANT-IN-AID SYSTEM FOR INTERSTATE HIGHWAY CONSTRUCTION: AN ACCOUNTING OR ECONOMIC PROBLEM?
TAR JL 64 VOL: 39 PG:631 - 638 :: QUAL. :SEC. :N/A :FIN.METH.

MANN ,H ; FIRS: FELTON,S CIT: 0
ACCOUNTING FOR A BREWERY OF LOUISBOURG
CAR AU 90 VOL: 7 PG:261 - 277 :: REGRESS. :CASE :HIST. :FIN.METH.

MANZONI,J ; FIRS: MERCHANT,KA CIT: 0.5
THE ACHIEVABILITY OF BUDGET TARGETS IN PROFIT CENTERS: A FIELD STUDY
TAR JL 89 VOL: 64 PG:539 - 558 :: REGRESS. :FIELD :HIPS :BUDG.& PLAN.

MARAIS,ML CIT: 0.89
AN APPLICATION OF THE BOOTSTRAP METHOD TO THE ANALYSIS OF SQUARED, STANDARDIZED MARKET MODEL PREDICTION ERRORS
JAR ST 84 VOL: 22 PG:34 - 54 :: DES.STAT. :PRIM. :EMH :METHOD.

MARAIS,ML ; SEC: PATELL,JM ; THIR: WOLFSON,MA CIT: 0.56
THE EXPERIMENTAL DESIGN OF CLASSIFICATORY MODELS: AN APPLICATION OF RECURSIVE PARTITIONING AND BOOTSTRAPPING COMMERCIAL BANK LOAN CLASSIFICATIONS
JAR ST 84 VOL: 22 PG:87 - 114 :: OTH.QUANT. :PRIM. :OTH.STAT. :BUS.FAIL.

MARCH ,JG CIT: 0.83
AMBIGUITY AND ACCOUNTING: THE ELUSIVE LINK BETWEEN INFORMATION AND DECISION MAKING
AOS 02 87 VOL: 12 PG:153 - 168 :: DES.STAT. :INT. LOG. :THEORY :FIN.METH.

MARCHANT,G ; FIRS: ANDERSON,U CIT: 0
THE AUDITOR'S ASSESSMENT OF COMPETENCE AND INTEGRITY OF AUDITEE PERSONNEL
AUD 89 VOL: 8 PG:101 - 115 :: REGRESS. :LAB. :HIPS :JUDG.

MARCHANT,G ; FIRS: ANDERSON,U CIT: 0
THE AUDITOR'S ASSESSMENT OF COMPETENCE AND INTEGRITY OF AUDITEE PERSONNEL
AUD 89 VOL: 8 PG:101 - 115 :: REGRESS. :LAB. :HIPS :JUDG.

MARCINKO,D ; SEC: PETRI ,E CIT: 0.22
USE OF THE PRODUCTION FUNCTION IN CALCULATION OF STANDARD COST VARIANCES - AN EXTENSION
TAR JL 84 VOL: 59 PG:488 - 495 :: ANAL. :INT. LOG. :OTH. :VAR.

MARGHEIM,L ; FIRS: KELLY ,T CIT: 0.67
THE IMPACT OF TIME BUDGET PRESSURE, PERSONALITY, AND LEADERSHIP VARIABLES ON DYSFUNCTIONAL AUDIT BEHAVIOR
AUD SP 90 VOL: 9 PG:21 - 42 :: REGRESS. :SURV. :HIPS :AUD.BEH.

MARGHEIM,LL ; SEC: PANY ,K CIT: 0.57
QUALITY CONTROL, PREMATURE SIGNOFF, AND UNDERREPORTING OF TIME: SOME EMPIRICAL FINDINGS
AUD SP 86 VOL: 5 PG:50 - 63 :: REGRESS. :LAB. :OTH.BEH. :ORG.

MARGHEIM,LL CIT: 0.29
FURTHER EVIDENCE ON EXTERNAL AUDITORS' RELIANCE ON INTERNAL AUDITORS
JAR SP 86 VOL: 24 PG:194 - 205 :: REGRESS. :LAB. :OTH. :ORG.

MARIS ,BA ; FIRS: HUTH ,WL CIT: 0
LARGE AND SMALL FIRM STOCK PRICE RESPONSE TO "HEARD ON THE STREET" RECOMMENDATIONS
JAA WI 92 VOL: 7 PG:27 - 44 :: REGRESS. :PRIM. :TIME SER. :OTH.MANAG.

MARKOWITZ,HM CIT: 0
RISK ADJUSTMENT
JAA SP 90 VOL: 5 PG:213 - 225 :: DES.STAT. :INT. LOG. :OTH. :OTH.MANAG.

MARKS ,BR ; FIRS: BENSON,ED ; THIR: RAMAN ,KK CIT: 0
THE EFFECT OF VOLUNTARY GAAP COMPLIANCE AND FINANCIAL DISCLOSURE ON GOVERNMENTAL BORROWING COSTS
JAA SU 91 VOL: 6 PG:303 - 319 :: REGRESS. :PRIM. :INSTIT. :FIN.METH.

MARKS ,BR ; SEC: RAMAN ,KK CIT: 0
THE EFFECT OF UNFUNDED ACCUMULATED AND PROJECTED PENSION OBLIGATIONS ON GOVERNMENTAL BORROWING COSTS
CAR SP 88 VOL: 4 PG:595 - 608 :: REGRESS. :PRIM. :INSTIT. :PENS.

MARKS ,BR ; SEC: RAMAN ,KK CIT: 0
SOME ADDITIONAL EVIDENCE ON THE DETERMINANTS OF STATE AUDIT BUDGETS
AUD AU 87 VOL: 7 PG:106 - 117 :: REGRESS. :PRIM. :THEORY :AUD.

MARKS ,BR ; SEC: RAMAN ,KK CIT: 0.13
THE IMPORTANCE OF PENSION DATA FOR MUNICIPAL & STATE CREDITOR DECISIONS: REPLICATIONS & EXTENSIONS
JAR AU 85 VOL: 23 PG:878 - 886 :: REGRESS. :PRIM. :OTH.STAT. :PENS.

MARKUS,ML ; SEC: PFEFFER,J CIT: 0.8
POWER AND THE DESIGN AND IMPLEMENTATION OF ACCOUNTING AND CONTROL SYSTEMS
AOS 23 83 VOL: 8 PG:205 - 218 :: QUAL. :CASE :OTH. :MANAG.

MARPLE,RM CIT: 0
VALUE-ITIS
TAR JL 63 VOL: 38 PG:478 - 482 :: QUAL. :INT. LOG. :THEORY :FIN.METH.

MARQUES,E CIT: 0.06
HUMAN RESOURCE ACCOUNTING: SOME QUESTIONS AND REFLECTIONS
AOS 23 76 VOL: 1 PG:175 - 178 :: QUAL. :SURV. :THEORY :HRA

MARSHALL,RM ; FIRS: JACOBS,FH CIT: 0.17
A RECIPROCAL SERVICE COST APPROXIMATION
TAR JA 87 VOL: 62 PG:67 - 78 :: DES.STAT. :INT. LOG. :THEORY :COST.ALLOC.

MARSHALL,RM CIT: 0.18
INTERPRETING THE API
TAR JA 75 VOL: 50 PG:99 - 111 :: ANAL. :INT. LOG. :EMH :METHOD.

MARSHALL,RM CIT: 0.35
DETERMINING AN OPTIMAL ACCOUNTING INFORMATION SYSTEM FOR AN UNIDENTIFIED USER
JAR AU 72 VOL: 10 PG:286 - 307 :: ANAL. :INT. LOG. :INF.ECO./AG. :INFO.STRUC.

MARSTON,F ; SEC: HARRIS,RS CIT: 0
SUITABILITY OF LEASES AND DEBT IN CORPORATE CAPITAL STRUCTURES
JAA SP 88 VOL: 03 PG:147 - 164 :: REGRESS. :PRIM. :EMH :LEASES

MARTIN,A CIT: 0
AN EMPIRICAL TEST OF THE RELEVANCE OF ACCOUNTING INFORMATION FOR INVESTMENT DECISIONS
JAR ST 71 VOL: 9 PG:1 - 31 :: REGRESS. :PRIM. :HIPS :FIN.METH.

MARTIN,JD ; SEC: ANDERSON,PF ; THIR: KEOWN ,AJ CIT: 0
LEASE CAPITALIZATION AND STOCK PRICE STABILITY: IMPLICATIONS FOR ACCOUNTING
JAA WI 79 VOL: 2 PG:151 - 164 :: REGRESS. :PRIM. :EMH :LEASES

MARTIN,K ; FIRS: LEWELLEN,W ; SEC: LODERER,C CIT: 0.5
EXECUTIVE COMPENSATION AND EXECUTIVE INCENTIVE PROBLEMS: AN EMPIRICAL
JAE DE 87 VOL: 9 PG:287 - 310 :: REGRESS. :PRIM. :OTH.STAT. :EXEC.COMP.

MARTIN,RK ; FIRS: BIDDLE,GC CIT: 0.25
INFLATION, TAXES, AND OPTIMAL INVENTORY POLICIES
JAR SP 85 VOL: 23 PG:57 - 83 :: REGRESS. :SIM. :OTH.STAT. :INV.

MASCARENHAS,B ; FIRS: DHARAN,BG CIT: 0
DETERMINANTS OF ACCOUNTING CHANGE: AN INDUSTRY ANALYSIS OF DEPRECIATION CHANGE
JAA WI 92 VOL: 7 PG:1 - 21 :: REGRESS. :PRIM. :OTH.STAT. :OIL & GAS

MASCHMEYER,R ; FIRS: BALACHANDRAN,KR ; THIR: LIVINGSTONE,JL CIT: 0.08
PRODUCT WARRANTY PERIOD: A MARKOVIAN APPROACH TO ESTIMATION AND ANALYSIS OF REPAIR AND REPLACEMENT COSTS
TAR JA 81 VOL: 56 PG:115 - 124 :: MARKOV :INT. LOG. :OTH.STAT. :SPEC.ITEMS

MASON ,RO ; FIRS: MITROFF,II CIT: 0.2
CAN WE DESIGN SYSTEMS FOR MANAGING MESSES? OR, WHY SO MANY MANAGEMENT INFORMATION SYSTEMS ARE UNINFORMATIVE
AOS 23 83 VOL: 8 PG:195 - 204 :: QUAL. :INT. LOG. :OTH. :MAN.DEC.CHAR.

MASULIS,RW ; FIRS: DANN ,LY ; THIR: MAYERS,D CIT: 1
REPURCHASE TENDER OFFERS AND EARNINGS INFORMATION
JAE SE 91 VOL: 14 PG:217 - 251 :: REGRESS. :PRIM. :TIME SER. :BUS.COMB.

MATEER,WH CIT: 0
TAX ALLOCATION: A MACRO APPROACH
TAR JL 65 VOL: 40 PG:583 - 586 :: QUAL. :INT. LOG. :THEORY :N/A

MATHEWS,RL ; FIRS: BUCKLEY,JW ; SEC: KIRCHER,P CIT: 0.06
METHODOLOGY IN ACCOUNTING THEORY
TAR AP 68 VOL: 43 PG:274 - 283 :: QUAL. :INT. LOG. :THEORY :FIN.METH.

MATHEWS,RL CIT: 0.06
INCOME, PRICE CHANGES AND THE VALUATION CONTROVERSY IN ACCOUNTING
TAR JL 68 VOL: 43 PG:509 - 516 :: QUAL. :INT. LOG. :THEORY :VALUAT.(INFL.)

MATOLCSY,ZP CIT: 0.44
EVIDENCE ON THE JOINT AND MARGINAL INFORMATION CONTENT OF INFLATION ADJUSTED ACCOUNTING INCOME NUMBERS
JAR AU 84 VOL: 22 PG:555 - 569 :: ANAL. :INT. LOG. :OTH.STAT. :VALUAT.(INFL.)

MATSUMURA,EM ; SEC: TUCKER,RR CIT: 0
FRAUD DETECTION: A THEORETICAL FOUNDATION
TAR OC 92 VOL: 67 PG:753 - 782 :: DES.STAT. :INT. LOG. :INF.ECO./AG. :AUD.THEOR.

MATSUMURA,EM ; SEC: TSUI ,K-W ; THIR: WONG ,W-K CIT: 0.33
AN EXTENDED MULTINOMIAL-DIRICHLET MODEL FOR ERROR BOUNDS FOR DOLLAR-UNIT SAMPLING
CAR SP 90 VOL: 6 PG:485 - 500 :: DES.STAT. :SIM. :OTH.STAT. :SAMP.

MATSUMURA,EM ; FIRS: TSUI ,KW ; THIR: TSUI ,KL CIT: 0.5
MULTINOMINAL-DIRICHLET BOUNDS FOR DOLLAR UNIT SAMPLING IN AUDITING
TAR JA 85 VOL: 60 PG:76 - 96 :: DES.STAT. :SIM. :OTH.STAT. :SAMP.

MATSUMURA,EM ; SEC: TSUI ,KW CIT: 0.09
STEIN-TYPE POISSON ESTIMATORS IN AUDIT SAMPLING
JAR SP 82 VOL: 20 PG:162 - 170 :: CORR. :INT. LOG. :N/A :SAMP.

MATTESSICH,R CIT: 0.18
METHODOLOGICAL PRECONDITIONS AND PROBLEMS OF A GENERAL THEORY OF ACCOUNTING
TAR JL 72 VOL: 47 PG:469 - 487 :: QUAL. :INT. LOG. :THEORY :FIN.METH.

MATTESSICH,RV CIT: 0
FRITZ SCHMIDT (1882-1950) AND HIS PIONEERING WORK OF CURRENT VALUE ACCOUNTING IN COMPARISON TO EDWARDS AND BELL'S THEORY
CAR SP 86 VOL: 2 PG:157 - 178 :: DES.STAT. :SURV. :THEORY :VALUAT.(INFL.)

MATTINGLY,LA CIT: 0
FORMATION AND DEVELOPMENT OF THE INSTITUTE OF CERTIFIED PUBLIC ACCOUNTANTS OF GREECE
TAR OC 64 VOL: 39 PG:996 - 003 :: QUAL. :INT. LOG. :INSTIT. :OTH.MANAG.

MAURIELLO,JA CIT: 0
THE ALL-INCLUSIVE STATEMENT OF FUNDS
TAR AP 64 VOL: 39 PG:347 - 357 :: QUAL. :INT. LOG. :THEORY :INFO.STRUC.

MAURIELLO,JA CIT: 0
REALIZATION AS THE BASIS FOR ASSET CLASSIFICATION AND MEASUREMENT
TAR JA 63 VOL: 38 PG:26 - 28 :: QUAL. :INT. LOG. :THEORY :REV.REC.

MAUTZ ,RD ; FIRS: TILLER,MG CIT: 0
THE IMPACT OF STATE-MANDATED ACCOUNTING AND AUDITING REQUIREMENTS ON MUNICIPAL BOND RATINGS
JAA SU 85 VOL: 8 PG:293 - 304 :: REGRESS. :PRIM. :OTH.STAT. :LTD

MAUTZ ,RK ; SEC: PREVITS,GJ CIT: 0
ERIC KOHLER: AN ACCOUNTING ORIGINAL
TAR AP 77 VOL: 52 PG:301 - 307 :: QUAL. :INT. LOG. :HIST. :N/A

MAUTZ ,RK ; SEC: SKOUSEN,KF CIT: 0
SOME PROBLEMS IN EMPIRICAL RESEARCH IN ACCOUNTING
TAR JL 69 VOL: 44 PG:447 - 456 :: QUAL. :INT. LOG. :N/A :OTH.MANAG.

MAUTZ ,RK ; SEC: MINI ,DL CIT: 0.06
INTERNAL CONTROL EVALUATION AND AUDIT PROGRAM MODIFICATION
TAR AP 66 VOL: 41 PG:283 - 291 :: QUAL. :INT. LOG. :N/A :INT.CONT.

MAUTZ ,RK CIT: 0
CHALLENGES TO THE ACCOUNTING PROFESSION
TAR AP 65 VOL: 40 PG:299 - 311 :: QUAL. :INT. LOG. :INSTIT. :OTH.MANAG.

MAUTZ ,RK CIT: 0.12
ACCOUNTING AS A SOCIAL SCIENCE
TAR AP 63 VOL: 38 PG:317 - 325 :: QUAL. :INT. LOG. :THEORY :OTH.MANAG.

MAUTZJR,RD CIT: 0
INFLATION-ADJUSTED DISCLOSURES AND THE DETERMINATION OF ABILITY TO PAY IN COLLECTIVE BARGAINING
AOS 04 90 VOL: 15 PG:273 - 295 :: REGRESS. :SURV. :HIPS :DEC.AIDS

MAXIM ,LD ; SEC: CULLEN,PE ; THIR: COOK ,FX CIT: 0
OPTIMAL ACCEPTANCE SAMPLING PLANS FOR AUDITING BATCHED STOP AND GO VS. CONVENTIONAL SINGLE-STAGE ATTRIBUTES
TAR JA 76 VOL: 51 PG:97 - 109 :: ANAL. :INT. LOG. :OTH.STAT. :SAMP.

MAXWELL,WD ; FIRS: ZEFF ,SA CIT: 0
HOLDING GAINS ON FIXED ASSETS - A DEMURRER
TAR JA 65 VOL: 40 PG:65 - 75 :: QUAL. :INT. LOG. :THEORY :VALUAT.(INFL.)

MAY ,JH ; FIRS: BAIMAN,S ; THIR: MUKHERJI,A CIT: 0.33
OPTIMAL EMPLOYMENT CONTRACTS AND THE RETURNS TO MONITORING IN A PRINCIPAL-AGENT CONTEXT
CAR SP 90 VOL: 6 PG:761 - 799 :: DES.STAT. :INT. LOG. :INF.ECO./AG. :EXEC.COMP.

MAY ,PT CIT: 0
SYSTEM CONTROL: COMPUTERS THE WEAK LINK?
TAR JL 69 VOL: 44 PG:583 - 592 :: QUAL. :INT. LOG. :N/A :OTH.MANAG.

MAY ,RG ; SEC: SUNDEM,GL CIT: 0.59
RESEARCH FOR ACCOUNTING POLICY: AN OVERVIEW
TAR OC 76 VOL: 51 PG:747 - 763 :: QUAL. :INT. LOG. :THEORY :FIN.METH.

MAY ,RG ; SEC: SUNDEM,GL CIT: 0.35
COST OF INFORMATION AND SECURITY PRICES: MARKET ASSOCIATION TESTS FOR ACCOUNTING POLICY DECISIONS
TAR JA 73 VOL: 48 PG:80 - 94 :: ANAL. :INT. LOG. :EMH :INFO.STRUC.

MAY ,RG CIT: 1.76
THE INFLUENCE OF QUARTERLY EARNINGS ANNOUNCEMENTS ON INVESTOR DECISIONS AS REFLECTED IN COMMON STOCK PRICE CHANGES
JAR ST 71 VOL: 9 PG:119 - 163 :: REGRESS. :PRIM. :EMH :INT.REP.

MAYER-SOMMER,AP CIT: 0.36
UNDERSTANDING AND ACCEPTANCE OF THE EFFICIENT MARKETS HYPOTHESIS AND ITS ACCOUNTING IMPLICATIONS
TAR JA 79 VOL: 54 PG:88 - 106 :: DES.STAT. :SURV. :EMH :OTH.MANAG.

MAYERS,D ; FIRS: DANN ,LY ; SEC: MASULIS,RW CIT: 1
REPURCHASE TENDER OFFERS AND EARNINGS INFORMATION
JAE SE 91 VOL: 14 PG:217 - 251 :: REGRESS. :PRIM. :TIME SER. :BUS.COMB.

MAYNE ,LS ; FIRS: PHILIPS,GE CIT: 0
INCOME MEASURE AND BANK STOCK VALUES
JAR ST 70 VOL: 8 PG:178 - 188 :: REGRESS. :PRIM. :TIME SER. :VALUAT.(INFL.)

MAYPER,AG ; SEC: ADDY JR,ND CIT: 0
THE RELIABILITY OF THE DISCLOSURE OF AUDITOR CHANGES BY THE PUBLIC ACCOUNTING REPORT
AUD SP 91 VOL: 10 PG:136 - 144 :: REGRESS. :PRIM. :INSTIT. :ORG.

MAYPER,AG ; SEC: DOUCET,MS ; THIR: WARREN,CS CIT: 0.25
AUDITORS' MATERIALITY JUDGMENTS OF INTERNAL ACCOUNTING CONTROL WEAKNESSES
AUD AU 89 VOL: 9 PG:72 - 86 :: REGRESS. :LAB. :HIPS :MAT.

MAYPER,AG ; FIRS: GIROUX,GA ; THIR: DAFT ,RL CIT: 0
ORGANIZATION SIZE, BUDGET CYCLE, AND BUDGET RELATED INFLUENCE IN CITY GOVERNMENTS: AN EMPIRICAL STUDY
AOS 06 86 VOL: 11 PG:499 - 520 :: REGRESS. :SURV. :OTH.STAT. :BUDG.& PLAN.

MAYPER,AG CIT: 0
CONSENSUS OF AUDITORS' MATERIALITY JUDGMENTS OF INTERNAL ACCOUNTING CONTROL WEAKNESSES
JAR AU 82 VOL: 20 PG:773 - 783 :: NON-PAR. :LAB. :HIPS :MAT.

MAZUR ,MJ ; FIRS: BANKER,RD ; SEC: DATAR ,SM CIT: 0
TESTING THE OPTIMALITY OF A PERCENTAGE EVALUATION MEASURE FOR A GAIN SHARING CONTRACT
CAR SP 90 VOL: 6 PG:809 - 824 :: DES.STAT. :INT. LOG. :INF.ECO./AG. :EXEC.COMP.

MCAFEE,RP ; FIRS: BAILEY,AP ; THIR: WHINSTON,AB CIT: 0.17
AN APPLICATION OF COMPLEXITY THEORY TO THE ANALYSIS OF INTERNAL CONTROL SYSTEMS
AUD SU 81 VOL: 1 PG:38 - 52 :: ANAL. :INT. LOG. :OTH.STAT. :INT.CONT.

MCALLISTER,JP ; FIRS: DIRSMITH,MW ; SEC: COVALESKI,MA CIT: 0.5
OF PARADIGMS AND METAPHORS IN AUDITING THOUGHT
CAR AU 85 VOL: 2 PG:46 - 68 :: REGRESS. :SURV. :THEORY :AUD.TRAIN.

MCALLISTER,JP ; FIRS: DIRSMITH,MW CIT: 0.45
THE ORGANIC VS. THE MECHANISTIC AUDIT: PROBLEMS AND PITFALLS (PART II)
JAA AU 82 VOL: 6 PG:60 - 74 :: QUAL. :INT. LOG. :OTH. :AUD.

MCALLISTER,JP ; FIRS: DIRSMITH,MW CIT: 0.45
THE ORGANIC VS. THE MECHANISTIC AUDIT
JAA SP 82 VOL: 5 PG:214 - 228 :: QUAL. :INT. LOG. :OTH. :AUD.

MCBRIDE,HJ CIT: 0
ASSIGNING TAX LOADS TO PROSPECTIVE PROJECTS
TAR AP 63 VOL: 38 PG:363 - 370 :: ANAL. :INT. LOG. :OTH. :INT.CONT.

MCCARTHY,WE CIT: 0.18
THE REA ACCOUNTING MODEL: A GENERALIZED FRAMEWORK FOR ACCOUNTING SYSTEMS IN A SHARED DATA ENVIRONMENT
TAR JL 82 VOL: 57 PG:554 - 578 :: QUAL. :INT. LOG. :THEORY :N/A

MCCARTHY,WE CIT: 0.36
AN ENTITY-RELATIONSHIP VIEW OF ACCOUNTING MODELS
TAR OC 79 VOL: 54 PG:667 - 686 :: QUAL. :INT. LOG. :OTH. :N/A

MCCLELLAND,LA ; FIRS: WALKER,KB CIT: 0
MANAGEMENT FORECASTS AND STATISTICAL PREDICTION MODEL FORECASTS IN CORPORATE BUDGETING
JAR AU 91 VOL: 29 PG:371 - 381 :: REGRESS. :CASE :TIME SER. :BUDG.& PLAN.

MCCLENON,PR CIT: 0
COST FINDING THROUGH MULTIPLE CORRELATION ANALYSIS
TAR JL 63 VOL: 38 PG:540 - 547 :: CORR. :INT. LOG. :OTH.STAT. :COST.ALLOC.

MCCONNELL,DK CIT: 0.11
AUDITOR CHANGES AND RELATED DISAGREEMENTS
AUD SP 84 VOL: 3 PG:44 - 56 :: DES.STAT. :PRIM. :OTH.STAT. :AUD.

MCCONNELL,DK CIT: 0.22
ARE THE BIG 8 INCREASING THEIR SHARE OF THE NYSE, AMEX, AND OTC AUDIT MARKETS?
JAA WI 84 VOL: 7 PG:178 - 181 :: NON-PAR. :PRIM. :INSTIT. :AUD.

MCCOSH,AM ; SEC: RAHMAN,M CIT: 0.06
THE INFLUENCE OF ORGANIZATIONAL AND PERSONAL FACTORS ON THE USE OF ACCOUNTING INFORMATION: AN EMPIRICAL STUDY
AOS 04 76 VOL: 1 PG:339 - 356 :: DES.STAT. :LAB. :HIPS :MAN.DEC.CHAR.

MCCOSH,AM CIT: 0
ACCOUNTING CONSISTENCY - KEY TO STOCKHOLDER INFORMATION
TAR OC 67 VOL: 42 PG:693 - 700 :: ANAL. :SIM. :THEORY :FIN.METH.

MCCRAY,JH CIT: 0.67
A QUASI-BAYESIAN AUDIT RISK MODEL FOR DOLLAR UNIT SAMPLING
TAR JA 84 VOL: 59 PG:35 - 51 :: MIXED :SIM. :OTH.STAT. :SAMP.

MCDANIEL,LS CIT: 0.33
THE EFFECTS OF TIME PRESSURE AND AUDIT PROGRAM STRUCTURE ON AUDIT PERFORMANCE
JAR AU 90 VOL: 28 PG:267 - 285 :: REGRESS. :LAB. :HIPS :AUD.BEH.

MCDANIEL,LS ; FIRS: KINNEY-JR,WR CIT: 1
CHARACTERISTICS OF FIRMS CORRECTING PREVIOUSLY REPORTED QUARTERLY EARNINGS
JAE FB 89 VOL: 11 PG:71 - 93 :: REGRESS. :PRIM. :OTH.STAT. :AUD.

MCDONALD,B ; FIRS: BALVERS,RJ ; THIR: MILLER,RE CIT: 0.8
UNDERPRICING OF NEW ISSUES AND THE CHOICE OF AUDITOR AS A SIGNAL OF INVESTMENT BANKER REPUTATION
TAR OC 88 VOL: 63 PG:605 - 622 :: REGRESS. :PRIM. :MATH.PROG. :AUD.THEOR.

MCDONALD,B ; SEC: MORRIS,MH CIT: 0.33
THE RELEVANCE OF SFAS 33 INFLATION ACCOUNTING DISCLOSURES IN THE ADJUSTMENT OF STOCK PRICES TO INFLATION
TAR JL 84 VOL: 59 PG:432 - 446 :: REGRESS. :PRIM. :EMH :VALUAT.(INFL.)

MCDONALD,CL ; FIRS: LOREK ,KS ; THIR: PATZ ,DH CIT: 0.65
A COMPARATIVE EXAMINATION OF MANAGEMENT FORECASTS AND BOX-JENKINS FORECASTS OF EARNINGS
TAR AP 76 VOL: 51 PG:321 - 330 :: REGRESS. :PRIM. :TIME SER. :METHOD.

MCDONALD,CL CIT: 0.82
AN EMPIRICAL EXAMINATION OF THE RELIABILITY OF PUBLISHED PREDICTIONS OF FUTURE EARNINGS
TAR JL 73 VOL: 48 PG:502 - 510 :: DES.STAT. :PRIM. :OTH.STAT. :FOREC.

MCDONALD,DL ; SEC: PUXTY ,AG CIT: 0
AN INDUCEMENT-CONTRIBUTION APPROACH TO CORPORATE FINANCIAL REPORTING
AOS 12 79 VOL: 4 PG:53 - 66 :: QUAL. :INT. LOG. :THEORY :N/A

MCDONALD,DL CIT: 0.12
A TEST APPLICATION OF THE FEASIBILITY OF MARKET BASED MEASURES IN ACCOUNTING
JAR SP 68 VOL: 6 PG:38 - 49 :: NON-PAR. :LAB. :N/A :VALUAT.(INFL.)

MCDONALD,DL CIT: 0.06
FEASIBILITY CRITERIA FOR ACCOUNTING MEASURES
TAR OC 67 VOL: 42 PG:662 - 679 :: ANAL. :INT. LOG. :THEORY :OTH.FIN.ACC.

MCDONOUGH,JJ ; FIRS: ANSARI,SL CIT: 0.15
INTERSUBJECTIVITY - THE CHALLENGE AND OPPORTUNITY FOR ACCOUNTING
AOS 01 80 VOL: 5 PG:129 - 142 :: QUAL. :INT. LOG. :THEORY :N/A

MCDONOUGH,JJ ; FIRS: EPSTEIN,MJ ; SEC: FLAMHOLTZ,EG CIT: 0.41
CORPORATE SOCIAL ACCOUNTING IN THE U.S.A.: STATE OF THE ART AND FUTURE PROSPECTS
AOS 01 76 VOL: 1 PG:23 - 42 :: QUAL. :SEC. :THEORY :HRA

MCDONOUGH,JJ CIT: 0.06
THE ACCOUNTANT, DATA COLLECTION AND SOCIAL EXCHANGE
TAR OC 71 VOL: 46 PG:676 - 685 :: QUAL. :INT. LOG. :OTH.BEH. :MANAG.

MCELROY,JC ; FIRS: GOETZ-JR,JF ; SEC: MORROW,PC CIT: 0
THE EFFECT OF ACCOUNTING FIRM SIZE AND MEMBER RANK ON PROFESSIONALISM
AOS 02 91 VOL: 16 PG:159 - 165 :: REGRESS. :SURV. :OTH.BEH. :ORG.

MCENALLY,RW ; FIRS: JOY ,OM ; SEC: LITZENBERGER,RH CIT: 0.81
THE ADJUSTMENT OF STOCK PRICES TO ANNOUNCEMENTS OF UNANTICIPATED CHANGES IN QUARTERLY EARNINGS
JAR AU 77 VOL: 15 PG:207 - 225 :: REGRESS. :PRIM. :EMH :FIN.METH.

MCGAHRAN,KT CIT: 0
SEC DISCLOSURE REGULATION AND MANAGEMENT PERQUISITES
TAR JA 88 VOL: 63 PG:23 - 41 :: DES.STAT. :PRIM. :EMH :EXEC.COMP.

MCGEE ,VE ; FIRS: CASEY JR,CJ ; THIR: STICKNEY,CP CIT: 0.43
DISCRIMINATING BETWEEN REORGANIZED AND LIQUIDATED FIRMS IN BANKRUPTCY
TAR AP 86 VOL: 61 PG:249 - 262 :: REGRESS. :PRIM. :OTH.STAT. :BUS.FAIL.

MCGHEE,W ; SEC: SHIELDS,MD ; THIR: BIRNBERG,JG CIT: 1
THE EFFECTS OF PERSONALITY ON A SUBJECT'S INFORMATION PROCESSING
TAR JL 78 VOL: 53 PG:681 - 697 :: ANOVA :LAB. :HIPS :OTH.MANAG.

MCGRATH,NT ; FIRS: CARCELLO,JV ; SEC: HERMANSON,RH CIT: 0
AUDIT QUALITY ATTRIBUTES: THE PERCEPTIONS OF AUDIT PARTNERS, PREPARERS, AND FINANCIAL STATEMENT USERS
AUD SP 92 VOL: 11 PG:1 - 15 :: REGRESS. :SURV. :OTH.BEH. :OPER.AUD.

MCHUGH,AJ ; FIRS: DYER ,JC CIT: 0.47
THE TIMELINESS OF THE AUSTRALIAN ANNUAL REPORT
JAR AU 75 VOL: 13 PG:204 - 219 :: NON-PAR. :PRIM. :OTH.STAT. :TIM.

MCINNES,M ; SEC: RAMAKRISHNAN,RTS CIT: 0
A DECISION-THEORY MODEL OF MOTIVATION AND ITS USEFULNESS IN THE DIAGNOSIS OF MANAGEMENT CONTROL SYSTEMS
AOS 02 91 VOL: 16 PG:167 - 184 :: REGRESS. :SURV. :HIPS :MANAG.

MCINNES,M ; FIRS: BROWNELL,P CIT: 1.57
BUDGETARY PARTICIPATION, MOTIVATION, AND MANAGERIAL PERFORMANCE
TAR OC 86 VOL: 61 PG:587 - 600 :: REGRESS. :SURV. :OTH.BEH. :BUDG.& PLAN.

MCINTYRE,EV ; FIRS: BAILEY,CD CIT: 0
SOME EVIDENCE ON THE NATURE OF RELEARNING CURVES
TAR AP 92 VOL: 67 PG:368 - 378 :: REGRESS. :LAB. :HIPS :EDUC.

MCINTYRE,EV CIT: 0
INTERACTION EFFECTS OF INFLATION ACCOUNTING MODELS AND ACCOUNTING TECHNIQUES
TAR JL 82 VOL: 57 PG:607 - 618 :: ANAL. :INT. LOG. :THEORY :VALUAT.(INFL.)

MCINTYRE,EV CIT: 0.06
PRESENT VALUE DEPRECIATION AND THE DISAGGREGATION PROBLEM
TAR JA 77 VOL: 52 PG:162 - 171 :: ANAL. :INT. LOG. :THEORY :PP&E / DEPR

MCINTYRE,EV CIT: 0.35
CURRENT-COST FINANCIAL STATEMENTS AND COMMON-STOCK INVESTMENTS DECISIONS
TAR JL 73 VOL: 48 PG:575 - 585 :: ANOVA :LAB. :THEORY :VALUAT.(INFL.)

MCKEE ,AJ ; SEC: BELL ,TB ; THIR: BOATSMAN,JR CIT: 0.56
MANAGEMENT PREFERENCES OVER ACCOUNTING STANDARDS: A REPLICATION AND ADDITIONAL TESTS
TAR OC 84 VOL: 59 PG:647 - 659 :: OTH.QUANT. :PRIM. :INSTIT. :FASB SUBM.

MCKENNA,EF CIT: 0
AN ANALYSIS OF LEADERSHIP PATTERNS IN THE FINANCE FUNCTION
AOS 03 80 VOL: 5 PG:297 - 310 :: CORR. :LAB. :OTH.STAT. :MANAG.

MCKEOWN,J ; FIRS: HOPWOOD,W ; THIR: MUTCHLER,J CIT: 0.25
A TEST OF THE INCREMENTAL EXPLANATORY POWER OF OPINIONS QUALIFIED FOR CONSISTENCY AND UNCERTAINTY
TAR JA 89 VOL: 64 PG:28 - 48 :: REGRESS. :PRIM. :THEORY :BUS.FAIL.

MCKEOWN,J ; FIRS: HOPWOOD,W ; THIR: MUTCHLER,J CIT: 0
THE SENSITIVITY OF FINANCIAL DISTRESS PREDICTION MODELS TO DEPARTURES FROM NORMALITY
CAR AU 88 VOL: 5 PG:284 - 298 :: REGRESS. :PRIM. :OTH.STAT. :METHOD.

MCKEOWN,JC ; FIRS: CHENG ,CSA ; SEC: HOPWOOD,WS CIT: 1
NON-LINEARITY AND SPECIFICATION PROBLEMS IN UNEXPECTED EARNINGS RESPONSE REGRESSION MODEL
TAR JL 92 VOL: 67 PG:579 - 598 :: REGRESS. :PRIM. :EMH :METHOD.

MCKEOWN,JC ; SEC: MUTCHLER,JF ; THIR: HOPWOOD,W CIT: 0
TOWARDS AN EXPLANATION OF AUDITOR FAILURE TO MODIFY THE AUDIT OPINIONS OF BANKRUPT COMPANIES
AUD 91 VOL: 10 PG:1 - 13 :: REGRESS. :PRIM. :OTH.STAT. :BUS.FAIL.

MCKEOWN,JC ; FIRS: HOPWOOD,WS CIT: 0
EVIDENCE ON SURROGATES FOR EARNINGS EXPECTATIONS WITHIN A CAPITAL MARKET CONTEXT
JAA SU 90 VOL: 5 PG:339 - 363 :: REGRESS. :PRIM. :TIME SER. :FOREC.

MCKEOWN,JC ; SEC: SHALCHI,H CIT: 0.2
A COMPARATIVE EXAMINATION OF THE TIME-SERIES PROPERTIES AND PREDICTIVE ABILITY OF ANNUAL HISTORICAL COST AND GENERAL PRICE LEVEL
CAR SP 88 VOL: 4 PG:485 - 507 :: REGRESS. :PRIM. :TIME SER. :FIN.METH.

MCKEOWN,JC ; FIRS: HOPWOOD,WS CIT: 0.25
THE INCREMENTAL INFORMATIONAL CONTENT OF INTERIM EXPENSES OVER INTERIM SALES
JAR SP 85 VOL: 23 PG:161 - 174 :: REGRESS. :PRIM. :EMH :TAXES

MCKEOWN,JC ; FIRS: SILHAN,PA CIT: 0
FURTHER EVIDENCE ON THE USEFULNESS OF SIMULATED MERGERS
JAR SP 85 VOL: 23 PG:416 - 426 :: REGRESS. :PRIM. :TIME SER. :BUS.COMB.

MCKEOWN,JC ; FIRS: BUBLITZ,B ; SEC: FRECKA,TJ CIT: 1.38
MARKET ASSOCIATION TESTS AND FASB STATEMENT NO. 33 DISCLOSURES: A REEXAMINATION
JAR ST 85 VOL: 23 PG:1 - 23 :: REGRESS. :PRIM. :EMH :VALUAT.(INFL.)

MCKEOWN,JC ; FIRS: COLLINS,WA ; SEC: HOPWOOD,WS CIT: 0.44
THE PREDICTABILITY OF INTERIM EARNINGS OVER ALTERNATIVE QUARTERS
JAR AU 84 VOL: 22 PG:467 - 479 :: NON-PAR. :PRIM. :TIME SER. :INT.REP.

MCKEOWN,JC ; FIRS: HOPWOOD,WS ; THIR: NEWBOLD,P CIT: 0.55
THE ADDITIONAL INFORMATION CONTENT OF QUARTERLY EARNINGS REPORTS: INTERTEMPORAL DISAGGREGATION
JAR AU 82 VOL: 20 PG:343 - 349 :: REGRESS. :PRIM. :TIME SER. :FOREC.

MCKEOWN,JC ; FIRS: HOPWOOD,WS CIT: 0.42
AN EVALUATION OF UNIVARIATE TIME-SERIES EARNINGS MODELS AND THEIR GENERALIZATION TO A SINGLE INPUT TRANSFER FUNCTION
JAR AU 81 VOL: 19 PG:313 - 322 :: CORR. :PRIM. :TIME SER. :FOREC.

MCKEOWN,JC ; FIRS: ABDEL-KHALIK,AR CIT: 0.27
DISCLOSURE OF ESTIMATES OF HOLDING GAINS AND THE ASSESSMENT OF SYSTEMATIC RISK
JAR ST 78 VOL: 16 PG:46 - 77 :: ANOVA :PRIM. :EMH :VALUAT.(INFL.)

MCKEOWN,JC ; FIRS: ABDEL-KHALIK,AR CIT: 1.27
UNDERSTANDING ACCOUNTING CHANGES IN AN EFFICIENT MARKET: EVIDENCE OF DIFFERENTIAL REACTION
TAR OC 78 VOL: 53 PG:851 - 868 :: ANOVA :PRIM. :EMH :INV.

MCKEOWN,JC ; FIRS: ALBRECHT,WS ; SEC: LOOKABILL,LL CIT: 2.25
THE TIME-SERIES PROPERTIES OF ANNUAL EARNINGS
JAR AU 77 VOL: 15 PG:226 - 244 :: MIXED :PRIM. :TIME SER. :FOREC.

MCKEOWN,JC CIT: 0.06
COMPARATIVE APPLICATION OF MARKET AND COST BASED ACCOUNTING MODELS
JAR SP 73 VOL: 11 PG:62 - 99 :: REGRESS. :CASE :OTH. :VALUAT.(INFL.)

MCKEOWN,JC ; FIRS: BEDFORD,NM CIT: 0
COMPARATIVE ANALYSIS OF NET REALIZABLE VALUE AND REPLACEMENT COSTING
TAR AP 72 VOL: 47 PG:333 - 338 :: QUAL. :INT. LOG. :THEORY :VALUAT.(INFL.)

MCKEOWN,JC CIT: 0
ADDITIVITY OF NET REALIZABLE VALUES
TAR JL 72 VOL: 47 PG:527 - 532 :: ANAL. :INT. LOG. :THEORY :VALUAT.(INFL.)

MCKEOWN,JC CIT: 0.18
AN EMPIRICAL TEST OF A MODEL PROPOSED BY CHAMBERS
TAR JA 71 VOL: 46 PG:12 - 29 :: ANAL. :CASE :THEORY :VALUAT.(INFL.)

MCKINELY,S ; SEC: PANY ,K ; THIR: RECKERS,PMJ CIT: 0.13
AN EXAMINATION OF THE INFLUENCE OF CPA FIRM TYPE, SIZE, AND MAS PROVISION ON LOAN OFFICER DECISIONS & PERCEPTIONS
JAR AU 85 VOL: 23 PG:887 - 896 :: REGRESS. :LAB. :OTH.BEH. :ORG.

MCKINNEY,G ; FIRS: RONEN ,J CIT: 0.47
TRANSFER PRICING FOR DIVISIONAL AUTONOMY
JAR SP 70 VOL: 8 PG:99 - 112 :: ANAL. :INT. LOG. :OTH. :TRANS.PRIC.

MCKINNON,JL ; FIRS: HARRISON,GL CIT: 0.14
CULTURE AND ACCOUNTING CHANGE: A NEW PROSPECTIVE ON CORPORATE REPORTING REGULATION AND ACCOUNTING POLICY FORMULATION
AOS 03 86 VOL: 11 PG:233 - 252 :: DES.STAT. :INT. LOG. :INSTIT. :FASB SUBM.

MCLEAY,S CIT: 0.1
VALUE ADDED: A COMPARATIVE STUDY
AOS 01 83 VOL: 8 PG:31 - 56 :: DES.STAT. :PRIM. :OTH.STAT. :INT.DIFF.

MCNAIR,CJ CIT: 1
PROPER COMPROMISES: THE MANAGEMENT CONTROL DILEMMA IN PUBLIC ACCOUNTING AND ITS IMPACT ON AUDITOR BEHAVIOR
AOS 91 VOL: 16 PG:635 - 653 :: REGRESS. :FIELD :OTH.BEH. :ORG.

MCNAMEE,AH ; FIRS: CHOW ,CW ; THIR: PLUMLEE,RD CIT: 0.5
PRACTITIONERS' PERCEPTIONS OF AUDIT STEP DIFFICULTY AND CRITICALNESS: IMPLICATIONS FOR AUDIT RESEARCH
AUD SP 87 VOL: 6 PG:123 - 133 :: REGRESS. :SURV. :OTH.STAT. :AUD.THEOR.

MCNICHOLS,M CIT: 1.25
EVIDENCE OF INFORMATIONAL ASYMMETRIES FROM MANAGEMENT EARNINGS FORECASTS
TAR JA 89 VOL: 64 PG:1 - 27 :: REGRESS. :PRIM. :EMH :N/A

MCNICHOLS,M CIT: 0.6
A COMPARISON OF THE SKEWNESS OF STOCK RETURN DISTRIBUTIONS AT EARNINGS AND NON-EARNINGS ANNOUNCEMENT DATES
JAE JL 88 VOL: 10 PG:239 - 273 :: REGRESS. :SIM. :EMH :METHOD.

MCNICHOLS,M ; SEC: WILSON,GP CIT: 2.4
EVIDENCE OF EARNINGS MANAGEMENT FROM THE PROVISION FOR BAD DEBTS
JAR ST 88 VOL: 26 PG:1 - 40 :: REGRESS. :PRIM. :OTH.STAT. :LTD

MCNICHOLS,M ; SEC: MANEGOLD,JG CIT: 1
THE EFFECT OF THE INFORMATION ENVIRONMENT ON THE RELATIONSHIP BETWEEN FINANCIAL DISCLOSURE AND SECURITY PRICE VARIABILITY
JAE AP 83 VOL: 5 PG:49 - 74 :: MIXED :PRIM. :EMH :INT.REP.

MCQUEENEY,J ; FIRS: JACKSON-COX,J ; SEC: THIRKELL,JE CIT: 0.33
THE DISCLOSURE OF COMPANY INFORMATION TO TRADE UNIONS: THE RELEVANCE OF THE ACAS CODE OF PRACTICE ON DISCLOSURE
AOS 34 84 VOL: 9 PG:253 - 273 :: QUAL. :SURV. :INSTIT. :N/A

MCRAE ,TW CIT: 0.35
A CITATIONAL ANALYSIS OF THE ACCOUNTING INFORMATION NETWORK
JAR SP 74 VOL: 12 PG:80 - 92 :: DES.STAT. :SEC. :OTH. :METHOD.

MCRAE ,TW CIT: 0.06
OPPORTUNITY AND INCREMENTAL COST: AN ATTEMPT TO DEFINE IN SYSTEMS TERMS
TAR AP 70 VOL: 45 PG:315 - 321 :: QUAL. :SEC. :N/A :REL.COSTS

MCRAE ,TW CIT: 0
ACCOUNTANCY TRAINING IN SCOTLAND
JAR AU 65 VOL: 3 PG:255 - 260 :: QUAL. :INT. LOG. :OTH. :AUD.TRAIN.

MCROBERTS,HA ; SEC: HUDSON,J CIT: 0
AUDITING PROGRAM EVALUATIONS: THE CANADIAN CASE
AOS 04 85 VOL: 10 PG:493 - 502 :: REGRESS. :FIELD :INSTIT. :OPER.AUD.

MEADE ,JA CIT: 0
THE IMPACT OF DIFFERENT CAPITAL GAINS TAX REGIMES ON THE LOCK-IN EFFECT AND NEW RISKY INVESTMENT DECISIONS
TAR AP 90 VOL: 65 PG:406 - 431 :: REGRESS. :LAB. :HIPS :TAXES

MEANS ,KM CIT: 0
ACCOUNTING FOR INCOME TAXES: SFAS NO.96-UNEXPECTED RESULTS
JAA AU 89 VOL: 4 PG:571 - 579 :: REGRESS. :INT. LOG. :INSTIT. :TAXES

MEANS ,KM ; FIRS: HOLZMANN,OJ CIT: 0
ACCOUNTING FOR SAVINGS AND LOAN MERGERS: CONFLICT AND ACCOUNTING ERROR
JAA WI 84 VOL: 7 PG:138 - 150 :: QUAL. :INT. LOG. :THEORY :BUS.COMB.

MEAR ,R ; SEC: FIRTH ,MA CIT: 0
ASSESSING THE ACCURACY OF FINANCIAL ANALYST SECURITY RETURN PREDICTIONS
AOS 04 87 VOL: 12 PG:331 - 340 :: REGRESS. :PRIM. :HIPS :FOREC.

MEAR ,R ; SEC: FIRTH ,MA CIT: 0
CUE USAGE AND SELF-INSIGHT OF FINANCIAL ANALYSTS
TAR JA 87 VOL: 62 PG:176 - 182 :: REGRESS. :LAB. :HIPS :MAN.DEC.CHAR.

MEAR ,RWT ; SEC: FIRTH ,MA CIT: 0
A PARSIMONIOUS DESCRIPTION OF INDIVIDUAL DIFFERENCES IN FINANCIAL ANALYST JUDGMENT
JAA AU 90 VOL: 5 PG:501 - 520 :: REGRESS. :LAB. :HIPS :JUDG.

MEEK ,GK CIT: 0
U.S. SECURITIES MARKET RESPONSES TO ALTERNATE EARNINGS DISCLOSURES OF NON-U.S. MULTINATIONAL CORPORATIONS
TAR AP 83 VOL: 58 PG:394 - 402 :: ANOVA :PRIM. :EMH :FIN.METH.

MEHREZ,A ; SEC: BROWN ,JR ; THIR: KHOUJA,M CIT: 1
AGGREGATE EFFICIENCY MEASURES AND SIMPSON'S PARADOX
CAR AU 92 VOL: 9 PG:329 - 342 :: DES.STAT. :INT. LOG. :MATH.PROG. :MANAG.

MEHTA ,DR ; SEC: ANDREWS,VL CIT: 0
A NOTE ON INSTALLMENT REPORTING OF INCOME, PROFITABILITY, AND FUND FLOWS
JAR SP 68 VOL: 6 PG:50 - 57 :: DES.STAT. :SIM. :OTH.STAT. :TAXES

MEIXNER,WF ; SEC: WELKER,RB CIT: 0
JUDGMENT CONSENSUS AND AUDITOR EXPERIENCE: AN EXAMINATION OF ORGANIZATIONAL RELATIONS
AUD JL 88 VOL: 63 PG:505 - 513 :: CORR. :LAB. :OTH.BEH. :JUDG.

MELBERG,WF CIT: 0
BENISHAYAN TIMES SERIES AS MODELS FOR DEBT PROCESSES OVER TIME
TAR JA 72 VOL: 47 PG:116 - 133 :: ANAL. :INT. LOG. :TIME SER. :OTH.MANAG.

MELLMAN,M ; FIRS: LILIEN,S ; THIR: PASTENA,V CIT: 0.6
ACCOUNTING CHANGES: SUCCESSFUL VERSUS UNSUCCESSFUL FIRMS
TAR OC 88 VOL: 63 PG:642 - 656 :: REGRESS. :PRIM. :THEORY :ACC.CHNG.

MELLMAN,M ; SEC: SEILER,ME CIT: 0
STRUCTURE NEEDED FOR IMPLEMENTING MANDATED ACCOUNTING CHANGES
JAA AU 86 VOL: 1 PG:305 - 318 :: REGRESS. :PRIM. :INSTIT. :FASB SUBM.

MELLMAN,M CIT: 0
MARKETING COST ANALYSIS - DEVELOPMENT AND CURRENT PRACTICES
TAR JA 63 VOL: 38 PG:118 - 123 :: DES.STAT. :SURV. :OTH.STAT. :COST.ALLOC.

MELUMAD,N ; SEC: MOOKHERJEE,D ; THIR: REICHELSTEIN,S CIT: 0
A THEORY OF RESPONSIBILITY CENTERS
JAE DE 92 VOL: 15 PG:445 - 483 :: DES.STAT. :INT. LOG. :INF.ECO./AG. :RESP.ACC.

MELUMAD,N ; SEC: THOMAN,L CIT: 0
AN EQUILIBRIUM ANALYSIS OF OPTIMAL AUDIT CONTRACTS
CAR AU 90 VOL: 7 PG:22 - 55 :: DES.STAT. :INT. LOG. :INF.ECO./AG. :ORG.

MELUMAD,ND ; SEC: THOMAN,L CIT: 1.67
ON AUDITORS AND THE COURTS IN AN ADVERSE SELECTION SETTING
JAR SP 90 VOL: 28 PG:77 - 120 :: DES.STAT. :INT. LOG. :INF.ECO./AG. :LITIG.

MELUMAD,ND CIT: 0.75
ASYMMETRIC INFORMATION AND THE TERMINATION OF CONTRACTS IN AGENCIES
CAR SP 89 VOL: 5 PG:733 - 753 :: DES.STAT. :INT. LOG. :INF.ECO./AG. :EXEC.COMP.

MELUMAD,ND ; SEC: REICHELSTEIN,S CIT: 1
CENTRALIZATION VERSUS DELEGATION AND THE VALUE OF COMMUNICATION
JAR ST 87 VOL: 25 PG:1 - 18 :: DES.STAT. :INT. LOG. :INF.ECO./AG. :ORG.& ENVIR.

MENDELSON,H ; FIRS: AMIHUD,Y CIT: 0
INDEX AND INDEX-FUTURES RETURNS
JAA AU 89 VOL: 4 PG:415 - 431 :: REGRESS. :PRIM. :EMH :OTH.FIN.ACC.

MENDELSON,H ; FIRS: AMIHUD,Y CIT: 0
LIQUIDITY, VOLATILITY, AND EXCHANGE AUTOMATION
JAA AU 88 VOL: 3 PG:369 - 395 :: DES.STAT. :INT. LOG. :EMH :ORG.& ENVIR.

MENDENHALL,RR ; FIRS: AFFLECK-GRAVES,J ; SEC: DAVIS ,LR CIT: 0
FORECASTS OF EARNINGS PER SHARE: POSSIBLE SOURCES OF ANALYST SUPERIORITY AND BIAS
CAR SP 90 VOL: 6 PG:501 - 517 :: REGRESS. :LAB. :TIME SER. :FOREC.

MENDENHALL,RR ; SEC: NICHOLS,WD CIT: 0
BAD NEWS AND DIFFERENTIAL MARKET REACTIONS TO ANNOUNCEMENTS OF EARLIER-QUARTERS VERSUS FOURTH-QUARTER EARNINGS
JAR ST 88 VOL: 26 PG:63 - 90 :: REGRESS. :PRIM. :TIME SER. :INT.REP.

MENON ,K ; SEC: WILLIAMS,DD CIT: 0
AUDITOR CREDIBILITY AND INITIAL PUBLIC OFFERINGS
TAR AP 91 VOL: 66 PG:313 - 332 :: REGRESS. :PRIM. :EMH :PROB.ELIC.

MENON ,K ; SEC: SCHWARTZ,KB CIT: 0
AN EMPIRICAL INVESTIGATION OF AUDIT QUALIFICATION DECISIONS IN THE PRESENCE OF GOING CONCERN UNCERTAINTIES
CAR SP 87 VOL: 3 PG:302 - 315 :: REGRESS. :PRIM. :OTH.STAT. :BUS.FAIL.

MENON ,K ; FIRS: SCHWARTZ,KB CIT: 0.5
AUDITOR SWITCHES BY FAILING FIRMS
TAR AP 85 VOL: 60 PG:248 - 261 :: REGRESS. :PRIM. :N/A :BUS.FAIL.

MENON ,K ; FIRS: DAVIS ,SW ; THIR: MORGAN,G CIT: 0.55
THE IMAGES THAT HAVE SHAPED ACCOUNTING THEORY
AOS 04 82 VOL: 7 PG:307 - 318 :: QUAL. :INT. LOG. :THEORY :N/A

MENSAH,YM CIT: 0
EXERCISING BUDGETARY CONTROL IN AUTOMATED PRODUCTION ENVIRONMENTS
CAR AU 88 VOL: 5 PG:222 - 249 :: DES.STAT. :INT. LOG. :OTH.STAT. :BUDG.& PLAN.

MENSAH,YM CIT: 0
AN EXAMINATION OF THE STATIONARITY OF MULTIVARIATE BANKRUPTCY PREDICTION MODELS: A METHODOLOGICAL STUDY
JAR SP 84 VOL: 22 PG:380 - 395 :: OTH.QUANT. :PRIM. :OTH.STAT. :BUS.FAIL.

MENSAH,YM CIT: 0
THE USEFULNESS OF THE HOLDING GAINS AND LOSSES DISCLOSURE
JAA WI 83 VOL: 6 PG:130 - 141 :: OTH.QUANT. :PRIM. :THEORY :VALUAT.(INFL.)

MENSAH,YM CIT: 0.1
THE DIFFERENTIAL BANKRUPTCY PREDICTIVE ABILITY OF SPECIFIC PRICE LEVEL ADJUSTMENTS: SOME EMPIRICAL EVIDENCE
TAR AP 83 VOL: 58 PG:228 - 246 :: OTH.QUANT. :PRIM. :OTH.STAT. :BUS.FAIL.

MENSAH,YM CIT: 0.18
A DYNAMIC APPROACH TO THE EVALUATION OF INPUT-VARIABLE COST CENTER PERFORMANCE
TAR OC 82 VOL: 57 PG:681 - 700 :: ANAL. :INT. LOG. :N/A :N/A

MENZEFRICKE,U ; SEC: SMIELIAUSKAS,W CIT: 0.4
ON SAMPLE SIZE ALLOCATION IN AUDITING
CAR SP 88 VOL: 4 PG:314 - 336 :: DES.STAT. :SIM. :OTH.STAT. :SAMP.

MENZEFRICKE,U ; SEC: SMIELIAUSKAS,W CIT: 0.17
A COMPARISON OF THE STRATIFIED DIFFERENCE ESTIMATOR WITH SOME MONETARY-UNIT SAMPLING ESTIMATORS
CAR AU 87 VOL: 4 PG:240 - 250 :: DES.STAT. :SIM. :OTH.STAT. :SAMP.

MENZEFRICKE,U CIT: 0.33
USING DECISION THEORY FOR PLANNING AUDIT SAMPLE SIZE WITH DOLLAR UNIT SAMPLING
JAR AU 84 VOL: 22 PG:570 - 587 :: DES.STAT. :SIM. :OTH.STAT. :LIAB.

MENZEFRICKE,U ; SEC: SMIELIAUSKAS,W CIT: 0.78
A SIMULATION STUDY OF THE PERFORMANCE OF PARAMETRIC DOLLAR UNIT SAMPLING STATISTICAL PROCEDURES
JAR AU 84 VOL: 22 PG:588 - 604 :: DES.STAT. :SIM. :OTH.STAT. :LIAB.

MENZEFRICKE,U CIT: 0.7
ON SAMPLING PLAN SELECTION WITH DOLLAR-UNIT SAMPLING
JAR SP 83 VOL: 21 PG:96 - 105 :: ANAL. :INT. LOG. :OTH.STAT. :SAMP.

MEPHAM,MJ CIT: 0
ROBERT HAMILTON'S CONTRIBUTION TO ACCOUNTING
TAR JA 83 VOL: 58 PG:43 - 57 :: QUAL. :INT. LOG. :HIST. :N/A

MERCHANT,G CIT: 0.5
ANALOGICAL REASONING AND HYPOTHESIS GENERATION IN AUDITING
TAR JL 89 VOL: 64 PG:500 - 513 :: REGRESS. :FIELD :HIPS :AUD.BEH.

MERCHANT,KA CIT: 0
THE EFFECTS OF FINANCIAL CONTROLS ON DATA MANIPULATION AND MANAGEMENT MYOPIA
AOS 04 90 VOL: 15 PG:297 - 313 :: REGRESS. :SURV. :OTH.BEH. :BUDG.& PLAN.

MERCHANT,KA ; SEC: MANZONI,J CIT: 0.5
THE ACHIEVABILITY OF BUDGET TARGETS IN PROFIT CENTERS: A FIELD STUDY
TAR JL 89 VOL: 64 PG:539 - 558 :: REGRESS. :FIELD :HIPS :BUDG.& PLAN.

MERCHANT,KA CIT: 0.63
ORGANIZATIONAL CONTROLS AND DISCRETIONARY PROGRAM DECISION MAKING: A FIELD STUDY
AOS 01 85 VOL: 10 PG:67 - 86 :: REGRESS. :FIELD :OTH.BEH. :MANAG.

MERCHANT,KA CIT: 0.75
BUDGETING AND THE PROPENSITY TO CREATE BUDGETARY SLACK
AOS 02 85 VOL: 10 PG:201 - 210 :: REGRESS. :FIELD :OTH.BEH. :BUDG.& PLAN.

MERCHANT,KA CIT: 1.33
INFLUENCES ON DEPARTMENTAL BUDGETING: AN EMPIRICAL EXAMINATION OF A CONTINGENCY MODEL
AOS 34 84 VOL: 9 PG:291 - 309 :: OTH.QUANT. :SURV. :OTH.BEH. :N/A

MERCHANT,KA CIT: 2.25
THE DESIGN OF THE CORPORATE BUDGETING SYSTEM: INFLUENCES ON MANAGERIAL BEHAVIOR AND PERFORMANCE
TAR OC 81 VOL: 56 PG:813 - 829 :: CORR. :SURV. :OTH.BEH. :BUDG.& PLAN.

MERCHANT,KA ; FIRS: HARVEY,DW ; SEC: RHODE ,JG CIT: 0.14
ACCOUNTING AGGREGATION: USER PREFERENCES AND DECISION MAKING
AOS 03 79 VOL: 4 PG:187 - 210 :: ANOVA :LAB. :OTH.BEH. :N/A

MERCHANT,KA ; FIRS: GORDON,FE ; SEC: RHODE ,JG CIT: 0.19
THE EFFECTS OF SALARY AND HUMAN RESOURCE ACCOUNTING DISCLOSURES ON SMALL GROUP RELATIONS AND PERFORMANCE
AOS 04 77 VOL: 2 PG:295 - 306 :: ANOVA :LAB. :OTH.BEH. :HRA

MERINO,BD ; SEC: KOCH ,BS ; THIR: MACRITCHIE,KL CIT: 0
HISTORICAL ANALYSIS- A DIAGNOSTIC TOOL FOR EVENTS STUDIES: THE IMPACT OF T
TAR OC 87 VOL: 62 PG:748 - 762 :: REGRESS. :INT. LOG. :HIST. :FIN.METH.

MERINO,BD ; FIRS: TINKER,AM ; THIR: NEIMARK,M CIT: 3.18
THE NORMATIVE ORIGINS OF POSITIVE THEORIES: IDEOLOGY AND ACCOUNTING THOUGHT
AOS 02 82 VOL: 7 PG:167 - 200 :: QUAL. :INT. LOG. :THEORY :N/A

MERVILLE,LJ ; SEC: PETTY ,JW CIT: 0.13
TRANSFER PRICING FOR THE MULTINATIONAL FIRM
TAR OC 78 VOL: 53 PG:935 - 951 :: ANAL. :INT. LOG. :MATH.PROG. :TRANS.PRIC.

MESERVY,RD ; SEC: BAILEY JR,AD ; THIR: JOHNSON,PE CIT: 0.57
INTERNAL CONTROL EVALUATION: A COMPUTATIONAL MODEL OF THE REVIEW PROCESS
AUD AU 86 VOL: 6 PG:44 - 74 :: DES.STAT. :LAB. :EXP.SYST. :INT.CONT.

MESERVY,RD ; FIRS: BAILEY JR,AD ; SEC: DUKE ,GL ; THIR: GERLACH,JH ; FOUR: KO ,CE ; SIX: WHINSTON,AB CIT: 0.38
TICOM AND THE ANALYSIS OF INTERNAL CONTROLS
TAR AP 85 VOL: 60 PG:186 - 201 :: CORR. :INT. LOG. :OTH. :INT.CONT.

MESSIER JR,WF ; FIRS: KNECHEL,WR CIT: 0.33
SEQUENTIAL AUDITOR DECISION MAKING: INFORMATION SEARCH AND EVIDENCE EVALUATION
CAR SP 90 VOL: 6 PG:386 - 406 :: REGRESS. :LAB. :HIPS :AUD.BEH.

MESSIER JR,WF ; FIRS: KACHELMEIER,SJ CIT: 0.67
AN INVESTIGATION OF THE INFLUENCE OF A NONSTATISTICAL DECISION AID ON AUDITOR SAMPLE SIZE DECISIONS
TAR JA 90 VOL: 65 PG:209 - 226 :: REGRESS. :LAB. :HIPS :DEC.AIDS

MESSIER JR,WF ; FIRS: TUBBS ,RM ; THIR: KNECHEL,WR CIT: 1.67
RECENCY EFFECTS IN THE AUDITOR'S BELIEF-REVISION PROCESS
TAR AP 90 VOL: 65 PG:452 - 460 :: REGRESS. :LAB. :HIPS :AUD.BEH.

MESSIER JR,WF ; SEC: SCHNEIDER,A CIT: 0
A HIERARCHICAL APPROACH TO THE EXTERNAL AUDITOR'S EVALUATION OF THE INTERNAL AUDITING FUNCTION
CAR SP 88 VOL: 4 PG:337 - 353 :: REGRESS. :LAB. :HIPS :INT.AUD.

MESSIER JR,WF ; FIRS: BIGGS ,SF ; THIR: HANSEN,JV CIT: 0.5
A DESCRIPTIVE ANALYSIS OF COMPUTER AUDIT SPECIALISTS' DECISION MAKING
AUD SP 87 VOL: 6 PG:1 - 21 :: REGRESS. :LAB. :HIPS :EDP AUD.

MESSIER JR,WF ; SEC: HANSEN,JV CIT: 0.33
EXPERT SYSTEMS IN AUDITING: THE STATE OF THE ART
AUD AU 87 VOL: 7 PG:94 - 105 :: REGRESS. :SURV. :EXP.SYST. :JUDG.

MESSIER JR,WF ; FIRS: HANSEN,JV CIT: 0.57
A PRELIMINARY INVESTIGATION OF EDP-XPERT
AUD AU 86 VOL: 6 PG:109 - 123 :: ANAL. :LAB. :EXP.SYST. :EDP AUD.

MESSIER JR,WF CIT: 1.1
THE EFFECT OF EXPERIENCE AND FIRM TYPE ON MATERIALITY/DISCLOSURE JUDGMENTS
JAR AU 83 VOL: 21 PG:611 - 618 :: ANOVA :SIM. :HIPS :MAT.

MESSIER JR,WF ; FIRS: HOLSTRUM,GL CIT: 0.73
A REVIEW AND INTEGRATION OF EMPIRICAL RESEARCH ON MATERIALITY
AUD AU 82 VOL: 2 PG:45 - 63 :: QUAL. :SEC. :OTH. :MAT.

MESSIER JR,WF ; FIRS: JOHNSON,SB CIT: 0
THE NATURE OF ACCOUNTING STANDARDS SETTING: AN ALTERNATIVE EXPLANATION
JAA SP 82 VOL: 5 PG:195 - 213 :: QUAL. :INT. LOG. :INSTIT. :FASB SUBM.

MESSIER JR,WF ; FIRS: EMERY ,DR ; SEC: BARRON,FH CIT: 0.09
CONJOINT MEASUREMENT AND THE ANALYSIS OF NOISY DATA: A COMMENT
JAR AU 82 VOL: 20 PG:450 - 458 :: NON-PAR. :SIM. :HIPS :METHOD.

MEST ,DP ; FIRS: JENNINGS,R ; THIR: THOMPSON II,RB CIT: 0
INVESTOR REACTION TO DISCLOSURES OF 1974-75 LIFO ADOPTION DECISIONS
TAR AP 92 VOL: 67 PG:337 - 354 :: REGRESS. :PRIM. :INF.ECO./AG. :ACC.CHNG.

METCALF,RW CIT: 0
THE BASIC POSTULATES IN PERSPECTIVE
TAR JA 64 VOL: 39 PG:16 - 21 :: QUAL. :INT. LOG. :THEORY :OTH.FIN.ACC.

MEYER ,JW CIT: 2
SOCIAL ENVIRONMENTS AND ORGANIZATIONAL ACCOUNTING
AOS 45 86 VOL: 11 PG:345 - 356 :: ANOVA :INT. LOG. :THEORY :OTH.MANAG.

MEYER ,PE CIT: 0
A FRAMEWORK FOR UNDERSTANDING SUBSTANCE OVER FORM IN ACCOUNTING
TAR JA 76 VOL: 51 PG:80 - 89 :: QUAL. :SEC. :THEORY :FIN.METH.

MEYERS,SL CIT: 0.06
AN EXAMINATION OF THE RELATIONSHIP BETWEEN INTERPERIOD TAX ALLOCATION AND PRESENT-VALUE DEPRECIATION
TAR JA 73 VOL: 48 PG:44 - 49 :: QUAL. :INT. LOG. :THEORY :TAXES

MEYERS,SL CIT: 0.18
THE STATIONARITY PROBLEM IN THE USE OF THE MARKET MODEL OF SECURITY PRICE BEHAVIOR
TAR AP 73 VOL: 48 PG:318 - 322 :: REGRESS. :PRIM. :EMH :METHOD.

MIA ,L CIT: 0.75
THE IMPACT OF PARTICIPATION IN BUDGETING AND JOB DIFFICULTY ON MANAGERIAL PERFORMANCE AND WORK MOTIVATION: A RESEARCH NOTE
AOS 04 89 VOL: 14 PG:347 - 357 :: REGRESS. :SURV. :OTH.BEH. :BUDG.& PLAN.

MIA ,L CIT: 0.4
MANAGERIAL ATTITUDE, MOTIVATION AND THE EFFECTIVENESS OF BUDGET PARTICIPATION
AOS 05 88 VOL: 13 PG:465 - 475 :: REGRESS. :LAB. :OTH.BEH. :BUDG.& PLAN.

MIAN ,SL ; SEC: SMITH JR,CW CIT: 0.67
INCENTIVES FOR UNCONSOLIDATED FINANCIAL REPORTING
JAE JA 90 VOL: 12 PG:141 - 171 :: REGRESS. :PRIM. :OTH.STAT. :BUS.COMB.

MIAN ,SL ; SEC: SMITH JR,CW CIT: 0.33
INCENTIVES ASSOCIATED WITH CHANGES IN CONSOLIDATED REPORTING REQUIREMENTS
JAE OC 90 VOL: 13 PG:249 - 266 :: REGRESS. :PRIM. :OTH.STAT. :FASB SUBM.

MIELKE,DE ; SEC: SEIFERT,J CIT: 0
A SURVEY ON THE EFFECTS OF DEFEASING DEBT
JAA WI 87 VOL: 2 PG:65 - 78 :: REGRESS. :PRIM. :THEORY :LTD

MILANI,K CIT: 2
THE RELATIONSHIP OF PARTICIPATION IN BUDGET-SETTING TO INDUSTRIAL SUPERVISOR PERFORMANCE AND ATTITUDES: A FIELD STUDY
TAR AP 75 VOL: 50 PG:274 - 284 :: NON-PAR. :FIELD :OTH.BEH. :BUDG.& PLAN.

MILLAR,JA ; FIRS: HAYES ,RD CIT: 0
MEASURING PRODUCTION EFFICIENCY IN A NOT-FOR-PROFIT SETTING
TAR JL 90 VOL: 65 PG:505 - 519 :: ANOVA :LAB. :INF.ECO./AG. :OPER.AUD.

MILLAR,JA ; FIRS: GLEZEN,GW CIT: 0
AN EMPIRICAL INVESTIGATION OF STOCKHOLDER REACTION TO DISCLOSURES REQUIRED
JAR AU 85 VOL: 23 PG:859 - 870 :: REGRESS. :PRIM. :INSTIT. :ORG.

MILLAR,JA CIT: 0
SPLIT OR DIVIDEND: DO THE WORDS REALLY MATTER?
TAR JA 77 VOL: 52 PG:52 - 55 :: DES.STAT. :PRIM. :EMH :STK.DIV.

MILLER,BL ; FIRS: BUCKMAN,AG CIT: 0
OPTIMAL INVESTIGATION OF A MULTIPLE COST PROCESSES SYSTEM
JAR SP 82 VOL: 20 PG:28 - 41 :: ANAL. :INT. LOG. :OTH.STAT. :N/A

MILLER,D ; FIRS: GORDON,LA CIT: 1.53
A CONTINGENCY FRAMEWORK FOR THE DESIGN OF ACCOUNTING INFORMATION SYSTEMS
AOS 01 76 VOL: 1 PG:59 - 70 :: QUAL. :INT. LOG. :OTH.BEH. :INFO.STRUC.

MILLER,EM CIT: 0
WHY OVERSTATED EARNINGS AFFECT STOCK PRICES BUT NOT THE REVERSE - AN IMPORTANT ASYMMETRY
JAA AU 80 VOL: 4 PG:6 - 19 :: QUAL. :INT. LOG. :EMH :INFO.STRUC.

MILLER,H CIT: 0.47
ENVIRONMENTAL COMPLEXITY AND FINANCIAL REPORTS
TAR JA 72 VOL: 47 PG:31 - 37 :: QUAL. :INT. LOG. :HIPS :INFO.STRUC.

MILLER,HE CIT: 0
TEXTBOOKS OR RESEARCH
TAR JA 66 VOL: 41 PG:1 - 7 :: QUAL. :INT. LOG. :INSTIT. :OTH.MANAG.

MILLER,JC ; FIRS: FALK ,H CIT: 0.06
AMORTIZATION OF ADVERTISING EXPENDITURES
JAR SP 77 VOL: 15 PG:12 - 22 :: REGRESS. :PRIM. :OTH.STAT. :AMOR./DEPL.

MILLER,MC CIT: 0
GOODWILL - AN AGGREGATION ISSUE
TAR AP 73 VOL: 48 PG:280 - 291 :: QUAL. :INT. LOG. :THEORY :OTH. NON-C/A

MILLER,P ; SEC: HOPPER,T ; THIR: LAUGHLIN,R CIT: 0
THE NEW ACCOUNTING HISTORY: AN INTRODUCTION
AOS 05 91 VOL: 16 PG:395 - 403 :: REGRESS. :SEC. :HIST. :METHOD.

MILLER,P CIT: 0
ACCOUNTING INNOVATION BEYOND THE ENTERPRISE: PROBLEMATIZING INVESTMENT DECISIONS AND PROGRAMMING ECONOMIC GROWTH IN THE U.K. IN THE 1960s
AOS 91 VOL: 16 PG:733 - 762 :: REGRESS. :SEC. :HIST. :DEC.AIDS

MILLER,P CIT: 1
ON THE INTERRELATIONS BETWEEN ACCOUNTING AND THE STATE
AOS 04 90 VOL: 15 PG:315 - 338 :: REGRESS. :SEC. :HIST. :ORG.& ENVIR.

MILLER,P ; SEC: O'LEARY,T CIT: 0.67
MAKING ACCOUNTANCY PRACTICAL
AOS 05 90 VOL: 15 PG:479 - 498 :: REGRESS. :SEC. :HIST. :ORG.& ENVIR.

MILLER,P ; SEC: O'LEARY,T CIT: 4.83
ACCOUNTING AND THE CONSTRUCTION OF THE GOVERNABLE PERSON
AOS 03 87 VOL: 12 PG:235 - 265 :: DES.STAT. :INT. LOG. :HIST. :MANAG.

MILLER,RE ; FIRS: BALVERS,RJ ; SEC: MCDONALD,B CIT: 0.8
UNDERPRICING OF NEW ISSUES AND THE CHOICE OF AUDITOR AS A SIGNAL OF INVESTMENT BANKER REPUTATION
TAR OC 88 VOL: 63 PG:605 - 622 :: REGRESS. :PRIM. :MATH.PROG. :AUD.THEOR.

MILLIRON,VC CIT: 0.25
A BEHAVIOURAL STUDY OF THE MEANING AND INFLUENCE OF TAX COMPLEXITY
JAR AU 85 VOL: 23 PG:794 - 816 :: REGRESS. :LAB. :HIPS :TAXES

MILLS ,RH CIT: 0
INVESTMENT LOSS RESERVES FOR CORPORATE BOND INVESTORS
TAR JA 67 VOL: 42 PG:74 - 81 :: DES.STAT. :PRIM. :N/A :OTH. NON-C/A

MILTZ ,D ; SEC: CALOMME,GJ ; THIR: WILLIKENS,M CIT: 0
A RISK-BASED ALLOCATION OF INTERNAL AUDIT TIME: A CASE STUDY
AUD AU 91 VOL: 10 PG:49 - 61 :: REGRESS. :CASE :OTH.STAT. :RISK

MINCH ,RA ; FIRS: PETRI ,E CIT: 0
A DECISION MODEL FOR TAX PREFERENCE ITEMS
TAR AP 78 VOL: 53 PG:415 - 428 :: ANAL. :INT. LOG. :OTH.STAT. :OTH.MANAG.

MINCH ,RA ; FIRS: PETRI ,E CIT: 0.12
THE TREASURY STOCK METHOD AND CONVENTIONAL METHOD IN RECIPROCAL STOCKHOLDINGS - AN AMALGAMATION
TAR AP 74 VOL: 49 PG:330 - 341 :: ANAL. :INT. LOG. :N/A :SPEC.ITEMS

MINCH ,RA ; FIRS: PETRI ,E CIT: 0
EVALUATION OF RESOURCE ACQUISITION DECISIONS BY THE PARTITIONING OF HOLDING ACTIVITY
TAR JL 74 VOL: 49 PG:455 - 464 :: ANAL. :INT. LOG. :N/A :INV.

MINER ,JB ; FIRS: DALTON,FE CIT: 0.06
THE ROLE OF ACCOUNTING TRAINING IN TOP MANAGEMENT DECISION MAKING
TAR JA 70 VOL: 45 PG:134 - 139 :: ANOVA :LAB. :N/A :AUD.TRAIN.

MINI ,DL ; FIRS: MAUTZ ,RK CIT: 0.06
INTERNAL CONTROL EVALUATION AND AUDIT PROGRAM MODIFICATION
TAR AP 66 VOL: 41 PG:283 - 291 :: QUAL. :INT. LOG. :N/A :INT.CONT.

MIRVIS,PH ; SEC: LAWLER III,EE CIT: 0.2
SYSTEMS ARE NOT SOLUTIONS: ISSUES IN CREATING INFORMATION SYSTEMS THAT ACCOUNT FOR THE HUMAN ORGANIZATION
AOS 23 83 VOL: 8 PG:175 - 190 :: QUAL. :FIELD :OTH.BEH. :ORG.& ENVIR.

MIRVIS,PH ; FIRS: MACY ,BA CIT: 0.18
ACCOUNTING FOR THE COSTS AND BENEFITS OF HUMAN RESOURCE DEVELOPMENT PROGRAMS: AN INTERDISCIPLINARY APPROACH
AOS 23 76 VOL: 1 PG:179 - 194 :: QUAL. :CASE :OTH.BEH. :HRA

MISTER,WG ; FIRS: HARPER JR,RM ; THIR: STRAWSER,JR CIT: 0
THE IMPACT OF NEW PENSION DISCLOSURE RULES ON PERCEPTIONS OF DEBT
JAR AU 87 VOL: 25 PG:327 - 330 :: REGRESS. :LAB. :OTH.STAT. :PENS.

MITCHELL,GB CIT: 0
AFTER-TAX COST OF LEASING
TAR AP 70 VOL: 45 PG:308 - 314 :: ANAL. :INT. LOG. :N/A :REL.COSTS

MITROFF,II ; SEC: MASON ,RO CIT: 0.2
CAN WE DESIGN SYSTEMS FOR MANAGING MESSES? OR, WHY SO MANY MANAGEMENT INFORMATION SYSTEMS ARE UNINFORMATIVE
AOS 23 83 VOL: 8 PG:195 - 204 :: QUAL. :INT. LOG. :OTH. :MAN.DEC.CHAR.

MITTELSTAEDT,HF ; SEC: REGIER,PR ; THIR: CHEWNING,EG ; FOUR: PANY ,K CIT: 0
DO CONSISTENCY MODIFICATIONS PROVIDE INFORMATION TO EQUITY MARKETS?
AUD SP 92 VOL: 11 PG:83 - 98 :: REGRESS. :PRIM. :OTH.STAT. :OPIN.

MITTELSTAEDT,HF CIT: 0.75
AN EMPIRICAL ANALYSIS OF THE FACTORS UNDERLYING THE DECISION TO REMOVE EXCESS ASSETS FROM OVERFUNDED PENSION PLANS
JAE NV 89 VOL: 11 PG:399 - 418 :: REGRESS. :PRIM. :OTH.STAT. :PENS.

MLYNARCZYK,FA CIT: 0.12
AN EMPIRICAL STUDY OF ACCOUNTING METHODS AND STOCK PRICES
JAR ST 69 VOL: 7 PG:63 - 81 :: REGRESS. :PRIM. :EMH :FIN.METH.

MLYNARCZYK,FA ; FIRS: COMISKEY,EE CIT: 0
RECOGNITION OF INCOME BY FINANCE COMPANIES
TAR AP 68 VOL: 43 PG:248 - 256 :: ANAL. :SIM. :THEORY :REV.REC.

MOBLEY,SC CIT: 0.18
THE CHALLENGES OF SOCIO-ECONOMIC ACCOUNTING
TAR OC 70 VOL: 45 PG:762 - 768 :: QUAL. :INT. LOG. :THEORY :HRA

MOBLEY,SC CIT: 0
MEASURES OF INCOME
TAR AP 68 VOL: 43 PG:333 - 341 :: QUAL. :INT. LOG. :THEORY :REV.REC.

MOBLEY,SC CIT: 0
REVENUE EXPERIENCE AS A GUIDE TO ASSET VALUATION
TAR JA 67 VOL: 42 PG:114 - 123 :: ANAL. :INT. LOG. :THEORY :PP&E / DEPR

MOBLEY,SC CIT: 0
THE CONCEPT OF REALIZATION: A USEFUL DEVICE
TAR AP 66 VOL: 41 PG:292 - 296 :: QUAL. :INT. LOG. :THEORY :REV.REC.

MOCK ,TJ ; FIRS: KLERSEY,GF CIT: 0.25
VERBAL PROTOCOL RESEARCH IN AUDITING
AOS 02 89 VOL: 14 PG:133 - 151 :: REGRESS. :SEC. :HIPS :METHOD.

MOCK ,TJ ; FIRS: BIGGS ,SF ; THIR: WATKINS,PR CIT: 1.4
AUDITOR'S USE OF ANALYTICAL REVIEW IN AUDIT PROGRAM DESIGN
TAR JA 88 VOL: 63 PG:148 - 162 :: REGRESS. :LAB. :OTH.BEH. :ANAL.REV.

MOCK ,TJ ; FIRS: LIN ,WT ; THIR: WRIGHT,A CIT: 0.33
THE USE OF ANALYTIC HIERARCHY PROCESS AS AN AID IN PLANNING THE NATURE AND EXTENT OF AUDIT PROCEDURES
AUD AU 84 VOL: 4 PG:89 - 99 :: ANAL. :INT. LOG. :OTH.STAT. :PLAN.

MOCK ,TJ ; SEC: WILLINGHAM,JJ CIT: 0.1
AN IMPROVED METHOD OF DOCUMENTING AND EVALUATING A SYSTEM OF INTERNAL ACCOUNTING CONTROLS
AUD SP 83 VOL: 2 PG:91 - 99 :: QUAL. :INT. LOG. :OTH. :INT.CONT.

MOCK ,TJ ; FIRS: BIGGS ,SF CIT: 1.1
AN INVESTIGATION OF AUDITOR DECISION PROCESSES IN THE EVALUATION OF INTERNAL CONTROLS AND AUDIT SCOPE DECISIONS
JAR SP 83 VOL: 21 PG:234 - 255 :: DES.STAT. :LAB. :HIPS :INT.CONT.

MOCK ,TJ ; SEC: WRIGHT,A CIT: 0.09
EVALUATING THE EFFECTIVENESS OF AUDIT PROCEDURES
AUD AU 82 VOL: 2 PG:33 - 44 :: QUAL. :INT. LOG. :THEORY :OPER.AUD.

MOCK ,TJ ; SEC: VASARHELYI,MA CIT: 0
A SYNTHESIS OF THE INFORMATION ECONOMICS AND LENS MODELS
JAR AU 78 VOL: 16 PG:414 - 423 :: ANAL. :INT. LOG. :HIPS :METHOD.

MOCK ,TJ ; FIRS: GROVE ,HD ; THIR: EHRENREICH,K CIT: 0.06
A REVIEW OF HUMAN RESOURCE ACCOUNTING MEASUREMENT SYSTEMS FROM A MEASUREMENT THEORY PERSPECTIVE
AOS 03 77 VOL: 2 PG:219 - 236 :: QUAL. :SEC. :OTH.BEH. :HRA

MOCK ,TJ ; FIRS: DRIVER,MJ CIT: 1.65
HUMAN INFORMATION PROCESSING, DECISION STYLE THEORY, AND ACCOUNTING INFORMATION SYSTEMS
TAR JL 75 VOL: 50 PG:490 - 508 :: MIXED :LAB. :HIPS :INFO.STRUC.

MOCK ,TJ CIT: 0.24
THE VALUE OF BUDGET INFORMATION
TAR JL 73 VOL: 48 PG:520 - 534 :: REGRESS. :LAB. :OTH.BEH. :INFO.STRUC.

MOCK ,TJ ; SEC: ESTRIN,TL ; THIR: VASARHELYI,MA CIT: 0.71
LEARNING PATTERNS, DECISION APPROACH, AND VALUE OF INFORMATION
JAR SP 72 VOL: 10 PG:129 - 153 :: ANOVA :LAB. :HIPS :INFO.STRUC.

MOCK ,TJ CIT: 0.18
CONCEPTS OF INFORMATION VALUE AND ACCOUNTING
TAR OC 71 VOL: 46 PG:765 - 777 :: ANAL. :INT. LOG. :INF.ECO./AG. :INFO.STRUC.

MOCK ,TJ CIT: 0.29
COMPARATIVE VALUES OF INFORMATION STRUCTURES
JAR ST 69 VOL: 7 PG:124 - 159 :: ANOVA :LAB. :OTH.BEH. :INFO.STRUC.

MODIGLIANI,F ; FIRS: HEALY ,PM CIT: 0
DIVIDEND DECISIONS AND EARNINGS
JAA WI 90 VOL: 5 PG:3 - 25 :: REGRESS. :PRIM. :OTH.STAT. :CASH DIV.

MOECKEL,C ; FIRS: KAPLAN,SE ; THIR: WILLIAMS,JD CIT: 0
AUDITORS' HYPOTHESIS PLAUSIBILITY ASSESSMENTS IN AN ANALYTICAL REVIEW SETTING
AUD AU 92 VOL: 11 PG:50 - 65 :: REGRESS. :LAB. :HIPS :ANAL.REV.

MOECKEL,C ; SEC: WILLIAMS,JD CIT: 0
THE ROLE OF SOURCE AVAILABILITY IN INFERENCE VERIFICATION
CAR SP 90 VOL: 6 PG:850 - 858 :: REGRESS. :LAB. :HIPS :AUD.BEH.

MOECKEL,C CIT: 0.33
THE EFFECT OF EXPERIENCE ON AUDITORS' MEMORY ERRORS
JAR AU 90 VOL: 28 PG:368 - 387 :: REGRESS. :LAB. :HIPS :AUD.BEH.

MOECKEL,CL ; SEC: PLUMLEE,RD CIT: 1.75
AUDITORS' CONFIDENCE IN RECOGNITION OF AUDIT EVIDENCE
TAR OC 89 VOL: 64 PG:653 - 666 :: REGRESS. :LAB. :HIPS :AUD.BEH.

MOFFIE,RP ; FIRS: BLOCHER,E ; THIR: ZMUD ,RW CIT: 0.14
REPORT FORMAT AND TASK COMPLEXITY: INTERACTION IN RISK JUDGMENTS
AOS 06 86 VOL: 11 PG:457 - 470 :: REGRESS. :LAB. :HIPS :INFO.STRUC.

MOHRWEIS,CS ; FIRS: KELLY ,AS CIT: 0
BANKERS' AND INVESTORS' PERCEPTIONS OF THE AUDITOR'S ROLE IN FINANCIAL STATEMENT REPORTING: THE IMPACT OF SAS NO. 58
AUD AU 89 VOL: 9 PG:87 - 97 :: REGRESS. :LAB. :HIPS :FASB SUBM.

MOIZER,P ; SEC: TURLEY,S CIT: 0
SURROGATES FOR AUDIT FEES IN CONCENTRATION STUDIES
AUD AU 87 VOL: 7 PG:118 - 123 :: REGRESS. :PRIM. :OTH.STAT. :ORG.

MONAHAN,TF ; SEC: BARENBAUM,L CIT: 0
THE USE OF CONSTANT DOLLAR INFORMATION TO PREDICT BOND RATING CHANGES
JAA SU 83 VOL: 6 PG:325 - 340 :: OTH.QUANT. :PRIM. :OTH.STAT. :VALUAT.(INFL.)

MONCUR,RH ; FIRS: SWIERINGA,RJ CIT: 0.53
THE RELATIONSHIP BETWEEN MANAGERS' BUDGET-ORIENTED BEHAVIOR AND SELECTED ATTITUDE, POSITION, SIZE, AND PERFORMANCE MEASURES
JAR ST 72 VOL: 10 PG:194 - 209 :: OTH.QUANT. :FIELD :OTH.BEH. :BUDG.& PLAN.

MONSON,NP ; SEC: TRACY ,JA CIT: 0
STOCK RIGHTS AND ACCOUNTING WRONGS
TAR OC 64 VOL: 39 PG:890 - 893 :: ANAL. :INT. LOG. :THEORY :STK.DIV.

MOODY ,SM ; SEC: FLESHER,DL CIT: 0
ANALYSIS OF FASB VOTING PATTERNS: STATEMENT NOS. 1-86
JAA AU 86 VOL: 1 PG:319 - 330 :: REGRESS. :PRIM. :INSTIT. :FASB SUBM.

MOOKHERJEE,D ; FIRS: MELUMAD,N ; THIR: REICHELSTEIN,S CIT: 0
A THEORY OF RESPONSIBILITY CENTERS
JAE DE 92 VOL: 15 PG:445 - 483 :: DES.STAT. :INT. LOG. :INF.ECO./AG. :RESP.ACC.

MOON ,JE ; FIRS: FULMER,JG CIT: 0
TESTS FOR COMMON STOCK EQUIVALENCY
JAA AU 84 VOL: 8 PG:5 - 14 :: NON-PAR. :PRIM. :OTH.STAT. :FIN.METH.

MOON ,P CIT: 0
SOME EXPERIMENTAL EVIDENCE ON FUNCTIONAL FIXATION: A RESEARCH NOTE
AOS 03 90 VOL: 15 PG:193 - 198 :: REGRESS. :LAB. :HIPS :DEC.AIDS

MOONITZ,M CIT: 0.12
PRICE-LEVEL ACCOUNTING AND SCALES OF MEASUREMENT
TAR JL 70 VOL: 45 PG:465 - 475 :: QUAL. :INT. LOG. :THEORY :VALUAT.(INFL.)

MOONITZ,M CIT: 0.12
SOME REFLECTIONS ON THE INVESTMENT CREDIT EXPERIENCE
JAR SP 66 VOL: 4 PG:47 - 61 :: QUAL. :INT. LOG. :INSTIT. :TAXES

MOONITZ,M ; SEC: RUSS ,A CIT: 0.06
ACCRUAL ACCOUNTING FOR EMPLOYERS' PENSION COSTS
JAR AU 66 VOL: 4 PG:155 - 168 :: QUAL. :INT. LOG. :THEORY :PENS.

MOORE ,CL CIT: 0
THE PRESENT-VALUE METHOD AND THE REPLACEMENT DECISION
TAR JA 64 VOL: 39 PG:94 - 102 :: ANAL. :INT. LOG. :N/A :CAP.BUDG.

MOORE ,DC CIT: 0
ACCOUNTING ON TRIAL: THE CRITICAL LEGAL STUDIES MOVEMENT AND ITS LESSONS FOR RADICAL ACCOUNTING
AOS 91 VOL: 16 PG:163 - 791 :: REGRESS. :SEC. :THEORY :OTH.MANAG.

MOORE ,G ; SEC: RONEN ,J CIT: 0
EXTERNAL AUDIT AND ASYMMETRIC INFORMATION
AUD 90 VOL: 9 PG:234 - 242 :: DES.STAT. :INT. LOG. :INF.ECO./AG. :INFO.STRUC.

MOORE ,G ; SEC: SCOTT ,WR CIT: 0.25
AUDITORS' LEGAL LIABILITY, COLLUSION WITH MANAGEMENT, AND INVESTORS' LOSS
CAR SP 89 VOL: 5 PG:754 - 774 :: DES.STAT. :INT. LOG. :INF.ECO./AG. :LIAB.

MOORE ,G ; FIRS: KIM ,M CIT: 0.4
ECONOMIC VS. ACCOUNTING DEPRECIATION
JAE AP 88 VOL: 10 PG:111 - 125 :: REGRESS. :PRIM. :THEORY :PP&E / DEPR

MOORE ,G CIT: 0
DEPRECIATION, INFLATION AND CAPITAL REPLACEMENT
CAR SP 87 VOL: 3 PG:375 - 383 :: DES.STAT. :SIM. :OTH.STAT. :CAP.BUDG.

MOORE ,JC ; FIRS: WILLIAMS,JJ ; SEC: MACINTOSH,NB CIT: 0.33
BUDGET-RELATED BEHAVIOR IN PUBLIC SECTOR ORGANIZATIONS: SOME EMPIRICAL EVIDENCE
AOS 03 90 VOL: 15 PG:221 - 246 :: REGRESS. :SURV. :OTH.BEH. :BUDG.& PLAN.

MOORE ,ML ; SEC: STEECE,BM ; THIR: SWENSON,CW CIT: 0.17
AN ANALYSIS OF THE IMPACT OF STATE INCOME TAX RATES AND BASES ON FOREIGN INVESTMENT
TAR OC 87 VOL: 62 PG:671 - 685 :: REGRESS. :PRIM. :TIME SER. :TAXES

MOORE ,ML ; SEC: STEECE,BM ; THIR: SWENSON,CW CIT: 0
SOME EMPIRICAL EVIDENCE ON TAXPAYER RATIONALITY
TAR JA 85 VOL: 60 PG:18 - 32 :: REGRESS. :PRIM. :TIME SER. :TAXES

MOORE ,ML CIT: 0.59
MANAGEMENT CHANGES AND DISCRETIONARY ACCOUNTING DECISIONS
JAR SP 73 VOL: 11 PG:100 - 107 :: NON-PAR. :PRIM. :OTH. :ACC.CHNG.

MOORES,K ; SEC: STEADMAN,GT CIT: 0
THE COMPARATIVE VIEWPOINTS OF GROUPS OF ACCOUNTANTS: MORE ON THE ENTITY-PROPRIETARY DEBATE
AOS 01 86 VOL: 11 PG:19 - 34 :: REGRESS. :SURV. :INSTIT. :FASB SUBM.

MORENO,RG CIT: 0
THE UNIFICATION OF THE PROFESSIONAL TEACHING OF ACCOUNTING IN THE AMERICAS
TAR OC 64 VOL: 39 PG:990 - 995 :: QUAL. :INT. LOG. :INSTIT. :OTH.MANAG.

MOREY ,L CIT: 0
PROGRESS OF THE INDEPENDENT POST AUDIT PROGRAM IN ILLINOIS
TAR JA 63 VOL: 38 PG:102 - 108 :: QUAL. :INT. LOG. :N/A :AUD.

MORGAN,EA ; FIRS: WILLIAMS,JJ ; SEC: NEWTON,JD CIT: 0
THE INTEGRATION OF ZERO-BASE BUDGETING WITH MANAGEMENT-BY-OBJECTIVES: AN EMPIRICAL INQUIRY
AOS 04 85 VOL: 10 PG:457 - 478 :: REGRESS. :FIELD :OTH.BEH. :BUDG.& PLAN.

MORGAN,G CIT: 1.2
ACCOUNTING AS REALITY CONTRUCTION: TOWARDS A NEW EPISTEMOLOGY FOR ACCOUNTING PRACTICE
AOS 05 88 VOL: 13 PG:477 - 485 :: DES.STAT. :INT. LOG. :THEORY :OTH.MANAG.

MORGAN,G ; FIRS: DAVIS ,SW ; SEC: MENON ,K CIT: 0.55
THE IMAGES THAT HAVE SHAPED ACCOUNTING THEORY
AOS 04 82 VOL: 7 PG:307 - 318 :: QUAL. :INT. LOG. :THEORY :N/A

MORGENSON,DL ; FIRS: REILLY,FK ; THIR: WEST ,M CIT: 0.18
THE PREDICTIVE ABILITY OF ALTERNATIVE PARTS OF INTERIM FINANCIAL STATEMENTS
JAR ST 72 VOL: 10 PG:105 - 124 :: REGRESS. :PRIM. :EMH :INT.REP.

MORIARITY,S CIT: 0.64
COMMUNICATING FINANCIAL INFORMATION THROUGH MULTIDIMENSIONAL GRAPHICS
JAR SP 79 VOL: 17 PG:205 - 224 :: DES.STAT. :LAB. :OTH.BEH. :INFO.STRUC.

MORIARITY,S ; SEC: BARRON,FH CIT: 0.57
A JUDGMENT-BASED DEFINITION OF MATERIALITY
JAR ST 79 VOL: 17 PG:114 - 135 :: OTH.QUANT. :LAB. :OTH.STAT. :MAT.

MORIARITY,S ; SEC: BARRON,FH CIT: 0.88
MODELING THE MATERIALITY JUDGMENTS OF AUDIT PARTNERS
JAR AU 76 VOL: 14 PG:320 - 341 :: MIXED :LAB. :OTH.BEH. :MAT.

MORIARITY,S CIT: 0.29
ANOTHER APPROACH TO ALLOCATING JOINT COSTS
TAR OC 75 VOL: 50 PG:791 - 795 :: ANAL. :INT. LOG. :THEORY :COST.ALLOC.

MORRIS,D ; FIRS: CHENHALL,R CIT: 0
THE EFFECT OF COGNITIVE STYLE AND SPONSORSHIP BIAS ON THE TREATMENT OF OPPORTUNITY COSTS IN RESOURCE ALLOCATION DECISIONS
AOS 01 91 VOL: 16 PG:27 - 46 :: REGRESS. :LAB. :HIPS :COST.ALLOC.

MORRIS,D ; FIRS: CHENHALL,RH CIT: 0.86
THE IMPACT OF STRUCTURE, ENVIRONMENT, AND INTERDEPENDENCE ON THE PERCEIVED USEFULNESS OF MANAGEMENT ACCOUNTING SYSTEMS
TAR JA 86 VOL: 61 PG:16 - 35 :: REGRESS. :SURV. :OTH.STAT. :ORG.& ENVIR.

MORRIS,MH ; SEC: NICHOLS,WD CIT: 0.8
CONSISTENCY EXCEPTIONS: MATERIALITY JUDGMENTS AND AUDIT FIRM STRUCTURE
TAR AP 88 VOL: 63 PG:237 - 254 :: REGRESS. :PRIM. :EMH :MAT.

MORRIS,MH ; SEC: NICHOLS,WD CIT: 0
PENSION ACCOUNTING AND THE BALANCE SHEET: THE POTENTIAL EFFECT OF THE FASB'S PRELIMINARY VIEWS
JAA SU 84 VOL: 7 PG:293 - 305 :: MIXED :PRIM. :OTH.STAT. :PENS.

MORRIS,MH ; FIRS: MCDONALD,B CIT: 0.33
THE RELEVANCE OF SFAS 33 INFLATION ACCOUNTING DISCLOSURES IN THE ADJUSTMENT OF STOCK PRICES TO INFLATION
TAR JL 84 VOL: 59 PG:432 - 446 :: REGRESS. :PRIM. :EMH :VALUAT.(INFL.)

MORRISON,TA ; SEC: KACZKA,E CIT: 0.06
A NEW APPLICATION OF CALCULUS AND RISK ANALYSIS TO COST-VOLUME-PROFIT CHANGES
TAR AP 69 VOL: 44 PG:330 - 343 :: ANAL. :INT. LOG. :OTH.STAT. :C-V-P-A

MORRISON,TA ; SEC: BUZBY ,SL CIT: 0
EFFECT OF THE INVESTMENT TAX CREDIT ON THE CAPITALIZE-EXPENSE DECISION
TAR JL 68 VOL: 43 PG:517 - 521 :: ANAL. :INT. LOG. :N/A :TAX PLNG.

MORRISON,TA CIT: 0
TAXATION OF INTERNATIONAL INVESTMENTS
TAR OC 66 VOL: 41 PG:704 - 713 :: QUAL. :INT. LOG. :N/A :TAX PLNG.

MORRISSEY,LE ; FIRS: GREER JR,WR CIT: 0
ACCOUNTING RULE-MAKING IN A WORLD OF EFFICIENT MARKETS
JAA AU 78 VOL: 2 PG:49 - 57 :: QUAL. :INT. LOG. :INSTIT. :FIN.METH.

MORROW,PC ; FIRS: HOLT ,DL CIT: 0
RISK ASSESSMENT JUDGMENTS OF AUDITORS AND BANK LENDERS: A COMPARATIVE ANALYSIS OF CONFORMANCE TO BAYES' THEOREM
AOS 06 92 VOL: 17 PG:549 - 559 :: REGRESS. :LAB. :HIPS :RISK

MORROW,PC ; FIRS: GOETZ-JR,JF ; THIR: MCELROY,JC CIT: 0
THE EFFECT OF ACCOUNTING FIRM SIZE AND MEMBER RANK ON PROFESSIONALISM
AOS 02 91 VOL: 16 PG:159 - 165 :: REGRESS. :SURV. :OTH.BEH. :ORG.

MORSE ,D ; SEC: STEPHAN,J ; THIR: STICE ,EK CIT: 0.5
EARNIGS ANNOUNCEMENTS AND THE CONVERGENCE (OR DIVERGENCE) OF BELIEFS
TAR AP 91 VOL: 66 PG:376 - 388 :: REGRESS. :PRIM. :EMH :AUD.BEH.

MORSE ,D CIT: 0.22
AN ECONOMETRIC ANALYSIS OF THE CHOICE OF DAILY VERSUS MONTHLY RETURNS IN TESTS OF INFORMATION CONTENT
JAR AU 84 VOL: 22 PG:605 - 623 :: ANAL. :SEC. :EMH :METHOD.

MORSE ,D ; SEC: RICHARDSON,G CIT: 1.7
THE LIFO/FIFO DECISION
JAR SP 83 VOL: 21 PG:106 - 127 :: DES.STAT. :PRIM. :OTH.STAT. :INV.

MORSE ,D ; SEC: USHMAN,N CIT: 0.2
THE EFFECT OF INFORMATION ANNOUNCEMENTS ON THE MARKET MICROSTRUCTURE
TAR AP 83 VOL: 58 PG:247 - 258 :: ANOVA :PRIM. :OTH. :FIN.METH.

MORSE ,D CIT: 1.75
PRICE AND TRADING VOLUME REACTION SURROUNDING EARNINGS ANNOUNCEMENTS: A CLOSER EXAMINATION
JAR AU 81 VOL: 19 PG:374 - 383 :: REGRESS. :PRIM. :EMH :FIN.METH.

MORSE ,D ; FIRS: BEAVER,WH ; SEC: LAMBERT,RA CIT: 4.31
THE INFORMATION CONTENT OF SECURITY PRICES
JAE MR 80 VOL: 2 PG:3 - 28 :: REGRESS. :PRIM. :EMH :FOREC.

MORSE ,WJ CIT: 0.06
REPORTING PRODUCTION COSTS THAT FOLLOW THE LEARNING CURVE PHENOMENON
TAR OC 72 VOL: 47 PG:761 - 773 :: ANAL. :INT. LOG. :OTH.STAT. :COST.ALLOC.

MORTON,JR CIT: 0.12
QUALITATIVE OBJECTIVES OF FINANCIAL ACCOUNTING: A COMMENT ON RELEVANCE AND UNDERSTANDABILITY
JAR AU 74 VOL: 12 PG:288 - 298 :: NON-PAR. :SURV. :OTH.BEH. :FIN.METH.

MOSER ,DV CIT: 1
THE EFFECTS OF OUTPUT INTERFERENCE, AVAILABILITY, AND ACCOUNTING INFORMATION ON INVESTORS' PREDICTIVE JUDGMENTS
TAR JL 89 VOL: 64 PG:433 - 448 :: REGRESS. :LAB. :HIPS :AUD.BEH.

MOSES ,OD CIT: 0
ON BANKRUPTCY INDICATORS FROM ANALYSTS' EARNINGS FORECASTS
JAA SU 90 VOL: 5 PG:379 - 409 :: REGRESS. :PRIM. :OTH.STAT. :BUS.FAIL.

MOSES ,OD CIT: 0.33
INCOME SMOOTHING AND INCENTIVES: EMPIRICAL TESTS USING ACCOUNTING CHANGES
TAR AP 87 VOL: 62 PG:358 - 377 :: REGRESS. :PRIM. :EMH :ACC.CHNG.

MOST ,KS CIT: 0.11
DEPRECIATION EXPENSE AND THE EFFECT OF INFLATION
JAR AU 84 VOL: 22 PG:782 - 788 :: DES.STAT. :SURV. :THEORY :PP&E / DEPR

MOST ,KS CIT: 0
SOMBART'S PROPOSITIONS REVISITED
TAR OC 72 VOL: 47 PG:722 - 734 :: QUAL. :SEC. :HIST. :OTH.MANAG.

MOST ,KS CIT: 0
TWO FORMS OF EXPERIMENTAL ACCOUNTS
TAR JA 69 VOL: 44 PG:145 - 152 :: QUAL. :INT. LOG. :THEORY :INFO.STRUC.

MOST ,KS CIT: 0
THE VALUE OF INVENTORIES
JAR SP 67 VOL: 5 PG:39 - 50 :: QUAL. :SEC. :HIST. :INV.

MUELLER,FJ ; FIRS: BERG ,KB CIT: 0
ACCOUNTING FOR INVESTMENT CREDITS
TAR JL 63 VOL: 38 PG:554 - 561 :: QUAL. :INT. LOG. :THEORY :TAXES

MUELLER,GG CIT: 0
WHYS AND HOWS OF INTERNATIONAL ACCOUNTING
TAR AP 65 VOL: 40 PG:386 - 394 :: QUAL. :INT. LOG. :INSTIT. :FIN.METH.

MUELLER,GG CIT: 0
VALUING INVENTORIES AT OTHER THAN HISTORICAL COSTS - SOME INTERNATIONAL DIFFERENCES
JAR AU 64 VOL: 2 PG:148 - 157 :: QUAL. :INT. LOG. :THEORY :INT.DIFF.

MUELLER,GG CIT: 0
THE DIMENSIONS OF THE INTERNATIONAL ACCOUNTING PROBLEM
TAR JA 63 VOL: 38 PG:142 - 147 :: QUAL. :INT. LOG. :THEORY :INT.DIFF.

MUKHERJI,A ; FIRS: BAIMAN,S ; SEC: MAY ,JH CIT: 0.33
OPTIMAL EMPLOYMENT CONTRACTS AND THE RETURNS TO MONITORING IN A PRINCIPAL-AGENT CONTEXT
CAR SP 90 VOL: 6 PG:761 - 799 :: DES.STAT. :INT. LOG. :INF.ECO./AG. :EXEC.COMP.

MULFORD,CW ; SEC: COMISKEY,EE CIT: 0
INVESTMENT DECISIONS AND THE EQUITY ACCOUNTING STANDARD
TAR JL 86 VOL: 61 PG:519 - 525 :: REGRESS. :PRIM. :OTH.STAT. :BUS.COMB.

MULFORD,CW CIT: 0.25
THE IMPORTANCE OF A MARKET VALUE MEASUREMENT OF DEBT IN LEVERAGE
JAR AU 85 VOL: 23 PG:897 - 906 :: REGRESS. :PRIM. :EMH :LTD

MULKAY,M ; FIRS: PINCH ,T ; THIR: ASHMORE,M CIT: 1
CLINICAL BUDGETING: EXPERIMENTATION IN THE SOCIAL SCIENCES: A DRAMA IN FIVE ACTS
AOS 03 89 VOL: 14 PG:271 - 301 :: REGRESS. :SURV. :OTH.BEH. :BUDG.& PLAN.

MUNTER,P ; FIRS: COLLINS,F ; THIR: FINN ,DW CIT: 0.5
THE BUDGETING GAMES PEOPLE PLAY
TAR JA 87 VOL: 62 PG:29 - 49 :: REGRESS. :SURV. :OTH.BEH. :BUDG.& PLAN.

MUNTER,P ; SEC: RATCLIFFE,TA CIT: 0
AN ASSESSMENT OF USER REACTIONS TO LEASE ACCOUNTING DISCLOSURES
JAA WI 83 VOL: 6 PG:108 - 114 :: NON-PAR. :LAB. :THEORY :LEASES

MURDOCH,B CIT: 0.14
THE INFORMATION CONTENT OF FAS 33 RETURNS ON EQUITY
TAR AP 86 VOL: 61 PG:273 - 287 :: REGRESS. :PRIM. :EMH :VALUAT.(INFL.)

MURDOCK,RJ ; FIRS: SHANK ,JK CIT: 0.33
COMPARABILITY IN THE APPLICATION OF REPORTING STANDARDS: SOME FURTHER EVIDENCE
TAR OC 78 VOL: 53 PG:824 - 835 :: DES.STAT. :PRIM. :EMH :OPIN.

MURNIGHAN,JK ; SEC: BAZERMAN,MH CIT: 0
A PERSPECTIVE ON NEGOTIATION RESEARCH IN ACCOUNTING AND AUDITING
TAR JL 90 VOL: 65 PG:642 - 657 :: DES.STAT. :SEC. :OTH.BEH. :MANAG.

MURPHY,GJ CIT: 0.06
A NUMERICAL REPRESENTATION OF SOME ACCOUNTING CONVENTIONS
TAR AP 76 VOL: 51 PG:277 - 286 :: QUAL. :INT. LOG. :OTH.STAT. :OTH.FIN.ACC.

MURPHY,KJ CIT: 1.63
CORPORATE PERFORMANCE AND MANAGERIAL REMUNERATION: AN EMPIRICAL ANALYSIS
JAE AP 85 VOL: 7 PG:11 - 42 :: REGRESS. :PRIM. :OTH.STAT. :EXEC.COMP.

MURRAY,D.; FIRS: ELGERS,P CIT: 0
THE RELATIVE AND COMPLEMENTARY PERFORMANCE OF ANALYST AND SECURITY-PRICE-BASED MEASURES OF EXPECTED EARNINGS
JAE JN 92 VOL: 15 PG:303 - 316 :: REGRESS. :PRIM. :OTH.STAT. :FOREC.

MURRAY,D ; SEC: FRAZIER,KB CIT: 0.43
A WITHIN-SUBJECTS TEST OF EXPECTANCY THEORY IN A PUBLIC ACCOUNTING ENVIRONMENT
JAR AU 86 VOL: 24 PG:400 - 404 :: REGRESS. :LAB. :OTH.BEH. :INFO.STRUC.

MURRAY,D ; FIRS: BLOOM ,R ; SEC: ELGERS,PT CIT: 0.11
FUNCTIONAL FIXATION IN PRODUCT PRICING: A COMPARISON OF INDIVIDUALS AND GROUPS
AOS 01 84 VOL: 9 PG:1 - 11 :: MIXED :LAB. :HIPS :PP&E / DEPR

MURRAY,D ; SEC: JOHNSON,R CIT: 0
DIFFERENTIAL GAAP AND THE FASB'S CONCEPTUAL FRAMEWORK
JAA AU 83 VOL: 7 PG:4 - 15 :: QUAL. :INT. LOG. :THEORY :FASB SUBM.

MURRAY,D CIT: 0.3
THE EFFECT OF CERTAIN RESEARCH DESIGN CHOICES ON THE ASSESSMENT OF THE MARKET'S REACTION TO LIFO CHANGES: A METHODOLOGICAL STUDY
JAR SP 83 VOL: 21 PG:128 - 140 :: NON-PAR. :PRIM. :EMH :INV.

MURRAY,D CIT: 0
THE IRRELEVANCE OF LEASE CAPITALIZATION
JAA WI 82 VOL: 5 PG:154 - 159 :: REGRESS. :PRIM. :EMH :FIN.METH.

MURRAY,D ; FIRS: ELGERS,PT CIT: 0
THE IMPACT OF THE CHOICE OF MARKET INDEX ON THE EMPIRICAL EVALUATION OF ACCOUNTING DETERMINED RISK MEASURES
TAR AP 82 VOL: 57 PG:358 - 375 :: REGRESS. :PRIM. :EMH :N/A

MUTCHLER,J ; FIRS: HOPWOOD,W ; SEC: MCKEOWN,J CIT: 0.25
A TEST OF THE INCREMENTAL EXPLANATORY POWER OF OPINIONS QUALIFIED FOR CONSISTENCY AND UNCERTAINTY
TAR JA 89 VOL: 64 PG:28 - 48 :: REGRESS. :PRIM. :THEORY :BUS.FAIL.

MUTCHLER,J ; FIRS: HOPWOOD,W ; SEC: MCKEOWN,J CIT: 0
THE SENSITIVITY OF FINANCIAL DISTRESS PREDICTION MODELS TO DEPARTURES FROM NORMALITY
CAR AU 88 VOL: 5 PG:284 - 298 :: REGRESS. :PRIM. :OTH.STAT. :METHOD.

MUTCHLER,JF ; FIRS: MCKEOWN,JC ; THIR: HOPWOOD,W CIT: 0
TOWARDS AN EXPLANATION OF AUDITOR FAILURE TO MODIFY THE AUDIT OPINIONS OF BANKRUPT COMPANIES
AUD 91 VOL: 10 PG:1 - 13 :: REGRESS. :PRIM. :OTH.STAT. :BUS.FAIL.

MUTCHLER,JF ; SEC: WILLIAMS,DD CIT: 0
THE RELATIONSHIP BETWEEN AUDIT TECHNOLOGY, CLIENT RISK PROFILES, AND THE GOING-CONCERN OPINION DECISION
AUD AU 90 VOL: 9 PG:39 - 54 :: REGRESS. :PRIM. :INSTIT. :ORG.

MUTCHLER,JF CIT: 0
EMPIRICAL EVIDENCE REGARDING THE AUDITOR'S GOING-CONCERN OPINION DECISION
AUD AU 86 VOL: 6 PG:148 - :: DES.STAT. :PRIM. :OTH.STAT. :OPIN.

MUTCHLER,JF CIT: 0.88
A MULTIVARIATE ANALYSIS OF THE AUDITOR'S GOING-CONCERN OPINION DECISION
JAR AU 85 VOL: 23 PG:668 - 682 :: REGRESS. :PRIM. :OTH.STAT. :OPIN.

MUTCHLER,JF CIT: 0.56
AUDITORS' PERCEPTIONS OF THE GOING-CONCERN OPINION DECISION
AUD SP 84 VOL: 3 PG:17 - 30 :: DES.STAT. :SURV. :OTH. :OPIN.

MYERS ,BL ; FIRS: PEARSON,MA ; SEC: LINDGREN,JH CIT: 0.07
A PRELIMINARY ANALYSIS OF AUDSEC VOTING PATTERNS
JAA WI 79 VOL: 2 PG:122 - 134 :: OTH.QUANT. :PRIM. :INSTIT. :FASB SUBM.

MYNATT,PG ; FIRS: CREADY,WM CIT: 0.5
THE INFORMATION CONTENT OF ANNUAL REPORTS: A PRICE AND TRADING RESPONSE ANALYSIS
TAR AP 91 VOL: 66 PG:291 - 312 :: REGRESS. :PRIM. :EMH :N/A

NACHMAN,DA ; FIRS: FERRARA,WL ; SEC: HAYYA ,JC CIT: 0.24
NORMALCY OF PROFIT IN THE JAEDICKE-ROBICHEK MODEL
TAR AP 72 VOL: 47 PG:299 - 307 :: ANAL. :SIM. :OTH.STAT. :C-V-P-A

NACHTMANN,R ; FIRS: DORAN ,DT CIT: 0
THE ASSOCIATION OF STOCK DISTRIBUTION ANNOUNCEMENTS AND EARNINGS PERFORMANCE
JAA SP 88 VOL: 03 PG:113 - 132 :: REGRESS. :PRIM. :EMH :STK.DIV.

NACHTSHEIM,CJ ; FIRS: KO ,CE ; THIR: DUKE ,GL ; FOUR: BAILEY JR,AD CIT: 0
ON THE ROBUSTNESS OF MODEL-BASED SAMPLING IN AUDITING
AUD SP 88 VOL: 07 PG:119 - 136 :: DES.STAT. :SIM. :OTH.STAT. :SAMP.

NAGARAJAN,NJ ; FIRS: BAIMAN,S ; SEC: EVANS III,JH CIT: 0.5
COLLUSION IN AUDITING
JAR SP 91 VOL: 29 PG:1 - 18 :: DES.STAT. :INT. LOG. :INF.ECO./AG. :AUD.BEH.

NAGARAJAN,NJ ; FIRS: BALACHANDRAN,BV CIT: 0.5
IMPERFECT INFORMATION, INSURANCE, AND AUDITORS' LEGAL LIABILITY
CAR SP 87 VOL: 3 PG:281 - 301 :: DES.STAT. :INT. LOG. :INF.ECO./AG. :LIAB.

NAGARAJAN,NJ ; FIRS: JOHNSON,WB ; SEC: MAGEE ,RP ; FOUR: NEWMAN,HA CIT: 0.13
AN ANALYSIS OF THE STOCK PRICE REACTION TO SUDDEN EXECUTIVE DEATHS: IMPLICATIONS FOR THE MANAGEMENT LABOR MARKET
JAE AP 85 VOL: 7 PG:151 - 174 :: REGRESS. :PRIM. :EMH :OTH.MANAG.

NAHAPIET,JE CIT: 0.6
THE RHETORIC AND REALITY OF AN ACCOUNTING CHANGE: A STUDY OF RESOURCE ALLOCATION
AOS 04 88 VOL: 13 PG:333 - 358 :: REGRESS. :SURV. :INSTIT. :COST.ALLOC.

NAHAPIET,JE ; FIRS: BURCHELL,S ; SEC: CLUBB ,C ; THIR: HOPWOOD,AG ; FOUR: HUGHES,JS CIT: 4.92
THE ROLES OF ACCOUNTING IN ORGANIZATIONS AND SOCIETY
AOS 01 80 VOL: 5 PG:5 - 27 :: QUAL. :INT. LOG. :THEORY :N/A

NAHAPIET,JE ; FIRS: BANBURY,J CIT: 0.86
TOWARDS A FRAMEWORK FOR THE STUDY OF THE ANTECEDENTS AND CONSEQUENCES OF INFORMATION SYSTEMS IN ORGANIZATIONS
AOS 03 79 VOL: 4 PG:163 - 178 :: QUAL. :INT. LOG. :OTH. :N/A

NAINAR,SMK ; FIRS: ODAIYAPPA,R CIT: 0
ECONOMIC CONSEQUENCES OF SFAS NO.33-AN INSIDER-TRADING PERSPECTIVE
TAR JL 92 VOL: 67 PG:599 - 609 :: REGRESS. :PRIM. :EMH :VALUAT.(INFL.)

NAIR ,RD ; SEC: RITTENBERG,LE CIT: 0
MESSAGES PERCEIVED FROM AUDIT, REVIEW, AND COMPILATION REPORTS: EXTENSION
AUD AU 87 VOL: 7 PG:15 - 38 :: REGRESS. :LAB. :HIPS :AUD.THEOR.

NAIR ,RD ; SEC: RITTENBERG,LE CIT: 0
ACCOUNTING COSTS OF PRIVATELY HELD BUSINESSES
JAA SP 83 VOL: 6 PG:234 - 243 :: DES.STAT. :SURV. :OTH.BEH. :N/A

NAIR ,RD ; SEC: FRANK ,WG CIT: 0.23
THE IMPACT OF DISCLOSURE AND MEASUREMENT PRACTICES ON INTERNATIONAL ACCOUNTING CLASSIFICATIONS
TAR JL 80 VOL: 55 PG:426 - 450 :: OTH.QUANT. :PRIM. :OTH.STAT. :INT.DIFF.

NAIR ,RD CIT: 0.21
ECONOMIC ANALYSES AND ACCOUNTING TECHNIQUES: AN EMPIRICAL STUDY
JAR SP 79 VOL: 17 PG:225 - 242 :: DES.STAT. :PRIM. :OTH.STAT. :METHOD.

NAKANO,I CIT: 0
NOISE AND REDUNDANCY IN ACCOUNTING COMMUNICATIONS
TAR OC 72 VOL: 47 PG:693 - 708 :: ANAL. :INT. LOG. :INF.ECO./AG. :VALUAT.(INFL.)

NALEBUFF,B ; FIRS: ANTLE ,R CIT: 0.5
CONSERVATISM AND AUDITOR-CLIENT NEGOTIATIONS
JAR ST 91 VOL: 29 PG:31 - 59 :: DES.STAT. :INT. LOG. :INF.ECO./AG. :FIN.METH.

NANNI JR,AJ CIT: 0.44
AN EXPLORATION OF THE MEDIATING EFFECTS OF AUDITOR EXPERIENCE AND POSITION IN INTERNAL ACCOUNTING CONTROL EVALUATION
AOS 02 84 VOL: 9 PG:149 - 163 :: ANOVA :LAB. :OTH.BEH. :INT.CONT.

NANTELL,TJ ; FIRS: MAHER ,MW CIT: 0
THE TAX EFFECTS OF INFLATION: DEPRECIATION, DEBT, AND MILLER'S EQUILIBRIUM TAX RATES
JAR SP 83 VOL: 21 PG:329 - 340 :: ANAL. :INT. LOG. :THEORY :VALUAT.(INFL.)

NANTELL,TJ ; FIRS: BRIGHAM,EF CIT: 0
NORMALIZATION VERSUS FLOW THROUGH FOR UTILITY COMPANIES USING LIBERALIZED TAX DEPRECIATION
TAR JL 74 VOL: 49 PG:436 - 447 :: ANAL. :SIM. :OTH.STAT. :TAXES

NARAYANAN,VK ; FIRS: GORDON,LA CIT: 0.89
MANAGEMENT ACCOUNTING SYSTEMS, PERCEIVED ENVIRONMENTAL UNCERTAINTY AND ORGANIZATION STRUCTURE: AN EMPIRICAL INVESTIGATION
AOS 01 84 VOL: 9 PG:33 - 47 :: CORR. :SURV. :OTH. :ORG.FORM

NASH ,JF ; FIRS: DILLON,RD CIT: 0.2
THE TRUE RELEVANCE OF RELEVANT COSTS
TAR JA 78 VOL: 53 PG:11 - 17 :: QUAL. :INT. LOG. :THEORY :REL.COSTS

NATH ,R ; FIRS: BIRNBERG,JG CIT: 0.47
LABORATORY EXPERIMENTATION IN ACCOUNTING RESEARCH
TAR JA 68 VOL: 43 PG:38 - 45 :: QUAL. :INT. LOG. :N/A :METHOD.

NATH ,R ; FIRS: BIRNBERG,JG CIT: 0.18
IMPLICATIONS OF BEHAVIOURAL SCIENCE FOR MANAGERIAL ACCOUNTING
TAR JL 67 VOL: 42 PG:468 - 479 :: QUAL. :SEC. :OTH.BEH. :MANAG.

NEIMARK,M ; FIRS: TINKER,T CIT: 1.5
THE ROLE OF ANNUAL REPORTS IN GENDER AND CLASS CONTRADICTIONS AT GENERAL MOTORS: 1917-1976
AOS 01 87 VOL: 12 PG:71 - 88 :: DES.STAT. :INT. LOG. :INSTIT. :ORG.& ENVIR.

NEIMARK,M ; SEC: TINKER,T CIT: 1.43
THE SOCIAL CONSTRUCTION OF MANAGEMENT CONTROL SYSTEMS
AOS 45 86 VOL: 11 PG:369 - 396 :: REGRESS. :INT. LOG. :THEORY :INT.CONT.

NEIMARK,M ; FIRS: TINKER,AM ; SEC: MERINO,BD CIT: 3.18
THE NORMATIVE ORIGINS OF POSITIVE THEORIES: IDEOLOGY AND ACCOUNTING THOUGHT
AOS 02 82 VOL: 7 PG:167 - 200 :: QUAL. :INT. LOG. :THEORY :N/A

NELSON,GK CIT: 0
CURRENT AND HISTORICAL COSTS IN FINANCIAL STATEMENTS
TAR JA 66 VOL: 41 PG:42 - 47 :: QUAL. :INT. LOG. :THEORY :VALUAT.(INFL.)

NELSON,J ; SEC: RONEN ,J ; THIR: WHITE ,L CIT: 0.2
LEGAL LIABILITIES AND THE MARKET FOR AUDITING SERVICES
JAA SU 88 VOL: 03 PG:255 - 296 :: DES.STAT. :INT. LOG. :INF.ECO./AG. :LIAB.

NETER ,J ; FIRS: PEEK ,LE ; THIR: WARREN,C CIT: 0
AICPA NONSTATISTICAL AUDIT SAMPLING GUIDELINES: A SIMULATION
AUD AU 91 VOL: 10 PG:33 - 48 :: DES.STAT. :SIM. :HIST. :SAMP.

NETER ,J ; FIRS: WURST ,J ; THIR: GODFREY,J CIT: 0
EFFECTIVENESS OF RECTIFICATION IN AUDIT SAMPLING
TAR AP 91 VOL: 66 PG:333 - 347 :: DES.STAT. :SIM. :OTH.STAT. :ERRORS

NETER ,J ; FIRS: KIM ,HS ; THIR: GODFREY,JT CIT: 0.17
BEHAVIOR OF STATISTICAL ESTIMATORS IN MULTILOCATION AUDIT SAMPLING
AUD SP 87 VOL: 6 PG:40 - 58 :: DES.STAT. :SIM. :OTH.STAT. :SAMP.

NETER ,J ; FIRS: PLANTE,R ; THIR: LEITCH,RA CIT: 0.25
COMPARATIVE PERFORMANCE OF MULTINOMIAL, CELL, AND STRINGER BOUNDS
AUD AU 85 VOL: 5 PG:40 - 56 :: DES.STAT. :SIM. :OTH.STAT. :SAMP.

NETER ,J ; SEC: KIM ,HS ; THIR: GRAHAM,LE CIT: 0.11
ON COMBINING STRINGER BOUNDS FOR INDEPENDENT MONETARY UNIT SAMPLES FROM SEVERAL POPULATIONS
AUD AU 84 VOL: 4 PG:75 - 88 :: ANAL. :INT. LOG. :OTH.STAT. :SAMP.

NETER ,J ; FIRS: GODFREY,JT CIT: 0.78
BAYESIAN BOUNDS FOR MONETARY UNIT SAMPLING IN ACCOUNTING AND AUDITING
JAR AU 84 VOL: 22 PG:497 - 525 :: ANAL. :SIM. :OTH.STAT. :SAMP.

NETER ,J ; FIRS: DUKE ,GL ; THIR: LEITCH,RA CIT: 1.09
POWER CHARACTERISTICS OF TEST STATISTICS IN THE AUDITING ENVIRONMENT: AN EMPIRICAL STUDY
JAR SP 82 VOL: 20 PG:42 - 67 :: MIXED :PRIM. :OTH.STAT. :ERRORS

NETER ,J ; FIRS: LEITCH,RA ; THIR: PLANTE,R ; FOUR: SINHA ,P CIT: 0.91
MODIFIED MULTINOMIAL BOUNDS FOR LARGER NUMBERS OF ERRORS IN AUDITS
TAR AP 82 VOL: 57 PG:384 - 400 :: DES.STAT. :SIM. :OTH.STAT. :SAMP.

NETER ,J ; FIRS: JOHNSON,JR ; SEC: LEITCH,RA CIT: 1.83
CHARACTERISTICS OF ERRORS IN ACCOUNTS RECEIVABLE AND INVENTORY AUDITS
TAR AP 81 VOL: 56 PG:270 - 293 :: DES.STAT. :PRIM. :OTH. :ERRORS

NETER ,J ; SEC: LEITCH,RA ; THIR: FIENBERG,SE CIT: 0.73
DOLLAR UNIT SAMPLING: MULTINOMIAL BOUNDS FOR TOTAL OVERSTATEMENT AND UNDERSTATEMENT ERRORS
TAR JA 78 VOL: 53 PG:77 - 93 :: NON-PAR. :SIM. :MATH.PROG. :SAMP.

NETER ,J ; FIRS: LOEBBECKE,JK CIT: 0.18
CONSIDERATIONS IN CHOOSING STATISTICAL SAMPLING PROCEDURES IN AUDITING
JAR ST 75 VOL: 13 PG:38 - 52 :: QUAL. :INT. LOG. :OTH.STAT. :SAMP.

NETER ,J ; FIRS: YU ,S CIT: 0.65
A STOCHASTIC MODEL OF THE INTERNAL CONTROL SYSTEM
JAR AU 73 VOL: 11 PG:273 - 295 :: ANAL. :INT. LOG. :OTH.STAT. :INT.CONT.

NETER ,J ; FIRS: DAVIDSON,HJ ; THIR: PETRAN,AS CIT: 0.12
ESTIMATING THE LIABILITY FOR UNREDEEMED STAMPS
JAR AU 67 VOL: 5 PG:186 - 207 :: ANAL. :INT. LOG. :OTH.STAT. :SPEC.ITEMS

NETHERCOTT,L ; FIRS: FERRIS,KR ; SEC: DILLARD,JF CIT: 0.08
A COMPARISON OF V-I-E MODEL PREDICTIONS: A CROSS-NATIONAL STUDY IN PROFESSIONAL ACCOUNTING FIRMS
AOS 04 80 VOL: 5 PG:361 - 368 :: DES.STAT. :LAB. :OTH.BEH. :INT.DIFF.

NEU ,D CIT: 1
THE SOCIAL CONSTRUCTION OF POSITIVE CHOICES
AOS 04 92 VOL: 17 PG:223 - 237 :: REGRESS. :PRIM. :INF.ECO./AG. :ORG.& ENVIR.

NEU ,D ; SEC: WRIGHT,M CIT: 0
BANK FAILURES, STIGMA MANAGEMENT AND THE ACCOUNTING ESTABLISHMENT
AOS 92 VOL: 17 PG:645 - 665 :: REGRESS. :CASE :OTH.BEH. :BUS.FAIL.

NEU ,D CIT: 1.5
NEW STOCK ISSUES AND THE INSTITUTIONAL PRODUCTION OF TRUST
AOS 02 91 VOL: 16 PG:185 - 200 :: REGRESS. :PRIM. :INSTIT. :ORG.& ENVIR.

NEU ,D CIT: 0.5
TRUST, CONTRACTING AND THE PROSPECTUS PROCESS
AOS 03 91 VOL: 16 PG:243 - 256 :: REGRESS. :PRIM. :INSTIT. :ORG.& ENVIR.

NEUBIG,RD CIT: 0
SALES GROWTH - FACT OR FICTION?
TAR JA 64 VOL: 39 PG:86 89 :: QUAL. :INT. LOG. :N/A :FIN.METH.

NEUBIG,RD ; FIRS: RABY ,WL CIT: 0
INTER-PERIOD TAX ALLOCATION OR BASIS ADJUSTMENT?
TAR JL 63 VOL: 38 PG:568 - 576 :: QUAL. :INT. LOG. :THEORY :TAXES

NEUMANN,BR ; FIRS: FRIEDMAN,LA CIT: 0.23
EFFECTS OF OPPORTUNITY COSTS ON PROJECT INVESTMENT DECISIONS: A REPLICATION AND EXTENSION
JAR AU 80 VOL: 18 PG:407 - 419 :: ANOVA :LAB. :OTH.BEH. :MANAG.

NEUMANN,BR CIT: 0
AN EMPIRICAL INVESTIGATION OF THE RELATIONSHIP BETWEEN AN AID HOSPITAL CLASSIFICATION MODEL AND ACCT. MEASURES OF PERFORMANCE
JAR SP 79 VOL: 17 PG:123 - 139 :: OTH.QUANT. :PRIM. :OTH.STAT. :MANAG.

NEUMANN,BR ; SEC: FRIEDMAN,LA CIT: 0.4
OPPORTUNITY COSTS: FURTHER EVIDENCE THROUGH AN EXPERIMENTAL REPLICATION
JAR AU 78 VOL: 16 PG:400 - 410 :: ANOVA :LAB. :OTH.BEH. :REL.COSTS

NEUMANN,FL ; FIRS: JOHNSTON,DJ ; SEC: LEMON ,WM CIT: 0
THE CANADIAN STUDY OF THE ROLE OF THE AUDITOR
JAA SP 80 VOL: 3 PG:251 - 263 :: QUAL. :INT. LOG. :THEORY :PROF.RESP.

NEUMANN,FL CIT: 0.06
THE INCIDENCE AND NATURE OF CONSISTENCY EXCEPTIONS
TAR JL 69 VOL: 44 PG:546 - 554 :: DES.STAT. :PRIM. :THEORY :ACC.CHNG.

NEUMANN,FL CIT: 0.41
THE AUDITING STANDARD OF CONSISTENCY
JAR ST 68 VOL: 6 PG:1 - 17 :: DES.STAT. :PRIM. :THEORY :MAT.

NEWBOLD,P ; FIRS: GENTRY,JA ; THIR: WHITFORD,DT CIT: 0.38
CLASSIFYING BANKRUPT FIRMS WITH FUNDS FLOW COMPONENTS
JAR SP 85 VOL: 23 PG:146 - 160 :: REGRESS. :PRIM. :OTH.STAT. :BUS.FAIL.

NEWBOLD,P ; FIRS: HOPWOOD,WS ; SEC: MCKEOWN,JC CIT: 0.55
THE ADDITIONAL INFORMATION CONTENT OF QUARTERLY EARNINGS REPORTS: INTERTEMPORAL DISAGGREGATION
JAR AU 82 VOL: 20 PG:343 - 349 :: REGRESS. :PRIM. :TIME SER. :FOREC.

NEWBOLD,P ; FIRS: HOPWOOD,WS ; THIR: SILHAN,PA CIT: 0.36
THE POTENTIAL FOR GAINS IN PREDICTIVE ABILITY THROUGH DISAGGREGATION: SEGMENTED ANNUAL EARNINGS
JAR AU 82 VOL: 20 PG:724 - 732 :: DES.STAT. :PRIM. :TIME SER. :SEG.REP.

NEWMAN,DP ; FIRS: FELLINGHAM,JC ; THIR: PATTERSON,ER CIT: 0.5
SAMPLING INFORMATION IN STRATEGIC AUDIT SETTINGS
AUD SP 89 VOL: 8 PG:1 - 21 :: DES.STAT. :INT. LOG. :INF.ECO./AG. :SAMP.

NEWMAN,DP ; FIRS: FELLINGHAM,JC CIT: 1
STRATEGIC CONSIDERATIONS IN AUDITING
TAR OC 85 VOL: 60 PG:634 - 650 :: REGRESS. :INT. LOG. :OTH.STAT. :PLAN.

NEWMAN,DP CIT: 0.33
AN INVESTIGATION OF THE DISTRIBUTION OF POWER IN THE APB AND FASB
JAR SP 81 VOL: 19 PG:247 - 262 :: MIXED :CASE :INSTIT. :FASB SUBM.

NEWMAN,DP CIT: 0.08
THE SEC'S INFLUENCE ON ACCOUNTING STANDARDS: THE POWER OF THE VETO
JAR ST 81 VOL: 19 PG:134 - 156 :: ANAL. :INT. LOG. :INSTIT. :FASB SUBM.

NEWMAN,DP CIT: 0
COALITION FORMATION IN THE APB AND THE FASB: SOME EVIDENCE ON THE SIZE PRINCIPLE
TAR OC 81 VOL: 56 PG:897 - 909 :: MIXED :PRIM. :INSTIT. :FASB SUBM.

NEWMAN,DP CIT: 0.23
PROSPECT THEORY: IMPLICATIONS FOR INFORMATION EVALUATION
AOS 02 80 VOL: 5 PG:217 - 230 :: ANAL. :INT. LOG. :HIPS :METHOD.

NEWMAN,HA CIT: 0.25
SELECTION OF SHORT-TERM ACCOUNTING-BASED BONUS PLANS
TAR OC 89 VOL: 64 PG:758 - 772 :: REGRESS. :PRIM. :TIME SER. :EXEC.COMP.

NEWMAN,HA ; FIRS: JOHNSON,WB ; SEC: MAGEE ,RP ; THIR: NAGARAJAN,NJ CIT: 0.13
AN ANALYSIS OF THE STOCK PRICE REACTION TO SUDDEN EXECUTIVE DEATHS: IMPLICATIONS FOR THE MANAGEMENT LABOR MARKET
JAE AP 85 VOL: 7 PG:151 - 174 :: REGRESS. :PRIM. :EMH :OTH.MANAG.

NEWMAN,P ; SEC: NOEL ,J CIT: 0.25
ERROR RATES, DETECTION RATES, AND PAYOFF FUNCTIONS IN AUDITING
AUD 89 VOL: 8 PG:50 - 63 :: DES.STAT. :INT. LOG. :INF.ECO./AG. :ERRORS

NEWTON,JD ; SEC: ASHTON,RH CIT: 0
THE ASSOCIATION BETWEEN AUDIT TECHNOLOGY AND AUDIT DELAY
AUD 89 VOL: 8 PG:22 - 37 :: REGRESS. :PRIM. :OTH.STAT. :TIM.

NEWTON,JD ; FIRS: ASHTON,RH ; SEC: GRAUL ,PR CIT: 0
AUDIT DELAY AND THE TIMELINESS OF CORPORATE REPORTING
CAR SP 89 VOL: 5 PG:657 - 673 :: REGRESS. :PRIM. :OTH.STAT. :TIM.

NEWTON,JD ; FIRS: ABDEL-KHALIK,AR ; SEC: GRAUL ,PR CIT: 0
REPORTING UNCERTAINTY AND ASSESSMENT OF RISK: REPLICATION AND EXTENSION IN
JAR AU 86 VOL: 24 PG:372 - 382 :: REGRESS. :LAB. :HIPS :OPIN.

NEWTON,JD ; FIRS: WILLIAMS,JJ ; THIR: MORGAN,EA CIT: 0
THE INTEGRATION OF ZERO-BASE BUDGETING WITH MANAGEMENT-BY-OBJECTIVES: AN EMPIRICAL INQUIRY
AOS 04 85 VOL: 10 PG:457 - 478 :: REGRESS. :FIELD :OTH.BEH. :BUDG.& PLAN.

NEWTON,SW ; FIRS: JOHNSON,GL CIT: 0
TAX CONSIDERATIONS IN EQUIPMENT REPLACEMENT DECISIONS
TAR OC 67 VOL: 42 PG:738 - 746 :: ANAL. :INT. LOG. :N/A :CAP.BUDG.

NEYHART,CA ; FIRS: CRAMER JR,JJ CIT: 0
A COMPREHENSIVE ACCOUNTING FRAMEWORK FOR EVALUATING EXECUTORY CONTRACTS
JAA WI 79 VOL: 2 PG:135 - 150 :: QUAL. :INT. LOG. :THEORY :N/A

NG ,DS ; SEC: STOECKENIUS,J CIT: 0.64
AUDITING: INCENTIVES AND TRUTHFUL REPORTING
JAR ST 79 VOL: 17 PG:1 - 24 :: ANAL. :INT. LOG. :INF.ECO./AG. :AUD.

NG ,DS CIT: 0.47
AN INFORMATION ECONOMICS ANALYSIS OF FINANCIAL REPORTING AND EXTERNAL AUDITING
TAR OC 78 VOL: 53 PG:910 - 920 :: ANAL. :INT. LOG. :INF.ECO./AG. :AUD.

NICHOLS,AC ; SEC: GRAWOIG,DE CIT: 0
ACCOUNTING REPORTS WITH TIME AS A VARIABLE
TAR OC 68 VOL: 43 PG:631 - 639 :: QUAL. :INT. LOG. :THEORY :OTH.MANAG.

NICHOLS,DR ; FIRS: CHANG ,OH CIT: 0
TAX INCENTIVES AND CAPITAL STRUCTURES: THE CASE OF THE DIVIDEND REINVESTMENT PLAN
JAR SP 92 VOL: 30 PG:109 - 125 :: REGRESS. :PRIM. :OTH.STAT. :TAXES

NICHOLS,DR CIT: 0
A MODEL OF AUDITORS' PRELIMINARY EVALUATIONS OF INTERNAL CONTROL FROM AUDIT DATA
TAR JA 87 VOL: 62 PG:183 - 190 :: REGRESS. :PRIM. :OTH.STAT. :INT.CONT.

NICHOLS,DR ; SEC: SMITH ,DB CIT: 0.4
AUDITOR CREDIBILITY AND AUDITOR CHANGES
JAR AU 83 VOL: 21 PG:534 - 544 :: REGRESS. :PRIM. :EMH :AUD.

NICHOLS,DR ; FIRS: SMITH ,DB CIT: 0.09
A MARKET TEST OF INVESTOR REACTION TO DISAGREEMENTS
JAE OC 82 VOL: 4 PG:109 - 120 :: DES.STAT. :SEC. :EMH :MAN.DEC.CHAR.

NICHOLS,DR ; SEC: TSAY ,JJ CIT: 0.43
SECURITY PRICE REACTIONS TO LONG-RANGE EXECUTIVE EARNINGS FORECASTS
JAR SP 79 VOL: 17 PG:140 - 155 :: REGRESS. :PRIM. :EMH :FOREC.

NICHOLS,DR ; SEC: TSAY ,JJ ; THIR: LARKIN,PD CIT: 0
INVESTOR TRADING RESPONSES TO DIFFERING CHARACTERISTICS OF VOLUNTARILY DISCLOSED EARNINGS FORECASTS
TAR AP 79 VOL: 54 PG:376 - 382 :: NON-PAR. :PRIM. :EMH :FOREC.

NICHOLS,DR ; SEC: PRICE ,KH CIT: 0.29
THE AUDITOR-FIRM CONFLICT: AN ANALYSIS USING CONCEPTS OF EXCHANGE THEORY
TAR AP 76 VOL: 51 PG:335 - 346 :: QUAL. :INT. LOG. :OTH.BEH. :AUD.

NICHOLS,WD ; FIRS: MENDENHALL,RR CIT: 0
BAD NEWS AND DIFFERENTIAL MARKET REACTIONS TO ANNOUNCEMENTS OF EARLIER-QUARTERS VERSUS FOURTH-QUARTER EARNINGS
JAR ST 88 VOL: 26 PG:63 - 90 :: REGRESS. :PRIM. :TIME SER. :INT.REP.

NICHOLS,WD ; FIRS: MORRIS,MH CIT: 0.8
CONSISTENCY EXCEPTIONS: MATERIALITY JUDGMENTS AND AUDIT FIRM STRUCTURE
TAR AP 88 VOL: 63 PG:237 - 254 :: REGRESS. :PRIM. :EMH :MAT.

NICHOLS,WD ; FIRS: MORRIS,MH CIT: 0
PENSION ACCOUNTING AND THE BALANCE SHEET: THE POTENTIAL EFFECT OF THE FASB'S PRELIMINARY VIEWS
JAA SU 84 VOL: 7 PG:293 - 305 :: MIXED :PRIM. :OTH.STAT. :PENS.

NICOL ,RE ; FIRS: SCHWAB,B CIT: 0.06
FROM DOUBLE-DECLINING-BALANCE TO SUM-OF-THE-YEAR'S DIGITS DEPRECIATION: AN OPTIMUM SWITCHING RULE
TAR AP 69 VOL: 44 PG:292 - 296 :: ANAL. :SIM. :OTH.STAT. :PP&E / DEPR

NIEBUHR,RE ; FIRS: NORRIS,DR CIT: 0.11
PROFESSIONALISM, ORGANIZATIONAL COMMITMENT AND JOB SATISFACTION IN AN ACCOUNTING ORGANIZATION
AOS 01 84 VOL: 9 PG:49 - 59 :: CORR. :SURV. :OTH.BEH. :PROF.RESP.

NIEHAUS,GR CIT: 0.75
OWNERSHIP STRUCTURE AND INVENTORY METHOD CHOICE
TAR AP 89 VOL: 64 PG:269 - 284 :: REGRESS. :PRIM. :HIPS :INV.

NIELSEN,CC CIT: 0
REPORTING JOINT-VENTURE CORPORATIONS
TAR OC 65 VOL: 40 PG:795 - 804 :: DES.STAT. :PRIM. :THEORY :BUS.COMB.

NIKOLAI,LA ; FIRS: HOWARD,TP CIT: 0.5
ATTITUDE MEASUREMENT AND PERCEPTIONS OF ACCOUNTING FACULTY PUBLICATION OUTLETS
TAR OC 83 VOL: 58 PG:765 - 776 :: DES.STAT. :SURV. :OTH. :METHOD.

NIKOLAI,LA ; SEC: ELAM ,R CIT: 0
THE POLLUTION CONTROL TAX INCENTIVE: A NON-INCENTIVE
TAR JA 79 VOL: 54 PG:119 - 131 :: ANAL. :SIM. :OTH.STAT. :TAXES

NILES ,MS ; FIRS: FELIX JR,WL CIT: 0
RESEARCH IN INTERNAL CONTROL EVALUATION
AUD SP 88 VOL: 07 PG:43 - 60 :: DES.STAT. :SEC. :THEORY :INT.CONT.

NIX ,HM ; SEC: WICHMANN JR,H CIT: 0
THE GOVERNMENTAL AUDIT REPORT
JAA SU 83 VOL: 6 PG:341 - 352 :: DES.STAT. :PRIM. :OTH. :OPIN.

NOBES ,CW CIT: 0
THE GALLERANI ACCOUNT BOOK OF 1305-1308
TAR AP 82 VOL: 57 PG:303 - 310 :: QUAL. :INT. LOG. :HIST. :N/A

NOEL ,J ; FIRS: HAN ,BH ; SEC: JENNINGS,R CIT: 0
COMMUNICATION OF NONEARNINGS INFORMATION AT THE FINANCIAL STATEMENTS RELEASE DATE
JAE MR 92 VOL: 15 PG:63 - 85 :: REGRESS. :PRIM. :EMH :BUS.FAIL.

NOEL ,J ; FIRS: BERNARD,VL CIT: 0
DO INVENTORY DISCLOSURES PREDICT SALES AND EARNINGS?
JAA SP 91 VOL: 6 PG:145 - 181 :: REGRESS. :PRIM. :OTH.STAT. :INV.

NOEL ,J ; FIRS: NEWMAN,P CIT: 0.25
ERROR RATES, DETECTION RATES, AND PAYOFF FUNCTIONS IN AUDITING
AUD 89 VOL: 8 PG:50 - 63 :: DES.STAT. :INT. LOG. :INF.ECO./AG. :ERRORS

NOEL ,J ; FIRS: BAIMAN,S ; SEC: EVANS III,JH CIT: 1.67
OPTIMAL CONTRACTS WITH A UTILITY-MAXIMIZING AUDITOR
JAR AU 87 VOL: 25 PG:217 - 244 :: ANAL. :INT. LOG. :INF.ECO./AG. :AUD.BEH.

NOEL ,J ; FIRS: BAIMAN,S CIT: 0.75
NONCONTROLLABLE COSTS AND RESPONSIBILITY ACCOUNTING
JAR AU 85 VOL: 23 PG:486 - 501 :: ANAL. :INT. LOG. :INF.ECO./AG. :RESP.ACC.

NOEL ,J ; FIRS: IJIRI ,Y CIT: 0.33
A RELIABILITY COMPARISON OF THE MEASUREMENT OF WEALTH, INCOME AND FORCE
TAR JA 84 VOL: 59 PG:52 - 63 :: ANAL. :INT. LOG. :THEORY :REV.REC.

NORDHAUSER,SL ; SEC: KRAMER,JL CIT: 0
REPEAL OF THE DEFERRAL PRIVILEGE FOR EARNINGS FROM DIRECT FOREIGN INVESTMENTS: AN ANALYSIS
TAR JA 81 VOL: 56 PG:54 - 69 :: ANAL. :INT. LOG. :OTH.STAT. :BUS.COMB.

NOREEN,E ; FIRS: BURGSTAHLER,D ; SEC: JIAMBALVO,J CIT: 0.25
CHANGES IN THE PROBABILITY OF BANKRUPTCY AND EQUITY VALUE
JAE JL 89 VOL: 11 PG:207 - 224 :: REGRESS. :PRIM. :OTH.STAT. :BUS.FAIL.

NOREEN,EW CIT: 1.4
THE ECONOMICS OF ETHICS: A NEW PERSPECTIVE ON AGENCY THEORY
AOS 04 88 VOL: 13 PG:359 - 369 :: DES.STAT. :INT. LOG. :INF.ECO./AG. :ORG.& ENVIR.

NOREEN,EW CIT: 1.4
AN EMPIRICAL COMPARISON OF PROBIT AND OLS REGRESSION HYPOTHESIS TESTS
JAR SP 88 VOL: 26 PG:119 - 133 :: REGRESS. :PRIM. :OTH.STAT. :METHOD.

NOREEN,EW ; FIRS: BURGSTAHLER,D CIT: 0
DETECTING CONTEMPORANEOUS SECURITY MARKET REACTIONS TO A SEQUENCE OF
JAR SP 86 VOL: 24 PG:170 - 186 :: REGRESS. :PRIM. :EMH :METHOD.

NOREEN,EW ; FIRS: BLANCHARD,GA ; SEC: CHOW ,CW CIT: 0
INFORMATION ASYMMETRY, INCENTIVE SCHEMES, AND INFORMATION BIASING: THE CASE OF HOSPITAL BUDGETING UNDER RATE REGULATION
TAR JA 86 VOL: 61 PG:1 - 15 :: REGRESS. :PRIM. :N/A :BUDG.& PLAN.

NOREEN,EW ; FIRS: BOWEN ,RM ; THIR: LACEY ,JM CIT: 4
DETERMINANTS OF THE CORPORATE DECISION TO CAPITALIZE INTEREST
JAE AG 81 VOL: 3 PG:151 - 179 :: DES.STAT. :INT. LOG. :INF.ECO./AG. :SPEC.ITEMS

NOREEN,EW ; SEC: WOLFSON,MA CIT: 0.33
EQUILIBRIUM WARRANT PRICING MODELS AND ACCOUNTING FOR EXECUTIVE STOCK OPTIONS
JAR AU 81 VOL: 19 PG:384 - 398 :: CORR. :PRIM. :EMH :N/A

NOREEN,EW ; SEC: SEPE ,J CIT: 1.08
MARKET REACTIONS TO ACCOUNTING POLICY DELIBERATIONS: THE INFLATION ACCOUNTING CASE
TAR AP 81 VOL: 56 PG:253 - 269 :: CORR. :PRIM. :EMH :VALUAT.(INFL.)

NORGAARD,CT CIT: 0
EXTENDING THE BOUNDARIES OF THE ATTEST FUNCTION
TAR JL 72 VOL: 47 PG:433 - 442 :: QUAL. :SEC. :INSTIT. :OPIN.

NORMAN,M ; FIRS: HESSEL,CA CIT: 0
FINANCIAL CHARACTERISTICS OF NEGLECTED AND INSTITUTIONALLY HELD STOCKS
JAA SU 92 VOL: 7 PG:313 - 330 :: REGRESS. :PRIM. :OTH.STAT. :ORG.& ENVIR.

NORMOLLE,D ; FIRS: HORWITZ,B CIT: 0
FEDERAL AGENCY R&D CONTRACT AWARDS AND THE FASB RULE FOR PRIVATELY-FUNDED R&D
TAR JL 88 VOL: 63 PG:414 - 435 :: REGRESS. :PRIM. :OTH.STAT. :R & D

NORRIS,DR ; SEC: NIEBUHR,RE CIT: 0.11
PROFESSIONALISM, ORGANIZATIONAL COMMITMENT AND JOB SATISFACTION IN AN ACCOUNTING ORGANIZATION
AOS 01 84 VOL: 9 PG:49 - 59 :: CORR. :SURV. :OTH.BEH. :PROF.RESP.

NORTON,CL ; SEC: SMITH ,RE CIT: 0.29
A COMPARISON OF GENERAL PRICE LEVEL AND HISTORICAL COST FINANCIAL STATEMENTS IN THE PREDICTION OF BANKRUPTCY
TAR JA 79 VOL: 54 PG:72 - 87 :: OTH.QUANT. :PRIM. :OTH.STAT. :VALUAT.(INFL.)

NOUR ,A ; FIRS: GAMBLING,TE CIT: 0
A NOTE ON INPUT-OUTPUT ANALYSIS: ITS USES IN MACRO-ECONOMICS AND MICRO-ECONOMICS
TAR JA 70 VOL: 45 PG:98 - 102 :: ANAL. :INT. LOG. :OTH.STAT. :BUDG.& PLAN.

NUNAMAKER,TR ; FIRS: GAUMNITZ,BR ; THIR: SURDICK,JJ ; FOUR: THOMAS,MF CIT: 0.64
AUDITOR CONSENSUS IN INTERNAL CONTROL EVALUATION AND AUDIT PROGRAM PLANNING
JAR AU 82 VOL: 20 PG:745 - 755 :: CORR. :LAB. :HIPS :INT.CONT.

NURNBERG,H ; SEC: CIANCIOLO,ST CIT: 0
THE MEASUREMENT VALUATION ALLOWANCE: HELP FOR DEFERRED TAXES
JAA AU 85 VOL: 9 PG:50 - 59 :: DES.STAT. :INT. LOG. :THEORY :TAXES

NURNBERG,H CIT: 0
DISCOUNTING DEFERRED TAX LIABILITIES
TAR OC 72 VOL: 47 PG:655 - 665 :: QUAL. :INT. LOG. :THEORY :TAXES

NURNBERG,H CIT: 0
TAX ALLOCATION FOR DIFFERENCES IN ORIGINAL BASES
JAR AU 70 VOL: 8 PG:217 - 231 :: ANAL. :INT. LOG. :HIST. :TAXES

NURNBERG,H CIT: 0
A NOTE ON THE FINANCIAL REPORTING OF DEPRECIATION AND INCOME TAXES
JAR AU 69 VOL: 7 PG:257 - 261 :: REGRESS. :SIM. :OTH. :TAXES

NURNBERG,H CIT: 0.06
PRESENT VALUE DEPRECIATION AND INCOME TAX ALLOCATION
TAR OC 68 VOL: 43 PG:719 - 729 :: QUAL. :INT. LOG. :THEORY :PP&E / DEPR

NYSTROM,PC CIT: 0.06
MANAGERIAL RESISTANCE TO A MANAGEMENT SYSTEM
AOS 04 77 VOL: 2 PG:317 - 322 :: CORR. :SURV. :OTH.BEH. :N/A

O'BRIEN,JR CIT: 0
EXPERIMENTAL STOCK MARKETS WITH CONTROLLED RISK PREFERENCES
JAA SP 92 VOL: 7 PG:117 - 134 :: DES.STAT. :LAB. :INF.ECO./AG. :N/A

O'BRIEN,JR CIT: 0
EX POST DISCLOSURE AND THE COORDINATION OF INVESTORS' ADAPTIVE EXPECTATIONS
CAR AU 90 VOL: 7 PG:1 - 21 :: DES.STAT. :INT. LOG. :INF.ECO./AG. :INFO.STRUC.

O'BRIEN,PC CIT: 0.33
FORECAST ACCURACY OF INDIVIDUAL ANALYSTS IN NINE INDUSTRIES
JAR AU 90 VOL: 28 PG:286 - 304 :: REGRESS. :PRIM. :TIME SER. :FOREC.

O'BRIEN,PC ; SEC: BHUSHAN,R CIT: 0.67
ANALYST FOLLOWING AND INSTITUTIONAL OWNERSHIP
JAR ST 90 VOL: 28 PG:055 - 82 :: REGRESS. :PRIM. :INSTIT. :ORG.& ENVIR.

O'BRIEN,PC CIT: 4.8
ANALYSTS' FORECASTS AS EARNINGS EXPECTATIONS
JAE JA 88 VOL: 10 PG:53 - 83 :: REGRESS. :PRIM. :TIME SER. :FOREC.

O'CONNOR,MC CIT: 0.24
ON THE USEFULNESS OF FINANCIAL RATIOS TO INVESTORS IN COMMON STOCK
TAR AP 73 VOL: 48 PG:339 - 352 :: REGRESS. :PRIM. :EMH :PENS.

O'CONNOR,MC ; SEC: HAMRE ,JC CIT: 0
ALTERNATIVE METHODS OF ACCOUNTING FOR LONG-TERM NONSUBSIDIARY INTERCORPORATE INVESTMENTS IN COMMON STOCK
TAR AP 72 VOL: 47 PG:308 - 319 :: QUAL. :INT. LOG. :THEORY :BUS.COMB.

O'DONNELL,JL CIT: 0
FURTHER OBSERVATIONS ON REPORTED EARNINGS AND STOCK PRICES
TAR JL 68 VOL: 43 PG:549 - 553 :: DES.STAT. :PRIM. :N/A :TAXES

O'DONNELL,JL CIT: 0
RELATIONSHIPS BETWEEN REPORTED EARNINGS AND STOCK PRICES IN THE ELECTRIC UTILITY INDUSTRY
TAR JA 65 VOL: 40 PG:135 - 143 :: DES.STAT. :PRIM. :TIME SER. :PP&E / DEPR

O'KEEFE,TB ; FIRS: KING ,RD CIT: 0
LOBBYING ACTIVITIES AND INSIDER TRADING
TAR JA 86 VOL: 61 PG:76 - 90 :: REGRESS. :PRIM. :OTH.STAT. :OIL & GAS

O'LEARY,T ; FIRS: MILLER,P CIT: 0.67
MAKING ACCOUNTANCY PRACTICAL
AOS 05 90 VOL: 15 PG:479 - 498 :: REGRESS. :SEC. :HIST. :ORG.& ENVIR.

O'LEARY,T ; FIRS: MILLER,P CIT: 4.83
ACCOUNTING AND THE CONSTRUCTION OF THE GOVERNABLE PERSON
AOS 03 87 VOL: 12 PG:235 - 265 :: DES.STAT. :INT. LOG. :HIST. :MANAG.

O'LEARY,T CIT: 0.38
OBSERVATIONS ON CORPORATE FINANCIAL REPORTING IN THE NAME OF POLITICS
AOS 01 85 VOL: 10 PG:87 - 104 :: REGRESS. :INT. LOG. :INSTIT. :FASB SUBM.

ODAIYAPPA,R ; SEC: NAINAR,SMK CIT: 0
ECONOMIC CONSEQUENCES OF SFAS NO.33-AN INSIDER-TRADING PERSPECTIVE
TAR JL 92 VOL: 67 PG:599 - 609 :: REGRESS. :PRIM. :EMH :VALUAT.(INFL.)

OFER ,AR ; FIRS: BARAN ,A ; SEC: LAKONISHOK,J CIT: 0.15
THE INFORMATION CONTENT OF GENERAL PRICE LEVEL ADJUSTED EARNINGS: SOME EMPIRICAL EVIDENCE
TAR JA 80 VOL: 55 PG:22 - 35 :: REGRESS. :PRIM. :HIPS :VALUAT.(INFL.)

OGAN ,P ; SEC: ZIEBART,DA CIT: 0
CORPORATE REPORTING AND THE ACCOUNTING PROFESSION: AN INTERPRETIVE PARADIGM
JAA SU 91 VOL: 6 PG:387 - 406 :: DES.STAT. :INT. LOG. :INF.ECO./AG. :INFO.STRUC.

OGAN ,P CIT: 0.06
APPLICATION OF A HUMAN RESOURCE VALUE MODEL: A FIELD STUDY
AOS 23 76 VOL: 1 PG:195 - 218 :: QUAL. :FIELD :OTH.BEH. :HRA

OGAN ,P CIT: 0.18
A HUMAN RESOURCE VALUE MODEL FOR PROFESSIONAL SERVICE ORGANIZATIONS
TAR AP 76 VOL: 51 PG:306 - 320 :: QUAL. :INT. LOG. :N/A :HRA

OGDEN ,S ; SEC: BOUGEN,P CIT: 0.63
A RADICAL PERSPECTIVE ON THE DISCLOSURE OF ACCOUNTING INFORMATION TO TRADE UNIONS
AOS 02 85 VOL: 10 PG:211 - 226 :: DES.STAT. :INT. LOG. :INSTIT. :METHOD.

OGDEN ,SG ; FIRS: BOUGEN,PD ; THIR: OUTRAM,Q CIT: 0
THE APPEARANCE AND DISAPPEARANCE OF ACCOUNTING: WAGE DETERMINATION IN THE U.K. COAL INDUSTRY
AOS 03 90 VOL: 15 PG:149 - 170 :: REGRESS. :SEC. :HIST. :ORG.& ENVIR.

OHLSON,JA ; SEC: PENMAN,SH CIT: 0
DISAGGREGATED ACCOUNTING DATA AS EXPLANATORY VARIABLES FOR RETURNS
JAA AU 92 VOL: 7 PG:553 - 573 :: REGRESS. :PRIM. :EMH :FIN.METH.

OHLSON,JA ; FIRS: EASTON,PD ; SEC: HARRIS,TS CIT: 2
AGGREGATE ACCOUNTING EARNINGS CAN EXPLAIN MOST OF SECURITY RETURNS: THE CASTOFF LONG RETURN INTERVALS
JAE JN 92 VOL: 15 PG:119 - 142 :: REGRESS. :PRIM. :EMH :FIN.METH.

OHLSON,JA ; SEC: SHROFF,PK CIT: 0
CHANGES VERSUS LEVELS IN EARNINGS AS EXPLANATORY VARIABLES FOR RETURNS: SOME THEORETICAL CONSIDERATIONS
JAR AU 92 VOL: 30 PG:210 - 226 :: DES.STAT. :INT. LOG. :TIME SER. :FIN.METH.

OHLSON,JA ; FIRS: LANDSMAN,WR CIT: 0.33
EVALUATION OF MARKET EFFICIENCY FOR SUPPLEMENTARY ACCOUNTING DISCLOSURES: THE CASE OF PENSION ASSETS AND LIABILITIES
CAR AU 90 VOL: 7 PG:185 - 198 :: REGRESS. :PRIM. :EMH :PENS.

OHLSON,JA CIT: 1.67
A SYNTHESIS OF SECURITY VALUATION THEORY AND THE ROLE OF DIVIDENDS, CASH FLOWS, AND EARNINGS
CAR SP 90 VOL: 6 PG:648 - 676 :: DES.STAT. :INT. LOG. :EMH :VALUAT.(INFL.)

OHLSON,JA ; FIRS: HARRIS,TS CIT: 0.67
ACCOUNTING DISCLOSURES AND THE MARKET'S VALUATION OF OIL AND GAS PROPERTIES: EVALUATION OF MARKET EFFICIENCY AND FUNCTIONAL FIXA
TAR OC 90 VOL: 65 PG:764 - 780 :: REGRESS. :PRIM. :HIPS :OIL & GAS

OHLSON,JA CIT: 1.5
UNGARBLED EARNINGS AND DIVIDENDS: AN ANALYSIS AND EXTENSION OF THE BEAVER, LAMBERT, AND MORSE VALUATION MODEL
JAE JL 89 VOL: 11 PG:109 - 115 :: DES.STAT. :INT. LOG. :EMH :FIN.METH.

OHLSON,JA CIT: 0.17
ON THE NATURE OF INCOME MEASUREMENT: THE BASIC RESULTS
CAR AU 87 VOL: 4 PG:1 - 15 :: DES.STAT. :INT. LOG. :INF.ECO./AG. :OTH.FIN.ACC.

OHLSON,JA ; FIRS: HARRIS,TS CIT: 1.5
ACCOUNTING DISCLOSURES AND THE MARKET'S VALUATION OF OIL AND GAS PROPERTIES
TAR OC 87 VOL: 62 PG:651 - 670 :: REGRESS. :PRIM. :EMH :OIL & GAS

OHLSON,JA CIT: 1.1
PRICE-EARNINGS RATIOS AND EARNINGS CAPITALIZATION UNDER UNCERTAINTY
JAR SP 83 VOL: 21 PG:141 - 154 :: ANAL. :INT. LOG. :EMH :N/A

OHLSON,JA ; FIRS: FREEMAN,RN ; THIR: PENMAN,SH CIT: 1.27
BOOK RATE-OF-RETURN AND PREDICTION OF EARNINGS CHANGES: AN EMPIRICAL INVESTIGATION
JAR AU 82 VOL: 20 PG:639 - 653 :: REGRESS. :PRIM. :EMH :FOREC.

OHLSON,JA ; FIRS: LEV ,B CIT: 3.27
MARKET-BASED EMPIRICAL RESEARCH IN ACCOUNTING: A REVIEW, INTERPRETATION, AND EXTENSION
JAR ST 82 VOL: 20 PG:249 - 322 :: QUAL. :SEC. :EMH :METHOD.

OHLSON,JA ; SEC: BUCKMAN,AG CIT: 0.42
TOWARD A THEORY OF FINANCIAL ACCOUNTING: WELFARE AND PUBLIC INFORMATION
JAR AU 81 VOL: 19 PG:399 - 433 :: ANAL. :INT. LOG. :THEORY :N/A

OHLSON,JA CIT: 1.62
FINANCIAL RATIOS AND THE PROBABILISTIC PREDICTION OF BANKRUPTCY
JAR SP 80 VOL: 18 PG:109 - 131 :: MIXED :PRIM. :OTH.STAT. :BUS.FAIL.

OHLSON,JA ; FIRS: GARMAN,MB CIT: 1.15
INFORMATION AND THE SEQUENTIAL VALUATION OF ASSETS IN ARBITRAGE-FREE ECONOMIES
JAR AU 80 VOL: 18 PG:420 - 440 :: ANAL. :INT. LOG. :OTH. :OTH.MANAG.

OHLSON,JA CIT: 0.86
ON FINANCIAL DISCLOSURE AND THE BEHAVIOR OF SECURITY PRICES
JAE DE 79 VOL: 1 PG:211 - 232 :: ANAL. :INT. LOG. :EMH :INFO.STRUC.

OHLSON,JA ; SEC: PATELL,JM CIT: 0.14
AN INTRODUCTION TO RESIDUAL (API) ANALYSIS AND THE PRIVATE VALUE OF INFORMATION AND THE API AND DESIGN OF EXPERIMENTS
JAR AU 79 VOL: 17 PG:504 - 505 :: QUAL. :INT. LOG. :EMH :METHOD.

OHLSON,JA CIT: 0.07
RESIDUAL (API) ANALYSIS AND THE PRIVATE VALUE OF INFORMATION
JAR AU 79 VOL: 17 PG:506 - 527 :: ANAL. :INT. LOG. :EMH :METHOD.

OHLSON,JA CIT: 0.18
THE COMPLETE ORDERING OF INFORMATION ALTERNATIVES FOR A CLASS OF PORTFOLIO SELECTION MODELS
JAR AU 75 VOL: 13 PG:267 - 282 :: ANAL. :INT. LOG. :EMH :INFO.STRUC.

OHLSON,JA CIT: 0
ANALYSIS OF THE USEFULNESS OF ACCOUNTING DATA FOR THE PORTFOLIO DECISION: A DECISION-THEORY APPROACH
JAR ST 72 VOL: 10 PG:45 - 84 :: REGRESS. :PRIM. :EMH :FIN.METH.

OHLSON,PA ; FIRS: GARSTKA,SJ CIT: 0.57
RATIO ESTIMATION IN ACCOUNTING POPULATIONS WITH PROBABILITIES OF SAMPLE SELECTION PROPORTIONAL TO SIZE OF BOOK VALUES
JAR SP 79 VOL: 17 PG:23 - 59 :: DES.STAT. :SIM. :OTH.STAT. :SAMP.

OLIPHANT,WJ CIT: 0
THE SEARCH FOR ACCOUNTING PRINCIPLES
JAR ST 71 VOL: 9 PG:93 - 98 :: QUAL. :INT. LOG. :THEORY :N/A

OLIVER,BL CIT: 0.53
THE SEMANTIC DIFFERENTIAL: A DEVICE FOR MEASURING THE INTERPROFESSIONAL COMMUNICATION OF SELECTED ACCOUNTING CONCEPTS
JAR AU 74 VOL: 12 PG:299 - 316 :: ANOVA :SURV. :OTH.BEH. :FIN.METH.

OLIVER,BL CIT: 0.41
A STUDY OF CONFIDENCE INTERVAL FINANCIAL STATEMENTS
JAR SP 72 VOL: 10 PG:154 - 166 :: NON-PAR. :LAB. :OTH.BEH. :FIN.METH.

OLSEN ,C ; FIRS: THOMPSON,RB ; THIR: DIETRICH,JR CIT: 0.4
THE INFLUENCE OF ESTIMATION PERIOD NEWS EVENTS ON STANDARDIZED MARKET MODEL PREDICTION ERRORS
TAR JL 88 VOL: 63 PG:448 - 471 :: REGRESS. :PRIM. :EMH :METHOD.

OLSEN ,C ; FIRS: THOMPSON II,RB ; THIR: DIETRICH,JR CIT: 1.17
ATTRIBUTES OF NEWS ABOUT FIRMS: AN ANALYSIS OF FIRM-SPECIFIC NEWS REPORTED IN THE WALL STREET JOURNAL INDEX
JAR AU 87 VOL: 25 PG:245 - 274 :: REGRESS. :PRIM. :INSTIT. :INFO.STRUC.

OLSEN ,C CIT: 0.5
VALUATION IMPLICATIONS OF SFAS NO. 33 DATA FOR ELECTRIC UTILITY INVESTORS
JAR ST 85 VOL: 23 PG:28 - 53 :: REGRESS. :SURV. :EMH :VALUAT.(INFL.)

OLSEN ,C ; SEC: DIETRICH,JR CIT: 0.75
VERTICAL INFORMATION TRANSFERS: THE ASSOCIATION BETWEEN RETAILERS' SALES ANNOUNCEMENTS AND SUPPLIERS' SECURITY RETURNS
JAR ST 85 VOL: 23 PG:144 - 166 :: REGRESS. :PRIM. :EMH :FIN.METH.

OLSEN ,C ; FIRS: FOSTER,G ; THIR: SHEVLIN,T CIT: 2.89
EARNINGS RELEASES, ANOMALIES, AND THE BEHAVIOR OF SECURITY RETURNS
TAR OC 84 VOL: 59 PG:574 - 603 :: REGRESS. :PRIM. :EMH :FIN.METH.

OMER ,T ; FIRS: DALY ,BA CIT: 0
A COMMENT ON "A BEHAVIORAL STUDY OF THE MEANING AND INFLUENCE OF TAX COMPLEXITY"
JAR SP 90 VOL: 28 PG:193 - 197 :: REGRESS. :LAB. :OTH.BEH. :TAXES

ONSI ,M CIT: 1.18
FACTOR ANALYSIS OF BEHAVIOURAL VARIABLES AFFECTING BUDGETARY STOCK
TAR JL 73 VOL: 48 PG:535 - 548 :: OTH.QUANT. :SURV. :OTH.BEH. :MAN.DEC.CHAR.

ONSI ,M CIT: 0.06
A TRANSFER PRICING SYSTEM BASED ON OPPORTUNITY COST
TAR JL 70 VOL: 45 PG:535 - 543 :: ANAL. :INT. LOG. :MATH.PROG. :TRANS.PRIC.

ONSI ,M CIT: 0
QUANTITATIVE MODELS FOR ACCOUNTING CONTROL
TAR AP 67 VOL: 42 PG:321 - 330 :: ANAL. :INT. LOG. :OTH.STAT. :VAR.

OPHIR ,T ; FIRS: FALK ,H CIT: 0.18
THE INFLUENCE OF DIFFERENCES IN ACCOUNTING POLICIES ON INVESTMENT DECISIONS
JAR SP 73 VOL: 11 PG:108 - 116 :: DES.STAT. :LAB. :OTH.BEH. :FIN.METH.

OPHIR ,T ; FIRS: FALK ,H CIT: 0.12
THE EFFECT OF RISK ON USE OF FINANCIAL STATEMENTS BY INVESTMENT DECISION-MAKERS: A CASE STUDY
TAR AP 73 VOL: 48 PG:323 - 338 :: NON-PAR. :CASE :THEORY :N/A

OPHIR ,T ; FIRS: AHARONI,Y CIT: 0
ACCOUNTING FOR LINKED LOANS
JAR SP 67 VOL: 5 PG:1 - 26 :: QUAL. :INT. LOG. :THEORY :FIN.METH.

OPPONG,A CIT: 0.46
INFORMATION CONTENT OF ANNUAL EARNINGS ANNOUNCEMENTS REVISITED
JAR AU 80 VOL: 18 PG:574 - 584 :: REGRESS. :PRIM. :EMH :FIN.ST.TIM.

ORMISTON,MB ; FIRS: BOATSMAN,JR ; SEC: GRASSO,LP ; FOUR: RENEAU,JH CIT: 0
A PERSPECTIVE ON THE USE OF LABORATORY MARKET EXPERIMENTATION IN AUDITING RESEARCH
TAR JA 92 VOL: 67 PG:148 - 156 :: ANOVA :SEC. :INF.ECO./AG. :METHOD.

ORTEGREN,AK ; FIRS: KING ,TE CIT: 0
ACCOUNTING FOR HYBRID SECURITIES: THE CASE OF ADJUSTABLE RATE CONVERTIBLE NOTES
AUD JL 88 VOL: 63 PG:522 - 535 :: DES.STAT. :INT. LOG. :THEORY :SPEC.ITEMS

ORTMAN,RF CIT: 0.18
THE EFFECTS ON INVESTMENT ANALYSIS OF ALTERNATIVE REPORTING PROCEDURES FOR DIVERSIFIED FIRMS
TAR AP 75 VOL: 50 PG:298 - 304 :: DES.STAT. :FIELD :THEORY :SEG.REP.

OTLEY ,DT ; SEC: DIAS ,FJB CIT: 0.18
ACCOUNTING AGGREGATION AND DECISION-MAKING PERFORMANCE: AN EXPERIMENTAL INVESTIGATION
JAR SP 82 VOL: 20 PG:171 - 188 :: ANOVA :LAB. :HIPS :INFO.STRUC.

OTLEY ,DT ; SEC: BERRY ,AJ CIT: 1.08
CONTROL, ORGANIZATION AND ACCOUNTING
AOS 02 80 VOL: 5 PG:231 - 246 :: QUAL. :INT. LOG. :OTH.BEH. :N/A

OTLEY ,DT CIT: 2.62
THE CONTINGENCY THEORY OF MANAGEMENT ACCOUNTING: ACHIEVEMENT AND PROGNOSIS
AOS 04 80 VOL: 5 PG:413 - 428 :: QUAL. :INT. LOG. :OTH. :MANAG.

OTLEY ,DT CIT: 2.2
BUDGET USE AND MANAGERIAL PERFORMANCE
JAR SP 78 VOL: 16 PG:122 - 149 :: CORR. :FIELD :OTH.BEH. :BUDG.& PLAN.

OU ,JA CIT: 1.33
THE INFORMATION CONTENT OF NONEARNINGS ACCOUNTING NUMBERS AS EARNINGS
JAR SP 90 VOL: 28 PG:144 - 163 :: REGRESS. :PRIM. :EMH :FIN.METH.

OU ,JA ; SEC: CIT: 5
FINANCIAL STATEMENT ANALYSIS AND THE PREDICTION OF STOCK RETURNS
JAE NV 89 VOL: 11 PG:295 - 329 :: REGRESS. :PRIM. :EMH :FIN.METH.

OU ,JA ; SEC: PENMAN,SH CIT: 3.25
ACCOUNTING MEASUREMENT, PRICE-EARNINGS RATIO, AND THE INFORMATION CONTENT OF SECURITY PRICES
JAR ST 89 VOL: 27 PG:111 - 144 :: REGRESS. :PRIM. :EMH :FIN.METH.

OUTRAM,Q ; FIRS: BOUGEN,PD ; SEC: OGDEN ,SG CIT: 0
THE APPEARANCE AND DISAPPEARANCE OF ACCOUNTING: WAGE DETERMINATION IN THE U.K. COAL INDUSTRY
AOS 03 90 VOL: 15 PG:149 - 170 :: REGRESS. :SEC. :HIST. :ORG.& ENVIR.

OUTSLAY,E ; SEC: WHEELER,JE CIT: 0
SEPARATING THE ANNUITY AND INCOME TRANSFER ELEMENTS OF SOCIAL SECURITY
TAR OC 82 VOL: 57 PG:716 - 733 :: DES.STAT. :PRIM. :OTH.STAT. :TAXES

OVADIA,A ; SEC: RONEN ,J CIT: 0.1
ON THE VALUE OF CURRENT-COST INFORMATION
JAA WI 83 VOL: 6 PG:115 - 129 :: ANAL. :INT. LOG. :THEORY :VALUAT.(INFL.)

OVADIA,A ; SEC: RONEN ,J CIT: 0.08
GENERAL PRICE-LEVEL ADJUSTMENT AND REPLACEMENT COST ACCOUNTING AS SPECIAL CASES OF THE INDEX NUMBER PROBLEM
JAA WI 80 VOL: 3 PG:113 - 137 :: ANAL. :SEC. :TIME SER. :VALUAT.(INFL.)

OWEN ,DL ; FIRS: HARTE ,GF CIT: 0.5
FIGHTING DE-INDUSTRIALIZATION: THE ROLE OF LOCAL GOVERNMENT SOCIAL AUDITS
AOS 02 87 VOL: 12 PG:123 - 142 :: REGRESS. :INT. LOG. :THEORY :ORG.& ENVIR.

OWEN ,DL ; SEC: LLOYD ,AJ CIT: 0.38
THE USE OF FINANCIAL INFORMATION BY TRADE UNION NEGOTIATORS IN PLANT LEVEL COLLECTIVE BARGAINING
AOS 03 85 VOL: 10 PG:329 - 352 :: DES.STAT. :INT. LOG. :THEORY :ORG.& ENVIR.

OWEN ,J ; FIRS: KATZ ,BG CIT: 0
INITIAL PUBLIC OFFERINGS: AN EQUILIBRIUM MODEL OF PRICE DETERMINATION
JAA SU 87 VOL: 2 PG:266 - 298 :: DES.STAT. :INT. LOG. :THEORY :SPEC.ITEMS

OWEN ,J ; FIRS: BRIEF ,RP CIT: 0.12
A REFORMULATION OF THE ESTIMATION PROBLEM
JAR SP 73 VOL: 11 PG:1 - 15 :: ANAL. :INT. LOG. :OTH.STAT. :PP&E / DEPR

OWEN ,J ; FIRS: BRIEF ,RP CIT: 0.06
PRESENT VALUE MODELS AND THE MULTI-ASSET PROBLEM
TAR OC 73 VOL: 48 PG:690 - 695 :: QUAL. :INT. LOG. :THEORY :PP&E / DEPR

OWEN ,J ; FIRS: BRIEF ,RP CIT: 0.18
THE ESTIMATION PROBLEM IN FINANCIAL ACCOUNTING
JAR AU 70 VOL: 8 PG:167 - 177 :: ANAL. :INT. LOG. :OTH.STAT. :PP&E / DEPR

OWEN ,J ; FIRS: BRIEF ,RP CIT: 0
ON THE BIAS IN ACCOUNTING ALLOCATIONS UNDER UNCERTAINTY
JAR SP 69 VOL: 7 PG:12 - 16 :: ANAL. :INT. LOG. :OTH.STAT. :COST.ALLOC.

OWEN ,J ; FIRS: BRIEF ,RP CIT: 0
A LEAST SQUARES ALLOCATION MODEL
JAR AU 68 VOL: 6 PG:193 - 199 :: ANAL. :INT. LOG. :MATH.PROG. :COST.ALLOC.

OWEN ,J ; FIRS: BRIEF ,RP CIT: 0
DEPRECIATION AND CAPITAL GAINS: A NEW APPROACH
TAR AP 68 VOL: 43 PG:367 - 372 :: ANAL. :INT. LOG. :THEORY :PP&E / DEPR

OZAN ,T ; SEC: DYCKMAN,TR CIT: 0.24
A NORMATIVE MODEL FOR INVESTIGATION DECISIONS INVOLVING MULTI-ORIGIN COST VARIANCES
JAR SP 71 VOL: 9 PG:88 - 115 :: ANAL. :INT. LOG. :MATH.PROG. :VAR.

PADMARAJ,RA ; FIRS: BALACHANDRAN,BV CIT: 0
A GENERALIZED TRANSSHIPMENT MODEL FOR CASH MANAGEMENT
JAA WI 91 VOL: 6 PG:1 - 28 :: DES.STAT. :INT. LOG. :MATH.PROG. :COST.ALLOC.

PAGACH,D ; FIRS: FRANCIS,J ; THIR: STEPHAN,J CIT: 0
THE STOCK MARKET RESPONSE TO EARNINGS ANNOUNCEMENTS RELEASED DURING TRADING VERSUS NONTRADING PERIODS
JAR AU 92 VOL: 30 PG:165 - 184 :: REGRESS. :PRIM. :EMH :FIN.ST.TIM.

PAGE ,MJ ; FIRS: LEMKE ,KW CIT: 0
ECONOMIC DETERMINANTS OF ACCOUNTING POLICY CHOICE: THE CASE OF CURRENT COST ACCOUNTING IN THE U.K.
JAE MR 92 VOL: 15 PG:87 - 114 :: REGRESS. :PRIM. :OTH.STAT. :ACC.CHNG.

PAIK ,TY ; FIRS: KIRBY ,AJ ; SEC: REICHELSTEIN,S ; THIR: SEN ,PK CIT: 1.5
PARTICIPATION, SLACK, AND BUDGET-BASED PERFORMANCE EVALUATION
JAR SP 91 VOL: 29 PG:109 - 128 :: DES.STAT. :INT. LOG. :OTH.BEH. :BUDG.& PLAN.

PAINE ,NR CIT: 0
UNCERTAINTY AND CAPITAL BUDGETING
TAR AP 64 VOL: 39 PG:330 - 332 :: ANAL. :INT. LOG. :N/A :LTD

PALEPU,K ; FIRS: ASQUITH,P ; SEC: HEALY ,P CIT: 0
EARNINGS AND STOCK SPLITS
TAR JL 89 VOL: 64 PG:387 - 403 :: REGRESS. :PRIM. :EMH :STK.DIV.

PALEPU,KG ; FIRS: HEALY ,PM CIT: 1.33
EFFECTIVENESS OF ACCOUNTING-BASED DIVIDEND COVENANTS
JAE JA 90 VOL: 12 PG:97 - 123 :: REGRESS. :PRIM. :OTH.STAT. :CASH DIV.

PALEPU,KG ; FIRS: HEALY ,PM CIT: 0.67
EARNINGS AND RISK CHANGES SURROUNDING PRIMARY STOCK OFFERS
JAR SP 90 VOL: 28 PG:25 - 48 :: REGRESS. :PRIM. :EMH :INFO.STRUC.

PALEPU,KG ; FIRS: HEALY ,PM ; SEC: KANG ,SH CIT: 1.5
THE EFFECT OF ACCOUNTING PROCEDURE CHANGES ON CEOS' CASH SALARY AND
JAE AP 87 VOL: 9 PG:7 - 34 :: REGRESS. :PRIM. :OTH.STAT. :INV.

PALEPU,KG CIT: 1.43
PREDICTING TAKEOVER TARGETS: A METHODOLOGICAL AND EMPIRICAL ANALYSIS
JAE MR 86 VOL: 8 PG:3 - 36 :: REGRESS. :PRIM. :OTH.STAT. :BUS.COMB.

PALMON,D ; FIRS: GIVOLY,D CIT: 1.64
TIMELINESS OF ANNUAL EARNINGS ANNOUNCEMENTS: SOME EMPIRICAL EVIDENCE
TAR JL 82 VOL: 57 PG:486 - 508 :: REGRESS. :PRIM. :EMH :FIN.ST.TIM.

PALMON,D ; FIRS: GIVOLY,D CIT: 0
CLASSIFICATION OF CONVERTIBLE DEBT AS COMMON STOCK EQUIVALENTS: SOME EMPIRICAL EVIDENCE ON THE EFFECTS OF APB OPINION 15
JAR AU 81 VOL: 19 PG:530 - 543 :: CORR. :PRIM. :EMH :LTD

PALMON,D ; SEC: KWATINETZ,M CIT: 0.08
THE SIGNIFICANT ROLE INTERPRETATION PLAYS IN THE IMPLEMENTATION OF SFAS NO.13
JAA SP 80 VOL: 3 PG:207 - 226 :: QUAL. :INT. LOG. :THEORY :LEASES

PALMROSE,Z CIT: 0
AN ANALYSIS OF AUDITOR LITIGATION DISCLOSURES
AUD 91 VOL: 10 PG:54 - 71 :: REGRESS. :PRIM. :OTH.STAT. :LITIG.

PALMROSE,Z CIT: 0
TRIALS OF LEGAL DISPUTES INVOLVING INDEPENDENT AUDITORS: SOME EMPIRICAL EVIDENCE
JAR ST 91 VOL: 29 PG:149 - 193 :: REGRESS. :PRIM. :OTH.STAT. :LITIG.

PALMROSE,Z CIT: 0.75
THE RELATION OF AUDIT CONTRACT TYPE TO AUDIT FEES AND HOURS
TAR JL 89 VOL: 64 PG:488 - 499 :: REGRESS. :SURV. :MATH.PROG. :AUD.

PALMROSE,ZV CIT: 0
PUBLIC ACCOUNTING FIRMS AND THE ACQUISITION OF NONAUDIT SERVICES BY PUBLIC AND CLOSELY-HELD COMPANIES
AUD AU 88 VOL: 08 PG:63 - 71 :: REGRESS. :SURV. :INSTIT. :ORG.

PALMROSE,ZV CIT: 1.4
AN ANALYSIS OF AUDITOR LITIGATION AND AUDIT SERVICE QUALITY
TAR JA 88 VOL: 63 PG:55 - 73 :: REGRESS. :PRIM. :THEORY :LITIG.

PALMROSE,ZV CIT: 0.5
LITIGATION AND INDEPENDENT AUDITORS: THE ROLE OF BUSINESS FAILURES AND MANAGEMENT FRAUD
AUD SP 87 VOL: 6 PG:90 - 103 :: DES.STAT. :SURV. :THEORY :LITIG.

PALMROSE,ZV CIT: 1.86
AUDIT FEES AND AUDITOR SIZE: FURTHER EVIDENCE
JAR SP 86 VOL: 24 PG:97 - 110 :: REGRESS. :PRIM. :OTH.STAT. :OPER.AUD.

PALMROSE,ZV CIT: 0.43
THE EFFECT OF NONAUDIT SERVICES ON THE PRICING OF AUDIT SERVICES: FURTHER EVIDENCE
JAR AU 86 VOL: 24 PG:405 - 411 :: REGRESS. :PRIM. :OTH.STAT. :OPER.AUD.

PANKOFF,LD ; SEC: VIRGIL JR,RL CIT: 0.59
SOME PRELIMINARY FINDINGS FROM A LABORATORY EXPERIMENT ON THE USEFULNESS OF FINANCIAL ACCOUNTING INFORMATION TO SECURITY ANALYSTS
JAR ST 70 VOL: 8 PG:1 - 48 :: MIXED :LAB. :OTH.BEH. :FIN.METH.

PANKOFF,LD ; SEC: VIRGIL JR,RL CIT: 0.12
ON THE USEFULNESS OF FINANCIAL STATEMENT INFORMATION: A SUGGESTED RESEARCH APPROACH
TAR AP 70 VOL: 45 PG:269 - 279 :: DES.STAT. :LAB. :N/A :OTH.MANAG.

PANY ,K ; FIRS: MITTELSTAEDT,HF ; SEC: REGIER,PR ; THIR: CHEWNING,EG CIT: 0
DO CONSISTENCY MODIFICATIONS PROVIDE INFORMATION TO EQUITY MARKETS?
AUD SP 92 VOL: 11 PG:83 - 98 :: REGRESS. :PRIM. :OTH.STAT. :OPIN.

PANY ,K ; FIRS: WHEELER,S CIT: 0
ASSESSING THE PERFORMANCE OF ANALYTICAL PROCEDURES: A BEST CASE SCENARIO
TAR JL 90 VOL: 65 PG:557 - 577 :: DES.STAT. :SIM. :MATH.PROG. :ERRORS

PANY ,K ; FIRS: CHEWNING,G ; THIR: WHEELER,S CIT: 0.5
AUDITOR REPORTING DECISIONS INVOLVING ACCOUNTING PRINCIPLE CHANGES: SOME EVIDENCE ON MATERIALITY THRESHOLDS
JAR SP 89 VOL: 27 PG:78 - 96 :: REGRESS. :PRIM. :OTH.STAT. :MAT.

PANY ,K ; SEC: RECKERS,PMJ CIT: 0
WITHIN- VS. BETWEEN-SUBJECTS EXPERIMENTAL DESIGNS: A STUDY OF DEMAND
AUD AU 87 VOL: 7 PG:39 - 53 :: REGRESS. :LAB. :OTH.BEH. :INDEP.

PANY ,K ; FIRS: MARGHEIM,LL CIT: 0.57
QUALITY CONTROL, PREMATURE SIGNOFF, AND UNDERREPORTING OF TIME: SOME EMPIRICAL FINDINGS
AUD SP 86 VOL: 5 PG:50 - 63 :: REGRESS. :LAB. :OTH.BEH. :ORG.

PANY ,K ; FIRS: MCKINELY,S ; THIR: RECKERS,PMJ CIT: 0.13
AN EXAMINATION OF THE INFLUENCE OF CPA FIRM TYPE, SIZE, AND MAS PROVISION ONLOAN OFFICER DECISIONS & PERCEPTIONS
JAR AU 85 VOL: 23 PG:887 - 896 :: REGRESS. :LAB. :OTH.BEH. :ORG.

PANY ,K ; SEC: RECKERS,PMJ CIT: 0.33
NON-AUDIT SERVICES AND AUDITOR INDEPENDENCE - A CONTINUING PROBLEM
AUD SP 84 VOL: 3 PG:89 - 97 :: DES.STAT. :SURV. :OTH.STAT. :INDEP.

PANY ,K ; FIRS: JOHNSON,DA CIT: 0
FORECASTS, AUDITOR REVIEW, AND BANK LOAN DECISIONS
JAR AU 84 VOL: 22 PG:731 - 743 :: ANOVA :LAB. :OTH.BEH. :FOREC.

PANY ,K ; FIRS: JOHNSON,DA ; THIR: WHITE ,RA CIT: 0
AUDIT REPORTS AND THE LOAN DECISION: ACTIONS AND PERCEPTIONS
AUD SP 83 VOL: 2 PG:38 - 51 :: ANOVA :LAB. :OTH.BEH. :OPIN.

PANY ,K ; SEC: SMITH ,CH CIT: 0
AUDITOR ASSOCIATION WITH QUARTERLY FINANCIAL INFORMATION: AN EMPIRICAL TEST
JAR AU 82 VOL: 20 PG:472 - 481 :: ANOVA :LAB. :OTH.BEH. :OPIN.

PANY ,K ; SEC: RECKERS,PMJ CIT: 0.23
THE EFFECT OF GIFTS, DISCOUNTS, AND CLIENT SIZE ON PERCEIVED AUDITOR INDEPENDENCE
TAR JA 80 VOL: 55 PG:50 - 61 :: ANOVA :LAB. :OTH.BEH. :INDEP.

PARE ,PV ; FIRS: IMHOFF JR,EA CIT: 0.82
ANALYSIS AND COMPARISON OF EARNINGS FORECAST AGENTS
JAR AU 82 VOL: 20 PG:429 - 439 :: DES.STAT. :PRIM. :TIME SER. :METHOD.

PARK ,K ; FIRS: FEROZ ,EH ; THIR: PASTENA,VS CIT: 0.5
THE FINANCIAL AND MARKET EFFECTS OF THE SEC'S ACCOUNTING AND AUDITING ENFORCEMENT RELEASES
JAR ST 91 VOL: 29 PG:107 - 148 :: REGRESS. :PRIM. :EMH :ORG.& ENVIR.

PARK ,SH ; FIRS: MANES ,RP ; THIR: JENSEN,RE CIT: 0.09
RELEVANT COSTS OF INTERMEDIATE GOODS AND SERVICES
TAR JL 82 VOL: 57 PG:594 - 606 :: ANAL. :INT. LOG. :MATH.PROG. :N/A

PARKE ,R ; SEC: PETERSON,JL CIT: 0
INDICATORS OF SOCIAL CHANGE: DEVELOPMENTS IN THE U.S.A.
AOS 03 81 VOL: 6 PG:235 - 246 :: QUAL. :INT. LOG. :OTH. :HRA

PARKER,JE CIT: 0.69
IMPACT OF PRICE-LEVEL ACCOUNTING
TAR JA 77 VOL: 52 PG:69 - 96 :: DES.STAT. :PRIM. :THEORY :VALUAT.(INFL.)

PARKER,JE CIT: 0.06
TESTING COMPARABILITY AND OBJECTIVITY OF EXIT VALUE ACCOUNTING
TAR JL 75 VOL: 50 PG:512 - 524 :: ANOVA :SURV. :THEORY :OTH.FIN.ACC.

PARKER,LD ; FIRS: FLEISCHMAN,RK CIT: 0
BRITISH ENTREPRENEURS AND PRE-INDUSTRIAL REVOLUTION EVIDENCE OF COST MANAGEMENT
TAR AP 91 VOL: 66 PG:361 - 375 :: REGRESS. :PRIM. :HIST. :MANAG.

PARKER,LD ; FIRS: COWEN ,SS ; SEC: FERRERI,LB CIT: 0.33
THE IMPACT OF CORPORATE CHARACTERISTICS ON SOCIAL RESPONSIBILITY DISCLOSURE: A TYPOLOGY AND FREQUENCY-BASED ANALYSIS
AOS 02 87 VOL: 12 PG:111 - 122 :: REGRESS. :PRIM. :THEORY :HRA

PARKER,LD ; FIRS: LEWIS ,NR ; THIR: SUTCLIFFE,P CIT: 0
FINANCIAL REPORTING TO EMPLOYEES: THE PATTERN OF DEVELOPMENT 1919 TO 1979
AOS 34 84 VOL: 9 PG:275 - 289 :: DES.STAT. :SEC. :HIST. :HRA

PARKER,RH CIT: 0.12
DISCOUNTED CASH FLOW IN HISTORICAL PERSPECTIVE
JAR SP 68 VOL: 6 PG:58 - 71 :: QUAL. :SEC. :HIST. :CAP.BUDG.

PARKER,WM CIT: 0
BUSINESS COMBINATIONS AND ACCOUNTING VALUATION
JAR AU 66 VOL: 4 PG:149 - 154 :: QUAL. :INT. LOG. :THEORY :BUS.COMB.

PARKER,WM CIT: 0
THE TREATMENT OF SHORT-TERM CREDIT IN THE FUNDS STATEMENT
TAR OC 63 VOL: 38 PG:785 - 788 :: QUAL. :INT. LOG. :THEORY :N/A

PASTENA,V ; FIRS: GHICAS,D CIT: 0.5
THE ACQUISITION VALUE OF OIL AND GAS FIRMS: THE ROLE OF HISTORICAL COSTS, RESERVE RECOGNITION ACCOUNTING, AND ANALYSTS' APPRAISA
CAR AU 89 VOL: 6 PG:125 - 142 :: REGRESS. :PRIM. :EMH :OIL & GAS

PASTENA,V ; FIRS: EL-GAZZAR,S ; SEC: LILIEN,S CIT: 0.25
THE USE OF OFF-BALANCE SHEET FINANCING TO CIRCUMVENT FINANCIAL COVENANT RESTRICTIONS
JAA SP 89 VOL: 4 PG:217 - 231 :: REGRESS. :PRIM. :OTH.STAT. :SPEC.ITEMS

PASTENA,V ; FIRS: LILIEN,S ; SEC: MELLMAN,M CIT: 0.6
ACCOUNTING CHANGES: SUCCESSFUL VERSUS UNSUCCESSFUL FIRMS
TAR OC 88 VOL: 63 PG:642 - 656 :: REGRESS. :PRIM. :THEORY :ACC.CHNG.

PASTENA,V ; FIRS: HAW ,IM ; THIR: LILIEN,S CIT: 0
THE ASSOCIATION BETWEEN MARKET-BASED MERGER PREMIUMS AND FIRMS' FINANCIAL POSITION PRIOR TO MERGER
JAA WI 87 VOL: 2 PG:24 - 42 :: REGRESS. :PRIM. :EMH :BUS.COMB.

PASTENA,V ; FIRS: EL-GAZZAR,S ; SEC: LILIEN,S CIT: 0.86
ACCOUNTING FOR LEASES BY LESSEES
JAE OC 86 VOL: 8 PG:217 - 238 :: REGRESS. :PRIM. :OTH.STAT. :LEASES

PASTENA,V ; SEC: RULAND,W CIT: 0.71
THE MERGER/BANKRUPTCY ALTERNATIVE
TAR AP 86 VOL: 61 PG:288 - 301 :: REGRESS. :PRIM. :THEORY :BUS.COMB.

PASTENA,V ; FIRS: LILIEN,S CIT: 1.82
DETERMINANTS OF INTRAMETHOD CHOICE IN THE OIL AND GAS INDUSTRY
JAE DE 82 VOL: 4 PG:145 - 170 :: REGRESS. :PRIM. :OTH.STAT. :OIL & GAS

PASTENA,V ; SEC: RONEN ,J CIT: 0.43
SOME HYPOTHESES ON THE PATTERN OF MANAGEMENT'S INFORMAL DISCLOSURES
JAR AU 79 VOL: 17 PG:550 - 564 :: NON-PAR. :PRIM. :OTH. :OTH.MANAG.

PASTENA,VS ; FIRS: FEROZ ,EH ; SEC: PARK ,K CIT: 0.5
THE FINANCIAL AND MARKET EFFECTS OF THE SEC'S ACCOUNTING AND AUDITING ENFORCEMENT RELEASES
JAR ST 91 VOL: 29 PG:107 - 148 :: REGRESS. :PRIM. :EMH :ORG.& ENVIR.

PASTENA,VS ; FIRS: HAW ,I ; THIR: LILIEN,SB CIT: 0.33
MARKET MANIFESTATION OF NONPUBLIC INFORMATION PRIOR TO MERGERS: THE EFFECT PF OWNERSHIP STRUCTURE
TAR AP 90 VOL: 65 PG:432 - 451 :: REGRESS. :PRIM. :EMH :BUS.COMB.

PATELL,JM ; FIRS: MARAIS,ML ; THIR: WOLFSON,MA CIT: 0.56
THE EXPERIMENTAL DESIGN OF CLASSIFICATORY MODELS: AN APPLICATION OF RECURSIVE PARTITIONING AND BOOTSTRAPPING COMMERCIAL BANK LOA
JAR ST 84 VOL: 22 PG:87 - 114 :: OTH.QUANT. :PRIM. :OTH.STAT. :BUS.FAIL.

PATELL,JM ; FIRS: DEMSKI,JS ; THIR: WOLFSON,MA CIT: 1.56
DECENTRALIZED CHOICE OF MONITORING SYSTEMS
TAR JA 84 VOL: 59 PG:16 - 34 :: ANAL. :INT. LOG. :INF.ECO./AG. :MANAG.

PATELL,JM ; SEC: WOLFSON,MA CIT: 1.91
GOOD NEWS, BAD NEWS, AND THE INTRADAY TIMING OF CORPORATE DISCLOSURES
TAR JL 82 VOL: 57 PG:509 - 527 :: REGRESS. :PRIM. :EMH :FIN.ST.TIM.

PATELL,JM ; SEC: WOLFSON,MA CIT: 1.08
THE EX ANTE AND EX POST PRICE EFFECTS OF QUARTERLY EARNINGS ANNOUNCEMENTS REFLECTED IN OPTION AND STOCK PRICES
JAR AU 81 VOL: 19 PG:434 - 458 :: REGRESS. :PRIM. :EMH :FIN.METH.

PATELL,JM ; SEC: WOLFSON,MA CIT: 0.93
ANTICIPATED INFORMATION RELEASES REFLECTED IN CALL OPTION PRICES
JAE AG 79 VOL: 1 PG:117 - 140 :: ANOVA :PRIM. :EMH :INFO.STRUC.

PATELL,JM ; FIRS: OHLSON,JA CIT: 0.14
AN INTRODUCTION TO RESIDUAL (API) ANALYSIS AND THE PRIVATE VALUE OF INFORMATION AND THE API AND DESIGN OF EXPERIMENTS
JAR AU 79 VOL: 17 PG:504 - 505 :: QUAL. :INT. LOG. :EMH :METHOD.

PATELL,JM CIT: 0.5
THE API AND THE DESIGN OF EXPERIMENTS
JAR AU 79 VOL: 17 PG:528 - 549 :: ANAL. :INT. LOG. :EMH :METHOD.

PATELL,JM CIT: 5.18
CORPORATE FORECASTS OF EARNINGS PER SHARE AND STOCK PRICE BEHAVIOR: EMPIRICAL TESTS
JAR AU 76 VOL: 14 PG:246 - 276 :: REGRESS. :PRIM. :EMH :FOREC.

PATON ,WA CIT: 0
POSTSCRIPT ON TREASURY SHARES
TAR AP 69 VOL: 44 PG:276 - 283 :: QUAL. :INT. LOG. :THEORY :SPEC.ITEMS

PATON ,WA CIT: 0
OBSERVATIONS ON INFLATION FROM AN ACCOUNTING STANCE
JAR SP 68 VOL: 6 PG:72 - 85 :: QUAL. :INT. LOG. :THEORY :VALUAT.(INFL.)

PATON ,WA CIT: 0
SOME REFLECTIONS ON EDUCATION AND PROFESSORING
TAR JA 67 VOL: 42 PG:7 - 23 :: QUAL. :INT. LOG. :INSTIT. :OTH.MANAG.

PATON ,WA CIT: 0
ACCOUNTING AND UTILIZATION OF RESOURCES
JAR SP 63 VOL: 1 PG:44 - 72 :: QUAL. :INT. LOG. :THEORY :N/A

PATON ,WA CIT: 0.06
THE CASH FLOW ILLUSION
TAR AP 63 VOL: 38 PG:243 - 251 :: QUAL. :INT. LOG. :THEORY :FIN.METH.

PATRICK,AW ; SEC: QUITTMEYER,CL CIT: 0
THE CPA AND MANAGEMENT SERVICES
TAR JA 63 VOL: 38 PG:109 - 117 :: QUAL. :INT. LOG. :N/A :N/A

PATTEN,DM CIT: 0
INTRA-INDUSTRY ENVIRONMENTAL DISCLOSURES IN RESPONSE TO THE ALASKAN OIL SPILL: A NOTE ON LEGITIMACY THEORY
AOS 05 92 VOL: 17 PG:471 - 475 :: REGRESS. :PRIM. :OTH.STAT. :OIL & GAS

PATTEN,DM CIT: 0
THE MARKET REACTION TO SOCIAL RESPONSIBILITY DISCLOSURES: THE CASE OF THE SULLIVAN PRINCIPLES SIGNINGS
AOS 06 90 VOL: 15 PG:575 - 587 :: REGRESS. :PRIM. :EMH :HRA

PATTEN,RJ CIT: 0
INTRAPERIOD INCOME TAX ALLOCATION - A PRACTICAL CONCEPT
TAR OC 64 VOL: 39 PG:876 - 879 :: DES.STAT. :PRIM. :THEORY :TAXES

PATTERSON,ER ; FIRS: FELLINGHAM,JC ; SEC: NEWMAN,DP CIT: 0.5
SAMPLING INFORMATION IN STRATEGIC AUDIT SETTINGS
AUD SP 89 VOL: 8 PG:1 - 21 :: DES.STAT. :INT. LOG. :INF.ECO./AG. :SAMP.

PATTERSON,RG CIT: 0
MATERIALITY AND THE ECONOMIC ENVIRONMENT
TAR OC 67 VOL: 42 PG:772 - 774 :: QUAL. :INT. LOG. :THEORY :OTH.FIN.ACC.

PATTON,JM ; FIRS: LEWIS ,BL ; THIR: GREEN ,SL CIT: 0.2
THE EFFECTS OF INFORMATION CHOICE AND INFORMATION USE ON ANALYSTS' PREDICTIONS OF MUNICIPAL BOND RATING CHANGES
TAR AP 88 VOL: 63 PG:270 - 282 :: REGRESS. :LAB. :OTH.STAT. :FOREC.

PATTON,JM ; FIRS: EVANS III,JH CIT: 0.83
SIGNALING AND MONITORING IN PUBLIC-SECTOR ACCOUNTING
JAR ST 87 VOL: 25 PG:130 - 164 :: MIXED :SURV. :INF.ECO./AG. :FIN.METH.

PATTON,JM ; FIRS: EVANS III,JH ; SEC: LEWIS ,BL CIT: 0.14
AN ECONOMIC MODELING APPROACH TO CONTINGENCY THEORY AND MANAGEMENT CONTROL
AOS 06 86 VOL: 11 PG:483 - 498 :: DES.STAT. :INT. LOG. :INF.ECO./AG. :INT.CONT.

PATTON,JM ; FIRS: EVANS III,JH CIT: 1.1
AN ECONOMIC ANALYSIS OF PARTICIPATION IN THE MUNICIPAL FINANCE OFFICERS ASSOCIATION CERTIFICATE OF CONFORMANCE PROGRAM
JAE AG 83 VOL: 5 PG:151 - 175 :: OTH.QUANT. :PRIM. :INSTIT. :FIN.METH.

PATTON,JM CIT: 0.13
AN EXPERIMENTAL INVESTIGATION OF SOME EFFECTS OF CONSOLIDATING MUNICIPAL FINANCIAL REPORTS
TAR AP 78 VOL: 53 PG:402 - 414 :: ANOVA :LAB. :HIPS :BUS.COMB.

PATZ ,DH ; FIRS: LOREK ,KS ; SEC: MCDONALD,CL CIT: 0.65
A COMPARATIVE EXAMINATION OF MANAGEMENT FORECASTS AND BOX-JENKINS FORECASTS OF EARNINGS
TAR AP 76 VOL: 51 PG:321 - 330 :: REGRESS. :PRIM. :TIME SER. :METHOD.

PATZ ,DH ; SEC: BOATSMAN,JR CIT: 0.18
ACCOUNTING PRINCIPLE FORMULATION IN AN EFFICIENT MARKETS ENVIRONMENT
JAR AU 72 VOL: 10 PG:392 - 403 :: ANOVA :PRIM. :EMH :OIL & GAS

PEARSON,MA ; SEC: LINDGREN,JH ; THIR: MYERS ,BL CIT: 0.07
A PRELIMINARY ANALYSIS OF AUDSEC VOTING PATTERNS
JAA WI 79 VOL: 2 PG:122 - 134 :: OTH.QUANT. :PRIM. :INSTIT. :FASB SUBM.

PEASNELL,KV ; SEC: SKERRATT,CL CIT: 0.25
HOW WELL DOES A SINGLE INDEX REPRESENT THE NINETEEN SANDILANDS PLANT AND MACHINERY INDICES?
JAR SP 77 VOL: 15 PG:108 - 119 :: CORR. :PRIM. :THEORY :VALUAT.(INFL.)

PEASNELL,KV CIT: 0
A NOTE ON THE DISCOUNTED PRESENT VALUE CONCEPT
TAR JA 77 VOL: 52 PG:186 - 189 :: QUAL. :INT. LOG. :THEORY :VALUAT.(INFL.)

PEAVY ,JW ; SEC: EDGAR ,SM CIT: 0
RATING ELECTRIC UTILITY COMMERCIAL PAPER
JAA WI 85 VOL: 8 PG:125 - 135 :: REGRESS. :PRIM. :OTH.STAT. :LTD

PEDERSEN,PH ; FIRS: BJORN-ANDERSEN,N CIT: 0
COMPUTER FACILITATED CHANGES IN THE MANAGEMENT POWER STRUCTURE
AOS 02 80 VOL: 5 PG:203 - 216 :: QUAL. :CASE :OTH.BEH. :N/A

PEEK ,LE ; SEC: NETER ,J ; THIR: WARREN,C CIT: 0
AICPA NONSTATISTICAL AUDIT SAMPLING GUIDELINES: A SIMULATION
AUD AU 91 VOL: 10 PG:33 - 48 :: DES.STAT. :SIM. :HIST. :SAMP.

PEI ,BKW ; SEC: REED ,SA ; THIR: KOCH ,BS CIT: 0
AUDITOR BELIEF REVISIONS IN A PERFORMANCE AUDITING SETTING: AN APPLICATION OF THE BELIEF-ADJUSTMENT MODEL
AOS 02 92 VOL: 17 PG:169 - 183 :: REGRESS. :LAB. :HIPS :AUD.BEH.

PEI ,BKW ; SEC: DAVIS ,FG CIT: 0
THE IMPACT OF ORGANIZATIONAL STRUCTURE ON INTERNAL AUDITOR ORGANIZATIONAL-PROFESSIONAL CONFLICT AN ROLE STRESS: AN EXPLORATION O
AUD SP 89 VOL: 8 PG:101 - 112 :: REGRESS. :LAB. :HIPS :ORG.& ENVIR.

PEIRSON,CG ; FIRS: YOUNG ,TN CIT: 0
DEPRECIATION - FUTURE SERVICES BASIS
TAR AP 67 VOL: 42 PG:338 - 341 :: ANAL. :INT. LOG. :THEORY :PP&E / DEPR

PEIRSON,G CIT: 0
THREE KINDS OF ADJUSTMENTS FOR PRICE CHANGES
TAR OC 66 VOL: 41 PG:729 - 736 :: QUAL. :INT. LOG. :N/A :VALUAT.(INFL.)

PELES ,YC CIT: 0
ON DEVIATIONS FROM LEARNING CURVES
JAA SU 91 VOL: 6 PG:349 - 359 :: DES.STAT. :SIM. :OTH.STAT. :REL.COSTS

PELES ,YC CIT: 0
ON ACCOUNTING AND ECONOMIC METHODS OF DEPRECIATION
JAA SP 90 VOL: 5 PG:309 - 327 :: REGRESS. :PRIM. :OTH.STAT. :PP&E / DEPR

PELES ,YC CIT: 0
A NOTE ON YIELD VARIANCE AND MIX VARIANCE
TAR AP 86 VOL: 61 PG:325 - 329 :: DES.STAT. :INT. LOG. :THEORY :VAR.

PELES ,YC CIT: 0.12
AMORTIZATION OF ADVERTISING EXPENDITURES IN THE FINANCIAL STATEMENTS
JAR SP 70 VOL: 8 PG:128 - 137 :: REGRESS. :CASE :THEORY :OTH. NON-C/A

PENMAN,SH CIT: 0
RETURN TO FUNDAMENTALS
JAA AU 92 VOL: 7 PG:465 - 484 :: DES.STAT. :SEC. :THEORY :FIN.METH.

PENMAN,SH ; FIRS: OHLSON,JA CIT: 0
DISAGGREGATED ACCOUNTING DATA AS EXPLANATORY VARIABLES FOR RETURNS
JAA AU 92 VOL: 7 PG:553 - 573 :: REGRESS. :PRIM. :EMH :FIN.METH.

PENMAN,SH CIT: 0
FINANCIAL STATEMENT INFORMATION AND THE PRICING OF EARNINGS CHANGES
TAR JL 92 VOL: 67 PG:563 - 578 :: REGRESS. :PRIM. :EMH :ANAL.REV.

PENMAN,SH CIT: 0
AN EVALUATION OF ACCOUNTING RATE-OF-RETURN
JAA SP 91 VOL: 6 PG:233 - 255 :: REGRESS. :PRIM. :OTH.STAT. :FIN.METH.

PENMAN,SH ; FIRS: LEV ,B CIT: 1.33
VOLUNTARY FORECAST DISCLOSURE, NONDISCLOSURE, AND STOCK PRICES
JAR SP 90 VOL: 28 PG:49 - 76 :: REGRESS. :PRIM. :EMH :FOREC.

PENMAN,SH ; SEC: OU,J. CIT: 5
FINANCIAL STATEMENT ANALYSIS AND THE PREDICTION OF STOCK RETURNS
JAE NV 89 VOL: 11 PG:295 - 329 :: REGRESS. :PRIM. :EMH :FIN.METH.

PENMAN,SH ; FIRS: OU ,JA CIT: 3.25
ACCOUNTING MEASUREMENT, PRICE-EARNINGS RATIO, AND THE INFORMATION CONTENT OF SECURITY PRICES
JAR ST 89 VOL: 27 PG:111 - 144 :: REGRESS. :PRIM. :EMH :FIN.METH.

PENMAN,SH CIT: 0.22
ABNORMAL RETURNS TO INVESTMENT STRATEGIES BASED ON THE TIMING OF EARNINGS REPORTS
JAE DE 84 VOL: 6 PG:165 - 183 :: REGRESS. :PRIM. :EMH :FIN.ST.TIM.

PENMAN,SH ; FIRS: CHAMBERS,AE CIT: 3.33
TIMELINESS OF REPORTING AND THE STOCK PRICE REACTION TO EARNINGS ANNOUNCEMENTS
JAR SP 84 VOL: 22 PG:21 - 47 :: REGRESS. :PRIM. :EMH :FIN.ST.TIM.

PENMAN,SH ; FIRS: FREEMAN,RN ; SEC: OHLSON,JA CIT: 1.27
BOOK RATE-OF-RETURN AND PREDICTION OF EARNINGS CHANGES: AN EMPIRICAL INVESTIGATION
JAR AU 82 VOL: 20 PG:639 - 653 :: REGRESS. :PRIM. :EMH :FOREC.

PENMAN,SH CIT: 2.23
AN EMPIRICAL INVESTIGATION OF THE VOLUNTARY DISCLOSURE OF CORPORATE EARNINGS FORECASTS OF EARNINGS
JAR SP 80 VOL: 18 PG:132 - 160 :: REGRESS. :PRIM. :EMH :FOREC.

PENMAN,SH ; FIRS: EGGLETON,IRC ; THIR: TWOMBLY,JR CIT: 0.82
ACCOUNTING CHANGES AND STOCK PRICES: AN EXAMINATION OF SELECTED UNCONTROLLED VARIABLES
JAR SP 76 VOL: 14 PG:66 - 88 :: NON-PAR. :PRIM. :EMH :ACC.CHNG.

PENMAN,SH ; FIRS: GONEDES,NJ ; SEC: DOPUCH,N CIT: 2.41
DISCLOSURE RULES, INFORMATION-PRODUCTION, AND CAPITAL MARKET EQUILIBRIUM: THE CASE OF FORECAST DISCLOSURE RULES
JAR SP 76 VOL: 14 PG:89 - 137 :: NON-PAR. :PRIM. :EMH :FOREC.

PENMAN,SH CIT: 0.06
WHAT NET ASSET VALUE? - AN EXTENSION OF A FAMILIAR DEBATE
TAR AP 70 VOL: 45 PG:333 - 346 :: QUAL. :INT. LOG. :THEORY :VALUAT.(INFL.)

PENNACCHI,G ; FIRS: GORTON,G CIT: 0
ARE LOAN SALES REALLY OFF-BALANCE SHEET?
JAA SP 89 VOL: 4 PG:125 - 145 :: REGRESS. :PRIM. :TIME SER. :SPEC.ITEMS

PENNO ,M ; SEC: WATTS ,JS CIT: 0
AN INDEPENDENT AUDITOR'S EX POST CRITERIA FOR THE DISCLOSURE OF INFORMATION
JAR ST 91 VOL: 29 PG:194 - 216 :: DES.STAT. :INT. LOG. :INF.ECO./AG. :INFO.STRUC.

PENNO ,M CIT: 0.33
ACCOUNTING SYSTEMS, PARTICIPATION IN BUDGETING, AND PERFORMANCE EVALUATION
TAR AP 90 VOL: 65 PG:303 - 314 :: DES.STAT. :INT. LOG. :INF.ECO./AG. :BUDG.& PLAN.

PENNO ,M CIT: 0
AUDITING FOR PERFORMANCE EVALUATION
TAR JL 90 VOL: 65 PG:520 - 536 :: DES.STAT. :INT. LOG. :INF.ECO./AG. :AUD.

PENNO ,M CIT: 0.17
A NOTE ON THE VALUE OF INFORMATION GIVEN ASYMMETRIC INFORMATION AND SELF-REPORTING
CAR SP 87 VOL: 3 PG:368 - 374 :: DES.STAT. :INT. LOG. :INF.ECO./AG. :MANAG.

PENNO ,M CIT: 0.63
INFORMATIONAL ISSUES IN THE FINANCIAL REPORTING PROCESS
JAR SP 85 VOL: 23 PG:240 - 255 :: REGRESS. :INT. LOG. :INF.ECO./AG. :BUS.FAIL.

PENNO ,M CIT: 1.56
ASYMMETRY OF PRE-DECISION INFORMATION AND MANAGERIAL ACCOUNTING
JAR SP 84 VOL: 22 PG:177 - 191 :: ANAL. :INT. LOG. :INF.ECO./AG. :MANAG.

PERAGALLO,E CIT: 0
DEVELOPMENT OF THE COMPOUND ENTRY IN 15TH CENTURY LEDGER OF JACHOMO BADOER, A VENETIAN MERCHANT
TAR JA 83 VOL: 58 PG:98 - 104 :: QUAL. :INT. LOG. :HIST. :N/A

PERAGALLO,E CIT: 0.08
CLOSING PROCEDURES IN THE 15TH CENTURY LEDGER OF JACHOMO BADOER, A VENETIAN MERCHANT
TAR JL 81 VOL: 56 PG:587 - 595 :: QUAL. :INT. LOG. :HIST. :N/A

PERAGALLO,E CIT: 0.19
THE LEDGER OF JACHOMO BADOER: CONSTANTINOPLE SEPTEMBER 2, 1436 TO FEBRUARY 26, 1440
TAR OC 77 VOL: 52 PG:881 - 892 :: QUAL. :PRIM. :HIST. :FIN.METH.

PERAGALLO,E CIT: 0
A COMMENT ON VIGANO'S HISTORICAL DEVELOPMENT OF LEDGER BALANCING PROCESS ADJUSTMENTS AND FINANCIAL STATEMENTS DURING THE 15TH, 16TH, AND 17TH CENTURIES
TAR JL 71 VOL: 46 PG:529 - 534 :: QUAL. :SEC. :HIST. :FIN.METH.

PERBY ,M ; FIRS: CARLSSON,J ; SEC: EHN ,P ; THIR: ERLANDER,B ; FIFT: SANDBERG,A CIT: 0.07
PLANNING AND CONTROL FROM THE PERSPECTIVE OF LABOR: A SHORT REPRESENTATION OF THE DEMOS PROJECT
AOS 34 78 VOL: 3 PG:249 - 260 :: QUAL. :FIELD :OTH. :BUDG.& PLAN.

PERRITT,GW ; FIRS: AGRAWAL,SP ; SEC: HALLBAUER,RC CIT: 0
MEASUREMENT OF THE CURRENT COST OF EQUIVALENT PRODUCTIVE CAPACITY
JAA WI 80 VOL: 3 PG:163 - 173 :: ANAL. :INT. LOG. :OTH.STAT. :VALUAT.(INFL.)

PESANDO,JE ; SEC: CLARKE,CK CIT: 0
ECONOMIC MODELS OF THE LABOR MARKET AND PENSION ACCOUNTING: AN EXPLORATORY ANALYSIS
TAR OC 83 VOL: 58 PG:733 - 748 :: ANAL. :INT. LOG. :OTH.STAT. :PENS.

PETERS,JM CIT: 0
A COGNITIVE COMPUTATIONAL MODEL OF RISK HYPOTHESIS GENERATION
JAR ST 90 VOL: 28 PG:83 - 109 :: REGRESS. :CASE :EXP.SYST. :RISK

PETERS,JM ; SEC: LEWIS ,BL ; THIR: DHAR ,V CIT: 0
ASSESSING INHERENT RISK DURING AUDIT PLANNING: THE DEVELOPMENT OF A KNOWLEDGE BASED MODEL
AOS 04 89 VOL: 14 PG:359 - 378 :: ANOVA :SURV. :EXP.SYST. :PLAN.

PETERSEN,RJ CIT: 0
A PORTFOLIO ANALYSIS OF GENERAL PRICE LEVEL RESTATEMENT
TAR JL 75 VOL: 50 PG:525 - 532 :: NON-PAR. :PRIM. :EMH :VALUAT.(INFL.)

PETERSEN,RJ CIT: 0.47
INTERINDUSTRY ESTIMATION OF GENERAL PRICE-LEVEL IMPACT ON FINANCIAL INFORMATION
TAR JA 73 VOL: 48 PG:34 - 43 :: NON-PAR. :PRIM. :THEORY :VALUAT.(INFL.)

PETERSON,JL ; FIRS: PARKE ,R CIT: 0
INDICATORS OF SOCIAL CHANGE: DEVELOPMENTS IN THE U.S.A.
AOS 03 81 VOL: 6 PG:235 - 246 :: QUAL. :INT. LOG. :OTH. :HRA

PETERSON,RB ; FIRS: MAHER ,MW ; SEC: RAMANATHAN,KV CIT: 0.29
PREFERENCE CONGRUENCE, INFORMATION ACCURACY, AND EMPLOYEE PERFORMANCE: A FIELD STUDY
JAR AU 79 VOL: 17 PG:476 - 503 :: ANOVA :FIELD :OTH.BEH. :AUD.BEH.

PETERSON,WA CIT: 0
SIGNIFICANCE OF PROSPECTIVE INCOME DATA
TAR AP 66 VOL: 41 PG:275 - 282 :: QUAL. :INT. LOG. :THEORY :VALUAT.(INFL.)

PETRAN,AS ; FIRS: DAVIDSON,HJ ; SEC: NETER ,J CIT: 0.12
ESTIMATING THE LIABILITY FOR UNREDEEMED STAMPS
JAR AU 67 VOL: 5 PG:186 - 207 :: ANAL. :INT. LOG. :OTH.STAT. :SPEC.ITEMS

PETRI ,E ; FIRS: MARCINKO,D CIT: 0.22
USE OF THE PRODUCTION FUNCTION IN CALCULATION OF STANDARD COST VARIANCES - AN EXTENSION
TAR JL 84 VOL: 59 PG:488 - 495 :: ANAL. :INT. LOG. :OTH. :VAR.

PETRI ,E ; SEC: GELFAND,J CIT: 0
THE PRODUCTION FUNCTION: A NEW PERSPECTIVE IN CAPITAL MAINTENANCE
TAR AP 79 VOL: 54 PG:330 - 345 :: ANAL. :INT. LOG. :OTH. :OTH.MANAG.

PETRI ,E ; SEC: MINCH ,RA CIT: 0
A DECISION MODEL FOR TAX PREFERENCE ITEMS
TAR AP 78 VOL: 53 PG:415 - 428 :: ANAL. :INT. LOG. :OTH.STAT. :OTH.MANAG.

PETRI ,E ; FIRS: SEAGLE,JP CIT: 0
GIFT VS. ESTATE TRANSFER: THE METHOD OF EQUATED RATES
TAR JA 77 VOL: 52 PG:124 - 136 :: ANAL. :INT. LOG. :THEORY :N/A

PETRI ,E ; SEC: MINCH ,RA CIT: 0.12
THE TREASURY STOCK METHOD AND CONVENTIONAL METHOD IN RECIPROCAL STOCKHOLDINGS - AN AMALGAMATION
TAR AP 74 VOL: 49 PG:330 - 341 :: ANAL. :INT. LOG. :N/A :SPEC.ITEMS

PETRI ,E ; SEC: MINCH ,RA CIT: 0
EVALUATION OF RESOURCE ACQUISITION DECISIONS BY THE PARTITIONING OF HOLDING ACTIVITY
TAR JL 74 VOL: 49 PG:455 - 464 :: ANAL. :INT. LOG. :N/A :INV.

PETRI ,E CIT: 0
HOLDING GAINS AND LOSSES AS COST SAVINGS: A COMMENT ON SUPPLEMENTARY STATEMENT NO.2 ON INVENTORY VALUATION
TAR JL 73 VOL: 48 PG:483 - 488 :: ANAL. :INT. LOG. :THEORY :INV.

PETRONI,KR CIT: 0
OPTIMISTIC REPORTING IN THE PROPERTY-CASUALTY INSURANCE INDUSTRY
JAE DE 92 VOL: 15 PG:485 - 507 :: REGRESS. :PRIM. :OTH.STAT. :SPEC.ITEMS

PETRUZZI,CR ; FIRS: LEE ,CWJ CIT: 0.5
INVENTORY ACCOUNTING SWITCH AND UNCERTAINTY
JAR AU 89 VOL: 27 PG:277 - 296 :: REGRESS. :PRIM. :OTH.STAT. :INV.

PETTY ,JW ; FIRS: MERVILLE,LJ CIT: 0.13
TRANSFER PRICING FOR THE MULTINATIONAL FIRM
TAR OC 78 VOL: 53 PG:935 - 951 :: ANAL. :INT. LOG. :MATH.PROG. :TRANS.PRIC.

PFEFFER,J ; FIRS: MARKUS,ML CIT: 0.8
POWER AND THE DESIGN AND IMPLEMENTATION OF ACCOUNTING AND CONTROL SYSTEMS
AOS 23 83 VOL: 8 PG:205 - 218 :: QUAL. :CASE :OTH. :MANAG.

PFEIFFER,GM ; FIRS: BOWEN ,RM CIT: 0
THE YEAR-END LIFO PURCHASE DECISION: THE CASE OF FARMER BROTHERS COMPANY
TAR JA 89 VOL: 64 PG:152 - 171 :: REGRESS. :CASE :HIST. :INV.

PHILBRICK,D ; FIRS: DYCKMAN,TR ; THIR: STEPHAN,J CIT: 0.89
A COMPARISON OF EVENT STUDY METHODOLOGIES USING DAILY STOCK RETURNS: A SIMULATION APPROACH
JAR ST 84 VOL: 22 PG:1 - 30 :: REGRESS. :SIM. :OTH.BEH. :METHOD.

PHILBRICK,DR ; FIRS: ELLIOTT,JA CIT: 0
ACCOUNTING CHANGES AND EARNINGS PREDICTABILITY
TAR JA 90 VOL: 65 PG:157 - 174 :: REGRESS. :PRIM. :OTH. :ACC.CHNG.

PHILIPS,GE ; SEC: MAYNE ,LS CIT: 0
INCOME MEASURE AND BANK STOCK VALUES
JAR ST 70 VOL: 8 PG:178 - 188 :: REGRESS. :PRIM. :TIME SER. :VALUAT.(INFL.)

PHILIPS,GE CIT: 0
PENSION LIABILITIES AND ASSETS
TAR JA 68 VOL: 43 PG:10 - 17 :: QUAL. :INT. LOG. :THEORY :PENS.

PHILIPS,GE CIT: 0
THE ACCRETION CONCEPT OF INCOME
TAR JA 63 VOL: 38 PG:14 - 25 :: QUAL. :INT. LOG. :THEORY :REV.REC.

PHILIPS,GE CIT: 0
THE REVOLUTION IN ACCOUNTING THEORY
TAR OC 63 VOL: 38 PG:696 - 708 :: QUAL. :INT. LOG. :THEORY :N/A

PHILLIPS JR,TJ ; FIRS: FLORY ,SM ; THIR: REIDENBACH,RE ; FOUR: ROBIN ,DP CIT: 0
A MULTIDIMENSIONAL ANALYSIS OF SELECTED ETHICAL ISSUES IN ACCOUNTING
TAR AP 92 VOL: 67 PG:284 - 302 :: REGRESS. :SURV. :HIPS :JUDG.

PHILLIPS,LC CIT: 0
ACCOUNTING FOR BUSINESS COMBINATIONS
TAR AP 65 VOL: 40 PG:377 - 381 :: QUAL. :INT. LOG. :THEORY :BUS.COMB.

PICCIOTTO,S CIT: 0
INTERNATIONAL TAXATION AND INTRAFIRM PRICING IN TRANSNATIONAL CORPORATE GROUPS
AOS 92 VOL: 17 PG:759 - 792 :: REGRESS. :SEC. :THEORY :INT.DIFF.

PIERCE,BJ ; FIRS: HALL ,TW ; THIR: ROSS ,WR CIT: 0
PLANNING SAMPLE SIZES FOR STRINGER-METHOD MONETARY UNIT AND SINGLE-STAGE ATTRIBUTE SAMPLING PLANS
AUD SP 89 VOL: 8 PG:64 - 89 :: DES.STAT. :SIM. :OTH.STAT. :SAMP.

PIERCE,LT ; FIRS: WALKER,NR CIT: 0
THE PRICE WATERHOUSE AUDIT: A STATE OF THE ART APPROACH
AUD AU 88 VOL: 08 PG:1 - 22 :: DES.STAT. :INT. LOG. :THEORY :AUD.THEOR.

PILLSBURY,CM CIT: 0
LIMITED ASSURANCE ENGAGEMENTS
AUD SP 85 VOL: 4 PG:63 - 79 :: REGRESS. :LAB. :OTH.STAT. :OPIN.

PINCH ,T ; SEC: MULKAY,M ; THIR: ASHMORE,M CIT: 1
CLINICAL BUDGETING: EXPERIMENTATION IN THE SOCIAL SCIENCES: A DRAMA IN FIVE ACTS
AOS 03 89 VOL: 14 PG:271 - 301 :: REGRESS. :SURV. :OTH.BEH. :BUDG.& PLAN.

PINCHES,GE ; FIRS: HAKA ,SF ; SEC: GORDON,LA CIT: 0.63
SOPHISTICATED CAPITAL BUDGETING SELECTION TECHNIQUES AND FIRM PERFORMANCE
TAR OC 85 VOL: 60 PG:651 - 669 :: REGRESS. :PRIM. :EMH :CAP.BUDG.

PINCUS CIT: 0
THE EFFICACY OF A RED FLAGS QUESTIONNAIRE FOR ASSESSING THE POSSIBILITY OF FRAUD
AOS 02 89 VOL: 14 PG:153 - 163 :: REGRESS. :LAB. :HIPS :PROF.RESP.

PINCUS,KV CIT: 0
AUDIT JUDGMENT CONSENSUS: A MODEL FOR DICHOTOMOUS DECISIONS
AUD SP 90 VOL: 9 PG:1 - 20 :: DES.STAT. :SIM. :OTH.BEH. :JUDG.

PINCUS,KV CIT: 0
AUDITOR INDIVIDUAL DIFFERENCES AND FAIRNESS OF PRESENTATION JUDGMENTS
AUD AU 90 VOL: 9 PG:150 - 167 :: REGRESS. :LAB. :HIPS :AUD.BEH.

PINCUS,M ; FIRS: DOPUCH,N CIT: 1.2
EVIDENCE ON THE CHOICE OF INVENTORY ACCOUNTING METHODS: LIFO VERSUS FIFO
JAR SP 88 VOL: 26 PG:28 - 59 :: REGRESS. :PRIM. :OTH.STAT. :INV.

PINCUS,M ; FIRS: MADEO ,SA CIT: 0.25
STOCK MARKET BEHAVIOR AND TAX RULE CHANGES: THE CASE OF THE DISALLOWANCE OF CERTAIN INTEREST DEDUCTIONS CLAIMED BY BANKS
TAR JL 85 VOL: 60 PG:407 - 429 :: REGRESS. :LAB. :EMH :TAXES

PINCUS,M CIT: 1.3
INFORMATION CHARACTERISTICS OF EARNINGS ANNOUNCEMENTS AND STOCK MARKET BEHAVIOR
JAR SP 83 VOL: 21 PG:155 - 183 :: NON-PAR. :PRIM. :EMH :FOREC.

PLANTE,R ; SEC: NETER ,J ; THIR: LEITCH,RA CIT: 0.25
COMPARATIVE PERFORMANCE OF MULTINOMIAL, CELL, AND STRINGER BOUNDS
AUD AU 85 VOL: 5 PG:40 - 56 :: DES.STAT. :SIM. :OTH.STAT. :SAMP.

PLANTE,R ; FIRS: LEITCH,RA ; SEC: NETER ,J ; FOUR: SINHA ,P CIT: 0.91
MODIFIED MULTINOMIAL BOUNDS FOR LARGER NUMBERS OF ERRORS IN AUDITS
TAR AP 82 VOL: 57 PG:384 - 400 :: DES.STAT. :SIM. :OTH.STAT. :SAMP.

PLAUT ,SE ; FIRS: GLICK ,R CIT: 0
MONEY DEMAND AND OFF-BALANCE SHEET LIQUIDITY: EMPIRICAL ANALYSIS AND IMPLICATIONS FOR MONETARY POLICY
JAA SP 89 VOL: 4 PG:147 - 159 :: REGRESS. :PRIM. :OTH.STAT. :SPEC.ITEMS

PLUMLEE,RD ; FIRS: COLLINS,JH CIT: 0.5
THE TAXPAYER'S LABOR AND REPORTING DECISION: THE EFFECT OF AUDIT SCHEMES
TAR JL 91 VOL: 66 PG:559 - 576 :: REGRESS. :SEC. :INF.ECO./AG. :TAX PLNG.

PLUMLEE,RD ; FIRS: MOECKEL,CL CIT: 1.75
AUDITOR'S CONFIDENCE IN RECOGNITION OF AUDIT EVIDENCE
TAR OC 89 VOL: 64 PG:653 - 666 :: REGRESS. :LAB. :HIPS :AUD.BEH.

PLUMLEE,RD ; FIRS: CHOW ,CW ; SEC: MCNAMEE,AH CIT: 0.5
PRACTITIONERS' PERCEPTIONS OF AUDIT STEP DIFFICULTY AND CRITICALNESS: IMPLICATIONS FOR AUDIT RESEARCH
AUD SP 87 VOL: 6 PG:123 - 133 :: REGRESS. :SURV. :OTH.STAT. :AUD.THEOR.

PLUMLEE,RD CIT: 0.38
THE STANDARD OF OBJECTIVITY FOR INTERNAL AUDITORS: MEMORY AND BIAS EFFECT
JAR AU 85 VOL: 23 PG:683 - 699 :: REGRESS. :LAB. :HIPS :INT.AUD.

POLLOCK,J ; FIRS: ARANYA,N ; THIR: AMERNIC,J CIT: 0.25
AN EXAMINATION OF PROFESSIONAL COMMITMENT IN PUBLIC ACCOUNTING
AOS 04 81 VOL: 6 PG:271 - 280 :: MIXED :LAB. :OTH.BEH. :PROF.RESP.

POMERANZ,F CIT: 0
HOW THE AUDIT COMMITTEE SHOULD WORK
JAA AU 77 VOL: 1 PG:45 - 52 :: QUAL. :INT. LOG. :INSTIT. :OTH.MANAG.

PONDY ,LR ; FIRS: BOLAND,RJ CIT: 0.57
THE MICRO DYNAMICS OF A BUDGET-CUTTING PROCESS: MODES, MODELS AND STRUCTURE
AOS 45 86 VOL: 11 PG:403 - 422 :: REGRESS. :FIELD :HIPS :BUDG.& PLAN.

PONDY ,LR ; FIRS: BOLAND,RJ CIT: 2.1
ACCOUNTING IN ORGANIZATIONS: A UNION OF NATURAL AND RATIONAL PERSPECTIVES
AOS 23 83 VOL: 8 PG:223 - 234 :: QUAL. :CASE :OTH. :OTH.MANAG.

PONEMON,LA CIT: 0
ETHICAL REASONING AND SELECTION-SOCIALIZATION IN ACCOUNTING
AOS 04 92 VOL: 17 PG:239 - 258 :: REGRESS. :LAB. :OTH.BEH. :ORG.

PONEMON,LA CIT: 0
AUDITOR UNDERREPORTING OF TIME AND MORAL REASONING: AN EXPERIMENTAL-LAB STUDY
CAR AU 92 VOL: 9 PG:171 - 189 :: REGRESS. :LAB. :OTH.BEH. :AUD.BEH.

PONEMON,LA ; FIRS: ARNOLD,DF CIT: 0
INTERNAL AUDITORS' PERCEPTIONS OF WHISTLE-BLOWING AND THE INFLUENCE OF MORAL REASONING: AN EXPERIMENT
AUD AU 91 VOL: 10 PG:1 - 15 :: REGRESS. :LAB. :HIPS :PROF.RESP.

PONEMON,LA ; SEC: SCHICK,AG CIT: 0
FINANCIALLY DISTRESSED COMPANIES AND AUDITOR PERCEPTIONS OF THE TWELVE CHARACTERISTICS OF DECLINE
AUD AU 91 VOL: 10 PG:70 - 83 :: REGRESS. :LAB. :HIPS :BUS.FAIL.

PONEMON,LA ; SEC: GABHART,DRL CIT: 0.67
AUDITOR INDEPENDENCE JUDGMENTS: A COGNITIVE-DEVELOPMENTAL MODEL AND EXPERIMENTAL EVIDENCE
CAR AU 90 VOL: 7 PG:227 - 251 :: REGRESS. :LAB. :HIPS :INDEP.

PORCANO,TM CIT: 0
DISTRIBUTIVE JUSTICE AND TAX POLICY
TAR OC 84 VOL: 59 PG:619 - 636 :: REGRESS. :LAB. :OTH.BEH. :TAXES

PORTER,GA ; FIRS: EVERETT,JO CIT: 0
SAFE-HARBOR LEASING - UNRAVELING THE TAX IMPLICATIONS
JAA SP 84 VOL: 7 PG:241 - 256 :: MIXED :INT. LOG. :THEORY :LEASES

POSEY ,JM ; FIRS: CARPER,WB CIT: 0.06
THE VALIDITY OF SELECTED SURROGATE MEASURES OF HUMAN RESOURCE VALUE: A FIELD STUDY
AOS 23 76 VOL: 1 PG:143 - 152 :: NON-PAR. :SURV. :OTH.BEH. :HRA

POTTER,G ; FIRS: BANKER,RD ; SEC: COOPER,WW CIT: 0
A PERSPECTIVE ON RESEARCH IN GOVERNMENTAL ACCOUNTING
TAR JL 92 VOL: 67 PG:496 - 510 :: REGRESS. :SEC. :THEORY :N/A

POURCIAU,S ; FIRS: SMITH ,DB CIT: 0.4
A COMPARISON OF THE FINANCIAL CHARACTERISTICS OF DECEMBER AND NON-DECEMBER YEAR-END COMPANIES
JAE DE 88 VOL: 10 PG:335 - 344 :: REGRESS. :PRIM. :OTH. :FIN.ST.TIM.

POWELL,RM CIT: 0
CAREER CHOICES AMONG BETA ALPHA PSI MEMBERS
TAR JL 66 VOL: 41 PG:525 - 534 :: DES.STAT. :SURV. :INSTIT. :OTH.MANAG.

POWER ,M CIT: 0
AFTER CALCULATION? REFLECTIONS ON CRITIQUE OF ECONOMIC REASON BY ANDRE GORZ
AOS 05 92 VOL: 17 PG:477 - 499 :: DES.STAT. :SEC. :THEORY :ORG.& ENVIR.

POWER ,MK CIT: 0
FROM COMMON SENSE TO EXPERTISE: REFLECTIONS ON THE PREHISTORY OF AUDIT SAMPLING
AOS 01 92 VOL: 17 PG:37 - 62 :: REGRESS. :SEC. :HIST. :SAMP.

POWER ,MK CIT: 0
EDUCATING ACCOUNTANTS: TOWARDS A CRITICAL ETHNOGRAPHY
AOS 04 91 VOL: 16 PG:333 - 353 :: ANOVA :SEC. :HIPS :EDUC.

POWERS,M ; SEC: REVSINE,L CIT: 0
LESSOR'S ACCOUNTING AND RESIDUAL VALUES: COMDISCO, BARRON'S, AND GAAP
TAR AP 89 VOL: 64 PG:346 - 368 :: DES.STAT. :SIM. :OTH.STAT. :LEASES

POWNALL,G ; FIRS: KING ,R ; THIR: WAYMIRE,G CIT: 0
CORPORATE DISCLOSURE AND PRICE DISCOVERY ASSOCIATED WITH NYSE TEMPORARY TRADING HALTS
CAR SP 92 VOL: 8 PG:509 - 531 :: REGRESS. :PRIM. :EMH :INFO.STRUC.

POWNALL,G ; SEC: WAYMIRE,G CIT: 0.75
VOLUNTARY DISCLOSURE CREDIBILITY AND SECURITIES PRICES: EVIDENCE FROM MANAGEMENT EARNINGS FORECASTS, 1969-73
JAR AU 89 VOL: 27 PG:227 - 245 :: REGRESS. :PRIM. :EMH :FOREC.

POWNALL,G ; SEC: WAYMIRE,G CIT: 0
VOLUNTARY DISCLOSURE CHOICE AND EARNINGS INFORMATION TRANSFER
JAR ST 89 VOL: 27 PG:85 - 105 :: REGRESS. :PRIM. :EMH :FOREC.

POWNALL,G CIT: 0.29
AN EMPIRICAL ANALYSIS OF THE REGULATION OF THE DEFENSE CONTRACTING INDUSTRY: THE COST ACCOUNTING STANDARDS BOARD
JAR AU 86 VOL: 24 PG:291 - 315 :: REGRESS. :PRIM. :INSTIT. :FASB SUBM.

POWNALL,G ; FIRS: WAYMIRE,G CIT: 0
SOME EVIDENCE ON POTENTIAL EFFECTS OF CONTEMPORANEOUS EARN. DISCLOSURES IN TESTS OF CAPITAL MARKET EFFECTS ASSOC. WITH FASB EXPOSURE DRAFT NO. 19
JAR AU 83 VOL: 21 PG:629 - 643 :: REGRESS. :PRIM. :EMH :OIL & GAS

PRAKASH,P ; SEC: SUNDER,S CIT: 0.29
THE CASE AGAINST SEPARATION OF CURRENT OPERATING PROFIT AND HOLDING GAIN
TAR JA 79 VOL: 54 PG:1 - 22 :: QUAL. :INT. LOG. :THEORY :VALUAT.(INFL.)

PRAKASH,P ; FIRS: DITTMAN,DA CIT: 0.29
COST VARIANCE INVESTIGATION: MARKOVIAN CONTROL VERSUS OPTIMAL CONTROL
TAR AP 79 VOL: 54 PG:358 - 373 :: DES.STAT. :SIM. :OTH.STAT. :VAR.

PRAKASH,P ; FIRS: DITTMAN,DA CIT: 0.33
COST VARIANCE INVESTIGATION: MARKOVIAN CONTROL OF MARKOV PROCESSES
JAR SP 78 VOL: 16 PG:14 - 25 :: ANAL. :INT. LOG. :OTH.STAT. :VAR.

PRAKASH,P ; SEC: RAPPAPORT,A CIT: 1.38
INFORMATION INDUCTANCE AND ITS SIGNIFICANCE FOR ACCOUNTING
AOS 01 77 VOL: 2 PG:29 - 38 :: QUAL. :INT. LOG. :HIPS :N/A

PRAKASH,P ; SEC: RAPPAPORT,A CIT: 0.18
INFORMATIONAL INTERDEPENDENCIES: SYSTEM STRUCTURED INDUCED BY ACCOUNTING INFORMATION
TAR OC 75 VOL: 50 PG:723 - 734 :: QUAL. :INT. LOG. :INSTIT. :OTH.MANAG.

PRATER,GI CIT: 0
TIME-SHARING COMPUTERS IN ACCOUNTING EDUCATION
TAR OC 66 VOL: 41 PG:619 - 625 :: QUAL. :INT. LOG. :N/A :OTH.MANAG.

PRATT ,J ; SEC: BEAULIEU,P CIT: 0
ORGANIZATIONAL CULTURE IN PUBLIC ACCOUNTING: SIZE, TECHNOLOGY, RANK, AND FUNCTIONAL AREA
AOS 92 VOL: 17 PG:667 - 684 :: REGRESS. :SURV. :OTH.BEH. :ORG.

PRATT ,J ; FIRS: AWASTHI,V CIT: 0.67
THE EFFECTS OF MONETARY INCENTIVES ON EFFORT AND DECISION PERFORMANCE: THE ROLE OF COGNITIVE CHARACTERISTICS
TAR OC 90 VOL: 65 PG:797 - 811 :: REGRESS. :LAB. :HIPS :DEC.AIDS

PRATT ,J CIT: 0
SFAS NO. 2: AUDITOR EVALUATIONS AND INPUT TO THE HOME OFFICE
AOS 04 85 VOL: 10 PG:427 - 442 :: REGRESS. :SURV. :OTH.BEH. :R & D

PRATT ,J ; SEC: JIAMBALVO,J CIT: 0
DETERMINANTS OF LEADER BEHAVIOR IN AN AUDIT ENVIRONMENT
AOS 04 82 VOL: 7 PG:369 - 380 :: NON-PAR. :SURV. :HIPS :AUD.BEH.

PRATT ,J CIT: 0.18
POST-COGNITIVE STRUCTURE: ITS DETERMINANTS AND RELATIONSHIP TO PERCEIVED INFORMATION AND PREDICTIVE ACCURACY
JAR SP 82 VOL: 20 PG:189 - 209 :: CORR. :LAB. :HIPS :INFO.STRUC.

PRATT ,J ; FIRS: JIAMBALVO,J CIT: 0.09
TASK COMPLEXITY AND LEADERSHIP EFFECTIVENESS IN CPA FIRMS
TAR OC 82 VOL: 57 PG:734 - 750 :: ANOVA :LAB. :OTH.BEH. :ORG.

PRATT ,J ; SEC: JIAMBALVO,J CIT: 0.33
RELATIONSHIPS BETWEEN LEADER BEHAVIORS AND AUDIT TEAM PERFORMANCE
AOS 02 81 VOL: 6 PG:133 - 142 :: CORR. :FIELD :OTH.BEH. :AUD.BEH.

PRESS ,EG ; SEC: WEINTROP,JB CIT: 3.33
ACCOUNTING-BASED CONSTRAINTS IN PUBLIC AND PRIVATE DEBT AGREEMENTS: THEIR ASSOCIATION WITH LEVERAGE AND IMPACT ON ACCOUNTING CHOICE
JAE JA 90 VOL: 12 PG:65 - 95 :: REGRESS. :PRIM. :OTH.STAT. :LTD

PRESTON,A CIT: 0.43
INTERACTIONS AND ARRANGEMENTS IN THE PROCESS OF INFORMING
AOS 06 86 VOL: 11 PG:521 - 540 :: REGRESS. :CASE :OTH.BEH. :MANAG.

PRESTON,AM CIT: 0
THE BIRTH OF CLINICAL ACCOUNTING: A STUDY OF THE EMERGENCE AND TRANSFORMATIONS OF DISCOURSES ON COSTS AND PRACTICES OF ACCOUNTING IN US HOSPITALS
AOS 01 92 VOL: 17 PG:63 - 100 :: REGRESS. :SEC. :HIST. :ORG.& ENVIR.

PRESTON,AM ; SEC: COOPER,DJ ; THIR: COOMBS,RW CIT: 1
FABRICATING BUDGETS: A STUDY OF PRODUCTION OF MANAGEMENT BUDGETING IN THE NATIONAL HEALTH SERVICE
AOS 06 92 VOL: 17 PG:561 - 593 :: REGRESS. :CASE :OTH.BEH. :BUDG.& PLAN.

PRESTON,AM CIT: 0.25
THE TAXMAN COMETH: SOME OBSERVATIONS ON THE INTERRELATIONSHIP BETWEEN ACCOUNTING AND INLAND REVENUE PRACTICE
AOS 06 89 VOL: 14 PG:389 - 413 :: REGRESS. :FIELD :HIST. :ORG.& ENVIR.

PRESTON,LE CIT: 0
RESEARCH ON CORPORATE SOCIAL REPORTING: DIRECTIONS FOR DEVELOPMENT
AOS 03 81 VOL: 6 PG:255 - 262 :: QUAL. :INT. LOG. :OTH. :HRA

PRESTON,LE ; FIRS: DIERKES,M CIT: 0.38
CORPORATE SOCIAL ACCOUNTING REPORTING FOR THE PHYSICAL ENVIRONMENT: A CRITICAL REVIEW AND IMPLEMENTATION PROPOSAL
AOS 01 77 VOL: 2 PG:3 - 22 :: QUAL. :INT. LOG. :THEORY :HRA

PREVITS,GJ ; FIRS: MAUTZ ,RK CIT: 0
ERIC KOHLER: AN ACCOUNTING ORIGINAL
TAR AP 77 VOL: 52 PG:301 - 307 :: QUAL. :INT. LOG. :HIST. :N/A

PRICE ,KH ; FIRS: NICHOLS,DR CIT: 0.29
THE AUDITOR-FIRM CONFLICT: AN ANALYSIS USING CONCEPTS OF EXCHANGE THEORY
TAR AP 76 VOL: 51 PG:335 - 346 :: QUAL. :INT. LOG. :OTH.BEH. :AUD.

PRINCE,TR ; FIRS: GODFREY,JT CIT: 0.12
THE ACCOUNTING MODEL FROM AN INFORMATION SYSTEMS PERSPECTIVE
TAR JA 71 VOL: 46 PG:75 - 89 :: QUAL. :INT. LOG. :INF.ECO./AG. :MANAG.

PRINCE,TR CIT: 0
THE MOTIVATIONAL ASSUMPTION FOR ACCOUNTING THEORY
TAR JL 64 VOL: 39 PG:553 - 562 :: QUAL. :INT. LOG. :THEORY :FIN.METH.

PROBST,FR CIT: 0.18
PROBABILISTIC COST CONTROLS: A BEHAVIOURAL DIMENSION
TAR JA 71 VOL: 46 PG:113 - 118 :: DES.STAT. :FIELD :OTH.STAT. :RESP.ACC.

PURDY ,CR ; SEC: SMITH JR,JM ; THIR: GRAY ,J CIT: 0
THE VISIBILITY OF THE AUDITOR'S DISCLOSURE OF DEVIANCE FROM APB OPINION: AN EMPIRICAL TEST
JAR ST 69 VOL: 7 PG:1 - 18 :: ANOVA :LAB. :OTH.BEH. :INFO.STRUC.

PURDY ,CR CIT: 0
INDUSTRY PATTERNS OF CAPACITY OR VOLUME CHOICE: THEIR EXISTENCE AND RATIONALE
JAR AU 65 VOL: 3 PG:228 - 241 :: ANAL. :INT. LOG. :OTH. :N/A

PURDY ,D CIT: 0.08
THE PROVISION OF FINANCIAL INFORMATION TO EMPLOYEES: A STUDY OF THE REPORTING PRACTICES OF SOME LARGE PUBLIC COMPANIES IN THE UK
AOS 04 81 VOL: 6 PG:327 - 338 :: DES.STAT. :SURV. :OTH. :MANAG.

PURO ,M CIT: 0
DO LARGE ACCOUNTING FIRMS COLLUDE IN THE STANDARDS-SETTING PROCESS?
JAA SP 85 VOL: 8 PG:165 - 177 :: REGRESS. :PRIM. :INSTIT. :FASB SUBM.

PURO ,M CIT: 0.22
AUDIT FIRM LOBBYING BEFORE THE FINANCIAL ACCOUNTING STANDARDS BOARD: AN EMPIRICAL STUDY
JAR AU 84 VOL: 22 PG:624 - 646 :: OTH.QUANT. :PRIM. :INSTIT. :FASB SUBM.

PURVIS,SEC CIT: 0
THE EFFECT OF AUDIT DOCUMENTATION FORMAT ON DATA COLLECTION
AOS 06 89 VOL: 14 PG:551 - 563 :: REGRESS. :LAB. :HIPS :INT.CONT.

PUTNAM,K ; SEC: THOMAS,LR CIT: 0
DOES PREDICTABILITY CHANGE WHEN GAAP CHANGE?
JAA AU 84 VOL: 8 PG:15 - 23 :: MIXED :PRIM. :TIME SER. :FOREC.

PUTNEY,FB ; FIRS: IJIRI ,Y ; SEC: KINARD,JC CIT: 0.47
AN INTEGRATED EVALUATION SYSTEM FOR BUDGET FORECASTING AND OPERATING PERFORMANCE WITH A CLASSIFIED BUDGETING BIBLIOGRAPHY
JAR SP 68 VOL: 6 PG:1 - 28 :: QUAL. :SEC. :OTH.BEH. :BUDG.& PLAN.

PUXTY ,AG ; SEC: WILLMOTT,HC ; THIR: COOPER,DJ ; FOUR: LOWE ,T CIT: 1.33
MODES OF REGULATION IN ADVANCED CAPITALISM: LOCATING ACCOUNTANCY IN FOUR COUNTRIES
AOS 03 87 VOL: 12 PG:273 - 291 :: DES.STAT. :INT. LOG. :THEORY :ORG.& ENVIR.

PUXTY ,AG ; FIRS: MCDONALD,DL CIT: 0
AN INDUCEMENT-CONTRIBUTION APPROACH TO CORPORATE FINANCIAL REPORTING
AOS 12 79 VOL: 4 PG:53 - 66 :: QUAL. :INT. LOG. :THEORY :N/A

PYLE ,WC ; FIRS: BRUMMET,RL ; SEC: FLAMHOLTZ,EG CIT: 0.41
HUMAN RESOURCE MEASUREMENT - A CHALLENGE FOR ACCOUNTANTS
TAR AP 68 VOL: 43 PG:217 - 224 :: QUAL. :INT. LOG. :OTH.BEH. :HRA

PYO ,Y ; SEC: LUSTGARTEN,S CIT: 0
DIFFERENTIAL INTRA-INDUSTRY INFORMATION TRANSFER ASSOCIATED WITH MANAGEMENT EARNINGS FORECASTS
JAE DE 90 VOL: 13 PG:365 - 379 :: REGRESS. :PRIM. :EMH :FIN.METH.

QUITTMEYER,CL ; FIRS: PATRICK,AW CIT: 0
THE CPA AND MANAGEMENT SERVICES
TAR JA 63 VOL: 38 PG:109 - 117 :: QUAL. :INT. LOG. :N/A :N/A

RABY ,WL CIT: 0
TAX ALLOCATION AND NON-HISTORICAL FINANCIAL STATEMENTS
TAR JA 69 VOL: 44 PG:1 - 11 :: QUAL. :INT. LOG. :THEORY :VALUAT.(INFL.)

RABY ,WL CIT: 0
ETHICS IN TAX PRACTICE
TAR OC 66 VOL: 41 PG:714 - 720 :: QUAL. :INT. LOG. :N/A :ORG.

RABY ,WL ; SEC: NEUBIG,RD CIT: 0
INTER-PERIOD TAX ALLOCATION OR BASIS ADJUSTMENT?
TAR JL 63 VOL: 38 PG:568 - 576 :: QUAL. :INT. LOG. :THEORY :TAXES

RADCLIFFE,RC ; FIRS: MABERT,VA CIT: 0.06
A FORECASTING METHODOLOGY AS APPLIED TO FINANCIAL TIME SERIES
TAR JA 74 VOL: 49 PG:61 - 75 :: REGRESS. :INT. LOG. :TIME SER. :BUDG.& PLAN.

RADEBAUGH,LH ; FIRS: GRAY ,SJ CIT: 0
INTERNATIONAL SEGMENT DISCLOSURES BY U.S. AND U.K. MULTINATIONAL ENTERPRISES: A DESCRIPTIVE STUDY
JAR SP 84 VOL: 22 PG:351 - 360 :: DES.STAT. :PRIM. :THEORY :INT.DIFF.

RADOSEVICH,R ; FIRS: STERLING,RR CIT: 0.12
A VALUATION EXPERIMENT
JAR SP 69 VOL: 7 PG:90 - 95 :: DES.STAT. :LAB. :OTH. :AUD.

RAGHUNANDAN,K ; SEC: GRIMLUND,RA ; THIR: SCHEPANSKI,A CIT: 0
AUDITOR EVALUATION OF LOSS CONTINGENCIES
CAR SP 91 VOL: 7 PG:549 - 568 :: REGRESS. :LAB. :HIPS :VALUAT.(INFL.)

RAHMAN,M ; FIRS: MCCOSH,AM CIT: 0.06
THE INFLUENCE OF ORGANIZATIONAL AND PERSONAL FACTORS ON THE USE OF ACCOUNTING INFORMATION: AN EMPIRICAL STUDY
AOS 04 76 VOL: 1 PG:339 - 356 :: DES.STAT. :LAB. :HIPS :MAN.DEC.CHAR.

RAJAN ,MV CIT: 0
MANAGEMENT CONTROL SYSTEMS AND THE IMPLEMENTATION OF STRATEGIES
JAR AU 92 VOL: 30 PG:227 - 248 :: DES.STAT. :INT. LOG. :INF.ECO./AG. :EXEC.COMP.

RAJAN ,MV CIT: 1
COST ALLOCATION IN MULTIAGENT SETTINGS
TAR JL 92 VOL: 67 PG:527 - 545 :: DES.STAT. :INT. LOG. :OTH.BEH. :COST.ALLOC.

RAJAN ,MV ; FIRS: BANKER,RD ; SEC: DATAR ,SM CIT: 0.33
MEASUREMENT OF PRODUCTIVITY IMPROVEMENTS: AN EMPIRICAL ANALYSIS
JAA AU 87 VOL: 2 PG:319 - 347 :: DES.STAT. :FIELD :OTH.STAT. :MANAG.

RAMAGE,JG ; SEC: KRIEGER,AM ; THIR: SPERO ,LL CIT: 0.79
AN EMPIRICAL STUDY OF ERROR CHARACTERISTICS IN AUDIT POPULATIONS
JAR ST 79 VOL: 17 PG:72 - 102 :: DES.STAT. :PRIM. :OTH.STAT. :ERRORS

RAMAKRISHNAN,RT ; FIRS: BALACHANDRAN,BV CIT: 0.33
A THEORY OF AUDIT PARTNERSHIPS: AUDIT FIRM SIZE AND FEES
JAR SP 87 VOL: 25 PG:111 - 126 :: DES.STAT. :INT. LOG. :INF.ECO./AG. :ORG.

RAMAKRISHNAN,RT ; FIRS: BALACHANDRAN,BV CIT: 0.08
JOINT COST ALLOCATION: A UNIFIED APPROACH
TAR JA 81 VOL: 56 PG:85 - 96 :: ANAL. :INT. LOG. :MATH.PROG. :COST.ALLOC.

RAMAKRISHNAN,RT ; FIRS: BALACHANDRAN,BV CIT: 0.23
INTERNAL CONTROL AND EXTERNAL AUDITING FOR INCENTIVE COMPENSATION SCHEDULES
JAR ST 80 VOL: 18 PG:140 - 171 :: ANAL. :INT. LOG. :INF.ECO./AG. :AUD.

RAMAKRISHNAN,RTS ; SEC: THOMAS,JK CIT: 0
WHAT MATTERS FROM THE PAST: MARKET VALUE, BOOK VALUE, OR EARNINGS?
JAA AU 92 VOL: 7 PG:423 - 464 :: REGRESS. :PRIM. :EMH :FIN.METH.

RAMAKRISHNAN,RTS ; FIRS: MCINNES,M CIT: 0
A DECISION-THEORY MODEL OF MOTIVATION AND ITS USEFULNESS IN THE DIAGNOSIS OF MANAGEMENT CONTROL SYSTEMS
AOS 02 91 VOL: 16 PG:167 - 184 :: REGRESS. :SURV. :HIPS :MANAG.

RAMAN ,KK ; FIRS: BENSON,ED ; SEC: MARKS ,BR CIT: 0
THE EFFECT OF VOLUNTARY GAAP COMPLIANCE AND FINANCIAL DISCLOSURE ON GOVERNMENTAL BORROWING COSTS
JAA SU 91 VOL: 6 PG:303 - 319 :: REGRESS. :PRIM. :INSTIT. :FIN.METH.

RAMAN ,KK ; FIRS: INGRAM,RW ; THIR: WILSON,ER CIT: 0
THE INFORMATION IN GOVERNMENTAL ANNUAL REPORTS: A CONTEMPORANEOUS PRICE REACTION APPROACH
TAR AP 89 VOL: 64 PG:250 - 268 :: REGRESS. :INT. LOG. :EMH :LTD

RAMAN ,KK ; FIRS: MARKS ,BR CIT: 0
THE EFFECT OF UNFUNDED ACCUMULATED AND PROJECTED PENSION OBLIGATIONS ON GOVERNMENTAL BORROWING COSTS
CAR SP 88 VOL: 4 PG:595 - 608 :: REGRESS. :PRIM. :INSTIT. :PENS.

RAMAN ,KK ; FIRS: MARKS ,BR CIT: 0
SOME ADDITIONAL EVIDENCE ON THE DETERMINANTS OF STATE AUDIT BUDGETS
AUD AU 87 VOL: 7 PG:106 - 117 :: REGRESS. :PRIM. :THEORY :AUD.

RAMAN ,KK ; FIRS: MARKS ,BR CIT: 0.13
THE IMPORTANCE OF PENSION DATA FOR MUNICIPAL & STATE CREDITOR DECISIONS: REPLICATIONS & EXTENSIONS
JAR AU 85 VOL: 23 PG:878 - 886 :: REGRESS. :PRIM. :OTH.STAT. :PENS.

RAMAN ,KK CIT: 0
ALTERNATIVE ACCOUNTING MEASURES AS PREDICTORS OF MUNICIPAL FINANCIAL DISTRESS
JAA AU 82 VOL: 6 PG:44 - 50 :: OTH.QUANT. :PRIM. :THEORY :BUS.FAIL.

RAMAN ,KK CIT: 0
FINANCIAL REPORTING AND MUNICIPAL BOND RATINGS
JAA WI 82 VOL: 5 PG:144 - 153 :: OTH.QUANT. :PRIM. :THEORY :FIN.METH.

RAMAN ,KK CIT: 0
MUNICIPAL FINANCIAL REPORTING: MONITORING FULL ACCOUNTABILITY
JAA SU 81 VOL: 4 PG:352 - 359 :: QUAL. :INT. LOG. :THEORY :AUD.

RAMAN ,KK CIT: 0.42
FINANCIAL REPORTING AND MUNICIPAL BOND RATING CHANGES
TAR OC 81 VOL: 56 PG:910 - 926 :: OTH.QUANT. :PRIM. :OTH.STAT. :FIN.METH.

RAMAN ,KK CIT: 0.07
THE TIEBOUT HYPOTHESIS: IMPLICATIONS FOR MUNICIPAL FINANCIAL REPORTING
JAA AU 79 VOL: 3 PG:31 - 41 :: QUAL. :INT. LOG. :INSTIT. :FIN.METH.

RAMANAN,R ; FIRS: CREADY,WM CIT: 0
THE POWER OF TESTS EMPLOYING LOG-TRANSFORMED VOLUME IN DETECTING ABNORMAL TRADING
JAE JN 91 VOL: 14 PG:203 - 214 :: DES.STAT. :SIM. :OTH.STAT. :METHOD.

RAMANAN,R ; FIRS: ALLEN ,S CIT: 0
EARNINGS SURPRISES AND PRIOR INSIDER TRADING: TESTS OF JOINT INFORMATIVENESS
CAR SP 90 VOL: 6 PG:518 - 543 :: REGRESS. :PRIM. :EMH :INS.TRAD.

RAMANAN,R ; FIRS: BALACHANDRAN,BV CIT: 0
OPTIMAL INTERNAL CONTROL STRATEGY UNDER DYNAMIC CONDITIONS
JAA WI 88 VOL: 03 PG:1 - 13 :: DES.STAT. :INT. LOG. :INF.ECO./AG. :INT.CONT.

RAMANAN,R ; FIRS: JOHNSON,WB CIT: 0.4
DISCRETIONARY ACCOUNTING CHANGES FROM SUCCESSFUL EFFORTS TO FULL COST METHOD
TAR JA 88 VOL: 63 PG:96 - 110 :: REGRESS. :PRIM. :OTH.STAT. :OIL & GAS

RAMANATHAN,KV ; SEC: WEIS ,WL CIT: 0.08
SUPPLEMENTING COLLEGIATE FINANCIAL STATEMENTS WITH ACROSS-FUND AGGREGATIONS: AN EXPERIMENTAL INQUIRY
AOS 02 81 VOL: 6 PG:143 - 152 :: ANOVA :LAB. :THEORY :INFO.STRUC.

RAMANATHAN,KV ; FIRS: MAHER ,MW ; THIR: PETERSON,RB CIT: 0.29
PREFERENCE CONGRUENCE, INFORMATION ACCURACY, AND EMPLOYEE PERFORMANCE: A FIELD STUDY
JAR AU 79 VOL: 17 PG:476 - 503 :: ANOVA :FIELD :OTH.BEH. :AUD.BEH.

RAMANATHAN,KV CIT: 0.29
TOWARD A THEORY OF CORPORATE SOCIAL ACCOUNTING
TAR JL 76 VOL: 51 PG:516 - 528 :: QUAL. :INT. LOG. :INSTIT. :HRA

RAMANATHAN,KV ; SEC: RAPPAPORT,A CIT: 0
SIZE, GROWTH RATES, AND MERGER VALUATION
TAR OC 71 VOL: 46 PG:733 - 745 :: ANAL. :SIM. :OTH.STAT. :BUS.COMB.

RAMESH,K ; FIRS: ANTHONY,JH CIT: 1
ASSOCIATION BETWEEN ACCOUNTING PERFORMANCE MEASURES AND STOCK PRICES: A TEST OF THE LIFE CYCLE HYPOTHESIS
JAE JN 92 VOL: 15 PG:203 - 227 :: REGRESS. :PRIM. :EMH :FIN.METH.

RAMESH,K ; FIRS: HAN ,JCY ; SEC: WILD ,JJ CIT: 1.25
MANAGERS' EARNINGS FORECASTS AND INTRA-INDUSTRY INFORMATION TRANSFERS
JAE FB 89 VOL: 11 PG:3 - 33 :: REGRESS. :PRIM. :EMH :FOREC.

RAMESH,K ; FIRS: GREENBERG,RR ; SEC: JOHNSON,GL CIT: 0
EARNINGS VERSUS CASH FLOW AS A PREDICTOR OF FUTURE CASH FLOW MEASURES
JAA AU 86 VOL: 1 PG:266 - 277 :: REGRESS. :PRIM. :THEORY :SPEC.ITEMS

RANDALL,RH ; FIRS: CUSHING,BE ; SEC: SEARFOSS,DG CIT: 0.36
MATERIALITY ALLOCATION IN AUDIT PLANNING: A FEASIBILITY STUDY
JAR ST 79 VOL: 17 PG:172 - 216 :: DES.STAT. :FIELD :OTH.STAT. :PLAN.

RANSOM,CR CIT: 0
THE EX ANTE INFORMATION CONTENT OF ACCOUNTING INFORMATION SYSTEMS
JAR ST 85 VOL: 23 PG:124 - 143 :: REGRESS. :PRIM. :EMH :FIN.METH.

RAPPAPORT,A ; FIRS: PRAKASH,P CIT: 1.38
INFORMATION INDUCTANCE AND ITS SIGNIFICANCE FOR ACCOUNTING
AOS 01 77 VOL: 2 PG:29 - 38 :: QUAL. :INT. LOG. :HIPS :N/A

RAPPAPORT,A ; FIRS: PRAKASH,P CIT: 0.18
INFORMATIONAL INTERDEPENDENCIES: SYSTEM STRUCTURED INDUCED BY ACCOUNTING INFORMATION
TAR OC 75 VOL: 50 PG:723 - 734 :: QUAL. :INT. LOG. :INSTIT. :OTH.MANAG.

RAPPAPORT,A ; FIRS: RAMANATHAN,KV CIT: 0
SIZE, GROWTH RATES, AND MERGER VALUATION
TAR OC 71 VOL: 46 PG:733 - 745 :: ANAL. :SIM. :OTH.STAT. :BUS.COMB.

RAPPAPORT,A CIT: 0
INTEGER PROGRAMMING AND MANAGERIAL ANALYSIS
TAR AP 69 VOL: 44 PG:297 - 299 :: ANAL. :INT. LOG. :MATH.PROG. :LTD

RAPPAPORT,A ; FIRS: LAVALLE,IH CIT: 0
ON THE ECONOMICS OF ACQUIRING INFORMATION OF IMPERFECT RELIABILITY
TAR AP 68 VOL: 43 PG:225 - 230 :: ANAL. :INT. LOG. :INF.ECO./AG. :REL.COSTS

RAPPAPORT,A CIT: 0.06
SENSITIVITY ANALYSIS IN DECISION MAKING
TAR JL 67 VOL: 42 PG:441 - 456 :: ANAL. :INT. LOG. :MATH.PROG. :BUDG.& PLAN.

RAPPAPORT,A CIT: 0.06
LEASE CAPITALIZATION AND THE TRANSACTION CONCEPT
TAR AP 65 VOL: 40 PG:373 - 376 :: QUAL. :INT. LOG. :THEORY :LEASES

RAPPAPORT,A CIT: 0
ESTABLISHING OBJECTIVES FOR PUBLISHED CORPORATE ACCOUNTING REPORTS
TAR OC 64 VOL: 39 PG:951 - 962 :: QUAL. :INT. LOG. :INSTIT. :OTH.MANAG.

RASCH ,RH ; SEC: HARRELL,A CIT: 0
THE IMPACT OF PERSONAL CHARACTERISTICS ON THE TURNOVER BEHAVIOR OF ACCOUNTING PROFESSIONALS
AUD SP 90 VOL: 9 PG:90 - 102 :: REGRESS. :SURV. :OTH.BEH. :ORG.

RASP ,J ; FIRS: STONE ,M CIT: 0.5
TRADEOFFS IN THE CHOICE BETWEEN LOGIT AND OLS FOR ACCOUNTING CHOICE STUDIES
TAR JA 91 VOL: 66 PG:170 - 187 :: DES.STAT. :SIM. :MATH.PROG. :METHOD.

RATCLIFFE,TA ; FIRS: MUNTER,P CIT: 0
AN ASSESSMENT OF USER REACTIONS TO LEASE ACCOUNTING DISCLOSURES
JAA WI 83 VOL: 6 PG:108 - 114 :: NON-PAR. :LAB. :THEORY :LEASES

RATSCH,H CIT: 0
THE NEW PROFESSIONAL CODE FOR CERTIFIED ACCOUNTANTS AND LICENSED ACCOUNTANTS IN THE FEDERAL REPUBLIC OF GERMANY
TAR JA 64 VOL: 39 PG:140 - 144 :: QUAL. :INT. LOG. :INSTIT. :OTH.MANAG.

RAUN ,DL CIT: 0
THE LIMITATIONS OF PROFIT GRAPHS, BREAKEVEN ANALYSIS, AND BUDGETS
TAR OC 64 VOL: 39 PG:927 - 945 :: REGRESS. :INT. LOG. :TIME SER. :C-V-P-A

RAUN ,DL CIT: 0
THE APPLICATION OF MONTE CARLO ANALYSIS TO AN INVENTORY PROBLEM
TAR OC 63 VOL: 38 PG:754 - 758 :: ANAL. :INT. LOG. :OTH.STAT. :INV.

RAVENSCROFT,SP ; FIRS: BUCKLESS,FA CIT: 0
CONTRAST CODING: A REFINEMENT OF ANOVA IN BEHAVIORAL ANALYSIS
TAR OC 90 VOL: 65 PG:933 - 945 :: REGRESS. :SEC. :HIPS :METHOD.

RAVIV ,A CIT: 0.13
MANAGEMENT COMPENSATION AND THE MANAGERIAL LABOR MARKET: AN OVERVIEW
JAE AP 85 VOL: 7 PG:239 - 246 :: REGRESS. :INT. LOG. :THEORY :EXEC.COMP.

RAYBURN,J ; SEC: LENWAY,S CIT: 0
AN INVESTIGATION OF THE BEHAVIOR OF ACCRUALS IN THE SEMICONDUCTOR INDUSTRY: 1985
CAR AU 92 VOL: 9 PG:237 - 251 :: REGRESS. :PRIM. :OTH. :REV.REC.

RAYBURN,J CIT: 2.86
THE ASSOCIATION OF OPERATING CASH FLOW AND ACCRUALS WITH SECURITY RETURNS
JAR ST 86 VOL: 24 PG:112 - 137 :: REGRESS. :PRIM. :EMH :SPEC.ITEMS

RAYBURN,JD ; FIRS: COLLINS,DW ; SEC: KOTHARI,SP CIT: 4.33
FIRM SIZE AND THE INFORMATION CONTENT OF PRICES WITH RESPECT TO EARNINGS
JAE JL 87 VOL: 9 PG:111 - 138 :: REGRESS. :PRIM. :EMH :ORG.& ENVIR.

RAYMAN,RA CIT: 0
AN EXTENSION OF THE SYSTEM OF ACCOUNTS: THE SEGREGATION OF FUNDS AND VALUE
JAR SP 69 VOL: 7 PG:53 - 89 :: QUAL. :INT. LOG. :THEORY :FIN.METH.

READ ,WJ ; FIRS: TOMCZYK,S CIT: 0.25
DIRECT MEASUREMENT OF SUPPLIER CONCENTRATION IN THE MARKET FOR AUDIT SERVICES
AUD AU 89 VOL: 9 PG:98 - 106 :: REGRESS. :PRIM. :OTH.STAT. :ORG.

REBELE,JE ; SEC: HEINTZ,JA ; THIR: BRIDEN,GE CIT: 0
INDEPENDENT AUDITOR SENSITIVITY TO EVIDENCE RELIABILITY
AUD AU 88 VOL: 08 PG:43 - 52 :: REGRESS. :LAB. :OTH.BEH. :JUDG.

RECKERS,PMJ ; FIRS: ANDERSON,JC ; SEC: KAPLAN,SE CIT: 0
THE EFFECTS OF OUTPUT INTERFERENCE ON ANALYTICAL PROCEDURES JUDGMENTS
AUD AU 92 VOL: 11 PG:1 - 13 :: REGRESS. :LAB. :HIPS :ANAL.REV.

RECKERS,PMJ ; FIRS: JENNINGS,MM ; SEC: KNEER ,DC CIT: 0
SELECTED AUDITOR COMMUNICATIONS AND PERCEPTIONS OF LEGAL LIABILITY
CAR SP 91 VOL: 7 PG:449 - 465 :: REGRESS. :LAB. :HIPS :LIAB.

RECKERS,PMJ ; FIRS: KAPLAN,SE CIT: 0
AN EXAMINATION OF INFORMATION SEARCH DURING INITIAL AUDIT PLANNING
AOS 06 89 VOL: 14 PG:539 - 550 :: REGRESS. :LAB. :HIPS :PLAN.

RECKERS,PMJ ; FIRS: KAPLAN,SE ; THIR: ROARK ,SJ CIT: 0
AN ATTRIBUTION THEORY ANALYSIS OF TAX EVASION RELATED JUDGMENTS
AOS 04 88 VOL: 13 PG:371 - 379 :: REGRESS. :LAB. :OTH.BEH. :TAXES

RECKERS,PMJ ; FIRS: PANY ,K CIT: 0
WITHIN- VS. BETWEEN-SUBJECTS EXPERIMENTAL DESIGNS: A STUDY OF DEMAND
AUD AU 87 VOL: 7 PG:39 - 53 :: REGRESS. :LAB. :OTH.BEH. :INDEP.

RECKERS,PMJ ; FIRS: JENNINGS,M ; SEC: KNEER ,DC CIT: 0.33
A REEXAMINATION OF THE CONCEPT OF MATERIALITY: VIEWS OF AUDITORS, USERS AND OFFICERS OF THE COURT
AUD SP 87 VOL: 6 PG:104 - 115 :: REGRESS. :LAB. :OTH.BEH. :MAT.

RECKERS,PMJ ; FIRS: MCKINELY,S ; SEC: PANY ,K CIT: 0.13
AN EXAMINATION OF THE INFLUENCE OF CPA FIRM TYPE, SIZE, AND MAS PROVISION ONLOAN OFFICER DECISIONS & PERCEPTIONS
JAR AU 85 VOL: 23 PG:887 - 896 :: REGRESS. :LAB. :OTH.BEH. :ORG.

RECKERS,PMJ ; FIRS: KAPLAN,SE CIT: 0.78
AN EMPIRICAL EXAMINATION OF AUDITORS' INITIAL PLANNING PROCESSES
AUD AU 84 VOL: 4 PG:1 - 19 :: ANOVA :LAB. :OTH.BEH. :PLAN.

RECKERS,PMJ ; FIRS: PANY ,K CIT: 0.33
NON-AUDIT SERVICES AND AUDITOR INDEPENDENCE - A CONTINUING PROBLEM
AUD SP 84 VOL: 3 PG:89 - 97 :: DES.STAT. :SURV. :OTH.STAT. :INDEP.

RECKERS,PMJ ; SEC: SCHULTZ JR,JJ CIT: 0.09
INDIVIDUAL VERSUS GROUP ASSISTED AUDIT EVALUATIONS
AUD AU 82 VOL: 2 PG:64 - 74 :: ANOVA :LAB. :OTH.BEH. :JUDG.

RECKERS,PMJ ; SEC: STAGLIANO,AJ CIT: 0.17
NON-AUDIT SERVICES AND PERCEIVED INDEPENDENCE: SOME NEW EVIDENCE
AUD SU 81 VOL: 1 PG:23 - 37 :: ANOVA :LAB. :OTH.BEH. :INDEP.

RECKERS,PMJ ; FIRS: SCHULTZ JR,JJ CIT: 0.75
THE IMPACT OF GROUP PROCESSING ON SELECTED AUDIT DISCLOSURE DECISIONS
JAR AU 81 VOL: 19 PG:482 - 501 :: ANOVA :PRIM. :OTH.BEH. :AUD.BEH.

RECKERS,PMJ ; FIRS: PANY ,K CIT: 0.23
THE EFFECT OF GIFTS, DISCOUNTS, AND CLIENT SIZE ON PERCEIVED AUDITOR INDEPENDENCE
TAR JA 80 VOL: 55 PG:50 - 61 :: ANOVA :LAB. :OTH.BEH. :INDEP.

RECKERS,PMJ ; SEC: TAYLOR,ME CIT: 0.29
CONSISTENCY IN AUDITORS' EVALUATIONS OF INTERNAL ACCOUNTING CONTROLS
JAA AU 79 VOL: 3 PG:42 - 55 :: ANOVA :LAB. :OTH.BEH. :INT.CONT.

REDER ,RE ; FIRS: LARCKER,DF ; THIR: SIMON ,DT CIT: 0.3
TRADES BY INSIDERS AND MANDATED ACCOUNTING STANDARDS
TAR JL 83 VOL: 58 PG:606 - 620 :: NON-PAR. :INT. LOG. :EMH :OIL & GAS

REED ,SA ; FIRS: PEI ,BKW ; THIR: KOCH ,BS CIT: 0
AUDITOR BELIEF REVISIONS IN A PERFORMANCE AUDITING SETTING: AN APPLICATION OF THE BELIEF-ADJUSTMENT MODEL
AOS 02 92 VOL: 17 PG:169 - 183 :: REGRESS. :LAB. :HIPS :AUD.BEH.

REGIER,PR ; FIRS: MITTELSTAEDT,HF ; THIR: CHEWNING,EG ; FOUR: PANY ,K CIT: 0
DO CONSISTENCY MODIFICATIONS PROVIDE INFORMATION TO EQUITY MARKETS?
AUD SP 92 VOL: 11 PG:83 - 98 :: REGRESS. :PRIM. :OTH.STAT. :OPIN.

REICHELSTEIN,S ; FIRS: MELUMAD,N ; SEC: MOOKHERJEE,D CIT: 0
A THEORY OF RESPONSIBILITY CENTERS
JAE DE 92 VOL: 15 PG:445 - 483 :: DES.STAT. :INT. LOG. :INF.ECO./AG. :RESP.ACC.

REICHELSTEIN,S CIT: 2
CONSTRUCTING INCENTIVE SCHEMES FOR GOVERNMENT CONTRACTS: AN APPLICATION OF AGENCY THEORY
TAR OC 92 VOL: 67 PG:712 - 731 :: DES.STAT. :CASE :MATH.PROG. :COST.ALLOC.

REICHELSTEIN,S ; FIRS: KIRBY ,AJ ; THIR: SEN ,PK ; FOUR: PAIK ,TY CIT: 1.5
PARTICIPATION, SLACK, AND BUDGET-BASED PERFORMANCE EVALUATION
JAR SP 91 VOL: 29 PG:109 - 128 :: DES.STAT. :INT. LOG. :OTH.BEH. :BUDG.& PLAN.

REICHELSTEIN,S ; FIRS: MELUMAD,ND CIT: 1
CENTRALIZATION VERSUS DELEGATION AND THE VALUE OF COMMUNICATION
JAR ST 87 VOL: 25 PG:1 - 18 :: DES.STAT. :INT. LOG. :INF.ECO./AG. :ORG.& ENVIR.

REICHENSTEIN,WR ; FIRS: FARRELY,GE ; SEC: FERRIS,KR CIT: 0
PERCEIVED RISK, MARKET RISK, AND ACCOUNTING-DETERMINED RISK MEASURES
TAR AP 85 VOL: 60 PG:278 - 288 :: REGRESS. :SURV. :OTH.STAT. :FOREC.

REIDENBACH,RE ; FIRS: FLORY ,SM ; SEC: PHILLIPS JR,TJ ; FOUR: ROBIN ,DP CIT: 0
A MULTIDIMENSIONAL ANALYSIS OF SELECTED ETHICAL ISSUES IN ACCOUNTING
TAR AP 92 VOL: 67 PG:284 - 302 :: REGRESS. :SURV. :HIPS :JUDG.

REILLY,FK ; SEC: STETTLER,HF CIT: 0
FACTORS INFLUENCING SUCCESS ON THE CPA EXAMINATION
JAR AU 72 VOL: 10 PG:308 - 321 :: REGRESS. :PRIM. :OTH.STAT. :EDUC.

REILLY,FK ; SEC: MORGENSON,DL ; THIR: WEST ,M CIT: 0.18
THE PREDICTIVE ABILITY OF ALTERNATIVE PARTS OF INTERIM FINANCIAL STATEMENTS
JAR ST 72 VOL: 10 PG:105 - 124 :: REGRESS. :PRIM. :EMH :INT.REP.

REIMERS,JL ; SEC: BUTLER,SA CIT: 0
THE EFFECT OF OUTCOME KNOWLEDGE ON AUDITORS' JUDGMENTAL EVALUATIONS
AOS 02 92 VOL: 17 PG:185 - 194 :: REGRESS. :LAB. :HIPS :JUDG.

REITER,SA ; FIRS: ZIEBART,DA CIT: 0
BOND RATINGS, BOND YIELDS AND FINANCIAL INFORMATION
CAR AU 92 VOL: 9 PG:252 - 282 :: REGRESS. :PRIM. :INF.ECO./AG. :FIN.METH.

REITER,SA ; FIRS: FRANCIS,JR CIT: 1.33
DETERMINANTS OF CORPORATE PENSION FUNDING STRATEGY
JAE AP 87 VOL: 9 PG:35 - 59 :: REGRESS. :PRIM. :OTH.STAT. :PENS.

REITSPERGER,WD ; FIRS: DANIEL,SJ CIT: 0
LINKING QUALITY STRATEGY WITH MANAGEMENT CONTROL SYSTEMS: EMPIRICAL EVIDENCE FROM JAPANESE INDUSTRY
AOS 91 VOL: 16 PG:601 - 618 :: REGRESS. :FIELD :OTH.STAT. :MANAG.

REITSPERGER,WD ; FIRS: DANIEL,SJ CIT: 0
LINKING QUALITY STRATEGY WITH MANAGEMENT CONTROL SYSTEMS: EMPIRICAL EVIDENCE FROM JAPANESE INDUSTRY
AOS 91 VOL: 16 PG:601 - 618 :: REGRESS. :FIELD :OTH.STAT. :MANAG.

RENEAU,JH ; FIRS: BOATSMAN,JR ; SEC: GRASSO,LP ; THIR: ORMISTON,MB CIT: 0
A PERSPECTIVE ON THE USE OF LABORATORY MARKET EXPERIMENTATION IN AUDITING RESEARCH
TAR JA 92 VOL: 67 PG:148 - 156 :: ANOVA :SEC. :INF.ECO./AG. :METHOD.

RENEAU,JH ; FIRS: WONG-ON-WING,B ; THIR: WEST ,SG CIT: 0
AUDITORS' PERCEPTION OF MANAGEMENT: DETERMINANTS AND CONSEQUENCES
AOS 06 89 VOL: 14 PG:577 - 587 :: REGRESS. :LAB. :HIPS :JUDG.

RENEAU,JH ; FIRS: HARRISON,PD ; SEC: WEST ,SG CIT: 0.2
INITIAL ATTRIBUTIONS AND INFORMATION-SEEKING BY SUPERIORS AND SUBORDINATES IN PRODUCTION VARIANCE INVESTIGATIONS
TAR AP 88 VOL: 63 PG:307 - 320 :: REGRESS. :LAB. :OTH.BEH. :VAR.

RENEAU,JH CIT: 0.47
CAV BOUNDS IN DOLLAR UNIT SAMPLING: SOME SIMULATION RESULTS
TAR JL 78 VOL: 53 PG:669 - 680 :: ANAL. :SIM. :OTH.STAT. :SAMP.

REVSINE,L ; FIRS: POWERS,M CIT: 0
LESSOR'S ACCOUNTING AND RESIDUAL VALUES: COMDISCO, BARRON'S, AND GAAP
TAR AP 89 VOL: 64 PG:346 - 368 :: DES.STAT. :SIM. :OTH.STAT. :LEASES

REVSINE,L ; FIRS: LARCKER,DF CIT: 0.5
THE OIL AND GAS ACCOUNTING CONTROVERSY: AN ANALYSIS OF ECONOMIC CONSEQUENCES
TAR OC 83 VOL: 58 PG:706 - 732 :: REGRESS. :PRIM. :EMH :OIL & GAS

REVSINE,L CIT: 0
THE THEORY AND MEASUREMENT OF BUSINESS INCOME: A REVIEW ARTICLE
TAR AP 81 VOL: 56 PG:342 - 354 :: QUAL. :SEC. :THEORY :VALUAT.(INFL.)

REVSINE,L CIT: 0.21
TECHNOLOGICAL CHANGES AND REPLACEMENT COSTS: A BEGINNING
TAR AP 79 VOL: 54 PG:306 - 322 :: QUAL. :INT. LOG. :THEORY :VALUAT.(INFL.)

REVSINE,L ; FIRS: DITTMAN,DA ; SEC: JURIS ,HA CIT: 0.29
ON THE EXISTENCE OF UNRECORDED HUMAN ASSETS: AN ECONOMIC PERSPECTIVE
JAR SP 76 VOL: 14 PG:49 - 65 :: ANAL. :INT. LOG. :OTH.BEH. :HRA

REVSINE,L ; SEC: THIES ,JB CIT: 0.12
PRODUCTIVITY CHANGES AND ALTERNATIVE INCOME SERIES: A SIMULATION
TAR AP 76 VOL: 51 PG:255 - 268 :: ANAL. :SIM. :OTH.STAT. :DEC.AIDS

REVSINE,L CIT: 0.06
PREDICTIVE ABILITY, MARKET PRICES, AND OPERATING FLOWS
TAR JL 71 VOL: 46 PG:480 - 489 :: QUAL. :INT. LOG. :N/A :FIN.METH.

REVSINE,L CIT: 0.35
ON THE CORRESPONDENCE BETWEEN REPLACEMENT COST INCOME AND ECONOMIC INCOME
TAR JL 70 VOL: 45 PG:513 - 523 :: ANAL. :INT. LOG. :THEORY :VALUAT.(INFL.)

REVSINE,L CIT: 0.65
DATA EXPANSION AND CONCEPTUAL STRUCTURE
TAR OC 70 VOL: 45 PG:704 - 711 :: QUAL. :INT. LOG. :OTH.BEH. :INFO.STRUC.

REVSINE,L CIT: 0
SOME CONTROVERSY CONCERNING CONTROVERSIAL ACCOUNTING CHANGES
TAR AP 69 VOL: 44 PG:354 - 358 :: QUAL. :INT. LOG. :THEORY :TAXES

REYNOLDS,IN CIT: 0
A VANISHING ACCOUNTING ITEM - REPLACEMENT ACCOUNTING?
TAR AP 64 VOL: 39 PG:342 - 346 :: QUAL. :INT. LOG. :THEORY :PP&E / DEPR

RHODE ,JG ; FIRS: BENKE ,RL CIT: 0.31
THE JOB SATISFACTION OF HIGHER LEVEL EMPLOYEES IN LARGE CERTIFIED PUBLIC ACCOUNTING FIRMS
AOS 02 80 VOL: 5 PG:187 - 202 :: OTH.QUANT. :SURV. :OTH.BEH. :ORG.

RHODE ,JG ; FIRS: HARVEY,DW ; THIR: MERCHANT,KA CIT: 0.14
ACCOUNTING AGGREGATION: USER PREFERENCES AND DECISION MAKING
AOS 03 79 VOL: 4 PG:187 - 210 :: ANOVA :LAB. :OTH.BEH. :N/A

RHODE ,JG ; SEC: SORENSEN,JE ; THIR: LAWLER III,EE CIT: 0.69
SOURCES OF PROFESSIONAL STAFF TURNOVER IN PUBLIC ACCOUNTING FIRMS REVEALED BY THE EXIT INTERVIEW
AOS 02 77 VOL: 2 PG:165 - 176 :: NON-PAR. :SURV. :OTH. :ORG.

RHODE ,JG ; FIRS: GORDON,FE ; THIR: MERCHANT,KA CIT: 0.19
THE EFFECTS OF SALARY AND HUMAN RESOURCE ACCOUNTING DISCLOSURES ON SMALL GROUP RELATIONS AND PERFORMANCE
AOS 04 77 VOL: 2 PG:295 - 306 :: ANOVA :LAB. :OTH.BEH. :HRA

RHODE ,JG ; SEC: WHITSELL,GM ; THIR: KELSEY,RL CIT: 0.29
AN ANALYSIS OF CLIENT-INDUSTRY CONCENTRATIONS FOR LARGE PUBLIC ACCOUNTING FIRMS
TAR OC 74 VOL: 49 PG:772 - 787 :: DES.STAT. :PRIM. :INSTIT. :AUD.

RHODE ,JG ; FIRS: DECOSTER,DT CIT: 0.12
THE ACCOUNTANT'S STEREOTYPE: REAL OR IMAGINED, DESERVED OR UNWARRANTED
TAR OC 71 VOL: 46 PG:651 - 664 :: ANOVA :SURV. :OTH.BEH. :AUD.

RICCHIUTE,DN CIT: 0
WORKING-PAPER ORDER EFFECTS AND AUDITORS' GOING-CONCERN DECISIONS
TAR JA 92 VOL: 67 PG:46 - 58 :: REGRESS. :LAB. :HIPS :AUD.BEH.

RICCHIUTE,DN CIT: 0.33
AN EMPIRICAL ASSESSMENT OF THE IMPACT OF ALTERNATIVE TASK PRESENTATION MODES ON DECISION-MAKING RESEARCH IN AUDITING
JAR SP 84 VOL: 22 PG:341 - 350 :: NON-PAR. :LAB. :HIPS :METHOD.

RICCHIUTE,DN ; FIRS: FAIRCLOTH,AW CIT: 0
AMBIGUITY INTOLERANCE AND FINANCIAL REPORTING ALTERNATIVES
AOS 01 81 VOL: 6 PG:53 - 68 :: DES.STAT. :SURV. :HIPS :FIN.METH.

RICCHIUTE,DN CIT: 0.14
STANDARD SETTING AND THE ENTITY-PROPRIETARY DEBATE
AOS 12 79 VOL: 4 PG:67 - 76 :: DES.STAT. :LAB. :INSTIT. :AUD.BEH.

RICE ,SJ ; FIRS: CHOW ,CW CIT: 0.36
QUALIFIED AUDIT OPINIONS AND SHARE PRICES - AN INVESTIGATION
AUD WI 82 VOL: 1 PG:35 - 53 :: MIXED :PRIM. :EMH :OPIN.

RICE ,SJ ; FIRS: CHOW ,CW CIT: 1
QUALIFIED AUDIT OPINIONS AND AUDITOR SWITCHING
TAR AP 82 VOL: 57 PG:326 - 335 :: DES.STAT. :PRIM. :OTH. :OPIN.

RICE ,SJ CIT: 0.27
THE INFORMATION CONTENT OF FULLY DILUTED EARNINGS PER SHARE
TAR AP 78 VOL: 53 PG:429 - 438 :: REGRESS. :PRIM. :EMH :FIN.METH.

RICHARD,DL CIT: 0
DIFFICULTIES IN TAX ALLOCATION ON GENERAL PRICE-LEVEL INCREASES
TAR OC 68 VOL: 43 PG:730 - 737 :: QUAL. :INT. LOG. :THEORY :TAXES

RICHARDSON,A ; FIRS: GIBBINS,M ; THIR: WATERHOUSE,J CIT: 0.33
THE MANAGEMENT OF CORPORATE FINANCIAL DISCLOSURES: OPPORTUNISM, RITUALISM, POLICIES, AND PROCESSES
JAR SP 90 VOL: 28 PG:121 - 143 :: REGRESS. :SURV. :OTH.BEH. :INFO.STRUC.

RICHARDSON,AJ CIT: 0.33
ACCOUNTING KNOWLEDGE AND PROFESSIONAL PRIVILEGE: A REPLICATION AND EXTENSION
AOS 05 90 VOL: 15 PG:499 - 501 :: REGRESS. :PRIM. :INSTIT. :INT.DIFF.

RICHARDSON,AJ ; SEC: WILLIAMS,JJ CIT: 0
CANADIAN ACADEMIC ACCOUNTANTS' PRODUCTIVITY: A SURVEY OF 10 REFEREED PUBLICATIONS, 1976-1989
CAR AU 90 VOL: 7 PG:278 - 294 :: REGRESS. :SEC. :THEORY :METHOD.

RICHARDSON,AJ CIT: 1
CORPORATISM AND INTRAPROFESSIONAL HEGEMONY: A STUDY OF REGULATION AND INTERNAL SOCIAL ORDER
AOS 06 89 VOL: 14 PG:415 - 431 :: REGRESS. :SEC. :HIST. :ORG.& ENVIR.

RICHARDSON,AJ CIT: 0.6
ACCOUNTING KNOWLEDGE AND PROFESSIONAL PRIVILEGE
AOS 04 88 VOL: 13 PG:381 - 396 :: REGRESS. :PRIM. :INSTIT. :INT.DIFF.

RICHARDSON,AJ CIT: 1.5
ACCOUNTING AS A LEGITIMATING INSTITUTION
AOS 04 87 VOL: 12 PG:341 - 355 :: DES.STAT. :INT. LOG. :THEORY :FIN.METH.

RICHARDSON,AW CIT: 0
COMMENT ON: "DISTINGUISHING THE TWO FORMS OF THE CONSTANT PERCENTAGE LEARNING CURVE MODEL"
CAR SP 88 VOL: 4 PG:609 - 614 :: DES.STAT. :SIM. :THEORY :REL.COSTS

RICHARDSON,E ; FIRS: DONTOH,A CIT: 0
ON INTERIM INFORMATION AND THE INFORMATION CONTENT OF FIRM EARNINGS: A STATE VARIABLE APPROACH
CAR SP 88 VOL: 4 PG:450 - 469 :: ANOVA :PRIM. :EMH :INT.REP.

RICHARDSON,G ; FIRS: CLARKSON,PM ; SEC: DONTOH,A ; FOUR: SEFCIK,SE CIT: 0
THE VOLUNTARY INCLUSION OF EARNINGS FORECASTS IN IPO PROSPECTUSES
CAR SP 92 VOL: 8 PG:601 - 625 :: REGRESS. :PRIM. :TIME SER. :VALUAT.(INFL.)

RICHARDSON,G ; SEC: SEFCIK,SE ; THIR: THOMPSON,R CIT: 0
TRADING VOLUME REACTIONS TO A CHANGE IN DIVIDEND POLICY: THE CANADIAN APPROACH
CAR AU 88 VOL: 5 PG:299 - 317 :: REGRESS. :PRIM. :TIME SER. :CASH DIV.

RICHARDSON,G ; FIRS: ELLIOTT,JA ; THIR: DYCKMAN,TR ; FOUR: DUKES ,RE CIT: 1
THE IMPACT OF SFAS NO.2 ON FIRM EXPENDITURES ON RESEARCH AND DEVELOPMENT: REPLICATIONS AND EXTENSIONS
JAR SP 84 VOL: 22 PG:85 - 102 :: NON-PAR. :PRIM. :EMH :R & D

RICHARDSON,G ; FIRS: MORSE ,D CIT: 1.7
THE LIFO/FIFO DECISION
JAR SP 83 VOL: 21 PG:106 - 127 :: DES.STAT. :PRIM. :OTH.STAT. :INV.

RICHARDSON,GD ; FIRS: BROWN ,LD ; THIR: TRZCINKA,CA CIT: 0.5
STRONG-FORM EFFICIENCY ON THE TORONTO STOCK EXCHANGE: AN EXAMINATION OF ANALYST PRICE FORECASTS
CAR SP 91 VOL: 7 PG:323 - 346 :: REGRESS. :PRIM. :EMH :FOREC.

RICHARDSON,GD ; FIRS: BROWN ,LD ; THIR: SCHWAGER,SJ CIT: 1.5
AN INFORMATION INTERPRETATION OF FINANCIAL ANALYST SUPERIORITY IN FORECASTING EARNINGS
JAR SP 87 VOL: 25 PG:49 - 67 :: REGRESS. :PRIM. :TIME SER. :FOREC.

RICKS ,RB CIT: 0.06
YEAR TO SWITCH TO STRAIGHT LINE DEPRECIATION
TAR JL 64 VOL: 39 PG:685 - 688 :: ANAL. :INT. LOG. :N/A :PP&E / DEPR

RICKS ,WE ; FIRS: BIDDLE,GC CIT: 0.2
ANALYST FORECAST ERRORS AND STOCK PRICE BEHAVIOR NEAR THE EARNINGS ANNOUNCEMENT DATES OF LIFO ADOPTERS
JAR AU 88 VOL: 26 PG:169 - 194 :: REGRESS. :PRIM. :EMH :INV.

RICKS ,WE ; FIRS: BABER ,WR ; SEC: BROOKS,EH CIT: 0.67
AN EMPIRICAL INVESTIGATION OF THE MARKET FOR AUDIT SERVICES IN THE PUBLIC SECTOR
JAR AU 87 VOL: 25 PG:293 - 305 :: REGRESS. :PRIM. :OTH.STAT. :ORG.

RICKS ,WE ; FIRS: HUGHES,JS CIT: 1
ASSOCIATIONS BETWEEN FORECAST ERRORS AND EXCESS RETURNS NEAR TO EARNINGS ANNOUNCEMENTS
TAR JA 87 VOL: 62 PG:158 - 175 :: REGRESS. :PRIM. :EMH :FOREC.

RICKS ,WE ; FIRS: HUGHES,JS CIT: 0
MARKET REACTIONS TO MANDATED INTEREST CAPITALIZATION
CAR SP 86 VOL: 2 PG:222 - 241 :: REGRESS. :PRIM. :EMH :FIN.METH.

RICKS ,WE CIT: 0.71
FIRM SIZE EFFECTS AND THE ASSOCIATION BETWEEN EXCESS RETURNS AND LIFO
JAR SP 86 VOL: 24 PG:206 - 216 :: REGRESS. :PRIM. :EMH :INV.

RICKS ,WE ; FIRS: HOSKIN,RE ; SEC: HUGHES,JS CIT: 1.43
EVIDENCE ON THE INCREMENTAL INFORMATION CONTENT OF ADDITIONAL FIRM DISCLOSURES MADE CONCURRENTLY WITH EARNINGS
JAR ST 86 VOL: 24 PG:1 - 36 :: REGRESS. :PRIM. :EMH :SPEC.ITEMS

RICKS ,WE ; SEC: HUGHES,JS CIT: 0.25
MARKET REACTIONS TO A NON-DISCRETIONARY ACCOUNTING CHANGE: THE CASE OF LONG-TERM INVESTMENTS
TAR JA 85 VOL: 60 PG:33 - 52 :: ANOVA :PRIM. :EMH :ACC.CHNG.

RICKS ,WE ; FIRS: HUGHES,JS CIT: 0.89
ACCOUNTING FOR RETAIL LAND SALES: ANALYSIS OF A MANDATED CHANGE
JAE AG 84 VOL: 6 PG:101 - 132 :: REGRESS. :PRIM. :EMH :ACC.CHNG.

RICKS ,WE CIT: 2.27
THE MARKET'S RESPONSE TO THE 1974 LIFO ADOPTIONS
JAR AU 82 VOL: 20 PG:367 - 387 :: REGRESS. :PRIM. :EMH :INV.

RIDDLE JR,JR ; FIRS: BIDWELL III,CM CIT: 0
MARKET INEFFICIENCIES - OPPORTUNITIES FOR PROFITS
JAA SP 81 VOL: 4 PG:198 - 214 :: REGRESS. :PRIM. :EMH :INFO.STRUC.

RITTENBERG,LE ; FIRS: FARMER,TA ; THIR: TROMPETER,GM CIT: 0.5
AN INVESTIGATION OF THE IMPACT OF ECONOMIC AND ORGANIZATIONAL FACTORS
AUD AU 87 VOL: 7 PG:1 - 14 :: REGRESS. :LAB. :OTH.BEH. :INDEP.

RITTENBERG,LE ; FIRS: NAIR ,RD CIT: 0
MESSAGES PERCEIVED FROM AUDIT, REVIEW, AND COMPILATION REPORTS: EXTENSION
AUD AU 87 VOL: 7 PG:15 - 38 :: REGRESS. :LAB. :HIPS :AUD.THEOR.

RITTENBERG,LE ; FIRS: NAIR ,RD CIT: 0
ACCOUNTING COSTS OF PRIVATELY HELD BUSINESSES
JAA SP 83 VOL: 6 PG:234 - 243 :: DES.STAT. :SURV. :OTH.BEH. :N/A

RITTS ,BA CIT: 0.12
A STUDY OF THE IMPACT OF APB OPINIONS UPON PRACTICING CPAS
JAR SP 74 VOL: 12 PG:93 - 111 :: DES.STAT. :SURV. :THEORY :FASB SUBM.

RIVERA,JM ; FIRS: ELLIOTT,EL ; SEC: LARREA,J CIT: 0
ACCOUNTING AID TO DEVELOPING COUNTRIES: SOME ADDITIONAL CONSIDERATIONS
TAR OC 68 VOL: 43 PG:763 - 768 :: QUAL. :INT. LOG. :INSTIT. :OTH.MANAG.

RO ,B ; FIRS: KROSS ,W ; THIR: SCHROEDER,D CIT: 0.67
EARNINGS EXPECTATIONS: THE ANALYSTS' INFORMATION ADVANTAGE
TAR AP 90 VOL: 65 PG:461 - 476 :: REGRESS. :PRIM. :TIME SER. :FOREC.

RO ,BT CIT: 0
EARNINGS NEWS AND THE FIRM SIZE EFFECT
CAR AU 89 VOL: 6 PG:177 - 195 :: REGRESS. :PRIM. :EMH :FIN.METH.

RO ,BT ; FIRS: JANG ,HJ CIT: 0.25
TRADING VOLUME THEORIES AND THEIR IMPLICATIONS FOR EMPIRICAL INFORMATION CONTENT STUDIES
CAR AU 89 VOL: 6 PG:242 - 262 :: DES.STAT. :INT. LOG. :MATH.PROG. :METHOD.

RO ,BT CIT: 0.4
FIRM SIZE AND THE INFORMATION CONTENT OF ANNUAL EARNINGS ANNOUNCEMENTS
CAR SP 88 VOL: 4 PG:438 - 449 :: REGRESS. :PRIM. :EMH :FIN.METH.

RO ,BT CIT: 0.33
THE DISCLOSURE OF REPLACEMENT COST ACCOUNTING DATA AND ITS EFFECT ON TRANSACTION VOLUMES
TAR JA 81 VOL: 56 PG:70 - 84 :: ANOVA :PRIM. :EMH :VALUAT.(INFL.)

RO ,BT CIT: 1.15
THE ADJUSTMENT OF SECURITY RETURNS TO THE DISCLOSURE OF REPLACEMENT COST ACCOUNTING INFORMATION
JAE AG 80 VOL: 2 PG:159 - 189 :: REGRESS. :PRIM. :EMH :VALUAT.(INFL.)

RO ,BT CIT: 0.47
THE DISCLOSURES OF CAPITALIZED LEASE INFORMATION AND STOCK PRICES
JAR AU 78 VOL: 16 PG:315 - 340 :: REGRESS. :PRIM. :EMH :LEASES

ROAN ,J ; FIRS: LIANG ,T-P ; SEC: CHANDLER,JS ; THIR: HAN ,I CIT: 0
AN EMPIRICAL INVESTIGATION OF SOME DATA EFFECTS ON THE CLASSIFICATION ACCURACY OF PROBIT, ID3 AND NEURAL NETWORKS
CAR AU 92 VOL: 9 PG:306 - 328 :: DES.STAT. :PRIM. :OTH.STAT. :METHOD.

ROARK ,SJ ; FIRS: KAPLAN,SE ; SEC: RECKERS,PMJ CIT: 0
AN ATTRIBUTION THEORY ANALYSIS OF TAX EVASION RELATED JUDGMENTS
AOS 04 88 VOL: 13 PG:371 - 379 :: REGRESS. :LAB. :OTH.BEH. :TAXES

ROBBINS,SM CIT: 0
RISK ANALYSIS IN CAPITAL BUDGETING
JAA AU 77 VOL: 1 PG:5 - 18 :: ANAL. :INT. LOG. :OTH. :CAP.BUDG.

ROBBINS,WA ; SEC: AUSTIN,KR CIT: 0.14
DISCLOSURE QUALITY IN GOVERNMENT FINANCIAL REPORTS: AN ASSESSMENT OF THE APPROPRIATENESS OF A COMPOUND MEASURE
JAR AU 86 VOL: 24 PG:412 - 421 :: REGRESS. :SURV. :THEORY :METHOD.

ROBBINS,WA ; SEC: APOSTOLOU,NG ; THIR: STRAWSER,RH CIT: 0
MUNICIPAL ANNUAL REPORTS AND THE INFORMATION NEEDS OF INVESTORS
JAA SU 85 VOL: 8 PG:279 - 292 :: REGRESS. :PRIM. :THEORY :FIN.METH.

ROBERTS,DM CIT: 0
STRATIFIED SAMPLING USING A STOCHASTIC MODEL
JAR SP 86 VOL: 24 PG:111 - 126 :: DES.STAT. :SIM. :OTH.STAT. :SAMP.

ROBERTS,DM CIT: 0
CONTROLLING AUDIT RISK - A METHOD FOR OPTIMAL SAMPLE DESIGN
JAA AU 80 VOL: 4 PG:57 - 69 :: ANAL. :INT. LOG. :THEORY :SAMP.

ROBERTS,J ; SEC: COUTTS,JA CIT: 0
FEMINIZATION AND PROFESSIONALIZATION: A REVIEW OF AN EMERGING LITERATURE ON THE DEVELOPMENT OF ACCOUNTING IN THE UNITED KINGDOM
AOS 04 92 VOL: 17 PG:379 - 395 :: REGRESS. :SEC. :HIST. :ORG.& ENVIR.

ROBERTS,J CIT: 1.5
THE POSSIBILITIES OF ACCOUNTABILITY
AOS 04 91 VOL: 16 PG:355 - 368 :: DES.STAT. :INT. LOG. :THEORY :PROF.RESP.

ROBERTS,J CIT: 1
STRATEGY AND ACCOUNTING IN A U.K. CONGLOMERATE
AOS 02 90 VOL: 15 PG:107 - 126 :: REGRESS. :CASE :OTH. :ORG.& ENVIR.

ROBERTS,J ; SEC: SCAPENS,RW CIT: 2
ACCOUNTING SYSTEMS AND SYSTEMS OF ACCOUNTABILITY - UNDERSTANDING ACCOUNTING PRACTICES IN THEIR ORGANIZATIONAL CONTEXTS
AOS 04 85 VOL: 10 PG:443 - 456 :: DES.STAT. :INT. LOG. :THEORY :FIN.METH.

ROBERTS,RW CIT: 0
DETERMINANTS OF CORPORATE SOCIAL RESPONSIBILITY DISCLOSURE: AN APPLICATION OF STAKEHOLDER THEORY
AOS 06 92 VOL: 17 PG:595 - 612 :: REGRESS. :PRIM. :OTH.STAT. :ORG.& ENVIR.

ROBERTS,RW ; SEC: GLEZEN,GW ; THIR: JONES ,TW CIT: 0.67
DETERMINANTS OF AUDIT CHANGE IN THE PUBLIC SECTOR
JAR SP 90 VOL: 28 PG:220 - 228 :: REGRESS. :PRIM. :OTH.STAT. :ORG.

ROBERTSON,JC CIT: 0.11
A DEFENSE OF EXTANT AUDITING THEORY
AUD SP 84 VOL: 3 PG:57 - 67 :: QUAL. :INT. LOG. :THEORY :AUD.THEOR.

ROBERTSON,JC ; SEC: ALDERMAN,CW CIT: 0
COMPARATIVE AUDITING STANDARDS
JAA WI 81 VOL: 4 PG:144 - 161 :: QUAL. :INT. LOG. :THEORY :ORG.

ROBERTSON,JC ; FIRS: BOATSMAN,JR CIT: 1
POLICY-CAPTURING ON SELECTED MATERIALITY JUDGMENTS
TAR AP 74 VOL: 49 PG:342 - 352 :: OTH.QUANT. :LAB. :OTH.STAT. :OTH.FIN.ACC.

ROBERTSON,JC ; SEC: CLARKE,RW CIT: 0.12
VERIFICATION OF MANAGEMENT REPRESENTATIONS: A FIRST STEP TOWARD INDEPENDENT AUDITS OF MANAGEMENT
TAR JL 71 VOL: 46 PG:562 - 571 :: DES.STAT. :PRIM. :N/A :AUD.

ROBERTSON,JC ; FIRS: LANGENDERFER,HQ CIT: 0.06
A THEORETICAL STRUCTURE FOR INDEPENDENT AUDITS OF MANAGEMENT
TAR OC 69 VOL: 44 PG:777 - 787 :: QUAL. :INT. LOG. :INSTIT. :OTH.MANAG.

ROBICHEK,AA ; FIRS: JAEDICKE,RK CIT: 0.47
COST-VOLUME-PROFIT ANALYSIS UNDER CONDITIONS OF UNCERTAINTY
TAR OC 64 VOL: 39 PG:917 - 926 :: ANAL. :INT. LOG. :OTH.STAT. :C-V-P-A

ROBIN ,DP ; FIRS: FLORY ,SM ; SEC: PHILLIPS JR,TJ ; THIR: REIDENBACH,RE CIT: 0
A MULTIDIMENSIONAL ANALYSIS OF SELECTED ETHICAL ISSUES IN ACCOUNTING
TAR AP 92 VOL: 67 PG:284 - 302 :: REGRESS. :SURV. :HIPS :JUDG.

ROBINSON,CF ; FIRS: TEITLEBAUM,AD CIT: 0.29
THE REAL RISKS IN AUDIT SAMPLING
JAR ST 75 VOL: 13 PG:70 - 91 :: MIXED :INT. LOG. :OTH.STAT. :SAMP.

ROBINSON,JR ; SEC: SHANE ,PB CIT: 0
ACQUISITION ACCOUNTING METHOD AND BID PREMIA FOR TARGET FIRMS
TAR JA 90 VOL: 65 PG:25 - 48 :: REGRESS. :PRIM. :OTH.STAT. :BUS.COMB.

ROBINSON,LA ; SEC: HALL ,TP CIT: 0
SYSTEMS EDUCATION AND THE ACCOUNTING CURRICULUM
TAR JA 64 VOL: 39 PG:62 - 69 :: QUAL. :INT. LOG. :N/A :OTH.MANAG.

ROBSON,K CIT: 0
ACCOUNTING NUMBERS AS "INSCRIPTION": ACTION AT A DISTANCE AND THE DEVELOPMENT OF ACCOUNTING
AOS 92 VOL: 17 PG:685 - 708 :: DES.STAT. :INT. LOG. :THEORY :INFO.STRUC.

ROBSON,K CIT: 0.5
ON THE ARENAS OF ACCOUNTING CHANGE: THE PROCESS OF TRANSLATION
AOS 05 91 VOL: 16 PG:547 - 570 :: REGRESS. :SEC. :HIST. :ORG.& ENVIR.

ROCKNESS,HO ; SEC: SHIELDS,MD CIT: 0
AN EMPIRICAL ANALYSIS OF THE EXPENDITURE BUDGET IN RESEARCH AND DEVELOPMENT
CAR SP 88 VOL: 4 PG:568 - 581 :: REGRESS. :PRIM. :THEORY :R & D

ROCKNESS,HO ; SEC: SHIELDS,MD CIT: 0.67
ORGANIZATIONAL CONTROL SYSTEMS IN RESEARCH AND DEVELOPMENT
AOS 02 84 VOL: 9 PG:165 - 177 :: CORR. :SURV. :OTH.BEH. :R & D

ROCKNESS,HO CIT: 0.69
EXPECTANCY THEORY IN A BUDGETARY SETTING: AN EXPERIMENTAL EXAMINATION
TAR OC 77 VOL: 52 PG:893 - 903 :: ANOVA :LAB. :OTH.BEH. :BUDG.& PLAN.

ROCKNESS,J ; SEC: WILLIAMS,PF CIT: 0.2
A DESCRIPTIVE STUDY OF SOCIAL RESPONSIBILITY MUTUAL FUNDS
AOS 04 88 VOL: 13 PG:397 - 411 :: REGRESS. :SURV. :INSTIT. :HRA

RODEN ,PF CIT: 0
THE FINANCIAL IMPLICATIONS OF IN-SUBSTANCE DEFEASANCE
JAA WI 87 VOL: 2 PG:79 - 89 :: DES.STAT. :INT. LOG. :THEORY :LTD

RODGERS,RC ; FIRS: COOPER,WW ; SEC: HO ,JL ; THIR: HUNTER,JE CIT: 0
THE IMPACT OF THE FOREIGN CORRUPT PRACTICES ACT ON INTERNAL CONTROL PRACTICES
JAA AU 85 VOL: 9 PG:22 - 39 :: REGRESS. :SEC. :THEORY :INT.CONT.

RODGERS,W CIT: 0
THE EFFECTS OF ACCOUNTING INFORMATION ON INDIVIDUALS' PERCEPTUAL PROCESSES
JAA WI 92 VOL: 7 PG:67 - 95 :: REGRESS. :LAB. :HIPS :FIN.METH.

ROGERSON,WP CIT: 3
OVERHEAD ALLOCATION AND INCENTIVES FOR COST MINIMIZATION IN DEFENSE PROCUREMENT
TAR OC 92 VOL: 67 PG:671 - 690 :: REGRESS. :INT. LOG. :MATH.PROG. :OVER.ALLOC.

ROHRBACH,K ; FIRS: CHANDRA,R CIT: 0.33
A METHODOLOGICAL NOTE ON DETECTING A LOCATION SHIFT IN THE DISTRIBUTION OF ABNORMAL RETURNS: A NONPARAMETRIC APPROACH
CAR AU 90 VOL: 7 PG:123 - 141 :: DES.STAT. :SIM. :EMH :METHOD.

ROHRBACH,KJ ; FIRS: CHANDRA,R ; THIR: WILLINGER,GL CIT: 0
LONGITUDINAL RANK TESTS FOR DETECTING LOCATION SHIFT IN THE DISTRIBUTION OF ABNORMAL RETURNS: AN EXTENSION
CAR AU 92 VOL: 9 PG:296 - 305 :: DES.STAT. :SIM. :TIME SER. :METHOD.

ROHRBACH.KJ CIT: 0
MONETARY UNIT ACCEPTANCE SAMPLING
JAR SP 86 VOL: 24 PG:127 - 150 :: DES.STAT. :SIM. :OTH.STAT. :SAMP.

ROLLER,J ; SEC: WILLIAMS,TH CIT: 0
PROFESSIONAL SCHOOLS OF ACCOUNTING
TAR AP 67 VOL: 42 PG:349 - 355 :: QUAL. :INT. LOG. :INSTIT. :OTH.MANAG.

ROMNEY,MB ; FIRS: SOLOMON,I ; SEC: KROGSTAD,JL ; FOUR: TOMASSINI,LA CIT: 0.64
AUDITORS' PRIOR PROBABILITY DISTRIBUTIONS FOR ACCOUNT BALANCES
AOS 01 82 VOL: 7 PG:27 - 42 :: DES.STAT. :LAB. :HIPS :PROB.ELIC.

RONEN ,J ; FIRS: MOORE ,G CIT: 0
EXTERNAL AUDIT AND ASYMMETRIC INFORMATION
AUD 90 VOL: 9 PG:234 - 242 :: DES.STAT. :INT. LOG. :INF.ECO./AG. :INFO.STRUC.

RONEN ,J ; FIRS: JOHN ,K CIT: 0
EVOLUTION OF INFORMATION STRUCTURES, OPTIMAL CONTRACTS AND THE THEORY OF THE FIRM
JAA WI 90 VOL: 5 PG:61 - 95 :: DES.STAT. :INT. LOG. :INF.ECO./AG. :INFO.STRUC.

RONEN ,J ; SEC: SORTER,G CIT: 0
REFLECTIONS ON "REFLECTIONS ON THE FASB'S CONCEPTUAL FRAMEWORK FOR ACCOUNTING AND ON AUDITING"
JAA WI 89 VOL: 4 PG:67 - 77 :: REGRESS. :SEC. :INSTIT. :FASB SUBM.

RONEN ,J ; SEC: SONDHI,AC CIT: 0.25
DEBT CAPACITY AND FINANCIAL CONTRACTING: FINANCE SUBSIDIARIES
JAA SP 89 VOL: 4 PG:237 - 265 :: ANOVA :MIXED :OTH.STAT. :SPEC.ITEMS

RONEN ,J ; SEC: AHARONI,A CIT: 0.25
THE CHOICE AMONG ACCOUNTING ALTERNATIVES AND MANAGEMENT COMPENSATION: EFFECTS OF CORPORATE TAX
TAR JA 89 VOL: 64 PG:69 - 86 :: REGRESS. :SURV. :OTH.BEH. :TAX PLNG.

RONEN ,J ; FIRS: NELSON,J ; THIR: WHITE ,L CIT: 0.2
LEGAL LIABILITIES AND THE MARKET FOR AUDITING SERVICES
JAA SU 88 VOL: 03 PG:255 - 296 :: DES.STAT. :INT. LOG. :INF.ECO./AG. :LIAB.

RONEN ,J ; SEC: BALACHANDRAN,KR CIT: 0.4
AN APPROACH TO TRANSFER PRICING UNDER UNCERTAINTY
JAR AU 88 VOL: 26 PG:300 - 314 :: ANAL. :INT. LOG. :INF.ECO./AG. :TRANS.PRIC.

RONEN ,J ; FIRS: BILDERSEE,JS CIT: 0.17
STOCK RETURNS AND REAL ACTIVITY IN AN INFLATIONARY ENVIRONMENT: THE INFORMATIONAL IMPACT OF FAS NO. 33
CAR AU 87 VOL: 4 PG:89 - 110 :: REGRESS. :PRIM. :EMH :VALUAT.(INFL.)

RONEN ,J ; FIRS: OVADIA,A CIT: 0.1
ON THE VALUE OF CURRENT-COST INFORMATION
JAA WI 83 VOL: 6 PG:115 - 129 :: ANAL. :INT. LOG. :THEORY :VALUAT.(INFL.)

RONEN ,J ; SEC: LIVNAT,J CIT: 0.17
INCENTIVES FOR SEGMENT REPORTING
JAR AU 81 VOL: 19 PG:459 - 481 :: ANAL. :INT. LOG. :EMH :SEG.REP.

RONEN ,J ; FIRS: OVADIA,A CIT: 0.08
GENERAL PRICE-LEVEL ADJUSTMENT AND REPLACEMENT COST ACCOUNTING AS SPECIAL CASES OF THE INDEX NUMBER PROBLEM
JAA WI 80 VOL: 3 PG:113 - 137 :: ANAL. :SEC. :TIME SER. :VALUAT.(INFL.)

RONEN ,J ; SEC: SADAN ,S CIT: 0.15
ACCOUNTING CLASSIFICATION AS A TOOL FOR INCOME PREDICTION
JAA SU 80 VOL: 3 PG:339 - 353 :: DES.STAT. :SEC. :TIME SER. :FOREC.

RONEN ,J ; FIRS: PASTENA,V CIT: 0.43
SOME HYPOTHESES ON THE PATTERN OF MANAGEMENT'S INFORMAL DISCLOSURES
JAR AU 79 VOL: 17 PG:550 - 564 :: NON-PAR. :PRIM. :OTH. :OTH.MANAG.

RONEN ,J ; FIRS: KAMIN ,JY CIT: 0.2
THE SMOOTHING ON INCOME NUMBERS: SOME EMPIRICAL EVIDENCE OF SYSTEMATIC DIFFERENCES AMONG MANAGEMENT AND OWNER-CONTROLLED FIRMS
AOS 02 78 VOL: 3 PG:141 - 160 :: ANOVA :PRIM. :OTH.STAT. :N/A

RONEN ,J ; FIRS: GIVOLY,D ; THIR: SCHIFF,A CIT: 0.07
DOES AUDIT INVOLVEMENT AFFECT THE QUALITY OF INTERIM REPORT NUMBERS?
JAA SU 78 VOL: 1 PG:361 - 372 :: ANOVA :PRIM. :INSTIT. :AUD.

RONEN ,J CIT: 0.31
THE EFFECT OF INSIDER TRADING RULES ON INFORMATION GENERATION AND DISCLOSURE BY CORPORATIONS
TAR AP 77 VOL: 52 PG:438 - 449 :: QUAL. :INT. LOG. :THEORY :INS.TRAD.

RONEN ,J ; FIRS: BARNEA,A ; THIR: SADAN ,S CIT: 0.29
CLASSIFICATORY SMOOTHING OF INCOME WITH EXTRAORDINARY ITEMS
TAR JA 76 VOL: 51 PG:110 - 122 :: REGRESS. :PRIM. :TIME SER. :INFO.STRUC.

RONEN ,J ; SEC: SADAN ,S CIT: 0.18
CLASSIFICATION SMOOTHING: ALTERNATIVE INCOME MODELS
JAR SP 75 VOL: 13 PG:133 - 149 :: CORR. :PRIM. :THEORY :REV.REC.

RONEN ,J ; FIRS: BARNEA,A ; THIR: SADAN ,S CIT: 0.24
THE IMPLEMENTATION OF ACCOUNTING OBJECTIVES: AN APPLICATION TO EXTRAORDINARY ITEMS
TAR JA 75 VOL: 50 PG:58 - 68 :: ANAL. :INT. LOG. :THEORY :SPEC.ITEMS

RONEN ,J ; SEC: LIVINGSTONE,JL CIT: 1.65
AN EXPECTANCY THEORY APPROACH TO THE MOTIVATIONAL IMPACTS OF BUDGETS
TAR OC 75 VOL: 50 PG:671 - 685 :: QUAL. :INT. LOG. :OTH.BEH. :BUDG.& PLAN.

RONEN ,J ; FIRS: BECKER,S ; THIR: SORTER,GH CIT: 0.35
OPPORTUNITY COSTS - AN EXPERIMENTAL APPROACH
JAR AU 74 VOL: 12 PG:317 - 329 :: ANOVA :LAB. :OTH.BEH. :REL.COSTS

RONEN ,J CIT: 0.18
NONAGGREGATION VERSUS DISAGGREGATION OF VARIANCES
TAR JA 74 VOL: 49 PG:50 - 60 :: ANAL. :INT. LOG. :OTH.STAT. :VAR.

RONEN ,J ; FIRS: DOPUCH,N CIT: 0.47
THE EFFECTS OF ALTERNATIVE INVENTORY VALUATION METHODS - AN EXPERIMENTAL STUDY
JAR AU 73 VOL: 11 PG:191 - 211 :: DES.STAT. :LAB. :THEORY :INV.

RONEN ,J ; SEC: FALK ,G CIT: 0.12
ACCOUNTING AGGREGATION AND THE ENTROPY MEASURE: AN EXPERIMENTAL APPROACH
TAR OC 73 VOL: 48 PG:696 - 717 :: NON-PAR. :LAB. :INF.ECO./AG. :INFO.STRUC.

RONEN ,J CIT: 0.47
SOME EFFECTS OF SEQUENTIAL AGGREGATION IN ACCOUNTING ON DECISION-MAKING
JAR AU 71 VOL: 9 PG:307 - 332 :: ANOVA :LAB. :OTH.BEH. :INFO.STRUC.

RONEN ,J ; SEC: MCKINNEY,G CIT: 0.47
TRANSFER PRICING FOR DIVISIONAL AUTONOMY
JAR SP 70 VOL: 8 PG:99 - 112 :: ANAL. :INT. LOG. :OTH. :TRANS.PRIC.

RONEN ,J CIT: 0
CAPACITY AND OPERATING VARIANCES: AN EX POST APPROACH
JAR AU 70 VOL: 8 PG:232 - 252 :: ANAL. :INT. LOG. :OTH.STAT. :VAR.

RORKE ,CH CIT: 0
AN EARLY PRICING MODEL REGARDING THE VALUE OF A CAT: A HISTORICAL NOTE
AOS 03 82 VOL: 7 PG:305 - 306 :: QUAL. :INT. LOG. :THEORY :VALUAT.(INFL.)

ROSE ,H CIT: 0
SOURCES AND USES: A BRITISH VIEW
JAR AU 64 VOL: 2 PG:137 - 147 :: QUAL. :INT. LOG. :THEORY :INT.DIFF.

ROSE ,PS ; SEC: ANDREWS,WT ; THIR: GIROUX,GA CIT: 0
PREDICTING BUSINESS FAILURE: A MACROECONOMIC PERSPECTIVE
JAA AU 82 VOL: 6 PG:20 - 31 :: REGRESS. :PRIM. :TIME SER. :BUS.FAIL.

ROSE ,R ; SEC: BEAVER,WH ; THIR: BECKER,S ; FOUR: SORTER,GH CIT: 0.65
TOWARD AN EMPIRICAL MEASURE OF MATERIALITY
JAR ST 70 VOL: 8 PG:138 - 148 :: DES.STAT. :LAB. :OTH.BEH. :MAT.

ROSEN ,LS ; SEC: DECOSTER,DT CIT: 0
FUNDS STATEMENTS: A HISTORICAL PERSPECTIVE
TAR JA 69 VOL: 44 PG:124 - 136 :: QUAL. :SEC. :HIST. :FIN.METH.

ROSEN ,LS CIT: 0
REPLACEMENT-VALUE ACCOUNTING
TAR JA 67 VOL: 42 PG:106 - 113 :: QUAL. :INT. LOG. :THEORY :VALUAT.(INFL.)

ROSENBERG,D ; SEC: TOMKINS,L ; THIR: DAY ,P CIT: 0.18
A WORK ROLE PERSPECTIVE OF ACCOUNTANTS IN LOCAL GOVERNMENT SERVICE DEPARTMENTS
AOS 02 82 VOL: 7 PG:123 - 138 :: QUAL. :SURV. :OTH.BEH. :N/A

ROSENFELD,A ; FIRS: LEWELLEN,W ; SEC: LODERER,C CIT: 0.5
MERGER DECISIONS AND EXECUTIVE STOCK OWNERSHIP IN ACQUIRING FIRMS
JAE AP 85 VOL: 7 PG:209 - 232 :: REGRESS. :PRIM. :OTH.STAT. :BUS.COMB.

ROSENFELD,J ; FIRS: ALI ,A ; SEC: KLEIN ,A CIT: 0
ANALYSTS' USE OF INFORMATION ABOUT PERMANENT AND TRANSITORY EARNINGS COMPONENTS IN FORECASTING ANNUAL EPS
TAR JA 92 VOL: 67 PG:183 - 198 :: REGRESS. :PRIM. :TIME SER. :FOREC.

ROSENFIELD,P CIT: 0
REPORTING SUBJUNCTIVE GAINS AND LOSSES
TAR OC 69 VOL: 44 PG:788 - 797 :: QUAL. :INT. LOG. :THEORY :VALUAT.(INFL.)

ROSENFIELD,P ; SEC: STOREY,R CIT: 0.06
THE ACCOUNTING PRINCIPLES BOARD - A CORRECTION
TAR AP 66 VOL: 41 PG:327 - 330 :: QUAL. :INT. LOG. :INSTIT. :N/A

ROSENZWEIG,K CIT: 0.08
AN EXPLORATORY FIELD STUDY OF THE RELATIONSHIPS BETWEEN CONTROLLER'S DEPARTMENT AND OVERALL ORGANIZATIONAL CHARACTERISTICS
AOS 04 81 VOL: 6 PG:339 - 354 :: CORR. :SURV. :OTH.BEH. :MANAG.

ROSHWALB,A ; SEC: WRIGHT,RL CIT: 0
USING INFORMATION IN ADDITION TO BOOK VALUE IN SAMPLE DESIGNS FOR INVENTORY COST ESTIMATOR
TAR AP 91 VOL: 66 PG:348 - 360 :: DES.STAT. :INT. LOG. :MATH.PROG. :ERRORS

ROSHWALB,A ; SEC: WRIGHT,RL ; THIR: GODFREY,JT CIT: 0
A NEW APPROACH FOR STRATIFIED SAMPLING IN INVENTORY COST ESTIMATION
AUD AU 87 VOL: 7 PG:54 - 70 :: DES.STAT. :SIM. :OTH.STAT. :SAMP.

ROSMAN,A CIT: 0
FASB STATEMENT NO. 94: DO LENDERS CONTRACT ON CONSOLIDATED INFORMATION
JAA SP 92 VOL: 7 PG:251 - 267 :: REGRESS. :PRIM. :OTH.STAT. :BUS.COMB.

ROSS ,H CIT: 0
THE WONDERFUL WORLD OF ACCOUNTING
JAR ST 70 VOL: 8 PG:108 - 115 :: QUAL. :INT. LOG. :INSTIT. :FIN.METH.

ROSS ,WR ; FIRS: HALL ,TW ; SEC: PIERCE,BJ CIT: 0
PLANNING SAMPLE SIZES FOR STRINGER-METHOD MONETARY UNIT AND SINGLE-STAGE ATTRIBUTE SAMPLING PLANS
AUD SP 89 VOL: 8 PG:64 - 89 :: DES.STAT. :SIM. :OTH.STAT. :SAMP.

ROSS ,WR CIT: 0
PERT/COST RESOURCE ALLOCATION PROCEDURE
TAR JL 66 VOL: 41 PG:464 - 473 :: ANAL. :INT. LOG. :OTH.STAT. :BUDG.& PLAN.

ROTENBERG,W ; FIRS: KRINSKY,I CIT: 0
THE VALUATION OF INITIAL PUBLIC OFFERINGS
CAR SP 89 VOL: 5 PG:501 - 515 :: REGRESS. :PRIM. :EMH :VALUAT.(INFL.)

ROUSSEY,RS CIT: 0
AUDITING ENVIRONMENTAL LIABILITIES
AUD SP 92 VOL: 11 PG:47 - 57 :: DES.STAT. :SEC. :THEORY :ORG.& ENVIR.

ROUSSEY,RS ; FIRS: FELIX JR,WL ; SEC: GRIMLUND,RA ; THIR: KOSTER,FJ CIT: 0
ARTHUR ANDERSEN'S NEW MONETARY UNIT SAMPLING APPROACH
AUD AU 90 VOL: 9 PG:1 - 16 :: DES.STAT. :SIM. :EXP.SYST. :SAMP.

ROZEFF,MS ; FIRS: COLLINS,DW ; THIR: SALATKA,WK CIT: 0.73
THE SEC'S REJECTION OF SFAS NO.19: TESTS OF MARKET PRICE REVERSAL
TAR JA 82 VOL: 57 PG:1 - 17 :: CORR. :PRIM. :EMH :OIL & GAS

ROZEFF,MS ; FIRS: COLLINS,DW ; THIR: DHALIWAL,DS CIT: 3.33
THE ECONOMIC DETERMINANTS OF THE MARKET REACTION TO PROPOSED MANDATORY ACCOUNTING CHANGES IN THE OIL AND GAS INDUSTRY: A CROSS-S
JAE MR 81 VOL: 3 PG:37 - 71 :: REGRESS. :PRIM. :EMH :OIL & GAS

ROZEFF,MS ; FIRS: BROWN ,LD ; SEC: HUGHES,JS ; FOUR: VANDERWEIDE,JH CIT: 0.08
EXPECTATIONS DATA AND THE PREDICTIVE VALUE OF INTERIM REPORTING: A COMMENT
JAR SP 80 VOL: 18 PG:278 - 288 :: REGRESS. :PRIM. :TIME SER. :FOREC.

ROZEFF,MS ; FIRS: BROWN ,LD CIT: 2.07
UNIVARIATE TIME-SERIES MODELS OF QUARTERLY ACCOUNTING EARNINGS PER SHARE: A PROPOSED MODEL
JAR SP 79 VOL: 17 PG:179 - 189 :: MIXED :PRIM. :TIME SER. :FOREC.

ROZEFF,MS ; FIRS: BROWN ,LD CIT: 0.86
ADAPTIVE EXPECTATIONS, TIME-SERIES MODELS, AND ANALYST FORECAST REVISION
JAR AU 79 VOL: 17 PG:341 - 351 :: REGRESS. :PRIM. :TIME SER. :FOREC.

ROZEFF,MS ; FIRS: BROWN ,LD CIT: 0.21
THE PREDICTIVE VALUE OF INTERIM REPORTS FOR IMPROVING FORECASTS OF FUTURE QUARTERLY EARNINGS
TAR JL 79 VOL: 54 PG:585 - 591 :: NON-PAR. :INT. LOG. :TIME SER. :FOREC.

ROZEN ,E ; FIRS: DAVIS ,HZ ; SEC: KAHN ,N CIT: 0
LIFO INVENTORY LIQUIDATIONS: AN EMPIRICAL STUDY
JAR AU 84 VOL: 22 PG:480 - 490 :: NON-PAR. :PRIM. :OTH.STAT. :INV.

RUBENSTEIN,DB CIT: 0
BRIDGING THE GAP BETWEEN GREEN ACCOUNTING AND BLACK INK
AOS 05 92 VOL: 17 PG:501 - 508 :: DES.STAT. :INT. LOG. :THEORY :OTH. NON-C/A

RUBIN ,MA CIT: 0.8
MUNICIPAL AUDIT FEE DETERMINANTS
TAR AP 88 VOL: 63 PG:219 - 236 :: REGRESS. :PRIM. :INSTIT. :ORG.

RUE ,JC ; SEC: VOLKAN,AG CIT: 0
FINANCIAL AND ECONOMIC CONSEQUENCES OF THE NEW PENSION ACCOUNTING PROPOSALS:
IS THE GLOOM JUSTIFIED?
JAA SU 84 VOL: 7 PG:306 - 322 :: DES.STAT. :PRIM. :THEORY :PENS.

RULAND,RG ; FIRS: BERNARD,VL CIT: 0.17
THE INCREMENTAL INFORMATION CONTENT OF HISTORICAL COST OME NUMBERS:
TIME-SERIES ANALYSES FOR 1962-1980
TAR OC 87 VOL: 62 PG:707 - 722 :: REGRESS. :PRIM. :EMH :VALUAT.(INFL.)

RULAND,W ; SEC: TUNG ,S ; THIR: GEORGE,NE CIT: 0
FACTORS ASSOCIATED WITH THE DISCLOSURE OF MANAGERS' FORECASTS
TAR JL 90 VOL: 65 PG:710 - 721 :: REGRESS. :PRIM. :HIPS :FOREC.

RULAND,W ; FIRS: PASTENA,V CIT: 0.71
THE MERGER/BANKRUPTCY ALTERNATIVE
TAR AP 86 VOL: 61 PG:288 - 301 :: REGRESS. :PRIM. :THEORY :BUS.COMB.

RULAND,W ; FIRS: COGGER,KO CIT: 0.09
A NOTE ON ALTERNATIVE TESTS FOR INDEPENDENCE OF FINANCIAL TIME SERIES
JAR AU 82 VOL: 20 PG:733 - 737 :: CORR. :PRIM. :TIME SER. :METHOD.

RULAND,W CIT: 0.47
THE ACCURACY OF FORECASTS BY MANAGEMENT AND BY FINANCIAL ANALYSTS
TAR AP 78 VOL: 53 PG:439 - 447 :: DES.STAT. :PRIM. :TIME SER. :FOREC.

RUNDFELT,R CIT: 0
INSIDER TRADING: REGULATION IN EUROPE
JAA SP 86 VOL: 1 PG:125 - 130 :: DES.STAT. :INT. LOG. :THEORY :LITIG.

RUSS ,A ; FIRS: MOONITZ,M CIT: 0.06
ACCRUAL ACCOUNTING FOR EMPLOYERS' PENSION COSTS
JAR AU 66 VOL: 4 PG:155 - 168 :: QUAL. :INT. LOG. :THEORY :PENS.

RYAN ,S ; FIRS: BEAVER,WH ; SEC: EGER ,C ; FOUR: WOLFSON,M CIT: 1
FINANCIAL REPORTING, SUPPLEMENTAL DISCLOSURES, AND BANK SHARE PRICES
JAR AU 89 VOL: 27 PG:157 - 178 :: REGRESS. :PRIM. :OTH.STAT. :INFO.STRUC.

RYAN ,SG CIT: 0
HISTORICAL COST ACCRUAL METHODS AND THE ROLE OF BOOK VALUE AND EARNINGS IN
LINEAR VALUATION MODELS
JAA SP 91 VOL: 6 PG:257 - 287 :: REGRESS. :PRIM. :OTH.STAT. :FIN.METH.

RYAN ,SG ; FIRS: BEAVER,WH ; SEC: LAMBERT,RA CIT: 3.33
THE INFORMATION CONTENT OF SECURITY PRICES: A SECOND LOOK
JAE JL 87 VOL: 9 PG:139 - 157 :: REGRESS. :PRIM. :EMH :FOREC.

SADAN ,S ; FIRS: RONEN ,J CIT: 0.15
ACCOUNTING CLASSIFICATION AS A TOOL FOR INCOME PREDICTION
JAA SU 80 VOL: 3 PG:339 - 353 :: DES.STAT. :SEC. :TIME SER. :FOREC.

SADAN ,S ; FIRS: BARNEA,A ; SEC: RONEN ,J CIT: 0.29
CLASSIFICATORY SMOOTHING OF INCOME WITH EXTRAORDINARY ITEMS
TAR JA 76 VOL: 51 PG:110 - 122 :: REGRESS. :PRIM. :TIME SER. :INFO.STRUC.

SADAN ,S ; FIRS: RONEN ,J CIT: 0.18
CLASSIFICATION SMOOTHING: ALTERNATIVE INCOME MODELS
JAR SP 75 VOL: 13 PG:133 - 149 :: CORR. :PRIM. :THEORY :REV.REC.

SADAN ,S ; FIRS: BARNEA,A ; SEC: RONEN ,J CIT: 0.24
THE IMPLEMENTATION OF ACCOUNTING OBJECTIVES: AN APPLICATION TO EXTRAORDINARY ITEMS
TAR JA 75 VOL: 50 PG:58 - 68 :: ANAL. :INT. LOG. :THEORY :SPEC.ITEMS

SALAMON,GL ; FIRS: DHALIWAL,DS ; THIR: SMITH ,ED CIT: 2.18
THE EFFECT OF OWNER VERSUS MANAGEMENT CONTROL ON THE CHOICE OF ACCOUNTING METHODS
JAE JL 82 VOL: 4 PG:41 - 53 :: NON-PAR. :SEC. :TIME SER. :AMOR./DEPL.

SALAMON,GL ; FIRS: KINNEY JR,WR CIT: 0.18
REGRESSION ANALYSIS IN AUDITING: A COMPARISON OF ALTERNATIVE INVESTIGATION RULES
JAR AU 82 VOL: 20 PG:350 - 366 :: REGRESS. :SIM. :OTH.STAT. :ANAL.REV.

SALAMON,GL CIT: 0.09
CASH RECOVERY RATES AND MEASURES OF FIRM PROFITABILITY
TAR AP 82 VOL: 57 PG:292 - 302 :: CORR. :INT. LOG. :OTH.STAT. :N/A

SALAMON,GL CIT: 0.12
MODELS OF THE RELATIONSHIP BETWEEN THE ACCOUNTING AND INTERNAL RATE OF RETURN: AN EXAMINATION OF THE METHODOLOGY
JAR AU 73 VOL: 11 PG:296 - 303 :: ANAL. :INT. LOG. :OTH.STAT. :FIN.METH.

SALAMON,GL ; FIRS: LIVINGSTONE,JL CIT: 0.12
RELATIONSHIP BETWEEN THE ACCOUNTING AND THE INTERNAL RATE OF RETURN MEASURES: A SYNTHESIS AND AN ANALYSIS
JAR AU 70 VOL: 8 PG:199 - 216 :: DES.STAT. :SIM. :OTH.STAT. :FIN.METH.

SALATKA,WK CIT: 0.25
THE IMPACT OF SFAS NO. 8 ON EQUITY PRICES OF EARLY AND LATE ADOPTING FIRMS: AN EVENTS STUDY AND CROSS-SECTIONAL ANALYSIS
JAE FB 89 VOL: 11 PG:35 - 69 :: REGRESS. :PRIM. :EMH :FOR.CUR.

SALATKA,WK ; FIRS: COLLINS,DW ; SEC: ROZEFF,MS CIT: 0.73
THE SEC'S REJECTION OF SFAS NO.19: TESTS OF MARKET PRICE REVERSAL
TAR JA 82 VOL: 57 PG:1 - 17 :: CORR. :PRIM. :EMH :OIL & GAS

SALE ,JT ; FIRS: SCAPENS,RW CIT: 0.25
AN INTERNATIONAL STUDY OF ACCOUNTING PRACTICES IN DIVISIONALIZED COMPANIES AND THEIR ASSOCIATIONS WITH ORGANIZATIONAL VARIABLES
TAR AP 85 VOL: 60 PG:231 - 247 :: REGRESS. :SURV. :OTH.STAT. :ORG.& ENVIR.

SALGADO,AP CIT: 0
ACCOUNTING REPORTS IN CHILE
TAR AP 63 VOL: 38 PG:389 - 397 :: QUAL. :INT. LOG. :HIST. :FIN.METH.

SALMI ,T ; FIRS: KISTNER,KP CIT: 0
GENERAL PRICE LEVEL ACCOUNTING AND INVENTORY VALUATION: A COMMENT
JAR SP 80 VOL: 18 PG:297 - 311 :: ANAL. :INT. LOG. :THEORY :VALUAT.(INFL.)

SAMI ,H ; SEC: WELSH ,MJ CIT: 0
CHARACTERISTICS OF EARLY AND LATE ADOPTERS OF PENSION ACCOUNTING STANDARD SFAS 87
CAR AU 92 VOL: 9 PG:212 - 236 :: REGRESS. :PRIM. :OTH.STAT. :FASB SUBM.

SAMI ,H ; SEC: CURATOLA,AP ; THIR: TRAPNELL,JE CIT: 0
EVIDENCE ON THE PREDICTIVE ABILITY OF INFLATION-ADJUSTED EARNINGS MEASURES
CAR SP 89 VOL: 5 PG:556 - 574 :: REGRESS. :PRIM. :EMH :VALUAT.(INFL.)

SAMUELS,JM ; FIRS: MANES ,RP ; THIR: SMYTH ,DJ CIT: 0
INVENTORIES AND SALES: A CROSS SECTION STUDY
JAR ST 67 VOL: 5 PG:139 - 156 :: REGRESS. :PRIM. :THEORY :INV.

SAMUELS,JM CIT: 0.12
OPPORTUNITY COSTING: AN APPLICATION OF MATHEMATICAL PROGRAMMING
JAR AU 65 VOL: 3 PG:182 - 191 :: ANAL. :INT. LOG. :MATH.PROG. :REL.COSTS

SAMUELSON,LA CIT: 0
DISCREPANCIES BETWEEN THE ROLES OF BUDGETING
AOS 01 86 VOL: 11 PG:35 - 46 :: DES.STAT. :INT. LOG. :OTH.BEH. :BUDG.& PLAN.

SAMUELSON,RA CIT: 0
SHOULD REPLACEMENT-COST CHANGES BE INCLUDED IN INCOME?
TAR AP 80 VOL: 55 PG:254 - 268 :: ANAL. :INT. LOG. :THEORY :REV.REC.

SAMUELSON,RA CIT: 0.18
PREDICTION AND PRICE-LEVEL ADJUSTMENT
JAR AU 72 VOL: 10 PG:322 - 344 :: REGRESS. :PRIM. :TIME SER. :VALUAT.(INFL.)

SAN MIGUEL,JG ; SEC: GOVINDARAJAN,V CIT: 0
THE CONTINGENT RELATIONSHIP BETWEEN THE CONTROLLER AND INTERNAL AUDIT
FUNCTIONS IN LARGE ORGANIZATIONS
AOS 02 84 VOL: 9 PG:179 - 188 :: NON-PAR. :SURV. :OTH.BEH. :INT.AUD.

SAN MIGUEL,JG CIT: 0
THE BEHAVIOURAL SCIENCES AND CONCEPTS AND STANDARDS FOR MANAGEMENT PLANNING
AND CONTROL
AOS 02 77 VOL: 2 PG:177 - 186 :: QUAL. :INT. LOG. :OTH.BEH. :N/A

SAN MIGUEL,JG ; SEC: SHANK ,JK ; THIR: GOVINDARAJAN,V CIT: 0.06
EXTENDING CORPORATE ACCOUNTABILITY: A SURVEY AND FRAMEWORK FOR ANALYSIS
AOS 04 77 VOL: 2 PG:333 - 348 :: DES.STAT. :PRIM. :OTH. :AUD.

SAN MIGUEL,JG CIT: 0
THE RELIABILITY OF R&D DATA IN COMPUSTAT AND 10-K REPORTS
TAR JL 77 VOL: 52 PG:638 - 641 :: DES.STAT. :PRIM. :N/A :N/A

SAN MIGUEL,JG CIT: 0.65
HUMAN INFORMATION PROCESSING AND ITS RELEVANCE TO ACCOUNTING: A LABORATORY STUDY
AOS 04 76 VOL: 1 PG:357 - 374 :: OTH.QUANT. :LAB. :MATH.PROG. :MAN.DEC.CHAR.

SANDBERG,A ; FIRS: CARLSSON,J ; SEC: EHN ,P ; THIR: ERLANDER,B ; FOUR: PERBY ,M CIT: 0.07
PLANNING AND CONTROL FROM THE PERSPECTIVE OF LABOR: A SHORT REPRESENTATION OF
THE DEMOS PROJECT
AOS 34 78 VOL: 3 PG:249 - 260 :: QUAL. :FIELD :OTH. :BUDG.& PLAN.

SANGSTER,JM ; FIRS: BURNS ,JS ; SEC: JAEDICKE,RK CIT: 0
FINANCIAL REPORTING OF PURCHASE CONTRACTS USED TO GUARANTEE LARGE INVESTMENTS
TAR JA 63 VOL: 38 PG:1 - 13 :: QUAL. :INT. LOG. :THEORY :SPEC.ITEMS

SANNELLA,AJ CIT: 0
SEGMENT REPORTING: THE COST ALLOCATION ISSUE
JAA WI 91 VOL: 6 PG:75 - 102 :: REGRESS. :PRIM. :INF.ECO./AG. :SEG.REP.

SANNELLA,AJ CIT: 0
AN APPLICATION OF INCOME STRATEGY TO COST ALLOCATION AND SEGMENT REPORTING
JAA AU 86 VOL: 1 PG:288 - 304 :: REGRESS. :SURV. :THEORY :SEG.REP.

SANSING,RC CIT: 0
ACCOUNTING AND THE CREDIBILITY OF MANAGEMENT FORECASTS
CAR AU 92 VOL: 9 PG:33 - 45 :: DES.STAT. :INT. LOG. :INF.ECO./AG. :FOREC.

SAPIENZA,SR CIT: 0
BUSINESS COMBINATIONS AND ENTERPRISE EVALUATION
JAR SP 64 VOL: 2 PG:50 - 66 :: QUAL. :INT. LOG. :THEORY :BUS.COMB.

SAPIENZA,SR CIT: 0
AN EXAMINATION OF AICPA RESEARCH STUDY NO.5 - STANDARDS FOR POOLING
TAR JL 64 VOL: 39 PG:582 - 590 :: QUAL. :INT. LOG. :THEORY :BUS.COMB.

SAPIENZA,SR CIT: 0
BUSINESS COMBINATIONS - A CASE STUDY
TAR JA 63 VOL: 38 PG:91 - 101 :: QUAL. :CASE :THEORY :BUS.COMB.

SAPPINGTON,DEM ; FIRS: DEMSKI,JS CIT: 0
FULLY REVEALING INCOME MEASUREMENT
TAR AP 90 VOL: 65 PG:363 - 383 :: DES.STAT. :INT. LOG. :THEORY :VALUAT.(INFL.)

SAPPINGTON,DEM ; FIRS: DEMSKI,JS CIT: 0.75
HIERARCHICAL STRUCTURE AND RESPONSIBILITY ACCOUNTING
JAR SP 89 VOL: 27 PG:40 - 58 :: DES.STAT. :INT. LOG. :INF.ECO./AG. :EXEC.COMP.

SAPPINGTON,DEM ; FIRS: DEMSKI,JS CIT: 1.33
DELEGATED EXPERTISE
JAR SP 87 VOL: 25 PG:68 - 89 :: DES.STAT. :INT. LOG. :INF.ECO./AG. :MANAG.

SAPPINGTON,DEM ; FIRS: DEMSKI,JS CIT: 0.71
LINE-ITEM REPORTING, FACTOR ACQUISITION, AND SUBCONTRACTING
JAR AU 86 VOL: 24 PG:250 - 269 :: ANAL. :INT. LOG. :INF.ECO./AG. :INFO.STRUC.

SAULS ,EH CIT: 0.06
NONSAMPLING ERRORS IN ACCOUNTS RECEIVABLE CONFIRMATION
TAR JA 72 VOL: 47 PG:109 - 115 :: DES.STAT. :FIELD :N/A :SAMP.

SAULS ,EH CIT: 0.06
AN EXPERIMENT ON NONSAMPLING ERRORS
JAR ST 70 VOL: 8 PG:157 - 171 :: ANOVA :LAB. :OTH.BEH. :SAMP.

SAVICH,RS ; FIRS: GROVE ,HD CIT: 0.21
ATTITUDE RESEARCH IN ACCOUNTING: A MODEL FOR RELIABILITY AND VALIDITY CONSIDERATIONS
TAR JL 79 VOL: 54 PG:522 - 537 :: QUAL. :SEC. :OTH.BEH. :METHOD.

SAVICH,RS CIT: 0.44
THE USE OF ACCOUNTING INFORMATION IN DECISION MAKING
TAR JL 77 VOL: 52 PG:642 - 652 :: REGRESS. :LAB. :HIPS :MAN.DEC.CHAR.

SAVICH,RS ; FIRS: CRUMBLEY,DL CIT: 0
USE OF HUMAN RESOURCE ACCOUNTING IN TAXATION
TAR JA 75 VOL: 50 PG:112 - 117 :: QUAL. :INT. LOG. :THEORY :HRA

SAVOIE,LM CIT: 0
RAISING ACCOUNTING STANDARDS
JAR ST 69 VOL: 7 PG:55 - 62 :: QUAL. :INT. LOG. :THEORY :FASB SUBM.

SAWYERS,RB ; FIRS: LOUDDER,ML ; SEC: KHURANA,IK ; FOUR: CORDERY,C ; FIFT: JOHNSON,C ; SIX LOWE ,J CIT: 0
THE INFORMATION CONTENT OF AUDIT QUALIFICATIONS
AUD SP 92 VOL: 11 PG:69 - 82 :: REGRESS. :PRIM. :OTH.STAT. :OPIN.

SCAPENS,RW ; FIRS: MACINTOSH,NB CIT: 0.33
STRUCTURATION THEORY IN MANAGEMENT ACCOUNTING
AOS 05 90 VOL: 15 PG:455 - 477 :: REGRESS. :CASE :OTH.BEH. :HRA

SCAPENS,RW ; FIRS: ROBERTS,J CIT: 2
ACCOUNTING SYSTEMS AND SYSTEMS OF ACCOUNTABILITY - UNDERSTANDING ACCOUNTING PRACTICES IN THEIR ORGANIZATIONAL CONTEXTS
AOS 04 85 VOL: 10 PG:443 - 456 :: DES.STAT. :INT. LOG. :THEORY :FIN.METH.

SCAPENS,RW ; SEC: SALE ,JT CIT: 0.25
AN INTERNATIONAL STUDY OF ACCOUNTING PRACTICES IN DIVISIONALIZED COMPANIES AND THEIR ASSOCIATIONS WITH ORGANIZATIONAL VARIABLES
TAR AP 85 VOL: 60 PG:231 - 247 :: REGRESS. :SURV. :OTH.STAT. :ORG.& ENVIR.

SCAPENS,RW CIT: 0.07
A NEOCLASSICAL MEASURE OF PROFIT
TAR AP 78 VOL: 53 PG:448 - 469 :: ANAL. :INT. LOG. :THEORY :OTH. NON-C/A

SCHACHNER,L CIT: 0
ACCOUNTABILITY UNDER INDUSTRIAL DIVERSIFICATION
TAR AP 68 VOL: 43 PG:303 - 311 :: QUAL. :INT. LOG. :THEORY :AMOR./DEPL.

SCHACHTER,B CIT: 0
OPEN INTEREST IN STOCK OPTIONS AROUND QUARTERLY EARNINGS ANNOUNCEMENTS
JAR AU 88 VOL: 26 PG:353 - 372 :: REGRESS. :PRIM. :EMH :INT.REP.

SCHACHTER,B CIT: 0
OPEN INTEREST AND CONSENSUS AMONG INVESTORS
JAR AU 85 VOL: 23 PG:907 - 910 :: DES.STAT. :INT. LOG. :OTH.STAT. :N/A

SCHADEWALD,M ; FIRS: ANDERSON,MJ ; SEC: ANDERSON,U ; THIR: HELLELOID,R ; FOUR: JOYCE ,E CIT: 0
INTERNAL REVENUE SERVICE ACCESS TO TAX ACCRUAL WORKPAPERS: A LABORATORY INVESTIGATION
TAR OC 90 VOL: 65 PG:857 - 874 :: REGRESS. :LAB. :MATH.PROG. :AUD.

SCHADEWALD,MS ; FIRS: KACHELMEIER,SJ ; SEC: LIMBERG,ST CIT: 0
A LABORATORY MARKET EXAMINATION OF THE CONSUMER PRICE RESPONSE TO INFORMATION ABOUT PRODUCERS' COSTS AND PROFITS
TAR OC 91 VOL: 66 PG:694 - 717 :: REGRESS. :LAB. :HIPS :N/A

SCHAEFER,T ; FIRS: HOPWOOD,W CIT: 0
FIRM-SPECIFIC RESPONSIVENESS TO INPUT PRICE CHANGES AND THE INCREMENTAL INFORMATION IN CURRENT COST INCOME
TAR AP 89 VOL: 64 PG:313 - 328 :: REGRESS. :PRIM. :EMH :FIN.METH.

SCHAEFER,T ; SEC: KENNELLEY,M CIT: 0
ALTERNATIVE CASH FLOW MEASURES AND RISK-ADJUSTED RETURNS
JAA AU 86 VOL: 1 PG:278 - 287 :: REGRESS. :PRIM. :EMH :SPEC.ITEMS

SCHAEFER,TF ; FIRS: HOPWOOD,WS CIT: 0
INCREMENTAL INFORMATION CONTENT OF EARNINGS AND NONEARNINGS BASED FINANCIAL RATIOS
CAR AU 88 VOL: 5 PG:318 - 342 :: REGRESS. :PRIM. :EMH :FIN.METH.

SCHAEFER,TF ; FIRS: CHRISTIE,AA ; SEC: KENNELLEY,MD ; THIR: KING ,JW CIT: 1
TESTING FOR INCREMENTAL INFORMATION CONTENT IN THE PRESENCE OF COLLINEARITY
JAE DE 84 VOL: 6 PG:205 - 217 :: ANAL. :INT. LOG. :OTH.STAT. :METHOD.

SCHAEFER,TF CIT: 0.67
THE INFORMATION CONTENT OF CURRENT COST INCOME RELATIVE TO DIVIDENDS AND HISTORICAL COST INCOME
JAR AU 84 VOL: 22 PG:647 - 656 :: REGRESS. :PRIM. :EMH :VALUAT.(INFL.)

SCHATTKE,RW CIT: 0
AN ANALYSIS OF ACCOUNTING PRINCIPLES BOARD STATEMENT NO.4
TAR AP 72 VOL: 47 PG:233 - 244 :: QUAL. :INT. LOG. :THEORY :FIN.METH.

SCHATTKE,RW ; FIRS: LARSON,KD CIT: 0
CURRENT CASH EQUIVALENT, ADDITIVITY, AND FINANCIAL ACTION
TAR OC 66 VOL: 41 PG:634 - 641 :: QUAL. :INT. LOG. :THEORY :VALUAT.(INFL.)

SCHATTKE,RW CIT: 0
FINANCIAL REPORTING OF ANTITRUST ACTIONS
TAR OC 65 VOL: 40 PG:805 - 811 :: QUAL. :CASE :THEORY :FIN.METH.

SCHATZBERG,J ; FIRS: SMITH ,VL ; THIR: WALLER,WS CIT: 1
EXPERIMENTAL ECONOMICS AND AUDITING
AUD AU 87 VOL: 7 PG:71 - 93 :: DES.STAT. :INT. LOG. :OTH. :METHOD.

SCHATZBERG,JW CIT: 0
A LABORATORY MARKET INVESTIGATION OF LOW BALLING IN AUDIT PRICING
TAR AP 90 VOL: 65 PG:337 - 362 :: REGRESS. :LAB. :OTH.BEH. :INDEP.

SCHEINER,JH CIT: 0.11
AN EMPIRICAL ASSESSMENT OF THE IMPACT OF SEC NONAUDIT SERVICE DISCLOSURE REQUIREMENTS ON INDEPENDENT AUDITORS AND THEIR CLIENTS
JAR AU 84 VOL: 22 PG:789 - 797 :: DES.STAT. :PRIM. :INSTIT. :FASB SUBM.

SCHEINER,JH ; SEC: KIGER ,JE CIT: 0.09
AN EMPIRICAL INVESTIGATION OF AUDITOR INVOLVEMENT IN NON-AUDIT SERVICES
JAR AU 82 VOL: 20 PG:482 - 496 :: DES.STAT. :PRIM. :HIPS :PROF.RESP.

SCHEPANSKI,A ; FIRS: RAGHUNANDAN,K ; SEC: GRIMLUND,RA CIT: 0
AUDITOR EVALUATION OF LOSS CONTINGENCIES
CAR SP 91 VOL: 7 PG:549 - 568 :: REGRESS. :LAB. :HIPS :VALUAT.(INFL.)

SCHEPANSKI,A ; FIRS: MADEO ,SA ; THIR: UECKER,WC CIT: 0
MODELING JUDGMENTS OF TAXPAYER COMPLIANCE
TAR AP 87 VOL: 62 PG:323 - 342 :: REGRESS. :LAB. :OTH.STAT. :TAXES

SCHEPANSKI,A ; FIRS: UECKER,WC ; THIR: SHIN ,J CIT: 0.25
TOWARD A POSITIVE THEORY OF INFORMATION EVALUATION: RELEVANT TESTS OF COMPETING MODELS IN A PRINCIPAL-AGENCY SETTING
TAR JL 85 VOL: 60 PG:430 - 457 :: REGRESS. :LAB. :INF.ECO./AG. :MANAG.

SCHEPANSKI,A ; SEC: UECKER,WC CIT: 0.3
TOWARD A POSITIVE THEORY OF INFORMATION EVALUATION
TAR AP 83 VOL: 58 PG:259 - 283 :: ANAL. :INT. LOG. :INF.ECO./AG. :OTH.MANAG.

SCHEPANSKI,A CIT: 0.3
TESTS OF THEORIES OF INFORMATION PROCESSING BEHAVIOR IN CREDIT JUDGMENT
TAR JL 83 VOL: 58 PG:581 - 599 :: CORR. :LAB. :HIPS :N/A

SCHICK,AG ; FIRS: PONEMON,LA CIT: 0
FINANCIALLY DISTRESSED COMPANIES AND AUDITOR PERCEPTIONS OF THE TWELVE CHARACTERISTICS OF DECLINE
AUD AU 91 VOL: 10 PG:70 - 83 :: REGRESS. :LAB. :HIPS :BUS.FAIL.

SCHICK,AG ; SEC: GORDON,LA ; THIR: HAKA ,S CIT: 0
INFORMATION OVERLOAD: A TEMPORAL APPROACH
AOS 03 90 VOL: 15 PG:199 - 220 :: REGRESS. :SEC. :HIPS :DEC.AIDS

SCHICK,AG ; FIRS: GORDON,LA ; SEC: HAKA ,S CIT: 0.11
STRATEGIES FOR INFORMATION SYSTEMS IMPLEMENTATION: THE CASE OF ZERO BASE BUDGETING
AOS 02 84 VOL: 9 PG:111 - 123 :: NON-PAR. :PRIM. :OTH. :BUDG.& PLAN.

SCHIENEMAN,GS CIT: 0
THE ACCOUNTING PROFESSION FACING THE CHALLENGES OF A CHANGING WORLD
JAA SP 83 VOL: 6 PG:212 - 226 :: QUAL. :INT. LOG. :OTH. :PROF.RESP.

SCHIENEMAN,GS CIT: 0
INTERNATIONAL ACCOUNTING: ISSUES AND PERSPECTIVE
JAA AU 79 VOL: 3 PG:21 - 30 :: QUAL. :INT. LOG. :INSTIT. :INT.DIFF.

SCHIFF,A ; FIRS: KAHN ,N CIT: 0
TANGIBLE EQUITY CHANGE AND THE EVOLUTION OF THE FASB'S DEFINITION OF INCOME
JAA AU 85 VOL: 9 PG:40 - 49 :: REGRESS. :INT. LOG. :THEORY :REV.REC.

SCHIFF,A ; FIRS: FRIED ,D CIT: 0.42
CPA SWITCHES AND ASSOCIATED MARKET REACTIONS
TAR AP 81 VOL: 56 PG:326 - 341 :: NON-PAR. :PRIM. :EMH :OTH.MANAG.

SCHIFF,A ; FIRS: GIVOLY,D ; SEC: RONEN ,J CIT: 0.07
DOES AUDIT INVOLVEMENT AFFECT THE QUALITY OF INTERIM REPORT NUMBERS?
JAA SU 78 VOL: 1 PG:361 - 372 :: ANOVA :PRIM. :INSTIT. :AUD.

SCHIFF,M CIT: 0
A NOTE ON TRANSFER PRICING AND INDUSTRY SEGMENT REPORTING
JAA SP 79 VOL: 2 PG:224 - 231 :: DES.STAT. :PRIM. :OTH. :TRANS.PRIC.

SCHIFF,M ; SEC: SORTER,GH ; THIR: WIESEN,JL CIT: 0
THE EVOLVING ROLE OF CORPORATE AUDIT COMMITTEES
JAA AU 77 VOL: 1 PG:19 - 44 :: QUAL. :INT. LOG. :INSTIT. :OTH.MANAG.

SCHIFF,M ; SEC: LEWIN ,AY CIT: 1.29
THE IMPACT OF PEOPLE ON BUDGETS
TAR AP 70 VOL: 45 PG:259 - 268 :: QUAL. :INT. LOG. :OTH.BEH. :BUDG.& PLAN.

SCHIFF,M CIT: 0.24
ACCOUNTING TACTICS AND THE THEORY OF THE FIRM
JAR SP 66 VOL: 4 PG:62 - 67 :: QUAL. :CASE :THEORY :OTH. NON-C/A

SCHIPPER,K ; SEC: THOMPSON,R CIT: 0.63
THE IMPACT OF MERGER-RELATED REGULATIONS USING EXACT DISTRIBUTIONS OF TEST STATISTICS
JAR SP 85 VOL: 23 PG:408 - 415 :: DES.STAT. :PRIM. :EMH :BUS.COMB.

SCHIPPER,K ; SEC: THOMPSON,R CIT: 2.5
THE IMPACT OF MERGER-RELATED REGULATIONS ON THE SHAREHOLDERS OF ACQUIRING FIRMS
JAR SP 83 VOL: 21 PG:184 - 221 :: REGRESS. :PRIM. :EMH :BUS.COMB.

SCHIPPER,K CIT: 0.13
FINANCIAL DISTRESS IN PRIVATE COLLEGES
JAR ST 77 VOL: 15 PG:1 - 40 :: ANOVA :PRIM. :OTH.STAT. :BUS.FAIL.

SCHLOSSER,RE ; FIRS: BOWER ,JB CIT: 0
INTERNAL CONTROL - ITS TRUE NATURE
TAR AP 65 VOL: 40 PG:338 - 344 :: QUAL. :INT. LOG. :INSTIT. :INT.CONT.

SCHMIDT,RM ; FIRS: COUGHLAN,AT CIT: 1.25
EXECUTIVE COMPENSATION, MANAGEMENT TURNOVER, AND FIRM PERFORMANCE: AN EMPIRICAL INVESTIGATION
JAE AP 85 VOL: 7 PG:43 - 66 :: REGRESS. :PRIM. :OTH.STAT. :EXEC.COMP.

SCHNEE,EJ ; SEC: TAYLOR,ME CIT: 0
IRS ACCESS TO ACCOUNTANTS' WORK PAPERS - THE RULES MAY BE CHANGING
JAA AU 81 VOL: 5 PG:18 - 29 :: QUAL. :INT. LOG. :INSTIT. :PROF.RESP.

SCHNEIDER,A ; SEC: WILNER,N CIT: 0
A TEST OF AUDIT DETERRENT TO FINANCIAL REPORTING IRREGULARITES USING THE RANDOMIZED RESPONSE TECHNIQUE
TAR JL 90 VOL: 65 PG:668 - 681 :: REGRESS. :FIELD :HIPS :MAN.DEC.CHAR.

SCHNEIDER,A ; FIRS: MESSIER JR,WF CIT: 0
A HIERARCHICAL APPROACH TO THE EXTERNAL AUDITOR'S EVALUATION OF THE INTERNAL AUDITING FUNCTION
CAR SP 88 VOL: 4 PG:337 - 353 :: REGRESS. :LAB. :HIPS :INT.AUD.

SCHNEIDER,A CIT: 0.38
THE RELIANCE OF EXTERNAL AUDITORS ON THE INTERNAL AUDIT FUNCTION
JAR AU 85 VOL: 23 PG:911 - 919 :: REGRESS. :LAB. :OTH.BEH. :INT.AUD.

SCHNEIDER,A CIT: 0.33
MODELING EXTERNAL AUDITORS' EVALUATIONS OF INTERNAL AUDITING
JAR AU 84 VOL: 22 PG:657 - 678 :: NON-PAR. :LAB. :HIPS :INT.AUD.

SCHNEIDER,AJ CIT: 0
FLOW-GRAPH NOTATION IN ACCOUNTING
TAR AP 67 VOL: 42 PG:342 - 348 :: QUAL. :INT. LOG. :N/A :OTH.MANAG.

SCHNEPPER,JA CIT: 0
THE ACCOUNTANT'S LIABILITY UNDER RULE 10B-5 AND SECTION 10(B) OF THE SECURITIES EXCHANGE ACT OF 1934: THE HOLE IN HOCHFELDER
TAR JL 77 VOL: 52 PG:653 - 657 :: QUAL. :SEC. :N/A :LIAB.

SCHOLES,M ; FIRS: BEAVER,WH ; SEC: KETTLER,P CIT: 1.82
THE ASSOCIATION BETWEEN MARKET DETERMINED AND ACCOUNTING DETERMINED RISK MEA
TAR OC 70 VOL: 45 PG:654 - 682 :: REGRESS. :PRIM. :TIME SER. :FIN.METH.

SCHOLES,MS ; SEC: WOLFSON,MA CIT: 0
REPACKAGING OWNERSHIP RIGHTS AND MULTINATIONAL TAXATION: THE CASE OF WITHHOLDING TAXES
JAA AU 91 VOL: 6 PG:513 - 532 :: DES.STAT. :INT. LOG. :OTH.STAT. :TAXES

SCHOLES,MS ; SEC: TERRY ,E ; THIR: WOLFSON,MA CIT: 0
TAXES, TRADING, AND THE VALUE OF REAL ESTATE
JAA SU 89 VOL: 4 PG:317 - 340 :: REGRESS. :MIXED :OTH.STAT. :TAXES

SCHONFELD,HM ; FIRS: HOLZER,HP CIT: 0
THE FUNKTIONALE KONTORECHNUNG OF WALTER THOMS
TAR AP 64 VOL: 39 PG:405 - 413 :: QUAL. :INT. LOG. :THEORY :FIN.METH.

SCHONFELD,HM ; FIRS: HOLZER,HP CIT: 0
THE GERMAN SOLUTION OF THE POST-WAR PRICE LEVEL PROBLEM
TAR AP 63 VOL: 38 PG:377 - 381 :: QUAL. :INT. LOG. :HIST. :FIN.METH.

SCHONFELD,HM ; FIRS: HOLZER,HP CIT: 0
THE FRENCH APPROACH TO THE POST-WAR PRICE LEVEL PROBLEM
TAR AP 63 VOL: 38 PG:382 - 388 :: QUAL. :INT. LOG. :HIST. :FIN.METH.

SCHRADER,WJ ; FIRS: CRAMER JR,JJ CIT: 0
DEPRECIATION ACCOUNTING AND THE ANOMALOUS SELF-INSURANCE COST
TAR OC 70 VOL: 45 PG:698 - 703 :: QUAL. :INT. LOG. :THEORY :PP&E / DEPR

SCHREUDER,H ; FIRS: SOETERS,J CIT: 0.8
THE INTERACTION BETWEEN NATIONAL AND ORGANIZATIONAL CULTURES IN ACCOUNTING
AOS 01 88 VOL: 13 PG:75 - 85 :: REGRESS. :SURV. :OTH.BEH. :AUD.BEH.

SCHREUDER,H ; SEC: KLAASSEN,J CIT: 0.11
CONFIDENTIAL REVENUE AND PROFIT FORECASTS BY MANAGEMENT AND FINANCIAL ANALYSTS: EVIDENCE FROM THE NETHERLANDS
TAR JA 84 VOL: 59 PG:64 - 77 :: NON-PAR. :PRIM. :OTH.STAT. :FOREC.

SCHREUDER,H CIT: 0.08
EMPLOYEES AND THE CORPORATE SOCIAL REPORT: THE DUTCH CASE
TAR AP 81 VOL: 56 PG:294 - 308 :: NON-PAR. :SURV. :INSTIT. :HRA

SCHREUDER,H CIT: 0.21
CORPORATE SOCIAL REPORTING IN THE FEDERAL REPUBLIC OF GERMANY: AN OVERVIEW
AOS 12 79 VOL: 4 PG:109 - 122 :: QUAL. :INT. LOG. :THEORY :HRA

SCHRODERHEIM,G CIT: 0.06
USING MATHEMATICAL PROBABILITY TO ESTIMATE THE ALLOWANCE FOR DOUBTFUL ACCOUNTS
TAR JL 64 VOL: 39 PG:679 - 684 :: ANAL. :INT. LOG. :OTH.STAT. :OTH.C/A

SCHROEDER,D ; FIRS: KROSS ,W ; SEC: RO ,B CIT: 0.67
EARNINGS EXPECTATIONS: THE ANALYSTS' INFORMATION ADVANTAGE
TAR AP 90 VOL: 65 PG:461 - 476 :: REGRESS. :PRIM. :TIME SER. :FOREC.

SCHROEDER,DA ; FIRS: LYON ,JD CIT: 0
FIRM GROWTH AND THE VALUATION RELEVANCE OF EARNINGS LEVELS, EARNINGS INNOVATIONS, AND DIVIDENDS
JAA AU 92 VOL: 7 PG:531 - 552 :: REGRESS. :PRIM. :OTH.STAT. :VALUAT.(INFL.)

SCHROEDER,DA ; FIRS: KROSS ,W CIT: 1.56
AN EMPIRICAL INVESTIGATION OF THE EFFECT OF QUARTERLY EARNINGS ANNOUNCEMENT TIMING ON STOCK RETURNS
JAR SP 84 VOL: 22 PG:153 - 176 :: REGRESS. :PRIM. :EMH :FIN.ST.TIM.

SCHROEDER,MS ; FIRS: GRIMLUND,RA CIT: 0.6
ON THE CURRENT USE OF THE STRINGER METHOD OF MUS: SOME NEW DIRECTIONS
AUD AU 88 VOL: 08 PG:53 - 62 :: REGRESS. :SIM. :OTH.STAT. :SAMP.

SCHROEDER,MS ; SEC: SOLOMON,I ; THIR: VICKREY,DW CIT: 0.14
AUDIT QUALITY: THE PERCEPTIONS OF AUDIT-COMMITTEE CHAIRPERSONS AND AUDIT PARTNERS
AUD SP 86 VOL: 5 PG:86 - 94 :: REGRESS. :SURV. :OTH.BEH. :OPER.AUD.

SCHROEDER,RG ; SEC: IMDIEKE,LF CIT: 0.19
LOCAL-COSMOPOLITAN AND BUREAUCRATIC PERCEPTIONS IN PUBLIC ACCOUNTING FIRMS
AOS 01 77 VOL: 2 PG:39 - 46 :: DES.STAT. :INT. LOG. :OTH.STAT. :ORG.

SCHULTE JR,AA CIT: 0
MANAGEMENT SERVICES: A CHALLENGE TO AUDIT INDEPENDENCE?
TAR OC 66 VOL: 41 PG:721 - 728 :: QUAL. :INT. LOG. :N/A :INDEP.

SCHULTE JR,AA CIT: 0.18
COMPATIBILITY OF MANAGEMENT CONSULTING AND AUDITING
TAR JL 65 VOL: 40 PG:587 - 593 :: ANOVA :SURV. :INSTIT. :INDEP.

SCHULTZ JR,JJ ; FIRS: RECKERS,PMJ CIT: 0.09
INDIVIDUAL VERSUS GROUP ASSISTED AUDIT EVALUATIONS
AUD AU 82 VOL: 2 PG:64 - 74 :: ANOVA :LAB. :OTH.BEH. :JUDG.

SCHULTZ JR,JJ ; SEC: RECKERS,PMJ CIT: 0.75
THE IMPACT OF GROUP PROCESSING ON SELECTED AUDIT DISCLOSURE DECISIONS
JAR AU 81 VOL: 19 PG:482 - 501 :: ANOVA :PRIM. :OTH.BEH. :AUD.BEH.

SCHULTZ JR,JJ ; SEC: GUSTAVSON,SG CIT: 0.53
ACTUARIES' PERCEPTIONS OF VARIABLES AFFECTING THE INDEPENDENT AUDITOR'S LEGAL LIABILITY
TAR JL 78 VOL: 53 PG:626 - 641 :: ANOVA :LAB. :HIPS :LIAB.

SCHWAB,B ; SEC: NICOL ,RE CIT: 0.06
FROM DOUBLE-DECLINING-BALANCE TO SUM-OF-THE-YEAR'S DIGITS DEPRECIATION: AN OPTIMUM SWITCHING RULE
TAR AP 69 VOL: 44 PG:292 - 296 :: ANAL. :SIM. :OTH.STAT. :PP&E / DEPR

SCHWAGER,SJ ; FIRS: BROWN ,LD ; SEC: RICHARDSON,GD CIT: 1.5
AN INFORMATION INTERPRETATION OF FINANCIAL ANALYST SUPERIORITY IN FORECASTING EARNINGS
JAR SP 87 VOL: 25 PG:49 - 67 :: REGRESS. :PRIM. :TIME SER. :FOREC.

SCHWAN,ES CIT: 0.47
THE EFFECTS OF HUMAN RESOURCE ACCOUNTING DATA ON FINANCIAL DECISIONS: AN EMPIRICAL TEST
AOS 23 76 VOL: 1 PG:219 - 238 :: DES.STAT. :LAB. :OTH.BEH. :HRA

SCHWARTZ,A ; FIRS: LEV ,B CIT: 0.65
ON THE USE OF THE ECONOMIC CONCEPT OF HUMAN CAPITAL IN FINANCIAL STATEMENTS
TAR JA 71 VOL: 46 PG:103 - 112 :: ANAL. :INT. LOG. :THEORY :HRA

SCHWARTZ,BN CIT: 0
DEFERRED TAXES: COMPLIANCE AND UNDERSTANDABILITY
JAA SP 83 VOL: 6 PG:244 - 253 :: DES.STAT. :PRIM. :THEORY :TAXES

SCHWARTZ,BN CIT: 0
INCOME TAX ALLOCATION: IT IS TIME FOR A CHANGE
JAA SP 81 VOL: 4 PG:238 - 247 :: QUAL. :INT. LOG. :THEORY :TAXES

SCHWARTZ,BN ; FIRS: FLAHERTY,RE CIT: 0.08
EARNINGS PER SHARE: COMPLIANCE AND UNDERSTANDABILITY
JAA AU 80 VOL: 4 PG:47 - 56 :: DES.STAT. :SEC. :THEORY :INFO.STRUC.

SCHWARTZ,ES ; FIRS: HUGHES,PJ CIT: 0.4
THE LIFO/FIFO CHOICE: AN ASYMMETRIC INFORMATION APPROACH
JAR ST 88 VOL: 26 PG:41 - 62 :: ANOVA :INT. LOG. :INF.ECO./AG. :INV.

SCHWARTZ,KB ; FIRS: MENON ,K CIT: 0
AN EMPIRICAL INVESTIGATION OF AUDIT QUALIFICATION DECISIONS IN THE PRESENCE OF GOING CONCERN UNCERTAINTIES
CAR SP 87 VOL: 3 PG:302 - 315 :: REGRESS. :PRIM. :OTH.STAT. :BUS.FAIL.

SCHWARTZ,KB ; SEC: MENON ,K CIT: 0.5
AUDITOR SWITCHES BY FAILING FIRMS
TAR AP 85 VOL: 60 PG:248 - 261 :: REGRESS. :PRIM. :N/A :BUS.FAIL.

SCHWARTZ,KB CIT: 0.18
ACCOUNTING CHANGES BY CORPORATIONS FACING POSSIBLE INSOLVENCY
JAA AU 82 VOL: 6 PG:32 - 43 :: DES.STAT. :PRIM. :OTH.STAT. :ACC.CHNG.

SCHWEIKART,JA CIT: 0
THE RELEVANCE OF MANAGERIAL ACCOUNTING INFORMATION: A MULTINATIONAL ANALYSIS
AOS 06 86 VOL: 11 PG:541 - 554 :: REGRESS. :SURV. :THEORY :INT.DIFF.

SCHWEIKER,W ; FIRS: ARRINGTON,CE CIT: 0
THE RHETORIC AND RATIONALITY OF ACCOUNTING RESEARCH
AOS 06 92 VOL: 17 PG:511 - 533 :: REGRESS. :SEC. :OTH. :METHOD.

SCOTT ,RA CIT: 0
OWNERS' EQUITY, THE ANACHRONISTIC ELEMENT
TAR OC 79 VOL: 54 PG:750 - 763 :: QUAL. :INT. LOG. :THEORY :OTH.FIN.ACC.

SCOTT ,WR ; FIRS: MOORE ,G CIT: 0.25
AUDITORS' LEGAL LIABILITY, COLLUSION WITH MANAGEMENT, AND INVESTORS' LOSS
CAR SP 89 VOL: 5 PG:754 - 774 :: DES.STAT. :INT. LOG. :INF.ECO./AG. :LIAB.

SCOTT ,WR CIT: 0
ECONOMIC EFFECTS OF A MANDATED AUDIT IN A CONTINGENT-CLAIMS PRODUCTION ECONOMY
CAR SP 88 VOL: 4 PG:354 - 388 :: N/A :INT. LOG. :INF.ECO./AG. :EXEC.COMP.

SCOTT ,WR ; FIRS: BLAZENKO,GW CIT: 0.29
A MODEL OF STANDARD SETTING IN AUDITING
CAR AU 86 VOL: 3 PG:68 - 92 :: DES.STAT. :INT. LOG. :INF.ECO./AG. :AUD.

SCOTT ,WR CIT: 0.21
SCORING RULES FOR PROBABILISTIC REPORTING
JAR SP 79 VOL: 17 PG:156 - 178 :: ANAL. :INT. LOG. :INF.ECO./AG. :PROB.ELIC.

SCOTT ,WR CIT: 0.25
GROUP PREFERENCE ORDERINGS FOR AUDIT AND VALUATION ALTERNATIVES: THE SINGLE-PEAKEDNESS CONDITION
JAR SP 77 VOL: 15 PG:120 - 137 :: ANAL. :INT. LOG. :OTH.STAT. :AUD.

SCOTT ,WR CIT: 0.71
AUDITOR'S LOSS FUNCTIONS IMPLICIT IN CONSUMPTION-INVESTMENT MODELS
JAR ST 75 VOL: 13 PG:98 - 117 :: ANAL. :SIM. :OTH.STAT. :SAMP.

SCOTT ,WR CIT: 1.35
A BAYESIAN APPROACH TO ASSET VALUATION AND AUDIT SIZE
JAR AU 73 VOL: 11 PG:304 - 330 :: ANAL. :INT. LOG. :OTH.STAT. :SAMP.

SEAGLE,JP ; SEC: PETRI ,E CIT: 0
GIFT VS. ESTATE TRANSFER: THE METHOD OF EQUATED RATES
TAR JA 77 VOL: 52 PG:124 - 136 :: ANAL. :INT. LOG. :THEORY :N/A

SEAMAN,JL CIT: 0
LESSONS FROM THE INVESTMENT CREDIT
TAR JL 65 VOL: 40 PG:617 - 621 :: QUAL. :INT. LOG. :INSTIT. :TAXES

SEARFOSS,DG ; FIRS: CUSHING,BE ; THIR: RANDALL,RH CIT: 0.36
MATERIALITY ALLOCATION IN AUDIT PLANNING: A FEASIBILITY STUDY
JAR ST 79 VOL: 17 PG:172 - 216 :: DES.STAT. :FIELD :OTH.STAT. :PLAN.

SEARFOSS,DG CIT: 0.24
SOME BEHAVIOURAL ASPECTS OF BUDGETING FOR CONTROL: AN EMPIRICAL STUDY
AOS 04 76 VOL: 1 PG:375 - 388 :: OTH.QUANT. :FIELD :OTH.BEH. :BUDG.& PLAN.

SEELYE,AL CIT: 0
THE ROLE OF BUSINESS SCHOOLS IN A CHANGING ENVIRONMENT
TAR AP 63 VOL: 38 PG:302 - 309 :: QUAL. :INT. LOG. :INSTIT. :EDUC.

SEFCIK,SE ; FIRS: CLARKSON,PM ; SEC: DONTOH,A ; THIR: RICHARDSON,G CIT: 0
THE VOLUNTARY INCLUSION OF EARNINGS FORECASTS IN IPO PROSPECTUSES
CAR SP 92 VOL: 8 PG:601 - 625 :: REGRESS. :PRIM. :TIME SER. :VALUAT.(INFL.)

SEFCIK,SE ; FIRS: BLACCONIERE,WG ; SEC: BOWEN ,RM ; FOUR: STINSON,CH CIT: 0
DETERMINANTS OF THE USE OF REGULATORY ACCOUNTING PRINCIPLES BY SAVINGS AND LOANS
JAE JN 91 VOL: 14 PG:167 - 201 :: REGRESS. :PRIM. :OTH.STAT. :ACC.CHNG.

SEFCIK,SE ; FIRS: RICHARDSON,G ; THIR: THOMPSON,R CIT: 0
TRADING VOLUME REACTIONS TO A CHANGE IN DIVIDEND POLICY: THE CANADIAN APPROACH
CAR AU 88 VOL: 5 PG:299 - 317 :: REGRESS. :PRIM. :TIME SER. :CASH DIV.

SEFCIK,SE ; SEC: THOMPSON,R CIT: 0.86
AN APPROACH TO STAT. INFERENCE IN CROSS-SECTIONAL MODELS WITH SECURITY ABNORMAL RETURNS AS DEPENDENT VARIABLE
JAR AU 86 VOL: 24 PG:316 - 334 :: DES.STAT. :INT. LOG. :OTH.STAT. :METHOD.

SEGALL,J ; FIRS: GREEN ,D CIT: 0.47
THE PREDICTIVE POWER OF FIRST-QUARTER EARNINGS REPORTS: A REPLICATION
JAR ST 66 VOL: 4 PG:21 - 36 :: DES.STAT. :PRIM. :OTH.STAT. :INT.REP.

SEIDLER,LJ CIT: 0
THE COHEN COMMISSION AFTER ONE YEAR: A PERSONAL VIEW
JAA SU 79 VOL: 2 PG:285 - 293 :: QUAL. :INT. LOG. :INSTIT. :AUD.

SEIDLER,LJ CIT: 0.12
INTERNATIONAL ACCOUNTING - THE ULTIMATE THEORY COURSE
TAR OC 67 VOL: 42 PG:775 - 781 :: QUAL. :INT. LOG. :N/A :OTH.MANAG.

SEIFERT,J ; FIRS: MIELKE,DE CIT: 0
A SURVEY ON THE EFFECTS OF DEFEASING DEBT
JAA WI 87 VOL: 2 PG:65 - 78 :: REGRESS. :PRIM. :THEORY :LTD

SEILER,ME ; FIRS: MELLMAN,M CIT: 0
STRUCTURE NEEDED FOR IMPLEMENTING MANDATED ACCOUNTING CHANGES
JAA AU 86 VOL: 1 PG:305 - 318 :: REGRESS. :PRIM. :INSTIT. :FASB SUBM.

SEILER,RE ; SEC: BARTLETT,RW CIT: 0.18
PERSONALITY VARIABLES AS PREDICTORS OF BUDGET SYSTEM CHARACTERISTICS
AOS 04 82 VOL: 7 PG:381 - 404 :: OTH.QUANT. :SURV. :OTH.BEH. :BUDG.& PLAN.

SEILER,RE CIT: 0
ACCOUNTING, INFORMATION SYSTEMS, AND UNDERDEVELOPED NATIONS
TAR OC 66 VOL: 41 PG:652 - 656 :: QUAL. :INT. LOG. :INSTIT. :OTH.MANAG.

SELLING,T ; SEC: SHANK ,J CIT: 0.25
LINEAR VERSUS PROCESS TRACING APPROACHES TO JUDGMENT MODELLING: A NEW PERSPECTIVE ON CUE IMPORTANCE
AOS 02 89 VOL: 14 PG:65 - 77 :: REGRESS. :LAB. :HIPS :JUDG.

SELLING,T ; FIRS: CASEY JR,CJ CIT: 0.14
THE EFFECT OF TASK PREDICTABILITY AND PRIOR PROBABILITY DISCLOSURE ON JUDGMENT QUALITY AND CONFIDENCE
TAR AP 86 VOL: 61 PG:302 - 317 :: REGRESS. :LAB. :HIPS :BUS.FAIL.

SELTO ,FH ; FIRS: COOPER,JC CIT: 0
AN EXPERIMENTAL EXAMINATION OF THE EFFECTS OF SFAS NO. 2 ON R&D INVESTMENT DECISIONS
AOS 03 91 VOL: 16 PG:227 - 242 :: REGRESS. :LAB. :THEORY :R & D

SELTO ,FH ; SEC: CLOUSE,ML CIT: 0.25
AN INVESTIGATION OF MANAGERS' ADAPTATIONS TO SFAS NO. 2: ACCOUNTING FOR RESEARCH AND DEVELOPMENT COSTS
JAR AU 85 VOL: 23 PG:700 - 717 :: REGRESS. :PRIM. :EMH :R & D

SELTO ,FH ; SEC: GROVE ,HD CIT: 0
THE PREDICTIVE POWER OF VOTING POWER INDICES: FASB VOTING ON STATEMENTS OF FINANCIAL ACCOUNTING STANDARDS NOS. 45-69
JAR AU 83 VOL: 21 PG:619 - 622 :: NON-PAR. :PRIM. :INSTIT. :FASB SUBM.

SELTO ,FH CIT: 0.18
INTERNAL ADAPTATIONS TO EFFECTS OF CHANGES IN FINANCIAL ACCOUNTING STANDARDS
AOS 02 82 VOL: 7 PG:139 - 148 :: QUAL. :INT. LOG. :INSTIT. :N/A

SELTO ,FH ; SEC: GROVE ,HD CIT: 0.09
VOTING POWER INDICES AND THE SETTING OF FINANCIAL ACCOUNTING STANDARDS: EXTENSIONS
JAR AU 82 VOL: 20 PG:676 - 688 :: DES.STAT. :PRIM. :INSTIT. :FASB SUBM.

SEN ,PK ; FIRS: BAR-YOSEF,S CIT: 0
ON OPTIMAL CHOICE OF INVENTORY ACCOUNTING METHOD
TAR AP 92 VOL: 67 PG:320 - 336 :: DES.STAT. :INT. LOG. :INF.ECO./AG. :INV.

SEN ,PK ; FIRS: KIRBY ,AJ ; SEC: REICHELSTEIN,S ; FOUR: PAIK ,TY CIT: 1.5
PARTICIPATION, SLACK, AND BUDGET-BASED PERFORMANCE EVALUATION
JAR SP 91 VOL: 29 PG:109 - 128 :: DES.STAT. :INT. LOG. :OTH.BEH. :BUDG.& PLAN.

SEN ,PK ; FIRS: BALAKRISHNAN,R ; SEC: HARRIS,TS CIT: 0
THE PREDICTIVE ABILITY OF GEOGRAPHIC SEGMENT DISCLOSURES
JAR AU 90 VOL: 28 PG:305 - 325 :: REGRESS. :PRIM. :TIME SER. :SEG.REP.

SENATRA,PT CIT: 0.69
ROLE CONFLICT, ROLE AMBIGUITY, AND ORGANIZATIONAL CLIMATE IN A PUBLIC ACCOUNTING FIRM
TAR OC 80 VOL: 55 PG:594 - 603 :: REGRESS. :SURV. :OTH.BEH. :ORG.

SENGUPTA,R ; FIRS: HOUGHTON,KA CIT: 0
THE EFFECT OF PRIOR PROBABILITY DISCLOSURE AND INFORMATION SET CONSTRUCTION ON BANKERS' ABILITY TO PREDICT FAILURE
JAR AU 84 VOL: 22 PG:768 - 775 :: DES.STAT. :LAB. :HIPS :BUS.FAIL.

SENKOW,DW ; FIRS: DALEY ,LA ; THIR: VIGELAND,RL CIT: 0.4
ANALYSTS' FORECASTS, EARNINGS VARIABILITY, AND OPTION PRICING: EMPIRICAL EVIDENCE
TAR OC 88 VOL: 63 PG:563 - 585 :: REGRESS. :PRIM. :TIME SER. :FOREC.

SENNETTI,JT CIT: 0
TOWARD A MORE CONSISTENT MODEL FOR AUDIT RISK
AUD SP 90 VOL: 9 PG:103 - 112 :: DES.STAT. :INT. LOG. :THEORY :RISK

SEOW ,GS ; FIRS: BIDDLE,GC CIT: 1
THE ESTIMATION AND DETERMINANTS OF ASSOCIATIONS BETWEEN RETURNS AND EARNINGS: EVIDENCE FROM CROSS-INDUSTRY COMPARISONS
JAA SP 91 VOL: 6 PG:183 - 232 :: REGRESS. :PRIM. :EMH :FIN.METH.

SEPE ,J CIT: 0.18
THE IMPACT OF THE FASB'S 1974 GPL PROPOSAL ON THE SECURITY PRICE STRUCTURE
TAR JL 82 VOL: 57 PG:467 - 485 :: REGRESS. :PRIM. :EMH :VALUAT.(INFL.)

SEPE ,J ; FIRS: NOREEN,EW CIT: 1.08
MARKET REACTIONS TO ACCOUNTING POLICY DELIBERATIONS: THE INFLATION ACCOUNTING CASE
TAR AP 81 VOL: 56 PG:253 - 269 :: CORR. :PRIM. :EMH :VALUAT.(INFL.)

SERLIN,JE ; FIRS: LANDSITTEL,DL CIT: 0.09
EVALUATING THE MATERIALITY OF ERRORS IN FINANCIAL STATEMENTS
JAA SU 82 VOL: 5 PG:291 - 300 :: QUAL. :INT. LOG. :OTH. :MAT.

SHABAHANG,R ; FIRS: HORWITZ,BN CIT: 0.29
PUBLISHED CORPORATE ACCOUNTING DATA AND GENERAL WAGE INCREASES OF THE FIRM
TAR AP 71 VOL: 46 PG:243 - 252 :: CORR. :PRIM. :N/A :FIN.METH.

SHACKELFORD,DA CIT: 0
THE MARKET FOR TAX BENEFITS: EVIDENCE FROM LEVERAGED ESOPs
JAE JN 91 VOL: 14 PG:117 - 145 :: REGRESS. :PRIM. :EMH :TAXES

SHAFER,G ; SEC: SRIVASTAVA,R CIT: 0
THE BAYESIAN AND BELIEF-FUNCTION FORMALISMS-A GENERAL PERSPECTIVE FOR AUDITING
AUD 90 VOL: 9 PG:110 - 137 :: DES.STAT. :INT. LOG. :OTH.STAT. :AUD.BEH.

SHAFER,GR ; FIRS: SRIVASTAVA,RP CIT: 0
BELIEF-FUNCTION FORMULAS FOR AUDIT RISK
TAR AP 92 VOL: 67 PG:249 - 283 :: REGRESS. :INT. LOG. :MATH.PROG. :AUD.BEH.

SHAFTEL,TL ; FIRS: HANSEN,DR CIT: 0
SAMPLING FOR INTEGRATED AUDITING OBJECTIVES
TAR JA 77 VOL: 52 PG:109 - 123 :: ANAL. :INT. LOG. :MATH.PROG. :SAMP.

SHAH ,P ; FIRS: HAGERMAN,RL ; SEC: ZMIJEWSKI,ME CIT: 1.11
THE ASSOCIATION BETWEEN THE MAGNITUDE OF QUARTERLY EARNINGS FORECAST ERRORS AND RISK-ADJUSTED STOCK RETURNS
JAR AU 84 VOL: 22 PG:526 - 540 :: REGRESS. :PRIM. :EMH :FOREC.

SHALCHI,H ; FIRS: MCKEOWN,JC CIT: 0.2
A COMPARATIVE EXAMINATION OF THE TIME-SERIES PROPERTIES AND PREDICTIVE ABILITY OF ANNUAL HISTORICAL COST AND GENERAL PRICE LEVEL ADJUSTED EARNINGS
CAR SP 88 VOL: 4 PG:485 - 507 :: REGRESS. :PRIM. :TIME SER. :FIN.METH.

SHANE ,PB ; FIRS: ROBINSON,JR CIT: 0
ACQUISITION ACCOUNTING METHOD AND BID PREMIA FOR TARGET FIRMS
TAR JA 90 VOL: 65 PG:25 - 48 :: REGRESS. :PRIM. :OTH.STAT. :BUS.COMB.

SHANE ,PB ; FIRS: ETTREDGE,M ; THIR: SMITH ,D CIT: 0
AUDIT FIRM SIZE AND THE ASSOCIATION BETWEEN REPORTED EARNINGS AND SECURITY RETURNS
AUD SP 88 VOL: 07 PG:29 - 42 :: REGRESS. :PRIM. :EMH :AUD.THEOR.

SHANE ,PB ; SEC: SPICER,BH CIT: 0.6
MARKET RESPONSE TO ENVIRONMENTAL INFORMATION PRODUCED OUTSIDE THE FIRM
TAR JL 83 VOL: 58 PG:521 - 538 :: DES.STAT. :PRIM. :EMH :ORG.& ENVIR.

SHANK ,J ; FIRS: SELLING,T CIT: 0.25
LINEAR VERSUS PROCESS TRACING APPROACHES TO JUDGMENT MODELLING: A NEW PERSPECTIVE ON CUE IMPORTANCE
AOS 02 89 VOL: 14 PG:65 - 77 :: REGRESS. :LAB. :HIPS :JUDG.

SHANK ,JK ; FIRS: CREADY,WM CIT: 0
UNDERSTANDING ACCOUNTING CHANGES IN AN EFFICIENT MARKET: A COMMENT REPLICATION, AND RE-INTERPRETATION
TAR JL 87 VOL: 62 PG:589 - 596 :: REGRESS. :PRIM. :EMH :ACC.CHNG.

SHANK ,JK ; SEC: MURDOCK,RJ CIT: 0.33
COMPARABILITY IN THE APPLICATION OF REPORTING STANDARDS: SOME FURTHER EVIDENCE
TAR OC 78 VOL: 53 PG:824 - 835 :: DES.STAT. :PRIM. :EMH :OPIN.

SHANK ,JK ; FIRS: SAN MIGUEL,JG ; THIR: GOVINDARAJAN,V CIT: 0.06
EXTENDING CORPORATE ACCOUNTABILITY: A SURVEY AND FRAMEWORK FOR ANALYSIS
AOS 04 77 VOL: 2 PG:333 - 348 :: DES.STAT. :PRIM. :OTH. :AUD.

SHANK ,JK ; FIRS: CHURCHILL,NC CIT: 0.12
ACCOUNTING FOR AFFIRMATIVE ACTION PROGRAMS: A STOCHASTIC FLOW APPROACH
TAR OC 75 VOL: 50 PG:643 - 656 :: ANOVA :FIELD :OTH.STAT. :HRA

SHANK ,JK ; SEC: COPELAND,RM CIT: 0.29
CORPORATE PERSONALITY THEORY AND CHANGES IN ACCOUNTING METHODS: AN EMPIRICAL TEST
TAR JL 73 VOL: 48 PG:494 - 501 :: NON-PAR. :PRIM. :OTH.STAT. :ORG.FORM

SHANK ,JK ; FIRS: COPELAND,RM CIT: 0.35
LIFO AND THE DIFFUSION OF INNOVATION
JAR ST 71 VOL: 9 PG:196 - 224 :: DES.STAT. :PRIM. :THEORY :INV.

SHANK ,JK CIT: 0.06
INCOME DETERMINATION UNDER UNCERTAINTY: AN APPLICATION OF MARKOV CHAINS
TAR JA 71 VOL: 46 PG:57 - 74 :: MARKOV :CASE :OTH.STAT. :REV.REC.

SHANKER,L CIT: 0
MARGIN REQUIREMENTS AND HEDGING EFFECTIVENESS: AN ANALYSIS IN A RISK-RETURN FRAMEWORK
JAA SU 92 VOL: 7 PG:379 - 393 :: REGRESS. :PRIM. :EMH :ORG.& ENVIR.

SHANTEAU,J CIT: 0
COGNITIVE HEURISTICS AND BIASES IN BEHAVIORAL AUDITING: REVIEW, COMMENTS AND OBSERVATIONS
AOS 02 89 VOL: 14 PG:165 - 177 :: REGRESS. :SEC. :HIPS :AUD.BEH.

SHANTEAU,J ; FIRS: KROGSTAD,JL ; SEC: ETTENSON,RT CIT: 0.67
CONTEXT AND EXPERIENCE IN AUDITORS' MATERIALITY JUDGMENTS
AUD AU 84 VOL: 4 PG:54 - 74 :: ANOVA :LAB. :OTH.BEH. :MAT.

SHAPIRO,AC ; FIRS: CORNELL,B ; SEC: LANDSMAN,W CIT: 0
CROSS-SECTIONAL REGULARITIES IN THE RESPONSE OF STOCK PRICES TO BOND RATING CHANGES
JAA AU 89 VOL: 4 PG:460 - 479 :: REGRESS. :PRIM. :EMH :OTH.C/A

SHARPE,IG ; SEC: WALKER,RG CIT: 0.06
ASSET REVALUATIONS AND STOCK MARKET PRICES
JAR AU 75 VOL: 13 PG:293 - 310 :: REGRESS. :PRIM. :EMH :VALUAT.(INFL.)

SHASHUA,L ; FIRS: GOLDSCHMIDT,Y CIT: 0
DISTORTION OF INCOME BY SFAS NO.33
JAA AU 84 VOL: 8 PG:54 - 67 :: QUAL. :INT. LOG. :THEORY :VALUAT.(INFL.)

SHAW ,R ; FIRS: ASKARI,H ; SEC: CAIN ,P CIT: 0
A GOVERNMENT TAX SUBSIDY
TAR AP 76 VOL: 51 PG:331 - 334 :: DES.STAT. :PRIM. :N/A :TAX PLNG.

SHAW ,WH ; FIRS: KENNEDY,D ; SEC: LAKONISHOK,J CIT: 0
ACCOMODATING OUTLIERS AND NONLINEARITY IN DECISION MODELS
JAA SP 92 VOL: 7 PG:161 - 190 :: REGRESS. :PRIM. :OTH.STAT. :METHOD.

SHAW ,WH CIT: 0
MASTER LIMITED PARTNERSHIPS: AN EXAMINATION OF CHANGES IN DIVIDEND DISTRIBUTION POLICY
CAR SP 91 VOL: 7 PG:407 - 423 :: REGRESS. :PRIM. :EMH :CASH DIV.

SHAW ,WH ; FIRS: ELLIOTT,JA ; SEC: HANNA ,JD CIT: 0
TE EVALUATION BY THE FINANCIAL MARKETS OF CHANGES IN BANK LOAN LOSS RESERVE LEVELS
TAR OC 91 VOL: 66 PG:847 - 861 :: REGRESS. :PRIM. :EMH :OTH. NON-C/A

SHAW ,WH CIT: 0.2
MEASURING THE IMPACT OF THE SAFE HARBOR LEASE LAW ON SECURITY PRICES
JAR SP 88 VOL: 26 PG:60 - 81 :: REGRESS. :PRIM. :EMH :TAXES

SHAW ,WH CIT: 0
SAFE HARBOR OR MUDDY WATERS
TAR AP 87 VOL: 62 PG:385 - 400 :: REGRESS. :PRIM. :THEORY :LEASES

SHAW,WH ; FIRS: ELLIOTT,JA CIT: 0.2
WRITE-OFFS AS ACCOUNTING PROCEDURES TO MANAGE PERCEPTIONS
JAR ST 88 VOL: 26 PG:91 - 126 :: REGRESS. :PRIM. :EMH :REV.REC.

SHEARON,WT ; FIRS: FROGOT,V CIT: 0
BUDGETARY PARTICIPATION, LOCUS OF CONTROL, AND MEXICAN MANAGERIAL PERFORMANCE AND JOB SATISFACTION
TAR JA 91 VOL: 66 PG:80 - 99 :: REGRESS. :FIELD :OTH.BEH. :BUDG.& PLAN.

SHEARON,WT ; FIRS: SWANSON,EP ; THIR: THOMAS,LR CIT: 0
PREDICTING CURRENT COST OPERATING PROFIT USING COMPONENT MODELS INCORPORATING ANALYSTS' FORECASTS
TAR OC 85 VOL: 60 PG:681 - 691 :: REGRESS. :PRIM. :TIME SER. :VALUAT.(INFL.)

SHEHATA,M CIT: 0
SELF-SELECTION BIAS AND THE ECONOMIC CONSEQUENCES OF ACCOUNTING REGULATION: AN APPLICATION OF TWO-STAGE SWITCHING REGRESSION TO SFAS NO. 2
TAR OC 91 VOL: 66 PG:768 - 787 :: REGRESS. :PRIM. :THEORY :R & D

SHERER,MJ ; FIRS: COOPER,DJ CIT: 2.78
THE VALUE OF CORPORATE ACCOUNTING REPORTS: ARGUMENTS FOR A POLITICAL ECONOMY OF ACCOUNTING
AOS 34 84 VOL: 9 PG:207 - 232 :: QUAL. :SURV. :THEORY :N/A

SHERMAN,HD CIT: 0.11
DATA ENVELOPMENT ANALYSIS AS A NEW MANAGERIAL AUDIT METHODOLOGY - TEST AND EVALUATION
AUD AU 84 VOL: 4 PG:35 - 53 :: ANAL. :INT. LOG. :MATH.PROG. :OPER.AUD.

SHEVLIN,T ; FIRS: BOWEN ,RM ; SEC: JOHNSON,MF ; FOUR: SHORES,D CIT: 0
DETERMINANTS OF THE TRADING OF QUARTERLY EARNINGS ANNOUNCEMENTS
JAA AU 92 VOL: 7 PG:395 - 422 :: REGRESS. :PRIM. :TIME SER. :FIN.ST.TIM.

SHEVLIN,T CIT: 0
THE VALUATION OF R&D FIRMS WITH R&D LIMITED PARTNERSHIPS
TAR JA 91 VOL: 66 PG:1 - 22 :: REGRESS. :INT. LOG. :EMH :R & D

SHEVLIN,T ; FIRS: BOWEN ,RM ; SEC: JOHNSON,MF CIT: 0.25
INFORMATIONAL EFFICIENCY AND THE INFORMATION CONTENT OF EARNINGS DURING THE MARKET CRASH OF OCTOBER 1987
JAE JL 89 VOL: 11 PG:225 - 254 :: REGRESS. :PRIM. :EMH :FIN.METH.

SHEVLIN,T CIT: 0.33
TAXES AND OFF-BALANCE-SHEET FINANCING: RESEARCH AND DEVELOPMENT LIMITED PARTNERSHIPS
TAR JL 87 VOL: 62 PG:480 - 509 :: REGRESS. :PRIM. :OTH.STAT. :ORG.FORM

SHEVLIN,T ; FIRS: FOSTER,G ; SEC: OLSEN ,C CIT: 2.89
EARNINGS RELEASES, ANOMALIES, AND THE BEHAVIOR OF SECURITY RETURNS
TAR OC 84 VOL: 59 PG:574 - 603 :: REGRESS. :PRIM. :EMH :FIN.METH.

SHIBANO,T CIT: 0.67
ASSESSING AUDIT RISK FROM ERRORS AND IRREGULARITIES
JAR ST 90 VOL: 28 PG:110 - 147 :: DES.STAT. :INT. LOG. :INF.ECO./AG. :RISK

SHIELDS,D ; FIRS: EICHENSEHER,JW ; SEC: HAGIGI,M CIT: 0.25
MARKET REACTION TO AUDITOR CHANGES BY OTC COMPANIES
AUD AU 89 VOL: 9 PG:29 - 40 :: REGRESS. :PRIM. :EMH :OTH.MANAG.

SHIELDS,D CIT: 0
SMALL CPA FIRM PRODUCT DIFFERENTIATION IN THE SMALL BUSINESS MARKET
AOS 01 84 VOL: 9 PG:61 - 80 :: CORR. :SURV. :HIPS :ORG.FORM

SHIELDS,D ; FIRS: EICHENSEHER,JW CIT: 1.3
THE CORRELATES OF CPA-FIRM CHANGE FOR PUBLICLY-HELD CORPORATIONS
AUD SP 83 VOL: 2 PG:23 - 37 :: NON-PAR. :SURV. :OTH.BEH. :ORG.

SHIELDS,MD ; FIRS: CHOW ,CW ; THIR: CHAN ,YK CIT: 0
THE EFFECTS OF MANAGEMENT CONTROLS AND NATIONAL CULTURE ON MANUFACTURING PERFORMANCE: AN EXPERIMENTAL INVESTIGATION
AOS 03 91 VOL: 16 PG:209 - 226 :: REGRESS. :LAB. :OTH.STAT. :ORG.& ENVIR.

SHIELDS,MD ; SEC: WALLER,WS CIT: 0.2
A BEHAVIORAL STUDY OF ACCOUNTING VARIABLES IN PERFORMANCE-INCENTIVE CONTRACTS
AOS 06 88 VOL: 13 PG:581 - 594 :: REGRESS. :LAB. :INF.ECO./AG. :EXEC.COMP.

SHIELDS,MD ; FIRS: YOUNG ,SM ; THIR: WOLF ,G CIT: 0.4
MANUFACTURING CONTROLS AND PERFORMANCE: AN EXPERIMENT
AOS 06 88 VOL: 13 PG:607 - 618 :: REGRESS. :LAB. :OTH.BEH. :EXEC.COMP.

SHIELDS,MD ; SEC: SOLOMON,I ; THIR: WALLER,WS CIT: 0
AUDITORS' USAGE OF UNAUDITED BOOK VALUES WHEN MAKING PRESAMPLING AUDIT VALUE ESTIMATES
CAR AU 88 VOL: 5 PG:1 - 18 :: REGRESS. :LAB. :HIPS :PLAN.

SHIELDS,MD ; FIRS: ROCKNESS,HO CIT: 0
AN EMPIRICAL ANALYSIS OF THE EXPENDITURE BUDGET IN RESEARCH AND DEVELOPMENT
CAR SP 88 VOL: 4 PG:568 - 581 :: REGRESS. :PRIM. :THEORY :R & D

SHIELDS,MD ; SEC: SOLOMON,I ; THIR: WALLER,WS CIT: 0.33
EFFECTS OF ALTERNATIVE SAMPLE SPACE REPRESENTATIONS ON THE ACCURACY OF AUDITORS' UNCERTAINTY JUDGMENTS
AOS 04 87 VOL: 12 PG:375 - 385 :: REGRESS. :LAB. :HIPS :MAN.DEC.CHAR.

SHIELDS,MD ; FIRS: ROCKNESS,HO CIT: 0.67
ORGANIZATIONAL CONTROL SYSTEMS IN RESEARCH AND DEVELOPMENT
AOS 02 84 VOL: 9 PG:165 - 177 :: CORR. :SURV. :OTH.BEH. :R & D

SHIELDS,MD CIT: 0.22
A PREDECISIONAL APPROACH TO THE MEASUREMENT OF THE DEMAND FOR INFORMATION IN A PERFORMANCE REPORT
AOS 34 84 VOL: 9 PG:355 - 363 :: CORR. :LAB. :HIPS :MANAG.

SHIELDS,MD ; FIRS: BIRNBERG,JG CIT: 0.44
THE ROLE OF ATTENTION AND MEMORY IN ACCOUNTING DECISIONS
AOS 34 84 VOL: 9 PG:365 - 382 :: QUAL. :INT. LOG. :HIPS :N/A

SHIELDS,MD ; FIRS: LEWIS ,BL ; THIR: YOUNG ,SM CIT: 0.9
EVALUATING HUMAN JUDGMENTS AND DECISION AIDS
JAR SP 83 VOL: 21 PG:271 - 285 :: DES.STAT. :LAB. :HIPS :ORG.& ENVIR.

SHIELDS,MD ; FIRS: BAILEY,KE ; SEC: BYLINSKI,JH CIT: 0
EFFECTS OF AUDIT REPORT WORDING CHANGES ON THE PERCEIVED MESSAGE
JAR AU 83 VOL: 21 PG:355 - 370 :: OTH.QUANT. :LAB. :OTH.BEH. :OPIN.

SHIELDS,MD CIT: 0.9
EFFECTS OF INFORMATION SUPPLY AND DEMAND ON JUDGMENT ACCURACY: EVIDENCE FROM CORPORATE MANAGERS
TAR AP 83 VOL: 58 PG:284 - 303 :: ANOVA :LAB. :HIPS :DEC.AIDS

SHIELDS,MD ; SEC: BIRNBERG,JG ; THIR: FRIEZE,IH CIT: 0.42
ATTRIBUTIONS, COGNITIVE PROCESSES AND CONTROL SYSTEMS
AOS 01 81 VOL: 6 PG:69 - 96 :: ANOVA :LAB. :OTH.BEH. :BUDG.& PLAN.

SHIELDS,MD CIT: 0.85
SOME EFFECTS OF INFORMATION LOAD ON SEARCH PATTERNS USED TO ANALYZE PERFORMANCE REPORTS
AOS 04 80 VOL: 5 PG:429 - 442 :: ANOVA :LAB. :HIPS :INFO.STRUC.

SHIELDS,MD ; FIRS: MCGHEE,W ; THIR: BIRNBERG,JG CIT: 1
THE EFFECTS OF PERSONALITY ON A SUBJECT'S INFORMATION PROCESSING
TAR JL 78 VOL: 53 PG:681 - 697 :: ANOVA :LAB. :HIPS :OTH.MANAG.

SHIELDS,MD ; FIRS: BIRNBERG,JG ; SEC: FRIEZE,IH CIT: 0.38
THE ROLE OF ATTRIBUTION THEORY IN CONTROL SYSTEMS
AOS 03 77 VOL: 2 PG:189 - 200 :: QUAL. :INT. LOG. :OTH.BEH. :MANAG.

SHIH ,MSH ; SEC: SUNDER,S CIT: 0.33
DESIGN AND TESTS OF AN EFFICIENT SEARCH ALGORITHM FOR ACCURATE LINEAR VALUATION SYSTEMS
CAR AU 87 VOL: 4 PG:16 - 31 :: DES.STAT. :INT. LOG. :OTH.STAT. :VALUAT.(INFL.)

SHIH ,W CIT: 0.29
A GENERAL DECISION MODEL FOR COST-VOLUME-PROFIT ANALYSIS UNDER UNCERTAINTY
TAR OC 79 VOL: 54 PG:687 - 706 :: ANAL. :INT. LOG. :OTH.STAT. :C-V-P-A

SHILLINGLAW,G CIT: 0
THE CONCEPT OF ATTRIBUTABLE COST
JAR SP 63 VOL: 1 PG:73 - 85 :: QUAL. :INT. LOG. :THEORY :N/A

SHIN ,HC ; FIRS: BROCKETT,P ; SEC: CHARNES,A ; THIR: COOPER,WW CIT: 0
A CHANCE-CONSTRAINED PROGRAMMING APPROACH TO COST-VOLUME-PROFIT ANALYSIS
TAR JL 84 VOL: 59 PG:474 - 487 :: ANAL. :INT. LOG. :MATH.PROG. :C-V-P-A

SHIN ,J ; FIRS: UECKER,WC ; SEC: SCHEPANSKI,A CIT: 0.25
TOWARD A POSITIVE THEORY OF INFORMATION EVALUATION: RELEVANT TESTS OF COMPETING MODELS IN A PRINCIPAL-AGENCY SETTING
TAR JL 85 VOL: 60 PG:430 - 457 :: REGRESS. :LAB. :INF.ECO./AG. :MANAG.

SHOCKLEY,RA ; SEC: HOLT ,RN CIT: 0.4
A BEHAVIOURAL INVESTIGATION OF SUPPLIER DIFFERENTIATION IN THE MARKET FOR AUDIT SERVICES
JAR AU 83 VOL: 21 PG:545 - 564 :: OTH.QUANT. :LAB. :INSTIT. :ORG.

SHOCKLEY,RA CIT: 0.18
PERCEPTIONS OF AUDIT INDEPENDENCE: A CONCEPTUAL MODEL
JAA WI 82 VOL: 5 PG:126 - 143 :: QUAL. :INT. LOG. :OTH. :INDEP.

SHOCKLEY,RA CIT: 0.42
PERCEPTIONS OF AUDITORS' INDEPENDENCE: AN EMPIRICAL ANALYSIS
TAR OC 81 VOL: 56 PG:785 - 800 :: ANOVA :SURV. :OTH.BEH. :INDEP.

SHORES,D ; FIRS: BOWEN ,RM ; SEC: JOHNSON,MF ; THIR: SHEVLIN,T CIT: 0
DETERMINANTS OF THE TRADING OF QUARTERLY EARNINGS ANNOUNCEMENTS
JAA AU 92 VOL: 7 PG:395 - 422 :: REGRESS. :PRIM. :TIME SER. :FIN.ST.TIM.

SHORES,D CIT: 1
THE ASSOCIATION BETWEEN INTERIM INFORMATION AND SECURITY RETURNS SURROUNDING EARNINGS ANNOUNCEMENTS
JAR SP 90 VOL: 28 PG:164 - 181 :: REGRESS. :PRIM. :EMH :INT.REP.

SHORT ,DG ; FIRS: GRANOF,MH CIT: 0.22
WHY DO COMPANIES REJECT LIFO?
JAA SU 84 VOL: 7 PG:323 - 333 :: DES.STAT. :SURV. :THEORY :INV.

SHORT ,DG CIT: 0.13
THE IMPACT OF PRICE-LEVEL ADJUSTMENT IN THE CONTEXT OF RISK ASSESSMENT
JAR ST 78 VOL: 16 PG:259 - 272 :: OTH.QUANT. :PRIM. :EMH :VALUAT.(INFL.)

SHOVEN,JB ; FIRS: GRUNDFEST,JA CIT: 0
ADVERSE IMPLICATIONS OF A SECURITIES TRANSACTIONS EXCISE TAX
JAA AU 91 VOL: 6 PG:409 - 442 :: DES.STAT. :INT. LOG. :OTH. :ORG.& ENVIR.

SHPILBERG,D ; SEC: GRAHAM,LE CIT: 0.57
DEVELOPING EXPERTAX: AN EXPERT SYSTEM FOR CORPORATE TAX ACCRUAL
AUD AU 86 VOL: 6 PG:75 - 94 :: QUAL. :LAB. :EXP.SYST. :TAXES

SHRIVER,KA ; FIRS: HALL ,TW CIT: 0.33
ECONOMETRIC PROPERTIES OF ASSET VALUATION RULES UNDER PRICE MOVEMENT AND MEASUREMENT ERRORS: AN EMPIRICAL TEST
TAR JL 90 VOL: 65 PG:537 - 556 :: DES.STAT. :LAB. :INF.ECO./AG. :VALUAT.(INFL.)

SHRIVER,KA CIT: 0.5
AN EMPIRICAL EXAMINATION OF THE EFFECTS OF ALTERNATIVE MEASUREMENT TECHNIQUES ON CURRENT COST DATA
TAR JA 87 VOL: 62 PG:79 - 96 :: REGRESS. :FIELD :THEORY :VALUAT.(INFL.)

SHRIVER,KA CIT: 0.57
FURTHER EVIDENCE ON THE MARGINAL GAINS IN ACCURACY OF ALTERNATIVE LEVELS OF SPECIFICITY OF THE PRODUCER PRICE INDEXES
JAR SP 86 VOL: 24 PG:151 - 165 :: REGRESS. :PRIM. :THEORY :VALUAT.(INFL.)

SHRIVER,KA ; FIRS: DUGAN ,MT ; SEC: GENTRY,JA CIT: 0
THE X-11 MODEL: A NEW ANALYTICAL REVIEW TECHNIQUE FOR THE AUDITOR
AUD SP 85 VOL: 4 PG:11 - 22 :: DES.STAT. :INT. LOG. :TIME SER. :ANAL.REV.

SHROLL,PK ; FIRS: OHLSON,JA CIT: 0
CHANGES VERSUS LEVELS IN EARNINGS AS EXPLANATORY VARIABLES FOR RETURNS: SOME THEORETICAL CONSIDERATIONS
JAR AU 92 VOL: 30 PG:210 - 226 :: DES.STAT. :INT. LOG. :TIME SER. :FIN.METH.

SHWAYDER,KR CIT: 0.06
TWO WRONGS MAKING A RIGHT
JAR AU 73 VOL: 11 PG:259 - 272 :: ANAL. :SIM. :THEORY :PP&E / DEPR

SHWAYDER,KR CIT: 0
ACCOUNTING FOR EXCHANGE RATE FLUCTUATIONS
TAR OC 72 VOL: 47 PG:747 - 760 :: ANAL. :INT. LOG. :THEORY :SPEC.ITEMS

SHWAYDER,KR CIT: 0.06
EXPECTED AND UNEXPECTED PRICE LEVEL CHANGES
TAR AP 71 VOL: 46 PG:306 - 319 :: ANAL. :INT. LOG. :THEORY :VALUAT.(INFL.)

SHWAYDER,KR CIT: 0
A PROPOSED MODIFICATION TO RESIDUAL INCOME - INTEREST ADJUSTED INCOME
TAR AP 70 VOL: 45 PG:299 - 307 :: ANAL. :INT. LOG. :N/A :COST.ALLOC.

SHWAYDER,KR CIT: 0.06
THE CAPITAL MAINTENANCE RULE AND THE NET ASSET VALUATION RULE
TAR AP 69 VOL: 44 PG:304 - 316 :: ANAL. :INT. LOG. :THEORY :VALUAT.(INFL.)

SHWAYDER,KR CIT: 0
RELEVANCE
JAR SP 68 VOL: 6 PG:86 - 97 :: QUAL. :INT. LOG. :THEORY :FIN.METH.

SHWAYDER,KR CIT: 0
A NOTE ON A CONTRIBUTION MARGIN APPROACH TO THE ANALYSIS OF CAPACITY UTILIZATION
TAR JA 68 VOL: 43 PG:101 - 104 :: QUAL. :INT. LOG. :N/A :VAR.

SIEGEL,AF ; FIRS: BIDDLE,GC ; SEC: BRUTON,CM CIT: 0
COMPUTER-INTENSIVE METHODS IN AUDITING: BOOTSTRAP DIFFERENCE AND RATIO ESTIMATION
AUD AU 90 VOL: 9 PG:92 - 114 :: DES.STAT. :SIM. :OTH.STAT. :SAMP.

SIEGEL,JP ; FIRS: DERMER,JD CIT: 0.12
THE ROLE OF BEHAVIOURAL MEASURES IN ACCOUNTING FOR HUMAN RESOURCES
TAR JA 74 VOL: 49 PG:88 - 97 :: CORR. :LAB. :OTH.BEH. :HRA

SIEGEL,S ; FIRS: SORTER,GH ; THIR: SLAIN ,J CIT: 0.2
ACCOUNTANTS' LEGAL LIABILITY: A DETERMINANT OF THE ACCOUNTING MODEL
JAA SU 88 VOL: 03 PG:233 - 244 :: DES.STAT. :INT. LOG. :THEORY :LIAB.

SIGLOCH,BA ; FIRS: BUTTERWORTH,JE CIT: 0.06
A GENERALIZED MULTI-STAGE INPUT-OUTPUT MODEL AND SOME DERIVED EQUIVALENT SYSTEMS
TAR OC 71 VOL: 46 PG:701 - 716 :: ANAL. :INT. LOG. :MATH.PROG. :MANAG.

SILHAN,PA ; SEC: MCKEOWN,JC CIT: 0
FURTHER EVIDENCE ON THE USEFULNESS OF SIMULATED MERGERS
JAR SP 85 VOL: 23 PG:416 - 426 :: REGRESS. :PRIM. :TIME SER. :BUS.COMB.

SILHAN,PA CIT: 0
THE EFFECTS OF SEGMENTING QUARTERLY SALES AND MARGINS ON EXTRAPOLATIVE
FORECASTS OF CONGLOMERATE EARNINGS: EXTENSION AND REPLICATION
JAR SP 83 VOL: 21 PG:341 - 347 :: NON-PAR. :PRIM. :EMH :FOREC.

SILHAN,PA CIT: 0.55
SIMULATED MERGERS OF EXISTENT AUTONOMOUS FIRMS, A NEW APPROACH TO
SEGMENTATION RESEARCH
JAR SP 82 VOL: 20 PG:255 - 262 :: DES.STAT. :SIM. :OTH.STAT. :BUS.COMB.

SILHAN,PA ; FIRS: HOPWOOD,WS ; SEC: NEWBOLD,P CIT: 0.36
THE POTENTIAL FOR GAINS IN PREDICTIVE ABILITY THROUGH DISAGGREGATION:
SEGMENTED ANNUAL EARNINGS
JAR AU 82 VOL: 20 PG:724 - 732 :: DES.STAT. :PRIM. :TIME SER. :SEG.REP.

SIMIK ,SS ; FIRS: JOHNSON,GL CIT: 0.12
THE USE OF PROBABILITY INEQUALITIES IN MULTIPRODUCT C-V-P ANALYSIS UNDER UNCERTAINTY
JAR SP 74 VOL: 12 PG:67 - 79 :: ANAL. :INT. LOG. :OTH.STAT. :C-V-P-A

SIMIK ,SS ; FIRS: JOHNSON,GL CIT: 0.12
MULTIPRODUCT C-V-P ANALYSIS UNDER UNCERTAINTY
JAR AU 71 VOL: 9 PG:278 - 286 :: ANAL. :INT. LOG. :OTH.STAT. :C-V-P-A

SIMMONS,JK ; SEC: GRAY ,J CIT: 0.35
AN INVESTIGATION OF THE EFFECT OF DIFFERING ACCOUNTING FRAMEWORKS ON THE PREDICTION OF NET INCOME
TAR OC 69 VOL: 44 PG:757 - 776 :: ANAL. :SIM. :THEORY :VALUAT.(INFL.)

SIMMONS,JK CIT: 0
A CONCEPT OF COMPARABILITY IN FINANCIAL REPORTING
TAR OC 67 VOL: 42 PG:680 - 692 :: QUAL. :INT. LOG. :THEORY :FIN.METH.

SIMNETT,R ; SEC: TROTMAN,K CIT: 0
AUDITOR VERSUS MODEL: INFORMATION CHOICE AND INFORMATION PROCESSING
TAR JL 89 VOL: 64 PG:514 - 528 :: REGRESS. :FIELD :HIPS :BUS.FAIL.

SIMON ,DT ; FIRS: DAVIS ,LR CIT: 0
THE IMPACT OF SEC DISCIPLINARY ACTIONS ON AUDIT FEES
AUD SP 92 VOL: 11 PG:58 - 68 :: REGRESS. :PRIM. :INSTIT. :ORG.

SIMON ,DT ; FIRS: FRANCIS,JR ; SEC: ANDREWS JR,WT CIT: 0
VOLUNTARY PEER REVIEWS, AUDIT QUALITY, AND PROPOSALS FOR MANDATORY PEER REVIEWS
JAA SU 90 VOL: 5 PG:369 - 378 :: REGRESS. :MIXED :OTH.STAT. :OPER.AUD.

SIMON ,DT ; SEC: FRANCIS,JR CIT: 1.4
THE EFFECTS OF AUDITOR CHANGE ON AUDIT FEES: TESTS OF PRICE CUTTING AND PRICE RECOVERY
TAR AP 88 VOL: 63 PG:255 - 269 :: REGRESS. :PRIM. :OTH.STAT. :ORG.

SIMON ,DT ; FIRS: FRANCIS,JR CIT: 1.5
A TEST OF AUDIT PRICING IN THE SMALL-CLIENT SEGMENT OF THE U.S. AUDIT MARKET
TAR JA 87 VOL: 62 PG:145 - 157 :: REGRESS. :SURV. :OTH.STAT. :ORG.

SIMON ,DT CIT: 0.38
THE AUDIT SERVICES MARKET: ADDITIONAL EMPIRICAL EVIDENCE
AUD AU 85 VOL: 5 PG:71 - 78 :: REGRESS. :PRIM. :OTH.STAT. :ORG.

SIMON ,DT ; FIRS: LARCKER,DF ; SEC: REDER ,RE CIT: 0.3
TRADES BY INSIDERS AND MANDATED ACCOUNTING STANDARDS
TAR JL 83 VOL: 58 PG:606 - 620 :: NON-PAR. :INT. LOG. :EMH :OIL & GAS

SIMON ,HA CIT: 0
INFORMATION TECHNOLOGIES AND ORGANIZATIONS
TAR JL 90 VOL: 65 PG:658 - 667 :: REGRESS. :SURV. :EXP.SYST. :INFO.STRUC.

SIMON ,SI CIT: 0
FRAUD IN THE BALANCE SHEET
TAR AP 65 VOL: 40 PG:401 - 406 :: QUAL. :SEC. :INSTIT. :FIN.METH.

SIMON ,SI CIT: 0
COST ACCOUNTING AND THE LAW
TAR OC 64 VOL: 39 PG:884 - 889 :: QUAL. :SEC. :INSTIT. :MANAG.

SIMONDS,RR ; FIRS: COLLINS,DW CIT: 0.36
SEC LINE-OF-BUSINESS DISCLOSURE AND MARKET RISK ADJUSTMENTS
JAR AU 79 VOL: 17 PG:352 - 383 :: MIXED :PRIM. :EMH :SEG.REP.

SIMONS,R CIT: 0
THE ROLE OF MANAGEMENT CONTROL SYSTEMS IN CREATING COMPETITIVE ADVANTAGE: NEW PERSPECTIVES
AOS 02 90 VOL: 15 PG:127 - 143 :: ANOVA :SURV. :OTH. :ORG.& ENVIR.

SIMONS,R CIT: 0
ANALYSIS OF THE ORGANIZATIONAL CHARACTERISTICS RELATED TO TIGHT BUDGET GOALS
CAR AU 88 VOL: 5 PG:267 - 283 :: REGRESS. :SURV. :OTH.BEH. :BUDG.& PLAN.

SIMONS,R CIT: 0.83
ACCOUNTING CONTROL SYSTEMS AND BUSINESS STRATEGY: AN EMPIRICAL ANALYSIS
AOS 04 87 VOL: 12 PG:357 - 374 :: REGRESS. :SURV. :OTH.BEH. :BUDG.& PLAN.

SIMPSON,RH CIT: 0.06
AN EMPIRICAL STUDY OF POSSIBLE INCOME MANIPULATION
TAR OC 69 VOL: 44 PG:806 - 817 :: DES.STAT. :PRIM. :N/A :FIN.METH.

SIMUNIC,DA ; FIRS: FELTHAM,GA ; SEC: HUGHES,JS CIT: 0.5
EMPIRICAL ASSESSMENT OF THE IMPACT OF AUDITOR QUALITY ON THE VALUATION OF NEW ISSUES
JAE DE 91 VOL: 14 PG:375 - 399 :: REGRESS. :PRIM. :EMH :OPER.AUD.

SIMUNIC,DA ; SEC: STEIN ,MT CIT: 0
AUDIT RISK IN A CLIENT PORTFOLIO CONTEXT
CAR SP 90 VOL: 6 PG:329 - 343 :: DES.STAT. :INT. LOG. :INF.ECO./AG. :RISK

SIMUNIC,DA CIT: 0.56
AUDITING, CONSULTING, AND AUDITOR INDEPENDENCE
JAR AU 84 VOL: 22 PG:679 - 702 :: REGRESS. :PRIM. :OTH.STAT. :INDEP.

SIMUNIC,DA CIT: 2.23
THE PRICING OF AUDIT SERVICES: THEORY AND EVIDENCE
JAR SP 80 VOL: 18 PG:161 - 190 :: REGRESS. :FIELD :OTH.STAT. :AUD.BEH.

SINCLAIR,NA ; FIRS: CLINCH,GJ CIT: 0.67
INTRA-INDUSTRY INFORMATION RELEASES: A RECURSIVE SYSTEMS APPROACH
JAE AP 87 VOL: 9 PG:89 - 106 :: REGRESS. :PRIM. :EMH :FIN.METH.

SINGER,FA CIT: 0
PROGRESS IN PROGRAMMED INSTRUCTION
TAR OC 65 VOL: 40 PG:847 - 853 :: DES.STAT. :LAB. :N/A :OTH.MANAG.

SINGHVI,SS ; SEC: DESAI ,HB CIT: 0.35
AN EMPIRICAL ANALYSIS OF THE QUALITY OF CORPORATE FINANCIAL DISCLOSURE
TAR JA 71 VOL: 46 PG:129 - 138 :: DES.STAT. :PRIM. :N/A :INFO.STRUC.

SINHA ,P ; FIRS: LEITCH,RA ; SEC: NETER ,J ; THIR: PLANTE,R CIT: 0.91
MODIFIED MULTINOMIAL BOUNDS FOR LARGER NUMBERS OF ERRORS IN AUDITS
TAR AP 82 VOL: 57 PG:384 - 400 :: DES.STAT. :SIM. :OTH.STAT. :SAMP.

SINNING,KE ; FIRS: DYKXHOORN,HJ CIT: 0
PERCEPTIONS OF AUDITOR INDEPENDENCE: ITS PERCEIVED EFFECT ON THE LOAN AND INVESTMENT DECISIONS OF GERMAN FINANCIAL STATEMENT USE
AOS 04 82 VOL: 7 PG:337 - 348 :: ANOVA :LAB. :HIPS :INDEP.

SINNING,KE ; FIRS: DYKXHOORN,HJ CIT: 0
WIRTSCHAFTSPRUFER PERCEPTION OF AUDITOR INDEPENDENCE
TAR JA 81 VOL: 56 PG:97 - 107 :: NON-PAR. :SURV. :OTH.BEH. :INDEP.

SIVARAMAKRISHNAN,K ; FIRS: BAIMAN,S CIT: 0
THE VALUE OF PRIVATE PRE-DECISION INFORMATION IN A PRINCIPLE-AGENT CONTEXT
TAR OC 91 VOL: 66 PG:747 - 767 :: DES.STAT. :INT. LOG. :INF.ECO./AG. :MANAG.

SIVARAMAKRISHNAN,K ; FIRS: LYS ,T CIT: 0.4
EARNINGS EXPECTATIONS AND CAPITAL RESTRUCTURING: THE CASE OF EQUITY-FOR-DEBT SWAPS
JAR AU 88 VOL: 26 PG:273 - 299 :: REGRESS. :PRIM. :EMH :LTD

SKERRATT,CL ; FIRS: PEASNELL,KV CIT: 0.25
HOW WELL DOES A SINGLE INDEX REPRESENT THE NINETEEN SANDILANDS PLANT AND MACHINERY INDICES?
JAR SP 77 VOL: 15 PG:108 - 119 :: CORR. :PRIM. :THEORY :VALUAT.(INFL.)

SKERRATT,LC CIT: 0
THE BIAS IN CURRENT COST INCOME: AN EXTENSION
JAA SU 84 VOL: 7 PG:362 - 368 :: ANAL. :INT. LOG. :THEORY :VALUAT.(INFL.)

SKINNER,DJ CIT: 0.33
OPTIONS MARKETS AND THE INFORMATION CONTENT OF ACCOUNTING EARNINGS RELEASES
JAE OC 90 VOL: 13 PG:191 - 211 :: REGRESS. :PRIM. :EMH :FIN.METH.

SKINNER,RC CIT: 0.18
FIXED ASSET LIVES AND REPLACEMENT COST ACCOUNTING
JAR SP 82 VOL: 20 PG:210 - 226 :: DES.STAT. :PRIM. :THEORY :PP&E / DEPR

SKOUSEN,KF ; FIRS: MAUTZ ,RK CIT: 0
SOME PROBLEMS IN EMPIRICAL RESEARCH IN ACCOUNTING
TAR JL 69 VOL: 44 PG:447 - 456 :: QUAL. :INT. LOG. :N/A :OTH.MANAG.

SLAIN ,J ; FIRS: SORTER,GH ; SEC: SIEGEL,S CIT: 0.2
ACCOUNTANTS' LEGAL LIABILITY: A DETERMINANT OF THE ACCOUNTING MODEL
JAA SU 88 VOL: 03 PG:233 - 244 :: DES.STAT. :INT. LOG. :THEORY :LIAB.

SLAVIN,NS CIT: 0
THE ELIMINATION OF 'SCIENTER' IN DETERMINING THE AUDITOR'S STATUTORY LIABILITY
TAR AP 77 VOL: 52 PG:360 - 368 :: QUAL. :SEC. :THEORY :LIAB.

SLOAN ,RG ; FIRS: KOTHARI,SP CIT: 2
INFORMATION IN PRICES ABOUT FUTURE EARNINGS: IMPLICATIONS FOR EARNINGS RESPONSE COEFFICIENTS
JAE JN 92 VOL: 15 PG:143 - 171 :: REGRESS. :PRIM. :EMH :FIN.METH.

SLOAN ,RG ; FIRS: DECHOW,PM CIT: 0
EXECUTIVE INCENTIVES AND THE HORIZON PROBLEM: AN EMPIRICAL INVESTIGATION
JAE MR 91 VOL: 14 PG:1 - 89 :: REGRESS. :PRIM. :INF.ECO./AG. :R & D

SMIDT ,S ; FIRS: GOLDSCHMIDT,Y CIT: 0
VALUING THE FIRM'S DURABLE ASSETS FOR MANAGERIAL INFORMATION
TAR AP 69 VOL: 44 PG:317 - 329 :: QUAL. :INT. LOG. :THEORY :VALUAT.(INFL.)

SMIDT ,S ; FIRS: BIERMAN JR,H CIT: 0
ACCOUNTING FOR DEBT AND COSTS OF LIQUIDITY UNDER CONDITIONS OF UNCERTAINTY
JAR AU 67 VOL: 5 PG:144 - 153 :: ANAL. :INT. LOG. :THEORY :LTD

SMIELIAUSKAS,W CIT: 0
A REEVALUATION OF THE POSITIVE TESTING APPROACH IN AUDITING
AUD 90 VOL: 9 PG:149 - 166 :: DES.STAT. :SIM. :OTH.STAT. :SAMP.

SMIELIAUSKAS,W ; FIRS: CHAN ,H CIT: 0
FURTHER TESTS OF THE MODIFIED MOMENT BOUND IN AUDIT SAMPLING OF ACCOUNTING POPULATIONS
AUD AU 90 VOL: 9 PG:167 - 182 :: REGRESS. :SIM. :OTH.STAT. :SAMP.

SMIELIAUSKAS,W ; SEC: SMITH ,L CIT: 0
A THEORY OF EVIDENCE BASED ON AUDIT ASSERTIONS
CAR SP 90 VOL: 6 PG:407 - 426 :: DES.STAT. :INT. LOG. :THEORY :AUD.THEOR.

SMIELIAUSKAS,W CIT: 0
A NOTE ON BAYESIAN RISK MODELS OF AUDIT PRACTICE
CAR SP 89 VOL: 5 PG:720 - 732 :: DES.STAT. :INT. LOG. :OTH.STAT. :RISK

SMIELIAUSKAS,W ; FIRS: MENZEFRICKE,U CIT: 0.4
ON SAMPLE SIZE ALLOCATION IN AUDITING
CAR SP 88 VOL: 4 PG:314 - 336 :: DES.STAT. :SIM. :OTH.STAT. :SAMP.

SMIELIAUSKAS,W ; FIRS: HAM ,J ; SEC: LOSELL,D CIT: 0.33
SOME EMPIRICAL EVIDENCE ON THE STABILITY OF ACCOUNTING ERROR CHARACTERISTICS OVERTIME
CAR AU 87 VOL: 4 PG:210 - 226 :: REGRESS. :PRIM. :TIME SER. :ERRORS

SMIELIAUSKAS,W ; FIRS: MENZEFRICKE,U CIT: 0.17
A COMPARISON OF THE STRATIFIED DIFFERENCE ESTIMATOR WITH SOME MONETARY-UNIT SAMPLING ESTIMATORS
CAR AU 87 VOL: 4 PG:240 - 250 :: DES.STAT. :SIM. :OTH.STAT. :SAMP.

SMIELIAUSKAS,W CIT: 0.57
CONTROL OF SAMPLING RISKS IN AUDITING
CAR AU 86 VOL: 3 PG:102 - 124 :: DES.STAT. :SIM. :OTH.STAT. :SAMP.

SMIELIAUSKAS,W ; FIRS: HAM ,J ; SEC: LOSELL,D CIT: 0
A NOTE ON THE NEUTRALITY OF INTERNAL CONTROL SYSTEMS IN AUDIT PRACTICE
CAR SP 86 VOL: 2 PG:311 - 317 :: DES.STAT. :FIELD :HIST. :AUD.

SMIELIAUSKAS,W CIT: 0.14
A SIMULATION ANALYSIS OF THE POWER CHARACTERISTICS OF SOME POPULAR ESTIMATORS UNDER DIFFERENT RISK AND MATERIALITY LEVELS
JAR SP 86 VOL: 24 PG:217 - 230 :: DES.STAT. :SIM. :OTH.STAT. :SAMP.

SMIELIAUSKAS,W CIT: 0.43
A NOTE ON COMPARISON OF BAYESIAN WITH NON-BAYESIAN DOLLAR-UNIT SAMPLING BOUNDS FOR OVERSTATEMENT ERRORS IN AUDITS
TAR JA 86 VOL: 61 PG:118 - 128 :: DES.STAT. :INT. LOG. :OTH.STAT. :SAMP.

SMIELIAUSKAS,W CIT: 0.25
SENSITIVITY ANALYSIS OF THE REALIZED RISKS OF AUDITING WITH UNCERTAINTY CONCERNING INTERNAL CONTROL EVALUATIONS
JAR AU 85 VOL: 23 PG:718 - 739 :: REGRESS. :SIM. :OTH.STAT. :RISK

SMIELIAUSKAS,W ; FIRS: HAM ,J ; SEC: LOSELL,D CIT: 0.88
AN EMPIRICAL STUDY OF ERROR CHARACTERISTICS IN ACCOUNTING POPULATIONS
TAR JL 85 VOL: 60 PG:387 - 406 :: REGRESS. :PRIM. :OTH.STAT. :ERRORS

SMIELIAUSKAS,W ; FIRS: MENZEFRICKE,U CIT: 0.78
A SIMULATION STUDY OF THE PERFORMANCE OF PARAMETRIC DOLLAR UNIT SAMPLING STATISTICAL PROCEDURES
JAR AU 84 VOL: 22 PG:588 - 604 :: DES.STAT. :SIM. :OTH.STAT. :LIAB.

SMITH ,A ; FIRS: ANTLE ,R CIT: 2.43
AN EMPIRICAL INVESTIGATION OF THE RELATIVE PERFORMANCE EVALUATION OF
JAR SP 86 VOL: 24 PG:1 - 39 :: REGRESS. :PRIM. :OTH.STAT. :EXEC.COMP.

SMITH ,A ; FIRS: ANTLE ,R CIT: 1
MEASURING EXECUTIVE COMPENSATION: METHODS AND AN APPLICATION
JAR SP 85 VOL: 23 PG:296 - 325 :: REGRESS. :PRIM. :OTH.STAT. :EXEC.COMP.

SMITH ,AJ CIT: 0.58
THE SEC REVERSAL OF FASB STATEMENT NO.19: AN INVESTIGATION OF INFORMATION EFFECTS
JAR ST 81 VOL: 19 PG:174 - 211 :: CORR. :PRIM. :EMH :OIL & GAS

SMITH ,AJ ; FIRS: DYCKMAN,TR CIT: 2.21
FINANCIAL ACCOUNTING AND REPORTING BY OIL AND GAS PRODUCING COMPANIES: A
STUDY OF INFORMATION EFFECTS
JAE MR 79 VOL: 1 PG:45 - 75 :: NON-PAR. :PRIM. :EMH :OIL & GAS

SMITH ,CH ; FIRS: GAA ,JC CIT: 0
AUDITORS AND DECEPTIVE FINANCIAL STATEMENTS: ASSIGNING RESPONSIBILITY AND BLAME
CAR SP 85 VOL: 1 PG:219 - 241 :: ANOVA :SURV. :INSTIT. :ERRORS

SMITH ,CH ; FIRS: PANY ,K CIT: 0
AUDITOR ASSOCIATION WITH QUARTERLY FINANCIAL INFORMATION: AN EMPIRICAL TEST
JAR AU 82 VOL: 20 PG:472 - 481 :: ANOVA :LAB. :OTH.BEH. :OPIN.

SMITH ,CH ; FIRS: WILCOX,KA CIT: 0
ROLE DISCREPANCIES AND THE AUDITOR-CLIENT RELATIONSHIP
AOS 01 77 VOL: 2 PG:81 - 97 :: NON-PAR. :FIELD :OTH.STAT. :AUD.

SMITH ,CH ; FIRS: BIRD ,FA ; SEC: DAVIDSON,LF CIT: 0.12
PERCEPTIONS OF EXTERNAL ACCOUNTING TRANSFERS UNDER ENTITY AND PROPRIETARY THEORY
TAR AP 74 VOL: 49 PG:233 - 244 :: QUAL. :INT. LOG. :THEORY :FIN.METH.

SMITH ,CH ; SEC: LANIER,RA ; THIR: TAYLOR,ME CIT: 0.12
THE NEED FOR AND SCOPE OF THE AUDIT OF MANAGEMENT: A SURVEY OF ATTITUDES
TAR AP 72 VOL: 47 PG:270 - 283 :: DES.STAT. :SURV. :INSTIT. :AUD.

SMITH ,CW ; FIRS: KOTHARI,SP ; SEC: LYS ,T ; FOUR: WATTS ,RL CIT: 0.6
AUDITOR LIABILITY AND INFORMATION DISCLOSURE
JAA AU 88 VOL: 3 PG:307 - 340 :: DES.STAT. :INT. LOG. :OTH. :LIAB.

SMITH ,D ; FIRS: ETTREDGE,M ; SEC: SHANE ,PB CIT: 0
AUDIT FIRM SIZE AND THE ASSOCIATION BETWEEN REPORTED EARNINGS AND SECURITY
AUD SP 88 VOL: 07 PG:29 - 42 :: REGRESS. :PRIM. :EMH :AUD.THEOR.

SMITH ,DB ; SEC: POURCIAU,S CIT: 0.4
A COMPARISON OF THE FINANCIAL CHARACTERISTICS OF DECEMBER AND NON-DECEMBER
YEAR-END COMPANIES
JAE DE 88 VOL: 10 PG:335 - 344 :: REGRESS. :PRIM. :OTH. :FIN.ST.TIM.

SMITH ,DB CIT: 0
AN INVESTIGATION OF SECURITIES AND EXCHANGE COMMISSION REGULATION OF AUDITOR
CHANGE DISCLOSURES: THE CASE OF ACCOUNTING SERIES RELEASE NO. 165
JAR SP 88 VOL: 26 PG:134 - 145 :: REGRESS. :PRIM. :EMH :AUD.THEOR.

SMITH ,DB CIT: 0.29
AUDITOR SUBJECT TO OPINIONS, DISCLAIMERS, AND AUDITOR CHANGES
AUD AU 86 VOL: 6 PG:95 - 108 :: DES.STAT. :PRIM. :OTH.STAT. :OPIN.

SMITH ,DB ; SEC: STETTLER,HF ; THIR: BEEDLES,W CIT: 0.22
AN INVESTIGATION OF THE INFORMATION CONTENT OF FOREIGN SENSITIVE PAYMENT DISCLOSURES
JAE AG 84 VOL: 6 PG:153 - 162 :: REGRESS. :PRIM. :EMH :N/A

SMITH ,DB ; FIRS: NICHOLS,DR CIT: 0.4
AUDITOR CREDIBILITY AND AUDITOR CHANGES
JAR AU 83 VOL: 21 PG:534 - 544 :: REGRESS. :PRIM. :EMH :AUD.

SMITH ,DB ; SEC: NICHOLS,DR CIT: 0.09
A MARKET TEST OF INVESTOR REACTION TO DISAGREEMENTS
JAE OC 82 VOL: 4 PG:109 - 120 :: DES.STAT. :SEC. :EMH :MAN.DEC.CHAR.

SMITH ,ED ; FIRS: DHALIWAL,DS ; SEC: SALAMON,GL CIT: 2.18
THE EFFECT OF OWNER VERSUS MANAGEMENT CONTROL ON THE CHOICE OF ACCOUNTING METHODS
JAE JL 82 VOL: 4 PG:41 - 53 :: NON-PAR. :SEC. :TIME SER. :AMOR./DEPL.

SMITH ,ED CIT: 0.88
THE EFFECT OF SEPARATION OF OWNERSHIP FROM CONTROL ON ACCOUNTING POLICY DECISIONS
TAR OC 76 VOL: 51 PG:707 - 723 :: NON-PAR. :PRIM. :OTH. :FIN.METH.

SMITH ,G ; SEC: KROGSTAD,JL CIT: 0
SOURCES AND USES OF AUDITING: A JOURNAL OF PRACTICE & THEORY'S LITERATURE: THE FIRST DECADE
AUD AU 91 VOL: 10 PG:84 - 97 :: REGRESS. :SEC. :HIST. :AUD.

SMITH ,G CIT: 0
A TAXONOMY OF CONTENT AND CITATIONS IN AUDITING: A JOURNAL OF PRACTICE & THEORY
AUD AU 88 VOL: 08 PG:108 - 117 :: REGRESS. :SEC. :THEORY :METHOD.

SMITH ,G ; SEC: KROGSTAD,JL CIT: 0.11
IMPACT OF SOURCES AND AUTHORS ON AUDITING: A JOURNAL OF PRACTICE & THEORY - A CITATION ANALYSIS
AUD AU 84 VOL: 4 PG:107 - 117 :: DES.STAT. :SEC. :OTH.STAT. :METHOD.

SMITH ,JE ; SEC: SMITH ,NP CIT: 0.24
READABILITY: A MEASURE OF THE PERFORMANCE OF THE COMMUNICATION FUNCTION OF FINANCIAL REPORTING
TAR JL 71 VOL: 46 PG:552 - 561 :: NON-PAR. :PRIM. :N/A :OTH.MANAG.

SMITH ,JH ; FIRS: DEJONG,DV CIT: 0.11
THE DETERMINATION OF AUDIT RESPONSIBILITIES: AN APPLICATION OF AGENCY THEORY
AUD AU 84 VOL: 4 PG:20 - 34 :: QUAL. :INT. LOG. :INF.ECO./AG. :LIAB.

SMITH ,JH ; FIRS: LEMBKE,VC CIT: 0
REPLACEMENT COSTS: AN ANALYSIS OF FINANCIAL STATEMENT AND TAX POLICY EFFECTS
JAA WI 80 VOL: 3 PG:147 - 162 :: DES.STAT. :PRIM. :THEORY :VALUAT.(INFL.)

SMITH ,KA CIT: 0.12
THE RELATIONSHIP OF INTERNAL CONTROL EVALUATION AND AUDIT SAMPLE SIZE
TAR AP 72 VOL: 47 PG:260 - 269 :: ANAL. :INT. LOG. :OTH.STAT. :SAMP.

SMITH ,KJ ; FIRS: GORDON,LA CIT: 0
POSTAUDITING CAPITAL EXPENDITURES AND FIRM PERFORMANCE: THE ROLE OF ASYMMETRIC INFORMATION
AOS 92 VOL: 17 PG:741 - 757 :: REGRESS. :PRIM. :OTH.BEH. :CAP.BUDG.

SMITH ,L ; FIRS: SMIELIAUSKAS,W CIT: 0
A THEORY OF EVIDENCE BASED ON AUDIT ASSERTIONS
CAR SP 90 VOL: 6 PG:407 - 426 :: DES.STAT. :INT. LOG. :THEORY :AUD.THEOR.

SMITH ,LW ; FIRS: WIGGINS JR,CE CIT: 0.17
A GENERALIZED AUDIT SIMULATION TOOL FOR EVALUATING THE RELIABILITY OF INTERNAL CONTROLS
CAR SP 87 VOL: 3 PG:316 - 337 :: DES.STAT. :SIM. :OTH. :INT.CONT.

SMITH ,NP ; FIRS: SMITH ,JE CIT: 0.24
READABILITY: A MEASURE OF THE PERFORMANCE OF THE COMMUNICATION FUNCTION OF FINANCIAL REPORTING
TAR JL 71 VOL: 46 PG:552 - 561 :: NON-PAR. :PRIM. :N/A :OTH.MANAG.

SMITH ,RE ; FIRS: NORTON,CL CIT: 0.29
A COMPARISON OF GENERAL PRICE LEVEL AND HISTORICAL COST FINANCIAL STATEMENTS IN THE PREDICTION OF BANKRUPTCY
TAR JA 79 VOL: 54 PG:72 - 87 :: OTH.QUANT. :PRIM. :OTH.STAT. :VALUAT.(INFL.)

SMITH ,VL ; SEC: SCHATZBERG,J ; THIR: WALLER,WS CIT: 1
EXPERIMENTAL ECONOMICS AND AUDITING
AUD AU 87 VOL: 7 PG:71 - 93 :: DES.STAT. :INT. LOG. :OTH. :METHOD.

SMITH ,VL ; FIRS: MANES ,RP CIT: 0
ECONOMIC JOINT COST THEORY AND ACCOUNTING PRACTICE
TAR JA 65 VOL: 40 PG:31 - 35 :: ANAL. :INT. LOG. :N/A :COST.ALLOC.

SMITH JR,CW ; FIRS: MIAN ,SL CIT: 0.67
INCENTIVES FOR UNCONSOLIDATED FINANCIAL REPORTING
JAE JA 90 VOL: 12 PG:141 - 171 :: REGRESS. :PRIM. :OTH.STAT. :BUS.COMB.

SMITH JR,CW ; FIRS: MIAN ,SL CIT: 0.33
INCENTIVES ASSOCIATED WITH CHANGES IN CONSOLIDATED REPORTING REQUIREMENTS
JAE OC 90 VOL: 13 PG:249 - 266 :: REGRESS. :PRIM. :OTH.STAT. :FASB SUBM.

SMITH JR,JM ; FIRS: PURDY ,CR ; THIR: GRAY ,J CIT: 0
THE VISIBILITY OF THE AUDITOR'S DISCLOSURE OF DEVIANCE FROM APB OPINION: AN EMPIRICAL TEST
JAR ST 69 VOL: 7 PG:1 - 18 :: ANOVA :LAB. :OTH.BEH. :INFO.STRUC.

SMOLINSKI,EJ CIT: 0
THE ADJUNCT METHOD IN CONSOLIDATIONS
JAR AU 63 VOL: 1 PG:149 - 178 :: QUAL. :INT. LOG. :THEORY :BUS.COMB.

SMYTH ,DJ ; FIRS: MANES ,RP ; SEC: SAMUELS,JM CIT: 0
INVENTORIES AND SALES: A CROSS SECTION STUDY
JAR ST 67 VOL: 5 PG:139 - 156 :: REGRESS. :PRIM. :THEORY :INV.

SNAVELY,HJ CIT: 0.06
CURRENT COST FOR LONG-LIVED ASSETS: A CRITICAL VIEW
TAR AP 69 VOL: 44 PG:344 - 353 :: QUAL. :INT. LOG. :THEORY :VALUAT.(INFL.)

SNAVELY,HJ CIT: 0.12
ACCOUNTING INFORMATION CRITERIA
TAR AP 67 VOL: 42 PG:223 - 232 :: QUAL. :INT. LOG. :THEORY :FIN.METH.

SNG ,J ; FIRS: TROTMAN,KT CIT: 0
THE EFFECT OF HYPOTHESIS FRAMING, PRIOR EXPECTATIONS AND CUE DIAGNOSTICITY ON AUDITORS' INFORMATION CHOICE
AOS 06 89 VOL: 14 PG:565 - 576 :: REGRESS. :LAB. :HIPS :JUDG.

SNODGRASS,C ; FIRS: BIRNBERG,JG CIT: 0.6
CULTURE AND CONTROL: A FIELD STUDY
AOS 05 88 VOL: 13 PG:447 - 464 :: REGRESS. :SURV. :OTH.BEH. :INT.DIFF.

SNOWBALL,D ; FIRS: BAMBER,EM ; THIR: TUBBS ,RM CIT: 0.5
AUDIT STRUCTURE AND ITS RELATION TO ROLE CONFLICT AND ROLE AMBIGUITY: AN
TAR AP 89 VOL: 64 PG:285 - 299 :: REGRESS. :FIELD :HIPS :AUD.

SNOWBALL,D ; FIRS: BAMBER,EM CIT: 0
AN EXPERIMENTAL STUDY OF THE EFFECTS OF AUDIT STRUCTURE IN UNCERTAIN TASK ENVIRONMENTS
AUD JL 88 VOL: 63 PG:490 - 504 :: REGRESS. :LAB. :OTH.BEH. :JUDG.

SNOWBALL,D CIT: 0
ACCOUNTING LABORATORY EXPERIMENTS ON HUMAN JUDGMENT: SOME CHARACTERISTICS AND INFLUENCES
AOS 01 86 VOL: 11 PG:47 - 70 :: REGRESS. :SEC. :HIPS :METHOD.

SNOWBALL,D ; FIRS: ABDEL-KHALIK,AR ; THIR: WRAGGE,JH CIT: 0.4
THE EFFECTS OF CERTAIN INTERNAL AUDIT VARIABLES ON THE PLANNING OF EXTERNAL AUDIT PROGRAMS
TAR AP 83 VOL: 58 PG:215 - 227 :: ANOVA :LAB. :OTH.BEH. :INT.AUD.

SNOWBALL,D CIT: 0.54
SOME EFFECTS OF ACCOUNTING EXPERTISE AND INFORMATION LOAD: AN EMPIRICAL STUDY
AOS 03 80 VOL: 5 PG:323 - 340 :: ANOVA :LAB. :HIPS :AUD.BEH.

SOETERS,J ; SEC: SCHREUDER,H CIT: 0.8
THE INTERACTION BETWEEN NATIONAL AND ORGANIZATIONAL CULTURES IN ACCOUNTING
AOS 01 88 VOL: 13 PG:75 - 85 :: REGRESS. :SURV. :OTH.BEH. :AUD.BEH.

SOHN ,S ; FIRS: LYS ,T CIT: 1
THE ASSOCIATION BETWEEN REVISIONS OF FINANCIAL ANALYSTS' EARNINGS FORECASTS AND SECURITY-PRICE CHANGES
JAE DE 90 VOL: 13 PG:341 - 363 :: REGRESS. :PRIM. :OTH.STAT. :FOREC.

SOLOMON,I ; FIRS: BROWN ,CE CIT: 0.5
CONFIGURAL INFORMATION PROCESSING IN AUDITING: THE ROLE OF DOMAIN-SPECIFIC KNOWLEDGE
TAR JA 91 VOL: 66 PG:100 - 119 :: REGRESS. :LAB. :HIPS :AUD.

SOLOMON,I ; FIRS: BROWN ,CE CIT: 0.33
AUDITOR CONFIGURAL INFORMATION PROCESSING IN CONTROL RISK ASSESSMENT
AUD AU 90 VOL: 9 PG:17 - 38 :: REGRESS. :LAB. :HIPS :RISK

SOLOMON,I ; FIRS: SHIELDS,MD ; THIR: WALLER,WS CIT: 0
AUDITORS' USAGE OF UNAUDITED BOOK VALUES WHEN MAKING PRESAMPLING AUDIT VALUE ESTIMATES
CAR AU 88 VOL: 5 PG:1 - 18 :: REGRESS. :LAB. :HIPS :PLAN.

SOLOMON,I ; FIRS: SHIELDS,MD ; THIR: WALLER,WS CIT: 0.33
EFFECTS OF ALTERNATIVE SAMPLE SPACE REPRESENTATIONS ON THE ACCURACY OF AUDITORS' UNCERTAINTY JUDGMENTS
AOS 04 87 VOL: 12 PG:375 - 385 :: REGRESS. :LAB. :HIPS :MAN.DEC.CHAR.

SOLOMON,I ; FIRS: BROWN ,C CIT: 0.5
EFFECTS OF OUTCOME INFORMATION ON EVALUATIONS OF MANAGERIAL DECISIONS
TAR JL 87 VOL: 62 PG:564 - 577 :: REGRESS. :LAB. :OTH.BEH. :BUDG.& PLAN.

SOLOMON,I ; FIRS: SCHROEDER,MS ; THIR: VICKREY,DW CIT: 0.14
AUDIT QUALITY: THE PERCEPTIONS OF AUDIT-COMMITTEE CHAIRPERSONS AND AUDIT PARTNERS
AUD SP 86 VOL: 5 PG:86 - 94 :: REGRESS. :SURV. :OTH.BEH. :OPER.AUD.

SOLOMON,I ; FIRS: BECK ,PJ CIT: 0.38
EX POST SAMPLING RISKS AND DECISION RULE CHOICE IN SUBSTANTIVE TESTING
AUD SP 85 VOL: 4 PG:1 - 10 :: DES.STAT. :INT. LOG. :OTH.STAT. :SAMP.

SOLOMON,I ; FIRS: BECK ,PJ ; THIR: TOMASSINI,LA CIT: 0.38
SUBJECTIVE PRIOR PROBABILITY DISTRIBUTIONS AND AUDIT RISK
JAR SP 85 VOL: 23 PG:37 - 56 :: REGRESS. :INT. LOG. :OTH.BEH. :RISK

SOLOMON,I ; SEC: KROGSTAD,JL ; THIR: ROMNEY,MB ; FOUR: TOMASSINI,LA CIT: 0.64
AUDITORS' PRIOR PROBABILITY DISTRIBUTIONS FOR ACCOUNT BALANCES
AOS 01 82 VOL: 7 PG:27 - 42 :: DES.STAT. :LAB. :HIPS :PROB.ELIC.

SOLOMON,I CIT: 1
PROBABILITY ASSESSMENT BY INDIVIDUAL AUDITORS AND AUDIT TEAMS: AN EMPIRICAL INVESTIGATION
JAR AU 82 VOL: 20 PG:689 - 710 :: DES.STAT. :LAB. :HIPS :AUD.BEH.

SOLOMON,KI ; FIRS: KAPLAN,HG CIT: 0
REGULATION OF THE ACCOUNTING PROFESSION IN ISRAEL
TAR JA 64 VOL: 39 PG:145 - 149 :: QUAL. :INT. LOG. :INSTIT. :OTH.MANAG.

SOLOMONS,D CIT: 0
BREAKEVEN ANALYSIS UNDER ABSORPTION COSTING
TAR JL 68 VOL: 43 PG:447 - 452 :: ANAL. :INT. LOG. :N/A :C-V-P-A

SOMEYA,K CIT: 0
THE USE OF FUNDS STATEMENTS IN JAPAN
TAR OC 64 VOL: 39 PG:983 - 989 :: DES.STAT. :SURV. :INSTIT. :MANAG.

SOMMERFELD,RM CIT: 0
TAX IMPLICATIONS FOR THE VISITING PROFESSOR
TAR OC 67 VOL: 42 PG:747 - 750 :: QUAL. :INT. LOG. :N/A :TAXES

SONDHI,AC ; FIRS: RONEN ,J CIT: 0.25
DEBT CAPACITY AND FINANCIAL CONTRACTING: FINANCE SUBSIDIARIES
JAA SP 89 VOL: 4 PG:237 - 265 :: ANOVA :MIXED :OTH.STAT. :SPEC.ITEMS

SONG ,I ; FIRS: LOBO ,GJ CIT: 0.5
THE INCREMENTAL INFORMATION IN SFAS NO. 33 INCOME DISCLOSURES OVER HISTORICAL COST INCOME AND ITS CASH AND ACCRUAL COMPON
TAR AP 89 VOL: 64 PG:329 - 343 :: REGRESS. :PRIM. :EMH :FIN.METH.

SOPER ,FJ ; SEC: DOLPHIN,R CIT: 0.06
READABILITY AND CORPORATE ANNUAL REPORTS
TAR AP 64 VOL: 39 PG:358 - 362 :: DES.STAT. :PRIM. :N/A :OTH.MANAG.

SORENSEN,JE ; FIRS: RHODE ,JG ; THIR: LAWLER III,EE CIT: 0.69
SOURCES OF PROFESSIONAL STAFF TURNOVER IN PUBLIC ACCOUNTING FIRMS REVEALED BY THE EXIT INTERVIEW
AOS 02 77 VOL: 2 PG:165 - 176 :: NON-PAR. :SURV. :OTH. :ORG.

SORENSEN,JE ; SEC: GROVE ,HD CIT: 0.06
COST-OUTCOME AND COST-EFFECTIVENESS ANALYSIS: EMERGING NONPROFIT PERFORMANCE EVALUATION TECHNIQUES
TAR JL 77 VOL: 52 PG:658 - 675 :: ANAL. :SEC. :OTH.STAT. :REL.COSTS

SORENSEN,JE ; SEC: FRANKS,DD CIT: 0.18
THE RELATIVE CONTRIBUTION OF ABILITY, SELF-ESTEEM AND EVALUATIVE FEEDBACK TO PERFORMANCE: IMPLICATIONS FOR ACCOUNTING SYSTEMS
TAR OC 72 VOL: 47 PG:735 - 746 :: ANOVA :FIELD :OTH.BEH. :OTH.MANAG.

SORENSEN,JE CIT: 0.41
BAYESIAN ANALYSIS IN AUDITING
TAR JL 69 VOL: 44 PG:555 - 561 :: ANAL. :INT. LOG. :OTH.STAT. :SAMP.

SORENSEN,JE CIT: 0.71
PROFESSIONAL AND BUREAUCRATIC ORGANIZATION IN THE PUBLIC ACCOUNTING FIRM
TAR JL 67 VOL: 42 PG:553 - 565 :: ANOVA :SURV. :OTH.BEH. :AUD.BEH.

SORENSEN,R ; FIRS: GROVES,R ; SEC: MANES ,RP CIT: 0.06
THE APPLICATION OF THE HIRSCH-DANTZIG FIXED CHARGE ALGORITHM TO PROFIT PLANNING: A FORMAL STATEMENT OF PRODUCT PROFITABILITY A
TAR JL 70 VOL: 45 PG:481 - 489 :: ANAL. :INT. LOG. :MATH.PROG. :BUDG.& PLAN.

SORTER,G ; FIRS: RONEN ,J CIT: 0
REFLECTIONS ON "REFLECTIONS ON THE FASB'S CONCEPTUAL FRAMEWORK FOR ACCOUNTING AND ON AUDITING
JAA WI 89 VOL: 4 PG:67 - 77 :: REGRESS. :SEC. :INSTIT. :FASB SUBM.

SORTER,GH ; SEC: SIEGEL,S ; THIR: SLAIN ,J CIT: 0.2
ACCOUNTANTS' LEGAL LIABILITY: A DETERMINANT OF THE ACCOUNTING MODEL
JAA SU 88 VOL: 03 PG:233 - 244 :: DES.STAT. :INT. LOG. :THEORY :LIAB.

SORTER,GH ; SEC: INGBERMAN,M CIT: 0
THE IMPLICIT CRITERIA FOR THE RECOGNITION, QUANTIFICATION , AND REPORTING O F ACCOUNTING EVENTS
JAA SP 87 VOL: 2 PG:99 - 116 :: DES.STAT. :INT. LOG. :THEORY :REV.REC.

SORTER,GH CIT: 0
THE EMPHASIS ON CASH AND ITS IMPACT ON THE FUNDS STATEMENT - SENSE AND NONSENSE
JAA SP 82 VOL: 5 PG:188 - 194 :: QUAL. :INT. LOG. :THEORY :CASH

SORTER,GH ; FIRS: INGBERMAN,M CIT: 0
THE ROLE OF FINANCIAL STATEMENTS IN AN EFFICIENT MARKET
JAA AU 78 VOL: 2 PG:58 - 62 :: QUAL. :INT. LOG. :INSTIT. :FIN.METH.

SORTER,GH ; FIRS: SCHIFF,M ; THIR: WIESEN,JL CIT: 0
THE EVOLVING ROLE OF CORPORATE AUDIT COMMITTEES
JAA AU 77 VOL: 1 PG:19 - 44 :: QUAL. :INT. LOG. :INSTIT. :OTH.MANAG.

SORTER,GH ; FIRS: BECKER,S ; SEC: RONEN ,J CIT: 0.35
OPPORTUNITY COSTS - AN EXPERIMENTAL APPROACH
JAR AU 74 VOL: 12 PG:317 - 329 :: ANOVA :LAB. :OTH.BEH. :REL.COSTS

SORTER,GH ; SEC: GANS ,MS CIT: 0
OPPORTUNITIES AND IMPLICATIONS OF THE REPORT ON OBJECTIVES OF FINANCIAL STATEMENTS
JAR ST 74 VOL: 12 PG:1 - 12 :: QUAL. :INT. LOG. :THEORY :FIN.METH.

SORTER,GH ; FIRS: ROSE ,R ; SEC: BEAVER,WH ; THIR: BECKER,S CIT: 0.65
TOWARD AN EMPIRICAL MEASURE OF MATERIALITY
JAR ST 70 VOL: 8 PG:138 - 148 :: DES.STAT. :LAB. :OTH.BEH. :MAT.

SORTER,GH CIT: 0.82
AN EVENTS APPROACH TO BASIC ACCOUNTING THEORY
TAR JA 69 VOL: 44 PG:12 - 19 :: QUAL. :INT. LOG. :THEORY :INFO.STRUC.

SORTER,GH ; SEC: BECKER,S ; THIR: ARCHIBALD,TR ; FOUR: BEAVER,WH CIT: 0.35
CORPORATE PERSONALITY AS REFLECTED IN ACCOUNTING DECISIONS: SOME PRELIMINARY FINDINGS
JAR AU 64 VOL: 2 PG:183 - 196 :: ANOVA :SURV. :THEORY :ORG.FORM

SORTER,GH ; FIRS: HORNGREN,CT CIT: 0
AN EVALUATION OF SOME CRITICISMS OF RELEVANT COSTING
TAR AP 64 VOL: 39 PG:417 - 420 :: QUAL. :INT. LOG. :N/A :COST.ALLOC.

SOTTO ,R CIT: 0.1
SCIENTIFIC UTOPIA AND ACCOUNTING
AOS 01 83 VOL: 8 PG:57 - 72 :: QUAL. :INT. LOG. :THEORY :N/A

SOUDERS,TL ; FIRS: KILLOUGH,LN CIT: 0.24
A GOAL PROGRAMMING MODEL FOR PUBLIC ACCOUNTING FIRMS
TAR AP 73 VOL: 48 PG:268 - 279 :: ANAL. :INT. LOG. :MATH.PROG. :ORG.

SPACEK,L CIT: 0
A SUGGESTED SOLUTION TO THE PRINCIPLES DILEMMA
TAR AP 64 VOL: 39 PG:275 - 284 :: QUAL. :INT. LOG. :THEORY :OTH.FIN.ACC.

SPENCER,CH ; SEC: BARNISEL,TS CIT: 0
A DECADE OF PRICE-LEVEL CHANGES - THE EFFECT ON THE FINANCIAL STATEMENTS OF CUMMINS ENGINE COMPANY
TAR JA 65 VOL: 40 PG:144 - 153 :: DES.STAT. :CASE :THEORY :VALUAT.(INFL.)

SPENCER,MH CIT: 0
AXIOMATIC METHOD AND ACCOUNTING SCIENCE
TAR AP 63 VOL: 38 PG:310 - 316 :: QUAL. :INT. LOG. :THEORY :OTH.MANAG.

SPERO ,LL ; FIRS: RAMAGE,JG ; SEC: KRIEGER,AM CIT: 0.79
AN EMPIRICAL STUDY OF ERROR CHARACTERISTICS IN AUDIT POPULATIONS
JAR ST 79 VOL: 17 PG:72 - 102 :: DES.STAT. :PRIM. :OTH.STAT. :ERRORS

SPICER,BH CIT: 0.2
TOWARDS AN ORGANIZATIONAL THEORY OF THE TRANSFER PRICING PROCESS
AOS 03 88 VOL: 13 PG:303 - 322 :: DES.STAT. :INT. LOG. :THEORY :TRANS.PRIC.

SPICER,BH ; SEC: BALLEW,V CIT: 0.9
MANAGEMENT ACCOUNTING SYSTEMS AND THE ECONOMICS OF INTERNAL ORGANIZATION
AOS 01 83 VOL: 8 PG:73 - 98 :: QUAL. :INT. LOG. :THEORY :MANAG.

SPICER,BH ; FIRS: SHANE ,PB CIT: 0.6
MARKET RESPONSE TO ENVIRONMENTAL INFORMATION PRODUCED OUTSIDE THE FIRM
TAR JL 83 VOL: 58 PG:521 - 538 :: DES.STAT. :PRIM. :EMH :ORG.& ENVIR.

SPICER,BM CIT: 0.67
INVESTORS, CORPORATE SOCIAL PERFORMANCE AND INFORMATION DISCLOSURE: AN EMPIRICAL STUDY
TAR JA 78 VOL: 53 PG:94 - 111 :: NON-PAR. :PRIM. :OTH.STAT. :HRA

SPILLER JR,EA ; SEC: VIRGIL JR,RL CIT: 0.06
EFFECTIVENESS OF APB OPINION NO.19 IN IMPROVING FUNDS REPORTING
JAR SP 74 VOL: 12 PG:112 - 142 :: DES.STAT. :LAB. :THEORY :INFO.STRUC.

SPILLER JR,EA CIT: 0
THEORY AND PRACTICE IN THE DEVELOPMENT OF ACCOUNTING
TAR OC 64 VOL: 39 PG:850 - 859 :: QUAL. :INT. LOG. :THEORY :FIN.METH.

SPIRES,EE ; FIRS: DILLARD,JF ; SEC: KAUFFMAN,NL CIT: 0
EVIDENCE ORDER AND BELIEF REVISION IN MANAGEMENT ACCOUNTING DECISIONS
AOS 91 VOL: 16 PG:619 - 633 :: REGRESS. :LAB. :HIPS :AUD.BEH.

SPIRES,EE CIT: 0.5
AUDITORS' EVALUATION OF TEST-OF-CONTROL STRENGTH
TAR AP 91 VOL: 66 PG:259 - 276 :: REGRESS. :LAB. :HIPS :JUDG.

SPROUSE,RT CIT: 0
OBSERVATIONS CONCERNING THE REALIZATION CONCEPT
TAR JL 65 VOL: 40 PG:522 - 526 :: QUAL. :INT. LOG. :THEORY :VALUAT.(INFL.)

SPROUSE,RT CIT: 0
HISTORICAL COSTS AND CURRENT ASSETS - TRADITIONAL AND TREACHEROUS
TAR OC 63 VOL: 38 PG:687 - 695 :: QUAL. :INT. LOG. :THEORY :VALUAT.(INFL.)

SRINIDHI,B ; FIRS: HALPERIN,RM CIT: 0
U.S. INCOME TAX TRANSFER-PRICING RULES AND RESOURCE ALLOCATION: THE CASE OF DECENTRALIZED MULTINATIONAL FIRMS
TAR JA 91 VOL: 66 PG:141 - 157 :: REGRESS. :INT. LOG. :INF.ECO./AG. :TRANS.PRIC.

SRINIDHI,BN ; FIRS: BALACHANDRAN,KR CIT: 0
A RATIONALE FOR FIXED CHARGE APPLICATION
JAA SP 87 VOL: 2 PG:151 - 169 :: DES.STAT. :INT. LOG. :MATH.PROG. :COST.ALLOC.

SRINIDHI,BN ; FIRS: HALPERIN,R CIT: 0
THE EFFECTS OF THE U.S. INCOME TAX REGULATIONS' TRANSFER PRICING RULE
TAR OC 87 VOL: 62 PG:686 - 706 :: REGRESS. :INT. LOG. :THEORY :TRANS.PRIC.

SRINIDHI,BN ; SEC: VASARHELYI,MA CIT: 0
AUDITOR JUDGMENT CONCERNING ESTABLISHMENT OF SUBSTANTIVE TESTS BASED ON INTERNAL CONTROL RELIABILITY
AUD SP 86 VOL: 5 PG:64 - 76 :: REGRESS. :LAB. :OTH.STAT. :INT.CONT.

SRIVASTAVA,R ; FIRS: SHAFER,G CIT: 0
THE BAYESIAN AND BELIEF-FUNCTION FORMALISMS-A GENERAL PERSPECTIVE FOR AUDITING
AUD 90 VOL: 9 PG:110 - 137 :: DES.STAT. :INT. LOG. :OTH.STAT. :AUD.BEH.

SRIVASTAVA,RP ; SEC: SHAFER,GR CIT: 0
BELIEF-FUNCTION FORMULAS FOR AUDIT RISK
TAR AP 92 VOL: 67 PG:249 - 283 :: REGRESS. :INT. LOG. :MATH.PROG. :AUD.BEH.

SRIVASTAVA,RP CIT: 0
AUDITING FUNCTIONS FOR INTERNAL CONTROL SYSTEMS WITH INTERDEPENDENT DOCUMENTS AND CHANNELS
JAR AU 86 VOL: 24 PG:422 - 427 :: DES.STAT. :INT. LOG. :OTH.STAT. :INT.CONT.

ST.PIERRE,K CIT: 0
INDEPENDENCE AND AUDITOR SANCTIONS
JAA SP 84 VOL: 7 PG:257 - 263 :: QUAL. :INT. LOG. :OTH. :INDEP.

ST.PIERRE,K ; SEC: ANDERSON,JA CIT: 1.33
AN ANALYSIS OF THE FACTORS ASSOCIATED WITH LAWSUITS AGAINST PUBLIC ACCOUNTANTS
TAR AP 84 VOL: 59 PG:242 - 263 :: DES.STAT. :PRIM. :INSTIT. :LIAB.

ST.PIERRE,K ; SEC: ANDERSON,JA CIT: 0
AN ANALYSIS OF AUDIT FAILURES BASED ON DOCUMENTED LEGAL CASES
JAA SP 82 VOL: 5 PG:229 - 247 :: DES.STAT. :PRIM. :OTH. :ERRORS

STAATS,EB CIT: 0
AUDITING AS WE ENTER THE 21ST CENTURY - WHAT NEW CHALLENGES WILL HAVE TO BE MET
AUD SU 81 VOL: 1 PG:1 - 11 :: QUAL. :INT. LOG. :INSTIT. :AUD.

STAGLIANO,AJ ; FIRS: RECKERS,PMJ CIT: 0.17
NON-AUDIT SERVICES AND PERCEIVED INDEPENDENCE: SOME NEW EVIDENCE
AUD SU 81 VOL: 1 PG:23 - 37 :: ANOVA :LAB. :OTH.BEH. :INDEP.

STAHL ,MJ ; FIRS: HARRELL,AM CIT: 0
MCCLELLAND'S TRICHOTOMY OF NEEDS THEORY AND THE JOB SATISFACTION AND WORK PERFORMANCE OF CPA FIRM PROFESSIONALS
AOS 34 84 VOL: 9 PG:241 - 252 :: CORR. :LAB. :OTH.BEH. :AUD.BEH.

STALLMAN,JC CIT: 0.06
A FRAMEWORK FOR EVALUATING COST CONTROL PROCEDURES FOR A PROCESS
TAR OC 72 VOL: 47 PG:774 - 790 :: ANAL. :INT. LOG. :OTH.STAT. :MANAG.

STALLMAN,JC CIT: 0.29
TOWARD EXPERIMENTAL CRITERIA FOR JUDGING DISCLOSURE IMPROVEMENT
JAR ST 69 VOL: 7 PG:29 - 43 :: ANOVA :LAB. :OTH.STAT. :INFO.STRUC.

STANDISH,PEM ; SEC: UNG ,S CIT: 0
CORPORATE SIGNALING, ASSET REVALUATIONS, AND STOCK PRICES OF BRITISH COMPANIES
TAR OC 82 VOL: 57 PG:701 - 715 :: REGRESS. :PRIM. :EMH :VALUAT.(INFL.)

STANDISH,PEM CIT: 0
AN APPRAISAL OF THE TEACHING AND STUDY OF AUDITING
TAR JL 64 VOL: 39 PG:654 - 666 :: QUAL. :INT. LOG. :INSTIT. :OTH.MANAG.

STANLEY,CH CIT: 0
COST-BASIS VALUATIONS IN TRANSACTIONS BETWEEN ENTITIES
TAR JL 64 VOL: 39 PG:639 - 647 :: QUAL. :INT. LOG. :THEORY :VALUAT.(INFL.)

STARK ,A ; FIRS: GROJER,JE CIT: 0.25
SOCIAL ACCOUNTING: A SWEDISH ATTEMPT
AOS 04 77 VOL: 2 PG:349 - 385 :: QUAL. :CASE :THEORY :HRA

STARKS,L ; FIRS: JENNINGS,R CIT: 0.38
INFORMATION CONTENT AND THE SPEED OF STOCK PRICE ADJUSTMENT
JAR SP 85 VOL: 23 PG:336 - 350 :: REGRESS. :PRIM. :EMH :N/A

STAUBUS,GJ CIT: 0.25
AN INDUCED THEORY OF ACCOUNTING MEASUREMENT
TAR JA 85 VOL: 60 PG:53 - 75 :: DES.STAT. :INT. LOG. :THEORY :INFO.STRUC.

STAUBUS,GJ CIT: 0.06
THE EFFECTS OF PRICE-LEVEL RESTATEMENTS ON EARNINGS
TAR JL 76 VOL: 51 PG:574 - 589 :: QUAL. :INT. LOG. :THEORY :VALUAT.(INFL.)

STAUBUS,GJ CIT: 0
TESTING INVENTORY ACCOUNTING
TAR JL 68 VOL: 43 PG:413 - 424 :: ANOVA :PRIM. :N/A :INV.

STAUBUS,GJ CIT: 0.06
CURRENT CASH EQUIVALENT FOR ASSETS: A DISSENT
TAR OC 67 VOL: 42 PG:650 - 661 :: QUAL. :INT. LOG. :THEORY :VALUAT.(INFL.)

STAUBUS,GJ CIT: 0
ALTERNATIVE ASSET FLOW CONCEPTS
TAR JL 66 VOL: 41 PG:397 - 412 :: QUAL. :INT. LOG. :N/A :INFO.STRUC.

STAUBUS,GJ CIT: 0.12
THE ASSOCIATION OF FINANCIAL ACCOUNTING VARIABLES WITH COMMON STOCK VALUES
TAR JA 65 VOL: 40 PG:119 - 134 :: REGRESS. :PRIM. :TIME SER. :VALUAT.(INFL.)

STAUBUS,GJ CIT: 0
DIRECT, RELEVANT OR ABSORPTION COSTING?
TAR JA 63 VOL: 38 PG:64 - 74 :: QUAL. :INT. LOG. :THEORY :COST.ALLOC.

STEADMAN,GT ; FIRS: MOORES,K CIT: 0
THE COMPARATIVE VIEWPOINTS OF GROUPS OF ACCOUNTANTS: MORE ON THE ENTITY-PROPRIETARY DEBATE
AOS 01 86 VOL: 11 PG:19 - 34 :: REGRESS. :SURV. :INSTIT. :FASB SUBM.

STEECE,BM ; FIRS: MOORE ,ML ; THIR: SWENSON,CW CIT: 0.17
AN ANALYSIS OF THE IMPACT OF STATE INCOME TAX RATES AND BASES ON FOREIGN INVESTMENT
TAR OC 87 VOL: 62 PG:671 - 685 :: REGRESS. :PRIM. :TIME SER. :TAXES

STEECE,BM ; FIRS: MOORE ,ML ; THIR: SWENSON,CW CIT: 0
SOME EMPIRICAL EVIDENCE ON TAXPAYER RATIONALITY
TAR JA 85 VOL: 60 PG:18 - 32 :: REGRESS. :PRIM. :TIME SER. :TAXES

STEIN ,JL ; SEC: HONG ,BG CIT: 0
PRICE VOLATILITY AND SPECULATION
JAA SP 90 VOL: 5 PG:277 - 300 :: DES.STAT. :INT. LOG. :INF.ECO./AG. :OTH.MANAG.

STEIN ,MT ; FIRS: SIMUNIC,DA CIT: 0
AUDIT RISK IN A CLIENT PORTFOLIO CONTEXT
CAR SP 90 VOL: 6 PG:329 - 343 :: DES.STAT. :INT. LOG. :INF.ECO./AG. :RISK

STEINBART,PJ ; FIRS: LOEBBECKE,JK CIT: 0.33
AN INVESTIGATION OF THE USE OF PRELIMINARY ANALYTICAL REVIEW TO PROVIDE SUBSTANTIVE AUDIT EVIDENCE
AUD SP 87 VOL: 6 PG:74 - 89 :: REGRESS. :SIM. :OTH.STAT. :ANAL.REV.

STEINBART,PJ CIT: 0.5
MATERIALITY: A CASE STUDY USING EXPERT SYSTEMS
TAR JA 87 VOL: 62 PG:97 - 116 :: REGRESS. :INT. LOG. :EXP.SYST. :MAT.

STENING,BW ; FIRS: DAVISON,AG ; THIR: WAI ,WT CIT: 0
AUDITOR CONCENTRATION AND THE IMPACT OF INTERLOCKING DIRECTORATES
JAR SP 84 VOL: 22 PG:313 - 317 :: CORR. :PRIM. :OTH. :ORG.& ENVIR.

STEPHAN,J ; FIRS: FRANCIS,J ; SEC: PAGACH,D CIT: 0
THE STOCK MARKET RESPONSE TO EARNINGS ANNOUNCEMENTS RELEASED DURING TRADING VERSUS NONTRADING PERIODS
JAR AU 92 VOL: 30 PG:165 - 184 :: REGRESS. :PRIM. :EMH :FIN.ST.TIM.

STEPHAN,J ; FIRS: MORSE ,D ; THIR: STICE ,EK CIT: 0.5
EARNIGS ANNOUNCEMENTS AND THE CONVERGENCE (OR DIVERGENCE) OF BELIEFS
TAR AP 91 VOL: 66 PG:376 - 388 :: REGRESS. :PRIM. :EMH :AUD.BEH.

STEPHAN,J ; FIRS: DYCKMAN,TR ; SEC: PHILBRICK,D CIT: 0.89
A COMPARISON OF EVENT STUDY METHODOLOGIES USING DAILY STOCK RETURNS: A SIMULATION APPROACH
JAR ST 84 VOL: 22 PG:1 - 30 :: REGRESS. :SIM. :OTH.BEH. :METHOD.

STEPHENS,RG ; SEC: GOVINDARAJAN,V CIT: 0
ON ASSESSING A FIRM'S CASH GENERATING ABILITY
TAR JA 90 VOL: 65 PG:242 - 257 :: REGRESS. :CASE :HIPS :FIN.METH.

STEPHENS,RG CIT: 0.3
AN INVESTIGATION OF THE DESCRIPTIVENESS OF THE GENERAL THEORY OF EVIDENCE AND AUDITING
AUD AU 83 VOL: 3 PG:55 - 74 :: NON-PAR. :LAB. :OTH.STAT. :JUDG.

STERLING,RR ; SEC: TOLLEFSON,SO ; THIR: FLAHERTY,RE CIT: 0
EXCHANGE VALUATION: AN EMPIRICAL TEST
TAR OC 72 VOL: 47 PG:709 - 721 :: DES.STAT. :LAB. :THEORY :VALUAT.(INFL.)

STERLING,RR ; SEC: FLAHERTY,RE CIT: 0
THE ROLE OF LIQUIDITY IN EXCHANGE VALUATION
TAR JL 71 VOL: 46 PG:441 - 456 :: ANAL. :INT. LOG. :THEORY :VALUAT.(INFL.)

STERLING,RR CIT: 0.24
ON THEORY CONSTRUCTION AND VERIFICATION
TAR JL 70 VOL: 45 PG:444 - 457 :: QUAL. :INT. LOG. :THEORY :OTH.MANAG.

STERLING,RR ; SEC: RADOSEVICH,R CIT: 0.12
A VALUATION EXPERIMENT
JAR SP 69 VOL: 7 PG:90 - 95 :: DES.STAT. :LAB. :OTH. :AUD.

STERLING,RR CIT: 0.06
THE GOING CONCERN: AN EXAMINATION
TAR JL 68 VOL: 43 PG:481 - 502 :: QUAL. :INT. LOG. :THEORY :OTH.FIN.ACC.

STERLING,RR CIT: 0.06
ELEMENTS OF PURE ACCOUNTING THEORY
TAR JA 67 VOL: 42 PG:62 - 73 :: ANAL. :INT. LOG. :THEORY :FIN.METH.

STERNER,JA CIT: 0
AN EMPIRICAL EVALUATION OF SFAS NO.55
JAR AU 83 VOL: 21 PG:623 - 628 :: OTH.QUANT. :PRIM. :OTH.STAT. :REV.REC.

STETTLER,HF ; FIRS: SMITH ,DB ; THIR: BEEDLES,W CIT: 0.22
AN INVESTIGATION OF THE INFORMATION CONTENT OF FOREIGN SENSITIVE PAYMENT DISCLOSURES
JAE AG 84 VOL: 6 PG:153 - 162 :: REGRESS. :PRIM. :EMH :N/A

STETTLER,HF ; FIRS: REILLY,FK CIT: 0
FACTORS INFLUENCING SUCCESS ON THE CPA EXAMINATION
JAR AU 72 VOL: 10 PG:308 - 321 :: REGRESS. :PRIM. :OTH.STAT. :EDUC.

STETTLER,HF CIT: 0
ACCREDITATION OF COLLEGIATE ACCOUNTING PROGRAMS
TAR OC 65 VOL: 40 PG:723 - 730 :: QUAL. :INT. LOG. :INSTIT. :OTH.MANAG.

STEUER,RE ; FIRS: BALACHANDRAN,KR CIT: 0.09
AN INTERACTIVE MODEL FOR THE CPA FIRM AUDIT STAFF PLANNING PROBLEM WITH MULTIPLE OBJECTIVES
TAR JA 82 VOL: 57 PG:125 - 140 :: ANAL. :INT. LOG. :N/A :AUD.

STEVENS,JL ; SEC: JOSE ,ML CIT: 0
THE EFFECTS OF DIVIDEND PAYOUT, STABILITY, AND SMOOTHING ON FIRM VALUE
JAA SP 92 VOL: 7 PG:195 - 212 :: REGRESS. :PRIM. :EMH :CASH DIV.

STEVENSON,FL CIT: 0.33
NEW EVIDENCE ON LIFO ADOPTIONS: THE EFFECTS OF MORE PRECISE EVENT DATES
JAR AU 87 VOL: 25 PG:306 - 316 :: REGRESS. :PRIM. :EMH :INV.

STEVENSON,RA CIT: 0
CORPORATE STOCK REACQUISITIONS
TAR AP 66 VOL: 41 PG:312 - 317 :: QUAL. :CASE :N/A :INFO.STRUC.

STEVENSON,WC ; FIRS: WEBER ,RP CIT: 0.25
EVALUATIONS OF ACCOUNTING JOURNAL AND DEPARTMENT QUALITY
TAR JL 81 VOL: 56 PG:596 - 612 :: DES.STAT. :SIM. :OTH. :OTH.MANAG.

STEWART,JP ; FIRS: WILSON,ER CIT: 0.33
MUNICIPAL FINANCIAL REPORTING AND COMPETITION AMONG UNDERWRITERS FOR NEWS ISSUES OF GENERAL OBLIGATION BONDS
CAR SP 90 VOL: 6 PG:573 - 591 :: REGRESS. :PRIM. :EMH :LTD

STICE ,EK CIT: 0
THE MARKET REACTION TO 10-K AND 10-Q FILINGS AND TO SUBSEQUENT THE WALL STREET JOURNAL EARNINGS ANNOUNCEMENTS
TAR JA 91 VOL: 66 PG:42 - 55 :: REGRESS. :PRIM. :EMH :FIN.ST.TIM.

STICE ,EK ; FIRS: MORSE ,D ; SEC: STEPHAN,J CIT: 0.5
EARNIGS ANNOUNCEMENTS AND THE CONVERGENCE (OR DIVERGENCE) OF BELIEFS
TAR AP 91 VOL: 66 PG:376 - 388 :: REGRESS. :PRIM. :EMH :AUD.BEH.

STICE ,JD CIT: 0
USING FINANCIAL AND MARKET INFORMATION TO IDENTIFY PRE-ENGAGEMENT FACTORS ASSOCIATED WITH LAWSUITS AGAINST AUDITORS
TAR JL 91 VOL: 66 PG:516 - 534 :: DES.STAT. :PRIM. :THEORY :LITIG.

STICKEL,SE CIT: 0
COMMON STOCK RETURNS SURROUNDING EARNINGS FORECAST REVISIONS: MORE PUZZLING EVIDENCE
TAR AP 91 VOL: 66 PG:402 - 416 :: REGRESS. :PRIM. :EMH :AUD.BEH.

STICKEL,SE CIT: 0.75
THE TIMING OF AND INCENTIVES FOR ANNUAL EARNINGS FORECASTS NEAR INTERIM EARNINGS ANNOUNCEMENTS
JAE JL 89 VOL: 11 PG:275 - 292 :: REGRESS. :PRIM. :OTH.STAT. :FOREC.

STICKEL,SE CIT: 0
THE EFFECT OF PREFERRED STOCK RATING CHANGES ON PREFERRED AND COMMON STOCK PRICES
JAE OC 86 VOL: 8 PG:197 - 216 :: REGRESS. :PRIM. :EMH :LTD

STICKNEY,CP ; FIRS: CASEY JR,CJ ; SEC: MCGEE ,VE CIT: 0.43
DISCRIMINATING BETWEEN REORGANIZED AND LIQUIDATED FIRMS IN BANKRUPTCY
TAR AP 86 VOL: 61 PG:249 - 262 :: REGRESS. :PRIM. :OTH.STAT. :BUS.FAIL.

STICKNEY,CP ; FIRS: ALIBER,RZ CIT: 0.12
ACCOUNTING MEASURES OF FOREIGN EXCHANGE EXPOSURE: THE LONG AND SHORT OF IT
TAR JA 75 VOL: 50 PG:44 - 57 :: QUAL. :INT. LOG. :INSTIT. :FOR.CUR.

STIGLITZ,JE ; FIRS: GREENWALD,B CIT: 0
IMPACT OF THE CHANGING TAX ENVIRONMENT ON INVESTMENTS AND PRODUCTIVITY: FINANCIAL STRUCTURE AND THE CORPORATION INCOME TAX
JAA SU 89 VOL: 4 PG:281 - 297 :: DES.STAT. :INT. LOG. :INF.ECO./AG. :TAXES

STINSON,CH ; FIRS: BLACCONIERE,WG ; SEC: BOWEN ,RM ; THIR: SEFCIK,SE CIT: 0
DETERMINANTS OF THE USE OF REGULATORY ACCOUNTING PRINCIPLES BY SAVINGS AND LOANS
JAE JN 91 VOL: 14 PG:167 - 201 :: REGRESS. :PRIM. :OTH.STAT. :ACC.CHNG.

STINSON,CH ; FIRS: BARTH ,ME ; SEC: BEAVER,WH CIT: 1
SUPPLEMENTAL DATA AND THE STRUCTURE OF THRIFT SHARE PRICES
TAR JA 91 VOL: 66 PG:56 - 66 :: REGRESS. :PRIM. :TIME SER. :FIN.METH.

STOBER,TL CIT: 3
SUMMARY FINANCIAL STATEMENT MEASURES AND ANALYSTS' FORECASTS OF EARNINGS
JAE JN 92 VOL: 15 PG:347 - 372 :: REGRESS. :PRIM. :EMH :FOREC.

STOBER,TL ; FIRS: BERNARD,VL CIT: 1.25
THE NATURE AND AMOUNT OF INFORMATION IN CASH FLOWS AND ACCRUALS
TAR OC 89 VOL: 64 PG:624 - 652 :: REGRESS. :PRIM. :EMH :OTH.FIN.ACC.

STOBER,TL CIT: 0.71
THE INCREMENTAL INFORMATION CONTENT OF FINANCIAL STATEMENT DISCLOSURES: THE CASE OF LIFO INVENTORY LIQUIDATIONS
JAR ST 86 VOL: 24 PG:138 - 164 :: REGRESS. :PRIM. :EMH :INV.

STOCK ,D ; SEC: WATSON,CJ CIT: 0.44
HUMAN JUDGMENT ACCURACY, MULTIDIMENSIONAL GRAPHICS, AND HUMANS VERSUS MODELS
JAR SP 84 VOL: 22 PG:192 - 206 :: OTH.QUANT. :LAB. :HIPS :BUS.FAIL.

STOECKENIUS,J ; FIRS: NG ,DS CIT: 0.64
AUDITING: INCENTIVES AND TRUTHFUL REPORTING
JAR ST 79 VOL: 17 PG:1 - 24 :: ANAL. :INT. LOG. :INF.ECO./AG. :AUD.

STOELWINDER,JU ; FIRS: ABERNETHY,MA CIT: 0
BUDGET USE, TASK UNCERTAINTY, SYSTEM GOAL ORIENTATION AND SUBUNIT PERFORMANCE: A TEST OF THE 'FIT' HYPOTHESIS IN NOT-FOR-PROFIT
AOS 02 91 VOL: 16 PG:105 - 120 :: REGRESS. :SURV. :OTH.BEH. :BUDG.& PLAN.

STOKES,DJ ; FIRS: FRANCIS,JR CIT: 0.43
AUDIT PRICES, PRODUCT DIFFERENTIATION, AND SCALE ECONOMIES: FURTHER
JAR AU 86 VOL: 24 PG:383 - 393 :: REGRESS. :PRIM. :OTH.STAT. :OPER.AUD.

STONE ,DE CIT: 0
THE OBJECTIVE OF FINANCIAL REPORTING IN THE ANNUAL REPORT
TAR AP 67 VOL: 42 PG:331 - 337 :: QUAL. :INT. LOG. :INSTIT. :FIN.METH.

STONE ,M ; SEC: RASP ,J CIT: 0.5
TRADEOFFS IN THE CHOICE BETWEEN LOGIT AND OLS FOR ACCOUNTING CHOICE STUDIES
TAR JA 91 VOL: 66 PG:170 - 187 :: DES.STAT. :SIM. :MATH.PROG. :METHOD.

STONE ,M CIT: 0.83
A FINANCING EXPLANATION FOR OVERFUNDED PENSION PLAN TERMINATIONS
JAR AU 87 VOL: 25 PG:317 - 326 :: REGRESS. :PRIM. :OTH.STAT. :PENS.

STONE ,M ; SEC: BUBLITZ,B CIT: 0.11
AN ANALYSIS OF THE RELIABILITY OF THE FASB DATA BANK OF CHANGING PRICE AND PENSION INFORMATION
TAR JL 84 VOL: 59 PG:469 - 473 :: DES.STAT. :PRIM. :OTH. :METHOD.

STONE ,ML CIT: 0
PROBLEMS IN SEARCH OF SOLUTIONS THROUGH RESEARCH
JAR ST 68 VOL: 6 PG:59 - 66 :: QUAL. :INT. LOG. :INSTIT. :OTH.MANAG.

STONE ,WE CIT: 0
ABACISTS VERSUS ALGORISTS
JAR AU 72 VOL: 10 PG:345 - 350 :: QUAL. :INT. LOG. :HIST. :N/A

STONE ,WE CIT: 0
ANTECEDENTS OF THE ACCOUNTING PROFESSION
TAR AP 69 VOL: 44 PG:284 - 291 :: QUAL. :SEC. :HIST. :FIN.METH.

STONE ,WE CIT: 0.06
ACCOUNTING DOCTORAL PROGRAMS IN AACSB COLLEGES OF BUSINESS ADMINISTRATION
TAR JA 65 VOL: 40 PG:190 - 195 :: DES.STAT. :PRIM. :INSTIT. :OTH.MANAG.

STONE ,WE CIT: 0
LEGAL IMPLICATIONS OF INTRACOMPANY PRICING
TAR JA 64 VOL: 39 PG:38 - 42 :: QUAL. :INT. LOG. :N/A :TRANS.PRIC.

STOREY,J ; FIRS: HOPPER,T ; THIR: WILLMOTT,H CIT: 1.17
ACCOUNTING FOR ACCOUNTING: TOWARDS THE DEVELOPMENT OF A DIALECTICAL VIEW
AOS 05 87 VOL: 12 PG:437 - 456 :: DES.STAT. :INT. LOG. :THEORY :MANAG.

STOREY,R ; FIRS: ROSENFIELD,P CIT: 0.06
THE ACCOUNTING PRINCIPLES BOARD - A CORRECTION
TAR AP 66 VOL: 41 PG:327 - 330 :: QUAL. :INT. LOG. :INSTIT. :N/A

STOUGHTON,NM ; FIRS: DARROUGH,MN CIT: 1.33
FINANCIAL DISCLOSURE POLICY IN AN ENTRY GAME
JAE JA 90 VOL: 12 PG:219 - 243 :: DES.STAT. :INT. LOG. :INF.ECO./AG. :INFO.STRUC.

STRAND,KH ; FIRS: KROSS ,W ; SEC: CHAPMAN,G CIT: 0
FULLY DILUTED EARNINGS PER SHARE AND SECURITY RETURNS: SOME ADDITIONAL EVIDENCE
JAA AU 80 VOL: 4 PG:36 - 46 :: CORR. :SEC. :EMH :CASH DIV.

STRAWSER,JR CIT: 0
EXAMINATION OF THE EFFECT OF RISK MODEL COMPONENTS ON PERCEIVED AUDIT RISK
AUD SP 91 VOL: 10 PG:126 - 135 :: REGRESS. :LAB. :HIPS :RISK

STRAWSER,JR ; FIRS: HARPER JR,RM ; THIR: TANG ,K CIT: 0
ESTABLISHING INVESTIGATION THRESHOLDS FOR PRELIMINARY ANALYTICAL PROCEDURES
AUD AU 90 VOL: 9 PG:115 - 133 :: DES.STAT. :PRIM. :OTH.STAT. :ANAL.REV.

STRAWSER,JR ; FIRS: HARPER JR,RM ; SEC: MISTER,WG CIT: 0
THE IMPACT OF NEW PENSION DISCLOSURE RULES ON PERCEPTIONS OF DEBT
JAR AU 87 VOL: 25 PG:327 - 330 :: REGRESS. :LAB. :OTH.STAT. :PENS.

STRAWSER,RH ; FIRS: LICATA,MP ; THIR: WELKER,RB CIT: 0.14
A NOTE ON PARTICIPATION IN BUDGETING AND LOCUS OF CONTROL
TAR JA 86 VOL: 61 PG:112 - 117 :: REGRESS. :LAB. :OTH.BEH. :BUDG.& PLAN.

STRAWSER,RH ; FIRS: ROBBINS,WA ; SEC: APOSTOLOU,NG CIT: 0
MUNICIPAL ANNUAL REPORTS AND THE INFORMATION NEEDS OF INVESTORS
JAA SU 85 VOL: 8 PG:279 - 292 :: REGRESS. :PRIM. :THEORY :FIN.METH.

STRAWSER,RH ; FIRS: COPELAND,RM ; SEC: FRANCIA,AJ CIT: 0.53
STUDENTS AS SUBJECTS IN BEHAVIOURAL BUSINESS RESEARCH
TAR AP 73 VOL: 48 PG:365 - 374 :: QUAL. :SURV. :OTH.BEH. :METHOD.

STRAWSER,RH ; FIRS: CARPENTER,CG CIT: 0
A STUDY OF THE JOB SATISFACTION OF ACADEMIC ACCOUNTANTS
TAR JL 71 VOL: 46 PG:509 - 518 :: NON-PAR. :SURV. :INSTIT. :OTH.MANAG.

STREER,PJ CIT: 0
CONFORMING FINANCIAL AND TAX ACCOUNTING: WILL THE CONCEPTUAL FRAMEWORK HELP?
JAA SU 79 VOL: 2 PG:329 - 338 :: QUAL. :INT. LOG. :INSTIT. :FIN.METH.

STRINGER,KW CIT: 0.94
A STATISTICAL TECHNIQUE FOR ANALYTICAL REVIEW
JAR ST 75 VOL: 13 PG:1 - 9 :: QUAL. :INT. LOG. :OTH.STAT. :ANAL.REV.

STROCK,E ; FIRS: ESPAHBODI,H ; THIR: TEHRANIAN,H CIT: 0
IMPACT ON EQUITY PRICES OF PRONOUNCEMENTS RELATED TO NONPENSION POST
RETIREMENT BENEFITS
JAE DE 91 VOL: 14 PG:323 - 345 :: REGRESS. :PRIM. :EMH :PENS.

STROCK,E ; FIRS: ELGERS,P ; SEC: CALLAHAN,C CIT: 0.17
THE EFFECT OF EARNINGS YIELDS UPON THE ASSOCIATION BETWEEN UNEXPECTED
EARNINGS AND SECURITY RETURNS; A RE-EXAMINATION
TAR OC 87 VOL: 62 PG:763 - 773 :: REGRESS. :PRIM. :EMH :FIN.METH.

STRONG,JS CIT: 0
VALUATION EFFECTS OF HOLDING GAINS ON LONG-TERM DEBT
JAE OC 90 VOL: 13 PG:267 - 283 :: REGRESS. :PRIM. :OTH.STAT. :VALUAT.(INFL.)

STURROCK,T ; FIRS: THIES ,CF CIT: 0
WHAT DID INFLATION ACCOUNTING TELL US?
JAA AU 87 VOL: 2 PG:375 - 391 :: DES.STAT. :PRIM. :THEORY :VALUAT.(INFL.)

SUH ,YS CIT: 0.2
NONCONTROLLABLE COSTS AND OPTIMAL PERFORMANCE MEASUREMENTS
JAR SP 88 VOL: 26 PG:154 - 168 :: ANAL. :INT. LOG. :INF.ECO./AG. :REL.COSTS

SUH ,YS CIT: 1
COLLUSION AND NONCONTROLLABLE COST ALLOCATION
JAR ST 87 VOL: 25 PG:22 - 46 :: DES.STAT. :INT. LOG. :INF.ECO./AG. :COST.ALLOC.

SUMMERS,EL ; FIRS: CHEN ,K CIT: 0.17
A STUDY OF REPORTING PROBABILISTIC ACCOUNTING FIGURES
AOS 01 81 VOL: 6 PG:1 - 16 :: ANOVA :LAB. :HIPS :MANAG.

SUMMERS,EL CIT: 0.24
THE AUDIT STAFF ASSIGNMENT PROBLEM: A LINEAR PROGRAMMING ANALYSIS
TAR JL 72 VOL: 47 PG:443 - 453 :: ANAL. :INT. LOG. :MATH.PROG. :AUD.

SUMMERS,EL ; SEC: DESKINS,JW CIT: 0
A CLASSIFICATION SCHEMA OF METHODS FOR REPORTING EFFECTS OF RESOURCE PRICE CHANGES
JAR SP 70 VOL: 8 PG:113 - 117 :: QUAL. :INT. LOG. :THEORY :VALUAT.(INFL.)

SUMMERS,EL CIT: 0
OBSERVATION OF EFFECTS OF USING ALTERNATIVE REPORTING PRACTICES
TAR AP 68 VOL: 43 PG:257 - 265 :: ANOVA :PRIM. :N/A :FIN.METH.

SUMMERS,EL ; FIRS: CRUSE ,RB CIT: 0
ECONOMICS, ACCOUNTING PRACTICE AND ACCOUNTING RESEARCH STUDY NO.3
TAR JA 65 VOL: 40 PG:82 - 88 :: QUAL. :INT. LOG. :THEORY :FIN.METH.

SUMNERS,GE ; SEC: WHITE ,RA ; THIR: CLAY JR,RJ CIT: 0
THE USE OF ENGAGEMENT LETTERS IN AUDIT, REVIEW, AND COMPILATION ENGAGEMENTS: AN EMPIRICAL STUDY
AUD SP 87 VOL: 6 PG:116 - 122 :: REGRESS. :SURV. :OTH.BEH. :ORG.

SUNDEM,GL ; FIRS: BOWEN ,RM CIT: 0
EDITORIAL AND PUBLICATION LAGS IN THE ACCOUNTING AND FINANCE LITERATURE
TAR OC 82 VOL: 57 PG:778 - 784 :: DES.STAT. :PRIM. :OTH. :N/A

SUNDEM,GL CIT: 0.43
A GAME THEORY MODEL OF THE INFORMATION EVALUATOR AND THE DECISION MAKER
JAR SP 79 VOL: 17 PG:243 - 261 :: ANAL. :INT. LOG. :INF.ECO./AG. :INFO.STRUC.

SUNDEM,GL ; FIRS: MAY ,RG CIT: 0.59
RESEARCH FOR ACCOUNTING POLICY: AN OVERVIEW
TAR OC 76 VOL: 51 PG:747 - 763 :: QUAL. :INT. LOG. :THEORY :FIN.METH.

SUNDEM,GL CIT: 0.41
EVALUATING SIMPLIFIED CAPITAL BUDGETING MODELS USING A TIME-STATE PREFERENCE METRIC
TAR AP 74 VOL: 49 PG:306 - 320 :: ANAL. :INT. LOG. :N/A :CAP.BUDG.

SUNDEM,GL ; FIRS: MAY ,RG CIT: 0.35
COST OF INFORMATION AND SECURITY PRICES: MARKET ASSOCIATION TESTS FOR ACCOUNTING POLICY DECISIONS
TAR JA 73 VOL: 48 PG:80 - 94 :: ANAL. :INT. LOG. :EMH :INFO.STRUC.

SUNDER,S ; FIRS: LIM ,SS CIT: 0
EFFICIENCY OF ASSET VALUATION RULES UNDER PRICE MOVEMENT AND MEASUREMENT ERRORS
TAR OC 91 VOL: 66 PG:669 - 693 :: DES.STAT. :INT. LOG. :MATH.PROG. :VALUAT.(INFL.)

SUNDER,S CIT: 0
PROOF THAT IN AN EFFICIENT MARKET, EVENT STUDIES CAN PROVIDE NO SYSTEMATIC GUIDANCE REVISION OF ACCOUNTING STANDARDS AND DISCLOSURE POLICY FOR THE PURPOSE OF MAXIMIZING WEALTH
CAR SP 89 VOL: 5 PG:452 - 460 :: DES.STAT. :INT. LOG. :EMH :FASB SUBM.

SUNDER,S ; FIRS: DONEGAN,J CIT: 0
CONTRACT THEORETIC ANALYSIS OF OFF-BALANCE SHEET FINANCING
JAA SP 89 VOL: 4 PG:203 - 216 :: REGRESS. :SEC. :INSTIT. :OTH.C/A

SUNDER,S ; FIRS: SHIH ,MSH CIT: 0.33
DESIGN AND TESTS OF AN EFFICIENT SEARCH ALGORITHM FOR ACCURATE LINEAR VALUATION SYSTEMS
CAR AU 87 VOL: 4 PG:16 - 31 :: DES.STAT. :INT. LOG. :OTH.STAT. :VALUAT.(INFL.)

SUNDER,S ; FIRS: AMERSHI,AH CIT: 0.5
FAILURE OF STOCK PRICES TO DISCIPLINE MANAGERS IN A RATIONAL EXPECTATIONS
JAR AU 87 VOL: 25 PG:177 - 195 :: DES.STAT. :INT. LOG. :INF.ECO./AG. :INV.

SUNDER,S ; SEC: WAYMIRE,G CIT: 0.78
ACCURACY OF EXCHANGE VALUATION RULES: ADDITIVITY AND UNBIASED ESTIMATION
JAR SP 84 VOL: 22 PG:396 - 405 :: ANAL. :INT. LOG. :THEORY :SPEC.ITEMS

SUNDER,S CIT: 0.1
SIMPSON'S REVERSAL PARADOX AND COST ALLOCATION
JAR SP 83 VOL: 21 PG:222 - 233 :: ANAL. :INT. LOG. :OTH.STAT. :COST.ALLOC.

SUNDER,S ; SEC: WAYMIRE,G CIT: 0.8
MARGINAL GAINS IN ACCURACY OF VALUATION FROM INCREASINGLY SPECIFIC PRICE INDEXES: EMPIRICAL EVIDENCE FOR THE U.S. ECONOMY
JAR AU 83 VOL: 21 PG:565 - 580 :: MIXED :PRIM. :OTH.STAT. :VALUAT.(INFL.)

SUNDER,S ; FIRS: JOYCE ,EJ ; SEC: LIBBY ,R CIT: 0.09
USING THE FASB'S QUALITATIVE CHARACTERISTICS IN ACCOUNTING POLICY CHOICES
JAR AU 82 VOL: 20 PG:654 - 675 :: DES.STAT. :SURV. :INSTIT. :FASB SUBM.

SUNDER,S ; FIRS: DOPUCH,N CIT: 0.46
FASB'S STATEMENTS ON OBJECTIVES AND ELEMENTS OF FINANCIAL ACCOUNTING: A REVIEW
TAR JA 80 VOL: 55 PG:1 - 21 :: QUAL. :INT. LOG. :INSTIT. :FASB SUBM.

SUNDER,S ; FIRS: LEV ,B CIT: 0.79
METHODOLOGICAL ISSUES IN THE USE OF FINANCIAL RATIOS
JAE DE 79 VOL: 1 PG:187 - 210 :: QUAL. :INT. LOG. :OTH.STAT. :METHOD.

SUNDER,S ; FIRS: PRAKASH,P CIT: 0.29
THE CASE AGAINST SEPARATION OF CURRENT OPERATING PROFIT AND HOLDING GAIN
TAR JA 79 VOL: 54 PG:1 - 22 :: QUAL. :INT. LOG. :THEORY :VALUAT.(INFL.)

SUNDER,S CIT: 0.67
ACCURACY OF EXCHANGE VALUATION RULES
JAR AU 78 VOL: 16 PG:341 - 367 :: ANAL. :INT. LOG. :INSTIT. :VALUAT.(INFL.)

SUNDER,S CIT: 0.53
OPTIMAL CHOICE BETWEEN FIFO AND LIFO
JAR AU 76 VOL: 14 PG:277 - 300 :: ANAL. :INT. LOG. :INF.ECO./AG. :INV.

SUNDER,S CIT: 0.82
PROPERTIES OF ACCOUNTING NUMBERS UNDER FULL COSTING AND SUCCESSFUL-EFFORTS COSTING IN THE PETROLEUM INDUSTRY
TAR JA 76 VOL: 51 PG:1 - 18 :: ANAL. :INT. LOG. :OTH.STAT. :OIL & GAS

SUNDER,S CIT: 0.47
A NOTE ON ESTIMATING THE ECONOMIC IMPACT OF THE LIFO METHOD OF INVENTORY VALUATION
TAR AP 76 VOL: 51 PG:287 - 291 :: ANAL. :INT. LOG. :OTH.STAT. :INV.

SUNDER,S CIT: 1.47
STOCK PRICE AND RISK RELATED TO ACCOUNTING CHANGES IN INVENTORY VALUATION
TAR AP 75 VOL: 50 PG:305 - 315 :: REGRESS. :PRIM. :EMH :INV.

SUNDER,S CIT: 2
RELATIONSHIP BETWEEN ACCOUNTING CHANGES AND STOCK PRICES: PROBLEMS OF MEASUREMENT AND SOME EMPIRICAL EVIDENCE
JAR ST 73 VOL: 11 PG:1 - 45 :: REGRESS. :PRIM. :EMH :INV.

SURDICK,JJ ; FIRS: GAUMNITZ,BR ; SEC: NUNAMAKER,TR ; FOUR: THOMAS,MF CIT: 0.64
AUDITOR CONSENSUS IN INTERNAL CONTROL EVALUATION AND AUDIT PROGRAM PLANNING
JAR AU 82 VOL: 20 PG:745 - 755 :: CORR. :LAB. :HIPS :INT.CONT.

SURET ,J-M ; FIRS: L'HER ,JF CIT: 0.5
THE REACTION OF CANADIAN SECURITIES TO REVISIONS OF EARNINGS FORECASTS
CAR SP 91 VOL: 7 PG:378 - 406 :: REGRESS. :PRIM. :EMH :FOREC.

SUSSMAN,MR CIT: 0
PRESENT-VALUE SHORT CUTS
TAR AP 65 VOL: 40 PG:407 - 413 :: ANAL. :INT. LOG. :OTH.STAT. :OTH.MANAG.

SUTCLIFFE,P ; FIRS: LEWIS ,NR ; SEC: PARKER,LD CIT: 0
FINANCIAL REPORTING TO EMPLOYEES: THE PATTERN OF DEVELOPMENT 1919 TO 1979
AOS 34 84 VOL: 9 PG:275 - 289 :: DES.STAT. :SEC. :HIST. :HRA

SUTTON,TG CIT: 0.6
THE PROPOSED INTRODUCTION OF CURRENT COST ACCOUNTING IN THE U.K.: DETERMINANTS OF CORPORATE PREFERENCE
JAE AP 88 VOL: 10 PG:127 - 149 :: REGRESS. :PRIM. :THEORY :VALUAT.(INFL.)

SUTTON,TG CIT: 0.11
LOBBYING OF ACCOUNTING STANDARD-SETTING BODIES IN THE U.K. AND THE U.S.A.: A DOWNSIAN ANALYSIS
AOS 01 84 VOL: 9 PG:81 - 95 :: DES.STAT. :PRIM. :INSTIT. :FASB SUBM.

SVENSSON,G ; FIRS: JONSON,LC ; SEC: JONSSON,B CIT: 0
THE APPLICATION OF SOCIAL ACCOUNTING TO ABSENTEEISM AND PERSONNEL TURNOVER
AOS 34 78 VOL: 3 PG:261 - 268 :: DES.STAT. :CASE :OTH.BEH. :METHOD.

SWAMINATHAN,S CIT: 0.5
THE IMPACT OF SEC MANDATED SEGMENT DATA ON PRICE VARIABILITY AND DIVERGENCE OF BELIEFS
TAR JA 91 VOL: 66 PG:23 - 41 :: REGRESS. :PRIM. :EMH :SEG.REP.

SWANSON,EB CIT: 0.13
THE TWO FACES OF ORGANIZATIONAL INFORMATION
AOS 34 78 VOL: 3 PG:237 - 248 :: QUAL. :INT. LOG. :OTH. :N/A

SWANSON,EP CIT: 0.33
RELATIVE MEASUREMENT ERRORS IN VALUING PLANT AND EQUIPMENT UNDER CURRENT COST AND REPLACEMENT COST
TAR OC 90 VOL: 65 PG:911 - 924 :: REGRESS. :PRIM. :THEORY :VALUAT.(INFL.)

SWANSON,EP ; FIRS: THOMAS,LR CIT: 0
ADDITIONAL CONSIDERATIONS WHEN USING THE FASB DATA BANK OF CHANGING PRICE INFORMATION
TAR AP 86 VOL: 61 PG:330 - 336 :: ANAL. :PRIM. :THEORY :VALUAT.(INFL.)

SWANSON,EP ; SEC: SHEARON,WT ; THIR: THOMAS,LR CIT: 0
PREDICTING CURRENT COST OPERATING PROFIT USING COMPONENT MODELS INCORPORATING ANALYSTS' FORECASTS
TAR OC 85 VOL: 60 PG:681 - 691 :: REGRESS. :PRIM. :TIME SER. :VALUAT.(INFL.)

SWANSON,GA ; SEC: GARDNER,JC CIT: 0
NOT-FOR-PROFIT ACCOUNTING AND AUDITING IN THE EARLY EIGHTEENTH CENTURY: SOME ARCHIVAL EVIDENCE
TAR JL 88 VOL: 63 PG:436 - 447 :: REGRESS. :INT. LOG. :HIST. :AUD.

SWEENEY,JL ; FIRS: SWIERINGA,RJ ; SEC: GIBBINS,M ; THIR: LARSSON,L CIT: 1.41
EXPERIMENTS IN THE HEURISTICS OF HUMAN INFORMATION PROCESSING
JAR ST 76 VOL: 14 PG:159 - 187 :: MIXED :LAB. :HIPS :MANAG.

SWENSON,CW CIT: 0
AN ANALYSIS OF ACRS DURING INFLATIONARY PERIODS
TAR JA 87 VOL: 62 PG:117 - 136 :: REGRESS. :SIM. :TIME SER. :VALUAT.(INFL.)

SWENSON,CW ; FIRS: MOORE ,ML ; SEC: STEECE,BM CIT: 0.17
AN ANALYSIS OF THE IMPACT OF STATE INCOME TAX RATES AND BASES ON FOREIGN INVESTMENT
TAR OC 87 VOL: 62 PG:671 - 685 :: REGRESS. :PRIM. :TIME SER. :TAXES

SWENSON,CW ; FIRS: MOORE ,ML ; SEC: STEECE,BM CIT: 0
SOME EMPIRICAL EVIDENCE ON TAXPAYER RATIONALITY
TAR JA 85 VOL: 60 PG:18 - 32 :: REGRESS. :PRIM. :TIME SER. :TAXES

SWIERINGA,RJ CIT: 0
RECOGNITION AND MEASUREMENT ISSUES IN ACCOUNTING FOR SECURITIZED ASSETS
JAA SP 89 VOL: 4 PG:169 - 186 :: REGRESS. :SEC. :INSTIT. :OTH.C/A

SWIERINGA,RJ ; FIRS: HILTON,RW ; THIR: TURNER,MJ CIT: 0.2
PRODUCT PRICING, ACCOUNTING COSTS AND USE OF PRODUCT-COSTING SYSTEMS
TAR AP 88 VOL: 63 PG:195 - 218 :: REGRESS. :LAB. :OTH.BEH. :REL.COSTS

SWIERINGA,RJ ; SEC: WEICK ,KE CIT: 0.33
MANAGEMENT ACCOUNTING AND ACTION
AOS 03 87 VOL: 12 PG:293 - 308 :: DES.STAT. :INT. LOG. :HIST. :MANAG.

SWIERINGA,RJ ; FIRS: DYCKMAN,TR ; SEC: HOSKIN,RE CIT: 0.36
AN ACCOUNTING CHANGE AND INFORMATION PROCESSING CHANGES
AOS 01 82 VOL: 7 PG:1 - 12 :: REGRESS. :LAB. :HIPS :ACC.CHNG.

SWIERINGA,RJ ; SEC: WATERHOUSE,JH CIT: 0.36
ORGANIZATIONAL VIEWS OF TRANSFER PRICING
AOS 02 82 VOL: 7 PG:149 - 166 :: QUAL. :INT. LOG. :OTH. :TRANS.PRIC.

SWIERINGA,RJ ; SEC: WEICK ,KE CIT: 1.64
AN ASSESSMENT OF LABORATORY EXPERIMENTS IN ACCOUNTING
JAR ST 82 VOL: 20 PG:56 - 101 :: DES.STAT. :SEC. :OTH.BEH. :METHOD.

SWIERINGA,RJ ; FIRS: HILTON,RW ; THIR: HOSKIN,RE CIT: 0.58
PERCEPTION OF ACCURACY AS A DETERMINANT OF INFORMATION VALUE
JAR SP 81 VOL: 19 PG:86 - 108 :: ANOVA :LAB. :OTH.BEH. :MANAG.

SWIERINGA,RJ ; FIRS: HILTON,RW CIT: 0.42
PERCEPTION OF INITIAL UNCERTAINTY AS A DETERMINANT OF INFORMATION VALUE
JAR SP 81 VOL: 19 PG:109 - 119 :: ANOVA :LAB. :HIPS :OTH.MANAG.

SWIERINGA,RJ ; SEC: GIBBINS,M ; THIR: LARSSON,L ; FOUR: SWEENEY,JL CIT: 1.41
EXPERIMENTS IN THE HEURISTICS OF HUMAN INFORMATION PROCESSING
JAR ST 76 VOL: 14 PG:159 - 187 :: MIXED :LAB. :HIPS :MANAG.

SWIERINGA,RJ ; FIRS: DEMSKI,JS CIT: 0.47
A COOPERATIVE FORMULATION OF THE AUDIT CHOICE PROBLEM
TAR JL 74 VOL: 49 PG:506 - 513 :: ANAL. :INT. LOG. :OTH.STAT. :AUD.

SWIERINGA,RJ ; SEC: MONCUR,RH CIT: 0.53
THE RELATIONSHIP BETWEEN MANAGERS' BUDGET-ORIENTED BEHAVIOR AND SELECTED ATTITUDE, POSITION, SIZE, AND PERFORMANCE MEASURES
JAR ST 72 VOL: 10 PG:194 - 209 :: OTH.QUANT. :FIELD :OTH.BEH. :BUDG.& PLAN.

SWIERINGA,RJ ; FIRS: CARMICHAEL,DR CIT: 0.06
THE COMPATIBILITY OF AUDITING INDEPENDENCE AND MANAGEMENT SERVICES: AN IDENTIFICATION OF ISSUES
TAR OC 68 VOL: 43 PG:697 - 705 :: QUAL. :INT. LOG. :INSTIT. :INDEP.

TABOR ,RH ; FIRS: BELL ,TB CIT: 0
EMPIRICAL ANALYSIS OF AUDIT UNCERTAINTY QUALIFICATIONS
JAR AU 91 VOL: 29 PG:350 - 370 :: REGRESS. :PRIM. :OTH.STAT. :OPIN.

TABOR ,RH ; SEC: WILLIS,JT CIT: 0.25
EMPIRICAL EVIDENCE ON THE CHANGING ROLE OF ANALYTICAL REVIEW PROCEDURES
AUD SP 85 VOL: 4 PG:93 - 109 :: REGRESS. :PRIM. :OTH.STAT. :ANAL.REV.

TABOR ,RH CIT: 0.2
INTERNAL CONTROL EVALUATIONS AND AUDIT PROGRAM REVISIONS: SOME ADDITIONAL EVIDENCE
JAR SP 83 VOL: 21 PG:348 - 354 :: MIXED :LAB. :OTH.BEH. :INT.CONT.

TALMOR,E ; FIRS: LITZENBERGER,RH CIT: 0
THE IRRELEVANCY OF CORPORATE TAXES FOR CAPITAL STRUCTURE AND INVESTMENT DECISIONS
JAA SU 89 VOL: 4 PG:305 - 316 :: DES.STAT. :INT. LOG. :INF.ECO./AG. :TAXES

TALWAR,PP ; FIRS: ADESI ,GB CIT: 0
STATIONARITY TESTS OF THE MARKET MODEL FOR SECURITY RETURNS
JAA SU 92 VOL: 7 PG:369 - 378 :: DES.STAT. :SIM. :OTH.STAT. :METHOD.

TAMURA,H ; FIRS: FROST ,PA CIT: 0
ACCURACY OF AUXILIARY INFORMATION INTERVAL ESTIMATION IN STATISTICAL
JAR SP 86 VOL: 24 PG:57 - 75 :: DES.STAT. :SIM. :OTH.STAT. :SAMP.

TAMURA,H ; SEC: FROST ,PA CIT: 0.14
TIGHTENING CAV (DUS) BOUNDS BY USING A PARAMETRIC MODEL
JAR AU 86 VOL: 24 PG:364 - 371 :: DES.STAT. :SIM. :OTH.STAT. :SAMP.

TAMURA,H CIT: 0
ANALYSIS OF THE GARSTKA-OHLSON BOUNDS
AUD SP 85 VOL: 4 PG:133 - 142 :: DES.STAT. :INT. LOG. :OTH.STAT. :SAMP.

TAMURA,H ; FIRS: FROST ,PA CIT: 0.55
JACKKNIFED RATIO ESTIMATION IN STATISTICAL AUDITING
JAR SP 82 VOL: 20 PG:103 - 120 :: DES.STAT. :SIM. :OTH.STAT. :SAMP.

TANG ,K ; FIRS: HARPER JR,RM ; SEC: STRAWSER,JR CIT: 0
ESTABLISHING INVESTIGATION THRESHOLDS FOR PRELIMINARY ANALYTICAL PROCEDURES
AUD AU 90 VOL: 9 PG:115 - 133 :: DES.STAT. :PRIM. :OTH.STAT. :ANAL.REV.

TAUSSIG,RA CIT: 0.1
IMPACT OF SFAS NO.52 ON THE TRANSLATION OF FOREIGN FINANCIAL STATEMENTS OF COMPANIES IN HIGHLY INFLATIONARY ECONOMIES
JAA WI 83 VOL: 6 PG:142 - 156 :: DES.STAT. :SIM. :THEORY :N/A

TAUSSIG,RA ; SEC: HAYES ,SC CIT: 0
CASH TAKE-OVERS AND ACCOUNTING VALUATIONS
TAR JA 68 VOL: 43 PG:68 - 74 :: ANOVA :PRIM. :N/A :INV.

TAUSSIG,RA CIT: 0
INFORMATION REQUIREMENTS OF REPLACEMENT MODELS
JAR SP 64 VOL: 2 PG:67 - 79 :: ANAL. :INT. LOG. :THEORY :VALUAT.(INFL.)

TAUSSIG,RA CIT: 0.06
GOVERNMENTAL ACCOUNTING: FUND FLOW OR SERVICE COST?
TAR JL 63 VOL: 38 PG:562 - 567 :: QUAL. :INT. LOG. :INSTIT. :FIN.METH.

TAYLOR,KW ; FIRS: LEV ,B CIT: 0
ACCOUNTING RECOGNITION OF IMPUTED INTEREST ON EQUITY: AN EMPIRICAL INVESTIGATION
JAA SP 79 VOL: 2 PG:232 - 243 :: REGRESS. :PRIM. :EMH :FIN.METH.

TAYLOR,M ; FIRS: HARRELL,A ; THIR: CHEWNING,E CIT: 0.5
AN EXAMINATION OF MANAGEMENT'S ABILITY TO BIAS THE PROFESSIONAL OBJECTIVITY OF INTERNAL AUDITORS
AOS 03 89 VOL: 14 PG:259 - 269 :: REGRESS. :LAB. :HIPS :INT.AUD.

TAYLOR,M ; FIRS: HARRELL,AM ; SEC: CHEWNING,EG CIT: 0
ORGANIZATIONAL-PROFESSIONAL CONFLICT AND THE JOB SATISFACTION AND TURNOVER INTENTIONS OF INTERNAL AUDITORS
AUD SP 86 VOL: 5 PG:111 - 121 :: REGRESS. :SURV. :OTH.BEH. :AUD.TRAIL

TAYLOR,ME ; FIRS: SCHNEE,EJ CIT: 0
IRS ACCESS TO ACCOUNTANTS' WORK PAPERS - THE RULES MAY BE CHANGING
JAA AU 81 VOL: 5 PG:18 - 29 :: QUAL. :INT. LOG. :INSTIT. :PROF.RESP.

TAYLOR,ME ; FIRS: RECKERS,PMJ CIT: 0.29
CONSISTENCY IN AUDITORS' EVALUATIONS OF INTERNAL ACCOUNTING CONTROLS
JAA AU 79 VOL: 3 PG:42 - 55 :: ANOVA :LAB. :OTH.BEH. :INT.CONT.

TAYLOR,ME ; FIRS: SMITH ,CH ; SEC: LANIER,RA CIT: 0.12
THE NEED FOR AND SCOPE OF THE AUDIT OF MANAGEMENT: A SURVEY OF ATTITUDES
TAR AP 72 VOL: 47 PG:270 - 283 :: DES.STAT. :SURV. :INSTIT. :AUD.

TAYLOR,RD ; FIRS: WRIGHT,GB CIT: 0
REPORTING MATERIALITY FOR INVESTORS
JAA SU 82 VOL: 5 PG:301 - 309 :: DES.STAT. :SURV. :OTH. :MAT.

TAYLOR,RG CIT: 0
A LOOK AT PUBLISHED INTERIM REPORTS
TAR JA 65 VOL: 40 PG:89 - 96 :: QUAL. :INT. LOG. :INSTIT. :INT.REP.

TAYLOR,RL ; FIRS: COPELAND,RM ; THIR: BROWN ,SH CIT: 0.08
OBSERVATION ERROR AND BIAS IN ACCOUNTING RESEARCH
JAR SP 81 VOL: 19 PG:197 - 207 :: ANOVA :LAB. :OTH.BEH. :METHOD.

TAYLOR,WM ; SEC: WEYGANDT,JJ CIT: 0
ACCOUNTING FOR STOCK-BASED AWARDS USING THE MINIMUM VALUE METHOD
JAR AU 82 VOL: 20 PG:497 - 502 :: ANAL. :INT. LOG. :THEORY :SPEC.ITEMS

TEALL ,HD CIT: 0
INFORMATION CONTENT OF CANADIAN OIL AND GAS COMPANIES' HISTORIC COST EARNINGS AND RESERVES DISCLOSURES
CAR SP 92 VOL: 8 PG:561 - 579 :: REGRESS. :PRIM. :EMH :OIL & GAS

TEALL ,HD CIT: 0
INFORMATION CONTENT OF CANADIAN OIL AND GAS COMPANIES' HISTORIC COST EARNINGS AND RESERVES DISCLOSURES
CAR SP 92 VOL: 8 PG:561 - 579 :: REGRESS. :PRIM. :EMH :OIL & GAS

TEARNEY,MG ; FIRS: WOLK ,HI CIT: 0
INCOME TAX ALLOCATION AND LOSS CARRYFORWARDS: EXPLORING UNCHARTED GROUND
TAR AP 73 VOL: 48 PG:292 - 299 :: ANAL. :INT. LOG. :THEORY :SPEC.ITEMS

TEETS ,W CIT: 0
THE ASSOCIATION BETWEEN STOCK MARKET RESPONSES TO EARNINGS ANNOUNCEMENTS AND REGULATION OF ELECTRIC UTILITIES
JAR AU 92 VOL: 30 PG:274 - 285 :: REGRESS. :PRIM. :EMH :FIN.METH.

TEHRANIAN,H ; FIRS: ESPAHBODI,H ; SEC: STROCK,E CIT: 0
IMPACT ON EQUITY PRICES OF PRONOUNCEMENTS RELATED TO NONPENSION POST RETIREMENT BENEFITS
JAE DE 91 VOL: 14 PG:323 - 345 :: REGRESS. :PRIM. :EMH :PENS.

TEHRANIAN,H ; FIRS: ESPAHBODI,R CIT: 0.25
STOCK MARKET REACTIONS TO THE ISSUANCE OF FAS 33 AND ITS PRECEDING EXPOSURE DRAFTS
CAR SP 89 VOL: 5 PG:575 - 591 :: REGRESS. :PRIM. :EMH :VALUAT.(INFL.)

TEHRANIAN,H ; SEC: TRAVLOS,NG ; THIR: WAEGELEIN,JF CIT: 0.5
MANAGEMENT COMPENSATION CONTRACTS AND MERGER-INDUCED ABNORMAL RETURNS
JAR ST 87 VOL: 25 PG:51 - 76 :: ANOVA :PRIM. :OTH.STAT. :BUS.COMB.

TEHRANIAN,H ; SEC: WAEGELEIN,JF CIT: 0.25
MARKET REACTION TO SHORT-TERM EXECUTIVE COMPENSATION PLAN ADOPTION
JAE AP 85 VOL: 7 PG:131 - 144 :: REGRESS. :PRIM. :EMH :EXEC.COMP.

TEITLEBAUM,AD ; SEC: ROBINSON,CF CIT: 0.29
THE REAL RISKS IN AUDIT SAMPLING
JAR ST 75 VOL: 13 PG:70 - 91 :: MIXED :INT. LOG. :OTH.STAT. :SAMP.

TELSER,LG CIT: 0
THEORY OF CORPORATIONS: AN APPLICATION OF THE THEORY OF THE CORE
JAA SP 90 VOL: 5 PG:159 - 201 :: DES.STAT. :INT. LOG. :OTH. :ORG.& ENVIR.

TENNANT,KL ; FIRS: FERRIS,KR CIT: 0.33
AN INVESTIGATION OF THE IMPACT OF THE QUALITATIVE NATURE OF COMPLIANCE ERRORS ON INTERNAL CONTROL ASSESSMENTS
AUD SP 84 VOL: 3 PG:31 - 43 :: NON-PAR. :LAB. :OTH.STAT. :INT.CONT.

TENNYSON,BM ; FIRS: FRAZIER,KB ; SEC: INGRAM,RW CIT: 0.22
A METHODOLOGY FOR THE ANALYSIS OF NARRATIVE ACCOUNTING DISCLOSURES
JAR SP 84 VOL: 22 PG:318 - 331 :: OTH.QUANT. :PRIM. :OTH.STAT. :FOREC.

TEOH ,HY ; SEC: THONG ,G CIT: 0
ANOTHER LOOK AT CORPORATE SOCIAL RESPONSIBILITY AND REPORTING: AN EMPIRICAL STUDY IN A DEVELOPING COUNTRY
AOS 02 84 VOL: 9 PG:189 - 206 :: MIXED :SURV. :THEORY :HRA

TEOH ,SH CIT: 0
AUDITOR INDEPENDENCE, DISMISSAL THREATS, AND THE MARKET REACTION TO AUDITOR SWITCHES
JAR SP 92 VOL: 30 PG:1 - 23 :: DES.STAT. :INT. LOG. :INF.ECO./AG. :ORG.

TERRY ,E ; FIRS: SCHOLES,MS ; THIR: WOLFSON,MA CIT: 0
TAXES, TRADING, AND THE VALUE OF REAL ESTATE
JAA SU 89 VOL: 4 PG:317 - 340 :: REGRESS. :MIXED :OTH.STAT. :TAXES

THAKKAR,RB ; SEC: FINLEY,DR ; THIR: LIAO ,WM CIT: 0.11
A STOCHASTIC DEMAND CVP MODEL WITH RETURN ON INVESTMENT CRITERION
CAR AU 84 VOL: 1 PG:77 - 86 :: DES.STAT. :INT. LOG. :MATH.PROG. :C-V-P-A

THANE ,P CIT: 0
THE HISTORY OF THE GENDER DIVISION OF LABOUR IN BRITAIN: REFLECTIONS ON "HERSTORY' IN ACCOUNTING: THE FIRST EIGHTY YEARS"
AOS 04 92 VOL: 17 PG:299 - 312 :: REGRESS. :SEC. :HIST. :ORG.& ENVIR.

THEIL ,H ; FIRS: LEV ,B CIT: 0
A MAXIMUM ENTROPY APPROACH TO THE CHOICE OF ASSET DEPRECIATION
JAR AU 78 VOL: 16 PG:286 - 293 :: ANAL. :INT. LOG. :THEORY :PP&E / DEPR

THEIL ,H CIT: 0.06
HOW TO WORRY ABOUT INCREASED EXPENDITURES
TAR JA 69 VOL: 44 PG:27 - 37 :: ANAL. :INT. LOG. :INF.ECO./AG. :LIAB.

THEOBALD,M CIT: 0
EXCLUSION PERIOD AND MARKET MODEL PARAMETER NONSTATIONARITIES IN PRICE REACTION STUDIES
CAR AU 85 VOL: 2 PG:1 - 22 :: ANOVA :INT. LOG. :EMH :METHOD.

THIES ,CF ; SEC: STURROCK,T CIT: 0
WHAT DID INFLATION ACCOUNTING TELL US?
JAA AU 87 VOL: 2 PG:375 - 391 :: DES.STAT. :PRIM. :THEORY :VALUAT.(INFL.)

THIES ,JB ; FIRS: REVSINE,L CIT: 0.12
PRODUCTIVITY CHANGES AND ALTERNATIVE INCOME SERIES: A SIMULATION
TAR AP 76 VOL: 51 PG:255 - 268 :: ANAL. :SIM. :OTH.STAT. :DEC.AIDS

THIRKELL,JE ; FIRS: JACKSON-COX,J ; THIR: MCQUEENEY,J CIT: 0.33
THE DISCLOSURE OF COMPANY INFORMATION TO TRADE UNIONS: THE RELEVANCE OF THE ACAS CODE OF PRACTICE ON DISCLOSURE
AOS 34 84 VOL: 9 PG:253 - 273 :: QUAL. :SURV. :INSTIT. :N/A

THODE ,SF ; SEC: DRTINA,RE ; THIR: LARGAY III,JA CIT: 0
OPERATING CASH FLOWS: A GROWING NEED FOR SEPARATE REPORTING
JAA WI 86 VOL: 1 PG:46 - 61 :: REGRESS. :PRIM. :EMH :OTH.FIN.ACC.

THOMAN,L ; FIRS: MELUMAD,N CIT: 0
AN EQUILIBRIUM ANALYSIS OF OPTIMAL AUDIT CONTRACTS]
CAR AU 90 VOL: 7 PG:22 - 55 :: DES.STAT. :INT. LOG. :INF.ECO./AG. :ORG.

THOMAN,L ; FIRS: MELUMAD,ND CIT: 1.67
ON AUDITORS AND THE COURTS IN AN ADVERSE SELECTION SETTING
JAR SP 90 VOL: 28 PG:77 - 120 :: DES.STAT. :INT. LOG. :INF.ECO./AG. :LITIG.

THOMAS,AL CIT: 0.12
USEFUL ARBITRARY ALLOCATIONS (WITH A COMMENT ON THE NEUTRALITY OF FINANCIAL ACCOUNTING REPORTS)
TAR JL 71 VOL: 46 PG:472 - 479 :: ANAL. :INT. LOG. :THEORY :PP&E / DEPR

THOMAS,AL CIT: 0
THE AMORTIZATION PROBLEM: A SIMPLIFIED MODEL AND SOME UNANSWERED QUESTIONS
JAR SP 65 VOL: 3 PG:103 - 113 :: ANAL. :INT. LOG. :THEORY :PP&E / DEPR

THOMAS,AL CIT: 0
DISCOUNTED SERVICES AGAIN: THE HOMOGENEITY PROBLEM
TAR JA 64 VOL: 39 PG:1 - 11 :: ANAL. :INT. LOG. :THEORY :PP&E / DEPR

THOMAS,AL CIT: 0
VALUE-ITIS - AN IMPRACTICAL THEORIST'S REPLY
TAR JL 64 VOL: 39 PG:574 - 581 :: QUAL. :INT. LOG. :THEORY :VALUAT.(INFL.)

THOMAS,AP CIT: 0
THE CONTINGENCY THEORY OF CORPORATE REPORTING: SOME EMPIRICAL EVIDENCE
AOS 03 86 VOL: 11 PG:253 - 270 :: REGRESS. :PRIM. :THEORY :ORG.FORM

THOMAS,JK ; FIRS: RAMAKRISHNAN,RTS CIT: 0
WHAT MATTERS FROM THE PAST: MARKET VALUE, BOOK VALUE, OR EARNINGS?
JAA AU 92 VOL: 7 PG:423 - 464 :: REGRESS. :PRIM. :EMH :FIN.METH.

THOMAS,JK ; SEC: TUNG ,S CIT: 2
COST MANIPULATION INCENTIVES UNDER COST REIMBURSEMENT: PENSION COSTS FOR DEFENSE CONTRACTS
TAR OC 92 VOL: 67 PG:691 - 711 :: REGRESS. :PRIM. :OTH.BEH. :PENS.

THOMAS,JK ; FIRS: BERNARD,VL CIT: 2.67
EVIDENCE THAT STOCK PRICES DO NOT FULLY REFLECT THE IMPLICATIONS OF CURRENT EARNINGS FOR FUTURE EARNINGS
JAE DE 90 VOL: 13 PG:305 - 340 :: REGRESS. :PRIM. :EMH :FIN.METH.

THOMAS,JK CIT: 0.75
WHY DO FIRMS TERMINATE THEIR OVERFUNDED PENSION PLANS?
JAE NV 89 VOL: 11 PG:361 - 398 :: REGRESS. :PRIM. :TIME SER. :PENS.

THOMAS,JK ; FIRS: BERNARD,VL CIT: 3.5
POST-EARNINGS-ANNOUNCEMENT DRIFT: DELAYED PRICE RESPONSE OR RISK PREMIUM?
JAR ST 89 VOL: 27 PG:1 - 36 :: REGRESS. :PRIM. :EMH :FIN.METH.

THOMAS,JK CIT: 0
UNUSUAL PATTERNS IN REPORTED EARNINGS
TAR OC 89 VOL: 64 PG:773 - 787 :: REGRESS. :PRIM. :OTH.BEH. :OTH.FIN.ACC.

THOMAS,JK CIT: 1.2
CORPORATE TAXES AND DEFINED BENEFIT PENSION PLANS
JAE JL 88 VOL: 10 PG:199 - 237 :: REGRESS. :INT. LOG. :EMH :TAXES

THOMAS,JK ; FIRS: IMHOFF-JR,EA CIT: 0
ECONOMIC CONSEQUENCES OF ACCOUNTING STANDARDS: THE LEASE DISCLOSURE RULE CHANGE
JAE DE 88 VOL: 10 PG:277 - 310 :: REGRESS. :PRIM. :INSTIT. :LEASES

THOMAS,LR ; SEC: SWANSON,EP CIT: 0
ADDITIONAL CONSIDERATIONS WHEN USING THE FASB DATA BANK OF CHANGING PRICE INFORMATION
TAR AP 86 VOL: 61 PG:330 - 336 :: ANAL. :PRIM. :THEORY :VALUAT.(INFL.)

THOMAS,LR ; FIRS: SWANSON,EP ; SEC: SHEARON,WT CIT: 0
PREDICTING CURRENT COST OPERATING PROFIT USING COMPONENT MODELS INCORPORATING ANALYSTS' FORECASTS
TAR OC 85 VOL: 60 PG:681 - 691 :: REGRESS. :PRIM. :TIME SER. :VALUAT.(INFL.)

THOMAS,LR ; FIRS: PUTNAM,K CIT: 0
DOES PREDICTABILITY CHANGE WHEN GAAP CHANGE?
JAA AU 84 VOL: 8 PG:15 - 23 :: MIXED :PRIM. :TIME SER. :FOREC.

THOMAS,MF ; FIRS: GAUMNITZ,BR ; SEC: NUNAMAKER,TR ; THIR: SURDICK,JJ CIT: 0.64
AUDITOR CONSENSUS IN INTERNAL CONTROL EVALUATION AND AUDIT PROGRAM PLANNING
JAR AU 82 VOL: 20 PG:745 - 755 :: CORR. :LAB. :HIPS :INT.CONT.

THOMPSON II,RB ; FIRS: JENNINGS,R ; SEC: MEST ,DP CIT: 0
INVESTOR REACTION TO DISCLOSURES OF 1974-75 LIFO ADOPTION DECISIONS
TAR AP 92 VOL: 67 PG:337 - 354 :: REGRESS. :PRIM. :INF.ECO./AG. :ACC.CHNG.

THOMPSON II,RB ; SEC: OLSEN ,C ; THIR: DIETRICH,JR CIT: 1.17
ATTRIBUTES OF NEWS ABOUT FIRMS: AN ANALYSIS OF FIRM-SPECIFIC NEWS REPORTED IN THE WALL STREET JOURNAL INDEX
JAR AU 87 VOL: 25 PG:245 - 274 :: REGRESS. :PRIM. :INSTIT. :INFO.STRUC.

THOMPSON,G CIT: 0.5
IS ACCOUNTING RHETORICAL? METHODOLOGY, LUCA PACIOLI AND PRINTING
AOS 05 91 VOL: 16 PG:572 - 599 :: REGRESS. :SEC. :HIST. :ORG.& ENVIR.

THOMPSON,G CIT: 0.67
INFLATION ACCOUNTING IN A THEORY OF CALCULATION
AOS 05 87 VOL: 12 PG:523 - 543 :: DES.STAT. :INT. LOG. :THEORY :VALUAT.(INFL.)

THOMPSON,GL ; FIRS: KAPLAN,RS CIT: 0.47
OVERHEAD ALLOCATION VIA MATHEMATICAL PROGRAMMING MODELS
TAR AP 71 VOL: 46 PG:352 - 364 :: ANAL. :INT. LOG. :MATH.PROG. :OVER.ALLOC.

THOMPSON,GL ; FIRS: IJIRI ,Y CIT: 0
APPLICATIONS OF MATHEMATICAL CONTROL THEORY TO ACCOUNTING AND BUDGETING (THE CONTINUOUS WHEAT TRADING MODEL)
TAR AP 70 VOL: 45 PG:246 - 258 :: ANAL. :INT. LOG. :OTH.STAT. :BUDG.& PLAN.

THOMPSON,R ; FIRS: RICHARDSON,G ; SEC: SEFCIK,SE CIT: 0
TRADING VOLUME REACTIONS TO A CHANGE IN DIVIDEND POLICY: THE CANADIAN APPROACH
CAR AU 88 VOL: 5 PG:299 - 317 :: REGRESS. :PRIM. :TIME SER. :CASH DIV.

THOMPSON,R ; FIRS: LANEN ,WN CIT: 0.4
STOCK PRICE REACTIONS AS SURROGATES FOR THE NET CASH FLOW EFFECTS OF CORPORATE POLICY DECISIONS
JAE DE 88 VOL: 10 PG:311 - 334 :: REGRESS. :PRIM. :EMH :MAN.DEC.CHAR.

THOMPSON,R ; FIRS: SEFCIK,SE CIT: 0.86
AN APPROACH TO STAT. INFERENCE IN CROSS-SECTIONAL MODELS WITH SECURITY ABNORMAL RETURNS AS DEPENDENT VARIABLE
JAR AU 86 VOL: 24 PG:316 - 334 :: DES.STAT. :INT. LOG. :OTH.STAT. :METHOD.

THOMPSON,R ; FIRS: SCHIPPER,K CIT: 0.63
THE IMPACT OF MERGER-RELATED REGULATIONS USING EXACT DISTRIBUTIONS OF TEST
JAR SP 85 VOL: 23 PG:408 - 415 :: DES.STAT. :PRIM. :EMH :BUS.COMB.

THOMPSON,R ; FIRS: SCHIPPER,K CIT: 2.5
THE IMPACT OF MERGER-RELATED REGULATIONS ON THE SHAREHOLDERS OF ACQUIRING FIRMS
JAR SP 83 VOL: 21 PG:184 - 221 :: REGRESS. :PRIM. :EMH :BUS.COMB.

THOMPSON,RB ; SEC: OLSEN ,C ; THIR: DIETRICH,JR CIT: 0.4
THE INFLUENCE OF ESTIMATION PERIOD NEWS EVENTS ON STANDARDIZED MARKET MODEL PREDICTION ERRORS
TAR JL 88 VOL: 63 PG:448 - 471 :: REGRESS. :PRIM. :EMH :METHOD.

THOMPSON,WW ; SEC: KEMPER,EL CIT: 0
PROBABILITY MEASURES FOR ESTIMATED DATA
TAR JL 65 VOL: 40 PG:574 - 578 :: ANAL. :INT. LOG. :N/A :PROB.ELIC.

THOMSEN,CT ; FIRS: JENSEN,RE CIT: 0
STATISTICAL ANALYSIS IN COST MEASUREMENT AND CONTROL
TAR JA 68 VOL: 43 PG:83 - 93 :: ANAL. :INT. LOG. :OTH.STAT. :VAR.

THONG ,G ; FIRS: TEOH ,HY CIT: 0
ANOTHER LOOK AT CORPORATE SOCIAL RESPONSIBILITY AND REPORTING: AN EMPIRICAL STUDY IN A DEVELOPING COUNTRY
AOS 02 84 VOL: 9 PG:189 - 206 :: MIXED :SURV. :THEORY :HRA

THORNTON,DB CIT: 0
CAPITAL VALUES IN USE VS. REPLACEMENT COSTS: THEORY AND CANADIAN EVIDENCE
CAR AU 88 VOL: 5 PG:343 - 370 :: REGRESS. :PRIM. :OTH.STAT. :VALUAT.(INFL.)

THORNTON,DB CIT: 0.71
CURRENT COST DISCLOSURES AND NONDISCLOSURES: CANADIAN EVIDENCE
CAR AU 86 VOL: 3 PG:1 - 34 :: REGRESS. :PRIM. :OTH.STAT. :VALUAT.(INFL.)

THORNTON,DB CIT: 0.21
INFORMATION AND INSTITUTIONS IN THE CAPITAL MARKET
AOS 03 79 VOL: 4 PG:211 - 234 :: QUAL. :INT. LOG. :EMH :N/A

TIESSEN,P ; FIRS: MAHER ,MW ; THIR: COLSON,R ; FOUR: BROMAN,AJ CIT: 0
COMPETITION AND AUDIT FEES
TAR JA 92 VOL: 67 PG:199 - 211 :: REGRESS. :PRIM. :OTH. :ORG.

TIESSEN,P ; SEC: WATERHOUSE,JH CIT: 1.3
TOWARDS A DESCRIPTIVE THEORY OF MANAGEMENT ACCOUNTING
AOS 23 83 VOL: 8 PG:251 - 268 :: QUAL. :INT. LOG. :THEORY :MANAG.

TIESSEN,P ; FIRS: WATERHOUSE,JH CIT: 2.73
A CONTINGENCY FRAMEWORK FOR MANAGEMENT ACCOUNTING SYSTEMS RESEARCH
AOS 01 78 VOL: 3 PG:65 - 76 :: QUAL. :INT. LOG. :HIPS :METHOD.

TILLER,MG ; SEC: MAUTZ ,RD CIT: 0
THE IMPACT OF STATE-MANDATED ACCOUNTING AND AUDITING REQUIREMENTS ON MUNICIPAL BOND RATINGS
JAA SU 85 VOL: 8 PG:293 - 304 :: REGRESS. :PRIM. :OTH.STAT. :LTD

TILLER,MG CIT: 0.1
THE DISSONANCE MODEL OF PARTICIPATIVE BUDGETING: AN EMPIRICAL EXPLORATION
JAR AU 83 VOL: 21 PG:581 - 595 :: ANOVA :LAB. :OTH.BEH. :BUDG.& PLAN.

TINIC ,SM CIT: 0
A PERSPECTIVE ON THE STOCK MARKET'S FIXATION ON ACCOUNTING NUMBERS
TAR OC 90 VOL: 65 PG:781 - 796 :: REGRESS. :SEC. :EMH :OTH.FIN.ACC.

TINKER,AM ; SEC: MERINO,BD ; THIR: NEIMARK,M CIT: 3.18
THE NORMATIVE ORIGINS OF POSITIVE THEORIES: IDEOLOGY AND ACCOUNTING THOUGHT
AOS 02 82 VOL: 7 PG:167 - 200 :: QUAL. :INT. LOG. :THEORY :N/A

TINKER,AM CIT: 1.85
TOWARDS A POLITICAL ECONOMY OF ACCOUNTING: AN EMPIRICAL ILLUSTRATION OF THE CAMBRIDGE CONTROVERSIES
AOS 01 80 VOL: 5 PG:147 - 160 :: QUAL. :INT. LOG. :THEORY :N/A

TINKER,T CIT: 1.4
PANGLOSSIAN ACCOUNTING THEORIES: THE SCIENCE OF APOLOGIZING IN STYLE
AOS 02 88 VOL: 13 PG:165 - 189 :: DES.STAT. :INT. LOG. :THEORY :OTH.MANAG.

TINKER,T ; SEC: NEIMARK,M CIT: 1.5
THE ROLE OF ANNUAL REPORTS IN GENDER AND CLASS CONTRADICTIONS AT GENERAL MOTORS: 1917-1976
AOS 01 87 VOL: 12 PG:71 - 88 :: DES.STAT. :INT. LOG. :INSTIT. :ORG.& ENVIR.

TINKER,T ; FIRS: LEHMAN,C CIT: 2.5
THE REAL CULTURAL SIGNIFICANCE OF ACCOUNTS
AOS 05 87 VOL: 12 PG:503 - 522 :: DES.STAT. :SEC. :HIST. :OTH.MANAG.

TINKER,T ; FIRS: NEIMARK,M CIT: 1.43
THE SOCIAL CONSTRUCTION OF MANAGEMENT CONTROL SYSTEM
AOS 45 86 VOL: 11 PG:369 - 396 :: REGRESS. :INT. LOG. :THEORY :INT.CONT.

TITMAN,S ; FIRS: TRUEMAN,B CIT: 0.4
AN EXPLANATION FOR ACCOUNTING INCOME SMOOTHING
JAR ST 88 VOL: 26 PG:127 - 143 :: DES.STAT. :INT. LOG. :INF.ECO./AG. :REV.REC.

TITMAN,S ; SEC: TRUEMAN,B CIT: 2.14
INFORMATION QUALITY AND THE VALUATION OF NEW ISSUES
JAE JN 86 VOL: 8 PG:159 - 172 :: DES.STAT. :INT. LOG. :INF.ECO./AG. :VALUAT.(INFL.)

TOBA ,Y CIT: 0
A SEMANTIC MEANING ANALYSIS OF THE ULTIMATE PROPOSITION TO BE VERIFIED BY INDEPENDENT AUDITORS
TAR OC 80 VOL: 55 PG:604 - 619 :: ANAL. :INT. LOG. :THEORY :OPIN.

TOBA ,Y CIT: 0.41
A GENERAL THEORY OF EVIDENCE AS THE CONCEPTUAL FOUNDATION IN AUDITING THEORY
TAR JA 75 VOL: 50 PG:7 - 24 :: ANAL. :INT. LOG. :OTH.STAT. :AUD.

TOLLEFSON,SO ; FIRS: STERLING,RR ; THIR: FLAHERTY,RE CIT: 0
EXCHANGE VALUATION: AN EMPIRICAL TEST
TAR OC 72 VOL: 47 PG:709 - 721 :: DES.STAT. :LAB. :THEORY :VALUAT.(INFL.)

TOMASSINI,LA CIT: 0
THE CONTINUING EVOLUTION OF AUDITING SCIENCE: MEGATRENDS AND RESEARCH OPPORTUNITIES FOR THE 1990s
CAR SP 90 VOL: 6 PG:287 - 294 :: ANOVA :SEC. :THEORY :METHOD.

TOMASSINI,LA ; FIRS: HARRISON,KE CIT: 0.25
JUDGING THE PROBABILITY OF A CONTINGENT LOSS: AN EMPIRICAL STUDY
CAR SP 89 VOL: 5 PG:642 - 648 :: REGRESS. :LAB. :HIPS :PROB.ELIC.

TOMASSINI,LA ; FIRS: BECK ,PJ ; SEC: SOLOMON,I CIT: 0.38
SUBJECTIVE PRIOR PROBABILITY DISTRIBUTIONS AND AUDIT RISK
JAR SP 85 VOL: 23 PG:37 - 56 :: REGRESS. :INT. LOG. :OTH.BEH. :RISK

TOMASSINI,LA ; FIRS: HARRISON JR,WT ; THIR: DIETRICH,JR CIT: 0.2
THE USE OF CONTROL GROUPS IN CAPITAL MARKET RESEARCH
JAR SP 83 VOL: 21 PG:65 - 77 :: NON-PAR. :PRIM. :EMH :METHOD.

TOMASSINI,LA ; FIRS: SOLOMON,I ; SEC: KROGSTAD,JL ; THIR: ROMNEY,MB CIT: 0.64
AUDITORS' PRIOR PROBABILITY DISTRIBUTIONS FOR ACCOUNT BALANCES
AOS 01 82 VOL: 7 PG:27 - 42 :: DES.STAT. :LAB. :HIPS :PROB.ELIC.

TOMASSINI,LA CIT: 0.13
ASSESSING THE IMPACT OF HUMAN RESOURCE ACCOUNTING: AN EXPERIMENTAL STUDY OF MANAGERIAL DECISION PREFERENCES
TAR OC 77 VOL: 52 PG:904 - 913 :: ANOVA :LAB. :OTH.BEH. :HRA

TOMASSINI,LA CIT: 0.12
BEHAVIOURAL RESEARCH ON HUMAN RESOURCE ACCOUNTING: A CONTINGENCY FRAMEWORK
AOS 23 76 VOL: 1 PG:239 - 252 :: QUAL. :INT. LOG. :OTH.BEH. :HRA

TOMCZYK,S ; SEC: READ ,WJ CIT: 0.25
DIRECT MEASUREMENT OF SUPPLIER CONCENTRATION IN THE MARKET FOR AUDIT SERVICES
AUD AU 89 VOL: 9 PG:98 - 106 :: REGRESS. :PRIM. :OTH.STAT. :ORG.

TOMKINS,C ; SEC: GROVES,R CIT: 2.4
THE EVERYDAY ACCOUNTANT AND RESEARCHING HIS REALITY
AOS 04 83 VOL: 8 PG:361 - 374 :: QUAL. :INT. LOG. :THEORY :METHOD.

TOMKINS,L ; FIRS: ROSENBERG,D ; THIR: DAY ,P CIT: 0.18
A WORK ROLE PERSPECTIVE OF ACCOUNTANTS IN LOCAL GOVERNMENT SERVICE DEPARTMENTS
AOS 02 82 VOL: 7 PG:123 - 138 :: QUAL. :SURV. :OTH.BEH. :N/A

TOOLE ,HR ; FIRS: LEMBKE,VC CIT: 0
DIFFERENCES IN DEPRECIATION METHODS AND THE ANALYSIS OF SUPPLEMENTAL CURRENT-COST AND REPLACEMENT COST DATA
JAA WI 81 VOL: 4 PG:128 - 135 :: ANAL. :INT. LOG. :THEORY :VALUAT.(INFL.)

TOOLE ,HR ; FIRS: LOY ,LD CIT: 0.08
ACCOUNTING FOR DISCOUNTED CONVERTIBLE BOND EXCHANGES: A SURVEY OF RESULTS
JAA SP 80 VOL: 3 PG:227 - 243 :: DES.STAT. :PRIM. :OTH. :METHOD.

TOPIOL,J CIT: 0
ACCOUNTING FOR PUBLIC HEALTH NURSING ASSOCIATIONS
TAR JA 66 VOL: 41 PG:83 - 91 :: QUAL. :INT. LOG. :N/A :FIN.METH.

TORABZADEH,KM ; SEC: BERTIN,WJ CIT: 0
ABNORMAL RETURNS TO STOCKHOLDERS OF FIRMS ACQUIRED IN BUSINESS COMBINATIONS AND LEVERAGED BUYOUTS
JAA SP 92 VOL: 7 PG:231 - 240 :: REGRESS. :PRIM. :EMH :BUS.COMB.

TOWNSEND,LA CIT: 0
A CAREER IN BUSINESS ACCOUNTING
TAR JA 67 VOL: 42 PG:1 - 6 :: QUAL. :INT. LOG. :INSTIT. :OTH.MANAG.

TRACY ,JA CIT: 0.41
BAYESIAN STATISTICAL METHODS IN AUDITING
TAR JA 69 VOL: 44 PG:90 - 98 :: ANAL. :INT. LOG. :OTH.STAT. :SAMP.

TRACY ,JA CIT: 0.06
A DISSENT TO THE GENERAL PRICE-LEVEL ADJUSTMENT PROPOSAL
TAR JA 65 VOL: 40 PG:163 - 175 :: QUAL. :INT. LOG. :THEORY :VALUAT.(INFL.)

TRACY ,JA ; FIRS: MONSON,NP CIT: 0
STOCK RIGHTS AND ACCOUNTING WRONGS
TAR OC 64 VOL: 39 PG:890 - 893 :: ANAL. :INT. LOG. :THEORY :STK.DIV.

TRADER,RL ; SEC: HUSS ,HF CIT: 0
AN INVESTIGATION OF THE POSSIBLE EFFECTS OF NONSAMPLING ERROR ON INFERENCE IN AUDITING: A BAYESIAN ANALYSIS
CAR AU 87 VOL: 4 PG:227 - 239 :: DES.STAT. :SIM. :OTH.STAT. :ERRORS

TRADER,RL ; FIRS: HUSS ,HF CIT: 0.14
A NOTE ON OPT. SAM. SIZE IN COMPLIANCE TESTS USING A FORMAL BAYESIAN
JAR AU 86 VOL: 24 PG:394 - 399 :: DES.STAT. :SIM. :OTH.STAT. :SAMP.

TRAPNELL,JE ; FIRS: SAMI ,H ; SEC: CURATOLA,AP CIT: 0
EVIDENCE ON THE PREDICTIVE ABILITY OF INFLATION-ADJUSTED EARNINGS MEASURES
CAR SP 89 VOL: 5 PG:556 - 574 :: REGRESS. :PRIM. :EMH :VALUAT.(INFL.)

TRAPNELL,JE ; FIRS: WELSH ,MJ CIT: 0
LABOR MARKET MODELS AND EMPLOYER ACCOUNTING FOR PENSIONS
JAA WI 85 VOL: 8 PG:100 - 111 :: DES.STAT. :INT. LOG. :THEORY :PENS.

TRAVLOS,NG ; FIRS: TEHRANIAN,H ; THIR: WAEGELEIN,JF CIT: 0.5
MANAGEMENT COMPENSATION CONTRACTS AND MERGER-INDUCED ABNORMAL RETURNS
JAR ST 87 VOL: 25 PG:51 - 76 :: ANOVA :PRIM. :OTH.STAT. :BUS.COMB.

TRITSCHLER,CA CIT: 0.53
STATISTICAL CRITERIA FOR ASSET VALUATION BY SPECIFIC PRICE INDEX
TAR JA 69 VOL: 44 PG:99 - 123 :: CORR. :PRIM. :N/A :VALUAT.(INFL.)

TROMBLEY,MA CIT: 0.5
ACCOUNTING METHOD CHOICE IN THE SOFTWARE INDUSTRY: CHARACTERISTICS OF FIRMS ELECTING EARLY ADOPTION OF SFAS NO. 86
TAR JL 89 VOL: 64 PG:529 - 538 :: REGRESS. :PRIM. :THEORY :FIN.METH.

TROMPETER,GM ; FIRS: FARMER,TA ; SEC: RITTENBERG,LE CIT: 0.5
AN INVESTIGATION OF THE IMPACT OF ECONOMIC AND ORGANIZATIONAL FACTORS
AUD AU 87 VOL: 7 PG:1 - 14 :: REGRESS. :LAB. :OTH.BEH. :INDEP.

TROTMAN,K ; FIRS: SIMNETT,R CIT: 0
AUDITOR VERSUS MODEL: INFORMATION CHOICE AND INFORMATION PROCESSING
TAR JL 89 VOL: 64 PG:514 - 528 :: REGRESS. :FIELD :HIPS :BUS.FAIL.

TROTMAN,KT ; FIRS: CHOO ,F CIT: 0.5
THE RELATIONSHIP BETWEEN KNOWLEDGE STRUCTURE AND JUDGMENTS FOR EXPERIENCED AND INEXPERIENCED AUDITORS
TAR JL 91 VOL: 66 PG:464 - 485 :: REGRESS. :LAB. :HIPS :JUDG.

TROTMAN,KT ; SEC: SNG ,J CIT: 0
THE EFFECT OF HYPOTHESIS FRAMING, PRIOR EXPECTATIONS AND CUE DIAGNOSTICITY ON AUDITORS' INFORMATION CHOICE
AOS 06 89 VOL: 14 PG:565 - 576 :: REGRESS. :LAB. :HIPS :JUDG.

TROTMAN,KT ; SEC: YETTON,PW CIT: 0.25
THE EFFECT OF THE REVIEW PROCESS ON AUDITOR JUDGMENTS
JAR SP 85 VOL: 23 PG:256 - 267 :: REGRESS. :LAB. :OTH.BEH. :JUDG.

TROTMAN,KT CIT: 0.25
THE REVIEW PROCESS AND THE ACCURACY OF AUDITOR JUDGMENTS
JAR AU 85 VOL: 23 PG:740 - 752 :: REGRESS. :LAB. :HIPS :JUDG.

TROTMAN,KT ; SEC: YETTON,PW ; THIR: ZIMMER,I CIT: 0.3
INDIVIDUAL AND GROUP JUDGMENTS OF INTERNAL CONTROL SYSTEMS
JAR SP 83 VOL: 21 PG:286 - 292 :: CORR. :LAB. :HIPS :MANAG.

TROTMAN,KT ; SEC: BRADLEY,G CIT: 0.5
ASSOCIATIONS BETWEEN SOCIAL RESPONSIBILITY DISCLOSURE AND CHARACTERISTICS OF COMPANIES
AOS 04 81 VOL: 6 PG:355 - 362 :: NON-PAR. :PRIM. :OTH. :HRA

TRUEBLOOD,RM CIT: 0
ACCOUNTING PRINCIPLES: THE BOARD AND ITS PROBLEMS
JAR ST 66 VOL: 4 PG:183 - 191 :: QUAL. :INT. LOG. :INSTIT. :N/A

TRUEBLOOD,RM CIT: 0
EDUCATION FOR A CHANGING PROFESSION
JAR SP 63 VOL: 1 PG:86 - 95 :: QUAL. :INT. LOG. :OTH. :AUD.TRAIN.

TRUEMAN,B CIT: 0
ON THE INCENTIVES FOR SECURITY ANALYSTS TO REVISE THEIR EARNINGS FORECASTS
CAR AU 90 VOL: 7 PG:203 - 222 :: DES.STAT. :INT. LOG. :INF.ECO./AG. :FOREC.

TRUEMAN,B CIT: 0
THEORIES OF EARNINGS-ANNOUNCEMENT TIMING
JAE OC 90 VOL: 13 PG:285 - 301 :: DES.STAT. :INT. LOG. :EMH :TIM.

TRUEMAN,B ; SEC: TITMAN,S CIT: 0.4
AN EXPLANATION FOR ACCOUNTING INCOME SMOOTHING
JAR ST 88 VOL: 26 PG:127 - 143 :: DES.STAT. :INT. LOG. :INF.ECO./AG. :REV.REC.

TRUEMAN,B CIT: 1.14
WHY DO MANAGERS VOLUNTARILY RELEASE EARNINGS FORECASTS?
JAE MR 86 VOL: 8 PG:53 - 72 :: DES.STAT. :INT. LOG. :THEORY :FOREC.

TRUEMAN,B ; FIRS: TITMAN,S CIT: 2.14
INFORMATION QUALITY AND THE VALUATION OF NEW ISSUES
JAE JN 86 VOL: 8 PG:159 - 172 :: DES.STAT. :INT. LOG. :INF.ECO./AG. :VALUAT.(INFL.)

TRUMBULL,WP CIT: 0
DIFFERENCES BETWEEN FINANCIAL AND TAX DEPRECIATION
TAR JL 68 VOL: 43 PG:459 - 468 :: QUAL. :INT. LOG. :THEORY :TAXES

TRUMBULL,WP CIT: 0
WHEN IS A LIABILITY?
TAR JA 63 VOL: 38 PG:46 - 51 :: QUAL. :INT. LOG. :THEORY :SPEC.ITEMS

TRZCINKA,CA ; FIRS: BROWN ,LD ; SEC: RICHARDSON,GD CIT: 0.5
STRONG-FORM EFFICIENCY ON THE TORONTO STOCK EXCHANGE: AN EXAMINATION OF ANALYST PRICE FORECASTS
CAR SP 91 VOL: 7 PG:323 - 346 :: REGRESS. :PRIM. :EMH :FOREC.

TSAY ,JJ ; FIRS: NICHOLS,DR CIT: 0.43
SECURITY PRICE REACTIONS TO LONG-RANGE EXECUTIVE EARNINGS FORECASTS
JAR SP 79 VOL: 17 PG:140 - 155 :: REGRESS. :PRIM. :EMH :FOREC.

TSAY ,JJ ; FIRS: NICHOLS,DR ; THIR: LARKIN,PD CIT: 0
INVESTOR TRADING RESPONSES TO DIFFERING CHARACTERISTICS OF VOLUNTARILY DISCLOSED EARNINGS FORECASTS
TAR AP 79 VOL: 54 PG:376 - 382 :: NON-PAR. :PRIM. :EMH :FOREC.

TSCHIRHART,JT ; FIRS: HAMLEN,SS ; SEC: HAMLEN,WA CIT: 0.08
THE USE OF THE GENERALIZED SHAPLEY ALLOCATION IN JOINT COST ALLOCATION
TAR AP 80 VOL: 55 PG:269 - 287 :: ANAL. :INT. LOG. :OTH.STAT. :INT.CONT.

TSCHIRHART,JT ; FIRS: HAMLEN,SS ; SEC: HAMLEN,WA CIT: 0.63
THE USE OF CORE THEORY IN EVALUATING JOINT COST ALLOCATION SCHEMES
TAR JL 77 VOL: 52 PG:616 - 627 :: ANAL. :INT. LOG. :MATH.PROG. :COST.ALLOC.

TSE ,S ; FIRS: FREEMAN,R CIT: 0
AN EARNINGS PREDICTION APPROACH TO EXAMINING INTERCOMPANY INFORMATION TRANSFERS
JAE DE 92 VOL: 15 PG:509 - 523 :: REGRESS. :PRIM. :EMH :FIN.ST.TIM.

TSE ,S CIT: 0
LIFO LIQUIDATIONS
JAR SP 90 VOL: 28 PG:229 - 238 :: REGRESS. :PRIM. :EMH :INV.

TSE ,S ; FIRS: ATIASE,RK ; SEC: BAMBER,LS CIT: 0.5
TIMELINESS OF FINANCIAL REPORTING, THE FIRM SIZE EFFECT, AND STOCK PRICE REACTIONS TO ANNUAL EARNINGS ANNOUNCEMENTS
CAR SP 89 VOL: 5 PG:526 - 552 :: REGRESS. :PRIM. :EMH :FIN.ST.TIM.

TSE ,S CIT: 0
ATTRIBUTES OF INDUSTRY, INDUSTRY SEGMENT AND FIRM-SPECIFIC INFORMATION IN SECURITY VALUATION
CAR SP 89 VOL: 5 PG:592 - 614 :: REGRESS. :PRIM. :EMH :SEG.REP.

TSE ,S ; FIRS: FREEMAN,RN CIT: 1.75
THE MULTIPERIOD INFORMATION CONTENT OF ACCOUNTING EARNINGS: CONFIRMATIONS AND CONTRADICTIONS OF PREVIOUS EARNINGS REPORTS
JAR ST 89 VOL: 27 PG:49 - 79 :: REGRESS. :PRIM. :EMH :REV.REC.

TSE ,S CIT: 0.14
INTRA-YEAR TRENDS IN THE DEGREE OF ASSOC. BETWEEN ACCOUNTING NUMBERS AND SECURITY PRICES
TAR JL 86 VOL: 61 PG:475 - 497 :: REGRESS. :PRIM. :EMH :FIN.METH.

TSE ,SY ; FIRS: FREEMAN,RN CIT: 1
A NONLINEAR MODEL OF SECURITY PRICE RESPONSES TO UNEXPECTED EARNINGS
JAR AU 92 VOL: 30 PG:185 - 209 :: REGRESS. :PRIM. :EMH :REV.REC.

TSENG ,M ; FIRS: MAGEE ,RP CIT: 1.33
AUDIT PRICING AND INDEPENDENCE
TAR AP 90 VOL: 65 PG:315 - 336 :: DES.STAT. :INT. LOG. :INF.ECO./AG. :INDEP.

TSUI ,AS ; FIRS: FLAMHOLTZ,EG ; SEC: DAS ,TK CIT: 0.13
TOWARD AN INTEGRATIVE FRAMEWORK OF ORGANIZATIONAL CONTROL
AOS 01 85 VOL: 10 PG:35 - 50 :: DES.STAT. :INT. LOG. :OTH.BEH. :HRA

TSUI ,K-W ; FIRS: MATSUMURA,EM ; THIR: WONG ,W-K CIT: 0.33
AN EXTENDED MULTINOMIAL-DIRICHLET MODEL FOR ERROR BOUNDS FOR DOLLAR-UNIT SAMPLING
CAR SP 90 VOL: 6 PG:485 - 500 :: DES.STAT. :SIM. :OTH.STAT. :SAMP.

TSUI ,KL ; FIRS: TSUI ,KW ; SEC: MATSUMURA,EM CIT: 0.5
MULTINOMINAL-DIRICHLET BOUNDS FOR DOLLAR-UNIT SAMPLING IN AUDITING
TAR JA 85 VOL: 60 PG:76 - 96 :: DES.STAT. :SIM. :OTH.STAT. :SAMP.

TSUI ,KW ; SEC: MATSUMURA,EM ; THIR: TSUI ,KL CIT: 0.5
MULTINOMINAL-DIRICHLET BOUNDS FOR DOLLAR-UNIT SAMPLING IN AUDITING
TAR JA 85 VOL: 60 PG:76 - 96 :: DES.STAT. :SIM. :OTH.STAT. :SAMP.

TSUI ,KW ; FIRS: MATSUMURA,EM CIT: 0.09
STEIN-TYPE POISSON ESTIMATORS IN AUDIT SAMPLING
JAR SP 82 VOL: 20 PG:162 - 170 :: CORR. :INT. LOG. :N/A :SAMP.

TUBBS ,RM CIT: 0
THE EFFECT OF EXPERIENCE ON THE AUDITOR'S ORGANIZATION AND AMOUNT OF KNOWLEDGE
TAR OC 92 VOL: 67 PG:783 - 801 :: REGRESS. :FIELD :HIPS :ERRORS

TUBBS ,RM ; SEC: MESSIER JR,WF ; THIR: KNECHEL,WR CIT: 1.67
RECENCY EFFECTS IN THE AUDITOR'S BELIEF-REVISION PROCESS
TAR AP 90 VOL: 65 PG:452 - 460 :: REGRESS. :LAB. :HIPS :AUD.BEH.

TUBBS ,RM ; FIRS: BAMBER,EM ; SEC: SNOWBALL,D CIT: 0.5
AUDIT STRUCTURE AND ITS RELATION TO ROLE CONFLICT AND ROLE AMBIGUITY: AN
TAR AP 89 VOL: 64 PG:285 - 299 :: REGRESS. :FIELD :HIPS :AUD.

TUCKER,RR ; FIRS: MATSUMURA,EM CIT: 0
FRAUD DETECTION: A THEORETICAL FOUNDATION
TAR OC 92 VOL: 67 PG:753 - 782 :: DES.STAT. :INT. LOG. :INF.ECO./AG. :AUD.THEOR.

TUCKERMAN,B CIT: 0
OBJECTIVE CONSOLIDATION STANDARDS FOR FOREIGN SUBSIDIARIES
TAR JA 64 VOL: 39 PG:32 - 37 :: QUAL. :INT. LOG. :THEORY :BUS.COMB.

TUGGLE,FD ; FIRS: GORDON,LA ; SEC: LARCKER,DF CIT: 0.67
STRATEGIC DECISION PROCESSES AND THE DESIGN OF ACCOUNTING INFORMATION
SYSTEMS: CONCEPTUAL LINKAGES
AOS 34 78 VOL: 3 PG:203 - 214 :: QUAL. :INT. LOG. :OTH. :INFO.STRUC.

TUNG ,S ; FIRS: THOMAS,JK CIT: 2
COST MANIPULATION INCENTIVES UNDER COST REIMBURSEMENT: PENSION COSTS FOR
DEFENSE CONTRACTS
TAR OC 92 VOL: 67 PG:691 - 711 :: REGRESS. :PRIM. :OTH.BEH. :PENS.

TUNG ,S ; FIRS: RULAND,W ; THIR: GEORGE,NE CIT: 0
FACTORS ASSOCIATED WITH THE DISCLOSURE OF MANAGERS' FORECASTS
TAR JL 90 VOL: 65 PG:710 - 721 :: REGRESS. :PRIM. :HIPS :FOREC.

TURLEY,S ; FIRS: MOIZER,P CIT: 0
SURROGATES FOR AUDIT FEES IN CONCENTRATION STUDIES
AUD AU 87 VOL: 7 PG:118 - 123 :: REGRESS. :PRIM. :OTH.STAT. :ORG.

TURNER,MJ ; SEC: HILTON,RW CIT: 0.25
USE OF ACCOUNTING PRODUCT-COSTING SYSTEMS IN MAKING PRODUCTION DECISIONS
JAR AU 89 VOL: 27 PG:297 - 312 :: REGRESS. :LAB. :OTH.BEH. :REL.COSTS

TURNER,MJ ; FIRS: HILTON,RW ; SEC: SWIERINGA,RJ CIT: 0.2
PRODUCT PRICING, ACCOUNTING COSTS AND USE OF PRODUCT-COSTING SYSTEMS
TAR AP 88 VOL: 63 PG:195 - 218 :: REGRESS. :LAB. :OTH.BEH. :REL.COSTS

TUROPOLEC,L ; FIRS: BIRNBERG,JG ; THIR: YOUNG ,SM CIT: 1.7
THE ORGANIZATIONAL CONTEXT OF ACCOUNTING
AOS 23 83 VOL: 8 PG:111 - 130 :: QUAL. :SEC. :OTH.BEH. :REL.COSTS

TURPEN,RA CIT: 0.33
DIFFERENCTIAL PRICING ON AUDITORS' INITIAL ENGAGEMENTS: FURTHER EVIDENCE
AUD SP 90 VOL: 9 PG:60 - 76 :: REGRESS. :PRIM. :OTH.STAT. :ORG.

TWARK ,RD ; FIRS: BASI ,BA ; SEC: CAREY ,KJ CIT: 0.82
A COMPARISON OF THE ACCURACY OF CORPORATE AND SECURITY ANALYSTS' FORECASTS
TAR AP 76 VOL: 51 PG:244 - 254 :: ANOVA :PRIM. :TIME SER. :FOREC.

TWARK ,RD ; FIRS: KRATCHMAN,SH ; SEC: MALCOM,RE CIT: 0.06
AN INTRA-INDUSTRY COMPARISON OF ALTERNATIVE INCOME CONCEPTS AND RELATIVE PERFORMANCE EVALUATIONS
TAR OC 74 VOL: 49 PG:682 - 689 :: NON-PAR. :PRIM. :N/A :VALUAT.(INFL.)

TWOMBLY,JR ; FIRS: EGGLETON,IRC ; SEC: PENMAN,SH CIT: 0.82
ACCOUNTING CHANGES AND STOCK PRICES: AN EXAMINATION OF SELECTED UNCONTROLLED VARIABLES
JAR SP 76 VOL: 14 PG:66 - 88 :: NON-PAR. :PRIM. :EMH :ACC.CHNG.

TZUR ,J ; FIRS: HALPERIN,R CIT: 0.13
MONETARY COMPENSATION AND NONTAXABLE EMPLOYEE BENEFITS: AN ANALYTICAL PERSPECTIVE
TAR OC 85 VOL: 60 PG:670 - 680 :: REGRESS. :INT. LOG. :THEORY :EXEC.COMP.

UECKER,WC ; FIRS: DEJONG,DV ; SEC: FORSYTHE,R ; THIR: KIM ,JA CIT: 0.25
A LABORATORY INVESTIGATION OF ALTERNATIVE TRANSFER PRICING MECHANISMS
AOS 02 89 VOL: 14 PG:41 - 64 :: REGRESS. :LAB. :OTH.BEH. :TRANS.PRIC.

UECKER,WC ; FIRS: MADEO ,SA ; SEC: SCHEPANSKI,A CIT: 0
MODELING JUDGMENTS OF TAXPAYER COMPLIANCE
TAR AP 87 VOL: 62 PG:323 - 342 :: REGRESS. :LAB. :OTH.STAT. :TAXES

UECKER,WC ; FIRS: DEJONG,DV ; SEC: FORSYTHE,R CIT: 1.25
THE METHODOLOGY OF LABORATORY MARKETS AND ITS IMPLICATIONS FOR AGENCY RESEARCH IN ACCOUNTING AND AUDITING
JAR AU 85 VOL: 23 PG:753 - 793 :: REGRESS. :LAB. :INF.ECO./AG. :METHOD.

UECKER,WC ; FIRS: DEJONG,DV ; SEC: FORSYTHE,R ; THIR: LUNDHOLM,RJ CIT: 0.88
A LABORATORY INVESTIGATION OF THE MORAL HAZARD PROBLEM IN AN AGENCY RELATIONSHIP
JAR ST 85 VOL: 23 PG:81 - 120 :: REGRESS. :LAB. :INF.ECO./AG. :MAN.DEC.CHAR.

UECKER,WC ; SEC: SCHEPANSKI,A ; THIR: SHIN ,J CIT: 0.25
TOWARD A POSITIVE THEORY OF INFORMATION EVALUATION: RELEVANT TESTS OF COMPETING MODELS IN A PRINCIPAL-AGENCY SETTING
TAR JL 85 VOL: 60 PG:430 - 457 :: REGRESS. :LAB. :INF.ECO./AG. :MANAG.

UECKER,WC ; FIRS: SCHEPANSKI,A CIT: 0.3
TOWARD A POSITIVE THEORY OF INFORMATION EVALUATION
TAR AP 83 VOL: 58 PG:259 - 283 :: ANAL. :INT. LOG. :INF.ECO./AG. :OTH.MANAG.

UECKER,WC CIT: 0.09
THE QUALITY OF GROUP PERFORMANCE IN SIMPLIFIED INFORMATION EVALUATION
JAR AU 82 VOL: 20 PG:388 - 402 :: DES.STAT. :LAB. :OTH.BEH. :INFO.STRUC.

UECKER,WC ; FIRS: KINNEY JR,WR CIT: 1
MITIGATING THE CONSEQUENCES OF ANCHORING IN AUDITOR JUDGMENTS
TAR JA 82 VOL: 57 PG:55 - 69 :: DES.STAT. :LAB. :HIPS :ANAL.REV.

UECKER,WC ; SEC: BRIEF ,AP ; THIR: KINNEY JR,WR CIT: 0.33
PERCEPTION OF THE INTERNAL AND EXTERNAL AUDITOR AS A DETERRENT TO CORPORATE IRREGULARITIES
TAR JL 81 VOL: 56 PG:465 - 478 :: ANOVA :LAB. :OTH.BEH. :AUD.BEH.

UECKER,WC CIT: 0.38
THE EFFECTS OF KNOWLEDGE OF THE USER'S DECISION MODEL IN SIMPLIFIED INFORMATION EVALUATION
JAR SP 80 VOL: 18 PG:191 - 213 :: ANOVA :LAB. :HIPS :INFO.STRUC.

UECKER,WC CIT: 0.87
A BEHAVIOURAL STUDY OF INFORMATION SYSTEM CHOICE
JAR SP 78 VOL: 16 PG:169 - 189 :: ANOVA :LAB. :INF.ECO./AG. :INFO.STRUC.

UECKER,WC CIT: 0.06
AN INQUIRY INTO THE NEED FOR CURRENTLY FEASIBLE EXTENSIONS OF THE ATTEST FUNCTION IN CORPORATE ANNUAL REPORTS
AOS 01 77 VOL: 2 PG:47 - 58 :: OTH.QUANT. :LAB. :OTH.BEH. :FIN.METH.

UECKER,WC ; SEC: KINNEY JR,WR CIT: 0.69
JUDGMENTAL EVALUATION OF SAMPLE RESULTS: A STUDY OF THE TYPE AND SEVERITY OF ERRORS MADE BY PRACTICING CPAS
AOS 03 77 VOL: 2 PG:269 - 275 :: DES.STAT. :LAB. :OTH.STAT. :SAMP.

ULLMANN,AA CIT: 0
CORPORATE SOCIAL REPORTING: POLITICAL INTERESTS AND CONFLICTS IN GERMANY
AOS 12 79 VOL: 4 PG:123 - 134 :: QUAL. :INT. LOG. :INSTIT. :HRA

ULLMANN,AA CIT: 0.06
THE CORPORATE ENVIRONMENTAL ACCOUNTING SYSTEM: A MANAGEMENT TOOL FOR FIGHTING ENVIRONMENTAL DEGRADATION
AOS 01 76 VOL: 1 PG:71 - 80 :: QUAL. :INT. LOG. :THEORY :HRA

UNG ,S ; FIRS: STANDISH,PEM CIT: 0
CORPORATE SIGNALING, ASSET REVALUATIONS, AND STOCK PRICES OF BRITISH COMPANIES
TAR OC 82 VOL: 57 PG:701 - 715 :: REGRESS. :PRIM. :EMH :VALUAT.(INFL.)

UPHOFF,HL ; FIRS: ELLIOTT,JW CIT: 0.12
PREDICTING THE NEAR TERM PROFIT AND LOSS STATEMENT WITH AN ECONOMETRIC MODEL: A FEASIBILITY STUDY
JAR AU 72 VOL: 10 PG:259 - 274 :: MIXED :PRIM. :TIME SER. :BUDG.& PLAN.

USHMAN,N ; FIRS: MORSE ,D CIT: 0.2
THE EFFECT OF INFORMATION ANNOUNCEMENTS ON THE MARKET MICROSTRUCTURE
TAR AP 83 VOL: 58 PG:247 - 258 :: ANOVA :PRIM. :OTH. :FIN.METH.

USRY ,MF CIT: 0
COST ACCOUNTING ON THE CPA EXAMINATION
TAR OC 66 VOL: 41 PG:754 - 762 :: DES.STAT. :PRIM. :N/A :N/A

VAN DRUNEN,LD ; FIRS: BRICKLEY,JA CIT: 0.33
INTERNAL CORPORATE RESTRUCTURING: AN EMPIRICAL ANALYSIS
JAE JA 90 VOL: 12 PG:251 - 280 :: REGRESS. :PRIM. :OTH.STAT. :ORG.& ENVIR.

VAN NESS,G ; FIRS: GRAHAM,LE ; SEC: DAMENS,J CIT: 0
DEVELOPING RISK ADVISOR: AN EXPERT SYSTEM FOR RISK IDENTIFICATION
AUD SP 91 VOL: 10 PG:69 - 96 :: REGRESS. :LAB. :EXP.SYST. :RISK

VANCE ,LL CIT: 0
THE ROAD TO REFORM OF ACCOUNTING PRINCIPLES
TAR OC 69 VOL: 44 PG:692 - 703 :: QUAL. :INT. LOG. :HIST. :FIN.METH.

VANCE ,LL CIT: 0
WHAT THE EDITOR OF AN ACADEMIC JOURNAL EXPECTS FROM AUTHORS
TAR JA 66 VOL: 41 PG:48 - 51 :: QUAL. :INT. LOG. :N/A :OTH.MANAG.

VANDERWEIDE,JH ; FIRS: BROWN ,LD ; SEC: HUGHES,JS ; THIR: ROZEFF,MS CIT: 0.08
EXPECTATIONS DATA AND THE PREDICTIVE VALUE OF INTERIM REPORTING: A COMMENT
JAR SP 80 VOL: 18 PG:278 - 288 :: REGRESS. :PRIM. :TIME SER. :FOREC.

VANECEK,M ; FIRS: WHITE ,D CIT: 0
INTENDED USE: A UNIFORM TAX DEFINITION OF SOFTWARE
JAA SU 82 VOL: 5 PG:338 - 354 :: QUAL. :INT. LOG. :THEORY :TAXES

VASARHELYI,MA ; SEC: HALPER,FB CIT: 0
THE CONTINUOUS AUDIT OF ONLINE SYSTEMS
AUD SP 91 VOL: 10 PG:110 - 125 :: REGRESS. :LAB. :EXP.SYST. :INT.AUD.

VASARHELYI,MA ; FIRS: BROWN ,LD ; SEC: GARDNER,JC CIT: 0
ATTRIBUTES OF ARTICLES IMPACTING CONTEMPORARY ACCOUNTING LITERATURE
CAR SP 89 VOL: 5 PG:793 - 815 :: REGRESS. :SEC. :THEORY :METHOD.

VASARHELYI,MA ; FIRS: BROWN ,LD ; SEC: GARDNER,JC CIT: 0.5
AN ANALYSIS OF THE RESEARCH CONTRIBUTIONS OF ACCOUNTING, ORGANIZATIONS AND SOCIETY, 1976-1984
AOS 02 87 VOL: 12 PG:193 - 204 :: REGRESS. :SEC. :HIST. :METHOD.

VASARHELYI,MA ; FIRS: KNAUF ,JB CIT: 0
EMPIRICAL CHARACTERISTICS OF DEBENTURE CONVERSIONS: THE ISSUE OF EQUIVALENCY
JAA WI 87 VOL: 2 PG:43 - 64 :: REGRESS. :PRIM. :THEORY :LTD

VASARHELYI,MA ; FIRS: BAO ,BE ; SEC: BAO ,DA CIT: 0
A STOCHASTIC MODEL OF PROFESSIONAL ACCOUNTANT TURNOVER
AOS 03 86 VOL: 11 PG:289 - 296 :: DES.STAT. :PRIM. :OTH.BEH. :ORG.

VASARHELYI,MA ; FIRS: SRINIDHI,BN CIT: 0
AUDITOR JUDGMENT CONCERNING ESTABLISHMENT OF SUBSTANTIVE TESTS BASED ON INTERNAL CONTROL RELIABILITY
AUD SP 86 VOL: 5 PG:64 - 76 :: REGRESS. :LAB. :OTH.STAT. :INT.CONT.

VASARHELYI,MA ; SEC: BAILEY JR,AD ; THIR: CAMARDESSE JR,JE ; FOUR: GROOMER,SM ; FIFT: LAMPE ,JC CIT: 0
THE USAGE OF COMPUTERS IN AUDITING TEACHING AND RESEARCH
AUD SP 84 VOL: 3 PG:98 - 103 :: QUAL. :SIM. :OTH. :EDP AUD.

VASARHELYI,MA CIT: 0
AUTOMATION AND CHANGES IN THE AUDIT PROCESS
AUD AU 84 VOL: 4 PG:100 - 106 :: QUAL. :INT. LOG. :OTH. :AUD.

VASARHELYI,MA ; FIRS: MOCK ,TJ CIT: 0
A SYNTHESIS OF THE INFORMATION ECONOMICS AND LENS MODELS
JAR AU 78 VOL: 16 PG:414 - 423 :: ANAL. :INT. LOG. :HIPS :METHOD.

VASARHELYI,MA CIT: 0.5
MAN-MACHINE PLANNING SYSTEMS: A COGNITIVE STYLE EXAMINATION OF INTERACTIVE DECISION MAKING
JAR SP 77 VOL: 15 PG:138 - 153 :: ANOVA :LAB. :HIPS :MAN.DEC.CHAR.

VASARHELYI,MA ; FIRS: MOCK ,TJ ; SEC: ESTRIN,TL CIT: 0.71
LEARNING PATTERNS, DECISION APPROACH, AND VALUE OF INFORMATION
JAR SP 72 VOL: 10 PG:129 - 153 :: ANOVA :LAB. :HIPS :INFO.STRUC.

VATTER,W CIT: 0.06
INCOME MODELS, BOOK YIELD, AND THE RATE OF RETURN
TAR OC 66 VOL: 41 PG:681 - 698 :: ANAL. :INT. LOG. :THEORY :PP&E / DEPR

VATTER,WJ CIT: 0.21
STATE OF THE ART - NON-BUSINESS ACCOUNTING
TAR JL 79 VOL: 54 PG:563 - 573 :: QUAL. :SEC. :THEORY :N/A

VATTER,WJ CIT: 0
THE USE OF OPERATIONS RESEARCH IN AMERICAN COMPANIES
TAR OC 67 VOL: 42 PG:721 - 730 :: DES.STAT. :SURV. :N/A :OTH.MANAG.

VATTER,WJ CIT: 0.12
ACCOUNTING FOR LEASES
JAR AU 66 VOL: 4 PG:133 - 148 :: QUAL. :INT. LOG. :THEORY :LEASES

VATTER,WJ CIT: 0.18
POSTULATES AND PRINCIPLES
JAR AU 63 VOL: 1 PG:179 - 197 :: QUAL. :INT. LOG. :THEORY :N/A

VATTER,WJ CIT: 0.06
E(M3)I - AN EVALUATION
TAR JL 63 VOL: 38 PG:470 - 477 :: QUAL. :INT. LOG. :THEORY :FIN.METH.

VENEZIA,I ; FIRS: BERKOWITCH,E CIT: 0
TERM VS. WHOLE LIFE INSURANCE
JAA SP 92 VOL: 7 PG:241 - 250 :: DES.STAT. :INT. LOG. :INF.ECO./AG. :N/A

VERRECCHIA,RE ; FIRS: LAMBERT,RA ; SEC: LARCKER,DF CIT: 0.5
PORTFOLIO CONSIDERATIONS IN VALUING EXECUTIVE COMPENSATION
JAR SP 91 VOL: 29 PG:129 - 149 :: DES.STAT. :SIM. :INF.ECO./AG. :EXEC.COMP.

VERRECCHIA,RE ; FIRS: KIM ,O CIT: 1
TRADING VOLUME AND PRICE REACTIONS TO PUBLIC ANNOUNCEMENTS
JAR AU 91 VOL: 29 PG:302 - 321 :: DES.STAT. :INT. LOG. :INF.ECO./AG. :INFO.STRUC.

VERRECCHIA,RE CIT: 0.67
ENDOGENOUS PROPRIETARY COSTS THROUGH FIRM INTERDEPENDENCE
JAE JA 90 VOL: 12 PG:245 - 250 :: DES.STAT. :SEC. :INF.ECO./AG. :INFO.STRUC.

VERRECCHIA,RE ; FIRS: HOLTHAUSEN,RW CIT: 1.33
THE EFFECT OF INFORMEDNESS AND CONSENSUS ON PRICE AND VOLUME BEHAVIOR
TAR JA 90 VOL: 65 PG:191 - 208 :: DES.STAT. :INT. LOG. :INF.ECO./AG. :INFO.STRUC.

VERRECCHIA,RE ; FIRS: BEATTY,RP CIT: 0
THE EFFECT OF A MANDATED ACCOUNTING CHANGE ON THE CAPITALIZATION PROCESS
CAR SP 89 VOL: 5 PG:472 - 493 :: REGRESS. :PRIM. :TIME SER. :R & D

VERRECCHIA,RE ; FIRS: HOLTHAUSEN,RW CIT: 2.2
THE EFFECT OF SEQUENTIAL INFORMATION RELEASES ON THE VARIANCE OF PRICE CHANGES IN AN INTERTEMPORAL MULTI-ASSET MARKET
JAR SP 88 VOL: 26 PG:82 - 106 :: ANAL. :INT. LOG. :INF.ECO./AG. :INFO.STRUC.

VERRECCHIA,RE ; SEC: LANEN ,WN CIT: 0.17
OPERATING DECISIONS AND THE DISCLOSURE OF MANAGEMENT ACCOUNTING INFORMATION
JAR ST 87 VOL: 25 PG:165 - 189 :: ANAL. :INT. LOG. :THEORY :MANAG.

VERRECCHIA,RE CIT: 0.43
MANAGERIAL DISCRETION IN THE CHOICE AMONG FINANCIAL REPORTING ALTERNATIVES
JAE OC 86 VOL: 8 PG:175 - 196 :: DES.STAT. :INT. LOG. :INF.ECO./AG. :INFO.STRUC.

VERRECCHIA,RE CIT: 2.1
DISCRETIONARY DISCLOSURE
JAE DE 83 VOL: 5 PG:179 - 194 :: ANAL. :INT. LOG. :OTH. :INFO.STRUC.

VERRECCHIA,RE CIT: 0.64
THE USE OF MATHEMATICAL MODELS IN FINANCIAL ACCOUNTING
JAR ST 82 VOL: 20 PG:1 - 42 :: ANAL. :SEC. :EMH :FIN.METH.

VERRECCHIA,RE CIT: 0
AN ANALYSIS OF TWO COST ALLOCATION CASES
TAR JL 82 VOL: 57 PG:579 - 593 :: ANAL. :INT. LOG. :OTH.STAT. :COST.ALLOC.

VERRECCHIA,RE ; FIRS: BILLERA,LJ ; SEC: HEATH ,DC CIT: 0.25
A UNIQUE PROCEDURE FOR ALLOCATING COMMON COSTS FROM A PRODUCTION PROCESS
JAR SP 81 VOL: 19 PG:185 - 196 :: ANAL. :INT. LOG. :INF.ECO./AG. :N/A

VERRECCHIA,RE CIT: 0.33
ON THE RELATIONSHIP BETWEEN VOLUME REACTION AND CONSENSUS OF INVESTORS: IMPLICATIONS FOR INTERPRETING TESTS OF INFORMATION CONTENT
JAR SP 81 VOL: 19 PG:271 - 283 :: ANAL. :INT. LOG. :OTH.STAT. :FIN.METH.

VERRECCHIA,RE CIT: 0.54
THE RAPIDITY OF PRICE ADJUSTMENTS TO INFORMATION
JAE MR 80 VOL: 2 PG:63 - 92 :: ANAL. :INT. LOG. :INF.ECO./AG. :INFO.STRUC.

VERRECCHIA,RE CIT: 0.43
ON THE THEORY OF MARKET INFORMATION EFFICIENCY
JAE MR 79 VOL: 1 PG:77 - 90 :: ANAL. :INT. LOG. :INF.ECO./AG. :METHOD.

VERRECCHIA,RE CIT: 0.07
ON THE CHOICE OF ACCOUNTING METHOD FOR PARTNERSHIPS
JAR SP 78 VOL: 16 PG:150 - 168 :: ANAL. :INT. LOG. :INF.ECO./AG. :FIN.METH.

VICKREY,D CIT: 0
REFINED CONDITIONS FOR FULLY REVEALING INCOME DISCLOSURE
TAR JL 92 VOL: 67 PG:623 - 627 :: DES.STAT. :INT. LOG. :THEORY :INFO.STRUC.

VICKREY,D ; FIRS: FOSTER III,TW ; SEC: KOOGLER,PR CIT: 0
VALUATION OF EXECUTIVE STOCK OPTIONS AND THE FASB PROPOSAL
TAR JL 91 VOL: 66 PG:595 - 610 :: DES.STAT. :INT. LOG. :INF.ECO./AG. :EXEC.COMP.

VICKREY,DW ; FIRS: SCHROEDER,MS ; SEC: SOLOMON,I CIT: 0.14
AUDIT QUALITY: THE PERCEPTIONS OF AUDIT-COMMITTEE CHAIRPERSONS AND AUDIT PARTNERS
AUD SP 86 VOL: 5 PG:86 - 94 :: REGRESS. :SURV. :OTH.BEH. :OPER.AUD.

VICKREY,DW ; FIRS: FOSTER III,TW CIT: 0.07
THE INFORMATION CONTENT OF STOCK DIVIDEND ANNOUNCEMENTS
TAR AP 78 VOL: 53 PG:360 - 370 :: REGRESS. :PRIM. :EMH :STK.DIV.

VICKREY,DW ; FIRS: FOSTER III,TW CIT: 0.6
THE INCREMENTAL INFORMATION CONTENT OF THE 10-K
TAR OC 78 VOL: 53 PG:921 - 934 :: ANOVA :PRIM. :EMH :FIN.METH.

VICKREY,DW CIT: 0.12
GENERAL-PRICE-LEVEL-ADJUSTED HISTORICAL-COST STATEMENTS AND THE RATIO-SCALE VIEW
TAR JA 76 VOL: 51 PG:31 - 40 :: QUAL. :INT. LOG. :THEORY :OTH.FIN.ACC.

VICKREY,DW CIT: 0.12
IS ACCOUNTING A MEASUREMENT DISCIPLINE?
TAR OC 70 VOL: 45 PG:731 - 742 :: ANAL. :INT. LOG. :THEORY :OTH.FIN.ACC.

VIGELAND,RL ; FIRS: DALEY ,LA ; SEC: SENKOW,DW CIT: 0.4
ANALYSTS' FORECASTS, EARNINGS VARIABILITY, AND OPTION PRICING: EMPIRICAL EVIDENCE
TAR OC 88 VOL: 63 PG:563 - 585 :: REGRESS. :PRIM. :TIME SER. :FOREC.

VIGELAND,RL ; FIRS: DALEY ,LA CIT: 2
THE EFFECTS OF DEBT COVENANTS AND POLITICAL COSTS ON THE CHOICE OF ACCOUNTING METHODS: THE CASE OF ACCOUNTING FOR R & D COSTS
JAE DE 83 VOL: 5 PG:195 - 211 :: OTH.QUANT. :PRIM. :OTH.STAT. :R & D

VIGELAND,RL CIT: 0.09
DILUTION OF EARNINGS PER SHARE IN AN OPTION PRICING FRAMEWORK
TAR AP 82 VOL: 57 PG:348 - 357 :: ANAL. :INT. LOG. :THEORY :AUD.TRAIN.

VIGELAND,RL CIT: 0.42
THE MARKET REACTION TO STATEMENT OF FINANCIAL ACCOUNTING STANDARDS NO.2
TAR AP 81 VOL: 56 PG:309 - 325 :: ANOVA :PRIM. :EMH :R & D

VIRGIL JR,RL ; FIRS: SPILLER JR,EA CIT: 0.06
EFFECTIVENESS OF APB OPINION NO.19 IN IMPROVING FUNDS REPORTING
JAR SP 74 VOL: 12 PG:112 - 142 :: DES.STAT. :LAB. :THEORY :INFO.STRUC.

VIRGIL JR,RL ; FIRS: PANKOFF,LD CIT: 0.59
SOME PRELIMINARY FINDINGS FROM A LABORATORY EXPERIMENT ON THE USEFULNESS OF FINANCIAL ACCOUNTING INFORMATION TO SECURITY ANALYST
JAR ST 70 VOL: 8 PG:1 - 48 :: MIXED :LAB. :OTH.BEH. :FIN.METH.

VIRGIL JR,RL ; FIRS: PANKOFF,LD CIT: 0.12
ON THE USEFULNESS OF FINANCIAL STATEMENT INFORMATION: A SUGGESTED RESEARCH APPROACH
TAR AP 70 VOL: 45 PG:269 - 279 :: DES.STAT. :LAB. :N/A :OTH.MANAG.

VOGT ,RA CIT: 0
A CORPORATE STRATEGY FOR REALIZING EQUAL EMPLOYMENT OPPORTUNITY
AOS 01 77 VOL: 2 PG:59 - 80 :: QUAL. :INT. LOG. :HIPS :HRA

VOLKAN,AG ; FIRS: RUE ,JC CIT: 0
FINANCIAL AND ECONOMIC CONSEQUENCES OF THE NEW PENSION ACCOUNTING PROPOSALS: IS THE GLOOM JUSTIFIED?
JAA SU 84 VOL: 7 PG:306 - 322 :: DES.STAT. :PRIM. :THEORY :PENS.

VOSS ,WM CIT: 0
ACCELERATED DEPRECIATION AND DEFERRED TAX ALLOCATION
JAR AU 68 VOL: 6 PG:262 - 269 :: DES.STAT. :PRIM. :N/A :TAXES

VOSS ,WM ; FIRS: BEAVER,WH ; SEC: KENNELLY,JW CIT: 0.94
PREDICTIVE ABILITY AS A CRITERION FOR THE EVALUATION OF ACCOUNTING DATA
TAR OC 68 VOL: 43 PG:675 - 683 :: QUAL. :INT. LOG. :THEORY :FIN.METH.

WADE ,HH CIT: 0
ACCOUNTING FOR THE INVESTMENT CREDIT
TAR OC 63 VOL: 38 PG:714 - 718 :: QUAL. :INT. LOG. :THEORY :N/A

WAEGELEIN,JF ; FIRS: TEHRANIAN,H ; SEC: TRAVLOS,NG CIT: 0.5
MANAGEMENT COMPENSATION CONTRACTS AND MERGER-INDUCED ABNORMAL RETURNS
JAR ST 87 VOL: 25 PG:51 - 76 :: ANOVA :PRIM. :OTH.STAT. :BUS.COMB.

WAEGELEIN,JF ; FIRS: TEHRANIAN,H CIT: 0.25
MARKET REACTION TO SHORT-TERM EXECUTIVE COMPENSATION PLAN ADOPTION
JAE AP 85 VOL: 7 PG:131 - 144 :: REGRESS. :PRIM. :EMH :EXEC.COMP.

WAGGONER,JB CIT: 0
AUDITOR DETECTION RATES IN AN INTERNAL CONTROL TEST
AUD SP 90 VOL: 9 PG:77 - 89 :: REGRESS. :LAB. :OTH.BEH. :RISK

WAGNER,JW CIT: 0
EDP AND THE AUDITOR OF THE 1970'S
TAR JL 69 VOL: 44 PG:600 - 604 :: QUAL. :INT. LOG. :N/A :EDP AUD.

WAGNER,JW CIT: 0.12
DEFINING OBJECTIVITY IN ACCOUNTING
TAR JL 65 VOL: 40 PG:599 - 605 :: QUAL. :INT. LOG. :THEORY :OTH.FIN.ACC.

WAI ,WT ; FIRS: DAVISON,AG ; SEC: STENING,BW CIT: 0
AUDITOR CONCENTRATION AND THE IMPACT OF INTERLOCKING DIRECTORATES
JAR SP 84 VOL: 22 PG:313 - 317 :: CORR. :PRIM. :OTH. :ORG.& ENVIR.

WAKEMAN,LM CIT: 0
OPTIMAL TAX DEPRECIATION
JAE DE 80 VOL: 2 PG:213 - 237 :: ANAL. :INT. LOG. :THEORY :AMOR./DEPL.

WALKER,KB ; SEC: MCCLELLAND,LA CIT: 0
MANAGEMENT FORECASTS AND STATISTICAL PREDICTION MODEL FORECASTS IN CORPORATE BUDGETING
JAR AU 91 VOL: 29 PG:371 - 381 :: REGRESS. :CASE :TIME SER. :BUDG.& PLAN.

WALKER,M ; FIRS: BOARD ,JLG CIT: 0
INTERTEMPORAL AND CROSS-SECTIONAL VARIATION IN THE ASSOCIATION BETWEEN UNEXPECTED ACCOUNTING RATES OF RETURN AND ABNORMA
JAR SP 90 VOL: 28 PG:182 - 192 :: REGRESS. :PRIM. :EMH :METHOD.

WALKER,M CIT: 0
AGENCY THEORY: A FALSIFICATIONIST PERSPECTIVE
AOS 06 89 VOL: 14 PG:433 - 453 :: DES.STAT. :INT. LOG. :INF.ECO./AG. :METHOD.

WALKER,M CIT: 0
RISK ATTITUDES, VALUE-RESTRICTED PREFERENCES AND PUBLIC CHOICE OVER LOTTERIES AND INFORMATION SYSTEMS
TAR AP 84 VOL: 59 PG:278 - 286 :: ANAL. :INT. LOG. :OTH.STAT. :N/A

WALKER,NR ; SEC: PIERCE,LT CIT: 0
THE PRICE WATERHOUSE AUDIT: A STATE OF THE ART APPROACH
AUD AU 88 VOL: 08 PG:1 - 22 :: DES.STAT. :INT. LOG. :THEORY :AUD.THEOR.

WALKER,RG ; FIRS: SHARPE,IG CIT: 0.06
ASSET REVALUATIONS AND STOCK MARKET PRICES
JAR AU 75 VOL: 13 PG:293 - 310 :: REGRESS. :PRIM. :EMH :VALUAT.(INFL.)

WALKER,SP CIT: 0
THE DEFENSE OF PROFESSIONAL MONOPOLY: SCOTTISH CHARTERED ACCOUNTANTS AND "SATELLITES IN THE ACCOUNTANCY FIRMAMENT: 1854-1914"
AOS 03 91 VOL: 16 PG:257 - 283 :: REGRESS. :SEC. :HIST. :ORG.& ENVIR.

WALLACE,WA CIT: 0
PEER REVIEW FILINGS AND THEIR IMPLICATIONS IN EVALUATING SELF-REGULATION
AUD SP 91 VOL: 10 PG:53 - 68 :: REGRESS. :PRIM. :OTH.BEH. :OTH.MANAG.

WALLACE,WA ; SEC: KRUETZFELDT,RW CIT: 0
DISTINCTIVE CHARACTERISTICS OF ENTITIES WITH AN INTERNAL AUDIT DEPARTMENT AND THE ASSOCIATION OF THE QUALITY OF SUCH DEPARTMENTS
CAR SP 91 VOL: 7 PG:485 - 512 :: REGRESS. :PRIM. :OTH.STAT. :INT.AUD.

WALLACE,WA ; FIRS: KREUTZFELDT,RW CIT: 0
CONTROL RISK ASSESSMENTS: DO THEY RELATE TO ERRORS?
AUD 90 VOL: 9 PG:1 - 26 :: REGRESS. :PRIM. :OTH.STAT. :ERRORS

WALLACE,WA ; FIRS: KREUTZFELDT,RW CIT: 1.14
ERROR CHARACTERISTICS IN AUDIT POPULATIONS: THEIR PROFILE AND RELATIONSHIP TO ENVIRONMENTAL FACTORS
AUD AU 86 VOL: 6 PG:20 - 43 :: DES.STAT. :SURV. :OTH.STAT. :ERRORS

WALLACE,WA CIT: 0
THE ACCEPTABILITY OF REGRESSION ANALYSIS AS EVIDENCE IN A COURTROOM - IMPLICATIONS FOR THE AUDITOR
AUD SP 83 VOL: 2 PG:66 - 90 :: REGRESS. :INT. LOG. :OTH.STAT. :LIAB.

WALLACE,WA CIT: 0.83
THE ASSOCIATION BETWEEN MUNICIPAL MARKET MEASURES AND SELECTED FINANCIAL REPORTING PRACTICES
JAR AU 81 VOL: 19 PG:502 - 520 :: REGRESS. :PRIM. :EMH :FIN.METH.

WALLACH,SJR ; FIRS: GRIFFIN,PA CIT: 0
LATIN AMERICAN LENDING BY MAJOR U.S. BANKS: THE EFFECTS OF DISCLOSURES ABOUT NONACCRUAL LOANS AND LOAN LOSS PROVISIONS
TAR OC 91 VOL: 66 PG:830 - 846 :: REGRESS. :PRIM. :EMH :OTH. NON-C/A

WALLER,WS ; SEC: BISHOP,RA CIT: 0.33
AN EXPERIMENTAL STUDY OF INCENTIVE PAY SCHEMES, COMMUNICATION, AND INTRAFIRM RESOURCE ALLOCATION
TAR OC 90 VOL: 65 PG:812 - 836 :: REGRESS. :FIELD :INF.ECO./AG. :COST.ALLOC.

WALLER,WS ; SEC: FELIX JR,WL CIT: 0
AUDITORS' CAUSAL JUDGMENTS: EFFECTS OF FORWARD VS BACKWARD INFERENCE ON INFORMATION PROCESSING
AOS 02 89 VOL: 14 PG:179 - 200 :: REGRESS. :LAB. :HIPS :JUDG.

WALLER,WS CIT: 1.2
SLACK IN PARTICIPATIVE BUDGETING: THE JOINT EFFECT OF A TRUTH-INDUCING PAY SCHEME AND RISK PREFERENCES
AOS 01 88 VOL: 13 PG:87 - 98 :: REGRESS. :LAB. :OTH.BEH. :BUDG.& PLAN.

WALLER,WS ; FIRS: SHIELDS,MD CIT: 0.2
A BEHAVIORAL STUDY OF ACCOUNTING VARIABLES IN PERFORMANCE-INCENTIVE CONTRACTS
AOS 06 88 VOL: 13 PG:581 - 594 :: REGRESS. :LAB. :INF.ECO./AG. :EXEC.COMP.

WALLER,WS ; FIRS: SHIELDS,MD ; SEC: SOLOMON,I CIT: 0
AUDITORS' USAGE OF UNAUDITED BOOK VALUES WHEN MAKING PRESAMPLING AUDIT VALUE ESTIMATES
CAR AU 88 VOL: 5 PG:1 - 18 :: REGRESS. :LAB. :HIPS :PLAN.

WALLER,WS ; FIRS: CHOW ,CW ; SEC: COOPER,JC CIT: 0.8
PARTICIPATIVE BUDGETING: EFFECTS OF A TRUTH-INDUCING PAY SCHEME AND INFORMATION ASYMMETRY ON SLACK AND PERFORMANCE
TAR JA 88 VOL: 63 PG:111 - 122 :: REGRESS. :LAB. :OTH.BEH. :BUDG.& PLAN.

WALLER,WS ; FIRS: SHIELDS,MD ; SEC: SOLOMON,I CIT: 0.33
EFFECTS OF ALTERNATIVE SAMPLE SPACE REPRESENTATIONS ON THE ACCURACY OF AUDITORS' UNCERTAINTY JUDGMENTS
AOS 04 87 VOL: 12 PG:375 - 385 :: REGRESS. :LAB. :HIPS :MAN.DEC.CHAR.

WALLER,WS ; FIRS: SMITH ,VL ; SEC: SCHATZBERG,J CIT: 1
EXPERIMENTAL ECONOMICS AND AUDITING
AUD AU 87 VOL: 7 PG:71 - 93 :: DES.STAT. :INT. LOG. :OTH. :METHOD.

WALLER,WS ; SEC: FELIX JR,WL CIT: 0.5
AUDITORS' COVARIATION JUDGMENTS
TAR AP 87 VOL: 62 PG:275 - 292 :: REGRESS. :LAB. :HIPS :JUDG.

WALLER,WS CIT: 0.25
SELF-SELECTION AND THE PROBABILITY OF QUITTING: A CONTRACTING APPROACH TO EMPLOYEE TURNOVER IN PUBLIC ACCOUNTING
JAR AU 85 VOL: 23 PG:817 - 828 :: REGRESS. :LAB. :OTH.BEH. :ORG.

WALLER,WS ; SEC: CHOW ,CW CIT: 0.75
THE SELF-SELECTION AND EFFORT EFFECTS OF STANDARD-BASED EMPLOYEE CONTRACTS: A FRAMEWORK AND SOME EMPIRICAL EVIDENCE
TAR JL 85 VOL: 60 PG:458 - 476 :: REGRESS. :LAB. :OTH.BEH. :EXEC.COMP.

WALLER,WS ; SEC: FELIX JR,WL CIT: 2.22
THE AUDITOR AND LEARNING FROM EXPERIENCE: SOME CONJECTURES
AOS 34 84 VOL: 9 PG:383 - 406 :: QUAL. :INT. LOG. :HIPS :N/A

WALLER,WS ; FIRS: JIAMBALVO,J CIT: 0.11
DECOMPOSITION AND ASSESSMENTS OF AUDIT RISK
AUD SP 84 VOL: 3 PG:80 - 88 :: NON-PAR. :LAB. :OTH.STAT. :RISK

WALLER,WS ; SEC: FELIX JR,WL CIT: 0.22
THE EFFECTS OF INCOMPLETE OUTCOME FEEDBACK ON AUDITORS' SELF-PERCEPTIONS OF JUDGMENT ABILITY
TAR OC 84 VOL: 59 PG:637 - 646 :: ANOVA :LAB. :HIPS :JUDG.

WALLIN,DE CIT: 1
LEGAL RECOURSE AND THE DEMAND FOR AUDITING
TAR JA 92 VOL: 67 PG:121 - 147 :: REGRESS. :LAB. :OTH.BEH. :LIAB.

WALLIN,DE ; FIRS: KING ,RR CIT: 1
VOLUNTARY DISCLOSURES WHEN SELLER'S LEVEL OF INFORMATION IN UNKNOWN
JAR SP 91 VOL: 29 PG:96 - 108 :: REGRESS. :LAB. :OTH.BEH. :INFO.STRUC.

WALLIN,DE ; FIRS: KING ,RR CIT: 1
THE EFFECTS OF ANTIFRAUD RULES AND EX POST VERIFIABILITY ON MANAGERIAL DISCLOSURES
CAR SP 90 VOL: 6 PG:859 - 892 :: REGRESS. :LAB. :OTH.BEH. :RESP.ACC.

WALLIN,DE ; FIRS: DOPUCH,N ; SEC: KING ,RR CIT: 0.25
THE USE OF EXPERIMENTAL MARKETS IN AUDITING RESEARCH: SOME INITIAL FINDINGS
AUD 89 VOL: 8 PG:98 - 127 :: REGRESS. :LAB. :INF.ECO./AG. :MAN.DEC.CHAR.

WALTHER,LM CIT: 0.18
A COMPARISON OF ESTIMATED AND REPORTED HISTORICAL COST/CONSTANT DOLLAR DATA
TAR AP 82 VOL: 57 PG:376 - 383 :: DES.STAT. :PRIM. :OTH.STAT. :VALUAT.(INFL.)

WAND ,Y ; SEC: WEBER ,R CIT: 0
A MODEL OF CONTROL AND AUDIT PROCEDURE CHANGE IN EVOLVING DATA PROCESSING SYSTEMS
TAR JA 89 VOL: 64 PG:87 - 107 :: DES.STAT. :INT. LOG. :MATH.PROG. :EDP AUD.

WANG ,S ; FIRS: DHALIWAL,D CIT: 0
THE EFFECT OF BOOK INCOME ADJUSTMENT IN THE 1986 ALTERNATIVE MINIMUM TAX ON CORPORATE FINANCIAL REPORTING
JAE MR 92 VOL: 15 PG:7 - 25 :: REGRESS. :PRIM. :OTH.STAT. :TAXES

WANG ,S CIT: 0
THE RELATION BETWEEN FIRM SIZE AND EFFECTIVE TAX RATES: A TEST OF FIRMS' POLITICAL SUCCESS
TAR JA 91 VOL: 66 PG:158 - 169 :: REGRESS. :INT. LOG. :OTH. :TAX PLNG.

WARD ,BH CIT: 0.47
AN INVESTIGATION OF THE MATERIALITY CONSTRUCT IN AUDITING
JAR SP 76 VOL: 14 PG:138 - 152 :: NON-PAR. :LAB. :OTH.BEH. :MAT.

WARDELL,M ; SEC: WEISENFELD,LW CIT: 0
MANAGEMENT ACCOUNTING AND THE WORKPLACE IN THE UNITED STATES AND GREAT BRITAIN
AOS 91 VOL: 16 PG:655 - 670 :: REGRESS. :SEC. :HIST. :ORG.& ENVIR.

WARFIELD,TD ; SEC: LINSMEIER,TJ CIT: 0
TAX PLANNING, EARNINGS MANAGEMENT, AND THE DIFFERENTIAL INFORMATION CONTENT OF BANK EARNINGS COMPONENTS
TAR JL 92 VOL: 67 PG:546 - 562 :: REGRESS. :PRIM. :EMH :FIN.METH.

WARFIELD,TD ; SEC: WILD ,JJ CIT: 0
ACCOUNTING RECOGNITION AND THE RELEVANCE OF EARNINGS AS AN EXPLANATORY VARIABLE FOR RETURNS
TAR OC 92 VOL: 67 PG:821 - 842 :: REGRESS. :PRIM. :EMH :REV.REC.

WARREN,C ; FIRS: PEEK ,LE ; SEC: NETER ,J CIT: 0
AICPA NONSTATISTICAL AUDIT SAMPLING GUIDELINES: A SIMULATION
AUD AU 91 VOL: 10 PG:33 - 48 :: DES.STAT. :SIM. :HIST. :SAMP.

WARREN,CS ; FIRS: MAYPER,AG ; SEC: DOUCET,MS CIT: 0.25
AUDITORS' MATERIALITY JUDGMENTS OF INTERNAL ACCOUNTING CONTROL WEAKNESSES
AUD AU 89 VOL: 9 PG:72 - 86 :: REGRESS. :LAB. :HIPS :MAT.

WARREN,CS CIT: 0
UNIFORMITY OF AUDITING STANDARDS: A REPLICATION
JAR SP 80 VOL: 18 PG:312 - 324 :: ANOVA :PRIM. :INSTIT. :OPIN.

WARREN,CS CIT: 0.13
CHARACTERISTICS OF FIRMS REPORTING CONSISTENCY EXCEPTIONS - A CROSS SECTIONAL ANALYSIS
TAR JA 77 VOL: 52 PG:150 - 161 :: ANOVA :PRIM. :OTH.STAT. :ACC.CHNG.

WARREN,CS CIT: 0.24
UNIFORMITY OF AUDITING STANDARDS
JAR SP 75 VOL: 13 PG:162 - 176 :: ANOVA :PRIM. :OTH.STAT. :OPIN.

WARREN,CS CIT: 0
CONFIRMATION INFORMATIVENESS
JAR SP 74 VOL: 12 PG:158 - 177 :: ANOVA :FIELD :OTH.STAT. :OPER.AUD.

WASLEY,CE ; FIRS: KOTHARI,SP CIT: 0.5
MEASURING SECURITY PRICE PERFORMANCE IN SIZE-CLUSTERED SAMPLES
TAR AP 89 VOL: 64 PG:228 - 249 :: REGRESS. :SIM. :TIME SER. :OTH.FIN.ACC.

WASSERMAN,W ; FIRS: HANNUM,WH CIT: 0
GENERAL ADJUSTMENTS AND PRICE LEVEL MEASUREMENT
TAR AP 68 VOL: 43 PG:295 - 302 :: QUAL. :INT. LOG. :THEORY :VALUAT.(INFL.)

WATERHOUSE,J ; FIRS: GIBBINS,M ; SEC: RICHARDSON,A CIT: 0.33
THE MANAGEMENT OF CORPORATE FINANCIAL DISCLOSURES: OPPORTUNISM, RITUALISM, POLICIES, AND PROCESSES
JAR SP 90 VOL: 28 PG:121 - 143 :: REGRESS. :SURV. :OTH.BEH. :INFO.STRUC.

WATERHOUSE,JH ; FIRS: TIESSEN,P CIT: 1.3
TOWARDS A DESCRIPTIVE THEORY OF MANAGEMENT ACCOUNTING
AOS 23 83 VOL: 8 PG:251 - 268 :: QUAL. :INT. LOG. :THEORY :MANAG.

WATERHOUSE,JH ; FIRS: SWIERINGA,RJ CIT: 0.36
ORGANIZATIONAL VIEWS OF TRANSFER PRICING
AOS 02 82 VOL: 7 PG:149 - 166 :: QUAL. :INT. LOG. :OTH. :TRANS.PRIC.

WATERHOUSE,JH ; SEC: TIESSEN,P CIT: 2.73
A CONTINGENCY FRAMEWORK FOR MANAGEMENT ACCOUNTING SYSTEMS RESEARCH
AOS 01 78 VOL: 3 PG:65 - 76 :: QUAL. :INT. LOG. :HIPS :METHOD.

WATERHOUSE,JH ; FIRS: BRUNS JR,WJ CIT: 3.18
BUDGETARY CONTROL AND ORGANIZATION STRUCTURE
JAR AU 75 VOL: 13 PG:177 - 203 :: OTH.QUANT. :FIELD :OTH.BEH. :ORG.FORM

WATKINS,PR ; FIRS: BIGGS ,SF ; SEC: MOCK ,TJ CIT: 1.4
AUDITOR'S USE OF ANALYTICAL REVIEW IN AUDIT PROGRAM DESIGN
TAR JA 88 VOL: 63 PG:148 - 162 :: REGRESS. :LAB. :OTH.BEH. :ANAL.REV.

WATKINS,PR CIT: 0
MULTIDIMENSIONAL SCALING MEASUREMENT AND ACCOUNTING RESEARCH
JAR SP 84 VOL: 22 PG:406 - 411 :: OTH.QUANT. :INT. LOG. :OTH.STAT. :METHOD.

WATSON,CJ CIT: 0
MULTIVARIATE DISTRIBUTIONAL PROPERTIES, OUTLIERS, AND TRANSFORMATION OF FINANCIAL RATIOS
TAR JL 90 VOL: 65 PG:682 - 695 :: ANOVA :PRIM. :OTH.STAT. :METHOD.

WATSON,CJ ; FIRS: STOCK ,D CIT: 0.44
HUMAN JUDGMENT ACCURACY, MULTIDIMENSIONAL GRAPHICS, AND HUMANS VERSUS MODELS
JAR SP 84 VOL: 22 PG:192 - 206 :: OTH.QUANT. :LAB. :HIPS :BUS.FAIL.

WATSON,DJ ; FIRS: JIAMBALVO,J ; THIR: BAUMLER,JV CIT: 0.6
AN EXAMINATION OF PERFORMANCE EVALUATION DECISIONS IN CPA FIRM SUBUNITS
AOS 01 83 VOL: 8 PG:13 - 30 :: REGRESS. :LAB. :OTH.BEH. :ORG.

WATSON,DJ CIT: 0.47
THE STRUCTURE OF PROJECT TEAMS FACING DIFFERENTIATED ENVIRONMENTS: AN EXPLORATORY STUDY IN PUBLIC ACCOUNTING FIRMS
TAR AP 75 VOL: 50 PG:259 - 273 :: ANOVA :SURV. :OTH.BEH. :ORG.

WATSON,DJ ; SEC: BAUMLER,JV CIT: 0.65
TRANSFER PRICING: A BEHAVIOURAL CONTEXT
TAR JL 75 VOL: 50 PG:466 - 474 :: QUAL. :INT. LOG. :OTH.BEH. :TRANS.PRIC.

WATSON,R ; FIRS: KEASEY,K CIT: 0.25
CONSENSUS AND ACCURACY IN ACCOUNTING STUDIES OF DECISION-MAKING: A NOTE ON ANEW MEASURE OF CONSENSUS
AOS 04 89 VOL: 14 PG:337 - 345 :: REGRESS. :LAB. :HIPS :AUD.BEH.

WATTS ,JS ; FIRS: PENNO ,M CIT: 0
AN INDEPENDENT AUDITOR'S EX POST CRITERIA FOR THE DISCLOSURE OF INFORMATION
JAR ST 91 VOL: 29 PG:194 - 216 :: DES.STAT. :INT. LOG. :INF.ECO./AG. :INFO.STRUC.

WATTS ,RL ; SEC: ZIMMERMAN,JL CIT: 4.33
POSITIVE ACCOUNTING THEORY: A TEN YEAR PERSPECTIVE
TAR JA 90 VOL: 65 PG:131 - 156 :: DES.STAT. :SEC. :THEORY :METHOD.

WATTS ,RL ; FIRS: KOTHARI,SP ; SEC: LYS ,T ; THIR: SMITH ,CW CIT: 0.6
AUDITOR LIABILITY AND INFORMATION DISCLOSURE
JAA AU 88 VOL: 3 PG:307 - 340 :: DES.STAT. :INT. LOG. :OTH. :LIAB.

WATTS ,RL ; FIRS: LEFTWICH,RW ; THIR: ZIMMERMAN,JL CIT: 0.58
VOLUNTARY CORPORATE DISCLOSURE: THE CASE OF INTERIM REPORTING
JAR ST 81 VOL: 19 PG:50 - 77 :: ANAL. :PRIM. :OTH.STAT. :INT.REP.

WATTS ,RL ; SEC: ZIMMERMAN,JL CIT: 0.38
ON THE IRRELEVANCE OF REPLACEMENT COST DISCLOSURES FOR SECURITY PRICES
JAE AG 80 VOL: 2 PG:95 - 106 :: QUAL. :SEC. :OTH. :VALUAT.(INFL.)

WATTS ,RL ; SEC: ZIMMERMAN,JL CIT: 3.5
THE DEMAND FOR AND SUPPLY OF ACCOUNTING THEORIES: THE MARKET FOR EXCUSES
TAR AP 79 VOL: 54 PG:273 - 305 :: QUAL. :INT. LOG. :THEORY :FIN.METH.

WATTS ,RL ; SEC: ZIMMERMAN,JL CIT: 8.2
TOWARDS A POSITIVE THEORY OF THE DETERMINATION OF ACCOUNTING STANDARDS
TAR JA 78 VOL: 53 PG:112 - 134 :: OTH.QUANT. :PRIM. :OTH.STAT. :FASB SUBM.

WATTS ,RL ; SEC: LEFTWICH,RW CIT: 2.63
THE TIME SERIES OF ANNUAL ACCOUNTING EARNINGS
JAR AU 77 VOL: 15 PG:253 - 271 :: MIXED :PRIM. :TIME SER. :FOREC.

WATTS ,RL ; FIRS: BALL ,R ; SEC: LEV ,B CIT: 0.24
INCOME VARIATION AND BALANCE SHEET COMPOSITIONS
JAR SP 76 VOL: 14 PG:1 - 9 :: REGRESS. :PRIM. :OTH.STAT. :REV.REC.

WATTS ,RL ; FIRS: DOPUCH,N CIT: 0.94
USING TIME-SERIES MODELS TO ASSESS THE SIGNIFICANCE OF ACCOUNTING CHANGES
JAR SP 72 VOL: 10 PG:180 - 194 :: MIXED :PRIM. :TIME SER. :ACC.CHNG.

WAUGH ,JB CIT: 0
THE INTERPERIOD ALLOCATION OF CORPORATE INCOME TAXES: A PROPOSAL
TAR JL 68 VOL: 43 PG:535 - 539 :: QUAL. :INT. LOG. :THEORY :TAXES

WAYMIRE,G ; FIRS: KING ,R ; SEC: POWNALL,G CIT: 0
CORPORATE DISCLOSURE AND PRICE DISCOVERY ASSOCIATED WITH NYSE TEMPORARY TRADING HALTS
CAR SP 92 VOL: 8 PG:509 - 531 :: REGRESS. :PRIM. :EMH :INFO.STRUC.

WAYMIRE,G ; FIRS: POWNALL,G CIT: 0.75
VOLUNTARY DISCLOSURE CREDIBILITY AND SECURITIES PRICES: EVIDENCE FROM MANAGEMENT EARNINGS FORECASTS, 1969-73
JAR AU 89 VOL: 27 PG:227 - 245 :: REGRESS. :PRIM. :EMH :FOREC.

WAYMIRE,G ; FIRS: POWNALL,G CIT: 0
VOLUNTARY DISCLOSURE CHOICE AND EARNINGS INFORMATION TRANSFER
JAR ST 89 VOL: 27 PG:85 - 105 :: REGRESS. :PRIM. :EMH :FOREC.

WAYMIRE,G CIT: 0.29
ADDITIONAL EVIDENCE ON THE ACCURACY OF ANALYST FORECASTS BEFORE AND AFTER VOLUNTARY MANAGEMENT EARNINGS FORECASTS
TAR JA 86 VOL: 61 PG:129 - 142 :: REGRESS. :PRIM. :TIME SER. :FOREC.

WAYMIRE,G CIT: 0.5
EARNINGS VOLATILITY AND VOLUNTARY MANAGEMENT FORECAST DISCLOSURE
JAR SP 85 VOL: 23 PG:268 - 295 :: REGRESS. :PRIM. :OTH.STAT. :FOREC.

WAYMIRE,G ; FIRS: SUNDER,S CIT: 0.78
ACCURACY OF EXCHANGE VALUATION RULES: ADDITIVITY AND UNBIASED ESTIMATION
JAR SP 84 VOL: 22 PG:396 - 405 :: ANAL. :INT. LOG. :THEORY :SPEC.ITEMS

WAYMIRE,G CIT: 1.67
ADDITIONAL EVIDENCE ON THE INFORMATION CONTENT OF MANAGEMENT EARNINGS FORECASTS
JAR AU 84 VOL: 22 PG:703 - 718 :: REGRESS. :PRIM. :EMH :FOREC.

WAYMIRE,G ; FIRS: SUNDER,S CIT: 0.8
MARGINAL GAINS IN ACCURACY OF VALUATION FROM INCREASINGLY SPECIFIC PRICE INDEXES: EMPIRICAL EVIDENCE FOR THE U.S. ECONOMY
JAR AU 83 VOL: 21 PG:565 - 580 :: MIXED :PRIM. :OTH.STAT. :VALUAT.(INFL.)

WAYMIRE,G ; SEC: POWNALL,G CIT: 0
SOME EVIDENCE ON POTENTIAL EFFECTS OF CONTEMPORANEOUS EARN. DISCLOSURES IN TESTS OF CAPITAL MARKET EFFECTS ASSOC. WITH FASB EXPO
JAR AU 83 VOL: 21 PG:629 - 643 :: REGRESS. :PRIM. :EMH :OIL & GAS

WEBB ,J ; FIRS: BARNES,P CIT: 0.43
MANAGEMENT INFORMATION CHANGES AND FUNCTIONAL FIXATION: SOME EXPERIMENTAL EVIDENCE FROM THE PUBLIC SECTOR
AOS 01 86 VOL: 11 PG:1 - 18 :: REGRESS. :LAB. :HIPS :COST.ALLOC.

WEBER ,C CIT: 0
THE MATHEMATICS OF VARIANCE ANALYSIS
TAR JL 63 VOL: 38 PG:534 - 539 :: ANAL. :SEC. :OTH. :VAR.

WEBER ,R ; FIRS: WAND ,Y CIT: 0
A MODEL OF CONTROL AND AUDIT PROCEDURE CHANGE IN EVOLVING DATA PROCESSING SYSTEMS
TAR JA 89 VOL: 64 PG:87 - 107 :: DES.STAT. :INT. LOG. :MATH.PROG. :EDP AUD.

WEBER ,R ; FIRS: DAVIS ,GB CIT: 0.14
THE IMPACT OF ADVANCED COMPUTER SYSTEMS ON CONTROLS AND AUDIT PROCEDURES: A THEORY AND AN EMPIRICAL TEST
AUD SP 86 VOL: 5 PG:35 - 49 :: REGRESS. :LAB. :OTH.STAT. :EDP AUD.

WEBER ,R CIT: 0.14
DATA MODELS RESEARCH IN ACCOUNTING: AN EVALUATION OF WHOLESALE DISTRIBUTION SOFTWARE
TAR JL 86 VOL: 61 PG:498 - 518 :: REGRESS. :SURV. :OTH.STAT. :INFO.STRUC.

WEBER ,R CIT: 0.18
AUDIT TRAIL SYSTEM SUPPORT IN ADVANCED COMPUTER-BASED ACCOUNTING SYSTEMS
TAR AP 82 VOL: 57 PG:311 - 325 :: QUAL. :INT. LOG. :OTH. :AUD.TRAIL

WEBER ,R CIT: 0.85
SOME CHARACTERISTICS OF THE FREE RECALL OF COMPUTER CONTROLS BY EDP AUDITORS
JAR SP 80 VOL: 18 PG:214 - 241 :: NON-PAR. :LAB. :HIPS :AUD.BEH.

WEBER ,R CIT: 0.4
AUDITOR DECISION MAKING ON OVERALL SYSTEM RELIABILITY: ACCURACY, CONSENSUS, AND THE USEFULNESS OF A SIMULATION DECISION AID
JAR AU 78 VOL: 16 PG:368 - 388 :: REGRESS. :LAB. :HIPS :INT.CONT.

WEBER ,R ; FIRS: EVEREST,GL CIT: 0.25
A RELATIONAL APPROACH TO ACCOUNTING MODELS
TAR AP 77 VOL: 52 PG:340 - 359 :: ANAL. :INT. LOG. :OTH.STAT. :N/A

WEBER ,RP ; SEC: STEVENSON,WC CIT: 0.25
EVALUATIONS OF ACCOUNTING JOURNAL AND DEPARTMENT QUALITY
TAR JL 81 VOL: 56 PG:596 - 612 :: DES.STAT. :SIM. :OTH. :OTH.MANAG.

WEBER ,RP CIT: 0
MISLEADING TAX FIGURES - A PROBLEM FOR ACCOUNTANTS
TAR JA 77 VOL: 52 PG:172 - 185 :: ANAL. :INT. LOG. :THEORY :TAXES

WEICK ,KE ; FIRS: SWIERINGA,RJ CIT: 0.33
MANAGEMENT ACCOUNTING AND ACTION
AOS 03 87 VOL: 12 PG:293 - 308 :: DES.STAT. :INT. LOG. :HIST. :MANAG.

WEICK ,KE ; FIRS: SWIERINGA,RJ CIT: 1.64
AN ASSESSMENT OF LABORATORY EXPERIMENTS IN ACCOUNTING
JAR ST 82 VOL: 20 PG:56 - 101 :: DES.STAT. :SEC. :OTH.BEH. :METHOD.

WEIGAND,RE CIT: 0
THE ACCOUNTANT AND MARKETING CHANNELS
TAR JL 63 VOL: 38 PG:584 - 590 :: QUAL. :INT. LOG. :INSTIT. :OTH.MANAG.

WEIL ,RL ; FIRS: DAVIDSON,S CIT: 0.07
INCOME TAX IMPLICATIONS OF VARIOUS METHODS OF ACCOUNTING FOR CHANGING PRICES
JAR ST 78 VOL: 16 PG:154 - 233 :: DES.STAT. :PRIM. :OTH.STAT. :VALUAT.(INFL.)

WEIL ,RL CIT: 0
RECIPROCAL OR MUTUAL HOLDINGS: ALLOCATING EARNINGS AND SELECTING THE ACCOUNTING METHOD
TAR OC 73 VOL: 48 PG:749 - 758 :: QUAL. :INT. LOG. :THEORY :BUS.COMB.

WEINGARTEN,HM CIT: 0
THE EXCESS PRESENT VALUE INDEX - A THEORETICAL BASIS AND CRITIQUE
JAR AU 63 VOL: 1 PG:213 - 224 :: ANAL. :INT. LOG. :MATH.PROG. :N/A

WEINSTEIN,MG ; FIRS: BRENNER,VC ; SEC: CARMACK,CW CIT: 0
AN EMPIRICAL TEST OF THE MOTIVATION-HYGIENE THEORY
JAR AU 71 VOL: 9 PG:359 - 366 :: CORR. :SURV. :OTH.BEH. :AUD.BEH

WEINTROP,JB ; FIRS: PRESS ,EG CIT: 3.33
ACCOUNTING-BASED CONSTRAINTS IN PUBLIC AND PRIVATE DEBT AGREEMENTS: THEIR ASSOCIATION WITH LEVERAGE AND IMPACT ON ACCOUNTING CHOICE
JAE JA 90 VOL: 12 PG:65 - 95 :: REGRESS. :PRIM. :OTH.STAT. :LTD

WEIS ,WL ; FIRS: RAMANATHAN,KV CIT: 0.08
SUPPLEMENTING COLLEGIATE FINANCIAL STATEMENTS WITH ACROSS-FUND AGGREGATIONS: AN EXPERIMENTAL INQUIRY
AOS 02 81 VOL: 6 PG:143 - 152 :: ANOVA :LAB. :THEORY :INFO.STRUC.

WEISENFELD,LW ; FIRS: WARDELL,M CIT: 0
MANAGEMENT ACCOUNTING AND THE WORKPLACE IN THE UNITED STATES AND GREAT BRITAIN
AOS 91 VOL: 16 PG:655 - 670 :: REGRESS. :SEC. :HIST. :ORG.& ENVIR.

WEISER,HJ CIT: 0
ACCOUNTING EDUCATION - PRESENT AND FUTURE
TAR JL 66 VOL: 41 PG:518 - 524 :: QUAL. :INT. LOG. :INSTIT. :OTH.MANAG.

WELAM ,VP ; FIRS: KAPLAN,RS CIT: 0.47
OVERHEAD ALLOCATION WITH IMPERFECT MARKETS AND NONLINEAR TECHNOLOGY
TAR JL 74 VOL: 49 PG:477 - 484 :: ANAL. :INT. LOG. :MATH.PROG. :OVER.ALLOC.

WELCH ,PR CIT: 0
A GENERALIZED DISTRIBUTED LAG MODEL FOR PREDICTING QUARTERLY EARNINGS
JAR AU 84 VOL: 22 PG:744 - 757 :: NON-PAR. :PRIM. :TIME SER. :FOREC.

WELKE ,WR CIT: 0
ACCOUNTING SYSTEMS IN THE CURRICULUM
TAR AP 66 VOL: 41 PG:253 - 256 :: QUAL. :INT. LOG. :N/A :OTH.MANAG.

WELKER,RB ; FIRS: MEIXNER,WF CIT: 0
JUDGMENT CONSENSUS AND AUDITOR EXPERIENCE: AN EXAMINATION OF ORGANIZATIONAL RELATIONS
AUD JL 88 VOL: 63 PG:505 - 513 :: CORR. :LAB. :OTH.BEH. :JUDG.

WELKER,RB ; FIRS: LICATA,MP ; SEC: STRAWSER,RH CIT: 0.14
A NOTE ON PARTICIPATION IN BUDGETING AND LOCUS OF CONTROL
TAR JA 86 VOL: 61 PG:112 - 117 :: REGRESS. :LAB. :OTH.BEH. :BUDG.& PLAN.

WELKER,RB ; FIRS: APOSTOLOU,NG ; SEC: GIROUX,GA CIT: 0
THE INFORMATION CONTENT OF MUNICIPAL SPENDING RATE DATA
JAR AU 85 VOL: 23 PG:853 - 858 :: REGRESS. :PRIM. :INSTIT. :LTD

WELKER,RB ; FIRS: GROSSMAN,SD ; SEC: KRATCHMAN,SH CIT: 0
COMMENT: THE EFFECT OF REPLACEMENT COST DISCLOSURES ON SECURITY PRICES
JAA WI 81 VOL: 4 PG:136 - 143 :: DES.STAT. :PRIM. :EMH :VALUAT.(INFL.)

WELKER,RB CIT: 0.12
DISCRIMINANT ANALYSIS AS AN AID TO EMPLOYEE SELECTION
TAR JL 74 VOL: 49 PG:514 - 523 :: OTH.QUANT. :INT. LOG. :OTH.STAT. :AUD.

WELLING,P CIT: 0.06
A GOAL PROGRAMMING MODEL FOR HUMAN RESOURCE ACCOUNTING IN A CPA FIRM
AOS 04 77 VOL: 2 PG:307 - 316 :: ANAL. :SIM. :MATH.PROG. :HRA

WELLS ,MC CIT: 0.12
A REVOLUTION IN ACCOUNTING THOUGHT?
TAR JL 76 VOL: 51 PG:471 - 482 :: QUAL. :SEC. :HIST. :FIN.METH.

WELLS ,MC CIT: 0
A NOTE ON THE AMORTIZATION OF FIXED ASSETS
TAR AP 68 VOL: 43 PG:373 - 376 :: QUAL. :INT. LOG. :THEORY :PP&E / DEPR

WELLS ,MC ; SEC: COTTON,W CIT: 0
HOLDING GAINS ON FIXED ASSETS
TAR OC 65 VOL: 40 PG:829 - 833 :: QUAL. :INT. LOG. :THEORY :VALUAT.(INFL.)

WELSCH,GA CIT: 0
SOME CHALLENGES FOR ACCOUNTING EDUCATION
TAR OC 64 VOL: 39 PG:008 - 013 :: QUAL. :INT. LOG. :INSTIT. :OTH.MANAG.

WELSH ,MJ ; FIRS: SAMI ,H CIT: 0
CHARACTERISTICS OF EARLY AND LATE ADOPTERS OF PENSION ACCOUNTING STANDARD SFAS 87
CAR AU 92 VOL: 9 PG:212 - 236 :: REGRESS. :PRIM. :OTH.STAT. :FASB SUBM.

WELSH ,MJ ; SEC: TRAPNELL,JE CIT: 0
LABOR MARKET MODELS AND EMPLOYER ACCOUNTING FOR PENSIONS
JAA WI 85 VOL: 8 PG:100 - 111 :: DES.STAT. :INT. LOG. :THEORY :PENS.

WENSLEY,AKP ; FIRS: BORITZ,JE CIT: 0
EVALUATING EXPERT SYSTEMS WITH COMPLEX OUTPUTS: THE CASE OF AUDIT PLANNING
AUD AU 92 VOL: 11 PG:14 - 29 :: REGRESS. :LAB. :EXP.SYST. :PLAN.

WENSLEY,AKP ; SEC: CIT: 0
STRUCTURING THE ASSESSMENT OF AUDIT EVIDENCE-AN EXPERT SYSTEMS APPROACH
AUD 90 VOL: 9 PG:49 - 87 :: DES.STAT. :MIXED :EXP.SYST. :JUDG.

WERNER,CA ; SEC: KOSTOLANSKY,JW CIT: 0
ACCOUNTING LIABILITIES UNDER THE MULTIEMPLOYER PENSION PLAN AMENDMENTS ACT
JAA SP 84 VOL: 7 PG:212 - 224 :: QUAL. :INT. LOG. :THEORY :PENS.

WERNER,CA ; SEC: KOSTOLANSKY,JW CIT: 0
ACCOUNTING LIABILITIES UNDER ERISA
JAA AU 83 VOL: 7 PG:54 - 64 :: QUAL. :INT. LOG. :THEORY :PENS.

WESCOTT,SH CIT: 0.11
ACCOUNTING NUMBERS AND SOCIOECONOMIC VARIABLES AS PREDICTORS OF MUNICIPAL GENERAL OBLIGATION BOND RATINGS
JAR SP 84 VOL: 22 PG:412 - 423 :: OTH.QUANT. :PRIM. :OTH.STAT. :ORG.& ENVIR.

WEST ,M ; FIRS: REILLY,FK ; SEC: MORGENSON,DL CIT: 0.18
THE PREDICTIVE ABILITY OF ALTERNATIVE PARTS OF INTERIM FINANCIAL STATEMENTS
JAR ST 72 VOL: 10 PG:105 - 124 :: REGRESS. :PRIM. :EMH :INT.REP.

WEST ,RR ; FIRS: HOFSTEDT,TR CIT: 0.06
THE APB, YIELD INDICES, AND PREDICTIVE ABILITY
TAR AP 71 VOL: 46 PG:329 - 337 :: DES.STAT. :PRIM. :OTH.STAT. :PENS.

WEST ,RR CIT: 0.24
AN ALTERNATIVE APPROACH TO PREDICTING CORPORATE BOND RATINGS
JAR SP 70 VOL: 8 PG:118 - 125 :: REGRESS. :PRIM. :OTH.STAT. :METHOD.

WEST ,SG ; FIRS: WONG-ON-WING,B ; SEC: RENEAU,JH CIT: 0
AUDITORS' PERCEPTION OF MANAGEMENT: DETERMINANTS AND CONSEQUENCES
AOS 06 89 VOL: 14 PG:577 - 587 :: REGRESS. :LAB. :HIPS :JUDG.

WEST ,SG ; FIRS: HARRISON,PD ; THIR: RENEAU,JH CIT: 0.2
INITIAL ATTRIBUTIONS AND INFORMATION-SEEKING BY SUPERIORS AND SUBORDINATES IN PRODUCTION VARIANCE INVESTIGATIONS
TAR AP 88 VOL: 63 PG:307 - 320 :: REGRESS. :LAB. :OTH.BEH. :VAR.

WEYGANDT,JJ ; FIRS: HIRSCHEY,M CIT: 0.5
AMORTIZATION POLICY FOR ADVERTISING AND RESEARCH AND DEVELOPMENT EXPENDITURES
JAR SP 85 VOL: 23 PG:326 - 335 :: REGRESS. :PRIM. :TIME SER. :R & D

WEYGANDT,JJ ; FIRS: TAYLOR,WM CIT: 0
ACCOUNTING FOR STOCK-BASED AWARDS USING THE MINIMUM VALUE METHOD
JAR AU 82 VOL: 20 PG:497 - 502 :: ANAL. :INT. LOG. :THEORY :SPEC.ITEMS

WEYGANDT,JJ CIT: 0.13
VALUATION OF STOCK OPTION CONTRACTS
TAR JA 77 VOL: 52 PG:40 - 51 :: ANAL. :INT. LOG. :OTH.STAT. :VALUAT.(INFL.)

WEYGANDT,JJ ; FIRS: BOLLOM,WJ CIT: 0.06
AN EXAMINATION OF SOME INTERIM REPORTING THEORIES FOR A SEASONAL BUSINESS
TAR JA 72 VOL: 47 PG:75 - 84 :: QUAL. :SEC. :THEORY :INT.REP.

WEYGANDT,JJ ; FIRS: FRANK ,WG CIT: 0.06
A PREDICTION MODEL FOR CONVERTIBLE DEBENTURES
JAR SP 71 VOL: 9 PG:116 - 126 :: OTH.QUANT. :PRIM. :OTH. :LTD

WEYGANDT,JJ ; FIRS: LLOYD ,BM CIT: 0
MARKET VALUE INFORMATION FOR NON SUBSIDIARY INVESTMENTS
TAR OC 71 VOL: 46 PG:756 - 764 :: DES.STAT. :PRIM. :N/A :BUS.COMB.

WEYGANDT,JJ CIT: 0
THE CPA AND HIS DUTY TO SILENCE
TAR JA 70 VOL: 45 PG:69 - 75 :: QUAL. :SEC. :INSTIT. :INT.AUD.

WEYGANDT,JJ ; FIRS: FRANK ,WG CIT: 0.12
CONVERTIBLE DEBT AND EARNINGS PER SHARE: PRAGMATISM VS. GOOD THEORY
TAR AP 70 VOL: 45 PG:280 - 289 :: DES.STAT. :PRIM. :N/A :PENS.

WEYGANDT,JJ ; FIRS: IMDIEKE,LF CIT: 0
CLASSIFICATION OF CONVERTIBLE DEBT
TAR OC 69 VOL: 44 PG:798 - 805 :: QUAL. :INT. LOG. :THEORY :LTD

WHALEY,RE ; SEC: CHEUNG,JK CIT: 0.09
ANTICIPATION OF QUARTERLY EARNINGS ANNOUNCEMENTS: A TEST OF OPTION MARKET EFFICIENCY
JAE OC 82 VOL: 4 PG:57 - 83 :: REGRESS. :SEC. :EMH :INT.REP.

WHEELER,JE ; FIRS: OUTSLAY,E CIT: 0
SEPARATING THE ANNUITY AND INCOME TRANSFER ELEMENTS OF SOCIAL SECURITY
TAR OC 82 VOL: 57 PG:716 - 733 :: DES.STAT. :PRIM. :OTH.STAT. :TAXES

WHEELER,JT ; FIRS: ARANYA,N CIT: 0.14
ACCOUNTANTS' PERSONALITY TYPES AND THEIR COMMITMENT TO ORGANIZATION AND PROFESSION
CAR AU 86 VOL: 3 PG:184 - 199 :: REGRESS. :LAB. :OTH.BEH. :AUD.BEH.

WHEELER,JT CIT: 0
ACCOUNTING THEORY AND RESEARCH IN PERSPECTIVE
TAR JA 70 VOL: 45 PG:1 - 10 :: QUAL. :INT. LOG. :THEORY :OTH.MANAG.

WHEELER,S ; SEC: PANY ,K CIT: 0
ASSESSING THE PERFORMANCE OF ANALYTICAL PROCEDURES: A BEST CASE SCENARIO
TAR JL 90 VOL: 65 PG:557 - 577 :: DES.STAT. :SIM. :MATH.PROG. :ERRORS

WHEELER,S ; FIRS: CHEWNING,G ; SEC: PANY ,K CIT: 0.5
AUDITOR REPORTING DECISIONS INVOLVING ACCOUNTING PRINCIPLE CHANGES: SOME EVIDENCE ON MATERIALITY THRESHOLDS
JAR SP 89 VOL: 27 PG:78 - 96 :: REGRESS. :PRIM. :OTH.STAT. :MAT.

WHINSTON,AB ; FIRS: BAILEY JR,AD ; SEC: DUKE ,GL ; THIR: GERLACH,JH ; FOUR: KO ,CE FIFT: MESERVY,RD CIT: 0.38
TICOM AND THE ANALYSIS OF INTERNAL CONTROLS
TAR AP 85 VOL: 60 PG:186 - 201 :: CORR. :INT. LOG. :OTH. :INT.CONT

WHINSTON,AB ; FIRS: BAILEY,AP ; SEC: MCAFEE,RP CIT: 0.17
AN APPLICATION OF COMPLEXITY THEORY TO THE ANALYSIS OF INTERNAL CONTROL SYSTEMS
AUD SU 81 VOL: 1 PG:38 - 52 :: ANAL. :INT. LOG. :OTH.STAT. :INT.CONT.

WHINSTON,AB ; FIRS: CASH JR,JI ; SEC: BAILEY JR,AD CIT: 0.13
A SURVEY OF TECHNIQUES FOR AUDITING EDP-BASED ACCOUNTING INFORMATION SYSTEMS
TAR OC 77 VOL: 52 PG:813 - 832 :: QUAL. :SEC. :N/A :ANAL.REV.

WHINSTON,AB ; FIRS: HASEMAN,WD CIT: 0.41
DESIGN OF A MULTIDIMENSIONAL ACCOUNTING SYSTEM
TAR JA 76 VOL: 51 PG:65 - 79 :: ANAL. :INT. LOG. :N/A :MANAG.

WHINSTON,AB ; FIRS: LIEBERMAN,AZ CIT: 0.41
A STRUCTURING OF AN EVENTS-ACCOUNTING INFORMATION SYSTEM
TAR AP 75 VOL: 50 PG:246 - 258 :: QUAL. :INT. LOG. :OTH.STAT. :N/A

WHINSTON,AB ; FIRS: COLANTONI,CS ; SEC: MANES ,RP CIT: 0.41
A UNIFIED APPROACH TO THE THEORY OF ACCOUNTING AND INFORMATION SYSTEMS
TAR JA 71 VOL: 46 PG:90 - 102 :: QUAL. :INT. LOG. :N/A :MANAG.

WHINSTON,AB ; FIRS: COLANTONI,CS ; SEC: MANES ,RP CIT: 0.06
PROGRAMMING, PROFIT RATES AND PRICING DECISIONS
TAR JL 69 VOL: 44 PG:467 - 481 :: ANAL. :INT. LOG. :MATH.PROG. :REL.COSTS

WHITE ,CE ; FIRS: COVALESKI,MA ; SEC: DIRSMITH,MW CIT: 0.17
ECONOMIC CONSEQUENCES: THE RELATIONSHIP BETWEEN FINANCIAL REPORTING AND STRATEGIC PLANNING, MANAGEMENT AND OPERATING CONTROL DEC
CAR SP 87 VOL: 3 PG:408 - 429 :: REGRESS. :LAB. :HIPS :FIN.METH.

WHITE ,D ; SEC: VANECEK,M CIT: 0
INTENDED USE: A UNIFORM TAX DEFINITION OF SOFTWARE
JAA SU 82 VOL: 5 PG:338 - 354 :: QUAL. :INT. LOG. :THEORY :TAXES

WHITE ,GB ; FIRS: HEINTZ,JA CIT: 0
AUDITOR JUDGMENT IN ANALYTICAL REVIEW-SOME FURTHER EVIDENCE
AUD SP 89 VOL: 8 PG:22 - 39 :: REGRESS. :LAB. :HIPS :ANAL.REV.

WHITE ,GE CIT: 0.29
DISCRETIONARY ACCOUNTING DECISIONS AND INCOME NORMALIZATION
JAR AU 70 VOL: 8 PG:260 - 273 :: ANOVA :PRIM. :TIME SER. :FIN.METH.

WHITE ,GT ; FIRS: WYER ,JC ; THIR: JANSON,EC CIT: 0.2
AUDITS OF PUBLIC COMPANIES BY SMALLER CPA FIRMS: CLIENTS, REPORTS, AND QUALITY
AUD SP 88 VOL: 07 PG:164 - 173 :: REGRESS. :PRIM. :INSTIT. :ORG.

WHITE ,L ; FIRS: NELSON,J ; SEC: RONEN ,J CIT: 0.2
LEGAL LIABILITIES AND THE MARKET FOR AUDITING SERVICES
JAA SU 88 VOL: 03 PG:255 - 296 :: DES.STAT. :INT. LOG. :INF.ECO./AG. :LIAB.

WHITE ,LJ CIT: 0
THE VALUE OF MARKET VALUE ACCOUNTING FOR THE DEPOSIT INSURANCE SYSTEM
JAA SP 91 VOL: 6 PG:289 - 302 :: DES.STAT. :INT. LOG. :THEORY :VALUAT.(INFL.)

WHITE ,RA ; FIRS: SUMNERS,GE ; THIR: CLAY JR,RJ CIT: 0
THE USE OF ENGAGEMENT LETTERS IN AUDIT, REVIEW, AND COMPILATION ENGAGEMENTS: AN EMPIRICAL STUDY
AUD SP 87 VOL: 6 PG:116 - 122 :: REGRESS. :SURV. :OTH.BEH. :ORG.

WHITE ,RA ; FIRS: JOHNSON,DA ; SEC: PANY ,K CIT: 0
AUDIT REPORTS AND THE LOAN DECISION: ACTIONS AND PERCEPTIONS
AUD SP 83 VOL: 2 PG:38 - 51 :: ANOVA :LAB. :OTH.BEH. :OPIN.

WHITE ,RA CIT: 0.2
EMPLOYEE PREFERENCES FOR NONTAXABLE COMPENSATION OFFERED IN A CAFETERIA COMPENSATION PLAN: AN EMPIRICAL STUDY
TAR JL 83 VOL: 58 PG:539 - 561 :: ANOVA :SURV. :OTH.BEH. :TAXES

WHITE JR,CE ; FIRS: KUNITAKE,WK CIT: 0
ETHICS FOR INDEPENDENT AUDITORS
JAA SU 86 VOL: 1 PG:222 - 231 :: DES.STAT. :INT. LOG. :INSTIT. :PROF.RESP.

WHITE JR,CE CIT: 0.18
EFFECTS OF DISCRETIONARY ACCOUNTING POLICY ON VARIABLE AND DECLINING PERFORMANCE TRENDS
JAR AU 72 VOL: 10 PG:351 - 358 :: DES.STAT. :PRIM. :TIME SER. :ACC.CHNG.

WHITEHURST,FD CIT: 0
THE PREDICTABILITY OF INVESTOR CASH RETURN FROM HISTORICAL INCOME TRENDS OF COMMON STOCKS
TAR JL 70 VOL: 45 PG:553 - 564 :: CORR. :PRIM. :TIME SER. :CASH

WHITFORD,DT ; FIRS: GENTRY,JA ; SEC: NEWBOLD,P CIT: 0.38
CLASSIFYING BANKRUPT FIRMS WITH FUNDS FLOW COMPONENTS
JAR SP 85 VOL: 23 PG:146 - 160 :: REGRESS. :PRIM. :OTH.STAT. :BUS.FAIL.

WHITLEY,R CIT: 0.86
THE TRANSFORMATION OF BUSINESS FINANCE INTO FINANCIAL ECONOMICS: THE ROLES OF ACADEMIC EXPANSION AND CHANGES IN U.S. CAPITAL MARKETS
AOS 02 86 VOL: 11 PG:171 - 192 :: DES.STAT. :INT. LOG. :OTH. :OTH.MANAG.

WHITSELL,GM ; FIRS: RHODE ,JG ; THIR: KELSEY,RL CIT: 0.29
AN ANALYSIS OF CLIENT-INDUSTRY CONCENTRATIONS FOR LARGE PUBLIC ACCOUNTING FIRMS
TAR OC 74 VOL: 49 PG:772 - 787 :: DES.STAT. :PRIM. :INSTIT. :AUD.

WHITTENBURG,G ; FIRS: WHITTINGTON,OR CIT: 0.08
JUDICIAL CLASSIFICATION OF DEBT VERSUS EQUITY - AN EMPIRICAL STUDY
TAR JL 80 VOL: 55 PG:409 - 418 :: OTH.QUANT. :PRIM. :OTH.STAT. :N/A

WHITTINGTON,OR ; FIRS: CARMICHAEL,DR CIT: 0
THE AUDITOR'S CHANGING ROLE IN FINANCIAL REPORTING
JAA SU 84 VOL: 7 PG:347 - 361 :: QUAL. :INT. LOG. :OTH. :PROF.RESP.

WHITTINGTON,OR ; SEC: ADAMS ,SJ CIT: 0
TEMPORARY BREAKDOWNS OF INTERNAL CONTROL: IMPLICATIONS FOR EXTERNAL AND INTERNAL AUDITORS
JAA SU 82 VOL: 5 PG:310 - 319 :: QUAL. :INT. LOG. :OTH. :N/A

WHITTINGTON,OR ; SEC: WHITTENBURG,G CIT: 0.08
JUDICIAL CLASSIFICATION OF DEBT VERSUS EQUITY - AN EMPIRICAL STUDY
TAR JL 80 VOL: 55 PG:409 - 418 :: OTH.QUANT. :PRIM. :OTH.STAT. :N/A

WHITTRED,G CIT: 0.67
THE DERIVED DEMAND FOR CONSOLIDATED FINANCIAL REPORTING
JAE DE 87 VOL: 9 PG:259 - 285 :: REGRESS. :PRIM. :THEORY :BUS.COMB.

WHITTRED,GP ; SEC: ZIMMER,I CIT: 0.11
TIMELINESS OF FINANCIAL REPORTING AND FINANCIAL DISTRESS
TAR AP 84 VOL: 59 PG:287 - 295 :: DES.STAT. :PRIM. :OTH.STAT. :FIN.ST.TIM.

WHITTRED,GP CIT: 0.62
AUDIT QUALIFICATION AND THE TIMELINESS OF CORPORATE ANNUAL REPORTS
TAR OC 80 VOL: 55 PG:563 - 577 :: NON-PAR. :PRIM. :OTH. :OPIN.

WICHMANN JR,H ; FIRS: NIX ,HM CIT: 0
THE GOVERNMENTAL AUDIT REPORT
JAA SU 83 VOL: 6 PG:341 - 352 :: DES.STAT. :PRIM. :OTH. :OPIN.

WIELINGA,C ; FIRS: HERTOG,FD CIT: 0
CONTROL SYSTEMS IN DISSONANCE: THE COMPUTER AS AN INK BLOT
AOS 02 92 VOL: 17 PG:103 - 128 :: REGRESS. :CASE :OTH.BEH. :ORG.& ENVIR.

WIESEN,JL CIT: 0
REPORTING CONCEPTS FOR THE 1980s
JAA SU 81 VOL: 4 PG:309 - 324 :: QUAL. :INT. LOG. :INSTIT. :FASB SUBM.

WIESEN,JL ; SEC: ENG ,R CIT: 0
CORPORATE PERKS: DISCLOSURE AND TAX CONSIDERATIONS
JAA WI 79 VOL: 2 PG:101 - 121 :: QUAL. :INT. LOG. :THEORY :TAXES

WIESEN,JL ; FIRS: SCHIFF,M ; SEC: SORTER,GH CIT: 0
THE EVOLVING ROLE OF CORPORATE AUDIT COMMITTEES
JAA AU 77 VOL: 1 PG:19 - 44 :: QUAL. :INT. LOG. :INSTIT. :OTH.MANAG.

WIGGIN,CE ; FIRS: BENJAMIN,JJ ; SEC: GROSSMAN,SD CIT: 0
THE IMPACT OF FOREIGN CURRENCY TRANSLATION ON REPORTING DURING THE PHASE-IN OF SFAS NO.52
JAA SU 86 VOL: 1 PG:177 - 184 :: REGRESS. :PRIM. :THEORY :FOR.CUR.

WIGGINS JR,CE ; SEC: SMITH ,LW CIT: 0.17
A GENERALIZED AUDIT SIMULATION TOOL FOR EVALUATING THE RELIABILITY OF INTERNAL CONTROLS
CAR SP 87 VOL: 3 PG:316 - 337 :: DES.STAT. :SIM. :OTH. :INT.CONT.

WILCOX,JA CIT: 0.29
A PREDICTION OF BUSINESS FAILURE USING ACCOUNTING DATA
JAR ST 73 VOL: 11 PG:163 - 179 :: DES.STAT. :PRIM. :OTH.STAT. :BUS.FAIL.

WILCOX,KA ; SEC: SMITH ,CH CIT: 0
ROLE DISCREPANCIES AND THE AUDITOR-CLIENT RELATIONSHIP
AOS 01 77 VOL: 2 PG:81 - 97 :: NON-PAR. :FIELD :OTH.STAT. :AUD.

WILD ,JJ ; FIRS: WARFIELD,TD CIT: 0
ACCOUNTING RECOGNITION AND THE RELEVANCE OF EARNINGS AS AN EXPLANATORY VARIABLE FOR RETURNS
TAR OC 92 VOL: 67 PG:821 - 842 :: REGRESS. :PRIM. :EMH :REV.REC.

WILD ,JJ ; FIRS: HAN ,JCY CIT: 0
STOCK PRICE BEHAVIOR ASSOCIATED WITH MANAGERS' EARNINGS AND REVENUE FORECASTS
JAR SP 91 VOL: 29 PG:79 - 95 :: REGRESS. :PRIM. :EMH :FOREC.

WILD ,JJ ; FIRS: HAN ,JCY CIT: 0.33
UNEXPECTED EARNINGS AND INTRAINDUSTRY INFORMATION TRANSFERS: FURTHER EVIDENCE
JAR SP 90 VOL: 28 PG:211 - 219 :: REGRESS. :PRIM. :EMH :METHOD.

WILD ,JJ ; SEC: BIGGS ,SF CIT: 0
STRATEGIC CONSIDERATIONS FOR UNAUDITED ACCOUNT VALUES IN ANALYTICAL REVIEW
TAR JA 90 VOL: 65 PG:227 - 241 :: DES.STAT. :INT. LOG. :OTH. :ANAL.REV.

WILD ,JJ ; FIRS: HAN ,JCY ; THIR: RAMESH,K CIT: 1.25
MANAGERS' EARNINGS FORECASTS AND INTRA-INDUSTRY INFORMATION TRANSFERS
JAE FB 89 VOL: 11 PG:3 - 33 :: REGRESS. :PRIM. :EMH :FOREC.

WILD ,JJ CIT: 0
THE PREDICTION PERFORMANCE OF A STRUCTURAL MODEL OF ACCOUNTING NUMBERS
JAR SP 87 VOL: 25 PG:139 - 160 :: DES.STAT. :CASE :THEORY :FOREC.

WILD ,JJ ; FIRS: BIGGS ,SF CIT: 0.5
AN INVESTIGATION OF AUDITOR JUDGMENT IN ANALYTICAL REVIEW
TAR OC 85 VOL: 60 PG:607 - 633 :: REGRESS. :LAB. :HIPS :ANAL.REV.

WILD ,JJ ; FIRS: BIGGS ,SF CIT: 0.22
A NOTE ON THE PRACTICE OF ANALYTICAL REVIEW
AUD SP 84 VOL: 3 PG:68 - 79 :: CORR. :SURV. :OTH.STAT. :ANAL.REV.

WILDAVSKY,A CIT: 0.47
POLICY ANALYSIS IS WHAT INFORMATION SYSTEMS ARE NOT
AOS 01 78 VOL: 3 PG:77 - 88 :: QUAL. :INT. LOG. :OTH. :METHOD.

WILKERSON JR,JE CIT: 0
SELECTING EXPERIMENTAL AND COMPARISON SAMPLES FOR USE IN STUDIES OF AUDITOR REPORTING DECISIONS
JAR SP 87 VOL: 25 PG:161 - 167 :: DES.STAT. :PRIM. :OTH.STAT. :METHOD.

WILKINS,MS ; FIRS: FIELDS,LP CIT: 0
THE INFORMATION CONTENT OF WITHDRAWN AUDIT QUALIFICATIONS: NEW EVIDENCE ON THE VALUE OF "SUBJECT-TO" OPINIONS
AUD AU 91 VOL: 10 PG:62 - 69 :: REGRESS. :PRIM. :EMH :OPIN.

WILKINS,T ; SEC: ZIMMER,I CIT: 0.1
THE EFFECT OF LEASING AND DIFFERENT METHODS OF ACCOUNTING FOR LEASES ON CREDIT EVALUATIONS
TAR OC 83 VOL: 58 PG:749 - 764 :: ANOVA :LAB. :OTH.BEH. :LEASES

WILKINSON,JR ; SEC: DONEY ,LD CIT: 0.06
EXTENDING AUDIT AND REPORTING BOUNDARIES
TAR OC 65 VOL: 40 PG:753 - 756 :: QUAL. :INT. LOG. :INSTIT. :AUD.

WILKINSON,TL CIT: 0
CAN ACCOUNTING BE AN INTERNATIONAL LANGUAGE?
TAR JA 64 VOL: 39 PG:133 - 139 :: QUAL. :INT. LOG. :THEORY :INT.DIFF.

WILL ,H ; FIRS: AHITUV,N ; SEC: HALPERN,J CIT: 0.13
AUDIT PLANNING: AN ALGORITHMIC APPROACH
CAR AU 85 VOL: 2 PG:95 - 110 :: DES.STAT. :INT. LOG. :MATH.PROG. :PLAN.

WILL ,HJ CIT: 0.18
AUDITING IN SYSTEMS PERSPECTIVE
TAR OC 74 VOL: 49 PG:690 - 706 :: QUAL. :INT. LOG. :N/A :AUD.

WILLIAMS,D CIT: 0
REPORTING LOSS CARRYOVERS IN FINANCIAL STATEMENTS
TAR AP 66 VOL: 41 PG:226 - 234 :: QUAL. :INT. LOG. :THEORY :TAXES

WILLIAMS,DD ; FIRS: MENON ,K CIT: 0
AUDITOR CREDIBILITY AND INITIAL PUBLIC OFFERINGS
TAR AP 91 VOL: 66 PG:313 - 332 :: REGRESS. :PRIM. :EMH :PROB.ELIC.

WILLIAMS,DD ; FIRS: MUTCHLER,JF CIT: 0
THE RELATIONSHIP BETWEEN AUDIT TECHNOLOGY, CLIENT RISK PROFILES, AND THE GOING-CONCERN OPINION DECISION
AUD AU 90 VOL: 9 PG:39 - 54 :: REGRESS. :PRIM. :INSTIT. :ORG.

WILLIAMS,DD ; FIRS: HASKINS,ME CIT: 0
A CONTINGENT MODEL OF INTRA-BIG EIGHT AUDITOR CHANGES
AUD AU 90 VOL: 9 PG:55 - 74 :: REGRESS. :PRIM. :INSTIT. :ORG.

WILLIAMS,DD ; SEC: DIRSMITH,MW CIT: 0.2
THE EFFECTS OF AUDIT TECHNOLOGY ON AUDITOR EFFICIENCY: AUDITING AND THE TIMELINESS OF CLIENT EARNINGS ANNOUNCEMENTS
AOS 05 88 VOL: 13 PG:487 - 508 :: REGRESS. :PRIM. :INSTIT. :OPER.AUD.

WILLIAMS,DJ CIT: 0
SHAREHOLDERS BONDING IN FINANCIAL MUTUALS: AN EXPLORATORY STUDY OF THE RELATIVE EFFECTS OF ALTRUISM AND AGENCY
AOS 03 86 VOL: 11 PG:271 - 288 :: REGRESS. :PRIM. :INF.ECO./AG. :ORG.FORM

WILLIAMS,DJ ; SEC: LILLIS,A CIT: 0
EDP AUDITS OF OPERATING SYSTEMS - AN EXPLORATORY STUDY OF THE DETERMINANTS OF THE PRIOR PROBABILITY RISK
AUD SP 85 VOL: 4 PG:110 - 117 :: REGRESS. :SURV. :OTH.STAT. :EDP AUD.

WILLIAMS,JD ; FIRS: KAPLAN,SE ; SEC: MOECKEL,C CIT: 0
AUDITORS' HYPOTHESIS PLAUSIBILITY ASSESSMENTS IN AN ANALYTICAL REVIEW SETTING
AUD AU 92 VOL: 11 PG:50 - 65 :: REGRESS. :LAB. :HIPS :ANAL.REV.

WILLIAMS,JD ; FIRS: MOECKEL,C CIT: 0
THE ROLE OF SOURCE AVAILABILITY IN INFERENCE VERIFICATION
CAR SP 90 VOL: 6 PG:850 - 858 :: REGRESS. :LAB. :HIPS :AUD.BEH.

WILLIAMS,JJ ; SEC: MACINTOSH,NB ; THIR: MOORE ,JC CIT: 0.33
BUDGET-RELATED BEHAVIOR IN PUBLIC SECTOR ORGANIZATIONS: SOME EMPIRICAL EVIDENCE
AOS 03 90 VOL: 15 PG:221 - 246 :: REGRESS. :SURV. :OTH.BEH. :BUDG.& PLAN.

WILLIAMS,JJ ; FIRS: RICHARDSON,AJ CIT: 0
CANADIAN ACADEMIC ACCOUNTANTS' PRODUCTIVITY: A SURVEY OF 10 REFEREED PUBLICATIONS, 1976-1989
CAR AU 90 VOL: 7 PG:278 - 294 :: REGRESS. :SEC. :THEORY :METHOD.

WILLIAMS,JJ ; SEC: HININGS,CR CIT: 0
A NOTE ON MATCHING CONTROL SYSTEM IMPLICATIONS WITH ORGANIZATIONAL CHARACTERISTICS: ZBB AND MBO REVISITED
AOS 02 88 VOL: 13 PG:191 - 198 :: REGRESS. :SURV. :OTH.BEH. :BUDG.& PLAN.

WILLIAMS,JJ ; SEC: NEWTON,JD ; THIR: MORGAN,EA CIT: 0
THE INTEGRATION OF ZERO-BASE BUDGETING WITH MANAGEMENT-BY-OBJECTIVES: AN EMPIRICAL INQUIRY
AOS 04 85 VOL: 10 PG:457 - 478 :: REGRESS. :FIELD :OTH.BEH. :BUDG.& PLAN.

WILLIAMS,JJ CIT: 0
ZERO-BASE BUDGETING: PROSPECTS FOR DEVELOPING A SEMI-CONFUSING BUDGETING INFORMATION SYSTEM
AOS 02 81 VOL: 6 PG:153 - 166 :: QUAL. :INT. LOG. :THEORY :BUDG.& PLAN.

WILLIAMS,PF CIT: 0
THE LOGIC OF POSITIVE ACCOUNTING RESEARCH
AOS 06 89 VOL: 14 PG:455 - 468 :: REGRESS. :SEC. :THEORY :FIN.METH.

WILLIAMS,PF ; FIRS: ROCKNESS,J CIT: 0.2
A DESCRIPTIVE STUDY OF SOCIAL RESPONSIBILITY MUTUAL FUNDS
AOS 04 88 VOL: 13 PG:397 - 411 :: REGRESS. :SURV. :INSTIT. :HRA

WILLIAMS,PF CIT: 0.67
THE LEGITIMATE CONCERN WITH FAIRNESS
AOS 02 87 VOL: 12 PG:169 - 192 :: DES.STAT. :INT. LOG. :THEORY :FIN.METH.

WILLIAMS,PF CIT: 0.09
THE PREDICTIVE ABILITY PARADOX IN BEHAVIOURAL ACCOUNTING RESEARCH
AOS 04 82 VOL: 7 PG:405 - 410 :: ANAL. :INT. LOG. :OTH.BEH. :METHOD.

WILLIAMS,PF CIT: 0.08
THE EVALUATIVE RELEVANCE OF SOCIAL DATA
TAR JA 80 VOL: 55 PG:62 - 77 :: ANOVA :SURV. :OTH.STAT. :HRA

WILLIAMS,TH ; FIRS: ROLLER,J CIT: 0
PROFESSIONAL SCHOOLS OF ACCOUNTING
TAR AP 67 VOL: 42 PG:349 - 355 :: QUAL. :INT. LOG. :INSTIT. :OTH.MANAG.

WILLIAMS,TH ; SEC: GRIFFIN,CH CIT: 0
INCOME DEFINITION AND MEASUREMENT: A STRUCTURAL APPROACH
TAR OC 67 VOL: 42 PG:642 - 649 :: QUAL. :INT. LOG. :THEORY :OTH.MANAG.

WILLIAMS,TH ; SEC: GRIFFIN,CH CIT: 0.12
MATRIX THEORY AND COST ALLOCATION
TAR JL 64 VOL: 39 PG:671 - 678 :: ANAL. :INT. LOG. :MATH.PROG. :COST.ALLOC.

WILLIAMSON,JE CIT: 0
THE EFFECTS OF MEASUREMENT CONCEPTS ON THE INVESTMENT DECISIONS OF TRUSTEES
TAR JA 71 VOL: 46 PG:139 - 148 :: ANAL. :INT. LOG. :N/A :OTH.FIN.ACC.

WILLIAMSON,JP ; FIRS: BOWER ,RS ; SEC: HERRINGER,F CIT: 0
LEASE EVALUATION
TAR AP 66 VOL: 41 PG:257 - 265 :: ANAL. :INT. LOG. :OTH.STAT. :LEASES

WILLIKENS,M ; FIRS: MILTZ ,D ; SEC: CALOMME,GJ CIT: 0
A RISK-BASED ALLOCATION OF INTERNAL AUDIT TIME: A CASE STUDY
AUD AU 91 VOL: 10 PG:49 - 61 :: REGRESS. :CASE :OTH.STAT. :RISK

WILLINGER,GL ; FIRS: CHANDRA,R ; SEC: ROHRBACH,KJ CIT: 0
LONGITUDINAL RANK TESTS FOR DETECTING LOCATION SHIFT IN THE DISTRIBUTION OF ABNORMAL RETURNS: AN EXTENSION
CAR AU 92 VOL: 9 PG:296 - 305 :: DES.STAT. :SIM. :TIME SER. :METHOD.

WILLINGER,GL ; FIRS: BATHKE,AW ; SEC: LOREK ,KS CIT: 0
FIRM-SIZE AND THE PREDICTIVE ABILITY OF QUARTERLY EARNINGS DATA
TAR JA 89 VOL: 64 PG:49 - 68 :: REGRESS. :PRIM. :TIME SER. :INT.REP.

WILLINGER,GL CIT: 0
A CONTINGENT CLAIMS MODEL FOR PENSION COSTS
JAR SP 85 VOL: 23 PG:351 - 359 :: DES.STAT. :INT. LOG. :THEORY :PENS.

WILLINGHAM,JJ ; FIRS: LOEBBECKE,JK ; SEC: EINING,MM CIT: 0.5
AUDITORS' EXPERIENCE WITH MATERIAL IRREGULARITIES: FREQUENCY, NATURE, AND DETECTABILITY
AUD AU 89 VOL: 9 PG:1 - 28 :: REGRESS. :SURV. :OTH.STAT. :PLAN.

WILLINGHAM,JJ ; FIRS: ASHTON,RH ; THIR: ELLIOTT,RK CIT: 0.33
AN EMPIRICAL ANALYSIS OF AUDIT DELAY
JAR AU 87 VOL: 25 PG:275 - 292 :: REGRESS. :SURV. :INSTIT. :TIM.

WILLINGHAM,JJ ; SEC: WRIGHT,WF CIT: 0.38
FINANCIAL STATEMENT ERRORS AND INTERNAL CONTROL JUDGMENTS
AUD AU 85 VOL: 5 PG:57 - 70 :: REGRESS. :PRIM. :OTH.STAT. :ERRORS

WILLINGHAM,JJ ; FIRS: LIBBY ,R ; SEC: ARTMAN,JT CIT: 0.75
PROCESS SUSCEPTIBILITY, CONTROL RISK, AND AUDIT PLANNING
TAR AP 85 VOL: 60 PG:212 - 230 :: REGRESS. :LAB. :HIPS :INT.CONT.

WILLINGHAM,JJ ; FIRS: BLOCHER,E ; SEC: ESPOSITO,RS CIT: 0.1
AUDITOR'S ANALYTICAL REVIEW JUDGMENTS FOR PAYROLL EXPENSE
AUD AU 83 VOL: 3 PG:75 - 91 :: DES.STAT. :LAB. :OTH.BEH. :ANAL.REV.

WILLINGHAM,JJ ; FIRS: MOCK ,TJ CIT: 0.1
AN IMPROVED METHOD OF DOCUMENTING AND EVALUATING A SYSTEM OF INTERNAL ACCOUNTING CONTROLS
AUD SP 83 VOL: 2 PG:91 - 99 :: QUAL. :INT. LOG. :OTH. :INT.CONT.

WILLINGHAM,JJ CIT: 0
THE ACCOUNTING ENTITY: A CONCEPTUAL MODEL
TAR JL 64 VOL: 39 PG:543 - 552 :: QUAL. :INT. LOG. :THEORY :FIN.METH.

WILLINGHAM,JJ ; FIRS: GRAY ,J ; THIR: JOHNSTON,K CIT: 0
A BUSINESS GAME FOR THE INTRODUCTORY COURSE IN ACCOUNTING
TAR AP 63 VOL: 38 PG:336 - 346 :: QUAL. :INT. LOG. :OTH. :EDUC.

WILLIS,JT ; FIRS: TABOR ,RH CIT: 0.25
EMPIRICAL EVIDENCE ON THE CHANGING ROLE OF ANALYTICAL REVIEW PROCEDURES
AUD SP 85 VOL: 4 PG:93 - 109 :: REGRESS. :PRIM. :OTH.STAT. :ANAL.REV.

WILLMOTT,H ; FIRS: HOPPER,T ; SEC: STOREY,J CIT: 1.17
ACCOUNTING FOR ACCOUNTING: TOWARDS THE DEVELOPMENT OF A DIALECTICAL VIEW
AOS 05 87 VOL: 12 PG:437 - 456 :: DES.STAT. :INT. LOG. :THEORY :MANAG.

WILLMOTT,H CIT: 1.14
ORGANIZING THE PROFESSION: A THEORETICAL AND HISTORICAL EXAMINATION OF THE DEVELOPMENT OF THE MAJOR ACCOUNTING BODIES IN THE U.K
AOS 06 86 VOL: 11 PG:555 - 582 :: REGRESS. :PRIM. :INSTIT. :ORG.& ENVIR.

WILLMOTT,HC ; FIRS: PUXTY ,AG ; THIR: COOPER,DJ ; FOUR: LOWE ,T CIT: 1.33
MODES OF REGULATION IN ADVANCED CAPITALISM: LOCATING ACCOUNTANCY IN
AOS 03 87 VOL: 12 PG:273 - 291 :: DES.STAT. :INT. LOG. :THEORY :ORG.& ENVIR.

WILNER,N ; FIRS: SCHNEIDER,A CIT: 0
A TEST OF AUDIT DETERRENT TO FINANCIAL REPORTING IRREGULARITES USING THE RANDOMIZED RESPONSE TECHNIQUE
TAR JL 90 VOL: 65 PG:668 - 681 :: REGRESS. :FIELD :HIPS :MAN.DEC.CHAR.

WILNER,N ; SEC: BIRNBERG,JG CIT: 0.43
METHODOLOGICAL PROBLEMS IN FUNCTIONAL FIXATION RESEARCH: CRITICISM AND SUGGESTIONS
AOS 01 86 VOL: 11 PG:71 - 82 :: REGRESS. :INT. LOG. :HIPS :METHOD.

WILNER,N ; FIRS: JIAMBALVO,J CIT: 0.38
AUDITOR EVALUATION OF CONTINGENT CLAIMS
AUD AU 85 VOL: 5 PG:1 - 11 :: REGRESS. :SURV. :OTH.STAT. :AUD.

WILNER,N CIT: 0.36
SFAS 8 AND INFORMATION INDUCTANCE: AN EXPERIMENT
AOS 01 82 VOL: 7 PG:43 - 52 :: NON-PAR. :LAB. :OTH.BEH. :N/A

WILSON JR,TE ; SEC: GRIMLUND,RA CIT: 0.67
AN EXAMINATION OF THE IMPORTANCE OF AN AUDITOR'S REPUTATION
AUD SP 90 VOL: 9 PG:43 - 59 :: REGRESS. :PRIM. :THEORY :AUD.

WILSON,AC CIT: 0
THE EFFECT OF AUTOCORRELATION ON REGRESSION-BASED MODEL EFFICIENCY AND EFFECTIVENESS IN ANALYTICAL REVIEW
AUD SP 92 VOL: 11 PG:32 - 46 :: REGRESS. :SIM. :OTH.STAT. :ANAL.REV.

WILSON,AC CIT: 0
USE OF REGRESSION MODELS AS ANALYTICAL PROCEDURES: AN EMPIRICAL INVESTIGATION OF EFFECT OF DATA DISPERSION ON AUDITOR DECISIONS
JAA SU 91 VOL: 6 PG:365 - 381 :: REGRESS. :PRIM. :OTH.STAT. :ANAL.REV.

WILSON,AC ; SEC: GLEZEN,GW CIT: 0
REGRESSION ANALYSIS IN AUDITING: A COMPARISON OF ALTERNATIVE INVESTIGATION RULES-SOME FURTHER EVIDENCE
AUD SP 89 VOL: 8 PG:90 - 100 :: DES.STAT. :PRIM. :OTH.STAT. :ANAL.REV.

WILSON,AC ; SEC: HUDSON,D CIT: 0
AN EMPIRICAL STUDY OF REGRESSION ANALYSIS AS AN ANALYTICAL PROCEDURE
CAR AU 89 VOL: 6 PG:196 - 215 :: REGRESS. :PRIM. :THEORY :ANAL.REV.

WILSON,ER ; FIRS: FEROZ ,EH CIT: 0
MARKET SEGMENTATION AND THE ASSOCIATION BETWEEN MUNICIPAL FINANCIAL DISCLOSURE AND NET INTEREST COSTS
TAR JL 92 VOL: 67 PG:480 - 495 :: REGRESS. :PRIM. :INSTIT. :LTD

WILSON,ER ; SEC: STEWART,JP CIT: 0.33
MUNICIPAL FINANCIAL REPORTING AND COMPETITION AMONG UNDERWRITERS FOR NEWS ISSUES OF GENERAL OBLIGATION BONDS
CAR SP 90 VOL: 6 PG:573 - 591 :: REGRESS. :PRIM. :EMH :LTD

WILSON,ER ; FIRS: INGRAM,RW ; SEC: RAMAN ,KK CIT: 0
THE INFORMATION IN GOVERNMENTAL ANNUAL REPORTS: A CONTEMPORANEOUS PRICE REACTION APPROACH
TAR AP 89 VOL: 64 PG:250 - 268 :: REGRESS. :INT. LOG. :EMH :LTD

WILSON,ER ; FIRS: FRANCIS,JR CIT: 0.6
AUDITOR CHANGES: A JOINT TEST OF THEORIES RELATING TO AGENCY COSTS AND AUDITOR DIFFERENTIATION
TAR OC 88 VOL: 63 PG:663 - 682 :: REGRESS. :PRIM. :OTH.STAT. :ORG.

WILSON,ER ; SEC: HOWARD,TP CIT: 0.56
THE ASSOCIATION BETWEEN MUNICIPAL MARKET MEASURES AND SELECTED FINANCIAL REPORTING PRACTICES: ADDITIONAL EVIDENCE
JAR SP 84 VOL: 22 PG:207 - 224 :: REGRESS. :PRIM. :OTH.STAT. :N/A

WILSON GP CIT: 2.14
THE RELATIVE INFO. CONTENT OF ACCRUALS AND CASH FLOWS: COMBINED EVIDENCE AT THE ANNOUNCEMENT & ANNUAL REPORT RELEASE DATE
JAR ST 86 VOL: 24 PG:165 - 203 :: REGRESS. :PRIM. :EMH :SPEC.ITEMS

WILSON,GP ; FIRS: MCNICHOLS,M CIT: 2.4
EVIDENCE OF EARNINGS MANAGEMENT FROM THE PROVISION FOR BAD DEBTS
JAR ST 88 VOL: 26 PG:1 - 40 :: REGRESS. :PRIM. :OTH.STAT. :LTD

WILSON,GP CIT: 3
THE INCREMENTAL INFORMATION CONTENT OF THE ACCRUAL AND FUNDS COMPONENTS OF EARNINGS AFTER CONTROLLING FOR EARNINGS
TAR AP 87 VOL: 62 PG:293 - 322 :: REGRESS. :PRIM. :EMH :FIN.METH.

WINBORNE,MG ; SEC: KLEESPIE,DC CIT: 0
TAX ALLOCATION IN PERSPECTIVE
TAR OC 66 VOL: 41 PG:737 - 744 :: QUAL. :INT. LOG. :N/A :TAXES

WINBORNE,MG CIT: 0
THE OPERATING CYCLE CONCEPT - ACCEPTED?
TAR JL 64 VOL: 39 PG:622 - 626 :: DES.STAT. :SURV. :N/A :FIN.METH.

WINDAL,FW CIT: 0
LEGAL BACKGROUND FOR THE ACCOUNTING CONCEPT OF REALIZATION
TAR JA 63 VOL: 38 PG:29 - 36 :: QUAL. :INT. LOG. :THEORY :REV.REC.

WINJUM,JO CIT: 0
ACCOUNTING AND THE RISE OF CAPITALISM: AN ACCOUNTANT'S VIEW
JAR AU 71 VOL: 9 PG:333 - 350 :: QUAL. :INT. LOG. :HIST. :OTH.MANAG.

WINJUM,JO CIT: 0
THE JOURNAL OF THOMAS GRESHAM
TAR JA 71 VOL: 46 PG:149 - 155 :: QUAL. :SEC. :HIST. :FIN.METH.

WINJUM,JO CIT: 0
ACCOUNTING IN ITS AGE OF STAGNATION
TAR OC 70 VOL: 45 PG:743 - 761 :: QUAL. :SEC. :HIST. :FIN.METH.

WISEMAN,J CIT: 0.36
AN EVALUATION OF ENVIRONMENTAL DISCLOSURES MADE IN CORPORATE ANNUAL REPORTS
AOS 01 82 VOL: 7 PG:53 - 64 :: CORR. :PRIM. :OTH.STAT. :HRA

WOJDAK,JF CIT: 0.06
LEVELS OF OBJECTIVITY IN THE ACCOUNTING PROCESS
TAR JA 70 VOL: 45 PG:88 - 97 :: QUAL. :INT. LOG. :THEORY :OTH.FIN.ACC.

WOJDAK,JF ; FIRS: COPELAND,RM CIT: 0.12
INCOME MANIPULATION AND THE PURCHASE-POOLING CHOICE
JAR AU 69 VOL: 7 PG:188 - 195 :: DES.STAT. :PRIM. :OTH. :BUS.COMB.

WOJDAK,JF CIT: 0.06
A THEORETICAL FOUNDATION FOR LEASES AND OTHER EXECUTORY CONTRACTS
TAR JL 69 VOL: 44 PG:562 - 570 :: QUAL. :INT. LOG. :THEORY :LEASES

WOLF ,FM ; FIRS: GIBBINS,M CIT: 0.73
AUDITORS' SUBJECTIVE DECISION ENVIRONMENT - THE CASE OF A NORMAL EXTERNAL AUDIT
TAR JA 82 VOL: 57 PG:105 - 124 :: DES.STAT. :SURV. :OTH.BEH. :AUD.

WOLF ,FM ; FIRS: COOPER,DJ ; SEC: HAYES ,DC CIT: 1.08
ACCOUNTING IN ORGANIZED ANARCHIES: UNDERSTANDING AND DESIGNING ACCOUNTING SYSTEMS IN AMBIGUOUS SITUATIONS
AOS 03 81 VOL: 6 PG:175 - 192 :: QUAL. :INT. LOG. :THEORY :N/A

WOLF ,FM CIT: 0.17
THE NATURE OF MANAGERIAL WORK: AN INVESTIGATION OF THE WORK OF THE AUDIT MANAGER
TAR OC 81 VOL: 56 PG:861 - 881 :: DES.STAT. :SURV. :OTH.BEH. :ORG.

WOLF ,G ; FIRS: YOUNG ,SM ; SEC: SHIELDS,MD CIT: 0.4
MANUFACTURING CONTROLS AND PERFORMANCE: AN EXPERIMENT
AOS 06 88 VOL: 13 PG:607 - 618 :: REGRESS. :LAB. :OTH.BEH. :EXEC.COMP.

WOLFSON,M ; FIRS: BEAVER,WH ; SEC: EGER ,C ; THIR: RYAN ,S CIT: 1
FINANCIAL REPORTING, SUPPLEMENTAL DISCLOSURES, AND BANK SHARE PRICES
JAR AU 89 VOL: 27 PG:157 - 178 :: REGRESS. :PRIM. :OTH.STAT. :INFO.STRUC.

WOLFSON,MA ; FIRS: SCHOLES,MS CIT: 0
REPACKAGING OWNERSHIP RIGHTS AND MULTINATIONAL TAXATION: THE CASE OF WITHHOLDING TAXES
JAA AU 91 VOL: 6 PG:513 - 532 :: DES.STAT. :INT. LOG. :OTH.STAT. :TAXES

WOLFSON,MA ; FIRS: SCHOLES,MS ; SEC: TERRY ,E CIT: 0
TAXES, TRADING, AND THE VALUE OF REAL ESTATE
JAA SU 89 VOL: 4 PG:317 - 340 :: REGRESS. :MIXED :OTH.STAT. :TAXES

WOLFSON,MA ; FIRS: FELLINGHAM,JC CIT: 0.5
TAXES AND RISK SHARING
TAR JA 85 VOL: 60 PG:10 - 17 :: DES.STAT. :INT. LOG. :INF.ECO./AG. :TAXES

WOLFSON,MA ; FIRS: MARAIS,ML ; SEC: PATELL,JM CIT: 0.56
THE EXPERIMENTAL DESIGN OF CLASSIFICATORY MODELS: AN APPLICATION OF RECURSIVE PARTITIONING AND BOOTSTRAPPING COMMERCIAL BANK LOA
JAR ST 84 VOL: 22 PG:87 - 114 :: OTH.QUANT. :PRIM. :OTH.STAT. :BUS.FAIL.

WOLFSON,MA ; FIRS: DEMSKI,JS ; SEC: PATELL,JM CIT: 1.56
DECENTRALIZED CHOICE OF MONITORING SYSTEMS
TAR JA 84 VOL: 59 PG:16 - 34 :: ANAL. :INT. LOG. :INF.ECO./AG. :MANAG.

WOLFSON,MA ; FIRS: BEAVER,WH CIT: 0.09
FOREIGN CURRENCY TRANSLATION AND CHANGING PRICES IN PERFECT AND COMPLETE MARKETS
JAR AU 82 VOL: 20 PG:528 - 550 :: ANAL. :INT. LOG. :OTH.STAT. :VALUAT.(INFL.)

WOLFSON,MA ; FIRS: PATELL,JM CIT: 1.91
GOOD NEWS, BAD NEWS, AND THE INTRADAY TIMING OF CORPORATE DISCLOSURES
TAR JL 82 VOL: 57 PG:509 - 527 :: REGRESS. :PRIM. :EMH :FIN.ST.TIM.

WOLFSON,MA ; FIRS: NOREEN,EW CIT: 0.33
EQUILIBRIUM WARRANT PRICING MODELS AND ACCOUNTING FOR EXECUTIVE STOCK OPTIONS
JAR AU 81 VOL: 19 PG:384 - 398 :: CORR. :PRIM. :EMH :N/A

WOLFSON,MA ; FIRS: PATELL,JM CIT: 1.08
THE EX ANTE AND EX POST PRICE EFFECTS OF QUARTERLY EARNINGS ANNOUNCEMENTS REFLECTED IN OPTION AND STOCK PRICES
JAR AU 81 VOL: 19 PG:434 - 458 :: REGRESS. :PRIM. :EMH :FIN.METH.

WOLFSON,MA ; FIRS: PATELL,JM CIT: 0.93
ANTICIPATED INFORMATION RELEASES REFLECTED IN CALL OPTION PRICES
JAE AG 79 VOL: 1 PG:117 - 140 :: ANOVA :PRIM. :EMH :INFO.STRUC.

WOLK ,HI ; SEC: TEARNEY,MG CIT: 0
INCOME TAX ALLOCATION AND LOSS CARRY FORWARDS: EXPLORING UNCHARTED GROUND
TAR AP 73 VOL: 48 PG:292 - 299 :: ANAL. :INT. LOG. :THEORY :SPEC.ITEMS

WOLK ,HI ; SEC: HILLMAN,AP CIT: 0.12
MATERIALS MIX AND YIELD VARIANCES: A SUGGESTED IMPROVEMENT
TAR JL 72 VOL: 47 PG:549 - 555 :: ANAL. :INT. LOG. :MATH.PROG. :VAR.

WOLK ,HI CIT: 0
CURRENT VALUE DEPRECIATION: A CONCEPTUAL CLARIFICATION
TAR JL 70 VOL: 45 PG:544 - 552 :: ANAL. :INT. LOG. :THEORY :VALUAT.(INFL.)

WONG ,J CIT: 0.6
POLITICAL COSTS AND AN INTRAPERIOD ACCOUNTING CHOICE FOR EXPORT TAX CREDITS
JAE JA 88 VOL: 10 PG:37 - 51 :: REGRESS. :PRIM. :THEORY :TAXES

WONG ,J CIT: 0.6
ECONOMIC INCENTIVES FOR THE VOLUNTARY DISCLOSURE OF CURRENT COST FINANCIAL STATEMENTS
JAE AP 88 VOL: 10 PG:151 - 167 :: REGRESS. :PRIM. :THEORY :VALUAT.(INFL.)

WONG ,W-K ; FIRS: MATSUMURA,EM ; SEC: TSUI ,K-W CIT: 0.33
AN EXTENDED MULTINOMIAL-DIRICHLET MODEL FOR ERROR BOUNDS FOR DOLLAR-UNIT SAMPLING
CAR SP 90 VOL: 6 PG:485 - 500 :: DES.STAT. :SIM. :OTH.STAT. :SAMP.

WONG-BOREN,A ; FIRS: CHOW ,CW CIT: 0.17
VOLUNTARY FINANCIAL DISCLOSURE BY MEXICAN CORPORATIONS
TAR JL 87 VOL: 62 PG:533 - 541 :: REGRESS. :PRIM. :OTH.STAT. :FIN.METH.

WONG-ON-WING,B ; SEC: RENEAU,JH ; THIR: WEST ,SG CIT: 0
AUDITORS' PERCEPTION OF MANAGEMENT: DETERMINANTS AND CONSEQUENCES
AOS 06 89 VOL: 14 PG:577 - 587 :: REGRESS. :LAB. :HIPS :JUDG.

WOODS ,RS CIT: 0
SOME DIMENSIONS OF INTEGRATED SYSTEMS
TAR JL 64 VOL: 39 PG:598 - 614 :: QUAL. :INT. LOG. :N/A :OTH.MANAG.

WOOLSEY,SM CIT: 0
ACCOUNTING FOR INVESTMENT CREDIT
TAR OC 63 VOL: 38 PG:709 - 713 :: QUAL. :INT. LOG. :THEORY :N/A

WRAGGE,JH ; FIRS: ABDEL-KHALIK,AR ; SEC: SNOWBALL,D CIT: 0.4
THE EFFECTS OF CERTAIN INTERNAL AUDIT VARIABLES ON THE PLANNING OF EXTERNAL AUDIT PROGRAMS
TAR AP 83 VOL: 58 PG:215 - 227 :: ANOVA :LAB. :OTH.BEH. :INT.AUD.

WRIGHT,A ; FIRS: HARRELL,A CIT: 0
EMPIRICAL EVIDENCE ON THE VALIDITY AND RELIABILITY OF BEHAVIORALLY ANCHORED RATING SCALES FOR AUDITORS
AUD AU 90 VOL: 9 PG:134 - 149 :: REGRESS. :FIELD :OTH.BEH. :AUD.BEH.

WRIGHT,A ; SEC: ASHTON,RH CIT: 1
IDENTIFYING AUDIT ADJUSTMENTS WITH ATTENTION-DIRECTING PROCEDURES
TAR OC 89 VOL: 64 PG:710 - 728 :: DES.STAT. :SURV. :OTH.BEH. :ANAL.REV.

WRIGHT,A CIT: 0
THE IMPACT OF PRIOR WORKING PAPERS ON AUDITOR EVIDENTIAL PLANNING JUDGMENTS
AOS 06 88 VOL: 13 PG:595 - 605 :: REGRESS. :LAB. :OTH.BEH. :PLAN.

WRIGHT,A ; FIRS: ABDOLMOHAMMADI,MJ CIT: 3
AN EXAMINATION OF THE EFFECTS OF EXPERIENCE AND TASK COMPLEXITY ON AUDIT JUDGMENTS
TAR JA 87 VOL: 62 PG:1 - 13 :: REGRESS. :LAB. :OTH.BEH. :JUDG.

WRIGHT,A CIT: 0.14
PERFORMANCE EVALUATION OF STAFF AUDITORS: A BEHAVIOURALLY ANCHORED RATING SCALE
AUD SP 86 VOL: 5 PG:86 - 94 :: REGRESS. :LAB. :OTH.BEH. :OPER.AUD.

WRIGHT,A ; FIRS: LIN ,WT ; SEC: MOCK ,TJ CIT: 0.33
THE USE OF ANALYTIC HIERARCHY PROCESS AS AN AID IN PLANNING THE NATURE AND EXTENT OF AUDIT PROCEDURES
AUD AU 84 VOL: 4 PG:89 - 99 :: ANAL. :INT. LOG. :OTH.STAT. :PLAN.

WRIGHT,A CIT: 0
THE IMPACT OF CPA-FIRM SIZE ON AUDITOR DISCLOSURE PREFERENCES
TAR JL 83 VOL: 58 PG:621 - 632 :: DES.STAT. :LAB. :OTH.BEH. :ORG.

WRIGHT,A ; FIRS: MOCK ,TJ CIT: 0.09
EVALUATING THE EFFECTIVENESS OF AUDIT PROCEDURES
AUD AU 82 VOL: 2 PG:33 - 44 :: QUAL. :INT. LOG. :THEORY :OPER.AUD.

WRIGHT,A CIT: 0.18
AN INVESTIGATION OF THE ENGAGEMENT EVALUATION PROCESS FOR STAFF AUDITORS
JAR SP 82 VOL: 20 PG:227 - 239 :: ANOVA :LAB. :OTH.BEH. :AUD.

WRIGHT,CJ ; SEC: GROFF ,JE CIT: 0.29
USES OF INDEXES AND DATA BASES FOR INFORMATION RELEASE ANALYSIS
TAR JA 86 VOL: 61 PG:91 - 100 :: REGRESS. :PRIM. :EMH :METHOD.

WRIGHT,DW CIT: 0
AUGMENTING A SAMPLE SELECTED WITH PROBABILITIES PROPORTIONAL TO SIZE
AUD SP 91 VOL: 10 PG:145 - 158 :: DES.STAT. :INT. LOG. :OTH.STAT. :SAMP.

WRIGHT,FK CIT: 0.06
DUAL VARIABLES IN INVENTORY MEASUREMENT
TAR JA 70 VOL: 45 PG:129 - 133 :: ANAL. :INT. LOG. :MATH.PROG. :INV.

WRIGHT,FK CIT: 0
MEASURING ASSET SERVICES: A LINEAR PROGRAMMING APPROACH
JAR AU 68 VOL: 6 PG:222 - 236 :: ANAL. :INT. LOG. :MATH.PROG. :PP&E / DEPR

WRIGHT,FK CIT: 0
AN EVALUATION OF LADELLE'S THEORY OF DEPRECIATION
JAR AU 67 VOL: 5 PG:173 - 179 :: QUAL. :INT. LOG. :HIST. :PP&E / DEPR

WRIGHT,FK CIT: 0.06
DEPRECIATION AND OBSOLESCENCE IN CURRENT VALUE ACCOUNTING
JAR AU 65 VOL: 3 PG:167 - 181 :: QUAL. :INT. LOG. :THEORY :PP&E / DEPR

WRIGHT,FK CIT: 0
TOWARDS A GENERAL THEORY OF DEPRECIATION
JAR SP 64 VOL: 2 PG:80 - 90 :: ANAL. :INT. LOG. :THEORY :PP&E / DEPR

WRIGHT,FK CIT: 0
DEPRECIATION THEORY AND THE COST OF FUNDS
TAR JA 63 VOL: 38 PG:87 - 90 :: ANAL. :INT. LOG. :THEORY :PP&E / DEPR

WRIGHT,GB ; SEC: TAYLOR,RD CIT: 0
REPORTING MATERIALITY FOR INVESTORS
JAA SU 82 VOL: 5 PG:301 - 309 :: DES.STAT. :SURV. :OTH. :MAT.

WRIGHT,HW CIT: 0
ALLOCATION OF GENERAL AND ADMINISTRATIVE EXPENSES
TAR OC 66 VOL: 41 PG:626 - 633 :: QUAL. :INT. LOG. :THEORY :COST.ALLOC.

WRIGHT,M ; FIRS: NEU ,D CIT: 0
BANK FAILURES, STIGMA MANAGEMENT AND THE ACCOUNTING ESTABLISHMENT
AOS 92 VOL: 17 PG:645 - 665 :: REGRESS. :CASE :OTH.BEH. :BUS.FAIL.

WRIGHT,RL ; FIRS: ROSHWALB,A CIT: 0
USING INFORMATION IN ADDITION TO BOOK VALUE IN SAMPLE DESIGNS FOR INVENTORY COST ESTIMATOR
TAR AP 91 VOL: 66 PG:348 - 360 :: DES.STAT. :INT. LOG. :MATH.PROG. :ERRORS

WRIGHT,RL ; FIRS: ROSHWALB,A ; THIR: GODFREY,JT CIT: 0
A NEW APPROACH FOR STRATIFIED SAMPLING IN INVENTORY COST ESTIMATION
AUD AU 87 VOL: 7 PG:54 - 70 :: DES.STAT. :SIM. :OTH.STAT. :SAMP.

WRIGHT,WF CIT: 0
EMPIRICAL COMPARISON OF SUBJECTIVE PROBABILITY ELICITATION METHODS
CAR AU 88 VOL: 5 PG:47 - 57 :: REGRESS. :LAB. :HIPS :JUDG.

WRIGHT,WF ; FIRS: WILLINGHAM,JJ CIT: 0.38
FINANCIAL STATEMENT ERRORS AND INTERNAL CONTROL JUDGMENTS
AUD AU 85 VOL: 5 PG:57 - 70 :: REGRESS. :PRIM. :OTH.STAT. :ERRORS

WRIGHT,WF CIT: 0.18
COMPARISON OF THE LENS AND SUBJECTIVE PROBABILITY PARADIGMS FOR FINANCIAL RESEARCH PURPOSES
AOS 01 82 VOL: 7 PG:65 - 78 :: QUAL. :INT. LOG. :HIPS :METHOD.

WRIGHT,WF ; FIRS: HAMILTON,RE CIT: 1.36
INTERNAL CONTROL JUDGMENTS AND EFFECTS OF EXPERIENCE: REPLICATIONS AND EXTENSIONS
JAR AU 82 VOL: 20 PG:756 - 765 :: MIXED :LAB. :HIPS :INT.CONT.

WRIGHT,WF ; FIRS: BEAVER,WH ; SEC: CLARKE,R CIT: 4.93
THE ASSOCIATION BETWEEN UNSYSTEMATIC SECURITY RETURNS AND THE MAGNITUDE OF EARNINGS FORECAST ERRORS
JAR AU 79 VOL: 17 PG:316 - 340 :: NON-PAR. :PRIM. :EMH :FIN.METH.

WRIGHT,WF CIT: 0.19
SELF-INSIGHT INTO THE COGNITIVE PROCESSING OF FINANCIAL INFORMATION
AOS 04 77 VOL: 2 PG:323 - 332 :: CORR. :LAB. :HIPS :INFO.STRUC.

WRIGHT,WF CIT: 0.63
FINANCIAL INFORMATION PROCESSING MODELS: AN EMPIRICAL STUDY
TAR JL 77 VOL: 52 PG:676 - 689 :: REGRESS. :LAB. :HIPS :N/A

WU ,C ; FIRS: LEE ,CF CIT: 0
EXPECTATION FORMATION AND FINANCIAL RATIO ADJUSTMENT PROCESSES
TAR AP 88 VOL: 63 PG:292 - 306 :: DES.STAT. :PRIM. :OTH.STAT. :METHOD.

WURST ,J ; SEC: NETER ,J ; THIR: GODFREY,J CIT: 0
EFFECTIVENESS OF RECTIFICATION IN AUDIT SAMPLING
TAR AP 91 VOL: 66 PG:333 - 347 :: DES.STAT. :SIM. :OTH.STAT. :ERRORS

WYATT ,AR ; FIRS: KETZ ,JE CIT: 0
THE FASB IN A WORLD WITH PARTIALLY EFFICIENT MARKETS
JAA AU 83 VOL: 7 PG:29 - 43 :: QUAL. :INT. LOG. :EMH :OTH.MANAG.

WYATT ,AR CIT: 0
ACCOUNTING FOR BUSINESS COMBINATIONS: WHAT NEXT?
TAR JL 65 VOL: 40 PG:527 - 535 :: QUAL. :INT. LOG. :THEORY :BUS.COMB.

WYER ,JC ; SEC: WHITE ,GT ; THIR: JANSON,EC CIT: 0.2
AUDITS OF PUBLIC COMPANIES BY SMALLER CPA FIRMS: CLIENTS, REPORTS, AND QUALITY
AUD SP 88 VOL: 07 PG:164 - 173 :: REGRESS. :PRIM. :INSTIT. :ORG.

WYMAN ,HE CIT: 0
ANALYSIS OF GAINS OR LOSSES FROM FOREIGN MONETARY ITEMS: AN APPLICATION OF PURCHASING POWER PARITY CONCEPTS
TAR JL 76 VOL: 51 PG:545 - 558 :: ANAL. :INT. LOG. :THEORY :FIN.ST.TIM.

WYMAN ,HE CIT: 0.12
FINANCIAL LEASE EVALUATION UNDER CONDITIONS OF UNCERTAINTY
TAR JL 73 VOL: 48 PG:489 - 493 :: ANAL. :SIM. :N/A :LEASES

WYNDELTS,RW ; FIRS: JENSEN,HL CIT: 0
THROUGH THE LOOKING GLASS: AN EMPIRICAL LOOK AT DISCRIMINATION IN THE FEDERAL INCOME TAX RATE STRUCTURE
TAR OC 76 VOL: 51 PG:846 - 853 :: ANAL. :SIM. :INSTIT. :OTH.MANAG.

XIE ,JZ ; FIRS: FELTHAM,GA CIT: 1
VOLUNTARY FINANCIAL DISCLOSURE IN AN ENTRY GAME WITH CONTINUA OF TYPES
CAR AU 92 VOL: 9 PG:46 - 80 :: DES.STAT. :INT. LOG. :INF.ECO./AG. :INFO.STRUC.

YAMEY ,BS CIT: 0
THE INDEX TO THE LEDGER: SOME HISTORICAL NOTES
TAR JL 80 VOL: 55 PG:419 - 425 :: QUAL. :INT. LOG. :HIST. :N/A

YAMEY ,BS CIT: 0.07
COMPOUND JOURNAL ENTRIES IN EARLY TREATISES ON BOOKKEEPING
TAR AP 79 VOL: 54 PG:323 - 329 :: QUAL. :INT. LOG. :HIST. :OTH.MANAG.

YAMEY ,BS CIT: 0.06
FIFTEENTH AND SIXTEENTH CENTURY MANUSCRIPTS ON THE ART OF BOOKKEEPING
JAR SP 67 VOL: 5 PG:51 - 76 :: QUAL. :SEC. :HIST. :N/A

YAMEY ,BS CIT: 0.18
ACCOUNTING AND THE RISE OF CAPITALISM: FURTHER NOTES ON A THEME BY SOMBART
JAR AU 64 VOL: 2 PG:117 - 136 :: QUAL. :INT. LOG. :HIST. :N/A

YARDLEY,JA CIT: 0
LENDERS' AND CPAs' PERCEPTIONS OF THE ASSURANCE PROVIDED BY PRESCRIBED PROCEDURES
AUD AU 89 VOL: 9 PG:41 - 56 :: REGRESS. :LAB. :HIPS :JUDG.

YETTON,PW ; FIRS: TROTMAN,KT CIT: 0.25
THE EFFECT OF THE REVIEW PROCESS ON AUDITOR JUDGMENTS
JAR SP 85 VOL: 23 PG:256 - 267 :: REGRESS. :LAB. :OTH.BEH. :JUDG.

YETTON,PW ; FIRS: TROTMAN,KT ; THIR: ZIMMER,I CIT: 0.3
INDIVIDUAL AND GROUP JUDGMENTS OF INTERNAL CONTROL SYSTEMS
JAR SP 83 VOL: 21 PG:286 - 292 :: CORR. :LAB. :HIPS :MANAG.

YETTON,PY CIT: 0.12
THE INTERACTION BETWEEN A STANDARD TIME INCENTIVE PAYMENT SCHEME AND A SIMPLE ACCOUNTING INFORMATION SYSTEM
AOS 01 76 VOL: 1 PG:81 - 90 :: QUAL. :INT. LOG. :THEORY :REL.COSTS

YOON ,SS CIT: 0
THE AUDITOR'S OFF-EQUILIBRIUM BEHAVIORS
AUD 90 VOL: 9 PG:253 - 275 :: DES.STAT. :INT. LOG. :INF.ECO./AG. :INDEP.

YOUNG ,A CIT: 0
THE MARKET CRASH: CHANGES AND PERSPECTIVES
JAA WI 91 VOL: 6 PG:129 - 133 :: DES.STAT. :SEC. :OTH. :ORG.& ENVIR.

YOUNG ,AE CIT: 0
WALL STREET AFTER THE FALL
JAA SU 92 VOL: 7 PG:361 - 368 :: REGRESS. :INT. LOG. :HIST. :ORG.& ENVIR.

YOUNG ,AE ; FIRS: FRANKFURTER,GM CIT: 0
FINANCIAL THEORY: ITS MESSAGE TO THE ACCOUNTANT
JAA SU 83 VOL: 6 PG:314 - 324 :: QUAL. :INT. LOG. :OTH. :N/A

YOUNG ,AE CIT: 0
COMMON STOCK REPURCHASING: ANOTHER MEANS OF REDUCING CORPORATE SIZE
JAA SP 80 VOL: 3 PG:244 - 250 :: QUAL. :INT. LOG. :THEORY :METHOD.

YOUNG ,AE CIT: 0
ACCOUNTING FOR TREASURY STOCKS
JAA SP 78 VOL: 1 PG:217 - 230 :: DES.STAT. :PRIM. :THEORY :FIN.METH.

YOUNG ,AE ; FIRS: HORWITZ,BN CIT: 0
AN EMPIRICAL STUDY OF ACCOUNTING POLICY AND TENDER OFFERS
JAR SP 72 VOL: 10 PG:96 - 107 :: DES.STAT. :PRIM. :OTH.STAT. :BUS.COMB.

YOUNG ,AE ; FIRS: CHOTTINER,S CIT: 0.06
A TEST OF THE AICPA DIFFERENTIATION BETWEEN STOCK DIVIDENDS AND STOCK SPLITS
JAR AU 71 VOL: 9 PG:367 - 374 :: DES.STAT. :PRIM. :OTH. :STK.DIV.

YOUNG ,DW CIT: 0.14
ADMINISTRATIVE THEORY AND ADMINISTRATIVE SYSTEMS: A SYNTHESIS AMONG DIVERGING FIELDS OF INQUIRY
AOS 03 79 VOL: 4 PG:235 - 244 :: QUAL. :INT. LOG. :OTH. :N/A

YOUNG ,DW CIT: 0
ACCOUNTING FOR THE COST OF INTEREST: IMPLICATIONS FOR THE TIMBER INDUSTRY
TAR OC 76 VOL: 51 PG:788 - 799 :: QUAL. :CASE :THEORY :FIN.METH.

YOUNG ,R CIT: 0.14
A NOTE ON ECONOMICALLY OPTIMAL PERFORMANCE EVALUATION AND CONTROL SYSTEMS: THE OPTIMALITY OF TWO-TAILED INVESTIGATIONS
JAR SP 86 VOL: 24 PG:231 - 240 :: REGRESS. :INT. LOG. :OTH.STAT. :INT.CONT.

YOUNG ,RA ; FIRS: FELLINGHAM,JC CIT: 0
THE VALUE OF SELF-REPORTED COSTS IN REPEATED INVESTMENT DECISIONS
TAR OC 90 VOL: 65 PG:837 - 856 :: DES.STAT. :INT. LOG. :INF.ECO./AG. :DEC.AIDS

YOUNG ,RA ; FIRS: FELLINGHAM,JC CIT: 0
SPECIAL ALLOCATIONS, INVESTMENT DECISIONS, AND TRANSACTIONS COSTS IN PARTNERSHIPS
JAR AU 89 VOL: 27 PG:179 - 200 :: DES.STAT. :INT. LOG. :INF.ECO./AG. :ORG.FORM

YOUNG ,RA ; FIRS: ANDERSON,U CIT: 0
INTERNAL AUDIT PLANNING IN AN INTERACTIVE ENVIRONMENT
AUD AU 88 VOL: 08 PG:23 - 42 :: DES.STAT. :INT. LOG. :OTH.BEH. :TIM.

YOUNG ,SD CIT: 0
INTEREST GROUP POLITICS AND THE LICENSING OF PUBLIC ACCOUNTANTS
TAR OC 91 VOL: 66 PG:809 - 817 :: REGRESS. :PRIM. :INSTIT. :ORG.& ENVIR.

YOUNG ,SD CIT: 0
THE ECONOMIC THEORY OF REGULATION: EVIDENCE FROM THE UNIFORM CPA EXAMINATION
TAR AP 88 VOL: 63 PG:283 - 291 :: REGRESS. :PRIM. :OTH.STAT. :AUD.TRAIN.

YOUNG ,SD CIT: 0
INSIDER TRADING: WHY THE CONCERN?
JAA SP 85 VOL: 8 PG:178 - 183 :: DES.STAT. :INT. LOG. :INSTIT. :INS.TRAD.

YOUNG ,SM ; FIRS: JAWORKSI,BJ CIT: 0
DYSFUNCTIONAL BEHAVIOR AND MANAGEMENT CONTROL: AN EMPIRICAL STUDY OF MARKETING MANAGERS
AOS 01 92 VOL: 17 PG:17 - 35 :: REGRESS. :SURV. :OTH.BEH. :INT.CONT.

YOUNG ,SM ; SEC: SHIELDS,MD ; THIR: WOLF ,G CIT: 0.4
MANUFACTURING CONTROLS AND PERFORMANCE: AN EXPERIMENT
AOS 06 88 VOL: 13 PG:607 - 618 :: REGRESS. :LAB. :OTH.BEH. :EXEC.COMP.

YOUNG ,SM CIT: 0.88
PARTICIPATIVE BUDGETING: THE EFFECTS OF RISK AVERSION AND ASYMMETRIC INFORMATION ON BUDGETARY SLACK
JAR AU 85 VOL: 23 PG:829 - 842 :: REGRESS. :LAB. :INF.ECO./AG. :BUDG.& PLAN.

YOUNG ,SM ; FIRS: BIRNBERG,JG ; SEC: TUROPOLEC,L CIT: 1.7
THE ORGANIZATIONAL CONTEXT OF ACCOUNTING
AOS 23 83 VOL: 8 PG:111 - 130 :: QUAL. :SEC. :OTH.BEH. :REL.COSTS

YOUNG ,SM ; FIRS: LEWIS ,BL ; SEC: SHIELDS,MD CIT: 0.9
EVALUATING HUMAN JUDGMENTS AND DECISION AIDS
JAR SP 83 VOL: 21 PG:271 - 285 :: DES.STAT. :LAB. :HIPS :ORG.& ENVIR.

YOUNG ,TN ; SEC: PEIRSON,CG CIT: 0
DEPRECIATION - FUTURE SERVICES BASIS
TAR AP 67 VOL: 42 PG:338 - 341 :: ANAL. :INT. LOG. :THEORY :PP&E / DEPR

YU ,S ; SEC: NETER ,J CIT: 0.65
A STOCHASTIC MODEL OF THE INTERNAL CONTROL SYSTEM
JAR AU 73 VOL: 11 PG:273 - 295 :: ANAL. :INT. LOG. :OTH.STAT. :INT.CONT.

YU ,SC CIT: 0
A FLOW-OF-RESOURCES STATEMENT FOR BUSINESS ENTERPRISES
TAR JL 69 VOL: 44 PG:571 - 582 :: QUAL. :INT. LOG. :THEORY :FIN.METH.

YU ,SC CIT: 0
MICROACCOUNTING AND MACROACCOUNTING
TAR JA 66 VOL: 41 PG:8 - 20 :: QUAL. :INT. LOG. :THEORY :OTH.MANAG.

YUN ,K ; FIRS: JORGENSON,DW CIT: 0
THE EXCESS BURDEN OF TAXATION IN THE UNITED STATES
JAA AU 91 VOL: 6 PG:487 - 508 :: DES.STAT. :SIM. :TIME SER. :TAXES

ZALD ,MN CIT: 0.14
THE SOCIOLOGY OF ENTERPRISE, ACCOUNTING AND BUDGET RULES: IMPLICATIONS FOR ORGANIZATIONAL THEORY
AOS 45 86 VOL: 11 PG:321 - 326 :: ANOVA :INT. LOG. :THEORY :BUDG.& PLAN.

ZANNETOS,ZS CIT: 0
PROGRAMMED INSTRUCTION AND COMPUTER TECHNOLOGY
TAR JL 67 VOL: 42 PG:566 - 571 :: QUAL. :INT. LOG. :N/A :OTH.MANAG.

ZANNETOS,ZS CIT: 0.12
STANDARD COSTS AS A FIRST STEP TO PROBABILISTIC CONTROL: A THEORETICAL JUSTIFICATION, AND EXTENSION AND IMPLICATIONS
TAR AP 64 VOL: 39 PG:296 - 304 :: ANAL. :INT. LOG. :OTH.STAT. :VAR.

ZANNETOS,ZS CIT: 0
SOME THOUGHTS ON INTERNAL CONTROL SYSTEMS OF THE FIRM
TAR OC 64 VOL: 39 PG:860 - 868 :: QUAL. :INT. LOG. :N/A :INT.CONT.

ZANNETOS,ZS CIT: 0
MATHEMATICS AS A TOOL OF ACCOUNTING INSTRUCTION AND RESEARCH
TAR AP 63 VOL: 38 PG:326 - 335 :: QUAL. :INT. LOG. :OTH. :EDUC.

ZANNETOS,ZS CIT: 0
ON THE MATHEMATICS OF VARIANCE ANALYSIS
TAR JL 63 VOL: 38 PG:528 - 533 :: ANAL. :INT. LOG. :OTH. :VAR.

ZAROWIN,P ; FIRS: ALI ,A CIT: 2
PERMANENT VERSUS TRANSITORY COMPONENTS OF ANNUAL EARNINGS AND ESTIMATION ERROR IN EARNINGS RESPONSE COEFFICIENTS
JAE JN 92 VOL: 15 PG:249 - 264 :: REGRESS. :PRIM. :EMH :FIN.METH.

ZAROWIN,P CIT: 0
WHAT DETERMINES EARNINGS-PRICE RATIOS: REVISITED
JAA SU 90 VOL: 5 PG:439 - 454 :: REGRESS. :PRIM. :OTH.STAT. :FOREC.

ZAROWIN,P ; FIRS: AMIT ,R ; SEC: LIVNAT,J CIT: 0
A CLASSIFICATION OF MERGERS AND ACQUISITIONS BY MOTIVES: ANALYSIS OF MARKET RESPONSES
CAR AU 89 VOL: 6 PG:143 - 158 :: REGRESS. :PRIM. :EMH :BUS.COMB.

ZAROWIN,P CIT: 0
NON-LINEARITIES AND NOMINAL CONTRACTING EFFECTS: THE CASE OF THE DEPRECIATION TAX SHIELD
JAE AP 88 VOL: 10 PG:89 - 110 :: REGRESS. :PRIM. :THEORY :PP&E / DEPR

ZEFF ,SA CIT: 0
ARTHUR ANDERSEN & CO. AND THE TWO-PART OPINION IN THE AUDITORS' REPORT: 1946-1962
CAR SP 92 VOL: 8 PG:443 - 467 :: REGRESS. :CASE :HIST. :OPIN.

ZEFF ,SA CIT: 0.14
BIG EIGHT FIRMS AND THE ACCOUNTING LITERATURE: THE FALLOFF IN ADVOCACY WRITING
JAA SP 86 VOL: 1 PG:131 - 154 :: REGRESS. :SEC. :HIST. :ORG.& ENVIR.

ZEFF ,SA ; FIRS: DYCKMAN,TR CIT: 1
TWO DECADES OF THE JOURNAL OF ACCOUNTING RESEARCH
JAR SP 84 VOL: 22 PG:225 - 297 :: DES.STAT. :SEC. :INSTIT. :METHOD.

ZEFF ,SA CIT: 0.33
SOME JUNCTURES IN THE EVOLUTION OF THE PROCESS OF ESTABLISHING ACCOUNTING PRINCIPLES IN THE U.S.A.: 1917-1972
TAR JL 84 VOL: 59 PG:447 - 468 :: QUAL. :SEC. :HIST. :FIN.METH.

ZEFF ,SA CIT: 0
TRUTH IN ACCOUNTING: THE ORDEAL OF KENNETH MACNEAL
TAR JL 82 VOL: 57 PG:528 - 553 :: QUAL. :INT. LOG. :HIST. :N/A

ZEFF ,SA ; SEC: FOSSUM,RL CIT: 0.29
AN ANALYSIS OF LARGE AUDIT CLIENTS
TAR AP 67 VOL: 42 PG:298 - 320 :: DES.STAT. :PRIM. :INSTIT. :AUD.

ZEFF ,SA ; SEC: MAXWELL,WD CIT: 0
HOLDING GAINS ON FIXED ASSETS - A DEMURRER
TAR JA 65 VOL: 40 PG:65 - 75 :: QUAL. :INT. LOG. :THEORY :VALUAT.(INFL.)

ZEGHAL,D ; FIRS: ZIND ,RG CIT: 0
SOME CHARACTERISTICS OF THE CANADIAN AUDIT INDUSTRY
CAR AU 89 VOL: 6 PG:26 - 47 :: REGRESS. :PRIM. :INSTIT. :ORG.

ZHAO ,J ; FIRS: HUSS ,HF CIT: 0
AN INVESTIGATION OF ALTERNATIVE TREATMENTS OF DEFERRED TAXES IN BOND RATERS' JUDGMENTS
JAA WI 91 VOL: 6 PG:53 - 66 :: REGRESS. :PRIM. :OTH.BEH. :TAXES

ZIEBART,DA ; SEC: REITER,SA CIT: 0
BOND RATINGS, BOND YIELDS AND FINANCIAL INFORMATION
CAR AU 92 VOL: 9 PG:252 - 282 :: REGRESS. :PRIM. :INF.ECO./AG. :FIN.METH.

ZIEBART,DA ; FIRS: KIM ,DH CIT: 0
AN INVESTIGATION OF THE PRICE AND TRADING REACTIONS TO THE ISSUANCE OF SFAS NO. 52
JAA WI 91 VOL: 6 PG:35 - 47 :: REGRESS. :PRIM. :EMH :FOR.CUR.

ZIEBART,DA ; FIRS: OGAN ,P CIT: 0
CORPORATE REPORTING AND THE ACCOUNTING PROFESSION: AN INTERPRETIVE PARADIGM
JAA SU 91 VOL: 6 PG:387 - 406 :: DES.STAT. :INT. LOG. :INF.ECO./AG. :INFO.STRUC.

ZIEBART,DA CIT: 0
THE ASSOCIATION BETWEEN CONSENSUS OF BELIEFS AND TRADING ACTIVITY SURROUNDING EARNINGS ANNOUNCEMENTS
TAR AP 90 VOL: 65 PG:477 - 488 :: REGRESS. :PRIM. :EMH :FOREC.

ZIEBART,DA ; SEC: KIM ,DH CIT: 0.17
AN EXAMINATION OF THE MARKET REACTIONS ASSOCIATED WITH SFAS NO. 8 AND SFAS
TAR AP 87 VOL: 62 PG:343 - 357 :: REGRESS. :PRIM. :EMH :FOR.CUR.

ZIEBART,DA CIT: 0
CONTROL OF BETA RELIABILITY IN STUDIES OF ABNORMAL RETURN MAGNITUDE
JAR AU 85 VOL: 23 PG:920 - 926 :: DES.STAT. :PRIM. :EMH :METHOD.

ZIEGLER,RE ; FIRS: BEDFORD,NM CIT: 0.06
THE CONTRIBUTIONS OF A.C. LITTLETON TO ACCOUNTING THOUGHT AND PRACTICE
TAR JL 75 VOL: 50 PG:435 - 443 :: QUAL. :SEC. :THEORY :FIN.METH.

ZIMMER,I CIT: 1.29
ACCOUNTING FOR INTEREST BY REAL ESTATE DEVELOPERS
JAE MR 86 VOL: 8 PG:37 - 52 :: REGRESS. :PRIM. :THEORY :BUS.COMB.

ZIMMER,I ; FIRS: WHITTRED,GP CIT: 0.11
TIMELINESS OF FINANCIAL REPORTING AND FINANCIAL DISTRESS
TAR AP 84 VOL: 59 PG:287 - 295 :: DES.STAT. :PRIM. :OTH.STAT. :FIN.ST.TIM.

ZIMMER,I ; FIRS: TROTMAN,KT ; SEC: YETTON,PW CIT: 0.3
INDIVIDUAL AND GROUP JUDGMENTS OF INTERNAL CONTROL SYSTEMS
JAR SP 83 VOL: 21 PG:286 - 292 :: CORR. :LAB. :HIPS :MANAG.

ZIMMER,I ; FIRS: WILKINS,T CIT: 0.1
THE EFFECT OF LEASING AND DIFFERENT METHODS OF ACCOUNTING FOR LEASES ON CREDIT EVALUATIONS
TAR OC 83 VOL: 58 PG:749 - 764 :: ANOVA :LAB. :OTH.BEH. :LEASES

ZIMMERMAN,JL ; FIRS: WATTS ,RL CIT: 4.33
POSITIVE ACCOUNTING THEORY: A TEN YEAR PERSPECTIVE
TAR JA 90 VOL: 65 PG:131 - 156 :: DES.STAT. :SEC. :THEORY :METHOD.

ZIMMERMAN,JL ; FIRS: LIBERTY,SE CIT: 1.71
LABOR UNION CONTRACT NEGOTIATIONS AND ACCOUNTING CHOICES
TAR OC 86 VOL: 61 PG:692 - 712 :: REGRESS. :PRIM. :OTH.STAT. :INFO.STRUC.

ZIMMERMAN,JL ; FIRS: JENSEN,MC CIT: 0
MANAGEMENT COMPENSATION AND THE MANAGERIAL LABOR MARKET
JAE AP 85 VOL: 7 PG:3 - 10 :: REGRESS. :INT. LOG. :THEORY :EXEC.COMP.

ZIMMERMAN,JL CIT: 1.2
TAXES AND FIRM SIZE
JAE AG 83 VOL: 5 PG:119 - 149 :: ANOVA :PRIM. :THEORY :TAXES

ZIMMERMAN,JL ; FIRS: LEFTWICH,RW ; SEC: WATTS ,RL CIT: 0.58
VOLUNTARY CORPORATE DISCLOSURE: THE CASE OF INTERIM REPORTING
JAR ST 81 VOL: 19 PG:50 - 77 :: ANAL. :PRIM. :OTH.STAT. :INT.REP.

ZIMMERMAN,JL ; FIRS: WATTS ,RL CIT: 0.38
ON THE IRRELEVANCE OF REPLACEMENT COST DISCLOSURES FOR SECURITY PRICES
JAE AG 80 VOL: 2 PG:95 - 106 :: QUAL. :SEC. :OTH. :VALUAT.(INFL.)

ZIMMERMAN,JL ; FIRS: WATTS ,RL CIT: 3.5
THE DEMAND FOR AND SUPPLY OF ACCOUNTING THEORIES: THE MARKET FOR EXCUSES
TAR AP 79 VOL: 54 PG:273 - 305 :: QUAL. :INT. LOG. :THEORY :FIN.METH.

ZIMMERMAN,JL CIT: 1.86
THE COST AND BENEFITS OF COST ALLOCATIONS
TAR JL 79 VOL: 54 PG:504 - 521 :: ANAL. :INT. LOG. :INF.ECO./AG. :COST.ALLOC.

ZIMMERMAN,JL ; FIRS: WATTS ,RL CIT: 8.2
TOWARDS A POSITIVE THEORY OF THE DETERMINATION OF ACCOUNTING STANDARDS
TAR JA 78 VOL: 53 PG:112 - 134 :: OTH.QUANT. :PRIM. :OTH.STAT. :FASB SUBM.

ZIMMERMAN,JL CIT: 0.81
THE MUNICIPAL ACCOUNTING MAZE: AN ANALYSIS OF POLITICAL INCENTIVES
JAR ST 77 VOL: 15 PG:107 - 144 :: DES.STAT. :PRIM. :INF.ECO./AG. :OTH.MANAG.

ZIMMERMAN,JL CIT: 0.18
BUDGET UNCERTAINTY AND THE ALLOCATION DECISION IN A NONPROFIT ORGANIZATION
JAR AU 76 VOL: 14 PG:301 - 319 :: REGRESS. :CASE :OTH.STAT. :OVER.ALLOC.

ZIND ,RG ; SEC: ZEGHAL,D CIT: 0
SOME CHARACTERISTICS OF THE CANADIAN AUDIT INDUSTRY
CAR AU 89 VOL: 6 PG:26 - 47 :: REGRESS. :PRIM. :INSTIT. :ORG.

ZMIJEWSKI,ME ; FIRS: BROWN ,LD CIT: 0.17
THE EFFECT OF LABOR STRIKES ON SECURITY ANALYSTS' FORECAST SUPERIORITY AND ON THE ASSOCIATION BETWEEN RISK-ADJUSTED STOCK RETURNS AND UNEXPECTED EARNINGS
CAR AU 87 VOL: 4 PG:61 - 75 :: REGRESS. :PRIM. :TIME SER. :FOREC.

ZMIJEWSKI,ME ; FIRS: EASTON,PD CIT: 5.5
CROSS-SECTIONAL VARIATION IN THE STOCK MARKET RESPONSE TO ACCOUNTING EARNINGS ANNOUNCEMENTS
JAE JL 89 VOL: 11 PG:117 - 141 :: REGRESS. :PRIM. :EMH :FIN.METH.

ZMIJEWSKI,ME ; FIRS: BROWN ,LD ; SEC: GRIFFIN,PA ; THIR: HAGERMAN,RL CIT: 4.5
SECURITY ANALYST SUPERIORITY RELATIVE TO UNIVARIATE TIME-SERIES MODELS IN FORECASTING QUARTERLY EARNINGS
JAE AP 87 VOL: 9 PG:61 - 87 :: REGRESS. :PRIM. :TIME SER. :FOREC.

ZMIJEWSKI,ME ; FIRS: BROWN ,LD ; SEC: GRIFFIN,PA ; THIR: HAGERMAN,RL CIT: 5.17
AN EVALUATION OF ALTERNATIVE PROXIES FOR THE MARKET'S ASSESSMENT OF UNEXPECTED EARNINGS
JAE JL 87 VOL: 9 PG:159 - 193 :: REGRESS. :PRIM. :TIME SER. :METHOD.

ZMIJEWSKI,ME ; FIRS: HAGERMAN,RL ; THIR: SHAH ,P CIT: 1.11
THE ASSOCIATION BETWEEN THE MAGNITUDE OF QUARTERLY EARNINGS FORECAST ERRORS AND RISK-ADJUSTED STOCK RETURNS
JAR AU 84 VOL: 22 PG:526 - 540 :: REGRESS. :PRIM. :EMH :FOREC.

ZMIJEWSKI,ME CIT: 1.67
METHODOLOGICAL ISSUES RELATED TO THE ESTIMATION OF FINANCIAL DISTRESS PREDICTION MODELS
JAR ST 84 VOL: 22 PG:59 - 82 :: OTH.QUANT. :PRIM. :OTH.STAT. :BUS.FAIL.

ZMIJEWSKI,ME ; SEC: HAGERMAN,RL CIT: 3.33
AN INCOME STRATEGY APPROACH TO THE POSITIVE THEORY OF ACCOUNTING STANDARD SETTING/CHOICE
JAE AG 81 VOL: 3 PG:129 - 149 :: OTH.QUANT. :SEC. :OTH.STAT. :METHOD.

ZMIJEWSKI,ME ; FIRS: HAGERMAN,RL CIT: 3.79
SOME ECONOMIC DETERMINANTS OF ACCOUNTING POLICY CHOICE
JAE AG 79 VOL: 1 PG:141 - 161 :: OTH.QUANT. :PRIM. :OTH.STAT. :ACC.CHNG.

ZMUD ,RW ; FIRS: BLOCHER,E ; SEC: MOFFIE,RP CIT: 0.14
REPORT FORMAT AND TASK COMPLEXITY: INTERACTION IN RISK JUDGMENTS
AOS 06 86 VOL: 11 PG:457 - 470 :: REGRESS. :LAB. :HIPS :INFO.STRUC.

ZOLTNERS,AA ; FIRS: BALACHANDRAN,BV CIT: 0
AN INTERACTIVE AUDIT-STAFF SCHEDULING DECISION SUPPORT SYSTEM
TAR OC 81 VOL: 56 PG:801 - 812 :: ANAL. :INT. LOG. :OTH.STAT. :AUD.BEH.

PART II

Articles Classified in Four Ways

- MODE OF REASONING
- RESEARCH METHOD
- SCHOOL OF THOUGHT
- TREATMENT–Subject Area

CITE INDEX	FIRST AUTHOR	ISS-UE	YE-AR	JOUR-NAL	SECOND AUTHOR	THIRD AUTHOR	PAG BEG	PAG END
1.1 MODE OF REASONING (METHOD)=QUANTITATIVE: DESCRIPTIVE STATS								
6.00	HOPWOOD,AG	03	1987	AOS			207	234
4.83	MILLER,P	03	1987	AOS	O'LEARY,T		235	265
4.33	WATTS ,RL	JA	1990	TAR	ZIMMERMAN,JL		131	156
4.17	CHRISTIE,AA	DE	1987	JAE			231	258
4.14	LOFT ,A	02	1986	AOS			137	170
4.00	BOWEN ,RM	AG	1981	JAE	NOREEN,EW	LACEY ,JM	151	179
3.75	BURCHELL,S	04	1985	AOS	CLUBB ,C	HOPWOOD,AG	381	414
3.00	HOSKIN,KW	02	1986	AOS	MACVE ,RH		105	136
2.75	ARRINGTON,CE	02	1989	AOS	FRANCIS,JR		1	28
2.50	LEHMAN,C	05	1987	AOS	TINKER,T		503	522
2.20	LEFTWICH,RW	JA	1983	TAR			23	42
2.14	CHUA ,WF	OC	1986	TAR			601	632
2.14	HUGHES,PJ	JN	1986	JAE			119	142
2.14	TITMAN,S	JN	1986	JAE	TRUEMAN,B		159	172
2.00	DYE ,RA	SP	1992	JAR			27	52
2.00	REICHELSTEIN,S	OC	1992	TAR			712	731
2.00	ROBERTS,J	04	1985	AOS	SCAPENS,RW		443	456
1.83	JOHNSON,JR	AP	1981	TAR	LEITCH,RA	NETER ,J	270	293
1.80	HOSKIN,KW	01	1988	AOS	MACVE ,RH		37	73
1.70	MORSE ,D	SP	1983	JAR	RICHARDSON,G		106	127
1.67	GOVINDARAJAN,V	02	1984	AOS			125	135
1.67	MELUMAD,ND	SP	1990	JAR	THOMAN,L		77	120
1.67	OHLSON,JA	SP	1990	CAR			648	676
1.64	SWIERINGA,RJ	ST	1982	JAR	WEICK ,KE		56	101
1.50	DATAR ,SM	MR	1991	JAE	FELTHAM,GA	HUGHES,JS	3	49
1.50	KIRBY ,AJ	SP	1991	JAR	REICHELSTEIN,S	SEN ,PK	109	128
1.50	OHLSON,JA	JL	1989	JAE			109	115
1.50	RICHARDSON,AJ	04	1987	AOS			341	355
1.50	ROBERTS,J	04	1991	AOS			355	368
1.50	TINKER,T	01	1987	AOS	NEIMARK,M		71	88
1.45	HYLAS ,RE	OC	1982	TAR	ASHTON,RH		751	765
1.40	NOREEN,EW	04	1988	AOS			359	369
1.40	TINKER,T	02	1988	AOS			165	189
1.35	DECOSTER,DT	AU	1968	JAR	FERTAKIS,JP		237	246
1.33	BERG ,KB	SP	1990	CAR	COURSEY,D	DICKHAUT,J	825	849
1.33	DARROUGH,MN	JA	1990	JAE	STOUGHTON,NM		219	243
1.33	DEMSKI,JS	SP	1987	JAR	SAPPINGTON,DEM		68	89
1.33	HOLTHAUSEN,RW	JA	1990	TAR	VERRECCHIA,RE		91	208
1.33	MAGEE ,RP	AP	1990	TAR	TSENG ,M		315	336
1.33	PUXTY ,AG	03	1987	AOS	WILLMOTT,HC	COOPER,DJ	273	291
1.33	ST.PIERRE,K	AP	1984	TAR	ANDERSON,JA		242	263
1.24	BEAVER,WH	ST	1966	JAR			71	111
1.20	MORGAN,G	05	1988	AOS			477	485
1.18	CORLESS,JC	JL	1972	TAR			556	566
1.17	HOPPER,T	05	1987	AOS	STOREY,J	WILLMOTT,H	437	456
1.17	KNIGHTS,D	05	1987	AOS	COLLINSON,D		457	477
1.14	GIVOLY,D	DE	1979	JAE	LAKONISHOK,J		165	185
1.14	KINNEY JR,WR	ST	1979	JAR			148	165
1.14	KREUTZFELDT,RW	AU	1986	AUD	WALLACE,WA		20	43
1.14	TRUEMAN,B	MR	1986	JAE			53	72
1.10	BIGGS ,SF	SP	1983	JAR	MOCK ,TJ		234	255

CITE INDEX	FIRST AUTHOR	ISS-UE	YE-AR	JOUR-NAL	SECOND AUTHOR	THIRD AUTHOR	PAG BEG	PAG END
1.06	FELIX JR,WL	OC	1976	TAR			800	807
1.00	BANKER,RD	SP	1989	JAR	DATAR ,SM		21	39
1.00	BANKER,RD	SP	1992	CAR	DATAR ,SM		329	352
1.00	BANKER,RD	AU	1992	CAR			343	354
1.00	CHANDRA,R	SP	1990	CAR	BALACHANDRAN,BV		611	640
1.00	CHOUDHURY,N	06	1988	AOS			549	557
1.00	CHOW ,CW	AP	1982	TAR	RICE ,SJ		326	335
1.00	COVALESKI,MA	06	1990	AOS	DIRSMITH,MW		543	573
1.00	DYCKMAN,TR	SP	1984	JAR	ZEFF ,SA		225	297
1.00	DYE ,RA	JA	1990	TAR			1	24
1.00	DYE ,RA	AU	1990	JAR	BALACHANDRAN,BV	MAGEE ,RP	239	266
1.00	FELTHAM,GA	AU	1992	CAR	XIE ,JZ		46	80
1.00	GRAY ,B	05	1992	AOS			399	425
1.00	KANODIA,C	SP	1989	JAR	BUSHMAN,R	DICKHAUT,J	59	77
1.00	KIM ,O	AU	1991	JAR	VERRECCHIA,RE		302	321
1.00	KINNEY JR,WR	JA	1982	TAR	UECKER,WC		55	69
1.00	LAVOIE,D	06	1987	AOS			579	604
1.00	MEHREZ,A	AU	1992	CAR	BROWN ,JR	KHOUJA,M	329	342
1.00	MELUMAD,ND	ST	1987	JAR	REICHELSTEIN,S		1	18
1.00	RAJAN ,MV	JL	1992	TAR			527	545
1.00	SMITH ,VL	AU	1987	AUD	SCHATZBERG,J	WALLER,WS	71	93
1.00	SOLOMON,I	AU	1982	JAR			689	710
1.00	SUH ,YS	ST	1987	JAR			22	46
1.00	WRIGHT,A	OC	1989	TAR	ASHTON,RH		710	728
0.92	ABDEL-KHALIK,AR	AU	1980	JAR	EL-SHESHAI,KM		325	342
0.91	CHOW ,CW	AP	1982	TAR			272	291
0.91	LEITCH,RA	AP	1982	TAR	NETER ,J	PLANTE,R	384	400
0.90	LEWIS ,BL	SP	1983	JAR	SHIELDS,MD	YOUNG ,SM	271	285
0.89	MARAIS,ML	ST	1984	JAR			34	54
0.86	SEFCIK,SE	AU	1986	JAR	THOMPSON,R		316	334
0.86	WHITLEY,R	02	1986	AOS			171	192
0.83	BURRELL,G	01	1987	AOS			89	102
0.83	HOPWOOD,AG	01	1987	AOS			65	70
0.83	MARCH ,JG	02	1987	AOS			153	168
0.82	IMHOFF JR,EA	AU	1982	JAR	PARE ,PV		429	439
0.82	MCDONALD,CL	JL	1973	TAR			502	510
0.81	ZIMMERMAN,JL	ST	1977	JAR			107	144
0.80	DYE ,RA	AU	1988	JAR			195	235
0.80	KINNEY JR,WR	SP	1988	CAR			416	425
0.80	LANDSMAN,WR	OC	1988	TAR	MAGLIOLO,J		586	604
0.79	RAMAGE,JG	ST	1979	JAR	KRIEGER,AM	SPERO ,LL	72	102
0.78	MENZEFRICKE,U	AU	1984	JAR	SMIELIAUSKAS,W		588	604
0.76	CUSHING,BE	AU	1969	JAR			196	203
0.75	ANTLE ,R	SP	1989	CAR	DEMSKI,JS		423	451
0.75	CROSBY,MA	AP	1981	TAR			355	365
0.75	DEMSKI,JS	SP	1989	JAR	SAPPINGTON,DEM		40	58
0.75	LIBBY ,R	OC	1989	TAR	LIBBY ,PA		729	747
0.75	MELUMAD,ND	SP	1989	CAR			733	753
0.73	GIBBINS,M	JA	1982	TAR	WOLF ,FM		105	124
0.71	CHUA ,WF	06	1986	AOS			583	598
0.71	DWORIN,L	JA	1986	TAR	GRIMLUND,RA		36	57
0.71	GOSMAN,ML	JA	1973	TAR			1	11
0.69	PARKER,JE	JA	1977	TAR			69	96

CITE INDEX	FIRST AUTHOR	ISS-UE	YE-AR	JOUR-NAL	SECOND AUTHOR	THIRD AUTHOR	PAG BEG	PAG END
0.69	UECKER,WC	03	1977	AOS	KINNEY JR,WR		269	275
0.67	AMERSHI,AH	AU	1990	CAR	CHENG ,P		61	99
0.67	BEAVER,WH	JA	1987	TAR			137	144
0.67	BEGLEY,J	JA	1990	JAE			125	139
0.67	JORDAN,JS	SP	1990	CAR			903	921
0.67	SHIBANO,T	ST	1990	JAR			110	147
0.67	THOMPSON,G	05	1987	AOS			523	543
0.67	VERRECCHIA,RE	JA	1990	JAE			245	250
0.67	WILLIAMS,PF	02	1987	AOS			169	192
0.65	GAGNON,JM	ST	1967	JAR			187	204
0.65	HARIED,AA	SP	1973	JAR			117	145
0.65	ROSE ,R	ST	1970	JAR	BEAVER,WH	BECKER,S	138	148
0.64	MORIARITY,S	SP	1979	JAR			205	224
0.64	SOLOMON,I	01	1982	AOS	KROGSTAD,JL	ROMNEY,MB	27	42
0.63	OGDEN ,S	02	1985	AOS	BOUGEN,P		211	226
0.63	SCHIPPER,K	SP	1985	JAR	THOMPSON,R		408	415
0.60	AMERSHI,AH	SP	1988	CAR	CHENG ,P		515	563
0.60	FRECKA,TJ	JA	1983	TAR	HOPWOOD,WS		115	128
0.60	HINES ,RD	OC	1988	TAR			642	656
0.60	JUNG ,WO	SP	1988	JAR	KWON ,YK		146	153
0.60	KOTHARI,SP	AU	1988	JAA	LYS ,T	SMITH ,CW	307	340
0.60	SHANE ,PB	JL	1983	TAR	SPICER,BH		521	538
0.59	BUZBY ,SL	JL	1974	TAR			423	435
0.59	KENNEDY,HA	SP	1975	JAR			97	116
0.57	GARSTKA,SJ	SP	1979	JAR	OHLSON,PA		23	59
0.57	MESERVY,RD	AU	1986	AUD	BAILEY JR,AD	JOHNSON,PE	44	74
0.57	SMIELIAUSKAS,W	AU	1986	CAR			102	124
0.56	MUTCHLER,JF	SP	1984	AUD			17	30
0.55	FROST ,PA	SP	1982	JAR	TAMURA,H		103	120
0.55	SILHAN,PA	SP	1982	JAR			255	262
0.53	ARCHIBALD,TR	ST	1967	JAR			164	186
0.53	BEAVER,WH	JA	1968	TAR			113	122
0.50	ALM ,J	JL	1991	TAR			577	594
0.50	AMERSHI,AH	AU	1987	JAR	SUNDER,S		177	195
0.50	ANTLE ,R	ST	1991	JAR	DEMSKI,JS		1	30
0.50	ANTLE ,R	ST	1991	JAR	NALEBUFF,B		31	59
0.50	BAIMAN,S	SP	1991	JAR	EVANS III,JH	NAGARAJAN,NJ	1	18
0.50	BALACHANDRAN,BV	SP	1987	CAR	NAGARAJAN,NJ		281	301
0.50	BENSTON,GJ	AP	1985	JAE			67	84
0.50	BUSHMAN,RM	AU	1991	JAR			261	276
0.50	COLIGNON,R	02	1991	AOS	COVALESKI,M		141	157
0.50	DONTOH,A	AU	1989	JAA			480	511
0.50	FELLINGHAM,JC	JA	1985	TAR	WOLFSON,MA		10	17
0.50	FELLINGHAM,JC	SP	1989	AUD	NEWMAN,DP	PATTERSON,ER	1	21
0.50	GRIMLUND,RA	JL	1987	TAR	FELIX JR,WL		455	479
0.50	HOGARTH,RM	AP	1991	TAR			277	290
0.50	HOWARD,TP	OC	1983	TAR	NIKOLAI,LA		765	776
0.50	INDJEJIKIAN,RJ	AU	1991	JAR			277	301
0.50	KINNEY JR,WR	SP	1987	AUD			59	73
0.50	LAMBERT,RA	SP	1991	JAR	LARCKER,DF	VERRECCHIA,RE	129	149
0.50	PALMROSE,ZV	SP	1987	AUD			90	103
0.50	STONE ,M	JA	1991	TAR	RASP ,J		170	187
0.50	TSUI ,KW	JA	1985	TAR	MATSUMURA,EM	TSUI ,KL	76	96

CITE INDEX	FIRST AUTHOR	ISS-UE	YE-AR	JOUR-NAL	SECOND AUTHOR	THIRD AUTHOR	PAG BEG	PAG END
0.47	DOPUCH,N	AU	1973	JAR	RONEN ,J		191	211
0.47	GREEN ,D	ST	1966	JAR	SEGALL,J		21	36
0.47	RULAND,W	AP	1978	TAR			439	447
0.47	SCHWAN,ES	23	1976	AOS			219	238
0.45	DEANGELO,LE	DE	1982	JAE			171	203
0.43	SMIELIAUSKAS,W	JA	1986	TAR			118	128
0.43	VERRECCHIA,RE	OC	1986	JAE			175	196
0.41	BEAVER,WH	AU	1968	JAR			179	192
0.41	DICKHAUT,JW	SP	1975	JAR	EGGLETON,IRC		38	72
0.41	NEUMANN,FL	ST	1968	JAR			1	17
0.40	BANKER,RD	AU	1988	CAR	DATAR ,SM	MAINDIRATTA,A	96	124
0.40	KNECHEL,WR	JA	1988	TAR			74	95
0.40	MENZEFRICKE,U	SP	1988	CAR	SMIELIAUSKAS,W		314	336
0.40	TRUEMAN,B	ST	1988	JAR	TITMAN,S		127	143
0.38	ABDOLMOHAMMADI,MJ	AU	1985	CAR			76	94
0.38	AMERSHI,AH	SP	1985	CAR	DEMSKI,JS	FELLINGHAM,J	176	192
0.38	BECK ,PJ	SP	1985	AUD	SOLOMON,I		1	10
0.38	OWEN ,DL	03	1985	AOS	LLOYD ,AJ		329	352
0.36	ALDERMAN,CW	WI	1982	AUD	DEITRICK,JW		54	68
0.36	BURTON,JC	WI	1982	AUD	FAIRFIELD,P		1	22
0.36	CUSHING,BE	ST	1979	JAR	SEARFOSS,DG	RANDALL,RH	172	216
0.36	HOPWOOD,WS	AU	1982	JAR	NEWBOLD,P	SILHAN,PA	724	732
0.36	LIGHTNER,SM	AU	1982	AUD	ADAMS ,SJ	LIGHTNER,KM	1	12
0.36	MAYER-SOMMER,AP	JA	1979	TAR			88	106
0.35	COPELAND,RM	ST	1971	JAR	SHANK ,JK		196	224
0.35	MCRAE ,TW	SP	1974	JAR			80	92
0.35	SINGHVI,SS	JA	1971	TAR	DESAI ,HB		129	138
0.33	ABDEL-KHALIK,AR	AU	1990	CAR			142	172
0.33	BAIMAN,S	SP	1990	CAR	MAY ,JH	MUKHERJI,A	761	799
0.33	BAIMAN,S	04	1990	AOS			341	371
0.33	BALACHANDRAN,BV	AU	1987	CAR	LI ,L	MAGEE ,RP	164	185
0.33	BALACHANDRAN,BV	SP	1987	JAR	RAMAKRISHNAN,RT		111	126
0.33	BANKER,RD	AU	1987	JAA	DATAR ,SM	RAJAN ,MV	319	347
0.33	CHANDRA,R	AU	1990	CAR	ROHRBACH,K		123	141
0.33	CONROY,RM	JA	1987	TAR	HUGHES,JS		50	66
0.33	HALL ,TW	JL	1990	TAR	SHRIVER,KA		537	556
0.33	HIRST ,MK	OC	1987	TAR			774	784
0.33	HOLTHAUSEN,RW	JA	1990	JAE			207	218
0.33	HUGHES,MA	03	1990	AOS	KWON ,SO		179	191
0.33	LAUGHLIN,RC	05	1987	AOS			479	502
0.33	MATSUMURA,EM	SP	1990	CAR	TSUI ,K-W	WONG ,W-K	485	500
0.33	MENZEFRICKE,U	AU	1984	JAR			570	587
0.33	PANY ,K	SP	1984	AUD	RECKERS,PMJ		89	97
0.33	PENNO ,M	AP	1990	TAR			303	314
0.33	SHANK ,JK	OC	1978	TAR	MURDOCK,RJ		824	835
0.33	SHIH ,MSH	AU	1987	CAR	SUNDER,S		16	31
0.33	SWIERINGA,RJ	03	1987	AOS	WEICK ,KE		293	308
0.31	COOPER,DJ	03	1977	AOS	ESSEX ,S		201	218
0.29	BERNSTEIN,LA	JA	1967	TAR			86	95
0.29	BLAZENKO,GW	AU	1986	CAR	SCOTT ,WR		68	92
0.29	BORITZ,JE	AU	1986	AUD	BROCA ,DS		1	19
0.29	BUZBY ,SL	JA	1979	TAR	FALK ,H		23	37
0.29	DITTMAN,DA	AP	1979	TAR	PRAKASH,P		358	373

CITE INDEX	FIRST AUTHOR	ISS-UE	YE-AR	JOUR-NAL	SECOND AUTHOR	THIRD AUTHOR	PAG BEG	PAG END
0.29	GAA ,JC	JL	1986	TAR			435	454
0.29	HOFSTEDT,TR	01	1976	AOS			43	58
0.29	RHODE ,JG	OC	1974	TAR	WHITSELL,GM	KELSEY,RL	772	787
0.29	SMITH ,DB	AU	1986	AUD			95	108
0.29	WILCOX,JA	ST	1973	JAR			163	179
0.29	ZEFF ,SA	AP	1967	TAR	FOSSUM,RL		298	320
0.27	DANOS ,P	WI	1982	AUD	IMHOFF JR,EA		23	34
0.27	JIAMBALVO,J	SP	1982	JAR			152	161
0.25	AMERSHI,AH	AU	1989	CAR	CHENG ,P		72	90
0.25	BACHAR,J	AU	1989	CAR			216	241
0.25	CHEUNG,JK	SP	1989	CAR			625	641
0.25	ETZIONI,A	AU	1989	JAA			555	570
0.25	GOLDIN,HJ	SU	1985	JAA			269	278
0.25	JANG ,HJ	AU	1989	CAR	RO ,BT		242	262
0.25	LANDSMAN,WR	SP	1989	JAR	DAMODARAN,A		97	115
0.25	MOORE ,G	SP	1989	CAR	SCOTT ,WR		754	774
0.25	NEWMAN,P		1989	AUD	NOEL ,J		50	63
0.25	PLANTE,R	AU	1985	AUD	NETER ,J	LEITCH,RA	40	56
0.25	STAUBUS,GJ	JA	1985	TAR			53	75
0.25	WEBER ,RP	JL	1981	TAR	STEVENSON,WC		596	612
0.24	BARRETT,ME	SP	1976	JAR			10	26
0.24	CHANDRA,G	OC	1974	TAR			733	742
0.24	DASCHER,PE	AU	1970	JAR	MALCOM,RE		253	259
0.24	HEINTZ,JA	OC	1973	TAR			679	689
0.24	LIVINGSTONE,JL	AP	1967	TAR			233	240
0.23	HUSSEIN,ME	SU	1980	JAA	KETZ ,JE		354	367
0.22	BIGGS ,SF	34	1984	AOS			313	323
0.22	CAMPBELL,JE	34	1984	AOS			329	342
0.22	GRANOF,MH	SU	1984	JAA	SHORT ,DG		323	333
0.21	BLOCHER,E	JL	1979	TAR			563	573
0.21	NAIR ,RD	SP	1979	JAR			225	242
0.20	BUZBY ,SL	34	1978	AOS	FALK ,H		191	202
0.20	COHEN ,SI	AU	1988	CAR	LOEB ,M		70	95
0.20	DERMER,JD	01	1988	AOS			25	36
0.20	FELTHAM,GA	AU	1988	CAR	CHRISTENSEN,PO		133	169
0.20	GRIMLUND,RA	SP	1988	AUD			77	104
0.20	HOLDER,WW	SP	1983	AUD			100	108
0.20	KNECHEL,WR	AU	1988	AUD			87	107
0.20	MAGEE ,RP	JA	1988	TAR			42	54
0.20	NELSON,J	SU	1988	JAA	RONEN ,J	WHITE ,L	255	296
0.20	SORTER,GH	SU	1988	JAA	SIEGEL,S	SLAIN ,J	233	244
0.20	SPICER,BH	03	1988	AOS			303	322
0.19	GARSTKA,SJ	AU	1977	JAR			179	192
0.19	SCHROEDER,RG	01	1977	AOS	IMDIEKE,LF		39	46
0.18	BOWMAN,EH	01	1976	AOS	HAIRE ,M		11	22
0.18	CAPLAN,EM	AP	1968	TAR			342	362
0.18	EGGLETON,IRC	SP	1982	JAR			68	102
0.18	FALK ,H	SP	1973	JAR	OPHIR ,T		108	116
0.18	ORTMAN,RF	AP	1975	TAR			298	304
0.18	PROBST,FR	JA	1971	TAR			113	118
0.18	SCHWARTZ,KB	AU	1982	JAA			32	43
0.18	SKINNER,RC	SP	1982	JAR			210	226
0.18	WALTHER,LM	AP	1982	TAR			376	383

CITE INDEX	FIRST AUTHOR	ISS-UE	YE-AR	JOUR-NAL	SECOND AUTHOR	THIRD AUTHOR	PAG BEG	PAG END
0.18	WHITE JR,CE	AU	1972	JAR			351	358
0.17	BERRY ,LE	JA	1987	TAR	HARWOOD,GB	KATZ ,JL	14	28
0.17	COOPER,DJ	05	1987	AOS	HOPPER,TM		407	414
0.17	GAMBLING,T	04	1987	AOS			319	329
0.17	JACOBS,FH	JA	1987	TAR	MARSHALL,RM		67	78
0.17	KIM ,HS	SP	1987	AUD	NETER ,J	GODFREY,JT	40	58
0.17	MAHER ,MW	OC	1981	TAR			751	770
0.17	MENZEFRICKE,U	AU	1987	CAR	SMIELIAUSKAS,W		240	250
0.17	OHLSON,JA	AU	1987	CAR			1	15
0.17	PENNO ,M	SP	1987	CAR			368	374
0.17	WIGGINS JR,CE	SP	1987	CAR	SMITH ,LW		316	337
0.17	WOLF ,FM	OC	1981	TAR			861	881
0.15	RONEN ,J	SU	1980	JAA	SADAN ,S		339	353
0.14	ANDERSON,JC	JL	1986	TAR	KRAUSHAAR,JM		379	399
0.14	BROCKHOFF,K	12	1979	AOS			77	86
0.14	DERMER,JD	06	1986	AOS	LUCAS ,RG		471	482
0.14	DIERKES,M	12	1979	AOS			87	108
0.14	DUNMORE,PV	AU	1986	CAR			125	148
0.14	EVANS III,JH	06	1986	AOS	LEWIS ,BL	PATTON,JM	483	498
0.14	HARRISON,GL	03	1986	AOS	MCKINNON,JL		233	252
0.14	HUSS ,HF	AU	1986	JAR	TRADER,RL		394	399
0.14	RICCHIUTE,DN	12	1979	AOS			67	76
0.14	SMIELIAUSKAS,W	SP	1986	JAR			217	230
0.14	TAMURA,H	AU	1986	JAR	FROST ,PA		364	371
0.13	AHITUV,N	AU	1985	CAR	HALPERN,J	WILL ,H	95	110
0.13	BORITZ,JE	SP	1985	CAR			193	218
0.13	DIERKES,M	01	1985	AOS	ANTAL ,AB		29	34
0.13	FLAMHOLTZ,EG	01	1985	AOS	DAS ,TK	TSUI ,AS	35	50
0.13	GAMBLING,T	04	1985	AOS			415	426
0.13	KELLY ,LK	JA	1977	TAR			97	108
0.12	BRILOFF,AJ	JL	1966	TAR			484	495
0.12	CHURCHILL,NC	OC	1965	TAR	COOPER,WW		767	781
0.12	COPELAND,RM	AU	1969	JAR	WOJDAK,JF		188	195
0.12	DOPUCH,N	ST	1966	JAR	DRAKE ,DF		192	219
0.12	FRANK ,WG	AP	1970	TAR	WEYGANDT,JJ		280	289
0.12	GREENBALL,MN	SP	1968	JAR			114	129
0.12	KIGER ,JE	JA	1974	TAR			1	7
0.12	LINDHE,R	AU	1963	JAR			139	148
0.12	LIVINGSTONE,JL	AU	1970	JAR	SALAMON,GL		199	216
0.12	LOEB ,SE	JA	1972	TAR			1	10
0.12	PANKOFF,LD	AP	1970	TAR	VIRGIL JR,RL		269	279
0.12	RITTS ,BA	SP	1974	JAR			93	111
0.12	ROBERTSON,JC	JL	1971	TAR	CLARKE,RW		562	571
0.12	SMITH ,CH	AP	1972	TAR	LANIER,RA	TAYLOR,ME	270	283
0.12	STERLING,RR	SP	1969	JAR	RADOSEVICH,R		90	95
0.11	MCCONNELL,DK	SP	1984	AUD			44	56
0.11	MOST ,KS	AU	1984	JAR			782	788
0.11	SCHEINER,JH	AU	1984	JAR			789	797
0.11	SMITH ,G	AU	1984	AUD	KROGSTAD,JL		107	117
0.11	STONE ,M	JL	1984	TAR	BUBLITZ,B		469	473
0.11	SUTTON,TG	01	1984	AOS			81	95
0.11	THAKKAR,RB	AU	1984	CAR	FINLEY,DR	LIAO ,WM	77	86
0.11	WHITTRED,GP	AP	1984	TAR	ZIMMER,I		287	295

CITE INDEX	FIRST AUTHOR	ISS-UE	YE-AR	JOUR-NAL	SECOND AUTHOR	THIRD AUTHOR	PAG BEG	PAG END
0.10	BLOCHER,E	AU	1983	AUD	ESPOSITO,RS	WILLINGHAM,JJ	75	91
0.10	LAWRENCE,EC	AU	1983	JAR			606	610
0.10	MCLEAY,S	01	1983	AOS			31	56
0.10	TAUSSIG,RA	WI	1983	JAA			142	156
0.09	JOYCE ,EJ	AU	1982	JAR	LIBBY ,R	SUNDER,S	654	675
0.09	SCHEINER,JH	AU	1982	JAR	KIGER ,JE		482	496
0.09	SELTO ,FH	AU	1982	JAR	GROVE ,HD		676	688
0.09	SMITH ,DB	OC	1982	JAE	NICHOLS,DR		109	120
0.09	UECKER,WC	AU	1982	JAR			388	402
0.08	ALFORD,MR	SP	1981	JAA	EDMONDS,TP		255	264
0.08	FERRIS,KR	04	1980	AOS	DILLARD,JF	NETHERCOTT,L	361	368
0.08	FLAHERTY,RE	AU	1980	JAA	SCHWARTZ,BN		47	56
0.08	LOY ,LD	SP	1980	JAA	TOOLE ,HR		227	243
0.08	PURDY ,D	04	1981	AOS			327	338
0.07	BARLEV,B	AU	1979	JAR	LEVY ,H		305	315
0.07	CHAN ,JL	04	1979	AOS			273	282
0.07	DAVIDSON,S	ST	1978	JAR	WEIL ,RL		154	233
0.07	GRAY ,SJ	AU	1978	JAR			242	253
0.07	JACOBS,FH	SP	1978	JAR			190	203
0.06	BRUNS JR,WJ	ST	1966	JAR			1	14
0.06	CHOTTINER,S	AU	1971	JAR	YOUNG ,AE		367	374
0.06	DAVIDSON,S	AU	1966	JAR	KOHLMEIER,JM		183	212
0.06	FOGELBERG,G	AU	1971	JAR			215	235
0.06	FRANKFURTER,GM	AP	1972	TAR	HORWITZ,BN		245	259
0.06	HOFSTEDT,TR	AP	1971	TAR	WEST ,RR		329	337
0.06	MAGEE ,RP	JA	1977	TAR			190	199
0.06	MCCOSH,AM	04	1976	AOS	RAHMAN,M		339	356
0.06	NEUMANN,FL	JL	1969	TAR			546	554
0.06	SAN MIGUEL,JG	04	1977	AOS	SHANK ,JK	GOVINDARAJAN,V	333	348
0.06	SAULS ,EH	JA	1972	TAR			109	115
0.06	SIMPSON,RH	OC	1969	TAR			806	817
0.06	SOPER ,FJ	AP	1964	TAR	DOLPHIN,R		358	362
0.06	SPILLER JR,EA	SP	1974	JAR	VIRGIL JR,RL		112	142
0.06	STONE ,WE	JA	1965	TAR			190	195
0.00	ADESI ,GB	SU	1992	JAA	TALWAR,PP		369	378
0.00	AMERSHI,AH	JA	1990	TAR	BANKER,RD	DATAR ,SM	113	130
0.00	AMEY ,LR	AU	1988	CAR	GOFFIN,JL		174	198
0.00	AMIHUD,Y	AU	1988	JAA	MENDELSON,H		369	395
0.00	ANDERSON,U	AU	1988	AUD	YOUNG ,RA		23	42
0.00	ANTLE ,R	SP	1990	JAR	FELLINGHAM,J		1	24
0.00	ARGYRIS,C	06	1990	AOS			503	511
0.00	ARNETT,HE	JA	1965	TAR			54	64
0.00	ASHTON,RH	SU	1981	JAA	HYLAS ,RE		325	332
0.00	ASKARI,H	AP	1976	TAR	CAIN ,P	SHAW ,R	331	334
0.00	BABAD ,YM	SP	1989	CAR	BALACHANDRAN,BV		775	792
0.00	BABER ,WR	JA	1985	TAR			1	9
0.00	BACHAR,J	AU	1989	JAA			432	459
0.00	BAILEY JR,AD	SP	1968	JAR	GRAY ,J		98	105
0.00	BAIMAN,S	OC	1991	TAR	SIVARAMAKRISHNAN,K		747	767
0.00	BALACHANDRAN,BV	SP	1986	CAR			282	287
0.00	BALACHANDRAN,BV	WI	1988	JAA	RAMANAN,R		1	13
0.00	BALACHANDRAN,BV	WI	1991	JAA	PADMARAJ,RA		1	28
0.00	BALACHANDRAN,KR	02	1977	AOS	LIVINGSTONE,JL		153	164

CITE INDEX	FIRST AUTHOR	ISS-UE	YE-AR	JOUR-NAL	SECOND AUTHOR	THIRD AUTHOR	PAG BEG	PAG END
0.00	BALACHANDRAN,KR	SP	1987	JAA	SRINIDHI,BN		151	169
0.00	BALACHANDRAN,KR	WI	1992	JAA	MACHMEYER,RA		49	64
0.00	BALAKRISHNAN,R	AU	1990	CAR			105	122
0.00	BALAKRISHNAN,R	SP	1992	CAR			353	373
0.00	BALL ,R	JN	1992	JAE			309	345
0.00	BANKER,RD	JL	1988	JAE	DATAR ,SM	KEKRE ,	171	197
0.00	BANKER,RD	AU	1989	JAA	DATAR ,SM	KAPLAN,RS	528	554
0.00	BANKER,RD	SP	1990	CAR	DATAR ,SM	MAZUR ,MJ	809	824
0.00	BAO ,BE	03	1986	AOS	BAO ,DA	VASARHELYI,MA	289	296
0.00	BAR-YOSEF,S	AP	1992	TAR	SEN ,PK		320	336
0.00	BARKMAN,A	JA	1977	TAR			450	464
0.00	BARNIV,R	JL	1990	TAR			578	605
0.00	BARTON,RF	SP	1969	JAR			116	122
0.00	BAUMOL,WJ	WI	1990	JAA			105	117
0.00	BEACH ,LR	02	1989	AOS	FREDERICKSON,JR		101	112
0.00	BEAVER,WH	DE	1981	JAE	LANDSMAN,WR		233	241
0.00	BELL ,PW	SP	1987	CAR			338	367
0.00	BENISHAY,H	SU	1987	JAA			203	238
0.00	BENISHAY,H	WI	1992	JAA			97	112
0.00	BERKOWITCH,E	SP	1992	JAA	VENEZIA,I		241	250
0.00	BIDDLE,GC	AU	1990	AUD	BRUTON,CM	SIEGEL,AF	92	114
0.00	BIERMAN JR,H	SP	1985	JAA			184	194
0.00	BIERMAN JR,H	WI	1986	JAA			62	70
0.00	BOLAND,LA	AU	1992	CAR	GORDON,IM		142	170
0.00	BONETT,DG	SP	1990	CAR	CLUTE ,RD		432	445
0.00	BORITZ,JE		1990	AUD			49	87
0.00	BOWEN ,RM	OC	1982	TAR	SUNDEM,GL		778	784
0.00	BOWSHER,CA	WI	1986	JAA			7	16
0.00	BOYLE ,PP	SP	1985	CAR			116	144
0.00	BOZE ,KM	AU	1990	JAA			627	638
0.00	BRADBURY,ME	AP	1988	TAR	CALDERWOOD,SC		330	347
0.00	BRIEF ,RP	SP	1987	CAR	ANTON ,HR		394	407
0.00	BRIEF ,RP	AP	1992	TAR	LAWSON,RA		411	426
0.00	BROMWICH,M	02	1990	AOS			27	46
0.00	BROWN ,LD	SP	1986	CAR			252	258
0.00	BROWN ,LD	AU	1991	JAR	KIM ,SK		382	385
0.00	BROWN ,PR	SU	1982	JAA			282	290
0.00	BRUNSSON,N	02	1990	AOS			47	59
0.00	CALLEN,JL	SP	1988	JAA			87	108
0.00	CAMPBELL,DR	SP	1983	JAA			196	211
0.00	CHAN ,KHOC	1986	TAR	DODIN ,B			726	734
0.00	CHANDRA,R	AU	1992	CAR	ROHRBACH,KJ	WILLINGER,GL	296	305
0.00	CHEUNG,JK	SP	1990	CAR			724	737
0.00	CHEUNG,JK	SP	1990	CAR	HEANEY,J		738	760
0.00	CHOO ,F	06	1989	AOS			481	493
0.00	COASE ,RH	JA	1990	JAE			3	13
0.00	COE ,TL	SP	1979	JAA			244	253
0.00	CONROY,R	AU	1989	CAR	HUGHES,JS		159	176
0.00	CREADY,WM	JN	1991	JAE	RAMANAN,R		203	214
0.00	DANOS ,P	SP	1987	AUD	HOLT ,DL	BAILEY JR,AD	134	149
0.00	DARROUGH,MN	AU	1988	CAR			199	221
0.00	DEMSKI,JS	AP	1990	TAR	SAPPINGTON,DEM		363	383
0.00	DEMSKI,JS	AP	1990	TAR	SAPPINGTON,DEM		363	383

CITE INDEX	FIRST AUTHOR	ISS-UE	YE-AR	JOUR-NAL	SECOND AUTHOR	THIRD AUTHOR	PAG BEG	PAG END
0.00	DEMSKI,JS	JL	1992	TAR	SAPPINGTON,DEM		628	630
0.00	DEMSKI,JS	OC	1992	TAR	MAGEE ,RP		732	740
0.00	DERMER,J	02	1990	AOS			67	76
0.00	DEVINE,CT	ST	1966	JAR			160	176
0.00	DHARAN,BG	SP	1987	CAR			445	459
0.00	DHAVALE,DG	SP	1991	AUD			159	166
0.00	DOPUCH,N	SU	1988	JAA			245	250
0.00	DOPUCH,N	AU	1992	AUD			109	112
0.00	DUGAN ,MT	SP	1985	AUD	GENTRY,JA	SHRIVER,KA	11	22
0.00	DUKE ,D	WI	1991	JAA			135	142
0.00	DWORIN,L	SP	1989	CAR	GRIMLUND,RA		674	691
0.00	DYE ,RA	DE	1991	JAE			347	373
0.00	ELITZUR,RR	SP	1991	CAR			466	484
0.00	ENGSTROM,JH	SP	1984	JAA			197	211
0.00	FAIRCLOTH,AW	01	1981	AOS	RICCHIUTE,DN		53	68
0.00	FALK ,H	SP	1992	CAR			468	499
0.00	FEINSCHREIBER,R	SP	1969	JAR			17	21
0.00	FELIX JR,WL	SP	1988	AUD	NILES ,MS		43	60
0.00	FELIX JR,WL	AU	1990	AUD	GRIMLUND,RA	KOSTER,FJ	1	16
0.00	FELLINGHAM,JC	AU	1989	JAR	YOUNG ,RA		179	200
0.00	FELLINGHAM,JC	OC	1990	TAR	YOUNG ,RA		837	856
0.00	FELTHAM,GA	AU	1992	CAR	GIGLER,FB	HUGHES,JS	1	23
0.00	FINLEY,DR	SP	1987	AUD	BOOCKHOLDT,JL		22	39
0.00	FINLEY,DR	SP	1989	CAR			692	719
0.00	FIRMIN,PA	ST	1968	JAR	GOODMAN,SS	HENDRICKS,TE	122	155
0.00	FLAMHOLTZ,EG	04	1987	AOS			309	318
0.00	FOGARTY,TJ	02	1992	AOS			129	149
0.00	FOSTER III,TW	JL	1991	TAR	KOOGLER,PR	VICKREY,D	595	610
0.00	FREDRIKSON,EB	AU	1968	JAR			208	221
0.00	FRIEDLOB,GT	WI	1983	JAA			100	107
0.00	FRISHKOFF,P	AU	1984	JAA	FRISHKOFF,PA	BOUWMAN,MJ	44	53
0.00	FROST ,PA	SP	1986	JAR	TAMURA,H		57	75
0.00	GAMBLE,GO	SP	1986	JAA			102	117
0.00	GERLACH,JH	SP	1988	AUD			61	76
0.00	GIACCOTTO,C	SU	1992	JAA			291	310
0.00	GIBBONS,M	AU	1992	AUD			113	126
0.00	GOLDWASSER,DL	SU	1988	JAA			217	232
0.00	GORDON,LA	JL	1988	AUD	HAMER ,MH		514	521
0.00	GOVINDARAJ,S	AU	1992	JAA			485	508
0.00	GOVINDARAJAN,V	SU	1979	JAA			339	343
0.00	GOVINDARAJAN,V	04	1980	AOS			383	392
0.00	GRAY ,D	AU	1984	JAR			760	764
0.00	GRAY ,SJ	SP	1984	JAR	RADEBAUGH,LH		351	360
0.00	GREENBALL,MN	ST	1968	JAR			27	49
0.00	GREENWALD,B	SU	1989	JAA	STIGLITZ,JE		281	297
0.00	GRIMLUND,RA	AU	1985	JAR			575	594
0.00	GRIMLUND,RA	SP	1990	CAR			446	484
0.00	GROSSMAN,SD	WI	1981	JAA	KRATCHMAN,SH	WELKER,RB	136	143
0.00	GRUNDFEST,JA	AU	1991	JAA	SHOVEN,JB		409	442
0.00	HAKANSSON,NH	WI	1990	JAA			33	53
0.00	HALL ,TW	SP	1989	AUD	PIERCE,BJ	ROSS ,WR	64	89
0.00	HALPERIN,R	SU	1989	JAA	MAINDIRATTA,A		345	366
0.00	HAM ,J	SP	1986	CAR	LOSELL,D	SMIELIAUSKAS,W	311	317

CITE INDEX	FIRST AUTHOR	ISS-UE	YE-AR	JOUR-NAL	SECOND AUTHOR	THIRD AUTHOR	PAG BEG	PAG END
0.00	HARPER JR,RM	AU	1990	AUD	STRAWSER,JR	TANG ,K	115	133
0.00	HILTON,RW	AU	1986	CAR			50	67
0.00	HINES ,RD	04	1992	AOS			313	341
0.00	HOLDREN,GC	JA	1964	TAR			70	85
0.00	HONIG ,LE	SP	1978	JAA			231	236
0.00	HOOKS ,KL	04	1992	AOS			343	366
0.00	HORRIGAN,JO	JL	1965	TAR			558	568
0.00	HORWITZ,BN	SP	1972	JAR	YOUNG ,AE		96	107
0.00	HOUGHTON,KA	AU	1984	JAR	SENGUPTA,R		768	775
0.00	HOUGHTON,KA	SP	1984	JAR			361	368
0.00	HUNT-III,HG	05	1990	AOS	HOGLER,RL		437	454
0.00	HUSS ,HF	AU	1985	JAA			60	66
0.00	HUSSEIN,ME	AU	1986	AUD	BAVISHI,VB	GANGOLLY,JS	124	133
0.00	IJIRI ,Y	OC	1986	TAR			745	760
0.00	IVES ,M	SU	1985	JAA			253	268
0.00	JAMES ,C	SP	1989	JAA			111	124
0.00	JOHN ,K	WI	1990	JAA	RONEN ,J		61	95
0.00	JOHNSON,O	OC	1976	TAR			808	823
0.00	JONSON,LC	34	1978	AOS	JONSSON,B	SVENSSON,G	261	268
0.00	JONSSON,S	05	1988	AOS	GRONLUND,A		513	532
0.00	JORGENSON,DW	AU	1991	JAA	YUN ,K		487	508
0.00	JUNG ,WO	AU	1989	CAR			1	25
0.00	KAHN ,N	SU	1982	JAA			327	337
0.00	KATZ ,BG	SU	1987	JAA	OWEN ,J		266	298
0.00	KENNEDY,DB	SP	1992	CAR			419	442
0.00	KHOURY,SJ	SU	1990	JAA			459	473
0.00	KING ,RD	JL	1984	TAR			419	431
0.00	KING ,TE	JL	1988	AUD	ORTEGREN,AK		522	535
0.00	KNUTSON,PH	ST	1971	JAR			99	112
0.00	KO ,CE	SP	1988	AUD	NACHTSHEIM,CJ	DUKE ,GL	119	136
0.00	KORKIE,B	AU	1990	JAA	LAISS ,B		593	617
0.00	KREISER,L	AP	1977	TAR			427	437
0.00	KUBLIN,M	JL	1965	TAR			626	635
0.00	KUNITAKE,WK	SU	1986	JAA	WHITE JR,CE		222	231
0.00	LAMBERT,RA	JL	1989	TAR	LARCHER,DF		449	467
0.00	LANZILLOTTI,RF	WI	1990	JAA	ESQUIBEL,AK		125	142
0.00	LAU ,AHL	AU	1987	CAR	LAU ,HS		194	209
0.00	LEE ,CF	AP	1988	TAR	WU ,C		292	306
0.00	LEMBKE,VC	WI	1980	JAA	SMITH ,JH		147	162
0.00	LERE ,JC	AP	1986	TAR			318	324
0.00	LEV ,B	ST	1969	JAR			182	197
0.00	LEVY ,H	AU	1987	JAA	BYUN ,YH		355	369
0.00	LEWIS ,NR	34	1984	AOS	PARKER,LD	SUTCLIFFE,P	275	289
0.00	LIANG ,T-P	AU	1992	CAR	CHANDLER,JS	HAN ,I	306	328
0.00	LIM ,SS	OC	1991	TAR	SUNDER,S		669	693
0.00	LITZENBERGER,RH	SU	1989	JAA	TALMOR,E		305	316
0.00	LIVINGSTONE,JL	SP	1967	JAR			77	94
0.00	LLOYD ,BM	OC	1971	TAR	WEYGANDT,JJ		756	764
0.00	LOREK ,KS	AU	1992	AUD	BRANSON,BC	ICERMAN,RC	66	88
0.00	LOWE ,RE	OC	1965	TAR			839	846
0.00	LUDMAN,EA	SP	1986	JAA			118	124
0.00	LUNDHOLM,RJ	AU	1991	JAR			322	349
0.00	MACNAUGHTON,A	AU	1992	CAR			113	137

CITE INDEX	FIRST AUTHOR	ISS-UE	YE-AR	JOUR-NAL	SECOND AUTHOR	THIRD AUTHOR	PAG BEG	PAG END
0.00	MADDALA,GS	OC	1991	TAR			788	808
0.00	MARKOWITZ,HM	SP	1990	JAA			213	225
0.00	MATSUMURA,EM	OC	1992	TAR	TUCKER,RR		753	782
0.00	MATTESSICH,RV	SP	1986	CAR			157	178
0.00	MCGAHRAN,KT	JA	1988	TAR			23	41
0.00	MEHTA ,DR	SP	1968	JAR	ANDREWS,VL		50	57
0.00	MELLMAN,M	JA	1963	TAR			118	123
0.00	MELUMAD,N	AU	1990	CAR	THOMAN,L		22	55
0.00	MELUMAD,N	DE	1992	JAE	MOOKHERJEE,D	REICHELSTEIN,S	445	483
0.00	MENSAH,YM	AU	1988	CAR			222	249
0.00	MILLAR,JA	JA	1977	TAR			52	55
0.00	MILLS ,RH	JA	1967	TAR			74	81
0.00	MOORE ,G	SP	1987	CAR			375	383
0.00	MOORE ,G		1990	AUD	RONEN ,J		234	242
0.00	MURNIGHAN,JK	JL	1990	TAR	BAZERMAN,MH		642	657
0.00	MUTCHLER,JF	AU	1986	AUD			148	.
0.00	NAIR ,RD	SP	1983	JAA	RITTENBERG,LE		234	243
0.00	NIELSEN,CC	OC	1965	TAR			795	804
0.00	NIX ,HM	SU	1983	JAA	WICHMANN JR,H		341	352
0.00	NURNBERG,H	AU	1985	JAA	CIANCIOLO,ST		50	59
0.00	O'BRIEN,JR	AU	1990	CAR			1	21
0.00	O'BRIEN,JR	SP	1992	JAA			117	134
0.00	O'DONNELL,JL	JA	1965	TAR			135	143
0.00	O'DONNELL,JL	JL	1968	TAR			549	553
0.00	OGAN ,P	SU	1991	JAA	ZIEBART,DA		387	406
0.00	OHLSON,JA	AU	1992	JAR	SHROLL,PK		210	226
0.00	OUTSLAY,E	OC	1982	TAR	WHEELER,JE		716	733
0.00	PATTEN,RJ	OC	1964	TAR			876	879
0.00	PEEK ,LE	AU	1991	AUD	NETER ,J	WARREN,C	33	48
0.00	PELES ,YC	AP	1986	TAR			325	329
0.00	PELES ,YC	SU	1991	JAA			349	359
0.00	PENMAN,SH	AU	1992	JAA			465	484
0.00	PENNO ,M	JL	1990	TAR			520	536
0.00	PENNO ,M	ST	1991	JAR	WATTS ,JS		194	216
0.00	PINCUS,KV	SP	1990	AUD			1	20
0.00	POWELL,RM	JL	1966	TAR			525	534
0.00	POWER ,M	05	1992	AOS			477	499
0.00	POWERS,M	AP	1989	TAR	REVSINE,L		346	368
0.00	RAJAN ,MV	AU	1992	JAR			227	248
0.00	RICHARDSON,AW	SP	1988	CAR			609	614
0.00	ROBERTS,DM	SP	1986	JAR			111	126
0.00	ROBSON,K		1992	AOS			685	708
0.00	RODEN ,PF	WI	1987	JAA			79	89
0.00	ROHRBACH.KJ	SP	1986	JAR			127	150
0.00	ROSHWALB,A	AU	1987	AUD	WRIGHT,RL	GODFREY,JT	54	70
0.00	ROSHWALB,A	AP	1991	TAR	WRIGHT,RL		348	360
0.00	ROUSSEY,RS	SP	1992	AUD			47	57
0.00	RUBENSTEIN,DB	05	1992	AOS			501	508
0.00	RUE ,JC	SU	1984	JAA	VOLKAN,AG		306	322
0.00	RUNDFELT,R	SP	1986	JAA			125	130
0.00	SAMUELSON,LA	01	1986	AOS			35	46
0.00	SAN MIGUEL,JG	JL	1977	TAR			638	641
0.00	SANSING,RC	AU	1992	CAR			33	45

CITE INDEX	FIRST AUTHOR	ISS-UE	YE-AR	JOUR-NAL	SECOND AUTHOR	THIRD AUTHOR	PAG BEG	PAG END
0.00	SCHACHTER,B	AU	1985	JAR			907	910
0.00	SCHIFF,M	SP	1979	JAA			224	231
0.00	SCHOLES,MS	AU	1991	JAA	WOLFSON,MA		513	532
0.00	SCHWARTZ,BN	SP	1983	JAA			244	253
0.00	SENNETTI,JT	SP	1990	AUD			103	112
0.00	SHAFER,G		1990	AUD	SRIVASTAVA,R		110	137
0.00	SIMUNIC,DA	SP	1990	CAR	STEIN ,MT		329	343
0.00	SINGER,FA	OC	1965	TAR			847	853
0.00	SMIELIAUSKAS,W	SP	1989	CAR			720	732
0.00	SMIELIAUSKAS,W		1990	AUD			149	166
0.00	SMIELIAUSKAS,W	SP	1990	CAR	SMITH ,L		407	426
0.00	SOMEYA,K	OC	1964	TAR			983	989
0.00	SORTER,GH	SP	1987	JAA	INGBERMAN,M		99	116
0.00	SPENCER,CH	JA	1965	TAR	BARNISEL,TS		144	153
0.00	SRIVASTAVA,RP	AU	1986	JAR			422	427
0.00	ST.PIERRE,K	SP	1982	JAA	ANDERSON,JA		229	247
0.00	STEIN ,JL	SP	1990	JAA	HONG ,BG		277	300
0.00	STERLING,RR	OC	1972	TAR	TOLLEFSON,SO	FLAHERTY,RE	709	721
0.00	STICE ,JD	JL	1991	TAR			516	534
0.00	SUNDER,S	SP	1989	CAR			452	460
0.00	TAMURA,H	SP	1985	AUD			133	142
0.00	TELSER,LG	SP	1990	JAA			159	201
0.00	TEOH ,SH	SP	1992	JAR			1	23
0.00	THIES ,CF	AU	1987	JAA	STURROCK,T		375	391
0.00	TRADER,RL	AU	1987	CAR	HUSS ,HF		227	239
0.00	TRUEMAN,B	AU	1990	CAR			203	222
0.00	TRUEMAN,B	OC	1990	JAE			285	301
0.00	USRY ,MF	OC	1966	TAR			754	762
0.00	VATTER,WJ	OC	1967	TAR			721	730
0.00	VICKREY,D	JL	1992	TAR			623	627
0.00	VOSS ,WM	AU	1968	JAR			262	269
0.00	WALKER,M	06	1989	AOS			433	453
0.00	WALKER,NR	AU	1988	AUD	PIERCE,LT		1	22
0.00	WAND ,Y	JA	1989	TAR	WEBER ,R		87	107
0.00	WELSH ,MJ	WI	1985	JAA	TRAPNELL,JE		100	111
0.00	WENSLEY,AKP		1990	AUD			49	87
0.00	WHEELER,S	JL	1990	TAR	PANY ,K		557	577
0.00	WHITE ,LJ	SP	1991	JAA			289	302
0.00	WILD ,JJ	SP	1987	JAR			139	160
0.00	WILD ,JJ	JA	1990	TAR	BIGGS ,SF		227	241
0.00	WILKERSON JR,JE	SP	1987	JAR			161	167
0.00	WILLINGER,GL	SP	1985	JAR			351	359
0.00	WILSON,AC	SP	1989	AUD	GLEZEN,GW		90	100
0.00	WINBORNE,MG	JL	1964	TAR			622	626
0.00	WRIGHT,A	JL	1983	TAR			621	632
0.00	WRIGHT,DW	SP	1991	AUD			145	158
0.00	WRIGHT,GB	SU	1982	JAA	TAYLOR,RD		301	309
0.00	WURST ,J	AP	1991	TAR	NETER ,J	GODFREY,J	333	347
0.00	YOON ,SS		1990	AUD			253	275
0.00	YOUNG ,A	WI	1991	JAA			129	133
0.00	YOUNG ,AE	SP	1978	JAA			217	230
0.00	YOUNG ,SD	SP	1985	JAA			178	183
0.00	ZIEBART,DA	AU	1985	JAR			920	926

CITE INDEX	FIRST AUTHOR	ISS-UE	YE-AR	JOUR-NAL	SECOND AUTHOR	THIRD AUTHOR	PAG BEG	PAG END

1.2 MODE OF REASONING (METHOD)=QUANTITATIVE: REGRESSION

CITE INDEX	FIRST AUTHOR	ISS-UE	YE-AR	JOUR-NAL	SECOND AUTHOR	THIRD AUTHOR	PAG BEG	PAG END
6.00	HEALY ,PM	AP	1985	JAE			85	108
5.50	COLLINS,DW	JL	1989	JAE	KOTHARI,SP	143	181	
5.50	EASTON,PD	JL	1989	JAE	ZMIJEWSKI,ME	117	141	
5.35	BEAVER,WH	ST	1968	JAR			67	92
5.18	PATELL,JM	AU	1976	JAR			246	276
5.17	BROWN ,LD	JL	1987	JAE	GRIFFIN,PA	HAGERMAN,RL	159	193
5.00	OU ,JA	NV	1989	JAE			295	329
5.00	PENMAN,SH	NV	1989	JAE			295	329
4.88	ATIASE,RK	SP	1985	JAR			21	36
4.80	O'BRIEN,PC	JA	1988	JAE			53	83
4.50	BERNARD,VL	SP	1987	JAR			1	48
4.50	BROWN ,LD	AP	1987	JAE	GRIFFIN,PA	HAGERMAN,RL	61	87
4.50	FREEMAN,RN	JL	1987	JAE			195	228
4.33	COLLINS,DW	JL	1987	JAE	KOTHARI,SP	RAYBURN,JD	111	138
4.31	BEAVER,WH	MR	1980	JAE	LAMBERT,RA	MORSE ,D	3	28
3.67	LIPE ,R	JA	1990	TAR			49	71
3.50	BERNARD,VL	ST	1989	JAR	THOMAS,JK		1	36
3.50	EASTON,PD	SP	1991	JAR	HARRIS,TS		19	36
3.33	ARMSTRONG,P	05	1987	AOS			415	436
3.33	BEAVER,WH	JL	1987	JAE	LAMBERT,RA	RYAN ,SG	139	157
3.33	CHAMBERS,AE	SP	1984	JAR	PENMAN,SH		21	47
3.33	COLLINS,DW	MR	1981	JAE	ROZEFF,MS	DHALIWAL,DS	37	71
3.33	HOLTHAUSEN,RW	MR	1981	JAE			73	109
3.33	PRESS ,EG	JA	1990	JAE	WEINTROP,JB		65	95
3.25	OU ,JA	ST	1989	JAR	PENMAN,SH		111	144
3.00	ABDOLMOHAMMADI,MJ	JA	1987	TAR	WRIGHT,A		1	13
3.00	BERRY ,AJ	01	1985	AOS	CAPPS ,T	COOPER,D	3	28
3.00	DUKE ,JC	JA	1990	JAE	HUNT III,HG		45	63
3.00	GREIG ,AC	JN	1992	JAE			413	442
3.00	LIBBY ,R	AU	1985	JAR			648	667
3.00	ROGERSON,WP	OC	1992	TAR			671	690
3.00	STOBER,TL	JN	1992	JAE			347	372
3.00	WILSON,GP	AP	1987	TAR			293	322
2.89	FOSTER,G	OC	1984	TAR	OLSEN ,C	SHEVLIN,T	574	603
2.86	LIPE ,RC	ST	1986	JAR			37	68
2.86	RAYBURN,J	ST	1986	JAR			112	137
2.67	BERNARD,VL	DE	1990	JAE	THOMAS,JK		305	340
2.50	SCHIPPER,K	SP	1983	JAR	THOMPSON,R		184	221
2.43	ANTLE ,R	SP	1986	JAR	SMITH ,A		1	39
2.40	ASHTON,AH	OC	1988	TAR	ASHTON,RH		623	641
2.40	LARCKER,DF	AP	1983	JAE			3	30
2.40	MCNICHOLS,M	ST	1988	JAR	WILSON,GP		1	40
2.38	DYE ,RA	SP	1985	JAR			123	145
2.33	CHRISTIE,AA	JA	1990	JAE			15	36
2.33	LIBBY ,R	AU	1990	JAR	FREDERICK,DM		348	367
2.29	BALL ,R	ST	1972	JAR			1	38
2.27	RICKS ,WE	AU	1982	JAR			367	387
2.23	PENMAN,SH	SP	1980	JAR			132	160
2.23	SIMUNIC,DA	SP	1980	JAR			161	190
2.18	BROWNELL,P	SP	1982	JAR			12	27
2.14	KINNEY JR,WR	MR	1986	JAE			73	89

CITE INDEX	FIRST AUTHOR	ISS-UE	YE-AR	JOUR-NAL	SECOND AUTHOR	THIRD AUTHOR	PAG BEG	PAG END
2.14	WILSON GP	ST	1986	JAR			165	203
2.00	ALI ,A	JN	1992	JAE	ZAROWIN,P		249	264
2.00	EASTON,PD	JN	1992	JAE	HARRIS,TS	OHLSON,JA	119	142
2.00	FREDERICK,DM	AU	1986	JAR	LIBBY ,R		270	290
2.00	FREDERICK,DM	AP	1991	TAR			240	258
2.00	GRANT ,EB	SP	1980	JAR			255	268
2.00	HOLTHAUSEN,RW	JN	1992	JAE	LARCKER,DF		373	411
2.00	KOTHARI,SP	JN	1992	JAE	SLAON ,RG		143	171
2.00	LEV ,B	ST	1989	JAR			153	192
2.00	SUNDER,S	ST	1973	JAR			1	45
2.00	THOMAS,JK	OC	1992	TAR	TUNG ,S		691	711
1.93	LEV ,B	JL	1979	TAR			485	503
1.91	PATELL,JM	JL	1982	TAR	WOLFSON,MA		509	527
1.89	LYS ,T	AP	1984	JAE			39	65
1.88	GONEDES,NJ	AU	1975	JAR			220	256
1.86	PALMROSE,ZV	SP	1986	JAR			97	110
1.82	BEAVER,WH	OC	1970	TAR	KETTLER,P	SCHOLES,M	654	682
1.82	LILIEN,S	DE	1982	JAE	PASTENA,V		145	170
1.80	COVALESKI,MA	01	1988	AOS	DIRSMITH,MW	1	24	
1.76	MAY ,RG	ST	1971	JAR			119	163
1.75	ABDEL-KHALIK,AR	AU	1985	JAR			427	447
1.75	FREEMAN,RN	ST	1989	JAR	TSE ,S		49	79
1.75	MOECKEL,CL	OC	1989	TAR	PLUMLEE,RD		653	666
1.75	MORSE ,D	AU	1981	JAR			374	383
1.71	BAMBER,LS	SP	1986	JAR			40	56
1.71	LIBERTY,SE	OC	1986	TAR	ZIMMERMAN,JL		692	712
1.67	BONNER,SE	JA	1990	TAR			72	92
1.67	BOWEN ,RM	OC	1987	TAR	BURGSTAHLER,D	DALEY ,LA	723	747
1.67	COLLINS,DW	OC	1990	JAE	DeANGELO,L		213	247
1.67	LAMBERT,RA	ST	1987	JAR	LARCKER,DF		85	125
1.67	TUBBS ,RM	AP	1990	TAR	MESSIER JR,WF	KNECHEL,WR	452	460
1.67	WAYMIRE,G	AU	1984	JAR			703	718
1.64	GIVOLY,D	JL	1982	TAR	PALMON,D		486	508
1.63	MURPHY,KJ	AP	1985	JAE			11	42
1.62	BEAVER,WH	AG	1980	JAE	CHRISTIE,AA	GRIFFIN,PA	127	157
1.60	DEANGELO,LE	JA	1988	JAE			3	36
1.59	BEAVER,WH	AP	1972	TAR	DUKES ,RE		320	332
1.57	BROWNELL,P	OC	1986	TAR	MCINNES,M		587	600
1.56	DODD ,P	AP	1984	JAE	DOPUCH,N	HOLTHAUSEN,RW	3	38
1.56	KROSS ,W	SP	1984	JAR	SCHROEDER,DA		153	176
1.50	ARMSTRONG,P	02	1985	AOS			129	148
1.50	BAMBER,LS	JL	1987	TAR			510	532
1.50	BARTOV,E	SE	1991	JAE			275	293
1.50	BROWN ,LD	SP	1987	JAR	RICHARDSON,GD	SCHWAGER,SJ	49	67
1.50	BROWNELL,P	OC	1981	TAR			844	860
1.50	FRANCIS,JR	JA	1987	TAR	SIMON ,DT		145	157
1.50	HAND ,JRM	OC	1989	TAR			587	623
1.50	HARRIS,TS	OC	1987	TAR	OHLSON,JA		651	670
1.50	HEALY ,PM	AP	1987	JAE	KANG ,SH	PALEPU,KG	7	34
1.50	HUNT III,HG	AU	1985	JAR			448	467
1.50	NEU ,D	02	1991	AOS			185	200
1.47	SUNDER,S	AP	1975	TAR			305	315
1.43	AYRES ,FL	JN	1986	JAE			143	158

CITE INDEX	FIRST AUTHOR	ISS-UE	YE-AR	JOUR-NAL	SECOND AUTHOR	THIRD AUTHOR	PAG BEG	PAG END
1.43	DEANGELO,LE	JL	1986	TAR			400	420
1.43	HOSKIN,RE	ST	1986	JAR	HUGHES,JS	RICKS ,WE	1	36
1.43	JIAMBALVO,J	AU	1979	JAR			436	455
1.43	NEIMARK,M	45	1986	AOS	TINKER,T		369	396
1.43	PALEPU,KG	MR	1986	JAE			3	36
1.40	BIGGS ,SF	JA	1988	TAR	MOCK ,TJ	WATKINS,P	148	162
1.40	NOREEN,EW	SP	1988	JAR			119	133
1.40	PALMROSE,ZV	JA	1988	TAR			55	73
1.40	SIMON ,DT	AP	1988	TAR	FRANCIS,JR		255	269
1.38	BUBLITZ,B	ST	1985	JAR	FRECKA,TJ	MCKEOWN,JC	1	23
1.38	GOVINDARAJAN,V	01	1985	AOS	GUPTA ,AK		51	66
1.38	LEE ,CJ	AU	1985	JAR	HSIEH ,DA		468	485
1.33	FRANCIS,JR	AP	1987	JAE	REITER,SA		35	59
1.33	HEALY ,PM	A	1990	JAE	PALEPU,KG		97	123
1.33	LEV ,B	SP	1990	JAR	PENMAN,SH		49	76
1.33	OU ,JA	SP	1990	JAR			144	163
1.31	BROWN ,RM	SP	1980	JAR			38	63
1.29	ZIMMER,I	MR	1986	JAE			37	52
1.27	FREEMAN,RN	AU	1982	JAR	OHLSON,JA	PENMAN,SH	639	653
1.25	ASHTON,AH	AP	1985	TAR			173	185
1.25	BAIMAN,S	SP	1989	JAR	LEWIS ,BL		1	20
1.25	BEDARD,JC	02	1989	AOS			113	131
1.25	BERNARD,VL	OC	1989	TAR	STOBER,TL		624	652
1.25	CORNELL,B	OC	1989	TAR	LANDSMAN,WR		680	692
1.25	COUGHLAN,AT	AP	1985	JAE	SCHMIDT,RM		43	66
1.25	DEJONG,DV	AU	1985	JAR	FORSYTHE,R	UECKER,WC	753	793
1.25	HAN ,JCY	FB	1989	JAE	WILD ,JJ	RAMESH,K	3	33
1.25	MCNICHOLS,M	JA	1989	TAR			1	27
1.20	BUTT ,JL	AU	1988	JAR			315	330
1.20	DOPUCH,N	SP	1988	JAR	PINCUS,M		28	59
1.20	THOMAS,JK	JL	1988	JAE			199	237
1.20	WALLER,WS	01	1988	AOS			87	98
1.17	ANSARI,SL	06	1987	AOS	EUSKE ,KJ		549	570
1.17	THOMPSON II,RB	AU	1987	JAR	OLSEN ,C	DIETRICH,JR	245	274
1.15	RO ,BT	AG	1980	JAE			159	189
1.14	BROWNELL,P	AU	1986	JAR	HIRST ,MK		241	249
1.14	COVALESKI,MA	03	1986	AOS	DIRSMITH,MW		193	214
1.14	LANDSMAN,WR	OC	1986	TAR			662	691
1.14	WILLMOTT,H	06	1986	AOS			555	582
1.13	FERRIS,KR	JL	1977	TAR			605	615
1.13	HOPWOOD,AG	03	1985	AOS			361	376
1.12	FOSTER,G	SP	1973	JAR			25	37
1.11	HAGERMAN,RL	AU	1984	JAR	ZMIJEWSKI,ME	SHAH ,P	526	540
1.08	PATELL,JM	AU	1981	JAR	WOLFSON,MA		434	458
1.07	COLLINS,F	AP	1978	TAR			324	335
1.06	HARRISON,T	SP	1977	JAR			84	107
1.00	ANTHONY,JH	JN	1992	JAE	RAMESH,K		203	227
1.00	ANTLE ,R	SP	1985	JAR	SMITH ,A		296	325
1.00	BALL ,R	OC	1991	TAR	KOTHARI,SP		718	738
1.00	BARTH ,ME	JA	1991	TAR	BEAVER,WH	STINSON,CH	56	66
1.00	BEAVER,WH	AU	1989	JAR	EGER ,C	RYAN ,S	157	178
1.00	BHUSHAN,R	JL	1989	JAE			183	206
1.00	BIDDLE,GC	SP	1991	JAA	SEOW ,GS		183	232

CITE INDEX	FIRST AUTHOR	ISS-UE	YE-AR	JOUR-NAL	SECOND AUTHOR	THIRD AUTHOR	PAG BEG	PAG END
1.00	BOUWMAN,MJ	01	1987	AOS	FRISHKOFF,PA	FRISHKOFF,P	1	30
1.00	CHENG ,CSA	JL	1992	TAR	HOPWOOD,WS	MCKEOWN,JC	579	598
1.00	CUSHING,BE	AP	1992	TAR	LECLERE,MJ		355	367
1.00	DANN ,LY	SE	1991	JAE	MASULIS,RW	MAYERS,	217	251
1.00	DOPUCH,N	JL	1987	TAR	HOLTHAUSEN,RW	LEFTWICH,RW	431	454
1.00	DOPUCH,N	JA	1992	TAR	KING ,RR		97	120
1.00	DORAN ,BM	JL	1988	TAR	COLLINS,DW	DHALIWAL,DS	389	413
1.00	ELLIOTT,JA	AU	1982	JAR			617	638
1.00	FELLINGHAM,JC	OC	1985	TAR	NEWMAN,DP		634	650
1.00	FRANCIS,JR	AG	1984	JAE			133	151
1.00	FREEMAN,RN	AU	1992	JAR	TSE ,SY		185	209
1.00	HERTZER,M	SE	1991	JAE	JAIN ,PC		253	273
1.00	HILL ,JW	OC	1989	TAR	INGRAM,RW		667	679
1.00	HINES ,RD	04	1991	AOS			313	331
1.00	HUGHES,JS	JA	1987	TAR	RICKS ,WE		158	175
1.00	HUIZING,A	05	1992	AOS	DEKKER,HC		427	448
1.00	IMHOFF JR,EA	AP	1992	TAR	LOBO ,GJ		427	439
1.00	JANAKIRAMAN,SN	SP	1992	JAR	LAMBERT,RA	LARCKER,DF	53	69
1.00	JOHNSON,WB	JA	1990	JAE	LYS ,T		281	308
1.00	KING ,RR	SP	1990	CAR	WALLIN,DE		859	892
1.00	KING ,RR	SP	1991	JAR	WALLIN,DE		96	108
1.00	KINNEY-JR,WR	FB	1989	JAE	MCDANIEL,LS		71	93
1.00	KIRKHAM,LM	04	1992	AOS			287	297
1.00	LEE ,CMC	JN	1992	JAE			265	302
1.00	LEHMAN,CR	04	1992	AOS			261	285
1.00	LUSTGARTEN,S	OC	1982	JAE			121	141
1.00	LYS ,T	DE	1990	JAE	SOHN ,S		341	363
1.00	MCNAIR,CJ		1991	AOS			635	653
1.00	MILLER,P	04	1990	AOS			315	338
1.00	MOSER ,DV	JL	1989	TAR			433	448
1.00	NEU ,D	04	1992	AOS			223	237
1.00	PINCH ,T	03	1989	AOS	MULKAY,M	ASHMORE,	271	301
1.00	PRESTON,AM	06	1992	AOS	COOPER,DJ	COOMBS,RW	561	593
1.00	RICHARDSON,AJ	06	1989	AOS			415	431
1.00	ROBERTS,J	02	1990	AOS			107	126
1.00	SHORES,D	SP	1990	JAR			164	181
1.00	WALLIN,DE	JA	1992	TAR			121	147
0.94	GONEDES,NJ	AU	1973	JAR			212	237
0.94	GONEDES,NJ	SP	1974	JAR			26	62
0.89	DALEY ,LA	AP	1984	TAR			177	198
0.89	DYCKMAN,TR	ST	1984	JAR	PHILBRICK,D	STEPHAN,J	1	30
0.89	HUGHES,JS	AG	1984	JAE	RICKS ,WE		101	132
0.89	KELLOGG,RL	DE	1984	JAE			185	204
0.88	ARCHIBALD,TR	JA	1972	TAR			22	30
0.88	BROWN ,LD	AP	1985	TAR	GARDNER,JC		262	277
0.88	BROWNELL,P	AU	1985	JAR			502	512
0.88	DEJONG,DV	ST	1985	JAR	FORSYTHE,R	LUNDHOLM,RJ	81	120
0.88	HAM ,J	JL	1985	TAR	LOSELL,D	SMIELIAUSKAS,W	387	406
0.88	MUTCHLER,JF	AU	1985	JAR			668	682
0.88	YOUNG ,SM	AU	1985	JAR			829	842
0.87	KINNEY JR,WR	JA	1978	TAR			48	60
0.86	BROWN ,LD	AU	1979	JAR	ROZEFF,MS		341	351
0.86	CHENHALL,RH	JA	1986	TAR	MORRIS,D		16	35

CITE INDEX	FIRST AUTHOR	ISS-UE	YE-AR	JOUR-NAL	SECOND AUTHOR	THIRD AUTHOR	PAG BEG	PAG END
0.86	EL-GAZZAR,S	OC	1986	JAE	LILIEN,S	PASTENA,V	217	238
0.86	KAPLAN,RS	45	1986	AOS			429	452
0.83	ATIASE,RK	SP	1987	JAR			168	176
0.83	BAGINSKI,SP	AU	1987	JAR			196	216
0.83	JENNINGS,R	SP	1987	JAR			90	110
0.83	SIMONS,R	04	1987	AOS			357	374
0.83	STONE ,M	AU	1987	JAR			317	326
0.83	WALLACE,WA	AU	1981	JAR			502	520
0.82	JAIN ,PC	DE	1982	JAE			205	228
0.81	JOY ,OM	AU	1977	JAR	LITZENBERGER,RH	MCENALLY,RW	207	225
0.80	BALVERS,RJ	OC	1988	TAR	MCDONALD,B	MILLER,R	605	622
0.80	CHOW ,CW	JA	1988	TAR	COOPER,JC	WALLER,WS	111	122
0.80	MORRIS,MH	AP	1988	TAR	NICHOLS,WD		237	254
0.80	RUBIN ,MA	AP	1988	TAR			219	236
0.80	SOETERS,J	01	1988	AOS	SCHREUDER,H		75	85
0.75	BROWN ,LD	SP	1985	JAR	GARDNER,JC		84	109
0.75	BUTT ,JL	06	1989	AOS	CAMPBELL,TL		471	479
0.75	DEFEO ,VJ	AP	1989	TAR	LAMBER,RA	LARCKER,DF	201	227
0.75	FROST ,CA	OC	1989	TAR			788	808
0.75	LIBBY ,R	AP	1985	TAR	ARTMAN,JT	WILLINGHAM,JJ	212	230
0.75	LINDAHL,FW	AU	1989	JAR			201	226
0.75	MERCHANT,KA	02	1985	AOS			201	210
0.75	MIA ,L	04	1989	AOS			347	357
0.75	MITTELSTAEDT,HF	NV	1989	JAE			399	418
0.75	NIEHAUS,GR	AP	1989	TAR			269	284
0.75	OLSEN ,C	ST	1985	JAR	DIETRICH,JR		144	166
0.75	PALMROSE,Z	JL	1989	TAR			488	499
0.75	POWNALL,G	AU	1989	JAR	WAYMIRE,G		227	245
0.75	STICKEL,SE	JL	1989	JAE			275	292
0.75	THOMAS,JK	NV	1989	JAE			361	398
0.75	WALLER,WS	JL	1985	TAR	CHOW ,CW		458	476
0.71	BEAVER,WH	JL	1973	TAR	DUKES ,RE		549	559
0.71	BOWEN ,RM	OC	1986	TAR	BURGSTAHLER,D	DALEY ,LA	713	725
0.71	LOREK ,KS	SP	1979	JAR			190	204
0.71	MAGLIOLO,J	ST	1986	JAR			69	111
0.71	PASTENA,V	AP	1986	TAR	RULAND,W		288	301
0.71	RICKS ,WE	SP	1986	JAR			206	216
0.71	STOBER,TL	ST	1986	JAR			138	164
0.71	THORNTON,DB	AU	1986	CAR			1	34
0.69	SENATRA,PT	OC	1980	TAR			594	603
0.67	ABDEL-KHALIK,AR	SP	1990	CAR			295	322
0.67	ASHTON,RH	ST	1990	JAR			148	186
0.67	AWASTHI,V	OC	1990	TAR	PRATT ,J		797	811
0.67	BABER ,WR	AU	1987	JAR	BROOKS,EH	RICKS ,WE	293	305
0.67	BONNER,SE	ST	1990	JAR	LEWIS ,BL		1	28
0.67	BOWEN ,RM	JA	1981	TAR			1	22
0.67	CLINCH,GJ	AP	1987	JAE	SINCLAIR,NA		89	106
0.67	DEANGELO,LE	JA	1990	TAR			93	112
0.67	ELIAS ,N	JL	1990	TAR			606	623
0.67	ETTREDGE,M	SP	1990	JAR	GREENBERG,R		198	210
0.67	HARRIS,TS	OC	1990	TAR	OHLSON,JA		764	780
0.67	HASKINS,M	JL	1987	TAR			542	563
0.67	HASKINS,ME	SP	1990	CAR	BAGLIONI,AJ	COOPER,CL	361	385

CITE INDEX	FIRST AUTHOR	ISS-UE	YE-AR	JOUR-NAL	SECOND AUTHOR	THIRD AUTHOR	PAG BEG	PAG END
0.67	HEALY ,PM	SP	1990	JAR	PALEPU,KG		25	48
0.67	HEIMAN,VB	OC	1990	TAR			875	890
0.67	KACHELMEIER,SJ	JA	1990	TAR	MESSIER JR,WF		209	226
0.67	KELLY ,T	SP	1990	AUD	MARGHEIM,L		21	42
0.67	KROSS ,W	AP	1990	TAR	RO ,B	SCHROEDER,	461	476
0.67	MACINTOSH,NB	01	1987	AOS	DAFT ,RL		49	61
0.67	MALMQUIST,DH	JA	1990	JAE			173	205
0.67	MIAN ,SL	JA	1990	JAE	SMITH JR,CW		141	171
0.67	MILLER,P	05	1990	AOS	O'LEARY,T		479	498
0.67	O'BRIEN,PC	ST	1990	JAR	BHUSHAN,R		55	82
0.67	PONEMON,LA	AU	1990	CAR	GABHART,DRL		227	251
0.67	ROBERTS,RW	SP	1990	JAR	GLEZEN,GW	JONES ,TW	220	228
0.67	SCHAEFER,TF	AU	1984	JAR			647	656
0.67	WHITTRED,G	DE	1987	JAE			259	285
0.67	WILSON JR,TE	SP	1990	AUD	GRIMLUND,RA		43	59
0.65	LOREK ,KS	AP	1976	TAR	MCDONALD,CL	PATZ ,DH	321	330
0.63	BRICKLEY,JA	AP	1985	JAE	BHAGAT,S	LEASE ,RC	115	130
0.63	DIRSMITH,MW	02	1985	AOS	COVALESKI,MA		149	170
0.63	EASTON,PD	ST	1985	JAR			54	77
0.63	GIVOLY,D	JL	1985	TAR			372	386
0.63	HAKA ,SF	OC	1985	TAR	GORDON,LA	PINCHES,GE	651	669
0.63	MERCHANT,KA	01	1985	AOS			67	86
0.63	PENNO ,M	SP	1985	JAR			240	255
0.63	WRIGHT,WF	JL	1977	TAR			676	689
0.60	ABDEL-KHALIK,AR	SP	1978	JAR	ESPEJO,J		1	13
0.60	ABDEL-KHALIK,AR	ST	1988	JAR			144	181
0.60	BELL ,TB	SP	1983	JAR			1	17
0.60	BIRNBERG,JG	05	1988	AOS	SNODGRASS,C		447	464
0.60	FRANCIS,JR	OC	1988	TAR	WILSON,ER		663	682
0.60	GRIMLUND,RA	AU	1988	AUD	SCHROEDER,MS		53	62
0.60	HIRST ,MK	AU	1983	JAR			596	605
0.60	JIAMBALVO,J	01	1983	AOS	WATSON,DJ	BAUMLER,JV	13	30
0.60	JOHNSON,WB	AU	1988	JAR	DHALIWAL,DS		236	272
0.60	LILIEN,S	OC	1988	TAR	MELLMAN,M	PASTENA,V	642	656
0.60	LUKKA ,K	03	1988	AOS			281	301
0.60	MCNICHOLS,M	JL	1988	JAE			239	273
0.60	NAHAPIET,JE	04	1988	AOS			333	358
0.60	RICHARDSON,AJ	04	1988	AOS			381	396
0.60	SUTTON,TG	AP	1988	JAE			127	149
0.60	WONG ,J	JA	1988	JAE			37	51
0.60	WONG ,J	AP	1988	JAE			151	167
0.57	BOLAND,RJ	45	1986	AOS	PONDY ,LR		403	422
0.57	CHOO ,F	SP	1986	AUD			17	34
0.57	DANOS ,P	OC	1986	TAR	EICHENSEHER,JW		633	650
0.57	DOPUCH,N	JN	1986	JAE	HOLTHAUSEN,RW	LEFTWICH,RW	93	118
0.57	HASSELL,JM	JA	1986	TAR	JENNINGS,RH		58	75
0.57	JARRELL,GA	AG	1979	JAE			93	116
0.57	MARGHEIM,LL	SP	1986	AUD	PANY ,K		50	63
0.57	SHRIVER,KA	SP	1986	JAR			151	165
0.56	BATHKE,AW	AP	1984	TAR	LOREK ,KS		163	176
0.56	IMHOFF JR,EA	AU	1984	JAR	LOBO ,GJ		541	554
0.56	SIMUNIC,DA	AU	1984	JAR			679	702
0.56	WILSON,ER	SP	1984	JAR	HOWARD,TP		207	224

CITE INDEX	FIRST AUTHOR	ISS-UE	YE-AR	JOUR-NAL	SECOND AUTHOR	THIRD AUTHOR	PAG BEG	PAG END
0.55	BANKS ,DW	SP	1982	JAR	KINNEY JR,WR		240	254
0.55	DIETRICH,JR	JA	1982	TAR	KAPLAN,RS		18	38
0.55	HOPWOOD,WS	AU	1982	JAR	MCKEOWN,JC	NEWBOLD,P	343	349
0.53	BEIDLEMAN,CR	OC	1973	TAR			653	667
0.50	AJINKYA,BB	NV	1989	JAE	JAIN ,PC		331	359
0.50	ASHTON,RH	SP	1981	JAR			42	61
0.50	ATIASE,RK	SP	1989	CAR	BAMBER,LS	TSE ,S	526	552
0.50	BABER ,WR	DE	1983	JAE			213	227
0.50	BALAKRISHNAN,R	JA	1991	TAR			120	140
0.50	BAMBER,EM	AP	1989	TAR	SNOWBALL,D	TUBBS ,RM	285	299
0.50	BEATTY,RP	OC	1989	TAR			693	709
0.50	BECK ,PJ	JL	1989	TAR	JUNG ,W		468	487
0.50	BECK ,PJ	JL	1991	TAR	DAVIS ,JS	JUNG ,W	535	558
0.50	BEDARD,JC	JL	1991	TAR	BIGGS ,SF		622	642
0.50	BHUSHAN,R	JL	1989	JAE			255	274
0.50	BIGGS ,SF	OC	1985	TAR	WILD ,JJ		607	633
0.50	BIGGS ,SF	SP	1987	AUD	MESSIER JR,WF	HANSEN,JV	1	21
0.50	BOUGEN,PD	03	1989	AOS			203	234
0.50	BROWN ,C	JL	1987	TAR	SOLOMON,I		564	577
0.50	BROWN ,CE	JA	1991	TAR	SOLOMON,I		100	119
0.50	BROWN ,LD	02	1987	AOS	GARDNER,JC	VASARHELYI,MA	193	204
0.50	BROWN ,LD	SP	1991	CAR	RICHARDSON,GD	TRZCINKA,CA	323	346
0.50	BROWNELL,P	AU	1983	JAR			456	472
0.50	BRYER ,RA	05	1991	AOS			439	486
0.50	BUBLITZ,B	JA	1989	TAR	ETTREDGE,M		108	124
0.50	CHEWNING,G	SP	1989	JAR	PANY ,K	WHEELER,S	78	96
0.50	CHOO ,F	JL	1991	TAR	TROTMAN,KT		464	485
0.50	CHOW ,CW	SP	1987	AUD	MCNAMEE,AH	PLUMLEE,RD	123	133
0.50	CHURCH,BK	SP	1991	CAR			513	534
0.50	COHEN ,J	AU	1989	JAR	KIDA ,T		263	276
0.50	COLLINS,F	JA	1987	TAR	MUNTER,P	FINN ,DW	29	49
0.50	COLLINS,JH	JL	1991	TAR	PLUMLEE,RD		559	576
0.50	CREADY,WM	AP	1991	TAR	MYNATT,PG		291	312
0.50	DIRSMITH,MW	AU	1985	CAR	COVALESKI,MA	MCALLISTER,JP	46	68
0.50	DOPUCH,N	SP	1989	CAR			494	500
0.50	DUNK ,AS	04	1989	AOS			321	324
0.50	DYE ,RA	AU	1985	JAR			544	574
0.50	ELY ,KM	SP	1991	JAR			37	58
0.50	FARMER,TA	AU	1987	AUD	RITTENBERG,LE	TROMPETER,GM	1	14
0.50	FELTHAM,GA	DE	1991	JAE	HUGHES,JS	SIMUNIC,DA	375	399
0.50	FEROZ ,EH	ST	1991	JAR	PARK ,K	PASTENA,VS	107	148
0.50	FREEMAN,RN	SP	1983	JAR			42	64
0.50	GHICAS,D	AU	1989	CAR	PASTENA,V		125	142
0.50	HARRELL,A	03	1989	AOS	TAYLOR,M	CHEWNING,E	259	269
0.50	HARTE ,GF	02	1987	AOS	OWEN ,DL		123	142
0.50	HIRSCHEY,M	SP	1985	JAR	WEYGANDT,JJ		326	335
0.50	JOHNSON,PE	02	1989	AOS	JAMAL ,K	BERRYMAN,RG	83	99
0.50	JONES ,JJ	AU	1991	JAR			193	228
0.50	KOTHARI,SP	AP	1989	TAR	WASLEY,CE		228	249
0.50	L'HER ,JF	SP	1991	CAR	SURET ,J-M		378	406
0.50	LARCKER,DF	OC	1983	TAR	REVSINE,L		706	732
0.50	LEE ,CWJ	AU	1989	JAR	PETRUZZI,CR		277	296
0.50	LEWELLEN,W	AP	1985	JAE	LODERER,C	ROSENFELD,A	209	232

CITE INDEX	FIRST AUTHOR	ISS-UE	YE-AR	JOUR-NAL	SECOND AUTHOR	THIRD AUTHOR	PAG BEG	PAG END
0.50	LEWELLEN,W	DE	1987	JAE	LODERER,C	MARTIN,K	287	310
0.50	LOBO ,GJ	AP	1989	TAR	SONG ,I		329	343
0.50	LOBO ,GL	SP	1989	JAR	MAHMOUD,AAW		116	134
0.50	LOEBBECKE,JK	AU	1989	AUD	EINING,MM	WILLINGHAM,JJ	1	28
0.50	MERCHANT,G	JL	1989	TAR			500	513
0.50	MERCHANT,KA	JL	1989	TAR	MANZONI,J		539	558
0.50	MORSE ,D	AP	1991	TAR	STEPHAN,J	STICE ,EK	376	388
0.50	NEU ,D	03	1991	AOS			243	256
0.50	OLSEN ,C	ST	1985	JAR			28	53
0.50	ROBSON,K	05	1991	AOS			547	570
0.50	SCHWARTZ,KB	AP	1985	TAR	MENON ,K		248	261
0.50	SHRIVER,KA	JA	1987	TAR			79	96
0.50	SPIRES,EE	AP	1991	TAR			259	276
0.50	STEINBART,PJ	JA	1987	TAR			97	116
0.50	SWAMINATHAN,S	JA	1991	TAR			23	41
0.50	THOMPSON,G	05	1991	AOS			572	599
0.50	TROMBLEY,MA	JL	1989	TAR			529	538
0.50	WALLER,WS	AP	1987	TAR	FELIX JR,WL		275	292
0.50	WAYMIRE,G	SP	1985	JAR			268	295
0.47	LOOKABILL,LL	OC	1976	TAR			724	738
0.47	RO ,BT	AU	1978	JAR			315	340
0.46	OPPONG,A	AU	1980	JAR			574	584
0.45	ABDEL KHALIK,AR	OC	1982	TAR	AJINKYA,BB		661	680
0.45	EGER ,C	AU	1982	JAR	DICKHAUT,JW		711	723
0.44	SAVICH,RS	JL	1977	TAR			642	652
0.43	BARNES,P	01	1986	AOS	WEBB ,J		1	18
0.43	BURGSTAHLER,D	AP	1986	TAR	JIAMBALVO,J		233	248
0.43	CASEY JR,CJ	AP	1986	TAR	MCGEE ,VE	STICKNEY,CP	249	262
0.43	DHALIWAL,DS	OC	1986	TAR			651	661
0.43	FRANCIS,JR	AU	1986	JAR	STOKES,DJ		383	393
0.43	JAIN ,PC	SP	1986	JAR			76	96
0.43	MURRAY,D	AU	1986	JAR	FRAZIER,KB		400	404
0.43	NICHOLS,DR	SP	1979	JAR	TSAY ,JJ		140	155
0.43	PALMROSE,ZV	AU	1986	JAR			405	411
0.43	PRESTON,A	06	1986	AOS			521	540
0.43	WILNER,N	01	1986	AOS	BIRNBERG,JG		71	82
0.41	KLAMMER,T	AP	1973	TAR			353	364
0.40	CREADY,WM	SP	1988	JAR			1	27
0.40	DALEY ,LA	OC	1988	TAR	SENKOW,DW	VIGELAND,RL	563	585
0.40	DEAN ,RA	03	1988	AOS	FERRIS,KR	KONSTANS,C	235	250
0.40	HAW ,IM	AU	1988	JAR	LUSTGARTEN,S		331	352
0.40	ISELIN,ER	02	1988	AOS			147	164
0.40	JOHNSON,WB	JA	1988	TAR	RAMANAN,R		96	110
0.40	KIM ,KK	JL	1988	TAR			472	489
0.40	KIM ,M	AP	1988	JAE	MOORE ,G		111	125
0.40	LANEN ,WN	DE	1988	JAE	THOMPSON,R		311	334
0.40	LYS ,T	AU	1988	JAR	SIVARAMAKRISHNAN,K		273	299
0.40	MIA ,L	05	1988	AOS			465	475
0.40	NICHOLS,DR	AU	1983	JAR	SMITH ,DB		534	544
0.40	RO ,BT	SP	1988	CAR			438	449
0.40	SMITH ,DB	DE	1988	JAE	POURCIAU,S		335	344
0.40	THOMPSON,RB	JL	1988	TAR	OLSEN ,C	DIETRICH,JR	448	471
0.40	WEBER ,R	AU	1978	JAR			368	388

CITE INDEX	FIRST AUTHOR	ISS-UE	YE-AR	JOUR-NAL	SECOND AUTHOR	THIRD AUTHOR	PAG BEG	PAG END
0.40	YOUNG ,SM	06	1988	AOS	SHIELDS,MD	WOLF ,G	607	618
0.38	ANDERSON,MJ	AU	1985	JAR			843	852
0.38	BECK ,PJ	SP	1985	JAR	SOLOMON,I	TOMASSINI,LA	37	56
0.38	CASLER,DJ	SP	1985	JAR	HALL ,TW		110	122
0.38	DIRSMITH,MW	AU	1985	JAA	COVALESKI,MA		5	21
0.38	GENTRY,JA	SP	1985	JAR	NEWBOLD,P	WHITFORD,DT	146	160
0.38	JENNINGS,R	SP	1985	JAR	STARKS,L		336	350
0.38	JIAMBALVO,J	AU	1985	AUD	WILNER,N		1	11
0.38	KELLY ,R	AU	1985	JAR			619	632
0.38	KNAPP ,MC	AP	1985	TAR			202	211
0.38	LAMBERT,RA	AU	1985	JAR			633	647
0.38	O'LEARY,T	01	1985	AOS			87	104
0.38	PLUMLEE,RD	AU	1985	JAR			683	699
0.38	SCHNEIDER,A	AU	1985	JAR			911	919
0.38	SIMON ,DT	AU	1985	AUD			71	78
0.38	WILLINGHAM,JJ	AU	1985	AUD	WRIGHT,WF		57	70
0.36	DYCKMAN,TR	01	1982	AOS	HOSKIN,RE	SWIERINGA,RJ	1	12
0.36	KINNEY JR,WR	AU	1979	JAR			456	475
0.35	BENSTON,GJ	ST	1967	JAR			1	54
0.35	CAMMANN,C	04	1976	AOS			301	314
0.35	DEAKIN,EB	OC	1974	TAR	GRANOF,MH		764	771
0.33	ABDEL-KHALIK,AR	AU	1987	CAR	CHI ,C	GHICAS,D	32	60
0.33	AHARONY,J	SP	1987	CAR	BAR-YOSEF,S		430	444
0.33	ASHTON,RH	AU	1987	JAR	WILLINGHAM,JJ	ELLIOTT,RK	275	292
0.33	BENSTON,GJ	ST	1978	JAR	KRASNEY,MA		1	30
0.33	BRICKLEY,JA	JA	1990	JAE	VAN DRUNEN,LD		251	280
0.33	BRIERS,M	04	1990	AOS	HIRST ,M		373	398
0.33	BROWN ,CE	AU	1990	AUD	SOLOMON,I		17	38
0.33	CHALOS,P	JL	1990	TAR	HAKA ,S		624	641
0.33	COWEN ,SS	02	1987	AOS	FERRERI,LB	PARKER,LD	111	122
0.33	DENT ,JF	02	1990	AOS			3	25
0.33	ESPELAND,WN	02	1990	AOS	HIRSCH,PM		77	96
0.33	GIBBINS,M	SP	1990	JAR	RICHARDSON,A	WATERHOUSE,J	121	143
0.33	HAKA ,SF	01	1987	AOS			31	48
0.33	HAM ,J	AU	1987	CAR	LOSELL,D	SMIELIAUSKAS,W	210	226
0.33	HAN ,JCY	SP	1990	JAR	WILD ,JJ		211	219
0.33	HAW ,I	AP	1990	TAR	PASTENA,VS	LILIEN,SB	432	451
0.33	HSIEH ,S-J	SP	1990	CAR	FERRIS,KR	CHEN ,AH	550	572
0.33	JENNINGS,M	SP	1987	AUD	KNEER ,DC	RECKERS,PMJ	104	115
0.33	KNECHEL,WR	SP	1990	CAR	MESSIER JR,WF		386	406
0.33	LANDSMAN,WR	AU	1990	CAR	OHLSON,JA		185	198
0.33	LEFTWICH,R	JA	1990	JAE			37	44
0.33	LOEBBECKE,JK	SP	1987	AUD	STEINBART,PJ		74	89
0.33	MACINTOSH,NB	05	1990	AOS	SCAPENS,RW		455	477
0.33	MCDANIEL,LS	AU	1990	JAR			267	285
0.33	MCDONALD,B	JL	1984	TAR	MORRIS,MH		432	446
0.33	MESSIER JR,WF	AU	1987	AUD	HANSEN,JV		94	105
0.33	MIAN ,SL	OC	1990	JAE	SMITH JR,CW		249	266
0.33	MOECKEL,C	AU	1990	JAR			368	387
0.33	MOSES ,OD	AP	1987	TAR			358	377
0.33	O'BRIEN,PC	AU	1990	JAR			286	304
0.33	RICHARDSON,AJ	05	1990	AOS			499	501
0.33	SHEVLIN,T	JL	1987	TAR			480	509

CITE INDEX	FIRST AUTHOR	ISS-UE	YE-AR	JOUR-NAL	SECOND AUTHOR	THIRD AUTHOR	PAG BEG	PAG END
0.33	SHIELDS,MD	04	1987	AOS	SOLOMON,I	WALLER,WS	375	385
0.33	SKINNER,DJ	OC	1990	JAE			191	211
0.33	STEVENSON,FL	AU	1987	JAR			306	316
0.33	SWANSON,EP	OC	1990	TAR			911	924
0.33	TURPEN,RA	SP	1990	AUD			60	76
0.33	WALLER,WS	OC	1990	TAR	BISHOP,RA		812	836
0.33	WILLIAMS,JJ	03	1990	AOS	MACINTOSH,NB	MOORE ,JC	221	246
0.33	WILSON,ER	SP	1990	CAR	STEWART,JP		573	591
0.31	ANDERSON,JC	JL	1980	TAR	FRANKLE,AW		467	479
0.31	BELKAOUI,A	AU	1980	JAR			362	374
0.31	LEV ,B	AU	1980	JAR			524	550
0.30	CHOW ,CW	JL	1983	TAR			485	520
0.29	ABDOLMOHAMMADI,MJ	SP	1986	AUD			1	16
0.29	BARNEA,A	JA	1976	TAR	RONEN ,J	SADAN ,S	110	122
0.29	BILDERSEE,JS	JA	1975	TAR			81	98
0.29	BORITZ,JE	AU	1986	JAR			335	348
0.29	FOSTER,G	AU	1975	JAR			283	292
0.29	HAKA ,S	JL	1986	TAR	FRIEDMAN,L	JONES ,V	455	474
0.29	MARGHEIM,LL	SP	1986	JAR			194	205
0.29	POWNALL,G	AU	1986	JAR			291	315
0.29	WAYMIRE,G	JA	1986	TAR			129	142
0.29	WRIGHT,CJ	JA	1986	TAR	GROFF ,JE		91	100
0.27	BALLEW,V	JA	1982	TAR			88	104
0.27	INGRAM,RW	AU	1982	JAR	COPELAND,RM		766	772
0.27	JAGGI ,B	OC	1978	TAR			961	967
0.27	RICE ,SJ	AP	1978	TAR			429	438
0.25	ARRINGTON,CE	SP	1985	JAR	BAILEY,CD	HOPWOOD,WS	1	20
0.25	AYRES ,FL	AP	1989	TAR	JACKSON,BR	HITE ,PS	300	312
0.25	BIDDLE,GC	SP	1985	JAR	MARTIN,RK		57	83
0.25	BOWEN ,RM	JL	1989	JAE	JOHNSON,MF	SHEVLIN,T	225	254
0.25	BROWN ,C	03	1985	AOS			255	266
0.25	BUCHMAN,TA	03	1985	AOS			267	286
0.25	BURGSTAHLER,D	JL	1989	JAE	JIAMBALVO,J	NOREEN,E	207	224
0.25	BUTLER,SA	AU	1985	JAR			513	526
0.25	DAMOS ,P	03	1989	AOS	HOLT ,DL	IMHOFF JR,EA	235	246
0.25	DAROCA,FP	SP	1985	AUD	HOLDER,WW		80	92
0.25	DEAKIN,EB	JA	1989	TAR			137	151
0.25	DEJONG,DV	02	1989	AOS	FORSYTHE,R	KIM ,JA	41	64
0.25	DOPUCH,N		1989	AUD	KING ,RR	WALLIN,DE	98	127
0.25	EICHENSEHER,JW	AU	1989	AUD	HAGIGI,M	SHIELDS,D	29	40
0.25	EL-GAZZAR,S	SP	1989	JAA	LILIEN,S	PASTENA,V	217	231
0.25	ESPAHBODI,R	SP	1989	CAR	TEHRANIAN,H		575	591
0.25	FALK ,H	SP	1989	CAR			816	825
0.25	FIRTH ,MA	SP	1985	AUD			23	37
0.25	GORDON,LA	03	1989	AOS			247	258
0.25	HARRISON,KE	SP	1989	CAR	TOMASSINI,LA		642	648
0.25	HOPWOOD,W	JA	1989	TAR	MCKEOWN,J	MUTCHLER,J	28	48
0.25	HOPWOOD,WS	SP	1985	JAR	MCKEOWN,JC		161	174
0.25	INGRAM,RW	AU	1985	JAR			595	618
0.25	KEASEY,K	04	1989	AOS	WATSON,R		337	345
0.25	KLERSEY,GF	02	1989	AOS	MOCK ,TJ		133	151
0.25	KNECHEL,WR	SP	1985	AUD			38	62
0.25	LAMBERT,RA	AP	1985	JAE	LARCKER,DF		179	204

CITE INDEX	FIRST AUTHOR	ISS-UE	YE-AR	JOUR-NAL	SECOND AUTHOR	THIRD AUTHOR	PAG BEG	PAG END
0.25	LEE ,CJ	SP	1985	JAR			213	227
0.25	LEVITAN,AS	AU	1985	AUD	KNOBLETT,JA		26	39
0.25	LUCKETT,PF	06	1989	AOS	HIRST ,MK		379	387
0.25	MADEO ,SA	JL	1985	TAR	PINCUS,M		407	429
0.25	MAYPER,AG	AU	1989	AUD	DOUCET,MS	WARREN,CS	72	86
0.25	MILLIRON,VC	AU	1985	JAR			794	816
0.25	MULFORD,CW	AU	1985	JAR			897	906
0.25	NEWMAN,HA	OC	1989	TAR			758	772
0.25	PRESTON,AM	06	1989	AOS			389	413
0.25	RONEN ,J	JA	1989	TAR	AHARONI,A		69	86
0.25	SALATKA,WK	FB	1989	JAE			35	69
0.25	SCAPENS,RW	AP	1985	TAR	SALE ,JT		231	247
0.25	SELLING,T	02	1989	AOS	SHANK ,J		65	77
0.25	SELTO ,FH	AU	1985	JAR	CLOUSE,ML		700	717
0.25	SMIELIAUSKAS,W	AU	1985	JAR			718	739
0.25	TABOR ,RH	SP	1985	AUD	WILLIS,JT		93	109
0.25	TEHRANIAN,H	AP	1985	JAE	WAEGELEIN,JF		131	144
0.25	TOMCZYK,S	AU	1989	AUD	READ ,WJ		98	106
0.25	TROTMAN,KT	SP	1985	JAR	YETTON,PW		256	267
0.25	TROTMAN,KT	AU	1985	JAR			740	752
0.25	TURNER,MJ	AU	1989	JAR	HILTON,RW		297	312
0.25	UECKER,WC	JL	1985	TAR	SCHEPANSKI,A	SHIN ,J	430	457
0.25	WALLER,WS	AU	1985	JAR			817	828
0.24	BALL ,R	SP	1976	JAR	LEV ,B	WATTS ,RL	1	9
0.24	LEV ,B	AU	1969	JAR			290	299
0.24	MOCK ,TJ	JL	1973	TAR			520	534
0.24	O'CONNOR,MC	AP	1973	TAR			339	352
0.24	WEST ,RR	SP	1970	JAR			118	125
0.22	PENMAN,SH	DE	1984	JAE			165	183
0.22	SMITH ,DB	AG	1984	JAE	STETTLER,HF	BEEDLES,W	153	162
0.20	ANDERSON,MJ	05	1988	AOS			431	446
0.20	BIDDLE,GC	AU	1988	JAR	RICKS ,WE		169	194
0.20	CARSLAW,C	AP	1988	TAR			321	327
0.20	COLIGNON,R	06	1988	AOS	COVALESKI,M		559	579
0.20	ELLIOTT,JA	ST	1988	JAR	SHAW,WH		91	126
0.20	ENIS ,CR	02	1988	AOS			123	145
0.20	GORMLEY,RJ	SU	1988	JAA			185	212
0.20	HARRISON,PD	AP	1988	TAR	WEST ,SG	RENEAU,JH	307	320
0.20	HILTON,RW	AP	1988	TAR	SWIERINGA,RJ	TURNER,MJ	195	218
0.20	LEE ,CJ	AU	1988	CAR			371	388
0.20	LEWIS ,BL	AP	1988	TAR	PATTON,JM	GREEN ,SL	270	282
0.20	MCKEOWN,JC	SP	1988	CAR	SHALCHI,H		485	507
0.20	ROCKNESS,J	04	1988	AOS	WILLIAMS,PF		397	411
0.20	SHAW ,WH	SP	1988	JAR			60	81
0.20	SHIELDS,MD	06	1988	AOS	WALLER,WS		581	594
0.20	WILLIAMS,DD	05	1988	AOS	DIRSMITH,MW		487	508
0.20	WYER ,JC	SP	1988	AUD	WHITE ,GT	JANSON,EC	164	173
0.18	BALOFF,N	AU	1967	JAR	KENNELLY,JW		131	143
0.18	BENSTON,GJ	OC	1966	TAR			657	672
0.18	DAVIS ,RR	AU	1982	AUD			13	32
0.18	DEAKIN,EB	JL	1976	TAR			590	603
0.18	ESKEW ,RK	AP	1975	TAR			316	324
0.18	KINNEY JR,WR	AU	1982	JAR	SALAMON,GL		350	366

CITE INDEX	FIRST AUTHOR	ISS-UE	YE-AR	JOUR-NAL	SECOND AUTHOR	THIRD AUTHOR	PAG BEG	PAG END
0.18	MEYERS,SL	AP	1973	TAR			318	322
0.18	REILLY,FK	ST	1972	JAR	MORGENSON,DL	WEST ,M	105	124
0.18	SAMUELSON,RA	AU	1972	JAR			322	344
0.18	SEPE ,J	JL	1982	TAR			467	485
0.18	ZIMMERMAN,JL	AU	1976	JAR			301	319
0.17	BERNARD,VL	OC	1987	TAR	RULAND,RG		707	722
0.17	BILDERSEE,JS	AU	1987	CAR	RONEN ,J		89	110
0.17	BROWN ,LD	AU	1987	CAR	ZMIJEWSKI,MA		61	75
0.17	CHOW ,CW	JL	1987	TAR	WONG-BOREN,A		533	541
0.17	COVALESKI,MA	SP	1987	CAR	DIRSMITH,MW	WHITE ,CE	408	429
0.17	ELGERS,P	OC	1987	TAR	CALLAHAN,C	STROCK,E	763	773
0.17	HOLT ,DL	06	1987	AOS			571	578
0.17	HOUGHTON,KA	02	1987	AOS			143	152
0.17	MOORE ,ML	OC	1987	TAR	STEECE,BM	SWENSON,CW	671	685
0.17	ZIEBART,DA	AP	1987	TAR	KIM ,DH		343	357
0.15	BARAN ,A	JA	1980	TAR	LAKONISHOK,J	OFER ,AR	22	35
0.15	BOWMAN,RG	AP	1980	TAR			237	253
0.15	HARRELL,AM	04	1980	AOS	KLICK ,HD		393	400
0.14	ARANYA,N	AU	1986	CAR	WHEELER,JT		184	199
0.14	BLOCHER,E	06	1986	AOS	MOFFIE,RP	ZMUD ,RW	457	470
0.14	BUTLER,SA	JA	1986	TAR			101	111
0.14	CASEY JR,CJ	AP	1986	TAR	SELLING,T		302	317
0.14	CHESLEY,GR	SP	1986	CAR			179	199
0.14	DAVIS ,GB	SP	1986	AUD	WEBER ,R		35	49
0.14	FLESHER,DL	JL	1986	TAR	FLESHER,TK		421	434
0.14	HILKE ,JC	WI	1986	JAA			17	29
0.14	JAIN ,PC	SP	1986	JAR			187	193
0.14	LARSSON,S	SP	1986	CAR	CHESLEY,GR		259	282
0.14	LICATA,MP	JA	1986	TAR	STRAWSER,RH	WELKER,RB	112	117
0.14	MURDOCH,B	AP	1986	TAR			273	287
0.14	ROBBINS,WA	AU	1986	JAR	AUSTIN,KR		412	421
0.14	SCHROEDER,MS	SP	1986	AUD	SOLOMON,I	VICKREY,DW	86	94
0.14	TSE ,S	JL	1986	TAR			475	497
0.14	WEBER ,R	JL	1986	TAR			498	518
0.14	WRIGHT,A	SP	1986	AUD			86	94
0.14	YOUNG ,R	SP	1986	JAR			231	240
0.14	ZEFF ,SA	SP	1986	JAA			131	154
0.13	ANELL ,B	04	1985	AOS			479	492
0.13	BULLEN,ML	03	1985	AOS	FLAMHOLTZ,EG		287	302
0.13	CASEY JR,CJ	SP	1985	JAR	BARTCZAK,N		384	401
0.13	COX ,CT	OC	1985	TAR			692	701
0.13	CROSBY,MA	SP	1985	AUD			118	132
0.13	DYL ,EA	02	1985	AOS	LILLY ,MS		171	176
0.13	EICHENSEHER,JW	SP	1985	JAA			195	209
0.13	HALPERIN,R	OC	1985	TAR	TZUR ,J		670	680
0.13	JOHNSON,WB	AP	1985	JAE	MAGEE ,RP	NAGARAJAN,NJ	151	174
0.13	JONES ,CS	03	1985	AOS			303	328
0.13	JONES ,CS	02	1985	AOS			177	200
0.13	KAPLAN,SE	AU	1985	AUD			12	25
0.13	KAPLAN,SE	AU	1985	JAR			871	877
0.13	KNECHEL,WR	SP	1985	JAR			194	212
0.13	MARKS ,BR	AU	1985	JAR	RAMAN ,KK		878	886
0.13	MCKINELY,S	AU	1985	JAR	PANY ,K	RECKERS,PMJ	887	896

CITE INDEX	FIRST AUTHOR	ISS-UE	YE-AR	JOUR-NAL	SECOND AUTHOR	THIRD AUTHOR	PAG BEG	PAG END
0.13	RAVIV ,A	AP	1985	JAE			239	246
0.12	ABDEL-KHALIK,AR	OC	1975	TAR			657	670
0.12	GRIFFIN,PA	JL	1976	TAR			499	515
0.12	MLYNARCZYK,FA	ST	1969	JAR			63	81
0.12	PELES ,YC	SP	1970	JAR			128	137
0.12	STAUBUS,GJ	JA	1965	TAR			119	134
0.11	ASHTON,AH	JL	1984	TAR			361	375
0.11	BERNARD,VL	AU	1984	JAR			445	466
0.11	DIETRICH,JR	AP	1984	JAE			67	96
0.10	HALL ,TW	SU	1983	JAA			299	313
0.10	INGRAM,RW	JL	1983	TAR	CHEWNING,EG		562	580
0.09	WHALEY,RE	OC	1982	JAE	CHEUNG,JK		57	83
0.08	BROWN ,LD	SP	1980	JAR	HUGHES,JS	ROZEFF,MS	278	288
0.08	MANEGOLD,JG	AU	1981	JAR			360	373
0.07	ENGLEBRECHT,TD	JL	1979	TAR	JAMISON,RW		554	562
0.07	FOSTER III,TW	AP	1978	TAR	VICKREY,DW		360	370
0.07	HILLISON,WA	SP	1979	JAR			60	73
0.06	COMISKEY,EE	AP	1966	TAR			235	238
0.06	FALK ,H	SP	1977	JAR	MILLER,JC		12	22
0.06	JENSEN,RE	AP	1967	TAR			265	273
0.06	LIVINGSTONE,JL	AU	1969	JAR			245	256
0.06	MABERT,VA	JA	1974	TAR	RADCLIFFE,RC		61	75
0.06	MCKEOWN,JC	SP	1973	JAR			62	99
0.06	SHARPE,IG	AU	1975	JAR	WALKER,RG		293	310
0.00	ABARBANELL,JS	JN	1991	JAE			147	165
0.00	ABDEL-KHALIK,AR	SP	1986	CAR			242	251
0.00	ABDEL-KHALIK,AR	AU	1986	JAR	GRAUL ,PR	NEWTON,JD	372	382
0.00	ABDOLMOHAMMADI,MJ	AU	1986	CAR	BERGER,PD		149	165
0.00	ABDOLMOHAMMADI,MJ	SP	1991	CAR			535	548
0.00	ABERNETHY,MA	02	1991	AOS	STOELWINDER,JU		105	120
0.00	AFFLECK-GRAVES,J	SP	1990	CAR	DAVIS ,LR	MENDENHALL,RR	501	517
0.00	AJINKYA,BB	AP	1991	TAR	ATIASE,RK	GIFT ,MJ	389	401
0.00	ALFORD,AW	SP	1992	JAR			94	108
0.00	ALI ,A	JA	1992	TAR	KLEIN ,A	ROSENFELD,J	183	198
0.00	ALLEN ,S	SP	1990	CAR	RAMANAN,R		518	543
0.00	ALY ,IM	SP	1992	JAA	BARLOW,HA	JONES ,RW	217	230
0.00	AMIHUD,Y	AU	1989	JAA	MENDELSON,H		415	431
0.00	AMIT ,R	WI	1988	JAA	LIVNAT,J		19	43
0.00	AMIT ,R	AU	1989	CAR	LIVNAT,J	ZAROWIN,P	143	158
0.00	ANDERSON JR,KE	JL	1985	TAR			357	371
0.00	ANDERSON,JC	AU	1992	AUD	KAPLAN,SE	RECKERS,PMJ	1	13
0.00	ANDERSON,MJ	OC	1990	TAR	ANDERSON,U	HELLELOID,R	857	874
0.00	ANDERSON,U		1989	AUD	MARCHANT,G		101	115
0.00	ANTHONY,JH	SP	1987	CAR			460	475
0.00	APOSTOLOU,NG	AU	1985	JAR	GIROUX,GA	WELKER,RB	853	858
0.00	ARNOLD,DF	AU	1991	AUD	PONEMON,LA		1	15
0.00	ARNOLD,PJ	02	1991	AOS			121	140
0.00	ARRINGTON,CE	06	1992	AOS	SCHWEIKER,W		511	533
0.00	ASARE ,SK	AP	1992	TAR			379	393
0.00	ASHTON,RH	SP	1989	CAR	GRAUL ,PR	NEWTON,JD	657	673
0.00	ASQUITH,P	JL	1989	TAR	HEALY ,P	PALEPU,K	387	403
0.00	AYRES ,FL	SP	1986	JAR			166	169
0.00	BABER ,WR	SP	1985	JAR			360	369

CITE INDEX	FIRST AUTHOR	ISS-UE	YE-AR	JOUR-NAL	SECOND AUTHOR	THIRD AUTHOR	PAG BEG	PAG END
0.00	BABER ,WR	OC	1991	TAR	FAIRFIELD,PM	HAGGARD,JA	818	829
0.00	BAGINSKI,SP	JA	1990	TAR	HASSELL,JM		175	190
0.00	BAILEY,CD	SP	1986	AUD	BALLARD,G		77	85
0.00	BAILEY,CD	AP	1992	TAR	MCINTYRE,EV		368	378
0.00	BAILEY,D	06	1990	AOS			513	525
0.00	BALAKRISHNAN,R	AU	1990	JAR	HARRIS,TS	SEN ,PK	305	325
0.00	BALDWIN,J	SU	1992	JAA	GLEZEN,GW		269	285
0.00	BAMBER,EM	AU	1987	CAR	BYLINSKI,JH		127	143
0.00	BAMBER,EM	JL	1988	AUD	SNOWBALL,D		490	504
0.00	BAMBER,EM	SP	1988	AUD	BAMBER,LS	BYLINSKI,JH	137	149
0.00	BANKER,RD	JL	1992	TAR	COOPER,WW	POTTER,G	496	510
0.00	BAO ,BE	04	1989	AOS	BAO ,DA		303	319
0.00	BARLEV,B	SP	1986	CAR	FRIED ,D	LIVNAT,J	288	310
0.00	BARLEY,B	SU	1990	JAA	LIVNAT,J		411	433
0.00	BARTH ,ME	JL	1991	TAR			516	534
0.00	BARTH ,ME	MR	1992	JAE	BEAVER,WH	LANDSMAN,WR	27	61
0.00	BARTOV,E	JL	1992	TAR			610	622
0.00	BATHKE,AW	JA	1989	TAR	LOREK ,KS	WILLINGER,GL	49	68
0.00	BEATTY,RP	WI	1985	JAA	JOHNSON,SB		112	124
0.00	BEATTY,RP	SP	1989	CAR	VERRECCHIA,RE		472	493
0.00	BEATTY,RP	AU	1992	JAA	HAND ,JRM		509	530
0.00	BECK ,PJ	AU	1992	CAR	DAVIS ,JS	JUNG ,W-O	86	112
0.00	BEDARD,JC	AU	1989	AUD			57	71
0.00	BEDARD,JC		1991	AUD	BIGGS ,SF		77	90
0.00	BELKAOUI,A	AU	1985	CAR			111	123
0.00	BELL ,TB	AU	1991	JAR	TABOR ,RH		350	370
0.00	BENJAMIN,JJ	SU	1986	JAA	GROSSMAN,SD	WIGGIN,CE	177	184
0.00	BENSON,ED	SU	1991	JAA	MARKS ,BR	RAMAN ,KK	303	319
0.00	BERNARD,VL	SP	1991	JAA	NOEL ,J		145	181
0.00	BIDWELL III,CM	SP	1981	JAA	RIDDLE JR,JR		198	214
0.00	BILDERSEE,JS	SU	1987	JAA	KAHN ,N		239	256
0.00	BINDER,JJ	SP	1985	JAR			370	383
0.00	BLACCONIERE,WG	MR	1991	JAE			91	113
0.00	BLACCONIERE,WG	JN	1991	JAE	BOWEN ,RM	SEFCIK,SE	167	201
0.00	BLANCHARD,GA	JA	1986	TAR	CHOW ,CW	NOREEN,EW	1	15
0.00	BLOCHER,E	AU	1985	AUD	BYLINSKI,JH		79	90
0.00	BLOCHER,E	SP	1988	AUD	COOPER,JC		1	28
0.00	BOARD ,JLG	SP	1990	JAR	WALKER,M		182	192
0.00	BONNIER,KA	FB	1989	JAE	BRUNER,RF		95	106
0.00	BORITZ,JE	SP	1988	CAR	GABER ,BG	LEMON ,WM	392	411
0.00	BORITZ,JE	AU	1992	AUD	WENSLEY,AKP		14	29
0.00	BOUGEN,PD	03	1990	AOS	OGDEN ,SG	OUTRAM,Q	149	170
0.00	BOWEN ,RM	JA	1989	TAR	PFEIFFER,GM		152	171
0.00	BOWEN ,RM	AU	1992	JAA	JOHNSON,MF	SHEVLIN,T	395	422
0.00	BRANCH,B	SP	1981	JAA	BERKOWITZ,B		215	219
0.00	BRICKER,R	AU	1989	JAR			246	262
0.00	BRIEF ,RP	JA	1969	TAR			20	26
0.00	BROWN ,BC	SU	1986	JAA	BRANDI,JT		185	205
0.00	BROWN ,C	AU	1987	CAR			111	126
0.00	BROWN ,LD	SP	1989	CAR	GARDNER,JC	VASARHELYI,MA	793	815
0.00	BROWN ,LD	OC	1992	TAR	HAN ,JCY		862	875
0.00	BROWNELL,P		1991	AOS	DUNK ,AS		693	703
0.00	BUCKLESS,FA	OC	1990	TAR	RAVENSCROFT,SP		933	945

CITE INDEX	FIRST AUTHOR	ISS-UE	YE-AR	JOUR-NAL	SECOND AUTHOR	THIRD AUTHOR	PAG BEG	PAG END
0.00	BURGSTAHLER,D	SP	1986	JAR	NOREEN,EW		170	186
0.00	CAHAN ,SF	JA	1992	TAR			77	96
0.00	CARCELLO,JV	SP	1992	AUD	HERMANSON,RH	MCGRATH,NT	1	15
0.00	CARPENTER,BW		1992	AOS	DIRSMITH,MW		709	739
0.00	CARPENTER,VL		1992	AOS	FEROZ ,EH		613	643
0.00	CASSIDY,DB	AU	1976	JAR			212	229
0.00	CASTER,P	AU	1990	AUD			75	91
0.00	CHALOS,P	AU	1985	JAR			527	543
0.00	CHALOS,P	SP	1991	CAR	CHERIAN,J	HARRIS,D	431	448
0.00	CHAN ,H	AU	1990	AUD	SMIELIAUSKAS,W		167	182
0.00	CHANEY,PK	SP	1992	CAR	JETER ,DC		540	560
0.00	CHANG ,OH	SP	1992	JAR	NICHOLS,DR		109	125
0.00	CHARITOU,A	AU	1990	JAA	KETZ ,JE		475	497
0.00	CHEN ,JT	SP	1985	CAR	MANES ,RP		242	252
0.00	CHEN ,KCW	AU	1992	AUD	CHURCH,BK		30	49
0.00	CHENG ,TT	AU	1986	CAR			226	241
0.00	CHENHALL,R	01	1991	AOS	MORRIS,D		27	46
0.00	CHENHALL,RH	AP	1986	TAR			263	272
0.00	CHEWNING,EG	06	1990	AOS	HARRELL,AM		527	542
0.00	CHIU ,JS	OC	1966	TAR	DECOSTER,DT		673	680
0.00	CHOI ,SK	JN	1992	JAE	JETER ,DC		229	247
0.00	CHOW ,CW	03	1991	AOS	SHIELDS,MD	CHAN ,YK	209	226
0.00	CHOW,CW	01	1991	AOS	COOPER,JC	HADDAD,K	47	60
0.00	CHUNG ,DY	AU	1988	CAR	LINDSAY,WD		19	46
0.00	CLARK ,TN	ST	1977	JAR			54	94
0.00	CLARKSON,PM	SP	1992	CAR	DONTOH,A	RICHARDSON,G	601	625
0.00	CLINCH,G	SP	1991	JAR			59	78
0.00	CLINCH,G	OC	1992	TAR	MAGLIOLO,J		843	861
0.00	COGLITORE,F	SP	1988	AUD	BERRYMAN,RG		150	163
0.00	COLBERT,JL	02	1988	AOS			111	121
0.00	COLLINS,KM	06	1992	AOS	KILLOUGH,LN		535	547
0.00	COOPER,JC	03	1991	AOS	SELTO ,FH		227	242
0.00	COOPER,WW	AU	1985	JAA	HO ,JL	HUNTER,JE	22	39
0.00	CORNELL,B	AU	1989	JAA	LANDSMAN,W	SHAPIRO,AC	460	479
0.00	COTTELL JR,PG	WI	1986	JAA			30	45
0.00	CREADY,WM	JL	1987	TAR	SHANK ,JK		589	596
0.00	CZARNIAWSKA-,B	04	1988	AOS			415	430
0.00	CZARNIAWSKA-JOERGES	02	1989	AOS	JACOBSSON,B		29	39
0.00	DALY ,BA	SP	1990	JAR	OMER ,T		193	197
0.00	DAMOS ,P	AU	1989	CAR	EICHENSEHER,JW	HOLT ,DL	91	109
0.00	DANIEL,SJ	SP	1988	AUD			174	181
0.00	DANIEL,SJ		1991	AOS	REITSPERGER,WD		601	618
0.00	DAS ,H	03	1986	AOS			215	232
0.00	DAVIS ,LR	06	1989	AOS			495	508
0.00	DAVIS ,LR	SP	1992	AUD	SIMON ,DT		58	68
0.00	DAVIS ,ML	AP	1988	TAR	LARGAY III,JA		348	363
0.00	DAVIS ,ML	JL	1990	TAR			696	709
0.00	DECHOW,PM	MR	1991	JAE	SLOAN ,RG		1	89
0.00	DEFOND,ML	JL	1991	TAR	JIAMBALVO,J		643	655
0.00	DEFOND,ML	SP	1992	AUD			16	31
0.00	DEIS JR,DR	JL	1992	TAR	GIROUX,GA		462	479
0.00	DEMPSEY,SJ	OC	1989	TAR			748	757
0.00	DEMSKI,JS	SP	1969	JAR			96	115

CITE INDEX	FIRST AUTHOR	ISS-UE	YE-AR	JOUR-NAL	SECOND AUTHOR	THIRD AUTHOR	PAG BEG	PAG END
0.00	DENT ,AS		1991	AOS			705	732
0.00	DESANCTIS,G	06	1989	AOS	JARVENPAA,SL		509	525
0.00	DHALIWAL,D	MR	1992	JAE	WANG ,S		7	25
0.00	DHARAN,BG	WI	1992	JAA	MASCARENHAS,B		1	21
0.00	DILLA ,WN	JL	1989	TAR			404	432
0.00	DILLARD,JF		1991	AOS	KAUFFMAN,NL	SPIRES,EE	619	633
0.00	DIRSMITH,MW	01	1991	AOS	HASKINS,ME		61	90
0.00	DONEGAN,J	SP	1989	JAA	SUNDER,S		203	216
0.00	DOPUCH,N	ST	1991	JAR	KING ,RR		60	106
0.00	DORAN ,DT	SP	1988	JAA	NACHTMANN,R		113	132
0.00	DUNK ,AS	03	1990	AOS			171	178
0.00	DUNK ,AS	04	1992	AOS			195	203
0.00	ELGERS,P	JN	1992	JAE	MURRAY,D		303	316
0.00	ELGERS,PT	JL	1980	TAR			389	408
0.00	ELGERS,PT	AP	1982	TAR	MURRAY,D		358	375
0.00	ELLIOTT,JA	JA	1990	TAR	PHILBRICK,DR		157	174
0.00	ELLIOTT,JA	OC	1991	TAR	HANNA ,JD	SHAW ,WH	847	861
0.00	ELNICKI,RA	ST	1977	JAR			209	218
0.00	EMBY ,C	SP	1988	CAR	GIBBINS,M		287	313
0.00	ENGLE ,TJ	WI	1991	JAA			109	121
0.00	ENGSTROM,JH	SU	1985	JAA			305	318
0.00	ESPAHBODI,H	DE	1991	JAE	STROCK,E	TEHRANIAN,H	323	345
0.00	ETTREDGE,M	SP	1988	AUD	SHANE ,PB	SMITH ,D	29	42
0.00	EZZAMEL,M	05	1990	AOS	BOURN ,M		399	424
0.00	FARRELY,GE	AP	1985	TAR	FERRIS,KR	REICHENSTEIN,WR	278	288
0.00	FELIX JR,WL	JA	1972	TAR			52	63
0.00	FELTHAM,GA	AU	1984	CAR			87	98
0.00	FELTON,S	AU	1990	CAR	MANN ,H		261	277
0.00	FEROZ ,EH	JL	1992	TAR	WILSON,ER		480	495
0.00	FERRIS,KR	03	1982	AOS			225	230
0.00	FIELDS,LP	AU	1991	AUD	WILKINS,MS		62	69
0.00	FIRTH ,MA	AU	1981	JAR			521	529
0.00	FISHER,MH		1990	AUD			184	223
0.00	FLEISCHMAN,RK	AP	1991	TAR	PARKER,LD		361	375
0.00	FLORY ,SM	AP	1992	TAR	PHILLIPS JR,TJ	REIDENBACH,RE	284	302
0.00	FOSTER,G	JA	1990	JAE	GUPTA ,M		309	337
0.00	FRANCIS,J	OC	1990	TAR			891	911
0.00	FRANCIS,J	AU	1990	JAR			326	347
0.00	FRANCIS,J	AU	1992	JAR	PAGACH,D	STEPHAN,J	165	184
0.00	FRANCIS,JR	SU	1990	JAA	ANDREWS JR,WT	SIMON ,DT	369	378
0.00	FRECKA,TJ	SP	1983	JAR	LEE ,CF		308	316
0.00	FREDERICKSON,JR	OC	1992	TAR			647	670
0.00	FREEMAN,R	DE	1992	JAE	TSE ,S		509	523
0.00	FREEMAN,RN	ST	1978	JAR			111	145
0.00	FRIED ,D	WI	1987	JAA	HOSLER,C		5	23
0.00	FROGOT,V	JA	1991	TAR	SHEARON,WT		80	99
0.00	GALLHOFER,S	05	1991	AOS	HASLAM,J		487	520
0.00	GAVER ,JJ	JA	1992	TAR	GAVER ,KM	BATTISTEL,GP	172	182
0.00	GAVER ,JJ	SP	1992	JAA			137	156
0.00	GEIGER,MA	SP	1989	AUD			40	63
0.00	GHICAS,DC	AP	1990	TAR			384	405
0.00	GIROUX,GA	06	1986	AOS	MAYPER,AG	DAFT ,RL	499	520
0.00	GIVOLY,D	SP	1987	JAA	LAKONISHOK,J		117	137

CITE INDEX	FIRST AUTHOR	ISS-UE	YE-AR	JOUR-NAL	SECOND AUTHOR	THIRD AUTHOR	PAG BEG	PAG END
0.00	GIVOLY,D	AP	1992	TAR	HAYN ,C		394	410
0.00	GLEZEN,GW	AU	1985	JAR	MILLAR,JA		859	870
0.00	GLICK ,R	SP	1989	JAA	PLAUT ,SE		147	159
0.00	GOETZ-JR,JF	02	1991	AOS	MORROW,PC	MCELROY,JC	159	165
0.00	GONEDES,NJ	ST	1969	JAR			90	113
0.00	GONEDES,NJ	JL	1971	TAR			535	551
0.00	GORDON,DA	AU	1990	JAA	GORDON,MJ		573	588
0.00	GORDON,LA		1992	AOS	SMITH ,KJ		741	757
0.00	GORTON,G	SP	1989	JAA	PENNACCHI,G		125	145
0.00	GRAHAM,LE	SP	1991	AUD	DAMENS,J	VAN NESS,G	69	96
0.00	GREENBERG,RR	AU	1986	JAA	JOHNSON,GL	RAMESH,K	266	277
0.00	GRIFFIN,PA	OC	1991	TAR	WALLACH,SJR		830	846
0.00	GUENTHER,DA	JA	1992	TAR			17	45
0.00	HACKENBRACK,K	SP	1992	JAR			126	136
0.00	HALL ,TW	SP	1985	JAA	CASLER,DJ		210	224
0.00	HALPERIN,R	AP	1987	TAR	LANEN ,WN		378	384
0.00	HALPERIN,R	OC	1987	TAR	SRINIDHI,BN		686	706
0.00	HALPERIN,RM	JA	1991	TAR	SRINIDHI,B		141	157
0.00	HAN ,BH	MR	1992	JAE	JENNINGS,R	NOEL ,J	63	85
0.00	HAN ,JCY	SP	1991	JAR	WILD ,JJ		79	95
0.00	HAND ,JRM	OC	1990	TAR			739	763
0.00	HAND ,JRM	OC	1991	TAR			739	746
0.00	HARMON,WK	AU	1984	JAA			24	34
0.00	HARPER JR,RM	AU	1987	JAR	MISTER,WG	STRAWSER,JR	327	330
0.00	HARRELL,A	AU	1990	AUD	WRIGHT,A		134	149
0.00	HARRELL,AM	SP	1986	AUD	CHEWNING,EG	TAYLOR,M	111	121
0.00	HARRELL,AM	SP	1988	AUD	EICKHOFF,R		105	118
0.00	HARRISON,GL	01	1992	AOS			1	15
0.00	HASKINS,ME	AU	1990	AUD	WILLIAMS,DD		55	74
0.00	HASSELL,JM	06	1989	AOS	ARRINGTON,CE		527	537
0.00	HAW ,I	SE	1991	JAE	JUNG ,K	LILIEN,SB	295	320
0.00	HAW ,I	SU	1991	JAA	KIM ,W		325	344
0.00	HAW ,IM	WI	1987	JAA	PASTENA,V	LILIEN,S	24	42
0.00	HEALY ,PM	WI	1990	JAA	MODIGLIANI,F		3	25
0.00	HECK ,JL	OC	1986	TAR	BREMSER,WG		735	744
0.00	HEINTZ,JA	SP	1989	AUD	WHITE ,GB		22	39
0.00	HERTOG,FD	02	1992	AOS	WIELINGA,C		103	128
0.00	HESSEL,CA	SU	1992	JAA	NORMAN,M		313	330
0.00	HINES JR,JR	AU	1991	JAA			447	479
0.00	HIRST ,MK	05	1990	AOS	LOWY ,SM		425	436
0.00	HOLT ,DL	06	1992	AOS	MORROW,PC		549	559
0.00	HOPWOOD,W	AU	1988	CAR	MCKEOWN,J	MUTCHLER,J	284	298
0.00	HOPWOOD,W	AP	1989	TAR	SCHAEFER,T		313	328
0.00	HOPWOOD,WS	AU	1988	CAR	SCHAEFER,TF		318	342
0.00	HOPWOOD,WS	SU	1990	JAA	MCKEOWN,JC		339	363
0.00	HORVITZ,JS	WI	1985	JAA	COLDWELL,S		86	99
0.00	HORWITZ,B	JL	1988	TAR	NORMOLLE,D		414	435
0.00	HOUGHTON,CW	SP	1991	AUD	FOGARTY,JA		1	21
0.00	HOUGHTON,KA	03	1988	AOS			263	280
0.00	HUGHES,JS	SP	1986	CAR	RICKS ,WE		222	241
0.00	HUIZING,A	05	1992	AOS	DEKKER,HC		449	458
0.00	HUSS ,HF	AU	1991	AUD	JACOBS,FA		16	32
0.00	HUSS ,HF	WI	1991	JAA	ZHAO ,J		53	66

CITE INDEX	FIRST AUTHOR	ISS-UE	YE-AR	JOUR-NAL	SECOND AUTHOR	THIRD AUTHOR	PAG BEG	PAG END
0.00	HUTH ,WL	WI	1992	JAA	MARIS ,BA		27	44
0.00	ICERMAN,RC	AU	1990	JAA	HILLISON,WA		527	543
0.00	ICERMAN,RC	SP	1991	AUD	HILLISON,WA		22	34
0.00	IMHOFF JR,EA	SU	1981	JAA			333	351
0.00	IMHOFF JR,EA	SP	1988	AUD			182	191
0.00	IMHOFF-JR,EA	DE	1988	JAE	THOMAS,JK		277	310
0.00	IMOISILI,OA	04	1989	AOS			325	335
0.00	INGRAM,RW	AU	1986	CAR			200	221
0.00	INGRAM,RW	AP	1989	TAR	RAMAN ,KK	WILSON,ER	250	268
0.00	ISMAIL,BE	AU	1987	CAR			76	88
0.00	ISMAIL,BE	JA	1989	TAR	KIM ,MK		125	136
0.00	JACKSON,MW	05	1992	AOS			459	469
0.00	JAIN ,PC	JL	1983	TAR			633	638
0.00	JAWORKSI,BJ	01	1992	AOS	YOUNG ,SM		17	35
0.00	JEFFREY,C	OC	1992	TAR			802	820
0.00	JENNINGS,MM	SP	1991	CAR	KNEER ,DC	RECKERS,PMJ	449	465
0.00	JENNINGS,R	OC	1990	TAR			925	932
0.00	JENNINGS,R	AP	1992	TAR	MEST ,DP	THOMPSON II,RB	337	354
0.00	JENSEN,MC	AP	1985	JAE	ZIMMERMAN,JL		3	10
0.00	JOHNSON,O	04	1992	AOS			205	222
0.00	JOHNSON,VE		1991	AUD	KAPLAN,SE		96	107
0.00	JONES ,CP	AU	1990	JAA	BUBLITZ,B		549	566
0.00	JONES ,CS	02	1992	AOS			151	168
0.00	JONSSON,S	05	1991	AOS			521	546
0.00	KACHELMEIER,SJ	OC	1991	TAR	LIMBERG,ST	SCHADEWALD,MS	694	717
0.00	KACHELMEIER,SJ		1991	AUD			25	48
0.00	KAHN ,N	AU	1985	JAA	SCHIFF,A		40	49
0.00	KANPP ,MC	SP	1991	AUD			35	52
0.00	KAPLAN,RS	SP	1983	AUD			52	65
0.00	KAPLAN,SE	04	1988	AOS	RECKERS,PMJ	ROARK ,SJ	371	379
0.00	KAPLAN,SE	06	1989	AOS	RECKERS,PMJ		539	550
0.00	KAPLAN,SE	AU	1992	AUD	MOECKEL,C	WILLIAMS,JD	50	65
0.00	KELLY ,AS	AU	1989	AUD	MOHRWEIS,CS		87	97
0.00	KENNEDY,D	SP	1992	JAA	LAKONISHOK,J	SHAW ,WH	161	190
0.00	KENNEDY,DT	SU	1992	JAA	HYON ,YH		335	356
0.00	KHURANA,I	JL	1991	TAR			611	621
0.00	KIM ,DC	AP	1992	TAR			303	319
0.00	KIM ,DH	WI	1991	JAA	ZIEBART,DA		35	47
0.00	KING ,R	SP	1992	CAR	POWNALL,G	WAYMIRE,G	509	531
0.00	KING ,RD	JA	1986	TAR	O'KEEFE,TB		76	90
0.00	KIRBY ,AJ	SP	1992	CAR			374	408
0.00	KISSINGER,JN	SP	1986	JAA			90	101
0.00	KNAPP ,MC	JL	1987	TAR			578	588
0.00	KNAUF ,JB	WI	1987	JAA	VASARHELYI,MA		43	64
0.00	KOONCE,L	JA	1992	TAR			59	76
0.00	KOTHARI,SP	JN	1992	JAE			173	202
0.00	KRAMER,SS	JA	1982	TAR			70	87
0.00	KREN ,L	JL	1992	TAR			511	526
0.00	KREUTZFELDT,RW		1990	AUD	WALLACE,WA		1	26
0.00	KRINSKY,I	SP	1989	CAR	ROTENBERG,W		501	515
0.00	KRIPKE,H	WI	1989	JAA			3	65
0.00	LABELLE,R	SP	1990	CAR			677	698
0.00	LAMBERT,JC	SP	1991	AUD	LAMBERT III,SJ	CALDERON,TG	97	109

CITE INDEX	FIRST AUTHOR	ISS-UE	YE-AR	JOUR-NAL	SECOND AUTHOR	THIRD AUTHOR	PAG BEG	PAG END
0.00	LANEN ,WN	SP	1992	JAR	LARCKER,DF		70	93
0.00	LANG ,M	AU	1991	JAR			229	257
0.00	LAU ,AH	SP	1987	JAR			127	138
0.00	LEMKE ,KW	MR	1992	JAE	PAGE ,MJ		87	114
0.00	LEV ,B	SP	1979	JAA	TAYLOR,KW		232	243
0.00	LEVY ,H	SP	1990	JAA			235	270
0.00	LEWIS ,BL	SP	1985	JAR	BELL ,J		228	239
0.00	LIBBY ,R	AU	1992	JAR	LIPE ,MG		249	273
0.00	LICHTENBERG,FR	OC	1992	TAR			741	752
0.00	LIVINGSTONE,JL	ST	1967	JAR			93	123
0.00	LIVNAT,J	AU	1981	JAR			350	359
0.00	LOFT ,A	04	1992	AOS			367	378
0.00	LORD ,AT	AU	1992	AUD			89	108
0.00	LOREK ,KS	SP	1983	JAR	ICERMAN,JD	ABDULKADER,AA	317	328
0.00	LOUDDER,ML	SP	1992	AUD	KHURANA,IK	SAWYERS,RB	69	82
0.00	LOVATA,LM	AU	1988	AUD			72	86
0.00	LUCAS ,HC	OC	1975	TAR			735	746
0.00	LUCKETT,PF	04	1991	AOS	EGGLETON,IRC		371	394
0.00	LUNDHOLM,RJ	JL	1991	TAR			486	515
0.00	LYON ,JD	AU	1992	JAA	SCHROEDER,DA		531	552
0.00	MADEO ,SA	AP	1987	TAR	SCHEPANSKI,A	UECKER,WC	323	342
0.00	MAHER ,JJ	OC	1987	TAR			785	798
0.00	MAHER ,MW	JA	1992	TAR	TIESSEN,P	COLSON,R	199	211
0.00	MAINES,LA	ST	1990	JAR			29	54
0.00	MAKSY ,MM	OC	1988	TAR			683	699
0.00	MANEGOLD,JG	SU	1986	JAA			206	221
0.00	MANES ,RP	ST	1967	JAR	SAMUELS,JM	SMYTH ,DJ	139	156
0.00	MARKS ,BR	AU	1987	AUD	RAMAN ,KK		106	117
0.00	MARKS ,BR	SP	1988	CAR	RAMAN ,KK		595	608
0.00	MARSTON,F	SP	1988	JAA	HARRIS,RS		147	164
0.00	MARTIN,A	ST	1971	JAR			1	31
0.00	MARTIN,JD	WI	1979	JAA	ANDERSON,PF	KEOWN ,AJ	151	164
0.00	MAUTZ-JR,RD	04	1990	AOS			273	295
0.00	MAYPER,AG	SP	1991	AUD	ADDY JR,ND		136	144
0.00	MCINNES,M	02	1991	AOS	RAMAKRISHNAN,RTS		167	184
0.00	MCKEOWN,JC		1991	AUD	MUTCHLER,JF	HOPWOOD,W	1	13
0.00	MCROBERTS,HA	04	1985	AOS	HUDSON,J		493	502
0.00	MEADE ,JA	AP	1990	TAR			406	431
0.00	MEANS ,KM	AU	1989	JAA			571	579
0.00	MEAR ,R	JA	1987	TAR	FIRTH ,MA		176	182
0.00	MEAR ,R	04	1987	AOS	FIRTH ,MA		331	340
0.00	MEAR ,RWT	AU	1990	JAA	FIRTH ,MA		501	520
0.00	MELLMAN,M	AU	1986	JAA	SEILER,ME		305	318
0.00	MENDENHALL,RR	ST	1988	JAR	NICHOLS,WD		63	90
0.00	MENON ,K	SP	1987	CAR	SCHWARTZ,KB		302	315
0.00	MENON ,K	AP	1991	TAR	WILLIAMS,DD		313	332
0.00	MERCHANT,KA	04	1990	AOS			297	313
0.00	MERINO,BD	OC	1987	TAR	KOCH ,BS	MACRITCHIE,KL	748	762
0.00	MESSIER JR,WF	SP	1988	CAR	SCHNEIDER,A		337	353
0.00	MIELKE,DE	WI	1987	JAA	SEIFERT,J		65	78
0.00	MILLER,P	05	1991	AOS	HOPPER,T	LAUGHLIN,R	395	403
0.00	MILLER,P		1991	AOS			733	762
0.00	MILTZ ,D	AU	1991	AUD	CALOMME,GJ	WILLIKENS,M	49	61

CITE INDEX	FIRST AUTHOR	ISS-UE	YE-AR	JOUR-NAL	SECOND AUTHOR	THIRD AUTHOR	PAG BEG	PAG END
0.00	MITTELSTAEDT,HF	SP	1992	AUD	REGIER,PR	CHEWNING,EG	83	98
0.00	MOECKEL,C	SP	1990	CAR	WILLIAMS,JD		850	858
0.00	MOIZER,P	AU	1987	AUD	TURLEY,S		118	123
0.00	MOODY ,SM	AU	1986	JAA	FLESHER,DL		319	330
0.00	MOON ,P	03	1990	AOS			193	198
0.00	MOORE ,DC		1991	AOS			163	791
0.00	MOORE ,ML	JA	1985	TAR	STEECE,BM	SWENSON,CW	18	32
0.00	MOORES,K	01	1986	AOS	STEADMAN,GT		19	34
0.00	MOSES ,OD	SU	1990	JAA			379	409
0.00	MULFORD,CW	JL	1986	TAR	COMISKEY,EE		519	525
0.00	MURRAY,D	WI	1982	JAA			154	159
0.00	MUTCHLER,JF	AU	1990	AUD	WILLIAMS,DD		39	54
0.00	NAIR ,RD	AU	1987	AUD	RITTENBERG,LE		15	38
0.00	NEU ,D		1992	AOS	WRIGHT,M		645	665
0.00	NEWTON,JD		1989	AUD	ASHTON,RH		22	37
0.00	NICHOLS,DR	JA	1987	TAR			183	190
0.00	NURNBERG,H	AU	1969	JAR			257	261
0.00	ODAIYAPPA,R	JL	1992	TAR	NAINAR,SMK		599	609
0.00	OHLSON,JA	ST	1972	JAR			45	84
0.00	OHLSON,JA	AU	1992	JAA	PENMAN,SH		553	573
0.00	PALMROSE,Z		1991	AUD			54	71
0.00	PALMROSE,Z	ST	1991	JAR			149	193
0.00	PALMROSE,ZV	AU	1988	AUD			63	71
0.00	PANY ,K	AU	1987	AUD	RECKERS,PMJ		39	53
0.00	PATTEN,DM	06	1990	AOS			575	587
0.00	PATTEN,DM	05	1992	AOS			471	475
0.00	PEAVY ,JW	WI	1985	JAA	EDGAR ,SM		125	135
0.00	PEI ,BKW	SP	1989	AUD	DAVIS ,FG		101	112
0.00	PEI ,BKW	02	1992	AOS	REED ,SA	KOCH ,BS	169	183
0.00	PELES ,YC	SP	1990	JAA			309	327
0.00	PENMAN,SH	SP	1991	JAA			233	255
0.00	PENMAN,SH	JL	1992	TAR			563	578
0.00	PETERS,JM	ST	1990	JAR			83	109
0.00	PETRONI,KR	DE	1992	JAE			485	507
0.00	PHILIPS,GE	ST	1970	JAR	MAYNE ,LS		178	188
0.00	PICCIOTTO,S		1992	AOS			759	792
0.00	PILLSBURY,CM	SP	1985	AUD			63	79
0.00	PINCUS	02	1989	AOS			153	163
0.00	PINCUS,KV	AU	1990	AUD			150	167
0.00	PONEMON,LA	AU	1991	AUD	SCHICK,AG		70	83
0.00	PONEMON,LA	AU	1992	CAR			171	189
0.00	PONEMON,LA	04	1992	AOS			239	258
0.00	PORCANO,TM	OC	1984	TAR			619	636
0.00	POWER ,MK	01	1992	AOS			37	62
0.00	POWNALL,G	ST	1989	JAR	WAYMIRE,G		85	105
0.00	PRATT ,J	04	1985	AOS			427	442
0.00	PRATT ,J		1992	AOS	BEAULIEU,P		667	684
0.00	PRESTON,AM	01	1992	AOS			63	100
0.00	PURO ,M	SP	1985	JAA			165	177
0.00	PURVIS,SEC	06	1989	AOS			551	563
0.00	PYO ,Y	DE	1990	JAE	LUSTGARTEN,S		365	379
0.00	RAGHUNANDAN,K	SP	1991	CAR	GRIMLUND,RA	SCHEPANSKI,A	549	568
0.00	RAMAKRISHNAN,RTS	AU	1992	JAA	THOMAS,JK		423	464

CITE INDEX	FIRST AUTHOR	ISS-UE	YE-AR	JOUR-NAL	SECOND AUTHOR	THIRD AUTHOR	PAG BEG	PAG END
0.00	RANSOM,CR	ST	1985	JAR			124	143
0.00	RASCH ,RH	SP	1990	AUD	HARRELL,A		90	102
0.00	RAUN ,DL	OC	1964	TAR			927	945
0.00	RAYBURN,J	AU	1992	CAR	LENWAY,S		237	251
0.00	REBELE,JE	AU	1988	AUD	HEINTZ,JA	BRIDEN,GE	43	52
0.00	REILLY,FK	AU	1972	JAR	STETTLER,HF		308	321
0.00	REIMERS,JL	02	1992	AOS	BUTLER,SA		185	194
0.00	RICCHIUTE,DN	JA	1992	TAR			46	58
0.00	RICHARDSON,AJ	AU	1990	CAR	WILLIAMS,JJ		278	294
0.00	RICHARDSON,G	AU	1988	CAR	SEFCIK,SE	THOMPSON,R	299	317
0.00	RO ,BT	AU	1989	CAR			177	195
0.00	ROBBINS,WA	SU	1985	JAA	APOSTOLOU,NG	STRAWSER,RH	279	292
0.00	ROBERTS,J	04	1992	AOS	COUTTS,JA		379	395
0.00	ROBERTS,RW	06	1992	AOS			595	612
0.00	ROBINSON,JR	JA	1990	TAR	SHANE ,PB		25	48
0.00	ROCKNESS,HO	SP	1988	CAR	SHIELDS,MD		568	581
0.00	RODGERS,W	WI	1992	JAA			67	95
0.00	RONEN ,J	WI	1989	JAA	SORTER,G		67	77
0.00	ROSE ,PS	AU	1982	JAA	ANDREWS,WT	GIROUX,GA	20	31
0.00	ROSMAN,A	SP	1992	JAA			251	267
0.00	RULAND,W	JL	1990	TAR	TUNG ,S	GEORGE,NE	710	721
0.00	RYAN ,SG	SP	1991	JAA			257	287
0.00	SAMI ,H	SP	1989	CAR	CURATOLA,AP	TRAPNELL,JE	556	574
0.00	SAMI ,H	AU	1992	CAR	WELSH ,MJ		212	236
0.00	SANNELLA,AJ	AU	1986	JAA			288	304
0.00	SANNELLA,AJ	WI	1991	JAA			75	102
0.00	SCHACHTER,B	AU	1988	JAR			353	372
0.00	SCHAEFER,T	AU	1986	JAA	KENNELLEY,M		278	287
0.00	SCHATZBERG,JW	AP	1990	TAR			337	362
0.00	SCHICK,AG	03	1990	AOS	GORDON,LA	HAKA ,S	199	220
0.00	SCHNEIDER,A	JL	1990	TAR	WILNER,N		668	681
0.00	SCHOLES,MS	SU	1989	JAA	TERRY ,E	WOLFSON,MA	317	340
0.00	SCHWEIKART,JA	06	1986	AOS			541	554
0.00	SHACKELFORD,DA	JN	1991	JAE			117	145
0.00	SHANKER,L	SU	1992	JAA			379	393
0.00	SHANTEAU,J	02	1989	AOS			165	177
0.00	SHAW ,WH	AP	1987	TAR			385	400
0.00	SHAW ,WH	SP	1991	CAR			407	423
0.00	SHEHATA,M	OC	1991	TAR			768	787
0.00	SHEVLIN,T	JA	1991	TAR			1	22
0.00	SHIELDS,MD	AU	1988	CAR	SOLOMON,I	WALLER,WS	1	18
0.00	SILHAN,PA	SP	1985	JAR	MCKEOWN,JC		416	426
0.00	SIMNETT,R	JL	1989	TAR	TROTMAN,K		514	528
0.00	SIMON ,HA	JL	1990	TAR			658	667
0.00	SIMONS,R	AU	1988	CAR			267	283
0.00	SMITH ,DB	SP	1988	JAR			134	145
0.00	SMITH ,G	AU	1988	AUD			108	117
0.00	SMITH ,G	AU	1991	AUD	KROGSTAD,JL		84	97
0.00	SNOWBALL,D	01	1986	AOS			47	70
0.00	SRINIDHI,BN	SP	1986	AUD	VASARHELYI,MA		64	76
0.00	SRIVASTAVA,RP	AP	1992	TAR	SHAFER,GR		249	283
0.00	STANDISH,PEM	OC	1982	TAR	UNG ,S		701	715
0.00	STEPHENS,RG	JA	1990	TAR	GOVINDARAJAN,V		242	257

CITE INDEX	FIRST AUTHOR	ISS-UE	YE-AR	JOUR-NAL	SECOND AUTHOR	THIRD AUTHOR	PAG BEG	PAG END
0.00	STEVENS,JL	SP	1992	JAA	JOSE ,ML		195	212
0.00	STICE ,EK	JA	1991	TAR			42	55
0.00	STICKEL,SE	OC	1986	JAE			197	216
0.00	STICKEL,SE	AP	1991	TAR			402	416
0.00	STRAWSER,JR	SP	1991	AUD			126	135
0.00	STRONG,JS	OC	1990	JAE			267	283
0.00	SUMNERS,GE	SP	1987	AUD	WHITE ,RA	CLAY JR,RJ	116	122
0.00	SWANSON,EP	OC	1985	TAR	SHEARON,WT	THOMAS,LR	681	691
0.00	SWANSON,GA	JL	1988	TAR	GARDNER,JC		436	447
0.00	SWENSON,CW	JA	1987	TAR			117	136
0.00	SWIERINGA,RJ	SP	1989	JAA			169	186
0.00	TEALL ,HD	SP	1992	CAR			561	579
0.00	TEALL ,HD	SP	1992	CAR			561	579
0.00	TEETS ,W	AU	1992	JAR			274	285
0.00	THANE ,P	04	1992	AOS			299	312
0.00	THODE ,SF	WI	1986	JAA	DRTINA,RE	LARGAY III,JA	46	61
0.00	THOMAS,AP	03	1986	AOS			253	270
0.00	THOMAS,JK	OC	1989	TAR			773	787
0.00	THORNTON,DB	AU	1988	CAR			343	370
0.00	TILLER,MG	SU	1985	JAA	MAUTZ ,RD		293	304
0.00	TINIC ,SM	OC	1990	TAR			781	796
0.00	TORABZADEH,KM	SP	1992	JAA	BERTIN,WJ		231	240
0.00	TROTMAN,KT	06	1989	AOS	SNG ,J		565	576
0.00	TSE ,S	SP	1989	CAR			592	614
0.00	TSE ,S	SP	1990	JAR			229	238
0.00	TUBBS ,RM	OC	1992	TAR			783	801
0.00	VASARHELYI,MA	SP	1991	AUD	HALPER,FB		110	125
0.00	WAGGONER,JB	SP	1990	AUD			77	89
0.00	WALKER,KB	AU	1991	JAR	MCCLELLAND,LA		371	381
0.00	WALKER,SP	03	1991	AOS			257	283
0.00	WALLACE,WA	SP	1983	AUD			66	90
0.00	WALLACE,WA	SP	1991	AUD			53	68
0.00	WALLACE,WA	SP	1991	CAR	KRUETZFELDT,RW		485	512
0.00	WALLER,WS	02	1989	AOS	FELIX JR,WL		179	200
0.00	WANG ,S	JA	1991	TAR			158	169
0.00	WARDELL,M		1991	AOS	WEISENFELD,LW		655	670
0.00	WARFIELD,TD	JL	1992	TAR	LINSMEIER,TJ		546	562
0.00	WARFIELD,TD	OC	1992	TAR	WILD ,JJ		821	842
0.00	WAYMIRE,G	AU	1983	JAR	POWNALL,G		629	643
0.00	WILLIAMS,DJ	SP	1985	AUD	LILLIS,A		110	117
0.00	WILLIAMS,DJ	03	1986	AOS			271	288
0.00	WILLIAMS,JJ	04	1985	AOS	NEWTON,JD	MORGAN,EA	457	478
0.00	WILLIAMS,JJ	02	1988	AOS	HININGS,CR		191	198
0.00	WILLIAMS,PF	06	1989	AOS			455	468
0.00	WILSON,AC	AU	1989	CAR	HUDSON,D		196	215
0.00	WILSON,AC	SU	1991	JAA			365	381
0.00	WILSON,AC	SP	1992	AUD			32	46
0.00	WONG-ON-WING,B	06	1989	AOS	RENEAU,JH	WEST ,SG	577	587
0.00	WRIGHT,A	06	1988	AOS			595	605
0.00	WRIGHT,WF	AU	1988	CAR			47	57
0.00	YARDLEY,JA	AU	1989	AUD			41	56
0.00	YOUNG ,AE	SU	1992	JAA			361	368
0.00	YOUNG ,SD	AP	1988	TAR			283	291

CITE INDEX	FIRST AUTHOR	ISS-UE	YE-AR	JOUR-NAL	SECOND AUTHOR	THIRD AUTHOR	PAG BEG	PAG END
0.00	YOUNG ,SD	OC	1991	TAR			809	817
0.00	ZAROWIN,P	AP	1988	JAE			89	110
0.00	ZAROWIN,P	SU	1990	JAA			439	454
0.00	ZEFF ,SA	SP	1992	CAR			443	467
0.00	ZIEBART,DA	AP	1990	TAR			477	488
0.00	ZIEBART,DA	AU	1992	CAR	REITER,SA		252	282
0.00	ZIND ,RG	AU	1989	CAR	ZEGHAL,D		26	47

1.3 MODE OF REASONING (METHOD)=QUANTITATIVE: ANOVA

CITE INDEX	FIRST AUTHOR	ISS-UE	YE-AR	JOUR-NAL	SECOND AUTHOR	THIRD AUTHOR	PAG BEG	PAG END
2.35	JOYCE ,EJ	ST	1976	JAR			29	60
2.00	MEYER ,JW	45	1986	AOS			345	356
1.80	HINES ,RD	03	1988	AOS			251	261
1.58	JOYCE ,EJ	SP	1981	JAR	BIDDLE,GC		120	145
1.56	AJINKYA,BB	AU	1984	JAR	GIFT ,MJ		425	444
1.42	JOYCE ,EJ	AU	1981	JAR	BIDDLE,GC		323	349
1.41	LIBBY ,R	JL	1975	TAR			475	489
1.31	COLLINS,WA	AU	1980	JAR	HOPWOOD,WS		390	406
1.27	ABDEL-KHALIK,AR	OC	1978	TAR	MCKEOWN,JC		851	868
1.20	ZIMMERMAN,JL	AG	1983	JAE			119	149
1.10	KELLER,SB	AU	1983	AUD	DAVIDSON,LF		1	22
1.10	MESSIER JR,WF	AU	1983	JAR			611	618
1.00	ASHTON,AH	AP	1991	TAR			218	239
1.00	CHOW ,CW	OC	1983	TAR			667	685
1.00	MCGHEE,W	JL	1978	TAR	SHIELDS,MD	BIRNBERG,JG	681	697
0.93	BENBASAT,I	OC	1979	TAR	DEXTER,AS		735	749
0.93	CRICHFIELD,T	JL	1978	TAR	DYCKMAN,TR	LAKONISHOK,J	651	668
0.93	PATELL,JM	AG	1979	JAE	WOLFSON,MA		117	140
0.90	SHIELDS,MD	AP	1983	TAR			284	303
0.88	BAREFIELD,RM	AU	1972	JAR			229	242
0.87	UECKER,WC	SP	1978	JAR			169	189
0.85	CASEY JR,CJ	JA	1980	TAR			36	49
0.85	LEWIS ,BL	AU	1980	JAR			594	602
0.85	SHIELDS,MD	04	1980	AOS			429	442
0.82	BASI ,BA	AP	1976	TAR	CAREY ,KJ	TWARK ,RD	244	254
0.82	CHERRINGTON,DJ	ST	1973	JAR	CHERRINGTON,JO		225	253
0.82	ELIAS ,N	ST	1972	JAR			215	233
0.82	KINNEY JR,WR	SP	1971	JAR			127	136
0.78	ARANYA,N	JA	1984	TAR	FERRIS,KR		1	15
0.78	KAPLAN,SE	AU	1984	AUD	RECKERS,PMJ		1	19
0.78	KIDA ,TE	SP	1984	JAR			332	340
0.75	SCHULTZ JR,JJ	AU	1981	JAR	RECKERS,PMJ		482	501
0.73	DANOS ,P	AU	1982	JAR	EICHENSEHER,JW		604	616
0.71	ABDEL-KHALIK,AR	ST	1973	JAR			104	138
0.71	DICKHAUT,JW	JA	1973	TAR			61	79
0.71	FORAN ,MF	OC	1974	TAR	DECOSTER,DT		751	763
0.71	MOCK ,TJ	SP	1972	JAR	ESTRIN,TL	VASARHELYI,MA	129	153
0.71	SORENSEN,JE	JL	1967	TAR			553	565
0.69	ROCKNESS,HO	OC	1977	TAR			893	903
0.67	KROGSTAD,JL	AU	1984	AUD	ETTENSON,RT	SHANTEAU,J	54	74
0.65	HOFSTEDT,TR	OC	1972	TAR			679	692
0.63	HARRELL,AM	OC	1977	TAR			833	841
0.60	CHENHALL,RH	03	1988	AOS	BROWNELL,P		225	233

CITE INDEX	FIRST AUTHOR	ISS-UE	YE-AR	JOUR-NAL	SECOND AUTHOR	THIRD AUTHOR	PAG BEG	PAG END
0.60	FOSTER III,TW	OC	1978	TAR	VICKREY,DW		921	934
0.59	CHESLEY,GR	SP	1976	JAR			27	48
0.58	HILTON,RW	SP	1981	JAR	SWIERINGA,RJ	HOSKIN,RE	86	108
0.58	LARCKER,DF	JL	1981	TAR			519	538
0.57	LIBBY ,R	ST	1979	JAR			35	57
0.55	HALL ,TW	SP	1982	JAR			139	151
0.54	SNOWBALL,D	03	1980	AOS			323	340
0.53	FIRTH ,MA	JL	1978	TAR			642	650
0.53	OLIVER,BL	AU	1974	JAR			299	316
0.53	SCHULTZ JR,JJ	JL	1978	TAR	GUSTAVSON,SG		626	641
0.50	ARMSTRONG,P	01	1991	AOS			1	25
0.50	TEHRANIAN,H	ST	1987	JAR	TRAVLOS,NG	WAEGELEIN,JF	51	76
0.50	VASARHELYI,MA	SP	1977	JAR			138	153
0.47	COOK ,DM	ST	1967	JAR			213	224
0.47	MAGEE ,RP	AU	1974	JAR			270	287
0.47	MAGEE ,RP	AU	1978	JAR	DICKHAUT,JW		294	314
0.47	RONEN ,J	AU	1971	JAR			307	332
0.47	WATSON,DJ	AP	1975	TAR			259	273
0.45	DANOS ,P	JA	1982	TAR	IMHOFF JR,EA		39	54
0.44	BENSTON,GJ	AU	1984	CAR			47	57
0.44	NANNI JR,AJ	02	1984	AOS			149	163
0.43	BROWN ,PR	AU	1986	AUD	KARAN ,V		134	147
0.42	HILTON,RW	SP	1981	JAR	SWIERINGA,RJ		109	119
0.42	KESSLER,L	SP	1981	JAR	ASHTON,RH		146	162
0.42	SHIELDS,MD	01	1981	AOS	BIRNBERG,JG	FRIEZE,IH	69	96
0.42	SHOCKLEY,RA	OC	1981	TAR			785	800
0.42	VIGELAND,RL	AP	1981	TAR			309	325
0.41	ANSARI,SL	AU	1976	JAR			189	211
0.41	JENSEN,RE	AU	1966	JAR			224	238
0.40	ABDEL-KHALIK,AR	AP	1983	TAR	SNOWBALL,D	WRAGGE,JH	215	227
0.40	CHESLEY,GR	AU	1978	JAR			225	241
0.40	HOSKIN,RE	SP	1983	JAR			78	95
0.40	HUGHES,PJ	ST	1988	JAR	SCHWARTZ,ES		41	62
0.40	INGRAM,RW	AU	1978	JAR			270	285
0.40	NEUMANN,BR	AU	1978	JAR	FRIEDMAN,LA		400	410
0.38	BOWMAN,RG	SP	1980	JAR			242	254
0.38	UECKER,WC	SP	1980	JAR			191	213
0.35	BECKER,S	AU	1974	JAR	RONEN ,J	SORTER,GH	317	329
0.35	EGGLETON,IRC	ST	1976	JAR			68	131
0.35	LAVIN ,D	JA	1976	TAR			41	50
0.35	MCINTYRE,EV	JL	1973	TAR			575	585
0.35	SORTER,GH	AU	1964	JAR	BECKER,S	ARCHIBALD,TR	183	196
0.33	BROWN ,C	SP	1981	JAR			62	85
0.33	CHAMBERS,RJ	AU	1984	CAR			1	22
0.33	DANOS ,P	OC	1984	TAR	HOLT ,DL	IMHOFF JR,EA	547	573
0.33	GUL ,FA	AP	1984	TAR			264	277
0.33	RO ,BT	JA	1981	TAR			70	84
0.33	UECKER,WC	JL	1981	TAR	BRIEF ,AP	KINNEY JR,WR	465	478
0.31	BELKAOUI,A	03	1980	AOS			263	284
0.30	BROWNELL,P	04	1983	AOS			307	322
0.29	COMISKEY,EE	AP	1971	TAR			279	285
0.29	COVALESKI,M	45	1986	AOS	AIKEN ,ME		297	320
0.29	DEAKIN,EB	JA	1976	TAR			90	96

CITE INDEX	FIRST AUTHOR	ISS-UE	YE-AR	JOUR-NAL	SECOND AUTHOR	THIRD AUTHOR	PAG BEG	PAG END
0.29	FIRTH ,MA	04	1979	AOS			283	296
0.29	MAHER ,MW	AU	1979	JAR	RAMANATHAN,KV	PETERSON,RB	476	503
0.29	MOCK ,TJ	ST	1969	JAR			124	159
0.29	RECKERS,PMJ	AU	1979	JAA	TAYLOR,ME		42	55
0.29	STALLMAN,JC	ST	1969	JAR			29	43
0.29	WHITE ,GE	AU	1970	JAR			260	273
0.27	ABDEL-KHALIK,AR	ST	1978	JAR	MCKEOWN,JC		46	77
0.27	ASHTON,AH	AU	1982	JAR			415	428
0.27	HICKS JR,JO	AP	1978	TAR			371	388
0.27	KEYS ,DE	AU	1978	JAR			389	399
0.25	RICKS ,WE	JA	1985	TAR	HUGHES,JS		33	52
0.25	RONEN ,J	SP	1989	JAA	SONDHI,AC		237	265
0.24	BREMSER,WG	JL	1975	TAR			563	573
0.24	HOLSTRUM,GL	AU	1971	JAR			268	277
0.24	WARREN,CS	SP	1975	JAR			162	176
0.23	AJINKYA,BB	AU	1980	JAR			343	361
0.23	FRIEDMAN,LA	AU	1980	JAR	NEUMANN,BR		407	419
0.23	PANY ,K	JA	1980	TAR	RECKERS,PMJ		50	61
0.22	KIDA ,TE	SP	1984	JAR			145	152
0.22	WALLER,WS	OC	1984	TAR	FELIX JR,WL		637	646
0.21	ADELBERG,AH	AU	1979	JAR			565	592
0.20	BAMBER,EM	AU	1983	JAR			396	412
0.20	BASU ,S	JL	1978	TAR			599	625
0.20	HIRSCH JR,ML	AU	1978	JAR			254	269
0.20	JOHNSON,WB	JA	1983	TAR			78	97
0.20	KAMIN ,JY	02	1978	AOS	RONEN ,J		141	160
0.20	MORSE ,D	AP	1983	TAR	USHMAN,N		247	258
0.20	WHITE ,RA	JL	1983	TAR			539	561
0.19	GORDON,FE	04	1977	AOS	RHODE ,JG	MERCHANT,KA	295	306
0.18	BENBASAT,I	SP	1982	JAR	DEXTER,AS		1	11
0.18	CHASTEEN,LG	JL	1971	TAR			504	508
0.18	COPELAND,RM	JL	1968	TAR	LICASTRO,RD		540	545
0.18	DASCHER,PE	SP	1971	JAR	COPELAND,RM		32	39
0.18	LENGERMANN,JJ	OC	1971	TAR			665	675
0.18	OTLEY ,DT	SP	1982	JAR	DIAS ,FJB		171	188
0.18	PATZ ,DH	AU	1972	JAR	BOATSMAN,JR		392	403
0.18	SCHULTE JR,AA	JL	1965	TAR			587	593
0.18	SORENSEN,JE	OC	1972	TAR	FRANKS,DD		735	746
0.18	WRIGHT,A	SP	1982	JAR			227	239
0.17	CHEN ,K	01	1981	AOS	SUMMERS,EL		1	16
0.17	RECKERS,PMJ	SU	1981	AUD	STAGLIANO,AJ		23	37
0.15	GRAY ,SJ	SP	1980	JAR			64	76
0.14	DEFEO ,VJ	AU	1986	JAR			349	363
0.14	ESKEW ,RK	JA	1979	TAR			107	118
0.14	HARVEY,DW	03	1979	AOS	RHODE ,JG	MERCHANT,KA	187	210
0.14	ZALD ,MN	45	1986	AOS			321	326
0.13	LIN ,WT	JA	1978	TAR			61	76
0.13	PATTON,JM	AP	1978	TAR			402	414
0.13	SCHIPPER,K	ST	1977	JAR			1	40
0.13	TOMASSINI,LA	OC	1977	TAR			904	913
0.13	WARREN,CS	JA	1977	TAR			150	161
0.12	CHURCHILL,NC	OC	1975	TAR	SHANK ,JK		643	656
0.12	DECOSTER,DT	OC	1971	TAR	RHODE ,JG		651	664

CITE INDEX	FIRST AUTHOR	ISS-UE	YE-AR	JOUR-NAL	SECOND AUTHOR	THIRD AUTHOR	PAG BEG	PAG END
0.11	CHAMBERS,RJ	AU	1984	CAR			58	63
0.11	DAROCA,FP	01	1984	AOS			13	32
0.10	BROWN ,C	AU	1983	JAR			413	431
0.10	DANOS ,P	AU	1983	JAR	IMHOFF JR,EA		473	494
0.10	TILLER,MG	AU	1983	JAR			581	595
0.10	WILKINS,T	OC	1983	TAR	ZIMMER,I		749	764
0.09	JIAMBALVO,J	OC	1982	TAR	PRATT ,J		734	750
0.09	RECKERS,PMJ	AU	1982	AUD	SCHULTZ JR,JJ		64	74
0.08	COPELAND,RM	SP	1981	JAR	TAYLOR,RL	BROWN ,SH	197	207
0.08	FIRTH ,MA	JL	1980	TAR			451	466
0.08	KOCH ,BS	JL	1981	TAR			574	586
0.08	RAMANATHAN,KV	02	1981	AOS	WEIS ,WL		143	152
0.08	WILLIAMS,PF	JA	1980	TAR			62	77
0.07	GIVOLY,D	SU	1978	JAA	RONEN ,J	SCHIFF,A	361	372
0.06	ALY ,HF	JA	1971	TAR	DUBOFF,JI		119	128
0.06	BOLLOM,WJ	JA	1973	TAR			12	22
0.06	CULPEPPER,RC	AP	1970	TAR			322	332
0.06	DALTON,FE	JA	1970	TAR	MINER ,JB		134	139
0.06	PARKER,JE	JL	1975	TAR			512	524
0.06	SAULS ,EH	ST	1970	JAR			157	171
0.00	AMEY ,LR	AU	1984	CAR			64	76
0.00	ASHTON,RH	SU	1981	AUD	HYLAS ,RE		12	22
0.00	BOATSMAN,JR	JA	1992	TAR	GRASSO,LP	ORMISTON,MB	148	156
0.00	BRENNAN,MJ	JA	1991	TAR			67	79
0.00	CHURCHILL,NC	WI	1982	AUD	COOPER,WW	GOVINDARAJAN,V	69	91
0.00	DEJONG,DV	JA	1992	TAR	FORSYTHE,R		157	171
0.00	DEMSKI,JS	AU	1985	CAR			69	75
0.00	DONTOH,A	SP	1988	CAR	RICHARDSON,E		450	469
0.00	DYKXHOORN,HJ	04	1982	AOS	SINNING,KE		337	348
0.00	FERRIS,KR	01	1982	AOS			13	26
0.00	GAA ,JC	SP	1985	CAR	SMITH ,CH		219	241
0.00	HASSELBACK,JR	AP	1976	TAR			269	276
0.00	HAYES ,RD	JL	1990	TAR	MILLAR,JA		505	519
0.00	HOPPER,T	05	1991	AOS	ARMSTRONG,P		405	438
0.00	JOHNSON,DA	SP	1983	AUD	PANY ,K	WHITE ,RA	38	51
0.00	JOHNSON,DA	AU	1984	JAR	PANY ,K		731	743
0.00	JOHNSON,WB	04	1982	AOS			349	368
0.00	KHEMAKHEM,A	JL	1968	TAR			522	534
0.00	LIVINGSTONE,JL	JL	1967	TAR			544	552
0.00	MEEK ,GK	AP	1983	TAR			394	402
0.00	PANY ,K	AU	1982	JAR	SMITH ,CH		472	481
0.00	PETERS,JM	04	1989	AOS	LEWIS ,BL	DHAR ,V	359	378
0.00	POWER ,MK	04	1991	AOS			333	353
0.00	PURDY ,CR	ST	1969	JAR	SMITH JR,JM	GRAY ,J	1	18
0.00	SIMONS,R	02	1990	AOS			127	143
0.00	STAUBUS,GJ	JL	1968	TAR			413	424
0.00	SUMMERS,EL	AP	1968	TAR			257	265
0.00	TAUSSIG,RA	JA	1968	TAR	HAYES ,SC		68	74
0.00	THEOBALD,M	AU	1985	CAR			1	22
0.00	TOMASSINI,LA	SP	1990	CAR			287	294
0.00	WARREN,CS	SP	1974	JAR			158	177
0.00	WARREN,CS	SP	1980	JAR			312	324
0.00	WATSON,CJ	JL	1990	TAR			682	695

CITE INDEX	FIRST AUTHOR	ISS-UE	YE-AR	JOUR-NAL	SECOND AUTHOR	THIRD AUTHOR	PAG BEG	PAG END
1.4 MODE OF REASONING (METHOD)=QUANTITATIVE: FACT.ANAL,MDA,LOGIT,PROBIT,DIS.								
8.20	WATTS ,RL	JA	1978	TAR	ZIMMERMAN,JL		112	134
3.79	HAGERMAN,RL	AG	1979	JAE	ZMIJEWSKI,ME		141	161
3.33	ZMIJEWSKI,ME	AG	1981	JAE	HAGERMAN,RL		129	149
3.18	BRUNS JR,WJ	AU	1975	JAR	WATERHOUSE,JH		177	203
2.73	FRIED ,D	OC	1982	JAE	GIVOLY,D		85	107
2.56	HAYES ,DC	JA	1977	TAR			22	39
2.00	DALEY ,LA	DE	1983	JAE	VIGELAND,RL		195	211
1.67	ZMIJEWSKI,ME	ST	1984	JAR			59	82
1.33	MERCHANT,KA	34	1984	AOS			291	309
1.24	DEAKIN,EB	SP	1972	JAR			167	179
1.18	ONSI ,M	JL	1973	TAR			535	548
1.10	EVANS III,JH	AG	1983	JAE	PATTON,JM		151	175
1.00	BOATSMAN,JR	AP	1974	TAR	ROBERTSON,JC		342	352
1.00	DEAKIN,EB	OC	1979	TAR			722	734
0.65	SAN MIGUEL,JG	04	1976	AOS			357	374
0.64	LIBBY ,R	SP	1979	JAR			99	122
0.58	BROWN ,PR	SP	1981	JAR			232	246
0.57	DILLARD,JF	03	1979	AOS	FERRIS,KR		179	186
0.57	MORIARITY,S	ST	1979	JAR	BARRON,FH		114	135
0.56	BALDWIN,BA	JL	1984	TAR			376	389
0.56	MARAIS,ML	ST	1984	JAR	PATELL,JM	WOLFSON,MA	87	114
0.56	MCKEE ,AJ	OC	1984	TAR	BELL ,TB	BOATSMAN,JR	647	659
0.53	FRISHKOFF,P	ST	1970	JAR			116	129
0.53	SWIERINGA,RJ	ST	1972	JAR	MONCUR,RH		194	209
0.44	ARRINGTON,CE	SP	1984	JAR	HILLISON,WA	JENSEN,RE	298	312
0.44	STOCK ,D	SP	1984	JAR	WATSON,CJ		192	206
0.42	RAMAN ,KK	OC	1981	TAR			910	926
0.40	FLAMHOLTZ,EG	02	1978	AOS	COOK ,E		115	140
0.40	LARCKER,DF	JA	1983	TAR	LESSIG,VP		58	77
0.40	SHOCKLEY,RA	AU	1983	JAR	HOLT ,RN		545	564
0.36	ALTMAN,EI	AU	1982	JAA			4	19
0.36	COPELAND,RM	AU	1982	JAR	INGRAM,RW		275	289
0.31	BENKE ,RL	02	1980	AOS	RHODE ,JG		187	202
0.31	HOLT ,RN	03	1980	AOS	CARROLL,R		285	296
0.29	BLUM ,M	SP	1974	JAR			1	25
0.29	CLANCY,DK	12	1979	AOS	COLLINS,F		21	30
0.29	NORTON,CL	JA	1979	TAR	SMITH ,RE		72	87
0.25	INGRAM,RW	OC	1981	TAR	COPELAND,RM		830	843
0.24	SEARFOSS,DG	04	1976	AOS			375	388
0.23	NAIR ,RD	JL	1980	TAR	FRANK ,WG		426	450
0.22	FRAZIER,KB	SP	1984	JAR	INGRAM,RW	TENNYSON,BM	318	331
0.22	PURO ,M	AU	1984	JAR			624	646
0.21	DILLARD,JF	12	1979	AOS			31	38
0.20	KETZ ,JE	ST	1978	JAR			273	284
0.18	GUPTA ,MC	SP	1972	JAR	HUEFNER,RJ		77	95
0.18	SEILER,RE	04	1982	AOS	BARTLETT,RW		381	404
0.14	FRANK ,WG	AU	1979	JAR			593	605
0.13	SHORT ,DG	ST	1978	JAR			259	272
0.12	HARMELINK,PJ	SP	1973	JAR			146	158
0.12	WELKER,RB	JL	1974	TAR			514	523
0.11	WESCOTT,SH	SP	1984	JAR			412	423

CITE INDEX	FIRST AUTHOR	ISS-UE	YE-AR	JOUR-NAL	SECOND AUTHOR	THIRD AUTHOR	PAG BEG	PAG END
0.10	CASEY JR,CJ	SP	1983	JAR			300	307
0.10	GOMBOLA,MJ	JA	1983	TAR	KETZ ,JE		105	114
0.10	MENSAH,YM	AP	1983	TAR			228	246
0.08	BELKAOUI,A	04	1981	AOS			281	290
0.08	KELLY ,LK	03	1980	AOS			311	322
0.08	WHITTINGTON,OR	JL	1980	TAR	WHITTENBURG,G		409	418
0.07	MADEO ,SA	JL	1979	TAR			538	553
0.07	PEARSON,MA	WI	1979	JAA	LINDGREN,JH	MYERS ,BL	122	134
0.06	FRANK ,WG	SP	1971	JAR	WEYGANDT,JJ		116	126
0.06	JENSEN,RE	JA	1971	TAR			36	56
0.06	LUSK ,EJ	JL	1972	TAR			567	575
0.06	UECKER,WC	01	1977	AOS			47	58
0.00	BAILEY,KE	AU	1983	JAR	BYLINSKI,JH	SHIELDS,MD	355	370
0.00	FIRTH ,MA	SP	1973	JAR			16	24
0.00	MENSAH,YM	WI	1983	JAA			130	141
0.00	MENSAH,YM	SP	1984	JAR			380	395
0.00	MONAHAN,TF	SU	1983	JAA	BARENBAUM,L		325	340
0.00	NEUMANN,BR	SP	1979	JAR			123	139
0.00	RAMAN ,KK	WI	1982	JAA			144	153
0.00	RAMAN ,KK	AU	1982	JAA			44	50
0.00	STERNER,JA	AU	1983	JAR			623	628
0.00	WATKINS,PR	SP	1984	JAR			406	411

1.5 MODE OF REASONING (METHOD)=QUANTITATIVE: MARKOV

CITE INDEX	FIRST AUTHOR	ISS-UE	YE-AR	JOUR-NAL	SECOND AUTHOR	THIRD AUTHOR	PAG BEG	PAG END
0.29	JAGGI ,B	AP	1974	TAR	LAU ,HS		321	329
0.12	GONEDES,NJ	AU	1971	JAR			236	252
0.08	BALACHANDRAN,KR	JA	1981	TAR	MASCHMEYER,R	LIVINGSTONE,JL	115	124
0.06	SHANK ,JK	JA	1971	TAR			57	74

1.6 MODE OF REASONING (METHOD)=QUANTITATIVE: NON-PARAMETRIC

CITE INDEX	FIRST AUTHOR	ISS-UE	YE-AR	JOUR-NAL	SECOND AUTHOR	THIRD AUTHOR	PAG BEG	PAG END
8.35	BALL ,R	AU	1968	JAR	BROWN ,P		159	178
4.93	BEAVER,WH	AU	1979	JAR	CLARKE,R	WRIGHT,WF	316	340
2.64	COLLINS,DW	MR	1979	JAE	DENT ,WT		3	44
2.41	GONEDES,NJ	SP	1976	JAR	DOPUCH,N	PENMAN,SH	89	137
2.21	DYCKMAN,TR	MR	1979	JAE	SMITH ,AJ		45	75
2.18	DHALIWAL,DS	JL	1982	JAE	SALAMON,GL	SMITH ,ED	41	53
2.00	MILANI,K	AP	1975	TAR			274	284
1.85	ASHTON,RH	SP	1980	JAR	KRAMER,SS		1	15
1.85	BIDDLE,GC	ST	1980	JAR			235	280
1.38	DUKES ,RE	ST	1980	JAR	DYCKMAN,TR	ELLIOTT,JA	1	26
1.30	EICHENSEHER,JW	SP	1983	AUD	SHIELDS,D		23	37
1.30	PINCUS,M	SP	1983	JAR			155	183
1.29	KAPLAN,RS	AU	1973	JAR			238	258
1.06	HOPWOOD,AG	JL	1974	TAR			485	495
1.00	ABDEL-KHALIK,AR	OC	1974	TAR		743	750	
1.00	ASHTON,RH	ST	1976	JAR			1	17
1.00	ELLIOTT,JA	SP	1984	JAR	RICHARDSON,G	DYCKMAN,TR	85	102
0.88	SMITH ,ED	OC	1976	TAR			707	723
0.85	WEBER ,R	SP	1980	JAR			214	241
0.82	EGGLETON,IRC	SP	1976	JAR	PENMAN,SH	TWOMBLY,JR	66	88
0.77	HORWITZ,BN	ST	1980	JAR	KOLODNY,R		38	74

CITE INDEX	FIRST AUTHOR	ISS-UE	YE-AR	JOUR-NAL	SECOND AUTHOR	THIRD AUTHOR	PAG BEG	PAG END
0.73	NETER ,J	JA	1978	TAR	LEITCH,RA	FIENBERG,SE	77	93
0.69	ASHTON,RH	SP	1980	JAR	BROWN ,PR		269	277
0.69	KIDA ,TE	AU	1980	JAR			506	523
0.69	RHODE ,JG	02	1977	AOS	SORENSEN,JE	LAWLER III,EE	165	176
0.67	SPICER,BM	JA	1978	TAR			94	111
0.62	WHITTRED,GP	OC	1980	TAR			563	577
0.59	COPELAND,RM	ST	1968	JAR			101	116
0.59	MOORE ,ML	SP	1973	JAR			100	107
0.56	CHESLEY,GR	SP	1977	JAR			1	11
0.53	IMHOFF JR,EA	OC	1978	TAR			836	850
0.50	TROTMAN,KT	04	1981	AOS	BRADLEY,G		355	362
0.47	DYER ,JC	AU	1975	JAR	MCHUGH,AJ		204	219
0.47	LUSK ,EJ	ST	1973	JAR			191	202
0.47	PETERSEN,RJ	JA	1973	TAR			34	43
0.47	WARD ,BH	SP	1976	JAR			138	152
0.44	COLLINS,WA	AU	1984	JAR	HOPWOOD,WS	MCKEOWN,JC	467	479
0.43	PASTENA,V	AU	1979	JAR	RONEN ,J		550	564
0.42	FRIED ,D	AP	1981	TAR	SCHIFF,A		326	341
0.41	DERSTINE,RP	AU	1974	JAR	HUEFNER,RJ		216	234
0.41	DYCKMAN,TR	SP	1964	JAR			91	107
0.41	ELAM ,R	JA	1975	TAR			25	43
0.41	FLAMHOLTZ,EG	23	1976	AOS			153	166
0.41	KIGER ,JE	SP	1972	JAR			113	128
0.41	OLIVER,BL	SP	1972	JAR			154	166
0.36	WILNER,N	01	1982	AOS			43	52
0.33	DHARAN,BG	AP	1984	TAR			199	217
0.33	FERRIS,KR	SP	1984	AUD	TENNANT,KL		31	43
0.33	RICCHIUTE,DN	SP	1984	JAR			341	350
0.33	SCHNEIDER,A	AU	1984	JAR			657	678
0.30	BROWN ,PR	AU	1983	JAR			444	455
0.30	LARCKER,DF	JL	1983	TAR	REDER ,RE	SIMON ,DT	606	620
0.30	MURRAY,D	SP	1983	JAR			128	140
0.30	STEPHENS,RG	AU	1983	AUD			55	74
0.29	BARRETT,ME	ST	1971	JAR			50	65
0.29	SHANK ,JK	JL	1973	TAR	COPELAND,RM		494	501
0.24	BAREFIELD,RM	AP	1972	TAR	COMISKEY,EE		291	298
0.24	BRENNER,VC	AU	1970	JAR			159	166
0.24	BRUNS JR,WJ	AP	1965	TAR			345	357
0.24	DYCKMAN,TR	AP	1964	TAR			285	295
0.24	FLAMHOLTZ,EG	ST	1972	JAR			241	266
0.24	SMITH ,JE	JL	1971	TAR	SMITH ,NP		552	561
0.22	KIDA ,TE	02	1984	AOS			137	147
0.22	MCCONNELL,DK	WI	1984	JAA			178	181
0.21	BROWN ,LD	JL	1979	TAR	ROZEFF,MS		585	591
0.20	HARRISON JR,WT	SP	1983	JAR	TOMASSINI,LA	DIETRICH,JR	65	77
0.18	BAREFIELD,RM	AU	1971	JAR	COMISKEY,EE		351	358
0.18	CHOI ,FD	AU	1973	JAR			159	175
0.18	FRANK ,WG	SP	1969	JAR			123	136
0.18	GAGNON,JM	SP	1971	JAR			52	72
0.12	ACLAND,D	23	1976	AOS			133	142
0.12	COPELAND,RM	SP	1968	JAR	FREDERICKS,W		106	113
0.12	FALK ,H	AP	1973	TAR	OPHIR ,T		323	338
0.12	MCDONALD,DL	SP	1968	JAR			38	49

CITE INDEX	FIRST AUTHOR	ISS-UE	YE-AR	JOUR-NAL	SECOND AUTHOR	THIRD AUTHOR	PAG BEG	PAG END
0.12	MORTON,JR	AU	1974	JAR			288	298
0.12	RONEN ,J	OC	1973	TAR	FALK ,G		696	717
0.11	GORDON,LA	02	1984	AOS	HAKA ,S	SCHICK,AG	111	123
0.11	JIAMBALVO,J	SP	1984	AUD	WALLER,WS		80	88
0.11	SCHREUDER,H	JA	1984	TAR	KLAASSEN,J		64	77
0.10	BROWN ,LD	AU	1983	JAR			432	443
0.09	DIRSMITH,MW	04	1982	AOS	LEWIS ,BL		319	336
0.09	EMERY ,DR	AU	1982	JAR	BARRON,FH	MESSIER JR,WF	450	458
0.08	HOPPER,TM	04	1980	AOS			401	412
0.08	HORWITZ,BN	WI	1981	JAA	KOLODNY,R		102	113
0.08	SCHREUDER,H	AP	1981	TAR			294	308
0.06	ARNOLD,DF	JA	1973	TAR	HUMANN,TE		23	33
0.06	BUZBY ,SL	SP	1975	JAR			16	37
0.06	CARPER,WB	23	1976	AOS	POSEY ,JM		143	152
0.06	CUMMING,J	ST	1973	JAR			60	95
0.06	ESTES ,RW	AU	1968	JAR			200	207
0.06	GREER JR,WR	JL	1974	TAR			496	505
0.06	KRATCHMAN,SH	OC	1974	TAR	MALCOM,RE	TWARK ,RD	682	689
0.00	BUCHMAN,TA	AU	1983	AUD			92	103
0.00	CARPENTER,CG	JL	1971	TAR	STRAWSER,RH		509	518
0.00	CHAN ,JL	AP	1978	TAR			309	323
0.00	DAVIS ,HZ	AU	1982	JAR	KAHN ,N		738	744
0.00	DAVIS ,HZ	AU	1984	JAR	KAHN ,N	ROZEN ,E	480	490
0.00	DHARAN,BG	SP	1983	JAR			256	270
0.00	DYKXHOORN,HJ	JA	1981	TAR	SINNING,KE		97	107
0.00	FALK ,H	OC	1975	TAR	HEINTZ,JA		758	779
0.00	FULMER,JG	AU	1984	JAA	MOON ,JE		5	14
0.00	GARSOMBKE,HP	SU	1983	JAA	ALLEN ,G		285	298
0.00	GREENBERG,R	AU	1984	JAR			719	730
0.00	GUL ,FA	34	1984	AOS			233	239
0.00	IMHOFF JR,EA	OC	1978	TAR			869	881
0.00	KROSS ,W	AU	1982	JAR			459	471
0.00	MAYPER,AG	AU	1982	JAR			773	783
0.00	MUNTER,P	WI	1983	JAA	RATCLIFFE,TA		108	114
0.00	NICHOLS,DR	AP	1979	TAR	TSAY ,JJ	LARKIN,PD	376	382
0.00	PETERSEN,RJ	JL	1975	TAR			525	532
0.00	PRATT ,J	04	1982	AOS	JIAMBALVO,J		369	380
0.00	SAN MIGUEL,JG	02	1984	AOS	GOVINDARAJAN,V		179	188
0.00	SELTO ,FH	AU	1983	JAR	GROVE ,HD		619	622
0.00	SILHAN,PA	SP	1983	JAR			341	347
0.00	WELCH ,PR	AU	1984	JAR			744	757
0.00	WILCOX,KA	01	1977	AOS	SMITH ,CH		81	97

1.7 MODE OF REASONING (METHOD)=QUANTITATIVE: CORRELATION

CITE INDEX	FIRST AUTHOR	ISS-UE	YE-AR	JOUR-NAL	SECOND AUTHOR	THIRD AUTHOR	PAG BEG	PAG END
2.25	MERCHANT,KA	OC	1981	TAR			813	829
2.20	OTLEY ,DT	SP	1978	JAR			122	149
2.17	FOSTER,G	DE	1981	JAE			201	232
1.93	KENIS ,I	OC	1979	TAR			707	721
1.24	DERMER,JD	JL	1973	TAR			511	519
1.12	KHANDWALLA,PN	AU	1972	JAR			275	285
1.08	NOREEN,EW	AP	1981	TAR	SEPE ,J		253	269
0.94	BROWN ,P	ST	1967	JAR	BALL ,R		55	77

CITE INDEX	FIRST AUTHOR	ISS-UE	YE-AR	JOUR-NAL	SECOND AUTHOR	THIRD AUTHOR	PAG BEG	PAG END
0.89	GORDON,LA	01	1984	AOS	NARAYANAN,VK		33	47
0.73	COLLINS,DW	JA	1982	TAR	ROZEFF,MS	SALATKA,WK	1	17
0.67	ROCKNESS,HO	02	1984	AOS	SHIELDS,MD		165	177
0.65	HARIED,AA	AU	1972	JAR			376	391
0.64	GAUMNITZ,BR	AU	1982	JAR	NUNAMAKER,TR	SURDICK,JJ	745	755
0.58	SMITH ,AJ	ST	1981	JAR			174	211
0.53	HORRIGAN,JO	ST	1966	JAR			44	62
0.53	TRITSCHLER,CA	JA	1969	TAR			99	123
0.50	COVALESKI,MA	04	1983	AOS	DIRSMITH,MW		323	340
0.47	DAILY ,RA	OC	1971	TAR			686	692
0.42	HOPWOOD,WS	AU	1981	JAR	MCKEOWN,JC		313	322
0.41	HENDRICKS,JA	AP	1976	TAR			292	305
0.40	LEV ,B	AP	1983	JAE			31	48
0.38	BAILEY JR,AD	AP	1985	TAR	DUKE ,GL	GERLACH,JH	186	201
0.36	WISEMAN,J	01	1982	AOS			53	64
0.35	LEV ,B	AP	1974	TAR	KUNITZKY,S		259	270
0.33	NOREEN,EW	AU	1981	JAR	WOLFSON,MA		384	398
0.33	PRATT ,J	02	1981	AOS	JIAMBALVO,J		133	142
0.30	FERRIS,KR	01	1983	AOS	LARCKER,DF		1	12
0.30	SCHEPANSKI,A	JL	1983	TAR			581	599
0.30	TROTMAN,KT	SP	1983	JAR	YETTON,PW	ZIMMER,I	286	292
0.29	HORWITZ,BN	AP	1971	TAR	SHABAHANG,R		243	252
0.29	IJIRI ,Y	SP	1971	JAR	KAPLAN,RS		73	87
0.27	ARANYA,N	03	1982	AOS	LACHMAN,R	AMERNIC,J	201	216
0.25	PEASNELL,KV	SP	1977	JAR	SKERRATT,CL		108	119
0.24	ABDEL-KHALIK,AR	AP	1974	TAR			271	283
0.22	BIGGS ,SF	SP	1984	AUD	WILD ,JJ		68	79
0.22	SHIELDS,MD	34	1984	AOS			355	363
0.19	WRIGHT,WF	04	1977	AOS			323	332
0.18	PRATT ,J	SP	1982	JAR			189	209
0.18	RONEN ,J	SP	1975	JAR	SADAN ,S		133	149
0.17	FERRIS,KR	04	1981	AOS			317	326
0.13	FERRIS,KR	01	1977	AOS			23	28
0.12	DERMER,JD	JA	1974	TAR	SIEGEL,JP		88	97
0.12	JOHNSON,O	AU	1967	JAR			164	172
0.12	KINNEY JR,WR	AP	1972	TAR			339	345
0.11	LOREK ,KS	SP	1984	JAR	BATHKE,AW		369	379
0.11	NORRIS,DR	01	1984	AOS	NIEBUHR,RE		49	59
0.09	COGGER,KO	AU	1982	JAR	RULAND,W		733	737
0.09	MATSUMURA,EM	SP	1982	JAR	TSUI ,KW		162	170
0.09	SALAMON,GL	AP	1982	TAR			292	302
0.08	ROSENZWEIG,K	04	1981	AOS			339	354
0.06	NYSTROM,PC	04	1977	AOS			317	322
0.00	ANDERSON JR,TN	AU	1982	JAR	KIDA ,TE		403	414
0.00	BRENNER,VC	AU	1971	JAR	CARMACK,CW	WEINSTEIN,MG	359	366
0.00	CLARK ,JJ	OC	1973	TAR	ELGERS,PT		668	678
0.00	DAVISON,AG	SP	1984	JAR	STENING,BW	WAI ,WT	313	317
0.00	GIVOLY,D	AU	1981	JAR	PALMON,D		530	543
0.00	HARRELL,AM	34	1984	AOS	STAHL ,MJ		241	252
0.00	KROSS ,W	AU	1980	JAA	CHAPMAN,G	STRAND,KH	36	46
0.00	MCCLENON,PR	JL	1963	TAR			540	547
0.00	MCKENNA,EF	03	1980	AOS			297	310
0.00	MEIXNER,WF	JL	1988	AUD	WELKER,RB		505	513

CITE INDEX	FIRST AUTHOR	ISS-UE	YE-AR	JOUR-NAL	SECOND AUTHOR	THIRD AUTHOR	PAG BEG	PAG END
0.00	SHIELDS,D	01	1984	AOS			61	80
0.00	WHITEHURST,FD	JL	1970	TAR			553	564

1.8 MODE OF REASONING (METHOD)=QUANTITATIVE: ANALYTICAL

CITE INDEX	FIRST AUTHOR	ISS-UE	YE-AR	JOUR-NAL	SECOND AUTHOR	THIRD AUTHOR	PAG BEG	PAG END
4.12	GONEDES,NJ	ST	1974	JAR	DOPUCH,N		48	129
3.15	FOSTER,G	MR	1980	JAE			29	62
2.80	DEMSKI,JS	AP	1978	TAR	FELTHAM,GA		336	359
2.50	BAIMAN,S	AU	1983	JAR	EVANS III,JH		371	395
2.25	DEANGELO,LE	AG	1981	JAE			113	127
2.20	HOLTHAUSEN,RW	SP	1988	JAR	VERRECCHIA,RE		82	106
2.10	VERRECCHIA,RE	DE	1983	JAE			179	194
2.00	LEV ,B	JA	1988	TAR			1	22
1.92	BAIMAN,S	ST	1980	JAR	DEMSKI,JS		184	220
1.86	ZIMMERMAN,JL	JL	1979	TAR			504	521
1.67	BAIMAN,S	AU	1987	JAR	EVANS III,JH	NOEL ,J	217	244
1.56	DEMSKI,JS	JA	1984	TAR	PATELL,JM	WOLFSON,MA	16	34
1.56	PENNO ,M	SP	1984	JAR			177	191
1.50	DYE ,RA	AU	1983	JAR			514	533
1.50	GJESDAL,F	SP	1981	JAR			208	231
1.35	SCOTT ,WR	AU	1973	JAR			304	330
1.30	CUSHING,BE	AU	1983	AUD	LOEBBECKE,JK		23	41
1.29	KINNEY JR,WR	SP	1975	JAR			117	132
1.19	FELIX JR,WL	SP	1977	JAR	GRIMLUND,RA		23	41
1.18	CHRISTENSEN,J	AU	1982	JAR			589	603
1.15	GARMAN,MB	AU	1980	JAR	OHLSON,JA		420	440
1.10	OHLSON,JA	SP	1983	JAR			141	154
1.08	BEAVER,WH	SP	1981	JAR			163	184
1.00	ANTLE ,R	SP	1984	JAR			1	20
1.00	CHRISTIE,AA	DE	1984	JAE	KENNELLEY,MD	KING ,JW	205	217
0.94	KINNEY JR,WR	ST	1975	JAR			14	29
0.89	LAMBERT,RA	OC	1984	TAR			604	618
0.86	OHLSON,JA	DE	1979	JAE			211	232
0.82	SUNDER,S	JA	1976	TAR			1	18
0.81	HAKANSSON,NH	AP	1977	TAR			396	416
0.78	GODFREY,JT	AU	1984	JAR	NETER ,J		497	525
0.78	SUNDER,S	SP	1984	JAR	WAYMIRE,G		396	405
0.77	HILTON,RW	AU	1980	JAR			477	505
0.76	DEMSKI,JS	AP	1974	TAR			221	232
0.76	FELTHAM,GA	OC	1970	TAR	DEMSKI,JS		623	640
0.75	BAIMAN,S	AU	1985	JAR	NOEL ,J		486	501
0.73	ANTLE ,R	AU	1982	JAR			504	527
0.71	BEAVER,WH	ST	1974	JAR	DEMSKI,JS		170	187
0.71	DEMSKI,JS	AU	1986	JAR	SAPPINGTON,DEM		250	269
0.71	SCOTT ,WR	ST	1975	JAR			98	117
0.70	MENZEFRICKE,U	SP	1983	JAR			96	105
0.67	SUNDER,S	AU	1978	JAR			341	367
0.65	BENSTON,GJ	JL	1969	TAR			515	532
0.65	CUSHING,BE	JA	1974	TAR			24	41
0.65	IJIRI ,Y	JL	1966	TAR	JAEDICKE,RK		474	483
0.65	KAPLAN,RS	SP	1973	JAR			38	46
0.65	LEV ,B	JA	1971	TAR	SCHWARTZ,A		103	112
0.65	MAGEE ,RP	JL	1976	TAR			529	544

CITE INDEX	FIRST AUTHOR	ISS-UE	YE-AR	JOUR-NAL	SECOND AUTHOR	THIRD AUTHOR	PAG BEG	PAG END
0.65	YU ,S	AU	1973	JAR	NETER ,J		273	295
0.64	GRIMLUND,RA	AU	1982	JAR			316	342
0.64	NG ,DS	ST	1979	JAR	STOECKENIUS,J	1	24	
0.64	VERRECCHIA,RE	ST	1982	JAR			1	42
0.63	HAMLEN,SS	JL	1977	TAR	HAMLEN,WA	TSCHIRHART,JT	616	627
0.62	MAGEE ,RP	AU	1980	JAR			551	573
0.59	DEMSKI,JS	AU	1976	JAR			230	245
0.59	ITAMI ,H	SP	1975	JAR			73	96
0.59	KAPLAN,RS	SP	1969	JAR			32	43
0.58	LEFTWICH,RW	ST	1981	JAR	WATTS ,RL	ZIMMERMAN,JL	50	77
0.57	HANSEN,JV	AU	1986	AUD	MESSIER JR,WF		109	123
0.54	EVANS III,JH	ST	1980	JAR			108	128
0.54	VERRECCHIA,RE	MR	1980	JAE			63	92
0.53	BAIMAN,S	SP	1975	JAR			1	15
0.53	BUTTERWORTH,JE	SP	1972	JAR			1	27
0.53	DEMSKI,JS	AU	1972	JAR			243	258
0.53	DYCKMAN,TR	AU	1969	JAR			215	244
0.53	KAPLAN,RS	ST	1975	JAR			126	133
0.53	SUNDER,S	AU	1976	JAR			277	300
0.50	JENSEN,DL	OC	1977	TAR			842	856
0.50	KINNEY JR,WR	SP	1983	AUD			13	22
0.50	PATELL,JM	AU	1979	JAR			528	549
0.47	BODNAR,G	OC	1975	TAR			747	757
0.47	DEMSKI,JS	JL	1974	TAR	SWIERINGA,RJ		506	513
0.47	FELTHAM,GA	OC	1968	TAR			684	696
0.47	JAEDICKE,RK	OC	1964	TAR	ROBICHEK,AA		917	926
0.47	KAPLAN,RS	AP	1971	TAR	THOMPSON,GL		352	364
0.47	KAPLAN,RS	JL	1974	TAR	WELAM ,VP		477	484
0.47	NG ,DS	OC	1978	TAR			910	920
0.47	RENEAU,JH	JL	1978	TAR			669	680
0.47	RONEN ,J	SP	1970	JAR	MCKINNEY,G		99	112
0.47	SUNDER,S	AP	1976	TAR			287	291
0.46	CROSBY,MA	AU	1980	JAR			585	593
0.44	MATOLCSY,ZP	AU	1984	JAR			555	569
0.43	ATKINSON,AA	SP	1979	JAR			1	22
0.43	SUNDEM,GL	SP	1979	JAR			243	261
0.43	VERRECCHIA,RE	MR	1979	JAE			77	90
0.42	HAKANSSON,NH	ST	1981	JAR			1	35
0.42	OHLSON,JA	AU	1981	JAR	BUCKMAN,AG		399	433
0.41	HASEMAN,WD	JA	1976	TAR	WHINSTON,AB		65	79
0.41	HILLIARD,JE	JA	1975	TAR	LEITCH,RA		69	80
0.41	SORENSEN,JE	JL	1969	TAR			555	561
0.41	SUNDEM,GL	AP	1974	TAR			306	320
0.41	TOBA ,Y	JA	1975	TAR			7	24
0.41	TRACY ,JA	JA	1969	TAR			90	98
0.40	KETZ ,JE	OC	1978	TAR			952	960
0.40	LOEB ,M	SP	1978	JAR	MAGAT ,WA		103	121
0.40	LUNDHOLM,RJ	SP	1988	JAR			107	118
0.40	RONEN ,J	AU	1988	JAR	BALACHANDRAN,KR		300	314
0.38	CUSHING,BE	AP	1977	TAR			308	321
0.38	GONEDES,NJ	AU	1980	JAR			441	476
0.36	GODFREY,JT	AU	1982	JAR	ANDREWS,RW		304	315
0.35	BUZBY ,SL	JA	1974	TAR			42	49

CITE INDEX	FIRST AUTHOR	ISS-UE	YE-AR	JOUR-NAL	SECOND AUTHOR	THIRD AUTHOR	PAG BEG	PAG END
0.35	DEMSKI,JS	OC	1967	TAR			701	712
0.35	DEMSKI,JS	SP	1972	JAR			58	76
0.35	GONEDES,NJ	AU	1974	JAR	IJIRI ,Y		251	269
0.35	LIAO ,M	OC	1975	TAR			780	790
0.35	MARSHALL,RM	AU	1972	JAR			286	307
0.35	MAY ,RG	JA	1973	TAR	SUNDEM,GL		80	94
0.35	REVSINE,L	JL	1970	TAR			513	523
0.35	SIMMONS,JK	OC	1969	TAR	GRAY ,J		757	776
0.33	BEAVER,WH	JA	1981	TAR			23	37
0.33	DITTMAN,DA	SP	1978	JAR	PRAKASH,P		14	25
0.33	IJIRI ,Y	JA	1984	TAR	NOEL ,J		52	63
0.33	LIN ,WT	AU	1984	AUD	MOCK ,TJ	WRIGHT,A	89	99
0.33	VERRECCHIA,RE	SP	1981	JAR			271	283
0.31	HAMLEN,SS	OC	1980	TAR			578	593
0.30	SCHEPANSKI,A	AP	1983	TAR	UECKER,WC		259	283
0.29	DITTMAN,DA	SP	1976	JAR	JURIS ,HA	REVSINE,L	49	65
0.29	HALPERIN,R	JA	1979	TAR			58	71
0.29	HILTON,RW	AU	1979	JAR			411	435
0.29	KANODIA,CS	SP	1979	JAR			74	98
0.29	KAPLAN,RS	OC	1973	TAR			738	748
0.29	LEV ,B	AU	1968	JAR			247	261
0.29	MORIARITY,S	OC	1975	TAR			791	795
0.29	SHIH ,W	OC	1979	TAR			687	706
0.27	KOTTAS,JF	AP	1978	TAR	LAU ,AH	LAU ,HS	389	401
0.25	BILLERA,LJ	SP	1981	JAR	HEATH ,DC	VERRECCHIA,RE	185	196
0.25	EVEREST,GL	AP	1977	TAR	WEBER ,R		340	359
0.25	HEIMANN,SR	AU	1977	JAR	CHESLEY,GR		193	206
0.25	HUGHES,JS	JA	1977	TAR			56	68
0.25	KANODIA,CS	SP	1985	JAR			175	193
0.25	KAPLAN,RS	AP	1977	TAR			369	378
0.25	KISSINGER,JN	AP	1977	TAR			322	339
0.25	SCOTT ,WR	SP	1977	JAR			120	137
0.24	ABDEL-KHALIK,AR	JL	1971	TAR			457	471
0.24	BARNEA,A	JA	1975	TAR	RONEN ,J	SADAN ,S	58	68
0.24	FERRARA,WL	AP	1972	TAR	HAYYA ,JC	NACHMAN,DA	299	307
0.24	FRIEDMAN,A	AU	1974	JAR	LEV ,B		235	250
0.24	IJIRI ,Y	OC	1969	TAR	KAPLAN,RS		743	756
0.24	IJIRI ,Y	OC	1973	TAR	ITAMI ,H		724	737
0.24	KILLOUGH,LN	AP	1973	TAR	SOUDERS,TL		268	279
0.24	OZAN ,T	SP	1971	JAR	DYCKMAN,TR		88	115
0.24	SUMMERS,EL	JL	1972	TAR			443	453
0.23	BALACHANDRAN,BV	ST	1980	JAR	RAMAKRISHNAN,RT		140	171
0.23	COHEN ,MA	AU	1980	JAR	HALPERIN,R		375	389
0.23	NEWMAN,DP	02	1980	AOS			217	230
0.22	MARCINKO,D	JL	1984	TAR	PETRI ,E		488	495
0.22	MORSE ,D	AU	1984	JAR			605	623
0.21	SCOTT ,WR	SP	1979	JAR			156	178
0.20	CALLEN,JL	AP	1978	TAR			303	308
0.20	CHEN ,JT	JL	1983	TAR			600	605
0.20	DHARAN,BG	SP	1983	JAR			18	41
0.20	DICKHAUT,JW	AU	1983	JAR	LERE ,JC		495	513
0.20	SUH ,YS	SP	1988	JAR			154	168
0.18	BRIEF ,RP	AU	1970	JAR	OWEN ,J		167	177

CITE INDEX	FIRST AUTHOR	ISS-UE	YE-AR	JOUR-NAL	SECOND AUTHOR	THIRD AUTHOR	PAG BEG	PAG END
0.18	DEMSKI,JS	JA	1970	TAR			76	87
0.18	DEMSKI,JS	AU	1970	JAR			178	198
0.18	DOPUCH,N	SP	1964	JAR	DRAKE ,DF		10	24
0.18	EAVES ,BC	JL	1966	TAR			426	442
0.18	FRIBERG,RA	JA	1973	TAR			50	60
0.18	GIBBINS,M	SP	1982	JAR			121	138
0.18	HARTLEY,RV	OC	1971	TAR			746	755
0.18	HASSELDINE,CR	JL	1967	TAR			497	515
0.18	MAGEE ,RP	AU	1975	JAR			257	266
0.18	MARSHALL,RM	JA	1975	TAR			99	111
0.18	MCKEOWN,JC	JA	1971	TAR			12	29
0.18	MENSAH,YM	OC	1982	TAR			681	700
0.18	MOCK ,TJ	OC	1971	TAR			765	777
0.18	OHLSON,JA	AU	1975	JAR			267	282
0.18	RONEN ,J	JA	1974	TAR			50	60
0.17	BAILEY,AP	SU	1981	AUD	MCAFEE,RP	WHINSTON,AB	38	52
0.17	BOATSMAN,JR	JA	1981	TAR	BASKIN,EF		38	53
0.17	COGGER,KO	AU	1981	JAR			285	298
0.17	RONEN ,J	AU	1981	JAR	LIVNAT,J		459	481
0.17	VERRECCHIA,RE	ST	1987	JAR	LANEN ,WN		165	189
0.15	BROMWICH,M	AP	1980	TAR			288	300
0.13	HUGHES,JS	OC	1978	TAR			882	894
0.13	MAGEE ,RP	OC	1977	TAR			869	880
0.13	MERVILLE,LJ	OC	1978	TAR	PETTY ,JW		935	951
0.13	WEYGANDT,JJ	JA	1977	TAR			40	51
0.12	BAREFIELD,RM	JL	1970	TAR			490	501
0.12	BEAVER,WH	AU	1974	JAR	DUKES ,RE		205	215
0.12	BENISHAY,H	SP	1965	JAR			114	132
0.12	BRIEF ,RP	SP	1973	JAR	OWEN ,J		1	15
0.12	CHAMBERS,RJ	AU	1965	JAR			242	252
0.12	CHURCHILL,NC	OC	1964	TAR			894	904
0.12	DAVIDSON,HJ	AU	1967	JAR	NETER ,J	PETRAN,AS	186	207
0.12	DEMSKI,JS	OC	1969	TAR			669	679
0.12	DEMSKI,JS	AP	1971	TAR			268	278
0.12	DEMSKI,JS	AU	1973	JAR			176	190
0.12	DOPUCH,N	JL	1967	TAR	BIRNBERG,JG	DEMSKI,JS	526	536
0.12	GORDON,MJ	JL	1970	TAR			427	443
0.12	GREER JR,WR	JA	1970	TAR			103	114
0.12	HINOMOTO,H	AU	1971	JAR			253	267
0.12	IJIRI ,Y	AU	1963	JAR	LEVY ,FK	LYON ,RC	198	212
0.12	IJIRI ,Y	SP	1965	JAR	JAEDICKE,RK	LIVINGSTONE,JL	63	74
0.12	IJIRI ,Y	AP	1976	TAR			227	243
0.12	JEN ,FC	AP	1970	TAR	HUEFNER,RJ		290	298
0.12	JOHNSON,GL	AU	1971	JAR	SIMIK ,SS		278	286
0.12	JOHNSON,GL	SP	1974	JAR	SIMIK ,SS		67	79
0.12	JOHNSON,O	OC	1970	TAR			641	653
0.12	KORNBLUTH,JS	AP	1974	TAR			284	295
0.12	LEV ,B	SP	1970	JAR			78	94
0.12	LIM ,R	OC	1966	TAR			642	651
0.12	LIVINGSTONE,JL	JL	1968	TAR			503	508
0.12	LUH ,FS	JA	1968	TAR			123	132
0.12	PETRI ,E	AP	1974	TAR	MINCH ,RA		330	341
0.12	REVSINE,L	AP	1976	TAR	THIES ,JB		255	268

CITE INDEX	FIRST AUTHOR	ISS-UE	YE-AR	JOUR-NAL	SECOND AUTHOR	THIRD AUTHOR	PAG BEG	PAG END
0.12	SALAMON,GL	AU	1973	JAR			296	303
0.12	SAMUELS,JM	AU	1965	JAR			182	191
0.12	SMITH ,KA	AP	1972	TAR			260	269
0.12	THOMAS,AL	JL	1971	TAR			472	479
0.12	VICKREY,DW	OC	1970	TAR			731	742
0.12	WILLIAMS,TH	JL	1964	TAR	GRIFFIN,CH		671	678
0.12	WOLK ,HI	JL	1972	TAR	HILLMAN,AP		549	555
0.12	WYMAN ,HE	JL	1973	TAR			489	493
0.12	ZANNETOS,ZS	AP	1964	TAR			296	304
0.11	LEE ,CJ	AU	1984	JAR			776	781
0.11	NETER ,J	AU	1984	AUD	KIM ,HS	GRAHAM,LE	75	88
0.11	SHERMAN,HD	AU	1984	AUD			35	53
0.10	OVADIA,A	WI	1983	JAA	RONEN ,J		115	129
0.10	SUNDER,S	SP	1983	JAR			222	233
0.09	BALACHANDRAN,KR	JA	1982	TAR	STEUER,RE		125	140
0.09	BEAVER,WH	AU	1982	JAR	WOLFSON,MA		528	550
0.09	COHEN ,SI	AP	1982	TAR	LOEB ,M		336	347
0.09	EMERY ,GW	AU	1982	JAR	COGGER,KO		290	303
0.09	MANES ,RP	JL	1982	TAR	PARK ,SH	JENSEN,RE	594	606
0.09	VIGELAND,RL	AP	1982	TAR			348	357
0.09	WILLIAMS,PF	04	1982	AOS			405	410
0.08	BALACHANDRAN,BV	JA	1981	TAR	RAMAKRISHNAN,RT		85	96
0.08	FRIED ,D	SU	1981	JAA			295	308
0.08	FRIED ,D	JL	1981	TAR	LIVNAT,J		493	509
0.08	GANGOLLY,JS	AU	1981	JAR			299	312
0.08	HAMLEN,SS	AP	1980	TAR	HAMLEN,WA	TSCHIRHART,JT	269	287
0.08	NEWMAN,DP	ST	1981	JAR			134	156
0.08	OVADIA,A	WI	1980	JAA	RONEN ,J		113	137
0.07	OHLSON,JA	AU	1979	JAR			506	527
0.07	SCAPENS,RW	AP	1978	TAR			448	469
0.07	VERRECCHIA,RE	SP	1978	JAR			150	168
0.06	AIKEN ,ME	JL	1975	TAR	BLACKETT,LA	ISAACS,G	544	562
0.06	AMATO ,HN	OC	1976	TAR	ANDERSON,EE	HARVEY,DW	854	862
0.06	BAILEY JR,AD	JL	1973	TAR			560	574
0.06	BAXTER,WT	AU	1971	JAR	CARRIER,NH		189	214
0.06	BIERMAN JR,H	AP	1966	TAR			271	274
0.06	BIERMAN JR,H	JL	1974	TAR			448	454
0.06	BODNAR,G	OC	1977	TAR	LUSK ,EJ		857	868
0.06	BRADFORD,WD	AP	1974	TAR			296	305
0.06	BULLOCK,CL	JA	1974	TAR			98	103
0.06	BUTTERWORTH,JE	OC	1971	TAR	SIGLOCH,BA		701	716
0.06	CHARNES,A	SP	1963	JAR	COOPER,WW	IJIRI ,Y	16	43
0.06	CHARNES,A	JA	1967	TAR	COOPER,WW		24	52
0.06	CHARNES,A	JA	1972	TAR	COLANTONI,CS	COOPER,WW	85	108
0.06	COLANTONI,CS	JL	1969	TAR	MANES ,RP	WHINSTON,AB	467	481
0.06	COOK ,JS	OC	1976	TAR	HOLZMANN,OJ		778	787
0.06	CORCORAN,AW	JA	1973	TAR	LEININGER,WE		105	114
0.06	DICKENS,RL	AP	1964	TAR	BLACKBURN,JO		312	329
0.06	DREBIN,AR	JA	1965	TAR			154	162
0.06	FELTHAM,GA	JA	1970	TAR			11	26
0.06	FRANK ,WG	JL	1967	TAR	MANES ,RP		516	525
0.06	GONEDES,NJ	SP	1970	JAR			1	20
0.06	GREENBALL,MN	AU	1969	JAR			262	289

CITE INDEX	FIRST AUTHOR	ISS-UE	YE-AR	JOUR-NAL	SECOND AUTHOR	THIRD AUTHOR	PAG BEG	PAG END
0.06	GROVES,R	JL	1970	TAR	MANES ,RP	SORENSEN,R	481	489
0.06	GYNTHER,MM	OC	1968	TAR			706	718
0.06	HARTLEY,RV	AP	1970	TAR			223	234
0.06	HARVEY,DW	OC	1976	TAR			838	845
0.06	HEIMANN,SR	JA	1976	TAR	LUSK ,EJ		51	64
0.06	HUEFNER,RJ	OC	1971	TAR			717	732
0.06	IJIRI ,Y	SP	1970	JAR	KAPLAN,RS		34	46
0.06	JENSEN,DL	JL	1974	TAR			465	476
0.06	JOHNSON,O	SP	1968	JAR			29	37
0.06	KINNEY JR,WR	SP	1969	JAR			44	52
0.06	LARSON,KD	OC	1969	TAR	GONEDES,NJ		720	728
0.06	LEMKE ,KW	SP	1970	JAR			47	77
0.06	LIVINGSTONE,JL	JA	1969	TAR			48	64
0.06	MANES ,RP	SP	1966	JAR			87	100
0.06	MCDONALD,DL	OC	1967	TAR			662	679
0.06	MCINTYRE,EV	JA	1977	TAR			162	171
0.06	MORRISON,TA	AP	1969	TAR	KACZKA,E		330	343
0.06	MORSE ,WJ	OC	1972	TAR			761	773
0.06	ONSI ,M	JL	1970	TAR			535	543
0.06	RAPPAPORT,A	JL	1967	TAR			441	456
0.06	RICKS ,RB	JL	1964	TAR			685	688
0.06	SCHRODERHEIM,G	JL	1964	TAR			679	684
0.06	SCHWAB,B	AP	1969	TAR	NICOL ,RE		292	296
0.06	SHWAYDER,KR	AP	1969	TAR			304	316
0.06	SHWAYDER,KR	AP	1971	TAR			306	319
0.06	SHWAYDER,KR	AU	1973	JAR			259	272
0.06	SORENSEN,JE	JL	1977	TAR	GROVE ,HD		658	675
0.06	STALLMAN,JC	OC	1972	TAR			774	790
0.06	STERLING,RR	JA	1967	TAR			62	73
0.06	THEIL ,H	JA	1969	TAR			27	37
0.06	VATTER,W	OC	1966	TAR			681	698
0.06	WELLING,P	04	1977	AOS			307	316
0.06	WRIGHT,FK	JA	1970	TAR			129	133
0.00	ABRANOVIC,WA	OC	1976	TAR			863	874
0.00	AGRAWAL,SP	OC	1977	TAR			789	809
0.00	AGRAWAL,SP	WI	1980	JAA	HALLBAUER,RC	PERRITT,GW	163	173
0.00	ALVEY ,KL	JA	1963	TAR			124	125
0.00	ANDERSON,JA	JL	1975	TAR			509	511
0.00	BAINBRIDGE,DR	SU	1984	JAA			334	346
0.00	BALACHANDRAN,BV	OC	1981	TAR	ZOLTNERS,AA		801	812
0.00	BARLEV,B	AP	1983	TAR			385	393
0.00	BASTABLE,CW	SP	1981	JAA	BEAMS ,FA		248	254
0.00	BEJA ,A	AU	1977	JAR	AHARONI,Y		169	178
0.00	BERANEK,W	OC	1964	TAR			914	916
0.00	BIERMAN JR,H	OC	1967	TAR			731	737
0.00	BIERMAN JR,H	AU	1967	JAR	SMIDT ,S		144	153
0.00	BIERMAN JR,H	OC	1968	TAR			657	661
0.00	BIERMAN JR,H	OC	1970	TAR			690	697
0.00	BIERMAN JR,H	OC	1971	TAR			693	700
0.00	BOATSMAN,JR	AU	1984	JAA	DOWELL,CD	KIMBRELL,JI	35	43
0.00	BOWER ,RS	AP	1966	TAR	HERRINGER,F	WILLIAMSON,JP	257	265
0.00	BRIEF ,RP	AU	1968	JAR	OWEN ,J		193	199
0.00	BRIEF ,RP	AP	1968	TAR	OWEN ,J		367	372

CITE INDEX	FIRST AUTHOR	ISS-UE	YE-AR	JOUR-NAL	SECOND AUTHOR	THIRD AUTHOR	PAG BEG	PAG END
0.00	BRIEF ,RP	SP	1969	JAR	OWEN ,J		12	16
0.00	BRIGHAM,EF	JA	1968	TAR			46	61
0.00	BRIGHAM,EF	JL	1974	TAR	NANTELL,TJ		436	447
0.00	BROCKETT,P	JL	1984	TAR	CHARNES,A	COOPER,WW	474	487
0.00	BRUNDAGE,MV	JL	1969	TAR	LIVINGSTONE,JL		539	545
0.00	BUCKMAN,AG	SP	1982	JAR	MILLER,BL		28	41
0.00	BURGHER,PH	JA	1964	TAR			103	120
0.00	BURT ,OR	SP	1972	JAR			28	57
0.00	BYRNE ,R	JA	1968	TAR	CHARNES,A	COOPER,WW	18	37
0.00	CALL ,DV	OC	1969	TAR			711	719
0.00	CARLSON,ML	JL	1981	TAR	LAMB ,JW		554	573
0.00	CARSBERG,BV	AU	1969	JAR			165	182
0.00	CASPARI,JA	OC	1976	TAR			739	746
0.00	CERF ,AR	JL	1975	TAR			451	465
0.00	CHAMBERS,RJ	JL	1972	TAR			488	509
0.00	CHARNES,A	AP	1964	TAR	DAVIDSON,HJ	KORTANEK,KO	241	250
0.00	CHARNES,A	04	1976	AOS	COLANTONI,CS	COOPER,WW	315	338
0.00	CHASTEEN,LG	OC	1973	TAR			764	767
0.00	CHUMACHENKO,NG	OC	1968	TAR			753	762
0.00	COMISKEY,EE	AP	1968	TAR	MLYNARCZYK,FA		248	256
0.00	CORCORAN,AW	AU	1965	JAR	KWANG ,CW		206	217
0.00	CORCORAN,AW	AP	1969	TAR			359	374
0.00	CURLEY,AJ	JL	1971	TAR			519	528
0.00	DAVIS ,GB	SP	1963	JAR			96	101
0.00	DAVIS ,PM	JA	1966	TAR			121	126
0.00	DEMING,WE	SP	1979	JAA			197	208
0.00	DESKINS,JW	JA	1965	TAR			76	81
0.00	DOPUCH,N	OC	1963	TAR			745	753
0.00	DREBIN,AR	JL	1966	TAR			413	425
0.00	DREBIN,AR	SP	1966	JAR			68	86
0.00	DREBIN,AR	AU	1969	JAR			204	214
0.00	DUVALL,RM	JL	1965	TAR	BULLOCH,J		569	573
0.00	FARAG ,SM	AP	1968	TAR			312	320
0.00	FERRARA,WL	JA	1966	TAR			106	114
0.00	FERRARA,WL	JL	1977	TAR			597	604
0.00	FOGLER,HR	JA	1972	TAR			134	143
0.00	GAMBLING,TE	JA	1970	TAR	NOUR ,A		98	102
0.00	GLOVER,F	AP	1969	TAR			300	303
0.00	GODFREY,JT	AP	1971	TAR			286	297
0.00	GONEDES,NJ	AP	1971	TAR			320	328
0.00	HAKANSSON,NH	JL	1969	TAR			495	514
0.00	HAKANSSON,NH	SP	1969	JAR			11	31
0.00	HANSEN,DR	JA	1977	TAR	SHAFTEL,TL		109	123
0.00	HEEBINK,DV	JA	1964	TAR			90	93
0.00	HOBBS ,JB	OC	1964	TAR			905	913
0.00	IJIRI ,Y	JA	1965	TAR			36	53
0.00	IJIRI ,Y	AP	1970	TAR	THOMPSON,GL		246	258
0.00	JARRETT,JE	SP	1972	JAR			108	112
0.00	JARRETT,JE	SP	1974	JAR			63	66
0.00	JENSEN,HL	OC	1976	TAR	WYNDELTS,RW		846	853
0.00	JENSEN,RE	JA	1968	TAR	THOMSEN,CT		83	93
0.00	JENSEN,RE	JL	1968	TAR			425	446
0.00	JOHNSON,GL	JL	1966	TAR			510	517

CITE INDEX	FIRST AUTHOR	ISS-UE	YE-AR	JOUR-NAL	SECOND AUTHOR	THIRD AUTHOR	PAG BEG	PAG END
0.00	JOHNSON,GL	OC	1967	TAR	NEWTON,SW		738	746
0.00	KISTNER,KP	SP	1980	JAR	SALMI ,T		297	311
0.00	LANGHOLM,O	AU	1965	JAR			218	227
0.00	LAU ,AH	SP	1978	JAR	LAU ,HS		80	102
0.00	LAVALLE,IH	AP	1968	TAR	RAPPAPORT,A		225	230
0.00	LEA ,RB	AP	1972	TAR			346	350
0.00	LEE ,LC	AP	1969	TAR	BEDFORD,NM		256	275
0.00	LEMBKE,VC	WI	1981	JAA	TOOLE ,HR		128	135
0.00	LEV ,B	OC	1969	TAR			704	710
0.00	LEV ,B	JL	1970	TAR			532	534
0.00	LEV ,B	AU	1978	JAR	THEIL ,H		286	293
0.00	LILLESTOL,J	SP	1981	JAR			263	267
0.00	LOWE ,HD	AP	1963	TAR			293	301
0.00	LUNESKI,C	OC	1967	TAR			767	771
0.00	MAHER ,MW	SP	1983	JAR	NANTELL,TJ		329	340
0.00	MAITRE,P	34	1978	AOS			227	236
0.00	MANES ,RP	JA	1965	TAR	SMITH ,VL		31	35
0.00	MAXIM ,LD	JA	1976	TAR	CULLEN,PE	COOK ,FX	97	109
0.00	MCBRIDE,HJ	AP	1963	TAR			363	370
0.00	MCCOSH,AM	OC	1967	TAR			693	700
0.00	MCINTYRE,EV	JL	1982	TAR			607	618
0.00	MCKEOWN,JC	JL	1972	TAR			527	532
0.00	MELBERG,WF	JA	1972	TAR			116	133
0.00	MITCHELL,GB	AP	1970	TAR			308	314
0.00	MOBLEY,SC	JA	1967	TAR			114	123
0.00	MOCK ,TJ	AU	1978	JAR	VASARHELYI,MA		414	423
0.00	MONSON,NP	OC	1964	TAR	TRACY ,JA		890	893
0.00	MOORE ,CL	JA	1964	TAR			94	102
0.00	MORRISON,TA	JL	1968	TAR	BUZBY ,SL		517	521
0.00	NAKANO,I	OC	1972	TAR			693	708
0.00	NIKOLAI,LA	JA	1979	TAR	ELAM ,R		119	131
0.00	NORDHAUSER,SL	JA	1981	TAR	KRAMER,JL		54	69
0.00	NURNBERG,H	AU	1970	JAR			217	231
0.00	ONSI ,M	AP	1967	TAR			321	330
0.00	PAINE ,NR	AP	1964	TAR			330	332
0.00	PESANDO,JE	OC	1983	TAR	CLARKE,CK		733	748
0.00	PETRI ,E	JL	1973	TAR			483	488
0.00	PETRI ,E	JL	1974	TAR	MINCH ,RA		455	464
0.00	PETRI ,E	AP	1978	TAR	MINCH ,RA		415	428
0.00	PETRI ,E	AP	1979	TAR	GELFAND,J		330	345
0.00	PURDY ,CR	AU	1965	JAR			228	241
0.00	RAMANATHAN,KV	OC	1971	TAR	RAPPAPORT,A		733	745
0.00	RAPPAPORT,A	AP	1969	TAR			297	299
0.00	RAUN ,DL	OC	1963	TAR			754	758
0.00	ROBBINS,SM	AU	1977	JAA			5	18
0.00	ROBERTS,DM	AU	1980	JAA			57	69
0.00	RONEN ,J	AU	1970	JAR			232	252
0.00	ROSS ,WR	JL	1966	TAR			464	473
0.00	SAMUELSON,RA	AP	1980	TAR			254	268
0.00	SEAGLE,JP	JA	1977	TAR	PETRI ,E		124	136
0.00	SHWAYDER,KR	AP	1970	TAR			299	307
0.00	SHWAYDER,KR	OC	1972	TAR			747	760
0.00	SKERRATT,LC	SU	1984	JAA			362	368

CITE INDEX	FIRST AUTHOR	ISS-UE	YE-AR	JOUR-NAL	SECOND AUTHOR	THIRD AUTHOR	PAG BEG	PAG END
0.00	SOLOMONS,D	JL	1968	TAR			447	452
0.00	STERLING,RR	JL	1971	TAR	FLAHERTY,RE		441	456
0.00	SUSSMAN,MR	AP	1965	TAR			407	413
0.00	TAUSSIG,RA	SP	1964	JAR			67	79
0.00	TAYLOR,WM	AU	1982	JAR	WEYGANDT,JJ		497	502
0.00	THOMAS,AL	JA	1964	TAR			1	11
0.00	THOMAS,AL	SP	1965	JAR			103	113
0.00	THOMAS,LR	AP	1986	TAR	SWANSON,EP		330	336
0.00	THOMPSON,WW	JL	1965	TAR	KEMPER,EL		574	578
0.00	TOBA ,Y	OC	1980	TAR			604	619
0.00	VERRECCHIA,RE	JL	1982	TAR			579	593
0.00	WAKEMAN,LM	DE	1980	JAE			213	237
0.00	WALKER,M	AP	1984	TAR			278	286
0.00	WEBER ,C	JL	1963	TAR			534	539
0.00	WEBER ,RP	JA	1977	TAR			172	185
0.00	WEINGARTER,HM	AU	1963	JAR			213	224
0.00	WILLIAMSON,JE	JA	1971	TAR			139	148
0.00	WOLK ,HI	JL	1970	TAR			544	552
0.00	WOLK ,HI	AP	1973	TAR	TEARNEY,MG		292	299
0.00	WRIGHT,FK	JA	1963	TAR			87	90
0.00	WRIGHT,FK	SP	1964	JAR			80	90
0.00	WRIGHT,FK	AU	1968	JAR			222	236
0.00	WYMAN ,HE	JL	1976	TAR			545	558
0.00	YOUNG ,TN	AP	1967	TAR	PEIRSON,CG		338	341
0.00	ZANNETOS,ZS	JL	1963	TAR			528	533

1.9 MODE OF REASONING (METHOD)=MIXED

CITE INDEX	FIRST AUTHOR	ISS-UE	YE-AR	JOUR-NAL	SECOND AUTHOR	THIRD AUTHOR	PAG BEG	PAG END
4.31	FOSTER,G	JA	1977	TAR			1	21
3.58	LEFTWICH,RW	MR	1981	JAE			3	36
2.82	BALL ,R	ST	1982	JAR	FOSTER,G		161	234
2.71	ASHTON,RH	SP	1974	JAR			143	157
2.63	WATTS ,RL	AU	1977	JAR	LEFTWICH,RW		253	271
2.55	BEAVER,WH	JL	1982	JAE	GRIFFIN,PA	LANDSMAN,WR	15	39
2.36	BIDDLE,GC	AU	1982	JAR	LINDAHL,FW		551	588
2.25	ALBRECHT,WS	AU	1977	JAR	LOOKABILL,LL	MCKEOWN,JC	226	244
2.19	GRIFFIN,PA	SP	1977	JAR			71	83
2.18	HOPWOOD,AG	ST	1972	JAR			156	182
2.07	BROWN ,LD	SP	1979	JAR	ROZEFF,MS		179	189
1.65	DRIVER,MJ	JL	1975	TAR	MOCK ,TJ		490	508
1.62	OHLSON,JA	SP	1980	JAR			109	131
1.53	GONEDES,NJ	SP	1978	JAR			26	79
1.44	COLLINS,DW	SP	1984	JAR	DENT ,WT		48	84
1.41	SWIERINGA,RJ	ST	1976	JAR	GIBBINS,M	LARSSON,L	159	187
1.36	HAMILTON,RE	AU	1982	JAR	WRIGHT,WF		756	765
1.35	BEAVER,WH	ST	1970	JAR			62	99
1.31	GHEYARA,K	AG	1980	JAE	BOATSMAN,JR		107	125
1.09	DUKE ,GL	SP	1982	JAR	NETER ,J	LEITCH,RA	42	67
1.06	LIBBY ,R	SP	1975	JAR			150	161
1.00	EICHENSEHER,JW	JL	1981	TAR	DANOS ,P		479	492
1.00	MCNICHOLS,M	AP	1983	JAE	MANEGOLD,JG		49	74
0.94	DOPUCH,N	SP	1972	JAR	WATTS ,RL		180	194
0.93	HONG ,H	JA	1978	TAR	KAPLAN,RS	MANDELKER,G	31	47

CITE INDEX	FIRST AUTHOR	ISS-UE	YE-AR	JOUR-NAL	SECOND AUTHOR	THIRD AUTHOR	PAG BEG	PAG END
0.89	DWORIN,L	AP	1984	TAR	GRIMLUND,RA		218	241
0.88	MORIARITY,S	AU	1976	JAR	BARRON,FH		320	341
0.83	EVANS III,JH	ST	1987	JAR	PATTON,JM		130	164
0.81	HOFSTEDT,TR	AP	1977	TAR	HUGHES,GD		379	395
0.80	SUNDER,S	AU	1983	JAR	WAYMIRE,G		565	580
0.67	MCCRAY,JH	JA	1984	TAR			35	51
0.59	PANKOFF,LD	ST	1970	JAR	VIRGIL JR,RL		1	48
0.56	BOUWMAN,MJ	34	1984	AOS			325	327
0.56	INGRAM,RW	SP	1984	JAR			126	144
0.47	DEMSKI,JS	JL	1972	TAR	FELTHAM,GA		533	548
0.47	FOSTER,G	OC	1975	TAR			686	698
0.41	BASKIN,EF	JA	1972	TAR			38	51
0.38	FELTHAM,GA	SP	1977	JAR			42	70
0.36	CHOW ,CW	WI	1982	AUD	RICE ,SJ		35	53
0.36	COLLINS,DW	AU	1979	JAR	SIMONDS,RR		352	383
0.35	COATES,R	ST	1972	JAR			132	144
0.33	NEWMAN,DP	SP	1981	JAR			247	262
0.29	DOWNES,D	AP	1973	TAR	DYCKMAN,TR		300	317
0.29	TEITLEBAUM,AD	ST	1975	JAR	ROBINSON,CF		70	91
0.25	ARANYA,N	04	1981	AOS	POLLOCK,J	AMERNIC,J	271	280
0.25	DILLARD,JF	01	1981	AOS			17	26
0.25	HUSSEIN,ME	01	1981	AOS			27	38
0.24	HAGERMAN,RL	OC	1975	TAR			699	709
0.24	KOCHANEK,RF	AP	1974	TAR			245	258
0.24	LOEB ,SE	AU	1971	JAR			287	306
0.23	HOPWOOD,WS	SP	1980	JAR			77	90
0.23	IJIRI ,Y	SP	1980	JAR	LEITCH,RA		91	108
0.20	FINLEY,DR	AU	1983	AUD			104	116
0.20	TABOR ,RH	SP	1983	JAR			348	354
0.18	BROWNELL,P	OC	1982	TAR			766	777
0.15	BECK ,PJ	SP	1980	JAR			16	37
0.12	ELLIOTT,JW	AU	1972	JAR	UPHOFF,HL		259	274
0.12	GREENBALL,MN	ST	1971	JAR			172	190
0.11	BLOOM ,R	01	1984	AOS	ELGERS,PT	MURRAY,D	1	11
0.10	ABDEL-KHALIK,AR	SP	1983	JAR			293	296
0.08	CHARNES,A	01	1980	AOS	COOPER,WW		87	107
0.08	HOPWOOD,WS	SP	1980	JAR			289	296
0.07	AGGARWAL,R	SP	1978	JAA			197	216
0.07	DAVIS ,DW	JA	1978	TAR	BOATSMAN,JR	BASKIN,EF	1	10
0.06	ALBRECHT,WS	OC	1976	TAR			824	837
0.00	BAILEY,WT	OC	1981	TAR			882	896
0.00	BIERMAN JR,H	AU	1964	JAR			229	235
0.00	COOPER,T	WI	1980	JAA			138	146
0.00	EVERETT,JO	SP	1984	JAA	PORTER,GA		241	256
0.00	FALK ,H	AU	1972	JAR			359	375
0.00	HAWKINS,CA	SP	1984	JAA	GIRARD,D		225	240
0.00	KINNEY JR,WR	AU	1981	JAA			5	17
0.00	KISSINGER,JN	AU	1983	AUD			42	54
0.00	MORRIS,MH	SU	1984	JAA	NICHOLS,WD		293	305
0.00	NEWMAN,DP	OC	1981	TAR			897	909
0.00	PUTNAM,K	AU	1984	JAA	THOMAS,LR		15	23
0.00	TEOH ,HY	02	1984	AOS	THONG ,G		189	206

CITE INDEX	FIRST AUTHOR	ISS-UE	YE-AR	JOUR-NAL	SECOND AUTHOR	THIRD AUTHOR	PAG BEG	PAG END
1.10 MODE OF REASONING (METHOD)=QUALITATIVE								
5.20	HOLTHAUSEN,RW	AG	1983	JAE	LEFTWICH,RW		77	117
4.92	BURCHELL,S	01	1980	AOS	CLUBB ,C	HOPWOOD,AG	5	27
3.50	WATTS ,RL	AP	1979	TAR	ZIMMERMAN,JL		273	305
3.27	LEV ,B	ST	1982	JAR	OHLSON,JA		249	322
3.18	TINKER,AM	02	1982	AOS	MERINO,BD	NEIMARK,M	167	200
3.11	GIBBINS,M	SP	1984	JAR			103	125
3.10	HOPWOOD,AG	23	1983	AOS			287	305
3.00	KAPLAN,RS	JL	1984	TAR			390	418
2.78	COOPER,DJ	34	1984	AOS	SHERER,MJ		207	232
2.73	WATERHOUSE,JH	01	1978	AOS	TIESSEN,P		65	76
2.62	OTLEY ,DT	04	1980	AOS			413	428
2.55	LIBBY ,R	03	1982	AOS	LEWIS ,BL		231	286
2.50	LIBBY ,R	03	1977	AOS	LEWIS ,BL		245	268
2.40	TOMKINS,C	04	1983	AOS	GROVES,R		361	374
2.30	KAPLAN,RS	OC	1983	TAR			686	705
2.22	WALLER,WS	34	1984	AOS	FELIX JR,WL		383	406
2.20	HOPWOOD,AG	01	1978	AOS			3	14
2.10	BOLAND,RJ	23	1983	AOS	PONDY ,LR		223	234
2.08	DEANGELO,LE	DE	1981	JAE			183	199
2.00	CHRISTENSON,C	JA	1983	TAR			1	22
1.93	HEDBERG,B	01	1978	AOS	JONSSON,S		47	64
1.91	FELIX JR,WL	AP	1982	TAR	KINNEY JR,WR		245	271
1.85	TINKER,AM	01	1980	AOS			147	160
1.80	COOPER,DJ	23	1983	AOS			269	286
1.70	BIRNBERG,JG	23	1983	AOS	TUROPOLEC,L	YOUNG ,SM	111	130
1.65	RONEN ,J	OC	1975	TAR	LIVINGSTONE,JL		671	685
1.53	GORDON,LA	01	1976	AOS	MILLER,D		59	70
1.50	BEAVER,WH	JA	1979	TAR	DEMSKI,JS		38	46
1.50	HAYES ,DC	23	1983	AOS			241	250
1.38	PRAKASH,P	01	1977	AOS	RAPPAPORT,A		29	38
1.30	TIESSEN,P	23	1983	AOS	WATERHOUSE,JH		251	268
1.29	SCHIFF,M	AP	1970	TAR	LEWIN ,AY		259	268
1.25	COLVILLE,I	02	1981	AOS			119	132
1.17	EINHORN,HJ	SP	1981	JAR	HOGARTH,RM		1	31
1.10	ELLIOTT,RK	SP	1983	AUD			1	12
1.08	COOPER,DJ	03	1981	AOS	HAYES ,DC	WOLF ,FM	175	192
1.08	OTLEY ,DT	02	1980	AOS	BERRY ,AJ		231	246
1.06	ARGYRIS,C	02	1977	AOS			113	124
1.06	DEMSKI,JS	OC	1973	TAR			718	723
1.06	GAMBLING,TE	02	1977	AOS			141	152
1.00	BOLAND,RJ	04	1979	AOS			259	272
1.00	CHESLEY,GR	AP	1975	TAR			325	337
1.00	DEMSKI,JS	ST	1982	JAR	KREPS ,DM		117	148
0.94	BEAVER,WH	OC	1968	TAR	KENNELLY,JW	VOSS ,WM	675	683
0.94	EINHORN,HJ	ST	1976	JAR			196	206
0.94	STRINGER,KW	ST	1975	JAR			1	9
0.92	HIRST ,MK	OC	1981	TAR			771	784
0.90	JOHNSON,HT	23	1983	AOS			139	146
0.90	SPICER,BH	01	1983	AOS	BALLEW,V		73	98
0.88	ANSARI,SL	02	1977	AOS			101	112
0.88	ASHTON,RH	OC	1974	TAR			719	732

CITE INDEX	FIRST AUTHOR	ISS-UE	YE-AR	JOUR-NAL	SECOND AUTHOR	THIRD AUTHOR	PAG BEG	PAG END
0.88	GORDON,MJ	AP	1964	TAR			251	263
0.86	BANBURY,J	03	1979	AOS	NAHAPIET,JE		163	178
0.83	MACINTOSH,NB	01	1981	AOS			39	52
0.82	SORTER,GH	JA	1969	TAR			12	19
0.80	MARKUS,ML	23	1983	AOS	PFEFFER,J		205	218
0.79	LEV ,B	DE	1979	JAE	SUNDER,S		187	210
0.78	GROBSTEIN,M	SP	1984	AUD	CRAIG ,PW		1	16
0.76	ABDEL-KHALIK,AR	JA	1974	TAR	LUSK ,EJ		8	23
0.75	LIBBY ,R	AU	1977	JAR	FISHBURN,PC		272	292
0.73	HOLSTRUM,GL	AU	1982	AUD	MESSIER JR,WF		45	63
0.71	CHANDLER,AD	12	1979	AOS	DAEMS ,H		3	20
0.70	FLAMHOLTZ,EG	23	1983	AOS			153	170
0.67	BARIFF,ML	01	1978	AOS	GALBRAITH,JR		15	28
0.67	GORDON,LA	34	1978	AOS	LARCKER,DF	TUGGLE,FD	203	214
0.65	CAPLAN,EM	JL	1966	TAR			496	509
0.65	REVSINE,L	OC	1970	TAR			704	711
0.65	WATSON,DJ	JL	1975	TAR	BAUMLER,JV		466	474
0.62	GINZBERG,MJ	04	1980	AOS			369	382
0.62	LEFTWICH,RW	DE	1980	JAE			193	211
0.59	FLAMHOLTZ,EG	AP	1971	TAR			253	267
0.59	MAY ,RG	OC	1976	TAR	SUNDEM,GL		747	763
0.57	ANSARI,SL	03	1979	AOS			149	162
0.57	SHPILBERG,D	AU	1986	AUD	GRAHAM,LE		75	94
0.55	DAVIS ,SW	04	1982	AOS	MENON ,K	MORGAN,G	307	318
0.53	ASHTON,RH	OC	1975	TAR			710	722
0.53	COPELAND,RM	AP	1973	TAR	FRANCIA,AJ	STRAWSER,RH	365	374
0.50	GONEDES,NJ	AU	1979	JAR	DOPUCH,N		384	410
0.50	JOHNSON,HT	JL	1981	TAR			510	518
0.47	BELKAOUI,A	02	1978	AOS			97	104
0.47	BIRNBERG,JG	JA	1968	TAR	NATH ,R		38	45
0.47	DRAKE ,DF	AU	1965	JAR	DOPUCH,N		192	205
0.47	HERTOG,JF	01	1978	AOS			29	46
0.47	IJIRI ,Y	SP	1968	JAR	KINARD,JC	PUTNEY,FB	1	28
0.47	MILLER,H	JA	1972	TAR			31	37
0.47	WILDAVSKY,A	01	1978	AOS			77	88
0.46	DOPUCH,N	JA	1980	TAR	SUNDER,S		1	21
0.45	COLLINS,F	02	1982	AOS			107	122
0.45	DIRSMITH,MW	SP	1982	JAA	MCALLISTER,JP		214	228
0.45	DIRSMITH,MW	AU	1982	JAA	MCALLISTER,JP		60	74
0.45	HITE ,GL	JL	1982	JAE	LONG ,MS		3	14
0.45	JONSSON,S	03	1982	AOS			287	304
0.44	BIRNBERG,JG	34	1984	AOS	SHIELDS,MD		365	382
0.42	EWUSI-MENSAH,K	04	1981	AOS			301	316
0.42	HOFSTEDE,G	03	1981	AOS			193	216
0.41	BENSTON,GJ	AP	1963	TAR			347	354
0.41	BRUMMET,RL	AP	1968	TAR	FLAMHOLTZ,EG	PYLE ,WC	217	224
0.41	COLANTONI,CS	JA	1971	TAR	MANES ,RP	WHINSTON,AB	90	102
0.41	EPSTEIN,MJ	01	1976	AOS	FLAMHOLTZ,EG	MCDONOUGH,JJ	23	42
0.41	ESTES ,RW	AP	1972	TAR			284	290
0.41	GONEDES,NJ	JA	1972	TAR			11	21
0.41	LIEBERMAN,AZ	AP	1975	TAR	WHINSTON,AB		246	258
0.38	BAKER ,CR	JL	1977	TAR			576	586
0.38	BIRNBERG,JG	03	1977	AOS	FRIEZE,IH	SHIELDS,MD	189	200

CITE INDEX	FIRST AUTHOR	ISS-UE	YE-AR	JOUR-NAL	SECOND AUTHOR	THIRD AUTHOR	PAG BEG	PAG END
0.38	DIERKES,M	01	1977	AOS	PRESTON,LE		3	22
0.38	WATTS ,RL	AG	1980	JAE	ZIMMERMAN,JL		95	106
0.36	DIRSMITH,MW	12	1979	AOS	JABLONSKY,SF		39	52
0.36	HAGG ,J	12	1979	AOS	HEDLUND,G		135	143
0.36	MCCARTHY,WE	OC	1979	TAR			667	686
0.36	SWIERINGA,RJ	02	1982	AOS	WATERHOUSE,JH		149	166
0.35	CARMICHAEL,DR	AP	1970	TAR			235	245
0.35	FLAMHOLTZ,EG	OC	1972	TAR			666	678
0.35	GOLDMAN,A	OC	1974	TAR	BARLEV,B		707	718
0.35	HOFSTEDT,TR	JA	1970	TAR	KINARD,JC		38	54
0.33	JACKSON-COX,J	34	1984	AOS	THIRKELL,JE	MCQUEENEY,J	253	273
0.33	JOYCE ,EJ	AU	1981	JAR	LIBBY ,R		544	550
0.33	ZEFF ,SA	JL	1984	TAR			447	468
0.31	RONEN ,J	AP	1977	TAR			438	449
0.29	ASHTON,RH	04	1976	AOS			289	300
0.29	BRUNS JR,WJ	JL	1968	TAR			469	480
0.29	CHEN ,RS	JL	1975	TAR			533	543
0.29	FERTAKIS,JP	OC	1969	TAR			680	691
0.29	GOLEMBIEWSKI,RT	AP	1964	TAR			333	341
0.29	JAIN ,TN	JA	1973	TAR			95	104
0.29	NICHOLS,DR	AP	1976	TAR	PRICE ,KH		335	346
0.29	PRAKASH,P	JA	1979	TAR	SUNDER,S		1	22
0.29	RAMANATHAN,KV	JL	1976	TAR			516	528
0.27	CHERNS,AB	02	1978	AOS			105	114
0.27	DIRSMITH,MW	34	1978	AOS	JABLONSKY,SF		215	226
0.25	ASHTON,RH	JL	1977	TAR			567	575
0.25	GROJER,JE	04	1977	AOS	STARK ,A		349	385
0.24	BARTON,AD	OC	1974	TAR			664	681
0.24	CRUMBLEY,DL	OC	1973	TAR			759	763
0.24	GYNTHER,RS	AP	1967	TAR			274	290
0.24	JOHNSON,HT	JL	1975	TAR			444	450
0.24	SCHIFF,M	SP	1966	JAR			62	67
0.24	STERLING,RR	JL	1970	TAR			444	457
0.21	GROVE ,HD	JL	1979	TAR	SAVICH,RS		522	537
0.21	REVSINE,L	AP	1979	TAR			306	322
0.21	SCHREUDER,H	12	1979	AOS			109	122
0.21	THORNTON,DB	03	1979	AOS			211	234
0.21	VATTER,WJ	JL	1979	TAR			563	573
0.20	DILLON,RD	JA	1978	TAR	NASH ,JF		11	17
0.20	IJIRI ,Y	SU	1978	JAA			331	348
0.20	KILMANN,RH	04	1983	AOS			341	360
0.20	MIRVIS,PH	23	1983	AOS	LAWLER III,EE		175	190
0.20	MITROFF,II	23	1983	AOS	MASON ,RO		195	204
0.19	ADAR ,Z	JA	1977	TAR	BARNEA,A	LEV ,B	137	149
0.19	COPPOCK,R	02	1977	AOS			125	130
0.19	LAVIN ,D	03	1977	AOS			237	244
0.19	PERAGALLO,E	OC	1977	TAR			881	892
0.18	ANTON ,HR	SP	1964	JAR			1	9
0.18	BIRNBERG,JG	JL	1967	TAR	NATH ,R		468	479
0.18	CHAMBERS,RJ	AP	1964	TAR			264	274
0.18	CHAMBERS,RJ	OC	1965	TAR			731	741
0.18	CYERT ,RM	ST	1974	JAR	IJIRI ,Y		29	42
0.18	GERBOTH,DL	JL	1973	TAR			475	482

CITE INDEX	FIRST AUTHOR	ISS-UE	YE-AR	JOUR-NAL	SECOND AUTHOR	THIRD AUTHOR	PAG BEG	PAG END
0.18	LOEBBECKE,JK	ST	1975	JAR	NETER ,J		38	52
0.18	MACY ,BA	23	1976	AOS	MIRVIS,PH		179	194
0.18	MATTESSICH,R	JL	1972	TAR			469	487
0.18	MCCARTHY,WE	JL	1982	TAR			554	578
0.18	MOBLEY,SC	OC	1970	TAR			762	768
0.18	OGAN ,P	AP	1976	TAR			306	320
0.18	PRAKASH,P	OC	1975	TAR	RAPPAPORT,A		723	734
0.18	ROSENBERG,D	02	1982	AOS	TOMKINS,L	DAY ,P	123	138
0.18	SELTO ,FH	02	1982	AOS			139	148
0.18	SHOCKLEY,RA	WI	1982	JAA			126	143
0.18	VATTER,WJ	AU	1963	JAR			179	197
0.18	WEBER ,R	AP	1982	TAR			311	325
0.18	WILL ,HJ	OC	1974	TAR			690	706
0.18	WRIGHT,WF	01	1982	AOS			65	78
0.18	YAMEY ,BS	AU	1964	JAR			117	136
0.17	BOLAND,RJ	02	1981	AOS			109	118
0.17	DYCKMAN,TR	04	1981	AOS			291	300
0.15	ANSARI,SL	01	1980	AOS	MCDONOUGH,JJ		129	142
0.14	OHLSON,JA	AU	1979	JAR	PATELL,JM		504	505
0.14	YOUNG ,DW	03	1979	AOS			235	244
0.13	ANDERSON,JA	AP	1977	TAR			417	426
0.13	BROMWICH,M	JL	1977	TAR			587	596
0.13	CASH JR,JI	OC	1977	TAR	BAILEY JR,AD	WHINSTON,AB	813	832
0.13	LESSEM,R	04	1977	AOS			279	294
0.13	SWANSON,EB	34	1978	AOS			237	248
0.12	ALIBER,RZ	JA	1975	TAR	STICKNEY,CP		44	57
0.12	ANDERSON,HM	JL	1970	TAR	GIESE ,J	BOOKER,J	524	531
0.12	BAILEY JR,AD	JL	1976	TAR	BOE ,WJ		559	573
0.12	BALL ,R	SP	1971	JAR			1	31
0.12	BERNHARDT,I	SP	1970	JAR	COPELAND,RM		95	98
0.12	BIERMAN JR,H	JL	1963	TAR			501	507
0.12	BIRD ,FA	AP	1974	TAR	DAVIDSON,LF	SMITH ,CH	233	244
0.12	BRIEF ,RP	SP	1965	JAR			12	31
0.12	BRIEF ,RP	AP	1975	TAR			285	297
0.12	CAUSEY JR,DY	JA	1976	TAR			19	30
0.12	CHAMBERS,RJ	SP	1963	JAR			3	15
0.12	CHAMBERS,RJ	SP	1965	JAR			32	62
0.12	CHAMBERS,RJ	JL	1966	TAR			443	457
0.12	CHAMBERS,RJ	OC	1967	TAR			751	757
0.12	DEVINE,CT	AU	1963	JAR			127	138
0.12	DOCKWEILER,RC	OC	1969	TAR			729	742
0.12	EDWARDS,EO	AP	1975	TAR			235	245
0.12	GODFREY,JT	JA	1971	TAR	PRINCE,TR		75	89
0.12	GOETZ ,BE	JA	1967	TAR			53	61
0.12	GREEN ,D	JA	1966	TAR			52	64
0.12	GYNTHER,RS	OC	1970	TAR			712	730
0.12	HANSON,EI	AP	1966	TAR			239	243
0.12	HORNGREN,CT	AP	1965	TAR			323	333
0.12	KNUTSON,PH	JA	1970	TAR			55	68
0.12	LARSON,KD	JA	1969	TAR			38	47
0.12	LEMKE ,KW	JA	1966	TAR			32	41
0.12	LORIG ,AN	JL	1964	TAR			563	573
0.12	MAUTZ ,RK	AP	1963	TAR			317	325

CITE INDEX	FIRST AUTHOR	ISS-UE	YE-AR	JOUR-NAL	SECOND AUTHOR	THIRD AUTHOR	PAG BEG	PAG END
0.12	MOONITZ,M	SP	1966	JAR			47	61
0.12	MOONITZ,M	JL	1970	TAR			465	475
0.12	PARKER,RH	SP	1968	JAR			58	71
0.12	SEIDLER,LJ	OC	1967	TAR			775	781
0.12	SNAVELY,HJ	AP	1967	TAR			223	232
0.12	TOMASSINI,LA	23	1976	AOS			239	252
0.12	VATTER,WJ	AU	1966	JAR			133	148
0.12	VICKREY,DW	JA	1976	TAR			31	40
0.12	WAGNER,JW	JL	1965	TAR			599	605
0.12	WELLS ,MC	JL	1976	TAR			471	482
0.12	YETTON,PY	01	1976	AOS			81	90
0.11	DEJONG,DV	AU	1984	AUD	SMITH ,JH		20	34
0.11	ROBERTSON,JC	SP	1984	AUD			57	67
0.10	MOCK ,TJ	SP	1983	AUD	WILLINGHAM,JJ		91	99
0.10	SOTTO ,R	01	1983	AOS			57	72
0.09	BENSTON,GJ	02	1982	AOS			87	106
0.09	LANDSITTEL,DL	SU	1982	JAA	SERLIN,JE		291	300
0.09	MOCK ,TJ	AU	1982	AUD	WRIGHT,A		33	44
0.08	BAKER ,CR	SP	1980	JAA			197	206
0.08	CHAMBERS,RJ	01	1980	AOS			167	180
0.08	FLAMHOLTZ,EG	01	1980	AOS			31	42
0.08	PALMON,D	SP	1980	JAA	KWATINETZ,M		207	226
0.08	PERAGALLO,E	JL	1981	TAR			587	595
0.07	AMEY ,LR	04	1979	AOS			247	258
0.07	CARLSSON,J	34	1978	AOS	EHN ,P	ERLANDER,B	249	260
0.07	HAKANSSON,NH	JL	1978	TAR			717	725
0.07	KOTTAS,JF	JL	1978	TAR	LAU ,HS		698	707
0.07	RAMAN ,KK	AU	1979	JAA			31	41
0.07	YAMEY ,BS	AP	1979	TAR			323	329
0.06	ABEL ,R	SP	1969	JAR			1	11
0.06	ALFRED,AM	AU	1964	JAR			172	182
0.06	ARNETT,HE	AP	1967	TAR			291	297
0.06	ARNOLD,DF	AU	1977	JAR	HUEFNER,RJ		245	252
0.06	BALADOUNI,V	AP	1966	TAR			215	225
0.06	BEDFORD,NM	JL	1968	TAR	IINO ,T		453	458
0.06	BEDFORD,NM	JL	1975	TAR	ZIEGLER,RE		435	443
0.06	BIRD ,PA	SP	1965	JAR			1	11
0.06	BIRNBERG,JG	OC	1965	TAR			814	820
0.06	BIRNBERG,JG	01	1976	AOS	GANDHI,NM		5	10
0.06	BOLLOM,WJ	JA	1972	TAR	WEYGANDT,JJ		75	84
0.06	BRADISH,RD	OC	1965	TAR			757	766
0.06	BRIEF ,RP	SP	1967	JAR			27	38
0.06	BRIEF ,RP	OC	1973	TAR	OWEN ,J		690	695
0.06	BRILOFF,AJ	JA	1964	TAR			12	15
0.06	BUCKLEY,JW	AP	1968	TAR	KIRCHER,P	MATHEWS,RL	274	283
0.06	BURKE ,EJ	OC	1964	TAR			837	849
0.06	CARMICHAEL,DR	OC	1968	TAR	SWIERINGA,RJ		697	705
0.06	CARSBERG,BV	SP	1966	JAR			1	15
0.06	CHURCHILL,NC	ST	1966	JAR			128	156
0.06	CLARKE,RW	OC	1968	TAR			769	776
0.06	COOPER,WW	OC	1968	TAR	DOPUCH,N	KELLER,TF	640	648
0.06	COWAN ,TK	OC	1965	TAR			788	794
0.06	CURRY ,DW	JL	1971	TAR			490	503

CITE INDEX	FIRST AUTHOR	ISS-UE	YE-AR	JOUR-NAL	SECOND AUTHOR	THIRD AUTHOR	PAG BEG	PAG END
0.06	DAVIDSON,S	AU	1963	JAR			117	126
0.06	ECKEL ,LG	OC	1976	TAR			764	777
0.06	FEKRAT,MA	AP	1972	TAR			351	355
0.06	FIELD ,JE	JL	1969	TAR			593	599
0.06	FIRMIN,PA	JA	1968	TAR	LINN ,JJ		75	82
0.06	FLOWER,JF	SP	1966	JAR			16	36
0.06	FRANCIS,ME	AP	1973	TAR			245	257
0.06	FREMGEN,JM	OC	1968	TAR			649	656
0.06	GAMBLING,TE	23	1976	AOS			167	174
0.06	GREEN ,D	SP	1964	JAR			35	49
0.06	GREENE,ED	AP	1963	TAR			355	362
0.06	GROVE ,HD	03	1977	AOS	MOCK ,TJ	EHRENREICH,K	219	236
0.06	HEATH ,LC	JL	1972	TAR			458	468
0.06	HECK ,WR	JL	1963	TAR			577	578
0.06	HICKS ,EL	AU	1964	JAR			158	171
0.06	HORNGREN,CT	JA	1971	TAR			1	11
0.06	HORRIGAN,JO	AP	1968	TAR			284	294
0.06	HUME ,LJ	SP	1970	JAR			21	33
0.06	ISELIN,ER	AP	1968	TAR			231	238
0.06	JAENICKE,HR	JA	1970	TAR			115	128
0.06	JOHNSON,O	JA	1972	TAR			64	74
0.06	KEISTER JR,OR	AP	1963	TAR			371	376
0.06	KEMP ,PS	OC	1965	TAR			782	787
0.06	KING ,RR	JA	1974	TAR	BARON ,CD		76	87
0.06	LANGENDERFER,HQ	OC	1969	TAR	ROBERTSON,JC		777	787
0.06	LARSON,KD	JL	1967	TAR			480	488
0.06	MARQUES,E	23	1976	AOS			175	178
0.06	MATHEWS,RL	JL	1968	TAR			509	516
0.06	MAUTZ ,RK	AP	1966	TAR	MINI ,DL		283	291
0.06	MCDONOUGH,JJ	OC	1971	TAR			676	685
0.06	MCRAE ,TW	AP	1970	TAR			315	321
0.06	MEYERS,SL	JA	1973	TAR			44	49
0.06	MOONITZ,M	AU	1966	JAR	RUSS ,A		155	168
0.06	MURPHY,GJ	AP	1976	TAR			277	286
0.06	NURNBERG,H	OC	1968	TAR			719	729
0.06	OGAN ,P	23	1976	AOS			195	218
0.06	PATON ,WA	AP	1963	TAR			243	251
0.06	PENMAN,SH	AP	1970	TAR			333	346
0.06	RAPPAPORT,A	AP	1965	TAR			373	376
0.06	REVSINE,L	JL	1971	TAR			480	489
0.06	ROSENFIELD,P	AP	1966	TAR	STOREY,R		327	330
0.06	SNAVELY,HJ	AP	1969	TAR			344	353
0.06	STAUBUS,GJ	OC	1967	TAR			650	661
0.06	STAUBUS,GJ	JL	1976	TAR			574	589
0.06	STERLING,RR	JL	1968	TAR			481	502
0.06	TAUSSIG,RA	JL	1963	TAR			562	567
0.06	TRACY ,JA	JA	1965	TAR			163	175
0.06	ULLMANN,AA	01	1976	AOS			71	80
0.06	VATTER,WJ	JL	1963	TAR			470	477
0.06	WILKINSON,JR	OC	1965	TAR	DONEY ,LD		753	756
0.06	WOJDAK,JF	JL	1969	TAR			562	570
0.06	WOJDAK,JF	JA	1970	TAR			88	97
0.06	WRIGHT,FK	AU	1965	JAR			167	181

CITE INDEX	FIRST AUTHOR	ISS-UE	YE-AR	JOUR-NAL	SECOND AUTHOR	THIRD AUTHOR	PAG BEG	PAG END
0.06	YAMEY ,BS	SP	1967	JAR			51	76
0.00	ABDEL-KHALIK,AR	SP	1966	JAR			37	46
0.00	ABDEL-MAGID,MF	AP	1979	TAR			346	357
0.00	ADAMS ,KD	WI	1984	JAA			151	163
0.00	AHARONI,Y	SP	1967	JAR	OPHIR ,T		1	26
0.00	ALLYN ,RG	JA	1964	TAR			121	127
0.00	ALLYN ,RG	AP	1966	TAR			303	311
0.00	ANDERSON,HM	OC	1963	TAR	GRIFFIN,FB		813	818
0.00	ANDERSON,JJ	JL	1967	TAR			583	588
0.00	ANDERSON,JM	AU	1964	JAR			236	238
0.00	ARNETT,HE	OC	1963	TAR			733	741
0.00	ARNETT,HE	JL	1969	TAR			482	494
0.00	BACKER,M	JL	1969	TAR			533	538
0.00	BAGGETT,WD	SP	1983	JAA			227	233
0.00	BAKER ,RE	JA	1964	TAR			52	61
0.00	BAKER ,RE	JA	1966	TAR			98	105
0.00	BARRETT,WB	JA	1968	TAR			105	112
0.00	BEAMS ,FA	AP	1969	TAR			382	388
0.00	BEAVER,WH	DE	1984	JAE	GRIFFIN,PA	LANDSMAN,WR	219	223
0.00	BEDFORD,NM	JA	1967	TAR			82	85
0.00	BEDFORD,NM	AP	1972	TAR	MCKEOWN,JC		333	338
0.00	BEECHY,TH	AP	1969	TAR			375	381
0.00	BENNINGER,LJ	JL	1965	TAR			547	557
0.00	BENSTON,GJ	JL	1976	TAR			483	498
0.00	BERG ,KB	JL	1963	TAR	MUELLER,FJ		554	561
0.00	BERKOW,WF	AP	1964	TAR			377	386
0.00	BIERMAN JR,H	JA	1963	TAR			61	63
0.00	BIERMAN JR,H	JL	1965	TAR			541	546
0.00	BIERMAN JR,H	JA	1968	TAR	LIU ,E		62	67
0.00	BIERMAN JR,H	JA	1969	TAR			65	78
0.00	BIERMAN JR,H	AP	1969	TAR	DAVIDSON,S		239	246
0.00	BIRNBERG,JG	OC	1964	TAR			963	971
0.00	BIRNBERG,JG	01	1980	AOS			71	80
0.00	BJORN ANDERSEN,N	02	1980	AOS	PEDERSEN,PH		203	216
0.00	BLAKELY,EJ	JA	1963	TAR	KNUTSON,PH		75	86
0.00	BOER ,G	JA	1966	TAR			92	97
0.00	BOGART,FO	OC	1965	TAR			834	838
0.00	BOTTS ,RR	OC	1963	TAR			789	795
0.00	BOURN ,AM	AU	1966	JAR			213	223
0.00	BOUTELL,WS	AP	1964	TAR			305	311
0.00	BOWEN ,EK	OC	1967	TAR			782	787
0.00	BOWER ,JB	AP	1965	TAR	SCHLOSSER,RE		338	344
0.00	BRAVENEC,LL	02	1977	AOS	EPSTEIN,MJ	CRUMBLEY,DL	131	140
0.00	BRIEF ,RP	OC	1977	TAR			810	812
0.00	BRIGHTON,GD	JA	1969	TAR			137	144
0.00	BRILOFF,AJ	JL	1967	TAR			489	496
0.00	BRUGEMAN,DC	OC	1963	TAR	BRIGHTON,GD		764	770
0.00	BRUGGE,WG	JL	1963	TAR			596	600
0.00	BUBLITZ,B	WI	1984	JAA	KEE ,R		123	137
0.00	BUCKLEY,JW	JA	1966	TAR			75	82
0.00	BUCKLEY,JW	JL	1967	TAR			572	582
0.00	BUCKLEY,JW	01	1980	AOS			49	64
0.00	BURKE ,WL	OC	1963	TAR			802	812

CITE INDEX	FIRST AUTHOR	ISS-UE	YE-AR	JOUR-NAL	SECOND AUTHOR	THIRD AUTHOR	PAG BEG	PAG END
0.00	BURNS ,JS	JA	1963	TAR	JAEDICKE,RK	SANGSTER,JM	1	13
0.00	CAMPFIELD,WL	JL	1963	TAR			521	527
0.00	CAMPFIELD,WL	JL	1965	TAR			594	598
0.00	CAMPFIELD,WL	OC	1970	TAR			683	689
0.00	CAREY ,JL	JA	1968	TAR			1	9
0.00	CAREY ,JL	JA	1969	TAR			79	85
0.00	CARLISLE,HM	JA	1966	TAR			115	120
0.00	CARMICHAEL,DR	SU	1979	JAA			294	306
0.00	CARMICHAEL,DR	SU	1984	JAA	WHITTINGTON,OR		347	361
0.00	CARSON,AB	AP	1965	TAR			334	337
0.00	CARTER,WK	JA	1981	TAR			108	114
0.00	CAUSEY JR,DY	AP	1973	TAR			258	267
0.00	CHAMBERS,RJ	AP	1967	TAR			241	253
0.00	CHAMBERS,RJ	AP	1968	TAR			239	247
0.00	CHAMBERS,RJ	OC	1979	TAR			764	775
0.00	CHAN ,KH	WI	1984	JAA	CHENG ,TT		164	177
0.00	CHATFIELD,M	JA	1975	TAR			1	6
0.00	CHURCHMAN,CW	JA	1971	TAR			30	35
0.00	COHEN ,MF	JA	1965	TAR			1	8
0.00	COPELAND,TE	AU	1978	JAA			33	48
0.00	CORBIN,DA	OC	1963	TAR			742	744
0.00	CORBIN,DA	OC	1967	TAR			635	641
0.00	COWAN ,TK	JA	1965	TAR			9	20
0.00	COWAN ,TK	JA	1968	TAR			94	100
0.00	COWIE ,JB	JA	1970	TAR	FREMGEN,JM		27	37
0.00	CRAMER JR,JJ	OC	1964	TAR			869	875
0.00	CRAMER JR,JJ	JL	1965	TAR			606	616
0.00	CRAMER JR,JJ	OC	1970	TAR	SCHRADER,WJ		698	703
0.00	CRAMER JR,JJ	WI	1979	JAA	NEYHART,CA		135	150
0.00	CRANDALL,RH	JL	1969	TAR			457	466
0.00	CRUMBLEY,DL	JL	1968	TAR			554	564
0.00	CRUMBLEY,DL	JA	1975	TAR	SAVICH,RS		112	117
0.00	CRUSE ,RB	JA	1965	TAR	SUMMERS,EL		82	88
0.00	CUSHING,BE	OC	1968	TAR			668	671
0.00	DAVIDSON,S	AP	1963	TAR			278	284
0.00	DEAN ,J	AP	1963	TAR	HARRISS,CL		229	242
0.00	DECOSTER,DT	AP	1966	TAR			297	302
0.00	DEFLIESE,PL	JL	1965	TAR			517	521
0.00	DEINZER,HT	JA	1966	TAR			21	31
0.00	DEITRICK,JW	SU	1979	JAA	ALDERMAN,CW		316	328
0.00	DEMARIS,EJ	JA	1963	TAR			37	45
0.00	DERY ,D	03	1982	AOS			217	224
0.00	DEWHIRST,JF	AP	1971	TAR			365	373
0.00	DILLARD,JF	34	1984	AOS			343	354
0.00	DOWELL,CD	AU	1981	JAA	HALL ,JA		30	40
0.00	DREBIN,AR	JL	1963	TAR			579	583
0.00	DREBIN,AR	SP	1964	JAR			25	34
0.00	DRINKWATER,D	JL	1965	TAR	EDWARDS,JD		579	582
0.00	EDEY ,HC	AP	1963	TAR			262	265
0.00	EIGEN ,MM	JL	1965	TAR			536	540
0.00	ELLIOTT,EL	OC	1968	TAR	LARREA,J	RIVERA,JM	763	768
0.00	FAGERBERG,P	JL	1972	TAR			454	457
0.00	FARMAN,WL	JA	1963	TAR	HOU ,C		133	141

CITE INDEX	FIRST AUTHOR	ISS-UE	YE-AR	JOUR-NAL	SECOND AUTHOR	THIRD AUTHOR	PAG BEG	PAG END
0.00	FARMAN,WL	AP	1964	TAR			392	404
0.00	FERRARA,WL	OC	1963	TAR			719	722
0.00	FERTAKIS,JP	JL	1970	TAR			509	512
0.00	FESS ,PE	OC	1963	TAR			723	732
0.00	FESS ,PE	AP	1966	TAR			266	270
0.00	FIRMIN,PA	AP	1963	TAR			270	277
0.00	FISHER,M	SU	1978	JAA			349	360
0.00	FITZGERALD,RD	AU	1979	JAA	KELLEY,EM		5	20
0.00	FLESHER,DL	04	1979	AOS	FLESHER,TK		297	304
0.00	FORD ,A	OC	1969	TAR			818	822
0.00	FORD ,A	AP	1975	TAR			338	344
0.00	FRANK ,WG	OC	1965	TAR			854	862
0.00	FRANKFURTER,GM	SU	1983	JAA	YOUNG ,AE		314	324
0.00	FREMGEN,JM	JA	1964	TAR			43	51
0.00	FREMGEN,JM	JL	1967	TAR			457	467
0.00	FRIEDMAN,LA	JA	1978	TAR			18	30
0.00	FRIEDMAN,LA	OC	1978	TAR			895	909
0.00	FU ,P	SP	1971	JAR			40	51
0.00	FURLONG,WL	AP	1966	TAR			244	252
0.00	GAMBLE,GO	SP	1981	JAA			220	237
0.00	GAMBLE,GO	SU	1982	JAA			320	326
0.00	GIBBS ,G	OC	1964	TAR			4	7
0.00	GIBSON,JL	JL	1963	TAR			492	500
0.00	GIBSON,RW	JA	1965	TAR			196	203
0.00	GILLES JR,LH	OC	1963	TAR			776	784
0.00	GIVENS,HR	JL	1966	TAR			458	463
0.00	GLATZER,W	03	1981	AOS			219	234
0.00	GOETZ ,BE	JL	1967	TAR			435	440
0.00	GOGGANS,TP	JL	1964	TAR			627	630
0.00	GOLDBERG,L	JL	1963	TAR			457	469
0.00	GOLDSCHMIDT,Y	AP	1969	TAR	SMIDT ,S		317	329
0.00	GOLDSCHMIDT,Y	AU	1984	JAA	SHASHUA,L		54	67
0.00	GOMBERG,M	JL	1964	TAR	FARBER,A		615	617
0.00	GORMLEY,RJ	SU	1980	JAA			293	312
0.00	GORMLEY,RJ	AU	1982	JAA			51	59
0.00	GRADY ,P	JA	1965	TAR			21	30
0.00	GRAESE,CE	AP	1964	TAR			387	391
0.00	GRAY ,J	AP	1963	TAR	WILLINGHAM,JJ	JOHNSTON,K	336	346
0.00	GREER ,HC	JA	1964	TAR			22	31
0.00	GREER JR,WR	AU	1978	JAA	MORRISSEY,LE		49	57
0.00	GROSS ,H	OC	1966	TAR			745	753
0.00	GUTBERLET,LG	SU	1980	JAA			313	338
0.00	GUTBERLET,LG	AU	1983	JAA			16	28
0.00	GYNTHER,RS	AP	1969	TAR			247	255
0.00	HAFNER,GF	OC	1964	TAR			979	982
0.00	HAIN ,HP	OC	1966	TAR			699	703
0.00	HAIN ,HP	AU	1967	JAR			154	163
0.00	HANNUM,WH	AP	1968	TAR	WASSERMAN,W		295	302
0.00	HANSEN,ES	ST	1977	JAR			156	201
0.00	HARTLEY,RV	AP	1968	TAR			321	332
0.00	HASEMAN,WC	OC	1968	TAR			738	752
0.00	HATFIELD,HR	AU	1966	JAR			169	182
0.00	HEARD ,JE	03	1981	AOS	BOLCE ,WJ		247	254

CITE INDEX	FIRST AUTHOR	ISS-UE	YE-AR	JOUR-NAL	SECOND AUTHOR	THIRD AUTHOR	PAG BEG	PAG END
0.00	HEIN ,LW	JL	1963	TAR			508	520
0.00	HEIN ,LW	AP	1963	TAR			252	261
0.00	HEINS ,EB	AP	1966	TAR			323	326
0.00	HELMKAMP,JG	JL	1969	TAR			605	610
0.00	HENDRICKSON,HS	AP	1968	TAR			363	366
0.00	HENDRIKSEN,ES	JL	1963	TAR			483	491
0.00	HENNESSY,VC	SU	1978	JAA			317	330
0.00	HERBERT,L	JL	1971	TAR			433	440
0.00	HICKS ,SA	JL	1978	TAR			708	716
0.00	HILL ,HP	WI	1982	JAA			99	109
0.00	HIRSCH,AJ	OC	1964	TAR			972	978
0.00	HIRSCHMAN,RW	JA	1965	TAR			176	183
0.00	HOLDER,WW	WI	1982	JAA	EUDY ,KH		110	125
0.00	HOLMES,W	JA	1979	TAR			47	57
0.00	HOLZER,HP	AP	1963	TAR	SCHONFELD,HM		377	381
0.00	HOLZER,HP	AP	1963	TAR	SCHONFELD,HM		382	388
0.00	HOLZER,HP	AP	1964	TAR	SCHONFELD,HM		405	413
0.00	HOLZMANN,OJ	WI	1984	JAA	MEANS ,KM		138	150
0.00	HORNE ,JC	JA	1963	TAR			56	60
0.00	HORNGREN,CT	AP	1964	TAR	SORTER,GH		417	420
0.00	HORNGREN,CT	AP	1967	TAR			254	264
0.00	HORNGREN,CT	JA	1969	TAR			86	89
0.00	HORVITZ,JS	WI	1981	JAA	HAINKEL,M		114	127
0.00	HORWITZ,BN	OC	1963	TAR			819	826
0.00	HORWITZ,BN	AU	1980	JAA	KOLODNY,R		20	35
0.00	HORWITZ,RM	JL	1964	TAR			618	621
0.00	HUDSON,RR	OC	1963	TAR			796	801
0.00	HYLTON,DP	JL	1964	TAR			667	670
0.00	HYLTON,DP	OC	1965	TAR			824	828
0.00	IJIRI ,Y	OC	1968	TAR			662	667
0.00	IJIRI ,Y	JL	1972	TAR			510	526
0.00	IJIRI ,Y	01	1980	AOS	KELLY ,EC		115	123
0.00	IMDIEKE,LF	OC	1969	TAR	WEYGANDT,JJ		798	805
0.00	IMKE ,FJ	AP	1966	TAR			318	322
0.00	INGBERMAN,M	AU	1978	JAA	SORTER,GH		58	62
0.00	INGBERMAN,M	WI	1980	JAA			101	112
0.00	JACOBSEN,LE	AP	1963	TAR			285	292
0.00	JACOBSEN,LE	AU	1964	JAR			221	228
0.00	JENKINS,DO	JL	1964	TAR			648	653
0.00	JENSEN,RE	JL	1970	TAR			502	508
0.00	JENTZ ,GA	JL	1966	TAR			535	541
0.00	JENTZ ,GA	AP	1967	TAR			362	365
0.00	JERSTON,JE	OC	1965	TAR			812	813
0.00	JEYNES,PH	JA	1965	TAR			105	118
0.00	JOHNSON,GL	OC	1965	TAR			821	823
0.00	JOHNSON,O	SP	1965	JAR			75	85
0.00	JOHNSON,O	JL	1968	TAR			546	548
0.00	JOHNSON,O	OC	1974	TAR	GUNN ,S		649	663
0.00	JOHNSON,O	ST	1981	JAR			89	119
0.00	JOHNSON,SB	SP	1982	JAA	MESSIER JR,WF		195	213
0.00	JOHNSTON,DJ	SP	1980	JAA	LEMON ,WM	NEUMANN,FL	251	263
0.00	JOLIVET,V	JL	1964	TAR			689	692
0.00	KABBES,SM	AP	1965	TAR			395	400

CITE INDEX	FIRST AUTHOR	ISS-UE	YE-AR	JOUR-NAL	SECOND AUTHOR	THIRD AUTHOR	PAG BEG	PAG END
0.00	KALINSKI,BD	JL	1963	TAR			591	595
0.00	KAPLAN,HG	JA	1964	TAR	SOLOMON,KI		145	149
0.00	KARLINSKY,SS	WI	1983	JAA			157	167
0.00	KARLINSKY,SS	AU	1983	JAA			65	76
0.00	KAUFMAN,F	OC	1967	TAR			713	720
0.00	KAY ,RS	SU	1979	JAA			307	315
0.00	KEISTER JR,OR	AP	1964	TAR			414	416
0.00	KELL ,WG	AP	1968	TAR			266	273
0.00	KELLER,TF	JA	1965	TAR			184	189
0.00	KEMP ,PS	JA	1963	TAR			126	132
0.00	KETZ ,JE	AU	1983	JAA	WYATT ,AR		29	43
0.00	KING ,TE	SP	1979	JAA			209	223
0.00	KIRCHER,P	OC	1965	TAR			742	752
0.00	KIRCHER,P	JL	1967	TAR			537	543
0.00	KISTLER,LH	OC	1967	TAR			758	766
0.00	KOHLER,EL	AP	1963	TAR			266	269
0.00	KOLLARITSCH,FP	AP	1965	TAR			382	385
0.00	KRIPKE,H	AU	1978	JAA			4	32
0.00	LAIBSTAIN,S	AP	1971	TAR			342	351
0.00	LAMDEN,CW	JA	1964	TAR			128	132
0.00	LARGAY III,JA	JA	1973	TAR			115	119
0.00	LARGAY III,JA	AU	1983	JAA			44	53
0.00	LARSON,KD	OC	1966	TAR	SCHATTKE,RW		634	641
0.00	LAUVER,RC	JA	1966	TAR			65	74
0.00	LAWLER,J	ST	1967	JAR			86	92
0.00	LEA ,RB	SU	1981	AUD			53	94
0.00	LEE ,GA	SP	1973	JAR			47	61
0.00	LEE ,GA	JL	1981	TAR			539	553
0.00	LEE ,SS	JL	1965	TAR			622	625
0.00	LEMBKE,VC	JL	1970	TAR			458	464
0.00	LENTILHON,RW	OC	1964	TAR			880	883
0.00	LESSARD,DR	JL	1977	TAR	LORANGE,P		628	637
0.00	LEWIS ,CD	JA	1967	TAR			96	105
0.00	LI ,DH	OC	1963	TAR			771	775
0.00	LI ,DH	JA	1963	TAR			52	55
0.00	LI ,DH	SP	1963	JAR			102	107
0.00	LI ,DH	OC	1964	TAR			946	950
0.00	LINOWES,DF	JA	1965	TAR			97	104
0.00	LITTLETON,AC	JL	1970	TAR			476	480
0.00	LIVOCK,DM	SP	1965	JAR			86	102
0.00	LONGSTRETH,B	WI	1984	JAA			110	122
0.00	LORIG ,AN	OC	1963	TAR			759	763
0.00	LOUDERBACK,JG	AP	1971	TAR			298	305
0.00	LOWE ,HD	AP	1967	TAR			356	360
0.00	LUNESKI,C	JL	1964	TAR			591	597
0.00	LYNN ,ES	AP	1964	TAR			371	376
0.00	MACKENZIE,O	AP	1964	TAR			363	370
0.00	MANES ,RP	JL	1964	TAR			631	638
0.00	MARPLE,RM	JL	1963	TAR			478	482
0.00	MATEER,WH	JL	1965	TAR			583	586
0.00	MATTINGLY,LA	OC	1964	TAR			996	3
0.00	MAURIELLO,JA	JA	1963	TAR			26	28
0.00	MAURIELLO,JA	AP	1964	TAR			347	357

CITE INDEX	FIRST AUTHOR	ISS-UE	YE-AR	JOUR-NAL	SECOND AUTHOR	THIRD AUTHOR	PAG BEG	PAG END
0.00	MAUTZ ,RK	AP	1965	TAR			299	311
0.00	MAUTZ ,RK	JL	1969	TAR	SKOUSEN,KF		447	456
0.00	MAUTZ ,RK	AP	1977	TAR	PREVITS,GJ		301	307
0.00	MAY ,PT	JL	1969	TAR			583	592
0.00	MCDONALD,DL	12	1979	AOS	PUXTY ,AG		53	66
0.00	MCRAE ,TW	AU	1965	JAR			255	260
0.00	MEPHAM,MJ	JA	1983	TAR			43	57
0.00	METCALF,RW	JA	1964	TAR			16	21
0.00	MEYER ,PE	JA	1976	TAR			80	89
0.00	MILLER,EM	AU	1980	JAA			6	19
0.00	MILLER,HE	JA	1966	TAR			1	7
0.00	MILLER,MC	AP	1973	TAR			280	291
0.00	MOBLEY,SC	AP	1966	TAR			292	296
0.00	MOBLEY,SC	AP	1968	TAR			333	341
0.00	MORENO,RG	OC	1964	TAR			990	995
0.00	MOREY ,L	JA	1963	TAR			102	108
0.00	MORRISON,TA	OC	1966	TAR			704	713
0.00	MOST ,KS	SP	1967	JAR			39	50
0.00	MOST ,KS	JA	1969	TAR			145	152
0.00	MOST ,KS	OC	1972	TAR			722	734
0.00	MUELLER,GG	JA	1963	TAR			142	147
0.00	MUELLER,GG	AU	1964	JAR			148	157
0.00	MUELLER,GG	AP	1965	TAR			386	394
0.00	MURRAY,D	AU	1983	JAA	JOHNSON,R		4	15
0.00	NELSON,GK	JA	1966	TAR			42	47
0.00	NEUBIG,RD	JA	1964	TAR			86	89
0.00	NICHOLS,AC	OC	1968	TAR	GRAWOIG,DE		631	639
0.00	NOBES ,CW	AP	1982	TAR			303	310
0.00	NORGAARD,CT	JL	1972	TAR			433	442
0.00	NURNBERG,H	OC	1972	TAR			655	665
0.00	O'CONNOR,MC	AP	1972	TAR	HAMRE ,JC		308	319
0.00	OLIPHANT,WJ	ST	1971	JAR			93	98
0.00	PARKE ,R	03	1981	AOS	PETERSON,JL		235	246
0.00	PARKER,WM	OC	1963	TAR			785	788
0.00	PARKER,WM	AU	1966	JAR			149	154
0.00	PATON ,WA	SP	1963	JAR			44	72
0.00	PATON ,WA	JA	1967	TAR			7	23
0.00	PATON ,WA	SP	1968	JAR			72	85
0.00	PATON ,WA	AP	1969	TAR			276	283
0.00	PATRICK,AW	JA	1963	TAR	QUITTMEYER,CL		109	117
0.00	PATTERSON,RG	OC	1967	TAR			772	774
0.00	PEASNELL,KV	JA	1977	TAR			186	189
0.00	PEIRSON,G	OC	1966	TAR			729	736
0.00	PERAGALLO,E	JL	1971	TAR			529	534
0.00	PERAGALLO,E	JA	1983	TAR			98	104
0.00	PETERSON,WA	AP	1966	TAR			275	282
0.00	PHILIPS,GE	OC	1963	TAR			696	708
0.00	PHILIPS,GE	JA	1963	TAR			14	25
0.00	PHILIPS,GE	JA	1968	TAR			10	17
0.00	PHILLIPS,LC	AP	1965	TAR			377	381
0.00	POMERANZ,F	AU	1977	JAA			45	52
0.00	PRATER,GI	OC	1966	TAR			619	625
0.00	PRESTON,LE	03	1981	AOS			255	262

CITE INDEX	FIRST AUTHOR	ISS-UE	YE-AR	JOUR-NAL	SECOND AUTHOR	THIRD AUTHOR	PAG BEG	PAG END
0.00	PRINCE,TR	JL	1964	TAR			553	562
0.00	RABY ,WL	JL	1963	TAR	NEUBIG,RD		568	576
0.00	RABY ,WL	OC	1966	TAR			714	720
0.00	RABY ,WL	JA	1969	TAR			1	11
0.00	RAMAN ,KK	SU	1981	JAA			352	359
0.00	RAPPAPORT,A	OC	1964	TAR			951	962
0.00	RATSCH,H	JA	1964	TAR			140	144
0.00	RAYMAN,RA	SP	1969	JAR			53	89
0.00	REVSINE,L	AP	1969	TAR			354	358
0.00	REVSINE,L	AP	1981	TAR			342	354
0.00	REYNOLDS,IN	AP	1964	TAR			342	346
0.00	RICHARD,DL	OC	1968	TAR			730	737
0.00	ROBERTSON,JC	WI	1981	JAA	ALDERMAN,CW		144	161
0.00	ROBINSON,LA	JA	1964	TAR	HALL ,TP		62	69
0.00	ROLLER,J	AP	1967	TAR	WILLIAMS,TH		349	355
0.00	RORKE ,CH	03	1982	AOS			305	306
0.00	ROSE ,H	AU	1964	JAR			137	147
0.00	ROSEN ,LS	JA	1967	TAR			106	113
0.00	ROSEN ,LS	JA	1969	TAR	DECOSTER,DT		124	136
0.00	ROSENFIELD,P	OC	1969	TAR			788	797
0.00	ROSS ,H	ST	1970	JAR			108	115
0.00	SALGADO,AP	AP	1963	TAR			389	397
0.00	SAN MIGUEL,JG	02	1977	AOS			177	186
0.00	SAPIENZA,SR	JA	1963	TAR			91	101
0.00	SAPIENZA,SR	JL	1964	TAR			582	590
0.00	SAPIENZA,SR	SP	1964	JAR			50	66
0.00	SAVOIE,LM	ST	1969	JAR			55	62
0.00	SCHACHNER,L	AP	1968	TAR			303	311
0.00	SCHATTKE,RW	OC	1965	TAR			805	811
0.00	SCHATTKE,RW	AP	1972	TAR			233	244
0.00	SCHIENEMAN,GS	AU	1979	JAA			21	30
0.00	SCHIENEMAN,GS	SP	1983	JAA			212	226
0.00	SCHIFF,M	AU	1977	JAA	SORTER,GH	WIESEN,JL	19	44
0.00	SCHNEE,EJ	AU	1981	JAA	TAYLOR,ME		18	29
0.00	SCHNEIDER,AJ	AP	1967	TAR			342	348
0.00	SCHNEPPER,JA	JL	1977	TAR			653	657
0.00	SCHULTE JR,AA	OC	1966	TAR			721	728
0.00	SCHWARTZ,BN	SP	1981	JAA			238	247
0.00	SCOTT ,RA	OC	1979	TAR			750	763
0.00	SEAMAN,JL	JL	1965	TAR			617	621
0.00	SEELYE,AL	AP	1963	TAR			302	309
0.00	SEIDLER,LJ	SU	1979	JAA			285	293
0.00	SEILER,RE	OC	1966	TAR			652	656
0.00	SHILLINGLAW,G	SP	1963	JAR			73	85
0.00	SHWAYDER,KR	JA	1968	TAR			101	104
0.00	SHWAYDER,KR	SP	1968	JAR			86	97
0.00	SIMMONS,JK	OC	1967	TAR			680	692
0.00	SIMON ,SI	OC	1964	TAR			884	889
0.00	SIMON ,SI	AP	1965	TAR			401	406
0.00	SLAVIN,NS	AP	1977	TAR			360	368
0.00	SMOLINSKI,EJ	AU	1963	JAR			149	178
0.00	SOMMERFELD,RM	OC	1967	TAR			747	750
0.00	SORTER,GH	ST	1974	JAR	GANS ,MS		1	12

CITE INDEX	FIRST AUTHOR	ISS-UE	YE-AR	JOUR-NAL	SECOND AUTHOR	THIRD AUTHOR	PAG BEG	PAG END
0.00	SORTER,GH	SP	1982	JAA			188	194
0.00	SPACEK,L	AP	1964	TAR			275	284
0.00	SPENCER,MH	AP	1963	TAR			310	316
0.00	SPILLER JR,EA	OC	1964	TAR			850	859
0.00	SPROUSE,RT	OC	1963	TAR			687	695
0.00	SPROUSE,RT	JL	1965	TAR			522	526
0.00	ST.PIERRE,K	SP	1984	JAA			257	263
0.00	STAATS,EB	SU	1981	AUD			1	11
0.00	STANDISH,PEM	JL	1964	TAR			654	666
0.00	STANLEY,CH	JL	1964	TAR			639	647
0.00	STAUBUS,GJ	JA	1963	TAR			64	74
0.00	STAUBUS,GJ	JL	1966	TAR			397	412
0.00	STETTLER,HF	OC	1965	TAR			723	730
0.00	STEVENSON,RA	AP	1966	TAR			312	317
0.00	STONE ,DE	AP	1967	TAR			331	337
0.00	STONE ,ML	ST	1968	JAR			59	66
0.00	STONE ,WE	JA	1964	TAR			38	42
0.00	STONE ,WE	AP	1969	TAR			284	291
0.00	STONE ,WE	AU	1972	JAR			345	350
0.00	STREER,PJ	SU	1979	JAA			329	338
0.00	SUMMERS,EL	SP	1970	JAR	DESKINS,JW		113	117
0.00	TAYLOR,RG	JA	1965	TAR			89	96
0.00	THOMAS,AL	JL	1964	TAR			574	581
0.00	TOPIOL,J	JA	1966	TAR			83	91
0.00	TOWNSEND,LA	JA	1967	TAR			1	6
0.00	TRUEBLOOD,RM	SP	1963	JAR			86	95
0.00	TRUEBLOOD,RM	ST	1966	JAR			183	191
0.00	TRUMBULL,WP	JA	1963	TAR			46	51
0.00	TRUMBULL,WP	JL	1968	TAR			459	468
0.00	TUCKERMAN,B	JA	1964	TAR			32	37
0.00	ULLMANN,AA	12	1979	AOS			123	134
0.00	VANCE ,LL	JA	1966	TAR			48	51
0.00	VANCE ,LL	OC	1969	TAR			692	703
0.00	VASARHELYI,MA	AU	1984	AUD			100	106
0.00	VASARHELYI,MA	SP	1984	AUD	BAILEY JR,AD	CAMARDESSE JR,JE	98	103
0.00	VOGT ,RA	01	1977	AOS			59	80
0.00	WADE ,HH	OC	1963	TAR			714	718
0.00	WAGNER,JW	JL	1969	TAR			600	604
0.00	WAUGH ,JB	JL	1968	TAR			535	539
0.00	WEIGAND,RE	JL	1963	TAR			584	590
0.00	WEIL ,RL	OC	1973	TAR			749	758
0.00	WEISER,HJ	JL	1966	TAR			518	524
0.00	WELKE ,WR	AP	1966	TAR			253	256
0.00	WELLS ,MC	OC	1965	TAR	COTTON,W		829	833
0.00	WELLS ,MC	AP	1968	TAR			373	376
0.00	WELSCH,GA	OC	1964	TAR			8	13
0.00	WERNER,CA	AU	1983	JAA	KOSTOLANSKY,JW		54	64
0.00	WERNER,CA	SP	1984	JAA	KOSTOLANSKY,JW		212	224
0.00	WEYGANDT,JJ	JA	1970	TAR			69	75
0.00	WHEELER,JT	JA	1970	TAR			1	10
0.00	WHITE ,D	SU	1982	JAA	VANECEK,M		338	354
0.00	WHITTINGTON,OR	SU	1982	JAA	ADAMS ,SJ		310	319
0.00	WIESEN,JL	WI	1979	JAA	ENG ,R		101	121

CITE INDEX	FIRST AUTHOR	ISS-UE	YE-AR	JOUR-NAL	SECOND AUTHOR	THIRD AUTHOR	PAG BEG	PAG END
0.00	WIESEN,JL	SU	1981	JAA			309	324
0.00	WILKINSON,TL	JA	1964	TAR			133	139
0.00	WILLIAMS,D	AP	1966	TAR			226	234
0.00	WILLIAMS,JJ	02	1981	AOS			153	166
0.00	WILLIAMS,TH	OC	1967	TAR	GRIFFIN,CH		642	649
0.00	WILLINGHAM,JJ	JL	1964	TAR			543	552
0.00	WINBORNE,MG	OC	1966	TAR	KLEESPIE,DC		737	744
0.00	WINDAL,FW	JA	1963	TAR			29	36
0.00	WINJUM,JO	OC	1970	TAR			743	761
0.00	WINJUM,JO	AU	1971	JAR			333	350
0.00	WINJUM,JO	JA	1971	TAR			149	155
0.00	WOODS ,RS	JL	1964	TAR			598	614
0.00	WOOLSEY,SM	OC	1963	TAR			709	713
0.00	WRIGHT,FK	AU	1967	JAR			173	179
0.00	WRIGHT,HW	OC	1966	TAR			626	633
0.00	WYATT ,AR	JL	1965	TAR			527	535
0.00	YAMEY ,BS	JL	1980	TAR			419	425
0.00	YOUNG ,AE	SP	1980	JAA			244	250
0.00	YOUNG ,DW	OC	1976	TAR			788	799
0.00	YU ,SC	JA	1966	TAR			8	20
0.00	YU ,SC	JL	1969	TAR			571	582
0.00	ZANNETOS,ZS	AP	1963	TAR			326	335
0.00	ZANNETOS,ZS	OC	1964	TAR			860	868
0.00	ZANNETOS,ZS	JL	1967	TAR			566	571
0.00	ZEFF ,SA	JA	1965	TAR	MAXWELL,WD		65	75
0.00	ZEFF ,SA	JL	1982	TAR			528	553

2.1 RESEARCH METHOD=ANALYTICAL – INTERNAL LOGIC

CITE INDEX	FIRST AUTHOR	ISS-UE	YE-AR	JOUR-NAL	SECOND AUTHOR	THIRD AUTHOR	PAG BEG	PAG END
6.00	HOPWOOD,AG	03	1987	AOS			207	234
4.92	BURCHELL,S	01	1980	AOS	CLUBB ,C	HOPWOOD,AG	5	27
4.83	MILLER,P	03	1987	AOS	O'LEARY,T		235	265
4.17	CHRISTIE,AA	DE	1987	JAE			231	258
4.14	LOFT ,A	02	1986	AOS			137	170
4.00	BOWEN ,RM	AG	1981	JAE	NOREEN,EW	LACEY ,JM	151	179
3.75	BURCHELL,S	04	1985	AOS	CLUBB ,C	HOPWOOD,AG	381	414
3.50	WATTS ,RL	AP	1979	TAR	ZIMMERMAN,JL		273	305
3.33	ARMSTRONG,P	05	1987	AOS			415	436
3.18	TINKER,AM	02	1982	AOS	MERINO,BD	NEIMARK,M	167	200
3.11	GIBBINS,M	SP	1984	JAR			103	125
3.10	HOPWOOD,AG	23	1983	AOS			287	305
3.00	HOSKIN,KW	02	1986	AOS	MACVE ,RH		105	136
3.00	KAPLAN,RS	JL	1984	TAR			390	418
3.00	ROGERSON,WP	OC	1992	TAR			671	690
2.80	DEMSKI,JS	AP	1978	TAR	FELTHAM,GA		336	359
2.73	WATERHOUSE,JH	01	1978	AOS	TIESSEN,P		65	76
2.62	OTLEY ,DT	04	1980	AOS			413	428
2.50	BAIMAN,S	AU	1983	JAR	EVANS III,JH		371	395
2.40	TOMKINS,C	04	1983	AOS	GROVES,R		361	374
2.38	DYE ,RA	SP	1985	JAR			123	145
2.30	KAPLAN,RS	OC	1983	TAR			686	705
2.25	DEANGELO,LE	AG	1981	JAE			113	127
2.22	WALLER,WS	34	1984	AOS	FELIX JR,WL		383	406

CITE INDEX	FIRST AUTHOR	ISS-UE	YE-AR	JOUR-NAL	SECOND AUTHOR	THIRD AUTHOR	PAG BEG	PAG END
2.20	HOLTHAUSEN,RW	SP	1988	JAR	VERRECCHIA,RE		82	106
2.14	CHUA ,WF	OC	1986	TAR			601	632
2.14	HUGHES,PJ	JN	1986	JAE			119	142
2.14	TITMAN,S	JN	1986	JAE	TRUEMAN,B		159	172
2.10	VERRECCHIA,RE	DE	1983	JAE			179	194
2.08	DEANGELO,LE	DE	1981	JAE			183	199
2.00	DYE ,RA	SP	1992	JAR			27	52
2.00	LEV ,B	JA	1988	TAR			1	22
2.00	MEYER ,JW	45	1986	AOS			345	356
2.00	ROBERTS,J	04	1985	AOS	SCAPENS,RW		443	456
1.93	HEDBERG,B	01	1978	AOS	JONSSON,S		47	64
1.92	BAIMAN,S	ST	1980	JAR	DEMSKI,JS		184	220
1.86	ZIMMERMAN,JL	JL	1979	TAR			504	521
1.85	TINKER,AM	01	1980	AOS			147	160
1.80	HINES ,RD	03	1988	AOS			251	261
1.80	HOSKIN,KW	01	1988	AOS	MACVE ,RH		37	73
1.67	BAIMAN,S	AU	1987	JAR	EVANS III,JH	NOEL ,J	217	244
1.67	MELUMAD,ND	SP	1990	JAR	THOMAN,L		77	120
1.67	OHLSON,JA	SP	1990	CAR			648	676
1.65	RONEN ,J	OC	1975	TAR	LIVINGSTONE,JL		671	685
1.56	DEMSKI,JS	JA	1984	TAR	PATELL,JM	WOLFSON,MA	16	34
1.56	PENNO ,M	SP	1984	JAR			177	191
1.53	GORDON,LA	01	1976	AOS	MILLER,D		59	70
1.50	ARMSTRONG,P	02	1985	AOS			129	148
1.50	BEAVER,WH	JA	1979	TAR	DEMSKI,JS		38	46
1.50	DATAR ,SM	MR	1991	JAE	FELTHAM,GA	HUGHES,JS	3	49
1.50	DYE ,RA	AU	1983	JAR			514	533
1.50	GJESDAL,F	SP	1981	JAR			208	231
1.50	HAYES ,DC	23	1983	AOS			241	250
1.50	KIRBY ,AJ	SP	1991	JAR	REICHELSTEIN,S	SEN ,PK	109	128
1.50	OHLSON,JA	JL	1989	JAE			109	115
1.50	RICHARDSON,AJ	04	1987	AOS			341	355
1.50	ROBERTS,J	04	1991	AOS			355	368
1.50	TINKER,T	01	1987	AOS	NEIMARK,M		71	88
1.43	NEIMARK,M	45	1986	AOS	TINKER,T		369	396
1.40	NOREEN,EW	04	1988	AOS			359	369
1.40	TINKER,T	02	1988	AOS			165	189
1.38	PRAKASH,P	01	1977	AOS	RAPPAPORT,A		29	38
1.35	SCOTT ,WR	AU	1973	JAR			304	330
1.33	DARROUGH,MN	JA	1990	JAE	STOUGHTON,NM		219	243
1.33	DEMSKI,JS	SP	1987	JAR	SAPPINGTON,DEM		68	89
1.33	HOLTHAUSEN,RW	JA	1990	TAR	VERRECCHIA,RE		191	208
1.33	MAGEE ,RP	AP	1990	TAR	TSENG ,M		315	336
1.33	PUXTY ,AG	03	1987	AOS	WILLMOTT,HC	COOPER,DJ	273	291
1.30	TIESSEN,P	23	1983	AOS	WATERHOUSE,JH		251	268
1.29	KINNEY JR,WR	SP	1975	JAR			117	132
1.29	SCHIFF,M	AP	1970	TAR	LEWIN ,AY		259	268
1.25	COLVILLE,I	02	1981	AOS			119	132
1.20	MORGAN,G	05	1988	AOS			477	485
1.20	THOMAS,JK	JL	1988	JAE			199	237
1.19	FELIX JR,WL	SP	1977	JAR	GRIMLUND,RA		23	41
1.18	CHRISTENSEN,J	AU	1982	JAR			589	603
1.17	HOPPER,T	05	1987	AOS	STOREY,J	WILLMOTT,H	437	456

CITE INDEX	FIRST AUTHOR	ISS-UE	YE-AR	JOUR-NAL	SECOND AUTHOR	THIRD AUTHOR	PAG BEG	PAG END
1.17	KNIGHTS,D	05	1987	AOS	COLLINSON,D		457	477
1.15	GARMAN,MB	AU	1980	JAR	OHLSON,JA		420	440
1.14	TRUEMAN,B	MR	1986	JAE			53	72
1.13	HOPWOOD,AG	03	1985	AOS			361	376
1.10	ELLIOTT,RK	SP	1983	AUD			1	12
1.10	OHLSON,JA	SP	1983	JAR			141	154
1.08	BEAVER,WH	SP	1981	JAR			163	184
1.08	COOPER,DJ	03	1981	AOS	HAYES ,DC	WOLF ,FM	175	192
1.08	OTLEY ,DT	02	1980	AOS	BERRY ,AJ		231	246
1.06	ARGYRIS,C	02	1977	AOS			113	124
1.06	DEMSKI,JS	OC	1973	TAR			718	723
1.06	GAMBLING,TE	02	1977	AOS			141	152
1.00	ANTLE ,R	SP	1984	JAR			1	20
1.00	BANKER,RD	SP	1989	JAR	DATAR ,SM		21	39
1.00	BANKER,RD	SP	1992	CAR	DATAR ,SM		329	352
1.00	BANKER,RD	AU	1992	CAR			343	354
1.00	BOLAND,RJ	04	1979	AOS			259	272
1.00	CHOUDHURY,N	06	1988	AOS			549	557
1.00	CHRISTIE,AA	DE	1984	JAE	KENNELLEY,MD	KING ,JW	205	217
1.00	COVALESKI,MA	06	1990	AOS	DIRSMITH,MW		543	573
1.00	DYE ,RA	JA	1990	TAR			1	24
1.00	DYE ,RA	AU	1990	JAR	BALACHANDRAN,BV	MAGEE ,RP	239	266
1.00	FELLINGHAM,JC	OC	1985	TAR	NEWMAN,DP		634	650
1.00	FELTHAM,GA	AU	1992	CAR	XIE ,JZ		46	80
1.00	GRAY ,B	05	1992	AOS			399	425
1.00	KANODIA,C	SP	1989	JAR	BUSHMAN,R	DICKHAUT,J	59	77
1.00	KIM ,O	AU	1991	JAR	VERRECCHIA,RE		302	321
1.00	LAVOIE,D	06	1987	AOS			579	604
1.00	MEHREZ,A	AU	1992	CAR	BROWN ,JR	KHOUJA,M	329	342
1.00	MELUMAD,ND	ST	1987	JAR	REICHELSTEIN,S		1	18
1.00	RAJAN ,MV	JL	1992	TAR			527	545
1.00	SMITH ,VL	AU	1987	AUD	SCHATZBERG,J	WALLER,WS	71	93
1.00	SUH ,YS	ST	1987	JAR			22	46
0.94	BEAVER,WH	OC	1968	TAR	KENNELLY,JW	VOSS ,WM	675	683
0.94	EINHORN,HJ	ST	1976	JAR			196	206
0.94	KINNEY JR,WR	ST	1975	JAR			14	29
0.94	STRINGER,KW	ST	1975	JAR			1	9
0.92	HIRST ,MK	OC	1981	TAR			771	784
0.90	JOHNSON,HT	23	1983	AOS			139	146
0.90	SPICER,BH	01	1983	AOS	BALLEW,V		73	98
0.89	LAMBERT,RA	OC	1984	TAR			604	618
0.88	ANSARI,SL	02	1977	AOS			101	112
0.88	ASHTON,RH	OC	1974	TAR			719	732
0.88	GORDON,MJ	AP	1964	TAR			251	263
0.86	BANBURY,J	03	1979	AOS	NAHAPIET,JE		163	178
0.86	KAPLAN,RS	45	1986	AOS			429	452
0.86	OHLSON,JA	DE	1979	JAE			211	232
0.86	SEFCIK,SE	AU	1986	JAR	THOMPSON,R		316	334
0.86	WHITLEY,R	02	1986	AOS			171	192
0.83	BURRELL,G	01	1987	AOS			89	102
0.83	HOPWOOD,AG	01	1987	AOS			65	70
0.83	MACINTOSH,NB	01	1981	AOS			39	52
0.83	MARCH ,JG	02	1987	AOS			153	168

CITE INDEX	FIRST AUTHOR	ISS-UE	YE-AR	JOUR-NAL	SECOND AUTHOR	THIRD AUTHOR	PAG BEG	PAG END
0.82	SORTER,GH	JA	1969	TAR			12	19
0.82	SUNDER,S	JA	1976	TAR			1	18
0.81	HAKANSSON,NH	AP	1977	TAR			396	416
0.80	DYE ,RA	AU	1988	JAR			195	235
0.80	KINNEY JR,WR	SP	1988	CAR			416	425
0.80	LANDSMAN,WR	OC	1988	TAR	MAGLIOLO,J		586	604
0.79	LEV ,B	DE	1979	JAE	SUNDER,S		187	210
0.78	GROBSTEIN,M	SP	1984	AUD	CRAIG ,PW		1	16
0.78	SUNDER,S	SP	1984	JAR	WAYMIRE,G		396	405
0.77	HILTON,RW	AU	1980	JAR			477	505
0.76	DEMSKI,JS	AP	1974	TAR			221	232
0.76	FELTHAM,GA	OC	1970	TAR	DEMSKI,JS		623	640
0.75	ANTLE ,R	SP	1989	CAR	DEMSKI,JS		423	451
0.75	BAIMAN,S	AU	1985	JAR	NOEL ,J		486	501
0.75	DEMSKI,JS	SP	1989	JAR	SAPPINGTON,DEM		40	58
0.75	MELUMAD,ND	SP	1989	CAR			733	753
0.73	ANTLE ,R	AU	1982	JAR			504	527
0.71	CHANDLER,AD	12	1979	AOS	DAEMS ,H		3	20
0.71	CHUA ,WF	06	1986	AOS			583	598
0.71	DEMSKI,JS	AU	1986	JAR	SAPPINGTON,DEM		250	269
0.70	MENZEFRICKE,U	SP	1983	JAR			96	105
0.67	AMERSHI,AH	AU	1990	CAR	CHENG ,P		61	99
0.67	BARIFF,ML	01	1978	AOS	GALBRAITH,JR		15	28
0.67	BEAVER,WH	JA	1987	TAR			137	144
0.67	GORDON,LA	34	1978	AOS	LARCKER,DF	TUGGLE,FD	203	214
0.67	JORDAN,JS	SP	1990	CAR			903	921
0.67	SHIBANO,T	ST	1990	JAR			110	147
0.67	SUNDER,S	AU	1978	JAR			341	367
0.67	THOMPSON,G	05	1987	AOS			523	543
0.67	WILLIAMS,PF	02	1987	AOS			169	192
0.65	CAPLAN,EM	JL	1966	TAR			496	509
0.65	CUSHING,BE	JA	1974	TAR			24	41
0.65	IJIRI ,Y	JL	1966	TAR	JAEDICKE,RK		474	483
0.65	KAPLAN,RS	SP	1973	JAR			38	46
0.65	LEV ,B	JA	1971	TAR	SCHWARTZ,A		103	112
0.65	REVSINE,L	OC	1970	TAR			704	711
0.65	WATSON,DJ	JL	1975	TAR	BAUMLER,JV		466	474
0.65	YU ,S	AU	1973	JAR	NETER ,J		273	295
0.64	GRIMLUND,RA	AU	1982	JAR			316	342
0.64	NG ,DS	ST	1979	JAR	STOECKENIUS,J		1	24
0.63	DIRSMITH,MW	02	1985	AOS	COVALESKI,MA		149	170
0.63	HAMLEN,SS	JL	1977	TAR	HAMLEN,WA	TSCHIRHART,JT	616	627
0.63	OGDEN ,S	02	1985	AOS	BOUGEN,P		211	226
0.63	PENNO ,M	SP	1985	JAR			240	255
0.62	GINZBERG,MJ	04	1980	AOS			369	382
0.62	LEFTWICH,RW	DE	1980	JAE			193	211
0.62	MAGEE ,RP	AU	1980	JAR			551	573
0.60	AMERSHI,AH	SP	1988	CAR	CHENG ,P		515	563
0.60	HINES ,RD	OC	1988	TAR			642	656
0.60	JUNG ,WO	SP	1988	JAR	KWON ,YK		146	153
0.60	KOTHARI,SP	AU	1988	JAA	LYS ,T	SMITH ,CW	307	340
0.59	DEMSKI,JS	AU	1976	JAR			230	245
0.59	FLAMHOLTZ,EG	AP	1971	TAR			253	267

CITE INDEX	FIRST AUTHOR	ISS-UE	YE-AR	JOUR-NAL	SECOND AUTHOR	THIRD AUTHOR	PAG BEG	PAG END
0.59	ITAMI ,H	SP	1975	JAR			73	96
0.59	KAPLAN,RS	SP	1969	JAR			32	43
0.59	MAY ,RG	OC	1976	TAR	SUNDEM,GL		747	763
0.57	ANSARI,SL	03	1979	AOS			149	162
0.55	DAVIS ,SW	04	1982	AOS	MENON ,K	MORGAN,G	307	318
0.54	EVANS III,JH	ST	1980	JAR			108	128
0.54	VERRECCHIA,RE	MR	1980	JAE			63	92
0.53	BAIMAN,S	SP	1975	JAR			1	15
0.53	BUTTERWORTH,JE	SP	1972	JAR			1	27
0.53	DEMSKI,JS	AU	1972	JAR			243	258
0.53	DYCKMAN,TR	AU	1969	JAR			215	244
0.53	KAPLAN,RS	ST	1975	JAR			126	133
0.53	SUNDER,S	AU	1976	JAR			277	300
0.50	AMERSHI,AH	AU	1987	JAR	SUNDER,S		177	195
0.50	ANTLE ,R	ST	1991	JAR	DEMSKI,JS		1	30
0.50	ANTLE ,R	ST	1991	JAR	NALEBUFF,B		31	59
0.50	BABER ,WR	DE	1983	JAE			213	227
0.50	BAIMAN,S	SP	1991	JAR	EVANS III,JH	NAGARAJAN,NJ	1	18
0.50	BALACHANDRAN,BV	SP	1987	CAR	NAGARAJAN,NJ		281	301
0.50	BALAKRISHNAN,R	JA	1991	TAR			120	140
0.50	BECK ,PJ	JL	1989	TAR	JUNG ,W		468	487
0.50	BUSHMAN,RM	AU	1991	JAR			261	276
0.50	DONTOH,A	AU	1989	JAA			480	511
0.50	DOPUCH,N	SP	1989	CAR			494	500
0.50	DYE ,RA	AU	1985	JAR			544	574
0.50	FELLINGHAM,JC	JA	1985	TAR	WOLFSON,MA		10	17
0.50	FELLINGHAM,JC	SP	1989	AUD	NEWMAN,DP	PATTERSON,ER	1	21
0.50	GONEDES,NJ	AU	1979	JAR	DOPUCH,N		384	410
0.50	HARTE ,GF	02	1987	AOS	OWEN ,DL		123	142
0.50	INDJEJIKIAN,RJ	AU	1991	JAR			277	301
0.50	JENSEN,DL	OC	1977	TAR			842	856
0.50	JOHNSON,HT	JL	1981	TAR			510	518
0.50	KINNEY JR,WR	SP	1983	AUD			13	22
0.50	PATELL,JM	AU	1979	JAR			528	549
0.50	STEINBART,PJ	JA	1987	TAR			97	116
0.47	BELKAOUI,A	02	1978	AOS			97	104
0.47	BIRNBERG,JG	JA	1968	TAR	NATH ,R		38	45
0.47	BODNAR,G	OC	1975	TAR			747	757
0.47	DEMSKI,JS	JL	1974	TAR	SWIERINGA,RJ		506	513
0.47	DRAKE ,DF	AU	1965	JAR	DOPUCH,N		192	205
0.47	FELTHAM,GA	OC	1968	TAR			684	696
0.47	HERTOG,JF	01	1978	AOS			29	46
0.47	JAEDICKE,RK	OC	1964	TAR	ROBICHEK,AA		917	926
0.47	KAPLAN,RS	AP	1971	TAR	THOMPSON,GL		352	364
0.47	KAPLAN,RS	JL	1974	TAR	WELAM ,VP		477	484
0.47	MILLER,H	JA	1972	TAR			31	37
0.47	NG ,DS	OC	1978	TAR			910	920
0.47	RONEN ,J	SP	1970	JAR	MCKINNEY,G		99	112
0.47	SUNDER,S	AP	1976	TAR			287	291
0.47	WILDAVSKY,A	01	1978	AOS			77	88
0.46	CROSBY,MA	AU	1980	JAR			585	593
0.46	DOPUCH,N	JA	1980	TAR	SUNDER,S		1	21
0.45	DIRSMITH,MW	SP	1982	JAA	MCALLISTER,JP		214	228

CITE INDEX	FIRST AUTHOR	ISS-UE	YE-AR	JOUR-NAL	SECOND AUTHOR	THIRD AUTHOR	PAG BEG	PAG END
0.45	DIRSMITH,MW	AU	1982	JAA	MCALLISTER,JP		60	74
0.45	HITE ,GL	JL	1982	JAE	LONG ,MS		3	14
0.44	BIRNBERG,JG	34	1984	AOS	SHIELDS,MD		365	382
0.44	MATOLCSY,ZP	AU	1984	JAR			555	569
0.43	ATKINSON,AA	SP	1979	JAR			1	22
0.43	SMIELIAUSKAS,W	JA	1986	TAR			118	128
0.43	SUNDEM,GL	SP	1979	JAR			243	261
0.43	VERRECCHIA,RE	MR	1979	JAE			77	90
0.43	VERRECCHIA,RE	OC	1986	JAE			175	196
0.43	WILNER,N	01	1986	AOS	BIRNBERG,JG		71	82
0.42	EWUSI-MENSAH,K	04	1981	AOS			301	316
0.42	HAKANSSON,NH	ST	1981	JAR			1	35
0.42	HOFSTEDE,G	03	1981	AOS			193	216
0.42	OHLSON,JA	AU	1981	JAR	BUCKMAN,AG		399	433
0.41	BENSTON,GJ	AP	1963	TAR			347	354
0.41	BRUMMET,RL	AP	1968	TAR	FLAMHOLTZ,EG	PYLE ,WC	217	224
0.41	COLANTONI,CS	JA	1971	TAR	MANES ,RP	WHINSTON,AB	90	102
0.41	ESTES ,RW	AP	1972	TAR			284	290
0.41	GONEDES,NJ	JA	1972	TAR			11	21
0.41	HASEMAN,WD	JA	1976	TAR	WHINSTON,AB		65	79
0.41	HILLIARD,JE	JA	1975	TAR	LEITCH,RA		69	80
0.41	LIEBERMAN,AZ	AP	1975	TAR	WHINSTON,AB		246	258
0.41	SORENSEN,JE	JL	1969	TAR			555	561
0.41	SUNDEM,GL	AP	1974	TAR			306	320
0.41	TOBA ,Y	JA	1975	TAR			7	24
0.41	TRACY ,JA	JA	1969	TAR			90	98
0.40	BANKER,RD	AU	1988	CAR	DATAR ,SM	MAINDIRATTA,A	96	124
0.40	HUGHES,PJ	ST	1988	JAR	SCHWARTZ,ES		41	62
0.40	LOEB ,M	SP	1978	JAR	MAGAT ,WA		103	121
0.40	LUNDHOLM,RJ	SP	1988	JAR			107	118
0.40	RONEN ,J	AU	1988	JAR	BALACHANDRAN,KR		300	314
0.40	TRUEMAN,B	ST	1988	JAR	TITMAN,S		127	143
0.38	ABDOLMOHAMMADI,MJ	AU	1985	CAR			76	94
0.38	AMERSHI,AH	SP	1985	CAR	DEMSKI,JS	FELLINGHAM,J	176	192
0.38	BAILEY JR,AD	AP	1985	TAR	DUKE ,GL	GERLACH,JH	186	201
0.38	BECK ,PJ	SP	1985	JAR	SOLOMON,I	TOMASSINI,LA	37	56
0.38	BECK ,PJ	SP	1985	AUD	SOLOMON,I		1	10
0.38	BIRNBERG,JG	03	1977	AOS	FRIEZE,IH	SHIELDS,MD	189	200
0.38	CUSHING,BE	AP	1977	TAR			308	321
0.38	DIERKES,M	01	1977	AOS	PRESTON,LE		3	22
0.38	GONEDES,NJ	AU	1980	JAR			441	476
0.38	LAMBERT,RA	AU	1985	JAR			633	647
0.38	O'LEARY,T	01	1985	AOS			87	104
0.38	OWEN ,DL	03	1985	AOS	LLOYD ,AJ		329	352
0.36	BURTON,JC	WI	1982	AUD	FAIRFIELD,P		1	22
0.36	DIRSMITH,MW	12	1979	AOS	JABLONSKY,SF		39	52
0.36	GODFREY,JT	AU	1982	JAR	ANDREWS,RW		304	315
0.36	HAGG ,J	12	1979	AOS	HEDLUND,G		135	143
0.36	MCCARTHY,WE	OC	1979	TAR			667	686
0.36	SWIERINGA,RJ	02	1982	AOS	WATERHOUSE,JH		149	166
0.35	BUZBY ,SL	JA	1974	TAR			42	49
0.35	CARMICHAEL,DR	AP	1970	TAR			235	245
0.35	DEAKIN,EB	OC	1974	TAR	GRANOF,MH		764	771

CITE INDEX	FIRST AUTHOR	ISS-UE	YE-AR	JOUR-NAL	SECOND AUTHOR	THIRD AUTHOR	PAG BEG	PAG END
0.35	DEMSKI,JS	OC	1967	TAR			701	712
0.35	DEMSKI,JS	SP	1972	JAR			58	76
0.35	FLAMHOLTZ,EG	OC	1972	TAR			666	678
0.35	GOLDMAN,A	OC	1974	TAR	BARLEV,B		707	718
0.35	GONEDES,NJ	AU	1974	JAR	IJIRI ,Y		251	269
0.35	HOFSTEDT,TR	JA	1970	TAR	KINARD,JC		38	54
0.35	LIAO ,M	OC	1975	TAR			780	790
0.35	MARSHALL,RM	AU	1972	JAR			286	307
0.35	MAY ,RG	JA	1973	TAR	SUNDEM,GL		80	94
0.35	REVSINE,L	JL	1970	TAR			513	523
0.33	BAIMAN,S	SP	1990	CAR	MAY ,JH	MUKHERJI,A	761	799
0.33	BALACHANDRAN,BV	AU	1987	CAR	LI ,L	MAGEE ,RP	164	185
0.33	BALACHANDRAN,BV	SP	1987	JAR	RAMAKRISHNAN,RT		111	126
0.33	BEAVER,WH	JA	1981	TAR			23	37
0.33	CONROY,RM	JA	1987	TAR	HUGHES,JS		50	66
0.33	DITTMAN,DA	SP	1978	JAR	PRAKASH,P		14	25
0.33	HIRST ,MK	OC	1987	TAR			774	784
0.33	IJIRI ,Y	JA	1984	TAR	NOEL ,J		52	63
0.33	JOYCE ,EJ	AU	1981	JAR	LIBBY ,R		544	550
0.33	LAUGHLIN,RC	05	1987	AOS			479	502
0.33	LIN ,WT	AU	1984	AUD	MOCK ,TJ	WRIGHT,A	89	99
0.33	PENNO ,M	AP	1990	TAR			303	314
0.33	SHIH ,MSH	AU	1987	CAR	SUNDER,S		16	31
0.33	SWIERINGA,RJ	03	1987	AOS	WEICK ,KE		293	308
0.33	VERRECCHIA,RE	SP	1981	JAR			271	283
0.31	HAMLEN,SS	OC	1980	TAR			578	593
0.31	RONEN ,J	AP	1977	TAR			438	449
0.30	LARCKER,DF	JL	1983	TAR	REDER ,RE	SIMON ,DT	606	620
0.30	SCHEPANSKI,A	AP	1983	TAR	UECKER,WC		259	283
0.29	ASHTON,RH	04	1976	AOS			289	300
0.29	BERNSTEIN,LA	JA	1967	TAR			86	95
0.29	BLAZENKO,GW	AU	1986	CAR	SCOTT ,WR		68	92
0.29	BRUNS JR,WJ	JL	1968	TAR			469	480
0.29	CHEN ,RS	JL	1975	TAR			533	543
0.29	COVALESKI,M	45	1986	AOS	AIKEN ,ME		297	320
0.29	DITTMAN,DA	SP	1976	JAR	JURIS ,HA	REVSINE,L	49	65
0.29	FERTAKIS,JP	OC	1969	TAR			680	691
0.29	GAA ,JC	JL	1986	TAR			435	454
0.29	GOLEMBIEWSKI,RT	AP	1964	TAR			333	341
0.29	HALPERIN,R	JA	1979	TAR			58	71
0.29	HILTON,RW	AU	1979	JAR			411	435
0.29	IJIRI ,Y	SP	1971	JAR	KAPLAN,RS		73	87
0.29	JAGGI ,B	AP	1974	TAR	LAU ,HS		321	329
0.29	JAIN ,TN	JA	1973	TAR			95	104
0.29	KANODIA,CS	SP	1979	JAR			74	98
0.29	KAPLAN,RS	OC	1973	TAR			738	748
0.29	LEV ,B	AU	1968	JAR			247	261
0.29	MORIARITY,S	OC	1975	TAR			791	795
0.29	NICHOLS,DR	AP	1976	TAR	PRICE ,KH		335	346
0.29	PRAKASH,P	JA	1979	TAR	SUNDER,S		1	22
0.29	RAMANATHAN,KV	JL	1976	TAR			516	528
0.29	SHIH ,W	OC	1979	TAR			687	706
0.29	TEITLEBAUM,AD	ST	1975	JAR	ROBINSON,CF		70	91

CITE INDEX	FIRST AUTHOR	ISS-UE	YE-AR	JOUR-NAL	SECOND AUTHOR	THIRD AUTHOR	PAG BEG	PAG END
0.27	CHERNS,AB	02	1978	AOS			105	114
0.27	DIRSMITH,MW	34	1978	AOS	JABLONSKY,SF		215	226
0.27	KOTTAS,JF	AP	1978	TAR	LAU ,AH	LAU ,HS	389	401
0.25	AMERSHI,AH	AU	1989	CAR	CHENG ,P		72	90
0.25	ASHTON,RH	JL	1977	TAR			567	575
0.25	BACHAR,J	AU	1989	CAR			216	241
0.25	BILLERA,LJ	SP	1981	JAR	HEATH ,DC	VERRECCHIA,RE	185	196
0.25	CHEUNG,JK	SP	1989	CAR			625	641
0.25	ETZIONI,A	AU	1989	JAA			555	570
0.25	EVEREST,GL	AP	1977	TAR	WEBER ,R		340	359
0.25	GOLDIN,HJ	SU	1985	JAA			269	278
0.25	HEIMANN,SR	AU	1977	JAR	CHESLEY,GR		193	206
0.25	HUGHES,JS	JA	1977	TAR			56	68
0.25	JANG ,HJ	AU	1989	CAR	RO ,BT		242	262
0.25	KANODIA,CS	SP	1985	JAR			175	193
0.25	KAPLAN,RS	AP	1977	TAR			369	378
0.25	KISSINGER,JN	AP	1977	TAR			322	339
0.25	MOORE ,G	SP	1989	CAR	SCOTT ,WR		754	774
0.25	NEWMAN,P		1989	AUD	NOEL ,J		50	63
0.25	SCOTT ,WR	SP	1977	JAR			120	137
0.25	STAUBUS,GJ	JA	1985	TAR			53	75
0.24	ABDEL-KHALIK,AR	JL	1971	TAR			457	471
0.24	BARNEA,A	JA	1975	TAR	RONEN ,J	SADAN ,S	58	68
0.24	BARTON,AD	OC	1974	TAR			664	681
0.24	CRUMBLEY,DL	OC	1973	TAR			759	763
0.24	FRIEDMAN,A	AU	1974	JAR	LEV ,B		235	250
0.24	GYNTHER,RS	AP	1967	TAR			274	290
0.24	IJIRI ,Y	OC	1969	TAR	KAPLAN,RS		743	756
0.24	IJIRI ,Y	OC	1973	TAR	ITAMI ,H		724	737
0.24	JOHNSON,HT	JL	1975	TAR			444	450
0.24	KILLOUGH,LN	AP	1973	TAR	SOUDERS,TL		268	279
0.24	OZAN ,T	SP	1971	JAR	DYCKMAN,TR		88	115
0.24	STERLING,RR	JL	1970	TAR			444	457
0.24	SUMMERS,EL	JL	1972	TAR			443	453
0.23	BALACHANDRAN,BV	ST	1980	JAR	RAMAKRISHNAN,RT		140	171
0.23	IJIRI ,Y	SP	1980	JAR	LEITCH,RA		91	108
0.23	NEWMAN,DP	02	1980	AOS			217	230
0.22	MARCINKO,D	JL	1984	TAR	PETRI ,E		488	495
0.21	BROWN ,LD	JL	1979	TAR	ROZEFF,MS		585	591
0.21	REVSINE,L	AP	1979	TAR			306	322
0.21	SCHREUDER,H	12	1979	AOS			109	122
0.21	SCOTT ,WR	SP	1979	JAR			156	178
0.21	THORNTON,DB	03	1979	AOS			211	234
0.20	CALLEN,JL	AP	1978	TAR			303	308
0.20	CHEN ,JT	JL	1983	TAR			600	605
0.20	COHEN ,SI	AU	1988	CAR	LOEB ,M		70	95
0.20	DERMER,JD	01	1988	AOS			25	36
0.20	DICKHAUT,JW	AU	1983	JAR	LERE ,JC		495	513
0.20	DILLON,RD	JA	1978	TAR	NASH ,JF		11	17
0.20	FELTHAM,GA	AU	1988	CAR	CHRISTENSEN,PO		133	169
0.20	FINLEY,DR	AU	1983	AUD			104	116
0.20	IJIRI ,Y	SU	1978	JAA			331	348
0.20	KILMANN,RH	04	1983	AOS			341	360

CITE INDEX	FIRST AUTHOR	ISS-UE	YE-AR	JOUR-NAL	SECOND AUTHOR	THIRD AUTHOR	PAG BEG	PAG END
0.20	MAGEE ,RP	JA	1988	TAR			42	54
0.20	MITROFF,II	23	1983	AOS	MASON ,RO		195	204
0.20	NELSON,J	SU	1988	JAA	RONEN ,J	WHITE ,L	255	296
0.20	SORTER,GH	SU	1988	JAA	SIEGEL,S	SLAIN ,J	233	244
0.20	SPICER,BH	03	1988	AOS			303	322
0.20	SUH ,YS	SP	1988	JAR			154	168
0.19	ADAR ,Z	JA	1977	TAR	BARNEA,A	LEV ,B	137	149
0.19	COPPOCK,R	02	1977	AOS			125	130
0.19	SCHROEDER,RG	01	1977	AOS	IMDIEKE,LF		39	46
0.18	ANTON ,HR	SP	1964	JAR			1	9
0.18	BENSTON,GJ	OC	1966	TAR			657	672
0.18	BRIEF ,RP	AU	1970	JAR	OWEN ,J		167	177
0.18	CHAMBERS,RJ	AP	1964	TAR			264	274
0.18	CHAMBERS,RJ	OC	1965	TAR			731	741
0.18	CYERT ,RM	ST	1974	JAR	IJIRI ,Y		29	42
0.18	DEMSKI,JS	AU	1970	JAR			178	198
0.18	DOPUCH,N	SP	1964	JAR	DRAKE ,DF		10	24
0.18	EAVES ,BC	JL	1966	TAR			426	442
0.18	FRIBERG,RA	JA	1973	TAR			50	60
0.18	GERBOTH,DL	JL	1973	TAR			475	482
0.18	GIBBINS,M	SP	1982	JAR			121	138
0.18	HARTLEY,RV	OC	1971	TAR			746	755
0.18	HASSELDINE,CR	JL	1967	TAR			497	515
0.18	LOEBBECKE,JK	ST	1975	JAR	NETER ,J		38	52
0.18	MAGEE ,RP	AU	1975	JAR			257	266
0.18	MARSHALL,RM	JA	1975	TAR			99	111
0.18	MATTESSICH,R	JL	1972	TAR			469	487
0.18	MCCARTHY,WE	JL	1982	TAR			554	578
0.18	MENSAH,YM	OC	1982	TAR			681	700
0.18	MOBLEY,SC	OC	1970	TAR			762	768
0.18	MOCK ,TJ	OC	1971	TAR			765	777
0.18	OGAN ,P	AP	1976	TAR			306	320
0.18	OHLSON,JA	AU	1975	JAR			267	282
0.18	PRAKASH,P	OC	1975	TAR	RAPPAPORT,A		723	734
0.18	RONEN ,J	JA	1974	TAR			50	60
0.18	SELTO ,FH	02	1982	AOS			139	148
0.18	SHOCKLEY,RA	WI	1982	JAA			126	143
0.18	VATTER,WJ	AU	1963	JAR			179	197
0.18	WEBER ,R	AP	1982	TAR			311	325
0.18	WILL ,HJ	OC	1974	TAR			690	706
0.18	WRIGHT,WF	01	1982	AOS			65	78
0.18	YAMEY ,BS	AU	1964	JAR			117	136
0.17	BAILEY,AP	SU	1981	AUD	MCAFEE,RP	WHINSTON,AB	38	52
0.17	BOATSMAN,JR	JA	1981	TAR	BASKIN,EF		38	53
0.17	BOLAND,RJ	02	1981	AOS			109	118
0.17	COGGER,KO	AU	1981	JAR			285	298
0.17	COOPER,DJ	05	1987	AOS	HOPPER,TM		407	414
0.17	DYCKMAN,TR	04	1981	AOS			291	300
0.17	GAMBLING,T	04	1987	AOS			319	329
0.17	JACOBS,FH	JA	1987	TAR	MARSHALL,RM		67	78
0.17	OHLSON,JA	AU	1987	CAR			1	15
0.17	PENNO ,M	SP	1987	CAR			368	374
0.17	RONEN ,J	AU	1981	JAR	LIVNAT,J		459	481

CITE INDEX	FIRST AUTHOR	ISS-UE	YE-AR	JOUR-NAL	SECOND AUTHOR	THIRD AUTHOR	PAG BEG	PAG END
0.17	VERRECCHIA,RE	ST	1987	JAR	LANEN ,WN		165	189
0.15	ANSARI,SL	01	1980	AOS	MCDONOUGH,JJ		129	142
0.15	BROMWICH,M	AP	1980	TAR			288	300
0.14	DERMER,JD	06	1986	AOS	LUCAS ,RG		471	482
0.14	DUNMORE,PV	AU	1986	CAR			125	148
0.14	EVANS III,JH	06	1986	AOS	LEWIS ,BL	PATTON,JM	483	498
0.14	HARRISON,GL	03	1986	AOS	MCKINNON,JL		233	252
0.14	JAIN ,PC	SP	1986	JAR			187	193
0.14	OHLSON,JA	AU	1979	JAR	PATELL,JM		504	505
0.14	YOUNG ,DW	03	1979	AOS			235	244
0.14	YOUNG ,R	SP	1986	JAR			231	240
0.14	ZALD ,MN	45	1986	AOS			321	326
0.13	AHITUV,N	AU	1985	CAR	HALPERN,J	WILL ,H	95	110
0.13	ANDERSON,JA	AP	1977	TAR			417	426
0.13	BROMWICH,M	JL	1977	TAR			587	596
0.13	DIERKES,M	01	1985	AOS	ANTAL ,AB		29	34
0.13	FLAMHOLTZ,EG	01	1985	AOS	DAS ,TK	TSUI ,AS	35	50
0.13	GAMBLING,T	04	1985	AOS			415	426
0.13	HALPERIN,R	OC	1985	TAR	TZUR ,J		670	680
0.13	HUGHES,JS	OC	1978	TAR			882	894
0.13	MERVILLE,LJ	OC	1978	TAR	PETTY ,JW		935	951
0.13	RAVIV ,A	AP	1985	JAE			239	246
0.13	SWANSON,EB	34	1978	AOS			237	248
0.13	WEYGANDT,JJ	JA	1977	TAR			40	51
0.12	ALIBER,RZ	JA	1975	TAR	STICKNEY,CP		44	57
0.12	ANDERSON,HM	JL	1970	TAR	GIESE ,J	BOOKER,J	524	531
0.12	BAILEY JR,AD	JL	1976	TAR	BOE ,WJ		559	573
0.12	BAREFIELD,RM	JL	1970	TAR			490	501
0.12	BEAVER,WH	AU	1974	JAR	DUKES ,RE		205	215
0.12	BENISHAY,H	SP	1965	JAR			114	132
0.12	BERNHARDT,I	SP	1970	JAR	COPELAND,RM		95	98
0.12	BIERMAN JR,H	JL	1963	TAR			501	507
0.12	BIRD ,FA	AP	1974	TAR	DAVIDSON,LF	SMITH ,CH	233	244
0.12	BRIEF ,RP	SP	1965	JAR			12	31
0.12	BRIEF ,RP	SP	1973	JAR	OWEN ,J		1	15
0.12	BRIEF ,RP	AP	1975	TAR			285	297
0.12	CHAMBERS,RJ	SP	1963	JAR			3	15
0.12	CHAMBERS,RJ	SP	1965	JAR			32	62
0.12	CHAMBERS,RJ	AU	1965	JAR			242	252
0.12	CHAMBERS,RJ	JL	1966	TAR			443	457
0.12	CHAMBERS,RJ	OC	1967	TAR			751	757
0.12	CHURCHILL,NC	OC	1964	TAR			894	904
0.12	DAVIDSON,HJ	AU	1967	JAR	NETER ,J	PETRAN,AS	186	207
0.12	DEMSKI,JS	OC	1969	TAR			669	679
0.12	DEMSKI,JS	AU	1973	JAR			176	190
0.12	DEVINE,CT	AU	1963	JAR			127	138
0.12	DOPUCH,N	JL	1967	TAR	BIRNBERG,JG	DEMSKI,JS	526	536
0.12	EDWARDS,EO	AP	1975	TAR			235	245
0.12	GODFREY,JT	JA	1971	TAR	PRINCE,TR		75	89
0.12	GOETZ ,BE	JA	1967	TAR			53	61
0.12	GONEDES,NJ	AU	1971	JAR			236	252
0.12	GORDON,MJ	JL	1970	TAR			427	443
0.12	GREEN ,D	JA	1966	TAR			52	64

CITE INDEX	FIRST AUTHOR	ISS-UE	YE-AR	JOUR-NAL	SECOND AUTHOR	THIRD AUTHOR	PAG BEG	PAG END
0.12	GREER JR,WR	JA	1970	TAR			103	114
0.12	GYNTHER,RS	OC	1970	TAR			712	730
0.12	HANSON,EI	AP	1966	TAR			239	243
0.12	HINOMOTO,H	AU	1971	JAR			253	267
0.12	HORNGREN,CT	AP	1965	TAR			323	333
0.12	IJIRI ,Y	AU	1963	JAR	LEVY ,FK	LYON ,RC	198	212
0.12	IJIRI ,Y	SP	1965	JAR	JAEDICKE,RK	LIVINGSTONE,JL	63	74
0.12	IJIRI ,Y	AP	1976	TAR			227	243
0.12	JEN ,FC	AP	1970	TAR	HUEFNER,RJ		290	298
0.12	JOHNSON,GL	AU	1971	JAR	SIMIK ,SS		278	286
0.12	JOHNSON,GL	SP	1974	JAR	SIMIK ,SS		67	79
0.12	JOHNSON,O	OC	1970	TAR			641	653
0.12	KNUTSON,PH	JA	1970	TAR			55	68
0.12	KORNBLUTH,JS	AP	1974	TAR			284	295
0.12	LARSON,KD	JA	1969	TAR			38	47
0.12	LEMKE ,KW	JA	1966	TAR			32	41
0.12	LEV ,B	SP	1970	JAR			78	94
0.12	LIM ,R	OC	1966	TAR			642	651
0.12	LIVINGSTONE,JL	JL	1968	TAR			503	508
0.12	LORIG ,AN	JL	1964	TAR			563	573
0.12	LUH ,FS	JA	1968	TAR			123	132
0.12	MAUTZ ,RK	AP	1963	TAR			317	325
0.12	MOONITZ,M	SP	1966	JAR			47	61
0.12	MOONITZ,M	JL	1970	TAR			465	475
0.12	PETRI ,E	AP	1974	TAR	MINCH ,RA		330	341
0.12	SALAMON,GL	AU	1973	JAR			296	303
0.12	SAMUELS,JM	AU	1965	JAR			182	191
0.12	SEIDLER,LJ	OC	1967	TAR			775	781
0.12	SMITH ,KA	AP	1972	TAR			260	269
0.12	SNAVELY,HJ	AP	1967	TAR			223	232
0.12	THOMAS,AL	JL	1971	TAR			472	479
0.12	TOMASSINI,LA	23	1976	AOS			239	252
0.12	VATTER,WJ	AU	1966	JAR			133	148
0.12	VICKREY,DW	OC	1970	TAR			731	742
0.12	VICKREY,DW	JA	1976	TAR			31	40
0.12	WAGNER,JW	JL	1965	TAR			599	605
0.12	WELKER,RB	JL	1974	TAR			514	523
0.12	WILLIAMS,TH	JL	1964	TAR	GRIFFIN,CH		671	678
0.12	WOLK ,HI	JL	1972	TAR	HILLMAN,AP		549	555
0.12	YETTON,PY	01	1976	AOS			81	90
0.12	ZANNETOS,ZS	AP	1964	TAR			296	304
0.11	DEJONG,DV	AU	1984	AUD	SMITH ,JH		20	34
0.11	LEE ,CJ	AU	1984	JAR			776	781
0.11	NETER ,J	AU	1984	AUD	KIM ,HS	GRAHAM,LE	75	88
0.11	ROBERTSON,JC	SP	1984	AUD			57	67
0.11	SHERMAN,HD	AU	1984	AUD			35	53
0.11	THAKKAR,RB	AU	1984	CAR	FINLEY,DR	LIAO ,WM	77	86
0.10	MOCK ,TJ	SP	1983	AUD	WILLINGHAM,JJ		91	99
0.10	OVADIA,A	WI	1983	JAA	RONEN ,J		115	129
0.10	SOTTO ,R	01	1983	AOS			57	72
0.10	SUNDER,S	SP	1983	JAR			222	233
0.09	BALACHANDRAN,KR	JA	1982	TAR	STEUER,RE		125	140
0.09	BEAVER,WH	AU	1982	JAR	WOLFSON,MA		528	550

CITE INDEX	FIRST AUTHOR	ISS-UE	YE-AR	JOUR-NAL	SECOND AUTHOR	THIRD AUTHOR	PAG BEG	PAG END
0.09	COHEN ,SI	AP	1982	TAR	LOEB ,M		336	347
0.09	LANDSITTEL,DL	SU	1982	JAA	SERLIN,JE		291	300
0.09	MANES ,RP	JL	1982	TAR	PARK ,SH	JENSEN,RE	594	606
0.09	MATSUMURA,EM	SP	1982	JAR	TSUI ,KW		162	170
0.09	MOCK ,TJ	AU	1982	AUD	WRIGHT,A		33	44
0.09	SALAMON,GL	AP	1982	TAR			292	302
0.09	VIGELAND,RL	AP	1982	TAR			348	357
0.09	WILLIAMS,PF	04	1982	AOS			405	410
0.08	BAKER ,CR	SP	1980	JAA			197	206
0.08	BALACHANDRAN,BV	JA	1981	TAR	RAMAKRISHNAN,RT		85	96
0.08	BALACHANDRAN,KR	JA	1981	TAR	MASCHMEYER,R	LIVINGSTONE,JL	115	124
0.08	CHAMBERS,RJ	01	1980	AOS			167	180
0.08	FLAMHOLTZ,EG	01	1980	AOS			31	42
0.08	FRIED ,D	SU	1981	JAA			295	308
0.08	FRIED ,D	JL	1981	TAR	LIVNAT,J		493	509
0.08	GANGOLLY,JS	AU	1981	JAR			299	312
0.08	HAMLEN,SS	AP	1980	TAR	HAMLEN,WA	TSCHIRHART,JT	269	287
0.08	NEWMAN,DP	ST	1981	JAR			134	156
0.08	PALMON,D	SP	1980	JAA	KWATINETZ,M		207	226
0.08	PERAGALLO,E	JL	1981	TAR			587	595
0.07	AGGARWAL,R	SP	1978	JAA			197	216
0.07	AMEY ,LR	04	1979	AOS			247	258
0.07	HAKANSSON,NH	JL	1978	TAR			717	725
0.07	KOTTAS,JF	JL	1978	TAR	LAU ,HS		698	707
0.07	OHLSON,JA	AU	1979	JAR			506	527
0.07	RAMAN ,KK	AU	1979	JAA			31	41
0.07	SCAPENS,RW	AP	1978	TAR			448	469
0.07	VERRECCHIA,RE	SP	1978	JAR			150	168
0.07	YAMEY ,BS	AP	1979	TAR			323	329
0.06	AIKEN ,ME	JL	1975	TAR	BLACKETT,LA	ISAACS,G	544	562
0.06	ALFRED,AM	AU	1964	JAR			172	182
0.06	AMATO ,HN	OC	1976	TAR	ANDERSON,EE	HARVEY,DW	854	862
0.06	ARNETT,HE	AP	1967	TAR			291	297
0.06	BAILEY JR,AD	JL	1973	TAR			560	574
0.06	BALADOUNI,V	AP	1966	TAR			215	225
0.06	BAXTER,WT	AU	1971	JAR	CARRIER,NH		189	214
0.06	BEDFORD,NM	JL	1968	TAR	IINO ,T		453	458
0.06	BIERMAN JR,H	AP	1966	TAR			271	274
0.06	BIERMAN JR,H	JL	1974	TAR			448	454
0.06	BIRD ,PA	SP	1965	JAR			1	11
0.06	BIRNBERG,JG	OC	1965	TAR			814	820
0.06	BIRNBERG,JG	01	1976	AOS	GANDHI,NM		5	10
0.06	BODNAR,G	OC	1977	TAR	LUSK ,EJ		857	868
0.06	BRADFORD,WD	AP	1974	TAR			296	305
0.06	BRIEF ,RP	OC	1973	TAR	OWEN ,J		690	695
0.06	BRILOFF,AJ	JA	1964	TAR			12	15
0.06	BUCKLEY,JW	AP	1968	TAR	KIRCHER,P	MATHEWS,RL	274	283
0.06	BULLOCK,CL	JA	1974	TAR			98	103
0.06	BURKE ,EJ	OC	1964	TAR			837	849
0.06	BUTTERWORTH,JE	OC	1971	TAR	SIGLOCH,BA		701	716
0.06	CARMICHAEL,DR	OC	1968	TAR	SWIERINGA,RJ		697	705
0.06	CARSBERG,BV	SP	1966	JAR			1	15
0.06	CHARNES,A	SP	1963	JAR	COOPER,WW	IJIRI ,Y	16	43

CITE INDEX	FIRST AUTHOR	ISS-UE	YE-AR	JOUR-NAL	SECOND AUTHOR	THIRD AUTHOR	PAG BEG	PAG END
0.06	CHARNES,A	JA	1967	TAR	COOPER,WW		24	52
0.06	CHARNES,A	JA	1972	TAR	COLANTONI,CS	COOPER,WW	85	108
0.06	CLARKE,RW	OC	1968	TAR			769	776
0.06	COLANTONI,CS	JL	1969	TAR	MANES ,RP	WHINSTON,AB	467	481
0.06	COMISKEY,EE	AP	1966	TAR			235	238
0.06	COOK ,JS	OC	1976	TAR	HOLZMANN,OJ		778	787
0.06	COOPER,WW	OC	1968	TAR	DOPUCH,N	KELLER,TF	640	648
0.06	CORCORAN,AW	JA	1973	TAR	LEININGER,WE		105	114
0.06	COWAN ,TK	OC	1965	TAR			788	794
0.06	CURRY ,DW	JL	1971	TAR			490	503
0.06	DAVIDSON,S	AU	1963	JAR			117	126
0.06	DICKENS,RL	AP	1964	TAR	BLACKBURN,JO		312	329
0.06	DREBIN,AR	JA	1965	TAR			154	162
0.06	ECKEL ,LG	OC	1976	TAR			764	777
0.06	FEKRAT,MA	AP	1972	TAR			351	355
0.06	FELTHAM,GA	JA	1970	TAR			11	26
0.06	FIELD ,JE	JL	1969	TAR			593	599
0.06	FIRMIN,PA	JA	1968	TAR	LINN ,JJ		75	82
0.06	FRANCIS,ME	AP	1973	TAR			245	257
0.06	FRANK ,WG	JL	1967	TAR	MANES ,RP		516	525
0.06	FREMGEN,JM	OC	1968	TAR			649	656
0.06	GAMBLING,TE	23	1976	AOS			167	174
0.06	GONEDES,NJ	SP	1970	JAR			1	20
0.06	GREEN ,D	SP	1964	JAR			35	49
0.06	GREENBALL,MN	AU	1969	JAR			262	289
0.06	GREENE,ED	AP	1963	TAR			355	362
0.06	GROVES,R	JL	1970	TAR	MANES ,RP	SORENSEN,R	481	489
0.06	HARTLEY,RV	AP	1970	TAR			223	234
0.06	HARVEY,DW	OC	1976	TAR			838	845
0.06	HEATH ,LC	JL	1972	TAR			458	468
0.06	HECK ,WR	JL	1963	TAR			577	578
0.06	HEIMANN,SR	JA	1976	TAR	LUSK ,EJ		51	64
0.06	HICKS ,EL	AU	1964	JAR			158	171
0.06	HORNGREN,CT	JA	1971	TAR			1	11
0.06	HUEFNER,RJ	OC	1971	TAR			717	732
0.06	IJIRI ,Y	SP	1970	JAR	KAPLAN,RS		34	46
0.06	ISELIN,ER	AP	1968	TAR			231	238
0.06	JAENICKE,HR	JA	1970	TAR			115	128
0.06	JENSEN,DL	JL	1974	TAR			465	476
0.06	JENSEN,RE	AP	1967	TAR			265	273
0.06	JOHNSON,O	SP	1968	JAR			29	37
0.06	JOHNSON,O	JA	1972	TAR			64	74
0.06	KEISTER JR,OR	AP	1963	TAR			371	376
0.06	KEMP ,PS	OC	1965	TAR			782	787
0.06	KING ,RR	JA	1974	TAR	BARON ,CD		76	87
0.06	KINNEY JR,WR	SP	1969	JAR			44	52
0.06	LANGENDERFER,HQ	OC	1969	TAR	ROBERTSON,JC		777	787
0.06	LARSON,KD	JL	1967	TAR			480	488
0.06	LARSON,KD	OC	1969	TAR	GONEDES,NJ		720	728
0.06	LEMKE ,KW	SP	1970	JAR			47	77
0.06	LIVINGSTONE,JL	JA	1969	TAR			48	64
0.06	LUSK ,EJ	JL	1972	TAR			567	575
0.06	MABERT,VA	JA	1974	TAR	RADCLIFFE,RC		61	75

CITE INDEX	FIRST AUTHOR	ISS-UE	YE-AR	JOUR-NAL	SECOND AUTHOR	THIRD AUTHOR	PAG BEG	PAG END
0.06	MANES ,RP	SP	1966	JAR			87	100
0.06	MATHEWS,RL	JL	1968	TAR			509	516
0.06	MAUTZ ,RK	AP	1966	TAR	MINI ,DL		283	291
0.06	MCDONALD,DL	OC	1967	TAR			662	679
0.06	MCDONOUGH,JJ	OC	1971	TAR			676	685
0.06	MCINTYRE,EV	JA	1977	TAR			162	171
0.06	MEYERS,SL	JA	1973	TAR			44	49
0.06	MOONITZ,M	AU	1966	JAR	RUSS ,A		155	168
0.06	MORRISON,TA	AP	1969	TAR	KACZKA,E		330	343
0.06	MORSE ,WJ	OC	1972	TAR			761	773
0.06	MURPHY,GJ	AP	1976	TAR			277	286
0.06	NURNBERG,H	OC	1968	TAR			719	729
0.06	ONSI ,M	JL	1970	TAR			535	543
0.06	PATON ,WA	AP	1963	TAR			243	251
0.06	PENMAN,SH	AP	1970	TAR			333	346
0.06	RAPPAPORT,A	AP	1965	TAR			373	376
0.06	RAPPAPORT,A	JL	1967	TAR			441	456
0.06	REVSINE,L	JL	1971	TAR			480	489
0.06	RICKS ,RB	JL	1964	TAR			685	688
0.06	ROSENFIELD,P	AP	1966	TAR	STOREY,R		327	330
0.06	SCHRODERHEIM,G	JL	1964	TAR			679	684
0.06	SHWAYDER,KR	AP	1969	TAR			304	316
0.06	SHWAYDER,KR	AP	1971	TAR			306	319
0.06	SNAVELY,HJ	AP	1969	TAR			344	353
0.06	STALLMAN,JC	OC	1972	TAR			774	790
0.06	STAUBUS,GJ	OC	1967	TAR			650	661
0.06	STAUBUS,GJ	JL	1976	TAR			574	589
0.06	STERLING,RR	JA	1967	TAR			62	73
0.06	STERLING,RR	JL	1968	TAR			481	502
0.06	TAUSSIG,RA	JL	1963	TAR			562	567
0.06	THEIL ,H	JA	1969	TAR			27	37
0.06	TRACY ,JA	JA	1965	TAR			163	175
0.06	ULLMANN,AA	01	1976	AOS			71	80
0.06	VATTER,W	OC	1966	TAR			681	698
0.06	VATTER,WJ	JL	1963	TAR			470	477
0.06	WILKINSON,JR	OC	1965	TAR	DONEY ,LD		753	756
0.06	WOJDAK,JF	JL	1969	TAR			562	570
0.06	WOJDAK,JF	JA	1970	TAR			88	97
0.06	WRIGHT,FK	AU	1965	JAR			167	181
0.06	WRIGHT,FK	JA	1970	TAR			129	133
0.00	ABDEL-KHALIK,AR	SP	1966	JAR			37	46
0.00	ABDEL-MAGID,MF	AP	1979	TAR			346	357
0.00	ABRANOVIC,WA	OC	1976	TAR			863	874
0.00	ADAMS ,KD	WI	1984	JAA			151	163
0.00	AGRAWAL,SP	OC	1977	TAR			789	809
0.00	AGRAWAL,SP	WI	1980	JAA	HALLBAUER,RC	PERRITT,GW	163	173
0.00	AHARONI,Y	SP	1967	JAR	OPHIR ,T		1	26
0.00	ALLYN ,RG	JA	1964	TAR			121	127
0.00	ALLYN ,RG	AP	1966	TAR			303	311
0.00	ALVEY ,KL	JA	1963	TAR			124	125
0.00	AMERSHI,AH	JA	1990	TAR	BANKER,RD	DATAR ,SM	113	130
0.00	AMEY ,LR	AU	1984	CAR			64	76
0.00	AMEY ,LR	AU	1988	CAR	GOFFIN,JL		174	198

CITE INDEX	FIRST AUTHOR	ISS-UE	YE-AR	JOUR-NAL	SECOND AUTHOR	THIRD AUTHOR	PAG BEG	PAG END
0.00	AMIHUD,Y	AU	1988	JAA	MENDELSON,H		369	395
0.00	ANDERSON,HM	OC	1963	TAR	GRIFFIN,FB		813	818
0.00	ANDERSON,JA	JL	1975	TAR			509	511
0.00	ANDERSON,JJ	JL	1967	TAR			583	588
0.00	ANDERSON,JM	AU	1964	JAR			236	238
0.00	ANDERSON,U	AU	1988	AUD	YOUNG ,RA		23	42
0.00	ANTLE ,R	SP	1990	JAR	FELLINGHAM,J		1	24
0.00	ARGYRIS,C	06	1990	AOS			503	511
0.00	ARNETT,HE	OC	1963	TAR			733	741
0.00	ARNETT,HE	JL	1969	TAR			482	494
0.00	BABAD ,YM	SP	1989	CAR	BALACHANDRAN,BV		775	792
0.00	BABER ,WR	JA	1985	TAR			1	9
0.00	BABER ,WR	SP	1985	JAR			360	369
0.00	BACHAR,J	AU	1989	JAA			432	459
0.00	BACKER,M	JL	1969	TAR			533	538
0.00	BAGGETT,WD	SP	1983	JAA			227	233
0.00	BAIMAN,S	OC	1991	TAR	SIVARAMAKRISHNAN,K		747	767
0.00	BAINBRIDGE,DR	SU	1984	JAA			334	346
0.00	BAKER ,RE	JA	1964	TAR			52	61
0.00	BAKER ,RE	JA	1966	TAR			98	105
0.00	BALACHANDRAN,BV	OC	1981	TAR	ZOLTNERS,AA		801	812
0.00	BALACHANDRAN,BV	WI	1988	JAA	RAMANAN,R		1	13
0.00	BALACHANDRAN,BV	WI	1991	JAA	PADMARAJ,RA		1	28
0.00	BALACHANDRAN,KR	SP	1987	JAA	SRINIDHI,BN		151	169
0.00	BALACHANDRAN,KR	WI	1992	JAA	MACHMEYER,RA		49	64
0.00	BALAKRISHNAN,R	AU	1990	CAR			105	122
0.00	BALAKRISHNAN,R	SP	1992	CAR			353	373
0.00	BANKER,RD	JL	1988	JAE	DATAR ,SM	KEKRE ,S	171	197
0.00	BANKER,RD	SP	1990	CAR	DATAR ,SM	MAZUR ,MJ	809	824
0.00	BAR-YOSEF,S	AP	1992	TAR	SEN ,PK		320	336
0.00	BARLEV,B	AP	1983	TAR			385	393
0.00	BARLEV,B	SP	1986	CAR	FRIED ,D	LIVNAT,J	288	310
0.00	BARRETT,WB	JA	1968	TAR			105	112
0.00	BASTABLE,CW	SP	1981	JAA	BEAMS ,FA		248	254
0.00	BAUMOL,WJ	WI	1990	JAA			105	117
0.00	BEAMS ,FA	AP	1969	TAR			382	388
0.00	BEAVER,WH	DE	1984	JAE	GRIFFIN,PA	LANDSMAN,WR	219	223
0.00	BEDFORD,NM	JA	1967	TAR			82	85
0.00	BEDFORD,NM	AP	1972	TAR	MCKEOWN,JC		333	338
0.00	BEECHY,TH	AP	1969	TAR			375	381
0.00	BEJA ,A	AU	1977	JAR	AHARONI,Y		169	178
0.00	BELL ,PW	SP	1987	CAR			338	367
0.00	BENISHAY,H	SU	1987	JAA			203	238
0.00	BENISHAY,H	WI	1992	JAA			97	112
0.00	BENNINGER,LJ	JL	1965	TAR			547	557
0.00	BENSTON,GJ	JL	1976	TAR			483	498
0.00	BERANEK,W	OC	1964	TAR			914	916
0.00	BERG ,KB	JL	1963	TAR	MUELLER,FJ		554	561
0.00	BERKOW,WF	AP	1964	TAR			377	386
0.00	BERKOWITCH,E	SP	1992	JAA	VENEZIA,I		241	250
0.00	BIERMAN JR,H	JA	1963	TAR			61	63
0.00	BIERMAN JR,H	AU	1964	JAR			229	235
0.00	BIERMAN JR,H	JL	1965	TAR			541	546

CITE INDEX	FIRST AUTHOR	ISS-UE	YE-AR	JOUR-NAL	SECOND AUTHOR	THIRD AUTHOR	PAG BEG	PAG END
0.00	BIERMAN JR,H	OC	1967	TAR			731	737
0.00	BIERMAN JR,H	AU	1967	JAR	SMIDT ,S		144	153
0.00	BIERMAN JR,H	OC	1968	TAR			657	661
0.00	BIERMAN JR,H	JA	1968	TAR	LIU ,E		62	67
0.00	BIERMAN JR,H	JA	1969	TAR			65	78
0.00	BIERMAN JR,H	AP	1969	TAR	DAVIDSON,S		239	246
0.00	BIERMAN JR,H	OC	1970	TAR			690	697
0.00	BIERMAN JR,H	OC	1971	TAR			693	700
0.00	BIERMAN JR,H	SP	1985	JAA			184	194
0.00	BIERMAN JR,H	WI	1986	JAA			62	70
0.00	BIRNBERG,JG	OC	1964	TAR			963	971
0.00	BIRNBERG,JG	01	1980	AOS			71	80
0.00	BLAKELY,EJ	JA	1963	TAR	KNUTSON,PH		75	86
0.00	BOATSMAN,JR	AU	1984	JAA	DOWELL,CD	KIMBRELL,JI	35	43
0.00	BOER ,G	JA	1966	TAR			92	97
0.00	BOGART,FO	OC	1965	TAR			834	838
0.00	BOTTS ,RR	OC	1963	TAR			789	795
0.00	BOURN ,AM	AU	1966	JAR			213	223
0.00	BOUTELL,WS	AP	1964	TAR			305	311
0.00	BOWEN ,EK	OC	1967	TAR			782	787
0.00	BOWER ,JB	AP	1965	TAR	SCHLOSSER,RE		338	344
0.00	BOWER ,RS	AP	1966	TAR	HERRINGER,F	WILLIAMSON,JP	257	265
0.00	BOWSHER,CA	WI	1986	JAA			7	16
0.00	BOYLE ,PP	SP	1985	CAR			116	144
0.00	BRADBURY,ME	AP	1988	TAR	CALDERWOOD,SC		330	347
0.00	BRAVENEC,LL	02	1977	AOS	EPSTEIN,MJ	CRUMBLEY,DL	131	140
0.00	BRIEF ,RP	AU	1968	JAR	OWEN ,J		193	199
0.00	BRIEF ,RP	AP	1968	TAR	OWEN ,J		367	372
0.00	BRIEF ,RP	SP	1969	JAR	OWEN ,J		12	16
0.00	BRIEF ,RP	SP	1987	CAR	ANTON ,HR		394	407
0.00	BRIEF ,RP	AP	1992	TAR	LAWSON,RA		411	426
0.00	BRILOFF,AJ	JL	1967	TAR			489	496
0.00	BROCKETT,P	JL	1984	TAR	CHARNES,A	COOPER,WW	474	487
0.00	BRUGEMAN,DC	OC	1963	TAR	BRIGHTON,GD		764	770
0.00	BRUGGE,WG	JL	1963	TAR			596	600
0.00	BRUNSSON,N	02	1990	AOS			47	59
0.00	BUBLITZ,B	WI	1984	JAA	KEE ,R		123	137
0.00	BUCKLEY,JW	JL	1967	TAR			572	582
0.00	BUCKMAN,AG	SP	1982	JAR	MILLER,BL		28	41
0.00	BURGHER,PH	JA	1964	TAR			103	120
0.00	BURKE ,WL	OC	1963	TAR			802	812
0.00	BURNS ,JS	JA	1963	TAR	JAEDICKE,RK	SANGSTER,JM	1	13
0.00	BURT ,OR	SP	1972	JAR			28	57
0.00	BYRNE ,R	JA	1968	TAR	CHARNES,A	COOPER,WW	18	37
0.00	CALL ,DV	OC	1969	TAR			711	719
0.00	CALLEN,JL	SP	1988	JAA			87	108
0.00	CAMPFIELD,WL	JL	1963	TAR			521	527
0.00	CAMPFIELD,WL	JL	1965	TAR			594	598
0.00	CAMPFIELD,WL	OC	1970	TAR			683	689
0.00	CAREY ,JL	JA	1968	TAR			1	9
0.00	CAREY ,JL	JA	1969	TAR			79	85
0.00	CARLISLE,HM	JA	1966	TAR			115	120
0.00	CARLSON,ML	JL	1981	TAR	LAMB ,JW		554	573

CITE INDEX	FIRST AUTHOR	ISS-UE	YE-AR	JOUR-NAL	SECOND AUTHOR	THIRD AUTHOR	PAG BEG	PAG END
0.00	CARMICHAEL,DR	SU	1979	JAA			294	306
0.00	CARMICHAEL,DR	SU	1984	JAA	WHITTINGTON,OR		347	361
0.00	CARSBERG,BV	AU	1969	JAR			165	182
0.00	CARSON,AB	AP	1965	TAR			334	337
0.00	CARTER,WK	JA	1981	TAR			108	114
0.00	CASPARI,JA	OC	1976	TAR			739	746
0.00	CAUSEY JR,DY	AP	1973	TAR			258	267
0.00	CERF ,AR	JL	1975	TAR			451	465
0.00	CHAMBERS,RJ	AP	1967	TAR			241	253
0.00	CHAMBERS,RJ	AP	1968	TAR			239	247
0.00	CHAMBERS,RJ	JL	1972	TAR			488	509
0.00	CHAMBERS,RJ	OC	1979	TAR			764	775
0.00	CHAN ,KH	WI	1984	JAA	CHENG ,TT		164	177
0.00	CHAN ,KH	OC	1986	TAR	DODIN ,B		726	734
0.00	CHARNES,A	AP	1964	TAR	DAVIDSON,HJ	KORTANEK,KO	241	250
0.00	CHARNES,A	04	1976	AOS	COLANTONI,CS	COOPER,WW	315	338
0.00	CHASTEEN,LG	OC	1973	TAR			764	767
0.00	CHEUNG,JK	SP	1990	CAR			724	737
0.00	CHEUNG,JK	SP	1990	CAR	HEANEY,J		738	760
0.00	CHIU ,JS	OC	1966	TAR	DECOSTER,DT		673	680
0.00	CHUMACHENKO,NG	OC	1968	TAR			753	762
0.00	CHURCHMAN,CW	JA	1971	TAR			30	35
0.00	CONROY,R	AU	1989	CAR	HUGHES,JS		159	176
0.00	CORBIN,DA	OC	1963	TAR			742	744
0.00	CORBIN,DA	OC	1967	TAR			635	641
0.00	CORCORAN,AW	AU	1965	JAR	KWANG ,CW		206	217
0.00	CORCORAN,AW	AP	1969	TAR			359	374
0.00	COWAN ,TK	JA	1965	TAR			9	20
0.00	COWAN ,TK	JA	1968	TAR			94	100
0.00	COWIE ,JB	JA	1970	TAR	FREMGEN,JM		27	37
0.00	CRAMER JR,JJ	OC	1964	TAR			869	875
0.00	CRAMER JR,JJ	JL	1965	TAR			606	616
0.00	CRAMER JR,JJ	OC	1970	TAR	SCHRADER,WJ		698	703
0.00	CRAMER JR,JJ	WI	1979	JAA	NEYHART,CA		135	150
0.00	CRANDALL,RH	JL	1969	TAR			457	466
0.00	CRUMBLEY,DL	JL	1968	TAR			554	564
0.00	CRUMBLEY,DL	JA	1975	TAR	SAVICH,RS		112	117
0.00	CRUSE ,RB	JA	1965	TAR	SUMMERS,EL		82	88
0.00	CURLEY,AJ	JL	1971	TAR			519	528
0.00	CUSHING,BE	OC	1968	TAR			668	671
0.00	DANOS ,P	SP	1987	AUD	HOLT ,DL	BAILEY JR,AD	134	149
0.00	DARROUGH,MN	AU	1988	CAR			199	221
0.00	DAVIS ,GB	SP	1963	JAR			96	101
0.00	DAVIS ,PM	JA	1966	TAR			121	126
0.00	DEAN ,J	AP	1963	TAR	HARRISS,CL		229	242
0.00	DECOSTER,DT	AP	1966	TAR			297	302
0.00	DEFLIESE,PL	JL	1965	TAR			517	521
0.00	DEINZER,HT	JA	1966	TAR			21	31
0.00	DEITRICK,JW	SU	1979	JAA	ALDERMAN,CW		316	328
0.00	DEMARIS,EJ	JA	1963	TAR			37	45
0.00	DEMING,WE	SP	1979	JAA			197	208
0.00	DEMSKI,JS	AP	1990	TAR	SAPPINGTON,DEM		363	383
0.00	DEMSKI,JS	AP	1990	TAR	SAPPINGTON,DEM		363	383

CITE INDEX	FIRST AUTHOR	ISS-UE	YE-AR	JOUR-NAL	SECOND AUTHOR	THIRD AUTHOR	PAG BEG	PAG END
0.00	DEMSKI,JS	JL	1992	TAR	SAPPINGTON,DEM		628	630
0.00	DERY ,D	03	1982	AOS			217	224
0.00	DESKINS,JW	JA	1965	TAR			76	81
0.00	DEWHIRST,JF	AP	1971	TAR			365	373
0.00	DHAVALE,DG	SP	1991	AUD			159	166
0.00	DILLARD,JF	34	1984	AOS			343	354
0.00	DOPUCH,N	OC	1963	TAR			745	753
0.00	DOPUCH,N	SU	1988	JAA			245	250
0.00	DOPUCH,N	AU	1992	AUD			109	112
0.00	DREBIN,AR	JL	1963	TAR			579	583
0.00	DREBIN,AR	SP	1964	JAR			25	34
0.00	DREBIN,AR	JL	1966	TAR			413	425
0.00	DREBIN,AR	SP	1966	JAR			68	86
0.00	DREBIN,AR	AU	1969	JAR			204	214
0.00	DRINKWATER,D	JL	1965	TAR	EDWARDS,JD		579	582
0.00	DUGAN ,MT	SP	1985	AUD	GENTRY,JA	SHRIVER,KA	11	22
0.00	DUVALL,RM	JL	1965	TAR	BULLOCH,J		569	573
0.00	DYE ,RA	DE	1991	JAE			347	373
0.00	EDEY ,HC	AP	1963	TAR			262	265
0.00	EIGEN ,MM	JL	1965	TAR			536	540
0.00	ELITZUR,RR	SP	1991	CAR			466	484
0.00	ELLIOTT,EL	OC	1968	TAR	LARREA,J	RIVERA,JM	763	768
0.00	ENGSTROM,JH	SP	1984	JAA			197	211
0.00	EVERETT,JO	SP	1984	JAA	PORTER,GA		241	256
0.00	FAGERBERG,P	JL	1972	TAR			454	457
0.00	FALK ,H	SP	1992	CAR			468	499
0.00	FARAG ,SM	AP	1968	TAR			312	320
0.00	FARMAN,WL	JA	1963	TAR	HOU ,C		133	141
0.00	FARMAN,WL	AP	1964	TAR			392	404
0.00	FELLINGHAM,JC	AU	1989	JAR	YOUNG ,RA		179	200
0.00	FELLINGHAM,JC	OC	1990	TAR	YOUNG ,RA		837	856
0.00	FELTHAM,GA	AU	1992	CAR	GIGLER,FB	HUGHES,JS	1	23
0.00	FERRARA,WL	OC	1963	TAR			719	722
0.00	FERRARA,WL	JA	1966	TAR			106	114
0.00	FERTAKIS,JP	JL	1970	TAR			509	512
0.00	FESS ,PE	OC	1963	TAR			723	732
0.00	FESS ,PE	AP	1966	TAR			266	270
0.00	FIRMIN,PA	AP	1963	TAR			270	277
0.00	FISHER,M	SU	1978	JAA			349	360
0.00	FITZGERALD,RD	AU	1979	JAA	KELLEY,EM		5	20
0.00	FLESHER,DL	04	1979	AOS	FLESHER,TK		297	304
0.00	FOGLER,HR	JA	1972	TAR			134	143
0.00	FORD ,A	OC	1969	TAR			818	822
0.00	FORD ,A	AP	1975	TAR			338	344
0.00	FOSTER III,TW	JL	1991	TAR	KOOGLER,PR	VICKREY,D	595	610
0.00	FRANK ,WG	OC	1965	TAR			854	862
0.00	FRANKFURTER,GM	SU	1983	JAA	YOUNG ,AE		314	324
0.00	FREMGEN,JM	JA	1964	TAR			43	51
0.00	FREMGEN,JM	JL	1967	TAR			457	467
0.00	FRIEDMAN,LA	JA	1978	TAR			18	30
0.00	FRIEDMAN,LA	OC	1978	TAR			895	909
0.00	FURLONG,WL	AP	1966	TAR			244	252
0.00	GAMBLE,GO	SP	1981	JAA			220	237

CITE INDEX	FIRST AUTHOR	ISS-UE	YE-AR	JOUR-NAL	SECOND AUTHOR	THIRD AUTHOR	PAG BEG	PAG END
0.00	GAMBLE,GO	SU	1982	JAA			320	326
0.00	GAMBLE,GO	SP	1986	JAA			102	117
0.00	GAMBLING,TE	JA	1970	TAR	NOUR ,A		98	102
0.00	GIBBONS,M	AU	1992	AUD			113	126
0.00	GIBSON,RW	JA	1965	TAR			196	203
0.00	GILLES JR,LH	OC	1963	TAR			776	784
0.00	GIVENS,HR	JL	1966	TAR			458	463
0.00	GLATZER,W	03	1981	AOS			219	234
0.00	GLOVER,F	AP	1969	TAR			300	303
0.00	GODFREY,JT	AP	1971	TAR			286	297
0.00	GOETZ ,BE	JL	1967	TAR			435	440
0.00	GOGGANS,TP	JL	1964	TAR			627	630
0.00	GOLDBERG,L	JL	1963	TAR			457	469
0.00	GOLDSCHMIDT,Y	AP	1969	TAR	SMIDT ,S		317	329
0.00	GOLDSCHMIDT,Y	AU	1984	JAA	SHASHUA,L		54	67
0.00	GOLDWASSER,DL	SU	1988	JAA			217	232
0.00	GOMBERG,M	JL	1964	TAR	FARBER,A		615	617
0.00	GONEDES,NJ	AP	1971	TAR			320	328
0.00	GORDON,LA	JL	1988	AUD	HAMER ,MH		514	521
0.00	GORMLEY,RJ	SU	1980	JAA			293	312
0.00	GORMLEY,RJ	AU	1982	JAA			51	59
0.00	GOVINDARAJ,S	AU	1992	JAA			485	508
0.00	GRAESE,CE	AP	1964	TAR			387	391
0.00	GRAY ,J	AP	1963	TAR	WILLINGHAM,JJ	JOHNSTON,K	336	346
0.00	GREENWALD,B	SU	1989	JAA	STIGLITZ,JE		281	297
0.00	GREER ,HC	JA	1964	TAR			22	31
0.00	GREER JR,WR	AU	1978	JAA	MORRISSEY,LE		49	57
0.00	GROSS ,H	OC	1966	TAR			745	753
0.00	GRUNDFEST,JA	AU	1991	JAA	SHOVEN,JB		409	442
0.00	GUTBERLET,LG	SU	1980	JAA			313	338
0.00	GUTBERLET,LG	AU	1983	JAA			16	28
0.00	GYNTHER,RS	AP	1969	TAR			247	255
0.00	HAFNER,GF	OC	1964	TAR			979	982
0.00	HAKANSSON,NH	JL	1969	TAR			495	514
0.00	HAKANSSON,NH	SP	1969	JAR			11	31
0.00	HAKANSSON,NH	WI	1990	JAA			33	53
0.00	HALPERIN,R	OC	1987	TAR	SRINIDHI,BN		686	706
0.00	HALPERIN,R	SU	1989	JAA	MAINDIRATTA,A		345	366
0.00	HALPERIN,RM	JA	1991	TAR	SRINIDHI,B		141	157
0.00	HANNUM,WH	AP	1968	TAR	WASSERMAN,W		295	302
0.00	HANSEN,DR	JA	1977	TAR	SHAFTEL,TL		109	123
0.00	HARTLEY,RV	AP	1968	TAR			321	332
0.00	HASEMAN,WC	OC	1968	TAR			738	752
0.00	HASSELBACK,JR	AP	1976	TAR			269	276
0.00	HATFIELD,HR	AU	1966	JAR			169	182
0.00	HAWKINS,CA	SP	1984	JAA	GIRARD,D		225	240
0.00	HEARD ,JE	03	1981	AOS	BOLCE ,WJ		247	254
0.00	HEEBINK,DV	JA	1964	TAR			90	93
0.00	HEIN ,LW	JL	1963	TAR			508	520
0.00	HEIN ,LW	AP	1963	TAR			252	261
0.00	HELMKAMP,JG	JL	1969	TAR			605	610
0.00	HENDRICKSON,HS	AP	1968	TAR			363	366
0.00	HENDRIKSEN,ES	JL	1963	TAR			483	491

CITE INDEX	FIRST AUTHOR	ISS-UE	YE-AR	JOUR-NAL	SECOND AUTHOR	THIRD AUTHOR	PAG BEG	PAG END
0.00	HENNESSY,VC	SU	1978	JAA			317	330
0.00	HERBERT,L	JL	1971	TAR			433	440
0.00	HICKS ,SA	JL	1978	TAR			708	716
0.00	HILL ,HP	WI	1982	JAA			99	109
0.00	HILTON,RW	AU	1986	CAR			50	67
0.00	HIRSCH,AJ	OC	1964	TAR			972	978
0.00	HIRSCHMAN,RW	JA	1965	TAR			176	183
0.00	HOBBS ,JB	OC	1964	TAR			905	913
0.00	HOLDER,WW	WI	1982	JAA	EUDY ,KH		110	125
0.00	HOLZER,HP	AP	1963	TAR	SCHONFELD,HM		377	381
0.00	HOLZER,HP	AP	1963	TAR	SCHONFELD,HM		382	388
0.00	HOLZER,HP	AP	1964	TAR	SCHONFELD,HM		405	413
0.00	HOLZMANN,OJ	WI	1984	JAA	MEANS ,KM		138	150
0.00	HORNE ,JC	JA	1963	TAR			56	60
0.00	HORNGREN,CT	AP	1964	TAR	SORTER,GH		417	420
0.00	HORNGREN,CT	AP	1967	TAR			254	264
0.00	HORNGREN,CT	JA	1969	TAR			86	89
0.00	HORWITZ,BN	OC	1963	TAR			819	826
0.00	HORWITZ,BN	AU	1980	JAA	KOLODNY,R		20	35
0.00	HORWITZ,RM	JL	1964	TAR			618	621
0.00	HUDSON,RR	OC	1963	TAR			796	801
0.00	HUSS ,HF	AU	1985	JAA			60	66
0.00	HYLTON,DP	JL	1964	TAR			667	670
0.00	HYLTON,DP	OC	1965	TAR			824	828
0.00	IJIRI ,Y	JA	1965	TAR			36	53
0.00	IJIRI ,Y	OC	1968	TAR			662	667
0.00	IJIRI ,Y	AP	1970	TAR	THOMPSON,GL		246	258
0.00	IJIRI ,Y	JL	1972	TAR			510	526
0.00	IJIRI ,Y	01	1980	AOS	KELLY ,EC		115	123
0.00	IJIRI ,Y	OC	1986	TAR			745	760
0.00	IMDIEKE,LF	OC	1969	TAR	WEYGANDT,JJ		798	805
0.00	IMKE ,FJ	AP	1966	TAR			318	322
0.00	INGBERMAN,M	AU	1978	JAA	SORTER,GH		58	62
0.00	INGBERMAN,M	WI	1980	JAA			101	112
0.00	INGRAM,RW	AP	1989	TAR	RAMAN ,KK	WILSON,ER	250	268
0.00	IVES ,M	SU	1985	JAA			253	268
0.00	JACOBSEN,LE	AP	1963	TAR			285	292
0.00	JACOBSEN,LE	AU	1964	JAR			221	228
0.00	JAMES ,C	SP	1989	JAA			111	124
0.00	JARRETT,JE	SP	1972	JAR			108	112
0.00	JARRETT,JE	SP	1974	JAR			63	66
0.00	JENKINS,DO	JL	1964	TAR			648	653
0.00	JENSEN,MC	AP	1985	JAE	ZIMMERMAN,JL		3	10
0.00	JENSEN,RE	JA	1968	TAR	THOMSEN,CT		83	93
0.00	JENSEN,RE	JL	1968	TAR			425	446
0.00	JENSEN,RE	JL	1970	TAR			502	508
0.00	JENTZ ,GA	JL	1966	TAR			535	541
0.00	JERSTON,JE	OC	1965	TAR			812	813
0.00	JEYNES,PH	JA	1965	TAR			105	118
0.00	JOHN ,K	WI	1990	JAA	RONEN ,J		61	95
0.00	JOHNSON,GL	OC	1965	TAR			821	823
0.00	JOHNSON,GL	JL	1966	TAR			510	517
0.00	JOHNSON,GL	OC	1967	TAR	NEWTON,SW		738	746

CITE INDEX	FIRST AUTHOR	ISS-UE	YE-AR	JOUR-NAL	SECOND AUTHOR	THIRD AUTHOR	PAG BEG	PAG END
0.00	JOHNSON,O	SP	1965	JAR			75	85
0.00	JOHNSON,O	JL	1968	TAR			546	548
0.00	JOHNSON,O	OC	1974	TAR	GUNN ,S		649	663
0.00	JOHNSON,O	ST	1981	JAR			89	119
0.00	JOHNSON,SB	SP	1982	JAA	MESSIER JR,WF		195	213
0.00	JOHNSTON,DJ	SP	1980	JAA	LEMON ,WM	NEUMANN,FL	251	263
0.00	JOLIVET,V	JL	1964	TAR			689	692
0.00	JUNG ,WO	AU	1989	CAR			1	25
0.00	KABBES,SM	AP	1965	TAR			395	400
0.00	KAHN ,N	AU	1985	JAA	SCHIFF,A		40	49
0.00	KALINSKI,BD	JL	1963	TAR			591	595
0.00	KAPLAN,HG	JA	1964	TAR	SOLOMON,KI		145	149
0.00	KARLINSKY,SS	WI	1983	JAA			157	167
0.00	KARLINSKY,SS	AU	1983	JAA			65	76
0.00	KATZ ,BG	SU	1987	JAA	OWEN ,J		266	298
0.00	KAUFMAN,F	OC	1967	TAR			713	720
0.00	KAY ,RS	SU	1979	JAA			307	315
0.00	KEISTER JR,OR	AP	1964	TAR			414	416
0.00	KELL ,WG	AP	1968	TAR			266	273
0.00	KELLER,TF	JA	1965	TAR			184	189
0.00	KEMP ,PS	JA	1963	TAR			126	132
0.00	KETZ ,JE	AU	1983	JAA	WYATT ,AR		29	43
0.00	KHOURY,SJ	SU	1990	JAA			459	473
0.00	KHURANA,I	JL	1991	TAR			611	621
0.00	KING ,TE	SP	1979	JAA			209	223
0.00	KING ,TE	JL	1988	AUD	ORTEGREN,AK		522	535
0.00	KIRCHER,P	OC	1965	TAR			742	752
0.00	KIRCHER,P	JL	1967	TAR			537	543
0.00	KISSINGER,JN	SP	1986	JAA			90	101
0.00	KISTNER,KP	SP	1980	JAR	SALMI ,T		297	311
0.00	KOHLER,EL	AP	1963	TAR			266	269
0.00	KOLLARITSCH,FP	AP	1965	TAR			382	385
0.00	KORKIE,B	AU	1990	JAA	LAISS ,B		593	617
0.00	KRIPKE,H	AU	1978	JAA			4	32
0.00	KUNITAKE,WK	SU	1986	JAA	WHITE JR,CE		222	231
0.00	LAIBSTAIN,S	AP	1971	TAR			342	351
0.00	LAMBERT,RA	JL	1989	TAR	LARCHER,DF		449	467
0.00	LAMDEN,CW	JA	1964	TAR			128	132
0.00	LANGHOLM,O	AU	1965	JAR			218	227
0.00	LANZILLOTTI,RF	WI	1990	JAA	ESQUIBEL,AK		125	142
0.00	LARGAY III,JA	JA	1973	TAR			115	119
0.00	LARGAY III,JA	AU	1983	JAA			44	53
0.00	LARSON,KD	OC	1966	TAR	SCHATTKE,RW		634	641
0.00	LAU ,AH	SP	1978	JAR	LAU ,HS		80	102
0.00	LAU ,AHL	AU	1987	CAR	LAU ,HS		194	209
0.00	LAUVER,RC	JA	1966	TAR			65	74
0.00	LAVALLE,IH	AP	1968	TAR	RAPPAPORT,A		225	230
0.00	LEA ,RB	AP	1972	TAR			346	350
0.00	LEA ,RB	SU	1981	AUD			53	94
0.00	LEE ,GA	SP	1973	JAR			47	61
0.00	LEE ,GA	JL	1981	TAR			539	553
0.00	LEE ,LC	AP	1969	TAR	BEDFORD,NM		256	275
0.00	LEE ,SS	JL	1965	TAR			622	625

CITE INDEX	FIRST AUTHOR	ISS-UE	YE-AR	JOUR-NAL	SECOND AUTHOR	THIRD AUTHOR	PAG BEG	PAG END
0.00	LEMBKE,VC	JL	1970	TAR			458	464
0.00	LEMBKE,VC	WI	1981	JAA	TOOLE ,HR		128	135
0.00	LENTILHON,RW	OC	1964	TAR			880	883
0.00	LERE ,JC	AP	1986	TAR			318	324
0.00	LESSARD,DR	JL	1977	TAR	LORANGE,P		628	637
0.00	LEV ,B	OC	1969	TAR			704	710
0.00	LEV ,B	JL	1970	TAR			532	534
0.00	LEV ,B	AU	1978	JAR	THEIL ,H		286	293
0.00	LI ,DH	OC	1963	TAR			771	775
0.00	LI ,DH	JA	1963	TAR			52	55
0.00	LI ,DH	SP	1963	JAR			102	107
0.00	LI ,DH	OC	1964	TAR			946	950
0.00	LIM ,SS	OC	1991	TAR	SUNDER,S		669	693
0.00	LINOWES,DF	JA	1965	TAR			97	104
0.00	LITTLETON,AC	JL	1970	TAR			476	480
0.00	LITZENBERGER,RH	SU	1989	JAA	TALMOR,E		305	316
0.00	LIVOCK,DM	SP	1965	JAR			86	102
0.00	LONGSTRETH,B	WI	1984	JAA			110	122
0.00	LORIG ,AN	OC	1963	TAR			759	763
0.00	LOUDERBACK,JG	AP	1971	TAR			298	305
0.00	LOWE ,HD	AP	1963	TAR			293	301
0.00	LOWE ,HD	AP	1967	TAR			356	360
0.00	LUDMAN,EA	SP	1986	JAA			118	124
0.00	LUNDHOLM,RJ	AU	1991	JAR			322	349
0.00	LUNESKI,C	JL	1964	TAR			591	597
0.00	LUNESKI,C	OC	1967	TAR			767	771
0.00	LYNN ,ES	AP	1964	TAR			371	376
0.00	MACKENZIE,O	AP	1964	TAR			363	370
0.00	MACNAUGHTON,A	AU	1992	CAR			113	137
0.00	MAHER ,MW	SP	1983	JAR	NANTELL,TJ		329	340
0.00	MAITRE,P	34	1978	AOS			227	236
0.00	MAKSY ,MM	OC	1988	TAR			683	699
0.00	MANES ,RP	JA	1965	TAR	SMITH ,VL		31	35
0.00	MARKOWITZ,HM	SP	1990	JAA			213	225
0.00	MARPLE,RM	JL	1963	TAR			478	482
0.00	MATEER,WH	JL	1965	TAR			583	586
0.00	MATSUMURA,EM	OC	1992	TAR	TUCKER,RR		753	782
0.00	MATTINGLY,LA	OC	1964	TAR			996	3
0.00	MAURIELLO,JA	JA	1963	TAR			26	28
0.00	MAURIELLO,JA	AP	1964	TAR			347	357
0.00	MAUTZ ,RK	AP	1965	TAR			299	311
0.00	MAUTZ ,RK	JL	1969	TAR	SKOUSEN,KF		447	456
0.00	MAUTZ ,RK	AP	1977	TAR	PREVITS,GJ		301	307
0.00	MAXIM ,LD	JA	1976	TAR	CULLEN,PE	COOK ,FX	97	109
0.00	MAY ,PT	JL	1969	TAR			583	592
0.00	MCBRIDE,HJ	AP	1963	TAR			363	370
0.00	MCCLENON,PR	JL	1963	TAR			540	547
0.00	MCDONALD,DL	12	1979	AOS	PUXTY ,AG		53	66
0.00	MCINTYRE,EV	JL	1982	TAR			607	618
0.00	MCKEOWN,JC	JL	1972	TAR			527	532
0.00	MCRAE ,TW	AU	1965	JAR			255	260
0.00	MEANS ,KM	AU	1989	JAA			571	579
0.00	MELBERG,WF	JA	1972	TAR			116	133

CITE INDEX	FIRST AUTHOR	ISS-UE	YE-AR	JOUR-NAL	SECOND AUTHOR	THIRD AUTHOR	PAG BEG	PAG END
0.00	MELUMAD,N	AU	1990	CAR	THOMAN,L		22	55
0.00	MELUMAD,N	DE	1992	JAE	MOOKHERJEE,D	REICHELSTEIN,S	445	483
0.00	MENSAH,YM	AU	1988	CAR			222	249
0.00	MEPHAM,MJ	JA	1983	TAR			43	57
0.00	MERINO,BD	OC	1987	TAR	KOCH ,BS	MACRITCHIE,KL	748	762
0.00	METCALF,RW	JA	1964	TAR			16	21
0.00	MILLER,EM	AU	1980	JAA			6	19
0.00	MILLER,HE	JA	1966	TAR			1	7
0.00	MILLER,MC	AP	1973	TAR			280	291
0.00	MITCHELL,GB	AP	1970	TAR			308	314
0.00	MOBLEY,SC	AP	1966	TAR			292	296
0.00	MOBLEY,SC	JA	1967	TAR			114	123
0.00	MOBLEY,SC	AP	1968	TAR			333	341
0.00	MOCK ,TJ	AU	1978	JAR	VASARHELYI,MA		414	423
0.00	MONSON,NP	OC	1964	TAR	TRACY ,JA		890	893
0.00	MOORE ,CL	JA	1964	TAR			94	102
0.00	MOORE ,G		1990	AUD	RONEN ,J		234	242
0.00	MORENO,RG	OC	1964	TAR			990	995
0.00	MOREY ,L	JA	1963	TAR			102	108
0.00	MORRISON,TA	OC	1966	TAR			704	713
0.00	MORRISON,TA	JL	1968	TAR	BUZBY ,SL		517	521
0.00	MOST ,KS	JA	1969	TAR			145	152
0.00	MUELLER,GG	JA	1963	TAR			142	147
0.00	MUELLER,GG	AU	1964	JAR			148	157
0.00	MUELLER,GG	AP	1965	TAR			386	394
0.00	MURRAY,D	AU	1983	JAA	JOHNSON,R		4	15
0.00	NAKANO,I	OC	1972	TAR			693	708
0.00	NELSON,GK	JA	1966	TAR			42	47
0.00	NEUBIG,RD	JA	1964	TAR			86	89
0.00	NICHOLS,AC	OC	1968	TAR	GRAWOIG,DE		631	639
0.00	NOBES ,CW	AP	1982	TAR			303	310
0.00	NORDHAUSER,SL	JA	1981	TAR	KRAMER,JL		54	69
0.00	NURNBERG,H	AU	1970	JAR			217	231
0.00	NURNBERG,H	OC	1972	TAR			655	665
0.00	NURNBERG,H	AU	1985	JAA	CIANCIOLO,ST		50	59
0.00	O'BRIEN,JR	AU	1990	CAR			1	21
0.00	O'CONNOR,MC	AP	1972	TAR	HAMRE ,JC		308	319
0.00	OGAN ,P	SU	1991	JAA	ZIEBART,DA		387	406
0.00	OHLSON,JA	AU	1992	JAR	SHROLL,PK		210	226
0.00	OLIPHANT,WJ	ST	1971	JAR			93	98
0.00	ONSI ,M	AP	1967	TAR			321	330
0.00	PAINE ,NR	AP	1964	TAR			330	332
0.00	PARKE ,R	03	1981	AOS	PETERSON,JL		235	246
0.00	PARKER,WM	OC	1963	TAR			785	788
0.00	PARKER,WM	AU	1966	JAR			149	154
0.00	PATON ,WA	SP	1963	JAR			44	72
0.00	PATON ,WA	JA	1967	TAR			7	23
0.00	PATON ,WA	SP	1968	JAR			72	85
0.00	PATON ,WA	AP	1969	TAR			276	283
0.00	PATRICK,AW	JA	1963	TAR	QUITTMEYER,CL		109	117
0.00	PATTERSON,RG	OC	1967	TAR			772	774
0.00	PEASNELL,KV	JA	1977	TAR			186	189
0.00	PEIRSON,G	OC	1966	TAR			729	736

CITE INDEX	FIRST AUTHOR	ISS-UE	YE-AR	JOUR-NAL	SECOND AUTHOR	THIRD AUTHOR	PAG BEG	PAG END
0.00	PELES ,YC	AP	1986	TAR			325	329
0.00	PENNO ,M	JL	1990	TAR			520	536
0.00	PENNO ,M	ST	1991	JAR	WATTS ,JS		194	216
0.00	PERAGALLO,E	JA	1983	TAR			98	104
0.00	PESANDO,JE	OC	1983	TAR	CLARKE,CK		733	748
0.00	PETERSON,WA	AP	1966	TAR			275	282
0.00	PETRI ,E	JL	1973	TAR			483	488
0.00	PETRI ,E	JL	1974	TAR	MINCH ,RA		455	464
0.00	PETRI ,E	AP	1978	TAR	MINCH ,RA		415	428
0.00	PETRI ,E	AP	1979	TAR	GELFAND,J		330	345
0.00	PHILIPS,GE	OC	1963	TAR			696	708
0.00	PHILIPS,GE	JA	1963	TAR			14	25
0.00	PHILIPS,GE	JA	1968	TAR			10	17
0.00	PHILLIPS,LC	AP	1965	TAR			377	381
0.00	POMERANZ,F	AU	1977	JAA			45	52
0.00	PRATER,GI	OC	1966	TAR			619	625
0.00	PRESTON,LE	03	1981	AOS			255	262
0.00	PRINCE,TR	JL	1964	TAR			553	562
0.00	PURDY ,CR	AU	1965	JAR			228	241
0.00	RABY ,WL	JL	1963	TAR	NEUBIG,RD		568	576
0.00	RABY ,WL	OC	1966	TAR			714	720
0.00	RABY ,WL	JA	1969	TAR			1	11
0.00	RAJAN ,MV	AU	1992	JAR			227	248
0.00	RAMAN ,KK	SU	1981	JAA			352	359
0.00	RAPPAPORT,A	OC	1964	TAR			951	962
0.00	RAPPAPORT,A	AP	1969	TAR			297	299
0.00	RATSCH,H	JA	1964	TAR			140	144
0.00	RAUN ,DL	OC	1963	TAR			754	758
0.00	RAUN ,DL	OC	1964	TAR			927	945
0.00	RAYMAN,RA	SP	1969	JAR			53	89
0.00	REVSINE,L	AP	1969	TAR			354	358
0.00	REYNOLDS,IN	AP	1964	TAR			342	346
0.00	RICHARD,DL	OC	1968	TAR			730	737
0.00	ROBBINS,SM	AU	1977	JAA			5	18
0.00	ROBERTS,DM	AU	1980	JAA			57	69
0.00	ROBERTSON,JC	WI	1981	JAA	ALDERMAN,CW		144	161
0.00	ROBINSON,LA	JA	1964	TAR	HALL ,TP		62	69
0.00	ROBSON,K		1992	AOS			685	708
0.00	RODEN ,PF	WI	1987	JAA			79	89
0.00	ROLLER,J	AP	1967	TAR	WILLIAMS,TH		349	355
0.00	RONEN ,J	AU	1970	JAR			232	252
0.00	RORKE ,CH	03	1982	AOS			305	306
0.00	ROSE ,H	AU	1964	JAR			137	147
0.00	ROSEN ,LS	JA	1967	TAR			106	113
0.00	ROSENFIELD,P	OC	1969	TAR			788	797
0.00	ROSHWALB,A	AP	1991	TAR	WRIGHT,RL		348	360
0.00	ROSS ,H	ST	1970	JAR			108	115
0.00	ROSS ,WR	JL	1966	TAR			464	473
0.00	RUBENSTEIN,DB	05	1992	AOS			501	508
0.00	RUNDFELT,R	SP	1986	JAA			125	130
0.00	SALGADO,AP	AP	1963	TAR			389	397
0.00	SAMUELSON,LA	01	1986	AOS			35	46
0.00	SAMUELSON,RA	AP	1980	TAR			254	268

CITE INDEX	FIRST AUTHOR	ISS-UE	YE-AR	JOUR-NAL	SECOND AUTHOR	THIRD AUTHOR	PAG BEG	PAG END
0.00	SAN MIGUEL,JG	02	1977	AOS			177	186
0.00	SANSING,RC	AU	1992	CAR			33	45
0.00	SAPIENZA,SR	JL	1964	TAR			582	590
0.00	SAPIENZA,SR	SP	1964	JAR			50	66
0.00	SAVOIE,LM	ST	1969	JAR			55	62
0.00	SCHACHNER,L	AP	1968	TAR			303	311
0.00	SCHACHTER,B	AU	1985	JAR			907	910
0.00	SCHATTKE,RW	AP	1972	TAR			233	244
0.00	SCHIENEMAN,GS	AU	1979	JAA			21	30
0.00	SCHIENEMAN,GS	SP	1983	JAA			212	226
0.00	SCHIFF,M	AU	1977	JAA	SORTER,GH	WIESEN,JL	19	44
0.00	SCHNEE,EJ	AU	1981	JAA	TAYLOR,ME		18	29
0.00	SCHNEIDER,AJ	AP	1967	TAR			342	348
0.00	SCHOLES,MS	AU	1991	JAA	WOLFSON,MA		513	532
0.00	SCHULTE JR,AA	OC	1966	TAR			721	728
0.00	SCHWARTZ,BN	SP	1981	JAA			238	247
0.00	SCOTT ,RA	OC	1979	TAR			750	763
0.00	SCOTT ,WR	SP	1988	CAR			354	388
0.00	SEAGLE,JP	JA	1977	TAR	PETRI ,E		124	136
0.00	SEAMAN,JL	JL	1965	TAR			617	621
0.00	SEELYE,AL	AP	1963	TAR			302	309
0.00	SEIDLER,LJ	SU	1979	JAA			285	293
0.00	SEILER,RE	OC	1966	TAR			652	656
0.00	SENNETTI,JT	SP	1990	AUD			103	112
0.00	SHAFER,G		1990	AUD	SRIVASTAVA,R		110	137
0.00	SHEVLIN,T	JA	1991	TAR			1	22
0.00	SHILLINGLAW,G	SP	1963	JAR			73	85
0.00	SHWAYDER,KR	JA	1968	TAR			101	104
0.00	SHWAYDER,KR	SP	1968	JAR			86	97
0.00	SHWAYDER,KR	AP	1970	TAR			299	307
0.00	SHWAYDER,KR	OC	1972	TAR			747	760
0.00	SIMMONS,JK	OC	1967	TAR			680	692
0.00	SIMUNIC,DA	SP	1990	CAR	STEIN ,MT		329	343
0.00	SKERRATT,LC	SU	1984	JAA			362	368
0.00	SMIELIAUSKAS,W	SP	1989	CAR			720	732
0.00	SMIELIAUSKAS,W	SP	1990	CAR	SMITH ,L		407	426
0.00	SMOLINSKI,EJ	AU	1963	JAR			149	178
0.00	SOLOMONS,D	JL	1968	TAR			447	452
0.00	SOMMERFELD,RM	OC	1967	TAR			747	750
0.00	SORTER,GH	ST	1974	JAR	GANS ,MS		1	12
0.00	SORTER,GH	SP	1982	JAA			188	194
0.00	SORTER,GH	SP	1987	JAA	INGBERMAN,M		99	116
0.00	SPACEK,L	AP	1964	TAR			275	284
0.00	SPENCER,MH	AP	1963	TAR			310	316
0.00	SPILLER JR,EA	OC	1964	TAR			850	859
0.00	SPROUSE,RT	OC	1963	TAR			687	695
0.00	SPROUSE,RT	JL	1965	TAR			522	526
0.00	SRIVASTAVA,RP	AU	1986	JAR			422	427
0.00	SRIVASTAVA,RP	AP	1992	TAR	SHAFER,GR		249	283
0.00	ST.PIERRE,K	SP	1984	JAA			257	263
0.00	STAATS,EB	SU	1981	AUD			1	11
0.00	STANDISH,PEM	JL	1964	TAR			654	666
0.00	STANLEY,CH	JL	1964	TAR			639	647

CITE INDEX	FIRST AUTHOR	ISS-UE	YE-AR	JOUR-NAL	SECOND AUTHOR	THIRD AUTHOR	PAG BEG	PAG END
0.00	STAUBUS,GJ	JA	1963	TAR			64	74
0.00	STAUBUS,GJ	JL	1966	TAR			397	412
0.00	STEIN ,JL	SP	1990	JAA	HONG ,BG		277	300
0.00	STERLING,RR	JL	1971	TAR	FLAHERTY,RE		441	456
0.00	STETTLER,HF	OC	1965	TAR			723	730
0.00	STONE ,DE	AP	1967	TAR			331	337
0.00	STONE ,ML	ST	1968	JAR			59	66
0.00	STONE ,WE	JA	1964	TAR			38	42
0.00	STONE ,WE	AU	1972	JAR			345	350
0.00	STREER,PJ	SU	1979	JAA			329	338
0.00	SUMMERS,EL	SP	1970	JAR	DESKINS,JW		113	117
0.00	SUNDER,S	SP	1989	CAR			452	460
0.00	SUSSMAN,MR	AP	1965	TAR			407	413
0.00	SWANSON,GA	JL	1988	TAR	GARDNER,JC		436	447
0.00	TAMURA,H	SP	1985	AUD			133	142
0.00	TAUSSIG,RA	SP	1964	JAR			67	79
0.00	TAYLOR,RG	JA	1965	TAR			89	96
0.00	TAYLOR,WM	AU	1982	JAR	WEYGANDT,JJ		497	502
0.00	TELSER,LG	SP	1990	JAA			159	201
0.00	TEOH ,SH	SP	1992	JAR			1	23
0.00	THEOBALD,M	AU	1985	CAR			1	22
0.00	THOMAS,AL	JL	1964	TAR			574	581
0.00	THOMAS,AL	JA	1964	TAR			1	11
0.00	THOMAS,AL	SP	1965	JAR			103	113
0.00	THOMPSON,WW	JL	1965	TAR	KEMPER,EL		574	578
0.00	TOBA ,Y	OC	1980	TAR			604	619
0.00	TOPIOL,J	JA	1966	TAR			83	91
0.00	TOWNSEND,LA	JA	1967	TAR			1	6
0.00	TRUEBLOOD,RM	SP	1963	JAR			86	95
0.00	TRUEBLOOD,RM	ST	1966	JAR			183	191
0.00	TRUEMAN,B	AU	1990	CAR			203	222
0.00	TRUEMAN,B	OC	1990	JAE			285	301
0.00	TRUMBULL,WP	JA	1963	TAR			46	51
0.00	TRUMBULL,WP	JL	1968	TAR			459	468
0.00	TUCKERMAN,B	JA	1964	TAR			32	37
0.00	ULLMANN,AA	12	1979	AOS			123	134
0.00	VANCE ,LL	JA	1966	TAR			48	51
0.00	VANCE ,LL	OC	1969	TAR			692	703
0.00	VASARHELYI,MA	AU	1984	AUD			100	106
0.00	VERRECCHIA,RE	JL	1982	TAR			579	593
0.00	VICKREY,D	JL	1992	TAR			623	627
0.00	VOGT ,RA	01	1977	AOS			59	80
0.00	WADE ,HH	OC	1963	TAR			714	718
0.00	WAGNER,JW	JL	1969	TAR			600	604
0.00	WAKEMAN,LM	DE	1980	JAE			213	237
0.00	WALKER,M	AP	1984	TAR			278	286
0.00	WALKER,M	06	1989	AOS			433	453
0.00	WALKER,NR	AU	1988	AUD	PIERCE,LT		1	22
0.00	WALLACE,WA	SP	1983	AUD			66	90
0.00	WAND ,Y	JA	1989	TAR	WEBER ,R		87	107
0.00	WANG ,S	JA	1991	TAR			158	169
0.00	WATKINS,PR	SP	1984	JAR			406	411
0.00	WAUGH ,JB	JL	1968	TAR			535	539

CITE INDEX	FIRST AUTHOR	ISS-UE	YE-AR	JOUR-NAL	SECOND AUTHOR	THIRD AUTHOR	PAG BEG	PAG END
0.00	WEBER ,RP	JA	1977	TAR			172	185
0.00	WEIGAND,RE	JL	1963	TAR			584	590
0.00	WEIL ,RL	OC	1973	TAR			749	758
0.00	WEINGARTER,HM	AU	1963	JAR			213	224
0.00	WEISER,HJ	JL	1966	TAR			518	524
0.00	WELKE ,WR	AP	1966	TAR			253	256
0.00	WELLS ,MC	OC	1965	TAR	COTTON,W		829	833
0.00	WELLS ,MC	AP	1968	TAR			373	376
0.00	WELSCH,GA	OC	1964	TAR			8	13
0.00	WELSH ,MJ	WI	1985	JAA	TRAPNELL,JE		100	111
0.00	WERNER,CA	AU	1983	JAA	KOSTOLANSKY,JW		54	64
0.00	WERNER,CA	SP	1984	JAA	KOSTOLANSKY,JW		212	224
0.00	WHEELER,JT	JA	1970	TAR			1	10
0.00	WHITE ,D	SU	1982	JAA	VANECEK,M		338	354
0.00	WHITE ,LJ	SP	1991	JAA			289	302
0.00	WHITTINGTON,OR	SU	1982	JAA	ADAMS ,SJ		310	319
0.00	WIESEN,JL	WI	1979	JAA	ENG ,R		101	121
0.00	WIESEN,JL	SU	1981	JAA			309	324
0.00	WILD ,JJ	JA	1990	TAR	BIGGS ,SF		227	241
0.00	WILKINSON,TL	JA	1964	TAR			133	139
0.00	WILLIAMS,D	AP	1966	TAR			226	234
0.00	WILLIAMS,JJ	02	1981	AOS			153	166
0.00	WILLIAMS,TH	OC	1967	TAR	GRIFFIN,CH		642	649
0.00	WILLIAMSON,JE	JA	1971	TAR			139	148
0.00	WILLINGER,GL	SP	1985	JAR			351	359
0.00	WILLINGHAM,JJ	JL	1964	TAR			543	552
0.00	WINBORNE,MG	OC	1966	TAR	KLEESPIE,DC		737	744
0.00	WINDAL,FW	JA	1963	TAR			29	36
0.00	WINJUM,JO	AU	1971	JAR			333	350
0.00	WOLK ,HI	JL	1970	TAR			544	552
0.00	WOLK ,HI	AP	1973	TAR	TEARNEY,MG		292	299
0.00	WOODS ,RS	JL	1964	TAR			598	614
0.00	WOOLSEY,SM	OC	1963	TAR			709	713
0.00	WRIGHT,DW	SP	1991	AUD			145	158
0.00	WRIGHT,FK	JA	1963	TAR			87	90
0.00	WRIGHT,FK	SP	1964	JAR			80	90
0.00	WRIGHT,FK	AU	1967	JAR			173	179
0.00	WRIGHT,FK	AU	1968	JAR			222	236
0.00	WRIGHT,HW	OC	1966	TAR			626	633
0.00	WYATT ,AR	JL	1965	TAR			527	535
0.00	WYMAN ,HE	JL	1976	TAR			545	558
0.00	YAMEY ,BS	JL	1980	TAR			419	425
0.00	YOON ,SS		1990	AUD			253	275
0.00	YOUNG ,AE	SP	1980	JAA			244	250
0.00	YOUNG ,AE	SU	1992	JAA			361	368
0.00	YOUNG ,SD	SP	1985	JAA			178	183
0.00	YOUNG ,TN	AP	1967	TAR	PEIRSON,CG		338	341
0.00	YU ,SC	JA	1966	TAR			8	20
0.00	YU ,SC	JL	1969	TAR			571	582
0.00	ZANNETOS,ZS	JL	1963	TAR			528	533
0.00	ZANNETOS,ZS	AP	1963	TAR			326	335
0.00	ZANNETOS,ZS	OC	1964	TAR			860	868
0.00	ZANNETOS,ZS	JL	1967	TAR			566	571

CITE INDEX	FIRST AUTHOR	ISS-UE	YE-AR	JOUR-NAL	SECOND AUTHOR	THIRD AUTHOR	PAG BEG	PAG END
0.00	ZEFF ,SA	JA	1965	TAR	MAXWELL,WD		65	75
0.00	ZEFF ,SA	JL	1982	TAR			528	553

2.2 RESEARCH METHOD=ANALYTICAL – SIMULATION

CITE INDEX	FIRST AUTHOR	ISS-UE	YE-AR	JOUR-NAL	SECOND AUTHOR	THIRD AUTHOR	PAG BEG	PAG END
1.44	COLLINS,DW	SP	1984	JAR	DENT ,WT		48	84
1.29	KAPLAN,RS	AU	1973	JAR			238	258
1.10	MESSIER JR,WF	AU	1983	JAR			611	618
0.91	LEITCH,RA	AP	1982	TAR	NETER ,J	PLANTE,R	384	400
0.89	DWORIN,L	AP	1984	TAR	GRIMLUND,RA		218	241
0.89	DYCKMAN,TR	ST	1984	JAR	PHILBRICK,D	STEPHAN,J	1	30
0.78	GODFREY,JT	AU	1984	JAR	NETER ,J		497	525
0.78	MENZEFRICKE,U	AU	1984	JAR	SMIELIAUSKAS,W		588	604
0.73	NETER ,J	JA	1978	TAR	LEITCH,RA	FIENBERG,SE	77	93
0.71	DWORIN,L	JA	1986	TAR	GRIMLUND,RA		36	57
0.71	SCOTT ,WR	ST	1975	JAR			98	117
0.67	MCCRAY,JH	JA	1984	TAR			35	51
0.65	MAGEE ,RP	JL	1976	TAR			529	544
0.60	GRIMLUND,RA	AU	1988	AUD	SCHROEDER,MS		53	62
0.60	MCNICHOLS,M	JL	1988	JAE			239	273
0.57	GARSTKA,SJ	SP	1979	JAR	OHLSON,PA		23	59
0.57	SMIELIAUSKAS,W	AU	1986	CAR			102	124
0.55	FROST ,PA	SP	1982	JAR	TAMURA,H		103	120
0.55	SILHAN,PA	SP	1982	JAR			255	262
0.50	GRIMLUND,RA	JL	1987	TAR	FELIX JR,WL		455	479
0.50	KOTHARI,SP	AP	1989	TAR	WASLEY,CE		228	249
0.50	LAMBERT,RA	SP	1991	JAR	LARCKER,DF	VERRECCHIA,RE	129	149
0.50	STONE ,M	JA	1991	TAR	RASP ,J		170	187
0.50	TSUI ,KW	JA	1985	TAR	MATSUMURA,EM	TSUI ,KL	76	96
0.47	DEMSKI,JS	JL	1972	TAR	FELTHAM,GA		533	548
0.47	RENEAU,JH	JL	1978	TAR			669	680
0.40	KNECHEL,WR	JA	1988	TAR			74	95
0.40	MENZEFRICKE,U	SP	1988	CAR	SMIELIAUSKAS,W		314	336
0.38	CASLER,DJ	SP	1985	JAR	HALL ,TW		110	122
0.38	FELTHAM,GA	SP	1977	JAR			42	70
0.36	KINNEY JR,WR	AU	1979	JAR			456	475
0.35	SIMMONS,JK	OC	1969	TAR	GRAY ,J		757	776
0.33	CHANDRA,R	AU	1990	CAR	ROHRBACH,K		123	141
0.33	LOEBBECKE,JK	SP	1987	AUD	STEINBART,PJ		74	89
0.33	MATSUMURA,EM	SP	1990	CAR	TSUI ,K-W	WONG ,W-K	485	500
0.33	MENZEFRICKE,U	AU	1984	JAR			570	587
0.29	BORITZ,JE	AU	1986	AUD	BROCA ,DS		1	19
0.29	DITTMAN,DA	AP	1979	TAR	PRAKASH,P		358	373
0.25	BIDDLE,GC	SP	1985	JAR	MARTIN,RK		57	83
0.25	KNECHEL,WR	SP	1985	AUD			38	62
0.25	PLANTE,R	AU	1985	AUD	NETER ,J	LEITCH,RA	40	56
0.25	SMIELIAUSKAS,W	AU	1985	JAR			718	739
0.25	WEBER ,RP	JL	1981	TAR	STEVENSON,WC		596	612
0.24	FERRARA,WL	AP	1972	TAR	HAYYA ,JC	NACHMAN,DA	299	307
0.23	COHEN ,MA	AU	1980	JAR	HALPERIN,R		375	389
0.20	DHARAN,BG	SP	1983	JAR			18	41
0.20	GRIMLUND,RA	SP	1988	AUD			77	104
0.20	KNECHEL,WR	AU	1988	AUD			87	107

CITE INDEX	FIRST AUTHOR	ISS-UE	YE-AR	JOUR-NAL	SECOND AUTHOR	THIRD AUTHOR	PAG BEG	PAG END
0.19	GARSTKA,SJ	AU	1977	JAR			179	192
0.18	DEMSKI,JS	JA	1970	TAR			76	87
0.18	KINNEY JR,WR	AU	1982	JAR	SALAMON,GL		350	366
0.17	KIM ,HS	SP	1987	AUD	NETER ,J	GODFREY,JT	40	58
0.17	MENZEFRICKE,U	AU	1987	CAR	SMIELIAUSKAS,W		240	250
0.17	WIGGINS JR,CE	SP	1987	CAR	SMITH ,LW		316	337
0.15	BECK ,PJ	SP	1980	JAR			16	37
0.14	ANDERSON,JC	JL	1986	TAR	KRAUSHAAR,JM		379	399
0.14	HUSS ,HF	AU	1986	JAR	TRADER,RL		394	399
0.14	SMIELIAUSKAS,W	SP	1986	JAR			217	230
0.14	TAMURA,H	AU	1986	JAR	FROST ,PA		364	371
0.13	KNECHEL,WR	SP	1985	JAR			194	212
0.13	LIN ,WT	JA	1978	TAR			61	76
0.13	MAGEE ,RP	OC	1977	TAR			869	880
0.12	DEMSKI,JS	AP	1971	TAR			268	278
0.12	GREENBALL,MN	SP	1968	JAR			114	129
0.12	LIVINGSTONE,JL	AU	1970	JAR	SALAMON,GL		199	216
0.12	REVSINE,L	AP	1976	TAR	THIES ,JB		255	268
0.12	WYMAN ,HE	JL	1973	TAR			489	493
0.10	TAUSSIG,RA	WI	1983	JAA			142	156
0.09	EMERY ,DR	AU	1982	JAR	BARRON,FH	MESSIER JR,WF	450	458
0.06	ABEL ,R	SP	1969	JAR			1	11
0.06	DAVIDSON,S	AU	1966	JAR	KOHLMEIER,JM		183	212
0.06	FRANKFURTER,GM	AP	1972	TAR	HORWITZ,BN		245	259
0.06	GYNTHER,MM	OC	1968	TAR			706	718
0.06	LIVINGSTONE,JL	AU	1969	JAR			245	256
0.06	MAGEE ,RP	JA	1977	TAR			190	199
0.06	SCHWAB,B	AP	1969	TAR	NICOL ,RE		292	296
0.06	SHWAYDER,KR	AU	1973	JAR			259	272
0.06	WELLING,P	04	1977	AOS			307	316
0.00	ADESI ,GB	SU	1992	JAA	TALWAR,PP		369	378
0.00	BAILEY JR,AD	SP	1968	JAR	GRAY ,J		98	105
0.00	BARKMAN,A	JA	1977	TAR			450	464
0.00	BIDDLE,GC	AU	1990	AUD	BRUTON,CM	SIEGEL,AF	92	114
0.00	BONETT,DG	SP	1990	CAR	CLUTE ,RD		432	445
0.00	BRIGHAM,EF	JA	1968	TAR			46	61
0.00	BRIGHAM,EF	JL	1974	TAR	NANTELL,TJ		436	447
0.00	BRUNDAGE,MV	JL	1969	TAR	LIVINGSTONE,JL		539	545
0.00	CHAN ,H	AU	1990	AUD	SMIELIAUSKAS,W		167	182
0.00	CHANDRA,R	AU	1992	CAR	ROHRBACH,KJ	WILLINGER,GL	296	305
0.00	COGLITORE,F	SP	1988	AUD	BERRYMAN,RG		150	163
0.00	COMISKEY,EE	AP	1968	TAR	MLYNARCZYK,FA		248	256
0.00	CREADY,WM	JN	1991	JAE	RAMANAN,R		203	214
0.00	DEMSKI,JS	SP	1969	JAR			96	115
0.00	DHARAN,BG	SP	1987	CAR			445	459
0.00	DWORIN,L	SP	1989	CAR	GRIMLUND,RA		674	691
0.00	FEINSCHREIBER,R	SP	1969	JAR			17	21
0.00	FELIX JR,WL	AU	1990	AUD	GRIMLUND,RA	KOSTER,FJ	1	16
0.00	FERRARA,WL	JL	1977	TAR			597	604
0.00	FINLEY,DR	SP	1987	AUD	BOOCKHOLDT,JL		22	39
0.00	FINLEY,DR	SP	1989	CAR			692	719
0.00	FIRMIN,PA	ST	1968	JAR	GOODMAN,SS	HENDRICKS,TE	122	155
0.00	FRANCIS,J	OC	1990	TAR			891	911

CITE INDEX	FIRST AUTHOR	ISS-UE	YE-AR	JOUR-NAL	SECOND AUTHOR	THIRD AUTHOR	PAG BEG	PAG END
0.00	FREDRIKSON,EB	AU	1968	JAR			208	221
0.00	FROST ,PA	SP	1986	JAR	TAMURA,H		57	75
0.00	GERLACH,JH	SP	1988	AUD			61	76
0.00	GREENBALL,MN	ST	1968	JAR			27	49
0.00	GRIMLUND,RA	AU	1985	JAR			575	594
0.00	GRIMLUND,RA	SP	1990	CAR			446	484
0.00	HALL ,TW	SP	1989	AUD	PIERCE,BJ	ROSS ,WR	64	89
0.00	JENSEN,HL	OC	1976	TAR	WYNDELTS,RW		846	853
0.00	JORGENSON,DW	AU	1991	JAA	YUN ,K		487	508
0.00	KENNEDY,DB	SP	1992	CAR			419	442
0.00	KINNEY JR,WR		1989	AUD			67	84
0.00	KO ,CE	SP	1988	AUD	NACHTSHEIM,CJ	DUKE ,GL	119	136
0.00	LILLESTOL,J	SP	1981	JAR			263	267
0.00	MCCOSH,AM	OC	1967	TAR			693	700
0.00	MEHTA ,DR	SP	1968	JAR	ANDREWS,VL		50	57
0.00	MOORE ,G	SP	1987	CAR			375	383
0.00	NIKOLAI,LA	JA	1979	TAR	ELAM ,R		119	131
0.00	NURNBERG,H	AU	1969	JAR			257	261
0.00	PEEK ,LE	AU	1991	AUD	NETER ,J	WARREN,C	33	48
0.00	PELES ,YC	SU	1991	JAA			349	359
0.00	PINCUS,KV	SP	1990	AUD			1	20
0.00	POWERS,M	AP	1989	TAR	REVSINE,L		346	368
0.00	RAMANATHAN,KV	OC	1971	TAR	RAPPAPORT,A		733	745
0.00	RICHARDSON,AW	SP	1988	CAR			609	614
0.00	ROBERTS,DM	SP	1986	JAR			111	126
0.00	ROHRBACH.KJ	SP	1986	JAR			127	150
0.00	ROSHWALB,A	AU	1987	AUD	WRIGHT,RL	GODFREY,JT	54	70
0.00	SMIELIAUSKAS,W		1990	AUD			149	166
0.00	SWENSON,CW	JA	1987	TAR			117	136
0.00	TRADER,RL	AU	1987	CAR	HUSS ,HF		227	239
0.00	VASARHELYI,MA	SP	1984	AUD	BAILEY JR,AD	CAMARDESSE JR,JE	98	103
0.00	WHEELER,S	JL	1990	TAR	PANY ,K		557	577
0.00	WILSON,AC	SP	1992	AUD			32	46
0.00	WURST ,J	AP	1991	TAR	NETER ,J	GODFREY,J	333	347

2.3 RESEARCH METHOD=ARCHIVAL – PRIMARY

CITE INDEX	FIRST AUTHOR	ISS-UE	YE-AR	JOUR-NAL	SECOND AUTHOR	THIRD AUTHOR	PAG BEG	PAG END
8.35	BALL ,R	AU	1968	JAR	BROWN ,P		159	178
8.20	WATTS ,RL	JA	1978	TAR	ZIMMERMAN,JL		112	134
6.00	HEALY ,PM	AP	1985	JAE			85	108
5.50	COLLINS,DW	JL	1989	JAE	KOTHARI,SP		143	181
5.50	EASTON,PD	JL	1989	JAE	ZMIJEWSKI,ME		117	141
5.35	BEAVER,WH	ST	1968	JAR			67	92
5.18	PATELL,JM	AU	1976	JAR			246	276
5.17	BROWN ,LD	JL	1987	JAE	GRIFFIN,PA	HAGERMAN,RL	159	193
5.00	OU ,JA	NV	1989	JAE			295	329
5.00	PENMAN,SH	NV	1989	JAE			295	329
4.93	BEAVER,WH	AU	1979	JAR	CLARKE,R	WRIGHT,WF	316	340
4.88	ATIASE,RK	SP	1985	JAR			21	36
4.80	O'BRIEN,PC	JA	1988	JAE			53	83
4.50	BERNARD,VL	SP	1987	JAR			1	48
4.50	BROWN ,LD	AP	1987	JAE	GRIFFIN,PA	HAGERMAN,RL	61	87
4.50	FREEMAN,RN	JL	1987	JAE			195	228

CITE INDEX	FIRST AUTHOR	ISS-UE	YE-AR	JOUR-NAL	SECOND AUTHOR	THIRD AUTHOR	PAG BEG	PAG END
4.33	COLLINS,DW	JL	1987	JAE	KOTHARI,SP	RAYBURN,JD	111	138
4.31	BEAVER,WH	MR	1980	JAE	LAMBERT,RA	MORSE ,D	3	28
4.31	FOSTER,G	JA	1977	TAR			1	21
3.79	HAGERMAN,RL	AG	1979	JAE	ZMIJEWSKI,ME		141	161
3.67	LIPE ,R	JA	1990	TAR			49	71
3.58	LEFTWICH,RW	MR	1981	JAE			3	36
3.50	BERNARD,VL	ST	1989	JAR	THOMAS,JK		1	36
3.50	EASTON,PD	SP	1991	JAR	HARRIS,TS		19	36
3.33	BEAVER,WH	JL	1987	JAE	LAMBERT,RA	RYAN ,SG	139	157
3.33	CHAMBERS,AE	SP	1984	JAR	PENMAN,SH		21	47
3.33	COLLINS,DW	MR	1981	JAE	ROZEFF,MS	DHALIWAL,DS	37	71
3.33	HOLTHAUSEN,RW	MR	1981	JAE			73	109
3.33	PRESS ,EG	JA	1990	JAE	WEINTROP,JB		65	95
3.25	OU ,JA	ST	1989	JAR	PENMAN,SH		111	144
3.00	DUKE ,JC	JA	1990	JAE	HUNT III,HG		45	63
3.00	GREIG ,AC	JN	1992	JAE			413	442
3.00	STOBER,TL	JN	1992	JAE			347	372
3.00	WILSON,GP	AP	1987	TAR			293	322
2.89	FOSTER,G	OC	1984	TAR	OLSEN ,C	SHEVLIN,T	574	603
2.86	LIPE ,RC	ST	1986	JAR			37	68
2.86	RAYBURN,J	ST	1986	JAR			112	137
2.67	BERNARD,VL	DE	1990	JAE	THOMAS,JK		305	340
2.64	COLLINS,DW	MR	1979	JAE	DENT ,WT		3	44
2.63	WATTS ,RL	AU	1977	JAR	LEFTWICH,RW		253	271
2.55	BEAVER,WH	JL	1982	JAE	GRIFFIN,PA	LANDSMAN,WR	15	39
2.50	SCHIPPER,K	SP	1983	JAR	THOMPSON,R		184	221
2.43	ANTLE ,R	SP	1986	JAR	SMITH ,A		1	39
2.41	GONEDES,NJ	SP	1976	JAR	DOPUCH,N	PENMAN,SH	89	137
2.40	LARCKER,DF	AP	1983	JAE			3	30
2.40	MCNICHOLS,M	ST	1988	JAR	WILSON,GP		1	40
2.36	BIDDLE,GC	AU	1982	JAR	LINDAHL,FW		551	588
2.29	BALL ,R	ST	1972	JAR			1	38
2.27	RICKS ,WE	AU	1982	JAR			367	387
2.25	ALBRECHT,WS	AU	1977	JAR	LOOKABILL,LL	MCKEOWN,JC	226	244
2.23	PENMAN,SH	SP	1980	JAR			132	160
2.21	DYCKMAN,TR	MR	1979	JAE	SMITH ,AJ		45	75
2.20	LEFTWICH,RW	JA	1983	TAR			23	42
2.19	GRIFFIN,PA	SP	1977	JAR			71	83
2.17	FOSTER,G	DE	1981	JAE			201	232
2.14	KINNEY JR,WR	MR	1986	JAE			73	89
2.14	WILSON GP	ST	1986	JAR			165	203
2.07	BROWN ,LD	SP	1979	JAR	ROZEFF,MS		179	189
2.00	ALI ,A	JN	1992	JAE	ZAROWIN,P		249	264
2.00	DALEY ,LA	DE	1983	JAE	VIGELAND,RL		195	211
2.00	EASTON,PD	JN	1992	JAE	HARRIS,TS	OHLSON,JA	119	142
2.00	GRANT ,EB	SP	1980	JAR			255	268
2.00	HOLTHAUSEN,RW	JN	1992	JAE	LARCKER,DF		373	411
2.00	KOTHARI,SP	JN	1992	JAE	SLAON ,RG		143	171
2.00	SUNDER,S	ST	1973	JAR			1	45
2.00	THOMAS,JK	OC	1992	TAR	TUNG ,S		691	711
1.93	LEV ,B	JL	1979	TAR			485	503
1.91	PATELL,JM	JL	1982	TAR	WOLFSON,MA		509	527
1.89	LYS ,T	AP	1984	JAE			39	65

CITE INDEX	FIRST AUTHOR	ISS-UE	YE-AR	JOUR-NAL	SECOND AUTHOR	THIRD AUTHOR	PAG BEG	PAG END
1.88	GONEDES,NJ	AU	1975	JAR			220	256
1.86	PALMROSE,ZV	SP	1986	JAR			97	110
1.85	BIDDLE,GC	ST	1980	JAR			235	280
1.83	JOHNSON,JR	AP	1981	TAR	LEITCH,RA	NETER ,J	270	293
1.82	BEAVER,WH	OC	1970	TAR	KETTLER,P	SCHOLES,M	654	682
1.82	LILIEN,S	DE	1982	JAE	PASTENA,V		145	170
1.76	MAY ,RG	ST	1971	JAR			119	163
1.75	ABDEL-KHALIK,AR	AU	1985	JAR			427	447
1.75	FREEMAN,RN	ST	1989	JAR	TSE ,S		49	79
1.75	MORSE ,D	AU	1981	JAR			374	383
1.71	BAMBER,LS	SP	1986	JAR			40	56
1.71	LIBERTY,SE	OC	1986	TAR	ZIMMERMAN,JL		692	712
1.70	MORSE ,D	SP	1983	JAR	RICHARDSON,G		106	127
1.67	BOWEN ,RM	OC	1987	TAR	BURGSTAHLER,D	DALEY ,LA	723	747
1.67	COLLINS,DW	OC	1990	JAE	DeANGELO,L		213	247
1.67	LAMBERT,RA	ST	1987	JAR	LARCKER,DF		85	125
1.67	WAYMIRE,G	AU	1984	JAR			703	718
1.67	ZMIJEWSKI,ME	ST	1984	JAR			59	82
1.64	GIVOLY,D	JL	1982	TAR	PALMON,D		486	508
1.63	MURPHY,KJ	AP	1985	JAE			11	42
1.62	BEAVER,WH	AG	1980	JAE	CHRISTIE,AA	GRIFFIN,PA	127	157
1.62	OHLSON,JA	SP	1980	JAR			109	131
1.60	DEANGELO,LE	JA	1988	JAE			3	36
1.59	BEAVER,WH	AP	1972	TAR	DUKES ,RE		320	332
1.56	AJINKYA,BB	AU	1984	JAR	GIFT ,MJ		425	444
1.56	DODD ,P	AP	1984	JAE	DOPUCH,N	HOLTHAUSEN,RW	3	38
1.56	KROSS ,W	SP	1984	JAR	SCHROEDER,DA		153	176
1.53	GONEDES,NJ	SP	1978	JAR			26	79
1.50	BAMBER,LS	JL	1987	TAR			510	532
1.50	BARTOV,E	SE	1991	JAE			275	293
1.50	BROWN ,LD	SP	1987	JAR	RICHARDSON,GD	SCHWAGER,SJ	49	67
1.50	HAND ,JRM	OC	1989	TAR			587	623
1.50	HARRIS,TS	OC	1987	TAR	OHLSON,JA		651	670
1.50	HEALY ,PM	AP	1987	JAE	KANG ,SH	PALEPU,KG	7	34
1.50	HUNT III,HG	AU	1985	JAR			448	467
1.50	NEU ,D	02	1991	AOS			185	200
1.47	SUNDER,S	AP	1975	TAR			305	315
1.43	AYRES ,FL	JN	1986	JAE			143	158
1.43	DEANGELO,LE	JL	1986	TAR			400	420
1.43	HOSKIN,RE	ST	1986	JAR	HUGHES,JS	RICKS ,WE	1	36
1.43	PALEPU,KG	MR	1986	JAE			3	36
1.40	NOREEN,EW	SP	1988	JAR			119	133
1.40	PALMROSE,ZV	JA	1988	TAR			55	73
1.40	SIMON ,DT	AP	1988	TAR	FRANCIS,JR		255	269
1.38	BUBLITZ,B	ST	1985	JAR	FRECKA,TJ	MCKEOWN,JC	1	23
1.38	DUKES ,RE	ST	1980	JAR	DYCKMAN,TR	ELLIOTT,JA	1	26
1.38	LEE ,CJ	AU	1985	JAR	HSIEH ,DA		468	485
1.35	BEAVER,WH	ST	1970	JAR			62	99
1.33	FRANCIS,JR	AP	1987	JAE	REITER,SA		35	59
1.33	HEALY ,PM	JA	1990	JAE	PALEPU,KG		97	123
1.33	LEV ,B	SP	1990	JAR	PENMAN,SH		49	76
1.33	OU ,JA	SP	1990	JAR			144	163
1.33	ST.PIERRE,K	AP	1984	TAR	ANDERSON,JA		242	263

CITE INDEX	FIRST AUTHOR	ISS-UE	YE-AR	JOUR-NAL	SECOND AUTHOR	THIRD AUTHOR	PAG BEG	PAG END
1.31	BROWN ,RM	SP	1980	JAR			38	63
1.31	COLLINS,WA	AU	1980	JAR	HOPWOOD,WS		390	406
1.31	GHEYARA,K	AG	1980	JAE	BOATSMAN,JR		107	125
1.30	PINCUS,M	SP	1983	JAR			155	183
1.29	ZIMMER,I	MR	1986	JAE			37	52
1.27	ABDEL-KHALIK,AR	OC	1978	TAR	MCKEOWN,JC		851	868
1.27	FREEMAN,RN	AU	1982	JAR	OHLSON,JA	PENMAN,SH	639	653
1.25	BERNARD,VL	OC	1989	TAR	STOBER,TL		624	652
1.25	CORNELL,B	OC	1989	TAR	LANDSMAN,WR		680	692
1.25	COUGHLAN,AT	AP	1985	JAE	SCHMIDT,RM		43	66
1.25	HAN ,JCY	FB	1989	JAE	WILD ,JJ	RAMESH,K	3	33
1.25	MCNICHOLS,M	JA	1989	TAR			1	27
1.24	BEAVER,WH	ST	1966	JAR			71	111
1.24	DEAKIN,EB	SP	1972	JAR			167	179
1.20	DOPUCH,N	SP	1988	JAR	PINCUS,M		28	59
1.20	ZIMMERMAN,JL	AG	1983	JAE			119	149
1.17	THOMPSON II,RB	AU	1987	JAR	OLSEN ,C	DIETRICH,JR	245	274
1.15	RO ,BT	AG	1980	JAE			159	189
1.14	GIVOLY,D	DE	1979	JAE	LAKONISHOK,J		165	185
1.14	KINNEY JR,WR	ST	1979	JAR			148	165
1.14	LANDSMAN,WR	OC	1986	TAR			662	691
1.14	WILLMOTT,H	06	1986	AOS			555	582
1.12	FOSTER,G	SP	1973	JAR			25	37
1.11	HAGERMAN,RL	AU	1984	JAR	ZMIJEWSKI,ME	SHAH ,P	526	540
1.10	EVANS III,JH	AG	1983	JAE	PATTON,JM		151	175
1.10	KELLER,SB	AU	1983	AUD	DAVIDSON,LF		1	22
1.09	DUKE ,GL	SP	1982	JAR	NETER ,J	LEITCH,RA	42	67
1.08	NOREEN,EW	AP	1981	TAR	SEPE ,J		253	269
1.08	PATELL,JM	AU	1981	JAR	WOLFSON,MA		434	458
1.06	HARRISON,T	SP	1977	JAR			84	107
1.00	ANTHONY,JH	JN	1992	JAE	RAMESH,K		203	227
1.00	ANTLE ,R	SP	1985	JAR	SMITH ,A		296	325
1.00	BALL ,R	OC	1991	TAR	KOTHARI,SP		718	738
1.00	BARTH ,ME	JA	1991	TAR	BEAVER,WH	STINSON,CH	56	66
1.00	BEAVER,WH	AU	1989	JAR	EGER ,C	RYAN ,S	157	178
1.00	BHUSHAN,R	JL	1989	JAE			183	206
1.00	BIDDLE,GC	SP	1991	JAA	SEOW ,GS		183	232
1.00	CHENG ,CSA	JL	1992	TAR	HOPWOOD,WS	MCKEOWN,JC	579	598
1.00	CHOW ,CW	AP	1982	TAR	RICE ,SJ		326	335
1.00	DANN ,LY	SE	1991	JAE	MASULIS,RW	MAYERS,D	217	251
1.00	DEAKIN,EB	OC	1979	TAR			722	734
1.00	DOPUCH,N	JL	1987	TAR	HOLTHAUSEN,RW	LEFTWICH,RW	431	454
1.00	DORAN ,BM	JL	1988	TAR	COLLINS,DW	DHALIWAL,DS	389	413
1.00	EICHENSEHER,JW	JL	1981	TAR	DANOS ,P		479	492
1.00	ELLIOTT,JA	AU	1982	JAR			617	638
1.00	ELLIOTT,JA	SP	1984	JAR	RICHARDSON,G	DYCKMAN,TR	85	102
1.00	FRANCIS,JR	AG	1984	JAE			133	151
1.00	FREEMAN,RN	AU	1992	JAR	TSE ,SY		185	209
1.00	HERTZER,M	SE	1991	JAE	JAIN ,PC		253	273
1.00	HILL ,JW	OC	1989	TAR	INGRAM,RW		667	679
1.00	HUGHES,JS	JA	1987	TAR	RICKS ,WE		158	175
1.00	IMHOFF JR,EA	AP	1992	TAR	LOBO ,GJ		427	439
1.00	JANAKIRAMAN,SN	SP	1992	JAR	LAMBERT,RA	LARCKER,DF	53	69

CITE INDEX	FIRST AUTHOR	ISS-UE	YE-AR	JOUR-NAL	SECOND AUTHOR	THIRD AUTHOR	PAG BEG	PAG END
1.00	JOHNSON,WB	JA	1990	JAE	LYS ,T		281	308
1.00	KINNEY-JR,WR	FB	1989	JAE	MCDANIEL,LS		71	93
1.00	LEE ,CMC	JN	1992	JAE			265	302
1.00	LUSTGARTEN,S	OC	1982	JAE			121	141
1.00	LYS ,T	DE	1990	JAE	SOHN ,S		341	363
1.00	MCNICHOLS,M	AP	1983	JAE	MANEGOLD,JG		49	74
1.00	NEU ,D	04	1992	AOS			223	237
1.00	SHORES,D	SP	1990	JAR			164	181
0.94	BROWN ,P	ST	1967	JAR	BALL ,R		55	77
0.94	DOPUCH,N	SP	1972	JAR	WATTS ,RL		180	194
0.94	GONEDES,NJ	AU	1973	JAR			212	237
0.94	GONEDES,NJ	SP	1974	JAR			26	62
0.93	CRICHFIELD,T	JL	1978	TAR	DYCKMAN,TR	LAKONISHOK,J	651	668
0.93	HONG ,H	JA	1978	TAR	KAPLAN,RS	MANDELKER,	31	47
0.93	PATELL,JM	AG	1979	JAE	WOLFSON,MA		117	140
0.91	CHOW ,CW	AP	1982	TAR			272	291
0.89	DALEY ,LA	AP	1984	TAR			177	198
0.89	HUGHES,JS	AG	1984	JAE	RICKS ,WE		101	132
0.89	KELLOGG,RL	DE	1984	JAE			185	204
0.89	MARAIS,ML	ST	1984	JAR			34	54
0.88	ARCHIBALD,TR	JA	1972	TAR			22	30
0.88	HAM ,J	JL	1985	TAR	LOSELL,D	SMIELIAUSKAS,W	387	406
0.88	MUTCHLER,JF	AU	1985	JAR			668	682
0.88	SMITH ,ED	OC	1976	TAR			707	723
0.87	KINNEY JR,WR	JA	1978	TAR			48	60
0.86	BROWN ,LD	AU	1979	JAR	ROZEFF,MS		341	351
0.86	EL-GAZZAR,S	OC	1986	JAE	LILIEN,S	PASTENA,V	217	238
0.83	ATIASE,RK	SP	1987	JAR			168	176
0.83	BAGINSKI,SP	AU	1987	JAR			196	216
0.83	JENNINGS,R	SP	1987	JAR			90	110
0.83	STONE ,M	AU	1987	JAR			317	326
0.83	WALLACE,WA	AU	1981	JAR			502	520
0.82	BASI ,BA	AP	1976	TAR	CAREY ,KJ	TWARK ,RD	244	254
0.82	EGGLETON,IRC	SP	1976	JAR	PENMAN,SH	TWOMBLY,JR	66	88
0.82	IMHOFF JR,EA	AU	1982	JAR	PARE ,PV		429	439
0.82	JAIN ,PC	DE	1982	JAE			205	228
0.82	KINNEY JR,WR	SP	1971	JAR			127	136
0.82	MCDONALD,CL	JL	1973	TAR			502	510
0.81	JOY ,OM	AU	1977	JAR	LITZENBERGER,RH	MCENALLY,RW	207	225
0.81	ZIMMERMAN,JL	ST	1977	JAR			107	144
0.80	BALVERS,RJ	OC	1988	TAR	MCDONALD,B	MILLER,RE	605	622
0.80	MORRIS,MH	AP	1988	TAR	NICHOLS,WD		237	254
0.80	RUBIN ,MA	AP	1988	TAR			219	236
0.80	SUNDER,S	AU	1983	JAR	WAYMIRE,G		565	580
0.79	RAMAGE,JG	ST	1979	JAR	KRIEGER,AM	SPERO ,LL	72	102
0.77	HORWITZ,BN	ST	1980	JAR	KOLODNY,R		38	74
0.76	CUSHING,BE	AU	1969	JAR			196	203
0.75	DEFEO ,VJ	AP	1989	TAR	LAMBER,RA	LARCKER,DF	201	227
0.75	FROST ,CA	OC	1989	TAR			788	808
0.75	LINDAHL,FW	AU	1989	JAR			201	226
0.75	MITTELSTAEDT,HF	NV	1989	JAE			399	418
0.75	NIEHAUS,GR	AP	1989	TAR			269	284
0.75	OLSEN ,C	ST	1985	JAR	DIETRICH,JR		144	166

CITE INDEX	FIRST AUTHOR	ISS-UE	YE-AR	JOUR-NAL	SECOND AUTHOR	THIRD AUTHOR	PAG BEG	PAG END
0.75	POWNALL,G	AU	1989	JAR	WAYMIRE,G		227	245
0.75	SCHULTZ JR,JJ	AU	1981	JAR	RECKERS,PMJ		482	501
0.75	STICKEL,SE	JL	1989	JAE			275	292
0.75	THOMAS,JK	NV	1989	JAE			361	398
0.73	COLLINS,DW	JA	1982	TAR	ROZEFF,MS	SALATKA,WK	1	17
0.73	DANOS ,P	AU	1982	JAR	EICHENSEHER,JW		604	616
0.71	BEAVER,WH	JL	1973	TAR	DUKES ,RE		549	559
0.71	BOWEN ,RM	OC	1986	TAR	BURGSTAHLER,D	DALEY ,LA	713	725
0.71	GOSMAN,ML	JA	1973	TAR			1	11
0.71	LOREK ,KS	SP	1979	JAR			190	204
0.71	MAGLIOLO,J	ST	1986	JAR			69	111
0.71	PASTENA,V	AP	1986	TAR	RULAND,W		288	301
0.71	RICKS ,WE	SP	1986	JAR			206	216
0.71	STOBER,TL	ST	1986	JAR			138	164
0.71	THORNTON,DB	AU	1986	CAR			1	34
0.69	PARKER,JE	JA	1977	TAR			69	96
0.67	ABDEL-KHALIK,AR	SP	1990	CAR			295	322
0.67	BABER ,WR	AU	1987	JAR	BROOKS,EH	RICKS ,WE	293	305
0.67	BOWEN ,RM	JA	1981	TAR			1	22
0.67	CLINCH,GJ	AP	1987	JAE	SINCLAIR,NA		89	106
0.67	ETTREDGE,M	SP	1990	JAR	GREENBERG,R		198	210
0.67	HARRIS,TS	OC	1990	TAR	OHLSON,JA		764	780
0.67	HEALY ,PM	SP	1990	JAR	PALEPU,KG		25	48
0.67	KROSS ,W	AP	1990	TAR	RO ,B	SCHROEDER,D	461	476
0.67	MALMQUIST,DH	JA	1990	JAE			173	205
0.67	MIAN ,SL	JA	1990	JAE	SMITH JR,CW		141	171
0.67	O'BRIEN,PC	ST	1990	JAR	BHUSHAN,R		55	82
0.67	ROBERTS,RW	SP	1990	JAR	GLEZEN,GW	JONES ,TW	220	228
0.67	SCHAEFER,TF	AU	1984	JAR			647	656
0.67	SPICER,BM	JA	1978	TAR			94	111
0.67	WHITTRED,G	DE	1987	JAE			259	285
0.67	WILSON JR,TE	SP	1990	AUD	GRIMLUND,RA		43	59
0.65	BENSTON,GJ	JL	1969	TAR			515	532
0.65	GAGNON,JM	ST	1967	JAR			187	204
0.65	LOREK ,KS	AP	1976	TAR	MCDONALD,CL	PATZ ,DH	321	330
0.63	BRICKLEY,JA	AP	1985	JAE	BHAGAT,S	LEASE ,RC	115	130
0.63	EASTON,PD	ST	1985	JAR			54	77
0.63	GIVOLY,D	JL	1985	TAR			372	386
0.63	HAKA ,SF	OC	1985	TAR	GORDON,LA	PINCHES,GE	651	669
0.63	SCHIPPER,K	SP	1985	JAR	THOMPSON,R		408	415
0.62	WHITTRED,GP	OC	1980	TAR			563	577
0.60	ABDEL-KHALIK,AR	ST	1988	JAR			144	181
0.60	BELL ,TB	SP	1983	JAR			1	17
0.60	FOSTER III,TW	OC	1978	TAR	VICKREY,DW		921	934
0.60	FRANCIS,JR	OC	1988	TAR	WILSON,ER		663	682
0.60	JOHNSON,WB	AU	1988	JAR	DHALIWAL,DS		236	272
0.60	LILIEN,S	OC	1988	TAR	MELLMAN,M	PASTENA,V	642	656
0.60	RICHARDSON,AJ	04	1988	AOS			381	396
0.60	SHANE ,PB	JL	1983	TAR	SPICER,BH		521	538
0.60	SUTTON,TG	AP	1988	JAE			127	149
0.60	WONG ,J	JA	1988	JAE			37	51
0.60	WONG ,J	AP	1988	JAE			151	167
0.59	COPELAND,RM	ST	1968	JAR			101	116

CITE INDEX	FIRST AUTHOR	ISS-UE	YE-AR	JOUR-NAL	SECOND AUTHOR	THIRD AUTHOR	PAG BEG	PAG END
0.59	MOORE ,ML	SP	1973	JAR			100	107
0.58	BROWN ,PR	SP	1981	JAR			232	246
0.58	LEFTWICH,RW	ST	1981	JAR	WATTS ,RL	ZIMMERMAN,JL	50	77
0.58	SMITH ,AJ	ST	1981	JAR			174	211
0.57	DANOS ,P	OC	1986	TAR	EICHENSEHER,JW		633	650
0.57	DOPUCH,N	JN	1986	JAE	HOLTHAUSEN,RW	LEFTWICH,RW	93	118
0.57	HASSELL,JM	JA	1986	TAR	JENNINGS,RH		58	75
0.57	SHRIVER,KA	SP	1986	JAR			151	165
0.56	BALDWIN,BA	JL	1984	TAR			376	389
0.56	BATHKE,AW	AP	1984	TAR	LOREK ,KS		163	176
0.56	IMHOFF JR,EA	AU	1984	JAR	LOBO ,GJ		541	554
0.56	INGRAM,RW	SP	1984	JAR			126	144
0.56	MARAIS,ML	ST	1984	JAR	PATELL,JM	WOLFSON,MA	87	114
0.56	MCKEE ,AJ	OC	1984	TAR	BELL ,TB	BOATSMAN,JR	647	659
0.56	SIMUNIC,DA	AU	1984	JAR			679	702
0.56	WILSON,ER	SP	1984	JAR	HOWARD,TP		207	224
0.55	BANKS ,DW	SP	1982	JAR	KINNEY JR,WR		240	254
0.55	DIETRICH,JR	JA	1982	TAR	KAPLAN,RS		18	38
0.55	HALL ,TW	SP	1982	JAR			139	151
0.55	HOPWOOD,WS	AU	1982	JAR	MCKEOWN,JC	NEWBOLD,P	343	349
0.53	ARCHIBALD,TR	ST	1967	JAR			164	186
0.53	BEAVER,WH	JA	1968	TAR			113	122
0.53	BEIDLEMAN,CR	OC	1973	TAR			653	667
0.53	FIRTH ,MA	JL	1978	TAR			642	650
0.53	FRISHKOFF,P	ST	1970	JAR			116	129
0.53	HORRIGAN,JO	ST	1966	JAR			44	62
0.53	IMHOFF JR,EA	OC	1978	TAR			836	850
0.53	TRITSCHLER,CA	JA	1969	TAR			99	123
0.50	AJINKYA,BB	NV	1989	JAE	JAIN ,PC		331	359
0.50	ATIASE,RK	SP	1989	CAR	BAMBER,LS	TSE ,S	526	552
0.50	BEATTY,RP	OC	1989	TAR			693	709
0.50	BENSTON,GJ	AP	1985	JAE			67	84
0.50	BHUSHAN,R	JL	1989	JAE			255	274
0.50	BROWN ,LD	SP	1991	CAR	RICHARDSON,GD	TRZCINKA,CA	323	346
0.50	BUBLITZ,B	JA	1989	TAR	ETTREDGE,M		108	124
0.50	CHEWNING,G	SP	1989	JAR	PANY ,K	WHEELER,S	78	96
0.50	CREADY,WM	AP	1991	TAR	MYNATT,PG		291	312
0.50	ELY ,KM	SP	1991	JAR			37	58
0.50	FELTHAM,GA	DE	1991	JAE	HUGHES,JS	SIMUNIC,DA	375	399
0.50	FEROZ ,EH	ST	1991	JAR	PARK ,K	PASTENA,VS	107	148
0.50	FREEMAN,RN	SP	1983	JAR			42	64
0.50	GHICAS,D	AU	1989	CAR	PASTENA,V		125	142
0.50	HIRSCHEY,M	SP	1985	JAR	WEYGANDT,JJ		326	335
0.50	JONES ,JJ	AU	1991	JAR			193	228
0.50	L'HER ,JF	SP	1991	CAR	SURET ,J-M		378	406
0.50	LARCKER,DF	OC	1983	TAR	REVSINE,L		706	732
0.50	LEE ,CWJ	AU	1989	JAR	PETRUZZI,CR		277	296
0.50	LEWELLEN,W	AP	1985	JAE	LODERER,C	ROSENFELD,A	209	232
0.50	LEWELLEN,W	DE	1987	JAE	LODERER,C	MARTIN,K	287	310
0.50	LOBO ,GJ	AP	1989	TAR	SONG ,I		329	343
0.50	LOBO ,GL	SP	1989	JAR	MAHMOUD,AAW		116	134
0.50	MORSE ,D	AP	1991	TAR	STEPHAN,J	STICE ,EK	376	388
0.50	NEU ,D	03	1991	AOS			243	256

CITE INDEX	FIRST AUTHOR	ISS-UE	YE-AR	JOUR-NAL	SECOND AUTHOR	THIRD AUTHOR	PAG BEG	PAG END
0.50	SCHWARTZ,KB	AP	1985	TAR	MENON ,K		248	261
0.50	SWAMINATHAN,S	JA	1991	TAR			23	41
0.50	TEHRANIAN,H	ST	1987	JAR	TRAVLOS,NG	WAEGELEIN,JF	51	76
0.50	TROMBLEY,MA	JL	1989	TAR			529	538
0.50	TROTMAN,KT	04	1981	AOS	BRADLEY,G		355	362
0.50	WAYMIRE,G	SP	1985	JAR			268	295
0.47	DAILY ,RA	OC	1971	TAR			686	692
0.47	DYER ,JC	AU	1975	JAR	MCHUGH,AJ		204	219
0.47	FOSTER,G	OC	1975	TAR			686	698
0.47	GREEN ,D	ST	1966	JAR	SEGALL,J		21	36
0.47	LOOKABILL,LL	OC	1976	TAR			724	738
0.47	MAGEE ,RP	AU	1974	JAR			270	287
0.47	PETERSEN,RJ	JA	1973	TAR			34	43
0.47	RO ,BT	AU	1978	JAR			315	340
0.47	RULAND,W	AP	1978	TAR			439	447
0.46	OPPONG,A	AU	1980	JAR			574	584
0.45	ABDEL-KHALIK,AR	OC	1982	TAR	AJINKYA,BB		661	680
0.44	COLLINS,WA	AU	1984	JAR	HOPWOOD,WS	MCKEOWN,JC	467	479
0.43	CASEY JR,CJ	AP	1986	TAR	MCGEE ,VE	STICKNEY,CP	249	262
0.43	DHALIWAL,DS	OC	1986	TAR			651	661
0.43	FRANCIS,JR	AU	1986	JAR	STOKES,DJ		383	393
0.43	JAIN ,PC	SP	1986	JAR			76	96
0.43	NICHOLS,DR	SP	1979	JAR	TSAY ,JJ		140	155
0.43	PALMROSE,ZV	AU	1986	JAR			405	411
0.43	PASTENA,V	AU	1979	JAR	RONEN ,J		550	564
0.42	FRIED ,D	AP	1981	TAR	SCHIFF,A		326	341
0.42	HOPWOOD,WS	AU	1981	JAR	MCKEOWN,JC		313	322
0.42	RAMAN ,KK	OC	1981	TAR			910	926
0.42	VIGELAND,RL	AP	1981	TAR			309	325
0.41	BASKIN,EF	JA	1972	TAR			38	51
0.41	BEAVER,WH	AU	1968	JAR			179	192
0.41	DERSTINE,RP	AU	1974	JAR	HUEFNER,RJ		216	234
0.41	ELAM ,R	JA	1975	TAR			25	43
0.41	KIGER ,JE	SP	1972	JAR			113	128
0.41	NEUMANN,FL	ST	1968	JAR			1	17
0.40	CREADY,WM	SP	1988	JAR			1	27
0.40	DALEY ,LA	OC	1988	TAR	SENKOW,DW	VIGELAND,RL	563	585
0.40	HAW ,IM	AU	1988	JAR	LUSTGARTEN,S		331	352
0.40	INGRAM,RW	AU	1978	JAR			270	285
0.40	JOHNSON,WB	JA	1988	TAR	RAMANAN,R		96	110
0.40	KIM ,M	AP	1988	JAE	MOORE ,G		111	125
0.40	LANEN ,WN	DE	1988	JAE	THOMPSON,R		311	334
0.40	LEV ,B	AP	1983	JAE			31	48
0.40	LYS ,T	AU	1988	JAR	SIVARAMAKRISHNAN,K		273	299
0.40	NICHOLS,DR	AU	1983	JAR	SMITH ,DB		534	544
0.40	RO ,BT	SP	1988	CAR			438	449
0.40	SMITH ,DB	DE	1988	JAE	POURCIAU,S		335	344
0.40	THOMPSON,RB	JL	1988	TAR	OLSEN ,C	DIETRICH,JR	448	471
0.38	BOWMAN,RG	SP	1980	JAR			242	254
0.38	GENTRY,JA	SP	1985	JAR	NEWBOLD,P	WHITFORD,DT	146	160
0.38	JENNINGS,R	SP	1985	JAR	STARKS,L		336	350
0.38	KELLY ,R	AU	1985	JAR			619	632
0.38	SIMON ,DT	AU	1985	AUD			71	78

CITE INDEX	FIRST AUTHOR	ISS-UE	YE-AR	JOUR-NAL	SECOND AUTHOR	THIRD AUTHOR	PAG BEG	PAG END
0.38	WILLINGHAM,JJ	AU	1985	AUD	WRIGHT,WF		57	70
0.36	ALTMAN,EI	AU	1982	JAA			4	19
0.36	CHOW ,CW	WI	1982	AUD	RICE ,SJ		35	53
0.36	COLLINS,DW	AU	1979	JAR	SIMONDS,RR		352	383
0.36	COPELAND,RM	AU	1982	JAR	INGRAM,RW		275	289
0.36	HOPWOOD,WS	AU	1982	JAR	NEWBOLD,P	SILHAN,PA	724	732
0.36	WISEMAN,J	01	1982	AOS			53	64
0.35	BENSTON,GJ	ST	1967	JAR			1	54
0.35	COATES,R	ST	1972	JAR			132	144
0.35	COPELAND,RM	ST	1971	JAR	SHANK ,JK		196	224
0.35	LEV ,B	AP	1974	TAR	KUNITZKY,S		259	270
0.35	SINGHVI,SS	JA	1971	TAR	DESAI ,HB		129	138
0.33	ABDEL-KHALIK,AR	AU	1987	CAR	CHI ,C	GHICAS,D	32	60
0.33	ABDEL-KHALIK,AR	AU	1990	CAR			142	172
0.33	AHARONY,J	SP	1987	CAR	BAR-YOSEF,S		430	444
0.33	BRICKLEY,JA	JA	1990	JAE	VAN DRUNEN,LD		251	280
0.33	COWEN ,SS	02	1987	AOS	FERRERI,LB	PARKER,LD	111	122
0.33	DHARAN,BG	AP	1984	TAR			199	217
0.33	HAM ,J	AU	1987	CAR	LOSELL,D	SMIELIAUSKAS,W	210	226
0.33	HAN ,JCY	SP	1990	JAR	WILD ,JJ		211	219
0.33	HAW ,I	AP	1990	TAR	PASTENA,VS	LILIEN,SB	432	451
0.33	HSIEH ,S-J	SP	1990	CAR	FERRIS,KR	CHEN ,AH	550	572
0.33	LANDSMAN,WR	AU	1990	CAR	OHLSON,JA		185	198
0.33	MCDONALD,B	JL	1984	TAR	MORRIS,MH		432	446
0.33	MIAN ,SL	OC	1990	JAE	SMITH JR,CW		249	266
0.33	MOSES ,OD	AP	1987	TAR			358	377
0.33	NOREEN,EW	AU	1981	JAR	WOLFSON,MA		384	398
0.33	O'BRIEN,PC	AU	1990	JAR			286	304
0.33	RICHARDSON,AJ	05	1990	AOS			499	501
0.33	RO ,BT	JA	1981	TAR			70	84
0.33	SHANK ,JK	OC	1978	TAR	MURDOCK,RJ		824	835
0.33	SHEVLIN,T	JL	1987	TAR			480	509
0.33	SKINNER,DJ	OC	1990	JAE			191	211
0.33	STEVENSON,FL	AU	1987	JAR			306	316
0.33	SWANSON,EP	OC	1990	TAR			911	924
0.33	TURPEN,RA	SP	1990	AUD			60	76
0.33	WILSON,ER	SP	1990	CAR	STEWART,JP		573	591
0.31	ANDERSON,JC	JL	1980	TAR	FRANKLE,AW		467	479
0.31	LEV ,B	AU	1980	JAR			524	550
0.30	CHOW ,CW	JL	1983	TAR			485	520
0.30	MURRAY,D	SP	1983	JAR			128	140
0.29	BARNEA,A	JA	1976	TAR	RONEN ,J	SADAN ,S	110	122
0.29	BILDERSEE,JS	JA	1975	TAR			81	98
0.29	BLUM ,M	SP	1974	JAR			1	25
0.29	COMISKEY,EE	AP	1971	TAR			279	285
0.29	DEAKIN,EB	JA	1976	TAR			90	96
0.29	FOSTER,G	AU	1975	JAR			283	292
0.29	HORWITZ,BN	AP	1971	TAR	SHABAHANG,R		243	252
0.29	NORTON,CL	JA	1979	TAR	SMITH ,RE		72	87
0.29	POWNALL,G	AU	1986	JAR			291	315
0.29	RHODE ,JG	OC	1974	TAR	WHITSELL,GM	KELSEY,RL	772	787
0.29	SHANK ,JK	JL	1973	TAR	COPELAND,RM		494	501
0.29	SMITH ,DB	AU	1986	AUD			95	108

CITE INDEX	FIRST AUTHOR	ISS-UE	YE-AR	JOUR-NAL	SECOND AUTHOR	THIRD AUTHOR	PAG BEG	PAG END
0.29	WAYMIRE,G	JA	1986	TAR			129	142
0.29	WHITE ,GE	AU	1970	JAR			260	273
0.29	WILCOX,JA	ST	1973	JAR			163	179
0.29	WRIGHT,CJ	JA	1986	TAR	GROFF ,JE		91	100
0.29	ZEFF ,SA	AP	1967	TAR	FOSSUM,RL		298	320
0.27	ABDEL-KHALIK,AR	ST	1978	JAR	MCKEOWN,JC		46	77
0.27	INGRAM,RW	AU	1982	JAR	COPELAND,RM		766	772
0.27	JAGGI ,B	OC	1978	TAR			961	967
0.27	RICE ,SJ	AP	1978	TAR			429	438
0.25	BOWEN ,RM	JL	1989	JAE	JOHNSON,MF	SHEVLIN,T	225	254
0.25	BURGSTAHLER,D	JL	1989	JAE	JIAMBALVO,J	NOREEN,E	207	224
0.25	DEAKIN,EB	JA	1989	TAR			137	151
0.25	EICHENSEHER,JW	AU	1989	AUD	HAGIGI,M	SHIELDS,D	29	40
0.25	EL-GAZZAR,S	SP	1989	JAA	LILIEN,S	PASTENA,V	217	231
0.25	ESPAHBODI,R	SP	1989	CAR	TEHRANIAN,H		575	591
0.25	FIRTH ,MA	SP	1985	AUD			23	37
0.25	GORDON,LA	03	1989	AOS			247	258
0.25	HOPWOOD,W	JA	1989	TAR	MCKEOWN,J	MUTCHLER,J	28	48
0.25	HOPWOOD,WS	SP	1985	JAR	MCKEOWN,JC		161	174
0.25	INGRAM,RW	OC	1981	TAR	COPELAND,RM		830	843
0.25	INGRAM,RW	AU	1985	JAR			595	618
0.25	LAMBERT,RA	AP	1985	JAE	LARCKER,DF		179	204
0.25	LANDSMAN,WR	SP	1989	JAR	DAMODARAN,A		97	115
0.25	LEE ,CJ	SP	1985	JAR			213	227
0.25	LEVITAN,AS	AU	1985	AUD	KNOBLETT,JA		26	39
0.25	MULFORD,CW	AU	1985	JAR			897	906
0.25	NEWMAN,HA	OC	1989	TAR			758	772
0.25	PEASNELL,KV	SP	1977	JAR	SKERRATT,CL		108	119
0.25	RICKS ,WE	JA	1985	TAR	HUGHES,JS		33	52
0.25	SALATKA,WK	FB	1989	JAE			35	69
0.25	SELTO ,FH	AU	1985	JAR	CLOUSE,ML		700	717
0.25	TABOR ,RH	SP	1985	AUD	WILLIS,JT		93	109
0.25	TEHRANIAN,H	AP	1985	JAE	WAEGELEIN,JF		131	144
0.25	TOMCZYK,S	AU	1989	AUD	READ ,WJ		98	106
0.24	BALL ,R	SP	1976	JAR	LEV ,B	WATTS ,RL	1	9
0.24	BAREFIELD,RM	AP	1972	TAR	COMISKEY,EE		291	298
0.24	BARRETT,ME	SP	1976	JAR			10	26
0.24	BREMSER,WG	JL	1975	TAR			563	573
0.24	DASCHER,PE	AU	1970	JAR	MALCOM,RE		253	259
0.24	HAGERMAN,RL	OC	1975	TAR			699	709
0.24	KOCHANEK,RF	AP	1974	TAR			245	258
0.24	LEV ,B	AU	1969	JAR			290	299
0.24	LIVINGSTONE,JL	AP	1967	TAR			233	240
0.24	O'CONNOR,MC	AP	1973	TAR			339	352
0.24	SMITH ,JE	JL	1971	TAR	SMITH ,NP		552	561
0.24	WARREN,CS	SP	1975	JAR			162	176
0.24	WEST ,RR	SP	1970	JAR			118	125
0.23	AJINKYA,BB	AU	1980	JAR			343	361
0.23	HOPWOOD,WS	SP	1980	JAR			77	90
0.23	NAIR ,RD	JL	1980	TAR	FRANK ,WG		426	450
0.22	FRAZIER,KB	SP	1984	JAR	INGRAM,RW	TENNYSON,BM	318	331
0.22	MCCONNELL,DK	WI	1984	JAA			178	181
0.22	PENMAN,SH	DE	1984	JAE			165	183

CITE INDEX	FIRST AUTHOR	ISS-UE	YE-AR	JOUR-NAL	SECOND AUTHOR	THIRD AUTHOR	PAG BEG	PAG END
0.22	PURO ,M	AU	1984	JAR			624	646
0.22	SMITH ,DB	AG	1984	JAE	STETTLER,HF	BEEDLES,W	153	162
0.21	ADELBERG,AH	AU	1979	JAR			565	592
0.21	NAIR ,RD	SP	1979	JAR			225	242
0.20	BASU ,S	JL	1978	TAR			599	625
0.20	BIDDLE,GC	AU	1988	JAR	RICKS ,WE		169	194
0.20	CARSLAW,C	AP	1988	TAR			321	327
0.20	ELLIOTT,JA	ST	1988	JAR	SHAW,WH		91	126
0.20	GORMLEY,RJ	SU	1988	JAA			185	212
0.20	HARRISON JR,WT	SP	1983	JAR	TOMASSINI,LA	DIETRICH,JR	65	77
0.20	KAMIN ,JY	02	1978	AOS	RONEN ,J		141	160
0.20	KETZ ,JE	ST	1978	JAR			273	284
0.20	LEE ,CJ	AU	1988	CAR			371	388
0.20	MCKEOWN,JC	SP	1988	CAR	SHALCHI,H		485	507
0.20	MORSE ,D	AP	1983	TAR	USHMAN,N		247	258
0.20	SHAW ,WH	SP	1988	JAR			60	81
0.20	WILLIAMS,DD	05	1988	AOS	DIRSMITH,MW		487	508
0.20	WYER ,JC	SP	1988	AUD	WHITE ,GT	JANSON,EC	164	173
0.19	PERAGALLO,E	OC	1977	TAR			881	892
0.18	BAREFIELD,RM	AU	1971	JAR	COMISKEY,EE		351	358
0.18	BOWMAN,EH	01	1976	AOS	HAIRE ,M		11	22
0.18	CHASTEEN,LG	JL	1971	TAR			504	508
0.18	CHOI ,FD	AU	1973	JAR			159	175
0.18	COPELAND,RM	JL	1968	TAR	LICASTRO,RD		540	545
0.18	DAVIS ,RR	AU	1982	AUD			13	32
0.18	DEAKIN,EB	JL	1976	TAR			590	603
0.18	ESKEW ,RK	AP	1975	TAR			316	324
0.18	FRANK ,WG	SP	1969	JAR			123	136
0.18	GAGNON,JM	SP	1971	JAR			52	72
0.18	GUPTA ,MC	SP	1972	JAR	HUEFNER,RJ		77	95
0.18	MEYERS,SL	AP	1973	TAR			318	322
0.18	PATZ ,DH	AU	1972	JAR	BOATSMAN,JR		392	403
0.18	REILLY,FK	ST	1972	JAR	MORGENSON,DL	WEST ,M	105	124
0.18	RONEN ,J	SP	1975	JAR	SADAN ,S		133	149
0.18	SAMUELSON,RA	AU	1972	JAR			322	344
0.18	SCHWARTZ,KB	AU	1982	JAA			32	43
0.18	SEPE ,J	JL	1982	TAR			467	485
0.18	SKINNER,RC	SP	1982	JAR			210	226
0.18	WALTHER,LM	AP	1982	TAR			376	383
0.18	WHITE JR,CE	AU	1972	JAR			351	358
0.17	BERNARD,VL	OC	1987	TAR	RULAND,RG		707	722
0.17	BILDERSEE,JS	AU	1987	CAR	RONEN ,J		89	110
0.17	BROWN ,LD	AU	1987	CAR	ZMIJEWSKI,MA		61	75
0.17	CHOW ,CW	JL	1987	TAR	WONG-BOREN,A		533	541
0.17	ELGERS,P	OC	1987	TAR	CALLAHAN,C	STROCK,E	763	773
0.17	MAHER ,MW	OC	1981	TAR			751	770
0.17	MOORE ,ML	OC	1987	TAR	STEECE,BM	SWENSON,CW	671	685
0.17	ZIEBART,DA	AP	1987	TAR	KIM ,DH		343	357
0.15	BARAN ,A	JA	1980	TAR	LAKONISHOK,J	OFER ,AR	22	35
0.15	BOWMAN,RG	AP	1980	TAR			237	253
0.15	GRAY ,SJ	SP	1980	JAR			64	76
0.14	BROCKHOFF,K	12	1979	AOS			77	86
0.14	DEFEO ,VJ	AU	1986	JAR			349	363

CITE INDEX	FIRST AUTHOR	ISS-UE	YE-AR	JOUR-NAL	SECOND AUTHOR	THIRD AUTHOR	PAG BEG	PAG END
0.14	DIERKES,M	12	1979	AOS			87	108
0.14	ESKEW ,RK	JA	1979	TAR			107	118
0.14	FRANK ,WG	AU	1979	JAR			593	605
0.14	MURDOCH,B	AP	1986	TAR			273	287
0.14	TSE ,S	JL	1986	TAR			475	497
0.13	ANELL ,B	04	1985	AOS			479	492
0.13	CASEY JR,CJ	SP	1985	JAR	BARTCZAK,N		384	401
0.13	COX ,CT	OC	1985	TAR			692	701
0.13	EICHENSEHER,JW	SP	1985	JAA			195	209
0.13	JOHNSON,WB	AP	1985	JAE	MAGEE ,RP	NAGARAJAN,NJ	151	174
0.13	LESSEM,R	04	1977	AOS			279	294
0.13	MARKS ,BR	AU	1985	JAR	RAMAN ,KK		878	886
0.13	SCHIPPER,K	ST	1977	JAR			1	40
0.13	SHORT ,DG	ST	1978	JAR			259	272
0.13	WARREN,CS	JA	1977	TAR			150	161
0.12	ABDEL-KHALIK,AR	OC	1975	TAR			657	670
0.12	COPELAND,RM	SP	1968	JAR	FREDERICKS,W		106	113
0.12	COPELAND,RM	AU	1969	JAR	WOJDAK,JF		188	195
0.12	DOPUCH,N	ST	1966	JAR	DRAKE ,DF		192	219
0.12	ELLIOTT,JW	AU	1972	JAR	UPHOFF,HL		259	274
0.12	FRANK ,WG	AP	1970	TAR	WEYGANDT,JJ		280	289
0.12	GREENBALL,MN	ST	1971	JAR			172	190
0.12	GRIFFIN,PA	JL	1976	TAR			499	515
0.12	HARMELINK,PJ	SP	1973	JAR			146	158
0.12	JOHNSON,O	AU	1967	JAR			164	172
0.12	KIGER ,JE	JA	1974	TAR			1	7
0.12	KINNEY JR,WR	AP	1972	TAR			339	345
0.12	LINDHE,R	AU	1963	JAR			139	148
0.12	LOEB ,SE	JA	1972	TAR			1	10
0.12	MLYNARCZYK,FA	ST	1969	JAR			63	81
0.12	ROBERTSON,JC	JL	1971	TAR	CLARKE,RW		562	571
0.12	STAUBUS,GJ	JA	1965	TAR			119	134
0.11	BERNARD,VL	AU	1984	JAR			445	466
0.11	DIETRICH,JR	AP	1984	JAE			67	96
0.11	GORDON,LA	02	1984	AOS	HAKA ,S	SCHICK,AG	111	123
0.11	LOREK ,KS	SP	1984	JAR	BATHKE,AW		369	379
0.11	MCCONNELL,DK	SP	1984	AUD			44	56
0.11	SCHEINER,JH	AU	1984	JAR			789	797
0.11	SCHREUDER,H	JA	1984	TAR	KLAASSEN,J		64	77
0.11	STONE ,M	JL	1984	TAR	BUBLITZ,B		469	473
0.11	SUTTON,TG	01	1984	AOS			81	95
0.11	WESCOTT,SH	SP	1984	JAR			412	423
0.11	WHITTRED,GP	AP	1984	TAR	ZIMMER,I		287	295
0.10	ABDEL-KHALIK,AR	SP	1983	JAR			293	296
0.10	BROWN ,LD	AU	1983	JAR			432	443
0.10	CASEY JR,CJ	SP	1983	JAR			300	307
0.10	HALL ,TW	SU	1983	JAA			299	313
0.10	INGRAM,RW	JL	1983	TAR	CHEWNING,EG		562	580
0.10	LAWRENCE,EC	AU	1983	JAR			606	610
0.10	MCLEAY,S	01	1983	AOS			31	56
0.10	MENSAH,YM	AP	1983	TAR			228	246
0.09	COGGER,KO	AU	1982	JAR	RULAND,W		733	737
0.09	EMERY ,GW	AU	1982	JAR	COGGER,KO		290	303

CITE INDEX	FIRST AUTHOR	ISS-UE	YE-AR	JOUR-NAL	SECOND AUTHOR	THIRD AUTHOR	PAG BEG	PAG END
0.09	SCHEINER,JH	AU	1982	JAR	KIGER ,JE		482	496
0.09	SELTO ,FH	AU	1982	JAR	GROVE ,HD		676	688
0.08	BROWN ,LD	SP	1980	JAR	HUGHES,JS	ROZEFF,MS	278	288
0.08	CHARNES,A	01	1980	AOS	COOPER,WW		87	107
0.08	HOPWOOD,WS	SP	1980	JAR			289	296
0.08	KELLY ,LK	03	1980	AOS			311	322
0.08	LOY ,LD	SP	1980	JAA	TOOLE ,HR		227	243
0.08	MANEGOLD,JG	AU	1981	JAR			360	373
0.08	WHITTINGTON,OR	JL	1980	TAR	WHITTENBURG,G		409	418
0.07	BARLEV,B	AU	1979	JAR	LEVY ,H		305	315
0.07	CHAN ,JL	04	1979	AOS			273	282
0.07	DAVIDSON,S	ST	1978	JAR	WEIL ,RL		154	233
0.07	DAVIS ,DW	JA	1978	TAR	BOATSMAN,JR	BASKIN,EF	1	10
0.07	ENGLEBRECHT,TD	JL	1979	TAR	JAMISON,RW		554	562
0.07	FOSTER III,TW	AP	1978	TAR	VICKREY,DW		360	370
0.07	GIVOLY,D	SU	1978	JAA	RONEN ,J	SCHIFF,A	361	372
0.07	GRAY ,SJ	AU	1978	JAR			242	253
0.07	HILLISON,WA	SP	1979	JAR			60	73
0.07	MADEO ,SA	JL	1979	TAR			538	553
0.07	PEARSON,MA	WI	1979	JAA	LINDGREN,JH	MYERS ,BL	122	134
0.06	ARNOLD,DF	JA	1973	TAR	HUMANN,TE		23	33
0.06	CHOTTINER,S	AU	1971	JAR	YOUNG ,AE		367	374
0.06	CULPEPPER,RC	AP	1970	TAR			322	332
0.06	FALK ,H	SP	1977	JAR	MILLER,JC		12	22
0.06	FRANK ,WG	SP	1971	JAR	WEYGANDT,JJ		116	126
0.06	HOFSTEDT,TR	AP	1971	TAR	WEST ,RR		329	337
0.06	HUME ,LJ	SP	1970	JAR			21	33
0.06	JENSEN,RE	JA	1971	TAR			36	56
0.06	KRATCHMAN,SH	OC	1974	TAR	MALCOM,RE	TWARK ,RD	682	689
0.06	NEUMANN,FL	JL	1969	TAR			546	554
0.06	SAN MIGUEL,JG	04	1977	AOS	SHANK ,JK	GOVINDARAJAN,V	333	348
0.06	SHARPE,IG	AU	1975	JAR	WALKER,RG		293	310
0.06	SIMPSON,RH	OC	1969	TAR			806	817
0.06	SOPER ,FJ	AP	1964	TAR	DOLPHIN,R		358	362
0.06	STONE ,WE	JA	1965	TAR			190	195
0.00	ABARBANELL,JS	JN	1991	JAE			147	165
0.00	AJINKYA,BB	AP	1991	TAR	ATIASE,RK	GIFT ,MJ	389	401
0.00	ALFORD,AW	SP	1992	JAR			94	108
0.00	ALI ,A	JA	1992	TAR	KLEIN ,A	ROSENFELD,J	183	198
0.00	ALLEN ,S	SP	1990	CAR	RAMANAN,R		518	543
0.00	ALY ,IM	SP	1992	JAA	BARLOW,HA	JONES ,RW	217	230
0.00	AMIHUD,Y	AU	1989	JAA	MENDELSON,H		415	431
0.00	AMIT ,R	WI	1988	JAA	LIVNAT,J		19	43
0.00	AMIT ,R	AU	1989	CAR	LIVNAT,J	ZAROWIN,P	143	158
0.00	ANDERSON JR,KE	JL	1985	TAR			357	371
0.00	ANTHONY,JH	SP	1987	CAR			460	475
0.00	APOSTOLOU,NG	AU	1985	JAR	GIROUX,GA	WELKER,RB	853	858
0.00	ARNETT,HE	JA	1965	TAR			54	64
0.00	ARNOLD,PJ	02	1991	AOS			121	140
0.00	ASHTON,RH	SP	1989	CAR	GRAUL ,PR	NEWTON,JD	657	673
0.00	ASKARI,H	AP	1976	TAR	CAIN ,P	SHAW ,R	331	334
0.00	ASQUITH,P	JL	1989	TAR	HEALY ,P	PALEPU,K	387	403
0.00	AYRES ,FL	SP	1986	JAR			166	169

CITE INDEX	FIRST AUTHOR	ISS-UE	YE-AR	JOUR-NAL	SECOND AUTHOR	THIRD AUTHOR	PAG BEG	PAG END
0.00	BABER ,WR	OC	1991	TAR	FAIRFIELD,PM	HAGGARD,JA	818	829
0.00	BAGINSKI,SP	JA	1990	TAR	HASSELL,JM		175	190
0.00	BALACHANDRAN,KR	02	1977	AOS	LIVINGSTONE,JL		153	164
0.00	BALAKRISHNAN,R	AU	1990	JAR	HARRIS,TS	SEN ,PK	305	325
0.00	BALDWIN,J	SU	1992	JAA	GLEZEN,GW		269	285
0.00	BAO ,BE	03	1986	AOS	BAO ,DA	VASARHELYI,MA	289	296
0.00	BAO ,BE	04	1989	AOS	BAO ,DA		303	319
0.00	BARLEY,B	SU	1990	JAA	LIVNAT,J		411	433
0.00	BARTH ,ME	JL	1991	TAR			516	534
0.00	BARTH ,ME	MR	1992	JAE	BEAVER,WH	LANDSMAN,WR	27	61
0.00	BARTOV,E	JL	1992	TAR			610	622
0.00	BATHKE,AW	JA	1989	TAR	LOREK ,KS	WILLINGER,GL	49	68
0.00	BEATTY,RP	WI	1985	JAA	JOHNSON,SB		112	124
0.00	BEATTY,RP	SP	1989	CAR	VERRECCHIA,RE		472	493
0.00	BEATTY,RP	AU	1992	JAA	HAND ,JRM		509	530
0.00	BEAVER,WH	DE	1981	JAE	LANDSMAN,WR		233	241
0.00	BELL ,TB	AU	1991	JAR	TABOR ,RH		350	370
0.00	BENJAMIN,JJ	SU	1986	JAA	GROSSMAN,SD	WIGGIN,CE	177	184
0.00	BENSON,ED	SU	1991	JAA	MARKS ,BR	RAMAN ,KK	303	319
0.00	BERNARD,VL	SP	1991	JAA	NOEL ,J		145	181
0.00	BIDWELL III,CM	SP	1981	JAA	RIDDLE JR,JR		198	214
0.00	BILDERSEE,JS	SU	1987	JAA	KAHN ,N		239	256
0.00	BINDER,JJ	SP	1985	JAR			370	383
0.00	BLACCONIERE,WG	MR	1991	JAE			91	113
0.00	BLACCONIERE,WG	JN	1991	JAE	BOWEN ,RM	SEFCIK,SE	167	201
0.00	BLANCHARD,GA	JA	1986	TAR	CHOW ,CW	NOREEN,EW	1	15
0.00	BOARD ,JLG	SP	1990	JAR	WALKER,M		182	192
0.00	BONNIER,KA	FB	1989	JAE	BRUNER,RF		95	106
0.00	BOWEN ,RM	OC	1982	TAR	SUNDEM,GL		778	784
0.00	BOWEN ,RM	AU	1992	JAA	JOHNSON,MF	SHEVLIN,T	395	422
0.00	BRIEF ,RP	JA	1969	TAR			20	26
0.00	BROWN ,BC	SU	1986	JAA	BRANDI,JT		185	205
0.00	BROWN ,LD	AU	1991	JAR	KIM ,SK		382	385
0.00	BROWN ,LD	OC	1992	TAR	HAN ,JCY		862	875
0.00	BROWN ,PR	SU	1982	JAA			282	290
0.00	BURGSTAHLER,D	SP	1986	JAR	NOREEN,EW		170	186
0.00	CAHAN ,SF	JA	1992	TAR			77	96
0.00	CAMPBELL,DR	SP	1983	JAA			196	211
0.00	CASSIDY,DB	AU	1976	JAR			212	229
0.00	CHALOS,P	SP	1991	CAR	CHERIAN,J	HARRIS,D	431	448
0.00	CHANEY,PK	SP	1992	CAR	JETER ,DC		540	560
0.00	CHANG ,OH	SP	1992	JAR	NICHOLS,DR		109	125
0.00	CHARITOU,A	AU	1990	JAA	KETZ ,JE		475	497
0.00	CHEN ,KCW	AU	1992	AUD	CHURCH,BK		30	49
0.00	CHENG ,TT	AU	1986	CAR			226	241
0.00	CHOI ,SK	JN	1992	JAE	JETER ,DC		229	247
0.00	CHUNG ,DY	AU	1988	CAR	LINDSAY,WD		19	46
0.00	CHURCHILL,NC	WI	1982	AUD	COOPER,WW	GOVINDARAJAN,V	69	91
0.00	CLARK ,TN	ST	1977	JAR			54	94
0.00	CLARKSON,PM	SP	1992	CAR	DONTOH,A	RICHARDSON,G	601	625
0.00	CLINCH,G	SP	1991	JAR			59	78
0.00	CLINCH,G	OC	1992	TAR	MAGLIOLO,J		843	861
0.00	COE ,TL	SP	1979	JAA			244	253

CITE INDEX	FIRST AUTHOR	ISS-UE	YE-AR	JOUR-NAL	SECOND AUTHOR	THIRD AUTHOR	PAG BEG	PAG END
0.00	CORNELL,B	AU	1989	JAA	LANDSMAN,W	SHAPIRO,AC	460	479
0.00	CREADY,WM	JL	1987	TAR	SHANK ,JK		589	596
0.00	DAVIS ,HZ	AU	1982	JAR	KAHN ,N		738	744
0.00	DAVIS ,HZ	AU	1984	JAR	KAHN ,N	ROZEN ,E	480	490
0.00	DAVIS ,LR	SP	1992	AUD	SIMON ,DT		58	68
0.00	DAVIS ,ML	AP	1988	TAR	LARGAY III,JA		348	363
0.00	DAVIS ,ML	JL	1990	TAR			696	709
0.00	DAVISON,AG	SP	1984	JAR	STENING,BW	WAI ,WT	313	317
0.00	DECHOW,PM	MR	1991	JAE	SLOAN ,RG		1	89
0.00	DEFOND,ML	SP	1992	AUD			16	31
0.00	DEMPSEY,SJ	OC	1989	TAR			748	757
0.00	DHALIWAL,D	MR	1992	JAE	WANG ,S		7	25
0.00	DHARAN,BG	SP	1983	JAR			256	270
0.00	DHARAN,BG	WI	1992	JAA	MASCARENHAS,B		1	21
0.00	DONTOH,A	SP	1988	CAR	RICHARDSON,E		450	469
0.00	DORAN ,DT	SP	1988	JAA	NACHTMANN,R		113	132
0.00	DUKE ,D	WI	1991	JAA			135	142
0.00	ELGERS,P	JN	1992	JAE	MURRAY,D		303	316
0.00	ELGERS,PT	JL	1980	TAR			389	408
0.00	ELGERS,PT	AP	1982	TAR	MURRAY,D		358	375
0.00	ELLIOTT,JA	JA	1990	TAR	PHILBRICK,DR		157	174
0.00	ELLIOTT,JA	OC	1991	TAR	HANNA ,JD	SHAW ,WH	847	861
0.00	ELNICKI,RA	ST	1977	JAR			209	218
0.00	ESPAHBODI,H	DE	1991	JAE	STROCK,E	TEHRANIAN,H	323	345
0.00	ETTREDGE,M	SP	1988	AUD	SHANE ,PB	SMITH ,D	29	42
0.00	FALK ,H	OC	1975	TAR	HEINTZ,JA		758	779
0.00	FELIX JR,WL	JA	1972	TAR			52	63
0.00	FEROZ ,EH	JL	1992	TAR	WILSON,ER		480	495
0.00	FIELDS,LP	AU	1991	AUD	WILKINS,MS		62	69
0.00	FIRTH ,MA	SP	1973	JAR			16	24
0.00	FIRTH ,MA	AU	1981	JAR			521	529
0.00	FLEISCHMAN,RK	AP	1991	TAR	PARKER,LD		361	375
0.00	FRANCIS,J	AU	1990	JAR			326	347
0.00	FRANCIS,J	AU	1992	JAR	PAGACH,D	STEPHAN,J	165	184
0.00	FRECKA,TJ	SP	1983	JAR	LEE ,CF		308	316
0.00	FREEMAN,R	DE	1992	JAE	TSE ,S		509	523
0.00	FREEMAN,RN	ST	1978	JAR			111	145
0.00	FRIED ,D	WI	1987	JAA	HOSLER,C		5	23
0.00	FRIEDLOB,GT	WI	1983	JAA			100	107
0.00	FU ,P	SP	1971	JAR			40	51
0.00	FULMER,JG	AU	1984	JAA	MOON ,JE		5	14
0.00	GARSOMBKE,HP	SU	1983	JAA	ALLEN ,G		285	298
0.00	GAVER ,JJ	JA	1992	TAR	GAVER ,KM	BATTISTEL,GP	172	182
0.00	GAVER ,JJ	SP	1992	JAA			137	156
0.00	GHICAS,DC	AP	1990	TAR			384	405
0.00	GIACCOTTO,C	SU	1992	JAA			291	310
0.00	GIVOLY,D	AU	1981	JAR	PALMON,D		530	543
0.00	GIVOLY,D	SP	1987	JAA	LAKONISHOK,J		117	137
0.00	GIVOLY,D	AP	1992	TAR	HAYN ,C		394	410
0.00	GLEZEN,GW	AU	1985	JAR	MILLAR,JA		859	870
0.00	GLICK ,R	SP	1989	JAA	PLAUT ,SE		147	159
0.00	GONEDES,NJ	ST	1969	JAR			90	113
0.00	GONEDES,NJ	JL	1971	TAR			535	551

CITE INDEX	FIRST AUTHOR	ISS-UE	YE-AR	JOUR-NAL	SECOND AUTHOR	THIRD AUTHOR	PAG BEG	PAG END
0.00	GORDON,DA	AU	1990	JAA	GORDON,MJ		573	588
0.00	GORDON,LA		1992	AOS	SMITH ,KJ		741	757
0.00	GORTON,G	SP	1989	JAA	PENNACCHI,G		125	145
0.00	GOVINDARAJAN,V	SU	1979	JAA			339	343
0.00	GOVINDARAJAN,V	04	1980	AOS			383	392
0.00	GRAY ,D	AU	1984	JAR			760	764
0.00	GRAY ,SJ	SP	1984	JAR	RADEBAUGH,LH		351	360
0.00	GREENBERG,R	AU	1984	JAR			719	730
0.00	GREENBERG,RR	AU	1986	JAA	JOHNSON,GL	RAMESH,K	266	277
0.00	GRIFFIN,PA	OC	1991	TAR	WALLACH,SJR		830	846
0.00	GROSSMAN,SD	WI	1981	JAA	KRATCHMAN,SH	WELKER,RB	136	143
0.00	GUENTHER,DA	JA	1992	TAR			17	45
0.00	HAIN ,HP	OC	1966	TAR			699	703
0.00	HALL ,TW	SP	1985	JAA	CASLER,DJ		210	224
0.00	HALPERIN,R	AP	1987	TAR	LANEN ,WN		378	384
0.00	HAN ,BH	MR	1992	JAE	JENNINGS,R	NOEL ,J	63	85
0.00	HAN ,JCY	SP	1991	JAR	WILD ,JJ		79	95
0.00	HAND ,JRM	OC	1990	TAR			739	763
0.00	HAND ,JRM	OC	1991	TAR			739	746
0.00	HANSEN,ES	ST	1977	JAR			156	201
0.00	HARMON,WK	AU	1984	JAA			24	34
0.00	HARPER JR,RM	AU	1990	AUD	STRAWSER,JR	TANG ,K	115	133
0.00	HASKINS,ME	AU	1990	AUD	WILLIAMS,DD		55	74
0.00	HAW ,I	SE	1991	JAE	JUNG ,K	LILIEN,SB	295	320
0.00	HAW ,I	SU	1991	JAA	KIM ,W		325	344
0.00	HAW ,IM	WI	1987	JAA	PASTENA,V	LILIEN,S	24	42
0.00	HEALY ,PM	WI	1990	JAA	MODIGLIANI,F		3	25
0.00	HESSEL,CA	SU	1992	JAA	NORMAN,M		313	330
0.00	HOLDREN,GC	JA	1964	TAR			70	85
0.00	HOPWOOD,W	AU	1988	CAR	MCKEOWN,J	MUTCHLER,J	284	298
0.00	HOPWOOD,W	AP	1989	TAR	SCHAEFER,T		313	328
0.00	HOPWOOD,WS	AU	1988	CAR	SCHAEFER,TF		318	342
0.00	HOPWOOD,WS	SU	1990	JAA	MCKEOWN,JC		339	363
0.00	HORRIGAN,JO	JL	1965	TAR			558	568
0.00	HORWITZ,B	JL	1988	TAR	NORMOLLE,D		414	435
0.00	HORWITZ,BN	SP	1972	JAR	YOUNG ,AE		96	107
0.00	HOUGHTON,CW	SP	1991	AUD	FOGARTY,JA		1	21
0.00	HOUGHTON,KA	SP	1984	JAR			361	368
0.00	HUGHES,JS	SP	1986	CAR	RICKS ,WE		222	241
0.00	HUSS ,HF	WI	1991	JAA	ZHAO ,J		53	66
0.00	HUSSEIN,ME	AU	1986	AUD	BAVISHI,VB	GANGOLLY,JS	124	133
0.00	HUTH ,WL	WI	1992	JAA	MARIS ,BA		27	44
0.00	ICERMAN,RC	SP	1991	AUD	HILLISON,WA		22	34
0.00	IMHOFF JR,EA	SU	1981	JAA			333	351
0.00	IMHOFF-JR,EA	DE	1988	JAE	THOMAS,JK		277	310
0.00	INGRAM,RW	AU	1986	CAR			200	221
0.00	ISMAIL,BE	AU	1987	CAR			76	88
0.00	ISMAIL,BE	JA	1989	TAR	KIM ,MK		125	136
0.00	JAIN ,PC	JL	1983	TAR			633	638
0.00	JENNINGS,R	AP	1992	TAR	MEST ,DP	THOMPSON II,RB	337	354
0.00	JOHNSON,O	OC	1976	TAR			808	823
0.00	JONES ,CP	AU	1990	JAA	BUBLITZ,B		549	566
0.00	KAHN ,N	SU	1982	JAA			327	337

CITE INDEX	FIRST AUTHOR	ISS-UE	YE-AR	JOUR-NAL	SECOND AUTHOR	THIRD AUTHOR	PAG BEG	PAG END
0.00	KENNEDY,D	SP	1992	JAA	LAKONISHOK,J	SHAW ,WH	161	190
0.00	KENNEDY,DT	SU	1992	JAA	HYON ,YH		335	356
0.00	KIM ,DH	WI	1991	JAA	ZIEBART,DA		35	47
0.00	KING ,R	SP	1992	CAR	POWNALL,G	WAYMIRE,G	509	531
0.00	KING ,RD	JL	1984	TAR			419	431
0.00	KING ,RD	JA	1986	TAR	O'KEEFE,TB		76	90
0.00	KISSINGER,JN	AU	1983	AUD			42	54
0.00	KNAUF ,JB	WI	1987	JAA	VASARHELYI,MA		43	64
0.00	KNUTSON,PH	ST	1971	JAR			99	112
0.00	KOTHARI,SP	JN	1992	JAE			173	202
0.00	KRAMER,SS	JA	1982	TAR			70	87
0.00	KREUTZFELDT,RW		1990	AUD	WALLACE,WA		1	26
0.00	KRINSKY,I	SP	1989	CAR	ROTENBERG,W		501	515
0.00	KROSS ,W	AU	1982	JAR			459	471
0.00	LABELLE,R	SP	1990	CAR			677	698
0.00	LANEN ,WN	SP	1992	JAR	LARCKER,DF		70	93
0.00	LANG ,M	AU	1991	JAR			229	257
0.00	LAU ,AH	SP	1987	JAR			127	138
0.00	LEE ,CF	AP	1988	TAR	WU ,C		292	306
0.00	LEMBKE,VC	WI	1980	JAA	SMITH ,JH		147	162
0.00	LEMKE ,KW	MR	1992	JAE	PAGE ,MJ		87	114
0.00	LEV ,B	ST	1969	JAR			182	197
0.00	LEV ,B	SP	1979	JAA	TAYLOR,KW		232	243
0.00	LEVY ,H	AU	1987	JAA	BYUN ,YH		355	369
0.00	LEVY ,H	SP	1990	JAA			235	270
0.00	LIANG ,T-P	AU	1992	CAR	CHANDLER,JS	HAN ,I	306	328
0.00	LICHTENBERG,FR	OC	1992	TAR			741	752
0.00	LIVINGSTONE,JL	JL	1967	TAR			544	552
0.00	LIVINGSTONE,JL	ST	1967	JAR			93	123
0.00	LIVINGSTONE,JL	SP	1967	JAR			77	94
0.00	LIVNAT,J	AU	1981	JAR			350	359
0.00	LLOYD ,BM	OC	1971	TAR	WEYGANDT,JJ		756	764
0.00	LOREK ,KS	SP	1983	JAR	ICERMAN,JD	ABDULKADER,AA	317	328
0.00	LOREK ,KS	AU	1992	AUD	BRANSON,BC	ICERMAN,RC	66	88
0.00	LOUDDER,ML	SP	1992	AUD	KHURANA,IK	SAWYERS,RB	69	82
0.00	LYON ,JD	AU	1992	JAA	SCHROEDER,DA		531	552
0.00	MAHER ,JJ	OC	1987	TAR			785	798
0.00	MAHER ,MW	JA	1992	TAR	TIESSEN,P	COLSON,R	199	211
0.00	MANEGOLD,JG	SU	1986	JAA			206	221
0.00	MANES ,RP	ST	1967	JAR	SAMUELS,JM	SMYTH ,DJ	139	156
0.00	MARKS ,BR	AU	1987	AUD	RAMAN ,KK		106	117
0.00	MARKS ,BR	SP	1988	CAR	RAMAN ,KK		595	608
0.00	MARSTON,F	SP	1988	JAA	HARRIS,RS		147	164
0.00	MARTIN,A	ST	1971	JAR			1	31
0.00	MARTIN,JD	WI	1979	JAA	ANDERSON,PF	KEOWN ,AJ	151	164
0.00	MAYPER,AG	SP	1991	AUD	ADDY JR,ND		136	144
0.00	MCGAHRAN,KT	JA	1988	TAR			23	41
0.00	MCKEOWN,JC		1991	AUD	MUTCHLER,JF	HOPWOOD,W	1	13
0.00	MEAR ,R	04	1987	AOS	FIRTH ,MA		331	340
0.00	MEEK ,GK	AP	1983	TAR			394	402
0.00	MELLMAN,M	AU	1986	JAA	SEILER,ME		305	318
0.00	MENDENHALL,RR	ST	1988	JAR	NICHOLS,WD		63	90
0.00	MENON ,K	SP	1987	CAR	SCHWARTZ,KB		302	315

CITE INDEX	FIRST AUTHOR	ISS-UE	YE-AR	JOUR-NAL	SECOND AUTHOR	THIRD AUTHOR	PAG BEG	PAG END
0.00	MENON ,K	AP	1991	TAR	WILLIAMS,DD		313	332
0.00	MENSAH,YM	WI	1983	JAA			130	141
0.00	MENSAH,YM	SP	1984	JAR			380	395
0.00	MIELKE,DE	WI	1987	JAA	SEIFERT,J		65	78
0.00	MILLAR,JA	JA	1977	TAR			52	55
0.00	MILLS ,RH	JA	1967	TAR			74	81
0.00	MITTELSTAEDT,HF	SP	1992	AUD	REGIER,PR	CHEWNING,EG	83	98
0.00	MOIZER,P	AU	1987	AUD	TURLEY,S		118	123
0.00	MONAHAN,TF	SU	1983	JAA	BARENBAUM,L		325	340
0.00	MOODY ,SM	AU	1986	JAA	FLESHER,DL		319	330
0.00	MOORE ,ML	JA	1985	TAR	STEECE,BM	SWENSON,CW	18	32
0.00	MORRIS,MH	SU	1984	JAA	NICHOLS,WD		293	305
0.00	MOSES ,OD	SU	1990	JAA			379	409
0.00	MULFORD,CW	JL	1986	TAR	COMISKEY,EE		519	525
0.00	MURRAY,D	WI	1982	JAA			154	159
0.00	MUTCHLER,JF	AU	1986	AUD			148	.
0.00	MUTCHLER,JF	AU	1990	AUD	WILLIAMS,DD		39	54
0.00	NEUMANN,BR	SP	1979	JAR			123	139
0.00	NEWMAN,DP	OC	1981	TAR			897	909
0.00	NEWTON,JD		1989	AUD	ASHTON,RH		22	37
0.00	NICHOLS,DR	AP	1979	TAR	TSAY ,JJ	LARKIN,PD	376	382
0.00	NICHOLS,DR	JA	1987	TAR			183	190
0.00	NIELSEN,CC	OC	1965	TAR			795	804
0.00	NIX ,JIM	SU	1983	JAA	WICHMANN JR,H		341	352
0.00	O'DONNELL,JL	JA	1965	TAR			135	143
0.00	O'DONNELL,JL	JL	1968	TAR			549	553
0.00	ODAIYAPPA,R	JL	1992	TAR	NAINAR,SMK		599	609
0.00	OHLSON,JA	ST	1972	JAR			45	84
0.00	OHLSON,JA	AU	1992	JAA	PENMAN,SH		553	573
0.00	OUTSLAY,E	OC	1982	TAR	WHEELER,JE		716	733
0.00	PALMROSE,Z		1991	AUD			54	71
0.00	PALMROSE,Z	ST	1991	JAR			149	193
0.00	PATTEN,DM	06	1990	AOS			575	587
0.00	PATTEN,DM	05	1992	AOS			471	475
0.00	PATTEN,RJ	OC	1964	TAR			876	879
0.00	PEAVY ,JW	WI	1985	JAA	EDGAR ,SM		125	135
0.00	PELES ,YC	SP	1990	JAA			309	327
0.00	PENMAN,SH	SP	1991	JAA			233	255
0.00	PENMAN,SH	JL	1992	TAR			563	578
0.00	PETERSEN,RJ	JL	1975	TAR			525	532
0.00	PETRONI,KR	DE	1992	JAE			485	507
0.00	PHILIPS,GE	ST	1970	JAR	MAYNE ,LS		178	188
0.00	POWNALL,G	ST	1989	JAR	WAYMIRE,G		85	105
0.00	PURO ,M	SP	1985	JAA			165	177
0.00	PUTNAM,K	AU	1984	JAA	THOMAS,LR		15	23
0.00	PYO ,Y	DE	1990	JAE	LUSTGARTEN,S		365	379
0.00	RAMAKRISHNAN,RTS	AU	1992	JAA	THOMAS,JK		423	464
0.00	RAMAN ,KK	WI	1982	JAA			144	153
0.00	RAMAN ,KK	AU	1982	JAA			44	50
0.00	RANSOM,CR	ST	1985	JAR			124	143
0.00	RAYBURN,J	AU	1992	CAR	LENWAY,S		237	251
0.00	REILLY,FK	AU	1972	JAR	STETTLER,HF		308	321
0.00	RICHARDSON,G	AU	1988	CAR	SEFCIK,SE	THOMPSON,R	299	317

CITE INDEX	FIRST AUTHOR	ISS-UE	YE-AR	JOUR-NAL	SECOND AUTHOR	THIRD AUTHOR	PAG BEG	PAG END
0.00	RO ,BT	AU	1989	CAR			177	195
0.00	ROBBINS,WA	SU	1985	JAA	APOSTOLOU,NG	STRAWSER,RH	279	292
0.00	ROBERTS,RW	06	1992	AOS			595	612
0.00	ROBINSON,JR	JA	1990	TAR	SHANE ,PB		25	48
0.00	ROCKNESS,HO	SP	1988	CAR	SHIELDS,MD		568	581
0.00	ROSE ,PS	AU	1982	JAA	ANDREWS,WT	GIROUX,GA	20	31
0.00	ROSMAN,A	SP	1992	JAA			251	267
0.00	RUE ,JC	SU	1984	JAA	VOLKAN,AG		306	322
0.00	RULAND,W	JL	1990	TAR	TUNG ,S	GEORGE,NE	710	721
0.00	RYAN ,SG	SP	1991	JAA			257	287
0.00	SAMI ,H	SP	1989	CAR	CURATOLA,AP	TRAPNELL,JE	556	574
0.00	SAMI ,H	AU	1992	CAR	WELSH ,MJ		212	236
0.00	SAN MIGUEL,JG	JL	1977	TAR			638	641
0.00	SANNELLA,AJ	WI	1991	JAA			75	102
0.00	SCHACHTER,B	AU	1988	JAR			353	372
0.00	SCHAEFER,T	AU	1986	JAA	KENNELLEY,M		278	287
0.00	SCHIFF,M	SP	1979	JAA			224	231
0.00	SCHWARTZ,BN	SP	1983	JAA			244	253
0.00	SELTO ,FH	AU	1983	JAR	GROVE ,HD		619	622
0.00	SHACKELFORD,DA	JN	1991	JAE			117	145
0.00	SHANKER,L	SU	1992	JAA			379	393
0.00	SHAW ,WH	AP	1987	TAR			385	400
0.00	SHAW ,WH	SP	1991	CAR			407	423
0.00	SHEHATA,M	OC	1991	TAR			768	787
0.00	SILHAN,PA	SP	1983	JAR			341	347
0.00	SILHAN,PA	SP	1985	JAR	MCKEOWN,JC		416	426
0.00	SMITH ,DB	SP	1988	JAR			134	145
0.00	ST.PIERRE,K	SP	1982	JAA	ANDERSON,JA		229	247
0.00	STANDISH,PEM	OC	1982	TAR	UNG ,S		701	715
0.00	STAUBUS,GJ	JL	1968	TAR			413	424
0.00	STERNER,JA	AU	1983	JAR			623	628
0.00	STEVENS,JL	SP	1992	JAA	JOSE ,ML		195	212
0.00	STICE ,EK	JA	1991	TAR			42	55
0.00	STICE ,JD	JL	1991	TAR			516	534
0.00	STICKEL,SE	OC	1986	JAE			197	216
0.00	STICKEL,SE	AP	1991	TAR			402	416
0.00	STRONG,JS	OC	1990	JAE			267	283
0.00	SUMMERS,EL	AP	1968	TAR			257	265
0.00	SWANSON,EP	OC	1985	TAR	SHEARON,WT	THOMAS,LR	681	691
0.00	TAUSSIG,RA	JA	1968	TAR	HAYES ,SC		68	74
0.00	TEALL ,HD	SP	1992	CAR			561	579
0.00	TEALL ,HD	SP	1992	CAR			561	579
0.00	TEETS ,W	AU	1992	JAR			274	285
0.00	THIES ,CF	AU	1987	JAA	STURROCK,T		375	391
0.00	THODE ,SF	WI	1986	JAA	DRTINA,RE	LARGAY III,JA	46	61
0.00	THOMAS,AP	03	1986	AOS			253	270
0.00	THOMAS,JK	OC	1989	TAR			773	787
0.00	THOMAS,LR	AP	1986	TAR	SWANSON,EP		330	336
0.00	THORNTON,DB	AU	1988	CAR			343	370
0.00	TILLER,MG	SU	1985	JAA	MAUTZ ,RD		293	304
0.00	TORABZADEH,KM	SP	1992	JAA	BERTIN,WJ		231	240
0.00	TSE ,S	SP	1989	CAR			592	614
0.00	TSE ,S	SP	1990	JAR			229	238

CITE INDEX	FIRST AUTHOR	ISS-UE	YE-AR	JOUR-NAL	SECOND AUTHOR	THIRD AUTHOR	PAG BEG	PAG END
0.00	USRY ,MF	OC	1966	TAR			754	762
0.00	VOSS ,WM	AU	1968	JAR			262	269
0.00	WALLACE,WA	SP	1991	AUD			53	68
0.00	WALLACE,WA	SP	1991	CAR	KRUETZFELDT,RW		485	512
0.00	WARFIELD,TD	JL	1992	TAR	LINSMEIER,TJ		546	562
0.00	WARFIELD,TD	OC	1992	TAR	WILD ,JJ		821	842
0.00	WARREN,CS	SP	1980	JAR			312	324
0.00	WATSON,CJ	JL	1990	TAR			682	695
0.00	WAYMIRE,G	AU	1983	JAR	POWNALL,G		629	643
0.00	WELCH ,PR	AU	1984	JAR			744	757
0.00	WHITEHURST,FD	JL	1970	TAR			553	564
0.00	WILKERSON JR,JE	SP	1987	JAR			161	167
0.00	WILLIAMS,DJ	03	1986	AOS			271	288
0.00	WILSON,AC	SP	1989	AUD	GLEZEN,GW		90	100
0.00	WILSON,AC	AU	1989	CAR	HUDSON,D		196	215
0.00	WILSON,AC	SU	1991	JAA			365	381
0.00	YOUNG ,AE	SP	1978	JAA			217	230
0.00	YOUNG ,SD	AP	1988	TAR			283	291
0.00	YOUNG ,SD	OC	1991	TAR			809	817
0.00	ZAROWIN,P	AP	1988	JAE			89	110
0.00	ZAROWIN,P	SU	1990	JAA			439	454
0.00	ZIEBART,DA	AU	1985	JAR			920	926
0.00	ZIEBART,DA	AP	1990	TAR			477	488
0.00	ZIEBART,DA	AU	1992	CAR	REITER,SA		252	282
0.00	ZIND ,RG	AU	1989	CAR	ZEGHAL,D		26	47

2.4 RESEARCH METHOD=ARCHIVAL – SECONDARY

CITE INDEX	FIRST AUTHOR	ISS-UE	YE-AR	JOUR-NAL	SECOND AUTHOR	THIRD AUTHOR	PAG BEG	PAG END
5.20	HOLTHAUSEN,RW	AG	1983	JAE	LEFTWICH,RW		77	117
4.33	WATTS ,RL	JA	1990	TAR	ZIMMERMAN,JL		131	156
4.12	GONEDES,NJ	ST	1974	JAR	DOPUCH,N		48	129
3.33	ZMIJEWSKI,ME	AG	1981	JAE	HAGERMAN,RL		129	149
3.27	LEV ,B	ST	1982	JAR	OHLSON,JA		249	322
3.15	FOSTER,G	MR	1980	JAE			29	62
2.82	BALL ,R	ST	1982	JAR	FOSTER,G		161	234
2.75	ARRINGTON,CE	02	1989	AOS	FRANCIS,JR		1	28
2.73	FRIED ,D	OC	1982	JAE	GIVOLY,D		85	107
2.55	LIBBY ,R	03	1982	AOS	LEWIS ,BL		231	286
2.50	LEHMAN,C	05	1987	AOS	TINKER,T		503	522
2.50	LIBBY ,R	03	1977	AOS	LEWIS ,BL		245	268
2.33	CHRISTIE,AA	JA	1990	JAE			15	36
2.20	HOPWOOD,AG	01	1978	AOS			3	14
2.18	DHALIWAL,DS	JL	1982	JAE	SALAMON,GL	SMITH ,ED	41	53
2.00	CHRISTENSON,C	JA	1983	TAR			1	22
2.00	LEV ,B	ST	1989	JAR			153	192
1.91	FELIX JR,WL	AP	1982	TAR	KINNEY JR,WR		245	271
1.80	COOPER,DJ	23	1983	AOS			269	286
1.70	BIRNBERG,JG	23	1983	AOS	TUROPOLEC,L	YOUNG ,SM	111	130
1.64	SWIERINGA,RJ	ST	1982	JAR	WEICK ,KE		56	101
1.33	BERG ,KB	SP	1990	CAR	COURSEY,D	DICKHAUT,J	825	849
1.30	CUSHING,BE	AU	1983	AUD	LOEBBECKE,JK		23	41
1.25	BEDARD,JC	02	1989	AOS			113	131
1.17	EINHORN,HJ	SP	1981	JAR	HOGARTH,RM		1	31

CITE INDEX	FIRST AUTHOR	ISS-UE	YE-AR	JOUR-NAL	SECOND AUTHOR	THIRD AUTHOR	PAG BEG	PAG END
1.00	CHANDRA,R	SP	1990	CAR	BALACHANDRAN,BV		611	640
1.00	CHESLEY,GR	AP	1975	TAR			325	337
1.00	DEMSKI,JS	ST	1982	JAR	KREPS ,DM		117	148
1.00	DYCKMAN,TR	SP	1984	JAR	ZEFF ,SA		225	297
1.00	HINES ,RD	04	1991	AOS			313	331
1.00	KIRKHAM,LM	04	1992	AOS			287	297
1.00	LEHMAN,CR	04	1992	AOS			261	285
1.00	MILLER,P	04	1990	AOS			315	338
1.00	RICHARDSON,AJ	06	1989	AOS			415	431
0.88	BROWN ,LD	AP	1985	TAR	GARDNER,JC		262	277
0.76	ABDEL-KHALIK,AR	JA	1974	TAR	LUSK ,EJ		8	23
0.75	BROWN ,LD	SP	1985	JAR	GARDNER,JC		84	109
0.75	LIBBY ,R	AU	1977	JAR	FISHBURN,PC		272	292
0.73	HOLSTRUM,GL	AU	1982	AUD	MESSIER JR,WF		45	63
0.71	BEAVER,WH	ST	1974	JAR	DEMSKI,JS		170	187
0.67	BEGLEY,J	JA	1990	JAE			125	139
0.67	MILLER,P	05	1990	AOS	O'LEARY,T		479	498
0.67	VERRECCHIA,RE	JA	1990	JAE			245	250
0.64	VERRECCHIA,RE	ST	1982	JAR			1	42
0.57	JARRELL,GA	AG	1979	JAE			93	116
0.53	ASHTON,RH	OC	1975	TAR			710	722
0.50	ARMSTRONG,P	01	1991	AOS			1	25
0.50	BROWN ,LD	02	1987	AOS	GARDNER,JC	VASARHELYI,MA	193	204
0.50	BRYER ,RA	05	1991	AOS			439	486
0.50	COLIGNON,R	02	1991	AOS	COVALESKI,M		141	157
0.50	COLLINS,JH	JL	1991	TAR	PLUMLEE,RD		559	576
0.50	HOGARTH,RM	AP	1991	TAR			277	290
0.50	JOHNSON,PE	02	1989	AOS	JAMAL ,K	BERRYMAN,RG	83	99
0.50	ROBSON,K	05	1991	AOS			547	570
0.50	THOMPSON,G	05	1991	AOS			572	599
0.47	IJIRI ,Y	SP	1968	JAR	KINARD,JC	PUTNEY,FB	1	28
0.45	DEANGELO,LE	DE	1982	JAE			171	203
0.44	BENSTON,GJ	AU	1984	CAR			47	57
0.41	EPSTEIN,MJ	01	1976	AOS	FLAMHOLTZ,EG	MCDONOUGH,JJ	23	42
0.40	KETZ ,JE	OC	1978	TAR			952	960
0.38	WATTS ,RL	AG	1980	JAE	ZIMMERMAN,JL		95	106
0.35	MCRAE ,TW	SP	1974	JAR			80	92
0.33	BAIMAN,S	04	1990	AOS			341	371
0.33	BRIERS,M	04	1990	AOS	HIRST ,M		373	398
0.33	CHAMBERS,RJ	AU	1984	CAR			1	22
0.33	DENT ,JF	02	1990	AOS			3	25
0.33	ESPELAND,WN	02	1990	AOS	HIRSCH,PM		77	96
0.33	HOLTHAUSEN,RW	JA	1990	JAE			207	218
0.33	HUGHES,MA	03	1990	AOS	KWON ,SO		179	191
0.33	LEFTWICH,R	JA	1990	JAE			37	44
0.33	ZEFF ,SA	JL	1984	TAR			447	468
0.29	DOWNES,D	AP	1973	TAR	DYCKMAN,TR		300	317
0.29	HOFSTEDT,TR	01	1976	AOS			43	58
0.25	FALK ,H	SP	1989	CAR			816	825
0.25	KLERSEY,GF	02	1989	AOS	MOCK ,TJ		133	151
0.23	HUSSEIN,ME	SU	1980	JAA	KETZ ,JE		354	367
0.22	MORSE ,D	AU	1984	JAR			605	623
0.21	GROVE ,HD	JL	1979	TAR	SAVICH,RS		522	537

CITE INDEX	FIRST AUTHOR	ISS-UE	YE-AR	JOUR-NAL	SECOND AUTHOR	THIRD AUTHOR	PAG BEG	PAG END
0.21	VATTER,WJ	JL	1979	TAR			563	573
0.19	LAVIN ,D	03	1977	AOS			237	244
0.18	BIRNBERG,JG	JL	1967	TAR	NATH ,R		468	479
0.15	RONEN ,J	SU	1980	JAA	SADAN ,S		339	353
0.14	FLESHER,DL	JL	1986	TAR	FLESHER,TK		421	434
0.14	ZEFF ,SA	SP	1986	JAA			131	154
0.13	CASH JR,JI	OC	1977	TAR	BAILEY JR,AD	WHINSTON,AB	813	832
0.13	CROSBY,MA	SP	1985	AUD			118	132
0.13	DYL ,EA	02	1985	AOS	LILLY ,MS		171	176
0.12	BALL ,R	SP	1971	JAR			1	31
0.12	CAUSEY JR,DY	JA	1976	TAR			19	30
0.12	PARKER,RH	SP	1968	JAR			58	71
0.12	WELLS ,MC	JL	1976	TAR			471	482
0.11	CHAMBERS,RJ	AU	1984	CAR			58	63
0.11	SMITH ,G	AU	1984	AUD	KROGSTAD,JL		107	117
0.09	SMITH ,DB	OC	1982	JAE	NICHOLS,DR		109	120
0.09	WHALEY,RE	OC	1982	JAE	CHEUNG,JK		57	83
0.08	ALFORD,MR	SP	1981	JAA	EDMONDS,TP		255	264
0.08	FLAHERTY,RE	AU	1980	JAA	SCHWARTZ,BN		47	56
0.08	OVADIA,A	WI	1980	JAA	RONEN ,J		113	137
0.06	BEDFORD,NM	JL	1975	TAR	ZIEGLER,RE		435	443
0.06	BOLLOM,WJ	JA	1972	TAR	WEYGANDT,JJ		75	84
0.06	BRIEF ,RP	SP	1967	JAR			27	38
0.06	GROVE ,HD	03	1977	AOS	MOCK ,TJ	EHRENREICH,K	219	236
0.06	HORRIGAN,JO	AP	1968	TAR			284	294
0.06	MCRAE ,TW	AP	1970	TAR			315	321
0.06	SORENSEN,JE	JL	1977	TAR	GROVE ,HD		658	675
0.06	YAMEY ,BS	SP	1967	JAR			51	76
0.00	ABDEL-KHALIK,AR	SP	1986	CAR			242	251
0.00	ARRINGTON,CE	06	1992	AOS	SCHWEIKER,W		511	533
0.00	BAILEY,D	06	1990	AOS			513	525
0.00	BALACHANDRAN,BV	SP	1986	CAR			282	287
0.00	BALL ,R	JN	1992	JAE			309	345
0.00	BANKER,RD	JL	1992	TAR	COOPER,WW	POTTER,G	496	510
0.00	BEACH ,LR	02	1989	AOS	FREDERICKSON,JR		101	112
0.00	BOATSMAN,JR	JA	1992	TAR	GRASSO,LP	ORMISTON,MB	148	156
0.00	BOLAND,LA	AU	1992	CAR	GORDON,IM		142	170
0.00	BOUGEN,PD	03	1990	AOS	OGDEN ,SG	OUTRAM,Q	149	170
0.00	BRANCH,B	SP	1981	JAA	BERKOWITZ,B		215	219
0.00	BRENNAN,MJ	JA	1991	TAR			67	79
0.00	BRICKER,R	AU	1989	JAR			246	262
0.00	BRIEF ,RP	OC	1977	TAR			810	812
0.00	BRIGHTON,GD	JA	1969	TAR			137	144
0.00	BROMWICH,M	02	1990	AOS			27	46
0.00	BROWN ,LD	SP	1986	CAR			252	258
0.00	BROWN ,LD	SP	1989	CAR	GARDNER,JC	VASARHELYI,MA	793	815
0.00	BUCKLESS,FA	OC	1990	TAR	RAVENSCROFT,SP		933	945
0.00	BUCKLEY,JW	JA	1966	TAR			75	82
0.00	BUCKLEY,JW	01	1980	AOS			49	64
0.00	CHATFIELD,M	JA	1975	TAR			1	6
0.00	CHEN ,JT	SP	1985	CAR	MANES ,RP		242	252
0.00	CHOO ,F	06	1989	AOS			481	493
0.00	COASE ,RH	JA	1990	JAE			3	13

CITE INDEX	FIRST AUTHOR	ISS-UE	YE-AR	JOUR-NAL	SECOND AUTHOR	THIRD AUTHOR	PAG BEG	PAG END
0.00	COHEN ,MF	JA	1965	TAR			1	8
0.00	COOPER,T	WI	1980	JAA			138	146
0.00	COOPER,WW	AU	1985	JAA	HO ,JL	HUNTER,JE	22	39
0.00	COPELAND,TE	AU	1978	JAA			33	48
0.00	CZARNIAWSKA-JOERGES	02	1989	AOS	JACOBSSON,B		29	39
0.00	DAVIDSON,S	AP	1963	TAR			278	284
0.00	DEJONG,DV	JA	1992	TAR	FORSYTHE,R		157	171
0.00	DEMSKI,JS	AU	1985	CAR			69	75
0.00	DEMSKI,JS	OC	1992	TAR	MAGEE ,RP		732	740
0.00	DERMER,J	02	1990	AOS			67	76
0.00	DONEGAN,J	SP	1989	JAA	SUNDER,S		203	216
0.00	FELIX JR,WL	SP	1988	AUD	NILES ,MS		43	60
0.00	FELTHAM,GA	AU	1984	CAR			87	98
0.00	FOGARTY,TJ	02	1992	AOS			129	149
0.00	GALLHOFER,S	05	1991	AOS	HASLAM,J		487	520
0.00	GIBBS ,G	OC	1964	TAR			4	7
0.00	GRADY ,P	JA	1965	TAR			21	30
0.00	HAIN ,HP	AU	1967	JAR			154	163
0.00	HECK ,JL	OC	1986	TAR	BREMSER,WG		735	744
0.00	HINES ,RD	04	1992	AOS			313	341
0.00	HOLMES,W	JA	1979	TAR			47	57
0.00	HOOKS ,KL	04	1992	AOS			343	366
0.00	HOPPER,T	05	1991	AOS	ARMSTRONG,P		405	438
0.00	HUNT-III,HG	05	1990	AOS	HOGLER,RL		437	454
0.00	JACKSON,MW	05	1992	AOS			459	469
0.00	JENNINGS,R	OC	1990	TAR			925	932
0.00	JENTZ ,GA	AP	1967	TAR			362	365
0.00	JOHNSON,O	04	1992	AOS			205	222
0.00	JONSSON,S	05	1991	AOS			521	546
0.00	KINNEY JR,WR	AU	1981	JAA			5	17
0.00	KRIPKE,H	WI	1989	JAA			3	65
0.00	KROSS ,W	AU	1980	JAA	CHAPMAN,G	STRAND,KH	36	46
0.00	LEWIS ,CD	JA	1967	TAR			96	105
0.00	LEWIS ,NR	34	1984	AOS	PARKER,LD	SUTCLIFFE,P	275	289
0.00	LOFT ,A	04	1992	AOS			367	378
0.00	LUCKETT,PF	04	1991	AOS	EGGLETON,IRC		371	394
0.00	MADDALA,GS	OC	1991	TAR			788	808
0.00	MANES ,RP	JL	1964	TAR			631	638
0.00	MEYER ,PE	JA	1976	TAR			80	89
0.00	MILLER,P	05	1991	AOS	HOPPER,T	LAUGHLIN,R	395	403
0.00	MILLER,P		1991	AOS			733	762
0.00	MOORE ,DC		1991	AOS			163	791
0.00	MOST ,KS	SP	1967	JAR			39	50
0.00	MOST ,KS	OC	1972	TAR			722	734
0.00	MURNIGHAN,JK	JL	1990	TAR	BAZERMAN,MH		642	657
0.00	NORGAARD,CT	JL	1972	TAR			433	442
0.00	PENMAN,SH	AU	1992	JAA			465	484
0.00	PERAGALLO,E	JL	1971	TAR			529	534
0.00	PICCIOTTO,S		1992	AOS			759	792
0.00	POWER ,M	05	1992	AOS			477	499
0.00	POWER ,MK	04	1991	AOS			333	353
0.00	POWER ,MK	01	1992	AOS			37	62
0.00	PRESTON,AM	01	1992	AOS			63	100

CITE INDEX	FIRST AUTHOR	ISS-UE	YE-AR	JOUR-NAL	SECOND AUTHOR	THIRD AUTHOR	PAG BEG	PAG END
0.00	REVSINE,L	AP	1981	TAR			342	354
0.00	RICHARDSON,AJ	AU	1990	CAR	WILLIAMS,JJ		278	294
0.00	ROBERTS,J	04	1992	AOS	COUTTS,JA		379	395
0.00	RONEN ,J	WI	1989	JAA	SORTER,G		67	77
0.00	ROSEN ,LS	JA	1969	TAR	DECOSTER,DT		124	136
0.00	ROUSSEY,RS	SP	1992	AUD			47	57
0.00	SCHICK,AG	03	1990	AOS	GORDON,LA	HAKA ,S	199	220
0.00	SCHNEPPER,JA	JL	1977	TAR			653	657
0.00	SHANTEAU,J	02	1989	AOS			165	177
0.00	SIMON ,SI	OC	1964	TAR			884	889
0.00	SIMON ,SI	AP	1965	TAR			401	406
0.00	SLAVIN,NS	AP	1977	TAR			360	368
0.00	SMITH ,G	AU	1988	AUD			108	117
0.00	SMITH ,G	AU	1991	AUD	KROGSTAD,JL		84	97
0.00	SNOWBALL,D	01	1986	AOS			47	70
0.00	STONE ,WE	AP	1969	TAR			284	291
0.00	SWIERINGA,RJ	SP	1989	JAA			169	186
0.00	THANE ,P	04	1992	AOS			299	312
0.00	TINIC ,SM	OC	1990	TAR			781	796
0.00	TOMASSINI,LA	SP	1990	CAR			287	294
0.00	WALKER,SP	03	1991	AOS			257	283
0.00	WARDELL,M		1991	AOS	WEISENFELD,LW		655	670
0.00	WEBER ,C	JL	1963	TAR			534	539
0.00	WEYGANDT,JJ	JA	1970	TAR			69	75
0.00	WILLIAMS,PF	06	1989	AOS			455	468
0.00	WINJUM,JO	OC	1970	TAR			743	761
0.00	WINJUM,JO	JA	1971	TAR			149	155
0.00	YOUNG ,A	WI	1991	JAA			129	133

2.5 RESEARCH METHOD=EMPIRICAL - CASE

CITE INDEX	FIRST AUTHOR	ISS-UE	YE-AR	JOUR-NAL	SECOND AUTHOR	THIRD AUTHOR	PAG BEG	PAG END
2.10	BOLAND,RJ	23	1983	AOS	PONDY ,LR		223	234
2.00	REICHELSTEIN,S	OC	1992	TAR			712	731
1.80	COVALESKI,MA	01	1988	AOS	DIRSMITH,MW		1	24
1.00	HUIZING,A	05	1992	AOS	DEKKER,HC		427	448
1.00	PRESTON,AM	06	1992	AOS	COOPER,DJ	COOMBS,RW	561	593
1.00	ROBERTS,J	02	1990	AOS			107	126
0.80	MARKUS,ML	23	1983	AOS	PFEFFER,J		205	218
0.60	LUKKA ,K	03	1988	AOS			281	301
0.50	BOUGEN,PD	03	1989	AOS			203	234
0.50	KINNEY JR,WR	SP	1987	AUD			59	73
0.45	JONSSON,S	03	1982	AOS			287	304
0.43	PRESTON,A	06	1986	AOS			521	540
0.38	BAKER ,CR	JL	1977	TAR			576	586
0.35	CAMMANN,C	04	1976	AOS			301	314
0.33	MACINTOSH,NB	05	1990	AOS	SCAPENS,RW		455	477
0.33	NEWMAN,DP	SP	1981	JAR			247	262
0.25	GROJER,JE	04	1977	AOS	STARK ,A		349	385
0.24	SCHIFF,M	SP	1966	JAR			62	67
0.21	BLOCHER,E	JL	1979	TAR			563	573
0.20	COLIGNON,R	06	1988	AOS	COVALESKI,M		559	579
0.18	BALOFF,N	AU	1967	JAR	KENNELLY,JW		131	143
0.18	MACY ,BA	23	1976	AOS	MIRVIS,PH		179	194

CITE INDEX	FIRST AUTHOR	ISS-UE	YE-AR	JOUR-NAL	SECOND AUTHOR	THIRD AUTHOR	PAG BEG	PAG END
0.18	MCKEOWN,JC	JA	1971	TAR			12	29
0.18	ZIMMERMAN,JL	AU	1976	JAR			301	319
0.12	DOCKWEILER,RC	OC	1969	TAR			729	742
0.12	FALK ,H	AP	1973	TAR	OPHIR ,T		323	338
0.12	PELES ,YC	SP	1970	JAR			128	137
0.06	ALBRECHT,WS	OC	1976	TAR			824	837
0.06	ALY ,HF	JA	1971	TAR	DUBOFF,JI		119	128
0.06	CHURCHILL,NC	ST	1966	JAR			128	156
0.06	FLOWER,JF	SP	1966	JAR			16	36
0.06	FOGELBERG,G	AU	1971	JAR			215	235
0.06	MCKEOWN,JC	SP	1973	JAR			62	99
0.06	SHANK ,JK	JA	1971	TAR			57	74
0.00	BANKER,RD	AU	1989	JAA	DATAR ,SM	KAPLAN,RS	528	554
0.00	BJORN-ANDERSEN,N	02	1980	AOS	PEDERSEN,PH		203	216
0.00	BOWEN ,RM	JA	1989	TAR	PFEIFFER,GM		152	171
0.00	CHAN ,JL	AP	1978	TAR			309	323
0.00	CLARK ,JJ	OC	1973	TAR	ELGERS,PT		668	678
0.00	CZARNIAWSKA-,B	04	1988	AOS			415	430
0.00	DENT ,AS		1991	AOS			705	732
0.00	EZZAMEL,M	05	1990	AOS	BOURN ,M		399	424
0.00	FELTON,S	AU	1990	CAR	MANN ,H		261	277
0.00	GIBSON,JL	JL	1963	TAR			492	500
0.00	HERTOG,FD	02	1992	AOS	WIELINGA,C		103	128
0.00	HINES JR,JR	AU	1991	JAA			447	479
0.00	HORVITZ,JS	WI	1981	JAA	HAINKEL,M		114	127
0.00	HORVITZ,JS	WI	1985	JAA	COLDWELL,S		86	99
0.00	HUIZING,A	05	1992	AOS	DEKKER,HC		449	458
0.00	JONSON,LC	34	1978	AOS	JONSSON,B	SVENSSON,G	261	268
0.00	JONSSON,S	05	1988	AOS	GRONLUND,A		513	532
0.00	KAPLAN,RS	SP	1983	AUD			52	65
0.00	KISTLER,LH	OC	1967	TAR			758	766
0.00	MILTZ ,D	AU	1991	AUD	CALOMME,GJ	WILLIKENS,M	49	61
0.00	NEU ,D		1992	AOS	WRIGHT,M		645	665
0.00	PETERS,JM	ST	1990	JAR			83	109
0.00	SAPIENZA,SR	JA	1963	TAR			91	101
0.00	SCHATTKE,RW	OC	1965	TAR			805	811
0.00	SPENCER,CH	JA	1965	TAR	BARNISEL,TS		144	153
0.00	STEPHENS,RG	JA	1990	TAR	GOVINDARAJAN,V		242	257
0.00	STEVENSON,RA	AP	1966	TAR			312	317
0.00	WALKER,KB	AU	1991	JAR	MCCLELLAND,LA		371	381
0.00	WILD ,JJ	SP	1987	JAR			139	160
0.00	YOUNG ,DW	OC	1976	TAR			788	799
0.00	ZEFF ,SA	SP	1992	CAR			443	467

2.6 RESEARCH METHOD=EMPIRICAL – FIELD

CITE INDEX	FIRST AUTHOR	ISS-UE	YE-AR	JOUR-NAL	SECOND AUTHOR	THIRD AUTHOR	PAG BEG	PAG END
3.18	BRUNS JR,WJ	AU	1975	JAR	WATERHOUSE,JH		177	203
3.00	BERRY ,AJ	01	1985	AOS	CAPPS ,T	COOPER,D	3	28
2.56	HAYES ,DC	JA	1977	TAR			22	39
2.23	SIMUNIC,DA	SP	1980	JAR			161	190
2.20	OTLEY ,DT	SP	1978	JAR			122	149
2.18	HOPWOOD,AG	ST	1972	JAR			156	182
2.00	FREDERICK,DM	AP	1991	TAR			240	258

CITE INDEX	FIRST AUTHOR	ISS-UE	YE-AR	JOUR-NAL	SECOND AUTHOR	THIRD AUTHOR	PAG BEG	PAG END
2.00	MILANI,K	AP	1975	TAR			274	284
1.45	HYLAS ,RE	OC	1982	TAR	ASHTON,RH		751	765
1.13	FERRIS,KR	JL	1977	TAR			605	615
1.07	COLLINS,F	AP	1978	TAR			324	335
1.06	HOPWOOD,AG	JL	1974	TAR			485	495
1.00	MCNAIR,CJ		1991	AOS			635	653
0.75	LIBBY ,R	OC	1989	TAR	LIBBY ,PA		729	747
0.75	MERCHANT,KA	02	1985	AOS			201	210
0.70	FLAMHOLTZ,EG	23	1983	AOS			153	170
0.67	HEIMAN,VB	OC	1990	TAR			875	890
0.63	MERCHANT,KA	01	1985	AOS			67	86
0.57	BOLAND,RJ	45	1986	AOS	PONDY ,LR		403	422
0.53	SWIERINGA,RJ	ST	1972	JAR	MONCUR,RH		194	209
0.50	BAMBER,EM	AP	1989	TAR	SNOWBALL,D	TUBBS ,RM	285	299
0.50	MERCHANT,G	JL	1989	TAR			500	513
0.50	MERCHANT,KA	JL	1989	TAR	MANZONI,J		539	558
0.50	SHRIVER,KA	JA	1987	TAR			79	96
0.40	FLAMHOLTZ,EG	02	1978	AOS	COOK ,E		115	140
0.36	CUSHING,BE	ST	1979	JAR	SEARFOSS,DG	RANDALL,RH	172	216
0.33	BANKER,RD	AU	1987	JAA	DATAR ,SM	RAJAN ,MV	319	347
0.33	PRATT ,J	02	1981	AOS	JIAMBALVO,J		133	142
0.33	WALLER,WS	OC	1990	TAR	BISHOP,RA		812	836
0.29	MAHER ,MW	AU	1979	JAR	RAMANATHAN,KV	PETERSON,RB	476	503
0.25	AYRES ,FL	AP	1989	TAR	JACKSON,BR	HITE ,PS	300	312
0.25	PRESTON,AM	06	1989	AOS			389	413
0.24	ABDEL-KHALIK,AR	AP	1974	TAR			271	283
0.24	FLAMHOLTZ,EG	ST	1972	JAR			241	266
0.24	SEARFOSS,DG	04	1976	AOS			375	388
0.20	MIRVIS,PH	23	1983	AOS	LAWLER III,EE		175	190
0.18	BROWNELL,P	OC	1982	TAR			766	777
0.18	ORTMAN,RF	AP	1975	TAR			298	304
0.18	PROBST,FR	JA	1971	TAR			113	118
0.18	SORENSEN,JE	OC	1972	TAR	FRANKS,DD		735	746
0.12	CHURCHILL,NC	OC	1965	TAR	COOPER,WW		767	781
0.12	CHURCHILL,NC	OC	1975	TAR	SHANK ,JK		643	656
0.11	ASHTON,AH	JL	1984	TAR			361	375
0.08	HOPPER,TM	04	1980	AOS			401	412
0.07	CARLSSON,J	34	1978	AOS	EHN ,P	ERLANDER,B	249	260
0.07	JACOBS,FH	SP	1978	JAR			190	203
0.06	ARNOLD,DF	AU	1977	JAR	HUEFNER,RJ		245	252
0.06	OGAN ,P	23	1976	AOS			195	218
0.06	SAULS ,EH	JA	1972	TAR			109	115
0.00	ASARE ,SK	AP	1992	TAR			379	393
0.00	ASHTON,RH	SU	1981	JAA	HYLAS ,RE		325	332
0.00	ASHTON,RH	SU	1981	AUD	HYLAS ,RE		12	22
0.00	BARNIV,R	JL	1990	TAR			578	605
0.00	DANIEL,SJ		1991	AOS	REITSPERGER,WD		601	618
0.00	DEFOND,ML	JL	1991	TAR	JIAMBALVO,J		643	655
0.00	DIRSMITH,MW	01	1991	AOS	HASKINS,ME		61	90
0.00	ENGLE ,TJ	WI	1991	JAA			109	121
0.00	FALK ,H	AU	1972	JAR			359	375
0.00	FLAMHOLTZ,EG	04	1987	AOS			309	318
0.00	FOSTER,G	JA	1990	JAE	GUPTA ,M		309	337

CITE INDEX	FIRST AUTHOR	ISS-UE	YE-AR	JOUR-NAL	SECOND AUTHOR	THIRD AUTHOR	PAG BEG	PAG END
0.00	FROGOT,V	JA	1991	TAR	SHEARON,WT		80	99
0.00	HAM ,J	SP	1986	CAR	LOSELL,D	SMIELIAUSKAS,W	311	317
0.00	HARRELL,A	AU	1990	AUD	WRIGHT,A		134	149
0.00	HUSS ,HF	AU	1991	AUD	JACOBS,FA		16	32
0.00	ICERMAN,RC	AU	1990	JAA	HILLISON,WA		527	543
0.00	LUCAS ,HC	OC	1975	TAR			735	746
0.00	MCROBERTS,HA	04	1985	AOS	HUDSON,J		493	502
0.00	SCHNEIDER,A	JL	1990	TAR	WILNER,N		668	681
0.00	SIMNETT,R	JL	1989	TAR	TROTMAN,K		514	528
0.00	TUBBS ,RM	OC	1992	TAR			783	801
0.00	WARREN,CS	SP	1974	JAR			158	177
0.00	WILCOX,KA	01	1977	AOS	SMITH ,CH		81	97
0.00	WILLIAMS,JJ	04	1985	AOS	NEWTON,JD	MORGAN,EA	457	478

2.7 RESEARCH METHOD=EMPIRICAL – LAB

CITE INDEX	FIRST AUTHOR	ISS-UE	YE-AR	JOUR-NAL	SECOND AUTHOR	THIRD AUTHOR	PAG BEG	PAG END
3.00	ABDOLMOHAMMADI,MJ	JA	1987	TAR	WRIGHT,A		1	13
3.00	LIBBY ,R	AU	1985	JAR			648	667
2.71	ASHTON,RH	SP	1974	JAR			143	157
2.40	ASHTON,AH	OC	1988	TAR	ASHTON,RH		623	641
2.35	JOYCE ,EJ	ST	1976	JAR			29	60
2.33	LIBBY ,R	AU	1990	JAR	FREDERICK,DM		348	367
2.18	BROWNELL,P	SP	1982	JAR			12	27
2.00	FREDERICK,DM	AU	1986	JAR	LIBBY ,R		270	290
1.85	ASHTON,RH	SP	1980	JAR	KRAMER,SS		1	15
1.75	MOECKEL,CL	OC	1989	TAR	PLUMLEE,RD		653	666
1.67	BONNER,SE	JA	1990	TAR			72	92
1.67	TUBBS ,RM	AP	1990	TAR	MESSIER JR,WF	KNECHEL,WR	452	460
1.65	DRIVER,MJ	JL	1975	TAR	MOCK ,TJ		490	508
1.58	JOYCE ,EJ	SP	1981	JAR	BIDDLE,GC		120	145
1.50	BROWNELL,P	OC	1981	TAR			844	860
1.43	JIAMBALVO,J	AU	1979	JAR			436	455
1.42	JOYCE ,EJ	AU	1981	JAR	BIDDLE,GC		323	349
1.41	LIBBY ,R	JL	1975	TAR			475	489
1.41	SWIERINGA,RJ	ST	1976	JAR	GIBBINS,M	LARSSON,L	159	187
1.40	BIGGS ,SF	JA	1988	TAR	MOCK ,TJ	WATKINS,PR	148	162
1.36	HAMILTON,RE	AU	1982	JAR	WRIGHT,WF		756	765
1.25	ASHTON,AH	AP	1985	TAR			173	185
1.25	BAIMAN,S	SP	1989	JAR	LEWIS ,BL		1	20
1.25	DEJONG,DV	AU	1985	JAR	FORSYTHE,R	UECKER,WC	753	793
1.24	DERMER,JD	JL	1973	TAR			511	519
1.20	BUTT ,JL	AU	1988	JAR			315	330
1.20	WALLER,WS	01	1988	AOS			87	98
1.18	CORLESS,JC	JL	1972	TAR			556	566
1.10	BIGGS ,SF	SP	1983	JAR	MOCK ,TJ		234	255
1.06	FELIX JR,WL	OC	1976	TAR			800	807
1.06	LIBBY ,R	SP	1975	JAR			150	161
1.00	ABDEL-KHALIK,AR	OC	1974	TAR			743	750
1.00	ASHTON,AH	AP	1991	TAR			218	239
1.00	ASHTON,RH	ST	1976	JAR			1	17
1.00	BOATSMAN,JR	AP	1974	TAR	ROBERTSON,JC		342	352
1.00	BOUWMAN,MJ	01	1987	AOS	FRISHKOFF,PA	FRISHKOFF,P	1	30
1.00	CHOW ,CW	OC	1983	TAR			667	685

CITE INDEX	FIRST AUTHOR	ISS-UE	YE-AR	JOUR-NAL	SECOND AUTHOR	THIRD AUTHOR	PAG BEG	PAG END
1.00	DOPUCH,N	JA	1992	TAR	KING ,RR		97	120
1.00	KING ,RR	SP	1990	CAR	WALLIN,DE		859	892
1.00	KING ,RR	SP	1991	JAR	WALLIN,DE		96	108
1.00	KINNEY JR,WR	JA	1982	TAR	UECKER,WC		55	69
1.00	MCGHEE,W	JL	1978	TAR	SHIELDS,MD	BIRNBERG,JG	681	697
1.00	MOSER ,DV	JL	1989	TAR			433	448
1.00	SOLOMON,I	AU	1982	JAR			689	710
1.00	WALLIN,DE	JA	1992	TAR			121	147
0.93	BENBASAT,I	OC	1979	TAR	DEXTER,AS		735	749
0.92	ABDEL-KHALIK,AR	AU	1980	JAR	EL-SHESHAI,KM		325	342
0.90	LEWIS ,BL	SP	1983	JAR	SHIELDS,MD	YOUNG ,SM	271	285
0.90	SHIELDS,MD	AP	1983	TAR			284	303
0.88	BAREFIELD,RM	AU	1972	JAR			229	242
0.88	DEJONG,DV	ST	1985	JAR	FORSYTHE,R	LUNDHOLM,RJ	81	120
0.88	MORIARITY,S	AU	1976	JAR	BARRON,FH		320	341
0.88	YOUNG ,SM	AU	1985	JAR			829	842
0.87	UECKER,WC	SP	1978	JAR			169	189
0.85	CASEY JR,CJ	JA	1980	TAR			36	49
0.85	LEWIS ,BL	AU	1980	JAR			594	602
0.85	SHIELDS,MD	04	1980	AOS			429	442
0.85	WEBER ,R	SP	1980	JAR			214	241
0.82	CHERRINGTON,DJ	ST	1973	JAR	CHERRINGTON,JO		225	253
0.82	ELIAS ,N	ST	1972	JAR			215	233
0.81	HOFSTEDT,TR	AP	1977	TAR	HUGHES,GD		379	395
0.80	CHOW ,CW	JA	1988	TAR	COOPER,JC	WALLER,WS	111	122
0.78	KAPLAN,SE	AU	1984	AUD	RECKERS,PMJ		1	19
0.78	KIDA ,TE	SP	1984	JAR			332	340
0.75	BUTT ,JL	06	1989	AOS	CAMPBELL,TL		471	479
0.75	CROSBY,MA	AP	1981	TAR			355	365
0.75	LIBBY ,R	AP	1985	TAR	ARTMAN,JT	WILLINGHAM,JJ	212	230
0.75	WALLER,WS	JL	1985	TAR	CHOW ,CW		458	476
0.71	ABDEL-KHALIK,AR	ST	1973	JAR			104	138
0.71	DICKHAUT,JW	JA	1973	TAR			61	79
0.71	FORAN ,MF	OC	1974	TAR	DECOSTER,DT		751	763
0.71	MOCK ,TJ	SP	1972	JAR	ESTRIN,TL	VASARHELYI,MA	129	153
0.69	ASHTON,RH	SP	1980	JAR	BROWN ,PR		269	277
0.69	KIDA ,TE	AU	1980	JAR			506	523
0.69	ROCKNESS,HO	OC	1977	TAR			893	903
0.69	UECKER,WC	03	1977	AOS	KINNEY JR,WR		269	275
0.67	ASHTON,RH	ST	1990	JAR			148	186
0.67	AWASTHI,V	OC	1990	TAR	PRATT ,J		797	811
0.67	BONNER,SE	ST	1990	JAR	LEWIS ,BL		1	28
0.67	ELIAS ,N	JL	1990	TAR			606	623
0.67	HASKINS,ME	SP	1990	CAR	BAGLIONI,AJ	COOPER,CL	361	385
0.67	KACHELMEIER,SJ	JA	1990	TAR	MESSIER JR,WF		209	226
0.67	KROGSTAD,JL	AU	1984	AUD	ETTENSON,RT	SHANTEAU,J	54	74
0.67	PONEMON,LA	AU	1990	CAR	GABHART,DRL		227	251
0.65	HARIED,AA	AU	1972	JAR			376	391
0.65	HOFSTEDT,TR	OC	1972	TAR			679	692
0.65	ROSE ,R	ST	1970	JAR	BEAVER,WH	BECKER,S	138	148
0.65	SAN MIGUEL,JG	04	1976	AOS			357	374
0.64	GAUMNITZ,BR	AU	1982	JAR	NUNAMAKER,TR	SURDICK,JJ	745	755
0.64	LIBBY ,R	SP	1979	JAR			99	122

CITE INDEX	FIRST AUTHOR	ISS-UE	YE-AR	JOUR-NAL	SECOND AUTHOR	THIRD AUTHOR	PAG BEG	PAG END
0.64	MORIARITY,S	SP	1979	JAR			205	224
0.64	SOLOMON,I	01	1982	AOS	KROGSTAD,JL	ROMNEY,MB	27	42
0.63	HARRELL,AM	OC	1977	TAR			833	841
0.63	WRIGHT,WF	JL	1977	TAR			676	689
0.60	ABDEL-KHALIK,AR	SP	1978	JAR	ESPEJO,J		1	13
0.60	FRECKA,TJ	JA	1983	TAR	HOPWOOD,WS		115	128
0.60	JIAMBALVO,J	01	1983	AOS	WATSON,DJ	BAUMLER,JV	13	30
0.59	CHESLEY,GR	SP	1976	JAR			27	48
0.59	KENNEDY,HA	SP	1975	JAR			97	116
0.59	PANKOFF,LD	ST	1970	JAR	VIRGIL JR,RL		1	48
0.58	HILTON,RW	SP	1981	JAR	SWIERINGA,RJ	HOSKIN,RE	86	108
0.58	LARCKER,DF	JL	1981	TAR			519	538
0.57	HANSEN,JV	AU	1986	AUD	MESSIER JR,WF		109	123
0.57	LIBBY ,R	ST	1979	JAR			35	57
0.57	MARGHEIM,LL	SP	1986	AUD	PANY ,K		50	63
0.57	MESERVY,RD	AU	1986	AUD	BAILEY JR,AD	JOHNSON,PE	44	74
0.57	MORIARITY,S	ST	1979	JAR	BARRON,FH		114	135
0.57	SHPILBERG,D	AU	1986	AUD	GRAHAM,LE		75	94
0.56	BOUWMAN,MJ	34	1984	AOS			325	327
0.56	CHESLEY,GR	SP	1977	JAR			1	11
0.54	SNOWBALL,D	03	1980	AOS			323	340
0.53	SCHULTZ JR,JJ	JL	1978	TAR	GUSTAVSON,SG		626	641
0.50	ASHTON,RH	SP	1981	JAR			42	61
0.50	BECK ,PJ	JL	1991	TAR	DAVIS ,JS	JUNG ,W	535	558
0.50	BEDARD,JC	JL	1991	TAR	BIGGS ,SF		622	642
0.50	BIGGS ,SF	OC	1985	TAR	WILD ,JJ		607	633
0.50	BIGGS ,SF	SP	1987	AUD	MESSIER JR,WF	HANSEN,JV	1	21
0.50	BROWN ,C	JL	1987	TAR	SOLOMON,I		564	577
0.50	BROWN ,CE	JA	1991	TAR	SOLOMON,I		100	119
0.50	CHOO ,F	JL	1991	TAR	TROTMAN,KT		464	485
0.50	CHURCH,BK	SP	1991	CAR			513	534
0.50	COHEN ,J	AU	1989	JAR	KIDA ,T		263	276
0.50	FARMER,TA	AU	1987	AUD	RITTENBERG,LE	TROMPETER,GM	1	14
0.50	HARRELL,A	03	1989	AOS	TAYLOR,M	CHEWNING,E	259	269
0.50	SPIRES,EE	AP	1991	TAR			259	276
0.50	VASARHELYI,MA	SP	1977	JAR			138	153
0.50	WALLER,WS	AP	1987	TAR	FELIX JR,WL		275	292
0.47	COOK ,DM	ST	1967	JAR			213	224
0.47	DOPUCH,N	AU	1973	JAR	RONEN ,J		191	211
0.47	LUSK ,EJ	ST	1973	JAR			191	202
0.47	MAGEE ,RP	AU	1978	JAR	DICKHAUT,JW		294	314
0.47	RONEN ,J	AU	1971	JAR			307	332
0.47	SCHWAN,ES	23	1976	AOS			219	238
0.47	WARD ,BH	SP	1976	JAR			138	152
0.45	DANOS ,P	JA	1982	TAR	IMHOFF JR,EA		39	54
0.45	EGER ,C	AU	1982	JAR	DICKHAUT,JW		711	723
0.44	ARRINGTON,CE	SP	1984	JAR	HILLISON,WA	JENSEN,RE	298	312
0.44	NANNI JR,AJ	02	1984	AOS			149	163
0.44	SAVICH,RS	JL	1977	TAR			642	652
0.44	STOCK ,D	SP	1984	JAR	WATSON,CJ		192	206
0.43	BARNES,P	01	1986	AOS	WEBB ,J		1	18
0.43	BROWN ,PR	AU	1986	AUD	KARAN ,V		134	147
0.43	BURGSTAHLER,D	AP	1986	TAR	JIAMBALVO,J		233	248

CITE INDEX	FIRST AUTHOR	ISS-UE	YE-AR	JOUR-NAL	SECOND AUTHOR	THIRD AUTHOR	PAG BEG	PAG END
0.43	MURRAY,D	AU	1986	JAR	FRAZIER,KB		400	404
0.42	HILTON,RW	SP	1981	JAR	SWIERINGA,RJ		109	119
0.42	KESSLER,L	SP	1981	JAR	ASHTON,RH		146	162
0.42	SHIELDS,MD	01	1981	AOS	BIRNBERG,JG	FRIEZE,IH	69	96
0.41	ANSARI,SL	AU	1976	JAR			189	211
0.41	DICKHAUT,JW	SP	1975	JAR	EGGLETON,IRC		38	72
0.41	DYCKMAN,TR	SP	1964	JAR			91	107
0.41	FLAMHOLTZ,EG	23	1976	AOS			153	166
0.41	HENDRICKS,JA	AP	1976	TAR			292	305
0.41	JENSEN,RE	AU	1966	JAR			224	238
0.41	OLIVER,BL	SP	1972	JAR			154	166
0.40	ABDEL-KHALIK,AR	AP	1983	TAR	SNOWBALL,D	WRAGGE,JH	215	227
0.40	CHESLEY,GR	AU	1978	JAR			225	241
0.40	HOSKIN,RE	SP	1983	JAR			78	95
0.40	ISELIN,ER	02	1988	AOS			147	164
0.40	LARCKER,DF	JA	1983	TAR	LESSIG,VP		58	77
0.40	MIA ,L	05	1988	AOS			465	475
0.40	NEUMANN,BR	AU	1978	JAR	FRIEDMAN,LA		400	410
0.40	SHOCKLEY,RA	AU	1983	JAR	HOLT ,RN		545	564
0.40	WEBER ,R	AU	1978	JAR			368	388
0.40	YOUNG ,SM	06	1988	AOS	SHIELDS,MD	WOLF ,G	607	618
0.38	ANDERSON,MJ	AU	1985	JAR			843	852
0.38	KNAPP ,MC	AP	1985	TAR			202	211
0.38	PLUMLEE,RD	AU	1985	JAR			683	699
0.38	SCHNEIDER,A	AU	1985	JAR			911	919
0.38	UECKER,WC	SP	1980	JAR			191	213
0.36	DYCKMAN,TR	01	1982	AOS	HOSKIN,RE	SWIERINGA,RJ	1	12
0.36	WILNER,N	01	1982	AOS			43	52
0.35	BECKER,S	AU	1974	JAR	RONEN ,J	SORTER,GH	317	329
0.35	EGGLETON,IRC	ST	1976	JAR			68	131
0.35	MCINTYRE,EV	JL	1973	TAR			575	585
0.33	BROWN ,C	SP	1981	JAR			62	85
0.33	BROWN ,CE	AU	1990	AUD	SOLOMON,I		17	38
0.33	CHALOS,P	JL	1990	TAR	HAKA ,S		624	641
0.33	DANOS ,P	OC	1984	TAR	HOLT ,DL	IMHOFF JR,EA	547	573
0.33	FERRIS,KR	SP	1984	AUD	TENNANT,KL		31	43
0.33	GUL ,FA	AP	1984	TAR			264	277
0.33	HALL ,TW	JL	1990	TAR	SHRIVER,KA		537	556
0.33	JENNINGS,M	SP	1987	AUD	KNEER ,DC	RECKERS,PMJ	104	115
0.33	KNECHEL,WR	SP	1990	CAR	MESSIER JR,WF		386	406
0.33	MCDANIEL,LS	AU	1990	JAR			267	285
0.33	MOECKEL,C	AU	1990	JAR			368	387
0.33	RICCHIUTE,DN	SP	1984	JAR			341	350
0.33	SCHNEIDER,A	AU	1984	JAR			657	678
0.33	SHIELDS,MD	04	1987	AOS	SOLOMON,I	WALLER,WS	375	385
0.33	UECKER,WC	JL	1981	TAR	BRIEF ,AP	KINNEY JR,WR	465	478
0.31	BELKAOUI,A	03	1980	AOS			263	284
0.31	HOLT ,RN	03	1980	AOS	CARROLL,R		285	296
0.30	BROWN ,PR	AU	1983	JAR			444	455
0.30	SCHEPANSKI,A	JL	1983	TAR			581	599
0.30	STEPHENS,RG	AU	1983	AUD			55	74
0.30	TROTMAN,KT	SP	1983	JAR	YETTON,PW	ZIMMER,I	286	292

CITE INDEX	FIRST AUTHOR	ISSUE	YEAR	JOURNAL	SECOND AUTHOR	THIRD AUTHOR	PAG BEG	PAG END
0.29	ABDOLMOHAMMADI,MJ	SP	1986	AUD			1	16
0.29	BARRETT,ME	ST	1971	JAR			50	65
0.29	BORITZ,JE	AU	1986	JAR			335	348
0.29	FIRTH ,MA	04	1979	AOS			283	296
0.29	HAKA ,S	JL	1986	TAR	FRIEDMAN,L	JONES ,V	455	474
0.29	MARGHEIM,LL	SP	1986	JAR			194	205
0.29	MOCK ,TJ	ST	1969	JAR			124	159
0.29	RECKERS,PMJ	AU	1979	JAA	TAYLOR,ME		42	55
0.29	STALLMAN,JC	ST	1969	JAR			29	43
0.27	ASHTON,AH	AU	1982	JAR			415	428
0.27	BALLEW,V	JA	1982	TAR			88	104
0.27	DANOS ,P	WI	1982	AUD	IMHOFF JR,EA		23	34
0.27	JIAMBALVO,J	SP	1982	JAR			152	161
0.27	KEYS ,DE	AU	1978	JAR			389	399
0.25	ARANYA,N	04	1981	AOS	POLLOCK,J	AMERNIC,J	271	280
0.25	ARRINGTON,CE	SP	1985	JAR	BAILEY,CD	HOPWOOD,WS	1	20
0.25	BROWN ,C	03	1985	AOS			255	266
0.25	BUCHMAN,TA	03	1985	AOS			267	286
0.25	BUTLER,SA	AU	1985	JAR			513	526
0.25	DAMOS ,P	03	1989	AOS	HOLT ,DL	IMHOFF JR,EA	235	246
0.25	DEJONG,DV	02	1989	AOS	FORSYTHE,R	KIM ,JA	41	64
0.25	DOPUCH,N		1989	AUD	KING ,RR	WALLIN,DE	98	127
0.25	HARRISON,KE	SP	1989	CAR	TOMASSINI,LA		642	648
0.25	KEASEY,K	04	1989	AOS	WATSON,R		337	345
0.25	LUCKETT,PF	06	1989	AOS	HIRST ,MK		379	387
0.25	MADEO ,SA	JL	1985	TAR	PINCUS,M		407	429
0.25	MAYPER,AG	AU	1989	AUD	DOUCET,MS	WARREN,CS	72	86
0.25	MILLIRON,VC	AU	1985	JAR			794	816
0.25	SELLING,T	02	1989	AOS	SHANK ,J		65	77
0.25	TROTMAN,KT	SP	1985	JAR	YETTON,PW		256	267
0.25	TROTMAN,KT	AU	1985	JAR			740	752
0.25	TURNER,MJ	AU	1989	JAR	HILTON,RW		297	312
0.25	UECKER,WC	JL	1985	TAR	SCHEPANSKI,A	SHIN ,J	430	457
0.25	WALLER,WS	AU	1985	JAR			817	828
0.24	BRUNS JR,WJ	AP	1965	TAR			345	357
0.24	CHANDRA,G	OC	1974	TAR			733	742
0.24	DYCKMAN,TR	AP	1964	TAR			285	295
0.24	HEINTZ,JA	OC	1973	TAR			679	689
0.24	HOLSTRUM,GL	AU	1971	JAR			268	277
0.24	MOCK ,TJ	JL	1973	TAR			520	534
0.23	FRIEDMAN,LA	AU	1980	JAR	NEUMANN,BR		407	419
0.23	PANY ,K	JA	1980	TAR	RECKERS,PMJ		50	61
0.22	BIGGS ,SF	34	1984	AOS			313	323
0.22	CAMPBELL,JE	34	1984	AOS			329	342
0.22	KIDA ,TE	SP	1984	JAR			145	152
0.22	SHIELDS,MD	34	1984	AOS			355	363
0.22	WALLER,WS	OC	1984	TAR	FELIX JR,WL		637	646
0.20	ANDERSON,MJ	05	1988	AOS			431	446
0.20	BAMBER,EM	AU	1983	JAR			396	412
0.20	ENIS ,CR	02	1988	AOS			123	145
0.20	HARRISON,PD	AP	1988	TAR	WEST ,SG	RENEAU,JH	307	320
0.20	HILTON,RW	AP	1988	TAR	SWIERINGA,RJ	TURNER,MJ	195	218
0.20	HIRSCH JR,ML	AU	1978	JAR			254	269

CITE INDEX	FIRST AUTHOR	ISS-UE	YE-AR	JOUR-NAL	SECOND AUTHOR	THIRD AUTHOR	PAG BEG	PAG END
0.20	HOLDER,WW	SP	1983	AUD			100	108
0.20	JOHNSON,WB	JA	1983	TAR			78	97
0.20	LEWIS ,BL	AP	1988	TAR	PATTON,JM	GREEN ,SL	270	282
0.20	SHIELDS,MD	06	1988	AOS	WALLER,WS		581	594
0.20	TABOR ,RH	SP	1983	JAR			348	354
0.19	GORDON,FE	04	1977	AOS	RHODE ,JG	MERCHANT,KA	295	306
0.19	WRIGHT,WF	04	1977	AOS			323	332
0.18	BENBASAT,I	SP	1982	JAR	DEXTER,AS		1	11
0.18	DASCHER,PE	SP	1971	JAR	COPELAND,RM		32	39
0.18	EGGLETON,IRC	SP	1982	JAR			68	102
0.18	FALK ,H	SP	1973	JAR	OPHIR ,T		108	116
0.18	OTLEY ,DT	SP	1982	JAR	DIAS ,FJB		171	188
0.18	PRATT ,J	SP	1982	JAR			189	209
0.18	WRIGHT,A	SP	1982	JAR			227	239
0.17	CHEN ,K	01	1981	AOS	SUMMERS,EL		1	16
0.17	COVALESKI,MA	SP	1987	CAR	DIRSMITH,MW	WHITE ,CE	408	429
0.17	HOLT ,DL	06	1987	AOS			571	578
0.17	HOUGHTON,KA	02	1987	AOS			143	152
0.17	RECKERS,PMJ	SU	1981	AUD	STAGLIANO,AJ		23	37
0.15	HARRELL,AM	04	1980	AOS	KLICK ,HD		393	400
0.14	ARANYA,N	AU	1986	CAR	WHEELER,JT		184	199
0.14	BLOCHER,E	06	1986	AOS	MOFFIE,RP	ZMUD ,RW	457	470
0.14	BUTLER,SA	JA	1986	TAR			101	111
0.14	CASEY JR,CJ	AP	1986	TAR	SELLING,T		302	317
0.14	CHESLEY,GR	SP	1986	CAR			179	199
0.14	DAVIS ,GB	SP	1986	AUD	WEBER ,R		35	49
0.14	HARVEY,DW	03	1979	AOS	RHODE ,JG	MERCHANT,KA	187	210
0.14	LICATA,MP	JA	1986	TAR	STRAWSER,RH	WELKER,RB	112	117
0.14	RICCHIUTE,DN	12	1979	AOS			67	76
0.14	WRIGHT,A	SP	1986	AUD			86	94
0.13	BORITZ,JE	SP	1985	CAR			193	218
0.13	KAPLAN,SE	AU	1985	AUD			12	25
0.13	KAPLAN,SE	AU	1985	JAR			871	877
0.13	KELLY ,LK	JA	1977	TAR			97	108
0.13	MCKINELY,S	AU	1985	JAR	PANY ,K	RECKERS,PMJ	887	896
0.13	PATTON,JM	AP	1978	TAR			402	414
0.13	TOMASSINI,LA	OC	1977	TAR			904	913
0.12	ACLAND,D	23	1976	AOS			133	142
0.12	DERMER,JD	JA	1974	TAR	SIEGEL,JP		88	97
0.12	MCDONALD,DL	SP	1968	JAR			38	49
0.12	PANKOFF,LD	AP	1970	TAR	VIRGIL JR,RL		269	279
0.12	RONEN ,J	OC	1973	TAR	FALK ,G		696	717
0.12	STERLING,RR	SP	1969	JAR	RADOSEVICH,R		90	95
0.11	BLOOM ,R	01	1984	AOS	ELGERS,PT	MURRAY,D	1	11
0.11	DAROCA,FP	01	1984	AOS			13	32
0.11	JIAMBALVO,J	SP	1984	AUD	WALLER,WS		80	88
0.10	BLOCHER,E	AU	1983	AUD	ESPOSITO,RS	WILLINGHAM,JJ	75	91
0.10	BROWN ,C	AU	1983	JAR			413	431
0.10	DANOS ,P	AU	1983	JAR	IMHOFF JR,EA		473	494
0.10	GOMBOLA,MJ	JA	1983	TAR	KETZ ,JE		105	114
0.10	TILLER,MG	AU	1983	JAR			581	595
0.10	WILKINS,T	OC	1983	TAR	ZIMMER,I		749	764
0.09	JIAMBALVO,J	OC	1982	TAR	PRATT ,J		734	750

CITE INDEX	FIRST AUTHOR	ISS-UE	YE-AR	JOUR-NAL	SECOND AUTHOR	THIRD AUTHOR	PAG BEG	PAG END
0.09	RECKERS,PMJ	AU	1982	AUD	SCHULTZ JR,JJ		64	74
0.09	UECKER,WC	AU	1982	JAR			388	402
0.08	COPELAND,RM	SP	1981	JAR	TAYLOR,RL	BROWN ,SH	197	207
0.08	FERRIS,KR	04	1980	AOS	DILLARD,JF	NETHERCOTT,L	361	368
0.08	KOCH ,BS	JL	1981	TAR			574	586
0.08	RAMANATHAN,KV	02	1981	AOS	WEIS ,WL		143	152
0.06	BOLLOM,WJ	JA	1973	TAR			12	22
0.06	BRUNS JR,WJ	ST	1966	JAR			1	14
0.06	DALTON,FE	JA	1970	TAR	MINER ,JB		134	139
0.06	GREER JR,WR	JL	1974	TAR			496	505
0.06	MCCOSH,AM	04	1976	AOS	RAHMAN,M		339	356
0.06	SAULS ,EH	ST	1970	JAR			157	171
0.06	SPILLER JR,EA	SP	1974	JAR	VIRGIL JR,RL		112	142
0.06	UECKER,WC	01	1977	AOS			47	58
0.00	ABDEL-KHALIK,AR	AU	1986	JAR	GRAUL ,PR	NEWTON,JD	372	382
0.00	ABDOLMOHAMMADI,MJ	AU	1986	CAR	BERGER,PD		149	165
0.00	ABDOLMOHAMMADI,MJ	SP	1991	CAR			535	548
0.00	AFFLECK-GRAVES,J	SP	1990	CAR	DAVIS ,LR	MENDENHALL,RR	501	517
0.00	ANDERSON JR,TN	AU	1982	JAR	KIDA ,TE		403	414
0.00	ANDERSON,JC	AU	1992	AUD	KAPLAN,SE	RECKERS,PMJ	1	13
0.00	ANDERSON,MJ	OC	1990	TAR	ANDERSON,U	HELLELOID,R	857	874
0.00	ANDERSON,U		1989	AUD	MARCHANT,G		101	115
0.00	ARNOLD,DF	AU	1991	AUD	PONEMON,LA		1	15
0.00	BAILEY,CD	SP	1986	AUD	BALLARD,G		77	85
0.00	BAILEY,CD	AP	1992	TAR	MCINTYRE,EV		368	378
0.00	BAILEY,KE	AU	1983	JAR	BYLINSKI,JH	SHIELDS,MD	355	370
0.00	BAILEY,WT	OC	1981	TAR			882	896
0.00	BAMBER,EM	AU	1987	CAR	BYLINSKI,JH		127	143
0.00	BAMBER,EM	JL	1988	AUD	SNOWBALL,D		490	504
0.00	BAMBER,EM	SP	1988	AUD	BAMBER,LS	BYLINSKI,JH	137	149
0.00	BARTON,RF	SP	1969	JAR			116	122
0.00	BECK ,PJ	AU	1992	CAR	DAVIS ,JS	JUNG ,W-O	86	112
0.00	BEDARD,JC		1991	AUD	BIGGS ,SF		77	90
0.00	BELKAOUI,A	AU	1985	CAR			111	123
0.00	BLOCHER,E	AU	1985	AUD	BYLINSKI,JH		79	90
0.00	BLOCHER,E	SP	1988	AUD	COOPER,JC		1	28
0.00	BORITZ,JE	SP	1988	CAR	GABER ,BG	LEMON ,WM	392	411
0.00	BORITZ,JE	AU	1992	AUD	WENSLEY,AKP		14	29
0.00	BROWN ,C	AU	1987	CAR			111	126
0.00	CARPENTER,BW		1992	AOS	DIRSMITH,MW		709	739
0.00	CASTER,P	AU	1990	AUD			75	91
0.00	CHALOS,P	AU	1985	JAR			527	543
0.00	CHENHALL,R	01	1991	AOS	MORRIS,D		27	46
0.00	CHEWNING,EG	06	1990	AOS	HARRELL,AM		527	542
0.00	CHOW ,CW	03	1991	AOS	SHIELDS,MD	CHAN ,YK	209	226
0.00	CHOW,CW	01	1991	AOS	COOPER,JC	HADDAD,K	47	60
0.00	COLBERT,JL	02	1988	AOS			111	121
0.00	COLLINS,KM	06	1992	AOS	KILLOUGH,LN		535	547
0.00	COOPER,JC	03	1991	AOS	SELTO ,FH		227	242
0.00	DALY ,BA	SP	1990	JAR	OMER ,T		193	197
0.00	DANIEL,SJ	SP	1988	AUD			174	181
0.00	DAS ,H	03	1986	AOS			215	232
0.00	DAVIS ,LR	06	1989	AOS			495	508

CITE INDEX	FIRST AUTHOR	ISS-UE	YE-AR	JOUR-NAL	SECOND AUTHOR	THIRD AUTHOR	PAG BEG	PAG END
0.00	DESANCTIS,G	06	1989	AOS	JARVENPAA,SL		509	525
0.00	DILLA ,WN	JL	1989	TAR			404	432
0.00	DILLARD,JF		1991	AOS	KAUFFMAN,NL	SPIRES,EE	619	633
0.00	DOPUCH,N	ST	1991	JAR	KING ,RR		60	106
0.00	DYKXHOORN,HJ	04	1982	AOS	SINNING,KE		337	348
0.00	FISHER,MH		1990	AUD			184	223
0.00	FREDERICKSON,JR	OC	1992	TAR			647	670
0.00	FRISHKOFF,P	AU	1984	JAA	FRISHKOFF,PA	BOUWMAN,MJ	44	53
0.00	GRAHAM,LE	SP	1991	AUD	DAMENS,J	VAN NESS,G	69	96
0.00	GUL ,FA	34	1984	AOS			233	239
0.00	HACKENBRACK,K	SP	1992	JAR			126	136
0.00	HARPER JR,RM	AU	1987	JAR	MISTER,WG	STRAWSER,JR	327	330
0.00	HARRELL,AM	34	1984	AOS	STAHL ,MJ		241	252
0.00	HASSELL,JM	06	1989	AOS	ARRINGTON,CE		527	537
0.00	HAYES ,RD	JL	1990	TAR	MILLAR,JA		505	519
0.00	HEINTZ,JA	SP	1989	AUD	WHITE ,GB		22	39
0.00	HOLT ,DL	06	1992	AOS	MORROW,PC		549	559
0.00	HOUGHTON,KA	AU	1984	JAR	SENGUPTA,R		768	775
0.00	HOUGHTON,KA	03	1988	AOS			263	280
0.00	JEFFREY,C	OC	1992	TAR			802	820
0.00	JENNINGS,MM	SP	1991	CAR	KNEER ,DC	RECKERS,PMJ	449	465
0.00	JOHNSON,DA	SP	1983	AUD	PANY ,K	WHITE ,RA	38	51
0.00	JOHNSON,DA	AU	1984	JAR	PANY ,K		731	743
0.00	JOHNSON,VE		1991	AUD	KAPLAN,SE		96	107
0.00	JOHNSON,WB	04	1982	AOS			349	368
0.00	KACHELMEIER,SJ	OC	1991	TAR	LIMBERG,ST	SCHADEWALD,MS	694	717
0.00	KACHELMEIER,SJ		1991	AUD			25	48
0.00	KANPP ,MC	SP	1991	AUD			35	52
0.00	KAPLAN,SE	04	1988	AOS	RECKERS,PMJ	ROARK ,SJ	371	379
0.00	KAPLAN,SE	06	1989	AOS	RECKERS,PMJ		539	550
0.00	KAPLAN,SE	AU	1992	AUD	MOECKEL,C	WILLIAMS,JD	50	65
0.00	KELLY ,AS	AU	1989	AUD	MOHRWEIS,CS		87	97
0.00	KHEMAKHEM,A	JL	1968	TAR			522	534
0.00	KIM ,DC	AP	1992	TAR			303	319
0.00	KIRBY ,AJ	SP	1992	CAR			374	408
0.00	KNAPP ,MC	JL	1987	TAR			578	588
0.00	KOONCE,L	JA	1992	TAR			59	76
0.00	LEWIS ,BL	SP	1985	JAR	BELL ,J		228	239
0.00	LIBBY ,R	AU	1992	JAR	LIPE ,MG		249	273
0.00	LORD ,AT	AU	1992	AUD			89	108
0.00	LUNDHOLM,RJ	JL	1991	TAR			486	515
0.00	MADEO ,SA	AP	1987	TAR	SCHEPANSKI,A	UECKER,WC	323	342
0.00	MAINES,LA	ST	1990	JAR			29	54
0.00	MAYPER,AG	AU	1982	JAR			773	783
0.00	MCKENNA,EF	03	1980	AOS			297	310
0.00	MEADE ,JA	AP	1990	TAR			406	431
0.00	MEAR ,R	JA	1987	TAR	FIRTH ,MA		176	182
0.00	MEAR ,RWT	AU	1990	JAA	FIRTH ,MA		501	520
0.00	MEIXNER,WF	JL	1988	AUD	WELKER,RB		505	513
0.00	MESSIER JR,WF	SP	1988	CAR	SCHNEIDER,A		337	353
0.00	MOECKEL,C	SP	1990	CAR	WILLIAMS,JD		850	858
0.00	MOON ,P	03	1990	AOS			193	198
0.00	MUNTER,P	WI	1983	JAA	RATCLIFFE,TA		108	114

CITE INDEX	FIRST AUTHOR	ISS-UE	YE-AR	JOUR-NAL	SECOND AUTHOR	THIRD AUTHOR	PAG BEG	PAG END
0.00	NAIR ,RD	AU	1987	AUD	RITTENBERG,LE		15	38
0.00	O'BRIEN,JR	SP	1992	JAA			117	134
0.00	PANY ,K	AU	1982	JAR	SMITH ,CH		472	481
0.00	PANY ,K	AU	1987	AUD	RECKERS,PMJ		39	53
0.00	PEI ,BKW	SP	1989	AUD	DAVIS ,FG		101	112
0.00	PEI ,BKW	02	1992	AOS	REED ,SA	KOCH ,BS	169	183
0.00	PILLSBURY,CM	SP	1985	AUD			63	79
0.00	PINCUS	02	1989	AOS			153	163
0.00	PINCUS,KV	AU	1990	AUD			150	167
0.00	PONEMON,LA	AU	1991	AUD	SCHICK,AG		70	83
0.00	PONEMON,LA	AU	1992	CAR			171	189
0.00	PONEMON,LA	04	1992	AOS			239	258
0.00	PORCANO,TM	OC	1984	TAR			619	636
0.00	PURDY ,CR	ST	1969	JAR	SMITH JR,JM	GRAY ,J	1	18
0.00	PURVIS,SEC	06	1989	AOS			551	563
0.00	RAGHUNANDAN,K	SP	1991	CAR	GRIMLUND,RA	SCHEPANSKI,A	549	568
0.00	REBELE,JE	AU	1988	AUD	HEINTZ,JA	BRIDEN,GE	43	52
0.00	REIMERS,JL	02	1992	AOS	BUTLER,SA		185	194
0.00	RICCHIUTE,DN	JA	1992	TAR			46	58
0.00	RODGERS,W	WI	1992	JAA			67	95
0.00	SCHATZBERG,JW	AP	1990	TAR			337	362
0.00	SHIELDS,MD	AU	1988	CAR	SOLOMON,I	WALLER,WS	1	18
0.00	SINGER,FA	OC	1965	TAR			847	853
0.00	SRINIDHI,BN	SP	1986	AUD	VASARHELYI,MA		64	76
0.00	STERLING,RR	OC	1972	TAR	TOLLEFSON,SO	FLAHERTY,RE	709	721
0.00	STRAWSER,JR	SP	1991	AUD			126	135
0.00	TROTMAN,KT	06	1989	AOS	SNG ,J		565	576
0.00	VASARHELYI,MA	SP	1991	AUD	HALPER,FB		110	125
0.00	WAGGONER,JB	SP	1990	AUD			77	89
0.00	WALLER,WS	02	1989	AOS	FELIX JR,WL		179	200
0.00	WONG-ON-WING,B	06	1989	AOS	RENEAU,JH	WEST ,SG	577	587
0.00	WRIGHT,A	JL	1983	TAR			621	632
0.00	WRIGHT,A	06	1988	AOS			595	605
0.00	WRIGHT,WF	AU	1988	CAR			47	57
0.00	YARDLEY,JA	AU	1989	AUD			41	56

2.8 RESEARCH METHOD=OPINION – SURVEY

CITE INDEX	FIRST AUTHOR	ISS-UE	YE-AR	JOUR-NAL	SECOND AUTHOR	THIRD AUTHOR	PAG BEG	PAG END
2.78	COOPER,DJ	34	1984	AOS	SHERER,MJ		207	232
2.25	MERCHANT,KA	OC	1981	TAR			813	829
1.93	KENIS ,I	OC	1979	TAR			707	721
1.67	GOVINDARAJAN,V	02	1984	AOS			125	135
1.57	BROWNELL,P	OC	1986	TAR	MCINNES,M		587	600
1.50	FRANCIS,JR	JA	1987	TAR	SIMON ,DT		145	157
1.38	GOVINDARAJAN,V	01	1985	AOS	GUPTA ,AK		51	66
1.35	DECOSTER,DT	AU	1968	JAR	FERTAKIS,JP		237	246
1.33	MERCHANT,KA	34	1984	AOS			291	309
1.30	EICHENSEHER,JW	SP	1983	AUD	SHIELDS,D		23	37
1.18	ONSI ,M	JL	1973	TAR			535	548
1.17	ANSARI,SL	06	1987	AOS	EUSKE ,KJ		549	570
1.14	BROWNELL,P	AU	1986	JAR	HIRST ,MK		241	249
1.14	COVALESKI,MA	03	1986	AOS	DIRSMITH,MW		193	214
1.14	KREUTZFELDT,RW	AU	1986	AUD	WALLACE,WA		20	43

CITE INDEX	FIRST AUTHOR	ISS-UE	YE-AR	JOUR-NAL	SECOND AUTHOR	THIRD AUTHOR	PAG BEG	PAG END
1.12	KHANDWALLA,PN	AU	1972	JAR			275	285
1.00	PINCH ,T	03	1989	AOS	MULKAY,M	ASHMORE,M	271	301
1.00	WRIGHT,A	OC	1989	TAR	ASHTON,RH		710	728
0.89	GORDON,LA	01	1984	AOS	NARAYANAN,VK		33	47
0.88	BROWNELL,P	AU	1985	JAR			502	512
0.86	CHENHALL,RH	JA	1986	TAR	MORRIS,D		16	35
0.83	EVANS III,JH	ST	1987	JAR	PATTON,JM		130	164
0.83	SIMONS,R	04	1987	AOS			357	374
0.80	SOETERS,J	01	1988	AOS	SCHREUDER,H		75	85
0.78	ARANYA,N	JA	1984	TAR	FERRIS,KR		1	15
0.75	MIA ,L	04	1989	AOS			347	357
0.75	PALMROSE,Z	JL	1989	TAR			488	499
0.73	GIBBINS,M	JA	1982	TAR	WOLF ,FM		105	124
0.71	SORENSEN,JE	JL	1967	TAR			553	565
0.69	RHODE ,JG	02	1977	AOS	SORENSEN,JE	LAWLER III,EE	165	176
0.69	SENATRA,PT	OC	1980	TAR			594	603
0.67	HASKINS,M	JL	1987	TAR			542	563
0.67	KELLY ,T	SP	1990	AUD	MARGHEIM,L		21	42
0.67	MACINTOSH,NB	01	1987	AOS	DAFT ,RL		49	61
0.67	ROCKNESS,HO	02	1984	AOS	SHIELDS,MD		165	177
0.65	HARIED,AA	SP	1973	JAR			117	145
0.60	BIRNBERG,JG	05	1988	AOS	SNODGRASS,C		447	464
0.60	CHENHALL,RH	03	1988	AOS	BROWNELL,P		225	233
0.60	HIRST ,MK	AU	1983	JAR			596	605
0.60	NAHAPIET,JE	04	1988	AOS			333	358
0.59	BUZBY ,SL	JL	1974	TAR			423	435
0.57	CHOO ,F	SP	1986	AUD			17	34
0.57	DILLARD,JF	03	1979	AOS	FERRIS,KR		179	186
0.56	MUTCHLER,JF	SP	1984	AUD			17	30
0.53	COPELAND,RM	AP	1973	TAR	FRANCIA,AJ	STRAWSER,RH	365	374
0.53	OLIVER,BL	AU	1974	JAR			299	316
0.50	ALM ,J	JL	1991	TAR			577	594
0.50	BROWNELL,P	AU	1983	JAR			456	472
0.50	CHOW ,CW	SP	1987	AUD	MCNAMEE,AH	PLUMLEE,RD	123	133
0.50	COLLINS,F	JA	1987	TAR	MUNTER,P	FINN ,DW	29	49
0.50	COVALESKI,MA	04	1983	AOS	DIRSMITH,MW		323	340
0.50	DIRSMITH,MW	AU	1985	CAR	COVALESKI,MA	MCALLISTER,JP	46	68
0.50	DUNK ,AS	04	1989	AOS			321	324
0.50	HOWARD,TP	OC	1983	TAR	NIKOLAI,LA		765	776
0.50	LOEBBECKE,JK	AU	1989	AUD	EINING,MM	WILLINGHAM,JJ	1	28
0.50	OLSEN ,C	ST	1985	JAR			28	53
0.50	PALMROSE,ZV	SP	1987	AUD			90	103
0.47	WATSON,DJ	AP	1975	TAR			259	273
0.45	COLLINS,F	02	1982	AOS			107	122
0.42	SHOCKLEY,RA	OC	1981	TAR			785	800
0.41	KLAMMER,T	AP	1973	TAR			353	364
0.40	DEAN ,RA	03	1988	AOS	FERRIS,KR	KONSTANS,C	235	250
0.40	KIM ,KK	JL	1988	TAR			472	489
0.38	DIRSMITH,MW	AU	1985	JAA	COVALESKI,MA		5	21
0.38	JIAMBALVO,J	AU	1985	AUD	WILNER,N		1	11
0.36	ALDERMAN,CW	WI	1982	AUD	DEITRICK,JW		54	68
0.36	LIGHTNER,SM	AU	1982	AUD	ADAMS ,SJ	LIGHTNER,KM	1	12
0.36	MAYER-SOMMER,AP	JA	1979	TAR			88	106

CITE INDEX	FIRST AUTHOR	ISS-UE	YE-AR	JOUR-NAL	SECOND AUTHOR	THIRD AUTHOR	PAG BEG	PAG END
0.35	LAVIN ,D	JA	1976	TAR			41	50
0.35	SORTER,GH	AU	1964	JAR	BECKER,S	ARCHIBALD,TR	183	196
0.33	ASHTON,RH	AU	1987	JAR	WILLINGHAM,JJ	ELLIOTT,RK	275	292
0.33	BENSTON,GJ	ST	1978	JAR	KRASNEY,MA		1	30
0.33	GIBBINS,M	SP	1990	JAR	RICHARDSON,A	WATERHOUSE,J	121	143
0.33	HAKA ,SF	01	1987	AOS			31	48
0.33	JACKSON-COX,J	34	1984	AOS	THIRKELL,JE	MCQUEENEY,J	253	273
0.33	MESSIER JR,WF	AU	1987	AUD	HANSEN,JV		94	105
0.33	PANY ,K	SP	1984	AUD	RECKERS,PMJ		89	97
0.33	WILLIAMS,JJ	03	1990	AOS	MACINTOSH,NB	MOORE ,JC	221	246
0.31	BELKAOUI,A	AU	1980	JAR			362	374
0.31	BENKE ,RL	02	1980	AOS	RHODE ,JG		187	202
0.31	COOPER,DJ	03	1977	AOS	ESSEX ,S		201	218
0.30	BROWNELL,P	04	1983	AOS			307	322
0.30	FERRIS,KR	01	1983	AOS	LARCKER,DF		1	12
0.29	BUZBY ,SL	JA	1979	TAR	FALK ,H		23	37
0.29	CLANCY,DK	12	1979	AOS	COLLINS,F		21	30
0.27	ARANYA,N	03	1982	AOS	LACHMAN,R	AMERNIC,J	201	216
0.27	HICKS JR,JO	AP	1978	TAR			371	388
0.25	DAROCA,FP	SP	1985	AUD	HOLDER,WW		80	92
0.25	DILLARD,JF	01	1981	AOS			17	26
0.25	HUSSEIN,ME	01	1981	AOS			27	38
0.25	RONEN ,J	JA	1989	TAR	AHARONI,A		69	86
0.25	SCAPENS,RW	AP	1985	TAR	SALE ,JT		231	247
0.24	BRENNER,VC	AU	1970	JAR			159	166
0.24	LOEB ,SE	AU	1971	JAR			287	306
0.22	BIGGS ,SF	SP	1984	AUD	WILD ,JJ		68	79
0.22	GRANOF,MH	SU	1984	JAA	SHORT ,DG		323	333
0.22	KIDA ,TE	02	1984	AOS			137	147
0.21	DILLARD,JF	12	1979	AOS			31	38
0.20	BUZBY ,SL	34	1978	AOS	FALK ,H		191	202
0.20	ROCKNESS,J	04	1988	AOS	WILLIAMS,PF		397	411
0.20	WHITE ,RA	JL	1983	TAR			539	561
0.18	CAPLAN,EM	AP	1968	TAR			342	362
0.18	LENGERMANN,JJ	OC	1971	TAR			665	675
0.18	ROSENBERG,D	02	1982	AOS	TOMKINS,L	DAY ,P	123	138
0.18	SCHULTE JR,AA	JL	1965	TAR			587	593
0.18	SEILER,RE	04	1982	AOS	BARTLETT,RW		381	404
0.17	BERRY ,LE	JA	1987	TAR	HARWOOD,GB	KATZ ,JL	14	28
0.17	FERRIS,KR	04	1981	AOS			317	326
0.17	WOLF ,FM	OC	1981	TAR			861	881
0.14	HILKE ,JC	WI	1986	JAA			17	29
0.14	LARSSON,S	SP	1986	CAR	CHESLEY,GR		259	282
0.14	ROBBINS,WA	AU	1986	JAR	AUSTIN,KR		412	421
0.14	SCHROEDER,MS	SP	1986	AUD	SOLOMON,I	VICKREY,DW	86	94
0.14	WEBER ,R	JL	1986	TAR			498	518
0.13	BULLEN,ML	03	1985	AOS	FLAMHOLTZ,EG		287	302
0.13	FERRIS,KR	01	1977	AOS			23	28
0.13	JONES ,CS	03	1985	AOS			303	328
0.13	JONES ,CS	02	1985	AOS			177	200
0.12	BRILOFF,AJ	JL	1966	TAR			484	495
0.12	DECOSTER,DT	OC	1971	TAR	RHODE ,JG		651	664
0.12	MORTON,JR	AU	1974	JAR			288	298

CITE INDEX	FIRST AUTHOR	ISS-UE	YE-AR	JOUR-NAL	SECOND AUTHOR	THIRD AUTHOR	PAG BEG	PAG END
0.12	RITTS ,BA	SP	1974	JAR			93	111
0.12	SMITH ,CH	AP	1972	TAR	LANIER,RA	TAYLOR,ME	270	283
0.11	MOST ,KS	AU	1984	JAR			782	788
0.11	NORRIS,DR	01	1984	AOS	NIEBUHR,RE		49	59
0.09	BENSTON,GJ	02	1982	AOS			87	106
0.09	DIRSMITH,MW	04	1982	AOS	LEWIS ,BL		319	336
0.09	JOYCE ,EJ	AU	1982	JAR	LIBBY ,R	SUNDER,S	654	675
0.08	BELKAOUI,A	04	1981	AOS			281	290
0.08	FIRTH ,MA	JL	1980	TAR			451	466
0.08	HORWITZ,BN	WI	1981	JAA	KOLODNY,R		102	113
0.08	PURDY ,D	04	1981	AOS			327	338
0.08	ROSENZWEIG,K	04	1981	AOS			339	354
0.08	SCHREUDER,H	AP	1981	TAR			294	308
0.08	WILLIAMS,PF	JA	1980	TAR			62	77
0.06	BRADISH,RD	OC	1965	TAR			757	766
0.06	BUZBY ,SL	SP	1975	JAR			16	37
0.06	CARPER,WB	23	1976	AOS	POSEY ,JM		143	152
0.06	CUMMING,J	ST	1973	JAR			60	95
0.06	ESTES ,RW	AU	1968	JAR			200	207
0.06	MARQUES,E	23	1976	AOS			175	178
0.06	NYSTROM,PC	04	1977	AOS			317	322
0.06	PARKER,JE	JL	1975	TAR			512	524
0.00	ABERNETHY,MA	02	1991	AOS	STOELWINDER,JU		105	120
0.00	BEDARD,JC	AU	1989	AUD			57	71
0.00	BRENNER,VC	AU	1971	JAR	CARMACK,CW	WEINSTEIN,MG	359	366
0.00	BROWNELL,P		1991	AOS	DUNK ,AS		693	703
0.00	BUCHMAN,TA	AU	1983	AUD			92	103
0.00	CARCELLO,JV	SP	1992	AUD	HERMANSON,RH	MCGRATH,NT	1	15
0.00	CARPENTER,CG	JL	1971	TAR	STRAWSER,RH		509	518
0.00	CHENHALL,RH	AP	1986	TAR			263	272
0.00	COTTELL JR,PG	WI	1986	JAA			30	45
0.00	DAMOS ,P	AU	1989	CAR	EICHENSEHER,JW	HOLT ,DL	91	109
0.00	DEVINE,CT	ST	1966	JAR			160	176
0.00	DOWELL,CD	AU	1981	JAA	HALL ,JA		30	40
0.00	DUNK ,AS	03	1990	AOS			171	178
0.00	DUNK ,AS	04	1992	AOS			195	203
0.00	DYKXHOORN,HJ	JA	1981	TAR	SINNING,KE		97	107
0.00	EMBY ,C	SP	1988	CAR	GIBBINS,M		287	313
0.00	ENGSTROM,JH	SU	1985	JAA			305	318
0.00	FAIRCLOTH,AW	01	1981	AOS	RICCHIUTE,DN		53	68
0.00	FARRELY,GE	AP	1985	TAR	FERRIS,KR	REICHENSTEIN,WR	278	288
0.00	FERRIS,KR	01	1982	AOS			13	26
0.00	FERRIS,KR	03	1982	AOS			225	230
0.00	FLORY ,SM	AP	1992	TAR	PHILLIPS JR,TJ	REIDENBACH,RE	284	302
0.00	GAA ,JC	SP	1985	CAR	SMITH ,CH		219	241
0.00	GEIGER,MA	SP	1989	AUD			40	63
0.00	GIROUX,GA	06	1986	AOS	MAYPER,AG	DAFT ,RL	499	520
0.00	GOETZ-JR,JF	02	1991	AOS	MORROW,PC	MCELROY,JC	159	165
0.00	HARRELL,AM	SP	1986	AUD	CHEWNING,EG	TAYLOR,M	111	121
0.00	HARRELL,AM	SP	1988	AUD	EICKHOFF,R		105	118
0.00	HARRISON,GL	01	1992	AOS			1	15
0.00	HEINS ,EB	AP	1966	TAR			323	326
0.00	HIRST ,MK	05	1990	AOS	LOWY ,SM		425	436

CITE INDEX	FIRST AUTHOR	ISS-UE	YE-AR	JOUR-NAL	SECOND AUTHOR	THIRD AUTHOR	PAG BEG	PAG END
0.00	HONIG ,LE	SP	1978	JAA			231	236
0.00	IMHOFF JR,EA	OC	1978	TAR			869	881
0.00	IMHOFF JR,EA	SP	1988	AUD			182	191
0.00	IMOISILI,OA	04	1989	AOS			325	335
0.00	JAWORKSI,BJ	01	1992	AOS	YOUNG ,SM		17	35
0.00	JONES ,CS	02	1992	AOS			151	168
0.00	KREISER,L	AP	1977	TAR			427	437
0.00	KREN ,L	JL	1992	TAR			511	526
0.00	KUBLIN,M	JL	1965	TAR			626	635
0.00	LAMBERT,JC	SP	1991	AUD	LAMBERT III,SJ	CALDERON,TG	97	109
0.00	LAWLER,J	ST	1967	JAR			86	92
0.00	LOVATA,LM	AU	1988	AUD			72	86
0.00	LOWE ,RE	OC	1965	TAR			839	846
0.00	MATTESSICH,RV	SP	1986	CAR			157	178
0.00	MAUTZ-JR,RD	04	1990	AOS			273	295
0.00	MCINNES,M	02	1991	AOS	RAMAKRISHNAN,RTS		167	184
0.00	MELLMAN,M	JA	1963	TAR			118	123
0.00	MERCHANT,KA	04	1990	AOS			297	313
0.00	MOORES,K	01	1986	AOS	STEADMAN,GT		19	34
0.00	NAIR ,RD	SP	1983	JAA	RITTENBERG,LE		234	243
0.00	PALMROSE,ZV	AU	1988	AUD			63	71
0.00	PETERS,JM	04	1989	AOS	LEWIS ,BL	DHAR ,V	359	378
0.00	POWELL,RM	JL	1966	TAR			525	534
0.00	PRATT ,J	04	1982	AOS	JIAMBALVO,J		369	380
0.00	PRATT ,J	04	1985	AOS			427	442
0.00	PRATT ,J		1992	AOS	BEAULIEU,P		667	684
0.00	RASCH ,RH	SP	1990	AUD	HARRELL,A		90	102
0.00	SAN MIGUEL,JG	02	1984	AOS	GOVINDARAJAN,V		179	188
0.00	SANNELLA,AJ	AU	1986	JAA			288	304
0.00	SCHWEIKART,JA	06	1986	AOS			541	554
0.00	SHIELDS,D	01	1984	AOS			61	80
0.00	SIMON ,HA	JL	1990	TAR			658	667
0.00	SIMONS,R	AU	1988	CAR			267	283
0.00	SIMONS,R	02	1990	AOS			127	143
0.00	SOMEYA,K	OC	1964	TAR			983	989
0.00	SUMNERS,GE	SP	1987	AUD	WHITE ,RA	CLAY JR,RJ	116	122
0.00	TEOH ,HY	02	1984	AOS	THONG ,G		189	206
0.00	VATTER,WJ	OC	1967	TAR			721	730
0.00	WILLIAMS,DJ	SP	1985	AUD	LILLIS,A		110	117
0.00	WILLIAMS,JJ	02	1988	AOS	HININGS,CR		191	198
0.00	WINBORNE,MG	JL	1964	TAR			622	626
0.00	WRIGHT,GB	SU	1982	JAA	TAYLOR,RD		301	309

2.9 RESEARCH METHOD=OPINION – MIXED

CITE INDEX	FIRST AUTHOR	ISS-UE	YE-AR	JOUR-NAL	SECOND AUTHOR	THIRD AUTHOR	PAG BEG	PAG END
1.00	CUSHING,BE	AP	1992	TAR	LECLERE,MJ		355	367
0.67	DEANGELO,LE	JA	1990	TAR			93	112
0.25	RONEN ,J	SP	1989	JAA	SONDHI,AC		237	265
0.00	BORITZ,JE		1990	AUD			49	87
0.00	BOZE ,KM	AU	1990	JAA			627	638
0.00	CARPENTER,VL		1992	AOS	FEROZ ,EH		613	643
0.00	DEIS JR,DR	JL	1992	TAR	GIROUX,GA		462	479
0.00	FRANCIS,JR	SU	1990	JAA	ANDREWS JR,WT	SIMON ,DT	369	378

CITE INDEX	FIRST AUTHOR	ISS-UE	YE-AR	JOUR-NAL	SECOND AUTHOR	THIRD AUTHOR	PAG BEG	PAG END
0.00	SCHOLES,MS	SU	1989	JAA	TERRY ,E	WOLFSON,MA	317	340
0.00	WENSLEY,AKP		1990	AUD			49	87

3.1 SCHOOL OF THOUGHT=BEHAVIORAL – HIPS

CITE INDEX	FIRST AUTHOR	ISS-UE	YE-AR	JOUR-NAL	SECOND AUTHOR	THIRD AUTHOR	PAG BEG	PAG END
3.11	GIBBINS,M	SP	1984	JAR			103	125
3.00	LIBBY ,R	AU	1985	JAR			648	667
2.73	WATERHOUSE,JH	01	1978	AOS	TIESSEN,P		65	76
2.71	ASHTON,RH	SP	1974	JAR			143	157
2.55	LIBBY ,R	03	1982	AOS	LEWIS ,BL		231	286
2.50	LIBBY ,R	03	1977	AOS	LEWIS ,BL		245	268
2.40	ASHTON,AH	OC	1988	TAR	ASHTON,RH		623	641
2.35	JOYCE ,EJ	ST	1976	JAR			29	60
2.33	LIBBY ,R	AU	1990	JAR	FREDERICK,DM		348	367
2.22	WALLER,WS	34	1984	AOS	FELIX JR,WL		383	406
2.00	FREDERICK,DM	AU	1986	JAR	LIBBY ,R		270	290
2.00	FREDERICK,DM	AP	1991	TAR			240	258
1.85	ASHTON,RH	SP	1980	JAR	KRAMER,SS		1	15
1.75	MOECKEL,CL	OC	1989	TAR	PLUMLEE,RD		653	666
1.67	BONNER,SE	JA	1990	TAR			72	92
1.67	TUBBS ,RM	AP	1990	TAR	MESSIER JR,WF	KNECHEL,WR	452	460
1.65	DRIVER,MJ	JL	1975	TAR	MOCK ,TJ		490	508
1.42	JOYCE ,EJ	AU	1981	JAR	BIDDLE,GC		323	349
1.41	LIBBY ,R	JL	1975	TAR			475	489
1.41	SWIERINGA,RJ	ST	1976	JAR	GIBBINS,M	LARSSON,L	159	187
1.38	PRAKASH,P	01	1977	AOS	RAPPAPORT,A		29	38
1.36	HAMILTON,RE	AU	1982	JAR	WRIGHT,WF		756	765
1.25	ASHTON,AH	AP	1985	TAR			173	185
1.25	BAIMAN,S	SP	1989	JAR	LEWIS ,BL		1	20
1.25	BEDARD,JC	02	1989	AOS			113	131
1.17	EINHORN,HJ	SP	1981	JAR	HOGARTH,RM		1	31
1.10	BIGGS ,SF	SP	1983	JAR	MOCK ,TJ		234	255
1.10	MESSIER JR,WF	AU	1983	JAR			611	618
1.06	LIBBY ,R	SP	1975	JAR			150	161
1.00	ASHTON,AH	AP	1991	TAR			218	239
1.00	ASHTON,RH	ST	1976	JAR			1	17
1.00	BOUWMAN,MJ	01	1987	AOS	FRISHKOFF,PA	FRISHKOFF,P	1	30
1.00	KINNEY JR,WR	JA	1982	TAR	UECKER,WC		55	69
1.00	MCGHEE,W	JL	1978	TAR	SHIELDS,MD	BIRNBERG,JG	681	697
1.00	MOSER ,DV	JL	1989	TAR			433	448
1.00	SOLOMON,I	AU	1982	JAR			689	710
0.94	EINHORN,HJ	ST	1976	JAR			196	206
0.93	BENBASAT,I	OC	1979	TAR	DEXTER,AS		735	749
0.92	ABDEL-KHALIK,AR	AU	1980	JAR	EL-SHESHAI,KM		325	342
0.90	LEWIS ,BL	SP	1983	JAR	SHIELDS,MD	YOUNG ,SM	271	285
0.90	SHIELDS,MD	AP	1983	TAR			284	303
0.88	ASHTON,RH	OC	1974	TAR			719	732
0.88	BAREFIELD,RM	AU	1972	JAR			229	242
0.85	CASEY JR,CJ	JA	1980	TAR			36	49
0.85	LEWIS ,BL	AU	1980	JAR			594	602
0.85	SHIELDS,MD	04	1980	AOS			429	442
0.85	WEBER ,R	SP	1980	JAR			214	241
0.81	HOFSTEDT,TR	AP	1977	TAR	HUGHES,GD		379	395

CITE INDEX	FIRST AUTHOR	ISS-UE	YE-AR	JOUR-NAL	SECOND AUTHOR	THIRD AUTHOR	PAG BEG	PAG END
0.78	KIDA ,TE	SP	1984	JAR			332	340
0.77	HILTON,RW	AU	1980	JAR			477	505
0.75	BUTT ,JL	06	1989	AOS	CAMPBELL,TL		471	479
0.75	LIBBY ,R	AP	1985	TAR	ARTMAN,JT	WILLINGHAM,JJ	212	230
0.75	LIBBY ,R	OC	1989	TAR	LIBBY ,PA		729	747
0.75	NIEHAUS,GR	AP	1989	TAR			269	284
0.71	DICKHAUT,JW	JA	1973	TAR			61	79
0.71	MOCK ,TJ	SP	1972	JAR	ESTRIN,TL	VASARHELYI,MA	129	153
0.69	ASHTON,RH	SP	1980	JAR	BROWN ,PR		269	277
0.67	ASHTON,RH	ST	1990	JAR			148	186
0.67	AWASTHI,V	OC	1990	TAR	PRATT ,J		797	811
0.67	BONNER,SE	ST	1990	JAR	LEWIS ,BL		1	28
0.67	HARRIS,TS	OC	1990	TAR	OHLSON,JA		764	780
0.67	HASKINS,ME	SP	1990	CAR	BAGLIONI,AJ	COOPER,CL	361	385
0.67	HEIMAN,VB	OC	1990	TAR			875	890
0.67	KACHELMEIER,SJ	JA	1990	TAR	MESSIER JR,WF		209	226
0.67	KELLY ,T	SP	1990	AUD	MARGHEIM,L		21	42
0.67	PONEMON,LA	AU	1990	CAR	GABHART,DRL		227	251
0.64	GAUMNITZ,BR	AU	1982	JAR	NUNAMAKER,TR	SURDICK,JJ	745	755
0.64	LIBBY ,R	SP	1979	JAR			99	122
0.64	SOLOMON,I	01	1982	AOS	KROGSTAD,JL	ROMNEY,MB	27	42
0.63	HARRELL,AM	OC	1977	TAR			833	841
0.63	WRIGHT,WF	JL	1977	TAR			676	689
0.59	CHESLEY,GR	SP	1976	JAR			27	48
0.59	KENNEDY,HA	SP	1975	JAR			97	116
0.57	BOLAND,RJ	45	1986	AOS	PONDY ,LR		403	422
0.57	CHOO ,F	SP	1986	AUD			17	34
0.57	LIBBY ,R	ST	1979	JAR			35	57
0.56	BOUWMAN,MJ	34	1984	AOS			325	327
0.56	CHESLEY,GR	SP	1977	JAR			1	11
0.54	SNOWBALL,D	03	1980	AOS			323	340
0.53	ASHTON,RH	OC	1975	TAR			710	722
0.53	SCHULTZ JR,JJ	JL	1978	TAR	GUSTAVSON,SG		626	641
0.50	ASHTON,RH	SP	1981	JAR			42	61
0.50	BAMBER,EM	AP	1989	TAR	SNOWBALL,D	TUBBS ,RM	285	299
0.50	BEDARD,JC	JL	1991	TAR	BIGGS ,SF		622	642
0.50	BIGGS ,SF	OC	1985	TAR	WILD ,JJ		607	633
0.50	BIGGS ,SF	SP	1987	AUD	MESSIER JR,WF	HANSEN,JV	1	21
0.50	BROWN ,CE	JA	1991	TAR	SOLOMON,I		100	119
0.50	BUBLITZ,B	JA	1989	TAR	ETTREDGE,M		108	124
0.50	CHOO ,F	JL	1991	TAR	TROTMAN,KT		464	485
0.50	CHURCH,BK	SP	1991	CAR			513	534
0.50	COHEN ,J	AU	1989	JAR	KIDA ,T		263	276
0.50	HARRELL,A	03	1989	AOS	TAYLOR,M	CHEWNING,E	259	269
0.50	HOGARTH,RM	AP	1991	TAR			277	290
0.50	JOHNSON,PE	02	1989	AOS	JAMAL ,K	BERRYMAN,RG	83	99
0.50	MERCHANT,G	JL	1989	TAR			500	513
0.50	MERCHANT,KA	JL	1989	TAR	MANZONI,J		539	558
0.50	SPIRES,EE	AP	1991	TAR			259	276
0.50	VASARHELYI,MA	SP	1977	JAR			138	153
0.50	WALLER,WS	AP	1987	TAR	FELIX JR,WL		275	292
0.47	LUSK ,EJ	ST	1973	JAR			191	202
0.47	MAGEE ,RP	AU	1978	JAR	DICKHAUT,JW		294	314

CITE INDEX	FIRST AUTHOR	ISS-UE	YE-AR	JOUR-NAL	SECOND AUTHOR	THIRD AUTHOR	PAG BEG	PAG END
0.47	MILLER,H	JA	1972	TAR			31	37
0.45	EGER ,C	AU	1982	JAR	DICKHAUT,JW		711	723
0.44	ARRINGTON,CE	SP	1984	JAR	HILLISON,WA	JENSEN,RE	298	312
0.44	BIRNBERG,JG	34	1984	AOS	SHIELDS,MD		365	382
0.44	SAVICH,RS	JL	1977	TAR			642	652
0.44	STOCK ,D	SP	1984	JAR	WATSON,CJ		192	206
0.43	BARNES,P	01	1986	AOS	WEBB ,J		1	18
0.43	BURGSTAHLER,D	AP	1986	TAR	JIAMBALVO,J		233	248
0.43	WILNER,N	01	1986	AOS	BIRNBERG,JG		71	82
0.42	HILTON,RW	SP	1981	JAR	SWIERINGA,RJ		109	119
0.42	KESSLER,L	SP	1981	JAR	ASHTON,RH		146	162
0.41	DICKHAUT,JW	SP	1975	JAR	EGGLETON,IRC		38	72
0.41	JENSEN,RE	AU	1966	JAR			224	238
0.40	CHESLEY,GR	AU	1978	JAR			225	241
0.40	ISELIN,ER	02	1988	AOS			147	164
0.40	LARCKER,DF	JA	1983	TAR	LESSIG,VP		58	77
0.40	WEBER ,R	AU	1978	JAR			368	388
0.38	ANDERSON,MJ	AU	1985	JAR			843	852
0.38	PLUMLEE,RD	AU	1985	JAR			683	699
0.38	UECKER,WC	SP	1980	JAR			191	213
0.36	DYCKMAN,TR	01	1982	AOS	HOSKIN,RE	SWIERINGA,RJ	1	12
0.35	EGGLETON,IRC	ST	1976	JAR			68	131
0.33	BROWN ,C	SP	1981	JAR			62	85
0.33	BROWN ,CE	AU	1990	AUD	SOLOMON,I		17	38
0.33	GUL ,FA	AP	1984	TAR			264	277
0.33	JOYCE ,EJ	AU	1981	JAR	LIBBY ,R		544	550
0.33	KNECHEL,WR	SP	1990	CAR	MESSIER JR,WF		386	406
0.33	MCDANIEL,LS	AU	1990	JAR			267	285
0.33	MOECKEL,C	AU	1990	JAR			368	387
0.33	RICCHIUTE,DN	SP	1984	JAR			341	350
0.33	SCHNEIDER,A	AU	1984	JAR			657	678
0.33	SHIELDS,MD	04	1987	AOS	SOLOMON,I	WALLER,WS	375	385
0.31	HOLT ,RN	03	1980	AOS	CARROLL,R		285	296
0.30	BROWN ,PR	AU	1983	JAR			444	455
0.30	SCHEPANSKI,A	JL	1983	TAR			581	599
0.30	TROTMAN,KT	SP	1983	JAR	YETTON,PW	ZIMMER,I	286	292
0.29	BORITZ,JE	AU	1986	JAR			335	348
0.29	FIRTH ,MA	04	1979	AOS			283	296
0.29	HAKA ,S	JL	1986	TAR	FRIEDMAN,L	JONES ,V	455	474
0.29	JAIN ,TN	JA	1973	TAR			95	104
0.25	ASHTON,RH	JL	1977	TAR			567	575
0.25	AYRES ,FL	AP	1989	TAR	JACKSON,BR	HITE ,PS	300	312
0.25	BUTLER,SA	AU	1985	JAR			513	526
0.25	DAMOS ,P	03	1989	AOS	HOLT ,DL	IMHOFF JR,EA	235	246
0.25	HARRISON,KE	SP	1989	CAR	TOMASSINI,LA		642	648
0.25	KEASEY,K	04	1989	AOS	WATSON,R		337	345
0.25	KLERSEY,GF	02	1989	AOS	MOCK ,TJ		133	151
0.25	LUCKETT,PF	06	1989	AOS	HIRST ,MK		379	387
0.25	MAYPER,AG	AU	1989	AUD	DOUCET,MS	WARREN,CS	72	86
0.25	MILLIRON,VC	AU	1985	JAR			794	816
0.25	SELLING,T	02	1989	AOS	SHANK ,J		65	77
0.25	TROTMAN,KT	AU	1985	JAR			740	752
0.23	NEWMAN,DP	02	1980	AOS			217	230

CITE INDEX	FIRST AUTHOR	ISS-UE	YE-AR	JOUR-NAL	SECOND AUTHOR	THIRD AUTHOR	PAG BEG	PAG END
0.22	BIGGS ,SF	34	1984	AOS			313	323
0.22	CAMPBELL,JE	34	1984	AOS			329	342
0.22	KIDA ,TE	SP	1984	JAR			145	152
0.22	KIDA ,TE	02	1984	AOS			137	147
0.22	SHIELDS,MD	34	1984	AOS			355	363
0.22	WALLER,WS	OC	1984	TAR	FELIX JR,WL		637	646
0.20	ANDERSON,MJ	05	1988	AOS			431	446
0.20	BAMBER,EM	AU	1983	JAR			396	412
0.20	ENIS ,CR	02	1988	AOS			123	145
0.20	JOHNSON,WB	JA	1983	TAR			78	97
0.19	WRIGHT,WF	04	1977	AOS			323	332
0.18	BENBASAT,I	SP	1982	JAR	DEXTER,AS		1	11
0.18	EGGLETON,IRC	SP	1982	JAR			68	102
0.18	GIBBINS,M	SP	1982	JAR			121	138
0.18	OTLEY ,DT	SP	1982	JAR	DIAS ,FJB		171	188
0.18	PRATT ,J	SP	1982	JAR			189	209
0.18	WRIGHT,WF	01	1982	AOS			65	78
0.17	CHEN ,K	01	1981	AOS	SUMMERS,EL		1	16
0.17	COVALESKI,MA	SP	1987	CAR	DIRSMITH,MW	WHITE ,CE	408	429
0.17	HOLT ,DL	06	1987	AOS			571	578
0.15	BARAN ,A	JA	1980	TAR	LAKONISHOK,J	OFER ,AR	22	35
0.14	BLOCHER,E	06	1986	AOS	MOFFIE,RP	ZMUD ,RW	457	470
0.14	BUTLER,SA	JA	1986	TAR			101	111
0.14	CASEY JR,CJ	AP	1986	TAR	SELLING,T		302	317
0.14	CHESLEY,GR	SP	1986	CAR			179	199
0.14	LARSSON,S	SP	1986	CAR	CHESLEY,GR		259	282
0.13	BORITZ,JE	SP	1985	CAR			193	218
0.13	KAPLAN,SE	AU	1985	JAR			871	877
0.13	PATTON,JM	AP	1978	TAR			402	414
0.12	HANSON,EI	AP	1966	TAR			239	243
0.11	ASHTON,AH	JL	1984	TAR			361	375
0.11	BERNARD,VL	AU	1984	JAR			445	466
0.11	BLOOM ,R	01	1984	AOS	ELGERS,PT	MURRAY,D	1	11
0.10	BROWN ,C	AU	1983	JAR			413	431
0.09	DIRSMITH,MW	04	1982	AOS	LEWIS ,BL		319	336
0.09	EMERY ,DR	AU	1982	JAR	BARRON,FH	MESSIER JR,WF	450	458
0.09	SCHEINER,JH	AU	1982	JAR	KIGER ,JE		482	496
0.06	MCCOSH,AM	04	1976	AOS	RAHMAN,M		339	356
0.00	ABDEL-KHALIK,AR	AU	1986	JAR	GRAUL ,PR	NEWTON,JD	372	382
0.00	ABDOLMOHAMMADI,MJ	AU	1986	CAR	BERGER,PD		149	165
0.00	ABDOLMOHAMMADI,MJ	SP	1991	CAR			535	548
0.00	ANDERSON,JC	AU	1992	AUD	KAPLAN,SE	RECKERS,PMJ	1	13
0.00	ANDERSON,U		1989	AUD	MARCHANT,G		101	115
0.00	ARNOLD,DF	AU	1991	AUD	PONEMON,LA		1	15
0.00	ASARE ,SK	AP	1992	TAR			379	393
0.00	BAILEY,CD	AP	1992	TAR	MCINTYRE,EV		368	378
0.00	BALACHANDRAN,BV	SP	1986	CAR			282	287
0.00	BAMBER,EM	AU	1987	CAR	BYLINSKI,JH		127	143
0.00	BAMBER,EM	SP	1988	AUD	BAMBER,LS	BYLINSKI,JH	137	149
0.00	BEACH ,LR	02	1989	AOS	FREDERICKSON,JR		101	112
0.00	BEDARD,JC		1991	AUD	BIGGS ,SF		77	90
0.00	BELKAOUI,A	AU	1985	CAR			111	123
0.00	BIRNBERG,JG	01	1980	AOS			71	80

CITE INDEX	FIRST AUTHOR	ISS-UE	YE-AR	JOUR-NAL	SECOND AUTHOR	THIRD AUTHOR	PAG BEG	PAG END
0.00	BORITZ,JE	SP	1988	CAR	GABER ,BG	LEMON ,WM	392	411
0.00	BRUNSSON,N	02	1990	AOS			47	59
0.00	BUCKLESS,FA	OC	1990	TAR	RAVENSCROFT,SP		933	945
0.00	CARPENTER,BW		1992	AOS	DIRSMITH,MW		709	739
0.00	CASTER,P	AU	1990	AUD			75	91
0.00	CHAN ,JL	AP	1978	TAR			309	323
0.00	CHENHALL,R	01	1991	AOS	MORRIS,D		27	46
0.00	CHEWNING,EG	06	1990	AOS	HARRELL,AM		527	542
0.00	CHOO ,F	06	1989	AOS			481	493
0.00	COLBERT,JL	02	1988	AOS			111	121
0.00	DAVIS ,LR	06	1989	AOS			495	508
0.00	DESANCTIS,G	06	1989	AOS	JARVENPAA,SL		509	525
0.00	DILLARD,JF	34	1984	AOS			343	354
0.00	DILLARD,JF		1991	AOS	KAUFFMAN,NL	SPIRES,EE	619	633
0.00	DIRSMITH,MW	01	1991	AOS	HASKINS,ME		61	90
0.00	DOPUCH,N	AU	1992	AUD			109	112
0.00	DYKXHOORN,HJ	04	1982	AOS	SINNING,KE		337	348
0.00	EMBY ,C	SP	1988	CAR	GIBBINS,M		287	313
0.00	FAIRCLOTH,AW	01	1981	AOS	RICCHIUTE,DN		53	68
0.00	FLORY ,SM	AP	1992	TAR	PHILLIPS JR,TJ	REIDENBACH,RE	284	302
0.00	FRISHKOFF,P	AU	1984	JAA	FRISHKOFF,PA	BOUWMAN,MJ	44	53
0.00	GIBBONS,M	AU	1992	AUD			113	126
0.00	HACKENBRACK,K	SP	1992	JAR			126	136
0.00	HASSELL,JM	06	1989	AOS	ARRINGTON,CE		527	537
0.00	HEINTZ,JA	SP	1989	AUD	WHITE ,GB		22	39
0.00	HOLT ,DL	06	1992	AOS	MORROW,PC		549	559
0.00	HOUGHTON,KA	AU	1984	JAR	SENGUPTA,R		768	775
0.00	HUSS ,HF	AU	1991	AUD	JACOBS,FA		16	32
0.00	ICERMAN,RC	SP	1991	AUD	HILLISON,WA		22	34
0.00	JEFFREY,C	OC	1992	TAR			802	820
0.00	JENNINGS,MM	SP	1991	CAR	KNEER ,DC	RECKERS,PMJ	449	465
0.00	JOHNSON,VE		1991	AUD	KAPLAN,SE		96	107
0.00	JONES ,CS	02	1992	AOS			151	168
0.00	KACHELMEIER,SJ	OC	1991	TAR	LIMBERG,ST	SCHADEWALD,MS	694	717
0.00	KAPLAN,SE	06	1989	AOS	RECKERS,PMJ		539	550
0.00	KAPLAN,SE	AU	1992	AUD	MOECKEL,C	WILLIAMS,JD	50	65
0.00	KELLY ,AS	AU	1989	AUD	MOHRWEIS,CS		87	97
0.00	KIM ,DC	AP	1992	TAR			303	319
0.00	KOONCE,L	JA	1992	TAR			59	76
0.00	LEWIS ,BL	SP	1985	JAR	BELL ,J		228	239
0.00	LIBBY ,R	AU	1992	JAR	LIPE ,MG		249	273
0.00	LORD ,AT	AU	1992	AUD			89	108
0.00	LUCKETT,PF	04	1991	AOS	EGGLETON,IRC		371	394
0.00	MAINES,LA	ST	1990	JAR			29	54
0.00	MARTIN,A	ST	1971	JAR			1	31
0.00	MAUTZ-JR,RD	04	1990	AOS			273	295
0.00	MAYPER,AG	AU	1982	JAR			773	783
0.00	MCINNES,M	02	1991	AOS	RAMAKRISHNAN,RTS		167	184
0.00	MEADE ,JA	AP	1990	TAR			406	431
0.00	MEAR ,R	JA	1987	TAR	FIRTH ,MA		176	182
0.00	MEAR ,R	04	1987	AOS	FIRTH ,MA		331	340
0.00	MEAR ,RWT	AU	1990	JAA	FIRTH ,MA		501	520
0.00	MESSIER JR,WF	SP	1988	CAR	SCHNEIDER,A		337	353

CITE INDEX	FIRST AUTHOR	ISS-UE	YE-AR	JOUR-NAL	SECOND AUTHOR	THIRD AUTHOR	PAG BEG	PAG END
0.00	MOCK ,TJ	AU	1978	JAR	VASARHELYI,MA		414	423
0.00	MOECKEL,C	SP	1990	CAR	WILLIAMS,JD		850	858
0.00	MOON ,P	03	1990	AOS			193	198
0.00	NAIR ,RD	AU	1987	AUD	RITTENBERG,LE		15	38
0.00	PEI ,BKW	SP	1989	AUD	DAVIS ,FG		101	112
0.00	PEI ,BKW	02	1992	AOS	REED ,SA	KOCH ,BS	169	183
0.00	PINCUS	02	1989	AOS			153	163
0.00	PINCUS,KV	AU	1990	AUD			150	167
0.00	PONEMON,LA	AU	1991	AUD	SCHICK,AG		70	83
0.00	POWER ,MK	04	1991	AOS			333	353
0.00	PRATT ,J	04	1982	AOS	JIAMBALVO,J		369	380
0.00	PURVIS,SEC	06	1989	AOS			551	563
0.00	RAGHUNANDAN,K	SP	1991	CAR	GRIMLUND,RA	SCHEPANSKI,A	549	568
0.00	REIMERS,JL	02	1992	AOS	BUTLER,SA		185	194
0.00	RICCHIUTE,DN	JA	1992	TAR			46	58
0.00	RODGERS,W	WI	1992	JAA			67	95
0.00	RULAND,W	JL	1990	TAR	TUNG ,S	GEORGE,NE	710	721
0.00	SCHICK,AG	03	1990	AOS	GORDON,LA	HAKA ,S	199	220
0.00	SCHNEIDER,A	JL	1990	TAR	WILNER,N		668	681
0.00	SHANTEAU,J	02	1989	AOS			165	177
0.00	SHIELDS,D	01	1984	AOS			61	80
0.00	SHIELDS,MD	AU	1988	CAR	SOLOMON,I	WALLER,WS	1	18
0.00	SIMNETT,R	JL	1989	TAR	TROTMAN,K		514	528
0.00	SNOWBALL,D	01	1986	AOS			47	70
0.00	STEPHENS,RG	JA	1990	TAR	GOVINDARAJAN,V		242	257
0.00	STRAWSER,JR	SP	1991	AUD			126	135
0.00	TROTMAN,KT	06	1989	AOS	SNG ,J		565	576
0.00	TUBBS ,RM	OC	1992	TAR			783	801
0.00	VOGT ,RA	01	1977	AOS			59	80
0.00	WALLER,WS	02	1989	AOS	FELIX JR,WL		179	200
0.00	WONG-ON-WING,B	06	1989	AOS	RENEAU,JH	WEST ,SG	577	587
0.00	WRIGHT,WF	AU	1988	CAR			47	57
0.00	YARDLEY,JA	AU	1989	AUD			41	56

3.2 SCHOOL OF THOUGHT=BEHAVIORAL – OTHER

CITE INDEX	FIRST AUTHOR	ISS-UE	YE-AR	JOUR-NAL	SECOND AUTHOR	THIRD AUTHOR	PAG BEG	PAG END
3.18	BRUNS JR,WJ	AU	1975	JAR	WATERHOUSE,JH		177	203
3.00	ABDOLMOHAMMADI,MJ	JA	1987	TAR	WRIGHT,A		1	13
3.00	BERRY ,AJ	01	1985	AOS	CAPPS ,T	COOPER,D	3	28
2.25	MERCHANT,KA	OC	1981	TAR			813	829
2.20	OTLEY ,DT	SP	1978	JAR			122	149
2.18	BROWNELL,P	SP	1982	JAR			12	27
2.18	HOPWOOD,AG	ST	1972	JAR			156	182
2.00	MILANI,K	AP	1975	TAR			274	284
2.00	THOMAS,JK	OC	1992	TAR	TUNG ,S		691	711
1.93	KENIS ,I	OC	1979	TAR			707	721
1.70	BIRNBERG,JG	23	1983	AOS	TUROPOLEC,L	YOUNG ,SM	111	130
1.67	GOVINDARAJAN,V	02	1984	AOS			125	135
1.65	RONEN ,J	OC	1975	TAR	LIVINGSTONE,JL		671	685
1.64	SWIERINGA,RJ	ST	1982	JAR	WEICK ,KE		56	101
1.58	JOYCE ,EJ	SP	1981	JAR	BIDDLE,GC		120	145
1.57	BROWNELL,P	OC	1986	TAR	MCINNES,M		587	600
1.53	GORDON,LA	01	1976	AOS	MILLER,D		59	70

CITE INDEX	FIRST AUTHOR	ISS-UE	YE-AR	JOUR-NAL	SECOND AUTHOR	THIRD AUTHOR	PAG BEG	PAG END
1.50	BROWNELL,P	OC	1981	TAR			844	860
1.50	KIRBY ,AJ	SP	1991	JAR	REICHELSTEIN,S	SEN ,PK	109	128
1.43	JIAMBALVO,J	AU	1979	JAR			436	455
1.40	BIGGS ,SF	JA	1988	TAR	MOCK ,TJ	WATKINS,PR	148	162
1.38	GOVINDARAJAN,V	01	1985	AOS	GUPTA ,AK		51	66
1.35	DECOSTER,DT	AU	1968	JAR	FERTAKIS,JP		237	246
1.33	MERCHANT,KA	34	1984	AOS			291	309
1.30	EICHENSEHER,JW	SP	1983	AUD	SHIELDS,D		23	37
1.29	SCHIFF,M	AP	1970	TAR	LEWIN ,AY		259	268
1.25	COLVILLE,I	02	1981	AOS			119	132
1.24	DERMER,JD	JL	1973	TAR			511	519
1.20	BUTT ,JL	AU	1988	JAR			315	330
1.20	WALLER,WS	01	1988	AOS			87	98
1.18	ONSI ,M	JL	1973	TAR			535	548
1.17	ANSARI,SL	06	1987	AOS	EUSKE ,KJ		549	570
1.14	BROWNELL,P	AU	1986	JAR	HIRST ,MK		241	249
1.14	COVALESKI,MA	03	1986	AOS	DIRSMITH,MW		193	214
1.13	FERRIS,KR	JL	1977	TAR			605	615
1.08	OTLEY ,DT	02	1980	AOS	BERRY ,AJ		231	246
1.07	COLLINS,F	AP	1978	TAR			324	335
1.06	ARGYRIS,C	02	1977	AOS			113	124
1.06	HOPWOOD,AG	JL	1974	TAR			485	495
1.00	CHESLEY,GR	AP	1975	TAR			325	337
1.00	DOPUCH,N	JA	1992	TAR	KING ,RR		97	120
1.00	KING ,RR	SP	1990	CAR	WALLIN,DE		859	892
1.00	KING ,RR	SP	1991	JAR	WALLIN,DE		96	108
1.00	MCNAIR,CJ		1991	AOS			635	653
1.00	PINCH ,T	03	1989	AOS	MULKAY,M	ASHMORE,M	271	301
1.00	PRESTON,AM	06	1992	AOS	COOPER,DJ	COOMBS,RW	561	593
1.00	RAJAN ,MV	JL	1992	TAR			527	545
1.00	WALLIN,DE	JA	1992	TAR			121	147
1.00	WRIGHT,A	OC	1989	TAR	ASHTON,RH		710	728
0.92	HIRST ,MK	OC	1981	TAR			771	784
0.89	DYCKMAN,TR	ST	1984	JAR	PHILBRICK,D	STEPHAN,J	1	30
0.88	BROWNELL,P	AU	1985	JAR			502	512
0.88	MORIARITY,S	AU	1976	JAR	BARRON,FH		320	341
0.83	SIMONS,R	04	1987	AOS			357	374
0.82	CHERRINGTON,DJ	ST	1973	JAR	CHERRINGTON,JO		225	253
0.82	ELIAS ,N	ST	1972	JAR			215	233
0.80	CHOW ,CW	JA	1988	TAR	COOPER,JC	WALLER,WS	111	122
0.80	SOETERS,J	01	1988	AOS	SCHREUDER,H		75	85
0.78	ARANYA,N	JA	1984	TAR	FERRIS,KR		1	15
0.78	KAPLAN,SE	AU	1984	AUD	RECKERS,PMJ		1	19
0.75	CROSBY,MA	AP	1981	TAR			355	365
0.75	LIBBY ,R	AU	1977	JAR	FISHBURN,PC		272	292
0.75	MERCHANT,KA	02	1985	AOS			201	210
0.75	MIA ,L	04	1989	AOS			347	357
0.75	SCHULTZ JR,JJ	AU	1981	JAR	RECKERS,PMJ		482	501
0.75	WALLER,WS	JL	1985	TAR	CHOW ,CW		458	476
0.73	GIBBINS,M	JA	1982	TAR	WOLF ,FM		105	124
0.71	FORAN ,MF	OC	1974	TAR	DECOSTER,DT		751	763
0.71	GOSMAN,ML	JA	1973	TAR			1	11
0.71	SORENSEN,JE	JL	1967	TAR			553	565

CITE INDEX	FIRST AUTHOR	ISS-UE	YE-AR	JOUR-NAL	SECOND AUTHOR	THIRD AUTHOR	PAG BEG	PAG END
0.70	FLAMHOLTZ,EG	23	1983	AOS			153	170
0.69	KIDA ,TE	AU	1980	JAR			506	523
0.69	ROCKNESS,HO	OC	1977	TAR			893	903
0.69	SENATRA,PT	OC	1980	TAR			594	603
0.67	BARIFF,ML	01	1978	AOS	GALBRAITH,JR		15	28
0.67	ELIAS ,N	JL	1990	TAR			606	623
0.67	HASKINS,M	JL	1987	TAR			542	563
0.67	KROGSTAD,JL	AU	1984	AUD	ETTENSON,RT	SHANTEAU,J	54	74
0.67	MACINTOSH,NB	01	1987	AOS	DAFT ,RL		49	61
0.67	ROCKNESS,HO	02	1984	AOS	SHIELDS,MD		165	177
0.65	CAPLAN,EM	JL	1966	TAR			496	509
0.65	HARIED,AA	SP	1973	JAR			117	145
0.65	HOFSTEDT,TR	OC	1972	TAR			679	692
0.65	REVSINE,L	OC	1970	TAR			704	711
0.65	ROSE ,R	ST	1970	JAR	BEAVER,WH	BECKER,S	138	148
0.65	WATSON,DJ	JL	1975	TAR	BAUMLER,JV		466	474
0.64	MORIARITY,S	SP	1979	JAR			205	224
0.63	MERCHANT,KA	01	1985	AOS			67	86
0.60	BIRNBERG,JG	05	1988	AOS	SNODGRASS,C		447	464
0.60	HIRST ,MK	AU	1983	JAR			596	605
0.60	JIAMBALVO,J	01	1983	AOS	WATSON,DJ	BAUMLER,JV	13	30
0.60	LUKKA ,K	03	1988	AOS			281	301
0.59	FLAMHOLTZ,EG	AP	1971	TAR			253	267
0.59	PANKOFF,LD	ST	1970	JAR	VIRGIL JR,RL		1	48
0.58	HILTON,RW	SP	1981	JAR	SWIERINGA,RJ	HOSKIN,RE	86	108
0.58	LARCKER,DF	JL	1981	TAR			519	538
0.57	ANSARI,SL	03	1979	AOS			149	162
0.57	DILLARD,JF	03	1979	AOS	FERRIS,KR		179	186
0.57	MARGHEIM,LL	SP	1986	AUD	PANY ,K		50	63
0.53	COPELAND,RM	AP	1973	TAR	FRANCIA,AJ	STRAWSER,RH	365	374
0.53	OLIVER,BL	AU	1974	JAR			299	316
0.53	SWIERINGA,RJ	ST	1972	JAR	MONCUR,RH		194	209
0.50	ALM ,J	JL	1991	TAR			577	594
0.50	BROWN ,C	JL	1987	TAR	SOLOMON,I		564	577
0.50	BROWNELL,P	AU	1983	JAR			456	472
0.50	COLLINS,F	JA	1987	TAR	MUNTER,P	FINN ,DW	29	49
0.50	COVALESKI,MA	04	1983	AOS	DIRSMITH,MW		323	340
0.50	DUNK ,AS	04	1989	AOS			321	324
0.50	FARMER,TA	AU	1987	AUD	RITTENBERG,LE	TROMPETER,GM	1	14
0.47	COOK ,DM	ST	1967	JAR			213	224
0.47	HERTOG,JF	01	1978	AOS			29	46
0.47	IJIRI ,Y	SP	1968	JAR	KINARD,JC	PUTNEY,FB	1	28
0.47	RONEN ,J	AU	1971	JAR			307	332
0.47	SCHWAN,ES	23	1976	AOS			219	238
0.47	WARD ,BH	SP	1976	JAR			138	152
0.47	WATSON,DJ	AP	1975	TAR			259	273
0.46	CROSBY,MA	AU	1980	JAR			585	593
0.45	COLLINS,F	02	1982	AOS			107	122
0.45	DANOS ,P	JA	1982	TAR	IMHOFF JR,EA		39	54
0.44	NANNI JR,AJ	02	1984	AOS			149	163
0.43	MURRAY,D	AU	1986	JAR	FRAZIER,KB		400	404
0.43	PRESTON,A	06	1986	AOS			521	540
0.42	SHIELDS,MD	01	1981	AOS	BIRNBERG,JG	FRIEZE,IH	69	96

CITE INDEX	FIRST AUTHOR	ISS-UE	YE-AR	JOUR-NAL	SECOND AUTHOR	THIRD AUTHOR	PAG BEG	PAG END
0.42	SHOCKLEY,RA	OC	1981	TAR			785	800
0.41	ANSARI,SL	AU	1976	JAR			189	211
0.41	BENSTON,GJ	AP	1963	TAR			347	354
0.41	BRUMMET,RL	AP	1968	TAR	FLAMHOLTZ,EG	PYLE ,WC	217	224
0.41	DYCKMAN,TR	SP	1964	JAR			91	107
0.41	FLAMHOLTZ,EG	23	1976	AOS			153	166
0.41	OLIVER,BL	SP	1972	JAR			154	166
0.40	ABDEL-KHALIK,AR	AP	1983	TAR	SNOWBALL,D	WRAGGE,JH	215	227
0.40	DEAN ,RA	03	1988	AOS	FERRIS,KR	KONSTANS,C	235	250
0.40	FLAMHOLTZ,EG	02	1978	AOS	COOK ,E		115	140
0.40	HOSKIN,RE	SP	1983	JAR			78	95
0.40	KIM ,KK	JL	1988	TAR			472	489
0.40	MIA ,L	05	1988	AOS			465	475
0.40	NEUMANN,BR	AU	1978	JAR	FRIEDMAN,LA		400	410
0.40	YOUNG ,SM	06	1988	AOS	SHIELDS,MD	WOLF ,G	607	618
0.38	BAKER ,CR	JL	1977	TAR			576	586
0.38	BECK ,PJ	SP	1985	JAR	SOLOMON,I	TOMASSINI,LA	37	56
0.38	BIRNBERG,JG	03	1977	AOS	FRIEZE,IH	SHIELDS,MD	189	200
0.38	KNAPP ,MC	AP	1985	TAR			202	211
0.38	SCHNEIDER,A	AU	1985	JAR			911	919
0.36	ALDERMAN,CW	WI	1982	AUD	DEITRICK,JW		54	68
0.36	WILNER,N	01	1982	AOS			43	52
0.35	BECKER,S	AU	1974	JAR	RONEN ,J	SORTER,GH	317	329
0.35	CAMMANN,C	04	1976	AOS			301	314
0.35	CARMICHAEL,DR	AP	1970	TAR			235	245
0.35	FLAMHOLTZ,EG	OC	1972	TAR			666	678
0.35	HOFSTEDT,TR	JA	1970	TAR	KINARD,JC		38	54
0.33	BRIERS,M	04	1990	AOS	HIRST ,M		373	398
0.33	CHALOS,P	JL	1990	TAR	HAKA ,S		624	641
0.33	DANOS ,P	OC	1984	TAR	HOLT ,DL	IMHOFF JR,EA	547	573
0.33	GIBBINS,M	SP	1990	JAR	RICHARDSON,A	WATERHOUSE,J	121	143
0.33	HAKA ,SF	01	1987	AOS			31	48
0.33	HIRST ,MK	OC	1987	TAR			774	784
0.33	HUGHES,MA	03	1990	AOS	KWON ,SO		179	191
0.33	JENNINGS,M	SP	1987	AUD	KNEER ,DC	RECKERS,PMJ	104	115
0.33	MACINTOSH,NB	05	1990	AOS	SCAPENS,RW		455	477
0.33	PRATT ,J	02	1981	AOS	JIAMBALVO,J		133	142
0.33	UECKER,WC	JL	1981	TAR	BRIEF ,AP	KINNEY JR,WR	465	478
0.33	WILLIAMS,JJ	03	1990	AOS	MACINTOSH,NB	MOORE ,JC	221	246
0.31	BELKAOUI,A	AU	1980	JAR			362	374
0.31	BELKAOUI,A	03	1980	AOS			263	284
0.31	BENKE ,RL	02	1980	AOS	RHODE ,JG		187	202
0.31	COOPER,DJ	03	1977	AOS	ESSEX ,S		201	218
0.30	BROWNELL,P	04	1983	AOS			307	322
0.30	FERRIS,KR	01	1983	AOS	LARCKER,DF		1	12
0.29	ABDOLMOHAMMADI,MJ	SP	1986	AUD			1	16
0.29	ASHTON,RH	04	1976	AOS			289	300
0.29	BARRETT,ME	ST	1971	JAR			50	65
0.29	BRUNS JR,WJ	JL	1968	TAR			469	480
0.29	DITTMAN,DA	SP	1976	JAR	JURIS ,HA	REVSINE,L	49	65
0.29	FERTAKIS,JP	OC	1969	TAR			680	691
0.29	GOLEMBIEWSKI,RT	AP	1964	TAR			333	341
0.29	HOFSTEDT,TR	01	1976	AOS			43	58

CITE INDEX	FIRST AUTHOR	ISS-UE	YE-AR	JOUR-NAL	SECOND AUTHOR	THIRD AUTHOR	PAG BEG	PAG END
0.29	MAHER ,MW	AU	1979	JAR	RAMANATHAN,KV	PETERSON,RB	476	503
0.29	MOCK ,TJ	ST	1969	JAR			124	159
0.29	NICHOLS,DR	AP	1976	TAR	PRICE ,KH		335	346
0.29	RECKERS,PMJ	AU	1979	JAA	TAYLOR,ME		42	55
0.27	ARANYA,N	03	1982	AOS	LACHMAN,R	AMERNIC,J	201	216
0.27	ASHTON,AH	AU	1982	JAR			415	428
0.27	DANOS ,P	WI	1982	AUD	IMHOFF JR,EA		23	34
0.27	JIAMBALVO,J	SP	1982	JAR			152	161
0.25	ARANYA,N	04	1981	AOS	POLLOCK,J	AMERNIC,J	271	280
0.25	ARRINGTON,CE	SP	1985	JAR	BAILEY,CD	HOPWOOD,WS	1	20
0.25	BROWN ,C	03	1985	AOS			255	266
0.25	BUCHMAN,TA	03	1985	AOS			267	286
0.25	DEJONG,DV	02	1989	AOS	FORSYTHE,R	KIM ,JA	41	64
0.25	DILLARD,JF	01	1981	AOS			17	26
0.25	GORDON,LA	03	1989	AOS			247	258
0.25	RONEN ,J	JA	1989	TAR	AHARONI,A		69	86
0.25	TROTMAN,KT	SP	1985	JAR	YETTON,PW		256	267
0.25	TURNER,MJ	AU	1989	JAR	HILTON,RW		297	312
0.25	WALLER,WS	AU	1985	JAR			817	828
0.24	FLAMHOLTZ,EG	ST	1972	JAR			241	266
0.24	FRIEDMAN,A	AU	1974	JAR	LEV ,B		235	250
0.24	GYNTHER,RS	AP	1967	TAR			274	290
0.24	HOLSTRUM,GL	AU	1971	JAR			268	277
0.24	LOEB ,SE	AU	1971	JAR			287	306
0.24	MOCK ,TJ	JL	1973	TAR			520	534
0.24	SEARFOSS,DG	04	1976	AOS			375	388
0.23	FRIEDMAN,LA	AU	1980	JAR	NEUMANN,BR		407	419
0.23	PANY ,K	JA	1980	TAR	RECKERS,PMJ		50	61
0.21	ADELBERG,AH	AU	1979	JAR			565	592
0.21	BLOCHER,E	JL	1979	TAR			563	573
0.21	DILLARD,JF	12	1979	AOS			31	38
0.21	GROVE ,HD	JL	1979	TAR	SAVICH,RS		522	537
0.20	BUZBY ,SL	34	1978	AOS	FALK ,H		191	202
0.20	HARRISON,PD	AP	1988	TAR	WEST ,SG	RENEAU,JH	307	320
0.20	HILTON,RW	AP	1988	TAR	SWIERINGA,RJ	TURNER,MJ	195	218
0.20	MIRVIS,PH	23	1983	AOS	LAWLER III,EE		175	190
0.20	TABOR ,RH	SP	1983	JAR			348	354
0.20	WHITE ,RA	JL	1983	TAR			539	561
0.19	GORDON,FE	04	1977	AOS	RHODE ,JG	MERCHANT,KA	295	306
0.19	LAVIN ,D	03	1977	AOS			237	244
0.18	BIRNBERG,JG	JL	1967	TAR	NATH ,R		468	479
0.18	BROWNELL,P	OC	1982	TAR			766	777
0.18	CAPLAN,EM	AP	1968	TAR			342	362
0.18	DASCHER,PE	SP	1971	JAR	COPELAND,RM		32	39
0.18	FALK ,H	SP	1973	JAR	OPHIR ,T		108	116
0.18	LENGERMANN,JJ	OC	1971	TAR			665	675
0.18	MACY ,BA	23	1976	AOS	MIRVIS,PH		179	194
0.18	ROSENBERG,D	02	1982	AOS	TOMKINS,L	DAY ,P	123	138
0.18	SEILER,RE	04	1982	AOS	BARTLETT,RW		381	404
0.18	SORENSEN,JE	OC	1972	TAR	FRANKS,DD		735	746
0.18	WRIGHT,A	SP	1982	JAR			227	239
0.17	FERRIS,KR	04	1981	AOS			317	326
0.17	HOUGHTON,KA	02	1987	AOS			143	152

CITE INDEX	FIRST AUTHOR	ISS-UE	YE-AR	JOUR-NAL	SECOND AUTHOR	THIRD AUTHOR	PAG BEG	PAG END
0.17	RECKERS,PMJ	SU	1981	AUD	STAGLIANO,AJ		23	37
0.17	WOLF ,FM	OC	1981	TAR			861	881
0.15	HARRELL,AM	04	1980	AOS	KLICK ,HD		393	400
0.14	ARANYA,N	AU	1986	CAR	WHEELER,JT		184	199
0.14	HARVEY,DW	03	1979	AOS	RHODE ,JG	MERCHANT,KA	187	210
0.14	LICATA,MP	JA	1986	TAR	STRAWSER,RH	WELKER,RB	112	117
0.14	SCHROEDER,MS	SP	1986	AUD	SOLOMON,I	VICKREY,DW	86	94
0.14	WRIGHT,A	SP	1986	AUD			86	94
0.13	BULLEN,ML	03	1985	AOS	FLAMHOLTZ,EG		287	302
0.13	DIERKES,M	01	1985	AOS	ANTAL ,AB		29	34
0.13	FERRIS,KR	01	1977	AOS			23	28
0.13	FLAMHOLTZ,EG	01	1985	AOS	DAS ,TK	TSUI ,AS	35	50
0.13	MCKINELY,S	AU	1985	JAR	PANY ,K	RECKERS,PMJ	887	896
0.13	TOMASSINI,LA	OC	1977	TAR			904	913
0.12	ACLAND,D	23	1976	AOS			133	142
0.12	CHURCHILL,NC	OC	1965	TAR	COOPER,WW		767	781
0.12	DECOSTER,DT	OC	1971	TAR	RHODE ,JG		651	664
0.12	DERMER,JD	JA	1974	TAR	SIEGEL,JP		88	97
0.12	MORTON,JR	AU	1974	JAR			288	298
0.12	TOMASSINI,LA	23	1976	AOS			239	252
0.11	DAROCA,FP	01	1984	AOS			13	32
0.11	NORRIS,DR	01	1984	AOS	NIEBUHR,RE		49	59
0.10	BLOCHER,E	AU	1983	AUD	ESPOSITO,RS	WILLINGHAM,JJ	75	91
0.10	CASEY JR,CJ	SP	1983	JAR			300	307
0.10	DANOS ,P	AU	1983	JAR	IMHOFF JR,EA		473	494
0.10	TILLER,MG	AU	1983	JAR			581	595
0.10	WILKINS,T	OC	1983	TAR	ZIMMER,I		749	764
0.09	JIAMBALVO,J	OC	1982	TAR	PRATT ,J		734	750
0.09	RECKERS,PMJ	AU	1982	AUD	SCHULTZ JR,JJ		64	74
0.09	UECKER,WC	AU	1982	JAR			388	402
0.09	WILLIAMS,PF	04	1982	AOS			405	410
0.08	BELKAOUI,A	04	1981	AOS			281	290
0.08	COPELAND,RM	SP	1981	JAR	TAYLOR,RL	BROWN ,SH	197	207
0.08	FERRIS,KR	04	1980	AOS	DILLARD,JF	NETHERCOTT,L	361	368
0.08	HOPPER,TM	04	1980	AOS			401	412
0.08	ROSENZWEIG,K	04	1981	AOS			339	354
0.06	BODNAR,G	OC	1977	TAR	LUSK ,EJ		857	868
0.06	BRUNS JR,WJ	ST	1966	JAR			1	14
0.06	CARPER,WB	23	1976	AOS	POSEY ,JM		143	152
0.06	CUMMING,J	ST	1973	JAR			60	95
0.06	FIELD ,JE	JL	1969	TAR			593	599
0.06	GAMBLING,TE	23	1976	AOS			167	174
0.06	GROVE ,HD	03	1977	AOS	MOCK ,TJ	EHRENREICH,K	219	236
0.06	MCDONOUGH,JJ	OC	1971	TAR			676	685
0.06	NYSTROM,PC	04	1977	AOS			317	322
0.06	OGAN ,P	23	1976	AOS			195	218
0.06	SAULS ,EH	ST	1970	JAR			157	171
0.06	UECKER,WC	01	1977	AOS			47	58
0.00	ABERNETHY,MA	02	1991	AOS	STOELWINDER,JU		105	120
0.00	ANDERSON JR,TN	AU	1982	JAR	KIDA ,TE		403	414
0.00	ANDERSON,U	AU	1988	AUD	YOUNG ,RA		23	42
0.00	BAILEY,CD	SP	1986	AUD	BALLARD,G		77	85
0.00	BAILEY,KE	AU	1983	JAR	BYLINSKI,JH	SHIELDS,MD	355	370

CITE INDEX	FIRST AUTHOR	ISSUE	YEAR	JOURNAL	SECOND AUTHOR	THIRD AUTHOR	PAG BEG	PAG END
0.00	BAILEY,WT	OC	1981	TAR			882	896
0.00	BAMBER,EM	JL	1988	AUD	SNOWBALL,D		490	504
0.00	BAO ,BE	03	1986	AOS	BAO ,DA	VASARHELYI,MA	289	296
0.00	BARTON,RF	SP	1969	JAR			116	122
0.00	BECK ,PJ	AU	1992	CAR	DAVIS ,JS	JUNG ,W-O	86	112
0.00	BJORN-ANDERSEN,N	02	1980	AOS	PEDERSEN,PH		203	216
0.00	BLOCHER,E	AU	1985	AUD	BYLINSKI,JH		79	90
0.00	BLOCHER,E	SP	1988	AUD	COOPER,JC		1	28
0.00	BRENNER,VC	AU	1971	JAR	CARMACK,CW	WEINSTEIN,MG	359	366
0.00	BROWN ,C	AU	1987	CAR			111	126
0.00	BROWNELL,P		1991	AOS	DUNK ,AS		693	703
0.00	BUCHMAN,TA	AU	1983	AUD			92	103
0.00	CARCELLO,JV	SP	1992	AUD	HERMANSON,RH	MCGRATH,NT	1	15
0.00	CHALOS,P	AU	1985	JAR			527	543
0.00	CHALOS,P	SP	1991	CAR	CHERIAN,J	HARRIS,D	431	448
0.00	CHENHALL,RH	AP	1986	TAR			263	272
0.00	CHOW,CW	01	1991	AOS	COOPER,JC	HADDAD,K	47	60
0.00	COLLINS,KM	06	1992	AOS	KILLOUGH,LN		535	547
0.00	DALY ,BA	SP	1990	JAR	OMER ,T		193	197
0.00	DAMOS ,P	AU	1989	CAR	EICHENSEHER,JW	HOLT ,DL	91	109
0.00	DAS ,H	03	1986	AOS			215	232
0.00	DENT ,AS		1991	AOS			705	732
0.00	DUNK ,AS	03	1990	AOS			171	178
0.00	DUNK ,AS	04	1992	AOS			195	203
0.00	DYKXHOORN,HJ	JA	1981	TAR	SINNING,KE		97	107
0.00	FERRIS,KR	01	1982	AOS			13	26
0.00	FERRIS,KR	03	1982	AOS			225	230
0.00	FERTAKIS,JP	JL	1970	TAR			509	512
0.00	FISHER,MH		1990	AUD			184	223
0.00	FLAMHOLTZ,EG	04	1987	AOS			309	318
0.00	FOGARTY,TJ	02	1992	AOS			129	149
0.00	FROGOT,V	JA	1991	TAR	SHEARON,WT		80	99
0.00	GOETZ-JR,JF	02	1991	AOS	MORROW,PC	MCELROY,JC	159	165
0.00	GORDON,LA		1992	AOS	SMITH ,KJ		741	757
0.00	GUL ,FA	34	1984	AOS			233	239
0.00	HARRELL,A	AU	1990	AUD	WRIGHT,A		134	149
0.00	HARRELL,AM	34	1984	AOS	STAHL ,MJ		241	252
0.00	HARRELL,AM	SP	1986	AUD	CHEWNING,EG	TAYLOR,M	111	121
0.00	HARRELL,AM	SP	1988	AUD	EICKHOFF,R		105	118
0.00	HARRISON,GL	01	1992	AOS			1	15
0.00	HERTOG,FD	02	1992	AOS	WIELINGA,C		103	128
0.00	HIRST ,MK	05	1990	AOS	LOWY ,SM		425	436
0.00	HOUGHTON,KA	SP	1984	JAR			361	368
0.00	HOUGHTON,KA	03	1988	AOS			263	280
0.00	HUSS ,HF	WI	1991	JAA	ZHAO ,J		53	66
0.00	IMOISILI,OA	04	1989	AOS			325	335
0.00	JAWORKSI,BJ	01	1992	AOS	YOUNG ,SM		17	35
0.00	JENSEN,RE	JL	1970	TAR			502	508
0.00	JOHNSON,DA	SP	1983	AUD	PANY ,K	WHITE ,RA	38	51
0.00	JOHNSON,DA	AU	1984	JAR	PANY ,K		731	743
0.00	JOHNSON,WB	04	1982	AOS			349	368
0.00	JONSON,LC	34	1978	AOS	JONSSON,B	SVENSSON,G	261	268
0.00	KANPP ,MC	SP	1991	AUD			35	52

CITE INDEX	FIRST AUTHOR	ISS-UE	YE-AR	JOUR-NAL	SECOND AUTHOR	THIRD AUTHOR	PAG BEG	PAG END
0.00	KAPLAN,SE	04	1988	AOS	RECKERS,PMJ	ROARK ,SJ	371	379
0.00	KNAPP ,MC	JL	1987	TAR			578	588
0.00	KREN ,L	JL	1992	TAR			511	526
0.00	LAU ,AH	SP	1978	JAR	LAU ,HS		80	102
0.00	LUCAS ,HC	OC	1975	TAR			735	746
0.00	MEIXNER,WF	JL	1988	AUD	WELKER,RB		505	513
0.00	MERCHANT,KA	04	1990	AOS			297	313
0.00	MURNIGHAN,JK	JL	1990	TAR	BAZERMAN,MH		642	657
0.00	NAIR ,RD	SP	1983	JAA	RITTENBERG,LE		234	243
0.00	NEU ,D		1992	AOS	WRIGHT,M		645	665
0.00	PANY ,K	AU	1982	JAR	SMITH ,CH		472	481
0.00	PANY ,K	AU	1987	AUD	RECKERS,PMJ		39	53
0.00	PINCUS,KV	SP	1990	AUD			1	20
0.00	PONEMON,LA	AU	1992	CAR			171	189
0.00	PONEMON,LA	04	1992	AOS			239	258
0.00	PORCANO,TM	OC	1984	TAR			619	636
0.00	PRATT ,J	04	1985	AOS			427	442
0.00	PRATT ,J		1992	AOS	BEAULIEU,P		667	684
0.00	PURDY ,CR	ST	1969	JAR	SMITH JR,JM	GRAY ,J	1	18
0.00	RASCH ,RH	SP	1990	AUD	HARRELL,A		90	102
0.00	REBELE,JE	AU	1988	AUD	HEINTZ,JA	BRIDEN,GE	43	52
0.00	SAMUELSON,LA	01	1986	AOS			35	46
0.00	SAN MIGUEL,JG	02	1977	AOS			177	186
0.00	SAN MIGUEL,JG	02	1984	AOS	GOVINDARAJAN,V		179	188
0.00	SCHATZBERG,JW	AP	1990	TAR			337	362
0.00	SIMONS,R	AU	1988	CAR			267	283
0.00	SUMNERS,GE	SP	1987	AUD	WHITE ,RA	CLAY JR,RJ	116	122
0.00	THOMAS,JK	OC	1989	TAR			773	787
0.00	WAGGONER,JB	SP	1990	AUD			77	89
0.00	WALLACE,WA	SP	1991	AUD			53	68
0.00	WILLIAMS,JJ	04	1985	AOS	NEWTON,JD	MORGAN,EA	457	478
0.00	WILLIAMS,JJ	02	1988	AOS	HININGS,CR		191	198
0.00	WRIGHT,A	JL	1983	TAR			621	632
0.00	WRIGHT,A	06	1988	AOS			595	605

3.3 SCHOOL OF THOUGHT=STAT.MODEL – EMH

CITE INDEX	FIRST AUTHOR	ISS-UE	YE-AR	JOUR-NAL	SECOND AUTHOR	THIRD AUTHOR	PAG BEG	PAG END
8.35	BALL ,R	AU	1968	JAR	BROWN ,P		159	178
5.50	COLLINS,DW	JL	1989	JAE	KOTHARI,SP		143	181
5.50	EASTON,PD	JL	1989	JAE	ZMIJEWSKI,ME		117	141
5.35	BEAVER,WH	ST	1968	JAR			67	92
5.20	HOLTHAUSEN,RW	AG	1983	JAE	LEFTWICH,RW		77	117
5.18	PATELL,JM	AU	1976	JAR			246	276
5.00	OU ,JA	NV	1989	JAE			295	329
5.00	PENMAN,SH	NV	1989	JAE			295	329
4.93	BEAVER,WH	AU	1979	JAR	CLARKE,R	WRIGHT,WF	316	340
4.88	ATIASE,RK	SP	1985	JAR			21	36
4.50	BERNARD,VL	SP	1987	JAR			1	48
4.50	FREEMAN,RN	JL	1987	JAE			195	228
4.33	COLLINS,DW	JL	1987	JAE	KOTHARI,SP	RAYBURN,JD	111	138
4.31	BEAVER,WH	MR	1980	JAE	LAMBERT,RA	MORSE ,D	3	28
4.17	CHRISTIE,AA	DE	1987	JAE			231	258
4.12	GONEDES,NJ	ST	1974	JAR	DOPUCH,N		48	129

CITE INDEX	FIRST AUTHOR	ISS-UE	YE-AR	JOUR-NAL	SECOND AUTHOR	THIRD AUTHOR	PAG BEG	PAG END
3.67	LIPE ,R	JA	1990	TAR			49	71
3.58	LEFTWICH,RW	MR	1981	JAE			3	36
3.50	BERNARD,VL	ST	1989	JAR	THOMAS,JK		1	36
3.50	EASTON,PD	SP	1991	JAR	HARRIS,TS		19	36
3.33	BEAVER,WH	JL	1987	JAE	LAMBERT,RA	RYAN ,SG	139	157
3.33	CHAMBERS,AE	SP	1984	JAR	PENMAN,SH		21	47
3.33	COLLINS,DW	MR	1981	JAE	ROZEFF,MS	DHALIWAL,DS	37	71
3.33	HOLTHAUSEN,RW	MR	1981	JAE			73	109
3.27	LEV ,B	ST	1982	JAR	OHLSON,JA		249	322
3.25	OU ,JA	ST	1989	JAR	PENMAN,SH		111	144
3.15	FOSTER,G	MR	1980	JAE			29	62
3.00	GREIG ,AC	JN	1992	JAE			413	442
3.00	STOBER,TL	JN	1992	JAE			347	372
3.00	WILSON,GP	AP	1987	TAR			293	322
2.89	FOSTER,G	OC	1984	TAR	OLSEN ,C	SHEVLIN,T	574	603
2.86	LIPE ,RC	ST	1986	JAR			37	68
2.86	RAYBURN,J	ST	1986	JAR			112	137
2.67	BERNARD,VL	DE	1990	JAE	THOMAS,JK		305	340
2.64	COLLINS,DW	MR	1979	JAE	DENT ,WT		3	44
2.55	BEAVER,WH	JL	1982	JAE	GRIFFIN,PA	LANDSMAN,WR	15	39
2.50	SCHIPPER,K	SP	1983	JAR	THOMPSON,R		184	221
2.41	GONEDES,NJ	SP	1976	JAR	DOPUCH,N	PENMAN,SH	89	137
2.40	LARCKER,DF	AP	1983	JAE			3	30
2.36	BIDDLE,GC	AU	1982	JAR	LINDAHL,FW		551	588
2.33	CHRISTIE,AA	JA	1990	JAE			15	36
2.29	BALL ,R	ST	1972	JAR			1	38
2.27	RICKS ,WE	AU	1982	JAR			367	387
2.23	PENMAN,SH	SP	1980	JAR			132	160
2.21	DYCKMAN,TR	MR	1979	JAE	SMITH ,AJ		45	75
2.17	FOSTER,G	DE	1981	JAE			201	232
2.14	WILSON GP	ST	1986	JAR			165	203
2.00	ALI ,A	JN	1992	JAE	ZAROWIN,P		249	264
2.00	EASTON,PD	JN	1992	JAE	HARRIS,TS	OHLSON,JA	119	142
2.00	GRANT ,EB	SP	1980	JAR			255	268
2.00	HOLTHAUSEN,RW	JN	1992	JAE	LARCKER,DF		373	411
2.00	KOTHARI,SP	JN	1992	JAE	SLAON ,RG		143	171
2.00	LEV ,B	ST	1989	JAR			153	192
2.00	SUNDER,S	ST	1973	JAR			1	45
1.93	LEV ,B	JL	1979	TAR			485	503
1.91	PATELL,JM	JL	1982	TAR	WOLFSON,MA		509	527
1.89	LYS ,T	AP	1984	JAE			39	65
1.88	GONEDES,NJ	AU	1975	JAR			220	256
1.76	MAY ,RG	ST	1971	JAR			119	163
1.75	FREEMAN,RN	ST	1989	JAR	TSE ,S		49	79
1.75	MORSE ,D	AU	1981	JAR			374	383
1.71	BAMBER,LS	SP	1986	JAR			40	56
1.67	BOWEN ,RM	OC	1987	TAR	BURGSTAHLER,D	DALEY ,LA	723	747
1.67	LAMBERT,RA	ST	1987	JAR	LARCKER,DF		85	125
1.67	OHLSON,JA	SP	1990	CAR			648	676
1.67	WAYMIRE,G	AU	1984	JAR			703	718
1.64	GIVOLY,D	JL	1982	TAR	PALMON,D		486	508
1.62	BEAVER,WH	AG	1980	JAE	CHRISTIE,AA	GRIFFIN,PA	127	157
1.60	DEANGELO,LE	JA	1988	JAE			3	36

CITE INDEX	FIRST AUTHOR	ISS-UE	YE-AR	JOUR-NAL	SECOND AUTHOR	THIRD AUTHOR	PAG BEG	PAG END
1.59	BEAVER,WH	AP	1972	TAR	DUKES ,RE		320	332
1.56	AJINKYA,BB	AU	1984	JAR	GIFT ,MJ		425	444
1.56	DODD ,P	AP	1984	JAE	DOPUCH,N	HOLTHAUSEN,RW	3	38
1.56	KROSS ,W	SP	1984	JAR	SCHROEDER,DA		153	176
1.53	GONEDES,NJ	SP	1978	JAR			26	79
1.50	BAMBER,LS	JL	1987	TAR			510	532
1.50	BARTOV,E	SE	1991	JAE			275	293
1.50	HARRIS,TS	OC	1987	TAR	OHLSON,JA		651	670
1.50	HUNT III,HG	AU	1985	JAR			448	467
1.50	OHLSON,JA	JL	1989	JAE			109	115
1.47	SUNDER,S	AP	1975	TAR			305	315
1.44	COLLINS,DW	SP	1984	JAR	DENT ,WT		48	84
1.43	HOSKIN,RE	ST	1986	JAR	HUGHES,JS	RICKS ,WE	1	36
1.38	BUBLITZ,B	ST	1985	JAR	FRECKA,TJ	MCKEOWN,JC	1	23
1.33	LEV ,B	SP	1990	JAR	PENMAN,SH		49	76
1.33	OU ,JA	SP	1990	JAR			144	163
1.31	BROWN ,RM	SP	1980	JAR			38	63
1.31	GHEYARA,K	AG	1980	JAE	BOATSMAN,JR		107	125
1.30	PINCUS,M	SP	1983	JAR			155	183
1.27	ABDEL-KHALIK,AR	OC	1978	TAR	MCKEOWN,JC		851	868
1.27	FREEMAN,RN	AU	1982	JAR	OHLSON,JA	PENMAN,SH	639	653
1.25	BERNARD,VL	OC	1989	TAR	STOBER,TL		624	652
1.25	CORNELL,B	OC	1989	TAR	LANDSMAN,WR		680	692
1.25	HAN ,JCY	FB	1989	JAE	WILD ,JJ	RAMESH,K	3	33
1.25	MCNICHOLS,M	JA	1989	TAR			1	27
1.24	DEAKIN,EB	SP	1972	JAR			167	179
1.20	THOMAS,JK	JL	1988	JAE			199	237
1.15	RO ,BT	AG	1980	JAE			159	189
1.14	GIVOLY,D	DE	1979	JAE	LAKONISHOK,J		165	185
1.14	LANDSMAN,WR	OC	1986	TAR			662	691
1.12	FOSTER,G	SP	1973	JAR			25	37
1.11	HAGERMAN,RL	AU	1984	JAR	ZMIJEWSKI,ME	SHAH ,P	526	540
1.10	KELLER,SB	AU	1983	AUD	DAVIDSON,LF		1	22
1.10	OHLSON,JA	SP	1983	JAR			141	154
1.08	BEAVER,WH	SP	1981	JAR			163	184
1.08	NOREEN,EW	AP	1981	TAR	SEPE ,J		253	269
1.08	PATELL,JM	AU	1981	JAR	WOLFSON,MA		434	458
1.06	HARRISON,T	SP	1977	JAR			84	107
1.00	ANTHONY,JH	JN	1992	JAE	RAMESH,K		203	227
1.00	BALL ,R	OC	1991	TAR	KOTHARI,SP		718	738
1.00	BHUSHAN,R	JL	1989	JAE			183	206
1.00	BIDDLE,GC	SP	1991	JAA	SEOW ,GS		183	232
1.00	CHENG ,CSA	JL	1992	TAR	HOPWOOD,WS	MCKEOWN,JC	579	598
1.00	DOPUCH,N	JL	1987	TAR	HOLTHAUSEN,RW	LEFTWICH,RW	431	454
1.00	DORAN ,BM	JL	1988	TAR	COLLINS,DW	DHALIWAL,DS	389	413
1.00	ELLIOTT,JA	AU	1982	JAR			617	638
1.00	ELLIOTT,JA	SP	1984	JAR	RICHARDSON,G	DYCKMAN,TR	85	102
1.00	FREEMAN,RN	AU	1992	JAR	TSE ,SY		185	209
1.00	HERTZER,M	SE	1991	JAE	JAIN ,PC		253	273
1.00	HUGHES,JS	JA	1987	TAR	RICKS ,WE		158	175
1.00	IMHOFF JR,EA	AP	1992	TAR	LOBO ,GJ		427	439
1.00	LEE ,CMC	JN	1992	JAE			265	302
1.00	LUSTGARTEN,S	OC	1982	JAE			121	141

CITE INDEX	FIRST AUTHOR	ISS-UE	YE-AR	JOUR-NAL	SECOND AUTHOR	THIRD AUTHOR	PAG BEG	PAG END
1.00	MCNICHOLS,M	AP	1983	JAE	MANEGOLD,JG		49	74
1.00	SHORES,D	SP	1990	JAR			164	181
0.94	BROWN ,P	ST	1967	JAR	BALL ,R		55	77
0.94	GONEDES,NJ	SP	1974	JAR			26	62
0.93	HONG ,H	JA	1978	TAR	KAPLAN,RS	MANDELKER,G	31	47
0.93	PATELL,JM	AG	1979	JAE	WOLFSON,MA		117	140
0.89	HUGHES,JS	AG	1984	JAE	RICKS ,WE		101	132
0.89	KELLOGG,RL	DE	1984	JAE			185	204
0.89	LAMBERT,RA	OC	1984	TAR			604	618
0.89	MARAIS,ML	ST	1984	JAR			34	54
0.88	ARCHIBALD,TR	JA	1972	TAR			22	30
0.86	OHLSON,JA	DE	1979	JAE			211	232
0.83	ATIASE,RK	SP	1987	JAR			168	176
0.83	JENNINGS,R	SP	1987	JAR			90	110
0.83	WALLACE,WA	AU	1981	JAR			502	520
0.82	EGGLETON,IRC	SP	1976	JAR	PENMAN,SH	TWOMBLY,JR	66	88
0.82	JAIN ,PC	DE	1982	JAE			205	228
0.81	JOY ,OM	AU	1977	JAR	LITZENBERGER,RH	MCENALLY,RW	207	225
0.80	LANDSMAN,WR	OC	1988	TAR	MAGLIOLO,J		586	604
0.80	MORRIS,MH	AP	1988	TAR	NICHOLS,WD		237	254
0.75	FROST ,CA	OC	1989	TAR			788	808
0.75	OLSEN ,C	ST	1985	JAR	DIETRICH,JR		144	166
0.75	POWNALL,G	AU	1989	JAR	WAYMIRE,G		227	245
0.73	COLLINS,DW	JA	1982	TAR	ROZEFF,MS	SALATKA,WK	1	17
0.71	BEAVER,WH	JL	1973	TAR	DUKES ,RE		549	559
0.71	MAGLIOLO,J	ST	1986	JAR			69	111
0.71	RICKS ,WE	SP	1986	JAR			206	216
0.71	STOBER,TL	ST	1986	JAR			138	164
0.67	BEAVER,WH	JA	1987	TAR			137	144
0.67	BOWEN ,RM	JA	1981	TAR			1	22
0.67	CLINCH,GJ	AP	1987	JAE	SINCLAIR,NA		89	106
0.67	DEANGELO,LE	JA	1990	TAR			93	112
0.67	HEALY ,PM	SP	1990	JAR	PALEPU,KG		25	48
0.67	SCHAEFER,TF	AU	1984	JAR			647	656
0.64	VERRECCHIA,RE	ST	1982	JAR			1	42
0.63	BRICKLEY,JA	AP	1985	JAE	BHAGAT,S	LEASE ,RC	115	130
0.63	EASTON,PD	ST	1985	JAR			54	77
0.63	HAKA ,SF	OC	1985	TAR	GORDON,LA	PINCHES,GE	651	669
0.63	SCHIPPER,K	SP	1985	JAR	THOMPSON,R		408	415
0.60	BELL ,TB	SP	1983	JAR			1	17
0.60	CHENHALL,RH	03	1988	AOS	BROWNELL,P		225	233
0.60	FOSTER III,TW	OC	1978	TAR	VICKREY,DW		921	934
0.60	JOHNSON,WB	AU	1988	JAR	DHALIWAL,DS		236	272
0.60	MCNICHOLS,M	JL	1988	JAE			239	273
0.60	SHANE ,PB	JL	1983	TAR	SPICER,BH		521	538
0.58	SMITH ,AJ	ST	1981	JAR			174	211
0.57	DOPUCH,N	JN	1986	JAE	HOLTHAUSEN,RW	LEFTWICH,RW	93	118
0.56	IMHOFF JR,EA	AU	1984	JAR	LOBO ,GJ		541	554
0.55	BANKS ,DW	SP	1982	JAR	KINNEY JR,WR		240	254
0.53	FIRTH ,MA	JL	1978	TAR			642	650
0.50	AJINKYA,BB	NV	1989	JAE	JAIN ,PC		331	359
0.50	ATIASE,RK	SP	1989	CAR	BAMBER,LS	TSE ,S	526	552
0.50	BROWN ,LD	SP	1991	CAR	RICHARDSON,GD	TRZCINKA,CA	323	346

CITE INDEX	FIRST AUTHOR	ISS-UE	YE-AR	JOUR-NAL	SECOND AUTHOR	THIRD AUTHOR	PAG BEG	PAG END
0.50	CREADY,WM	AP	1991	TAR	MYNATT,PG		291	312
0.50	FELTHAM,GA	DE	1991	JAE	HUGHES,JS	SIMUNIC,DA	375	399
0.50	FEROZ ,EH	ST	1991	JAR	PARK ,K	PASTENA,VS	107	148
0.50	FREEMAN,RN	SP	1983	JAR			42	64
0.50	GHICAS,D	AU	1989	CAR	PASTENA,V		125	142
0.50	L'HER ,JF	SP	1991	CAR	SURET ,J-M		378	406
0.50	LARCKER,DF	OC	1983	TAR	REVSINE,L		706	732
0.50	LOBO ,GJ	AP	1989	TAR	SONG ,I		329	343
0.50	LOBO ,GL	SP	1989	JAR	MAHMOUD,AAW		116	134
0.50	MORSE ,D	AP	1991	TAR	STEPHAN,J	STICE ,EK	376	388
0.50	OLSEN ,C	ST	1985	JAR			28	53
0.50	PATELL,JM	AU	1979	JAR			528	549
0.50	SWAMINATHAN,S	JA	1991	TAR			23	41
0.47	FOSTER,G	OC	1975	TAR			686	698
0.47	MAGEE ,RP	AU	1974	JAR			270	287
0.47	RO ,BT	AU	1978	JAR			315	340
0.46	OPPONG,A	AU	1980	JAR			574	584
0.45	ABDEL-KHALIK,AR	OC	1982	TAR	AJINKYA,BB		661	680
0.43	DHALIWAL,DS	OC	1986	TAR			651	661
0.43	JAIN ,PC	SP	1986	JAR			76	96
0.43	NICHOLS,DR	SP	1979	JAR	TSAY ,JJ		140	155
0.42	FRIED ,D	AP	1981	TAR	SCHIFF,A		326	341
0.42	VIGELAND,RL	AP	1981	TAR			309	325
0.41	BASKIN,EF	JA	1972	TAR			38	51
0.41	GONEDES,NJ	JA	1972	TAR			11	21
0.41	KIGER ,JE	SP	1972	JAR			113	128
0.41	KLAMMER,T	AP	1973	TAR			353	364
0.40	CREADY,WM	SP	1988	JAR			1	27
0.40	HAW ,IM	AU	1988	JAR	LUSTGARTEN,S		331	352
0.40	LANEN ,WN	DE	1988	JAE	THOMPSON,R		311	334
0.40	LEV ,B	AP	1983	JAE			31	48
0.40	LYS ,T	AU	1988	JAR	SIVARAMAKRISHNAN,K		273	299
0.40	NICHOLS,DR	AU	1983	JAR	SMITH ,DB		534	544
0.40	RO ,BT	SP	1988	CAR			438	449
0.40	THOMPSON,RB	JL	1988	TAR	OLSEN ,C	DIETRICH,JR	448	471
0.38	BOWMAN,RG	SP	1980	JAR			242	254
0.38	JENNINGS,R	SP	1985	JAR	STARKS,L		336	350
0.36	CHOW ,CW	WI	1982	AUD	RICE ,SJ		35	53
0.36	COLLINS,DW	AU	1979	JAR	SIMONDS,RR		352	383
0.36	MAYER-SOMMER,AP	JA	1979	TAR			88	106
0.35	BENSTON,GJ	ST	1967	JAR			1	54
0.35	MAY ,RG	JA	1973	TAR	SUNDEM,GL		80	94
0.33	AHARONY,J	SP	1987	CAR	BAR-YOSEF,S		430	444
0.33	BEAVER,WH	JA	1981	TAR			23	37
0.33	CHANDRA,R	AU	1990	CAR	ROHRBACH,K		123	141
0.33	HAN ,JCY	SP	1990	JAR	WILD ,JJ		211	219
0.33	HAW ,I	AP	1990	TAR	PASTENA,VS	LILIEN,SB	432	451
0.33	HSIEH ,S-J	SP	1990	CAR	FERRIS,KR	CHEN ,AH	550	572
0.33	LANDSMAN,WR	AU	1990	CAR	OHLSON,JA		185	198
0.33	LEFTWICH,R	JA	1990	JAE			37	44
0.33	MCDONALD,B	JL	1984	TAR	MORRIS,MH		432	446
0.33	MOSES ,OD	AP	1987	TAR			358	377
0.33	NOREEN,EW	AU	1981	JAR	WOLFSON,MA		384	398

CITE INDEX	FIRST AUTHOR	ISS-UE	YE-AR	JOUR-NAL	SECOND AUTHOR	THIRD AUTHOR	PAG BEG	PAG END
0.33	RO ,BT	JA	1981	TAR			70	84
0.33	SHANK ,JK	OC	1978	TAR	MURDOCK,RJ		824	835
0.33	SKINNER,DJ	OC	1990	JAE			191	211
0.33	STEVENSON,FL	AU	1987	JAR			306	316
0.33	WILSON,ER	SP	1990	CAR	STEWART,JP		573	591
0.31	ANDERSON,JC	JL	1980	TAR	FRANKLE,AW		467	479
0.30	CHOW ,CW	JL	1983	TAR			485	520
0.30	LARCKER,DF	JL	1983	TAR	REDER ,RE	SIMON ,DT	606	620
0.30	MURRAY,D	SP	1983	JAR			128	140
0.29	BILDERSEE,JS	JA	1975	TAR			81	98
0.29	DOWNES,D	AP	1973	TAR	DYCKMAN,TR		300	317
0.29	FOSTER,G	AU	1975	JAR			283	292
0.29	WRIGHT,CJ	JA	1986	TAR	GROFF ,JE		91	100
0.27	ABDEL-KHALIK,AR	ST	1978	JAR	MCKEOWN,JC		46	77
0.27	JAGGI ,B	OC	1978	TAR			961	967
0.27	RICE ,SJ	AP	1978	TAR			429	438
0.25	BOWEN ,RM	JL	1989	JAE	JOHNSON,MF	SHEVLIN,T	225	254
0.25	EICHENSEHER,JW	AU	1989	AUD	HAGIGI,M	SHIELDS,D	29	40
0.25	ESPAHBODI,R	SP	1989	CAR	TEHRANIAN,H		575	591
0.25	HOPWOOD,WS	SP	1985	JAR	MCKEOWN,JC		161	174
0.25	INGRAM,RW	AU	1985	JAR			595	618
0.25	LAMBERT,RA	AP	1985	JAE	LARCKER,DF		179	204
0.25	LEE ,CJ	SP	1985	JAR			213	227
0.25	MADEO ,SA	JL	1985	TAR	PINCUS,M		407	429
0.25	MULFORD,CW	AU	1985	JAR			897	906
0.25	RICKS ,WE	JA	1985	TAR	HUGHES,JS		33	52
0.25	SALATKA,WK	FB	1989	JAE			35	69
0.25	SELTO ,FH	AU	1985	JAR	CLOUSE,ML		700	717
0.25	TEHRANIAN,H	AP	1985	JAE	WAEGELEIN,JF		131	144
0.24	HAGERMAN,RL	OC	1975	TAR			699	709
0.24	O'CONNOR,MC	AP	1973	TAR			339	352
0.23	AJINKYA,BB	AU	1980	JAR			343	361
0.22	MORSE ,D	AU	1984	JAR			605	623
0.22	PENMAN,SH	DE	1984	JAE			165	183
0.22	SMITH ,DB	AG	1984	JAE	STETTLER,HF	BEEDLES,W	153	162
0.21	THORNTON,DB	03	1979	AOS			211	234
0.20	BASU ,S	JL	1978	TAR			599	625
0.20	BIDDLE,GC	AU	1988	JAR	RICKS ,WE		169	194
0.20	ELLIOTT,JA	ST	1988	JAR	SHAW,WH		91	126
0.20	HARRISON JR,WT	SP	1983	JAR	TOMASSINI,LA	DIETRICH,JR	65	77
0.20	KETZ ,JE	ST	1978	JAR			273	284
0.20	LEE ,CJ	AU	1988	CAR			371	388
0.20	SHAW ,WH	SP	1988	JAR			60	81
0.18	DAVIS ,RR	AU	1982	AUD			13	32
0.18	DEAKIN,EB	JL	1976	TAR			590	603
0.18	ESKEW ,RK	AP	1975	TAR			316	324
0.18	MAGEE ,RP	AU	1975	JAR			257	266
0.18	MARSHALL,RM	JA	1975	TAR			99	111
0.18	MEYERS,SL	AP	1973	TAR			318	322
0.18	OHLSON,JA	AU	1975	JAR			267	282
0.18	PATZ ,DH	AU	1972	JAR	BOATSMAN,JR		392	403
0.18	REILLY,FK	ST	1972	JAR	MORGENSON,DL	WEST ,M	105	124
0.18	SEPE ,J	JL	1982	TAR			467	485

CITE INDEX	FIRST AUTHOR	ISS-UE	YE-AR	JOUR-NAL	SECOND AUTHOR	THIRD AUTHOR	PAG BEG	PAG END
0.17	BERNARD,VL	OC	1987	TAR	RULAND,RG		707	722
0.17	BILDERSEE,JS	AU	1987	CAR	RONEN ,J		89	110
0.17	BOATSMAN,JR	JA	1981	TAR	BASKIN,EF		38	53
0.17	ELGERS,P	OC	1987	TAR	CALLAHAN,C	STROCK,E	763	773
0.17	RONEN ,J	AU	1981	JAR	LIVNAT,J		459	481
0.17	ZIEBART,DA	AP	1987	TAR	KIM ,DH		343	357
0.15	BOWMAN,RG	AP	1980	TAR			237	253
0.14	DEFEO ,VJ	AU	1986	JAR			349	363
0.14	JAIN ,PC	SP	1986	JAR			187	193
0.14	MURDOCH,B	AP	1986	TAR			273	287
0.14	OHLSON,JA	AU	1979	JAR	PATELL,JM		504	505
0.14	TSE ,S	JL	1986	TAR			475	497
0.13	ANDERSON,JA	AP	1977	TAR			417	426
0.13	COX ,CT	OC	1985	TAR			692	701
0.13	JOHNSON,WB	AP	1985	JAE	MAGEE ,RP	NAGARAJAN,NJ	151	174
0.13	SHORT ,DG	ST	1978	JAR			259	272
0.12	GRIFFIN,PA	JL	1976	TAR			499	515
0.12	KINNEY JR,WR	AP	1972	TAR			339	345
0.12	MLYNARCZYK,FA	ST	1969	JAR			63	81
0.11	DIETRICH,JR	AP	1984	JAE			67	96
0.10	INGRAM,RW	JL	1983	TAR	CHEWNING,EG		562	580
0.10	LAWRENCE,EC	AU	1983	JAR			606	610
0.09	SMITH ,DB	OC	1982	JAE	NICHOLS,DR		109	120
0.09	WHALEY,RE	OC	1982	JAE	CHEUNG,JK		57	83
0.07	DAVIS ,DW	JA	1978	TAR	BOATSMAN,JR	BASKIN,EF	1	10
0.07	FOSTER III,TW	AP	1978	TAR	VICKREY,DW		360	370
0.07	HILLISON,WA	SP	1979	JAR			60	73
0.07	OHLSON,JA	AU	1979	JAR			506	527
0.06	SHARPE,IG	AU	1975	JAR	WALKER,RG		293	310
0.00	ABDEL-KHALIK,AR	SP	1986	CAR			242	251
0.00	AJINKYA,BB	AP	1991	TAR	ATIASE,RK	GIFT ,MJ	389	401
0.00	ALLEN ,S	SP	1990	CAR	RAMANAN,R		518	543
0.00	AMIHUD,Y	AU	1988	JAA	MENDELSON,H		369	395
0.00	AMIHUD,Y	AU	1989	JAA	MENDELSON,H		415	431
0.00	AMIT ,R	WI	1988	JAA	LIVNAT,J		19	43
0.00	AMIT ,R	AU	1989	CAR	LIVNAT,J	ZAROWIN,P	143	158
0.00	ASQUITH,P	JL	1989	TAR	HEALY ,P	PALEPU,K	387	403
0.00	BAGINSKI,SP	JA	1990	TAR	HASSELL,JM		175	190
0.00	BALL ,R	JN	1992	JAE			309	345
0.00	BARTH ,ME	MR	1992	JAE	BEAVER,WH	LANDSMAN,WR	27	61
0.00	BARTOV,E	JL	1992	TAR			610	622
0.00	BEATTY,RP	WI	1985	JAA	JOHNSON,SB		112	124
0.00	BEATTY,RP	AU	1992	JAA	HAND ,JRM		509	530
0.00	BEAVER,WH	DE	1981	JAE	LANDSMAN,WR		233	241
0.00	BIDWELL III,CM	SP	1981	JAA	RIDDLE JR,JR		198	214
0.00	BINDER,JJ	SP	1985	JAR			370	383
0.00	BLACCONIERE,WG	MR	1991	JAE			91	113
0.00	BOARD ,JLG	SP	1990	JAR	WALKER,M		182	192
0.00	BONNIER,KA	FB	1989	JAE	BRUNER,RF		95	106
0.00	BRENNAN,MJ	JA	1991	TAR			67	79
0.00	BROWN ,BC	SU	1986	JAA	BRANDI,JT		185	205
0.00	BROWN ,LD	SP	1986	CAR			252	258
0.00	BROWN ,LD	AU	1991	JAR	KIM ,SK		382	385

CITE INDEX	FIRST AUTHOR	ISS-UE	YE-AR	JOUR-NAL	SECOND AUTHOR	THIRD AUTHOR	PAG BEG	PAG END
0.00	BROWN ,LD	OC	1992	TAR	HAN ,JCY		862	875
0.00	BURGSTAHLER,D	SP	1986	JAR	NOREEN,EW		170	186
0.00	CASSIDY,DB	AU	1976	JAR			212	229
0.00	CHANEY,PK	SP	1992	CAR	JETER ,DC		540	560
0.00	CHARITOU,A	AU	1990	JAA	KETZ ,JE		475	497
0.00	CHOI ,SK	JN	1992	JAE	JETER ,DC		229	247
0.00	COOPER,T	WI	1980	JAA			138	146
0.00	COPELAND,TE	AU	1978	JAA			33	48
0.00	CORNELL,B	AU	1989	JAA	LANDSMAN,W	SHAPIRO,AC	460	479
0.00	CREADY,WM	JL	1987	TAR	SHANK ,JK		589	596
0.00	DONTOH,A	SP	1988	CAR	RICHARDSON,E		450	469
0.00	DORAN ,DT	SP	1988	JAA	NACHTMANN,R		113	132
0.00	ELGERS,PT	JL	1980	TAR			389	408
0.00	ELGERS,PT	AP	1982	TAR	MURRAY,D		358	375
0.00	ELLIOTT,JA	OC	1991	TAR	HANNA ,JD	SHAW ,WH	847	861
0.00	ESPAHBODI,H	DE	1991	JAE	STROCK,E	TEHRANIAN,H	323	345
0.00	ETTREDGE,M	SP	1988	AUD	SHANE ,PB	SMITH ,D	29	42
0.00	FIELDS,LP	AU	1991	AUD	WILKINS,MS		62	69
0.00	FIRTH ,MA	AU	1981	JAR			521	529
0.00	FRANCIS,J	AU	1992	JAR	PAGACH,D	STEPHAN,J	165	184
0.00	FRECKA,TJ	SP	1983	JAR	LEE ,CF		308	316
0.00	FREEMAN,R	DE	1992	JAE	TSE ,S		509	523
0.00	FREEMAN,RN	ST	1978	JAR			111	145
0.00	GAVER ,JJ	JA	1992	TAR	GAVER ,KM	BATTISTEL,GP	172	182
0.00	GIVOLY,D	AU	1981	JAR	PALMON,D		530	543
0.00	GIVOLY,D	SP	1987	JAA	LAKONISHOK,J		117	137
0.00	GIVOLY,D	AP	1992	TAR	HAYN ,C		394	410
0.00	GONEDES,NJ	ST	1969	JAR			90	113
0.00	GONEDES,NJ	JL	1971	TAR			535	551
0.00	GORDON,DA	AU	1990	JAA	GORDON,MJ		573	588
0.00	GOVINDARAJ,S	AU	1992	JAA			485	508
0.00	GRIFFIN,PA	OC	1991	TAR	WALLACH,SJR		830	846
0.00	GROSSMAN,SD	WI	1981	JAA	KRATCHMAN,SH	WELKER,RB	136	143
0.00	HALPERIN,R	AP	1987	TAR	LANEN ,WN		378	384
0.00	HAN ,BH	MR	1992	JAE	JENNINGS,R	NOEL ,J	63	85
0.00	HAN ,JCY	SP	1991	JAR	WILD ,JJ		79	95
0.00	HAND ,JRM	OC	1990	TAR			739	763
0.00	HAND ,JRM	OC	1991	TAR			739	746
0.00	HARMON,WK	AU	1984	JAA			24	34
0.00	HAW ,I	SU	1991	JAA	KIM ,W		325	344
0.00	HAW ,IM	WI	1987	JAA	PASTENA,V	LILIEN,S	24	42
0.00	HOPWOOD,W	AP	1989	TAR	SCHAEFER,T		313	328
0.00	HOPWOOD,WS	AU	1988	CAR	SCHAEFER,TF		318	342
0.00	HUGHES,JS	SP	1986	CAR	RICKS ,WE		222	241
0.00	INGRAM,RW	AP	1989	TAR	RAMAN ,KK	WILSON,ER	250	268
0.00	JAIN ,PC	JL	1983	TAR			633	638
0.00	JENNINGS,R	OC	1990	TAR			925	932
0.00	KETZ ,JE	AU	1983	JAA	WYATT ,AR		29	43
0.00	KIM ,DH	WI	1991	JAA	ZIEBART,DA		35	47
0.00	KING ,R	SP	1992	CAR	POWNALL,G	WAYMIRE,G	509	531
0.00	KORKIE,B	AU	1990	JAA	LAISS ,B		593	617
0.00	KOTHARI,SP	JN	1992	JAE			173	202
0.00	KRAMER,SS	JA	1982	TAR			70	87

CITE INDEX	FIRST AUTHOR	ISS-UE	YE-AR	JOUR-NAL	SECOND AUTHOR	THIRD AUTHOR	PAG BEG	PAG END
0.00	KRINSKY,I	SP	1989	CAR	ROTENBERG,W		501	515
0.00	KROSS ,W	AU	1980	JAA	CHAPMAN,G	STRAND,KH	36	46
0.00	KROSS ,W	AU	1982	JAR			459	471
0.00	LEV ,B	SP	1979	JAA	TAYLOR,KW		232	243
0.00	LEVY ,H	SP	1990	JAA			235	270
0.00	LIVNAT,J	AU	1981	JAR			350	359
0.00	LUNDHOLM,RJ	JL	1991	TAR			486	515
0.00	MARSTON,F	SP	1988	JAA	HARRIS,RS		147	164
0.00	MARTIN,JD	WI	1979	JAA	ANDERSON,PF	KEOWN ,AJ	151	164
0.00	MCGAHRAN,KT	JA	1988	TAR			23	41
0.00	MEEK ,GK	AP	1983	TAR			394	402
0.00	MENON ,K	AP	1991	TAR	WILLIAMS,DD		313	332
0.00	MILLAR,JA	JA	1977	TAR			52	55
0.00	MILLER,EM	AU	1980	JAA			6	19
0.00	MURRAY,D	WI	1982	JAA			154	159
0.00	NICHOLS,DR	AP	1979	TAR	TSAY ,JJ	LARKIN,PD	376	382
0.00	ODAIYAPPA,R	JL	1992	TAR	NAINAR,SMK		599	609
0.00	OHLSON,JA	ST	1972	JAR			45	84
0.00	OHLSON,JA	AU	1992	JAA	PENMAN,SH		553	573
0.00	PATTEN,DM	06	1990	AOS			575	587
0.00	PENMAN,SH	JL	1992	TAR			563	578
0.00	PETERSEN,RJ	JL	1975	TAR			525	532
0.00	POWNALL,G	ST	1989	JAR	WAYMIRE,G		85	105
0.00	PYO ,Y	DE	1990	JAE	LUSTGARTEN,S		365	379
0.00	RAMAKRISHNAN,RTS	AU	1992	JAA	THOMAS,JK		423	464
0.00	RANSOM,CR	ST	1985	JAR			124	143
0.00	RO ,BT	AU	1989	CAR			177	195
0.00	SAMI ,H	SP	1989	CAR	CURATOLA,AP	TRAPNELL,JE	556	574
0.00	SCHACHTER,B	AU	1988	JAR			353	372
0.00	SCHAEFER,T	AU	1986	JAA	KENNELLEY,M		278	287
0.00	SHACKELFORD,DA	JN	1991	JAE			117	145
0.00	SHANKER,L	SU	1992	JAA			379	393
0.00	SHAW ,WH	SP	1991	CAR			407	423
0.00	SHEVLIN,T	JA	1991	TAR			1	22
0.00	SILHAN,PA	SP	1983	JAR			341	347
0.00	SMITH ,DB	SP	1988	JAR			134	145
0.00	STANDISH,PEM	OC	1982	TAR	UNG ,S		701	715
0.00	STEVENS,JL	SP	1992	JAA	JOSE ,ML		195	212
0.00	STICE ,EK	JA	1991	TAR			42	55
0.00	STICKEL,SE	OC	1986	JAE			197	216
0.00	STICKEL,SE	AP	1991	TAR			402	416
0.00	SUNDER,S	SP	1989	CAR			452	460
0.00	TEALL ,HD	SP	1992	CAR			561	579
0.00	TEALL ,HD	SP	1992	CAR			561	579
0.00	TEETS ,W	AU	1992	JAR			274	285
0.00	THEOBALD,M	AU	1985	CAR			1	22
0.00	THODE ,SF	WI	1986	JAA	DRTINA,RE	LARGAY III,JA	46	61
0.00	TINIC ,SM	OC	1990	TAR			781	796
0.00	TORABZADEH,KM	SP	1992	JAA	BERTIN,WJ		231	240
0.00	TRUEMAN,B	OC	1990	JAE			285	301
0.00	TSE ,S	SP	1989	CAR			592	614
0.00	TSE ,S	SP	1990	JAR			229	238
0.00	WARFIELD,TD	JL	1992	TAR	LINSMEIER,TJ		546	562

CITE INDEX	FIRST AUTHOR	ISS-UE	YE-AR	JOUR-NAL	SECOND AUTHOR	THIRD AUTHOR	PAG BEG	PAG END
0.00	WARFIELD,TD	OC	1992	TAR	WILD ,JJ		821	842
0.00	WAYMIRE,G	AU	1983	JAR	POWNALL,G		629	643
0.00	ZIEBART,DA	AU	1985	JAR			920	926
0.00	ZIEBART,DA	AP	1990	TAR			477	488

3.4 SCHOOL OF THOUGHT=STAT.MODEL - TIME SERIES

CITE INDEX	FIRST AUTHOR	ISS-UE	YE-AR	JOUR-NAL	SECOND AUTHOR	THIRD AUTHOR	PAG BEG	PAG END
5.17	BROWN ,LD	JL	1987	JAE	GRIFFIN,PA	HAGERMAN,RL	159	193
4.80	O'BRIEN,PC	JA	1988	JAE			53	83
4.50	BROWN ,LD	AP	1987	JAE	GRIFFIN,PA	HAGERMAN,RL	61	87
4.31	FOSTER,G	JA	1977	TAR			1	21
2.73	FRIED ,D	OC	1982	JAE	GIVOLY,D		85	107
2.63	WATTS ,RL	AU	1977	JAR	LEFTWICH,RW		253	271
2.25	ALBRECHT,WS	AU	1977	JAR	LOOKABILL,LL	MCKEOWN,JC	226	244
2.25	DEANGELO,LE	AG	1981	JAE			113	127
2.19	GRIFFIN,PA	SP	1977	JAR			71	83
2.18	DHALIWAL,DS	JL	1982	JAE	SALAMON,GL	SMITH ,ED	41	53
2.07	BROWN ,LD	SP	1979	JAR	ROZEFF,MS		179	189
1.82	BEAVER,WH	OC	1970	TAR	KETTLER,P	SCHOLES,M	654	682
1.67	COLLINS,DW	OC	1990	JAE	DeANGELO,L		213	247
1.50	BROWN ,LD	SP	1987	JAR	RICHARDSON,GD	SCHWAGER,SJ	49	67
1.50	HAND ,JRM	OC	1989	TAR			587	623
1.35	BEAVER,WH	ST	1970	JAR			62	99
1.31	COLLINS,WA	AU	1980	JAR	HOPWOOD,WS		390	406
1.00	BARTH ,ME	JA	1991	TAR	BEAVER,WH	STINSON,CH	56	66
1.00	CHANDRA,R	SP	1990	CAR	BALACHANDRAN,BV		611	640
1.00	DANN ,LY	SE	1991	JAE	MASULIS,RW	MAYERS,D	217	251
0.94	DOPUCH,N	SP	1972	JAR	WATTS ,RL		180	194
0.94	GONEDES,NJ	AU	1973	JAR			212	237
0.93	CRICHFIELD,T	JL	1978	TAR	DYCKMAN,TR	LAKONISHOK,J	651	668
0.87	KINNEY JR,WR	JA	1978	TAR			48	60
0.86	BROWN ,LD	AU	1979	JAR	ROZEFF,MS		341	351
0.82	BASI ,BA	AP	1976	TAR	CAREY ,KJ	TWARK ,RD	244	254
0.82	IMHOFF JR,EA	AU	1982	JAR	PARE ,PV		429	439
0.82	KINNEY JR,WR	SP	1971	JAR			127	136
0.75	THOMAS,JK	NV	1989	JAE			361	398
0.71	LOREK ,KS	SP	1979	JAR			190	204
0.67	KROSS ,W	AP	1990	TAR	RO ,B	SCHROEDER,D	461	476
0.65	LOREK ,KS	AP	1976	TAR	MCDONALD,CL	PATZ ,DH	321	330
0.60	ABDEL-KHALIK,AR	SP	1978	JAR	ESPEJO,J		1	13
0.57	HASSELL,JM	JA	1986	TAR	JENNINGS,RH		58	75
0.56	BATHKE,AW	AP	1984	TAR	LOREK ,KS		163	176
0.55	HOPWOOD,WS	AU	1982	JAR	MCKEOWN,JC	NEWBOLD,P	343	349
0.53	BEIDLEMAN,CR	OC	1973	TAR			653	667
0.50	ELY ,KM	SP	1991	JAR			37	58
0.50	HIRSCHEY,M	SP	1985	JAR	WEYGANDT,JJ		326	335
0.50	KOTHARI,SP	AP	1989	TAR	WASLEY,CE		228	249
0.47	LOOKABILL,LL	OC	1976	TAR			724	738
0.47	RULAND,W	AP	1978	TAR			439	447
0.44	COLLINS,WA	AU	1984	JAR	HOPWOOD,WS	MCKEOWN,JC	467	479
0.42	HOPWOOD,WS	AU	1981	JAR	MCKEOWN,JC		313	322
0.41	BEAVER,WH	AU	1968	JAR			179	192
0.40	DALEY ,LA	OC	1988	TAR	SENKOW,DW	VIGELAND,RL	563	585

CITE INDEX	FIRST AUTHOR	ISS-UE	YE-AR	JOUR-NAL	SECOND AUTHOR	THIRD AUTHOR	PAG BEG	PAG END
0.36	HOPWOOD,WS	AU	1982	JAR	NEWBOLD,P	SILHAN,PA	724	732
0.35	COATES,R	ST	1972	JAR			132	144
0.35	LEV ,B	AP	1974	TAR	KUNITZKY,S		259	270
0.33	ABDEL-KHALIK,AR	AU	1990	CAR			142	172
0.33	HAM ,J	AU	1987	CAR	LOSELL,D	SMIELIAUSKAS,W	210	226
0.33	O'BRIEN,PC	AU	1990	JAR			286	304
0.31	LEV ,B	AU	1980	JAR			524	550
0.29	BARNEA,A	JA	1976	TAR	RONEN ,J	SADAN ,S	110	122
0.29	WAYMIRE,G	JA	1986	TAR			129	142
0.29	WHITE ,GE	AU	1970	JAR			260	273
0.25	LANDSMAN,WR	SP	1989	JAR	DAMODARAN,A		97	115
0.25	NEWMAN,HA	OC	1989	TAR			758	772
0.24	BAREFIELD,RM	AP	1972	TAR	COMISKEY,EE		291	298
0.24	DASCHER,PE	AU	1970	JAR	MALCOM,RE		253	259
0.24	LEV ,B	AU	1969	JAR			290	299
0.23	HOPWOOD,WS	SP	1980	JAR			77	90
0.21	BROWN ,LD	JL	1979	TAR	ROZEFF,MS		585	591
0.20	DHARAN,BG	SP	1983	JAR			18	41
0.20	MCKEOWN,JC	SP	1988	CAR	SHALCHI,H		485	507
0.18	BALOFF,N	AU	1967	JAR	KENNELLY,JW		131	143
0.18	BAREFIELD,RM	AU	1971	JAR	COMISKEY,EE		351	358
0.18	BENSTON,GJ	OC	1966	TAR			657	672
0.18	COPELAND,RM	JL	1968	TAR	LICASTRO,RD		540	545
0.18	SAMUELSON,RA	AU	1972	JAR			322	344
0.18	WHITE JR,CE	AU	1972	JAR			351	358
0.17	BROWN ,LD	AU	1987	CAR	ZMIJEWSKI,MA		61	75
0.17	COGGER,KO	AU	1981	JAR			285	298
0.17	MOORE ,ML	OC	1987	TAR	STEECE,BM	SWENSON,CW	671	685
0.15	RONEN ,J	SU	1980	JAA	SADAN ,S		339	353
0.12	ABDEL-KHALIK,AR	OC	1975	TAR			657	670
0.12	ELLIOTT,JW	AU	1972	JAR	UPHOFF,HL		259	274
0.12	GREENBALL,MN	ST	1971	JAR			172	190
0.12	JOHNSON,O	AU	1967	JAR			164	172
0.12	KIGER ,JE	JA	1974	TAR			1	7
0.12	STAUBUS,GJ	JA	1965	TAR			119	134
0.11	LOREK ,KS	SP	1984	JAR	BATHKE,AW		369	379
0.10	ABDEL-KHALIK,AR	SP	1983	JAR			293	296
0.09	COGGER,KO	AU	1982	JAR	RULAND,W		733	737
0.08	BROWN ,LD	SP	1980	JAR	HUGHES,JS	ROZEFF,MS	278	288
0.08	FRIED ,D	JL	1981	TAR	LIVNAT,J		493	509
0.08	HOPWOOD,WS	SP	1980	JAR			289	296
0.08	MANEGOLD,JG	AU	1981	JAR			360	373
0.08	OVADIA,A	WI	1980	JAA	RONEN ,J		113	137
0.07	BARLEV,B	AU	1979	JAR	LEVY ,H		305	315
0.06	JENSEN,RE	AP	1967	TAR			265	273
0.06	KINNEY JR,WR	SP	1969	JAR			44	52
0.06	MABERT,VA	JA	1974	TAR	RADCLIFFE,RC		61	75
0.00	AFFLECK-GRAVES,J	SP	1990	CAR	DAVIS ,LR	MENDENHALL,RR	501	517
0.00	ALI ,A	JA	1992	TAR	KLEIN ,A	ROSENFELD,J	183	198
0.00	BALAKRISHNAN,R	AU	1990	JAR	HARRIS,TS	SEN ,PK	305	325
0.00	BALDWIN,J	SU	1992	JAA	GLEZEN,GW		269	285
0.00	BARLEY,B	SU	1990	JAA	LIVNAT,J		411	433
0.00	BATHKE,AW	JA	1989	TAR	LOREK ,KS	WILLINGER,GL	49	68

CITE INDEX	FIRST AUTHOR	ISS-UE	YE-AR	JOUR-NAL	SECOND AUTHOR	THIRD AUTHOR	PAG BEG	PAG END
0.00	BEATTY,RP	SP	1989	CAR	VERRECCHIA,RE		472	493
0.00	BOWEN ,RM	AU	1992	JAA	JOHNSON,MF	SHEVLIN,T	395	422
0.00	BRIEF ,RP	JA	1969	TAR			20	26
0.00	CHANDRA,R	AU	1992	CAR	ROHRBACH,KJ	WILLINGER,GL	296	305
0.00	CHENG ,TT	AU	1986	CAR			226	241
0.00	CHIU ,JS	OC	1966	TAR	DECOSTER,DT		673	680
0.00	CLARKSON,PM	SP	1992	CAR	DONTOH,A	RICHARDSON,G	601	625
0.00	DEMPSEY,SJ	OC	1989	TAR			748	757
0.00	DHARAN,BG	SP	1983	JAR			256	270
0.00	DUGAN ,MT	SP	1985	AUD	GENTRY,JA	SHRIVER,KA	11	22
0.00	ELNICKI,RA	ST	1977	JAR			209	218
0.00	FELIX JR,WL	JA	1972	TAR			52	63
0.00	GIACCOTTO,C	SU	1992	JAA			291	310
0.00	GONEDES,NJ	AP	1971	TAR			320	328
0.00	GORTON,G	SP	1989	JAA	PENNACCHI,G		125	145
0.00	GREENBERG,R	AU	1984	JAR			719	730
0.00	HAW ,I	SE	1991	JAE	JUNG ,K	LILIEN,SB	295	320
0.00	HOPWOOD,WS	SU	1990	JAA	MCKEOWN,JC		339	363
0.00	HUTH ,WL	WI	1992	JAA	MARIS ,BA		27	44
0.00	ISMAIL,BE	AU	1987	CAR			76	88
0.00	ISMAIL,BE	JA	1989	TAR	KIM ,MK		125	136
0.00	JONES ,CP	AU	1990	JAA	BUBLITZ,B		549	566
0.00	JORGENSON,DW	AU	1991	JAA	YUN ,K		487	508
0.00	KHURANA,I	JL	1991	TAR			611	621
0.00	LANG ,M	AU	1991	JAR			229	257
0.00	LIVINGSTONE,JL	SP	1967	JAR			77	94
0.00	LOREK ,KS	SP	1983	JAR	ICERMAN,JD	ABDULKADER,AA	317	328
0.00	LOREK ,KS	AU	1992	AUD	BRANSON,BC	ICERMAN,RC	66	88
0.00	MELBERG,WF	JA	1972	TAR			116	133
0.00	MENDENHALL,RR	ST	1988	JAR	NICHOLS,WD		63	90
0.00	MOORE ,ML	JA	1985	TAR	STEECE,BM	SWENSON,CW	18	32
0.00	O'DONNELL,JL	JA	1965	TAR			135	143
0.00	OHLSON,JA	AU	1992	JAR	SHROLL,PK		210	226
0.00	PHILIPS,GE	ST	1970	JAR	MAYNE ,LS		178	188
0.00	PUTNAM,K	AU	1984	JAA	THOMAS,LR		15	23
0.00	RAUN ,DL	OC	1964	TAR			927	945
0.00	RICHARDSON,G	AU	1988	CAR	SEFCIK,SE	THOMPSON,R	299	317
0.00	ROSE ,PS	AU	1982	JAA	ANDREWS,WT	GIROUX,GA	20	31
0.00	SILHAN,PA	SP	1985	JAR	MCKEOWN,JC		416	426
0.00	SWANSON,EP	OC	1985	TAR	SHEARON,WT	THOMAS,LR	681	691
0.00	SWENSON,CW	JA	1987	TAR			117	136
0.00	WALKER,KB	AU	1991	JAR	MCCLELLAND,LA		371	381
0.00	WELCH ,PR	AU	1984	JAR			744	757
0.00	WHITEHURST,FD	JL	1970	TAR			553	564

3.5 SCHOOL OF THOUGHT=STAT.MODEL – INFO ECON./AGENCY

CITE INDEX	FIRST AUTHOR	ISS-UE	YE-AR	JOUR-NAL	SECOND AUTHOR	THIRD AUTHOR	PAG BEG	PAG END
4.00	BOWEN ,RM	AG	1981	JAE	NOREEN,EW	LACEY ,JM	151	179
2.80	DEMSKI,JS	AP	1978	TAR	FELTHAM,GA		336	359
2.50	BAIMAN,S	AU	1983	JAR	EVANS III,JH		371	395
2.38	DYE ,RA	SP	1985	JAR			123	145
2.20	HOLTHAUSEN,RW	SP	1988	JAR	VERRECCHIA,RE		82	106
2.14	HUGHES,PJ	JN	1986	JAE			119	142

CITE INDEX	FIRST AUTHOR	ISS-UE	YE-AR	JOUR-NAL	SECOND AUTHOR	THIRD AUTHOR	PAG BEG	PAG END
2.14	TITMAN,S	JN	1986	JAE	TRUEMAN,B		159	172
2.00	DYE ,RA	SP	1992	JAR			27	52
1.86	ZIMMERMAN,JL	JL	1979	TAR			504	521
1.67	BAIMAN,S	AU	1987	JAR	EVANS III,JH	NOEL ,J	217	244
1.67	MELUMAD,ND	SP	1990	JAR	THOMAN,L		77	120
1.56	DEMSKI,JS	JA	1984	TAR	PATELL,JM	WOLFSON,MA	16	34
1.56	PENNO ,M	SP	1984	JAR			177	191
1.50	BEAVER,WH	JA	1979	TAR	DEMSKI,JS		38	46
1.50	DATAR ,SM	MR	1991	JAE	FELTHAM,GA	HUGHES,JS	3	49
1.50	DYE ,RA	AU	1983	JAR			514	533
1.50	GJESDAL,F	SP	1981	JAR			208	231
1.50	HAYES ,DC	23	1983	AOS			241	250
1.40	NOREEN,EW	04	1988	AOS			359	369
1.33	BERG ,KB	SP	1990	CAR	COURSEY,D	DICKHAUT,J	825	849
1.33	DARROUGH,MN	JA	1990	JAE	STOUGHTON,NM		219	243
1.33	DEMSKI,JS	SP	1987	JAR	SAPPINGTON,DEM		68	89
1.33	HOLTHAUSEN,RW	JA	1990	TAR	VERRECCHIA,RE		191	208
1.33	MAGEE ,RP	AP	1990	TAR	TSENG ,M		315	336
1.29	KINNEY JR,WR	SP	1975	JAR			117	132
1.25	DEJONG,DV	AU	1985	JAR	FORSYTHE,R	UECKER,WC	753	793
1.18	CHRISTENSEN,J	AU	1982	JAR			589	603
1.00	ANTLE ,R	SP	1984	JAR			1	20
1.00	BANKER,RD	SP	1989	JAR	DATAR ,SM		21	39
1.00	BANKER,RD	SP	1992	CAR	DATAR ,SM		329	352
1.00	DYE ,RA	JA	1990	TAR			1	24
1.00	DYE ,RA	AU	1990	JAR	BALACHANDRAN,BV	MAGEE ,RP	239	266
1.00	FELTHAM,GA	AU	1992	CAR	XIE ,JZ		46	80
1.00	JANAKIRAMAN,SN	SP	1992	JAR	LAMBERT,RA	LARCKER,DF	53	69
1.00	JOHNSON,WB	JA	1990	JAE	LYS ,T		281	308
1.00	KANODIA,C	SP	1989	JAR	BUSHMAN,R	DICKHAUT,J	59	77
1.00	KIM ,O	AU	1991	JAR	VERRECCHIA,RE		302	321
1.00	MELUMAD,ND	ST	1987	JAR	REICHELSTEIN,S		1	18
1.00	NEU ,D	04	1992	AOS			223	237
1.00	SUH ,YS	ST	1987	JAR			22	46
0.91	CHOW ,CW	AP	1982	TAR			272	291
0.88	DEJONG,DV	ST	1985	JAR	FORSYTHE,R	LUNDHOLM,RJ	81	120
0.88	YOUNG ,SM	AU	1985	JAR			829	842
0.87	UECKER,WC	SP	1978	JAR			169	189
0.83	EVANS III,JH	ST	1987	JAR	PATTON,JM		130	164
0.81	ZIMMERMAN,JL	ST	1977	JAR			107	144
0.80	DYE ,RA	AU	1988	JAR			195	235
0.76	DEMSKI,JS	AP	1974	TAR			221	232
0.76	FELTHAM,GA	OC	1970	TAR	DEMSKI,JS		623	640
0.75	ANTLE ,R	SP	1989	CAR	DEMSKI,JS		423	451
0.75	BAIMAN,S	AU	1985	JAR	NOEL ,J		486	501
0.75	DEFEO ,VJ	AP	1989	TAR	LAMBER,RA	LARCKER,DF	201	227
0.75	DEMSKI,JS	SP	1989	JAR	SAPPINGTON,DEM		40	58
0.75	MELUMAD,ND	SP	1989	CAR			733	753
0.73	ANTLE ,R	AU	1982	JAR			504	527
0.71	DEMSKI,JS	AU	1986	JAR	SAPPINGTON,DEM		250	269
0.67	AMERSHI,AH	AU	1990	CAR	CHENG ,P		61	99
0.67	SHIBANO,T	ST	1990	JAR			110	147
0.67	VERRECCHIA,RE	JA	1990	JAE			245	250

CITE INDEX	FIRST AUTHOR	ISS-UE	YE-AR	JOUR-NAL	SECOND AUTHOR	THIRD AUTHOR	PAG BEG	PAG END
0.65	MAGEE ,RP	JL	1976	TAR			529	544
0.64	NG ,DS	ST	1979	JAR	STOECKENIUS,J		1	24
0.63	PENNO ,M	SP	1985	JAR			240	255
0.62	LEFTWICH,RW	DE	1980	JAE			193	211
0.62	MAGEE ,RP	AU	1980	JAR			551	573
0.60	ABDEL-KHALIK,AR	ST	1988	JAR			144	181
0.60	AMERSHI,AH	SP	1988	CAR	CHENG ,P		515	563
0.60	JUNG ,WO	SP	1988	JAR	KWON ,YK		146	153
0.59	DEMSKI,JS	AU	1976	JAR			230	245
0.59	ITAMI ,H	SP	1975	JAR			73	96
0.57	JARRELL,GA	AG	1979	JAE			93	116
0.54	EVANS III,JH	ST	1980	JAR			108	128
0.54	VERRECCHIA,RE	MR	1980	JAE			63	92
0.53	BAIMAN,S	SP	1975	JAR			1	15
0.53	BUTTERWORTH,JE	SP	1972	JAR			1	27
0.53	DEMSKI,JS	AU	1972	JAR			243	258
0.53	SUNDER,S	AU	1976	JAR			277	300
0.50	AMERSHI,AH	AU	1987	JAR	SUNDER,S		177	195
0.50	ANTLE ,R	ST	1991	JAR	DEMSKI,JS		1	30
0.50	ANTLE ,R	ST	1991	JAR	NALEBUFF,B		31	59
0.50	ARMSTRONG,P	01	1991	AOS			1	25
0.50	BAIMAN,S	SP	1991	JAR	EVANS III,JH	NAGARAJAN,NJ	1	18
0.50	BALACHANDRAN,BV	SP	1987	CAR	NAGARAJAN,NJ		281	301
0.50	BALAKRISHNAN,R	JA	1991	TAR			120	140
0.50	BECK ,PJ	JL	1989	TAR	JUNG ,W		468	487
0.50	BECK ,PJ	JL	1991	TAR	DAVIS ,JS	JUNG ,W	535	558
0.50	BUSHMAN,RM	AU	1991	JAR			261	276
0.50	COLLINS,JH	JL	1991	TAR	PLUMLEE,RD		559	576
0.50	DONTOH,A	AU	1989	JAA			480	511
0.50	FELLINGHAM,JC	JA	1985	TAR	WOLFSON,MA		10	17
0.50	FELLINGHAM,JC	SP	1989	AUD	NEWMAN,DP	PATTERSON,ER	1	21
0.50	INDJEJIKIAN,RJ	AU	1991	JAR			277	301
0.50	LAMBERT,RA	SP	1991	JAR	LARCKER,DF	VERRECCHIA,RE	129	149
0.47	DEMSKI,JS	JL	1972	TAR	FELTHAM,GA		533	548
0.47	NG ,DS	OC	1978	TAR			910	920
0.43	ATKINSON,AA	SP	1979	JAR			1	22
0.43	SUNDEM,GL	SP	1979	JAR			243	261
0.43	VERRECCHIA,RE	MR	1979	JAE			77	90
0.43	VERRECCHIA,RE	OC	1986	JAE			175	196
0.40	BANKER,RD	AU	1988	CAR	DATAR ,SM	MAINDIRATTA,A	96	124
0.40	HUGHES,PJ	ST	1988	JAR	SCHWARTZ,ES		41	62
0.40	LOEB ,M	SP	1978	JAR	MAGAT ,WA		103	121
0.40	LUNDHOLM,RJ	SP	1988	JAR			107	118
0.40	RONEN ,J	AU	1988	JAR	BALACHANDRAN,KR		300	314
0.40	TRUEMAN,B	ST	1988	JAR	TITMAN,S		127	143
0.38	AMERSHI,AH	SP	1985	CAR	DEMSKI,JS	FELLINGHAM,J	176	192
0.38	FELTHAM,GA	SP	1977	JAR			42	70
0.38	GONEDES,NJ	AU	1980	JAR			441	476
0.38	LAMBERT,RA	AU	1985	JAR			633	647
0.35	DEMSKI,JS	OC	1967	TAR			701	712
0.35	DEMSKI,JS	SP	1972	JAR			58	76
0.35	GONEDES,NJ	AU	1974	JAR	IJIRI ,Y		251	269
0.35	MARSHALL,RM	AU	1972	JAR			286	307

CITE INDEX	FIRST AUTHOR	ISS-UE	YE-AR	JOUR-NAL	SECOND AUTHOR	THIRD AUTHOR	PAG BEG	PAG END
0.33	ABDEL-KHALIK,AR	AU	1987	CAR	CHI ,C	GHICAS,D	32	60
0.33	BAIMAN,S	SP	1990	CAR	MAY ,JH	MUKHERJI,A	761	799
0.33	BAIMAN,S	04	1990	AOS			341	371
0.33	BALACHANDRAN,BV	AU	1987	CAR	LI ,L	MAGEE ,RP	164	185
0.33	BALACHANDRAN,BV	SP	1987	JAR	RAMAKRISHNAN,RT		111	126
0.33	CONROY,RM	JA	1987	TAR	HUGHES,JS		50	66
0.33	HALL ,TW	JL	1990	TAR	SHRIVER,KA		537	556
0.33	PENNO ,M	AP	1990	TAR			303	314
0.33	WALLER,WS	OC	1990	TAR	BISHOP,RA		812	836
0.30	SCHEPANSKI,A	AP	1983	TAR	UECKER,WC		259	283
0.29	BLAZENKO,GW	AU	1986	CAR	SCOTT ,WR		68	92
0.29	HILTON,RW	AU	1979	JAR			411	435
0.29	LEV ,B	AU	1968	JAR			247	261
0.25	AMERSHI,AH	AU	1989	CAR	CHENG ,P		72	90
0.25	BACHAR,J	AU	1989	CAR			216	241
0.25	BILLERA,LJ	SP	1981	JAR	HEATH ,DC	VERRECCHIA,RE	185	196
0.25	DOPUCH,N		1989	AUD	KING ,RR	WALLIN,DE	98	127
0.25	KANODIA,CS	SP	1985	JAR			175	193
0.25	MOORE ,G	SP	1989	CAR	SCOTT ,WR		754	774
0.25	NEWMAN,P		1989	AUD	NOEL ,J		50	63
0.25	UECKER,WC	JL	1985	TAR	SCHEPANSKI,A	SHIN ,J	430	457
0.24	ABDEL-KHALIK,AR	AP	1974	TAR			271	283
0.23	BALACHANDRAN,BV	ST	1980	JAR	RAMAKRISHNAN,RT		140	171
0.21	SCOTT ,WR	SP	1979	JAR			156	178
0.20	COHEN ,SI	AU	1988	CAR	LOEB ,M		70	95
0.20	DICKHAUT,JW	AU	1983	JAR	LERE ,JC		495	513
0.20	FELTHAM,GA	AU	1988	CAR	CHRISTENSEN,PO		133	169
0.20	MAGEE ,RP	JA	1988	TAR			42	54
0.20	NELSON,J	SU	1988	JAA	RONEN ,J	WHITE ,L	255	296
0.20	SHIELDS,MD	06	1988	AOS	WALLER,WS		581	594
0.20	SUH ,YS	SP	1988	JAR			154	168
0.18	DEMSKI,JS	AU	1970	JAR			178	198
0.18	MOCK ,TJ	OC	1971	TAR			765	777
0.17	OHLSON,JA	AU	1987	CAR			1	15
0.17	PENNO ,M	SP	1987	CAR			368	374
0.14	EVANS III,JH	06	1986	AOS	LEWIS ,BL	PATTON,JM	483	498
0.13	MAGEE ,RP	OC	1977	TAR			869	880
0.12	BERNHARDT,I	SP	1970	JAR	COPELAND,RM		95	98
0.12	DEMSKI,JS	OC	1969	TAR			669	679
0.12	DEMSKI,JS	AP	1971	TAR			268	278
0.12	GODFREY,JT	JA	1971	TAR	PRINCE,TR		75	89
0.12	LEV ,B	SP	1970	JAR			78	94
0.12	RONEN ,J	OC	1973	TAR	FALK ,G		696	717
0.11	DEJONG,DV	AU	1984	AUD	SMITH ,JH		20	34
0.07	VERRECCHIA,RE	SP	1978	JAR			150	168
0.06	THEIL ,H	JA	1969	TAR			27	37
0.00	AMERSHI,AH	JA	1990	TAR	BANKER,RD	DATAR ,SM	113	130
0.00	AMEY ,LR	AU	1988	CAR	GOFFIN,JL		174	198
0.00	ANTHONY,JH	SP	1987	CAR			460	475
0.00	ANTLE ,R	SP	1990	JAR	FELLINGHAM,J		1	24
0.00	BABER ,WR	JA	1985	TAR			1	9
0.00	BABER ,WR	OC	1991	TAR	FAIRFIELD,PM	HAGGARD,JA	818	829
0.00	BACHAR,J	AU	1989	JAA			432	459

CITE INDEX	FIRST AUTHOR	ISS-UE	YE-AR	JOUR-NAL	SECOND AUTHOR	THIRD AUTHOR	PAG BEG	PAG END
0.00	BAIMAN,S	OC	1991	TAR	SIVARAMAKRISHNAN,K		747	767
0.00	BALACHANDRAN,BV	WI	1988	JAA	RAMANAN,R		1	13
0.00	BALAKRISHNAN,R	AU	1990	CAR			105	122
0.00	BALAKRISHNAN,R	SP	1992	CAR			353	373
0.00	BANKER,RD	SP	1990	CAR	DATAR ,SM	MAZUR ,MJ	809	824
0.00	BAR-YOSEF,S	AP	1992	TAR	SEN ,PK		320	336
0.00	BENISHAY,H	SU	1987	JAA			203	238
0.00	BENISHAY,H	WI	1992	JAA			97	112
0.00	BERKOWITCH,E	SP	1992	JAA	VENEZIA,I		241	250
0.00	BOATSMAN,JR	JA	1992	TAR	GRASSO,LP	ORMISTON,MB	148	156
0.00	CONROY,R	AU	1989	CAR	HUGHES,JS		159	176
0.00	CRANDALL,RH	JL	1969	TAR			457	466
0.00	CUSHING,BE	OC	1968	TAR			668	671
0.00	DARROUGH,MN	AU	1988	CAR			199	221
0.00	DECHOW,PM	MR	1991	JAE	SLOAN ,RG		1	89
0.00	DEFOND,ML	JL	1991	TAR	JIAMBALVO,J		643	655
0.00	DEFOND,ML	SP	1992	AUD			16	31
0.00	DEJONG,DV	JA	1992	TAR	FORSYTHE,R		157	171
0.00	DEMSKI,JS	OC	1992	TAR	MAGEE ,RP		732	740
0.00	DILLA ,WN	JL	1989	TAR			404	432
0.00	DYE ,RA	DE	1991	JAE			347	373
0.00	FELLINGHAM,JC	AU	1989	JAR	YOUNG ,RA		179	200
0.00	FELLINGHAM,JC	OC	1990	TAR	YOUNG ,RA		837	856
0.00	FELTHAM,GA	AU	1992	CAR	GIGLER,FB	HUGHES,JS	1	23
0.00	FOSTER III,TW	JL	1991	TAR	KOOGLER,PR	VICKREY,D	595	610
0.00	FREDERICKSON,JR	OC	1992	TAR			647	670
0.00	GREENWALD,B	SU	1989	JAA	STIGLITZ,JE		281	297
0.00	HAKANSSON,NH	JL	1969	TAR			495	514
0.00	HAKANSSON,NH	WI	1990	JAA			33	53
0.00	HALPERIN,R	SU	1989	JAA	MAINDIRATTA,A		345	366
0.00	HALPERIN,RM	JA	1991	TAR	SRINIDHI,B		141	157
0.00	HAYES ,RD	JL	1990	TAR	MILLAR,JA		505	519
0.00	HILTON,RW	AU	1986	CAR			50	67
0.00	HUNT-III,HG	05	1990	AOS	HOGLER,RL		437	454
0.00	JENNINGS,R	AP	1992	TAR	MEST ,DP	THOMPSON II,RB	337	354
0.00	JOHN ,K	WI	1990	JAA	RONEN ,J		61	95
0.00	KACHELMEIER,SJ		1991	AUD			25	48
0.00	KIRBY ,AJ	SP	1992	CAR			374	408
0.00	LANEN ,WN	SP	1992	JAR	LARCKER,DF		70	93
0.00	LAVALLE,IH	AP	1968	TAR	RAPPAPORT,A		225	230
0.00	LEE ,LC	AP	1969	TAR	BEDFORD,NM		256	275
0.00	LEV ,B	OC	1969	TAR			704	710
0.00	LICHTENBERG,FR	OC	1992	TAR			741	752
0.00	LITZENBERGER,RH	SU	1989	JAA	TALMOR,E		305	316
0.00	LUNDHOLM,RJ	AU	1991	JAR			322	349
0.00	MACNAUGHTON,A	AU	1992	CAR			113	137
0.00	MATSUMURA,EM	OC	1992	TAR	TUCKER,RR		753	782
0.00	MELUMAD,N	AU	1990	CAR	THOMAN,L		22	55
0.00	MELUMAD,N	DE	1992	JAE	MOOKHERJEE,D	REICHELSTEIN,S	445	483
0.00	MOORE ,G		1990	AUD	RONEN ,J		234	242
0.00	NAKANO,I	OC	1972	TAR			693	708
0.00	O'BRIEN,JR	AU	1990	CAR			1	21
0.00	O'BRIEN,JR	SP	1992	JAA			117	134

CITE INDEX	FIRST AUTHOR	ISS-UE	YE-AR	JOUR-NAL	SECOND AUTHOR	THIRD AUTHOR	PAG BEG	PAG END
0.00	OGAN ,P	SU	1991	JAA	ZIEBART,DA		387	406
0.00	PENNO ,M	JL	1990	TAR			520	536
0.00	PENNO ,M	ST	1991	JAR	WATTS ,JS		194	216
0.00	RAJAN ,MV	AU	1992	JAR			227	248
0.00	SANNELLA,AJ	WI	1991	JAA			75	102
0.00	SANSING,RC	AU	1992	CAR			33	45
0.00	SCOTT ,WR	SP	1988	CAR			354	388
0.00	SIMUNIC,DA	SP	1990	CAR	STEIN ,MT		329	343
0.00	STEIN ,JL	SP	1990	JAA	HONG ,BG		277	300
0.00	TEOH ,SH	SP	1992	JAR			1	23
0.00	TRUEMAN,B	AU	1990	CAR			203	222
0.00	WALKER,M	06	1989	AOS			433	453
0.00	WILLIAMS,DJ	03	1986	AOS			271	288
0.00	YOON ,SS		1990	AUD			253	275
0.00	ZIEBART,DA	AU	1992	CAR	REITER,SA		252	282

3.6 SCHOOL OF THOUGHT=STAT.MODEL – MATH. PROGRAMMING

CITE INDEX	FIRST AUTHOR	ISS-UE	YE-AR	JOUR-NAL	SECOND AUTHOR	THIRD AUTHOR	PAG BEG	PAG END
3.00	ROGERSON,WP	OC	1992	TAR			671	690
2.00	REICHELSTEIN,S	OC	1992	TAR			712	731
1.00	BANKER,RD	AU	1992	CAR			343	354
1.00	MEHREZ,A	AU	1992	CAR	BROWN ,JR	KHOUJA,M	329	342
0.80	BALVERS,RJ	OC	1988	TAR	MCDONALD,B	MILLER,RE	605	622
0.75	PALMROSE,Z	JL	1989	TAR			488	499
0.73	NETER ,J	JA	1978	TAR	LEITCH,RA	FIENBERG,SE	77	93
0.67	JORDAN,JS	SP	1990	CAR			903	921
0.65	SAN MIGUEL,JG	04	1976	AOS			357	374
0.63	HAMLEN,SS	JL	1977	TAR	HAMLEN,WA	TSCHIRHART,JT	616	627
0.59	KAPLAN,RS	SP	1969	JAR			32	43
0.53	DYCKMAN,TR	AU	1969	JAR			215	244
0.50	JENSEN,DL	OC	1977	TAR			842	856
0.50	STONE ,M	JA	1991	TAR	RASP ,J		170	187
0.47	KAPLAN,RS	AP	1971	TAR	THOMPSON,GL		352	364
0.47	KAPLAN,RS	JL	1974	TAR	WELAM ,VP		477	484
0.38	ABDOLMOHAMMADI,MJ	AU	1985	CAR			76	94
0.31	HAMLEN,SS	OC	1980	TAR			578	593
0.29	KANODIA,CS	SP	1979	JAR			74	98
0.29	KAPLAN,RS	OC	1973	TAR			738	748
0.27	KOTTAS,JF	AP	1978	TAR	LAU ,AH	LAU ,HS	389	401
0.25	CHEUNG,JK	SP	1989	CAR			625	641
0.25	HEIMANN,SR	AU	1977	JAR	CHESLEY,GR		193	206
0.25	JANG ,HJ	AU	1989	CAR	RO ,BT		242	262
0.24	KILLOUGH,LN	AP	1973	TAR	SOUDERS,TL		268	279
0.24	OZAN ,T	SP	1971	JAR	DYCKMAN,TR		88	115
0.24	SUMMERS,EL	JL	1972	TAR			443	453
0.23	COHEN ,MA	AU	1980	JAR	HALPERIN,R		375	389
0.18	DOPUCH,N	SP	1964	JAR	DRAKE ,DF		10	24
0.18	HARTLEY,RV	OC	1971	TAR			746	755
0.13	AHITUV,N	AU	1985	CAR	HALPERN,J	WILL ,H	95	110
0.13	CASEY JR,CJ	SP	1985	JAR	BARTCZAK,N		384	401
0.13	LIN ,WT	JA	1978	TAR			61	76
0.13	MERVILLE,LJ	OC	1978	TAR	PETTY ,JW		935	951

CITE INDEX	FIRST AUTHOR	ISS-UE	YE-AR	JOUR-NAL	SECOND AUTHOR	THIRD AUTHOR	PAG BEG	PAG END
0.12	BAILEY JR,AD	JL	1976	TAR	BOE ,WJ		559	573
0.12	BAREFIELD,RM	JL	1970	TAR			490	501
0.12	CHURCHILL,NC	OC	1964	TAR			894	904
0.12	HINOMOTO,H	AU	1971	JAR			253	267
0.12	IJIRI ,Y	AU	1963	JAR	LEVY ,FK	LYON ,RC	198	212
0.12	KORNBLUTH,JS	AP	1974	TAR			284	295
0.12	LIVINGSTONE,JL	JL	1968	TAR			503	508
0.12	SAMUELS,JM	AU	1965	JAR			182	191
0.12	WILLIAMS,TH	JL	1964	TAR	GRIFFIN,CH		671	678
0.12	WOLK ,HI	JL	1972	TAR	HILLMAN,AP		549	555
0.11	SHERMAN,HD	AU	1984	AUD			35	53
0.11	THAKKAR,RB	AU	1984	CAR	FINLEY,DR	LIAO ,WM	77	86
0.09	MANES ,RP	JL	1982	TAR	PARK ,SH	JENSEN,RE	594	606
0.08	BALACHANDRAN,BV	JA	1981	TAR	RAMAKRISHNAN,RT		85	96
0.06	BAILEY JR,AD	JL	1973	TAR			560	574
0.06	BUTTERWORTH,JE	OC	1971	TAR	SIGLOCH,BA		701	716
0.06	CHARNES,A	SP	1963	JAR	COOPER,WW	IJIRI ,Y	16	43
0.06	CHARNES,A	JA	1967	TAR	COOPER,WW		24	52
0.06	CHARNES,A	JA	1972	TAR	COLANTONI,CS	COOPER,WW	85	108
0.06	COLANTONI,CS	JL	1969	TAR	MANES ,RP	WHINSTON,AB	467	481
0.06	CORCORAN,AW	JA	1973	TAR	LEININGER,WE		105	114
0.06	FELTHAM,GA	JA	1970	TAR			11	26
0.06	FRANK ,WG	JL	1967	TAR	MANES ,RP		516	525
0.06	GONEDES,NJ	SP	1970	JAR			1	20
0.06	GROVES,R	JL	1970	TAR	MANES ,RP	SORENSEN,R	481	489
0.06	HARTLEY,RV	AP	1970	TAR			223	234
0.06	LIVINGSTONE,JL	JA	1969	TAR			48	64
0.06	MAGEE ,RP	JA	1977	TAR			190	199
0.06	ONSI ,M	JL	1970	TAR			535	543
0.06	RAPPAPORT,A	JL	1967	TAR			441	456
0.06	WELLING,P	04	1977	AOS			307	316
0.06	WRIGHT,FK	JA	1970	TAR			129	133
0.00	AMEY ,LR	AU	1984	CAR			64	76
0.00	ANDERSON,MJ	OC	1990	TAR	ANDERSON,U	HELLELOID,R	857	874
0.00	BABAD ,YM	SP	1989	CAR	BALACHANDRAN,BV		775	792
0.00	BALACHANDRAN,BV	WI	1991	JAA	PADMARAJ,RA		1	28
0.00	BALACHANDRAN,KR	SP	1987	JAA	SRINIDHI,BN		151	169
0.00	BARLEV,B	SP	1986	CAR	FRIED ,D	LIVNAT,J	288	310
0.00	BARNIV,R	JL	1990	TAR			578	605
0.00	BOYLE ,PP	SP	1985	CAR			116	144
0.00	BRIEF ,RP	AU	1968	JAR	OWEN ,J		193	199
0.00	BROCKETT,P	JL	1984	TAR	CHARNES,A	COOPER,WW	474	487
0.00	BYRNE ,R	JA	1968	TAR	CHARNES,A	COOPER,WW	18	37
0.00	CARSBERG,BV	AU	1969	JAR			165	182
0.00	CHAN ,KH	OC	1986	TAR	DODIN ,B		726	734
0.00	CHARNES,A	04	1976	AOS	COLANTONI,CS	COOPER,WW	315	338
0.00	CHEN ,JT	SP	1985	CAR	MANES ,RP		242	252
0.00	CHEUNG,JK	SP	1990	CAR			724	737
0.00	CLINCH,G	OC	1992	TAR	MAGLIOLO,J		843	861
0.00	DAVIS ,GB	SP	1963	JAR			96	101
0.00	DOPUCH,N	OC	1963	TAR			745	753
0.00	FARAG ,SM	AP	1968	TAR			312	320
0.00	FOGLER,HR	JA	1972	TAR			134	143

CITE INDEX	FIRST AUTHOR	ISS-UE	YE-AR	JOUR-NAL	SECOND AUTHOR	THIRD AUTHOR	PAG BEG	PAG END
0.00	FRANCIS,J	OC	1990	TAR			891	911
0.00	GLOVER,F	AP	1969	TAR			300	303
0.00	GODFREY,JT	AP	1971	TAR			286	297
0.00	HANSEN,DR	JA	1977	TAR	SHAFTEL,TL		109	123
0.00	HARTLEY,RV	AP	1968	TAR			321	332
0.00	JENSEN,RE	JL	1968	TAR			425	446
0.00	JUNG ,WO	AU	1989	CAR			1	25
0.00	KINNEY JR,WR		1989	AUD			67	84
0.00	LAMBERT,RA	JL	1989	TAR	LARCHER,DF		449	467
0.00	LEA ,RB	AP	1972	TAR			346	350
0.00	LIM ,SS	OC	1991	TAR	SUNDER,S		669	693
0.00	RAPPAPORT,A	AP	1969	TAR			297	299
0.00	ROSHWALB,A	AP	1991	TAR	WRIGHT,RL		348	360
0.00	SRIVASTAVA,RP	AP	1992	TAR	SHAFER,GR		249	283
0.00	WAND ,Y	JA	1989	TAR	WEBER ,R		87	107
0.00	WEINGARTER,HM	AU	1963	JAR			213	224
0.00	WHEELER,S	JL	1990	TAR	PANY ,K		557	577
0.00	WRIGHT,FK	AU	1968	JAR			222	236

3.7 SCHOOL OF THOUGHT=STAT.MODEL – OTHER

CITE INDEX	FIRST AUTHOR	ISS-UE	YE-AR	JOUR-NAL	SECOND AUTHOR	THIRD AUTHOR	PAG BEG	PAG END
8.20	WATTS ,RL	JA	1978	TAR	ZIMMERMAN,JL		112	134
6.00	HEALY ,PM	AP	1985	JAE			85	108
3.79	HAGERMAN,RL	AG	1979	JAE	ZMIJEWSKI,ME		141	161
3.33	PRESS ,EG	JA	1990	JAE	WEINTROP,JB		65	95
3.33	ZMIJEWSKI,ME	AG	1981	JAE	HAGERMAN,RL		129	149
3.00	DUKE ,JC	JA	1990	JAE	HUNT III,HG		45	63
2.56	HAYES ,DC	JA	1977	TAR			22	39
2.43	ANTLE ,R	SP	1986	JAR	SMITH ,A		1	39
2.40	MCNICHOLS,M	ST	1988	JAR	WILSON,GP		1	40
2.23	SIMUNIC,DA	SP	1980	JAR			161	190
2.00	DALEY ,LA	DE	1983	JAE	VIGELAND,RL		195	211
1.86	PALMROSE,ZV	SP	1986	JAR			97	110
1.82	LILIEN,S	DE	1982	JAE	PASTENA,V		145	170
1.75	ABDEL-KHALIK,AR	AU	1985	JAR			427	447
1.71	LIBERTY,SE	OC	1986	TAR	ZIMMERMAN,JL		692	712
1.70	MORSE ,D	SP	1983	JAR	RICHARDSON,G		106	127
1.67	ZMIJEWSKI,ME	ST	1984	JAR			59	82
1.63	MURPHY,KJ	AP	1985	JAE			11	42
1.62	OHLSON,JA	SP	1980	JAR			109	131
1.50	FRANCIS,JR	JA	1987	TAR	SIMON ,DT		145	157
1.50	HEALY ,PM	AP	1987	JAE	KANG ,SH	PALEPU,KG	7	34
1.43	AYRES ,FL	JN	1986	JAE			143	158
1.43	PALEPU,KG	MR	1986	JAE			3	36
1.40	NOREEN,EW	SP	1988	JAR			119	133
1.40	SIMON ,DT	AP	1988	TAR	FRANCIS,JR		255	269
1.38	LEE ,CJ	AU	1985	JAR	HSIEH ,DA		468	485
1.35	SCOTT ,WR	AU	1973	JAR			304	330
1.33	FRANCIS,JR	AP	1987	JAE	REITER,SA		35	59
1.33	HEALY ,PM	JA	1990	JAE	PALEPU,KG		97	123
1.30	CUSHING,BE	AU	1983	AUD	LOEBBECKE,JK		23	41
1.29	KAPLAN,RS	AU	1973	JAR			238	258
1.25	COUGHLAN,AT	AP	1985	JAE	SCHMIDT,RM		43	66

CITE INDEX	FIRST AUTHOR	ISS-UE	YE-AR	JOUR-NAL	SECOND AUTHOR	THIRD AUTHOR	PAG BEG	PAG END
1.24	BEAVER,WH	ST	1966	JAR			71	111
1.20	DOPUCH,N	SP	1988	JAR	PINCUS,M		28	59
1.19	FELIX JR,WL	SP	1977	JAR	GRIMLUND,RA		23	41
1.18	CORLESS,JC	JL	1972	TAR			556	566
1.14	KINNEY JR,WR	ST	1979	JAR			148	165
1.14	KREUTZFELDT,RW	AU	1986	AUD	WALLACE,WA		20	43
1.09	DUKE ,GL	SP	1982	JAR	NETER ,J	LEITCH,RA	42	67
1.06	FELIX JR,WL	OC	1976	TAR			800	807
1.00	ANTLE ,R	SP	1985	JAR	SMITH ,A		296	325
1.00	BEAVER,WH	AU	1989	JAR	EGER ,C	RYAN ,S	157	178
1.00	BOATSMAN,JR	AP	1974	TAR	ROBERTSON,JC		342	352
1.00	CHOW ,CW	OC	1983	TAR			667	685
1.00	CHRISTIE,AA	DE	1984	JAE	KENNELLEY,MD	KING ,JW	205	217
1.00	CUSHING,BE	AP	1992	TAR	LECLERE,MJ		355	367
1.00	DEAKIN,EB	OC	1979	TAR			722	734
1.00	DEMSKI,JS	ST	1982	JAR	KREPS ,DM		117	148
1.00	EICHENSEHER,JW	JL	1981	TAR	DANOS ,P		479	492
1.00	FELLINGHAM,JC	OC	1985	TAR	NEWMAN,DP		634	650
1.00	FRANCIS,JR	AG	1984	JAE			133	151
1.00	KINNEY-JR,WR	FB	1989	JAE	MCDANIEL,LS		71	93
1.00	LYS ,T	DE	1990	JAE	SOHN ,S		341	363
0.94	KINNEY JR,WR	ST	1975	JAR			14	29
0.94	STRINGER,KW	ST	1975	JAR			1	9
0.91	LEITCH,RA	AP	1982	TAR	NETER ,J	PLANTE,R	384	400
0.89	DALEY ,LA	AP	1984	TAR			177	198
0.89	DWORIN,L	AP	1984	TAR	GRIMLUND,RA		218	241
0.88	BROWN ,LD	AP	1985	TAR	GARDNER,JC		262	277
0.88	HAM ,J	JL	1985	TAR	LOSELL,D	SMIELIAUSKAS,W	387	406
0.88	MUTCHLER,JF	AU	1985	JAR			668	682
0.86	CHENHALL,RH	JA	1986	TAR	MORRIS,D		16	35
0.86	EL-GAZZAR,S	OC	1986	JAE	LILIEN,S	PASTENA,V	217	238
0.86	SEFCIK,SE	AU	1986	JAR	THOMPSON,R		316	334
0.83	BAGINSKI,SP	AU	1987	JAR			196	216
0.83	STONE ,M	AU	1987	JAR			317	326
0.82	MCDONALD,CL	JL	1973	TAR			502	510
0.82	SUNDER,S	JA	1976	TAR			1	18
0.80	SUNDER,S	AU	1983	JAR	WAYMIRE,G		565	580
0.79	LEV ,B	DE	1979	JAE	SUNDER,S		187	210
0.79	RAMAGE,JG	ST	1979	JAR	KRIEGER,AM	SPERO ,LL	72	102
0.78	GODFREY,JT	AU	1984	JAR	NETER ,J		497	525
0.78	MENZEFRICKE,U	AU	1984	JAR	SMIELIAUSKAS,W		588	604
0.75	LINDAHL,FW	AU	1989	JAR			201	226
0.75	MITTELSTAEDT,HF	NV	1989	JAE			399	418
0.75	STICKEL,SE	JL	1989	JAE			275	292
0.73	DANOS ,P	AU	1982	JAR	EICHENSEHER,JW		604	616
0.71	BOWEN ,RM	OC	1986	TAR	BURGSTAHLER,D	DALEY ,LA	713	725
0.71	DWORIN,L	JA	1986	TAR	GRIMLUND,RA		36	57
0.71	SCOTT ,WR	ST	1975	JAR			98	117
0.71	THORNTON,DB	AU	1986	CAR			1	34
0.70	MENZEFRICKE,U	SP	1983	JAR			96	105
0.69	UECKER,WC	03	1977	AOS	KINNEY JR,WR		269	275
0.67	ABDEL-KHALIK,AR	SP	1990	CAR			295	322
0.67	BABER ,WR	AU	1987	JAR	BROOKS,EH	RICKS ,WE	293	305

CITE INDEX	FIRST AUTHOR	ISS-UE	YE-AR	JOUR-NAL	SECOND AUTHOR	THIRD AUTHOR	PAG BEG	PAG END
0.67	ETTREDGE,M	SP	1990	JAR	GREENBERG,R		198	210
0.67	MALMQUIST,DH	JA	1990	JAE			173	205
0.67	MCCRAY,JH	JA	1984	TAR			35	51
0.67	MIAN ,SL	JA	1990	JAE	SMITH JR,CW		141	171
0.67	ROBERTS,RW	SP	1990	JAR	GLEZEN,GW	JONES ,TW	220	228
0.67	SPICER,BM	JA	1978	TAR			94	111
0.65	CUSHING,BE	JA	1974	TAR			24	41
0.65	HARIED,AA	AU	1972	JAR			376	391
0.65	IJIRI ,Y	JL	1966	TAR	JAEDICKE,RK		474	483
0.65	KAPLAN,RS	SP	1973	JAR			38	46
0.65	YU ,S	AU	1973	JAR	NETER ,J		273	295
0.64	GRIMLUND,RA	AU	1982	JAR			316	342
0.60	FRANCIS,JR	OC	1988	TAR	WILSON,ER		663	682
0.60	FRECKA,TJ	JA	1983	TAR	HOPWOOD,WS		115	128
0.60	GRIMLUND,RA	AU	1988	AUD	SCHROEDER,MS		53	62
0.58	LEFTWICH,RW	ST	1981	JAR	WATTS ,RL	ZIMMERMAN,JL	50	77
0.57	DANOS ,P	OC	1986	TAR	EICHENSEHER,JW		633	650
0.57	GARSTKA,SJ	SP	1979	JAR	OHLSON,PA		23	59
0.57	MORIARITY,S	ST	1979	JAR	BARRON,FH		114	135
0.57	SMIELIAUSKAS,W	AU	1986	CAR			102	124
0.56	BALDWIN,BA	JL	1984	TAR			376	389
0.56	MARAIS,ML	ST	1984	JAR	PATELL,JM	WOLFSON,MA	87	114
0.56	SIMUNIC,DA	AU	1984	JAR			679	702
0.56	WILSON,ER	SP	1984	JAR	HOWARD,TP		207	224
0.55	DIETRICH,JR	JA	1982	TAR	KAPLAN,RS		18	38
0.55	FROST ,PA	SP	1982	JAR	TAMURA,H		103	120
0.55	HALL ,TW	SP	1982	JAR			139	151
0.55	SILHAN,PA	SP	1982	JAR			255	262
0.53	HORRIGAN,JO	ST	1966	JAR			44	62
0.53	KAPLAN,RS	ST	1975	JAR			126	133
0.50	BABER ,WR	DE	1983	JAE			213	227
0.50	BHUSHAN,R	JL	1989	JAE			255	274
0.50	CHEWNING,G	SP	1989	JAR	PANY ,K	WHEELER,S	78	96
0.50	CHOW ,CW	SP	1987	AUD	MCNAMEE,AH	PLUMLEE,RD	123	133
0.50	GRIMLUND,RA	JL	1987	TAR	FELIX JR,WL		455	479
0.50	JONES ,JJ	AU	1991	JAR			193	228
0.50	KINNEY JR,WR	SP	1983	AUD			13	22
0.50	KINNEY JR,WR	SP	1987	AUD			59	73
0.50	LEE ,CWJ	AU	1989	JAR	PETRUZZI,CR		277	296
0.50	LEWELLEN,W	AP	1985	JAE	LODERER,C	ROSENFELD,A	209	232
0.50	LEWELLEN,W	DE	1987	JAE	LODERER,C	MARTIN,K	287	310
0.50	LOEBBECKE,JK	AU	1989	AUD	EINING,MM	WILLINGHAM,JJ	1	28
0.50	TEHRANIAN,H	ST	1987	JAR	TRAVLOS,NG	WAEGELEIN,JF	51	76
0.50	TSUI ,KW	JA	1985	TAR	MATSUMURA,EM	TSUI ,KL	76	96
0.50	WAYMIRE,G	SP	1985	JAR			268	295
0.47	BODNAR,G	OC	1975	TAR			747	757
0.47	DEMSKI,JS	JL	1974	TAR	SWIERINGA,RJ		506	513
0.47	DYER ,JC	AU	1975	JAR	MCHUGH,AJ		204	219
0.47	GREEN ,D	ST	1966	JAR	SEGALL,J		21	36
0.47	JAEDICKE,RK	OC	1964	TAR	ROBICHEK,AA		917	926
0.47	RENEAU,JH	JL	1978	TAR			669	680
0.47	SUNDER,S	AP	1976	TAR			287	291
0.44	MATOLCSY,ZP	AU	1984	JAR			555	569

CITE INDEX	FIRST AUTHOR	ISS-UE	YE-AR	JOUR-NAL	SECOND AUTHOR	THIRD AUTHOR	PAG BEG	PAG END
0.43	CASEY JR,CJ	AP	1986	TAR	MCGEE ,VE	STICKNEY,CP	249	262
0.43	FRANCIS,JR	AU	1986	JAR	STOKES,DJ		383	393
0.43	PALMROSE,ZV	AU	1986	JAR			405	411
0.43	SMIELIAUSKAS,W	JA	1986	TAR			118	128
0.42	RAMAN ,KK	OC	1981	TAR			910	926
0.41	HILLIARD,JE	JA	1975	TAR	LEITCH,RA		69	80
0.41	LIEBERMAN,AZ	AP	1975	TAR	WHINSTON,AB		246	258
0.41	SORENSEN,JE	JL	1969	TAR			555	561
0.41	TOBA ,Y	JA	1975	TAR			7	24
0.41	TRACY ,JA	JA	1969	TAR			90	98
0.40	INGRAM,RW	AU	1978	JAR			270	285
0.40	JOHNSON,WB	JA	1988	TAR	RAMANAN,R		96	110
0.40	KETZ ,JE	OC	1978	TAR			952	960
0.40	KNECHEL,WR	JA	1988	TAR			74	95
0.40	MENZEFRICKE,U	SP	1988	CAR	SMIELIAUSKAS,W		314	336
0.38	BECK ,PJ	SP	1985	AUD	SOLOMON,I		1	10
0.38	CASLER,DJ	SP	1985	JAR	HALL ,TW		110	122
0.38	GENTRY,JA	SP	1985	JAR	NEWBOLD,P	WHITFORD,DT	146	160
0.38	JIAMBALVO,J	AU	1985	AUD	WILNER,N		1	11
0.38	SIMON ,DT	AU	1985	AUD			71	78
0.38	WILLINGHAM,JJ	AU	1985	AUD	WRIGHT,WF		57	70
0.36	ALTMAN,EI	AU	1982	JAA			4	19
0.36	COPELAND,RM	AU	1982	JAR	INGRAM,RW		275	289
0.36	CUSHING,BE	ST	1979	JAR	SEARFOSS,DG	RANDALL,RH	172	216
0.36	GODFREY,JT	AU	1982	JAR	ANDREWS,RW		304	315
0.36	KINNEY JR,WR	AU	1979	JAR			456	475
0.36	LIGHTNER,SM	AU	1982	AUD	ADAMS ,SJ	LIGHTNER,KM	1	12
0.36	WISEMAN,J	01	1982	AOS			53	64
0.35	BUZBY ,SL	JA	1974	TAR			42	49
0.35	DEAKIN,EB	OC	1974	TAR	GRANOF,MH		764	771
0.35	LIAO ,M	OC	1975	TAR			780	790
0.33	BANKER,RD	AU	1987	JAA	DATAR ,SM	RAJAN ,MV	319	347
0.33	BENSTON,GJ	ST	1978	JAR	KRASNEY,MA		1	30
0.33	BRICKLEY,JA	JA	1990	JAE	VAN DRUNEN,LD		251	280
0.33	DHARAN,BG	AP	1984	TAR			199	217
0.33	DITTMAN,DA	SP	1978	JAR	PRAKASH,P		14	25
0.33	FERRIS,KR	SP	1984	AUD	TENNANT,KL		31	43
0.33	LIN ,WT	AU	1984	AUD	MOCK ,TJ	WRIGHT,A	89	99
0.33	LOEBBECKE,JK	SP	1987	AUD	STEINBART,PJ		74	89
0.33	MATSUMURA,EM	SP	1990	CAR	TSUI ,K-W	WONG ,W-K	485	500
0.33	MENZEFRICKE,U	AU	1984	JAR			570	587
0.33	MIAN ,SL	OC	1990	JAE	SMITH JR,CW		249	266
0.33	PANY ,K	SP	1984	AUD	RECKERS,PMJ		89	97
0.33	SHEVLIN,T	JL	1987	TAR			480	509
0.33	SHIH ,MSH	AU	1987	CAR	SUNDER,S		16	31
0.33	TURPEN,RA	SP	1990	AUD			60	76
0.33	VERRECCHIA,RE	SP	1981	JAR			271	283
0.30	STEPHENS,RG	AU	1983	AUD			55	74
0.29	BLUM ,M	SP	1974	JAR			1	25
0.29	BORITZ,JE	AU	1986	AUD	BROCA ,DS		1	19
0.29	DEAKIN,EB	JA	1976	TAR			90	96
0.29	DITTMAN,DA	AP	1979	TAR	PRAKASH,P		358	373
0.29	JAGGI ,B	AP	1974	TAR	LAU ,HS		321	329

CITE INDEX	FIRST AUTHOR	ISS-UE	YE-AR	JOUR-NAL	SECOND AUTHOR	THIRD AUTHOR	PAG BEG	PAG END
0.29	NORTON,CL	JA	1979	TAR	SMITH ,RE		72	87
0.29	SHANK ,JK	JL	1973	TAR	COPELAND,RM		494	501
0.29	SHIH ,W	OC	1979	TAR			687	706
0.29	SMITH ,DB	AU	1986	AUD			95	108
0.29	STALLMAN,JC	ST	1969	JAR			29	43
0.29	TEITLEBAUM,AD	ST	1975	JAR	ROBINSON,CF		70	91
0.29	WILCOX,JA	ST	1973	JAR			163	179
0.27	BALLEW,V	JA	1982	TAR			88	104
0.27	INGRAM,RW	AU	1982	JAR	COPELAND,RM		766	772
0.27	KEYS ,DE	AU	1978	JAR			389	399
0.25	BIDDLE,GC	SP	1985	JAR	MARTIN,RK		57	83
0.25	BURGSTAHLER,D	JL	1989	JAE	JIAMBALVO,J	NOREEN,E	207	224
0.25	EL-GAZZAR,S	SP	1989	JAA	LILIEN,S	PASTENA,V	217	231
0.25	EVEREST,GL	AP	1977	TAR	WEBER ,R		340	359
0.25	FIRTH ,MA	SP	1985	AUD			23	37
0.25	HUGHES,JS	JA	1977	TAR			56	68
0.25	KNECHEL,WR	SP	1985	AUD			38	62
0.25	LEVITAN,AS	AU	1985	AUD	KNOBLETT,JA		26	39
0.25	PLANTE,R	AU	1985	AUD	NETER ,J	LEITCH,RA	40	56
0.25	RONEN ,J	SP	1989	JAA	SONDHI,AC		237	265
0.25	SCAPENS,RW	AP	1985	TAR	SALE ,JT		231	247
0.25	SCOTT ,WR	SP	1977	JAR			120	137
0.25	SMIELIAUSKAS,W	AU	1985	JAR			718	739
0.25	TABOR ,RH	SP	1985	AUD	WILLIS,JT		93	109
0.25	TOMCZYK,S	AU	1989	AUD	READ ,WJ		98	106
0.24	BALL ,R	SP	1976	JAR	LEV ,B	WATTS ,RL	1	9
0.24	FERRARA,WL	AP	1972	TAR	HAYYA ,JC	NACHMAN,DA	299	307
0.24	IJIRI ,Y	OC	1969	TAR	KAPLAN,RS		743	756
0.24	IJIRI ,Y	OC	1973	TAR	ITAMI ,H		724	737
0.24	KOCHANEK,RF	AP	1974	TAR			245	258
0.24	WARREN,CS	SP	1975	JAR			162	176
0.24	WEST ,RR	SP	1970	JAR			118	125
0.23	HUSSEIN,ME	SU	1980	JAA	KETZ ,JE		354	367
0.23	IJIRI ,Y	SP	1980	JAR	LEITCH,RA		91	108
0.23	NAIR ,RD	JL	1980	TAR	FRANK ,WG		426	450
0.22	BIGGS ,SF	SP	1984	AUD	WILD ,JJ		68	79
0.22	FRAZIER,KB	SP	1984	JAR	INGRAM,RW	TENNYSON,BM	318	331
0.21	NAIR ,RD	SP	1979	JAR			225	242
0.20	CALLEN,JL	AP	1978	TAR			303	308
0.20	CHEN ,JT	JL	1983	TAR			600	605
0.20	FINLEY,DR	AU	1983	AUD			104	116
0.20	GRIMLUND,RA	SP	1988	AUD			77	104
0.20	HIRSCH JR,ML	AU	1978	JAR			254	269
0.20	KAMIN ,JY	02	1978	AOS	RONEN ,J		141	160
0.20	KNECHEL,WR	AU	1988	AUD			87	107
0.20	LEWIS ,BL	AP	1988	TAR	PATTON,JM	GREEN ,SL	270	282
0.19	GARSTKA,SJ	AU	1977	JAR			179	192
0.19	SCHROEDER,RG	01	1977	AOS	IMDIEKE,LF		39	46
0.18	BRIEF ,RP	AU	1970	JAR	OWEN ,J		167	177
0.18	DEMSKI,JS	JA	1970	TAR			76	87
0.18	FRIBERG,RA	JA	1973	TAR			50	60
0.18	GUPTA ,MC	SP	1972	JAR	HUEFNER,RJ		77	95
0.18	HASSELDINE,CR	JL	1967	TAR			497	515

CITE INDEX	FIRST AUTHOR	ISS-UE	YE-AR	JOUR-NAL	SECOND AUTHOR	THIRD AUTHOR	PAG BEG	PAG END
0.18	KINNEY JR,WR	AU	1982	JAR	SALAMON,GL		350	366
0.18	LOEBBECKE,JK	ST	1975	JAR	NETER ,J		38	52
0.18	PROBST,FR	JA	1971	TAR			113	118
0.18	RONEN ,J	JA	1974	TAR			50	60
0.18	SCHWARTZ,KB	AU	1982	JAA			32	43
0.18	WALTHER,LM	AP	1982	TAR			376	383
0.18	ZIMMERMAN,JL	AU	1976	JAR			301	319
0.17	BAILEY,AP	SU	1981	AUD	MCAFEE,RP	WHINSTON,AB	38	52
0.17	BERRY ,LE	JA	1987	TAR	HARWOOD,GB	KATZ ,JL	14	28
0.17	CHOW ,CW	JL	1987	TAR	WONG-BOREN,A		533	541
0.17	KIM ,HS	SP	1987	AUD	NETER ,J	GODFREY,JT	40	58
0.17	MENZEFRICKE,U	AU	1987	CAR	SMIELIAUSKAS,W		240	250
0.15	BECK ,PJ	SP	1980	JAR			16	37
0.14	ANDERSON,JC	JL	1986	TAR	KRAUSHAAR,JM		379	399
0.14	DAVIS ,GB	SP	1986	AUD	WEBER ,R		35	49
0.14	DUNMORE,PV	AU	1986	CAR			125	148
0.14	ESKEW ,RK	JA	1979	TAR			107	118
0.14	HUSS ,HF	AU	1986	JAR	TRADER,RL		394	399
0.14	SMIELIAUSKAS,W	SP	1986	JAR			217	230
0.14	TAMURA,H	AU	1986	JAR	FROST ,PA		364	371
0.14	WEBER ,R	JL	1986	TAR			498	518
0.14	YOUNG ,R	SP	1986	JAR			231	240
0.13	CROSBY,MA	SP	1985	AUD			118	132
0.13	KAPLAN,SE	AU	1985	AUD			12	25
0.13	KNECHEL,WR	SP	1985	JAR			194	212
0.13	MARKS ,BR	AU	1985	JAR	RAMAN ,KK		878	886
0.13	SCHIPPER,K	ST	1977	JAR			1	40
0.13	WARREN,CS	JA	1977	TAR			150	161
0.13	WEYGANDT,JJ	JA	1977	TAR			40	51
0.12	BEAVER,WH	AU	1974	JAR	DUKES ,RE		205	215
0.12	BRIEF ,RP	SP	1973	JAR	OWEN ,J		1	15
0.12	CHURCHILL,NC	OC	1975	TAR	SHANK ,JK		643	656
0.12	DAVIDSON,HJ	AU	1967	JAR	NETER ,J	PETRAN,AS	186	207
0.12	DEMSKI,JS	AU	1973	JAR			176	190
0.12	DOPUCH,N	JL	1967	TAR	BIRNBERG,JG	DEMSKI,JS	526	536
0.12	GONEDES,NJ	AU	1971	JAR			236	252
0.12	GREENBALL,MN	SP	1968	JAR			114	129
0.12	GREER JR,WR	JA	1970	TAR			103	114
0.12	JEN ,FC	AP	1970	TAR	HUEFNER,RJ		290	298
0.12	JOHNSON,GL	AU	1971	JAR	SIMIK ,SS		278	286
0.12	JOHNSON,GL	SP	1974	JAR	SIMIK ,SS		67	79
0.12	LIM ,R	OC	1966	TAR			642	651
0.12	LIVINGSTONE,JL	AU	1970	JAR	SALAMON,GL		199	216
0.12	LUH ,FS	JA	1968	TAR			123	132
0.12	REVSINE,L	AP	1976	TAR	THIES ,JB		255	268
0.12	SALAMON,GL	AU	1973	JAR			296	303
0.12	SMITH ,KA	AP	1972	TAR			260	269
0.12	WELKER,RB	JL	1974	TAR			514	523
0.12	ZANNETOS,ZS	AP	1964	TAR			296	304
0.11	JIAMBALVO,J	SP	1984	AUD	WALLER,WS		80	88
0.11	MCCONNELL,DK	SP	1984	AUD			44	56
0.11	NETER ,J	AU	1984	AUD	KIM ,HS	GRAHAM,LE	75	88
0.11	SCHREUDER,H	JA	1984	TAR	KLAASSEN,J		64	77

CITE INDEX	FIRST AUTHOR	ISS-UE	YE-AR	JOUR-NAL	SECOND AUTHOR	THIRD AUTHOR	PAG BEG	PAG END
0.11	SMITH ,G	AU	1984	AUD	KROGSTAD,JL		107	117
0.11	WESCOTT,SH	SP	1984	JAR			412	423
0.11	WHITTRED,GP	AP	1984	TAR	ZIMMER,I		287	295
0.10	BROWN ,LD	AU	1983	JAR			432	443
0.10	GOMBOLA,MJ	JA	1983	TAR	KETZ ,JE		105	114
0.10	MCLEAY,S	01	1983	AOS			31	56
0.10	MENSAH,YM	AP	1983	TAR			228	246
0.10	SUNDER,S	SP	1983	JAR			222	233
0.09	BEAVER,WH	AU	1982	JAR	WOLFSON,MA		528	550
0.09	COHEN ,SI	AP	1982	TAR	LOEB ,M		336	347
0.09	EMERY ,GW	AU	1982	JAR	COGGER,KO		290	303
0.09	SALAMON,GL	AP	1982	TAR			292	302
0.08	BALACHANDRAN,KR	JA	1981	TAR	MASCHMEYER,R	LIVINGSTONE,JL	115	124
0.08	CHARNES,A	01	1980	AOS	COOPER,WW		87	107
0.08	FRIED ,D	SU	1981	JAA			295	308
0.08	GANGOLLY,JS	AU	1981	JAR			299	312
0.08	HAMLEN,SS	AP	1980	TAR	HAMLEN,WA	TSCHIRHART,JT	269	287
0.08	KELLY ,LK	03	1980	AOS			311	322
0.08	WHITTINGTON,OR	JL	1980	TAR	WHITTENBURG,G		409	418
0.08	WILLIAMS,PF	JA	1980	TAR			62	77
0.07	DAVIDSON,S	ST	1978	JAR	WEIL ,RL		154	233
0.07	ENGLEBRECHT,TD	JL	1979	TAR	JAMISON,RW		554	562
0.07	JACOBS,FH	SP	1978	JAR			190	203
0.07	KOTTAS,JF	JL	1978	TAR	LAU ,HS		698	707
0.07	MADEO ,SA	JL	1979	TAR			538	553
0.06	ALBRECHT,WS	OC	1976	TAR			824	837
0.06	ALY ,HF	JA	1971	TAR	DUBOFF,JI		119	128
0.06	ARNOLD,DF	JA	1973	TAR	HUMANN,TE		23	33
0.06	COMISKEY,EE	AP	1966	TAR			235	238
0.06	DAVIDSON,S	AU	1966	JAR	KOHLMEIER,JM		183	212
0.06	FALK ,H	SP	1977	JAR	MILLER,JC		12	22
0.06	GREENBALL,MN	AU	1969	JAR			262	289
0.06	GYNTHER,MM	OC	1968	TAR			706	718
0.06	HARVEY,DW	OC	1976	TAR			838	845
0.06	HEIMANN,SR	JA	1976	TAR	LUSK ,EJ		51	64
0.06	HOFSTEDT,TR	AP	1971	TAR	WEST ,RR		329	337
0.06	HUEFNER,RJ	OC	1971	TAR			717	732
0.06	IJIRI ,Y	SP	1970	JAR	KAPLAN,RS		34	46
0.06	JENSEN,RE	JA	1971	TAR			36	56
0.06	LEMKE ,KW	SP	1970	JAR			47	77
0.06	LIVINGSTONE,JL	AU	1969	JAR			245	256
0.06	LUSK ,EJ	JL	1972	TAR			567	575
0.06	MANES ,RP	SP	1966	JAR			87	100
0.06	MORRISON,TA	AP	1969	TAR	KACZKA,E		330	343
0.06	MORSE ,WJ	OC	1972	TAR			761	773
0.06	MURPHY,GJ	AP	1976	TAR			277	286
0.06	SCHRODERHEIM,G	JL	1964	TAR			679	684
0.06	SCHWAB,B	AP	1969	TAR	NICOL ,RE		292	296
0.06	SHANK ,JK	JA	1971	TAR			57	74
0.06	SORENSEN,JE	JL	1977	TAR	GROVE ,HD		658	675
0.06	STALLMAN,JC	OC	1972	TAR			774	790
0.00	ABARBANELL,JS	JN	1991	JAE			147	165
0.00	ABDEL-MAGID,MF	AP	1979	TAR			346	357

CITE INDEX	FIRST AUTHOR	ISS-UE	YE-AR	JOUR-NAL	SECOND AUTHOR	THIRD AUTHOR	PAG BEG	PAG END
0.00	ABRANOVIC,WA	OC	1976	TAR			863	874
0.00	ADESI ,GB	SU	1992	JAA	TALWAR,PP		369	378
0.00	AGRAWAL,SP	WI	1980	JAA	HALLBAUER,RC	PERRITT,GW	163	173
0.00	ALFORD,AW	SP	1992	JAR			94	108
0.00	ALY ,IM	SP	1992	JAA	BARLOW,HA	JONES ,RW	217	230
0.00	ASHTON,RH	SP	1989	CAR	GRAUL ,PR	NEWTON,JD	657	673
0.00	BABER ,WR	SP	1985	JAR			360	369
0.00	BALACHANDRAN,BV	OC	1981	TAR	ZOLTNERS,AA		801	812
0.00	BALACHANDRAN,KR	02	1977	AOS	LIVINGSTONE,JL		153	164
0.00	BALACHANDRAN,KR	WI	1992	JAA	MACHMEYER,RA		49	64
0.00	BANKER,RD	JL	1988	JAE	DATAR ,SM	KEKRE ,S	171	197
0.00	BANKER,RD	AU	1989	JAA	DATAR ,SM	KAPLAN,RS	528	554
0.00	BAO ,BE	04	1989	AOS	BAO ,DA		303	319
0.00	BARKMAN,A	JA	1977	TAR			450	464
0.00	BEAVER,WH	DE	1984	JAE	GRIFFIN,PA	LANDSMAN,WR	219	223
0.00	BELL ,TB	AU	1991	JAR	TABOR ,RH		350	370
0.00	BERNARD,VL	SP	1991	JAA	NOEL ,J		145	181
0.00	BIDDLE,GC	AU	1990	AUD	BRUTON,CM	SIEGEL,AF	92	114
0.00	BILDERSEE,JS	SU	1987	JAA	KAHN ,N		239	256
0.00	BLACCONIERE,WG	JN	1991	JAE	BOWEN ,RM	SEFCIK,SE	167	201
0.00	BOATSMAN,JR	AU	1984	JAA	DOWELL,CD	KIMBRELL,JI	35	43
0.00	BONETT,DG	SP	1990	CAR	CLUTE ,RD		432	445
0.00	BOWER ,RS	AP	1966	TAR	HERRINGER,F	WILLIAMSON,JP	257	265
0.00	BRANCH,B	SP	1981	JAA	BERKOWITZ,B		215	219
0.00	BRIEF ,RP	SP	1969	JAR	OWEN ,J		12	16
0.00	BRIEF ,RP	SP	1987	CAR	ANTON ,HR		394	407
0.00	BRIEF ,RP	AP	1992	TAR	LAWSON,RA		411	426
0.00	BRIGHAM,EF	JA	1968	TAR			46	61
0.00	BRIGHAM,EF	JL	1974	TAR	NANTELL,TJ		436	447
0.00	BUCKMAN,AG	SP	1982	JAR	MILLER,BL		28	41
0.00	BURGHER,PH	JA	1964	TAR			103	120
0.00	CALLEN,JL	SP	1988	JAA			87	108
0.00	CHAN ,H	AU	1990	AUD	SMIELIAUSKAS,W		167	182
0.00	CHANG ,OH	SP	1992	JAR	NICHOLS,DR		109	125
0.00	CHARNES,A	AP	1964	TAR	DAVIDSON,HJ	KORTANEK,KO	241	250
0.00	CHEN ,KCW	AU	1992	AUD	CHURCH,BK		30	49
0.00	CHOW ,CW	03	1991	AOS	SHIELDS,MD	CHAN ,YK	209	226
0.00	CHUNG ,DY	AU	1988	CAR	LINDSAY,WD		19	46
0.00	CHURCHILL,NC	WI	1982	AUD	COOPER,WW	GOVINDARAJAN,V	69	91
0.00	CLARK ,JJ	OC	1973	TAR	ELGERS,PT		668	678
0.00	CLARK ,TN	ST	1977	JAR			54	94
0.00	CLINCH,G	SP	1991	JAR			59	78
0.00	CREADY,WM	JN	1991	JAE	RAMANAN,R		203	214
0.00	DANIEL,SJ		1991	AOS	REITSPERGER,WD		601	618
0.00	DAVIS ,HZ	AU	1982	JAR	KAHN ,N		738	744
0.00	DAVIS ,HZ	AU	1984	JAR	KAHN ,N	ROZEN ,E	480	490
0.00	DEMING,WE	SP	1979	JAA			197	208
0.00	DEMSKI,JS	SP	1969	JAR			96	115
0.00	DHALIWAL,D	MR	1992	JAE	WANG ,S		7	25
0.00	DHARAN,BG	SP	1987	CAR			445	459
0.00	DHARAN,BG	WI	1992	JAA	MASCARENHAS,B		1	21
0.00	DHAVALE,DG	SP	1991	AUD			159	166
0.00	DOPUCH,N	ST	1991	JAR	KING ,RR		60	106

CITE INDEX	FIRST AUTHOR	ISS-UE	YE-AR	JOUR-NAL	SECOND AUTHOR	THIRD AUTHOR	PAG BEG	PAG END
0.00	DREBIN,AR	SP	1966	JAR			68	86
0.00	DUVALL,RM	JL	1965	TAR	BULLOCH,J		569	573
0.00	DWORIN,L	SP	1989	CAR	GRIMLUND,RA		674	691
0.00	ELGERS,P	JN	1992	JAE	MURRAY,D		303	316
0.00	FALK ,H	AU	1972	JAR			359	375
0.00	FARRELY,GE	AP	1985	TAR	FERRIS,KR	REICHENSTEIN,WR	278	288
0.00	FERRARA,WL	JL	1977	TAR			597	604
0.00	FINLEY,DR	SP	1987	AUD	BOOCKHOLDT,JL		22	39
0.00	FINLEY,DR	SP	1989	CAR			692	719
0.00	FIRMIN,PA	ST	1968	JAR	GOODMAN,SS	HENDRICKS,TE	122	155
0.00	FOSTER,G	JA	1990	JAE	GUPTA ,M		309	337
0.00	FRANCIS,J	AU	1990	JAR			326	347
0.00	FRANCIS,JR	SU	1990	JAA	ANDREWS JR,WT	SIMON ,DT	369	378
0.00	FROST ,PA	SP	1986	JAR	TAMURA,H		57	75
0.00	FULMER,JG	AU	1984	JAA	MOON ,JE		5	14
0.00	GAMBLING,TE	JA	1970	TAR	NOUR ,A		98	102
0.00	GAVER ,JJ	SP	1992	JAA			137	156
0.00	GERLACH,JH	SP	1988	AUD			61	76
0.00	GHICAS,DC	AP	1990	TAR			384	405
0.00	GIROUX,GA	06	1986	AOS	MAYPER,AG	DAFT ,RL	499	520
0.00	GLICK ,R	SP	1989	JAA	PLAUT ,SE		147	159
0.00	GRIMLUND,RA	AU	1985	JAR			575	594
0.00	GRIMLUND,RA	SP	1990	CAR			446	484
0.00	HAKANSSON,NH	SP	1969	JAR			11	31
0.00	HALL ,TW	SP	1989	AUD	PIERCE,BJ	ROSS ,WR	64	89
0.00	HARPER JR,RM	AU	1987	JAR	MISTER,WG	STRAWSER,JR	327	330
0.00	HARPER JR,RM	AU	1990	AUD	STRAWSER,JR	TANG ,K	115	133
0.00	HEALY ,PM	WI	1990	JAA	MODIGLIANI,F		3	25
0.00	HESSEL,CA	SU	1992	JAA	NORMAN,M		313	330
0.00	HINES JR,JR	AU	1991	JAA			447	479
0.00	HOBBS ,JB	OC	1964	TAR			905	913
0.00	HOPWOOD,W	AU	1988	CAR	MCKEOWN,J	MUTCHLER,J	284	298
0.00	HORWITZ,B	JL	1988	TAR	NORMOLLE,D		414	435
0.00	HORWITZ,BN	SP	1972	JAR	YOUNG ,AE		96	107
0.00	ICERMAN,RC	AU	1990	JAA	HILLISON,WA		527	543
0.00	IJIRI ,Y	AP	1970	TAR	THOMPSON,GL		246	258
0.00	IMHOFF JR,EA	SU	1981	JAA			333	351
0.00	JAMES ,C	SP	1989	JAA			111	124
0.00	JARRETT,JE	SP	1972	JAR			108	112
0.00	JENSEN,RE	JA	1968	TAR	THOMSEN,CT		83	93
0.00	JOHNSON,GL	JL	1966	TAR			510	517
0.00	KAHN ,N	SU	1982	JAA			327	337
0.00	KAPLAN,RS	SP	1983	AUD			52	65
0.00	KENNEDY,D	SP	1992	JAA	LAKONISHOK,J	SHAW ,WH	161	190
0.00	KENNEDY,DB	SP	1992	CAR			419	442
0.00	KENNEDY,DT	SU	1992	JAA	HYON ,YH		335	356
0.00	KHOURY,SJ	SU	1990	JAA			459	473
0.00	KING ,RD	JL	1984	TAR			419	431
0.00	KING ,RD	JA	1986	TAR	O'KEEFE,TB		76	90
0.00	KINNEY JR,WR	AU	1981	JAA			5	17
0.00	KO ,CE	SP	1988	AUD	NACHTSHEIM,CJ	DUKE ,GL	119	136
0.00	KREUTZFELDT,RW		1990	AUD	WALLACE,WA		1	26
0.00	LABELLE,R	SP	1990	CAR			677	698

CITE INDEX	FIRST AUTHOR	ISS-UE	YE-AR	JOUR-NAL	SECOND AUTHOR	THIRD AUTHOR	PAG BEG	PAG END
0.00	LAMBERT,JC	SP	1991	AUD	LAMBERT III,SJ	CALDERON,TG	97	109
0.00	LAU ,AH	SP	1987	JAR			127	138
0.00	LAU ,AHL	AU	1987	CAR	LAU ,HS		194	209
0.00	LEE ,CF	AP	1988	TAR	WU ,C		292	306
0.00	LEMKE ,KW	MR	1992	JAE	PAGE ,MJ		87	114
0.00	LEV ,B	ST	1969	JAR			182	197
0.00	LIANG ,T-P	AU	1992	CAR	CHANDLER,JS	HAN ,I	306	328
0.00	LILLESTOL,J	SP	1981	JAR			263	267
0.00	LIVINGSTONE,JL	ST	1967	JAR			93	123
0.00	LOUDDER,ML	SP	1992	AUD	KHURANA,IK	SAWYERS,RB	69	82
0.00	LYON ,JD	AU	1992	JAA	SCHROEDER,DA		531	552
0.00	MADEO ,SA	AP	1987	TAR	SCHEPANSKI,A	UECKER,WC	323	342
0.00	MAHER ,JJ	OC	1987	TAR			785	798
0.00	MAXIM ,LD	JA	1976	TAR	CULLEN,PE	COOK ,FX	97	109
0.00	MCCLENON,PR	JL	1963	TAR			540	547
0.00	MCKENNA,EF	03	1980	AOS			297	310
0.00	MCKEOWN,JC		1991	AUD	MUTCHLER,JF	HOPWOOD,W	1	13
0.00	MEHTA ,DR	SP	1968	JAR	ANDREWS,VL		50	57
0.00	MELLMAN,M	JA	1963	TAR			118	123
0.00	MENON ,K	SP	1987	CAR	SCHWARTZ,KB		302	315
0.00	MENSAH,YM	SP	1984	JAR			380	395
0.00	MENSAH,YM	AU	1988	CAR			222	249
0.00	MILTZ ,D	AU	1991	AUD	CALOMME,GJ	WILLIKENS,M	49	61
0.00	MITTELSTAEDT,HF	SP	1992	AUD	REGIER,PR	CHEWNING,EG	83	98
0.00	MOIZER,P	AU	1987	AUD	TURLEY,S		118	123
0.00	MONAHAN,TF	SU	1983	JAA	BARENBAUM,L		325	340
0.00	MOORE ,G	SP	1987	CAR			375	383
0.00	MORRIS,MH	SU	1984	JAA	NICHOLS,WD		293	305
0.00	MOSES ,OD	SU	1990	JAA			379	409
0.00	MULFORD,CW	JL	1986	TAR	COMISKEY,EE		519	525
0.00	MUTCHLER,JF	AU	1986	AUD			148	.
0.00	NEUMANN,BR	SP	1979	JAR			123	139
0.00	NEWTON,JD		1989	AUD	ASHTON,RH		22	37
0.00	NICHOLS,DR	JA	1987	TAR			183	190
0.00	NIKOLAI,LA	JA	1979	TAR	ELAM ,R		119	131
0.00	NORDHAUSER,SL	JA	1981	TAR	KRAMER,JL		54	69
0.00	ONSI ,M	AP	1967	TAR			321	330
0.00	OUTSLAY,E	OC	1982	TAR	WHEELER,JE		716	733
0.00	PALMROSE,Z		1991	AUD			54	71
0.00	PALMROSE,Z	ST	1991	JAR			149	193
0.00	PATTEN,DM	05	1992	AOS			471	475
0.00	PEAVY ,JW	WI	1985	JAA	EDGAR ,SM		125	135
0.00	PELES ,YC	SP	1990	JAA			309	327
0.00	PELES ,YC	SU	1991	JAA			349	359
0.00	PENMAN,SH	SP	1991	JAA			233	255
0.00	PESANDO,JE	OC	1983	TAR	CLARKE,CK		733	748
0.00	PETRI ,E	AP	1978	TAR	MINCH ,RA		415	428
0.00	PETRONI,KR	DE	1992	JAE			485	507
0.00	PILLSBURY,CM	SP	1985	AUD			63	79
0.00	POWERS,M	AP	1989	TAR	REVSINE,L		346	368
0.00	RAMANATHAN,KV	OC	1971	TAR	RAPPAPORT,A		733	745
0.00	RAUN ,DL	OC	1963	TAR			754	758
0.00	REILLY,FK	AU	1972	JAR	STETTLER,HF		308	321

CITE INDEX	FIRST AUTHOR	ISS-UE	YE-AR	JOUR-NAL	SECOND AUTHOR	THIRD AUTHOR	PAG BEG	PAG END
0.00	ROBERTS,DM	SP	1986	JAR			111	126
0.00	ROBERTS,RW	06	1992	AOS			595	612
0.00	ROBINSON,JR	JA	1990	TAR	SHANE ,PB		25	48
0.00	ROHRBACH.KJ	SP	1986	JAR			127	150
0.00	RONEN ,J	AU	1970	JAR			232	252
0.00	ROSHWALB,A	AU	1987	AUD	WRIGHT,RL	GODFREY,JT	54	70
0.00	ROSMAN,A	SP	1992	JAA			251	267
0.00	ROSS ,WR	JL	1966	TAR			464	473
0.00	RYAN ,SG	SP	1991	JAA			257	287
0.00	SAMI ,H	AU	1992	CAR	WELSH ,MJ		212	236
0.00	SCHACHTER,B	AU	1985	JAR			907	910
0.00	SCHOLES,MS	SU	1989	JAA	TERRY ,E	WOLFSON,MA	317	340
0.00	SCHOLES,MS	AU	1991	JAA	WOLFSON,MA		513	532
0.00	SHAFER,G		1990	AUD	SRIVASTAVA,R		110	137
0.00	SMIELIAUSKAS,W	SP	1989	CAR			720	732
0.00	SMIELIAUSKAS,W		1990	AUD			149	166
0.00	SRINIDHI,BN	SP	1986	AUD	VASARHELYI,MA		64	76
0.00	SRIVASTAVA,RP	AU	1986	JAR			422	427
0.00	STERNER,JA	AU	1983	JAR			623	628
0.00	STRONG,JS	OC	1990	JAE			267	283
0.00	SUSSMAN,MR	AP	1965	TAR			407	413
0.00	TAMURA,H	SP	1985	AUD			133	142
0.00	THORNTON,DB	AU	1988	CAR			343	370
0.00	TILLER,MG	SU	1985	JAA	MAUTZ ,RD		293	304
0.00	TRADER,RL	AU	1987	CAR	HUSS ,HF		227	239
0.00	VERRECCHIA,RE	JL	1982	TAR			579	593
0.00	WALKER,M	AP	1984	TAR			278	286
0.00	WALLACE,WA	SP	1983	AUD			66	90
0.00	WALLACE,WA	SP	1991	CAR	KRUETZFELDT,RW		485	512
0.00	WARREN,CS	SP	1974	JAR			158	177
0.00	WATKINS,PR	SP	1984	JAR			406	411
0.00	WATSON,CJ	JL	1990	TAR			682	695
0.00	WILCOX,KA	01	1977	AOS	SMITH ,CH		81	97
0.00	WILKERSON JR,JE	SP	1987	JAR			161	167
0.00	WILLIAMS,DJ	SP	1985	AUD	LILLIS,A		110	117
0.00	WILSON,AC	SP	1989	AUD	GLEZEN,GW		90	100
0.00	WILSON,AC	SU	1991	JAA			365	381
0.00	WILSON,AC	SP	1992	AUD			32	46
0.00	WRIGHT,DW	SP	1991	AUD			145	158
0.00	WURST ,J	AP	1991	TAR	NETER ,J	GODFREY,J	333	347
0.00	YOUNG ,SD	AP	1988	TAR			283	291
0.00	ZAROWIN,P	SU	1990	JAA			439	454

3.8 SCHOOL OF THOUGHT=ACCOUNTING THEORY

CITE INDEX	FIRST AUTHOR	ISS-UE	YE-AR	JOUR-NAL	SECOND AUTHOR	THIRD AUTHOR	PAG BEG	PAG END
4.92	BURCHELL,S	01	1980	AOS	CLUBB ,C	HOPWOOD,AG	5	27
4.33	WATTS ,RL	JA	1990	TAR	ZIMMERMAN,JL		131	156
3.75	BURCHELL,S	04	1985	AOS	CLUBB ,C	HOPWOOD,AG	381	414
3.50	WATTS ,RL	AP	1979	TAR	ZIMMERMAN,JL		273	305
3.18	TINKER,AM	02	1982	AOS	MERINO,BD	NEIMARK,M	167	200
3.10	HOPWOOD,AG	23	1983	AOS			287	305
3.00	KAPLAN,RS	JL	1984	TAR			390	418
2.78	COOPER,DJ	34	1984	AOS	SHERER,MJ		207	232

CITE INDEX	FIRST AUTHOR	ISS-UE	YE-AR	JOUR-NAL	SECOND AUTHOR	THIRD AUTHOR	PAG BEG	PAG END
2.75	ARRINGTON,CE	02	1989	AOS	FRANCIS,JR		1	28
2.40	TOMKINS,C	04	1983	AOS	GROVES,R		361	374
2.30	KAPLAN,RS	OC	1983	TAR			686	705
2.20	LEFTWICH,RW	JA	1983	TAR			23	42
2.14	CHUA ,WF	OC	1986	TAR			601	632
2.08	DEANGELO,LE	DE	1981	JAE			183	199
2.00	LEV ,B	JA	1988	TAR			1	22
2.00	MEYER ,JW	45	1986	AOS			345	356
2.00	ROBERTS,J	04	1985	AOS	SCAPENS,RW		443	456
1.85	TINKER,AM	01	1980	AOS			147	160
1.80	COVALESKI,MA	01	1988	AOS	DIRSMITH,MW		1	24
1.80	HINES ,RD	03	1988	AOS			251	261
1.80	HOSKIN,KW	01	1988	AOS	MACVE ,RH		37	73
1.50	RICHARDSON,AJ	04	1987	AOS			341	355
1.50	ROBERTS,J	04	1991	AOS			355	368
1.43	DEANGELO,LE	JL	1986	TAR			400	420
1.43	NEIMARK,M	45	1986	AOS	TINKER,T		369	396
1.40	PALMROSE,ZV	JA	1988	TAR			55	73
1.40	TINKER,T	02	1988	AOS			165	189
1.38	DUKES ,RE	ST	1980	JAR	DYCKMAN,TR	ELLIOTT,JA	1	26
1.33	PUXTY ,AG	03	1987	AOS	WILLMOTT,HC	COOPER,DJ	273	291
1.30	TIESSEN,P	23	1983	AOS	WATERHOUSE,JH		251	268
1.29	ZIMMER,I	MR	1986	JAE			37	52
1.20	MORGAN,G	05	1988	AOS			477	485
1.20	ZIMMERMAN,JL	AG	1983	JAE			119	149
1.17	HOPPER,T	05	1987	AOS	STOREY,J	WILLMOTT,H	437	456
1.17	KNIGHTS,D	05	1987	AOS	COLLINSON,D		457	477
1.14	TRUEMAN,B	MR	1986	JAE			53	72
1.08	COOPER,DJ	03	1981	AOS	HAYES ,DC	WOLF ,FM	175	192
1.06	DEMSKI,JS	OC	1973	TAR			718	723
1.06	GAMBLING,TE	02	1977	AOS			141	152
1.00	CHOUDHURY,N	06	1988	AOS			549	557
1.00	COVALESKI,MA	06	1990	AOS	DIRSMITH,MW		543	573
1.00	GRAY ,B	05	1992	AOS			399	425
1.00	LAVOIE,D	06	1987	AOS			579	604
0.94	BEAVER,WH	OC	1968	TAR	KENNELLY,JW	VOSS ,WM	675	683
0.90	SPICER,BH	01	1983	AOS	BALLEW,V		73	98
0.88	GORDON,MJ	AP	1964	TAR			251	263
0.86	KAPLAN,RS	45	1986	AOS			429	452
0.83	MARCH ,JG	02	1987	AOS			153	168
0.82	SORTER,GH	JA	1969	TAR			12	19
0.81	HAKANSSON,NH	AP	1977	TAR			396	416
0.80	KINNEY JR,WR	SP	1988	CAR			416	425
0.78	SUNDER,S	SP	1984	JAR	WAYMIRE,G		396	405
0.71	BEAVER,WH	ST	1974	JAR	DEMSKI,JS		170	187
0.71	CHUA ,WF	06	1986	AOS			583	598
0.71	PASTENA,V	AP	1986	TAR	RULAND,W		288	301
0.69	PARKER,JE	JA	1977	TAR			69	96
0.67	BEGLEY,J	JA	1990	JAE			125	139
0.67	THOMPSON,G	05	1987	AOS			523	543
0.67	WHITTRED,G	DE	1987	JAE			259	285
0.67	WILLIAMS,PF	02	1987	AOS			169	192
0.67	WILSON JR,TE	SP	1990	AUD	GRIMLUND,RA		43	59

CITE INDEX	FIRST AUTHOR	ISS-UE	YE-AR	JOUR-NAL	SECOND AUTHOR	THIRD AUTHOR	PAG BEG	PAG END
0.65	GAGNON,JM	ST	1967	JAR			187	204
0.65	LEV ,B	JA	1971	TAR	SCHWARTZ,A		103	112
0.60	HINES ,RD	OC	1988	TAR			642	656
0.60	LILIEN,S	OC	1988	TAR	MELLMAN,M	PASTENA,V	642	656
0.60	SUTTON,TG	AP	1988	JAE			127	149
0.60	WONG ,J	JA	1988	JAE			37	51
0.60	WONG ,J	AP	1988	JAE			151	167
0.59	MAY ,RG	OC	1976	TAR	SUNDEM,GL		747	763
0.57	SHRIVER,KA	SP	1986	JAR			151	165
0.55	DAVIS ,SW	04	1982	AOS	MENON ,K	MORGAN,G	307	318
0.53	ARCHIBALD,TR	ST	1967	JAR			164	186
0.53	FRISHKOFF,P	ST	1970	JAR			116	129
0.50	BENSTON,GJ	AP	1985	JAE			67	84
0.50	BOUGEN,PD	03	1989	AOS			203	234
0.50	COLIGNON,R	02	1991	AOS	COVALESKI,M		141	157
0.50	DIRSMITH,MW	AU	1985	CAR	COVALESKI,MA	MCALLISTER,JP	46	68
0.50	DYE ,RA	AU	1985	JAR			544	574
0.50	GONEDES,NJ	AU	1979	JAR	DOPUCH,N		384	410
0.50	HARTE ,GF	02	1987	AOS	OWEN ,DL		123	142
0.50	PALMROSE,ZV	SP	1987	AUD			90	103
0.50	SHRIVER,KA	JA	1987	TAR			79	96
0.50	TROMBLEY,MA	JL	1989	TAR			529	538
0.47	DOPUCH,N	AU	1973	JAR	RONEN ,J		191	211
0.47	DRAKE ,DF	AU	1965	JAR	DOPUCH,N		192	205
0.47	FELTHAM,GA	OC	1968	TAR			684	696
0.47	PETERSEN,RJ	JA	1973	TAR			34	43
0.45	DEANGELO,LE	DE	1982	JAE			171	203
0.45	HITE ,GL	JL	1982	JAE	LONG ,MS		3	14
0.44	BENSTON,GJ	AU	1984	CAR			47	57
0.42	OHLSON,JA	AU	1981	JAR	BUCKMAN,AG		399	433
0.41	EPSTEIN,MJ	01	1976	AOS	FLAMHOLTZ,EG	MCDONOUGH,JJ	23	42
0.41	HENDRICKS,JA	AP	1976	TAR			292	305
0.41	NEUMANN,FL	ST	1968	JAR			1	17
0.40	KIM ,M	AP	1988	JAE	MOORE ,G		111	125
0.38	DIERKES,M	01	1977	AOS	PRESTON,LE		3	22
0.38	KELLY ,R	AU	1985	JAR			619	632
0.38	OWEN ,DL	03	1985	AOS	LLOYD ,AJ		329	352
0.35	COPELAND,RM	ST	1971	JAR	SHANK ,JK		196	224
0.35	MCINTYRE,EV	JL	1973	TAR			575	585
0.35	REVSINE,L	JL	1970	TAR			513	523
0.35	SIMMONS,JK	OC	1969	TAR	GRAY ,J		757	776
0.35	SORTER,GH	AU	1964	JAR	BECKER,S	ARCHIBALD,TR	183	196
0.33	CHAMBERS,RJ	AU	1984	CAR			1	22
0.33	COWEN ,SS	02	1987	AOS	FERRERI,LB	PARKER,LD	111	122
0.33	HOLTHAUSEN,RW	JA	1990	JAE			207	218
0.33	IJIRI ,Y	JA	1984	TAR	NOEL ,J		52	63
0.33	LAUGHLIN,RC	05	1987	AOS			479	502
0.33	SWANSON,EP	OC	1990	TAR			911	924
0.31	RONEN ,J	AP	1977	TAR			438	449
0.29	BERNSTEIN,LA	JA	1967	TAR			86	95
0.29	CHEN ,RS	JL	1975	TAR			533	543
0.29	CLANCY,DK	12	1979	AOS	COLLINS,F		21	30
0.29	COVALESKI,M	45	1986	AOS	AIKEN ,ME		297	320

CITE INDEX	FIRST AUTHOR	ISS-UE	YE-AR	JOUR-NAL	SECOND AUTHOR	THIRD AUTHOR	PAG BEG	PAG END
0.29	GAA ,JC	JL	1986	TAR			435	454
0.29	MORIARITY,S	OC	1975	TAR			791	795
0.29	PRAKASH,P	JA	1979	TAR	SUNDER,S		1	22
0.27	DIRSMITH,MW	34	1978	AOS	JABLONSKY,SF		215	226
0.25	FALK ,H	SP	1989	CAR			816	825
0.25	GOLDIN,HJ	SU	1985	JAA			269	278
0.25	GROJER,JE	04	1977	AOS	STARK ,A		349	385
0.25	HOPWOOD,W	JA	1989	TAR	MCKEOWN,J	MUTCHLER,J	28	48
0.25	KAPLAN,RS	AP	1977	TAR			369	378
0.25	KISSINGER,JN	AP	1977	TAR			322	339
0.25	PEASNELL,KV	SP	1977	JAR	SKERRATT,CL		108	119
0.25	STAUBUS,GJ	JA	1985	TAR			53	75
0.24	BARNEA,A	JA	1975	TAR	RONEN ,J	SADAN ,S	58	68
0.24	BARRETT,ME	SP	1976	JAR			10	26
0.24	BARTON,AD	OC	1974	TAR			664	681
0.24	HEINTZ,JA	OC	1973	TAR			679	689
0.24	LIVINGSTONE,JL	AP	1967	TAR			233	240
0.24	SCHIFF,M	SP	1966	JAR			62	67
0.24	STERLING,RR	JL	1970	TAR			444	457
0.22	GRANOF,MH	SU	1984	JAA	SHORT ,DG		323	333
0.21	REVSINE,L	AP	1979	TAR			306	322
0.21	SCHREUDER,H	12	1979	AOS			109	122
0.21	VATTER,WJ	JL	1979	TAR			563	573
0.20	COLIGNON,R	06	1988	AOS	COVALESKI,M		559	579
0.20	DILLON,RD	JA	1978	TAR	NASH ,JF		11	17
0.20	IJIRI ,Y	SU	1978	JAA			331	348
0.20	KILMANN,RH	04	1983	AOS			341	360
0.20	SORTER,GH	SU	1988	JAA	SIEGEL,S	SLAIN ,J	233	244
0.20	SPICER,BH	03	1988	AOS			303	322
0.19	ADAR ,Z	JA	1977	TAR	BARNEA,A	LEV ,B	137	149
0.18	ANTON ,HR	SP	1964	JAR			1	9
0.18	BOWMAN,EH	01	1976	AOS	HAIRE ,M		11	22
0.18	CHAMBERS,RJ	AP	1964	TAR			264	274
0.18	CHAMBERS,RJ	OC	1965	TAR			731	741
0.18	CYERT ,RM	ST	1974	JAR	IJIRI ,Y		29	42
0.18	EAVES ,BC	JL	1966	TAR			426	442
0.18	MATTESSICH,R	JL	1972	TAR			469	487
0.18	MCCARTHY,WE	JL	1982	TAR			554	578
0.18	MCKEOWN,JC	JA	1971	TAR			12	29
0.18	MOBLEY,SC	OC	1970	TAR			762	768
0.18	ORTMAN,RF	AP	1975	TAR			298	304
0.18	RONEN ,J	SP	1975	JAR	SADAN ,S		133	149
0.18	SKINNER,RC	SP	1982	JAR			210	226
0.18	VATTER,WJ	AU	1963	JAR			179	197
0.17	COOPER,DJ	05	1987	AOS	HOPPER,TM		407	414
0.17	DYCKMAN,TR	04	1981	AOS			291	300
0.17	GAMBLING,T	04	1987	AOS			319	329
0.17	JACOBS,FH	JA	1987	TAR	MARSHALL,RM		67	78
0.17	VERRECCHIA,RE	ST	1987	JAR	LANEN ,WN		165	189
0.15	ANSARI,SL	01	1980	AOS	MCDONOUGH,JJ		129	142
0.14	BROCKHOFF,K	12	1979	AOS			77	86
0.14	DERMER,JD	06	1986	AOS	LUCAS ,RG		471	482
0.14	DIERKES,M	12	1979	AOS			87	108

CITE INDEX	FIRST AUTHOR	ISS-UE	YE-AR	JOUR-NAL	SECOND AUTHOR	THIRD AUTHOR	PAG BEG	PAG END
0.14	HILKE ,JC	WI	1986	JAA			17	29
0.14	ROBBINS,WA	AU	1986	JAR	AUSTIN,KR		412	421
0.14	ZALD ,MN	45	1986	AOS			321	326
0.13	ANELL ,B	04	1985	AOS			479	492
0.13	BROMWICH,M	JL	1977	TAR			587	596
0.13	GAMBLING,T	04	1985	AOS			415	426
0.13	HALPERIN,R	OC	1985	TAR	TZUR ,J		670	680
0.13	HUGHES,JS	OC	1978	TAR			882	894
0.13	JONES ,CS	03	1985	AOS			303	328
0.13	JONES ,CS	02	1985	AOS			177	200
0.13	KELLY ,LK	JA	1977	TAR			97	108
0.13	LESSEM,R	04	1977	AOS			279	294
0.13	RAVIV ,A	AP	1985	JAE			239	246
0.12	BENISHAY,H	SP	1965	JAR			114	132
0.12	BIERMAN JR,H	JL	1963	TAR			501	507
0.12	BIRD ,FA	AP	1974	TAR	DAVIDSON,LF	SMITH ,CH	233	244
0.12	BRIEF ,RP	AP	1975	TAR			285	297
0.12	CHAMBERS,RJ	SP	1963	JAR			3	15
0.12	CHAMBERS,RJ	SP	1965	JAR			32	62
0.12	CHAMBERS,RJ	AU	1965	JAR			242	252
0.12	CHAMBERS,RJ	JL	1966	TAR			443	457
0.12	CHAMBERS,RJ	OC	1967	TAR			751	757
0.12	COPELAND,RM	SP	1968	JAR	FREDERICKS,W		106	113
0.12	DEVINE,CT	AU	1963	JAR			127	138
0.12	DOCKWEILER,RC	OC	1969	TAR			729	742
0.12	DOPUCH,N	ST	1966	JAR	DRAKE ,DF		192	219
0.12	EDWARDS,EO	AP	1975	TAR			235	245
0.12	FALK ,H	AP	1973	TAR	OPHIR ,T		323	338
0.12	GYNTHER,RS	OC	1970	TAR			712	730
0.12	HORNGREN,CT	AP	1965	TAR			323	333
0.12	IJIRI ,Y	SP	1965	JAR	JAEDICKE,RK	LIVINGSTONE,JL	63	74
0.12	IJIRI ,Y	AP	1976	TAR			227	243
0.12	JOHNSON,O	OC	1970	TAR			641	653
0.12	KNUTSON,PH	JA	1970	TAR			55	68
0.12	LARSON,KD	JA	1969	TAR			38	47
0.12	LEMKE ,KW	JA	1966	TAR			32	41
0.12	LINDHE,R	AU	1963	JAR			139	148
0.12	LORIG ,AN	JL	1964	TAR			563	573
0.12	MAUTZ ,RK	AP	1963	TAR			317	325
0.12	MOONITZ,M	JL	1970	TAR			465	475
0.12	PELES ,YC	SP	1970	JAR			128	137
0.12	RITTS ,BA	SP	1974	JAR			93	111
0.12	SNAVELY,HJ	AP	1967	TAR			223	232
0.12	THOMAS,AL	JL	1971	TAR			472	479
0.12	VATTER,WJ	AU	1966	JAR			133	148
0.12	VICKREY,DW	OC	1970	TAR			731	742
0.12	VICKREY,DW	JA	1976	TAR			31	40
0.12	WAGNER,JW	JL	1965	TAR			599	605
0.12	YETTON,PY	01	1976	AOS			81	90
0.11	CHAMBERS,RJ	AU	1984	CAR			58	63
0.11	MOST ,KS	AU	1984	JAR			782	788
0.11	ROBERTSON,JC	SP	1984	AUD			57	67
0.10	HALL ,TW	SU	1983	JAA			299	313

CITE INDEX	FIRST AUTHOR	ISS-UE	YE-AR	JOUR-NAL	SECOND AUTHOR	THIRD AUTHOR	PAG BEG	PAG END
0.10	OVADIA,A	WI	1983	JAA	RONEN ,J		115	129
0.10	SOTTO ,R	01	1983	AOS			57	72
0.10	TAUSSIG,RA	WI	1983	JAA			142	156
0.09	BENSTON,GJ	02	1982	AOS			87	106
0.09	MOCK ,TJ	AU	1982	AUD	WRIGHT,A		33	44
0.09	VIGELAND,RL	AP	1982	TAR			348	357
0.08	ALFORD,MR	SP	1981	JAA	EDMONDS,TP		255	264
0.08	CHAMBERS,RJ	01	1980	AOS			167	180
0.08	FLAHERTY,RE	AU	1980	JAA	SCHWARTZ,BN		47	56
0.08	FLAMHOLTZ,EG	01	1980	AOS			31	42
0.08	HORWITZ,BN	WI	1981	JAA	KOLODNY,R		102	113
0.08	KOCH ,BS	JL	1981	TAR			574	586
0.08	PALMON,D	SP	1980	JAA	KWATINETZ,M		207	226
0.08	RAMANATHAN,KV	02	1981	AOS	WEIS ,WL		143	152
0.07	AGGARWAL,R	SP	1978	JAA			197	216
0.07	CHAN ,JL	04	1979	AOS			273	282
0.07	GRAY ,SJ	AU	1978	JAR			242	253
0.07	HAKANSSON,NH	JL	1978	TAR			717	725
0.07	SCAPENS,RW	AP	1978	TAR			448	469
0.06	AIKEN ,ME	JL	1975	TAR	BLACKETT,LA	ISAACS,G	544	562
0.06	ALFRED,AM	AU	1964	JAR			172	182
0.06	ARNETT,HE	AP	1967	TAR			291	297
0.06	ARNOLD,DF	AU	1977	JAR	HUEFNER,RJ		245	252
0.06	BAXTER,WT	AU	1971	JAR	CARRIER,NH		189	214
0.06	BEDFORD,NM	JL	1968	TAR	IINO ,T		453	458
0.06	BEDFORD,NM	JL	1975	TAR	ZIEGLER,RE		435	443
0.06	BIERMAN JR,H	AP	1966	TAR			271	274
0.06	BIRD ,PA	SP	1965	JAR			1	11
0.06	BIRNBERG,JG	OC	1965	TAR			814	820
0.06	BIRNBERG,JG	01	1976	AOS	GANDHI,NM		5	10
0.06	BOLLOM,WJ	JA	1972	TAR	WEYGANDT,JJ		75	84
0.06	BOLLOM,WJ	JA	1973	TAR			12	22
0.06	BRADFORD,WD	AP	1974	TAR			296	305
0.06	BRIEF ,RP	OC	1973	TAR	OWEN ,J		690	695
0.06	BRILOFF,AJ	JA	1964	TAR			12	15
0.06	BUCKLEY,JW	AP	1968	TAR	KIRCHER,P	MATHEWS,RL	274	283
0.06	BULLOCK,CL	JA	1974	TAR			98	103
0.06	BURKE ,EJ	OC	1964	TAR			837	849
0.06	BUZBY ,SL	SP	1975	JAR			16	37
0.06	CHURCHILL,NC	ST	1966	JAR			128	156
0.06	COOK ,JS	OC	1976	TAR	HOLZMANN,OJ		778	787
0.06	COOPER,WW	OC	1968	TAR	DOPUCH,N	KELLER,TF	640	648
0.06	CURRY ,DW	JL	1971	TAR			490	503
0.06	DAVIDSON,S	AU	1963	JAR			117	126
0.06	DICKENS,RL	AP	1964	TAR	BLACKBURN,JO		312	329
0.06	DREBIN,AR	JA	1965	TAR			154	162
0.06	ECKEL ,LG	OC	1976	TAR			764	777
0.06	FEKRAT,MA	AP	1972	TAR			351	355
0.06	FOGELBERG,G	AU	1971	JAR			215	235
0.06	FRANCIS,ME	AP	1973	TAR			245	257
0.06	FRANKFURTER,GM	AP	1972	TAR	HORWITZ,BN		245	259
0.06	FREMGEN,JM	OC	1968	TAR			649	656
0.06	GREEN ,D	SP	1964	JAR			35	49

CITE INDEX	FIRST AUTHOR	ISS-UE	YE-AR	JOUR-NAL	SECOND AUTHOR	THIRD AUTHOR	PAG BEG	PAG END
0.06	HEATH ,LC	JL	1972	TAR			458	468
0.06	HECK ,WR	JL	1963	TAR			577	578
0.06	HICKS ,EL	AU	1964	JAR			158	171
0.06	ISELIN,ER	AP	1968	TAR			231	238
0.06	JOHNSON,O	SP	1968	JAR			29	37
0.06	KING ,RR	JA	1974	TAR	BARON ,CD		76	87
0.06	LARSON,KD	JL	1967	TAR			480	488
0.06	MARQUES,E	23	1976	AOS			175	178
0.06	MATHEWS,RL	JL	1968	TAR			509	516
0.06	MCDONALD,DL	OC	1967	TAR			662	679
0.06	MCINTYRE,EV	JA	1977	TAR			162	171
0.06	MEYERS,SL	JA	1973	TAR			44	49
0.06	MOONITZ,M	AU	1966	JAR	RUSS ,A		155	168
0.06	NEUMANN,FL	JL	1969	TAR			546	554
0.06	NURNBERG,H	OC	1968	TAR			719	729
0.06	PARKER,JE	JL	1975	TAR			512	524
0.06	PATON ,WA	AP	1963	TAR			243	251
0.06	PENMAN,SH	AP	1970	TAR			333	346
0.06	RAPPAPORT,A	AP	1965	TAR			373	376
0.06	SHWAYDER,KR	AP	1969	TAR			304	316
0.06	SHWAYDER,KR	AP	1971	TAR			306	319
0.06	SHWAYDER,KR	AU	1973	JAR			259	272
0.06	SNAVELY,HJ	AP	1969	TAR			344	353
0.06	SPILLER JR,EA	SP	1974	JAR	VIRGIL JR,RL		112	142
0.06	STAUBUS,GJ	OC	1967	TAR			650	661
0.06	STAUBUS,GJ	JL	1976	TAR			574	589
0.06	STERLING,RR	JA	1967	TAR			62	73
0.06	STERLING,RR	JL	1968	TAR			481	502
0.06	TRACY ,JA	JA	1965	TAR			163	175
0.06	ULLMANN,AA	01	1976	AOS			71	80
0.06	VATTER,W	OC	1966	TAR			681	698
0.06	VATTER,WJ	JL	1963	TAR			470	477
0.06	WOJDAK,JF	JL	1969	TAR			562	570
0.06	WOJDAK,JF	JA	1970	TAR			88	97
0.06	WRIGHT,FK	AU	1965	JAR			167	181
0.00	ADAMS ,KD	WI	1984	JAA			151	163
0.00	AGRAWAL,SP	OC	1977	TAR			789	809
0.00	AHARONI,Y	SP	1967	JAR	OPHIR ,T		1	26
0.00	ALVEY ,KL	JA	1963	TAR			124	125
0.00	ANDERSON JR,KE	JL	1985	TAR			357	371
0.00	ANDERSON,HM	OC	1963	TAR	GRIFFIN,FB		813	818
0.00	ANDERSON,JM	AU	1964	JAR			236	238
0.00	ARGYRIS,C	06	1990	AOS			503	511
0.00	ARNETT,HE	OC	1963	TAR			733	741
0.00	ARNETT,HE	JA	1965	TAR			54	64
0.00	AYRES ,FL	SP	1986	JAR			166	169
0.00	BAINBRIDGE,DR	SU	1984	JAA			334	346
0.00	BAKER ,RE	JA	1964	TAR			52	61
0.00	BANKER,RD	JL	1992	TAR	COOPER,WW	POTTER,G	496	510
0.00	BARRETT,WB	JA	1968	TAR			105	112
0.00	BARTH ,ME	JL	1991	TAR			516	534
0.00	BEAMS ,FA	AP	1969	TAR			382	388
0.00	BEDARD,JC	AU	1989	AUD			57	71

CITE INDEX	FIRST AUTHOR	ISS-UE	YE-AR	JOUR-NAL	SECOND AUTHOR	THIRD AUTHOR	PAG BEG	PAG END
0.00	BEDFORD,NM	JA	1967	TAR			82	85
0.00	BEDFORD,NM	AP	1972	TAR	MCKEOWN,JC		333	338
0.00	BEJA ,A	AU	1977	JAR	AHARONI,Y		169	178
0.00	BELL ,PW	SP	1987	CAR			338	367
0.00	BENJAMIN,JJ	SU	1986	JAA	GROSSMAN,SD	WIGGIN,CE	177	184
0.00	BENNINGER,LJ	JL	1965	TAR			547	557
0.00	BERG ,KB	JL	1963	TAR	MUELLER,FJ		554	561
0.00	BIERMAN JR,H	JA	1963	TAR			61	63
0.00	BIERMAN JR,H	AU	1964	JAR			229	235
0.00	BIERMAN JR,H	JL	1965	TAR			541	546
0.00	BIERMAN JR,H	OC	1967	TAR			731	737
0.00	BIERMAN JR,H	AU	1967	JAR	SMIDT ,S		144	153
0.00	BIERMAN JR,H	OC	1968	TAR			657	661
0.00	BIERMAN JR,H	JA	1968	TAR	LIU ,E		62	67
0.00	BIERMAN JR,H	AP	1969	TAR	DAVIDSON,S		239	246
0.00	BIERMAN JR,H	OC	1971	TAR			693	700
0.00	BIERMAN JR,H	SP	1985	JAA			184	194
0.00	BIERMAN JR,H	WI	1986	JAA			62	70
0.00	BLAKELY,EJ	JA	1963	TAR	KNUTSON,PH		75	86
0.00	BOLAND,LA	AU	1992	CAR	GORDON,IM		142	170
0.00	BOTTS ,RR	OC	1963	TAR			789	795
0.00	BOZE ,KM	AU	1990	JAA			627	638
0.00	BRADBURY,ME	AP	1988	TAR	CALDERWOOD,SC		330	347
0.00	BRAVENEC,LL	02	1977	AOS	EPSTEIN,MJ	CRUMBLEY,DL	131	140
0.00	BRICKER,R	AU	1989	JAR			246	262
0.00	BRIEF ,RP	AP	1968	TAR	OWEN ,J		367	372
0.00	BRILOFF,AJ	JL	1967	TAR			489	496
0.00	BROWN ,LD	SP	1989	CAR	GARDNER,JC	VASARHELYI,MA	793	815
0.00	BRUGEMAN,DC	OC	1963	TAR	BRIGHTON,GD		764	770
0.00	BRUGGE,WG	JL	1963	TAR			596	600
0.00	BUCKLEY,JW	01	1980	AOS			49	64
0.00	BURKE ,WL	OC	1963	TAR			802	812
0.00	BURNS ,JS	JA	1963	TAR	JAEDICKE,RK	SANGSTER,JM	1	13
0.00	BURT ,OR	SP	1972	JAR			28	57
0.00	CARLSON,ML	JL	1981	TAR	LAMB ,JW		554	573
0.00	CARSON,AB	AP	1965	TAR			334	337
0.00	CARTER,WK	JA	1981	TAR			108	114
0.00	CASPARI,JA	OC	1976	TAR			739	746
0.00	CERF ,AR	JL	1975	TAR			451	465
0.00	CHAMBERS,RJ	AP	1967	TAR			241	253
0.00	CHAMBERS,RJ	AP	1968	TAR			239	247
0.00	CHAMBERS,RJ	JL	1972	TAR			488	509
0.00	CHAN ,KH	WI	1984	JAA	CHENG ,TT		164	177
0.00	CHEUNG,JK	SP	1990	CAR	HEANEY,J		738	760
0.00	COGLITORE,F	SP	1988	AUD	BERRYMAN,RG		150	163
0.00	COMISKEY,EE	AP	1968	TAR	MLYNARCZYK,FA		248	256
0.00	COOPER,JC	03	1991	AOS	SELTO ,FH		227	242
0.00	COOPER,WW	AU	1985	JAA	HO ,JL	HUNTER,JE	22	39
0.00	CORBIN,DA	OC	1963	TAR			742	744
0.00	CORBIN,DA	OC	1967	TAR			635	641
0.00	CORCORAN,AW	AU	1965	JAR	KWANG ,CW		206	217
0.00	COTTELL JR,PG	WI	1986	JAA			30	45
0.00	COWAN ,TK	JA	1965	TAR			9	20

CITE INDEX	FIRST AUTHOR	ISS-UE	YE-AR	JOUR-NAL	SECOND AUTHOR	THIRD AUTHOR	PAG BEG	PAG END
0.00	COWAN ,TK	JA	1968	TAR			94	100
0.00	CRAMER JR,JJ	OC	1970	TAR	SCHRADER,WJ		698	703
0.00	CRAMER JR,JJ	WI	1979	JAA	NEYHART,CA		135	150
0.00	CRUMBLEY,DL	JA	1975	TAR	SAVICH,RS		112	117
0.00	CRUSE ,RB	JA	1965	TAR	SUMMERS,EL		82	88
0.00	DANOS ,P	SP	1987	AUD	HOLT ,DL	BAILEY JR,AD	134	149
0.00	DAVIS ,ML	AP	1988	TAR	LARGAY III,JA		348	363
0.00	DAVIS ,ML	JL	1990	TAR			696	709
0.00	DEAN ,J	AP	1963	TAR	HARRISS,CL		229	242
0.00	DEFLIESE,PL	JL	1965	TAR			517	521
0.00	DEINZER,HT	JA	1966	TAR			21	31
0.00	DEMARIS,EJ	JA	1963	TAR			37	45
0.00	DEMSKI,JS	AU	1985	CAR			69	75
0.00	DEMSKI,JS	AP	1990	TAR	SAPPINGTON,DEM		363	383
0.00	DEMSKI,JS	AP	1990	TAR	SAPPINGTON,DEM		363	383
0.00	DEMSKI,JS	JL	1992	TAR	SAPPINGTON,DEM		628	630
0.00	DEWHIRST,JF	AP	1971	TAR			365	373
0.00	DOWELL,CD	AU	1981	JAA	HALL ,JA		30	40
0.00	DREBIN,AR	JL	1963	TAR			579	583
0.00	DREBIN,AR	SP	1964	JAR			25	34
0.00	DREBIN,AR	JL	1966	TAR			413	425
0.00	DRINKWATER,D	JL	1965	TAR	EDWARDS,JD		579	582
0.00	EIGEN ,MM	JL	1965	TAR			536	540
0.00	ELITZUR,RR	SP	1991	CAR			466	484
0.00	ENGSTROM,JH	SP	1984	JAA			197	211
0.00	ENGSTROM,JH	SU	1985	JAA			305	318
0.00	EVERETT,JO	SP	1984	JAA	PORTER,GA		241	256
0.00	FALK ,H	SP	1992	CAR			468	499
0.00	FARMAN,WL	JA	1963	TAR	HOU ,C		133	141
0.00	FELIX JR,WL	SP	1988	AUD	NILES ,MS		43	60
0.00	FELTHAM,GA	AU	1984	CAR			87	98
0.00	FERRARA,WL	OC	1963	TAR			719	722
0.00	FESS ,PE	OC	1963	TAR			723	732
0.00	FESS ,PE	AP	1966	TAR			266	270
0.00	FIRMIN,PA	AP	1963	TAR			270	277
0.00	FORD ,A	OC	1969	TAR			818	822
0.00	FREDRIKSON,EB	AU	1968	JAR			208	221
0.00	FREMGEN,JM	JA	1964	TAR			43	51
0.00	FREMGEN,JM	JL	1967	TAR			457	467
0.00	FRIED ,D	WI	1987	JAA	HOSLER,C		5	23
0.00	FRIEDLOB,GT	WI	1983	JAA			100	107
0.00	FRIEDMAN,LA	JA	1978	TAR			18	30
0.00	FRIEDMAN,LA	OC	1978	TAR			895	909
0.00	GAMBLE,GO	SP	1981	JAA			220	237
0.00	GAMBLE,GO	SU	1982	JAA			320	326
0.00	GARSOMBKE,HP	SU	1983	JAA	ALLEN ,G		285	298
0.00	GIBSON,JL	JL	1963	TAR			492	500
0.00	GILLES JR,LH	OC	1963	TAR			776	784
0.00	GIVENS,HR	JL	1966	TAR			458	463
0.00	GOLDBERG,L	JL	1963	TAR			457	469
0.00	GOLDSCHMIDT,Y	AP	1969	TAR	SMIDT ,S		317	329
0.00	GOLDSCHMIDT,Y	AU	1984	JAA	SHASHUA,L		54	67
0.00	GOMBERG,M	JL	1964	TAR	FARBER,A		615	617

CITE INDEX	FIRST AUTHOR	ISS-UE	YE-AR	JOUR-NAL	SECOND AUTHOR	THIRD AUTHOR	PAG BEG	PAG END
0.00	GORDON,LA	JL	1988	AUD	HAMER ,MH		514	521
0.00	GORMLEY,RJ	SU	1980	JAA			293	312
0.00	GOVINDARAJAN,V	SU	1979	JAA			339	343
0.00	GOVINDARAJAN,V	04	1980	AOS			383	392
0.00	GRADY ,P	JA	1965	TAR			21	30
0.00	GRAY ,D	AU	1984	JAR			760	764
0.00	GRAY ,SJ	SP	1984	JAR	RADEBAUGH,LH		351	360
0.00	GREENBALL,MN	ST	1968	JAR			27	49
0.00	GREENBERG,RR	AU	1986	JAA	JOHNSON,GL	RAMESH,K	266	277
0.00	GREER ,HC	JA	1964	TAR			22	31
0.00	GUTBERLET,LG	SU	1980	JAA			313	338
0.00	GUTBERLET,LG	AU	1983	JAA			16	28
0.00	GYNTHER,RS	AP	1969	TAR			247	255
0.00	HALL ,TW	SP	1985	JAA	CASLER,DJ		210	224
0.00	HALPERIN,R	OC	1987	TAR	SRINIDHI,BN		686	706
0.00	HANNUM,WH	AP	1968	TAR	WASSERMAN,W		295	302
0.00	HASEMAN,WC	OC	1968	TAR			738	752
0.00	HATFIELD,HR	AU	1966	JAR			169	182
0.00	HAWKINS,CA	SP	1984	JAA	GIRARD,D		225	240
0.00	HENDRICKSON,HS	AP	1968	TAR			363	366
0.00	HENDRIKSEN,ES	JL	1963	TAR			483	491
0.00	HENNESSY,VC	SU	1978	JAA			317	330
0.00	HILL ,HP	WI	1982	JAA			99	109
0.00	HINES ,RD	04	1992	AOS			313	341
0.00	HIRSCH,AJ	OC	1964	TAR			972	978
0.00	HIRSCHMAN,RW	JA	1965	TAR			176	183
0.00	HOLDER,WW	WI	1982	JAA	EUDY ,KH		110	125
0.00	HOLZER,HP	AP	1964	TAR	SCHONFELD,HM		405	413
0.00	HOLZMANN,OJ	WI	1984	JAA	MEANS ,KM		138	150
0.00	HORNE ,JC	JA	1963	TAR			56	60
0.00	HORVITZ,JS	WI	1985	JAA	COLDWELL,S		86	99
0.00	HORWITZ,BN	OC	1963	TAR			819	826
0.00	HORWITZ,BN	AU	1980	JAA	KOLODNY,R		20	35
0.00	HORWITZ,RM	JL	1964	TAR			618	621
0.00	HOUGHTON,CW	SP	1991	AUD	FOGARTY,JA		1	21
0.00	HUDSON,RR	OC	1963	TAR			796	801
0.00	HUSS ,HF	AU	1985	JAA			60	66
0.00	HYLTON,DP	OC	1965	TAR			824	828
0.00	IJIRI ,Y	JA	1965	TAR			36	53
0.00	IJIRI ,Y	OC	1968	TAR			662	667
0.00	IJIRI ,Y	JL	1972	TAR			510	526
0.00	IJIRI ,Y	01	1980	AOS	KELLY ,EC		115	123
0.00	IJIRI ,Y	OC	1986	TAR			745	760
0.00	IMDIEKE,LF	OC	1969	TAR	WEYGANDT,JJ		798	805
0.00	IMKE ,FJ	AP	1966	TAR			318	322
0.00	IVES ,M	SU	1985	JAA			253	268
0.00	JACOBSEN,LE	AP	1963	TAR			285	292
0.00	JARRETT,JE	SP	1974	JAR			63	66
0.00	JENKINS,DO	JL	1964	TAR			648	653
0.00	JENSEN,MC	AP	1985	JAE	ZIMMERMAN,JL		3	10
0.00	JERSTON,JE	OC	1965	TAR			812	813
0.00	JOHNSON,GL	OC	1965	TAR			821	823
0.00	JOHNSON,O	SP	1965	JAR			75	85

CITE INDEX	FIRST AUTHOR	ISS-UE	YE-AR	JOUR-NAL	SECOND AUTHOR	THIRD AUTHOR	PAG BEG	PAG END
0.00	JOHNSON,O	JL	1968	TAR			546	548
0.00	JOHNSON,O	OC	1976	TAR			808	823
0.00	JOHNSTON,DJ	SP	1980	JAA	LEMON ,WM	NEUMANN,FL	251	263
0.00	JOLIVET,V	JL	1964	TAR			689	692
0.00	JONSSON,S	05	1988	AOS	GRONLUND,A		513	532
0.00	KAHN ,N	AU	1985	JAA	SCHIFF,A		40	49
0.00	KARLINSKY,SS	WI	1983	JAA			157	167
0.00	KARLINSKY,SS	AU	1983	JAA			65	76
0.00	KATZ ,BG	SU	1987	JAA	OWEN ,J		266	298
0.00	KELLER,TF	JA	1965	TAR			184	189
0.00	KEMP ,PS	JA	1963	TAR			126	132
0.00	KING ,TE	SP	1979	JAA			209	223
0.00	KING ,TE	JL	1988	AUD	ORTEGREN,AK		522	535
0.00	KIRCHER,P	OC	1965	TAR			742	752
0.00	KIRCHER,P	JL	1967	TAR			537	543
0.00	KISSINGER,JN	SP	1986	JAA			90	101
0.00	KISTNER,KP	SP	1980	JAR	SALMI ,T		297	311
0.00	KNAUF ,JB	WI	1987	JAA	VASARHELYI,MA		43	64
0.00	KNUTSON,PH	ST	1971	JAR			99	112
0.00	LAIBSTAIN,S	AP	1971	TAR			342	351
0.00	LANGHOLM,O	AU	1965	JAR			218	227
0.00	LARGAY III,JA	AU	1983	JAA			44	53
0.00	LARSON,KD	OC	1966	TAR	SCHATTKE,RW		634	641
0.00	LAUVER,RC	JA	1966	TAR			65	74
0.00	LAWLER,J	ST	1967	JAR			86	92
0.00	LEE ,SS	JL	1965	TAR			622	625
0.00	LEMBKE,VC	JL	1970	TAR			458	464
0.00	LEMBKE,VC	WI	1980	JAA	SMITH ,JH		147	162
0.00	LEMBKE,VC	WI	1981	JAA	TOOLE ,HR		128	135
0.00	LENTILHON,RW	OC	1964	TAR			880	883
0.00	LERE ,JC	AP	1986	TAR			318	324
0.00	LESSARD,DR	JL	1977	TAR	LORANGE,P		628	637
0.00	LEV ,B	AU	1978	JAR	THEIL ,H		286	293
0.00	LI ,DH	OC	1963	TAR			771	775
0.00	LI ,DH	JA	1963	TAR			52	55
0.00	LI ,DH	SP	1963	JAR			102	107
0.00	LI ,DH	OC	1964	TAR			946	950
0.00	LITTLETON,AC	JL	1970	TAR			476	480
0.00	LORIG ,AN	OC	1963	TAR			759	763
0.00	LOUDERBACK,JG	AP	1971	TAR			298	305
0.00	LOWE ,HD	AP	1963	TAR			293	301
0.00	LUDMAN,EA	SP	1986	JAA			118	124
0.00	MADDALA,GS	OC	1991	TAR			788	808
0.00	MAHER ,MW	SP	1983	JAR	NANTELL,TJ		329	340
0.00	MAITRE,P	34	1978	AOS			227	236
0.00	MAKSY ,MM	OC	1988	TAR			683	699
0.00	MANEGOLD,JG	SU	1986	JAA			206	221
0.00	MANES ,RP	ST	1967	JAR	SAMUELS,JM	SMYTH ,DJ	139	156
0.00	MARKS ,BR	AU	1987	AUD	RAMAN ,KK		106	117
0.00	MARPLE,RM	JL	1963	TAR			478	482
0.00	MATEER,WH	JL	1965	TAR			583	586
0.00	MATTESSICH,RV	SP	1986	CAR			157	178
0.00	MAURIELLO,JA	JA	1963	TAR			26	28

CITE INDEX	FIRST AUTHOR	ISS-UE	YE-AR	JOUR-NAL	SECOND AUTHOR	THIRD AUTHOR	PAG BEG	PAG END
0.00	MAURIELLO,JA	AP	1964	TAR			347	357
0.00	MCCOSH,AM	OC	1967	TAR			693	700
0.00	MCDONALD,DL	12	1979	AOS	PUXTY ,AG		53	66
0.00	MCINTYRE,EV	JL	1982	TAR			607	618
0.00	MCKEOWN,JC	JL	1972	TAR			527	532
0.00	MENSAH,YM	WI	1983	JAA			130	141
0.00	METCALF,RW	JA	1964	TAR			16	21
0.00	MEYER ,PE	JA	1976	TAR			80	89
0.00	MIELKE,DE	WI	1987	JAA	SEIFERT,J		65	78
0.00	MILLER,MC	AP	1973	TAR			280	291
0.00	MOBLEY,SC	AP	1966	TAR			292	296
0.00	MOBLEY,SC	JA	1967	TAR			114	123
0.00	MOBLEY,SC	AP	1968	TAR			333	341
0.00	MONSON,NP	OC	1964	TAR	TRACY ,JA		890	893
0.00	MOORE ,DC		1991	AOS			163	791
0.00	MOST ,KS	JA	1969	TAR			145	152
0.00	MUELLER,GG	JA	1963	TAR			142	147
0.00	MUELLER,GG	AU	1964	JAR			148	157
0.00	MUNTER,P	WI	1983	JAA	RATCLIFFE,TA		108	114
0.00	MURRAY,D	AU	1983	JAA	JOHNSON,R		4	15
0.00	NELSON,GK	JA	1966	TAR			42	47
0.00	NICHOLS,AC	OC	1968	TAR	GRAWOIG,DE		631	639
0.00	NIELSEN,CC	OC	1965	TAR			795	804
0.00	NURNBERG,H	OC	1972	TAR			655	665
0.00	NURNBERG,H	AU	1985	JAA	CIANCIOLO,ST		50	59
0.00	O'CONNOR,MC	AP	1972	TAR	HAMRE ,JC		308	319
0.00	OLIPHANT,WJ	ST	1971	JAR			93	98
0.00	PARKER,WM	OC	1963	TAR			785	788
0.00	PARKER,WM	AU	1966	JAR			149	154
0.00	PATON ,WA	SP	1963	JAR			44	72
0.00	PATON ,WA	SP	1968	JAR			72	85
0.00	PATON ,WA	AP	1969	TAR			276	283
0.00	PATTEN,RJ	OC	1964	TAR			876	879
0.00	PATTERSON,RG	OC	1967	TAR			772	774
0.00	PEASNELL,KV	JA	1977	TAR			186	189
0.00	PELES ,YC	AP	1986	TAR			325	329
0.00	PENMAN,SH	AU	1992	JAA			465	484
0.00	PETERSON,WA	AP	1966	TAR			275	282
0.00	PETRI ,E	JL	1973	TAR			483	488
0.00	PHILIPS,GE	OC	1963	TAR			696	708
0.00	PHILIPS,GE	JA	1963	TAR			14	25
0.00	PHILIPS,GE	JA	1968	TAR			10	17
0.00	PHILLIPS,LC	AP	1965	TAR			377	381
0.00	PICCIOTTO,S		1992	AOS			759	792
0.00	POWER ,M	05	1992	AOS			477	499
0.00	PRINCE,TR	JL	1964	TAR			553	562
0.00	RABY ,WL	JL	1963	TAR	NEUBIG,RD		568	576
0.00	RABY ,WL	JA	1969	TAR			1	11
0.00	RAMAN ,KK	SU	1981	JAA			352	359
0.00	RAMAN ,KK	WI	1982	JAA			144	153
0.00	RAMAN ,KK	AU	1982	JAA			44	50
0.00	RAYMAN,RA	SP	1969	JAR			53	89
0.00	REVSINE,L	AP	1969	TAR			354	358

CITE INDEX	FIRST AUTHOR	ISS-UE	YE-AR	JOUR-NAL	SECOND AUTHOR	THIRD AUTHOR	PAG BEG	PAG END
0.00	REVSINE,L	AP	1981	TAR			342	354
0.00	REYNOLDS,IN	AP	1964	TAR			342	346
0.00	RICHARD,DL	OC	1968	TAR			730	737
0.00	RICHARDSON,AJ	AU	1990	CAR	WILLIAMS,JJ		278	294
0.00	RICHARDSON,AW	SP	1988	CAR			609	614
0.00	ROBBINS,WA	SU	1985	JAA	APOSTOLOU,NG	STRAWSER,RH	279	292
0.00	ROBERTS,DM	AU	1980	JAA			57	69
0.00	ROBERTSON,JC	WI	1981	JAA	ALDERMAN,CW		144	161
0.00	ROBSON,K		1992	AOS			685	708
0.00	ROCKNESS,HO	SP	1988	CAR	SHIELDS,MD		568	581
0.00	RODEN ,PF	WI	1987	JAA			79	89
0.00	RORKE ,CH	03	1982	AOS			305	306
0.00	ROSE ,H	AU	1964	JAR			137	147
0.00	ROSEN ,LS	JA	1967	TAR			106	113
0.00	ROSENFIELD,P	OC	1969	TAR			788	797
0.00	ROUSSEY,RS	SP	1992	AUD			47	57
0.00	RUBENSTEIN,DB	05	1992	AOS			501	508
0.00	RUE ,JC	SU	1984	JAA	VOLKAN,AG		306	322
0.00	RUNDFELT,R	SP	1986	JAA			125	130
0.00	SAMUELSON,RA	AP	1980	TAR			254	268
0.00	SANNELLA,AJ	AU	1986	JAA			288	304
0.00	SAPIENZA,SR	JA	1963	TAR			91	101
0.00	SAPIENZA,SR	JL	1964	TAR			582	590
0.00	SAPIENZA,SR	SP	1964	JAR			50	66
0.00	SAVOIE,LM	ST	1969	JAR			55	62
0.00	SCHACHNER,L	AP	1968	TAR			303	311
0.00	SCHATTKE,RW	OC	1965	TAR			805	811
0.00	SCHATTKE,RW	AP	1972	TAR			233	244
0.00	SCHWARTZ,BN	SP	1981	JAA			238	247
0.00	SCHWARTZ,BN	SP	1983	JAA			244	253
0.00	SCHWEIKART,JA	06	1986	AOS			541	554
0.00	SCOTT ,RA	OC	1979	TAR			750	763
0.00	SEAGLE,JP	JA	1977	TAR	PETRI ,E		124	136
0.00	SENNETTI,JT	SP	1990	AUD			103	112
0.00	SHAW ,WH	AP	1987	TAR			385	400
0.00	SHEHATA,M	OC	1991	TAR			768	787
0.00	SHILLINGLAW,G	SP	1963	JAR			73	85
0.00	SHWAYDER,KR	SP	1968	JAR			86	97
0.00	SHWAYDER,KR	OC	1972	TAR			747	760
0.00	SIMMONS,JK	OC	1967	TAR			680	692
0.00	SKERRATT,LC	SU	1984	JAA			362	368
0.00	SLAVIN,NS	AP	1977	TAR			360	368
0.00	SMIELIAUSKAS,W	SP	1990	CAR	SMITH ,L		407	426
0.00	SMITH ,G	AU	1988	AUD			108	117
0.00	SMOLINSKI,EJ	AU	1963	JAR			149	178
0.00	SORTER,GH	ST	1974	JAR	GANS ,MS		1	12
0.00	SORTER,GH	SP	1982	JAA			188	194
0.00	SORTER,GH	SP	1987	JAA	INGBERMAN,M		99	116
0.00	SPACEK,L	AP	1964	TAR			275	284
0.00	SPENCER,CH	JA	1965	TAR	BARNISEL,TS		144	153
0.00	SPENCER,MH	AP	1963	TAR			310	316
0.00	SPILLER JR,EA	OC	1964	TAR			850	859
0.00	SPROUSE,RT	OC	1963	TAR			687	695

CITE INDEX	FIRST AUTHOR	ISS-UE	YE-AR	JOUR-NAL	SECOND AUTHOR	THIRD AUTHOR	PAG BEG	PAG END
0.00	SPROUSE,RT	JL	1965	TAR			522	526
0.00	STANLEY,CH	JL	1964	TAR			639	647
0.00	STAUBUS,GJ	JA	1963	TAR			64	74
0.00	STERLING,RR	JL	1971	TAR	FLAHERTY,RE		441	456
0.00	STERLING,RR	OC	1972	TAR	TOLLEFSON,SO	FLAHERTY,RE	709	721
0.00	STICE ,JD	JL	1991	TAR			516	534
0.00	SUMMERS,EL	SP	1970	JAR	DESKINS,JW		113	117
0.00	TAUSSIG,RA	SP	1964	JAR			67	79
0.00	TAYLOR,WM	AU	1982	JAR	WEYGANDT,JJ		497	502
0.00	TEOH ,HY	02	1984	AOS	THONG ,G		189	206
0.00	THIES ,CF	AU	1987	JAA	STURROCK,T		375	391
0.00	THOMAS,AL	JL	1964	TAR			574	581
0.00	THOMAS,AL	JA	1964	TAR			1	11
0.00	THOMAS,AL	SP	1965	JAR			103	113
0.00	THOMAS,AP	03	1986	AOS			253	270
0.00	THOMAS,LR	AP	1986	TAR	SWANSON,EP		330	336
0.00	TOBA ,Y	OC	1980	TAR			604	619
0.00	TOMASSINI,LA	SP	1990	CAR			287	294
0.00	TRUMBULL,WP	JA	1963	TAR			46	51
0.00	TRUMBULL,WP	JL	1968	TAR			459	468
0.00	TUCKERMAN,B	JA	1964	TAR			32	37
0.00	VICKREY,D	JL	1992	TAR			623	627
0.00	WADE ,HH	OC	1963	TAR			714	718
0.00	WAKEMAN,LM	DE	1980	JAE			213	237
0.00	WALKER,NR	AU	1988	AUD	PIERCE,LT		1	22
0.00	WAUGH ,JB	JL	1968	TAR			535	539
0.00	WEBER ,RP	JA	1977	TAR			172	185
0.00	WEIL ,RL	OC	1973	TAR			749	758
0.00	WELLS ,MC	OC	1965	TAR	COTTON,W		829	833
0.00	WELLS ,MC	AP	1968	TAR			373	376
0.00	WELSH ,MJ	WI	1985	JAA	TRAPNELL,JE		100	111
0.00	WERNER,CA	AU	1983	JAA	KOSTOLANSKY,JW		54	64
0.00	WERNER,CA	SP	1984	JAA	KOSTOLANSKY,JW		212	224
0.00	WHEELER,JT	JA	1970	TAR			1	10
0.00	WHITE ,D	SU	1982	JAA	VANECEK,M		338	354
0.00	WHITE ,LJ	SP	1991	JAA			289	302
0.00	WIESEN,JL	WI	1979	JAA	ENG ,R		101	121
0.00	WILD ,JJ	SP	1987	JAR			139	160
0.00	WILKINSON,TL	JA	1964	TAR			133	139
0.00	WILLIAMS,D	AP	1966	TAR			226	234
0.00	WILLIAMS,JJ	02	1981	AOS			153	166
0.00	WILLIAMS,PF	06	1989	AOS			455	468
0.00	WILLIAMS,TH	OC	1967	TAR	GRIFFIN,CH		642	649
0.00	WILLINGER,GL	SP	1985	JAR			351	359
0.00	WILLINGHAM,JJ	JL	1964	TAR			543	552
0.00	WILSON,AC	AU	1989	CAR	HUDSON,D		196	215
0.00	WINDAL,FW	JA	1963	TAR			29	36
0.00	WOLK ,HI	JL	1970	TAR			544	552
0.00	WOLK ,HI	AP	1973	TAR	TEARNEY,MG		292	299
0.00	WOOLSEY,SM	OC	1963	TAR			709	713
0.00	WRIGHT,FK	JA	1963	TAR			87	90
0.00	WRIGHT,FK	SP	1964	JAR			80	90
0.00	WRIGHT,HW	OC	1966	TAR			626	633

CITE INDEX	FIRST AUTHOR	ISS-UE	YE-AR	JOUR-NAL	SECOND AUTHOR	THIRD AUTHOR	PAG BEG	PAG END
0.00	WYATT ,AR	JL	1965	TAR			527	535
0.00	WYMAN ,HE	JL	1976	TAR			545	558
0.00	YOUNG ,AE	SP	1978	JAA			217	230
0.00	YOUNG ,AE	SP	1980	JAA			244	250
0.00	YOUNG ,DW	OC	1976	TAR			788	799
0.00	YOUNG ,TN	AP	1967	TAR	PEIRSON,CG		338	341
0.00	YU ,SC	JA	1966	TAR			8	20
0.00	YU ,SC	JL	1969	TAR			571	582
0.00	ZAROWIN,P	AP	1988	JAE			89	110
0.00	ZEFF ,SA	JA	1965	TAR	MAXWELL,WD		65	75

3.9 SCHOOL OF THOUGHT=ACCOUNTING HISTORY

CITE INDEX	FIRST AUTHOR	ISS-UE	YE-AR	JOUR-NAL	SECOND AUTHOR	THIRD AUTHOR	PAG BEG	PAG END
6.00	HOPWOOD,AG	03	1987	AOS			207	234
4.83	MILLER,P	03	1987	AOS	O'LEARY,T		235	265
4.14	LOFT ,A	02	1986	AOS			137	170
3.33	ARMSTRONG,P	05	1987	AOS			415	436
3.00	HOSKIN,KW	02	1986	AOS	MACVE ,RH		105	136
2.50	LEHMAN,C	05	1987	AOS	TINKER,T		503	522
1.00	HILL ,JW	OC	1989	TAR	INGRAM,RW		667	679
1.00	HUIZING,A	05	1992	AOS	DEKKER,HC		427	448
1.00	KIRKHAM,LM	04	1992	AOS			287	297
1.00	LEHMAN,CR	04	1992	AOS			261	285
1.00	MILLER,P	04	1990	AOS			315	338
1.00	RICHARDSON,AJ	06	1989	AOS			415	431
0.90	JOHNSON,HT	23	1983	AOS			139	146
0.75	BROWN ,LD	SP	1985	JAR	GARDNER,JC		84	109
0.71	CHANDLER,AD	12	1979	AOS	DAEMS ,H		3	20
0.67	MILLER,P	05	1990	AOS	O'LEARY,T		479	498
0.50	BROWN ,LD	02	1987	AOS	GARDNER,JC	VASARHELYI,MA	193	204
0.50	BRYER ,RA	05	1991	AOS			439	486
0.50	DOPUCH,N	SP	1989	CAR			494	500
0.50	JOHNSON,HT	JL	1981	TAR			510	518
0.50	ROBSON,K	05	1991	AOS			547	570
0.50	THOMPSON,G	05	1991	AOS			572	599
0.33	ESPELAND,WN	02	1990	AOS	HIRSCH,PM		77	96
0.33	SWIERINGA,RJ	03	1987	AOS	WEICK ,KE		293	308
0.33	ZEFF ,SA	JL	1984	TAR			447	468
0.25	PRESTON,AM	06	1989	AOS			389	413
0.24	JOHNSON,HT	JL	1975	TAR			444	450
0.19	PERAGALLO,E	OC	1977	TAR			881	892
0.18	YAMEY ,BS	AU	1964	JAR			117	136
0.14	FLESHER,DL	JL	1986	TAR	FLESHER,TK		421	434
0.14	ZEFF ,SA	SP	1986	JAA			131	154
0.12	BRIEF ,RP	SP	1965	JAR			12	31
0.12	PARKER,RH	SP	1968	JAR			58	71
0.12	WELLS ,MC	JL	1976	TAR			471	482
0.08	PERAGALLO,E	JL	1981	TAR			587	595
0.07	YAMEY ,BS	AP	1979	TAR			323	329
0.06	BRIEF ,RP	SP	1967	JAR			27	38
0.06	CARSBERG,BV	SP	1966	JAR			1	15
0.06	HORRIGAN,JO	AP	1968	TAR			284	294
0.06	HUME ,LJ	SP	1970	JAR			21	33

CITE INDEX	FIRST AUTHOR	ISS-UE	YE-AR	JOUR-NAL	SECOND AUTHOR	THIRD AUTHOR	PAG BEG	PAG END
0.06	KEISTER JR,OR	AP	1963	TAR			371	376
0.06	YAMEY ,BS	SP	1967	JAR			51	76
0.00	BAILEY,D	06	1990	AOS			513	525
0.00	BOER ,G	JA	1966	TAR			92	97
0.00	BOUGEN,PD	03	1990	AOS	OGDEN ,SG	OUTRAM,Q	149	170
0.00	BOWEN ,RM	JA	1989	TAR	PFEIFFER,GM		152	171
0.00	BRIEF ,RP	OC	1977	TAR			810	812
0.00	BRIGHTON,GD	JA	1969	TAR			137	144
0.00	CARPENTER,VL		1992	AOS	FEROZ ,EH		613	643
0.00	CHAMBERS,RJ	OC	1979	TAR			764	775
0.00	CHATFIELD,M	JA	1975	TAR			1	6
0.00	COASE ,RH	JA	1990	JAE			3	13
0.00	CZARNIAWSKA-,B	04	1988	AOS			415	430
0.00	CZARNIAWSKA-JOERGES	02	1989	AOS	JACOBSSON,B		29	39
0.00	DAVIDSON,S	AP	1963	TAR			278	284
0.00	FELTON,S	AU	1990	CAR	MANN ,H		261	277
0.00	FLEISCHMAN,RK	AP	1991	TAR	PARKER,LD		361	375
0.00	FLESHER,DL	04	1979	AOS	FLESHER,TK		297	304
0.00	FU ,P	SP	1971	JAR			40	51
0.00	GALLHOFER,S	05	1991	AOS	HASLAM,J		487	520
0.00	HAIN ,HP	OC	1966	TAR			699	703
0.00	HAIN ,HP	AU	1967	JAR			154	163
0.00	HAM ,J	SP	1986	CAR	LOSELL,D	SMIELIAUSKAS,W	311	317
0.00	HECK ,JL	OC	1986	TAR	BREMSER,WG		735	744
0.00	HEIN ,LW	JL	1963	TAR			508	520
0.00	HERBERT,L	JL	1971	TAR			433	440
0.00	HOLMES,W	JA	1979	TAR			47	57
0.00	HOLZER,HP	AP	1963	TAR	SCHONFELD,HM		377	381
0.00	HOLZER,HP	AP	1963	TAR	SCHONFELD,HM		382	388
0.00	HOOKS ,KL	04	1992	AOS			343	366
0.00	HOPPER,T	05	1991	AOS	ARMSTRONG,P		405	438
0.00	INGBERMAN,M	WI	1980	JAA			101	112
0.00	JACKSON,MW	05	1992	AOS			459	469
0.00	JACOBSEN,LE	AU	1964	JAR			221	228
0.00	JONSSON,S	05	1991	AOS			521	546
0.00	KEISTER JR,OR	AP	1964	TAR			414	416
0.00	LEE ,GA	SP	1973	JAR			47	61
0.00	LEE ,GA	JL	1981	TAR			539	553
0.00	LEWIS ,NR	34	1984	AOS	PARKER,LD	SUTCLIFFE,P	275	289
0.00	LIVOCK,DM	SP	1965	JAR			86	102
0.00	LOFT ,A	04	1992	AOS			367	378
0.00	MAUTZ ,RK	AP	1977	TAR	PREVITS,GJ		301	307
0.00	MEPHAM,MJ	JA	1983	TAR			43	57
0.00	MERINO,BD	OC	1987	TAR	KOCH ,BS	MACRITCHIE,KL	748	762
0.00	MILLER,P	05	1991	AOS	HOPPER,T	LAUGHLIN,R	395	403
0.00	MILLER,P		1991	AOS			733	762
0.00	MOST ,KS	SP	1967	JAR			39	50
0.00	MOST ,KS	OC	1972	TAR			722	734
0.00	NOBES ,CW	AP	1982	TAR			303	310
0.00	NURNBERG,H	AU	1970	JAR			217	231
0.00	PEEK ,LE	AU	1991	AUD	NETER ,J	WARREN,C	33	48
0.00	PERAGALLO,E	JL	1971	TAR			529	534
0.00	PERAGALLO,E	JA	1983	TAR			98	104

CITE INDEX	FIRST AUTHOR	ISS-UE	YE-AR	JOUR-NAL	SECOND AUTHOR	THIRD AUTHOR	PAG BEG	PAG END
0.00	POWER ,MK	01	1992	AOS			37	62
0.00	PRESTON,AM	01	1992	AOS			63	100
0.00	ROBERTS,J	04	1992	AOS	COUTTS,JA		379	395
0.00	ROSEN ,LS	JA	1969	TAR	DECOSTER,DT		124	136
0.00	SALGADO,AP	AP	1963	TAR			389	397
0.00	SMITH ,G	AU	1991	AUD	KROGSTAD,JL		84	97
0.00	STONE ,WE	AP	1969	TAR			284	291
0.00	STONE ,WE	AU	1972	JAR			345	350
0.00	SWANSON,GA	JL	1988	TAR	GARDNER,JC		436	447
0.00	THANE ,P	04	1992	AOS			299	312
0.00	VANCE ,LL	OC	1969	TAR			692	703
0.00	WALKER,SP	03	1991	AOS			257	283
0.00	WARDELL,M		1991	AOS	WEISENFELD,LW		655	670
0.00	WINJUM,JO	OC	1970	TAR			743	761
0.00	WINJUM,JO	AU	1971	JAR			333	350
0.00	WINJUM,JO	JA	1971	TAR			149	155
0.00	WRIGHT,FK	AU	1967	JAR			173	179
0.00	YAMEY ,BS	JL	1980	TAR			419	425
0.00	YOUNG ,AE	SU	1992	JAA			361	368
0.00	ZEFF ,SA	JL	1982	TAR			528	553
0.00	ZEFF ,SA	SP	1992	CAR			443	467

3.10 SCHOOL OF THOUGHT=INSTITUTIONAL

CITE INDEX	FIRST AUTHOR	ISS-UE	YE-AR	JOUR-NAL	SECOND AUTHOR	THIRD AUTHOR	PAG BEG	PAG END
2.14	KINNEY JR,WR	MR	1986	JAE			73	89
1.50	ARMSTRONG,P	02	1985	AOS			129	148
1.50	NEU ,D	02	1991	AOS			185	200
1.50	TINKER,T	01	1987	AOS	NEIMARK,M		71	88
1.33	ST.PIERRE,K	AP	1984	TAR	ANDERSON,JA		242	263
1.17	THOMPSON II,RB	AU	1987	JAR	OLSEN ,C	DIETRICH,JR	245	274
1.14	WILLMOTT,H	06	1986	AOS			555	582
1.13	HOPWOOD,AG	03	1985	AOS			361	376
1.10	EVANS III,JH	AG	1983	JAE	PATTON,JM		151	175
1.00	DYCKMAN,TR	SP	1984	JAR	ZEFF ,SA		225	297
1.00	HINES ,RD	04	1991	AOS			313	331
0.83	BURRELL,G	01	1987	AOS			89	102
0.83	HOPWOOD,AG	01	1987	AOS			65	70
0.80	RUBIN ,MA	AP	1988	TAR			219	236
0.67	O'BRIEN,PC	ST	1990	JAR	BHUSHAN,R		55	82
0.67	SUNDER,S	AU	1978	JAR			341	367
0.65	BENSTON,GJ	JL	1969	TAR			515	532
0.63	DIRSMITH,MW	02	1985	AOS	COVALESKI,MA		149	170
0.63	OGDEN ,S	02	1985	AOS	BOUGEN,P		211	226
0.60	NAHAPIET,JE	04	1988	AOS			333	358
0.60	RICHARDSON,AJ	04	1988	AOS			381	396
0.58	BROWN ,PR	SP	1981	JAR			232	246
0.56	INGRAM,RW	SP	1984	JAR			126	144
0.56	MCKEE ,AJ	OC	1984	TAR	BELL ,TB	BOATSMAN,JR	647	659
0.50	BEATTY,RP	OC	1989	TAR			693	709
0.50	NEU ,D	03	1991	AOS			243	256
0.46	DOPUCH,N	JA	1980	TAR	SUNDER,S		1	21
0.43	BROWN ,PR	AU	1986	AUD	KARAN ,V		134	147
0.42	HAKANSSON,NH	ST	1981	JAR			1	35

CITE INDEX	FIRST AUTHOR	ISS-UE	YE-AR	JOUR-NAL	SECOND AUTHOR	THIRD AUTHOR	PAG BEG	PAG END
0.41	ESTES ,RW	AP	1972	TAR			284	290
0.40	SHOCKLEY,RA	AU	1983	JAR	HOLT ,RN		545	564
0.38	CUSHING,BE	AP	1977	TAR			308	321
0.38	O'LEARY,T	01	1985	AOS			87	104
0.36	BURTON,JC	WI	1982	AUD	FAIRFIELD,P		1	22
0.35	GOLDMAN,A	OC	1974	TAR	BARLEV,B		707	718
0.35	LAVIN ,D	JA	1976	TAR			41	50
0.33	ASHTON,RH	AU	1987	JAR	WILLINGHAM,JJ	ELLIOTT,RK	275	292
0.33	JACKSON-COX,J	34	1984	AOS	THIRKELL,JE	MCQUEENEY,J	253	273
0.33	NEWMAN,DP	SP	1981	JAR			247	262
0.33	RICHARDSON,AJ	05	1990	AOS			499	501
0.29	BUZBY ,SL	JA	1979	TAR	FALK ,H		23	37
0.29	POWNALL,G	AU	1986	JAR			291	315
0.29	RAMANATHAN,KV	JL	1976	TAR			516	528
0.29	RHODE ,JG	OC	1974	TAR	WHITSELL,GM	KELSEY,RL	772	787
0.29	ZEFF ,SA	AP	1967	TAR	FOSSUM,RL		298	320
0.27	HICKS JR,JO	AP	1978	TAR			371	388
0.25	DAROCA,FP	SP	1985	AUD	HOLDER,WW		80	92
0.25	DEAKIN,EB	JA	1989	TAR			137	151
0.25	HUSSEIN,ME	01	1981	AOS			27	38
0.25	INGRAM,RW	OC	1981	TAR	COPELAND,RM		830	843
0.24	CRUMBLEY,DL	OC	1973	TAR			759	763
0.22	MCCONNELL,DK	WI	1984	JAA			178	181
0.22	PURO ,M	AU	1984	JAR			624	646
0.20	DERMER,JD	01	1988	AOS			25	36
0.20	GORMLEY,RJ	SU	1988	JAA			185	212
0.20	ROCKNESS,J	04	1988	AOS	WILLIAMS,PF		397	411
0.20	WILLIAMS,DD	05	1988	AOS	DIRSMITH,MW		487	508
0.20	WYER ,JC	SP	1988	AUD	WHITE ,GT	JANSON,EC	164	173
0.18	CHOI ,FD	AU	1973	JAR			159	175
0.18	GERBOTH,DL	JL	1973	TAR			475	482
0.18	PRAKASH,P	OC	1975	TAR	RAPPAPORT,A		723	734
0.18	SCHULTE JR,AA	JL	1965	TAR			587	593
0.18	SELTO ,FH	02	1982	AOS			139	148
0.17	MAHER ,MW	OC	1981	TAR			751	770
0.15	BROMWICH,M	AP	1980	TAR			288	300
0.14	FRANK ,WG	AU	1979	JAR			593	605
0.14	HARRISON,GL	03	1986	AOS	MCKINNON,JL		233	252
0.14	RICCHIUTE,DN	12	1979	AOS			67	76
0.13	DYL ,EA	02	1985	AOS	LILLY ,MS		171	176
0.12	ALIBER,RZ	JA	1975	TAR	STICKNEY,CP		44	57
0.12	ANDERSON,HM	JL	1970	TAR	GIESE ,J	BOOKER,J	524	531
0.12	BRILOFF,AJ	JL	1966	TAR			484	495
0.12	CAUSEY JR,DY	JA	1976	TAR			19	30
0.12	GOETZ ,BE	JA	1967	TAR			53	61
0.12	LOEB ,SE	JA	1972	TAR			1	10
0.12	MOONITZ,M	SP	1966	JAR			47	61
0.12	SMITH ,CH	AP	1972	TAR	LANIER,RA	TAYLOR,ME	270	283
0.11	SCHEINER,JH	AU	1984	JAR			789	797
0.11	SUTTON,TG	01	1984	AOS			81	95
0.09	JOYCE ,EJ	AU	1982	JAR	LIBBY ,R	SUNDER,S	654	675
0.09	SELTO ,FH	AU	1982	JAR	GROVE ,HD		676	688
0.08	BAKER ,CR	SP	1980	JAA			197	206

CITE INDEX	FIRST AUTHOR	ISS-UE	YE-AR	JOUR-NAL	SECOND AUTHOR	THIRD AUTHOR	PAG BEG	PAG END
0.08	NEWMAN,DP	ST	1981	JAR			134	156
0.08	SCHREUDER,H	AP	1981	TAR			294	308
0.07	GIVOLY,D	SU	1978	JAA	RONEN ,J	SCHIFF,A	361	372
0.07	PEARSON,MA	WI	1979	JAA	LINDGREN,JH	MYERS ,BL	122	134
0.07	RAMAN ,KK	AU	1979	JAA			31	41
0.06	BALADOUNI,V	AP	1966	TAR			215	225
0.06	BRADISH,RD	OC	1965	TAR			757	766
0.06	CARMICHAEL,DR	OC	1968	TAR	SWIERINGA,RJ		697	705
0.06	CLARKE,RW	OC	1968	TAR			769	776
0.06	COWAN ,TK	OC	1965	TAR			788	794
0.06	CULPEPPER,RC	AP	1970	TAR			322	332
0.06	FLOWER,JF	SP	1966	JAR			16	36
0.06	GREENE,ED	AP	1963	TAR			355	362
0.06	HORNGREN,CT	JA	1971	TAR			1	11
0.06	KEMP ,PS	OC	1965	TAR			782	787
0.06	LANGENDERFER,HQ	OC	1969	TAR	ROBERTSON,JC		777	787
0.06	ROSENFIELD,P	AP	1966	TAR	STOREY,R		327	330
0.06	STONE ,WE	JA	1965	TAR			190	195
0.06	TAUSSIG,RA	JL	1963	TAR			562	567
0.06	WILKINSON,JR	OC	1965	TAR	DONEY ,LD		753	756
0.00	ABDEL-KHALIK,AR	SP	1966	JAR			37	46
0.00	ALLYN ,RG	JA	1964	TAR			121	127
0.00	ALLYN ,RG	AP	1966	TAR			303	311
0.00	APOSTOLOU,NG	AU	1985	JAR	GIROUX,GA	WELKER,RB	853	858
0.00	ARNETT,HE	JL	1969	TAR			482	494
0.00	BACKER,M	JL	1969	TAR			533	538
0.00	BENSON,ED	SU	1991	JAA	MARKS ,BR	RAMAN ,KK	303	319
0.00	BENSTON,GJ	JL	1976	TAR			483	498
0.00	BOWER ,JB	AP	1965	TAR	SCHLOSSER,RE		338	344
0.00	BROWN ,PR	SU	1982	JAA			282	290
0.00	BUBLITZ,B	WI	1984	JAA	KEE ,R		123	137
0.00	CAMPFIELD,WL	JL	1963	TAR			521	527
0.00	CAMPFIELD,WL	JL	1965	TAR			594	598
0.00	CAREY ,JL	JA	1968	TAR			1	9
0.00	CAREY ,JL	JA	1969	TAR			79	85
0.00	CARMICHAEL,DR	SU	1979	JAA			294	306
0.00	CARPENTER,CG	JL	1971	TAR	STRAWSER,RH		509	518
0.00	CHURCHMAN,CW	JA	1971	TAR			30	35
0.00	COE ,TL	SP	1979	JAA			244	253
0.00	COHEN ,MF	JA	1965	TAR			1	8
0.00	CRAMER JR,JJ	JL	1965	TAR			606	616
0.00	DAVIS ,LR	SP	1992	AUD	SIMON ,DT		58	68
0.00	DEIS JR,DR	JL	1992	TAR	GIROUX,GA		462	479
0.00	DEITRICK,JW	SU	1979	JAA	ALDERMAN,CW		316	328
0.00	DESKINS,JW	JA	1965	TAR			76	81
0.00	DONEGAN,J	SP	1989	JAA	SUNDER,S		203	216
0.00	DOPUCH,N	SU	1988	JAA			245	250
0.00	EDEY ,HC	AP	1963	TAR			262	265
0.00	ELLIOTT,EL	OC	1968	TAR	LARREA,J	RIVERA,JM	763	768
0.00	FARMAN,WL	AP	1964	TAR			392	404
0.00	FEINSCHREIBER,R	SP	1969	JAR			17	21
0.00	FEROZ ,EH	JL	1992	TAR	WILSON,ER		480	495
0.00	FISHER,M	SU	1978	JAA			349	360

CITE INDEX	FIRST AUTHOR	ISS-UE	YE-AR	JOUR-NAL	SECOND AUTHOR	THIRD AUTHOR	PAG BEG	PAG END
0.00	FITZGERALD,RD	AU	1979	JAA	KELLEY,EM		5	20
0.00	GAA ,JC	SP	1985	CAR	SMITH ,CH		219	241
0.00	GAMBLE,GO	SP	1986	JAA			102	117
0.00	GEIGER,MA	SP	1989	AUD			40	63
0.00	GIBSON,RW	JA	1965	TAR			196	203
0.00	GLEZEN,GW	AU	1985	JAR	MILLAR,JA		859	870
0.00	GOGGANS,TP	JL	1964	TAR			627	630
0.00	GOLDWASSER,DL	SU	1988	JAA			217	232
0.00	GREER JR,WR	AU	1978	JAA	MORRISSEY,LE		49	57
0.00	HANSEN,ES	ST	1977	JAR			156	201
0.00	HASKINS,ME	AU	1990	AUD	WILLIAMS,DD		55	74
0.00	HASSELBACK,JR	AP	1976	TAR			269	276
0.00	HEIN ,LW	AP	1963	TAR			252	261
0.00	HORVITZ,JS	WI	1981	JAA	HAINKEL,M		114	127
0.00	HUSSEIN,ME	AU	1986	AUD	BAVISHI,VB	GANGOLLY,JS	124	133
0.00	IMHOFF JR,EA	OC	1978	TAR			869	881
0.00	IMHOFF JR,EA	SP	1988	AUD			182	191
0.00	IMHOFF-JR,EA	DE	1988	JAE	THOMAS,JK		277	310
0.00	INGBERMAN,M	AU	1978	JAA	SORTER,GH		58	62
0.00	INGRAM,RW	AU	1986	CAR			200	221
0.00	JENSEN,HL	OC	1976	TAR	WYNDELTS,RW		846	853
0.00	JENTZ ,GA	JL	1966	TAR			535	541
0.00	JOHNSON,O	OC	1974	TAR	GUNN ,S		649	663
0.00	JOHNSON,O	ST	1981	JAR			89	119
0.00	JOHNSON,O	04	1992	AOS			205	222
0.00	JOHNSON,SB	SP	1982	JAA	MESSIER JR,WF		195	213
0.00	KABBES,SM	AP	1965	TAR			395	400
0.00	KALINSKI,BD	JL	1963	TAR			591	595
0.00	KAPLAN,HG	JA	1964	TAR	SOLOMON,KI		145	149
0.00	KAUFMAN,F	OC	1967	TAR			713	720
0.00	KAY ,RS	SU	1979	JAA			307	315
0.00	KELL ,WG	AP	1968	TAR			266	273
0.00	KOHLER,EL	AP	1963	TAR			266	269
0.00	KOLLARITSCH,FP	AP	1965	TAR			382	385
0.00	KRIPKE,H	AU	1978	JAA			4	32
0.00	KRIPKE,H	WI	1989	JAA			3	65
0.00	KUBLIN,M	JL	1965	TAR			626	635
0.00	KUNITAKE,WK	SU	1986	JAA	WHITE JR,CE		222	231
0.00	LAMDEN,CW	JA	1964	TAR			128	132
0.00	LEA ,RB	SU	1981	AUD			53	94
0.00	LINOWES,DF	JA	1965	TAR			97	104
0.00	LONGSTRETH,B	WI	1984	JAA			110	122
0.00	LOWE ,HD	AP	1967	TAR			356	360
0.00	LOWE ,RE	OC	1965	TAR			839	846
0.00	LYNN ,ES	AP	1964	TAR			371	376
0.00	MACKENZIE,O	AP	1964	TAR			363	370
0.00	MARKS ,BR	SP	1988	CAR	RAMAN ,KK		595	608
0.00	MATTINGLY,LA	OC	1964	TAR			996	3
0.00	MAUTZ ,RK	AP	1965	TAR			299	311
0.00	MAYPER,AG	SP	1991	AUD	ADDY JR,ND		136	144
0.00	MCROBERTS,HA	04	1985	AOS	HUDSON,J		493	502
0.00	MEANS ,KM	AU	1989	JAA			571	579
0.00	MELLMAN,M	AU	1986	JAA	SEILER,ME		305	318

CITE INDEX	FIRST AUTHOR	ISS-UE	YE-AR	JOUR-NAL	SECOND AUTHOR	THIRD AUTHOR	PAG BEG	PAG END
0.00	MILLER,HE	JA	1966	TAR			1	7
0.00	MOODY ,SM	AU	1986	JAA	FLESHER,DL		319	330
0.00	MOORES,K	01	1986	AOS	STEADMAN,GT		19	34
0.00	MORENO,RG	OC	1964	TAR			990	995
0.00	MUELLER,GG	AP	1965	TAR			386	394
0.00	MUTCHLER,JF	AU	1990	AUD	WILLIAMS,DD		39	54
0.00	NEWMAN,DP	OC	1981	TAR			897	909
0.00	NORGAARD,CT	JL	1972	TAR			433	442
0.00	PALMROSE,ZV	AU	1988	AUD			63	71
0.00	PATON ,WA	JA	1967	TAR			7	23
0.00	POMERANZ,F	AU	1977	JAA			45	52
0.00	POWELL,RM	JL	1966	TAR			525	534
0.00	PURO ,M	SP	1985	JAA			165	177
0.00	RAPPAPORT,A	OC	1964	TAR			951	962
0.00	RATSCH,H	JA	1964	TAR			140	144
0.00	ROLLER,J	AP	1967	TAR	WILLIAMS,TH		349	355
0.00	RONEN ,J	WI	1989	JAA	SORTER,G		67	77
0.00	ROSS ,H	ST	1970	JAR			108	115
0.00	SCHIENEMAN,GS	AU	1979	JAA			21	30
0.00	SCHIFF,M	AU	1977	JAA	SORTER,GH	WIESEN,JL	19	44
0.00	SCHNEE,EJ	AU	1981	JAA	TAYLOR,ME		18	29
0.00	SEAMAN,JL	JL	1965	TAR			617	621
0.00	SEELYE,AL	AP	1963	TAR			302	309
0.00	SEIDLER,LJ	SU	1979	JAA			285	293
0.00	SEILER,RE	OC	1966	TAR			652	656
0.00	SELTO ,FH	AU	1983	JAR	GROVE ,HD		619	622
0.00	SIMON ,SI	OC	1964	TAR			884	889
0.00	SIMON ,SI	AP	1965	TAR			401	406
0.00	SOMEYA,K	OC	1964	TAR			983	989
0.00	STAATS,EB	SU	1981	AUD			1	11
0.00	STANDISH,PEM	JL	1964	TAR			654	666
0.00	STETTLER,HF	OC	1965	TAR			723	730
0.00	STONE ,DE	AP	1967	TAR			331	337
0.00	STONE ,ML	ST	1968	JAR			59	66
0.00	STREER,PJ	SU	1979	JAA			329	338
0.00	SWIERINGA,RJ	SP	1989	JAA			169	186
0.00	TAYLOR,RG	JA	1965	TAR			89	96
0.00	TOWNSEND,LA	JA	1967	TAR			1	6
0.00	TRUEBLOOD,RM	ST	1966	JAR			183	191
0.00	ULLMANN,AA	12	1979	AOS			123	134
0.00	WARREN,CS	SP	1980	JAR			312	324
0.00	WEIGAND,RE	JL	1963	TAR			584	590
0.00	WEISER,HJ	JL	1966	TAR			518	524
0.00	WELSCH,GA	OC	1964	TAR			8	13
0.00	WEYGANDT,JJ	JA	1970	TAR			69	75
0.00	WIESEN,JL	SU	1981	JAA			309	324
0.00	YOUNG ,SD	SP	1985	JAA			178	183
0.00	YOUNG ,SD	OC	1991	TAR			809	817
0.00	ZIND ,RG	AU	1989	CAR	ZEGHAL,D		26	47

3.11 SCHOOL OF THOUGHT=OTHER

CITE INDEX	FIRST AUTHOR	ISS-UE	YE-AR	JOUR-NAL	SECOND AUTHOR	THIRD AUTHOR	PAG BEG	PAG END
2.82	BALL ,R	ST	1982	JAR	FOSTER,G		161	234

CITE INDEX	FIRST AUTHOR	ISS-UE	YE-AR	JOUR-NAL	SECOND AUTHOR	THIRD AUTHOR	PAG BEG	PAG END
2.62	OTLEY ,DT	04	1980	AOS			413	428
2.20	HOPWOOD,AG	01	1978	AOS			3	14
2.10	BOLAND,RJ	23	1983	AOS	PONDY ,LR		223	234
2.10	VERRECCHIA,RE	DE	1983	JAE			179	194
2.00	CHRISTENSON,C	JA	1983	TAR			1	22
1.93	HEDBERG,B	01	1978	AOS	JONSSON,S		47	64
1.92	BAIMAN,S	ST	1980	JAR	DEMSKI,JS		184	220
1.91	FELIX JR,WL	AP	1982	TAR	KINNEY JR,WR		245	271
1.85	BIDDLE,GC	ST	1980	JAR			235	280
1.83	JOHNSON,JR	AP	1981	TAR	LEITCH,RA	NETER ,J	270	293
1.80	COOPER,DJ	23	1983	AOS			269	286
1.15	GARMAN,MB	AU	1980	JAR	OHLSON,JA		420	440
1.12	KHANDWALLA,PN	AU	1972	JAR			275	285
1.10	ELLIOTT,RK	SP	1983	AUD			1	12
1.00	BOLAND,RJ	04	1979	AOS			259	272
1.00	CHOW ,CW	AP	1982	TAR	RICE ,SJ		326	335
1.00	ROBERTS,J	02	1990	AOS			107	126
1.00	SMITH ,VL	AU	1987	AUD	SCHATZBERG,J	WALLER,WS	71	93
0.89	GORDON,LA	01	1984	AOS	NARAYANAN,VK		33	47
0.88	ANSARI,SL	02	1977	AOS			101	112
0.88	SMITH ,ED	OC	1976	TAR			707	723
0.86	BANBURY,J	03	1979	AOS	NAHAPIET,JE		163	178
0.86	WHITLEY,R	02	1986	AOS			171	192
0.83	MACINTOSH,NB	01	1981	AOS			39	52
0.80	MARKUS,ML	23	1983	AOS	PFEFFER,J		205	218
0.78	GROBSTEIN,M	SP	1984	AUD	CRAIG ,PW		1	16
0.77	HORWITZ,BN	ST	1980	JAR	KOLODNY,R		38	74
0.76	CUSHING,BE	AU	1969	JAR			196	203
0.73	HOLSTRUM,GL	AU	1982	AUD	MESSIER JR,WF		45	63
0.71	ABDEL-KHALIK,AR	ST	1973	JAR			104	138
0.69	RHODE ,JG	02	1977	AOS	SORENSEN,JE	LAWLER III,EE	165	176
0.67	GORDON,LA	34	1978	AOS	LARCKER,DF	TUGGLE,FD	203	214
0.62	GINZBERG,MJ	04	1980	AOS			369	382
0.62	WHITTRED,GP	OC	1980	TAR			563	577
0.60	KOTHARI,SP	AU	1988	JAA	LYS ,T	SMITH ,CW	307	340
0.59	MOORE ,ML	SP	1973	JAR			100	107
0.56	MUTCHLER,JF	SP	1984	AUD			17	30
0.53	IMHOFF JR,EA	OC	1978	TAR			836	850
0.50	HOWARD,TP	OC	1983	TAR	NIKOLAI,LA		765	776
0.50	TROTMAN,KT	04	1981	AOS	BRADLEY,G		355	362
0.47	BELKAOUI,A	02	1978	AOS			97	104
0.47	RONEN ,J	SP	1970	JAR	MCKINNEY,G		99	112
0.47	WILDAVSKY,A	01	1978	AOS			77	88
0.45	DIRSMITH,MW	SP	1982	JAA	MCALLISTER,JP		214	228
0.45	DIRSMITH,MW	AU	1982	JAA	MCALLISTER,JP		60	74
0.45	JONSSON,S	03	1982	AOS			287	304
0.43	PASTENA,V	AU	1979	JAR	RONEN ,J		550	564
0.42	EWUSI-MENSAH,K	04	1981	AOS			301	316
0.42	HOFSTEDE,G	03	1981	AOS			193	216
0.41	DERSTINE,RP	AU	1974	JAR	HUEFNER,RJ		216	234
0.41	ELAM ,R	JA	1975	TAR			25	43
0.40	SMITH ,DB	DE	1988	JAE	POURCIAU,S		335	344
0.38	BAILEY JR,AD	AP	1985	TAR	DUKE ,GL	GERLACH,JH	186	201

CITE INDEX	FIRST AUTHOR	ISS-UE	YE-AR	JOUR-NAL	SECOND AUTHOR	THIRD AUTHOR	PAG BEG	PAG END
0.38	DIRSMITH,MW	AU	1985	JAA	COVALESKI,MA		5	21
0.38	WATTS ,RL	AG	1980	JAE	ZIMMERMAN,JL		95	106
0.36	DIRSMITH,MW	12	1979	AOS	JABLONSKY,SF		39	52
0.36	HAGG ,J	12	1979	AOS	HEDLUND,G		135	143
0.36	MCCARTHY,WE	OC	1979	TAR			667	686
0.36	SWIERINGA,RJ	02	1982	AOS	WATERHOUSE,JH		149	166
0.35	MCRAE ,TW	SP	1974	JAR			80	92
0.33	DENT ,JF	02	1990	AOS			3	25
0.29	IJIRI ,Y	SP	1971	JAR	KAPLAN,RS		73	87
0.29	MARGHEIM,LL	SP	1986	JAR			194	205
0.27	CHERNS,AB	02	1978	AOS			105	114
0.25	ETZIONI,A	AU	1989	JAA			555	570
0.25	WEBER ,RP	JL	1981	TAR	STEVENSON,WC		596	612
0.24	BRENNER,VC	AU	1970	JAR			159	166
0.22	MARCINKO,D	JL	1984	TAR	PETRI ,E		488	495
0.20	CARSLAW,C	AP	1988	TAR			321	327
0.20	HOLDER,WW	SP	1983	AUD			100	108
0.20	MITROFF,II	23	1983	AOS	MASON ,RO		195	204
0.20	MORSE ,D	AP	1983	TAR	USHMAN,N		247	258
0.19	COPPOCK,R	02	1977	AOS			125	130
0.18	FRANK ,WG	SP	1969	JAR			123	136
0.18	GAGNON,JM	SP	1971	JAR			52	72
0.18	SHOCKLEY,RA	WI	1982	JAA			126	143
0.18	WEBER ,R	AP	1982	TAR			311	325
0.17	BOLAND,RJ	02	1981	AOS			109	118
0.17	WIGGINS JR,CE	SP	1987	CAR	SMITH ,LW		316	337
0.15	GRAY ,SJ	SP	1980	JAR			64	76
0.14	YOUNG ,DW	03	1979	AOS			235	244
0.13	EICHENSEHER,JW	SP	1985	JAA			195	209
0.13	SWANSON,EB	34	1978	AOS			237	248
0.12	BALL ,R	SP	1971	JAR			1	31
0.12	COPELAND,RM	AU	1969	JAR	WOJDAK,JF		188	195
0.12	HARMELINK,PJ	SP	1973	JAR			146	158
0.12	STERLING,RR	SP	1969	JAR	RADOSEVICH,R		90	95
0.11	GORDON,LA	02	1984	AOS	HAKA ,S	SCHICK,AG	111	123
0.11	LEE ,CJ	AU	1984	JAR			776	781
0.11	STONE ,M	JL	1984	TAR	BUBLITZ,B		469	473
0.10	MOCK ,TJ	SP	1983	AUD	WILLINGHAM,JJ		91	99
0.09	LANDSITTEL,DL	SU	1982	JAA	SERLIN,JE		291	300
0.08	FIRTH ,MA	JL	1980	TAR			451	466
0.08	LOY ,LD	SP	1980	JAA	TOOLE ,HR		227	243
0.08	PURDY ,D	04	1981	AOS			327	338
0.07	AMEY ,LR	04	1979	AOS			247	258
0.07	CARLSSON,J	34	1978	AOS	EHN ,P	ERLANDER,B	249	260
0.06	ABEL ,R	SP	1969	JAR			1	11
0.06	AMATO ,HN	OC	1976	TAR	ANDERSON,EE	HARVEY,DW	854	862
0.06	CHOTTINER,S	AU	1971	JAR	YOUNG ,AE		367	374
0.06	FRANK ,WG	SP	1971	JAR	WEYGANDT,JJ		116	126
0.06	MCKEOWN,JC	SP	1973	JAR			62	99
0.06	SAN MIGUEL,JG	04	1977	AOS	SHANK ,JK	GOVINDARAJAN,V	333	348
0.00	ARNOLD,PJ	02	1991	AOS			121	140
0.00	ARRINGTON,CE	06	1992	AOS	SCHWEIKER,W		511	533
0.00	ASHTON,RH	SU	1981	JAA	HYLAS ,RE		325	332

CITE INDEX	FIRST AUTHOR	ISS-UE	YE-AR	JOUR-NAL	SECOND AUTHOR	THIRD AUTHOR	PAG BEG	PAG END
0.00	ASHTON,RH	SU	1981	AUD	HYLAS ,RE		12	22
0.00	BAGGETT,WD	SP	1983	JAA			227	233
0.00	BARLEV,B	AP	1983	TAR			385	393
0.00	BASTABLE,CW	SP	1981	JAA	BEAMS ,FA		248	254
0.00	BAUMOL,WJ	WI	1990	JAA			105	117
0.00	BOURN ,AM	AU	1966	JAR			213	223
0.00	BOWEN ,RM	OC	1982	TAR	SUNDEM,GL		778	784
0.00	BOWSHER,CA	WI	1986	JAA			7	16
0.00	BROMWICH,M	02	1990	AOS			27	46
0.00	CAHAN ,SF	JA	1992	TAR			77	96
0.00	CAMPBELL,DR	SP	1983	JAA			196	211
0.00	CARMICHAEL,DR	SU	1984	JAA	WHITTINGTON,OR		347	361
0.00	CAUSEY JR,DY	AP	1973	TAR			258	267
0.00	DANIEL,SJ	SP	1988	AUD			174	181
0.00	DAVISON,AG	SP	1984	JAR	STENING,BW	WAI ,WT	313	317
0.00	DERMER,J	02	1990	AOS			67	76
0.00	DERY ,D	03	1982	AOS			217	224
0.00	DEVINE,CT	ST	1966	JAR			160	176
0.00	DREBIN,AR	AU	1969	JAR			204	214
0.00	DUKE ,D	WI	1991	JAA			135	142
0.00	ELLIOTT,JA	JA	1990	TAR	PHILBRICK,DR		157	174
0.00	ENGLE ,TJ	WI	1991	JAA			109	121
0.00	FIRTH ,MA	SP	1973	JAR			16	24
0.00	FORD ,A	AP	1975	TAR			338	344
0.00	FRANKFURTER,GM	SU	1983	JAA	YOUNG ,AE		314	324
0.00	GLATZER,W	03	1981	AOS			219	234
0.00	GORMLEY,RJ	AU	1982	JAA			51	59
0.00	GRAY ,J	AP	1963	TAR	WILLINGHAM,JJ	JOHNSTON,K	336	346
0.00	GRUNDFEST,JA	AU	1991	JAA	SHOVEN,JB		409	442
0.00	GUENTHER,DA	JA	1992	TAR			17	45
0.00	HEARD ,JE	03	1981	AOS	BOLCE ,WJ		247	254
0.00	HONIG ,LE	SP	1978	JAA			231	236
0.00	HUIZING,A	05	1992	AOS	DEKKER,HC		449	458
0.00	KISSINGER,JN	AU	1983	AUD			42	54
0.00	LANZILLOTTI,RF	WI	1990	JAA	ESQUIBEL,AK		125	142
0.00	LEVY ,H	AU	1987	JAA	BYUN ,YH		355	369
0.00	LOVATA,LM	AU	1988	AUD			72	86
0.00	MAHER ,MW	JA	1992	TAR	TIESSEN,P	COLSON,R	199	211
0.00	MARKOWITZ,HM	SP	1990	JAA			213	225
0.00	MCBRIDE,HJ	AP	1963	TAR			363	370
0.00	MCRAE ,TW	AU	1965	JAR			255	260
0.00	NIX ,HM	SU	1983	JAA	WICHMANN JR,H		341	352
0.00	NURNBERG,H	AU	1969	JAR			257	261
0.00	PARKE ,R	03	1981	AOS	PETERSON,JL		235	246
0.00	PETRI ,E	AP	1979	TAR	GELFAND,J		330	345
0.00	PRESTON,LE	03	1981	AOS			255	262
0.00	PURDY ,CR	AU	1965	JAR			228	241
0.00	RAYBURN,J	AU	1992	CAR	LENWAY,S		237	251
0.00	ROBBINS,SM	AU	1977	JAA			5	18
0.00	SCHIENEMAN,GS	SP	1983	JAA			212	226
0.00	SCHIFF,M	SP	1979	JAA			224	231
0.00	SIMONS,R	02	1990	AOS			127	143

CITE INDEX	FIRST AUTHOR	ISS-UE	YE-AR	JOUR-NAL	SECOND AUTHOR	THIRD AUTHOR	PAG BEG	PAG END
0.00	ST.PIERRE,K	SP	1982	JAA	ANDERSON,JA		229	247
0.00	ST.PIERRE,K	SP	1984	JAA			257	263
0.00	TELSER,LG	SP	1990	JAA			159	201
0.00	TRUEBLOOD,RM	SP	1963	JAR			86	95
0.00	VASARHELYI,MA	AU	1984	AUD			100	106
0.00	VASARHELYI,MA	SP	1984	AUD	BAILEY JR,AD	CAMARDESSE JR,JE	98	103
0.00	WANG ,S	JA	1991	TAR			158	169
0.00	WEBER ,C	JL	1963	TAR			534	539
0.00	WHITTINGTON,OR	SU	1982	JAA	ADAMS ,SJ		310	319
0.00	WILD ,JJ	JA	1990	TAR	BIGGS ,SF		227	241
0.00	WRIGHT,GB	SU	1982	JAA	TAYLOR,RD		301	309
0.00	YOUNG ,A	WI	1991	JAA			129	133
0.00	ZANNETOS,ZS	JL	1963	TAR			528	533
0.00	ZANNETOS,ZS	AP	1963	TAR			326	335

3.12 SCHOOL OF THOUGHT=EXPERT SYSTEMS

CITE INDEX	FIRST AUTHOR	ISS-UE	YE-AR	JOUR-NAL	SECOND AUTHOR	THIRD AUTHOR	PAG BEG	PAG END
0.57	HANSEN,JV	AU	1986	AUD	MESSIER JR,WF		109	123
0.57	MESERVY,RD	AU	1986	AUD	BAILEY JR,AD	JOHNSON,PE	44	74
0.57	SHPILBERG,D	AU	1986	AUD	GRAHAM,LE		75	94
0.50	STEINBART,PJ	JA	1987	TAR			97	116
0.33	MESSIER JR,WF	AU	1987	AUD	HANSEN,JV		94	105
0.00	BORITZ,JE		1990	AUD			49	87
0.00	BORITZ,JE	AU	1992	AUD	WENSLEY,AKP		14	29
0.00	EZZAMEL,M	05	1990	AOS	BOURN ,M		399	424
0.00	FELIX JR,WL	AU	1990	AUD	GRIMLUND,RA	KOSTER,FJ	1	16
0.00	GRAHAM,LE	SP	1991	AUD	DAMENS,J	VAN NESS,G	69	96
0.00	PETERS,JM	04	1989	AOS	LEWIS ,BL	DHAR ,V	359	378
0.00	PETERS,JM	ST	1990	JAR			83	109
0.00	SIMON ,HA	JL	1990	TAR			658	667
0.00	VASARHELYI,MA	SP	1991	AUD	HALPER,FB		110	125
0.00	WENSLEY,AKP		1990	AUD			49	87

4.1 TREATMENTS=FINANCIAL ACCOUNTING METHODS

CITE INDEX	FIRST AUTHOR	ISS-UE	YE-AR	JOUR-NAL	SECOND AUTHOR	THIRD AUTHOR	PAG BEG	PAG END
8.35	BALL ,R	AU	1968	JAR	BROWN ,P		159	178
5.50	COLLINS,DW	JL	1989	JAE	KOTHARI,SP		143	181
5.50	EASTON,PD	JL	1989	JAE	ZMIJEWSKI,ME		117	141
5.35	BEAVER,WH	ST	1968	JAR			67	92
5.00	OU ,JA	NV	1989	JAE			295	329
5.00	PENMAN,SH	NV	1989	JAE			295	329
4.93	BEAVER,WH	AU	1979	JAR	CLARKE,R	WRIGHT,WF	316	340
4.88	ATIASE,RK	SP	1985	JAR			21	36
4.50	FREEMAN,RN	JL	1987	JAE			195	228
4.12	GONEDES,NJ	ST	1974	JAR	DOPUCH,N		48	129
3.67	LIPE ,R	JA	1990	TAR			49	71
3.50	BERNARD,VL	ST	1989	JAR	THOMAS,JK		1	36
3.50	EASTON,PD	SP	1991	JAR	HARRIS,TS		19	36
3.50	WATTS ,RL	AP	1979	TAR	ZIMMERMAN,JL		273	305
3.33	ARMSTRONG,P	05	1987	AOS			415	436
3.25	OU ,JA	ST	1989	JAR	PENMAN,SH		111	144
3.00	GREIG ,AC	JN	1992	JAE			413	442
3.00	WILSON,GP	AP	1987	TAR			293	322

CITE INDEX	FIRST AUTHOR	ISS-UE	YE-AR	JOUR-NAL	SECOND AUTHOR	THIRD AUTHOR	PAG BEG	PAG END
2.89	FOSTER,G	OC	1984	TAR	OLSEN ,C	SHEVLIN,T	574	603
2.86	LIPE ,RC	ST	1986	JAR			37	68
2.82	BALL ,R	ST	1982	JAR	FOSTER,G		161	234
2.67	BERNARD,VL	DE	1990	JAE	THOMAS,JK		305	340
2.38	DYE ,RA	SP	1985	JAR			123	145
2.33	CHRISTIE,AA	JA	1990	JAE			15	36
2.17	FOSTER,G	DE	1981	JAE			201	232
2.00	ALI ,A	JN	1992	JAE	ZAROWIN,P		249	264
2.00	EASTON,PD	JN	1992	JAE	HARRIS,TS	OHLSON,JA	119	142
2.00	HOLTHAUSEN,RW	JN	1992	JAE	LARCKER,DF		373	411
2.00	KOTHARI,SP	JN	1992	JAE	SLAON ,RG		143	171
2.00	LEV ,B	JA	1988	TAR			1	22
2.00	LEV ,B	ST	1989	JAR			153	192
2.00	ROBERTS,J	04	1985	AOS	SCAPENS,RW		443	456
1.82	BEAVER,WH	OC	1970	TAR	KETTLER,P	SCHOLES,M	654	682
1.80	HINES ,RD	03	1988	AOS			251	261
1.75	MORSE ,D	AU	1981	JAR			374	383
1.71	BAMBER,LS	SP	1986	JAR			40	56
1.67	BOWEN ,RM	OC	1987	TAR	BURGSTAHLER,D	DALEY ,LA	723	747
1.50	BAMBER,LS	JL	1987	TAR			510	532
1.50	OHLSON,JA	JL	1989	JAE			109	115
1.50	RICHARDSON,AJ	04	1987	AOS			341	355
1.35	BEAVER,WH	ST	1970	JAR			62	99
1.33	OU ,JA	SP	1990	JAR			144	163
1.10	EVANS III,JH	AG	1983	JAE	PATTON,JM		151	175
1.08	PATELL,JM	AU	1981	JAR	WOLFSON,MA		434	458
1.06	DEMSKI,JS	OC	1973	TAR			718	723
1.00	ANTHONY,JH	JN	1992	JAE	RAMESH,K		203	227
1.00	BARTH ,ME	JA	1991	TAR	BEAVER,WH	STINSON,CH	56	66
1.00	BHUSHAN,R	JL	1989	JAE			183	206
1.00	BIDDLE,GC	SP	1991	JAA	SEOW ,GS		183	232
1.00	HILL ,JW	OC	1989	TAR	INGRAM,RW		667	679
1.00	HINES ,RD	04	1991	AOS			313	331
1.00	LAVOIE,D	06	1987	AOS			579	604
1.00	LEE ,CMC	JN	1992	JAE			265	302
0.94	BEAVER,WH	OC	1968	TAR	KENNELLY,JW	VOSS ,WM	675	683
0.94	GONEDES,NJ	AU	1973	JAR			212	237
0.94	GONEDES,NJ	SP	1974	JAR			26	62
0.88	ASHTON,RH	OC	1974	TAR			719	732
0.88	SMITH ,ED	OC	1976	TAR			707	723
0.83	EVANS III,JH	ST	1987	JAR	PATTON,JM		130	164
0.83	MARCH ,JG	02	1987	AOS			153	168
0.83	WALLACE,WA	AU	1981	JAR			502	520
0.81	JOY ,OM	AU	1977	JAR	LITZENBERGER,RH	MCENALLY,RW	207	225
0.76	DEMSKI,JS	AP	1974	TAR			221	232
0.75	OLSEN ,C	ST	1985	JAR	DIETRICH,JR		144	166
0.71	BEAVER,WH	ST	1974	JAR	DEMSKI,JS		170	187
0.67	BEGLEY,J	JA	1990	JAE			125	139
0.67	BOWEN ,RM	JA	1981	TAR			1	22
0.67	CLINCH,GJ	AP	1987	JAE	SINCLAIR,NA		89	106
0.67	WILLIAMS,PF	02	1987	AOS			169	192
0.65	HARIED,AA	SP	1973	JAR			117	145
0.64	VERRECCHIA,RE	ST	1982	JAR			1	42

CITE INDEX	FIRST AUTHOR	ISS-UE	YE-AR	JOUR-NAL	SECOND AUTHOR	THIRD AUTHOR	PAG BEG	PAG END
0.60	FOSTER III,TW	OC	1978	TAR	VICKREY,DW		921	934
0.59	MAY ,RG	OC	1976	TAR	SUNDEM,GL		747	763
0.59	PANKOFF,LD	ST	1970	JAR	VIRGIL JR,RL		1	48
0.53	BEIDLEMAN,CR	OC	1973	TAR			653	667
0.53	OLIVER,BL	AU	1974	JAR			299	316
0.50	ANTLE ,R	ST	1991	JAR	NALEBUFF,B		31	59
0.50	JONES ,JJ	AU	1991	JAR			193	228
0.50	LOBO ,GJ	AP	1989	TAR	SONG ,I		329	343
0.50	TROMBLEY,MA	JL	1989	TAR			529	538
0.47	FOSTER,G	OC	1975	TAR			686	698
0.47	MAGEE ,RP	AU	1974	JAR			270	287
0.42	RAMAN ,KK	OC	1981	TAR			910	926
0.41	GONEDES,NJ	JA	1972	TAR			11	21
0.41	OLIVER,BL	SP	1972	JAR			154	166
0.40	CREADY,WM	SP	1988	JAR			1	27
0.40	RO ,BT	SP	1988	CAR			438	449
0.38	CUSHING,BE	AP	1977	TAR			308	321
0.36	ALTMAN,EI	AU	1982	JAA			4	19
0.36	COPELAND,RM	AU	1982	JAR	INGRAM,RW		275	289
0.35	BENSTON,GJ	ST	1967	JAR			1	54
0.35	LEV ,B	AP	1974	TAR	KUNITZKY,S		259	270
0.33	BEAVER,WH	JA	1981	TAR			23	37
0.33	HOLTHAUSEN,RW	JA	1990	JAE			207	218
0.33	LEFTWICH,R	JA	1990	JAE			37	44
0.33	SKINNER,DJ	OC	1990	JAE			191	211
0.33	VERRECCHIA,RE	SP	1981	JAR			271	283
0.33	ZEFF ,SA	JL	1984	TAR			447	468
0.31	BELKAOUI,A	AU	1980	JAR			362	374
0.30	CHOW ,CW	JL	1983	TAR			485	520
0.29	BILDERSEE,JS	JA	1975	TAR			81	98
0.29	DEAKIN,EB	JA	1976	TAR			90	96
0.29	DOWNES,D	AP	1973	TAR	DYCKMAN,TR		300	317
0.29	FOSTER,G	AU	1975	JAR			283	292
0.29	HORWITZ,BN	AP	1971	TAR	SHABAHANG,R		243	252
0.29	JAIN ,TN	JA	1973	TAR			95	104
0.29	WHITE ,GE	AU	1970	JAR			260	273
0.27	INGRAM,RW	AU	1982	JAR	COPELAND,RM		766	772
0.27	RICE ,SJ	AP	1978	TAR			429	438
0.25	BOWEN ,RM	JL	1989	JAE	JOHNSON,MF	SHEVLIN,T	225	254
0.25	DEAKIN,EB	JA	1989	TAR			137	151
0.25	GOLDIN,HJ	SU	1985	JAA			269	278
0.24	ABDEL-KHALIK,AR	JL	1971	TAR			457	471
0.24	BAREFIELD,RM	AP	1972	TAR	COMISKEY,EE		291	298
0.24	DASCHER,PE	AU	1970	JAR	MALCOM,RE		253	259
0.24	GYNTHER,RS	AP	1967	TAR			274	290
0.24	HAGERMAN,RL	OC	1975	TAR			699	709
0.21	ADELBERG,AH	AU	1979	JAR			565	592
0.20	BASU ,S	JL	1978	TAR			599	625
0.20	IJIRI ,Y	SU	1978	JAA			331	348
0.20	MCKEOWN,JC	SP	1988	CAR	SHALCHI,H		485	507
0.20	MORSE ,D	AP	1983	TAR	USHMAN,N		247	258
0.19	PERAGALLO,E	OC	1977	TAR			881	892
0.18	CYERT ,RM	ST	1974	JAR	IJIRI ,Y		29	42

CITE INDEX	FIRST AUTHOR	ISS-UE	YE-AR	JOUR-NAL	SECOND AUTHOR	THIRD AUTHOR	PAG BEG	PAG END
0.18	DEAKIN,EB	JL	1976	TAR			590	603
0.18	EAVES ,BC	JL	1966	TAR			426	442
0.18	ESKEW ,RK	AP	1975	TAR			316	324
0.18	FALK ,H	SP	1973	JAR	OPHIR ,T		108	116
0.18	MATTESSICH,R	JL	1972	TAR			469	487
0.17	BOATSMAN,JR	JA	1981	TAR	BASKIN,EF		38	53
0.17	CHOW ,CW	JL	1987	TAR	WONG-BOREN,A		533	541
0.17	COOPER,DJ	05	1987	AOS	HOPPER,TM		407	414
0.17	COVALESKI,MA	SP	1987	CAR	DIRSMITH,MW	WHITE ,CE	408	429
0.17	ELGERS,P	OC	1987	TAR	CALLAHAN,C	STROCK,E	763	773
0.14	DEFEO ,VJ	AU	1986	JAR			349	363
0.14	ESKEW ,RK	JA	1979	TAR			107	118
0.14	FRANK ,WG	AU	1979	JAR			593	605
0.14	TSE ,S	JL	1986	TAR			475	497
0.12	BIERMAN JR,H	JL	1963	TAR			501	507
0.12	BIRD ,FA	AP	1974	TAR	DAVIDSON,LF	SMITH ,CH	233	244
0.12	CHAMBERS,RJ	JL	1966	TAR			443	457
0.12	DEMSKI,JS	AU	1973	JAR			176	190
0.12	DOPUCH,N	ST	1966	JAR	DRAKE ,DF		192	219
0.12	JOHNSON,O	OC	1970	TAR			641	653
0.12	LIVINGSTONE,JL	AU	1970	JAR	SALAMON,GL		199	216
0.12	LORIG ,AN	JL	1964	TAR			563	573
0.12	MLYNARCZYK,FA	ST	1969	JAR			63	81
0.12	MORTON,JR	AU	1974	JAR			288	298
0.12	SALAMON,GL	AU	1973	JAR			296	303
0.12	SNAVELY,HJ	AP	1967	TAR			223	232
0.12	WELLS ,MC	JL	1976	TAR			471	482
0.10	INGRAM,RW	JL	1983	TAR	CHEWNING,EG		562	580
0.09	DIRSMITH,MW	04	1982	AOS	LEWIS ,BL		319	336
0.07	BARLEV,B	AU	1979	JAR	LEVY ,H		305	315
0.07	DAVIS ,DW	JA	1978	TAR	BOATSMAN,JR	BASKIN,EF	1	10
0.07	HAKANSSON,NH	JL	1978	TAR			717	725
0.07	RAMAN ,KK	AU	1979	JAA			31	41
0.07	VERRECCHIA,RE	SP	1978	JAR			150	168
0.06	BEDFORD,NM	JL	1975	TAR	ZIEGLER,RE		435	443
0.06	BRADISH,RD	OC	1965	TAR			757	766
0.06	BRILOFF,AJ	JA	1964	TAR			12	15
0.06	BUCKLEY,JW	AP	1968	TAR	KIRCHER,P	MATHEWS,RL	274	283
0.06	CHARNES,A	JA	1972	TAR	COLANTONI,CS	COOPER,WW	85	108
0.06	COOPER,WW	OC	1968	TAR	DOPUCH,N	KELLER,TF	640	648
0.06	COWAN ,TK	OC	1965	TAR			788	794
0.06	CULPEPPER,RC	AP	1970	TAR			322	332
0.06	FRANKFURTER,GM	AP	1972	TAR	HORWITZ,BN		245	259
0.06	HORRIGAN,JO	AP	1968	TAR			284	294
0.06	KEMP ,PS	OC	1965	TAR			782	787
0.06	KING ,RR	JA	1974	TAR	BARON ,CD		76	87
0.06	LEMKE ,KW	SP	1970	JAR			47	77
0.06	PATON ,WA	AP	1963	TAR			243	251
0.06	REVSINE,L	JL	1971	TAR			480	489
0.06	SIMPSON,RH	OC	1969	TAR			806	817
0.06	STERLING,RR	JA	1967	TAR			62	73
0.06	TAUSSIG,RA	JL	1963	TAR			562	567
0.06	UECKER,WC	01	1977	AOS			47	58

CITE INDEX	FIRST AUTHOR	ISS-UE	YE-AR	JOUR-NAL	SECOND AUTHOR	THIRD AUTHOR	PAG BEG	PAG END
0.06	VATTER,WJ	JL	1963	TAR			470	477
0.00	ABDEL-KHALIK,AR	SP	1986	CAR			242	251
0.00	ABDEL-MAGID,MF	AP	1979	TAR			346	357
0.00	ADAMS ,KD	WI	1984	JAA			151	163
0.00	AHARONI,Y	SP	1967	JAR	OPHIR ,T		1	26
0.00	ANDERSON,JA	JL	1975	TAR			509	511
0.00	ANTHONY,JH	SP	1987	CAR			460	475
0.00	ARNETT,HE	JL	1969	TAR			482	494
0.00	BABAD ,YM	SP	1989	CAR	BALACHANDRAN,BV		775	792
0.00	BALL ,R	JN	1992	JAE			309	345
0.00	BARLEV,B	AP	1983	TAR			385	393
0.00	BARRETT,WB	JA	1968	TAR			105	112
0.00	BEAMS ,FA	AP	1969	TAR			382	388
0.00	BEDFORD,NM	JA	1967	TAR			82	85
0.00	BENSON,ED	SU	1991	JAA	MARKS ,BR	RAMAN ,KK	303	319
0.00	BIERMAN JR,H	JL	1965	TAR			541	546
0.00	BIERMAN JR,H	AP	1969	TAR	DAVIDSON,S		239	246
0.00	BOLAND,LA	AU	1992	CAR	GORDON,IM		142	170
0.00	BOYLE ,PP	SP	1985	CAR			116	144
0.00	BOZE ,KM	AU	1990	JAA			627	638
0.00	BROWN ,LD	SP	1986	CAR			252	258
0.00	BRUGGE,WG	JL	1963	TAR			596	600
0.00	BUCKLEY,JW	JA	1966	TAR			75	82
0.00	CAHAN ,SF	JA	1992	TAR			77	96
0.00	CARSON,AB	AP	1965	TAR			334	337
0.00	CARTER,WK	JA	1981	TAR			108	114
0.00	CHAMBERS,RJ	AP	1967	TAR			241	253
0.00	CHANEY,PK	SP	1992	CAR	JETER ,DC		540	560
0.00	COPELAND,TE	AU	1978	JAA			33	48
0.00	COWAN ,TK	JA	1965	TAR			9	20
0.00	COWAN ,TK	JA	1968	TAR			94	100
0.00	CRAMER JR,JJ	OC	1964	TAR			869	875
0.00	CRAMER JR,JJ	JL	1965	TAR			606	616
0.00	CRUSE ,RB	JA	1965	TAR	SUMMERS,EL		82	88
0.00	DEMSKI,JS	AU	1985	CAR			69	75
0.00	DUKE ,D	WI	1991	JAA			135	142
0.00	EDEY ,HC	AP	1963	TAR			262	265
0.00	ENGSTROM,JH	SU	1985	JAA			305	318
0.00	FAGERBERG,P	JL	1972	TAR			454	457
0.00	FAIRCLOTH,AW	01	1981	AOS	RICCHIUTE,DN		53	68
0.00	FALK ,H	OC	1975	TAR	HEINTZ,JA		758	779
0.00	FALK ,H	SP	1992	CAR			468	499
0.00	FELTON,S	AU	1990	CAR	MANN ,H		261	277
0.00	FREMGEN,JM	JL	1967	TAR			457	467
0.00	FULMER,JG	AU	1984	JAA	MOON ,JE		5	14
0.00	GIVENS,HR	JL	1966	TAR			458	463
0.00	GOMBERG,M	JL	1964	TAR	FARBER,A		615	617
0.00	GONEDES,NJ	ST	1969	JAR			90	113
0.00	GONEDES,NJ	JL	1971	TAR			535	551
0.00	GONEDES,NJ	AP	1971	TAR			320	328
0.00	GORDON,LA	JL	1988	AUD	HAMER ,MH		514	521
0.00	GOVINDARAJAN,V	SU	1979	JAA			339	343
0.00	GRADY ,P	JA	1965	TAR			21	30

CITE INDEX	FIRST AUTHOR	ISS-UE	YE-AR	JOUR-NAL	SECOND AUTHOR	THIRD AUTHOR	PAG BEG	PAG END
0.00	GREENBALL,MN	ST	1968	JAR			27	49
0.00	GREER ,HC	JA	1964	TAR			22	31
0.00	GREER JR,WR	AU	1978	JAA	MORRISSEY,LE		49	57
0.00	HAIN ,HP	OC	1966	TAR			699	703
0.00	HAND ,JRM	OC	1991	TAR			739	746
0.00	HARMON,WK	AU	1984	JAA			24	34
0.00	HEIN ,LW	AP	1963	TAR			252	261
0.00	HOLMES,W	JA	1979	TAR			47	57
0.00	HOLZER,HP	AP	1963	TAR	SCHONFELD,HM		377	381
0.00	HOLZER,HP	AP	1963	TAR	SCHONFELD,HM		382	388
0.00	HOLZER,HP	AP	1964	TAR	SCHONFELD,HM		405	413
0.00	HOPWOOD,W	AP	1989	TAR	SCHAEFER,T		313	328
0.00	HOPWOOD,WS	AU	1988	CAR	SCHAEFER,TF		318	342
0.00	HUGHES,JS	SP	1986	CAR	RICKS ,WE		222	241
0.00	IJIRI ,Y	JA	1965	TAR			36	53
0.00	INGBERMAN,M	AU	1978	JAA	SORTER,GH		58	62
0.00	INGRAM,RW	AU	1986	CAR			200	221
0.00	IVES ,M	SU	1985	JAA			253	268
0.00	JOHNSON,GL	OC	1965	TAR			821	823
0.00	JOHNSON,GL	JL	1966	TAR			510	517
0.00	JOHNSON,O	OC	1974	TAR	GUNN ,S		649	663
0.00	KABBES,SM	AP	1965	TAR			395	400
0.00	KEISTER JR,OR	AP	1964	TAR			414	416
0.00	KHEMAKHEM,A	JL	1968	TAR			522	534
0.00	KOHLER,EL	AP	1963	TAR			266	269
0.00	KOLLARITSCH,FP	AP	1965	TAR			382	385
0.00	KORKIE,B	AU	1990	JAA	LAISS ,B		593	617
0.00	KOTHARI,SP	JN	1992	JAE			173	202
0.00	KROSS ,W	AU	1982	JAR			459	471
0.00	LEMBKE,VC	JL	1970	TAR			458	464
0.00	LEV ,B	SP	1979	JAA	TAYLOR,KW		232	243
0.00	LONGSTRETH,B	WI	1984	JAA			110	122
0.00	LOUDERBACK,JG	AP	1971	TAR			298	305
0.00	MAITRE,P	34	1978	AOS			227	236
0.00	MAKSY ,MM	OC	1988	TAR			683	699
0.00	MANES ,RP	JL	1964	TAR			631	638
0.00	MARPLE,RM	JL	1963	TAR			478	482
0.00	MARTIN,A	ST	1971	JAR			1	31
0.00	MCCOSH,AM	OC	1967	TAR			693	700
0.00	MEEK ,GK	AP	1983	TAR			394	402
0.00	MERINO,BD	OC	1987	TAR	KOCH ,BS	MACRITCHIE,KL	748	762
0.00	MEYER ,PE	JA	1976	TAR			80	89
0.00	MUELLER,GG	AP	1965	TAR			386	394
0.00	MURRAY,D	WI	1982	JAA			154	159
0.00	NEUBIG,RD	JA	1964	TAR			86	89
0.00	OHLSON,JA	ST	1972	JAR			45	84
0.00	OHLSON,JA	AU	1992	JAR	SHROLL,PK		210	226
0.00	OHLSON,JA	AU	1992	JAA	PENMAN,SH		553	573
0.00	PENMAN,SH	SP	1991	JAA			233	255
0.00	PENMAN,SH	AU	1992	JAA			465	484
0.00	PERAGALLO,E	JL	1971	TAR			529	534
0.00	PRINCE,TR	JL	1964	TAR			553	562
0.00	PYO ,Y	DE	1990	JAE	LUSTGARTEN,S		365	379

CITE INDEX	FIRST AUTHOR	ISS-UE	YE-AR	JOUR-NAL	SECOND AUTHOR	THIRD AUTHOR	PAG BEG	PAG END
0.00	RAMAKRISHNAN,RTS	AU	1992	JAA	THOMAS,JK		423	464
0.00	RAMAN ,KK	WI	1982	JAA			144	153
0.00	RANSOM,CR	ST	1985	JAR			124	143
0.00	RAYMAN,RA	SP	1969	JAR			53	89
0.00	RO ,BT	AU	1989	CAR			177	195
0.00	ROBBINS,WA	SU	1985	JAA	APOSTOLOU,NG	STRAWSER,RH	279	292
0.00	RODGERS,W	WI	1992	JAA			67	95
0.00	ROSEN ,LS	JA	1969	TAR	DECOSTER,DT		124	136
0.00	ROSS ,H	ST	1970	JAR			108	115
0.00	RYAN ,SG	SP	1991	JAA			257	287
0.00	SALGADO,AP	AP	1963	TAR			389	397
0.00	SCHATTKE,RW	OC	1965	TAR			805	811
0.00	SCHATTKE,RW	AP	1972	TAR			233	244
0.00	SHWAYDER,KR	SP	1968	JAR			86	97
0.00	SIMMONS,JK	OC	1967	TAR			680	692
0.00	SIMON ,SI	AP	1965	TAR			401	406
0.00	SORTER,GH	ST	1974	JAR	GANS ,MS		1	12
0.00	SPILLER JR,EA	OC	1964	TAR			850	859
0.00	STEPHENS,RG	JA	1990	TAR	GOVINDARAJAN,V		242	257
0.00	STONE ,DE	AP	1967	TAR			331	337
0.00	STONE ,WE	AP	1969	TAR			284	291
0.00	STREER,PJ	SU	1979	JAA			329	338
0.00	SUMMERS,EL	AP	1968	TAR			257	265
0.00	TEETS ,W	AU	1992	JAR			274	285
0.00	TOPIOL,J	JA	1966	TAR			83	91
0.00	VANCE ,LL	OC	1969	TAR			692	703
0.00	WARFIELD,TD	JL	1992	TAR	LINSMEIER,TJ		546	562
0.00	WILLIAMS,PF	06	1989	AOS			455	468
0.00	WILLINGHAM,JJ	JL	1964	TAR			543	552
0.00	WINBORNE,MG	JL	1964	TAR			622	626
0.00	WINJUM,JO	OC	1970	TAR			743	761
0.00	WINJUM,JO	JA	1971	TAR			149	155
0.00	YOUNG ,AE	SP	1978	JAA			217	230
0.00	YOUNG ,DW	OC	1976	TAR			788	799
0.00	YU ,SC	JL	1969	TAR			571	582
0.00	ZIEBART,DA	AU	1992	CAR	REITER,SA		252	282

4.2 TREATMENTS=CASH

CITE INDEX	FIRST AUTHOR	ISS-UE	YE-AR	JOUR-NAL	SECOND AUTHOR	THIRD AUTHOR	PAG BEG	PAG END
0.00	FREDRIKSON,EB	AU	1968	JAR			208	221
0.00	FREEMAN,RN	ST	1978	JAR			111	145
0.00	GOVINDARAJAN,V	04	1980	AOS			383	392
0.00	ISMAIL,BE	AU	1987	CAR			76	88
0.00	SORTER,GH	SP	1982	JAA			188	194
0.00	WHITEHURST,FD	JL	1970	TAR			553	564

4.3 TREATMENTS=INVENTORY

CITE INDEX	FIRST AUTHOR	ISS-UE	YE-AR	JOUR-NAL	SECOND AUTHOR	THIRD AUTHOR	PAG BEG	PAG END
2.36	BIDDLE,GC	AU	1982	JAR	LINDAHL,FW		551	588
2.27	RICKS ,WE	AU	1982	JAR			367	387
2.00	SUNDER,S	ST	1973	JAR			1	45
1.85	BIDDLE,GC	ST	1980	JAR			235	280
1.75	ABDEL-KHALIK,AR	AU	1985	JAR			427	447

CITE INDEX	FIRST AUTHOR	ISS-UE	YE-AR	JOUR-NAL	SECOND AUTHOR	THIRD AUTHOR	PAG BEG	PAG END
1.70	MORSE ,D	SP	1983	JAR	RICHARDSON,G		106	127
1.50	HEALY ,PM	AP	1987	JAE	KANG ,SH	PALEPU,KG	7	34
1.50	HUNT III,HG	AU	1985	JAR			448	467
1.47	SUNDER,S	AP	1975	TAR			305	315
1.38	LEE ,CJ	AU	1985	JAR	HSIEH ,DA		468	485
1.31	BROWN ,RM	SP	1980	JAR			38	63
1.27	ABDEL-KHALIK,AR	OC	1978	TAR	MCKEOWN,JC		851	868
1.20	DOPUCH,N	SP	1988	JAR	PINCUS,M		28	59
1.00	CUSHING,BE	AP	1992	TAR	LECLERE,MJ		355	367
0.83	BAGINSKI,SP	AU	1987	JAR			196	216
0.75	LINDAHL,FW	AU	1989	JAR			201	226
0.75	NIEHAUS,GR	AP	1989	TAR			269	284
0.71	RICKS ,WE	SP	1986	JAR			206	216
0.71	STOBER,TL	ST	1986	JAR			138	164
0.60	JOHNSON,WB	AU	1988	JAR	DHALIWAL,DS		236	272
0.53	SUNDER,S	AU	1976	JAR			277	300
0.50	AMERSHI,AH	AU	1987	JAR	SUNDER,S		177	195
0.50	LEE ,CWJ	AU	1989	JAR	PETRUZZI,CR		277	296
0.47	DOPUCH,N	AU	1973	JAR	RONEN ,J		191	211
0.47	SUNDER,S	AP	1976	TAR			287	291
0.41	DERSTINE,RP	AU	1974	JAR	HUEFNER,RJ		216	234
0.41	DYCKMAN,TR	SP	1964	JAR			91	107
0.40	HUGHES,PJ	ST	1988	JAR	SCHWARTZ,ES		41	62
0.35	COPELAND,RM	ST	1971	JAR	SHANK ,JK		196	224
0.33	AHARONY,J	SP	1987	CAR	BAR-YOSEF,S		430	444
0.33	STEVENSON,FL	AU	1987	JAR			306	316
0.30	MURRAY,D	SP	1983	JAR			128	140
0.29	HALPERIN,R	JA	1979	TAR			58	71
0.25	BIDDLE,GC	SP	1985	JAR	MARTIN,RK		57	83
0.24	BRUNS JR,WJ	AP	1965	TAR			345	357
0.24	DYCKMAN,TR	AP	1964	TAR			285	295
0.23	COHEN ,MA	AU	1980	JAR	HALPERIN,R		375	389
0.22	GRANOF,MH	SU	1984	JAA	SHORT ,DG		323	333
0.20	BIDDLE,GC	AU	1988	JAR	RICKS ,WE		169	194
0.20	LEE ,CJ	AU	1988	CAR			371	388
0.18	CHASTEEN,LG	JL	1971	TAR			504	508
0.14	HILKE ,JC	WI	1986	JAA			17	29
0.06	BAILEY JR,AD	JL	1973	TAR			560	574
0.06	DREBIN,AR	JA	1965	TAR			154	162
0.06	WRIGHT,FK	JA	1970	TAR			129	133
0.00	BAINBRIDGE,DR	SU	1984	JAA			334	346
0.00	BAO ,BE	04	1989	AOS	BAO ,DA		303	319
0.00	BAR-YOSEF,S	AP	1992	TAR	SEN ,PK		320	336
0.00	BARLEV,B	SP	1986	CAR	FRIED ,D	LIVNAT,J	288	310
0.00	BERNARD,VL	SP	1991	JAA	NOEL ,J		145	181
0.00	BIERMAN JR,H	OC	1967	TAR			731	737
0.00	BOWEN ,RM	JA	1989	TAR	PFEIFFER,GM		152	171
0.00	COTTELL JR,PG	WI	1986	JAA			30	45
0.00	DAVIS ,HZ	AU	1982	JAR	KAHN ,N		738	744
0.00	DAVIS ,HZ	AU	1984	JAR	KAHN ,N	ROZEN ,E	480	490
0.00	DREBIN,AR	SP	1966	JAR			68	86
0.00	FIRMIN,PA	AP	1963	TAR			270	277
0.00	HALPERIN,R	AP	1987	TAR	LANEN ,WN		378	384

CITE INDEX	FIRST AUTHOR	ISSUE	YEAR	JOURNAL	SECOND AUTHOR	THIRD AUTHOR	PAG BEG	PAG END
0.00	HIRSCHMAN,RW	JA	1965	TAR			176	183
0.00	HOLDREN,GC	JA	1964	TAR			70	85
0.00	JUNG ,WO	AU	1989	CAR			1	25
0.00	LARGAY III,JA	JA	1973	TAR			115	119
0.00	MANES ,RP	ST	1967	JAR	SAMUELS,JM	SMYTH ,DJ	139	156
0.00	MOST ,KS	SP	1967	JAR			39	50
0.00	PETRI ,E	JL	1973	TAR			483	488
0.00	PETRI ,E	JL	1974	TAR	MINCH ,RA		455	464
0.00	RAUN ,DL	OC	1963	TAR			754	758
0.00	STAUBUS,GJ	JL	1968	TAR			413	424
0.00	TAUSSIG,RA	JA	1968	TAR	HAYES ,SC		68	74
0.00	TSE ,S	SP	1990	JAR			229	238

4.4 TREATMENTS=OTHER CURRENT ASSETS

CITE INDEX	FIRST AUTHOR	ISSUE	YEAR	JOURNAL	SECOND AUTHOR	THIRD AUTHOR	PAG BEG	PAG END
0.12	BENISHAY,H	SP	1965	JAR			114	132
0.12	HARMELINK,PJ	SP	1973	JAR			146	158
0.06	SCHRODERHEIM,G	JL	1964	TAR			679	684
0.00	ABRANOVIC,WA	OC	1976	TAR			863	874
0.00	CORNELL,B	AU	1989	JAA	LANDSMAN,W	SHAPIRO,AC	460	479
0.00	DONEGAN,J	SP	1989	JAA	SUNDER,S		203	216
0.00	GIACCOTTO,C	SU	1992	JAA			291	310
0.00	SWIERINGA,RJ	SP	1989	JAA			169	186

4.5 TREATMENTS=PROP, PLANT & EQUIP / DEPR

CITE INDEX	FIRST AUTHOR	ISSUE	YEAR	JOURNAL	SECOND AUTHOR	THIRD AUTHOR	PAG BEG	PAG END
1.59	BEAVER,WH	AP	1972	TAR	DUKES ,RE		320	332
0.88	ARCHIBALD,TR	JA	1972	TAR			22	30
0.71	BEAVER,WH	JL	1973	TAR	DUKES ,RE		549	559
0.57	JARRELL,GA	AG	1979	JAE			93	116
0.55	HALL ,TW	SP	1982	JAR			139	151
0.53	ARCHIBALD,TR	ST	1967	JAR			164	186
0.40	KIM ,M	AP	1988	JAE	MOORE ,G		111	125
0.29	COMISKEY,EE	AP	1971	TAR			279	285
0.24	IJIRI ,Y	OC	1969	TAR	KAPLAN,RS		743	756
0.18	BAREFIELD,RM	AU	1971	JAR	COMISKEY,EE		351	358
0.18	BRIEF ,RP	AU	1970	JAR	OWEN ,J		167	177
0.18	FRIBERG,RA	JA	1973	TAR			50	60
0.18	SKINNER,RC	SP	1982	JAR			210	226
0.12	BEAVER,WH	AU	1974	JAR	DUKES ,RE		205	215
0.12	BRIEF ,RP	SP	1973	JAR	OWEN ,J		1	15
0.12	JEN ,FC	AP	1970	TAR	HUEFNER,RJ		290	298
0.12	LINDHE,R	AU	1963	JAR			139	148
0.12	THOMAS,AL	JL	1971	TAR			472	479
0.11	BLOOM ,R	01	1984	AOS	ELGERS,PT	MURRAY,D	1	11
0.11	MOST ,KS	AU	1984	JAR			782	788
0.08	FRIED ,D	SU	1981	JAA			295	308
0.06	BIERMAN JR,H	AP	1966	TAR			271	274
0.06	BIERMAN JR,H	JL	1974	TAR			448	454
0.06	BRIEF ,RP	SP	1967	JAR			27	38
0.06	BRIEF ,RP	OC	1973	TAR	OWEN ,J		690	695
0.06	BULLOCK,CL	JA	1974	TAR			98	103
0.06	GREENE,ED	AP	1963	TAR			355	362

CITE INDEX	FIRST AUTHOR	ISS-UE	YE-AR	JOUR-NAL	SECOND AUTHOR	THIRD AUTHOR	PAG BEG	PAG END
0.06	GYNTHER,MM	OC	1968	TAR			706	718
0.06	IJIRI ,Y	SP	1970	JAR	KAPLAN,RS		34	46
0.06	JOHNSON,O	SP	1968	JAR			29	37
0.06	MCINTYRE,EV	JA	1977	TAR			162	171
0.06	NURNBERG,H	OC	1968	TAR			719	729
0.06	RICKS ,RB	JL	1964	TAR			685	688
0.06	SCHWAB,B	AP	1969	TAR	NICOL ,RE		292	296
0.06	SHWAYDER,KR	AU	1973	JAR			259	272
0.06	VATTER,W	OC	1966	TAR			681	698
0.06	WRIGHT,FK	AU	1965	JAR			167	181
0.00	BIERMAN JR,H	JA	1969	TAR			65	78
0.00	BRIEF ,RP	AP	1968	TAR	OWEN ,J		367	372
0.00	BRIEF ,RP	OC	1977	TAR			810	812
0.00	BRIEF ,RP	SP	1987	CAR	ANTON ,HR		394	407
0.00	BRIGHAM,EF	JA	1968	TAR			46	61
0.00	BURT ,OR	SP	1972	JAR			28	57
0.00	CARSBERG,BV	AU	1969	JAR			165	182
0.00	CORCORAN,AW	AU	1965	JAR	KWANG ,CW		206	217
0.00	CRAMER JR,JJ	OC	1970	TAR	SCHRADER,WJ		698	703
0.00	FEINSCHREIBER,R	SP	1969	JAR			17	21
0.00	HAWKINS,CA	SP	1984	JAA	GIRARD,D		225	240
0.00	HIRSCH,AJ	OC	1964	TAR			972	978
0.00	HORWITZ,BN	OC	1963	TAR			819	826
0.00	JOHNSON,O	JL	1968	TAR			546	548
0.00	LEV ,B	AU	1978	JAR	THEIL ,H		286	293
0.00	LIVINGSTONE,JL	ST	1967	JAR			93	123
0.00	LIVINGSTONE,JL	SP	1967	JAR			77	94
0.00	LOWE ,HD	AP	1963	TAR			293	301
0.00	MOBLEY,SC	JA	1967	TAR			114	123
0.00	O'DONNELL,JL	JA	1965	TAR			135	143
0.00	PELES ,YC	SP	1990	JAA			309	327
0.00	REYNOLDS,IN	AP	1964	TAR			342	346
0.00	THOMAS,AL	JA	1964	TAR			1	11
0.00	THOMAS,AL	SP	1965	JAR			103	113
0.00	WELLS ,MC	AP	1968	TAR			373	376
0.00	WRIGHT,FK	JA	1963	TAR			87	90
0.00	WRIGHT,FK	SP	1964	JAR			80	90
0.00	WRIGHT,FK	AU	1967	JAR			173	179
0.00	WRIGHT,FK	AU	1968	JAR			222	236
0.00	YOUNG ,TN	AP	1967	TAR	PEIRSON,CG		338	341
0.00	ZAROWIN,P	AP	1988	JAE			89	110

4.6 TREATMENTS=OTHER NON-CURRENT ASSETS

CITE INDEX	FIRST AUTHOR	ISS-UE	YE-AR	JOUR-NAL	SECOND AUTHOR	THIRD AUTHOR	PAG BEG	PAG END
0.24	SCHIFF,M	SP	1966	JAR			62	67
0.12	ABDEL-KHALIK,AR	OC	1975	TAR			657	670
0.12	PELES ,YC	SP	1970	JAR			128	137
0.07	SCAPENS,RW	AP	1978	TAR			448	469
0.06	CARSBERG,BV	SP	1966	JAR			1	15
0.00	BRIEF ,RP	JA	1969	TAR			20	26
0.00	DREBIN,AR	JL	1966	TAR			413	425
0.00	ELLIOTT,JA	OC	1991	TAR	HANNA ,JD	SHAW ,WH	847	861
0.00	GRIFFIN,PA	OC	1991	TAR	WALLACH,SJR		830	846

CITE INDEX	FIRST AUTHOR	ISS-UE	YE-AR	JOUR-NAL	SECOND AUTHOR	THIRD AUTHOR	PAG BEG	PAG END
0.00	GYNTHER,RS	AP	1969	TAR			247	255
0.00	JOHNSON,O	OC	1976	TAR			808	823
0.00	MILLER,MC	AP	1973	TAR			280	291
0.00	MILLS ,RH	JA	1967	TAR			74	81
0.00	RUBENSTEIN,DB	05	1992	AOS			501	508

4.7 TREATMENTS=LEASES

CITE INDEX	FIRST AUTHOR	ISS-UE	YE-AR	JOUR-NAL	SECOND AUTHOR	THIRD AUTHOR	PAG BEG	PAG END
0.86	EL-GAZZAR,S	OC	1986	JAE	LILIEN,S	PASTENA,V	217	238
0.47	RO ,BT	AU	1978	JAR			315	340
0.24	LEV ,B	AU	1969	JAR			290	299
0.15	BOWMAN,RG	AP	1980	TAR			237	253
0.12	VATTER,WJ	AU	1966	JAR			133	148
0.12	WYMAN ,HE	JL	1973	TAR			489	493
0.10	WILKINS,T	OC	1983	TAR	ZIMMER,I		749	764
0.08	BAKER ,CR	SP	1980	JAA			197	206
0.08	PALMON,D	SP	1980	JAA	KWATINETZ,M		207	226
0.06	RAPPAPORT,A	AP	1965	TAR			373	376
0.06	WOJDAK,JF	JL	1969	TAR			562	570
0.00	BEECHY,TH	AP	1969	TAR			375	381
0.00	BOWER ,RS	AP	1966	TAR	HERRINGER,F	WILLIAMSON,JP	257	265
0.00	CHASTEEN,LG	OC	1973	TAR			764	767
0.00	EVERETT,JO	SP	1984	JAA	PORTER,GA		241	256
0.00	IMHOFF-JR,EA	DE	1988	JAE	THOMAS,JK		277	310
0.00	MARSTON,F	SP	1988	JAA	HARRIS,RS		147	164
0.00	MARTIN,JD	WI	1979	JAA	ANDERSON,PF	KEOWN ,AJ	151	164
0.00	MUNTER,P	WI	1983	JAA	RATCLIFFE,TA		108	114
0.00	POWERS,M	AP	1989	TAR	REVSINE,L		346	368
0.00	SHAW ,WH	AP	1987	TAR			385	400

4.8 TREATMENTS=LONG TERM DEBT

CITE INDEX	FIRST AUTHOR	ISS-UE	YE-AR	JOUR-NAL	SECOND AUTHOR	THIRD AUTHOR	PAG BEG	PAG END
3.33	PRESS ,EG	JA	1990	JAE	WEINTROP,JB		65	95
3.00	DUKE ,JC	JA	1990	JAE	HUNT III,HG		45	63
2.40	MCNICHOLS,M	ST	1988	JAR	WILSON,GP		1	40
1.50	HAND ,JRM	OC	1989	TAR			587	623
0.75	DEFEO ,VJ	AP	1989	TAR	LAMBER,RA	LARCKER,DF	201	227
0.53	HORRIGAN,JO	ST	1966	JAR			44	62
0.40	LYS ,T	AU	1988	JAR	SIVARAMAKRISHNAN,K		273	299
0.38	BOWMAN,RG	SP	1980	JAR			242	254
0.33	WILSON,ER	SP	1990	CAR	STEWART,JP		573	591
0.25	INGRAM,RW	AU	1985	JAR			595	618
0.25	MULFORD,CW	AU	1985	JAR			897	906
0.11	DIETRICH,JR	AP	1984	JAE			67	96
0.06	ARNOLD,DF	JA	1973	TAR	HUMANN,TE		23	33
0.06	CURRY ,DW	JL	1971	TAR			490	503
0.06	FRANK ,WG	SP	1971	JAR	WEYGANDT,JJ		116	126
0.00	APOSTOLOU,NG	AU	1985	JAR	GIROUX,GA	WELKER,RB	853	858
0.00	BEATTY,RP	WI	1985	JAA	JOHNSON,SB		112	124
0.00	BIERMAN JR,H	AU	1967	JAR	SMIDT ,S		144	153
0.00	BIERMAN JR,H	OC	1968	TAR			657	661
0.00	BIERMAN JR,H	WI	1986	JAA			62	70
0.00	FEROZ ,EH	JL	1992	TAR	WILSON,ER		480	495

CITE INDEX	FIRST AUTHOR	ISS-UE	YE-AR	JOUR-NAL	SECOND AUTHOR	THIRD AUTHOR	PAG BEG	PAG END
0.00	FORD ,A	OC	1969	TAR			818	822
0.00	FRIED ,D	WI	1987	JAA	HOSLER,C		5	23
0.00	GIVOLY,D	AU	1981	JAR	PALMON,D		530	543
0.00	GLOVER,F	AP	1969	TAR			300	303
0.00	GORDON,DA	AU	1990	JAA	GORDON,MJ		573	588
0.00	HAND ,JRM	OC	1990	TAR			739	763
0.00	IMDIEKE,LF	OC	1969	TAR	WEYGANDT,JJ		798	805
0.00	INGRAM,RW	AP	1989	TAR	RAMAN ,KK	WILSON,ER	250	268
0.00	KAHN ,N	SU	1982	JAA			327	337
0.00	KING ,RD	JL	1984	TAR			419	431
0.00	KNAUF ,JB	WI	1987	JAA	VASARHELYI,MA		43	64
0.00	KNUTSON,PH	ST	1971	JAR			99	112
0.00	MIELKE,DE	WI	1987	JAA	SEIFERT,J		65	78
0.00	PAINE ,NR	AP	1964	TAR			330	332
0.00	PEAVY ,JW	WI	1985	JAA	EDGAR ,SM		125	135
0.00	RAPPAPORT,A	AP	1969	TAR			297	299
0.00	RODEN ,PF	WI	1987	JAA			79	89
0.00	STICKEL,SE	OC	1986	JAE			197	216
0.00	TILLER,MG	SU	1985	JAA	MAUTZ ,RD		293	304

4.9 TREATMENTS=TAXES

CITE INDEX	FIRST AUTHOR	ISS-UE	YE-AR	JOUR-NAL	SECOND AUTHOR	THIRD AUTHOR	PAG BEG	PAG END
1.20	THOMAS,JK	JL	1988	JAE			199	237
1.20	ZIMMERMAN,JL	AG	1983	JAE			119	149
0.60	WONG ,J	JA	1988	JAE			37	51
0.57	SHPILBERG,D	AU	1986	AUD	GRAHAM,LE		75	94
0.50	BECK ,PJ	JL	1989	TAR	JUNG ,W		468	487
0.50	FELLINGHAM,JC	JA	1985	TAR	WOLFSON,MA		10	17
0.45	HITE ,GL	JL	1982	JAE	LONG ,MS		3	14
0.25	AYRES ,FL	AP	1989	TAR	JACKSON,BR	HITE ,PS	300	312
0.25	CHEUNG,JK	SP	1989	CAR			625	641
0.25	HOPWOOD,WS	SP	1985	JAR	MCKEOWN,JC		161	174
0.25	MADEO ,SA	JL	1985	TAR	PINCUS,M		407	429
0.25	MILLIRON,VC	AU	1985	JAR			794	816
0.24	CRUMBLEY,DL	OC	1973	TAR			759	763
0.20	SHAW ,WH	SP	1988	JAR			60	81
0.20	WHITE ,RA	JL	1983	TAR			539	561
0.19	ADAR ,Z	JA	1977	TAR	BARNEA,A	LEV ,B	137	149
0.17	MOORE ,ML	OC	1987	TAR	STEECE,BM	SWENSON,CW	671	685
0.12	GRIFFIN,PA	JL	1976	TAR			499	515
0.12	MOONITZ,M	SP	1966	JAR			47	61
0.07	ENGLEBRECHT,TD	JL	1979	TAR	JAMISON,RW		554	562
0.07	MADEO ,SA	JL	1979	TAR			538	553
0.06	ALFRED,AM	AU	1964	JAR			172	182
0.06	GREENBALL,MN	AU	1969	JAR			262	289
0.06	LIVINGSTONE,JL	AU	1969	JAR			245	256
0.06	MEYERS,SL	JA	1973	TAR			44	49
0.00	ALVEY ,KL	JA	1963	TAR			124	125
0.00	ANDERSON JR,KE	JL	1985	TAR			357	371
0.00	BECK ,PJ	AU	1992	CAR	DAVIS ,JS	JUNG ,W-O	86	112
0.00	BERG ,KB	JL	1963	TAR	MUELLER,FJ		554	561
0.00	BIERMAN JR,H	SP	1985	JAA			184	194
0.00	BOGART,FO	OC	1965	TAR			834	838

CITE INDEX	FIRST AUTHOR	ISS-UE	YE-AR	JOUR-NAL	SECOND AUTHOR	THIRD AUTHOR	PAG BEG	PAG END
0.00	BRIGHAM,EF	JL	1974	TAR	NANTELL,TJ		436	447
0.00	CHANG ,OH	SP	1992	JAR	NICHOLS,DR		109	125
0.00	DALY ,BA	SP	1990	JAR	OMER ,T		193	197
0.00	DEAN ,J	AP	1963	TAR	HARRISS,CL		229	242
0.00	DHALIWAL,D	MR	1992	JAE	WANG ,S		7	25
0.00	DRINKWATER,D	JL	1965	TAR	EDWARDS,JD		579	582
0.00	GREENWALD,B	SU	1989	JAA	STIGLITZ,JE		281	297
0.00	HASSELBACK,JR	AP	1976	TAR			269	276
0.00	HICKS ,SA	JL	1978	TAR			708	716
0.00	HINES JR,JR	AU	1991	JAA			447	479
0.00	HORNE ,JC	JA	1963	TAR			56	60
0.00	HORWITZ,RM	JL	1964	TAR			618	621
0.00	HUSS ,HF	AU	1985	JAA			60	66
0.00	HUSS ,HF	WI	1991	JAA	ZHAO ,J		53	66
0.00	JERSTON,JE	OC	1965	TAR			812	813
0.00	JORGENSON,DW	AU	1991	JAA	YUN ,K		487	508
0.00	KAPLAN,SE	04	1988	AOS	RECKERS,PMJ	ROARK ,SJ	371	379
0.00	KARLINSKY,SS	WI	1983	JAA			157	167
0.00	KARLINSKY,SS	AU	1983	JAA			65	76
0.00	KELLER,TF	JA	1965	TAR			184	189
0.00	KRAMER,SS	JA	1982	TAR			70	87
0.00	LAIBSTAIN,S	AP	1971	TAR			342	351
0.00	LEWIS ,CD	JA	1967	TAR			96	105
0.00	LITZENBERGER,RH	SU	1989	JAA	TALMOR,E		305	316
0.00	LIVINGSTONE,JL	JL	1967	TAR			544	552
0.00	MACNAUGHTON,A	AU	1992	CAR			113	137
0.00	MADEO ,SA	AP	1987	TAR	SCHEPANSKI,A	UECKER,WC	323	342
0.00	MEADE ,JA	AP	1990	TAR			406	431
0.00	MEANS ,KM	AU	1989	JAA			571	579
0.00	MEHTA ,DR	SP	1968	JAR	ANDREWS,VL		50	57
0.00	MOORE ,ML	JA	1985	TAR	STEECE,BM	SWENSON,CW	18	32
0.00	NIKOLAI,LA	JA	1979	TAR	ELAM ,R		119	131
0.00	NURNBERG,H	AU	1969	JAR			257	261
0.00	NURNBERG,H	AU	1970	JAR			217	231
0.00	NURNBERG,H	OC	1972	TAR			655	665
0.00	NURNBERG,H	AU	1985	JAA	CIANCIOLO,ST		50	59
0.00	O'DONNELL,JL	JL	1968	TAR			549	553
0.00	OUTSLAY,E	OC	1982	TAR	WHEELER,JE		716	733
0.00	PATTEN,RJ	OC	1964	TAR			876	879
0.00	PORCANO,TM	OC	1984	TAR			619	636
0.00	RABY ,WL	JL	1963	TAR	NEUBIG,RD		568	576
0.00	REVSINE,L	AP	1969	TAR			354	358
0.00	RICHARD,DL	OC	1968	TAR			730	737
0.00	SCHOLES,MS	SU	1989	JAA	TERRY ,E	WOLFSON,MA	317	340
0.00	SCHOLES,MS	AU	1991	JAA	WOLFSON,MA		513	532
0.00	SCHWARTZ,BN	SP	1981	JAA			238	247
0.00	SCHWARTZ,BN	SP	1983	JAA			244	253
0.00	SEAMAN,JL	JL	1965	TAR			617	621
0.00	SHACKELFORD,DA	JN	1991	JAE			117	145
0.00	SOMMERFELD,RM	OC	1967	TAR			747	750
0.00	TRUMBULL,WP	JL	1968	TAR			459	468
0.00	VOSS ,WM	AU	1968	JAR			262	269
0.00	WAUGH ,JB	JL	1968	TAR			535	539

CITE INDEX	FIRST AUTHOR	ISS-UE	YE-AR	JOUR-NAL	SECOND AUTHOR	THIRD AUTHOR	PAG BEG	PAG END
0.00	WEBER ,RP	JA	1977	TAR			172	185
0.00	WHITE ,D	SU	1982	JAA	VANECEK,M		338	354
0.00	WIESEN,JL	WI	1979	JAA	ENG ,R		101	121
0.00	WILLIAMS,D	AP	1966	TAR			226	234
0.00	WINBORNE,MG	OC	1966	TAR	KLEESPIE,DC		737	744

4.10 TREATMENTS=OTHER LIABILITIES

CITE INDEX	FIRST AUTHOR	ISS-UE	YE-AR	JOUR-NAL	SECOND AUTHOR	THIRD AUTHOR	PAG BEG	PAG END
0.55	BANKS ,DW	SP	1982	JAR	KINNEY JR,WR		240	254
0.25	EL-GAZZAR,S	SP	1989	JAA	LILIEN,S	PASTENA,V	217	231
0.25	RONEN ,J	SP	1989	JAA	SONDHI,AC		237	265
0.13	HUGHES,JS	OC	1978	TAR			882	894
0.12	DAVIDSON,HJ	AU	1967	JAR	NETER ,J	PETRAN,AS	186	207
0.08	BALACHANDRAN,KR	JA	1981	TAR	MASCHMEYER,R	LIVINGSTONE,JL	115	124
0.06	AMATO ,HN	OC	1976	TAR	ANDERSON,EE	HARVEY,DW	854	862
0.06	HECK ,WR	JL	1963	TAR			577	578
0.00	BRIGHTON,GD	JA	1969	TAR			137	144
0.00	DREBIN,AR	JL	1963	TAR			579	583
0.00	ENGLE ,TJ	WI	1991	JAA			109	121
0.00	FRANCIS,J	AU	1990	JAR			326	347
0.00	GIVOLY,D	AP	1992	TAR	HAYN ,C		394	410
0.00	GLICK ,R	SP	1989	JAA	PLAUT ,SE		147	159
0.00	GORTON,G	SP	1989	JAA	PENNACCHI,G		125	145
0.00	HENNESSY,VC	SU	1978	JAA			317	330
0.00	JAMES ,C	SP	1989	JAA			111	124
0.00	KING ,TE	JL	1988	AUD	ORTEGREN,AK		522	535
0.00	PETRONI,KR	DE	1992	JAE			485	507
0.00	TRUMBULL,WP	JA	1963	TAR			46	51
0.00	WOLK ,HI	AP	1973	TAR	TEARNEY,MG		292	299

4.11 TREATMENTS=VALUATION (INFLATION)

CITE INDEX	FIRST AUTHOR	ISS-UE	YE-AR	JOUR-NAL	SECOND AUTHOR	THIRD AUTHOR	PAG BEG	PAG END
2.55	BEAVER,WH	JL	1982	JAE	GRIFFIN,PA	LANDSMAN,WR	15	39
2.14	TITMAN,S	JN	1986	JAE	TRUEMAN,B		159	172
1.67	OHLSON,JA	SP	1990	CAR			648	676
1.62	BEAVER,WH	AG	1980	JAE	CHRISTIE,AA	GRIFFIN,PA	127	157
1.50	DATAR ,SM	MR	1991	JAE	FELTHAM,GA	HUGHES,JS	3	49
1.38	BUBLITZ,B	ST	1985	JAR	FRECKA,TJ	MCKEOWN,JC	1	23
1.31	GHEYARA,K	AG	1980	JAE	BOATSMAN,JR		107	125
1.15	RO ,BT	AG	1980	JAE			159	189
1.08	NOREEN,EW	AP	1981	TAR	SEPE ,J		253	269
1.00	LUSTGARTEN,S	OC	1982	JAE			121	141
0.80	SUNDER,S	AU	1983	JAR	WAYMIRE,G		565	580
0.71	THORNTON,DB	AU	1986	CAR			1	34
0.69	PARKER,JE	JA	1977	TAR			69	96
0.67	DEANGELO,LE	JA	1990	TAR			93	112
0.67	SCHAEFER,TF	AU	1984	JAR			647	656
0.67	SUNDER,S	AU	1978	JAR			341	367
0.67	THOMPSON,G	05	1987	AOS			523	543
0.60	SUTTON,TG	AP	1988	JAE			127	149
0.60	WONG ,J	AP	1988	JAE			151	167
0.57	SHRIVER,KA	SP	1986	JAR			151	165
0.53	TRITSCHLER,CA	JA	1969	TAR			99	123

CITE INDEX	FIRST AUTHOR	ISS-UE	YE-AR	JOUR-NAL	SECOND AUTHOR	THIRD AUTHOR	PAG BEG	PAG END
0.50	FREEMAN,RN	SP	1983	JAR			42	64
0.50	OLSEN ,C	ST	1985	JAR			28	53
0.50	SHRIVER,KA	JA	1987	TAR			79	96
0.47	PETERSEN,RJ	JA	1973	TAR			34	43
0.44	MATOLCSY,ZP	AU	1984	JAR			555	569
0.40	HAW ,IM	AU	1988	JAR	LUSTGARTEN,S		331	352
0.40	KETZ ,JE	OC	1978	TAR			952	960
0.38	CASLER,DJ	SP	1985	JAR	HALL ,TW		110	122
0.38	WATTS ,RL	AG	1980	JAE	ZIMMERMAN,JL		95	106
0.35	MCINTYRE,EV	JL	1973	TAR			575	585
0.35	REVSINE,L	JL	1970	TAR			513	523
0.35	SIMMONS,JK	OC	1969	TAR	GRAY ,J		757	776
0.33	BENSTON,GJ	ST	1978	JAR	KRASNEY,MA		1	30
0.33	HALL ,TW	JL	1990	TAR	SHRIVER,KA		537	556
0.33	MCDONALD,B	JL	1984	TAR	MORRIS,MH		432	446
0.33	RO ,BT	JA	1981	TAR			70	84
0.33	SHIH ,MSH	AU	1987	CAR	SUNDER,S		16	31
0.33	SWANSON,EP	OC	1990	TAR			911	924
0.29	NORTON,CL	JA	1979	TAR	SMITH ,RE		72	87
0.29	PRAKASH,P	JA	1979	TAR	SUNDER,S		1	22
0.27	ABDEL-KHALIK,AR	ST	1978	JAR	MCKEOWN,JC		46	77
0.25	ESPAHBODI,R	SP	1989	CAR	TEHRANIAN,H		575	591
0.25	KAPLAN,RS	AP	1977	TAR			369	378
0.25	PEASNELL,KV	SP	1977	JAR	SKERRATT,CL		108	119
0.24	BARTON,AD	OC	1974	TAR			664	681
0.24	BRENNER,VC	AU	1970	JAR			159	166
0.24	HEINTZ,JA	OC	1973	TAR			679	689
0.24	LIVINGSTONE,JL	AP	1967	TAR			233	240
0.21	REVSINE,L	AP	1979	TAR			306	322
0.20	ENIS ,CR	02	1988	AOS			123	145
0.20	KETZ ,JE	ST	1978	JAR			273	284
0.18	CHAMBERS,RJ	OC	1965	TAR			731	741
0.18	FRANK ,WG	SP	1969	JAR			123	136
0.18	MCKEOWN,JC	JA	1971	TAR			12	29
0.18	SAMUELSON,RA	AU	1972	JAR			322	344
0.18	SEPE ,J	JL	1982	TAR			467	485
0.18	WALTHER,LM	AP	1982	TAR			376	383
0.17	BERNARD,VL	OC	1987	TAR	RULAND,RG		707	722
0.17	BILDERSEE,JS	AU	1987	CAR	RONEN ,J		89	110
0.15	BARAN ,A	JA	1980	TAR	LAKONISHOK,J	OFER ,AR	22	35
0.14	MURDOCH,B	AP	1986	TAR			273	287
0.13	BROMWICH,M	JL	1977	TAR			587	596
0.13	SHORT ,DG	ST	1978	JAR			259	272
0.13	WEYGANDT,JJ	JA	1977	TAR			40	51
0.12	CHAMBERS,RJ	SP	1965	JAR			32	62
0.12	CHAMBERS,RJ	AU	1965	JAR			242	252
0.12	CHAMBERS,RJ	OC	1967	TAR			751	757
0.12	DOCKWEILER,RC	OC	1969	TAR			729	742
0.12	EDWARDS,EO	AP	1975	TAR			235	245
0.12	GREENBALL,MN	SP	1968	JAR			114	129
0.12	GYNTHER,RS	OC	1970	TAR			712	730
0.12	HORNGREN,CT	AP	1965	TAR			323	333
0.12	IJIRI ,Y	AP	1976	TAR			227	243

CITE INDEX	FIRST AUTHOR	ISS-UE	YE-AR	JOUR-NAL	SECOND AUTHOR	THIRD AUTHOR	PAG BEG	PAG END
0.12	LEMKE ,KW	JA	1966	TAR			32	41
0.12	MCDONALD,DL	SP	1968	JAR			38	49
0.12	MOONITZ,M	JL	1970	TAR			465	475
0.12	STAUBUS,GJ	JA	1965	TAR			119	134
0.11	BERNARD,VL	AU	1984	JAR			445	466
0.10	OVADIA,A	WI	1983	JAA	RONEN ,J		115	129
0.09	BEAVER,WH	AU	1982	JAR	WOLFSON,MA		528	550
0.08	KELLY ,LK	03	1980	AOS			311	322
0.08	OVADIA,A	WI	1980	JAA	RONEN ,J		113	137
0.07	DAVIDSON,S	ST	1978	JAR	WEIL ,RL		154	233
0.07	HILLISON,WA	SP	1979	JAR			60	73
0.06	ARNOLD,DF	AU	1977	JAR	HUEFNER,RJ		245	252
0.06	BAXTER,WT	AU	1971	JAR	CARRIER,NH		189	214
0.06	BRADFORD,WD	AP	1974	TAR			296	305
0.06	COOK ,JS	OC	1976	TAR	HOLZMANN,OJ		778	787
0.06	DICKENS,RL	AP	1964	TAR	BLACKBURN,JO		312	329
0.06	ESTES ,RW	AU	1968	JAR			200	207
0.06	HEATH ,LC	JL	1972	TAR			458	468
0.06	ISELIN,ER	AP	1968	TAR			231	238
0.06	KRATCHMAN,SH	OC	1974	TAR	MALCOM,RE	TWARK ,RD	682	689
0.06	MATHEWS,RL	JL	1968	TAR			509	516
0.06	MCKEOWN,JC	SP	1973	JAR			62	99
0.06	PENMAN,SH	AP	1970	TAR			333	346
0.06	SHARPE,IG	AU	1975	JAR	WALKER,RG		293	310
0.06	SHWAYDER,KR	AP	1969	TAR			304	316
0.06	SHWAYDER,KR	AP	1971	TAR			306	319
0.06	SNAVELY,HJ	AP	1969	TAR			344	353
0.06	STAUBUS,GJ	OC	1967	TAR			650	661
0.06	STAUBUS,GJ	JL	1976	TAR			574	589
0.06	TRACY ,JA	JA	1965	TAR			163	175
0.00	AGRAWAL,SP	OC	1977	TAR			789	809
0.00	AGRAWAL,SP	WI	1980	JAA	HALLBAUER,RC	PERRITT,GW	163	173
0.00	ALFORD,AW	SP	1992	JAR			94	108
0.00	ARNETT,HE	OC	1963	TAR			733	741
0.00	BACHAR,J	AU	1989	JAA			432	459
0.00	BEDFORD,NM	AP	1972	TAR	MCKEOWN,JC		333	338
0.00	BEJA ,A	AU	1977	JAR	AHARONI,Y		169	178
0.00	BIERMAN JR,H	OC	1971	TAR			693	700
0.00	BOER ,G	JA	1966	TAR			92	97
0.00	CHAMBERS,RJ	AP	1968	TAR			239	247
0.00	CHARITOU,A	AU	1990	JAA	KETZ ,JE		475	497
0.00	CHEUNG,JK	SP	1990	CAR			724	737
0.00	CLARKSON,PM	SP	1992	CAR	DONTOH,A	RICHARDSON,G	601	625
0.00	COOPER,T	WI	1980	JAA			138	146
0.00	CORBIN,DA	OC	1963	TAR			742	744
0.00	CORBIN,DA	OC	1967	TAR			635	641
0.00	DEFLIESE,PL	JL	1965	TAR			517	521
0.00	DEMSKI,JS	AP	1990	TAR	SAPPINGTON,DEM		363	383
0.00	DEMSKI,JS	AP	1990	TAR	SAPPINGTON,DEM		363	383
0.00	DREBIN,AR	AU	1969	JAR			204	214
0.00	FRIEDMAN,LA	JA	1978	TAR			18	30
0.00	FRIEDMAN,LA	OC	1978	TAR			895	909
0.00	GAMBLE,GO	SU	1982	JAA			320	326

CITE INDEX	FIRST AUTHOR	ISS-UE	YE-AR	JOUR-NAL	SECOND AUTHOR	THIRD AUTHOR	PAG BEG	PAG END
0.00	GOLDSCHMIDT,Y	AP	1969	TAR	SMIDT ,S		317	329
0.00	GOLDSCHMIDT,Y	AU	1984	JAA	SHASHUA,L		54	67
0.00	GROSSMAN,SD	WI	1981	JAA	KRATCHMAN,SH	WELKER,RB	136	143
0.00	HAKANSSON,NH	SP	1969	JAR			11	31
0.00	HALL ,TW	SP	1985	JAA	CASLER,DJ		210	224
0.00	HANNUM,WH	AP	1968	TAR	WASSERMAN,W		295	302
0.00	HENDRIKSEN,ES	JL	1963	TAR			483	491
0.00	INGBERMAN,M	WI	1980	JAA			101	112
0.00	JARRETT,JE	SP	1974	JAR			63	66
0.00	JOLIVET,V	JL	1964	TAR			689	692
0.00	KISTNER,KP	SP	1980	JAR	SALMI ,T		297	311
0.00	KRINSKY,I	SP	1989	CAR	ROTENBERG,W		501	515
0.00	LARSON,KD	OC	1966	TAR	SCHATTKE,RW		634	641
0.00	LEE ,SS	JL	1965	TAR			622	625
0.00	LEMBKE,VC	WI	1980	JAA	SMITH ,JH		147	162
0.00	LEMBKE,VC	WI	1981	JAA	TOOLE ,HR		128	135
0.00	LIM ,SS	OC	1991	TAR	SUNDER,S		669	693
0.00	LYON ,JD	AU	1992	JAA	SCHROEDER,DA		531	552
0.00	MAHER ,MW	SP	1983	JAR	NANTELL,TJ		329	340
0.00	MATTESSICH,RV	SP	1986	CAR			157	178
0.00	MCINTYRE,EV	JL	1982	TAR			607	618
0.00	MCKEOWN,JC	JL	1972	TAR			527	532
0.00	MENSAH,YM	WI	1983	JAA			130	141
0.00	MONAHAN,TF	SU	1983	JAA	BARENBAUM,L		325	340
0.00	NAKANO,I	OC	1972	TAR			693	708
0.00	NELSON,GK	JA	1966	TAR			42	47
0.00	ODAIYAPPA,R	JL	1992	TAR	NAINAR,SMK		599	609
0.00	PATON ,WA	SP	1968	JAR			72	85
0.00	PEASNELL,KV	JA	1977	TAR			186	189
0.00	PEIRSON,G	OC	1966	TAR			729	736
0.00	PETERSEN,RJ	JL	1975	TAR			525	532
0.00	PETERSON,WA	AP	1966	TAR			275	282
0.00	PHILIPS,GE	ST	1970	JAR	MAYNE ,LS		178	188
0.00	RABY ,WL	JA	1969	TAR			1	11
0.00	RAGHUNANDAN,K	SP	1991	CAR	GRIMLUND,RA	SCHEPANSKI,A	549	568
0.00	REVSINE,L	AP	1981	TAR			342	354
0.00	RORKE ,CH	03	1982	AOS			305	306
0.00	ROSEN ,LS	JA	1967	TAR			106	113
0.00	ROSENFIELD,P	OC	1969	TAR			788	797
0.00	SAMI ,H	SP	1989	CAR	CURATOLA,AP	TRAPNELL,JE	556	574
0.00	SKERRATT,LC	SU	1984	JAA			362	368
0.00	SPENCER,CH	JA	1965	TAR	BARNISEL,TS		144	153
0.00	SPROUSE,RT	OC	1963	TAR			687	695
0.00	SPROUSE,RT	JL	1965	TAR			522	526
0.00	STANDISH,PEM	OC	1982	TAR	UNG ,S		701	715
0.00	STANLEY,CH	JL	1964	TAR			639	647
0.00	STERLING,RR	JL	1971	TAR	FLAHERTY,RE		441	456
0.00	STERLING,RR	OC	1972	TAR	TOLLEFSON,SO	FLAHERTY,RE	709	721
0.00	STRONG,JS	OC	1990	JAE			267	283
0.00	SUMMERS,EL	SP	1970	JAR	DESKINS,JW		113	117
0.00	SWANSON,EP	OC	1985	TAR	SHEARON,WT	THOMAS,LR	681	691
0.00	SWENSON,CW	JA	1987	TAR			117	136
0.00	TAUSSIG,RA	SP	1964	JAR			67	79

CITE INDEX	FIRST AUTHOR	ISS-UE	YE-AR	JOUR-NAL	SECOND AUTHOR	THIRD AUTHOR	PAG BEG	PAG END
0.00	THIES ,CF	AU	1987	JAA	STURROCK,T		375	391
0.00	THOMAS,AL	JL	1964	TAR			574	581
0.00	THOMAS,LR	AP	1986	TAR	SWANSON,EP		330	336
0.00	THORNTON,DB	AU	1988	CAR			343	370
0.00	WELLS ,MC	OC	1965	TAR	COTTON,W		829	833
0.00	WHITE ,LJ	SP	1991	JAA			289	302
0.00	WOLK ,HI	JL	1970	TAR			544	552
0.00	ZEFF ,SA	JA	1965	TAR	MAXWELL,WD		65	75

4.12 TREATMENTS=SPECIAL ITEMS

CITE INDEX	FIRST AUTHOR	ISS-UE	YE-AR	JOUR-NAL	SECOND AUTHOR	THIRD AUTHOR	PAG BEG	PAG END
4.00	BOWEN ,RM	AG	1981	JAE	NOREEN,EW	LACEY ,JM	151	179
2.86	RAYBURN,J	ST	1986	JAR			112	137
2.14	WILSON GP	ST	1986	JAR			165	203
1.88	GONEDES,NJ	AU	1975	JAR			220	256
1.43	HOSKIN,RE	ST	1986	JAR	HUGHES,JS	RICKS ,WE	1	36
0.82	JAIN ,PC	DE	1982	JAE			205	228
0.78	SUNDER,S	SP	1984	JAR	WAYMIRE,G		396	405
0.24	BARNEA,A	JA	1975	TAR	RONEN ,J	SADAN ,S	58	68
0.12	PETRI ,E	AP	1974	TAR	MINCH ,RA		330	341
0.10	GOMBOLA,MJ	JA	1983	TAR	KETZ ,JE		105	114
0.06	CUMMING,J	ST	1973	JAR			60	95
0.00	BURNS ,JS	JA	1963	TAR	JAEDICKE,RK	SANGSTER,JM	1	13
0.00	FURLONG,WL	AP	1966	TAR			244	252
0.00	GREENBERG,RR	AU	1986	JAA	JOHNSON,GL	RAMESH,K	266	277
0.00	GRIMLUND,RA	AU	1985	JAR			575	594
0.00	KATZ ,BG	SU	1987	JAA	OWEN ,J		266	298
0.00	MANEGOLD,JG	SU	1986	JAA			206	221
0.00	PATON ,WA	AP	1969	TAR			276	283
0.00	SCHAEFER,T	AU	1986	JAA	KENNELLEY,M		278	287
0.00	SHWAYDER,KR	OC	1972	TAR			747	760
0.00	TAYLOR,WM	AU	1982	JAR	WEYGANDT,JJ		497	502

4.13 TREATMENTS=REVENUE RECOGNITION

CITE INDEX	FIRST AUTHOR	ISS-UE	YE-AR	JOUR-NAL	SECOND AUTHOR	THIRD AUTHOR	PAG BEG	PAG END
1.75	FREEMAN,RN	ST	1989	JAR	TSE ,S		49	79
1.00	FREEMAN,RN	AU	1992	JAR	TSE ,SY		185	209
0.94	BROWN ,P	ST	1967	JAR	BALL ,R		55	77
0.89	LAMBERT,RA	OC	1984	TAR			604	618
0.80	DYE ,RA	AU	1988	JAR			195	235
0.75	ANTLE ,R	SP	1989	CAR	DEMSKI,JS		423	451
0.71	BOWEN ,RM	OC	1986	TAR	BURGSTAHLER,D	DALEY ,LA	713	725
0.59	COPELAND,RM	ST	1968	JAR			101	116
0.47	DRAKE ,DF	AU	1965	JAR	DOPUCH,N		192	205
0.40	TRUEMAN,B	ST	1988	JAR	TITMAN,S		127	143
0.33	IJIRI ,Y	JA	1984	TAR	NOEL ,J		52	63
0.24	BALL ,R	SP	1976	JAR	LEV ,B	WATTS ,RL	1	9
0.20	ELLIOTT,JA	ST	1988	JAR	SHAW,WH		91	126
0.18	RONEN ,J	SP	1975	JAR	SADAN ,S		133	149
0.08	KOCH ,BS	JL	1981	TAR			574	586
0.06	SHANK ,JK	JA	1971	TAR			57	74
0.00	BAKER ,RE	JA	1966	TAR			98	105
0.00	CERF ,AR	JL	1975	TAR			451	465

CITE INDEX	FIRST AUTHOR	ISS-UE	YE-AR	JOUR-NAL	SECOND AUTHOR	THIRD AUTHOR	PAG BEG	PAG END
0.00	COMISKEY,EE	AP	1968	TAR	MLYNARCZYK,FA		248	256
0.00	DEMARIS,EJ	JA	1963	TAR			37	45
0.00	DHARAN,BG	SP	1987	CAR			445	459
0.00	FRIEDLOB,GT	WI	1983	JAA			100	107
0.00	HENDRICKSON,HS	AP	1968	TAR			363	366
0.00	HUDSON,RR	OC	1963	TAR			796	801
0.00	HYLTON,DP	OC	1965	TAR			824	828
0.00	JACOBSEN,LE	AP	1963	TAR			285	292
0.00	KAHN ,N	AU	1985	JAA	SCHIFF,A		40	49
0.00	LITTLETON,AC	JL	1970	TAR			476	480
0.00	MAURIELLO,JA	JA	1963	TAR			26	28
0.00	MOBLEY,SC	AP	1966	TAR			292	296
0.00	MOBLEY,SC	AP	1968	TAR			333	341
0.00	PHILIPS,GE	JA	1963	TAR			14	25
0.00	RAYBURN,J	AU	1992	CAR	LENWAY,S		237	251
0.00	SAMUELSON,RA	AP	1980	TAR			254	268
0.00	SORTER,GH	SP	1987	JAA	INGBERMAN,M		99	116
0.00	STERNER,JA	AU	1983	JAR			623	628
0.00	WARFIELD,TD	OC	1992	TAR	WILD ,JJ		821	842
0.00	WINDAL,FW	JA	1963	TAR			29	36

4.14 TREATMENTS=ACCTG CHANGES

CITE INDEX	FIRST AUTHOR	ISS-UE	YE-AR	JOUR-NAL	SECOND AUTHOR	THIRD AUTHOR	PAG BEG	PAG END
3.79	HAGERMAN,RL	AG	1979	JAE	ZMIJEWSKI,ME		141	161
3.58	LEFTWICH,RW	MR	1981	JAE			3	36
2.29	BALL ,R	ST	1972	JAR			1	38
1.06	HARRISON,T	SP	1977	JAR			84	107
0.94	DOPUCH,N	SP	1972	JAR	WATTS ,RL		180	194
0.89	HUGHES,JS	AG	1984	JAE	RICKS ,WE		101	132
0.82	EGGLETON,IRC	SP	1976	JAR	PENMAN,SH	TWOMBLY,JR	66	88
0.76	CUSHING,BE	AU	1969	JAR			196	203
0.60	LILIEN,S	OC	1988	TAR	MELLMAN,M	PASTENA,V	642	656
0.59	MOORE ,ML	SP	1973	JAR			100	107
0.44	BENSTON,GJ	AU	1984	CAR			47	57
0.41	BASKIN,EF	JA	1972	TAR			38	51
0.36	DYCKMAN,TR	01	1982	AOS	HOSKIN,RE	SWIERINGA,RJ	1	12
0.33	ABDEL-KHALIK,AR	AU	1987	CAR	CHI ,C	GHICAS,D	32	60
0.33	CHAMBERS,RJ	AU	1984	CAR			1	22
0.33	MOSES ,OD	AP	1987	TAR			358	377
0.25	RICKS ,WE	JA	1985	TAR	HUGHES,JS		33	52
0.24	BREMSER,WG	JL	1975	TAR			563	573
0.18	SCHWARTZ,KB	AU	1982	JAA			32	43
0.18	WHITE JR,CE	AU	1972	JAR			351	358
0.13	WARREN,CS	JA	1977	TAR			150	161
0.11	CHAMBERS,RJ	AU	1984	CAR			58	63
0.10	BROWN ,LD	AU	1983	JAR			432	443
0.08	HORWITZ,BN	WI	1981	JAA	KOLODNY,R		102	113
0.06	NEUMANN,FL	JL	1969	TAR			546	554
0.00	BLACCONIERE,WG	MR	1991	JAE			91	113
0.00	BLACCONIERE,WG	JN	1991	JAE	BOWEN ,RM	SEFCIK,SE	167	201
0.00	CREADY,WM	JL	1987	TAR	SHANK ,JK		589	596
0.00	ELLIOTT,JA	JA	1990	TAR	PHILBRICK,DR		157	174
0.00	JENNINGS,R	AP	1992	TAR	MEST ,DP	THOMPSON II,RB	337	354

CITE INDEX	FIRST AUTHOR	ISS-UE	YE-AR	JOUR-NAL	SECOND AUTHOR	THIRD AUTHOR	PAG BEG	PAG END
0.00	LABELLE,R	SP	1990	CAR			677	698
0.00	LEMKE ,KW	MR	1992	JAE	PAGE ,MJ		87	114

4.15 TREATMENTS=BUSINESS COMBINATIONS

CITE INDEX	FIRST AUTHOR	ISS-UE	YE-AR	JOUR-NAL	SECOND AUTHOR	THIRD AUTHOR	PAG BEG	PAG END
2.50	SCHIPPER,K	SP	1983	JAR	THOMPSON,R		184	221
1.67	COLLINS,DW	OC	1990	JAE	DeANGELO,L		213	247
1.60	DEANGELO,LE	JA	1988	JAE			3	36
1.50	BARTOV,E	SE	1991	JAE			275	293
1.43	PALEPU,KG	MR	1986	JAE			3	36
1.29	ZIMMER,I	MR	1986	JAE			37	52
1.00	DANN ,LY	SE	1991	JAE	MASULIS,RW	MAYERS,D	217	251
1.00	HERTZER,M	SE	1991	JAE	JAIN ,PC		253	273
0.93	HONG ,H	JA	1978	TAR	KAPLAN,RS	MANDELKER,G	31	47
0.71	PASTENA,V	AP	1986	TAR	RULAND,W		288	301
0.67	MIAN ,SL	JA	1990	JAE	SMITH JR,CW		141	171
0.67	WHITTRED,G	DE	1987	JAE			259	285
0.65	GAGNON,JM	ST	1967	JAR			187	204
0.63	SCHIPPER,K	SP	1985	JAR	THOMPSON,R		408	415
0.55	SILHAN,PA	SP	1982	JAR			255	262
0.50	LEWELLEN,W	AP	1985	JAE	LODERER,C	ROSENFELD,A	209	232
0.50	TEHRANIAN,H	ST	1987	JAR	TRAVLOS,NG	WAEGELEIN,JF	51	76
0.33	HAW ,I	AP	1990	TAR	PASTENA,VS	LILIEN,SB	432	451
0.29	BLUM ,M	SP	1974	JAR			1	25
0.18	GAGNON,JM	SP	1971	JAR			52	72
0.13	JONES ,CS	03	1985	AOS			303	328
0.13	JONES ,CS	02	1985	AOS			177	200
0.13	PATTON,JM	AP	1978	TAR			402	414
0.12	COPELAND,RM	AU	1969	JAR	WOJDAK,JF		188	195
0.06	LARSON,KD	OC	1969	TAR	GONEDES,NJ		720	728
0.00	AMIT ,R	AU	1989	CAR	LIVNAT,J	ZAROWIN,P	143	158
0.00	BOATSMAN,JR	AU	1984	JAA	DOWELL,CD	KIMBRELL,JI	35	43
0.00	BRADBURY,ME	AP	1988	TAR	CALDERWOOD,SC		330	347
0.00	BRILOFF,AJ	JL	1967	TAR			489	496
0.00	CONROY,R	AU	1989	CAR	HUGHES,JS		159	176
0.00	CRUMBLEY,DL	JL	1968	TAR			554	564
0.00	CURLEY,AJ	JL	1971	TAR			519	528
0.00	DAVIS ,ML	AP	1988	TAR	LARGAY III,JA		348	363
0.00	DAVIS ,ML	JL	1990	TAR			696	709
0.00	EIGEN ,MM	JL	1965	TAR			536	540
0.00	HAW ,IM	WI	1987	JAA	PASTENA,V	LILIEN,S	24	42
0.00	HOLZMANN,OJ	WI	1984	JAA	MEANS ,KM		138	150
0.00	HORWITZ,BN	SP	1972	JAR	YOUNG ,AE		96	107
0.00	KHURANA,I	JL	1991	TAR			611	621
0.00	KING ,TE	SP	1979	JAA			209	223
0.00	LAUVER,RC	JA	1966	TAR			65	74
0.00	LEV ,B	JL	1970	TAR			532	534
0.00	LLOYD ,BM	OC	1971	TAR	WEYGANDT,JJ		756	764
0.00	MULFORD,CW	JL	1986	TAR	COMISKEY,EE		519	525
0.00	NIELSEN,CC	OC	1965	TAR			795	804
0.00	NORDHAUSER,SL	JA	1981	TAR	KRAMER,JL		54	69
0.00	O'CONNOR,MC	AP	1972	TAR	HAMRE ,JC		308	319
0.00	PARKER,WM	AU	1966	JAR			149	154

CITE INDEX	FIRST AUTHOR	ISS-UE	YE-AR	JOUR-NAL	SECOND AUTHOR	THIRD AUTHOR	PAG BEG	PAG END
0.00	PHILLIPS,LC	AP	1965	TAR			377	381
0.00	RAMANATHAN,KV	OC	1971	TAR	RAPPAPORT,A		733	745
0.00	ROBINSON,JR	JA	1990	TAR	SHANE ,PB		25	48
0.00	ROSMAN,A	SP	1992	JAA			251	267
0.00	SAPIENZA,SR	JA	1963	TAR			91	101
0.00	SAPIENZA,SR	JL	1964	TAR			582	590
0.00	SAPIENZA,SR	SP	1964	JAR			50	66
0.00	SILHAN,PA	SP	1985	JAR	MCKEOWN,JC		416	426
0.00	SMOLINSKI,EJ	AU	1963	JAR			149	178
0.00	TORABZADEH,KM	SP	1992	JAA	BERTIN,WJ		231	240
0.00	TUCKERMAN,B	JA	1964	TAR			32	37
0.00	WEIL ,RL	OC	1973	TAR			749	758
0.00	WYATT ,AR	JL	1965	TAR			527	535

4.16 TREATMENTS=INTERIM REPORTING

CITE INDEX	FIRST AUTHOR	ISS-UE	YE-AR	JOUR-NAL	SECOND AUTHOR	THIRD AUTHOR	PAG BEG	PAG END
2.00	GRANT ,EB	SP	1980	JAR			255	268
1.76	MAY ,RG	ST	1971	JAR			119	163
1.00	MCNICHOLS,M	AP	1983	JAE	MANEGOLD,JG		49	74
1.00	SHORES,D	SP	1990	JAR			164	181
0.81	HAKANSSON,NH	AP	1977	TAR			396	416
0.58	LEFTWICH,RW	ST	1981	JAR	WATTS ,RL	ZIMMERMAN,JL	50	77
0.47	GREEN ,D	ST	1966	JAR	SEGALL,J		21	36
0.44	COLLINS,WA	AU	1984	JAR	HOPWOOD,WS	MCKEOWN,JC	467	479
0.41	KIGER ,JE	SP	1972	JAR			113	128
0.35	COATES,R	ST	1972	JAR			132	144
0.18	REILLY,FK	ST	1972	JAR	MORGENSON,DL	WEST ,M	105	124
0.12	KIGER ,JE	JA	1974	TAR			1	7
0.09	WHALEY,RE	OC	1982	JAE	CHEUNG,JK		57	83
0.08	ALFORD,MR	SP	1981	JAA	EDMONDS,TP		255	264
0.06	BOLLOM,WJ	JA	1972	TAR	WEYGANDT,JJ		75	84
0.06	BOLLOM,WJ	JA	1973	TAR			12	22
0.06	BRUNS JR,WJ	ST	1966	JAR			1	14
0.06	FOGELBERG,G	AU	1971	JAR			215	235
0.06	GREEN ,D	SP	1964	JAR			35	49
0.00	BATHKE,AW	JA	1989	TAR	LOREK ,KS	WILLINGER,GL	49	68
0.00	BRENNAN,MJ	JA	1991	TAR			67	79
0.00	DONTOH,A	SP	1988	CAR	RICHARDSON,E		450	469
0.00	JONES ,CP	AU	1990	JAA	BUBLITZ,B		549	566
0.00	MENDENHALL,RR	ST	1988	JAR	NICHOLS,WD		63	90
0.00	SCHACHTER,B	AU	1988	JAR			353	372
0.00	TAYLOR,RG	JA	1965	TAR			89	96

4.17 TREATMENTS=AMORTIZATION/DEPLETION

CITE INDEX	FIRST AUTHOR	ISS-UE	YE-AR	JOUR-NAL	SECOND AUTHOR	THIRD AUTHOR	PAG BEG	PAG END
3.33	HOLTHAUSEN,RW	MR	1981	JAE			73	109
2.18	DHALIWAL,DS	JL	1982	JAE	SALAMON,GL	SMITH ,ED	41	53
0.06	FALK ,H	SP	1977	JAR	MILLER,JC		12	22
0.00	BIERMAN JR,H	AU	1964	JAR			229	235
0.00	GILLES JR,LH	OC	1963	TAR			776	784
0.00	SCHACHNER,L	AP	1968	TAR			303	311
0.00	WAKEMAN,LM	DE	1980	JAE			213	237

CITE INDEX	FIRST AUTHOR	ISS-UE	YE-AR	JOUR-NAL	SECOND AUTHOR	THIRD AUTHOR	PAG BEG	PAG END

4.18 TREATMENTS=SEGMENT REPORTS

CITE INDEX	FIRST AUTHOR	ISS-UE	YE-AR	JOUR-NAL	SECOND AUTHOR	THIRD AUTHOR	PAG BEG	PAG END
0.82	KINNEY JR,WR	SP	1971	JAR			127	136
0.56	BALDWIN,BA	JL	1984	TAR			376	389
0.50	SWAMINATHAN,S	JA	1991	TAR			23	41
0.36	COLLINS,DW	AU	1979	JAR	SIMONDS,RR		352	383
0.36	HOPWOOD,WS	AU	1982	JAR	NEWBOLD,P	SILHAN,PA	724	732
0.24	KOCHANEK,RF	AP	1974	TAR			245	258
0.23	AJINKYA,BB	AU	1980	JAR			343	361
0.18	DASCHER,PE	SP	1971	JAR	COPELAND,RM		32	39
0.18	ORTMAN,RF	AP	1975	TAR			298	304
0.17	RONEN ,J	AU	1981	JAR	LIVNAT,J		459	481
0.13	EICHENSEHER,JW	SP	1985	JAA			195	209
0.12	KINNEY JR,WR	AP	1972	TAR			339	345
0.00	BALAKRISHNAN,R	AU	1990	JAR	HARRIS,TS	SEN ,PK	305	325
0.00	FELTHAM,GA	AU	1992	CAR	GIGLER,FB	HUGHES,JS	1	23
0.00	HORWITZ,BN	AU	1980	JAA	KOLODNY,R		20	35
0.00	SANNELLA,AJ	AU	1986	JAA			288	304
0.00	SANNELLA,AJ	WI	1991	JAA			75	102
0.00	TSE ,S	SP	1989	CAR			592	614

4.19 TREATMENTS=FOREIGN CURRENCY

CITE INDEX	FIRST AUTHOR	ISS-UE	YE-AR	JOUR-NAL	SECOND AUTHOR	THIRD AUTHOR	PAG BEG	PAG END
1.43	AYRES ,FL	JN	1986	JAE			143	158
0.25	SALATKA,WK	FB	1989	JAE			35	69
0.17	ZIEBART,DA	AP	1987	TAR	KIM ,DH		343	357
0.12	ALIBER,RZ	JA	1975	TAR	STICKNEY,CP		44	57
0.10	HALL ,TW	SU	1983	JAA			299	313
0.07	AGGARWAL,R	SP	1978	JAA			197	216
0.00	AYRES ,FL	SP	1986	JAR			166	169
0.00	BENJAMIN,JJ	SU	1986	JAA	GROSSMAN,SD	WIGGIN,CE	177	184
0.00	BROWN ,BC	SU	1986	JAA	BRANDI,JT		185	205
0.00	CHENG ,TT	AU	1986	CAR			226	241
0.00	ELITZUR,RR	SP	1991	CAR			466	484
0.00	GRAY ,D	AU	1984	JAR			760	764
0.00	KIM ,DH	WI	1991	JAA	ZIEBART,DA		35	47
0.00	LARGAY III,JA	AU	1983	JAA			44	53

4.20 TREATMENTS=DIVIDENDS-CASH

CITE INDEX	FIRST AUTHOR	ISS-UE	YE-AR	JOUR-NAL	SECOND AUTHOR	THIRD AUTHOR	PAG BEG	PAG END
1.53	GONEDES,NJ	SP	1978	JAR			26	79
1.33	HEALY ,PM	JA	1990	JAE	PALEPU,KG		97	123
0.63	EASTON,PD	ST	1985	JAR			54	77
0.18	COPELAND,RM	JL	1968	TAR	LICASTRO,RD		540	545
0.00	HAW ,I	SU	1991	JAA	KIM ,W		325	344
0.00	HEALY ,PM	WI	1990	JAA	MODIGLIANI,F		3	25
0.00	KROSS ,W	AU	1980	JAA	CHAPMAN,G	STRAND,KH	36	46
0.00	RICHARDSON,G	AU	1988	CAR	SEFCIK,SE	THOMPSON,R	299	317
0.00	SHAW ,WH	SP	1991	CAR			407	423
0.00	STEVENS,JL	SP	1992	JAA	JOSE ,ML		195	212

4.21 TREATMENTS=DIVIDENDS-STOCK

CITE INDEX	FIRST AUTHOR	ISS-UE	YE-AR	JOUR-NAL	SECOND AUTHOR	THIRD AUTHOR	PAG BEG	PAG END
0.07	FOSTER III,TW	AP	1978	TAR	VICKREY,DW		360	370

CITE INDEX	FIRST AUTHOR	ISS-UE	YE-AR	JOUR-NAL	SECOND AUTHOR	THIRD AUTHOR	PAG BEG	PAG END
0.06	CHOTTINER,S	AU	1971	JAR	YOUNG ,AE		367	374
0.06	JAENICKE,HR	JA	1970	TAR			115	128
0.00	ASQUITH,P	JL	1989	TAR	HEALY ,P	PALEPU,K	387	403
0.00	DORAN ,DT	SP	1988	JAA	NACHTMANN,R		113	132
0.00	FIRTH ,MA	SP	1973	JAR			16	24
0.00	KISTLER,LH	OC	1967	TAR			758	766
0.00	MILLAR,JA	JA	1977	TAR			52	55
0.00	MONSON,NP	OC	1964	TAR	TRACY ,JA		890	893

4.22 TREATMENTS=PENSION (FUNDS)

CITE INDEX	FIRST AUTHOR	ISS-UE	YE-AR	JOUR-NAL	SECOND AUTHOR	THIRD AUTHOR	PAG BEG	PAG END
2.00	THOMAS,JK	OC	1992	TAR	TUNG ,S		691	711
1.33	FRANCIS,JR	AP	1987	JAE	REITER,SA		35	59
1.14	LANDSMAN,WR	OC	1986	TAR			662	691
0.89	DALEY ,LA	AP	1984	TAR			177	198
0.83	STONE ,M	AU	1987	JAR			317	326
0.75	MITTELSTAEDT,HF	NV	1989	JAE			399	418
0.75	THOMAS,JK	NV	1989	JAE			361	398
0.43	DHALIWAL,DS	OC	1986	TAR			651	661
0.33	HSIEH ,S-J	SP	1990	CAR	FERRIS,KR	CHEN ,AH	550	572
0.33	LANDSMAN,WR	AU	1990	CAR	OHLSON,JA		185	198
0.24	O'CONNOR,MC	AP	1973	TAR			339	352
0.13	MARKS ,BR	AU	1985	JAR	RAMAN ,KK		878	886
0.12	FRANK ,WG	AP	1970	TAR	WEYGANDT,JJ		280	289
0.06	HOFSTEDT,TR	AP	1971	TAR	WEST ,RR		329	337
0.06	MOONITZ,M	AU	1966	JAR	RUSS ,A		155	168
0.00	BAKER ,RE	JA	1964	TAR			52	61
0.00	BARTH ,ME	JL	1991	TAR			516	534
0.00	BARTH ,ME	MR	1992	JAE	BEAVER,WH	LANDSMAN,WR	27	61
0.00	BIERMAN JR,H	JA	1968	TAR	LIU ,E		62	67
0.00	DEWHIRST,JF	AP	1971	TAR			365	373
0.00	ENGSTROM,JH	SP	1984	JAA			197	211
0.00	ESPAHBODI,H	DE	1991	JAE	STROCK,E	TEHRANIAN,H	323	345
0.00	GHICAS,DC	AP	1990	TAR			384	405
0.00	HARPER JR,RM	AU	1987	JAR	MISTER,WG	STRAWSER,JR	327	330
0.00	HAW ,I	SE	1991	JAE	JUNG ,K	LILIEN,SB	295	320
0.00	JENKINS,DO	JL	1964	TAR			648	653
0.00	MAHER ,JJ	OC	1987	TAR			785	798
0.00	MARKS ,BR	SP	1988	CAR	RAMAN ,KK		595	608
0.00	MORRIS,MH	SU	1984	JAA	NICHOLS,WD		293	305
0.00	PESANDO,JE	OC	1983	TAR	CLARKE,CK		733	748
0.00	PHILIPS,GE	JA	1968	TAR			10	17
0.00	RUE ,JC	SU	1984	JAA	VOLKAN,AG		306	322
0.00	WELSH ,MJ	WI	1985	JAA	TRAPNELL,JE		100	111
0.00	WERNER,CA	AU	1983	JAA	KOSTOLANSKY,JW		54	64
0.00	WERNER,CA	SP	1984	JAA	KOSTOLANSKY,JW		212	224
0.00	WILLINGER,GL	SP	1985	JAR			351	359

4.23 TREATMENTS=OTHER – FIN.ACCGT

CITE INDEX	FIRST AUTHOR	ISS-UE	YE-AR	JOUR-NAL	SECOND AUTHOR	THIRD AUTHOR	PAG BEG	PAG END
1.50	BEAVER,WH	JA	1979	TAR	DEMSKI,JS		38	46
1.25	BERNARD,VL	OC	1989	TAR	STOBER,TL		624	652
1.00	BOATSMAN,JR	AP	1974	TAR	ROBERTSON,JC		342	352

CITE INDEX	FIRST AUTHOR	ISS-UE	YE-AR	JOUR-NAL	SECOND AUTHOR	THIRD AUTHOR	PAG BEG	PAG END
1.00	BOUWMAN,MJ	01	1987	AOS	FRISHKOFF,PA	FRISHKOFF,P	1	30
0.88	GORDON,MJ	AP	1964	TAR			251	263
0.65	IJIRI ,Y	JL	1966	TAR	JAEDICKE,RK		474	483
0.50	KOTHARI,SP	AP	1989	TAR	WASLEY,CE		228	249
0.25	ASHTON,RH	JL	1977	TAR			567	575
0.25	DAMOS ,P	03	1989	AOS	HOLT ,DL	IMHOFF JR,EA	235	246
0.18	CHAMBERS,RJ	AP	1964	TAR			264	274
0.17	OHLSON,JA	AU	1987	CAR			1	15
0.12	LARSON,KD	JA	1969	TAR			38	47
0.12	LIM ,R	OC	1966	TAR			642	651
0.12	VICKREY,DW	OC	1970	TAR			731	742
0.12	VICKREY,DW	JA	1976	TAR			31	40
0.12	WAGNER,JW	JL	1965	TAR			599	605
0.06	ARNETT,HE	AP	1967	TAR			291	297
0.06	BEDFORD,NM	JL	1968	TAR	IINO ,T		453	458
0.06	BURKE ,EJ	OC	1964	TAR			837	849
0.06	FREMGEN,JM	OC	1968	TAR			649	656
0.06	LARSON,KD	JL	1967	TAR			480	488
0.06	MCDONALD,DL	OC	1967	TAR			662	679
0.06	MURPHY,GJ	AP	1976	TAR			277	286
0.06	PARKER,JE	JL	1975	TAR			512	524
0.06	STERLING,RR	JL	1968	TAR			481	502
0.06	WOJDAK,JF	JA	1970	TAR			88	97
0.00	AMIHUD,Y	AU	1989	JAA	MENDELSON,H		415	431
0.00	AMIT ,R	WI	1988	JAA	LIVNAT,J		19	43
0.00	BARLEY,B	SU	1990	JAA	LIVNAT,J		411	433
0.00	BIRNBERG,JG	OC	1964	TAR			963	971
0.00	CHAMBERS,RJ	JL	1972	TAR			488	509
0.00	IJIRI ,Y	JL	1972	TAR			510	526
0.00	ISMAIL,BE	JA	1989	TAR	KIM ,MK		125	136
0.00	METCALF,RW	JA	1964	TAR			16	21
0.00	PATTERSON,RG	OC	1967	TAR			772	774
0.00	SCOTT ,RA	OC	1979	TAR			750	763
0.00	SPACEK,L	AP	1964	TAR			275	284
0.00	THODE ,SF	WI	1986	JAA	DRTINA,RE	LARGAY III,JA	46	61
0.00	THOMAS,JK	OC	1989	TAR			773	787
0.00	TINIC ,SM	OC	1990	TAR			781	796
0.00	WILLIAMSON,JE	JA	1971	TAR			139	148

4.24 REATMENTS=FIN. STATEMENT TIMING

CITE INDEX	FIRST AUTHOR	ISS-UE	YE-AR	JOUR-NAL	SECOND AUTHOR	THIRD AUTHOR	PAG BEG	PAG END
3.33	CHAMBERS,AE	SP	1984	JAR	PENMAN,SH		21	47
1.91	PATELL,JM	JL	1982	TAR	WOLFSON,MA		509	527
1.64	GIVOLY,D	JL	1982	TAR	PALMON,D		486	508
1.56	KROSS ,W	SP	1984	JAR	SCHROEDER,DA		153	176
1.00	BALL ,R	OC	1991	TAR	KOTHARI,SP		718	738
0.50	ATIASE,RK	SP	1989	CAR	BAMBER,LS	TSE ,S	526	552
0.46	OPPONG,A	AU	1980	JAR			574	584
0.40	SMITH ,DB	DE	1988	JAE	POURCIAU,S		335	344
0.24	ABDEL-KHALIK,AR	AP	1974	TAR			271	283
0.22	PENMAN,SH	DE	1984	JAE			165	183
0.11	WHITTRED,GP	AP	1984	TAR	ZIMMER,I		287	295
0.10	LAWRENCE,EC	AU	1983	JAR			606	610

CITE INDEX	FIRST AUTHOR	ISS-UE	YE-AR	JOUR-NAL	SECOND AUTHOR	THIRD AUTHOR	PAG BEG	PAG END
0.00	BOWEN ,RM	AU	1992	JAA	JOHNSON,MF	SHEVLIN,T	395	422
0.00	FRANCIS,J	AU	1992	JAR	PAGACH,D	STEPHAN,J	165	184
0.00	FREEMAN,R	DE	1992	JAE	TSE ,S		509	523
0.00	LANG ,M	AU	1991	JAR			229	257
0.00	STICE ,EK	JA	1991	TAR			42	55
0.00	WYMAN ,HE	JL	1976	TAR			545	558

4.25 TREATMENTS=R&D

CITE INDEX	FIRST AUTHOR	ISS-UE	YE-AR	JOUR-NAL	SECOND AUTHOR	THIRD AUTHOR	PAG BEG	PAG END
2.00	DALEY ,LA	DE	1983	JAE	VIGELAND,RL		195	211
1.38	DUKES ,RE	ST	1980	JAR	DYCKMAN,TR	ELLIOTT,JA	1	26
1.00	ELLIOTT,JA	SP	1984	JAR	RICHARDSON,G	DYCKMAN,TR	85	102
0.77	HORWITZ,BN	ST	1980	JAR	KOLODNY,R		38	74
0.67	ROCKNESS,HO	02	1984	AOS	SHIELDS,MD		165	177
0.50	BUBLITZ,B	JA	1989	TAR	ETTREDGE,M		108	124
0.50	HIRSCHEY,M	SP	1985	JAR	WEYGANDT,JJ		326	335
0.42	VIGELAND,RL	AP	1981	TAR			309	325
0.25	SELTO ,FH	AU	1985	JAR	CLOUSE,ML		700	717
0.12	JOHNSON,O	AU	1967	JAR			164	172
0.00	BABER ,WR	OC	1991	TAR	FAIRFIELD,PM	HAGGARD,JA	818	829
0.00	BEATTY,RP	SP	1989	CAR	VERRECCHIA,RE		472	493
0.00	CLINCH,G	SP	1991	JAR			59	78
0.00	COOPER,JC	03	1991	AOS	SELTO ,FH		227	242
0.00	DECHOW,PM	MR	1991	JAE	SLOAN ,RG		1	89
0.00	HORWITZ,B	JL	1988	TAR	NORMOLLE,D		414	435
0.00	PRATT ,J	04	1985	AOS			427	442
0.00	ROCKNESS,HO	SP	1988	CAR	SHIELDS,MD		568	581
0.00	SHEHATA,M	OC	1991	TAR			768	787
0.00	SHEVLIN,T	JA	1991	TAR			1	22

4.26 TREATMENTS=OIL & GAS

CITE INDEX	FIRST AUTHOR	ISS-UE	YE-AR	JOUR-NAL	SECOND AUTHOR	THIRD AUTHOR	PAG BEG	PAG END
3.33	COLLINS,DW	MR	1981	JAE	ROZEFF,MS	DHALIWAL,DS	37	71
3.15	FOSTER,G	MR	1980	JAE			29	62
2.64	COLLINS,DW	MR	1979	JAE	DENT ,WT		3	44
2.21	DYCKMAN,TR	MR	1979	JAE	SMITH ,AJ		45	75
1.93	LEV ,B	JL	1979	TAR			485	503
1.89	LYS ,T	AP	1984	JAE			39	65
1.82	LILIEN,S	DE	1982	JAE	PASTENA,V		145	170
1.50	HARRIS,TS	OC	1987	TAR	OHLSON,JA		651	670
1.00	DEAKIN,EB	OC	1979	TAR			722	734
1.00	DORAN ,BM	JL	1988	TAR	COLLINS,DW	DHALIWAL,DS	389	413
0.82	SUNDER,S	JA	1976	TAR			1	18
0.75	FROST ,CA	OC	1989	TAR			788	808
0.73	COLLINS,DW	JA	1982	TAR	ROZEFF,MS	SALATKA,WK	1	17
0.71	MAGLIOLO,J	ST	1986	JAR			69	111
0.67	HARRIS,TS	OC	1990	TAR	OHLSON,JA		764	780
0.67	MALMQUIST,DH	JA	1990	JAE			173	205
0.60	BELL ,TB	SP	1983	JAR			1	17
0.58	SMITH ,AJ	ST	1981	JAR			174	211
0.50	GHICAS,D	AU	1989	CAR	PASTENA,V		125	142
0.50	LARCKER,DF	OC	1983	TAR	REVSINE,L		706	732
0.45	DEANGELO,LE	DE	1982	JAE			171	203

CITE INDEX	FIRST AUTHOR	ISS-UE	YE-AR	JOUR-NAL	SECOND AUTHOR	THIRD AUTHOR	PAG BEG	PAG END
0.40	JOHNSON,WB	JA	1988	TAR	RAMANAN,R		96	110
0.33	DHARAN,BG	AP	1984	TAR			199	217
0.30	LARCKER,DF	JL	1983	TAR	REDER ,RE	SIMON ,DT	606	620
0.18	PATZ ,DH	AU	1972	JAR	BOATSMAN,JR		392	403
0.00	CLINCH,G	OC	1992	TAR	MAGLIOLO,J		843	861
0.00	DHARAN,BG	WI	1992	JAA	MASCARENHAS,B		1	21
0.00	GARSOMBKE,HP	SU	1983	JAA	ALLEN ,G		285	298
0.00	JAIN ,PC	JL	1983	TAR			633	638
0.00	KENNEDY,DT	SU	1992	JAA	HYON ,YH		335	356
0.00	KING ,RD	JA	1986	TAR	O'KEEFE,TB		76	90
0.00	PATTEN,DM	05	1992	AOS			471	475
0.00	TEALL ,HD	SP	1992	CAR			561	579
0.00	TEALL ,HD	SP	1992	CAR			561	579
0.00	WAYMIRE,G	AU	1983	JAR	POWNALL,G		629	643

4.27 TREATMENTS=AUDITING

CITE INDEX	FIRST AUTHOR	ISS-UE	YE-AR	JOUR-NAL	SECOND AUTHOR	THIRD AUTHOR	PAG BEG	PAG END
1.00	KINNEY-JR,WR	FB	1989	JAE	MCDANIEL,LS		71	93
0.91	CHOW ,CW	AP	1982	TAR			272	291
0.75	PALMROSE,Z	JL	1989	TAR			488	499
0.73	GIBBINS,M	JA	1982	TAR	WOLF ,FM		105	124
0.67	WILSON JR,TE	SP	1990	AUD	GRIMLUND,RA		43	59
0.64	NG ,DS	ST	1979	JAR	STOECKENIUS,J		1	24
0.54	EVANS III,JH	ST	1980	JAR			108	128
0.50	BABER ,WR	DE	1983	JAE			213	227
0.50	BAMBER,EM	AP	1989	TAR	SNOWBALL,D	TUBBS ,RM	285	299
0.50	BROWN ,CE	JA	1991	TAR	SOLOMON,I		100	119
0.47	DEMSKI,JS	JL	1974	TAR	SWIERINGA,RJ		506	513
0.47	NG ,DS	OC	1978	TAR			910	920
0.45	DANOS ,P	JA	1982	TAR	IMHOFF JR,EA		39	54
0.45	DIRSMITH,MW	SP	1982	JAA	MCALLISTER,JP		214	228
0.45	DIRSMITH,MW	AU	1982	JAA	MCALLISTER,JP		60	74
0.41	TOBA ,Y	JA	1975	TAR			7	24
0.40	NICHOLS,DR	AU	1983	JAR	SMITH ,DB		534	544
0.38	JIAMBALVO,J	AU	1985	AUD	WILNER,N		1	11
0.29	BLAZENKO,GW	AU	1986	CAR	SCOTT ,WR		68	92
0.29	NICHOLS,DR	AP	1976	TAR	PRICE ,KH		335	346
0.29	RHODE ,JG	OC	1974	TAR	WHITSELL,GM	KELSEY,RL	772	787
0.29	ZEFF ,SA	AP	1967	TAR	FOSSUM,RL		298	320
0.25	ARRINGTON,CE	SP	1985	JAR	BAILEY,CD	HOPWOOD,WS	1	20
0.25	SCOTT ,WR	SP	1977	JAR			120	137
0.24	SUMMERS,EL	JL	1972	TAR			443	453
0.23	BALACHANDRAN,BV	ST	1980	JAR	RAMAKRISHNAN,RT		140	171
0.22	MCCONNELL,DK	WI	1984	JAA			178	181
0.18	LENGERMANN,JJ	OC	1971	TAR			665	675
0.18	WILL ,HJ	OC	1974	TAR			690	706
0.18	WRIGHT,A	SP	1982	JAR			227	239
0.17	BERRY ,LE	JA	1987	TAR	HARWOOD,GB	KATZ ,JL	14	28
0.12	ANDERSON,HM	JL	1970	TAR	GIESE ,J	BOOKER,J	524	531
0.12	BRILOFF,AJ	JL	1966	TAR			484	495
0.12	CHURCHILL,NC	OC	1965	TAR	COOPER,WW		767	781
0.12	DECOSTER,DT	OC	1971	TAR	RHODE ,JG		651	664
0.12	ROBERTSON,JC	JL	1971	TAR	CLARKE,RW		562	571

CITE INDEX	FIRST AUTHOR	ISS-UE	YE-AR	JOUR-NAL	SECOND AUTHOR	THIRD AUTHOR	PAG BEG	PAG END
0.12	SMITH ,CH	AP	1972	TAR	LANIER,RA	TAYLOR,ME	270	283
0.12	STERLING,RR	SP	1969	JAR	RADOSEVICH,R		90	95
0.12	WELKER,RB	JL	1974	TAR			514	523
0.11	MCCONNELL,DK	SP	1984	AUD			44	56
0.09	BALACHANDRAN,KR	JA	1982	TAR	STEUER,RE		125	140
0.08	CHARNES,A	01	1980	AOS	COOPER,WW		87	107
0.07	GIVOLY,D	SU	1978	JAA	RONEN ,J	SCHIFF,A	361	372
0.06	CHURCHILL,NC	ST	1966	JAR			128	156
0.06	SAN MIGUEL,JG	04	1977	AOS	SHANK ,JK	GOVINDARAJAN,V	333	348
0.06	WILKINSON,JR	OC	1965	TAR	DONEY ,LD		753	756
0.00	ANDERSON,MJ	OC	1990	TAR	ANDERSON,U	HELLELOID,R	857	874
0.00	CAREY ,JL	JA	1968	TAR			1	9
0.00	CARMICHAEL,DR	SU	1979	JAA			294	306
0.00	COHEN ,MF	JA	1965	TAR			1	8
0.00	DAVIS ,GB	SP	1963	JAR			96	101
0.00	DEITRICK,JW	SU	1979	JAA	ALDERMAN,CW		316	328
0.00	GIBSON,RW	JA	1965	TAR			196	203
0.00	HAFNER,GF	OC	1964	TAR			979	982
0.00	HAM ,J	SP	1986	CAR	LOSELL,D	SMIELIAUSKAS,W	311	317
0.00	IJIRI ,Y	OC	1968	TAR			662	667
0.00	KAY ,RS	SU	1979	JAA			307	315
0.00	KNAPP ,MC	JL	1987	TAR			578	588
0.00	MARKS ,BR	AU	1987	AUD	RAMAN ,KK		106	117
0.00	MOREY ,L	JA	1963	TAR			102	108
0.00	PENNO ,M	JL	1990	TAR			520	536
0.00	RAMAN ,KK	SU	1981	JAA			352	359
0.00	SEIDLER,LJ	SU	1979	JAA			285	293
0.00	SMITH ,G	AU	1991	AUD	KROGSTAD,JL		84	97
0.00	STAATS,EB	SU	1981	AUD			1	11
0.00	SWANSON,GA	JL	1988	TAR	GARDNER,JC		436	447
0.00	VASARHELYI,MA	AU	1984	AUD			100	106
0.00	WILCOX,KA	01	1977	AOS	SMITH ,CH		81	97

4.28 TREATMENTS=OPINION

CITE INDEX	FIRST AUTHOR	ISS-UE	YE-AR	JOUR-NAL	SECOND AUTHOR	THIRD AUTHOR	PAG BEG	PAG END
1.56	DODD ,P	AP	1984	JAE	DOPUCH,N	HOLTHAUSEN,RW	3	38
1.10	KELLER,SB	AU	1983	AUD	DAVIDSON,LF		1	22
1.00	CHOW ,CW	AP	1982	TAR	RICE ,SJ		326	335
1.00	DOPUCH,N	JL	1987	TAR	HOLTHAUSEN,RW	LEFTWICH,RW	431	454
1.00	ELLIOTT,JA	AU	1982	JAR			617	638
0.88	MUTCHLER,JF	AU	1985	JAR			668	682
0.69	KIDA ,TE	AU	1980	JAR			506	523
0.64	LIBBY ,R	SP	1979	JAR			99	122
0.62	WHITTRED,GP	OC	1980	TAR			563	577
0.57	DOPUCH,N	JN	1986	JAE	HOLTHAUSEN,RW	LEFTWICH,RW	93	118
0.57	LIBBY ,R	ST	1979	JAR			35	57
0.56	MUTCHLER,JF	SP	1984	AUD			17	30
0.53	FIRTH ,MA	JL	1978	TAR			642	650
0.38	KNAPP ,MC	AP	1985	TAR			202	211
0.36	CHOW ,CW	WI	1982	AUD	RICE ,SJ		35	53
0.33	SHANK ,JK	OC	1978	TAR	MURDOCK,RJ		824	835
0.29	SMITH ,DB	AU	1986	AUD			95	108
0.25	KISSINGER,JN	AP	1977	TAR			322	339

CITE INDEX	FIRST AUTHOR	ISS-UE	YE-AR	JOUR-NAL	SECOND AUTHOR	THIRD AUTHOR	PAG BEG	PAG END
0.25	LEVITAN,AS	AU	1985	AUD	KNOBLETT,JA		26	39
0.24	WARREN,CS	SP	1975	JAR			162	176
0.18	DAVIS ,RR	AU	1982	AUD			13	32
0.06	CLARKE,RW	OC	1968	TAR			769	776
0.06	KINNEY JR,WR	SP	1969	JAR			44	52
0.00	ABDEL-KHALIK,AR	AU	1986	JAR	GRAUL ,PR	NEWTON,JD	372	382
0.00	BAILEY,KE	AU	1983	JAR	BYLINSKI,JH	SHIELDS,MD	355	370
0.00	BAILEY,WT	OC	1981	TAR			882	896
0.00	BELL ,TB	AU	1991	JAR	TABOR ,RH		350	370
0.00	CHEN ,KCW	AU	1992	AUD	CHURCH,BK		30	49
0.00	CHOI ,SK	JN	1992	JAE	JETER ,DC		229	247
0.00	DANOS ,P	SP	1987	AUD	HOLT ,DL	BAILEY JR,AD	134	149
0.00	FIELDS,LP	AU	1991	AUD	WILKINS,MS		62	69
0.00	JOHNSON,DA	SP	1983	AUD	PANY ,K	WHITE ,RA	38	51
0.00	LOUDDER,ML	SP	1992	AUD	KHURANA,IK	SAWYERS,RB	69	82
0.00	MITTELSTAEDT,HF	SP	1992	AUD	REGIER,PR	CHEWNING,EG	83	98
0.00	MUTCHLER,JF	AU	1986	AUD			148	.
0.00	NIX ,HM	SU	1983	JAA	WICHMANN JR,H		341	352
0.00	NORGAARD,CT	JL	1972	TAR			433	442
0.00	PANY ,K	AU	1982	JAR	SMITH ,CH		472	481
0.00	PILLSBURY,CM	SP	1985	AUD			63	79
0.00	TOBA ,Y	OC	1980	TAR			604	619
0.00	WARREN,CS	SP	1980	JAR			312	324
0.00	ZEFF ,SA	SP	1992	CAR			443	467

4.29 TREATMENTS=SAMPLING

CITE INDEX	FIRST AUTHOR	ISS-UE	YE-AR	JOUR-NAL	SECOND AUTHOR	THIRD AUTHOR	PAG BEG	PAG END
1.35	SCOTT ,WR	AU	1973	JAR			304	330
1.29	KAPLAN,RS	AU	1973	JAR			238	258
1.29	KINNEY JR,WR	SP	1975	JAR			117	132
1.19	FELIX JR,WL	SP	1977	JAR	GRIMLUND,RA		23	41
1.18	CORLESS,JC	JL	1972	TAR			556	566
0.94	KINNEY JR,WR	ST	1975	JAR			14	29
0.91	LEITCH,RA	AP	1982	TAR	NETER ,J	PLANTE,R	384	400
0.89	DWORIN,L	AP	1984	TAR	GRIMLUND,RA		218	241
0.78	GODFREY,JT	AU	1984	JAR	NETER ,J		497	525
0.73	NETER ,J	JA	1978	TAR	LEITCH,RA	FIENBERG,SE	77	93
0.71	DWORIN,L	JA	1986	TAR	GRIMLUND,RA		36	57
0.71	SCOTT ,WR	ST	1975	JAR			98	117
0.70	MENZEFRICKE,U	SP	1983	JAR			96	105
0.69	UECKER,WC	03	1977	AOS	KINNEY JR,WR		269	275
0.67	MCCRAY,JH	JA	1984	TAR			35	51
0.65	KAPLAN,RS	SP	1973	JAR			38	46
0.64	GRIMLUND,RA	AU	1982	JAR			316	342
0.60	GRIMLUND,RA	AU	1988	AUD	SCHROEDER,MS		53	62
0.57	GARSTKA,SJ	SP	1979	JAR	OHLSON,PA		23	59
0.57	SMIELIAUSKAS,W	AU	1986	CAR			102	124
0.55	FROST ,PA	SP	1982	JAR	TAMURA,H		103	120
0.53	KAPLAN,RS	ST	1975	JAR			126	133
0.50	FELLINGHAM,JC	SP	1989	AUD	NEWMAN,DP	PATTERSON,ER	1	21
0.50	GRIMLUND,RA	JL	1987	TAR	FELIX JR,WL		455	479
0.50	TSUI ,KW	JA	1985	TAR	MATSUMURA,EM	TSUI ,KL	76	96
0.47	RENEAU,JH	JL	1978	TAR			669	680

CITE INDEX	FIRST AUTHOR	ISS-UE	YE-AR	JOUR-NAL	SECOND AUTHOR	THIRD AUTHOR	PAG BEG	PAG END
0.43	SMIELIAUSKAS,W	JA	1986	TAR			118	128
0.41	SORENSEN,JE	JL	1969	TAR			555	561
0.41	TRACY ,JA	JA	1969	TAR			90	98
0.40	MENZEFRICKE,U	SP	1988	CAR	SMIELIAUSKAS,W		314	336
0.38	BECK ,PJ	SP	1985	AUD	SOLOMON,I		1	10
0.36	GODFREY,JT	AU	1982	JAR	ANDREWS,RW		304	315
0.36	KINNEY JR,WR	AU	1979	JAR			456	475
0.35	DEAKIN,EB	OC	1974	TAR	GRANOF,MH		764	771
0.33	MATSUMURA,EM	SP	1990	CAR	TSUI ,K-W	WONG ,W-K	485	500
0.29	ABDOLMOHAMMADI,MJ	SP	1986	AUD			1	16
0.29	IJIRI ,Y	SP	1971	JAR	KAPLAN,RS		73	87
0.29	TEITLEBAUM,AD	ST	1975	JAR	ROBINSON,CF		70	91
0.25	HEIMANN,SR	AU	1977	JAR	CHESLEY,GR		193	206
0.25	PLANTE,R	AU	1985	AUD	NETER ,J	LEITCH,RA	40	56
0.20	FINLEY,DR	AU	1983	AUD			104	116
0.20	GRIMLUND,RA	SP	1988	AUD			77	104
0.19	GARSTKA,SJ	AU	1977	JAR			179	192
0.18	LOEBBECKE,JK	ST	1975	JAR	NETER ,J		38	52
0.17	KIM ,HS	SP	1987	AUD	NETER ,J	GODFREY,JT	40	58
0.17	MENZEFRICKE,U	AU	1987	CAR	SMIELIAUSKAS,W		240	250
0.14	ANDERSON,JC	JL	1986	TAR	KRAUSHAAR,JM		379	399
0.14	DUNMORE,PV	AU	1986	CAR			125	148
0.14	HUSS ,HF	AU	1986	JAR	TRADER,RL		394	399
0.14	SMIELIAUSKAS,W	SP	1986	JAR			217	230
0.14	TAMURA,H	AU	1986	JAR	FROST ,PA		364	371
0.13	CROSBY,MA	SP	1985	AUD			118	132
0.12	SMITH ,KA	AP	1972	TAR			260	269
0.11	NETER ,J	AU	1984	AUD	KIM ,HS	GRAHAM,LE	75	88
0.09	MATSUMURA,EM	SP	1982	JAR	TSUI ,KW		162	170
0.06	ALY ,HF	JA	1971	TAR	DUBOFF,JI		119	128
0.06	SAULS ,EH	ST	1970	JAR			157	171
0.06	SAULS ,EH	JA	1972	TAR			109	115
0.00	BIDDLE,GC	AU	1990	AUD	BRUTON,CM	SIEGEL,AF	92	114
0.00	BLOCHER,E	AU	1985	AUD	BYLINSKI,JH		79	90
0.00	BONETT,DG	SP	1990	CAR	CLUTE ,RD		432	445
0.00	CHAN ,H	AU	1990	AUD	SMIELIAUSKAS,W		167	182
0.00	CHARNES,A	AP	1964	TAR	DAVIDSON,HJ	KORTANEK,KO	241	250
0.00	DEMING,WE	SP	1979	JAA			197	208
0.00	DHAVALE,DG	SP	1991	AUD			159	166
0.00	DWORIN,L	SP	1989	CAR	GRIMLUND,RA		674	691
0.00	FELIX JR,WL	AU	1990	AUD	GRIMLUND,RA	KOSTER,FJ	1	16
0.00	FINLEY,DR	SP	1987	AUD	BOOCKHOLDT,JL		22	39
0.00	FINLEY,DR	SP	1989	CAR			692	719
0.00	FROST ,PA	SP	1986	JAR	TAMURA,H		57	75
0.00	GRIMLUND,RA	SP	1990	CAR			446	484
0.00	HALL ,TW	SP	1989	AUD	PIERCE,BJ	ROSS ,WR	64	89
0.00	HANSEN,DR	JA	1977	TAR	SHAFTEL,TL		109	123
0.00	KO ,CE	SP	1988	AUD	NACHTSHEIM,CJ	DUKE ,GL	119	136
0.00	MAXIM ,LD	JA	1976	TAR	CULLEN,PE	COOK ,FX	97	109
0.00	PEEK ,LE	AU	1991	AUD	NETER ,J	WARREN,C	33	48
0.00	POWER ,MK	01	1992	AOS			37	62
0.00	ROBERTS,DM	AU	1980	JAA			57	69
0.00	ROBERTS,DM	SP	1986	JAR			111	126

CITE INDEX	FIRST AUTHOR	ISS-UE	YE-AR	JOUR-NAL	SECOND AUTHOR	THIRD AUTHOR	PAG BEG	PAG END
0.00	ROHRBACH.KJ	SP	1986	JAR			127	150
0.00	ROSHWALB,A	AU	1987	AUD	WRIGHT,RL	GODFREY,JT	54	70
0.00	SMIELIAUSKAS,W		1990	AUD			149	166
0.00	TAMURA,H	SP	1985	AUD			133	142
0.00	WRIGHT,DW	SP	1991	AUD			145	158

4.30 TREATMENTS=LIABILITY

CITE INDEX	FIRST AUTHOR	ISS-UE	YE-AR	JOUR-NAL	SECOND AUTHOR	THIRD AUTHOR	PAG BEG	PAG END
1.33	ST.PIERRE,K	AP	1984	TAR	ANDERSON,JA		242	263
1.00	DOPUCH,N	JA	1992	TAR	KING ,RR		97	120
1.00	WALLIN,DE	JA	1992	TAR			121	147
0.78	MENZEFRICKE,U	AU	1984	JAR	SMIELIAUSKAS,W		588	604
0.60	KOTHARI,SP	AU	1988	JAA	LYS ,T	SMITH ,CW	307	340
0.53	SCHULTZ JR,JJ	JL	1978	TAR	GUSTAVSON,SG		626	641
0.50	BALACHANDRAN,BV	SP	1987	CAR	NAGARAJAN,NJ		281	301
0.33	MENZEFRICKE,U	AU	1984	JAR			570	587
0.25	MOORE ,G	SP	1989	CAR	SCOTT ,WR		754	774
0.20	GORMLEY,RJ	SU	1988	JAA			185	212
0.20	NELSON,J	SU	1988	JAA	RONEN ,J	WHITE ,L	255	296
0.20	SORTER,GH	SU	1988	JAA	SIEGEL,S	SLAIN ,J	233	244
0.13	ANDERSON,JA	AP	1977	TAR			417	426
0.12	CAUSEY JR,DY	JA	1976	TAR			19	30
0.11	DEJONG,DV	AU	1984	AUD	SMITH ,JH		20	34
0.06	THEIL ,H	JA	1969	TAR			27	37
0.00	DOPUCH,N	SU	1988	JAA			245	250
0.00	GOLDWASSER,DL	SU	1988	JAA			217	232
0.00	JENNINGS,MM	SP	1991	CAR	KNEER ,DC	RECKERS,PMJ	449	465
0.00	LILLESTOL,J	SP	1981	JAR			263	267
0.00	SCHNEPPER,JA	JL	1977	TAR			653	657
0.00	SLAVIN,NS	AP	1977	TAR			360	368
0.00	WALLACE,WA	SP	1983	AUD			66	90

4.31 TREATMENTS=RISK

CITE INDEX	FIRST AUTHOR	ISS-UE	YE-AR	JOUR-NAL	SECOND AUTHOR	THIRD AUTHOR	PAG BEG	PAG END
1.30	CUSHING,BE	AU	1983	AUD	LOEBBECKE,JK		23	41
0.78	GROBSTEIN,M	SP	1984	AUD	CRAIG ,PW		1	16
0.67	SHIBANO,T	ST	1990	JAR			110	147
0.50	KINNEY JR,WR	SP	1983	AUD			13	22
0.38	BECK ,PJ	SP	1985	JAR	SOLOMON,I	TOMASSINI,LA	37	56
0.33	BROWN ,CE	AU	1990	AUD	SOLOMON,I		17	38
0.25	SMIELIAUSKAS,W	AU	1985	JAR			718	739
0.14	BUTLER,SA	JA	1986	TAR			101	111
0.11	JIAMBALVO,J	SP	1984	AUD	WALLER,WS		80	88
0.00	BARKMAN,A	JA	1977	TAR			450	464
0.00	DANIEL,SJ	SP	1988	AUD			174	181
0.00	GORMLEY,RJ	SU	1980	JAA			293	312
0.00	GRAHAM,LE	SP	1991	AUD	DAMENS,J	VAN NESS,G	69	96
0.00	HOLT ,DL	06	1992	AOS	MORROW,PC		549	559
0.00	HUSS ,HF	AU	1991	AUD	JACOBS,FA		16	32
0.00	KINNEY JR,WR		1989	AUD			67	84
0.00	MILTZ ,D	AU	1991	AUD	CALOMME,GJ	WILLIKENS,M	49	61
0.00	PETERS,JM	ST	1990	JAR			83	109
0.00	SENNETTI,JT	SP	1990	AUD			103	112

CITE INDEX	FIRST AUTHOR	ISS-UE	YE-AR	JOUR-NAL	SECOND AUTHOR	THIRD AUTHOR	PAG BEG	PAG END
0.00	SIMUNIC,DA	SP	1990	CAR	STEIN ,MT		329	343
0.00	SMIELIAUSKAS,W	SP	1989	CAR			720	732
0.00	STRAWSER,JR	SP	1991	AUD			126	135
0.00	WAGGONER,JB	SP	1990	AUD			77	89

4.32 TREATMENTS=INDEPENDENCE

CITE INDEX	FIRST AUTHOR	ISS-UE	YE-AR	JOUR-NAL	SECOND AUTHOR	THIRD AUTHOR	PAG BEG	PAG END
2.25	DEANGELO,LE	AG	1981	JAE			113	127
1.33	MAGEE ,RP	AP	1990	TAR	TSENG ,M		315	336
1.00	ANTLE ,R	SP	1984	JAR			1	20
0.67	PONEMON,LA	AU	1990	CAR	GABHART,DRL		227	251
0.56	SIMUNIC,DA	AU	1984	JAR			679	702
0.50	FARMER,TA	AU	1987	AUD	RITTENBERG,LE	TROMPETER,GM	1	14
0.42	SHOCKLEY,RA	OC	1981	TAR			785	800
0.35	GOLDMAN,A	OC	1974	TAR	BARLEV,B		707	718
0.35	LAVIN ,D	JA	1976	TAR			41	50
0.33	PANY ,K	SP	1984	AUD	RECKERS,PMJ		89	97
0.23	PANY ,K	JA	1980	TAR	RECKERS,PMJ		50	61
0.19	LAVIN ,D	03	1977	AOS			237	244
0.18	SCHULTE JR,AA	JL	1965	TAR			587	593
0.18	SHOCKLEY,RA	WI	1982	JAA			126	143
0.17	RECKERS,PMJ	SU	1981	AUD	STAGLIANO,AJ		23	37
0.08	FIRTH ,MA	JL	1980	TAR			451	466
0.06	CARMICHAEL,DR	OC	1968	TAR	SWIERINGA,RJ		697	705
0.00	DEIS JR,DR	JL	1992	TAR	GIROUX,GA		462	479
0.00	DOPUCH,N	ST	1991	JAR	KING ,RR		60	106
0.00	DYKXHOORN,HJ	JA	1981	TAR	SINNING,KE		97	107
0.00	DYKXHOORN,HJ	04	1982	AOS	SINNING,KE		337	348
0.00	IMHOFF JR,EA	OC	1978	TAR			869	881
0.00	KELL ,WG	AP	1968	TAR			266	273
0.00	PANY ,K	AU	1987	AUD	RECKERS,PMJ		39	53
0.00	SCHATZBERG,JW	AP	1990	TAR			337	362
0.00	SCHULTE JR,AA	OC	1966	TAR			721	728
0.00	ST.PIERRE,K	SP	1984	JAA			257	263
0.00	YOON ,SS		1990	AUD			253	275

4.33 TREATMENTS=ANALYTICAL REVIEW

CITE INDEX	FIRST AUTHOR	ISS-UE	YE-AR	JOUR-NAL	SECOND AUTHOR	THIRD AUTHOR	PAG BEG	PAG END
3.00	LIBBY ,R	AU	1985	JAR			648	667
1.40	BIGGS ,SF	JA	1988	TAR	MOCK ,TJ	WATKINS,PR	148	162
1.14	KINNEY JR,WR	ST	1979	JAR			148	165
1.00	KINNEY JR,WR	JA	1982	TAR	UECKER,WC		55	69
1.00	WRIGHT,A	OC	1989	TAR	ASHTON,RH		710	728
0.94	STRINGER,KW	ST	1975	JAR			1	9
0.87	KINNEY JR,WR	JA	1978	TAR			48	60
0.67	HEIMAN,VB	OC	1990	TAR			875	890
0.50	BIGGS ,SF	OC	1985	TAR	WILD ,JJ		607	633
0.50	COHEN ,J	AU	1989	JAR	KIDA ,T		263	276
0.50	KINNEY JR,WR	SP	1987	AUD			59	73
0.44	ARRINGTON,CE	SP	1984	JAR	HILLISON,WA	JENSEN,RE	298	312
0.40	KNECHEL,WR	JA	1988	TAR			74	95
0.33	LOEBBECKE,JK	SP	1987	AUD	STEINBART,PJ		74	89
0.31	LEV ,B	AU	1980	JAR			524	550

CITE INDEX	FIRST AUTHOR	ISS-UE	YE-AR	JOUR-NAL	SECOND AUTHOR	THIRD AUTHOR	PAG BEG	PAG END
0.25	DAROCA,FP	SP	1985	AUD	HOLDER,WW		80	92
0.25	TABOR ,RH	SP	1985	AUD	WILLIS,JT		93	109
0.22	BIGGS ,SF	SP	1984	AUD	WILD ,JJ		68	79
0.20	HOLDER,WW	SP	1983	AUD			100	108
0.20	KNECHEL,WR	AU	1988	AUD			87	107
0.18	KINNEY JR,WR	AU	1982	JAR	SALAMON,GL		350	366
0.13	CASH JR,JI	OC	1977	TAR	BAILEY JR,AD	WHINSTON,AB	813	832
0.10	BLOCHER,E	AU	1983	AUD	ESPOSITO,RS	WILLINGHAM,JJ	75	91
0.00	ANDERSON,JC	AU	1992	AUD	KAPLAN,SE	RECKERS,PMJ	1	13
0.00	BEDARD,JC		1991	AUD	BIGGS ,SF		77	90
0.00	BLOCHER,E	SP	1988	AUD	COOPER,JC		1	28
0.00	COGLITORE,F	SP	1988	AUD	BERRYMAN,RG		150	163
0.00	DUGAN ,MT	SP	1985	AUD	GENTRY,JA	SHRIVER,KA	11	22
0.00	HARPER JR,RM	AU	1990	AUD	STRAWSER,JR	TANG ,K	115	133
0.00	HEINTZ,JA	SP	1989	AUD	WHITE ,GB		22	39
0.00	IMHOFF JR,EA	SU	1981	JAA			333	351
0.00	KAPLAN,RS	SP	1983	AUD			52	65
0.00	KAPLAN,SE	AU	1992	AUD	MOECKEL,C	WILLIAMS,JD	50	65
0.00	KINNEY JR,WR	AU	1981	JAA			5	17
0.00	KOONCE,L	JA	1992	TAR			59	76
0.00	LOREK ,KS	AU	1992	AUD	BRANSON,BC	ICERMAN,RC	66	88
0.00	PENMAN,SH	JL	1992	TAR			563	578
0.00	WILD ,JJ	JA	1990	TAR	BIGGS ,SF		227	241
0.00	WILSON,AC	SP	1989	AUD	GLEZEN,GW		90	100
0.00	WILSON,AC	AU	1989	CAR	HUDSON,D		196	215
0.00	WILSON,AC	SU	1991	JAA			365	381
0.00	WILSON,AC	SP	1992	AUD			32	46

4.34 TREATMENTS=INTERNAL CONTROL

CITE INDEX	FIRST AUTHOR	ISS-UE	YE-AR	JOUR-NAL	SECOND AUTHOR	THIRD AUTHOR	PAG BEG	PAG END
2.71	ASHTON,RH	SP	1974	JAR			143	157
1.43	NEIMARK,M	45	1986	AOS	TINKER,T		369	396
1.36	HAMILTON,RE	AU	1982	JAR	WRIGHT,WF		756	765
1.10	BIGGS ,SF	SP	1983	JAR	MOCK ,TJ		234	255
0.75	LIBBY ,R	AP	1985	TAR	ARTMAN,JT	WILLINGHAM,JJ	212	230
0.69	ASHTON,RH	SP	1980	JAR	BROWN ,PR		269	277
0.67	HASKINS,M	JL	1987	TAR			542	563
0.65	CUSHING,BE	JA	1974	TAR			24	41
0.65	YU ,S	AU	1973	JAR	NETER ,J		273	295
0.64	GAUMNITZ,BR	AU	1982	JAR	NUNAMAKER,TR	SURDICK,JJ	745	755
0.57	MESERVY,RD	AU	1986	AUD	BAILEY JR,AD	JOHNSON,PE	44	74
0.47	BODNAR,G	OC	1975	TAR			747	757
0.44	NANNI JR,AJ	02	1984	AOS			149	163
0.40	WEBER ,R	AU	1978	JAR			368	388
0.38	BAILEY JR,AD	AP	1985	TAR	DUKE ,GL	GERLACH,JH	186	201
0.35	CARMICHAEL,DR	AP	1970	TAR			235	245
0.33	FERRIS,KR	SP	1984	AUD	TENNANT,KL		31	43
0.29	RECKERS,PMJ	AU	1979	JAA	TAYLOR,ME		42	55
0.25	KNECHEL,WR	SP	1985	AUD			38	62
0.20	TABOR ,RH	SP	1983	JAR			348	354
0.17	BAILEY,AP	SU	1981	AUD	MCAFEE,RP	WHINSTON,AB	38	52
0.17	WIGGINS JR,CE	SP	1987	CAR	SMITH ,LW		316	337
0.14	DERMER,JD	06	1986	AOS	LUCAS ,RG		471	482

CITE INDEX	FIRST AUTHOR	ISS-UE	YE-AR	JOUR-NAL	SECOND AUTHOR	THIRD AUTHOR	PAG BEG	PAG END
0.14	EVANS III,JH	06	1986	AOS	LEWIS ,BL	PATTON,JM	483	498
0.14	YOUNG ,R	SP	1986	JAR			231	240
0.13	KAPLAN,SE	AU	1985	JAR			871	877
0.10	MOCK ,TJ	SP	1983	AUD	WILLINGHAM,JJ		91	99
0.08	HAMLEN,SS	AP	1980	TAR	HAMLEN,WA	TSCHIRHART,JT	269	287
0.06	MAUTZ ,RK	AP	1966	TAR	MINI ,DL		283	291
0.00	BABER ,WR	SP	1985	JAR			360	369
0.00	BALACHANDRAN,BV	WI	1988	JAA	RAMANAN,R		1	13
0.00	BOWER ,JB	AP	1965	TAR	SCHLOSSER,RE		338	344
0.00	COOPER,WW	AU	1985	JAA	HO ,JL	HUNTER,JE	22	39
0.00	DAS ,H	03	1986	AOS			215	232
0.00	FELIX JR,WL	SP	1988	AUD	NILES ,MS		43	60
0.00	FISHER,M	SU	1978	JAA			349	360
0.00	GERLACH,JH	SP	1988	AUD			61	76
0.00	JAWORKSI,BJ	01	1992	AOS	YOUNG ,SM		17	35
0.00	JONES ,CS	02	1992	AOS			151	168
0.00	MCBRIDE,HJ	AP	1963	TAR			363	370
0.00	NICHOLS,DR	JA	1987	TAR			183	190
0.00	PURVIS,SEC	06	1989	AOS			551	563
0.00	SRINIDHI,BN	SP	1986	AUD	VASARHELYI,MA		64	76
0.00	SRIVASTAVA,RP	AU	1986	JAR			422	427
0.00	ZANNETOS,ZS	OC	1964	TAR			860	868

4.35 TREATMENTS=TIMING

CITE INDEX	FIRST AUTHOR	ISS-UE	YE-AR	JOUR-NAL	SECOND AUTHOR	THIRD AUTHOR	PAG BEG	PAG END
0.47	DYER ,JC	AU	1975	JAR	MCHUGH,AJ		204	219
0.33	ASHTON,RH	AU	1987	JAR	WILLINGHAM,JJ	ELLIOTT,RK	275	292
0.25	HUGHES,JS	JA	1977	TAR			56	68
0.00	ANDERSON,U	AU	1988	AUD	YOUNG ,RA		23	42
0.00	ASHTON,RH	SP	1989	CAR	GRAUL ,PR	NEWTON,JD	657	673
0.00	BARTOV,E	JL	1992	TAR			610	622
0.00	KISSINGER,JN	AU	1983	AUD			42	54
0.00	NEWTON,JD		1989	AUD	ASHTON,RH		22	37
0.00	TRUEMAN,B	OC	1990	JAE			285	301

4.36 TREATMENTS=MATERIALITY

CITE INDEX	FIRST AUTHOR	ISS-UE	YE-AR	JOUR-NAL	SECOND AUTHOR	THIRD AUTHOR	PAG BEG	PAG END
1.10	MESSIER JR,WF	AU	1983	JAR			611	618
0.88	MORIARITY,S	AU	1976	JAR	BARRON,FH		320	341
0.80	MORRIS,MH	AP	1988	TAR	NICHOLS,WD		237	254
0.73	HOLSTRUM,GL	AU	1982	AUD	MESSIER JR,WF		45	63
0.67	KROGSTAD,JL	AU	1984	AUD	ETTENSON,RT	SHANTEAU,J	54	74
0.65	ROSE ,R	ST	1970	JAR	BEAVER,WH	BECKER,S	138	148
0.57	MORIARITY,S	ST	1979	JAR	BARRON,FH		114	135
0.53	FRISHKOFF,P	ST	1970	JAR			116	129
0.50	CHEWNING,G	SP	1989	JAR	PANY ,K	WHEELER,S	78	96
0.50	STEINBART,PJ	JA	1987	TAR			97	116
0.47	WARD ,BH	SP	1976	JAR			138	152
0.41	NEUMANN,FL	ST	1968	JAR			1	17
0.33	JENNINGS,M	SP	1987	AUD	KNEER ,DC	RECKERS,PMJ	104	115
0.29	BERNSTEIN,LA	JA	1967	TAR			86	95
0.29	FIRTH ,MA	04	1979	AOS			283	296
0.25	MAYPER,AG	AU	1989	AUD	DOUCET,MS	WARREN,CS	72	86

CITE INDEX	FIRST AUTHOR	ISS-UE	YE-AR	JOUR-NAL	SECOND AUTHOR	THIRD AUTHOR	PAG BEG	PAG END
0.13	KELLY ,LK	JA	1977	TAR			97	108
0.09	LANDSITTEL,DL	SU	1982	JAA	SERLIN,JE		291	300
0.06	HICKS ,EL	AU	1964	JAR			158	171
0.00	CARPENTER,BW		1992	AOS	DIRSMITH,MW		709	739
0.00	FISHER,MH		1990	AUD			184	223
0.00	ICERMAN,RC	SP	1991	AUD	HILLISON,WA		22	34
0.00	MAYPER,AG	AU	1982	JAR			773	783
0.00	WRIGHT,GB	SU	1982	JAA	TAYLOR,RD		301	309

4.37 TREATMENTS=EDP AUDIT

CITE INDEX	FIRST AUTHOR	ISS-UE	YE-AR	JOUR-NAL	SECOND AUTHOR	THIRD AUTHOR	PAG BEG	PAG END
0.57	HANSEN,JV	AU	1986	AUD	MESSIER JR,WF		109	123
0.50	BIGGS ,SF	SP	1987	AUD	MESSIER JR,WF	HANSEN,JV	1	21
0.14	DAVIS ,GB	SP	1986	AUD	WEBER ,R		35	49
0.00	DOWELL,CD	AU	1981	JAA	HALL ,JA		30	40
0.00	LOVATA,LM	AU	1988	AUD			72	86
0.00	VASARHELYI,MA	SP	1984	AUD	BAILEY JR,AD	CAMARDESSE JR,JE	98	103
0.00	WAGNER,JW	JL	1969	TAR			600	604
0.00	WAND ,Y	JA	1989	TAR	WEBER ,R		87	107
0.00	WILLIAMS,DJ	SP	1985	AUD	LILLIS,A		110	117

4.38 TREATMENTS=ORGANIZATON

CITE INDEX	FIRST AUTHOR	ISS-UE	YE-AR	JOUR-NAL	SECOND AUTHOR	THIRD AUTHOR	PAG BEG	PAG END
1.50	FRANCIS,JR	JA	1987	TAR	SIMON ,DT		145	157
1.40	SIMON ,DT	AP	1988	TAR	FRANCIS,JR		255	269
1.30	EICHENSEHER,JW	SP	1983	AUD	SHIELDS,D		23	37
1.00	EICHENSEHER,JW	JL	1981	TAR	DANOS ,P		479	492
1.00	FRANCIS,JR	AG	1984	JAE			133	151
1.00	JOHNSON,WB	JA	1990	JAE	LYS ,T		281	308
1.00	MCNAIR,CJ		1991	AOS			635	653
0.80	RUBIN ,MA	AP	1988	TAR			219	236
0.73	DANOS ,P	AU	1982	JAR	EICHENSEHER,JW		604	616
0.69	RHODE ,JG	02	1977	AOS	SORENSEN,JE	LAWLER III,EE	165	176
0.69	SENATRA,PT	OC	1980	TAR			594	603
0.67	ABDEL-KHALIK,AR	SP	1990	CAR			295	322
0.67	BABER ,WR	AU	1987	JAR	BROOKS,EH	RICKS ,WE	293	305
0.67	ETTREDGE,M	SP	1990	JAR	GREENBERG,R		198	210
0.67	ROBERTS,RW	SP	1990	JAR	GLEZEN,GW	JONES ,TW	220	228
0.63	DIRSMITH,MW	02	1985	AOS	COVALESKI,MA		149	170
0.60	FRANCIS,JR	OC	1988	TAR	WILSON,ER		663	682
0.60	JIAMBALVO,J	01	1983	AOS	WATSON,DJ	BAUMLER,JV	13	30
0.57	MARGHEIM,LL	SP	1986	AUD	PANY ,K		50	63
0.50	ANTLE ,R	ST	1991	JAR	DEMSKI,JS		1	30
0.47	WATSON,DJ	AP	1975	TAR			259	273
0.40	SHOCKLEY,RA	AU	1983	JAR	HOLT ,RN		545	564
0.38	DIRSMITH,MW	AU	1985	JAA	COVALESKI,MA		5	21
0.38	SIMON ,DT	AU	1985	AUD			71	78
0.36	BURTON,JC	WI	1982	AUD	FAIRFIELD,P		1	22
0.36	LIGHTNER,SM	AU	1982	AUD	ADAMS ,SJ	LIGHTNER,KM	1	12
0.33	BALACHANDRAN,BV	SP	1987	JAR	RAMAKRISHNAN,RT		111	126
0.33	TURPEN,RA	SP	1990	AUD			60	76
0.31	BENKE ,RL	02	1980	AOS	RHODE ,JG		187	202
0.30	FERRIS,KR	01	1983	AOS	LARCKER,DF		1	12

CITE INDEX	FIRST AUTHOR	ISS-UE	YE-AR	JOUR-NAL	SECOND AUTHOR	THIRD AUTHOR	PAG BEG	PAG END
0.29	MARGHEIM,LL	SP	1986	JAR			194	205
0.27	BALLEW,V	JA	1982	TAR			88	104
0.25	DILLARD,JF	01	1981	AOS			17	26
0.25	FIRTH ,MA	SP	1985	AUD			23	37
0.25	TOMCZYK,S	AU	1989	AUD	READ ,WJ		98	106
0.25	WALLER,WS	AU	1985	JAR			817	828
0.24	KILLOUGH,LN	AP	1973	TAR	SOUDERS,TL		268	279
0.21	BLOCHER,E	JL	1979	TAR			563	573
0.20	WYER ,JC	SP	1988	AUD	WHITE ,GT	JANSON,EC	164	173
0.19	SCHROEDER,RG	01	1977	AOS	IMDIEKE,LF		39	46
0.17	WOLF ,FM	OC	1981	TAR			861	881
0.13	BULLEN,ML	03	1985	AOS	FLAMHOLTZ,EG		287	302
0.13	MCKINELY,S	AU	1985	JAR	PANY ,K	RECKERS,PMJ	887	896
0.09	JIAMBALVO,J	OC	1982	TAR	PRATT ,J		734	750
0.00	BAO ,BE	03	1986	AOS	BAO ,DA	VASARHELYI,MA	289	296
0.00	CHAN ,KH	OC	1986	TAR	DODIN ,B		726	734
0.00	CHUNG ,DY	AU	1988	CAR	LINDSAY,WD		19	46
0.00	COLLINS,KM	06	1992	AOS	KILLOUGH,LN		535	547
0.00	DAVIS ,LR	SP	1992	AUD	SIMON ,DT		58	68
0.00	DENT ,AS		1991	AOS			705	732
0.00	DYE ,RA	DE	1991	JAE			347	373
0.00	FERRIS,KR	01	1982	AOS			13	26
0.00	FOGARTY,TJ	02	1992	AOS			129	149
0.00	GLEZEN,GW	AU	1985	JAR	MILLAR,JA		859	870
0.00	GOETZ-JR,JF	02	1991	AOS	MORROW,PC	MCELROY,JC	159	165
0.00	HASKINS,ME	AU	1990	AUD	WILLIAMS,DD		55	74
0.00	IMHOFF JR,EA	SP	1988	AUD			182	191
0.00	LAMBERT,JC	SP	1991	AUD	LAMBERT III,SJ	CALDERON,TG	97	109
0.00	LEA ,RB	SU	1981	AUD			53	94
0.00	MAHER ,MW	JA	1992	TAR	TIESSEN,P	COLSON,R	199	211
0.00	MAYPER,AG	SP	1991	AUD	ADDY JR,ND		136	144
0.00	MELUMAD,N	AU	1990	CAR	THOMAN,L		22	55
0.00	MOIZER,P	AU	1987	AUD	TURLEY,S		118	123
0.00	MUTCHLER,JF	AU	1990	AUD	WILLIAMS,DD		39	54
0.00	PALMROSE,ZV	AU	1988	AUD			63	71
0.00	PONEMON,LA	04	1992	AOS			239	258
0.00	PRATT ,J		1992	AOS	BEAULIEU,P		667	684
0.00	RABY ,WL	OC	1966	TAR			714	720
0.00	RASCH ,RH	SP	1990	AUD	HARRELL,A		90	102
0.00	ROBERTSON,JC	WI	1981	JAA	ALDERMAN,CW		144	161
0.00	SUMNERS,GE	SP	1987	AUD	WHITE ,RA	CLAY JR,RJ	116	122
0.00	TEOH ,SH	SP	1992	JAR			1	23
0.00	WRIGHT,A	JL	1983	TAR			621	632
0.00	ZIND ,RG	AU	1989	CAR	ZEGHAL,D		26	47

4.39 TREATMENTS=INTERNAL AUDIT

CITE INDEX	FIRST AUTHOR	ISS-UE	YE-AR	JOUR-NAL	SECOND AUTHOR	THIRD AUTHOR	PAG BEG	PAG END
0.50	HARRELL,A	03	1989	AOS	TAYLOR,M	CHEWNING,E	259	269
0.43	BROWN ,PR	AU	1986	AUD	KARAN ,V		134	147
0.40	ABDEL-KHALIK,AR	AP	1983	TAR	SNOWBALL,D	WRAGGE,JH	215	227
0.38	PLUMLEE,RD	AU	1985	JAR			683	699
0.38	SCHNEIDER,A	AU	1985	JAR			911	919
0.33	SCHNEIDER,A	AU	1984	JAR			657	678

CITE INDEX	FIRST AUTHOR	ISS-UE	YE-AR	JOUR-NAL	SECOND AUTHOR	THIRD AUTHOR	PAG BEG	PAG END
0.30	BROWN ,PR	AU	1983	JAR			444	455
0.29	BORITZ,JE	AU	1986	AUD	BROCA ,DS		1	19
0.00	BUCHMAN,TA	AU	1983	AUD			92	103
0.00	BURGHER,PH	JA	1964	TAR			103	120
0.00	MESSIER JR,WF	SP	1988	CAR	SCHNEIDER,A		337	353
0.00	SAN MIGUEL,JG	02	1984	AOS	GOVINDARAJAN,V		179	188
0.00	VASARHELYI,MA	SP	1991	AUD	HALPER,FB		110	125
0.00	WALLACE,WA	SP	1991	CAR	KRUETZFELDT,RW		485	512
0.00	WEYGANDT,JJ	JA	1970	TAR			69	75

4.40 TREATMENTS=ERRORS

CITE INDEX	FIRST AUTHOR	ISS-UE	YE-AR	JOUR-NAL	SECOND AUTHOR	THIRD AUTHOR	PAG BEG	PAG END
1.83	JOHNSON,JR	AP	1981	TAR	LEITCH,RA	NETER ,J	270	293
1.45	HYLAS ,RE	OC	1982	TAR	ASHTON,RH		751	765
1.14	KREUTZFELDT,RW	AU	1986	AUD	WALLACE,WA		20	43
1.09	DUKE ,GL	SP	1982	JAR	NETER ,J	LEITCH,RA	42	67
0.88	HAM ,J	JL	1985	TAR	LOSELL,D	SMIELIAUSKAS,W	387	406
0.79	RAMAGE,JG	ST	1979	JAR	KRIEGER,AM	SPERO ,LL	72	102
0.50	BEDARD,JC	JL	1991	TAR	BIGGS ,SF		622	642
0.43	BURGSTAHLER,D	AP	1986	TAR	JIAMBALVO,J		233	248
0.38	WILLINGHAM,JJ	AU	1985	AUD	WRIGHT,WF		57	70
0.36	ALDERMAN,CW	WI	1982	AUD	DEITRICK,JW		54	68
0.33	HAM ,J	AU	1987	CAR	LOSELL,D	SMIELIAUSKAS,W	210	226
0.27	JIAMBALVO,J	SP	1982	JAR			152	161
0.25	NEWMAN,P		1989	AUD	NOEL ,J		50	63
0.13	KNECHEL,WR	SP	1985	JAR			194	212
0.00	DEFOND,ML	JL	1991	TAR	JIAMBALVO,J		643	655
0.00	GAA ,JC	SP	1985	CAR	SMITH ,CH		219	241
0.00	HOUGHTON,CW	SP	1991	AUD	FOGARTY,JA		1	21
0.00	ICERMAN,RC	AU	1990	JAA	HILLISON,WA		527	543
0.00	KREUTZFELDT,RW		1990	AUD	WALLACE,WA		1	26
0.00	ROSHWALB,A	AP	1991	TAR	WRIGHT,RL		348	360
0.00	ST.PIERRE,K	SP	1982	JAA	ANDERSON,JA		229	247
0.00	TRADER,RL	AU	1987	CAR	HUSS ,HF		227	239
0.00	TUBBS ,RM	OC	1992	TAR			783	801
0.00	WHEELER,S	JL	1990	TAR	PANY ,K		557	577
0.00	WURST ,J	AP	1991	TAR	NETER ,J	GODFREY,J	333	347

4.41 TREATMENTS=TRAIL

CITE INDEX	FIRST AUTHOR	ISS-UE	YE-AR	JOUR-NAL	SECOND AUTHOR	THIRD AUTHOR	PAG BEG	PAG END
0.25	AMERSHI,AH	AU	1989	CAR	CHENG ,P		72	90
0.18	WEBER ,R	AP	1982	TAR			311	325
0.00	HARRELL,AM	SP	1986	AUD	CHEWNING,EG	TAYLOR,M	111	121

4.42 TREATMENTS=JUDGMENT

CITE INDEX	FIRST AUTHOR	ISS-UE	YE-AR	JOUR-NAL	SECOND AUTHOR	THIRD AUTHOR	PAG BEG	PAG END
3.11	GIBBINS,M	SP	1984	JAR			103	125
3.00	ABDOLMOHAMMADI,MJ	JA	1987	TAR	WRIGHT,A		1	13
2.40	ASHTON,AH	OC	1988	TAR	ASHTON,RH		623	641
2.08	DEANGELO,LE	DE	1981	JAE			183	199
2.00	FREDERICK,DM	AU	1986	JAR	LIBBY ,R		270	290
1.20	BUTT ,JL	AU	1988	JAR			315	330
0.85	LEWIS ,BL	AU	1980	JAR			594	602

CITE INDEX	FIRST AUTHOR	ISS-UE	YE-AR	JOUR-NAL	SECOND AUTHOR	THIRD AUTHOR	PAG BEG	PAG END
0.78	KIDA ,TE	SP	1984	JAR			332	340
0.75	BUTT ,JL	06	1989	AOS	CAMPBELL,TL		471	479
0.75	LIBBY ,R	OC	1989	TAR	LIBBY ,PA		729	747
0.50	CHOO ,F	JL	1991	TAR	TROTMAN,KT		464	485
0.50	HOGARTH,RM	AP	1991	TAR			277	290
0.50	JOHNSON,PE	02	1989	AOS	JAMAL ,K	BERRYMAN,RG	83	99
0.50	SPIRES,EE	AP	1991	TAR			259	276
0.50	WALLER,WS	AP	1987	TAR	FELIX JR,WL		275	292
0.38	ABDOLMOHAMMADI,MJ	AU	1985	CAR			76	94
0.33	MESSIER JR,WF	AU	1987	AUD	HANSEN,JV		94	105
0.30	STEPHENS,RG	AU	1983	AUD			55	74
0.25	SELLING,T	02	1989	AOS	SHANK ,J		65	77
0.25	TROTMAN,KT	SP	1985	JAR	YETTON,PW		256	267
0.25	TROTMAN,KT	AU	1985	JAR			740	752
0.22	WALLER,WS	OC	1984	TAR	FELIX JR,WL		637	646
0.20	BAMBER,EM	AU	1983	JAR			396	412
0.17	HOLT ,DL	06	1987	AOS			571	578
0.14	CHESLEY,GR	SP	1986	CAR			179	199
0.14	LARSSON,S	SP	1986	CAR	CHESLEY,GR		259	282
0.13	BORITZ,JE	SP	1985	CAR			193	218
0.10	DANOS ,P	AU	1983	JAR	IMHOFF JR,EA		473	494
0.09	RECKERS,PMJ	AU	1982	AUD	SCHULTZ JR,JJ		64	74
0.00	ANDERSON,U		1989	AUD	MARCHANT,G		101	115
0.00	BALACHANDRAN,BV	SP	1986	CAR			282	287
0.00	BAMBER,EM	AU	1987	CAR	BYLINSKI,JH		127	143
0.00	BAMBER,EM	JL	1988	AUD	SNOWBALL,D		490	504
0.00	BORITZ,JE		1990	AUD			49	87
0.00	COLBERT,JL	02	1988	AOS			111	121
0.00	EMBY ,C	SP	1988	CAR	GIBBINS,M		287	313
0.00	FLORY ,SM	AP	1992	TAR	PHILLIPS JR,TJ	REIDENBACH,RE	284	302
0.00	HACKENBRACK,K	SP	1992	JAR			126	136
0.00	HASSELL,JM	06	1989	AOS	ARRINGTON,CE		527	537
0.00	JEFFREY,C	OC	1992	TAR			802	820
0.00	JOHNSON,VE		1991	AUD	KAPLAN,SE		96	107
0.00	LIBBY ,R	AU	1992	JAR	LIPE ,MG		249	273
0.00	MEAR ,RWT	AU	1990	JAA	FIRTH ,MA		501	520
0.00	MEIXNER,WF	JL	1988	AUD	WELKER,RB		505	513
0.00	PINCUS,KV	SP	1990	AUD			1	20
0.00	REBELE,JE	AU	1988	AUD	HEINTZ,JA	BRIDEN,GE	43	52
0.00	REIMERS,JL	02	1992	AOS	BUTLER,SA		185	194
0.00	TROTMAN,KT	06	1989	AOS	SNG ,J		565	576
0.00	WALLER,WS	02	1989	AOS	FELIX JR,WL		179	200
0.00	WENSLEY,AKP		1990	AUD			49	87
0.00	WONG-ON-WING,B	06	1989	AOS	RENEAU,JH	WEST ,SG	577	587
0.00	WRIGHT,WF	AU	1988	CAR			47	57
0.00	YARDLEY,JA	AU	1989	AUD			41	56

4.43 TREATMENTS=PLANNING

CITE INDEX	FIRST AUTHOR	ISS-UE	YE-AR	JOUR-NAL	SECOND AUTHOR	THIRD AUTHOR	PAG BEG	PAG END
2.35	JOYCE ,EJ	ST	1976	JAR			29	60
1.42	JOYCE ,EJ	AU	1981	JAR	BIDDLE,GC		323	349
1.00	FELLINGHAM,JC	OC	1985	TAR	NEWMAN,DP		634	650
0.78	KAPLAN,SE	AU	1984	AUD	RECKERS,PMJ		1	19

CITE INDEX	FIRST AUTHOR	ISS-UE	YE-AR	JOUR-NAL	SECOND AUTHOR	THIRD AUTHOR	PAG BEG	PAG END
0.50	LOEBBECKE,JK	AU	1989	AUD	EINING,MM	WILLINGHAM,JJ	1	28
0.36	CUSHING,BE	ST	1979	JAR	SEARFOSS,DG	RANDALL,RH	172	216
0.33	LIN ,WT	AU	1984	AUD	MOCK ,TJ	WRIGHT,A	89	99
0.29	BORITZ,JE	AU	1986	JAR			335	348
0.13	AHITUV,N	AU	1985	CAR	HALPERN,J	WILL ,H	95	110
0.13	KAPLAN,SE	AU	1985	AUD			12	25
0.00	BEDARD,JC	AU	1989	AUD			57	71
0.00	BORITZ,JE	AU	1992	AUD	WENSLEY,AKP		14	29
0.00	KAPLAN,SE	06	1989	AOS	RECKERS,PMJ		539	550
0.00	PETERS,JM	04	1989	AOS	LEWIS ,BL	DHAR ,V	359	378
0.00	SHIELDS,MD	AU	1988	CAR	SOLOMON,I	WALLER,WS	1	18
0.00	WRIGHT,A	06	1988	AOS			595	605

4.44 TREATMENTS=EFFICIENCY – OPERATIONAL

CITE INDEX	FIRST AUTHOR	ISS-UE	YE-AR	JOUR-NAL	SECOND AUTHOR	THIRD AUTHOR	PAG BEG	PAG END
1.86	PALMROSE,ZV	SP	1986	JAR			97	110
0.50	FELTHAM,GA	DE	1991	JAE	HUGHES,JS	SIMUNIC,DA	375	399
0.43	FRANCIS,JR	AU	1986	JAR	STOKES,DJ		383	393
0.43	PALMROSE,ZV	AU	1986	JAR			405	411
0.25	BACHAR,J	AU	1989	CAR			216	241
0.20	WILLIAMS,DD	05	1988	AOS	DIRSMITH,MW		487	508
0.14	SCHROEDER,MS	SP	1986	AUD	SOLOMON,I	VICKREY,DW	86	94
0.14	WRIGHT,A	SP	1986	AUD			86	94
0.11	SHERMAN,HD	AU	1984	AUD			35	53
0.09	MOCK ,TJ	AU	1982	AUD	WRIGHT,A		33	44
0.00	ASHTON,RH	SU	1981	JAA	HYLAS ,RE		325	332
0.00	CARCELLO,JV	SP	1992	AUD	HERMANSON,RH	MCGRATH,NT	1	15
0.00	CHURCHILL,NC	WI	1982	AUD	COOPER,WW	GOVINDARAJAN,V	69	91
0.00	DAMOS ,P	AU	1989	CAR	EICHENSEHER,JW	HOLT ,DL	91	109
0.00	DEFOND,ML	SP	1992	AUD			16	31
0.00	FRANCIS,JR	SU	1990	JAA	ANDREWS JR,WT	SIMON ,DT	369	378
0.00	HAYES ,RD	JL	1990	TAR	MILLAR,JA		505	519
0.00	KANPP ,MC	SP	1991	AUD			35	52
0.00	MCROBERTS,HA	04	1985	AOS	HUDSON,J		493	502
0.00	WARREN,CS	SP	1974	JAR			158	177

4.45 TREATMENTS=AUDIT THEORY

CITE INDEX	FIRST AUTHOR	ISS-UE	YE-AR	JOUR-NAL	SECOND AUTHOR	THIRD AUTHOR	PAG BEG	PAG END
1.10	ELLIOTT,RK	SP	1983	AUD			1	12
0.80	BALVERS,RJ	OC	1988	TAR	MCDONALD,B	MILLER,RE	605	622
0.50	CHOW ,CW	SP	1987	AUD	MCNAMEE,AH	PLUMLEE,RD	123	133
0.11	ROBERTSON,JC	SP	1984	AUD			57	67
0.00	ETTREDGE,M	SP	1988	AUD	SHANE ,PB	SMITH ,D	29	42
0.00	MATSUMURA,EM	OC	1992	TAR	TUCKER,RR		753	782
0.00	NAIR ,RD	AU	1987	AUD	RITTENBERG,LE		15	38
0.00	SMIELIAUSKAS,W	SP	1990	CAR	SMITH ,L		407	426
0.00	SMITH ,DB	SP	1988	JAR			134	145
0.00	WALKER,NR	AU	1988	AUD	PIERCE,LT		1	22

4.46 TREATMENTS=CONFIRMATIONS

CITE INDEX	FIRST AUTHOR	ISS-UE	YE-AR	JOUR-NAL	SECOND AUTHOR	THIRD AUTHOR	PAG BEG	PAG END
0.00	ASHTON,RH	SU	1981	AUD	HYLAS ,RE		12	22
0.00	BAILEY,CD	SP	1986	AUD	BALLARD,G		77	85

CITE INDEX	FIRST AUTHOR	ISS-UE	YE-AR	JOUR-NAL	SECOND AUTHOR	THIRD AUTHOR	PAG BEG	PAG END
0.00	CASTER,P	AU	1990	AUD			75	91

4.47 TREATMENTS=MANAGERIAL

CITE INDEX	FIRST AUTHOR	ISS-UE	YE-AR	JOUR-NAL	SECOND AUTHOR	THIRD AUTHOR	PAG BEG	PAG END
4.83	MILLER,P	03	1987	AOS	O'LEARY,T		235	265
3.00	BERRY ,AJ	01	1985	AOS	CAPPS ,T	COOPER,D	3	28
3.00	KAPLAN,RS	JL	1984	TAR			390	418
2.62	OTLEY ,DT	04	1980	AOS			413	428
2.55	LIBBY ,R	03	1982	AOS	LEWIS ,BL		231	286
2.50	BAIMAN,S	AU	1983	JAR	EVANS III,JH		371	395
2.50	LIBBY ,R	03	1977	AOS	LEWIS ,BL		245	268
1.92	BAIMAN,S	ST	1980	JAR	DEMSKI,JS		184	220
1.80	COOPER,DJ	23	1983	AOS			269	286
1.56	DEMSKI,JS	JA	1984	TAR	PATELL,JM	WOLFSON,MA	16	34
1.56	PENNO ,M	SP	1984	JAR			177	191
1.50	HAYES ,DC	23	1983	AOS			241	250
1.41	SWIERINGA,RJ	ST	1976	JAR	GIBBINS,M	LARSSON,L	159	187
1.38	GOVINDARAJAN,V	01	1985	AOS	GUPTA ,AK		51	66
1.33	DEMSKI,JS	SP	1987	JAR	SAPPINGTON,DEM		68	89
1.30	TIESSEN,P	23	1983	AOS	WATERHOUSE,JH		251	268
1.17	HOPPER,T	05	1987	AOS	STOREY,J	WILLMOTT,H	437	456
1.12	KHANDWALLA,PN	AU	1972	JAR			275	285
1.00	ASHTON,RH	ST	1976	JAR			1	17
1.00	BANKER,RD	AU	1992	CAR			343	354
1.00	BOLAND,RJ	04	1979	AOS			259	272
1.00	MEHREZ,A	AU	1992	CAR	BROWN ,JR	KHOUJA,M	329	342
0.90	JOHNSON,HT	23	1983	AOS			139	146
0.90	SPICER,BH	01	1983	AOS	BALLEW,V		73	98
0.80	MARKUS,ML	23	1983	AOS	PFEFFER,J		205	218
0.76	FELTHAM,GA	OC	1970	TAR	DEMSKI,JS		623	640
0.65	CAPLAN,EM	JL	1966	TAR			496	509
0.63	MERCHANT,KA	01	1985	AOS			67	86
0.59	DEMSKI,JS	AU	1976	JAR			230	245
0.59	ITAMI ,H	SP	1975	JAR			73	96
0.58	HILTON,RW	SP	1981	JAR	SWIERINGA,RJ	HOSKIN,RE	86	108
0.53	DEMSKI,JS	AU	1972	JAR			243	258
0.50	ASHTON,RH	SP	1981	JAR			42	61
0.50	BOUGEN,PD	03	1989	AOS			203	234
0.43	ATKINSON,AA	SP	1979	JAR			1	22
0.43	PRESTON,A	06	1986	AOS			521	540
0.41	COLANTONI,CS	JA	1971	TAR	MANES ,RP	WHINSTON,AB	90	102
0.41	HASEMAN,WD	JA	1976	TAR	WHINSTON,AB		65	79
0.38	BIRNBERG,JG	03	1977	AOS	FRIEZE,IH	SHIELDS,MD	189	200
0.35	DEMSKI,JS	OC	1967	TAR			701	712
0.33	BANKER,RD	AU	1987	JAA	DATAR ,SM	RAJAN ,MV	319	347
0.33	CONROY,RM	JA	1987	TAR	HUGHES,JS		50	66
0.33	JOYCE ,EJ	AU	1981	JAR	LIBBY ,R		544	550
0.33	SWIERINGA,RJ	03	1987	AOS	WEICK ,KE		293	308
0.31	HAMLEN,SS	OC	1980	TAR			578	593
0.30	TROTMAN,KT	SP	1983	JAR	YETTON,PW	ZIMMER,I	286	292
0.29	BRUNS JR,WJ	JL	1968	TAR			469	480
0.29	HOFSTEDT,TR	01	1976	AOS			43	58
0.25	KANODIA,CS	SP	1985	JAR			175	193

CITE INDEX	FIRST AUTHOR	ISS-UE	YE-AR	JOUR-NAL	SECOND AUTHOR	THIRD AUTHOR	PAG BEG	PAG END
0.25	UECKER,WC	JL	1985	TAR	SCHEPANSKI,A	SHIN ,J	430	457
0.23	FRIEDMAN,LA	AU	1980	JAR	NEUMANN,BR		407	419
0.22	SHIELDS,MD	34	1984	AOS			355	363
0.18	BIRNBERG,JG	JL	1967	TAR	NATH ,R		468	479
0.18	CAPLAN,EM	AP	1968	TAR			342	362
0.18	DEMSKI,JS	AU	1970	JAR			178	198
0.17	CHEN ,K	01	1981	AOS	SUMMERS,EL		1	16
0.17	PENNO ,M	SP	1987	CAR			368	374
0.17	VERRECCHIA,RE	ST	1987	JAR	LANEN ,WN		165	189
0.12	DEMSKI,JS	OC	1969	TAR			669	679
0.12	GODFREY,JT	JA	1971	TAR	PRINCE,TR		75	89
0.12	GONEDES,NJ	AU	1971	JAR			236	252
0.12	HINOMOTO,H	AU	1971	JAR			253	267
0.12	IJIRI ,Y	SP	1965	JAR	JAEDICKE,RK	LIVINGSTONE,JL	63	74
0.12	KORNBLUTH,JS	AP	1974	TAR			284	295
0.08	FLAMHOLTZ,EG	01	1980	AOS			31	42
0.08	PURDY ,D	04	1981	AOS			327	338
0.08	ROSENZWEIG,K	04	1981	AOS			339	354
0.07	AMEY ,LR	04	1979	AOS			247	258
0.06	BUTTERWORTH,JE	OC	1971	TAR	SIGLOCH,BA		701	716
0.06	CHARNES,A	JA	1967	TAR	COOPER,WW		24	52
0.06	FIELD ,JE	JL	1969	TAR			593	599
0.06	FLOWER,JF	SP	1966	JAR			16	36
0.06	GONEDES,NJ	SP	1970	JAR			1	20
0.06	HARVEY,DW	OC	1976	TAR			838	845
0.06	HEIMANN,SR	JA	1976	TAR	LUSK ,EJ		51	64
0.06	MCDONOUGH,JJ	OC	1971	TAR			676	685
0.06	STALLMAN,JC	OC	1972	TAR			774	790
0.00	AMERSHI,AH	JA	1990	TAR	BANKER,RD	DATAR ,SM	113	130
0.00	ARGYRIS,C	06	1990	AOS			503	511
0.00	BAIMAN,S	OC	1991	TAR	SIVARAMAKRISHNAN,K		747	767
0.00	BALACHANDRAN,KR	02	1977	AOS	LIVINGSTONE,JL		153	164
0.00	BENNINGER,LJ	JL	1965	TAR			547	557
0.00	BROMWICH,M	02	1990	AOS			27	46
0.00	CARLISLE,HM	JA	1966	TAR			115	120
0.00	CHAN ,JL	AP	1978	TAR			309	323
0.00	CHEN ,JT	SP	1985	CAR	MANES ,RP		242	252
0.00	CZARNIAWSKA-,B	04	1988	AOS			415	430
0.00	DANIEL,SJ		1991	AOS	REITSPERGER,WD		601	618
0.00	DAVIS ,PM	JA	1966	TAR			121	126
0.00	DEMSKI,JS	OC	1992	TAR	MAGEE ,RP		732	740
0.00	FIRMIN,PA	ST	1968	JAR	GOODMAN,SS	HENDRICKS,TE	122	155
0.00	FLEISCHMAN,RK	AP	1991	TAR	PARKER,LD		361	375
0.00	FREDERICKSON,JR	OC	1992	TAR			647	670
0.00	GIBSON,JL	JL	1963	TAR			492	500
0.00	HARTLEY,RV	AP	1968	TAR			321	332
0.00	HASEMAN,WC	OC	1968	TAR			738	752
0.00	HELMKAMP,JG	JL	1969	TAR			605	610
0.00	HOPPER,T	05	1991	AOS	ARMSTRONG,P		405	438
0.00	JONSSON,S	05	1988	AOS	GRONLUND,A		513	532
0.00	KHOURY,SJ	SU	1990	JAA			459	473
0.00	LEA ,RB	AP	1972	TAR			346	350
0.00	LUNESKI,C	JL	1964	TAR			591	597

CITE INDEX	FIRST AUTHOR	ISS-UE	YE-AR	JOUR-NAL	SECOND AUTHOR	THIRD AUTHOR	PAG BEG	PAG END
0.00	MCINNES,M	02	1991	AOS	RAMAKRISHNAN,RTS		167	184
0.00	MCKENNA,EF	03	1980	AOS			297	310
0.00	MURNIGHAN,JK	JL	1990	TAR	BAZERMAN,MH		642	657
0.00	NEUMANN,BR	SP	1979	JAR			123	139
0.00	SIMON ,SI	OC	1964	TAR			884	889
0.00	SOMEYA,K	OC	1964	TAR			983	989

4.48 TREATMENTS=TRANSFER PRICING

CITE INDEX	FIRST AUTHOR	ISS-UE	YE-AR	JOUR-NAL	SECOND AUTHOR	THIRD AUTHOR	PAG BEG	PAG END
1.00	BANKER,RD	SP	1992	CAR	DATAR ,SM		329	352
0.76	ABDEL-KHALIK,AR	JA	1974	TAR	LUSK ,EJ		8	23
0.67	AMERSHI,AH	AU	1990	CAR	CHENG ,P		61	99
0.65	WATSON,DJ	JL	1975	TAR	BAUMLER,JV		466	474
0.47	RONEN ,J	SP	1970	JAR	MCKINNEY,G		99	112
0.40	RONEN ,J	AU	1988	JAR	BALACHANDRAN,KR		300	314
0.36	SWIERINGA,RJ	02	1982	AOS	WATERHOUSE,JH		149	166
0.33	CHALOS,P	JL	1990	TAR	HAKA ,S		624	641
0.25	DEJONG,DV	02	1989	AOS	FORSYTHE,R	KIM ,JA	41	64
0.20	SPICER,BH	03	1988	AOS			303	322
0.18	DOPUCH,N	SP	1964	JAR	DRAKE ,DF		10	24
0.13	MERVILLE,LJ	OC	1978	TAR	PETTY ,JW		935	951
0.12	BAILEY JR,AD	JL	1976	TAR	BOE ,WJ		559	573
0.12	GORDON,MJ	JL	1970	TAR			427	443
0.06	ONSI ,M	JL	1970	TAR			535	543
0.00	GOETZ ,BE	JL	1967	TAR			435	440
0.00	HALPERIN,R	OC	1987	TAR	SRINIDHI,BN		686	706
0.00	HALPERIN,RM	JA	1991	TAR	SRINIDHI,B		141	157
0.00	LESSARD,DR	JL	1977	TAR	LORANGE,P		628	637
0.00	SCHIFF,M	SP	1979	JAA			224	231
0.00	STONE ,WE	JA	1964	TAR			38	42

4.49 TREATMENTS=BREAKEVEN, CVPA

CITE INDEX	FIRST AUTHOR	ISS-UE	YE-AR	JOUR-NAL	SECOND AUTHOR	THIRD AUTHOR	PAG BEG	PAG END
0.47	JAEDICKE,RK	OC	1964	TAR	ROBICHEK,AA		917	926
0.41	HILLIARD,JE	JA	1975	TAR	LEITCH,RA		69	80
0.35	BUZBY ,SL	JA	1974	TAR			42	49
0.35	LIAO ,M	OC	1975	TAR			780	790
0.29	HILTON,RW	AU	1979	JAR			411	435
0.29	SHIH ,W	OC	1979	TAR			687	706
0.27	KOTTAS,JF	AP	1978	TAR	LAU ,AH	LAU ,HS	389	401
0.24	FERRARA,WL	AP	1972	TAR	HAYYA ,JC	NACHMAN,DA	299	307
0.24	IJIRI ,Y	OC	1973	TAR	ITAMI ,H		724	737
0.18	MAGEE ,RP	AU	1975	JAR			257	266
0.12	JOHNSON,GL	AU	1971	JAR	SIMIK ,SS		278	286
0.12	JOHNSON,GL	SP	1974	JAR	SIMIK ,SS		67	79
0.11	THAKKAR,RB	AU	1984	CAR	FINLEY,DR	LIAO ,WM	77	86
0.07	KOTTAS,JF	JL	1978	TAR	LAU ,HS		698	707
0.06	CHARNES,A	SP	1963	JAR	COOPER,WW	IJIRI ,Y	16	43
0.06	MANES ,RP	SP	1966	JAR			87	100
0.06	MORRISON,TA	AP	1969	TAR	KACZKA,E		330	343
0.00	BROCKETT,P	JL	1984	TAR	CHARNES,A	COOPER,WW	474	487
0.00	CHEUNG,JK	SP	1990	CAR	HEANEY,J		738	760
0.00	LAU ,AHL	AU	1987	CAR	LAU ,HS		194	209

CITE INDEX	FIRST AUTHOR	ISS-UE	YE-AR	JOUR-NAL	SECOND AUTHOR	THIRD AUTHOR	PAG BEG	PAG END
0.00	RAUN ,DL	OC	1964	TAR			927	945
0.00	SOLOMONS,D	JL	1968	TAR			447	452

4.50 TREATMENTS=BUDGETING & PLANNING

CITE INDEX	FIRST AUTHOR	ISS-UE	YE-AR	JOUR-NAL	SECOND AUTHOR	THIRD AUTHOR	PAG BEG	PAG END
2.80	DEMSKI,JS	AP	1978	TAR	FELTHAM,GA		336	359
2.25	MERCHANT,KA	OC	1981	TAR			813	829
2.20	OTLEY ,DT	SP	1978	JAR			122	149
2.18	BROWNELL,P	SP	1982	JAR			12	27
2.00	MILANI,K	AP	1975	TAR			274	284
1.93	KENIS ,I	OC	1979	TAR			707	721
1.80	COVALESKI,MA	01	1988	AOS	DIRSMITH,MW		1	24
1.65	RONEN ,J	OC	1975	TAR	LIVINGSTONE,JL		671	685
1.57	BROWNELL,P	OC	1986	TAR	MCINNES,M		587	600
1.50	BROWNELL,P	OC	1981	TAR			844	860
1.50	KIRBY ,AJ	SP	1991	JAR	REICHELSTEIN,S	SEN ,PK	109	128
1.35	DECOSTER,DT	AU	1968	JAR	FERTAKIS,JP		237	246
1.29	SCHIFF,M	AP	1970	TAR	LEWIN ,AY		259	268
1.20	WALLER,WS	01	1988	AOS			87	98
1.18	CHRISTENSEN,J	AU	1982	JAR			589	603
1.14	BROWNELL,P	AU	1986	JAR	HIRST ,MK		241	249
1.14	COVALESKI,MA	03	1986	AOS	DIRSMITH,MW		193	214
1.07	COLLINS,F	AP	1978	TAR			324	335
1.06	HOPWOOD,AG	JL	1974	TAR			485	495
1.00	CHOW ,CW	OC	1983	TAR			667	685
1.00	PINCH ,T	03	1989	AOS	MULKAY,M	ASHMORE,M	271	301
1.00	PRESTON,AM	06	1992	AOS	COOPER,DJ	COOMBS,RW	561	593
0.88	BROWNELL,P	AU	1985	JAR			502	512
0.88	YOUNG ,SM	AU	1985	JAR			829	842
0.83	SIMONS,R	04	1987	AOS			357	374
0.82	CHERRINGTON,DJ	ST	1973	JAR	CHERRINGTON,JO		225	253
0.80	CHOW ,CW	JA	1988	TAR	COOPER,JC	WALLER,WS	111	122
0.75	MERCHANT,KA	02	1985	AOS			201	210
0.75	MIA ,L	04	1989	AOS			347	357
0.71	FORAN ,MF	OC	1974	TAR	DECOSTER,DT		751	763
0.70	FLAMHOLTZ,EG	23	1983	AOS			153	170
0.69	ROCKNESS,HO	OC	1977	TAR			893	903
0.62	MAGEE ,RP	AU	1980	JAR			551	573
0.60	CHENHALL,RH	03	1988	AOS	BROWNELL,P		225	233
0.60	LUKKA ,K	03	1988	AOS			281	301
0.57	ANSARI,SL	03	1979	AOS			149	162
0.57	BOLAND,RJ	45	1986	AOS	PONDY ,LR		403	422
0.53	ASHTON,RH	OC	1975	TAR			710	722
0.53	SWIERINGA,RJ	ST	1972	JAR	MONCUR,RH		194	209
0.50	BROWN ,C	JL	1987	TAR	SOLOMON,I		564	577
0.50	BROWNELL,P	AU	1983	JAR			456	472
0.50	COLLINS,F	JA	1987	TAR	MUNTER,P	FINN ,DW	29	49
0.50	COVALESKI,MA	04	1983	AOS	DIRSMITH,MW		323	340
0.50	DUNK ,AS	04	1989	AOS			321	324
0.50	MERCHANT,KA	JL	1989	TAR	MANZONI,J		539	558
0.47	COOK ,DM	ST	1967	JAR			213	224
0.47	DEMSKI,JS	JL	1972	TAR	FELTHAM,GA		533	548
0.47	IJIRI ,Y	SP	1968	JAR	KINARD,JC	PUTNEY,FB	1	28

CITE INDEX	FIRST AUTHOR	ISS-UE	YE-AR	JOUR-NAL	SECOND AUTHOR	THIRD AUTHOR	PAG BEG	PAG END
0.45	JONSSON,S	03	1982	AOS			287	304
0.42	HOFSTEDE,G	03	1981	AOS			193	216
0.42	KESSLER,L	SP	1981	JAR	ASHTON,RH		146	162
0.42	SHIELDS,MD	01	1981	AOS	BIRNBERG,JG	FRIEZE,IH	69	96
0.41	BENSTON,GJ	AP	1963	TAR			347	354
0.40	MIA ,L	05	1988	AOS			465	475
0.35	CAMMANN,C	04	1976	AOS			301	314
0.33	BRIERS,M	04	1990	AOS	HIRST ,M		373	398
0.33	HAKA ,SF	01	1987	AOS			31	48
0.33	HIRST ,MK	OC	1987	TAR			774	784
0.33	PENNO ,M	AP	1990	TAR			303	314
0.33	WILLIAMS,JJ	03	1990	AOS	MACINTOSH,NB	MOORE ,JC	221	246
0.30	BROWNELL,P	04	1983	AOS			307	322
0.29	KANODIA,CS	SP	1979	JAR			74	98
0.27	DIRSMITH,MW	34	1978	AOS	JABLONSKY,SF		215	226
0.24	HOLSTRUM,GL	AU	1971	JAR			268	277
0.24	SEARFOSS,DG	04	1976	AOS			375	388
0.20	COLIGNON,R	06	1988	AOS	COVALESKI,M		559	579
0.18	BENSTON,GJ	OC	1966	TAR			657	672
0.18	BROWNELL,P	OC	1982	TAR			766	777
0.18	EGGLETON,IRC	SP	1982	JAR			68	102
0.18	HARTLEY,RV	OC	1971	TAR			746	755
0.18	SEILER,RE	04	1982	AOS	BARTLETT,RW		381	404
0.14	LICATA,MP	JA	1986	TAR	STRAWSER,RH	WELKER,RB	112	117
0.14	ZALD ,MN	45	1986	AOS			321	326
0.13	LIN ,WT	JA	1978	TAR			61	76
0.12	DEMSKI,JS	AP	1971	TAR			268	278
0.12	ELLIOTT,JW	AU	1972	JAR	UPHOFF,HL		259	274
0.12	HANSON,EI	AP	1966	TAR			239	243
0.12	IJIRI ,Y	AU	1963	JAR	LEVY ,FK	LYON ,RC	198	212
0.11	ASHTON,AH	JL	1984	TAR			361	375
0.11	DAROCA,FP	01	1984	AOS			13	32
0.11	GORDON,LA	02	1984	AOS	HAKA ,S	SCHICK,AG	111	123
0.10	TILLER,MG	AU	1983	JAR			581	595
0.08	HOPPER,TM	04	1980	AOS			401	412
0.07	CARLSSON,J	34	1978	AOS	EHN ,P	ERLANDER,B	249	260
0.06	FELTHAM,GA	JA	1970	TAR			11	26
0.06	GROVES,R	JL	1970	TAR	MANES ,RP	SORENSEN,R	481	489
0.06	HARTLEY,RV	AP	1970	TAR			223	234
0.06	JENSEN,RE	AP	1967	TAR			265	273
0.06	MABERT,VA	JA	1974	TAR	RADCLIFFE,RC		61	75
0.06	RAPPAPORT,A	JL	1967	TAR			441	456
0.00	ABERNETHY,MA	02	1991	AOS	STOELWINDER,JU		105	120
0.00	BABER ,WR	JA	1985	TAR			1	9
0.00	BELKAOUI,A	AU	1985	CAR			111	123
0.00	BLANCHARD,GA	JA	1986	TAR	CHOW ,CW	NOREEN,EW	1	15
0.00	BROWNELL,P		1991	AOS	DUNK ,AS		693	703
0.00	BYRNE ,R	JA	1968	TAR	CHARNES,A	COOPER,WW	18	37
0.00	CHENHALL,RH	AP	1986	TAR			263	272
0.00	CHOW,CW	01	1991	AOS	COOPER,JC	HADDAD,K	47	60
0.00	CLARK ,JJ	OC	1973	TAR	ELGERS,PT		668	678
0.00	DUNK ,AS	03	1990	AOS			171	178
0.00	DUNK ,AS	04	1992	AOS			195	203

CITE INDEX	FIRST AUTHOR	ISS-UE	YE-AR	JOUR-NAL	SECOND AUTHOR	THIRD AUTHOR	PAG BEG	PAG END
0.00	FARAG ,SM	AP	1968	TAR			312	320
0.00	FERRARA,WL	JA	1966	TAR			106	114
0.00	FROGOT,V	JA	1991	TAR	SHEARON,WT		80	99
0.00	GAMBLING,TE	JA	1970	TAR	NOUR ,A		98	102
0.00	GIROUX,GA	06	1986	AOS	MAYPER,AG	DAFT ,RL	499	520
0.00	GODFREY,JT	AP	1971	TAR			286	297
0.00	HARRISON,GL	01	1992	AOS			1	15
0.00	HIRST ,MK	05	1990	AOS	LOWY ,SM		425	436
0.00	IJIRI ,Y	AP	1970	TAR	THOMPSON,GL		246	258
0.00	IMOISILI,OA	04	1989	AOS			325	335
0.00	JENSEN,RE	JL	1968	TAR			425	446
0.00	KIM ,DC	AP	1992	TAR			303	319
0.00	KREN ,L	JL	1992	TAR			511	526
0.00	LEV ,B	ST	1969	JAR			182	197
0.00	MENSAH,YM	AU	1988	CAR			222	249
0.00	MERCHANT,KA	04	1990	AOS			297	313
0.00	ROSS ,WR	JL	1966	TAR			464	473
0.00	SAMUELSON,LA	01	1986	AOS			35	46
0.00	SIMONS,R	AU	1988	CAR			267	283
0.00	WALKER,KB	AU	1991	JAR	MCCLELLAND,LA		371	381
0.00	WILLIAMS,JJ	02	1981	AOS			153	166
0.00	WILLIAMS,JJ	04	1985	AOS	NEWTON,JD	MORGAN,EA	457	478
0.00	WILLIAMS,JJ	02	1988	AOS	HININGS,CR		191	198

4.51 TREATMENTS=RELEVANT COSTS

CITE INDEX	FIRST AUTHOR	ISS-UE	YE-AR	JOUR-NAL	SECOND AUTHOR	THIRD AUTHOR	PAG BEG	PAG END
1.70	BIRNBERG,JG	23	1983	AOS	TUROPOLEC,L	YOUNG ,SM	111	130
0.40	HOSKIN,RE	SP	1983	JAR			78	95
0.40	NEUMANN,BR	AU	1978	JAR	FRIEDMAN,LA		400	410
0.35	BECKER,S	AU	1974	JAR	RONEN ,J	SORTER,GH	317	329
0.29	HAKA ,S	JL	1986	TAR	FRIEDMAN,L	JONES ,V	455	474
0.25	TURNER,MJ	AU	1989	JAR	HILTON,RW		297	312
0.20	DILLON,RD	JA	1978	TAR	NASH ,JF		11	17
0.20	HILTON,RW	AP	1988	TAR	SWIERINGA,RJ	TURNER,MJ	195	218
0.20	SUH ,YS	SP	1988	JAR			154	168
0.12	SAMUELS,JM	AU	1965	JAR			182	191
0.12	YETTON,PY	01	1976	AOS			81	90
0.06	COLANTONI,CS	JL	1969	TAR	MANES ,RP	WHINSTON,AB	467	481
0.06	JENSEN,DL	JL	1974	TAR			465	476
0.06	MCRAE ,TW	AP	1970	TAR			315	321
0.06	SORENSEN,JE	JL	1977	TAR	GROVE ,HD		658	675
0.00	AMEY ,LR	AU	1988	CAR	GOFFIN,JL		174	198
0.00	BALACHANDRAN,KR	WI	1992	JAA	MACHMEYER,RA		49	64
0.00	BANKER,RD	JL	1988	JAE	DATAR ,SM	KEKRE ,S	171	197
0.00	BANKER,RD	AU	1989	JAA	DATAR ,SM	KAPLAN,RS	528	554
0.00	BERKOW,WF	AP	1964	TAR			377	386
0.00	FERRARA,WL	OC	1963	TAR			719	722
0.00	FESS ,PE	OC	1963	TAR			723	732
0.00	GROSS ,H	OC	1966	TAR			745	753
0.00	LAVALLE,IH	AP	1968	TAR	RAPPAPORT,A		225	230
0.00	MITCHELL,GB	AP	1970	TAR			308	314
0.00	PELES ,YC	SU	1991	JAA			349	359
0.00	RICHARDSON,AW	SP	1988	CAR			609	614

CITE INDEX	FIRST AUTHOR	ISS-UE	YE-AR	JOUR-NAL	SECOND AUTHOR	THIRD AUTHOR	PAG BEG	PAG END
4.52 TREATMENTS=RESPONSIBTY ACCTG								
2.56	HAYES ,DC	JA	1977	TAR			22	39
1.00	KING ,RR	SP	1990	CAR	WALLIN,DE		859	892
0.75	BAIMAN,S	AU	1985	JAR	NOEL ,J		486	501
0.63	HARRELL,AM	OC	1977	TAR			833	841
0.18	PROBST,FR	JA	1971	TAR			113	118
0.08	BELKAOUI,A	04	1981	AOS			281	290
0.00	FERRARA,WL	JL	1977	TAR			597	604
0.00	GRAESE,CE	AP	1964	TAR			387	391
0.00	MELUMAD,N	DE	1992	JAE	MOOKHERJEE,D	REICHELSTEIN,S	445	483
4.53 TREATMENTS=COST ALLOCS								
4.14	LOFT ,A	02	1986	AOS			137	170
2.00	REICHELSTEIN,S	OC	1992	TAR			712	731
1.86	ZIMMERMAN,JL	JL	1979	TAR			504	521
1.17	ANSARI,SL	06	1987	AOS	EUSKE ,KJ		549	570
1.00	RAJAN ,MV	JL	1992	TAR			527	545
1.00	SUH ,YS	ST	1987	JAR			22	46
0.67	JORDAN,JS	SP	1990	CAR			903	921
0.63	HAMLEN,SS	JL	1977	TAR	HAMLEN,WA	TSCHIRHART,JT	616	627
0.60	NAHAPIET,JE	04	1988	AOS			333	358
0.43	BARNES,P	01	1986	AOS	WEBB ,J		1	18
0.33	BALACHANDRAN,BV	AU	1987	CAR	LI ,L	MAGEE ,RP	164	185
0.33	WALLER,WS	OC	1990	TAR	BISHOP,RA		812	836
0.29	KAPLAN,RS	OC	1973	TAR			738	748
0.29	MORIARITY,S	OC	1975	TAR			791	795
0.25	GORDON,LA	03	1989	AOS			247	258
0.20	CALLEN,JL	AP	1978	TAR			303	308
0.20	CHEN ,JT	JL	1983	TAR			600	605
0.20	COHEN ,SI	AU	1988	CAR	LOEB ,M		70	95
0.20	MAGEE ,RP	JA	1988	TAR			42	54
0.18	BALOFF,N	AU	1967	JAR	KENNELLY,JW		131	143
0.17	JACOBS,FH	JA	1987	TAR	MARSHALL,RM		67	78
0.13	MAGEE ,RP	OC	1977	TAR			869	880
0.12	CHURCHILL,NC	OC	1964	TAR			894	904
0.12	LIVINGSTONE,JL	JL	1968	TAR			503	508
0.12	WILLIAMS,TH	JL	1964	TAR	GRIFFIN,CH		671	678
0.10	SUNDER,S	SP	1983	JAR			222	233
0.09	COHEN ,SI	AP	1982	TAR	LOEB ,M		336	347
0.08	BALACHANDRAN,BV	JA	1981	TAR	RAMAKRISHNAN,RT		85	96
0.08	GANGOLLY,JS	AU	1981	JAR			299	312
0.06	CORCORAN,AW	JA	1973	TAR	LEININGER,WE		105	114
0.06	ECKEL ,LG	OC	1976	TAR			764	777
0.06	LIVINGSTONE,JL	JA	1969	TAR			48	64
0.06	MAGEE ,RP	JA	1977	TAR			190	199
0.06	MORSE ,WJ	OC	1972	TAR			761	773
0.00	BALACHANDRAN,BV	WI	1991	JAA	PADMARAJ,RA		1	28
0.00	BALACHANDRAN,KR	SP	1987	JAA	SRINIDHI,BN		151	169
0.00	BALAKRISHNAN,R	SP	1992	CAR			353	373
0.00	BRIEF ,RP	AU	1968	JAR	OWEN ,J		193	199
0.00	BRIEF ,RP	SP	1969	JAR	OWEN ,J		12	16

CITE INDEX	FIRST AUTHOR	ISS-UE	YE-AR	JOUR-NAL	SECOND AUTHOR	THIRD AUTHOR	PAG BEG	PAG END
0.00	CHAN ,KH	WI	1984	JAA	CHENG ,TT		164	177
0.00	CHENHALL,R	01	1991	AOS	MORRIS,D		27	46
0.00	CHIU ,JS	OC	1966	TAR	DECOSTER,DT		673	680
0.00	FREMGEN,JM	JA	1964	TAR			43	51
0.00	HORNGREN,CT	AP	1964	TAR	SORTER,GH		417	420
0.00	LAMBERT,RA	JL	1989	TAR	LARCHER,DF		449	467
0.00	LERE ,JC	AP	1986	TAR			318	324
0.00	LICHTENBERG,FR	OC	1992	TAR			741	752
0.00	MANES ,RP	JA	1965	TAR	SMITH ,VL		31	35
0.00	MCCLENON,PR	JL	1963	TAR			540	547
0.00	MELLMAN,M	JA	1963	TAR			118	123
0.00	SHWAYDER,KR	AP	1970	TAR			299	307
0.00	STAUBUS,GJ	JA	1963	TAR			64	74
0.00	VERRECCHIA,RE	JL	1982	TAR			579	593
0.00	WRIGHT,HW	OC	1966	TAR			626	633

4.54 TREATMENTS=CAPITAL BUDGETING

CITE INDEX	FIRST AUTHOR	ISS-UE	YE-AR	JOUR-NAL	SECOND AUTHOR	THIRD AUTHOR	PAG BEG	PAG END
0.63	HAKA ,SF	OC	1985	TAR	GORDON,LA	PINCHES,GE	651	669
0.58	LARCKER,DF	JL	1981	TAR			519	538
0.41	KLAMMER,T	AP	1973	TAR			353	364
0.41	SUNDEM,GL	AP	1974	TAR			306	320
0.12	GREER JR,WR	JA	1970	TAR			103	114
0.12	PARKER,RH	SP	1968	JAR			58	71
0.06	GREER JR,WR	JL	1974	TAR			496	505
0.06	LUSK ,EJ	JL	1972	TAR			567	575
0.00	BAILEY JR,AD	SP	1968	JAR	GRAY ,J		98	105
0.00	BERANEK,W	OC	1964	TAR			914	916
0.00	BRIEF ,RP	AP	1992	TAR	LAWSON,RA		411	426
0.00	FOGLER,HR	JA	1972	TAR			134	143
0.00	GORDON,LA		1992	AOS	SMITH ,KJ		741	757
0.00	HEEBINK,DV	JA	1964	TAR			90	93
0.00	JEYNES,PH	JA	1965	TAR			105	118
0.00	JOHNSON,GL	OC	1967	TAR	NEWTON,SW		738	746
0.00	MOORE ,CL	JA	1964	TAR			94	102
0.00	MOORE ,G	SP	1987	CAR			375	383
0.00	ROBBINS,SM	AU	1977	JAA			5	18

4.55 TREATMENTS=TAX (TAX PLANNING)

CITE INDEX	FIRST AUTHOR	ISS-UE	YE-AR	JOUR-NAL	SECOND AUTHOR	THIRD AUTHOR	PAG BEG	PAG END
0.50	ALM ,J	JL	1991	TAR			577	594
0.50	BECK ,PJ	JL	1991	TAR	DAVIS ,JS	JUNG ,W	535	558
0.50	COLLINS,JH	JL	1991	TAR	PLUMLEE,RD		559	576
0.25	RONEN ,J	JA	1989	TAR	AHARONI,A		69	86
0.00	ASKARI,H	AP	1976	TAR	CAIN ,P	SHAW ,R	331	334
0.00	BIERMAN JR,H	OC	1970	TAR			690	697
0.00	KISSINGER,JN	SP	1986	JAA			90	101
0.00	MORRISON,TA	OC	1966	TAR			704	713
0.00	MORRISON,TA	JL	1968	TAR	BUZBY ,SL		517	521
0.00	WANG ,S	JA	1991	TAR			158	169

4.56 TREATMENTS=OVERHEAD ALLOCS.

CITE INDEX	FIRST AUTHOR	ISS-UE	YE-AR	JOUR-NAL	SECOND AUTHOR	THIRD AUTHOR	PAG BEG	PAG END
3.00	ROGERSON,WP	OC	1992	TAR			671	690

CITE INDEX	FIRST AUTHOR	ISS-UE	YE-AR	JOUR-NAL	SECOND AUTHOR	THIRD AUTHOR	PAG BEG	PAG END
0.50	JENSEN,DL	OC	1977	TAR			842	856
0.47	KAPLAN,RS	AP	1971	TAR	THOMPSON,GL		352	364
0.47	KAPLAN,RS	JL	1974	TAR	WELAM ,VP		477	484
0.18	ZIMMERMAN,JL	AU	1976	JAR			301	319
0.06	BODNAR,G	OC	1977	TAR	LUSK ,EJ		857	868
0.06	FEKRAT,MA	AP	1972	TAR			351	355
0.00	BARTON,RF	SP	1969	JAR			116	122
0.00	DAVIDSON,S	AP	1963	TAR			278	284
0.00	FOSTER,G	JA	1990	JAE	GUPTA ,M		309	337
0.00	LENTILHON,RW	OC	1964	TAR			880	883

4.57 TREATMENTS=HRA-SOCIAL ACCTG

CITE INDEX	FIRST AUTHOR	ISS-UE	YE-AR	JOUR-NAL	SECOND AUTHOR	THIRD AUTHOR	PAG BEG	PAG END
3.75	BURCHELL,S	04	1985	AOS	CLUBB ,C	HOPWOOD,AG	381	414
1.17	KNIGHTS,D	05	1987	AOS	COLLINSON,D		457	477
0.82	ELIAS ,N	ST	1972	JAR			215	233
0.67	SPICER,BM	JA	1978	TAR			94	111
0.65	LEV ,B	JA	1971	TAR	SCHWARTZ,A		103	112
0.59	FLAMHOLTZ,EG	AP	1971	TAR			253	267
0.50	ARMSTRONG,P	01	1991	AOS			1	25
0.50	TROTMAN,KT	04	1981	AOS	BRADLEY,G		355	362
0.47	SCHWAN,ES	23	1976	AOS			219	238
0.41	BRUMMET,RL	AP	1968	TAR	FLAMHOLTZ,EG	PYLE ,WC	217	224
0.41	EPSTEIN,MJ	01	1976	AOS	FLAMHOLTZ,EG	MCDONOUGH,JJ	23	42
0.41	ESTES ,RW	AP	1972	TAR			284	290
0.41	FLAMHOLTZ,EG	23	1976	AOS			153	166
0.41	HENDRICKS,JA	AP	1976	TAR			292	305
0.40	INGRAM,RW	AU	1978	JAR			270	285
0.38	DIERKES,M	01	1977	AOS	PRESTON,LE		3	22
0.36	WISEMAN,J	01	1982	AOS			53	64
0.35	FLAMHOLTZ,EG	OC	1972	TAR			666	678
0.33	COWEN ,SS	02	1987	AOS	FERRERI,LB	PARKER,LD	111	122
0.33	MACINTOSH,NB	05	1990	AOS	SCAPENS,RW		455	477
0.31	ANDERSON,JC	JL	1980	TAR	FRANKLE,AW		467	479
0.31	BELKAOUI,A	03	1980	AOS			263	284
0.31	COOPER,DJ	03	1977	AOS	ESSEX ,S		201	218
0.29	BUZBY ,SL	JA	1979	TAR	FALK ,H		23	37
0.29	DITTMAN,DA	SP	1976	JAR	JURIS ,HA	REVSINE,L	49	65
0.29	JAGGI ,B	AP	1974	TAR	LAU ,HS		321	329
0.29	RAMANATHAN,KV	JL	1976	TAR			516	528
0.25	GROJER,JE	04	1977	AOS	STARK ,A		349	385
0.24	FLAMHOLTZ,EG	ST	1972	JAR			241	266
0.24	FRIEDMAN,A	AU	1974	JAR	LEV ,B		235	250
0.21	SCHREUDER,H	12	1979	AOS			109	122
0.20	ROCKNESS,J	04	1988	AOS	WILLIAMS,PF		397	411
0.19	GORDON,FE	04	1977	AOS	RHODE ,JG	MERCHANT,KA	295	306
0.18	BOWMAN,EH	01	1976	AOS	HAIRE ,M		11	22
0.18	MACY ,BA	23	1976	AOS	MIRVIS,PH		179	194
0.18	MOBLEY,SC	OC	1970	TAR			762	768
0.18	OGAN ,P	AP	1976	TAR			306	320
0.15	HARRELL,AM	04	1980	AOS	KLICK ,HD		393	400
0.14	BROCKHOFF,K	12	1979	AOS			77	86
0.14	DIERKES,M	12	1979	AOS			87	108

CITE INDEX	FIRST AUTHOR	ISS-UE	YE-AR	JOUR-NAL	SECOND AUTHOR	THIRD AUTHOR	PAG BEG	PAG END
0.13	DIERKES,M	01	1985	AOS	ANTAL ,AB		29	34
0.13	FLAMHOLTZ,EG	01	1985	AOS	DAS ,TK	TSUI ,AS	35	50
0.13	GAMBLING,T	04	1985	AOS			415	426
0.13	LESSEM,R	04	1977	AOS			279	294
0.13	TOMASSINI,LA	OC	1977	TAR			904	913
0.12	ACLAND,D	23	1976	AOS			133	142
0.12	CHURCHILL,NC	OC	1975	TAR	SHANK ,JK		643	656
0.12	DERMER,JD	JA	1974	TAR	SIEGEL,JP		88	97
0.12	TOMASSINI,LA	23	1976	AOS			239	252
0.09	BENSTON,GJ	02	1982	AOS			87	106
0.08	SCHREUDER,H	AP	1981	TAR			294	308
0.08	WILLIAMS,PF	JA	1980	TAR			62	77
0.07	CHAN ,JL	04	1979	AOS			273	282
0.06	BIRNBERG,JG	01	1976	AOS	GANDHI,NM		5	10
0.06	CARPER,WB	23	1976	AOS	POSEY ,JM		143	152
0.06	FRANCIS,ME	AP	1973	TAR			245	257
0.06	GAMBLING,TE	23	1976	AOS			167	174
0.06	GROVE ,HD	03	1977	AOS	MOCK ,TJ	EHRENREICH,K	219	236
0.06	MARQUES,E	23	1976	AOS			175	178
0.06	OGAN ,P	23	1976	AOS			195	218
0.06	ULLMANN,AA	01	1976	AOS			71	80
0.06	WELLING,P	04	1977	AOS			307	316
0.00	BRAVENEC,LL	02	1977	AOS	EPSTEIN,MJ	CRUMBLEY,DL	131	140
0.00	CHARNES,A	04	1976	AOS	COLANTONI,CS	COOPER,WW	315	338
0.00	CHURCHMAN,CW	JA	1971	TAR			30	35
0.00	CRUMBLEY,DL	JA	1975	TAR	SAVICH,RS		112	117
0.00	FARMAN,WL	AP	1964	TAR			392	404
0.00	FLAMHOLTZ,EG	04	1987	AOS			309	318
0.00	GLATZER,W	03	1981	AOS			219	234
0.00	GUL ,FA	34	1984	AOS			233	239
0.00	HEARD ,JE	03	1981	AOS	BOLCE ,WJ		247	254
0.00	LAU ,AH	SP	1978	JAR	LAU ,HS		80	102
0.00	LEWIS ,NR	34	1984	AOS	PARKER,LD	SUTCLIFFE,P	275	289
0.00	PARKE ,R	03	1981	AOS	PETERSON,JL		235	246
0.00	PATTEN,DM	06	1990	AOS			575	587
0.00	PRESTON,LE	03	1981	AOS			255	262
0.00	TEOH ,HY	02	1984	AOS	THONG ,G		189	206
0.00	ULLMANN,AA	12	1979	AOS			123	134
0.00	VOGT ,RA	01	1977	AOS			59	80

4.58 TREATMENTS=VARIANCES

CITE INDEX	FIRST AUTHOR	ISS-UE	YE-AR	JOUR-NAL	SECOND AUTHOR	THIRD AUTHOR	PAG BEG	PAG END
0.65	MAGEE ,RP	JL	1976	TAR			529	544
0.59	KAPLAN,RS	SP	1969	JAR			32	43
0.53	DYCKMAN,TR	AU	1969	JAR			215	244
0.47	MAGEE ,RP	AU	1978	JAR	DICKHAUT,JW		294	314
0.41	ANSARI,SL	AU	1976	JAR			189	211
0.38	LAMBERT,RA	AU	1985	JAR			633	647
0.33	BROWN ,C	SP	1981	JAR			62	85
0.33	DITTMAN,DA	SP	1978	JAR	PRAKASH,P		14	25
0.29	DITTMAN,DA	AP	1979	TAR	PRAKASH,P		358	373
0.25	BROWN ,C	03	1985	AOS			255	266
0.24	OZAN ,T	SP	1971	JAR	DYCKMAN,TR		88	115

CITE INDEX	FIRST AUTHOR	ISS-UE	YE-AR	JOUR-NAL	SECOND AUTHOR	THIRD AUTHOR	PAG BEG	PAG END
0.22	MARCINKO,D	JL	1984	TAR	PETRI ,E		488	495
0.20	HARRISON,PD	AP	1988	TAR	WEST ,SG	RENEAU,JH	307	320
0.18	DEMSKI,JS	JA	1970	TAR			76	87
0.18	HASSELDINE,CR	JL	1967	TAR			497	515
0.18	RONEN ,J	JA	1974	TAR			50	60
0.12	DOPUCH,N	JL	1967	TAR	BIRNBERG,JG	DEMSKI,JS	526	536
0.12	LUH ,FS	JA	1968	TAR			123	132
0.12	WOLK ,HI	JL	1972	TAR	HILLMAN,AP		549	555
0.12	ZANNETOS,ZS	AP	1964	TAR			296	304
0.07	JACOBS,FH	SP	1978	JAR			190	203
0.06	COMISKEY,EE	AP	1966	TAR			235	238
0.06	FRANK ,WG	JL	1967	TAR	MANES ,RP		516	525
0.00	BALAKRISHNAN,R	AU	1990	CAR			105	122
0.00	BROWN ,C	AU	1987	CAR			111	126
0.00	CALLEN,JL	SP	1988	JAA			87	108
0.00	CHUMACHENKO,NG	OC	1968	TAR			753	762
0.00	CUSHING,BE	OC	1968	TAR			668	671
0.00	DARROUGH,MN	AU	1988	CAR			199	221
0.00	DECOSTER,DT	AP	1966	TAR			297	302
0.00	DEMSKI,JS	SP	1969	JAR			96	115
0.00	HOBBS ,JB	OC	1964	TAR			905	913
0.00	HORNGREN,CT	AP	1967	TAR			254	264
0.00	HORNGREN,CT	JA	1969	TAR			86	89
0.00	JENSEN,RE	JA	1968	TAR	THOMSEN,CT		83	93
0.00	LEV ,B	OC	1969	TAR			704	710
0.00	ONSI ,M	AP	1967	TAR			321	330
0.00	PELES ,YC	AP	1986	TAR			325	329
0.00	RONEN ,J	AU	1970	JAR			232	252
0.00	SHWAYDER,KR	JA	1968	TAR			101	104
0.00	WEBER ,C	JL	1963	TAR			534	539
0.00	ZANNETOS,ZS	JL	1963	TAR			528	533

4.59 TREATMENTS=EXEC.COMPENSATION

CITE INDEX	FIRST AUTHOR	ISS-UE	YE-AR	JOUR-NAL	SECOND AUTHOR	THIRD AUTHOR	PAG BEG	PAG END
6.00	HEALY ,PM	AP	1985	JAE			85	108
2.43	ANTLE ,R	SP	1986	JAR	SMITH ,A		1	39
2.40	LARCKER,DF	AP	1983	JAE			3	30
2.00	DYE ,RA	SP	1992	JAR			27	52
1.67	LAMBERT,RA	ST	1987	JAR	LARCKER,DF		85	125
1.63	MURPHY,KJ	AP	1985	JAE			11	42
1.25	BAIMAN,S	SP	1989	JAR	LEWIS ,BL		1	20
1.25	COUGHLAN,AT	AP	1985	JAE	SCHMIDT,RM		43	66
1.00	ANTLE ,R	SP	1985	JAR	SMITH ,A		296	325
1.00	BANKER,RD	SP	1989	JAR	DATAR ,SM		21	39
1.00	JANAKIRAMAN,SN	SP	1992	JAR	LAMBERT,RA	LARCKER,DF	53	69
1.00	KANODIA,C	SP	1989	JAR	BUSHMAN,R	DICKHAUT,J	59	77
0.75	DEMSKI,JS	SP	1989	JAR	SAPPINGTON,DEM		40	58
0.75	MELUMAD,ND	SP	1989	CAR			733	753
0.75	WALLER,WS	JL	1985	TAR	CHOW ,CW		458	476
0.63	BRICKLEY,JA	AP	1985	JAE	BHAGAT,S	LEASE ,RC	115	130
0.60	ABDEL-KHALIK,AR	ST	1988	JAR			144	181
0.60	AMERSHI,AH	SP	1988	CAR	CHENG ,P		515	563
0.50	BENSTON,GJ	AP	1985	JAE			67	84

CITE INDEX	FIRST AUTHOR	ISS-UE	YE-AR	JOUR-NAL	SECOND AUTHOR	THIRD AUTHOR	PAG BEG	PAG END
0.50	LAMBERT,RA	SP	1991	JAR	LARCKER,DF	VERRECCHIA,RE	129	149
0.50	LEWELLEN,W	DE	1987	JAE	LODERER,C	MARTIN,K	287	310
0.40	BANKER,RD	AU	1988	CAR	DATAR ,SM	MAINDIRATTA,A	96	124
0.40	YOUNG ,SM	06	1988	AOS	SHIELDS,MD	WOLF ,G	607	618
0.33	BAIMAN,S	SP	1990	CAR	MAY ,JH	MUKHERJI,A	761	799
0.33	BAIMAN,S	04	1990	AOS			341	371
0.25	LAMBERT,RA	AP	1985	JAE	LARCKER,DF		179	204
0.25	NEWMAN,HA	OC	1989	TAR			758	772
0.25	TEHRANIAN,H	AP	1985	JAE	WAEGELEIN,JF		131	144
0.20	FELTHAM,GA	AU	1988	CAR	CHRISTENSEN,PO		133	169
0.20	SHIELDS,MD	06	1988	AOS	WALLER,WS		581	594
0.13	HALPERIN,R	OC	1985	TAR	TZUR ,J		670	680
0.13	RAVIV ,A	AP	1985	JAE			239	246
0.00	ANTLE ,R	SP	1990	JAR	FELLINGHAM,J		1	24
0.00	BANKER,RD	SP	1990	CAR	DATAR ,SM	MAZUR ,MJ	809	824
0.00	FOSTER III,TW	JL	1991	TAR	KOOGLER,PR	VICKREY,D	595	610
0.00	GAVER ,JJ	JA	1992	TAR	GAVER ,KM	BATTISTEL,GP	172	182
0.00	GAVER ,JJ	SP	1992	JAA			137	156
0.00	JENSEN,MC	AP	1985	JAE	ZIMMERMAN,JL		3	10
0.00	KIRBY ,AJ	SP	1992	CAR			374	408
0.00	LANEN ,WN	SP	1992	JAR	LARCKER,DF		70	93
0.00	MCGAHRAN,KT	JA	1988	TAR			23	41
0.00	RAJAN ,MV	AU	1992	JAR			227	248
0.00	SCOTT ,WR	SP	1988	CAR			354	388

4.60 TREATMENTS=OTHER

CITE INDEX	FIRST AUTHOR	ISS-UE	YE-AR	JOUR-NAL	SECOND AUTHOR	THIRD AUTHOR	PAG BEG	PAG END
2.50	LEHMAN,C	05	1987	AOS	TINKER,T		503	522
2.10	BOLAND,RJ	23	1983	AOS	PONDY ,LR		223	234
2.00	MEYER ,JW	45	1986	AOS			345	356
1.80	HOSKIN,KW	01	1988	AOS	MACVE ,RH		37	73
1.41	LIBBY ,R	JL	1975	TAR			475	489
1.40	TINKER,T	02	1988	AOS			165	189
1.20	MORGAN,G	05	1988	AOS			477	485
1.15	GARMAN,MB	AU	1980	JAR	OHLSON,JA		420	440
1.00	MCGHEE,W	JL	1978	TAR	SHIELDS,MD	BIRNBERG,JG	681	697
0.86	WHITLEY,R	02	1986	AOS			171	192
0.81	ZIMMERMAN,JL	ST	1977	JAR			107	144
0.77	HILTON,RW	AU	1980	JAR			477	505
0.75	LIBBY ,R	AU	1977	JAR	FISHBURN,PC		272	292
0.43	PASTENA,V	AU	1979	JAR	RONEN ,J		550	564
0.42	FRIED ,D	AP	1981	TAR	SCHIFF,A		326	341
0.42	HILTON,RW	SP	1981	JAR	SWIERINGA,RJ		109	119
0.36	MAYER-SOMMER,AP	JA	1979	TAR			88	106
0.35	HOFSTEDT,TR	JA	1970	TAR	KINARD,JC		38	54
0.33	LAUGHLIN,RC	05	1987	AOS			479	502
0.30	SCHEPANSKI,A	AP	1983	TAR	UECKER,WC		259	283
0.29	CHEN ,RS	JL	1975	TAR			533	543
0.29	GOLEMBIEWSKI,RT	AP	1964	TAR			333	341
0.25	EICHENSEHER,JW	AU	1989	AUD	HAGIGI,M	SHIELDS,D	29	40
0.25	WEBER ,RP	JL	1981	TAR	STEVENSON,WC		596	612
0.24	JOHNSON,HT	JL	1975	TAR			444	450
0.24	SMITH ,JE	JL	1971	TAR	SMITH ,NP		552	561

CITE INDEX	FIRST AUTHOR	ISS-UE	YE-AR	JOUR-NAL	SECOND AUTHOR	THIRD AUTHOR	PAG BEG	PAG END
0.24	STERLING,RR	JL	1970	TAR			444	457
0.18	PRAKASH,P	OC	1975	TAR	RAPPAPORT,A		723	734
0.18	SORENSEN,JE	OC	1972	TAR	FRANKS,DD		735	746
0.13	FERRIS,KR	01	1977	AOS			23	28
0.13	JOHNSON,WB	AP	1985	JAE	MAGEE ,RP	NAGARAJAN,NJ	151	174
0.12	GOETZ ,BE	JA	1967	TAR			53	61
0.12	GREEN ,D	JA	1966	TAR			52	64
0.12	LOEB ,SE	JA	1972	TAR			1	10
0.12	MAUTZ ,RK	AP	1963	TAR			317	325
0.12	PANKOFF,LD	AP	1970	TAR	VIRGIL JR,RL		269	279
0.12	SEIDLER,LJ	OC	1967	TAR			775	781
0.07	YAMEY ,BS	AP	1979	TAR			323	329
0.06	AIKEN ,ME	JL	1975	TAR	BLACKETT,LA	ISAACS,G	544	562
0.06	BALADOUNI,V	AP	1966	TAR			215	225
0.06	FIRMIN,PA	JA	1968	TAR	LINN ,JJ		75	82
0.06	HORNGREN,CT	JA	1971	TAR			1	11
0.06	HUEFNER,RJ	OC	1971	TAR			717	732
0.06	HUME ,LJ	SP	1970	JAR			21	33
0.06	KEISTER JR,OR	AP	1963	TAR			371	376
0.06	LANGENDERFER,HQ	OC	1969	TAR	ROBERTSON,JC		777	787
0.06	SOPER ,FJ	AP	1964	TAR	DOLPHIN,R		358	362
0.06	STONE ,WE	JA	1965	TAR			190	195
0.00	ALLYN ,RG	JA	1964	TAR			121	127
0.00	ALLYN ,RG	AP	1966	TAR			303	311
0.00	ANDERSON,JJ	JL	1967	TAR			583	588
0.00	BAUMOL,WJ	WI	1990	JAA			105	117
0.00	BOUTELL,WS	AP	1964	TAR			305	311
0.00	BOWEN ,EK	OC	1967	TAR			782	787
0.00	BRUNDAGE,MV	JL	1969	TAR	LIVINGSTONE,JL		539	545
0.00	BUCKLEY,JW	JL	1967	TAR			572	582
0.00	CALL ,DV	OC	1969	TAR			711	719
0.00	CAMPFIELD,WL	JL	1965	TAR			594	598
0.00	CAMPFIELD,WL	OC	1970	TAR			683	689
0.00	CAREY ,JL	JA	1969	TAR			79	85
0.00	CARPENTER,CG	JL	1971	TAR	STRAWSER,RH		509	518
0.00	CASPARI,JA	OC	1976	TAR			739	746
0.00	CLARK ,TN	ST	1977	JAR			54	94
0.00	COE ,TL	SP	1979	JAA			244	253
0.00	CORCORAN,AW	AP	1969	TAR			359	374
0.00	COWIE ,JB	JA	1970	TAR	FREMGEN,JM		27	37
0.00	CRANDALL,RH	JL	1969	TAR			457	466
0.00	DEINZER,HT	JA	1966	TAR			21	31
0.00	DUVALL,RM	JL	1965	TAR	BULLOCH,J		569	573
0.00	ELLIOTT,EL	OC	1968	TAR	LARREA,J	RIVERA,JM	763	768
0.00	ELNICKI,RA	ST	1977	JAR			209	218
0.00	FELTHAM,GA	AU	1984	CAR			87	98
0.00	FRANK ,WG	OC	1965	TAR			854	862
0.00	FU ,P	SP	1971	JAR			40	51
0.00	GIBBS ,G	OC	1964	TAR			4	7
0.00	GOGGANS,TP	JL	1964	TAR			627	630
0.00	GOLDBERG,L	JL	1963	TAR			457	469
0.00	HANSEN,ES	ST	1977	JAR			156	201
0.00	HEIN ,LW	JL	1963	TAR			508	520

CITE INDEX	FIRST AUTHOR	ISS-UE	YE-AR	JOUR-NAL	SECOND AUTHOR	THIRD AUTHOR	PAG BEG	PAG END
0.00	HEINS ,EB	AP	1966	TAR			323	326
0.00	HERBERT,L	JL	1971	TAR			433	440
0.00	HORRIGAN,JO	JL	1965	TAR			558	568
0.00	HUTH ,WL	WI	1992	JAA	MARIS ,BA		27	44
0.00	HYLTON,DP	JL	1964	TAR			667	670
0.00	IMKE ,FJ	AP	1966	TAR			318	322
0.00	JENSEN,HL	OC	1976	TAR	WYNDELTS,RW		846	853
0.00	JENTZ ,GA	JL	1966	TAR			535	541
0.00	JENTZ ,GA	AP	1967	TAR			362	365
0.00	KALINSKI,BD	JL	1963	TAR			591	595
0.00	KAPLAN,HG	JA	1964	TAR	SOLOMON,KI		145	149
0.00	KAUFMAN,F	OC	1967	TAR			713	720
0.00	KETZ ,JE	AU	1983	JAA	WYATT ,AR		29	43
0.00	KIRCHER,P	OC	1965	TAR			742	752
0.00	KIRCHER,P	JL	1967	TAR			537	543
0.00	KRIPKE,H	AU	1978	JAA			4	32
0.00	KUBLIN,M	JL	1965	TAR			626	635
0.00	LAMDEN,CW	JA	1964	TAR			128	132
0.00	LEE ,GA	SP	1973	JAR			47	61
0.00	LEE ,LC	AP	1969	TAR	BEDFORD,NM		256	275
0.00	LEVY ,H	AU	1987	JAA	BYUN ,YH		355	369
0.00	LI ,DH	OC	1964	TAR			946	950
0.00	LINOWES,DF	JA	1965	TAR			97	104
0.00	LOWE ,HD	AP	1967	TAR			356	360
0.00	LOWE ,RE	OC	1965	TAR			839	846
0.00	LUCAS ,HC	OC	1975	TAR			735	746
0.00	LUNESKI,C	OC	1967	TAR			767	771
0.00	LYNN ,ES	AP	1964	TAR			371	376
0.00	MACKENZIE,O	AP	1964	TAR			363	370
0.00	MARKOWITZ,HM	SP	1990	JAA			213	225
0.00	MATTINGLY,LA	OC	1964	TAR			996	3
0.00	MAUTZ ,RK	AP	1965	TAR			299	311
0.00	MAUTZ ,RK	JL	1969	TAR	SKOUSEN,KF		447	456
0.00	MAY ,PT	JL	1969	TAR			583	592
0.00	MELBERG,WF	JA	1972	TAR			116	133
0.00	MILLER,HE	JA	1966	TAR			1	7
0.00	MOORE ,DC		1991	AOS			163	791
0.00	MORENO,RG	OC	1964	TAR			990	995
0.00	MOST ,KS	OC	1972	TAR			722	734
0.00	NICHOLS,AC	OC	1968	TAR	GRAWOIG,DE		631	639
0.00	PATON ,WA	JA	1967	TAR			7	23
0.00	PETRI ,E	AP	1978	TAR	MINCH ,RA		415	428
0.00	PETRI ,E	AP	1979	TAR	GELFAND,J		330	345
0.00	POMERANZ,F	AU	1977	JAA			45	52
0.00	POWELL,RM	JL	1966	TAR			525	534
0.00	PRATER,GI	OC	1966	TAR			619	625
0.00	RAPPAPORT,A	OC	1964	TAR			951	962
0.00	RATSCH,H	JA	1964	TAR			140	144
0.00	ROBINSON,LA	JA	1964	TAR	HALL ,TP		62	69
0.00	ROLLER,J	AP	1967	TAR	WILLIAMS,TH		349	355
0.00	SCHIFF,M	AU	1977	JAA	SORTER,GH	WIESEN,JL	19	44
0.00	SCHNEIDER,AJ	AP	1967	TAR			342	348
0.00	SEILER,RE	OC	1966	TAR			652	656

CITE INDEX	FIRST AUTHOR	ISS-UE	YE-AR	JOUR-NAL	SECOND AUTHOR	THIRD AUTHOR	PAG BEG	PAG END
0.00	SINGER,FA	OC	1965	TAR			847	853
0.00	SPENCER,MH	AP	1963	TAR			310	316
0.00	STANDISH,PEM	JL	1964	TAR			654	666
0.00	STEIN ,JL	SP	1990	JAA	HONG ,BG		277	300
0.00	STETTLER,HF	OC	1965	TAR			723	730
0.00	STONE ,ML	ST	1968	JAR			59	66
0.00	SUSSMAN,MR	AP	1965	TAR			407	413
0.00	TOWNSEND,LA	JA	1967	TAR			1	6
0.00	VANCE ,LL	JA	1966	TAR			48	51
0.00	VATTER,WJ	OC	1967	TAR			721	730
0.00	WALLACE,WA	SP	1991	AUD			53	68
0.00	WEIGAND,RE	JL	1963	TAR			584	590
0.00	WEISER,HJ	JL	1966	TAR			518	524
0.00	WELKE ,WR	AP	1966	TAR			253	256
0.00	WELSCH,GA	OC	1964	TAR			8	13
0.00	WHEELER,JT	JA	1970	TAR			1	10
0.00	WILLIAMS,TH	OC	1967	TAR	GRIFFIN,CH		642	649
0.00	WINJUM,JO	AU	1971	JAR			333	350
0.00	WOODS ,RS	JL	1964	TAR			598	614
0.00	YU ,SC	JA	1966	TAR			8	20
0.00	ZANNETOS,ZS	JL	1967	TAR			566	571

4.61 TREATMENTS=SUBMISSN TO THE FASB ETC.

CITE INDEX	FIRST AUTHOR	ISS-UE	YE-AR	JOUR-NAL	SECOND AUTHOR	THIRD AUTHOR	PAG BEG	PAG END
8.20	WATTS ,RL	JA	1978	TAR	ZIMMERMAN,JL		112	134
3.00	HOSKIN,KW	02	1986	AOS	MACVE ,RH		105	136
2.20	LEFTWICH,RW	JA	1983	TAR			23	42
2.14	KINNEY JR,WR	MR	1986	JAE			73	89
1.13	HOPWOOD,AG	03	1985	AOS			361	376
0.71	CHUA ,WF	06	1986	AOS			583	598
0.58	BROWN ,PR	SP	1981	JAR			232	246
0.56	MCKEE ,AJ	OC	1984	TAR	BELL ,TB	BOATSMAN,JR	647	659
0.46	DOPUCH,N	JA	1980	TAR	SUNDER,S		1	21
0.38	KELLY ,R	AU	1985	JAR			619	632
0.38	O'LEARY,T	01	1985	AOS			87	104
0.33	MIAN ,SL	OC	1990	JAE	SMITH JR,CW		249	266
0.33	NEWMAN,DP	SP	1981	JAR			247	262
0.29	POWNALL,G	AU	1986	JAR			291	315
0.25	HUSSEIN,ME	01	1981	AOS			27	38
0.23	HUSSEIN,ME	SU	1980	JAA	KETZ ,JE		354	367
0.22	PURO ,M	AU	1984	JAR			624	646
0.15	BROMWICH,M	AP	1980	TAR			288	300
0.14	HARRISON,GL	03	1986	AOS	MCKINNON,JL		233	252
0.12	RITTS ,BA	SP	1974	JAR			93	111
0.11	SCHEINER,JH	AU	1984	JAR			789	797
0.11	SUTTON,TG	01	1984	AOS			81	95
0.09	JOYCE ,EJ	AU	1982	JAR	LIBBY ,R	SUNDER,S	654	675
0.09	SELTO ,FH	AU	1982	JAR	GROVE ,HD		676	688
0.08	NEWMAN,DP	ST	1981	JAR			134	156
0.07	PEARSON,MA	WI	1979	JAA	LINDGREN,JH	MYERS ,BL	122	134
0.00	BEATTY,RP	AU	1992	JAA	HAND ,JRM		509	530
0.00	BROWN ,PR	SU	1982	JAA			282	290
0.00	BUBLITZ,B	WI	1984	JAA	KEE ,R		123	137

CITE INDEX	FIRST AUTHOR	ISS-UE	YE-AR	JOUR-NAL	SECOND AUTHOR	THIRD AUTHOR	PAG BEG	PAG END
0.00	GAMBLE,GO	SP	1986	JAA			102	117
0.00	GEIGER,MA	SP	1989	AUD			40	63
0.00	GUTBERLET,LG	AU	1983	JAA			16	28
0.00	HILL ,HP	WI	1982	JAA			99	109
0.00	HOLDER,WW	WI	1982	JAA	EUDY ,KH		110	125
0.00	JOHNSON,SB	SP	1982	JAA	MESSIER JR,WF		195	213
0.00	KELLY ,AS	AU	1989	AUD	MOHRWEIS,CS		87	97
0.00	KRIPKE,H	WI	1989	JAA			3	65
0.00	MELLMAN,M	AU	1986	JAA	SEILER,ME		305	318
0.00	MOODY ,SM	AU	1986	JAA	FLESHER,DL		319	330
0.00	MOORES,K	01	1986	AOS	STEADMAN,GT		19	34
0.00	MURRAY,D	AU	1983	JAA	JOHNSON,R		4	15
0.00	NEWMAN,DP	OC	1981	TAR			897	909
0.00	PURO ,M	SP	1985	JAA			165	177
0.00	RONEN ,J	WI	1989	JAA	SORTER,G		67	77
0.00	SAMI ,H	AU	1992	CAR	WELSH ,MJ		212	236
0.00	SAVOIE,LM	ST	1969	JAR			55	62
0.00	SELTO ,FH	AU	1983	JAR	GROVE ,HD		619	622
0.00	SUNDER,S	SP	1989	CAR			452	460
0.00	WIESEN,JL	SU	1981	JAA			309	324

4.62 TREATMENTS=MANAGER DECISION CHARS.

CITE INDEX	FIRST AUTHOR	ISS-UE	YE-AR	JOUR-NAL	SECOND AUTHOR	THIRD AUTHOR	PAG BEG	PAG END
2.18	HOPWOOD,AG	ST	1972	JAR			156	182
1.50	DYE ,RA	AU	1983	JAR			514	533
1.24	DERMER,JD	JL	1973	TAR			511	519
1.18	ONSI ,M	JL	1973	TAR			535	548
0.88	DEJONG,DV	ST	1985	JAR	FORSYTHE,R	LUNDHOLM,RJ	81	120
0.65	SAN MIGUEL,JG	04	1976	AOS			357	374
0.50	BALAKRISHNAN,R	JA	1991	TAR			120	140
0.50	VASARHELYI,MA	SP	1977	JAR			138	153
0.45	EGER ,C	AU	1982	JAR	DICKHAUT,JW		711	723
0.44	SAVICH,RS	JL	1977	TAR			642	652
0.40	LANEN ,WN	DE	1988	JAE	THOMPSON,R		311	334
0.33	SHIELDS,MD	04	1987	AOS	SOLOMON,I	WALLER,WS	375	385
0.25	DOPUCH,N		1989	AUD	KING ,RR	WALLIN,DE	98	127
0.22	CAMPBELL,JE	34	1984	AOS			329	342
0.20	ANDERSON,MJ	05	1988	AOS			431	446
0.20	MITROFF,II	23	1983	AOS	MASON ,RO		195	204
0.17	HOUGHTON,KA	02	1987	AOS			143	152
0.09	SMITH ,DB	OC	1982	JAE	NICHOLS,DR		109	120
0.06	MCCOSH,AM	04	1976	AOS	RAHMAN,M		339	356
0.00	ANDERSON JR,TN	AU	1982	JAR	KIDA ,TE		403	414
0.00	DILLA ,WN	JL	1989	TAR			404	432
0.00	EZZAMEL,M	05	1990	AOS	BOURN ,M		399	424
0.00	HAIN ,HP	AU	1967	JAR			154	163
0.00	MEAR ,R	JA	1987	TAR	FIRTH ,MA		176	182
0.00	SCHNEIDER,A	JL	1990	TAR	WILNER,N		668	681

4.63 TREATMENTS=INFO STRCTRS (DISCL)

CITE INDEX	FIRST AUTHOR	ISS-UE	YE-AR	JOUR-NAL	SECOND AUTHOR	THIRD AUTHOR	PAG BEG	PAG END
2.20	HOLTHAUSEN,RW	SP	1988	JAR	VERRECCHIA,RE		82	106
2.14	HUGHES,PJ	JN	1986	JAE			119	142

CITE INDEX	FIRST AUTHOR	ISS-UE	YE-AR	JOUR-NAL	SECOND AUTHOR	THIRD AUTHOR	PAG BEG	PAG END
2.10	VERRECCHIA,RE	DE	1983	JAE			179	194
1.71	LIBERTY,SE	OC	1986	TAR	ZIMMERMAN,JL		692	712
1.65	DRIVER,MJ	JL	1975	TAR	MOCK ,TJ		490	508
1.53	GORDON,LA	01	1976	AOS	MILLER,D		59	70
1.50	GJESDAL,F	SP	1981	JAR			208	231
1.43	DEANGELO,LE	JL	1986	TAR			400	420
1.33	DARROUGH,MN	JA	1990	JAE	STOUGHTON,NM		219	243
1.33	HOLTHAUSEN,RW	JA	1990	TAR	VERRECCHIA,RE		191	208
1.17	THOMPSON II,RB	AU	1987	JAR	OLSEN ,C	DIETRICH,JR	245	274
1.00	BEAVER,WH	AU	1989	JAR	EGER ,C	RYAN ,S	157	178
1.00	DYE ,RA	JA	1990	TAR			1	24
1.00	FELTHAM,GA	AU	1992	CAR	XIE ,JZ		46	80
1.00	KIM ,O	AU	1991	JAR	VERRECCHIA,RE		302	321
1.00	KING ,RR	SP	1991	JAR	WALLIN,DE		96	108
0.93	BENBASAT,I	OC	1979	TAR	DEXTER,AS		735	749
0.93	PATELL,JM	AG	1979	JAE	WOLFSON,MA		117	140
0.88	BAREFIELD,RM	AU	1972	JAR			229	242
0.87	UECKER,WC	SP	1978	JAR			169	189
0.86	OHLSON,JA	DE	1979	JAE			211	232
0.85	SHIELDS,MD	04	1980	AOS			429	442
0.83	ATIASE,RK	SP	1987	JAR			168	176
0.82	SORTER,GH	JA	1969	TAR			12	19
0.81	HOFSTEDT,TR	AP	1977	TAR	HUGHES,GD		379	395
0.71	DEMSKI,JS	AU	1986	JAR	SAPPINGTON,DEM		250	269
0.71	DICKHAUT,JW	JA	1973	TAR			61	79
0.71	MOCK ,TJ	SP	1972	JAR	ESTRIN,TL	VASARHELYI,MA	129	153
0.67	GORDON,LA	34	1978	AOS	LARCKER,DF	TUGGLE,FD	203	214
0.67	HEALY ,PM	SP	1990	JAR	PALEPU,KG		25	48
0.67	VERRECCHIA,RE	JA	1990	JAE			245	250
0.65	BENSTON,GJ	JL	1969	TAR			515	532
0.65	HOFSTEDT,TR	OC	1972	TAR			679	692
0.65	REVSINE,L	OC	1970	TAR			704	711
0.64	MORIARITY,S	SP	1979	JAR			205	224
0.60	JUNG ,WO	SP	1988	JAR	KWON ,YK		146	153
0.59	BUZBY ,SL	JL	1974	TAR			423	435
0.54	VERRECCHIA,RE	MR	1980	JAE			63	92
0.53	BAIMAN,S	SP	1975	JAR			1	15
0.53	BUTTERWORTH,JE	SP	1972	JAR			1	27
0.50	BUSHMAN,RM	AU	1991	JAR			261	276
0.50	DONTOH,A	AU	1989	JAA			480	511
0.50	DYE ,RA	AU	1985	JAR			544	574
0.50	INDJEJIKIAN,RJ	AU	1991	JAR			277	301
0.50	LOBO ,GL	SP	1989	JAR	MAHMOUD,AAW		116	134
0.47	FELTHAM,GA	OC	1968	TAR			684	696
0.47	LUSK ,EJ	ST	1973	JAR			191	202
0.47	MILLER,H	JA	1972	TAR			31	37
0.47	RONEN ,J	AU	1971	JAR			307	332
0.43	MURRAY,D	AU	1986	JAR	FRAZIER,KB		400	404
0.43	SUNDEM,GL	SP	1979	JAR			243	261
0.43	VERRECCHIA,RE	OC	1986	JAE			175	196
0.42	HAKANSSON,NH	ST	1981	JAR			1	35
0.41	JENSEN,RE	AU	1966	JAR			224	238
0.40	ISELIN,ER	02	1988	AOS			147	164

CITE INDEX	FIRST AUTHOR	ISS-UE	YE-AR	JOUR-NAL	SECOND AUTHOR	THIRD AUTHOR	PAG BEG	PAG END
0.40	KIM ,KK	JL	1988	TAR			472	489
0.40	LUNDHOLM,RJ	SP	1988	JAR			107	118
0.38	FELTHAM,GA	SP	1977	JAR			42	70
0.38	GONEDES,NJ	AU	1980	JAR			441	476
0.38	UECKER,WC	SP	1980	JAR			191	213
0.35	DEMSKI,JS	SP	1972	JAR			58	76
0.35	MARSHALL,RM	AU	1972	JAR			286	307
0.35	MAY ,RG	JA	1973	TAR	SUNDEM,GL		80	94
0.35	SINGHVI,SS	JA	1971	TAR	DESAI ,HB		129	138
0.33	GIBBINS,M	SP	1990	JAR	RICHARDSON,A	WATERHOUSE,J	121	143
0.29	BARNEA,A	JA	1976	TAR	RONEN ,J	SADAN ,S	110	122
0.29	FERTAKIS,JP	OC	1969	TAR			680	691
0.29	LEV ,B	AU	1968	JAR			247	261
0.29	MOCK ,TJ	ST	1969	JAR			124	159
0.29	STALLMAN,JC	ST	1969	JAR			29	43
0.25	STAUBUS,GJ	JA	1985	TAR			53	75
0.24	CHANDRA,G	OC	1974	TAR			733	742
0.24	MOCK ,TJ	JL	1973	TAR			520	534
0.20	DICKHAUT,JW	AU	1983	JAR	LERE ,JC		495	513
0.20	HIRSCH JR,ML	AU	1978	JAR			254	269
0.19	WRIGHT,WF	04	1977	AOS			323	332
0.18	CHOI ,FD	AU	1973	JAR			159	175
0.18	MOCK ,TJ	OC	1971	TAR			765	777
0.18	OHLSON,JA	AU	1975	JAR			267	282
0.18	OTLEY ,DT	SP	1982	JAR	DIAS ,FJB		171	188
0.18	PRATT ,J	SP	1982	JAR			189	209
0.17	COGGER,KO	AU	1981	JAR			285	298
0.14	BLOCHER,E	06	1986	AOS	MOFFIE,RP	ZMUD ,RW	457	470
0.14	WEBER ,R	JL	1986	TAR			498	518
0.12	BERNHARDT,I	SP	1970	JAR	COPELAND,RM		95	98
0.12	COPELAND,RM	SP	1968	JAR	FREDERICKS,W		106	113
0.12	KNUTSON,PH	JA	1970	TAR			55	68
0.12	LEV ,B	SP	1970	JAR			78	94
0.12	RONEN ,J	OC	1973	TAR	FALK ,G		696	717
0.09	UECKER,WC	AU	1982	JAR			388	402
0.08	FLAHERTY,RE	AU	1980	JAA	SCHWARTZ,BN		47	56
0.08	RAMANATHAN,KV	02	1981	AOS	WEIS ,WL		143	152
0.06	BIRNBERG,JG	OC	1965	TAR			814	820
0.06	SPILLER JR,EA	SP	1974	JAR	VIRGIL JR,RL		112	142
0.00	ARNETT,HE	JA	1965	TAR			54	64
0.00	BACKER,M	JL	1969	TAR			533	538
0.00	BIDWELL III,CM	SP	1981	JAA	RIDDLE JR,JR		198	214
0.00	BILDERSEE,JS	SU	1987	JAA	KAHN ,N		239	256
0.00	CHALOS,P	SP	1991	CAR	CHERIAN,J	HARRIS,D	431	448
0.00	DEMSKI,JS	JL	1992	TAR	SAPPINGTON,DEM		628	630
0.00	FERTAKIS,JP	JL	1970	TAR			509	512
0.00	FESS ,PE	AP	1966	TAR			266	270
0.00	FRISHKOFF,P	AU	1984	JAA	FRISHKOFF,PA	BOUWMAN,MJ	44	53
0.00	HAKANSSON,NH	JL	1969	TAR			495	514
0.00	HAKANSSON,NH	WI	1990	JAA			33	53
0.00	HILTON,RW	AU	1986	CAR			50	67
0.00	IJIRI ,Y	01	1980	AOS	KELLY ,EC		115	123
0.00	IJIRI ,Y	OC	1986	TAR			745	760

CITE INDEX	FIRST AUTHOR	ISS-UE	YE-AR	JOUR-NAL	SECOND AUTHOR	THIRD AUTHOR	PAG BEG	PAG END
0.00	JENSEN,RE	JL	1970	TAR			502	508
0.00	JOHN ,K	WI	1990	JAA	RONEN ,J		61	95
0.00	KING ,R	SP	1992	CAR	POWNALL,G	WAYMIRE,G	509	531
0.00	LEWIS ,BL	SP	1985	JAR	BELL ,J		228	239
0.00	LUNDHOLM,RJ	JL	1991	TAR			486	515
0.00	LUNDHOLM,RJ	AU	1991	JAR			322	349
0.00	MAURIELLO,JA	AP	1964	TAR			347	357
0.00	MILLER,EM	AU	1980	JAA			6	19
0.00	MOORE ,G		1990	AUD	RONEN ,J		234	242
0.00	MOST ,KS	JA	1969	TAR			145	152
0.00	O'BRIEN,JR	AU	1990	CAR			1	21
0.00	OGAN ,P	SU	1991	JAA	ZIEBART,DA		387	406
0.00	PENNO ,M	ST	1991	JAR	WATTS ,JS		194	216
0.00	PURDY ,CR	ST	1969	JAR	SMITH JR,JM	GRAY ,J	1	18
0.00	ROBSON,K		1992	AOS			685	708
0.00	SIMON ,HA	JL	1990	TAR			658	667
0.00	STAUBUS,GJ	JL	1966	TAR			397	412
0.00	STEVENSON,RA	AP	1966	TAR			312	317
0.00	VICKREY,D	JL	1992	TAR			623	627

4.64 TREATMENTS=AUDITOR TRAINING

CITE INDEX	FIRST AUTHOR	ISS-UE	YE-AR	JOUR-NAL	SECOND AUTHOR	THIRD AUTHOR	PAG BEG	PAG END
0.50	DIRSMITH,MW	AU	1985	CAR	COVALESKI,MA	MCALLISTER,JP	46	68
0.09	VIGELAND,RL	AP	1982	TAR			348	357
0.06	DALTON,FE	JA	1970	TAR	MINER ,JB		134	139
0.00	KREISER,L	AP	1977	TAR			427	437
0.00	MCRAE ,TW	AU	1965	JAR			255	260
0.00	TRUEBLOOD,RM	SP	1963	JAR			86	95
0.00	YOUNG ,SD	AP	1988	TAR			283	291

4.65 TREATMENTS=INSIDER TRADING RULES

CITE INDEX	FIRST AUTHOR	ISS-UE	YE-AR	JOUR-NAL	SECOND AUTHOR	THIRD AUTHOR	PAG BEG	PAG END
0.31	RONEN ,J	AP	1977	TAR			438	449
0.00	ALLEN ,S	SP	1990	CAR	RAMANAN,R		518	543
0.00	YOUNG ,SD	SP	1985	JAA			178	183

4.66 TREATMENTS=PROBABLTY ELICITATION

CITE INDEX	FIRST AUTHOR	ISS-UE	YE-AR	JOUR-NAL	SECOND AUTHOR	THIRD AUTHOR	PAG BEG	PAG END
1.06	FELIX JR,WL	OC	1976	TAR			800	807
1.00	CHESLEY,GR	AP	1975	TAR			325	337
0.75	CROSBY,MA	AP	1981	TAR			355	365
0.64	SOLOMON,I	01	1982	AOS	KROGSTAD,JL	ROMNEY,MB	27	42
0.59	CHESLEY,GR	SP	1976	JAR			27	48
0.56	CHESLEY,GR	SP	1977	JAR			1	11
0.46	CROSBY,MA	AU	1980	JAR			585	593
0.40	CHESLEY,GR	AU	1978	JAR			225	241
0.35	GONEDES,NJ	AU	1974	JAR	IJIRI ,Y		251	269
0.27	KEYS ,DE	AU	1978	JAR			389	399
0.25	HARRISON,KE	SP	1989	CAR	TOMASSINI,LA		642	648
0.21	SCOTT ,WR	SP	1979	JAR			156	178
0.06	ALBRECHT,WS	OC	1976	TAR			824	837
0.00	ABDOLMOHAMMADI,MJ	AU	1986	CAR	BERGER,PD		149	165
0.00	JOHNSON,WB	04	1982	AOS			349	368

CITE INDEX	FIRST AUTHOR	ISS-UE	YE-AR	JOUR-NAL	SECOND AUTHOR	THIRD AUTHOR	PAG BEG	PAG END
0.00	MENON ,K	AP	1991	TAR	WILLIAMS,DD		313	332
0.00	THOMPSON,WW	JL	1965	TAR	KEMPER,EL		574	578

4.67 TREATMENTS=INTL DIFFERENCES

CITE INDEX	FIRST AUTHOR	ISS-UE	YE-AR	JOUR-NAL	SECOND AUTHOR	THIRD AUTHOR	PAG BEG	PAG END
0.60	BIRNBERG,JG	05	1988	AOS	SNODGRASS,C		447	464
0.60	RICHARDSON,AJ	04	1988	AOS			381	396
0.40	LOEB ,M	SP	1978	JAR	MAGAT ,WA		103	121
0.33	RICHARDSON,AJ	05	1990	AOS			499	501
0.24	BARRETT,ME	SP	1976	JAR			10	26
0.23	NAIR ,RD	JL	1980	TAR	FRANK ,WG		426	450
0.15	GRAY ,SJ	SP	1980	JAR			64	76
0.10	MCLEAY,S	01	1983	AOS			31	56
0.08	FERRIS,KR	04	1980	AOS	DILLARD,JF	NETHERCOTT,L	361	368
0.07	GRAY ,SJ	AU	1978	JAR			242	253
0.06	ABEL ,R	SP	1969	JAR			1	11
0.06	BIRD ,PA	SP	1965	JAR			1	11
0.06	DAVIDSON,S	AU	1966	JAR	KOHLMEIER,JM		183	212
0.00	FARMAN,WL	JA	1963	TAR	HOU ,C		133	141
0.00	FITZGERALD,RD	AU	1979	JAA	KELLEY,EM		5	20
0.00	GRAY ,SJ	SP	1984	JAR	RADEBAUGH,LH		351	360
0.00	HATFIELD,HR	AU	1966	JAR			169	182
0.00	HUSSEIN,ME	AU	1986	AUD	BAVISHI,VB	GANGOLLY,JS	124	133
0.00	MUELLER,GG	JA	1963	TAR			142	147
0.00	MUELLER,GG	AU	1964	JAR			148	157
0.00	PICCIOTTO,S		1992	AOS			759	792
0.00	ROSE ,H	AU	1964	JAR			137	147
0.00	SCHIENEMAN,GS	AU	1979	JAA			21	30
0.00	SCHWEIKART,JA	06	1986	AOS			541	554
0.00	WILKINSON,TL	JA	1964	TAR			133	139

4.68 TREATMENTS=FORM OF ORG. (PARTNER.)

CITE INDEX	FIRST AUTHOR	ISS-UE	YE-AR	JOUR-NAL	SECOND AUTHOR	THIRD AUTHOR	PAG BEG	PAG END
3.18	BRUNS JR,WJ	AU	1975	JAR	WATERHOUSE,JH		177	203
0.89	GORDON,LA	01	1984	AOS	NARAYANAN,VK		33	47
0.67	BARIFF,ML	01	1978	AOS	GALBRAITH,JR		15	28
0.47	HERTOG,JF	01	1978	AOS			29	46
0.35	SORTER,GH	AU	1964	JAR	BECKER,S	ARCHIBALD,TR	183	196
0.33	SHEVLIN,T	JL	1987	TAR			480	509
0.29	SHANK ,JK	JL	1973	TAR	COPELAND,RM		494	501
0.20	DERMER,JD	01	1988	AOS			25	36
0.20	KILMANN,RH	04	1983	AOS			341	360
0.00	FELLINGHAM,JC	AU	1989	JAR	YOUNG ,RA		179	200
0.00	GUENTHER,DA	JA	1992	TAR			17	45
0.00	HALPERIN,R	SU	1989	JAA	MAINDIRATTA,A		345	366
0.00	SHIELDS,D	01	1984	AOS			61	80
0.00	THOMAS,AP	03	1986	AOS			253	270
0.00	WILLIAMS,DJ	03	1986	AOS			271	288

4.69 TREATMENTS=AUDITOR BEHAVIOR

CITE INDEX	FIRST AUTHOR	ISS-UE	YE-AR	JOUR-NAL	SECOND AUTHOR	THIRD AUTHOR	PAG BEG	PAG END
2.33	LIBBY ,R	AU	1990	JAR	FREDERICK,DM		348	367
2.23	SIMUNIC,DA	SP	1980	JAR			161	190

CITE INDEX	FIRST AUTHOR	ISS-UE	YE-AR	JOUR-NAL	SECOND AUTHOR	THIRD AUTHOR	PAG BEG	PAG END
2.20	HOPWOOD,AG	01	1978	AOS			3	14
2.00	FREDERICK,DM	AP	1991	TAR			240	258
1.75	MOECKEL,CL	OC	1989	TAR	PLUMLEE,RD		653	666
1.67	BAIMAN,S	AU	1987	JAR	EVANS III,JH	NOEL ,J	217	244
1.67	BONNER,SE	JA	1990	TAR			72	92
1.67	TUBBS ,RM	AP	1990	TAR	MESSIER JR,WF	KNECHEL,WR	452	460
1.43	JIAMBALVO,J	AU	1979	JAR			436	455
1.25	BEDARD,JC	02	1989	AOS			113	131
1.25	CORNELL,B	OC	1989	TAR	LANDSMAN,WR		680	692
1.13	FERRIS,KR	JL	1977	TAR			605	615
1.00	ASHTON,AH	AP	1991	TAR			218	239
1.00	DYE ,RA	AU	1990	JAR	BALACHANDRAN,BV	MAGEE ,RP	239	266
1.00	MOSER ,DV	JL	1989	TAR			433	448
1.00	SOLOMON,I	AU	1982	JAR			689	710
0.85	WEBER ,R	SP	1980	JAR			214	241
0.80	SOETERS,J	01	1988	AOS	SCHREUDER,H		75	85
0.75	SCHULTZ JR,JJ	AU	1981	JAR	RECKERS,PMJ		482	501
0.73	ANTLE ,R	AU	1982	JAR			504	527
0.71	GOSMAN,ML	JA	1973	TAR			1	11
0.71	SORENSEN,JE	JL	1967	TAR			553	565
0.67	ASHTON,RH	ST	1990	JAR			148	186
0.67	BONNER,SE	ST	1990	JAR	LEWIS ,BL		1	28
0.67	HASKINS,ME	SP	1990	CAR	BAGLIONI,AJ	COOPER,CL	361	385
0.67	KELLY ,T	SP	1990	AUD	MARGHEIM,L		21	42
0.62	GINZBERG,MJ	04	1980	AOS			369	382
0.57	CHOO ,F	SP	1986	AUD			17	34
0.57	DILLARD,JF	03	1979	AOS	FERRIS,KR		179	186
0.54	SNOWBALL,D	03	1980	AOS			323	340
0.50	BAIMAN,S	SP	1991	JAR	EVANS III,JH	NAGARAJAN,NJ	1	18
0.50	BEATTY,RP	OC	1989	TAR			693	709
0.50	CHURCH,BK	SP	1991	CAR			513	534
0.50	MERCHANT,G	JL	1989	TAR			500	513
0.50	MORSE ,D	AP	1991	TAR	STEPHAN,J	STICE ,EK	376	388
0.40	DEAN ,RA	03	1988	AOS	FERRIS,KR	KONSTANS,C	235	250
0.38	BAKER ,CR	JL	1977	TAR			576	586
0.33	KNECHEL,WR	SP	1990	CAR	MESSIER JR,WF		386	406
0.33	MCDANIEL,LS	AU	1990	JAR			267	285
0.33	MOECKEL,C	AU	1990	JAR			368	387
0.33	PRATT ,J	02	1981	AOS	JIAMBALVO,J		133	142
0.33	UECKER,WC	JL	1981	TAR	BRIEF ,AP	KINNEY JR,WR	465	478
0.29	MAHER ,MW	AU	1979	JAR	RAMANATHAN,KV	PETERSON,RB	476	503
0.25	KEASEY,K	04	1989	AOS	WATSON,R		337	345
0.25	LUCKETT,PF	06	1989	AOS	HIRST ,MK		379	387
0.24	LOEB ,SE	AU	1971	JAR			287	306
0.22	KIDA ,TE	02	1984	AOS			137	147
0.21	DILLARD,JF	12	1979	AOS			31	38
0.17	FERRIS,KR	04	1981	AOS			317	326
0.14	ARANYA,N	AU	1986	CAR	WHEELER,JT		184	199
0.14	RICCHIUTE,DN	12	1979	AOS			67	76
0.06	JENSEN,RE	JA	1971	TAR			36	56
0.00	AJINKYA,BB	AP	1991	TAR	ATIASE,RK	GIFT ,MJ	389	401
0.00	ASARE ,SK	AP	1992	TAR			379	393
0.00	BALACHANDRAN,BV	OC	1981	TAR	ZOLTNERS,AA		801	812

CITE INDEX	FIRST AUTHOR	ISS-UE	YE-AR	JOUR-NAL	SECOND AUTHOR	THIRD AUTHOR	PAG BEG	PAG END
0.00	BAMBER,EM	SP	1988	AUD	BAMBER,LS	BYLINSKI,JH	137	149
0.00	BRENNER,VC	AU	1971	JAR	CARMACK,CW	WEINSTEIN,MG	359	366
0.00	BROWN ,LD	OC	1992	TAR	HAN ,JCY		862	875
0.00	CHEWNING,EG	06	1990	AOS	HARRELL,AM		527	542
0.00	DAVIS ,LR	06	1989	AOS			495	508
0.00	DILLARD,JF		1991	AOS	KAUFFMAN,NL	SPIRES,EE	619	633
0.00	FELIX JR,WL	JA	1972	TAR			52	63
0.00	HARRELL,A	AU	1990	AUD	WRIGHT,A		134	149
0.00	HARRELL,AM	34	1984	AOS	STAHL ,MJ		241	252
0.00	HARRELL,AM	SP	1988	AUD	EICKHOFF,R		105	118
0.00	KACHELMEIER,SJ		1991	AUD			25	48
0.00	LORD ,AT	AU	1992	AUD			89	108
0.00	LUCKETT,PF	04	1991	AOS	EGGLETON,IRC		371	394
0.00	MOECKEL,C	SP	1990	CAR	WILLIAMS,JD		850	858
0.00	PEI ,BKW	02	1992	AOS	REED ,SA	KOCH ,BS	169	183
0.00	PINCUS,KV	AU	1990	AUD			150	167
0.00	PONEMON,LA	AU	1992	CAR			171	189
0.00	PRATT ,J	04	1982	AOS	JIAMBALVO,J		369	380
0.00	RICCHIUTE,DN	JA	1992	TAR			46	58
0.00	SHAFER,G		1990	AUD	SRIVASTAVA,R		110	137
0.00	SHANTEAU,J	02	1989	AOS			165	177
0.00	SRIVASTAVA,RP	AP	1992	TAR	SHAFER,GR		249	283
0.00	STICKEL,SE	AP	1991	TAR			402	416

4.70 TREATMENTS=METHODOLOGY

CITE INDEX	FIRST AUTHOR	ISS-UE	YE-AR	JOUR-NAL	SECOND AUTHOR	THIRD AUTHOR	PAG BEG	PAG END
5.20	HOLTHAUSEN,RW	AG	1983	JAE	LEFTWICH,RW		77	117
5.17	BROWN ,LD	JL	1987	JAE	GRIFFIN,PA	HAGERMAN,RL	159	193
4.50	BERNARD,VL	SP	1987	JAR			1	48
4.33	WATTS ,RL	JA	1990	TAR	ZIMMERMAN,JL		131	156
4.17	CHRISTIE,AA	DE	1987	JAE			231	258
3.33	ZMIJEWSKI,ME	AG	1981	JAE	HAGERMAN,RL		129	149
3.27	LEV ,B	ST	1982	JAR	OHLSON,JA		249	322
2.75	ARRINGTON,CE	02	1989	AOS	FRANCIS,JR		1	28
2.73	WATERHOUSE,JH	01	1978	AOS	TIESSEN,P		65	76
2.40	TOMKINS,C	04	1983	AOS	GROVES,R		361	374
2.30	KAPLAN,RS	OC	1983	TAR			686	705
2.14	CHUA ,WF	OC	1986	TAR			601	632
2.00	CHRISTENSON,C	JA	1983	TAR			1	22
1.85	ASHTON,RH	SP	1980	JAR	KRAMER,SS		1	15
1.64	SWIERINGA,RJ	ST	1982	JAR	WEICK ,KE		56	101
1.44	COLLINS,DW	SP	1984	JAR	DENT ,WT		48	84
1.40	NOREEN,EW	SP	1988	JAR			119	133
1.33	BERG ,KB	SP	1990	CAR	COURSEY,D	DICKHAUT,J	825	849
1.25	DEJONG,DV	AU	1985	JAR	FORSYTHE,R	UECKER,WC	753	793
1.08	BEAVER,WH	SP	1981	JAR			163	184
1.00	ABDEL-KHALIK,AR	OC	1974	TAR			743	750
1.00	CHANDRA,R	SP	1990	CAR	BALACHANDRAN,BV		611	640
1.00	CHENG ,CSA	JL	1992	TAR	HOPWOOD,WS	MCKEOWN,JC	579	598
1.00	CHRISTIE,AA	DE	1984	JAE	KENNELLEY,MD	KING ,JW	205	217
1.00	COVALESKI,MA	06	1990	AOS	DIRSMITH,MW		543	573
1.00	DEMSKI,JS	ST	1982	JAR	KREPS ,DM		117	148
1.00	DYCKMAN,TR	SP	1984	JAR	ZEFF ,SA		225	297

CITE INDEX	FIRST AUTHOR	ISS-UE	YE-AR	JOUR-NAL	SECOND AUTHOR	THIRD AUTHOR	PAG BEG	PAG END
1.00	SMITH ,VL	AU	1987	AUD	SCHATZBERG,J	WALLER,WS	71	93
0.94	EINHORN,HJ	ST	1976	JAR			196	206
0.89	DYCKMAN,TR	ST	1984	JAR	PHILBRICK,D	STEPHAN,J	1	30
0.89	MARAIS,ML	ST	1984	JAR			34	54
0.88	BROWN ,LD	AP	1985	TAR	GARDNER,JC		262	277
0.86	KAPLAN,RS	45	1986	AOS			429	452
0.86	SEFCIK,SE	AU	1986	JAR	THOMPSON,R		316	334
0.82	IMHOFF JR,EA	AU	1982	JAR	PARE ,PV		429	439
0.80	KINNEY JR,WR	SP	1988	CAR			416	425
0.80	LANDSMAN,WR	OC	1988	TAR	MAGLIOLO,J		586	604
0.79	LEV ,B	DE	1979	JAE	SUNDER,S		187	210
0.75	BROWN ,LD	SP	1985	JAR	GARDNER,JC		84	109
0.67	BEAVER,WH	JA	1987	TAR			137	144
0.65	HARIED,AA	AU	1972	JAR			376	391
0.65	LOREK ,KS	AP	1976	TAR	MCDONALD,CL	PATZ ,DH	321	330
0.63	OGDEN ,S	02	1985	AOS	BOUGEN,P		211	226
0.62	LEFTWICH,RW	DE	1980	JAE			193	211
0.60	FRECKA,TJ	JA	1983	TAR	HOPWOOD,WS		115	128
0.60	HINES ,RD	OC	1988	TAR			642	656
0.60	MCNICHOLS,M	JL	1988	JAE			239	273
0.53	COPELAND,RM	AP	1973	TAR	FRANCIA,AJ	STRAWSER,RH	365	374
0.50	AJINKYA,BB	NV	1989	JAE	JAIN ,PC		331	359
0.50	BROWN ,LD	02	1987	AOS	GARDNER,JC	VASARHELYI,MA	193	204
0.50	DOPUCH,N	SP	1989	CAR			494	500
0.50	GONEDES,NJ	AU	1979	JAR	DOPUCH,N		384	410
0.50	HOWARD,TP	OC	1983	TAR	NIKOLAI,LA		765	776
0.50	PATELL,JM	AU	1979	JAR			528	549
0.50	STONE ,M	JA	1991	TAR	RASP ,J		170	187
0.47	BIRNBERG,JG	JA	1968	TAR	NATH ,R		38	45
0.47	WILDAVSKY,A	01	1978	AOS			77	88
0.43	JAIN ,PC	SP	1986	JAR			76	96
0.43	VERRECCHIA,RE	MR	1979	JAE			77	90
0.43	WILNER,N	01	1986	AOS	BIRNBERG,JG		71	82
0.40	FLAMHOLTZ,EG	02	1978	AOS	COOK ,E		115	140
0.40	LARCKER,DF	JA	1983	TAR	LESSIG,VP		58	77
0.40	LEV ,B	AP	1983	JAE			31	48
0.40	THOMPSON,RB	JL	1988	TAR	OLSEN ,C	DIETRICH,JR	448	471
0.38	ANDERSON,MJ	AU	1985	JAR			843	852
0.36	HAGG ,J	12	1979	AOS	HEDLUND,G		135	143
0.35	MCRAE ,TW	SP	1974	JAR			80	92
0.33	ABDEL-KHALIK,AR	AU	1990	CAR			142	172
0.33	CHANDRA,R	AU	1990	CAR	ROHRBACH,K		123	141
0.33	DENT ,JF	02	1990	AOS			3	25
0.33	HAN ,JCY	SP	1990	JAR	WILD ,JJ		211	219
0.33	HUGHES,MA	03	1990	AOS	KWON ,SO		179	191
0.33	RICCHIUTE,DN	SP	1984	JAR			341	350
0.29	WRIGHT,CJ	JA	1986	TAR	GROFF ,JE		91	100
0.27	ASHTON,AH	AU	1982	JAR			415	428
0.25	FALK ,H	SP	1989	CAR			816	825
0.25	JANG ,HJ	AU	1989	CAR	RO ,BT		242	262
0.25	KLERSEY,GF	02	1989	AOS	MOCK ,TJ		133	151
0.25	LANDSMAN,WR	SP	1989	JAR	DAMODARAN,A		97	115
0.25	LEE ,CJ	SP	1985	JAR			213	227

CITE INDEX	FIRST AUTHOR	ISS-UE	YE-AR	JOUR-NAL	SECOND AUTHOR	THIRD AUTHOR	PAG BEG	PAG END
0.24	WEST ,RR	SP	1970	JAR			118	125
0.23	HOPWOOD,WS	SP	1980	JAR			77	90
0.23	NEWMAN,DP	02	1980	AOS			217	230
0.22	MORSE ,D	AU	1984	JAR			605	623
0.21	GROVE ,HD	JL	1979	TAR	SAVICH,RS		522	537
0.21	NAIR ,RD	SP	1979	JAR			225	242
0.20	BUZBY ,SL	34	1978	AOS	FALK ,H		191	202
0.20	CARSLAW,C	AP	1988	TAR			321	327
0.20	HARRISON JR,WT	SP	1983	JAR	TOMASSINI,LA	DIETRICH,JR	65	77
0.18	GERBOTH,DL	JL	1973	TAR			475	482
0.18	GIBBINS,M	SP	1982	JAR			121	138
0.18	MARSHALL,RM	JA	1975	TAR			99	111
0.18	MEYERS,SL	AP	1973	TAR			318	322
0.18	WRIGHT,WF	01	1982	AOS			65	78
0.15	BECK ,PJ	SP	1980	JAR			16	37
0.14	JAIN ,PC	SP	1986	JAR			187	193
0.14	OHLSON,JA	AU	1979	JAR	PATELL,JM		504	505
0.14	ROBBINS,WA	AU	1986	JAR	AUSTIN,KR		412	421
0.13	DYL ,EA	02	1985	AOS	LILLY ,MS		171	176
0.12	BALL ,R	SP	1971	JAR			1	31
0.11	LEE ,CJ	AU	1984	JAR			776	781
0.11	SMITH ,G	AU	1984	AUD	KROGSTAD,JL		107	117
0.11	STONE ,M	JL	1984	TAR	BUBLITZ,B		469	473
0.10	ABDEL-KHALIK,AR	SP	1983	JAR			293	296
0.09	COGGER,KO	AU	1982	JAR	RULAND,W		733	737
0.09	EMERY ,DR	AU	1982	JAR	BARRON,FH	MESSIER JR,WF	450	458
0.09	WILLIAMS,PF	04	1982	AOS			405	410
0.08	COPELAND,RM	SP	1981	JAR	TAYLOR,RL	BROWN ,SH	197	207
0.08	LOY ,LD	SP	1980	JAA	TOOLE ,HR		227	243
0.07	OHLSON,JA	AU	1979	JAR			506	527
0.06	JOHNSON,O	JA	1972	TAR			64	74
0.00	ADESI ,GB	SU	1992	JAA	TALWAR,PP		369	378
0.00	ARRINGTON,CE	06	1992	AOS	SCHWEIKER,W		511	533
0.00	BEACH ,LR	02	1989	AOS	FREDERICKSON,JR		101	112
0.00	BEAVER,WH	DE	1984	JAE	GRIFFIN,PA	LANDSMAN,WR	219	223
0.00	BELL ,PW	SP	1987	CAR			338	367
0.00	BENISHAY,H	SU	1987	JAA			203	238
0.00	BENISHAY,H	WI	1992	JAA			97	112
0.00	BINDER,JJ	SP	1985	JAR			370	383
0.00	BOARD ,JLG	SP	1990	JAR	WALKER,M		182	192
0.00	BOATSMAN,JR	JA	1992	TAR	GRASSO,LP	ORMISTON,MB	148	156
0.00	BORITZ,JE	SP	1988	CAR	GABER ,BG	LEMON ,WM	392	411
0.00	BRICKER,R	AU	1989	JAR			246	262
0.00	BROWN ,LD	SP	1989	CAR	GARDNER,JC	VASARHELYI,MA	793	815
0.00	BROWN ,LD	AU	1991	JAR	KIM ,SK		382	385
0.00	BUCKLESS,FA	OC	1990	TAR	RAVENSCROFT,SP		933	945
0.00	BURGSTAHLER,D	SP	1986	JAR	NOREEN,EW		170	186
0.00	CHANDRA,R	AU	1992	CAR	ROHRBACH,KJ	WILLINGER,GL	296	305
0.00	CHOO ,F	06	1989	AOS			481	493
0.00	CREADY,WM	JN	1991	JAE	RAMANAN,R		203	214
0.00	DEJONG,DV	JA	1992	TAR	FORSYTHE,R		157	171
0.00	DHARAN,BG	SP	1983	JAR			256	270
0.00	DOPUCH,N	AU	1992	AUD			109	112

CITE INDEX	FIRST AUTHOR	ISS-UE	YE-AR	JOUR-NAL	SECOND AUTHOR	THIRD AUTHOR	PAG BEG	PAG END
0.00	GAMBLE,GO	SP	1981	JAA			220	237
0.00	GIBBONS,M	AU	1992	AUD			113	126
0.00	GOVINDARAJ,S	AU	1992	JAA			485	508
0.00	HECK ,JL	OC	1986	TAR	BREMSER,WG		735	744
0.00	HONIG ,LE	SP	1978	JAA			231	236
0.00	HOOKS ,KL	04	1992	AOS			343	366
0.00	HOPWOOD,W	AU	1988	CAR	MCKEOWN,J	MUTCHLER,J	284	298
0.00	HOUGHTON,KA	03	1988	AOS			263	280
0.00	JENNINGS,R	OC	1990	TAR			925	932
0.00	JONSON,LC	34	1978	AOS	JONSSON,B	SVENSSON,G	261	268
0.00	KENNEDY,D	SP	1992	JAA	LAKONISHOK,J	SHAW ,WH	161	190
0.00	KENNEDY,DB	SP	1992	CAR			419	442
0.00	LEE ,CF	AP	1988	TAR	WU ,C		292	306
0.00	LIANG ,T-P	AU	1992	CAR	CHANDLER,JS	HAN ,I	306	328
0.00	LIVNAT,J	AU	1981	JAR			350	359
0.00	MADDALA,GS	OC	1991	TAR			788	808
0.00	MILLER,P	05	1991	AOS	HOPPER,T	LAUGHLIN,R	395	403
0.00	MOCK ,TJ	AU	1978	JAR	VASARHELYI,MA		414	423
0.00	RICHARDSON,AJ	AU	1990	CAR	WILLIAMS,JJ		278	294
0.00	SMITH ,G	AU	1988	AUD			108	117
0.00	SNOWBALL,D	01	1986	AOS			47	70
0.00	THEOBALD,M	AU	1985	CAR			1	22
0.00	TOMASSINI,LA	SP	1990	CAR			287	294
0.00	WALKER,M	06	1989	AOS			433	453
0.00	WATKINS,PR	SP	1984	JAR			406	411
0.00	WATSON,CJ	JL	1990	TAR			682	695
0.00	WILKERSON JR,JE	SP	1987	JAR			161	167
0.00	YOUNG ,AE	SP	1980	JAA			244	250
0.00	ZIEBART,DA	AU	1985	JAR			920	926

4.71 TREATMENTS=BUSINESS FAILURE

CITE INDEX	FIRST AUTHOR	ISS-UE	YE-AR	JOUR-NAL	SECOND AUTHOR	THIRD AUTHOR	PAG BEG	PAG END
1.67	ZMIJEWSKI,ME	ST	1984	JAR			59	82
1.62	OHLSON,JA	SP	1980	JAR			109	131
1.24	BEAVER,WH	ST	1966	JAR			71	111
1.24	DEAKIN,EB	SP	1972	JAR			167	179
1.06	LIBBY ,R	SP	1975	JAR			150	161
0.92	ABDEL-KHALIK,AR	AU	1980	JAR	EL-SHESHAI,KM		325	342
0.85	CASEY JR,CJ	JA	1980	TAR			36	49
0.63	PENNO ,M	SP	1985	JAR			240	255
0.59	KENNEDY,HA	SP	1975	JAR			97	116
0.56	MARAIS,ML	ST	1984	JAR	PATELL,JM	WOLFSON,MA	87	114
0.55	DIETRICH,JR	JA	1982	TAR	KAPLAN,RS		18	38
0.53	BEAVER,WH	JA	1968	TAR			113	122
0.50	SCHWARTZ,KB	AP	1985	TAR	MENON ,K		248	261
0.44	STOCK ,D	SP	1984	JAR	WATSON,CJ		192	206
0.43	CASEY JR,CJ	AP	1986	TAR	MCGEE ,VE	STICKNEY,CP	249	262
0.41	BEAVER,WH	AU	1968	JAR			179	192
0.41	ELAM ,R	JA	1975	TAR			25	43
0.38	GENTRY,JA	SP	1985	JAR	NEWBOLD,P	WHITFORD,DT	146	160
0.31	HOLT ,RN	03	1980	AOS	CARROLL,R		285	296
0.29	WILCOX,JA	ST	1973	JAR			163	179
0.25	BUCHMAN,TA	03	1985	AOS			267	286

CITE INDEX	FIRST AUTHOR	ISS-UE	YE-AR	JOUR-NAL	SECOND AUTHOR	THIRD AUTHOR	PAG BEG	PAG END
0.25	BURGSTAHLER,D	JL	1989	JAE	JIAMBALVO,J	NOREEN,E	207	224
0.25	HOPWOOD,W	JA	1989	TAR	MCKEOWN,J	MUTCHLER,J	28	48
0.22	KIDA ,TE	SP	1984	JAR			145	152
0.20	JOHNSON,WB	JA	1983	TAR			78	97
0.14	CASEY JR,CJ	AP	1986	TAR	SELLING,T		302	317
0.14	FLESHER,DL	JL	1986	TAR	FLESHER,TK		421	434
0.13	ANELL ,B	04	1985	AOS			479	492
0.13	CASEY JR,CJ	SP	1985	JAR	BARTCZAK,N		384	401
0.13	SCHIPPER,K	ST	1977	JAR			1	40
0.10	MENSAH,YM	AP	1983	TAR			228	246
0.09	EMERY ,GW	AU	1982	JAR	COGGER,KO		290	303
0.00	ALY ,IM	SP	1992	JAA	BARLOW,HA	JONES ,RW	217	230
0.00	BALDWIN,J	SU	1992	JAA	GLEZEN,GW		269	285
0.00	BARNIV,R	JL	1990	TAR			578	605
0.00	CHALOS,P	AU	1985	JAR			527	543
0.00	HAN ,BH	MR	1992	JAE	JENNINGS,R	NOEL ,J	63	85
0.00	HOUGHTON,KA	AU	1984	JAR	SENGUPTA,R		768	775
0.00	HOUGHTON,KA	SP	1984	JAR			361	368
0.00	LAU ,AH	SP	1987	JAR			127	138
0.00	MCKEOWN,JC		1991	AUD	MUTCHLER,JF	HOPWOOD,W	1	13
0.00	MENON ,K	SP	1987	CAR	SCHWARTZ,KB		302	315
0.00	MENSAH,YM	SP	1984	JAR			380	395
0.00	MOSES ,OD	SU	1990	JAA			379	409
0.00	NEU ,D		1992	AOS	WRIGHT,M		645	665
0.00	PONEMON,LA	AU	1991	AUD	SCHICK,AG		70	83
0.00	RAMAN ,KK	AU	1982	JAA			44	50
0.00	ROSE ,PS	AU	1982	JAA	ANDREWS,WT	GIROUX,GA	20	31
0.00	SIMNETT,R	JL	1989	TAR	TROTMAN,K		514	528

4.72 TREATMENTS=EDUCATION

CITE INDEX	FIRST AUTHOR	ISS-UE	YE-AR	JOUR-NAL	SECOND AUTHOR	THIRD AUTHOR	PAG BEG	PAG END
0.00	ANDERSON,HM	OC	1963	TAR	GRIFFIN,FB		813	818
0.00	BAILEY,CD	AP	1992	TAR	MCINTYRE,EV		368	378
0.00	BOURN ,AM	AU	1966	JAR			213	223
0.00	FALK ,H	AU	1972	JAR			359	375
0.00	FERRIS,KR	03	1982	AOS			225	230
0.00	GRAY ,J	AP	1963	TAR	WILLINGHAM,JJ	JOHNSTON,K	336	346
0.00	POWER ,MK	04	1991	AOS			333	353
0.00	REILLY,FK	AU	1972	JAR	STETTLER,HF		308	321
0.00	SEELYE,AL	AP	1963	TAR			302	309
0.00	ZANNETOS,ZS	AP	1963	TAR			326	335

4.73 TREATMENTS=PROF. RESPONSIBLTS

CITE INDEX	FIRST AUTHOR	ISS-UE	YE-AR	JOUR-NAL	SECOND AUTHOR	THIRD AUTHOR	PAG BEG	PAG END
1.50	ROBERTS,J	04	1991	AOS			355	368
0.78	ARANYA,N	JA	1984	TAR	FERRIS,KR		1	15
0.71	ABDEL-KHALIK,AR	ST	1973	JAR			104	138
0.25	ARANYA,N	04	1981	AOS	POLLOCK,J	AMERNIC,J	271	280
0.11	NORRIS,DR	01	1984	AOS	NIEBUHR,RE		49	59
0.09	SCHEINER,JH	AU	1982	JAR	KIGER ,JE		482	496
0.00	ABDEL-KHALIK,AR	SP	1966	JAR			37	46
0.00	ARNOLD,DF	AU	1991	AUD	PONEMON,LA		1	15
0.00	CAMPBELL,DR	SP	1983	JAA			196	211

CITE INDEX	FIRST AUTHOR	ISS-UE	YE-AR	JOUR-NAL	SECOND AUTHOR	THIRD AUTHOR	PAG BEG	PAG END
0.00	CAMPFIELD,WL	JL	1963	TAR			521	527
0.00	CARMICHAEL,DR	SU	1984	JAA	WHITTINGTON,OR		347	361
0.00	DEVINE,CT	ST	1966	JAR			160	176
0.00	GORMLEY,RJ	AU	1982	JAA			51	59
0.00	GUTBERLET,LG	SU	1980	JAA			313	338
0.00	HORVITZ,JS	WI	1981	JAA	HAINKEL,M		114	127
0.00	JOHNSTON,DJ	SP	1980	JAA	LEMON ,WM	NEUMANN,FL	251	263
0.00	KUNITAKE,WK	SU	1986	JAA	WHITE JR,CE		222	231
0.00	PINCUS	02	1989	AOS			153	163
0.00	SCHIENEMAN,GS	SP	1983	JAA			212	226
0.00	SCHNEE,EJ	AU	1981	JAA	TAYLOR,ME		18	29

4.74 TREATMENTS=FORECASTS

CITE INDEX	FIRST AUTHOR	ISS-UE	YE-AR	JOUR-NAL	SECOND AUTHOR	THIRD AUTHOR	PAG BEG	PAG END
5.18	PATELL,JM	AU	1976	JAR			246	276
4.80	O'BRIEN,PC	JA	1988	JAE			53	83
4.50	BROWN ,LD	AP	1987	JAE	GRIFFIN,PA	HAGERMAN,RL	61	87
4.31	BEAVER,WH	MR	1980	JAE	LAMBERT,RA	MORSE ,D	3	28
4.31	FOSTER,G	JA	1977	TAR			1	21
3.33	BEAVER,WH	JL	1987	JAE	LAMBERT,RA	RYAN ,SG	139	157
3.00	STOBER,TL	JN	1992	JAE			347	372
2.73	FRIED ,D	OC	1982	JAE	GIVOLY,D		85	107
2.63	WATTS ,RL	AU	1977	JAR	LEFTWICH,RW		253	271
2.41	GONEDES,NJ	SP	1976	JAR	DOPUCH,N	PENMAN,SH	89	137
2.25	ALBRECHT,WS	AU	1977	JAR	LOOKABILL,LL	MCKEOWN,JC	226	244
2.23	PENMAN,SH	SP	1980	JAR			132	160
2.19	GRIFFIN,PA	SP	1977	JAR			71	83
2.07	BROWN ,LD	SP	1979	JAR	ROZEFF,MS		179	189
1.67	WAYMIRE,G	AU	1984	JAR			703	718
1.56	AJINKYA,BB	AU	1984	JAR	GIFT ,MJ		425	444
1.50	BROWN ,LD	SP	1987	JAR	RICHARDSON,GD	SCHWAGER,SJ	49	67
1.33	LEV ,B	SP	1990	JAR	PENMAN,SH		49	76
1.31	COLLINS,WA	AU	1980	JAR	HOPWOOD,WS		390	406
1.30	PINCUS,M	SP	1983	JAR			155	183
1.27	FREEMAN,RN	AU	1982	JAR	OHLSON,JA	PENMAN,SH	639	653
1.25	ASHTON,AH	AP	1985	TAR			173	185
1.25	HAN ,JCY	FB	1989	JAE	WILD ,JJ	RAMESH,K	3	33
1.14	GIVOLY,D	DE	1979	JAE	LAKONISHOK,J		165	185
1.14	TRUEMAN,B	MR	1986	JAE			53	72
1.12	FOSTER,G	SP	1973	JAR			25	37
1.11	HAGERMAN,RL	AU	1984	JAR	ZMIJEWSKI,ME	SHAH ,P	526	540
1.00	HUGHES,JS	JA	1987	TAR	RICKS ,WE		158	175
1.00	LYS ,T	DE	1990	JAE	SOHN ,S		341	363
0.93	CRICHFIELD,T	JL	1978	TAR	DYCKMAN,TR	LAKONISHOK,J	651	668
0.86	BROWN ,LD	AU	1979	JAR	ROZEFF,MS		341	351
0.83	JENNINGS,R	SP	1987	JAR			90	110
0.82	BASI ,BA	AP	1976	TAR	CAREY ,KJ	TWARK ,RD	244	254
0.82	MCDONALD,CL	JL	1973	TAR			502	510
0.75	POWNALL,G	AU	1989	JAR	WAYMIRE,G		227	245
0.75	STICKEL,SE	JL	1989	JAE			275	292
0.71	LOREK ,KS	SP	1979	JAR			190	204
0.67	KROSS ,W	AP	1990	TAR	RO ,B	SCHROEDER,D	461	476

CITE INDEX	FIRST AUTHOR	ISS-UE	YE-AR	JOUR-NAL	SECOND AUTHOR	THIRD AUTHOR	PAG BEG	PAG END
0.63	GIVOLY,D	JL	1985	TAR			372	386
0.60	ABDEL-KHALIK,AR	SP	1978	JAR	ESPEJO,J		1	13
0.57	HASSELL,JM	JA	1986	TAR	JENNINGS,RH		58	75
0.56	BATHKE,AW	AP	1984	TAR	LOREK ,KS		163	176
0.56	IMHOFF JR,EA	AU	1984	JAR	LOBO ,GJ		541	554
0.55	HOPWOOD,WS	AU	1982	JAR	MCKEOWN,JC	NEWBOLD,P	343	349
0.53	IMHOFF JR,EA	OC	1978	TAR			836	850
0.50	BHUSHAN,R	JL	1989	JAE			255	274
0.50	BROWN ,LD	SP	1991	CAR	RICHARDSON,GD	TRZCINKA,CA	323	346
0.50	L'HER ,JF	SP	1991	CAR	SURET ,J-M		378	406
0.50	WAYMIRE,G	SP	1985	JAR			268	295
0.47	DAILY ,RA	OC	1971	TAR			686	692
0.47	LOOKABILL,LL	OC	1976	TAR			724	738
0.47	RULAND,W	AP	1978	TAR			439	447
0.45	ABDEL-KHALIK,AR	OC	1982	TAR	AJINKYA,BB		661	680
0.43	NICHOLS,DR	SP	1979	JAR	TSAY ,JJ		140	155
0.42	HOPWOOD,WS	AU	1981	JAR	MCKEOWN,JC		313	322
0.40	DALEY ,LA	OC	1988	TAR	SENKOW,DW	VIGELAND,RL	563	585
0.33	DANOS ,P	OC	1984	TAR	HOLT ,DL	IMHOFF JR,EA	547	573
0.33	O'BRIEN,PC	AU	1990	JAR			286	304
0.29	WAYMIRE,G	JA	1986	TAR			129	142
0.27	DANOS ,P	WI	1982	AUD	IMHOFF JR,EA		23	34
0.27	JAGGI ,B	OC	1978	TAR			961	967
0.22	FRAZIER,KB	SP	1984	JAR	INGRAM,RW	TENNYSON,BM	318	331
0.21	BROWN ,LD	JL	1979	TAR	ROZEFF,MS		585	591
0.20	DHARAN,BG	SP	1983	JAR			18	41
0.20	LEWIS ,BL	AP	1988	TAR	PATTON,JM	GREEN ,SL	270	282
0.17	BROWN ,LD	AU	1987	CAR	ZMIJEWSKI,MA		61	75
0.15	RONEN ,J	SU	1980	JAA	SADAN ,S		339	353
0.13	COX ,CT	OC	1985	TAR			692	701
0.12	BAREFIELD,RM	JL	1970	TAR			490	501
0.11	LOREK ,KS	SP	1984	JAR	BATHKE,AW		369	379
0.11	SCHREUDER,H	JA	1984	TAR	KLAASSEN,J		64	77
0.08	BROWN ,LD	SP	1980	JAR	HUGHES,JS	ROZEFF,MS	278	288
0.08	HOPWOOD,WS	SP	1980	JAR			289	296
0.08	MANEGOLD,JG	AU	1981	JAR			360	373
0.00	ABARBANELL,JS	JN	1991	JAE			147	165
0.00	AFFLECK-GRAVES,J	SP	1990	CAR	DAVIS ,LR	MENDENHALL,RR	501	517
0.00	ALI ,A	JA	1992	TAR	KLEIN ,A	ROSENFELD,J	183	198
0.00	BAGINSKI,SP	JA	1990	TAR	HASSELL,JM		175	190
0.00	BRANCH,B	SP	1981	JAA	BERKOWITZ,B		215	219
0.00	DEMPSEY,SJ	OC	1989	TAR			748	757
0.00	DESANCTIS,G	06	1989	AOS	JARVENPAA,SL		509	525
0.00	ELGERS,P	JN	1992	JAE	MURRAY,D		303	316
0.00	ELGERS,PT	JL	1980	TAR			389	408
0.00	FARRELY,GE	AP	1985	TAR	FERRIS,KR	REICHENSTEIN,WR	278	288
0.00	GIVOLY,D	SP	1987	JAA	LAKONISHOK,J		117	137
0.00	GREENBERG,R	AU	1984	JAR			719	730
0.00	HAN ,JCY	SP	1991	JAR	WILD ,JJ		79	95
0.00	HOPWOOD,WS	SU	1990	JAA	MCKEOWN,JC		339	363
0.00	JOHNSON,DA	AU	1984	JAR	PANY ,K		731	743
0.00	LOREK ,KS	SP	1983	JAR	ICERMAN,JD	ABDULKADER,AA	317	328
0.00	MAINES,LA	ST	1990	JAR			29	54

CITE INDEX	FIRST AUTHOR	ISS-UE	YE-AR	JOUR-NAL	SECOND AUTHOR	THIRD AUTHOR	PAG BEG	PAG END
0.00	MEAR ,R	04	1987	AOS	FIRTH ,MA		331	340
0.00	NICHOLS,DR	AP	1979	TAR	TSAY ,JJ	LARKIN,PD	376	382
0.00	POWNALL,G	ST	1989	JAR	WAYMIRE,G		85	105
0.00	PUTNAM,K	AU	1984	JAA	THOMAS,LR		15	23
0.00	RULAND,W	JL	1990	TAR	TUNG ,S	GEORGE,NE	710	721
0.00	SANSING,RC	AU	1992	CAR			33	45
0.00	SILHAN,PA	SP	1983	JAR			341	347
0.00	TRUEMAN,B	AU	1990	CAR			203	222
0.00	WELCH ,PR	AU	1984	JAR			744	757
0.00	WILD ,JJ	SP	1987	JAR			139	160
0.00	ZAROWIN,P	SU	1990	JAA			439	454
0.00	ZIEBART,DA	AP	1990	TAR			477	488

4.75 TREATM=DECISION AIDS

CITE INDEX	FIRST AUTHOR	ISS-UE	YE-AR	JOUR-NAL	SECOND AUTHOR	THIRD AUTHOR	PAG BEG	PAG END
1.58	JOYCE ,EJ	SP	1981	JAR	BIDDLE,GC		120	145
0.90	SHIELDS,MD	AP	1983	TAR			284	303
0.67	AWASTHI,V	OC	1990	TAR	PRATT ,J		797	811
0.67	KACHELMEIER,SJ	JA	1990	TAR	MESSIER JR,WF		209	226
0.38	AMERSHI,AH	SP	1985	CAR	DEMSKI,JS	FELLINGHAM,J	176	192
0.25	BUTLER,SA	AU	1985	JAR			513	526
0.18	BENBASAT,I	SP	1982	JAR	DEXTER,AS		1	11
0.12	REVSINE,L	AP	1976	TAR	THIES ,JB		255	268
0.00	ABDOLMOHAMMADI,MJ	SP	1991	CAR			535	548
0.00	AMEY ,LR	AU	1984	CAR			64	76
0.00	BASTABLE,CW	SP	1981	JAA	BEAMS ,FA		248	254
0.00	BENSTON,GJ	JL	1976	TAR			483	498
0.00	DIRSMITH,MW	01	1991	AOS	HASKINS,ME		61	90
0.00	FELLINGHAM,JC	OC	1990	TAR	YOUNG ,RA		837	856
0.00	MAUTZ-JR,RD	04	1990	AOS			273	295
0.00	MILLER,P		1991	AOS			733	762
0.00	MOON ,P	03	1990	AOS			193	198
0.00	SCHICK,AG	03	1990	AOS	GORDON,LA	HAKA ,S	199	220

4.76 TREATMENTS=ORGANIZATION * ENVIRONMENT

CITE INDEX	FIRST AUTHOR	ISS-UE	YE-AR	JOUR-NAL	SECOND AUTHOR	THIRD AUTHOR	PAG BEG	PAG END
6.00	HOPWOOD,AG	03	1987	AOS			207	234
4.33	COLLINS,DW	JL	1987	JAE	KOTHARI,SP	RAYBURN,JD	111	138
3.10	HOPWOOD,AG	23	1983	AOS			287	305
1.67	GOVINDARAJAN,V	02	1984	AOS			125	135
1.50	ARMSTRONG,P	02	1985	AOS			129	148
1.50	NEU ,D	02	1991	AOS			185	200
1.50	TINKER,T	01	1987	AOS	NEIMARK,M		71	88
1.40	NOREEN,EW	04	1988	AOS			359	369
1.33	PUXTY ,AG	03	1987	AOS	WILLMOTT,HC	COOPER,DJ	273	291
1.14	WILLMOTT,H	06	1986	AOS			555	582
1.00	CHOUDHURY,N	06	1988	AOS			549	557
1.00	GRAY ,B	05	1992	AOS			399	425
1.00	HUIZING,A	05	1992	AOS	DEKKER,HC		427	448
1.00	KIRKHAM,LM	04	1992	AOS			287	297
1.00	LEHMAN,CR	04	1992	AOS			261	285
1.00	MELUMAD,ND	ST	1987	JAR	REICHELSTEIN,S		1	18
1.00	MILLER,P	04	1990	AOS			315	338

CITE INDEX	FIRST AUTHOR	ISS-UE	YE-AR	JOUR-NAL	SECOND AUTHOR	THIRD AUTHOR	PAG BEG	PAG END
1.00	NEU ,D	04	1992	AOS			223	237
1.00	RICHARDSON,AJ	06	1989	AOS			415	431
1.00	ROBERTS,J	02	1990	AOS			107	126
0.90	LEWIS ,BL	SP	1983	JAR	SHIELDS,MD	YOUNG ,SM	271	285
0.86	CHENHALL,RH	JA	1986	TAR	MORRIS,D		16	35
0.83	BURRELL,G	01	1987	AOS			89	102
0.83	HOPWOOD,AG	01	1987	AOS			65	70
0.67	ELIAS ,N	JL	1990	TAR			606	623
0.67	MACINTOSH,NB	01	1987	AOS	DAFT ,RL		49	61
0.67	MILLER,P	05	1990	AOS	O'LEARY,T		479	498
0.67	O'BRIEN,PC	ST	1990	JAR	BHUSHAN,R		55	82
0.60	HIRST ,MK	AU	1983	JAR			596	605
0.60	SHANE ,PB	JL	1983	TAR	SPICER,BH		521	538
0.57	DANOS ,P	OC	1986	TAR	EICHENSEHER,JW		633	650
0.56	INGRAM,RW	SP	1984	JAR			126	144
0.50	BRYER ,RA	05	1991	AOS			439	486
0.50	COLIGNON,R	02	1991	AOS	COVALESKI,M		141	157
0.50	ELY ,KM	SP	1991	JAR			37	58
0.50	FEROZ ,EH	ST	1991	JAR	PARK ,K	PASTENA,VS	107	148
0.50	HARTE ,GF	02	1987	AOS	OWEN ,DL		123	142
0.50	NEU ,D	03	1991	AOS			243	256
0.50	ROBSON,K	05	1991	AOS			547	570
0.50	THOMPSON,G	05	1991	AOS			572	599
0.38	OWEN ,DL	03	1985	AOS	LLOYD ,AJ		329	352
0.33	BRICKLEY,JA	JA	1990	JAE	VAN DRUNEN,LD		251	280
0.33	ESPELAND,WN	02	1990	AOS	HIRSCH,PM		77	96
0.29	COVALESKI,M	45	1986	AOS	AIKEN ,ME		297	320
0.29	GAA ,JC	JL	1986	TAR			435	454
0.25	ETZIONI,A	AU	1989	JAA			555	570
0.25	PRESTON,AM	06	1989	AOS			389	413
0.25	SCAPENS,RW	AP	1985	TAR	SALE ,JT		231	247
0.20	MIRVIS,PH	23	1983	AOS	LAWLER III,EE		175	190
0.17	GAMBLING,T	04	1987	AOS			319	329
0.14	ZEFF ,SA	SP	1986	JAA			131	154
0.11	WESCOTT,SH	SP	1984	JAR			412	423
0.10	BROWN ,C	AU	1983	JAR			413	431
0.00	AMIHUD,Y	AU	1988	JAA	MENDELSON,H		369	395
0.00	ARNOLD,PJ	02	1991	AOS			121	140
0.00	BAILEY,D	06	1990	AOS			513	525
0.00	BOUGEN,PD	03	1990	AOS	OGDEN ,SG	OUTRAM,Q	149	170
0.00	BOWSHER,CA	WI	1986	JAA			7	16
0.00	BRUNSSON,N	02	1990	AOS			47	59
0.00	CARPENTER,VL		1992	AOS	FEROZ ,EH		613	643
0.00	CHOW ,CW	03	1991	AOS	SHIELDS,MD	CHAN ,YK	209	226
0.00	COASE ,RH	JA	1990	JAE			3	13
0.00	CZARNIAWSKA-JOERGES	02	1989	AOS	JACOBSSON,B		29	39
0.00	DAVISON,AG	SP	1984	JAR	STENING,BW	WAI ,WT	313	317
0.00	DERMER,J	02	1990	AOS			67	76
0.00	GALLHOFER,S	05	1991	AOS	HASLAM,J		487	520
0.00	GRUNDFEST,JA	AU	1991	JAA	SHOVEN,JB		409	442
0.00	HERTOG,FD	02	1992	AOS	WIELINGA,C		103	128
0.00	HESSEL,CA	SU	1992	JAA	NORMAN,M		313	330
0.00	HINES ,RD	04	1992	AOS			313	341

CITE INDEX	FIRST AUTHOR	ISS-UE	YE-AR	JOUR-NAL	SECOND AUTHOR	THIRD AUTHOR	PAG BEG	PAG END
0.00	HUIZING,A	05	1992	AOS	DEKKER,HC		449	458
0.00	HUNT-III,HG	05	1990	AOS	HOGLER,RL		437	454
0.00	JACKSON,MW	05	1992	AOS			459	469
0.00	JONSSON,S	05	1991	AOS			521	546
0.00	LEVY ,H	SP	1990	JAA			235	270
0.00	LOFT ,A	04	1992	AOS			367	378
0.00	PEI ,BKW	SP	1989	AUD	DAVIS ,FG		101	112
0.00	POWER ,M	05	1992	AOS			477	499
0.00	PRESTON,AM	01	1992	AOS			63	100
0.00	ROBERTS,J	04	1992	AOS	COUTTS,JA		379	395
0.00	ROBERTS,RW	06	1992	AOS			595	612
0.00	ROUSSEY,RS	SP	1992	AUD			47	57
0.00	SHANKER,L	SU	1992	JAA			379	393
0.00	SIMONS,R	02	1990	AOS			127	143
0.00	TELSER,LG	SP	1990	JAA			159	201
0.00	THANE ,P	04	1992	AOS			299	312
0.00	WALKER,SP	03	1991	AOS			257	283
0.00	WARDELL,M		1991	AOS	WEISENFELD,LW		655	670
0.00	YOUNG ,A	WI	1991	JAA			129	133
0.00	YOUNG ,AE	SU	1992	JAA			361	368
0.00	YOUNG ,SD	OC	1991	TAR			809	817

4.77 TREATMENTS=LITIGATION

CITE INDEX	FIRST AUTHOR	ISS-UE	YE-AR	JOUR-NAL	SECOND AUTHOR	THIRD AUTHOR	PAG BEG	PAG END
1.67	MELUMAD,ND	SP	1990	JAR	THOMAN,L		77	120
1.40	PALMROSE,ZV	JA	1988	TAR			55	73
0.89	KELLOGG,RL	DE	1984	JAE			185	204
0.50	PALMROSE,ZV	SP	1987	AUD			90	103
0.00	HORVITZ,JS	WI	1985	JAA	COLDWELL,S		86	99
0.00	JOHNSON,O	04	1992	AOS			205	222
0.00	LANZILLOTTI,RF	WI	1990	JAA	ESQUIBEL,AK		125	142
0.00	LUDMAN,EA	SP	1986	JAA			118	124
0.00	PALMROSE,Z		1991	AUD			54	71
0.00	PALMROSE,Z	ST	1991	JAR			149	193
0.00	RUNDFELT,R	SP	1986	JAA			125	130
0.00	STICE ,JD	JL	1991	TAR			516	534

ABBREVIATIONS

5.1.1 CLASSIFICATIONS

1. Mode of Reasoning

1. 1. Quantitative: Descriptive Statistics (Des. Stat.)
1. 2. Quantitative: Regression (Regress.)
1. 3. Quantitative: ANOVA (ANOVA)
1. 4. Quantitative: Factor Analysis, Multiple Discriminant Analysis, Probit (Oth. Quant.)
1. 5. Quantitative: Markov (MARKOV)

1. 6. Quantitative: Non-Parametric (Non-Par.)
1. 7. Quantitative: Correlation (Corr.)
1. 8. Quantitative: Analytical (Anal.)
1. 9. Mixed Quantitative/qualitative (Mixed)
1. 10. Qualitative (Qual.)

2. Research Method

2. 1. Analytical-Internal Logic (Int. Log.)
2. 2. Analytical-Simulation (Sim.)
2. 3. Analytical-Primary (Prim.)
2. 4. Analytical-Secondary (Sec.)
2. 5. Empirical-Case (Case)
2. 6. Empirical-Field (Field)
2. 7. Empirical-Laboratory (Lab)
2. 8. Opinion-Survey (Surv.)

3. School of Thought

3. 1. Behavioral-Human Information Processing (HIPS)
3. 2. Behavioral-Other (Oth. Beh.)
3. 3. Statistical Modelling-Efficient Markets Hypothesis (EMH)
3. 4. Statistical Modelling-Time Series (Time Ser.)
3. 5. Statistical Modelling-Information Economics/agency (Inf. Eco./Ag.)
3. 6. Statistical Modelling-Math Programming (Math Prog.)
3. 7. Statistical Modelling-Other (Oth. Stat.)
3. 8. Accounting Theory (Theory)
3. 9. Accounting History (Hist.)
3. 10. Institutional (Install)
3. 11. Other (Oth.)

4. Treatment

4. 1. Financial Accounting Methods (Fin. Meth.)
4. 2. Cash (Cash)
4. 3. Inventory (Inv.)
4. 4. Other Current Assets (Oth. C/A)
4. 5. Property, Plant and Equipment/depreciation (P/P/A)
4. 6. Other Non-Current Assets (Oth. Non-C/A)
4. 7. Leases (Leases)
4. 8. Long Term Debt (LTD)
4. 9. Taxes (Taxes)
4. 10. Other Liabilities (Oth. L)
4. 11. Valuation [Inflation] (Val.)
4. 12. Special Items (Spec. Items)

4. 13. Revenue Recognition (Rev. Rec.)
4. 14. Accounting Changes (Acc. Chng.)
4. 15. Business Combinations (Bus. Comb.)
4. 16. Interim Reporting (Anal Rep.)
4. 17. Amortization/Depletion (Amor/Depl.)
4. 18. Segment Reports (Seg. Rep.)
4. 19. Foreign Currency (For. Cur.)
4. 20. Cash Dividends (Cash Div.)
4. 21. Stock Dividends (Stk. Div.)
4. 22. Pension (Pens.)
4. 23. Other Financial Accounting (Oth. Fin. Acc.)
4. 24. Financial Statement Timing (Fin. St. Tim.)
4. 25. Research and Development (R ~ D)
4. 26. Oil and Gas (Oil & Gas)
4. 27. Auditing (Aud.)
4. 28. Opinion (Opin.)
4. 29. Sampling (Swamp.)
4. 30. Liability (Liab.)
4. 31. Risk (Risk)
4. 32. Independence (Indep.)
4. 33. Analytical Review (Anal. Rev.)
4. 34. Internal Control (Int. Cont.)
4. 35. Timing (Tim.)
4. 36. Materiality (Mat.)
4. 37. EDP Audit (EDP Aud.)
4. 38. Organization (Org.)
4. 39. Internal Audit (Int. Aud.)
4. 40. Errors (Errors)
4. 41. Audit Trail (Trail)
4. 42. Judgment age.)
4. 43. Planning (Plan.)
4. 44. Efficiency - Operational (Oper.)
4. 45. Audit Theory (Aud. Theor.)
4. 46. Confirmations (Confirms.)
4. 47. Managerial (Manag.)
4. 48. Transfer Pricing (Trans. Pric.)
4. 49. Cost-Volume-Profit-Analysis (C-V-P-A)
4. 50. Budgeting and Planning (Budg. & Plan.)
4. 51. Relevant Costs (Rel. Costs)
4. 52. Responsibility Accounting (Resp. Acc.)
4. 53. Cost Allocation (Cost Alloc.)
4. 54. Capital Budgeting (Cap. Budg.)

4. 55. Tax [Tax Planning] (Tax)
4. 56. Overhead Allocation (Over. Alloc.)
4. 57. Human Resource Accounting-Social Accounting (HRA)
4. 58. Variances (Var.)
4. 59. Executive Compensation (Exec.Comp.)
4. 60. Managerial (Oth. Manag.)
4. 61. Submissions to the FASB (FASB Subm.)
4. 62. Manager Decision Characteristics (Man. Dec. Char.)
4. 63. Information Structures [Disclosures] (Info. Struc.)
4. 64. Auditor Training (Aud. Train.)
4. 65. Insider Trading Rules (Ins. Trad.)
4. 66. Probability Elicitation (Probe. Elic.)
4. 67. International Differences (Int. Diff.)
4. 68. Form of Organization [Partnerships, etc.] (Org. Form)
4. 69. Auditor Behavior (Aud. Beh.)
4. 70. Methodology (Method.)
4. 71. Business Failure (Bus. Fail.)
4. 72. Education (Educ.)
4. 73. Professional Responsibilities (Proof. Resp.)
4. 74. Forecasts (Fork.)
4. 75. Decision Aids (Dec. Aids)
4. 76. Organization and Environment (Org. & Envir.)
4. 77. Litigation (Litig.)

5.1.2 JOURNALS

AOS	Accounting, Organizations and Society
TAR	The Accounting Review
AUD	Auditing: A Journal of Theory and Practice
JAA	Journal of Accounting and Finance
CAR	Contemporary Accounting Research
JAE	Journal of Accounting and Economics
JAR	Journal of Accounting Research

5.1.3 ISSUES

AU	Fall/Autumn	MR	March
AG	August	OC	October
AP	April	SP	Spring
DE	December	ST	Supplement
JA	January	SU	Summer
JL	July	WI	Winter

GLOSSARY

5.2.1 . MODE OF REASONING (Key method of analysis)

Quantitative -Descriptive Statistics Relies primarily on the characteristics of the populations through frequencies, means and variances.

Quantitative -Regression Uses regression as the primary statistical method of analysis or inference.

Quantitative -ANOVA Uses analysis of variance (covariance) as the primary statistical method of analysis or inference.

Quantitative - Multivariate Clustering Methods Uses multivariate clustering methods as: factor analysis, MDA, discriminant analysis, log it, probit, principal factor, etc.

Quantitative -Markov Uses Markov chains as the primary statistical method of analysis or inference.

Quantitative -Non-parametric Uses non-parametric analysis as the primary statistical method. This may be descriptive, correlation, ANOVA, etc.

Quantitative -Correlation Uses correlations as the primary statistical method of analysis or inference.

Quantitative -Analytical Uses analytical methods for argument support.

Mixed -Quantitative/qualitative A combination of modes of reasoning.

Qualitative Relies primarily on qualitative and "a-priori" arguments to advance arguments.

5.2.2 RESEARCH METHOD

Analytical -Internal logic Involves all analytical papers plus individual opinion type of research such as the early "a-priori" papers.

Analytical -Simulation Computer-based simulation papers with random numbers, etc.

Archival -Primary Use of data compiled by others in magnetic or non-magnetic form such as COMPUSTAT, VALUE LINE or (for example) looking up 10K's on paper.

Archival -Secondary Primarily literature reviews. Looks at an issue primarily through the comparison of other studies.

Empirical -Case Examines a particular issue through the careful examination of a particular field situation which is only being observed but not interfered with.

Empirical -Field Examines a particular issue through a field situation where there is interference and a control group.

Empirical -Laboratory Uses the experimental methodology on a simulated environment with manipulation of variables. A questionnaire containing a hypothetical case is a laboratory study.

Opinion -Survey Questionnaires and/or interviews asking for opinions or facts about certain issues.

5.2.3 SCHOOL OF THOUGHT

Behavioral -HIPS Human Information Processing Studies including judgment, inference, bayesian revision, lens, cognitive style, etc.

Behavioral -Other Includes behavioral issues as budget-related issues, decision-maker attitudes, etc.

Statistical Modelling -Efficient Market Hypothesis (EMH) Security price and volume studies

Statistical Modelling -Time series, Econometrics Time series studies, forecasting, valuation models, etc.

Statistical Modelling -Information economics/ agency theory Typically analytical papers Modelling management processes.

Statistical Modelling -Mathematical programming Mathematical programming techniques such as linear programming, dynamic programming, etc.

Statistical Modelling -Other Studies using other types of statistical modelling or a mix of modelling approaches.

Accounting Theory Typically the development of accounting thought through "a priori" reasoning or other type of support.

Accounting History Studies dealing with the evolution of accounting thought.

Institutional Studies of accounting institutions such as the FASB, APB, and other accounting-related and standard-setting institutions.

Other Studies that do not easily fall into the above paradigms or belong to lesser-divulged paradigms.